The Palgrave Handbook of Screenwriting Studies

Rosamund Davies · Paolo Russo · Claus Tieber
Editors

The Palgrave Handbook of Screenwriting Studies

Editors
Rosamund Davies
School of Stage and Screen
University of Greenwich
London, UK

Paolo Russo
School of Arts
Oxford Brookes University
Oxford, UK

Claus Tieber
Institut für Theater-, Film- und Medienwissenschaft
University of Vienna
Vienna, Austria

ISBN 978-3-031-20768-6   ISBN 978-3-031-20769-3 (eBook)
https://doi.org/10.1007/978-3-031-20769-3

© The Editor(s) (if applicable) and The Author(s), under exclusive license to Springer Nature Switzerland AG 2023
Chapter 'Film Dramaturgy: A Practice and a Tool for Researcher' is licensed under the terms of the Creative Commons Attribution 4.0 International License (http://creativecommons.org/licenses/by/4.0/). For further details see license information in the chapter.
This work is subject to copyright. All rights are solely and exclusively licensed by the Publisher, whether the whole or part of the material is concerned, specifically the rights of translation, reprinting, reuse of illustrations, recitation, broadcasting, reproduction on microfilms or in any other physical way, and transmission or information storage and retrieval, electronic adaptation, computer software, or by similar or dissimilar methodology now known or hereafter developed.
The use of general descriptive names, registered names, trademarks, service marks, etc. in this publication does not imply, even in the absence of a specific statement, that such names are exempt from the relevant protective laws and regulations and therefore free for general use.
The publisher, the authors, and the editors are safe to assume that the advice and information in this book are believed to be true and accurate at the date of publication. Neither the publisher nor the authors or the editors give a warranty, expressed or implied, with respect to the material contained herein or for any errors or omissions that may have been made. The publisher remains neutral with regard to jurisdictional claims in published maps and institutional affiliations.

This Palgrave Macmillan imprint is published by the registered company Springer Nature Switzerland AG
The registered company address is: Gewerbestrasse 11, 6330 Cham, Switzerland

Foreword

Screenwriting seems an obvious concept: it must mean writing for the screen. However, what might be involved in a single-authored description of images and dialogue for an hour-and-one-half fictional drama seems weirdly minimal contrasted with a room of ever-shifting writers who produce 100-plus episodes for a multi-year television series or the online global exchanges of code for multiple people engaging in creating a digital game.

Not surprisingly, attention to how to write for the screen started as soon as films were being produced, with amateurs seeking guidance from "how-to" columns in entertainment newspapers published from 1905 on (*Variety* in the USA) and soon books, with early examples beginning in 1911. And, of course, the advice of these essays and books drew on centuries of theatrical drama.

Indeed, this volume is not so much a handbook as an encyclopaedia of methods and approaches to screenwriting in its very broadest meanings and uses. Moreover, not only is screenwriting as an action the focus of the *Handbook* but so is the screenplay which exists in many forms and is used by screen workers in many different ways. Thus, the *Handbook* wisely and astutely does not treat screenplays as simply an ingredient for something else (a film, a television series, a game experience) but as art objects in themselves.

Both the complexity of what might be involved in screenwriting and the variety of ways to approach what actually shows up on large and small screens deserve significant attention. Rosamund Davies, Paolo Russo and Claus Tieber admirably pilot *The Palgrave Handbook of Screenwriting Studies*. To navigate such a challenging subject, the editors have drawn on the talents of the major scholars of screenwriting studies, opening the conversation to forty-four people from six continents. This ultimately helps the reader see the similarities and the variations that occur as a consequence of different national and cultural practices.

As an encyclopaedia, the book is not a *set-in-stone outline* of screenwriting but rather an implicit call, even provocation, for further research and debate. Numerous essays introduce new ideas about screenwriting as a field, object, practice and process. This is due not only to the number of authors contributing but to the variety of perspectives these people offer. Essays develop issues not only about national and cultural differences but also about gendered, sexual and racial significances. Screenwriting in China, Japan, Latin America, India, South Africa, Nigeria, Syria, Lebanon and Australia is discussed besides the more expected discussions of the US and European industries.

Moreover, the single, lone writer is not the only process considered. Also described is the writers' room for serial writing, providing Petr Szczepanik's apt term for studying that to be "development analysis". Practices in writing animation, shorts and games are described. Considered are alternative ways to conceptualize characters (rather than the traditional *realism* goal), protagonists (rather than characters), the development of sensual responses from the spectator and transnational scripting (appealing to audiences across national borders).

As the editors note, while the study of screenwriting in popular and academic environments is now over a century old, and scholarly histories of the practices and objects have been published for fifty years, the inauguration of the Screenwriting Research Network (SRN) in 2008 has facilitated worldwide dialogue among practitioners and scholars. I was fortunate to serve on the SRN's first two committees awarding recognition for the best book and best article in the field (2019 and 2020–21). This *Handbook* is a delightful and provocative introduction and summary, setting practitioners and scholars on very good paths for the next century of writing and studying. It is a pleasure.

June 2023

Janet Staiger
Professor Emeritus
The University of Texas at Austin
Austin, USA

Preface

The general aim of a handbook is to gather expertise and compare approaches to demonstrate the state of the art in a certain field. Handbooks are published as new fields appear or new approaches in an established field gain importance. To publish the first handbook in an emergent field is therefore to make a statement about the stage of maturity that it has reached. Having actively participated in the research fora that contributed to such development, for us as editors this seemed to be the logical next step. So logical indeed that two of us shared this idea for some time, unbeknownst to each other. One was Paolo Russo, whose initial proposals even made it into David Bordwell and Kristin Thompson's blog: "We learned of a planned encyclopedia of screenwriting edited by Paolo Russo".[1] The other was Claus Tieber, who was looking for a co-editor to work on a project that could not be done solo. Once Claus contacted Paolo, the development of *The Palgrave Handbook of Screenwriting Studies* officially started.

In the early months of 2017, Paolo obtained a small grant that allowed him and Claus to exchange visits, in Vienna and in Oxford, respectively, to start workshopping the possible contents of the volume. As a first tentative shape began to emerge and the sheer scope of the prospective volume started to become apparent, so did the realization that enrolling the help of a third co-editor was necessary. Both Paolo and Claus suggested the same name: Rosamund Davies.

The team now complete, we initially estimated that the volume could comprise around twenty-five chapters. We were wrong: as soon as we started listing all the areas of interest, topics, a varied range of cultural perspectives and methodological approaches that we deemed essential to include, that number ballooned very quickly.

---

[1] Bordwell, David, and Kristin Thompson. 2013. "Screenplaying." *Observation on Film Art* Blog, 3 September. http://www.davidbordwell.net/blog/2013/09/03/screenplaying/. Accessed 1 August 2022.

Meanwhile, we were compiling a second list as we set out to involve the best expertise available globally. All three of us have been significantly involved with the Screenwriting Research Network since its early days in various capacities and this handbook would certainly not have been possible without it. The SRN membership has indeed provided us with an ample pool of scholars to pick from. However, we are well aware that the scholarship in screenwriting research is not limited to the network, and therefore, we always intended for this handbook to reach beyond it and accommodate a genuine cross- and inter-disciplinary approach as well as perspectives from practitioners.

The Palgrave Handbook of Screenwriting Studies thus consists of forty chapters penned by forty-four contributing authors from twenty-five countries and all six continents. Most contributors are academics—some of which also practitioners—affiliated to thirty-eight universities, and at various career stages: emerging, early career researchers feature alongside more established names. Three more contributors come from the industry. These contributions represent the richness of discourses, strands of inquiry and perspectives that have evolved and characterized screenwriting studies over the past few decades.

London, UK   Rosamund Davies
Oxford, UK   Paolo Russo
Vienna, Austria   Claus Tieber

Acknowledgements

This project has benefitted from a Collaborative Research & Travel Award granted by Oxford Brookes University that helped to take it off the ground in its initial stages.

We are grateful to all the members of the SRN and to the organizers of its annual conferences for their invaluable contribution to creating and maintaining such a productive and enjoyable environment over the years—which is no small feat. We owe a particular debt of gratitude to Ian W. Macdonald for facilitating the initial encounter between Claus and Paolo, and whose precious advice has helped us give shape to this project when it was still in its embryonic stage.

The bulk of the work for *The Palgrave Handbook of Screenwriting Studies*—i.e. researching, writing, editing—took place during the COVID-19 pandemic. This forced us to change our approach in substantial ways and the entire editorial process took place online via videoconferencing tools. Directly or indirectly, the pandemic has had an impact on all of us and many of our contributing authors or their families were affected by it. And sadly, our esteemed colleague, Professor Brian Winston, who was working on a chapter on scripting the documentary, passed away a few months before the completion of the volume. To each and every one of our authors goes our deepest gratitude for their contributing such a high standard in spite of and through these difficult times.

Last but not least, we wish to thank the whole Editorial Team at Palgrave Macmillan, and reserve a special mention for Lina Aboujieb, Executive Editor for Film and Television Studies, who firmly believed in this project from day one and graced us with utmost professionalism and unwavering support.

June 2023

Rosamund Davies
Paolo Russo
Claus Tieber

Contents

1	**Introduction**	1
	Rosamund Davies, Paolo Russo, and Claus Tieber	
	1.1 Scholarship and Directions in Screenwriting Studies	2
	1.2 About This Volume	5
	1.2.1 PART I: What—Screenwriting Ontology: Defining the Screenplay and Screenwriting	6
	1.2.2 PART II: When/Where—Screenwriting Historiography	8
	1.2.3 PART III: Who—Screenwriting and the Screen Industries	10
	1.2.4 Part IV: How—Approaches to Screen Storytelling	11
	1.2.5 PART V: How To—Researching and Teaching Screenwriting: Discourses and Methods	13
	References	14

Part I: What
Screenwriting Ontology: Defining the Screenplay and Screenwriting

2	**How to Think About Screenwriting**	21
	Ian W. Macdonald	
	2.1 Introduction: What Are We Studying Here?	21
	2.2 Scripting the Screen Idea	25
	2.3 The Domain of Screenwriting	27
	2.4 Cluster 1: Orthodox Creative Screenwriting	29
	2.5 Cluster 2: Critical Practice	32
	2.6 Cluster 3: Critical Analysis	34
	2.7 Screenwriting Studies	37
	References	38

3	**Screenplectics: Screenwriting as a Complex Adaptive System**		**45**
	Paolo Russo		
	3.1	Introduction	45
	3.2	Complexity in Narratology and Media Studies	47
	3.3	Core Features of Complex Systems	49
	3.4	Screenwriting as a Complex Adaptive System (SCAS)	50
	3.5	Modelling SCAS	53
		3.5.1 Cellular Automata Models	53
		3.5.2 Network Models	59
		3.5.3 4-D Topological Manifolds: Spacetime and the Block Universe Model	62
	3.6	Conclusions	67
	References		69
4	**Collaboration, Cooperation and Authorship in Screenwriting aka How Many People Does It Take to Create an Author?**		**73**
	Rosamund Davies		
	4.1	Introduction	73
	4.2	Script Development as Collective Practice	74
	4.3	Collaboration Versus Cooperation	75
	4.4	Prior Relationships and Group Identities	79
	4.5	Understandings of Authorship	81
	4.6	The Screenplay and the Production of Authorship	82
	4.7	Authorship and Voice	83
	4.8	Who Speaks as an Author?	84
	4.9	Authorship, Collaboration and Cooperation	87
	4.10	Conclusions	89
	References		89
5	**Acts of Reading: The Demands on Screenplay Reading**		**93**
	Rita Benis		
	5.1	Introduction	93
	5.2	Background	95
	5.3	Reading the Screenplay Text	98
	5.4	Love Calls You by Your Name	101
	5.5	Conclusion	106
	References		107
6	**The Reality of (Screen) Characters**		**111**
	Murray Smith		
	6.1	Introduction	111
	6.2	Just What Is a Character?	112
	6.3	The (Ir)reality of Characters	115
	6.4	Mimesis in Action	119
	6.5	The Artefact Strikes Back	122

	6.6	*Real Imaginings*	123
	6.7	*Conclusion*	127
	References		128
7	**"We Come to Realize": Screenwriting and Representations of Time**		131
	Adam Ganz		
	7.1	*Introduction*	131
	7.2	*The Effect of Sound*	135
	7.3	*Individual Techniques*	137
		7.3.1 *James Agee*	137
		7.3.2 *William Goldman*	142
		7.3.3 *Wes Craven*	144
	7.4	*Conclusion*	146
	References		147
8	**The Motion Picture Screenplay as Data: Quantifying the Stylistic Differences Between Dialogue and Scene Text**		151
	Warren Buckland		
	8.1	*Introduction*	151
	8.2	*Dialogue and Scene Text*	152
	8.3	*Method*	155
	8.4	*Results*	157
	8.5	*Discussion*	160
	8.6	*Conclusions*	165
	References		166
9	**Writer/Reader as Performer: Creating a Negotiated Narrative**		167
	Anna Zaluczkowska		
	9.1	*Introduction*	167
	9.2	*Theoretical Overview*	169
	9.3	*Projects*	172
	9.4	*Conclusion*	184
	References		186
10	**An Ontology of the Interactive Script**		189
	Rafael Leal		
	10.1	*Introduction*	189
	10.2	*A Complex Definition*	190
	10.3	*Servant of Two Masters*	192
	10.4	*Interactivity and Film Production*	195
	10.5	*The Poetics of Interactivity*	198
	10.6	*Conclusion*	203
	References		203

Part II: When/Where Screenwriting Historiography

11 Historiographies of Screenwriting   207
Steven Price
11.1 Introduction   207
11.2 Historiography and Academic Research   208
11.3 Histories of Screenwriting   210
11.4 Historiography of Screenplay Texts   213
11.5 Microhistories: Case Studies   217
11.6 Hidden and Future Histories   220
References   221

12 They Actually Had Scripts in Silent Films? Researching Screenwriting in the Silent Era   225
Tom Stempel
12.1 Getting Started   225
12.2 In the Belly of the Beast   227
12.3 Aftermath   233
References   235

13 Silent Screenwriting in Europe: Discourses on Authorship, Form, and Literature   237
Alexandra Ksenofontova
13.1 Introduction   237
13.2 Pre-War Screenwriting Discourse: The Famous Authors   238
13.3 The Second Half of the 1910s: Screenwriter vs. Director   244
13.4 The 1920s: Enter the (Published) Screenplay   248
13.5 Conclusion   253
References   255

14 When Women Wrote Hollywood: How Early Female Screenwriters Disappeared from the History of the Industry They Created. A Case Study of Four Female Screenwriters   259
Rosanne Welch
14.1 Introduction   259
14.2 Act One: How They Entered the Fledgling Industry…   260
    14.2.1 From the Theater   260
    14.2.2 From Journalism   262
    14.2.3 From Contests   262
14.3 Act Two: Why They Left the Now Mainstreamed Industry   263
    14.3.1 Studio Mismanagement (or Sabotage?) After Loss of Thalberg   264
    14.3.2 Mismanagement by Male Partners   265
    14.3.3 Forced to Work Outside the Hollywood Factory System   266

	14.4	Act Three: Why These Female Pioneers Disappeared from History	268
		14.4.1 Unreliable Male Narrators (Who Were Sometimes Partners)	268
		14.4.2 Unreliable Female Narrators	270
		14.4.3 Lack of Early Female Historians of Cinema	271
	14.5	Conclusion	271
	References		272
15	**Narrating with Music: Screenwriting Musical Numbers**		**277**
	Claus Tieber		
	15.1	Introduction	277
	15.2	Screenwriting and Music	278
	15.3	Story Conferences	278
	15.4	Screenplays	279
	15.5	Walter Reisch: The Great Waltz (1938)	280
	15.6	The Screenwriter as Musical Adviser	282
	15.7	Excursion: Music Changes Format	282
	15.8	Musical Numbers	283
	15.9	First the Song, then the Number	284
	15.10	Making the World a Stage for Music	285
	15.11	Music as Theme	289
	15.12	Conclusion	291
	References		292
16	**Women Screenwriters of Early Sinophone Cinema: 1916–1949**		**295**
	S. Louisa Wei		
	16.1	Introduction	295
	16.2	Early Women Screenwriters and Their Working Conditions	296
	16.3	Cases of Chinese Women's Screenplays and Films	300
		16.3.1 Marion E. Wong and The Curse of Quon Gwon (1916)	300
		16.3.2 Pu Shunqing and Cupid's Puppets (1925)	301
		16.3.3 Ai Xia and A Modern Girl (1933)	303
		16.3.4 Sheng Qinxian's Modern Women (1945)	305
		16.3.5 Eileen Chang's Unending Love (1947) and Long Live the Mistress (1948)	306
	16.4	Conclusion: Towards a Women's Cinema	307
	References		309

17	**A Historiography of Japanese Screenwriting** Lauri Kitsnik	**315**
17.1	Introduction	315
17.2	Screenwriting in Japanese Film Histories	316
	17.2.1 A Cursory History: "Sketches on Developmental History of Screenwriting" (1959)	318
	17.2.2 General Film Histories: Tanaka Jun'ichirō (1957) and Satō Tadao (1995)	321
17.3	A Comprehensive History of Screenwriting	323
	17.3.1 Structuring Principles	323
	17.3.2 Personalized Time Frames and National History	326
17.4	Conclusion	329
	References	330
18	**Writing Social Relevance: US Television Dramas in the Civil Rights Era** Caryn Murphy	**333**
18.1	Introduction	333
18.2	Integration Without Identification: The Defenders, "A Man Against Himself"	336
18.3	A Writer's Intent: The Nurses, "Express Stop from Lenox Ave"	338
18.4	Standards and Practices: Mr. Novak	340
18.5	Conclusion	345
	References	346
19	**Horror Bubbles: Andrés Caicedo's Weird Screenplays** Jerónimo Arellano	**349**
19.1	Introduction	349
19.2	Between Hollywood and McOndo	350
19.3	Caicedo's Screenplays	354
19.4	Caicedo and the Weird	358
19.5	Conclusion	361
	References	362
20	**Writers as Workers: The Making of a Film Trade Union in India** Rakesh Sengupta	**365**
20.1	Introduction	365
20.2	Precarity and Unionisation	367
	20.2.1 Creativity and Precarity	368
	20.2.2 Trade Unions in India	369
	20.2.3 Film Trade Union Movement in India	370
20.3	The Formation of FWA	371
	20.3.1 The Early years	372
	20.3.2 The Revival of FWA	373
	20.3.3 Differences and Disagreements	375

	20.4	Writers as Workers	377
		20.4.1 Supporting Precarious Writers	378
		20.4.2 Housing for Screenwriters	379
		20.4.3 Settling Disputes	380
		20.4.4 Minimum Wage	381
		20.4.5 Copyright Activism	381
		20.4.6 The Foundations for a Federation	382
	20.5	Conclusion	382
	References		383
21	The Evolving Depictions of Black South Africans in the Post-Apartheid Screenwriting Tradition		387
	Ziphozakhe Hlobo and Mpumelelo Skosana		
	21.1	Introduction	387
	21.2	Depictions	390
	21.3	The Dying Days of Apartheid	391
	21.4	A Hopeful Nation	395
	21.5	A Youthful Renaissance	398
	21.6	Finding a Place in the World	401
	21.7	Conclusion	404
	References		404

Part III: Who
Screenwriting and the Screen Industries

22	The International Writers' Room: A Transnational Approach to Serial Drama Development from an Italian Perspective		411
	Luisa Cotta Ramosino and Laura Cotta Ramosino		
	22.1	Introduction	411
	22.2	Writers, Showrunners and Producers: Differences Between the US and Europe	413
	22.3	Medici—Masters of Florence	414
	22.4	Devils	418
	22.5	Django	421
	22.6	Serial Eyes: Training New Authors for a New International Production Horizon	423
	22.7	Conclusions	426
	References		428
23	Writing Online Drama for Public Service Media in the Era of Streaming Platforms		431
	Petr Szczepanik and Dorota Vašíčková		
	23.1	Introduction	431
	23.2	Online-Only Content Development as a Site of Creative Innovation, "Youthification", and "Platformization" of Public Service Media	432

	23.3	Czech Public Service Television on a Journey Towards a VOD Platform	436
	23.4	TBH's Development	440
	23.5	Online-Only Content Development as an Accelerator of ČT's Institutional Change	446
	References		448
24	**Screenwriting for Children and Young Audiences**		453
	Eva Novrup Redvall		
	24.1	Introduction	453
	24.2	Books on Writing for Children and Young Audiences	454
	24.3	Screenwriting for Children and Young Audiences	456
	24.4	Screenwriting about Children and Young Audiences	458
	24.5	Screenwriting with Children and Young Audiences in an On-Demand Age	463
	24.6	Concluding Remarks and Cliffhangers	464
	References		466
25	**Imitations of Life? A Challenge for Black Screenwriters**		469
	Julius Ayodeji		
	25.1	Introduction	469
	25.2	Diversity Through the Screen	470
	25.3	Subtext, Dual Task Thinking and Double Consciousness	471
	25.4	The Screenplay and the Captivated Audience	474
	25.5	The Preservation of Self in Everyday Life: The Place of the Screenplay	475
		25.5.1 Strategy One: Passing—Denial	475
		25.5.2 Strategy Two: Assimilation—Enveloped	476
		25.5.3 Strategy Three: Mirroring—To See Oneself Through Others	478
	25.6	Conclusions	479
	References		480
26	**Beauties and Beasts: The Representation of National Identity Through Characterisation in Syrian-Lebanese Pan-Arab Dramas**		485
	Fadi G. Haddad and Alexander Dhoest		
	26.1	Introduction	485
	26.2	Characterisation: Schemata, Cognition, and Development	486
	26.3	National Culture in Representation: Syria and Lebanon	488
		26.3.1 Lebanon: A "Bridge Between the East and the West"	489
		26.3.2 Syria: The "Den of Arabism"	490
	26.4	Case Study: Syrian-Lebanese Dramas of Ramadan 2020	492
		26.4.1 Hawas [Obsession]	495
		26.4.2 Al-Saher [The Mentalist]	495

		26.4.3 Al-Nahhat (The Sculptor)	496
		26.4.4 Awlad Adam [Children of Adam]	497
	26.5	Discussion and Conclusion	499
	References		502
27	"That's a Chick's Movie!": How Women Are Excluded from Screenwriting Work		507
	Natalie Wreyford		
	27.1	Context	507
	27.2	Women's Interests	510
	27.3	Constructing Gender, Constructing Taste	512
	27.4	The Currency of Taste in the UK Film Labour Market	516
	27.5	Conclusion	521
	References		523
28	The Different American Legal Structures for Unionization of Writers for Stage and Screen		527
	Catherine L. Fisk		
	28.1	Introduction	527
	28.2	Origins and Evolution of the Guilds of Writers for Stage and Screen	529
	28.3	Independent Contractors and Copyright Law	530
	28.4	Independent Contractors and Labor and Antitrust Law	531
	28.5	Authors, Owners, and the Role of Mediating Institutions in Collaborative Creation	536
	28.6	Conclusion	538
	References		540

Part IV: How Approaches to Screen Storytelling

29	Random Access Memories: Screenwriting for Games		545
	Colin Harvey		
	29.1	Introduction	545
	29.2	Memory Games	546
	29.3	Terminology and Technology	547
	29.4	Storytelling in Video Games	548
	29.5	The Complexity of Games	550
	29.6	Characters	551
	29.7	Game Writers and Narrative Designers	553
	29.8	Case Study 1: Sniper Elite 4	554
	29.9	Case Study 2: Blood and Truth	557
	29.10	Conclusions	559
	References		560

30	\multicolumn{2}{l}{"Everybody Chips in Ten Cents, and Somehow It Seems to Add up to a Dollar": Exploring the Visual Toolbox of Animation Story Design}	563
	\multicolumn{2}{l}{Chris Pallant and Paul Wells}	
	30.1	Introduction	563
	30.2	The Animation Toolbox	565
	30.3	Micro-Narratives	569
	30.4	Frames of Reference	572
	30.5	Production Contexts	576
		30.5.1 The Feature Film	576
		30.5.2 The TV Episode	577
		30.5.3 The Independent Short Film	578
		30.5.4 Metamedia Writing	580
	30.6	Conclusions	581
	\multicolumn{2}{l}{References}	582
31	\multicolumn{2}{l}{The Short-Form Scripted Serial Drama: The Novice Showrunner's New Opportunity}	587
	\multicolumn{2}{l}{Debbie Danielpour}	
	31.1	Introduction	587
	31.2	Television Poetics	589
	31.3	Premium Prestige Long-Form Television Series	589
		31.3.1 Content	589
		31.3.2 Characters	590
		31.3.3 Structure	590
		31.3.4 Thematic Integrity of a Franchise	591
		31.3.5 Arc or Integrity of a Season	591
		31.3.6 Structure of Episodes	592
	31.4	The Short-Form Series	593
		31.4.1 Content and Characters	593
		31.4.2 Season Structure and Integrity	595
		31.4.3 Special	596
		31.4.4 The Stranger	598
		31.4.5 The Other F-Word	598
		31.4.6 Episode Structure	599
	31.5	Summary: Poetics of the Short-Form, Serialized Drama and Dramedy	601
		31.5.1 Content	602
		31.5.2 Character	602
		31.5.3 Structure	602
	\multicolumn{2}{l}{References}	603

32 The Plural Protagonist. Or: How to Be Many and Why 607
Ronald Geerts
- 32.1 Introduction 607
- 32.2 The Doxa as the Heritage of Realism 608
- 32.3 Universals and Archetypes 610
- 32.4 Thwarting the Doxa (From the Inside Out) 611
- 32.5 Beyond the Individual Character: The Plural Protagonist 613
- References 619

33 The Haptic Encounter: Scripting Female Subjectivity 623
Funke Oyebanjo
- 33.1 Introduction 623
- 33.2 Audiovisual Image: Viewership and Haptic Visuality 624
- 33.3 The Haptic Encounter 626
- 33.4 The Historical Drama 627
- 33.5 The Iyalode Character: Why Explore Efunsetan's Story? 630
- 33.6 The Haptic Encounter and Efunsetan's Story 631
  - 33.6.1 Internal Haptic Encounter Through the Frame 633
  - 33.6.2 External Haptic Encounter With the Frame 634
  - 33.6.3 Internal and External Haptic Encounters 636
- 33.7 The Haptic Encounter as Compassionate Involvement with Efunsetan 638
- 33.8 Conclusion 639
- References 640

34 Script Development from the Inside Looking Out: Telling a Transnational Story in the Australian Films 33 Postcards (Chan, 2011) and Strange Colours (Lodkina, 2017) 643
Margaret McVeigh
- 34.1 Introduction 643
- 34.2 What Does Script Development Mean? 644
- 34.3 Transnational Film Theory and Telling Stories for the Screen 645
- 34.4 Transnational Script Development 647
- 34.5 It's All in the Family: Script Development and the Transnational 649
- 34.6 Telling Transnational Stories and the Co-Production Model: 33 Postcards 650
- 34.7 Transnational Story Script Development: Strange Colours 654
- 34.8 Transnational Transformations 658
- References 659

35 Extended How? Narrative Structure in the Short and Long Versions of *The Lord of the Rings*, *Kingdom of Heaven*, and *Dances with Wolves* 663
Kristin Thompson
- 35.1 Models of Act Structure — 663
- 35.2 *Added Footage and Act Structure:* The Fellowship of the Ring — 666
- 35.3 *Added Footage and Act Structure:* The Two Towers — 669
- 35.4 *Added Footage and Act Structure:* The Return of the King — 673
- 35.5 *Added Footage and Act Structure:* Kingdom of Heaven — 676
- 35.6 *Added Footage and Act Structure:* Dances with Wolves — 680
- 35.7 Conclusion — 684
- References — 684

Part V: How To
Researching and Teaching Screenwriting: Discourses and Methods

36 Film Dramaturgy: A Practice and a Tool for the Researcher 689
Kerstin Stutterheim
- 36.1 Introduction — 689
- 36.2 Roots and Tradition — 690
- 36.3 Influential Dramaturgs — 693
- 36.4 Dramaturgy as Academic Discipline and Education — 694
- 36.5 The Merging of Dramaturgy for Theatre and for Film — 694
- 36.6 Dramaturgy and Screenwriting — 698
- 36.7 Dramaturgy as Tool for Analysis and Research — 702
- References — 703

37 Screenwriting Pedagogy in the United States: In Search of the Missing Pieces 709
Paul Joseph Gulino
- 37.1 Introduction — 709
- 37.2 Early Screenwriting Pedagogy — 709
- 37.3 Post-Studio Interregnum — 712
- 37.4 The Return of the Screenwriting Manual — 713
- 37.5 The Rise of the Film School — 716
- 37.6 Comparing the Craft of Screenwriting Across Eras — 718
  - 37.6.1 Hacksaw Ridge vs. Sergeant York — 720
  - 37.6.2 Sunset Boulevard vs. Hacks — 720
- 37.7 How to Teach Screenwriting — 722
- References — 723

38	Screenwriting Manuals and Pedagogy in Italy from the 1930s to the End of the Twentieth Century	725
	Mariapia Comand	
	38.1 Introduction	*725*
	38.2 Literacy and Ideology in the 1930s and 1940s	*726*
	38.3 The Pedagogy of Screenwriting During the Cold War	*729*
	38.4 From Script to Print Between the 1950s and 1970s	*732*
	38.5 Screenwriter-Professors. The 1980s and 1990s	*734*
	38.6 Conclusions	*737*
	References	*738*
39	Screenwriting, Short Film, and Pedagogy	743
	Díóg O'Connell	
	39.1 Introduction	*743*
	39.2 Narrative Aesthetics Explored	*745*
	39.3 Narrative Form Re-visited	*749*
	39.4 Case Study as Method in Pedagogy	*751*
	39.5 Conclusion	*754*
	References	*755*
40	Screenwriters in the Academy: The Opportunities of Research-Led Practice	759
	Craig Batty	
	40.1 Introduction	*759*
	40.2 Scene 1: The Creative Doctorate	*760*
	40.3 Scene 2: The Screenwriting Practice Doctorate	*762*
	40.4 Scene 3: Defining Screenwriting Practice Research	*763*
	40.5 Scene 4: Screenwriting Research as a Form of Script Development	*764*
	40.6 Scene 5: The Screenplay as a Research Artefact	*765*
	40.7 Scene 6: Screenwriters in the Academy	*768*
	40.8 Conclusion	*770*
	References	*770*

Author and Title Index 777

Subject Index 801

Editors and Contributors

About the Editors

Rosamund Davies has a background in professional practice in the film and television industries, in which she worked with both independent production companies and public funding bodies. As script editor and story consultant for Film London, she oversaw the development of around 100 projects.

She has been a Senior Lecturer in Creative and Media Writing at the University of Greenwich since 2001, founding and expanding the university's screenwriting provision. She also developed the Working in Creative Industries course, which became the basis for the book *Introducing the Creative Industries: Theory into Practice* (SAGE 2013), co-authored with Gauti Sigthorsson.

As an original member of the International Screenwriting Research Group, she has been active in the development of the field of Screenwriting Studies and her article "Screenwriting Strategies in Marguerite Duras's script for *Hiroshima, Mon Amour* (1960)" was included in the first ever issue of the *Journal of Screenwriting* (2010). Recent publications include "The Screenplay as Boundary Object" in *Journal of Screenwriting* 10 (2) and "Nordic Noir with an Icelandic Twist: Establishing a Shared Space for Collaboration Within European Coproduction" in *Script Development. Critical Approaches, Creative Practices, International Perspectives* (2021).

Paolo Russo is Senior Lecturer at Oxford Brookes University where he teaches Screenwriting, Story Development, Film Narratives and Film History, and co-leads CIRIN (Creative Industries Research & Innovation Network).

He published a *History of Italian Cinema* (2008), on Italian screenwriting and screenwriters (2014, 2015, 2016), about storylining in serial television drama (2017, 2018, 2019), complex screen narratives (2014), cyborgism and AI in film and TV dramas (2010, 2018), and about migration in film and television (2009, 2016, 2020, 2021).

He served as Chairperson and Secretary of the Screenwriting Research Network. He sits on the editorial boards of *Journal of Italian Cinema and Media Studies* (Intellect) and *L'avventura. International Journal of Italian Film and Media Landscapes* (Il Mulino). He served for several years on the editorial board of *New Review of Film Television Studies* (Routledge) and, briefly, of the *Journal of Screenwriting* (Intellect).

He is also a screenwriter. He was a writer on the animated series *Topo Gigio—The Series* (2020–) for RAI TV. He co-wrote the feature film *Tre giorni d'anarchia* (*Three Days of Anarchy*, 2006), premiered at 30+ international film festivals. He has also worked as a translator of screenplays and videogames, and as a script reader and editor for Italian and Hollywood majors and global companies.

Claus Tieber is currently the Principal Investigator of a research project about screenwriting musical numbers. He teaches Film Studies at universities in Vienna, Brno, Kiel, and Salamanca.

He sat on the Executive Council of the SRN for several years, most of them as Chairperson. He is a founding member of Netzwerk Drehbuchforschung, which promotes academic screenwriting research in German-speaking countries.

After working as a commissioning editor for TV movies at the Austrian Broadcast Company (ORF), he wrote his Habilitation (post-doc thesis) about the history of the American screenplay (*Schreiben für Hollywood: Das Drehbuch im Studiosystem*, Lit Verlag 2008) and switched from practice to research. His publications also include a monograph on storytelling in silent cinema (*Stummfilmdramaturgie. Erzählweisen des Amerikanischen Feature Films 1917–1927*) and an edited (with Anna K. Windisch) volume on film music in silent cinema (*The Sounds of Silent Films: New Perspectives on History, Theory and Practice*, Palgrave Macmillan, 2014).

Contributors

Jerónimo Arellano is Associate Professor of Latin American Literature at Brandeis University. He is the author of *Magical Realism and the History of the Emotions in Latin America* (Bucknell University Press, 2015) as well as a series of interconnected articles on Latin American screenwriting. In 2016, he edited a dossier of essays on comparative media studies for *Revista Hispánica Moderna*.

Julius Ayodeji is a Playwright and Senior Lecturer, predominantly teaching screenwriting and filmmaking at undergraduate and postgraduate levels. Currently, the Course Director for B.A. (Hons.) Filmmaking at Leeds Beckett University, he has also written and presented a number of papers for academic conferences around the world and acts as a script consultant. Currently developing a television series about travel and colonialism, over the last ten years he has written primarily for the stage with a number of productions and rehearsed readings of his work. He has also written a number of unproduced film scripts.

Craig Batty is Dean of Research at the University of South Australia. He is the author, co-author and editor of 15 books, including *The Palgrave Handbook of Script Development* (2021), *Script Development: Critical Approaches, Creative Practices, International Perspectives* (2021), *The Doctoral Experience: Student Stories from the Creative Arts and Humanities* (2019), *Writing for the Screen: Creative and Critical Approaches (2nd ed.)* (2019) and *Screen Production Research: Creative Practice as a Mode of Enquiry* (2018). He has published widely on the topics of screenwriting practice, screenwriting theory, creative practice research and doctoral supervision. He is also a screenwriter and script consultant, with experiences in short film, feature film, television and online drama—and this has led to his passion for practice-based research in screenwriting.

Rita Benis is an award-winning screenwriter who has worked in cinema since 2000 and collaborated with Teresa Villaverde, Margarida Gil, Inês Oliveira, António Cunha Telles, Jorge Cramez, among others. Researcher at Center for Comparative Studies (Faculty of Letters, University of Lisbon), she's currently finishing her doctorate on Manoel de Oliveira's screenplays. Master in Comparative Literature, she taught *Screenwriting* and *History of Cinema*. Member of the research project *Cinema and the World*, she co-edited the electronic magazine *Falso Movimento* (also published: Documenta 2015). She has translated books and published articles and books on the relationship between writing and image. Recently, she co-edited the Portuguese volume *Escrita e Imagem [Writing and image]* (Documenta, 2020) and wrote the chapter "How *Angelica* Became *The Strange Case of Angelica*: from the idea to the script to the book to the film", published in *Palgrave Handbook of Script Development*, edited by Craig Batty and Stayci Taylor (Springer, 2021).

Warren Buckland is Reader in Film Studies at Oxford Brookes University. He is the author or editor of several books, including *Wes Anderson's Symbolic Storyworld* (2019), *Hollywood Puzzle Films* (ed., 2014), *Film Theory: Rational Reconstructions* (2012) and *Puzzle Films: Complex Storytelling in Contemporary Cinema* (ed., 2009).

Mariapia Comand is Full Professor at the University of Udine where she teaches screenwriting (since 2002) and Italian Cinema. She is Director of the Digital Storytelling Lab and a member of the executive committee of the journal *L'avventura. International Journal of Italian Film and Media Landscape*. She is editor of the first history of Italian screenwriting (*Sulla carta. Storia e storie della sceneggiatura in Italia*, 2006).

Laura Cotta Ramosino was a consultant story editor for the first channel of Italian Public Broadcasting, for eleven years. She is now a creative producer at leading Italian production company Cattleya, for local and international projects. As a screenwriter, she is the author (with Luisa Cotta Ramosino and Paolo Marchesini) of TV series *Made in Italy,* about the birth of the Italian fashion system, which has been broadcast on Amazon. She has a Ph.D. in Ancient History and is the author (with Luisa Cotta Ramosino and Cristiano Dognini) of a study about the evolving image of Roman history in cinema and television. She has taught docudrama at the Centro Sperimentale di Cinematografia in Palermo and regularly collaborates with Catholic University of Milan's Masters in International Screenwriting and Production. She has written a number of essays on TV and cinema production.

Luisa Cotta Ramosino is Director, Original Series, at Netflix Italia. Previously, she was a freelance screenwriter and creative producer for leading Italian television companies. She has been involved in many international projects (among them *Medici-Masters of Florence, Leonardo* and *Devils*) and she has created and written (with Laura Cotta Ramosino and Paolo Marchesini) *Made in Italy*, a TV series about the birth of the Italian fashion system, which has been broadcast by Amazon. She has a Ph.D. in Applied Linguistics from the Università Cattolica del Sacro Cuore in Milan and attended a Masters in Media and Entertainment Management in New York. She collaborates with Catholic University of Milan's Masters in International Screenwriting and Production. She is the author of a book about the image of Roman history in cinema and television and a number of essays on Italian television productions.

Debbie Danielpour writes screenplays, fiction and libretti. A professor of fiction and screenwriting for over twenty years, she is now at Boston University where she is professor of screenwriting and associate chair of the department of film and television. Her seventh motion picture screenplay, *We're All Here,* is currently in pre-production with Rimer Films. She has written for television and consults for feature film production companies. Her short fiction and essays have been published in literary and academic journals, and her libretti include *Margaret Garner, The Great Good Thing* and *The King's Ear*. She has an AB from Harvard College, an M.A. in film production and screenwriting from San Francisco State University, and an MFA in fiction and literature from the Bennington Writing Seminars.

Alexander Dhoest is Professor and Chair of the Department of Communication Studies at the University of Antwerp (Belgium). He teaches and does research on popular culture and media (in particular TV drama), focusing specifically on issues of representation as well as national and cultural identity. He has published widely on these issues. His full profile, including a list of publications, is available at www.uantwerpen.be/alexander-dhoest.

Catherine L. Fisk is the Barbara Nachtrieb Armstrong Distinguished Professor of Law at the University of California, Berkeley. She is the author of five books, including *Writing for Hire: Unions, Hollywood, and Madison Avenue* (Harvard University Press 2016) and *Working Knowledge: Employee*

Innovation and the Rise of Corporate Intellectual Property, 1800–1930 (University of North Carolina Press 2009). She has worked with Brent Salter, "The Fragility of Labor Relations in American Theatre" (*Ohio State Law Journal* forthcoming 2022), and with Michael Szalay, "Story Work: Non-Proprietary Autonomy and Contemporary Television Writing" (*Television and New Media* 2016).

Adam Ganz is Professor of Screenwriting at Royal Holloway and head of the Writers Room at StoryFutures Academy, the National Centre for Immersive Storytelling. He is co-author (with Steven Price) of *Robert de Niro at Work: From Screenplay to Screen Performance* (2020) and has published widely on the screenplay. He also writes for film, TV and radio. *The Filmmaker's House*, co-written with Marc Isaacs, was described by *Sight and Sound* as "deeply empathetic and kind-hearted". In 2022, he was writer in residence at the University of Innsbruck.

Ronald Geerts teaches and researches screenwriting studies and theatre studies at the Vrije Universiteit Brussel and the Université Libre de Bruxelles. He also taught at the School of Arts RITCS, Brussels, and the University of Antwerp. He served on the executive council of the Screenwriting Research Network (SRN) and co-organized the 3rd International SRN Conference in 2011 in Brussels. His research interests lie on the crossroads between screenwriting, theatre and performance studies. He also combines his training as a camera and sound person, editor and screenwriter with his academic background in film and theatre studies. He has published on genetic screenwriting research, character dramaturgy, Belgian film and screenwriting and contemporary Flemish theatre in an international context. Recently, he co-edited the "Seriality" special issue of the *Journal of Literary and Intermedial Crossings* and a special issue of *Documenta* on the work of dramaturgy pioneer Marianne Van Kerkhoven.

Paul Joseph Gulino is an award-winning screenwriter and playwright, whose book, *Screenwriting: The Sequence Approach,* has been adopted as a textbook at schools and universities around the globe. His latest book, *The Science of Screenwriting: The Neuroscience Behind Storytelling Strategies,* was published in 2018. His credits include two produced screenplays and numerous commissioned works and script consultations; his plays have been produced in New York and Los Angeles. He has lectured in the US and Europe, most recently at the Story Academy in Sweden and for Disney Animation. He's been featured in interviews on Film Courage and on podcasts for Bulletproof Screenwriting, Trendfollowing, and Robot Breakfast. He studied screenwriting at Columbia University with František "Frank" Daniel and Milos Forman and taught screenwriting at the University of Southern California for five years before accepting a position at Chapman University in 1998, where he is currently a tenured professor.

Fadi G. Haddad is an assistant professor of production and storytelling at the American University in Dubai (United Arab Emirates) and a Ph.D. candidate in Film Studies and Visual Culture at the University of Antwerp (Belgium). Through a diverse experience across the filmmaking field since 2010, he has worked as a director, writer, editor and creative producer for several short and feature films. His doctoral research is focused on Pan-Arab television series and transnational Arab identity.

Colin Harvey is a writer and narrative designer working primarily in games but also prose, comics, radio and Virtual Reality. His credits include the screenplays for *Blood and Truth* (Sony, 2019) and *Sniper Elite 4* (2017), licensed tie-in material for the *Doctor Who* and *Highlander* ranges published by Big Finish Productions, comic stories for *2000AD* and *Commando*, and short fiction for Black Library's *Warhammer—Age of Sigmar* range. He is also the author of *Fantastic Transmedia* (Palgrave, 2015), an academic monograph exploring crossmedia storytelling in relation to a range of large- and small-scale science fiction and fantasy franchises including *Star Wars, The Lord of the Rings, Halo* and the Marvel Cinematic Universe. His Ph.D. explores the interrelationship of storytelling and play in video game media. He wrote and presented "The Origins of the Metaverse" for BBC Radio Four in March 2022.

Ziphozakhe Hlobo is a Nelson Mandela University Media Studies graduate. She currently works as a Production Analyst for the Kwa-Zulu Natal Film Commission and enjoys her work which includes managing the development of emerging filmmakers. She has written and produced various lifestyle and reality TV programmes commissioned by the SABC and Multichoice.

Lauri Kitsnik is Associate Professor at the Graduate School of Humanities and Social Sciences, Hiroshima University. His main research interests lie at the intersection of Japanese literary and audio-visual cultures. In particular, he has published essays on adaptation, documentary film, screenwriting and stardom. His writing has appeared in *arts, Asian Cinema, Film Studies, Japan Review, Japanese Studies, Journal of Japanese and Korean Cinema, Journal of Screenwriting, Screen* and several edited volumes, including *Women Screenwriters: An International Guide*.

Alexandra Ksenofontova is currently a postdoctoral researcher at the Cluster of Excellence "Temporal Communities: Doing Literature in a Global Perspective". She holds a Ph.D. in comparative literature from the Freie Universität Berlin. Her award-winning first book *The Modernist Screenplay: Experimental Writing for Silent Film* (Palgrave Macmillan, 2020) explores the conjunctions between literary modernism and the screenwriting of the European avant-gardes of the 1920s. She is the co-founder of the German research network *Drehbuchforschung* that seeks to increase the visibility of screenwriting research in the German-speaking academia. She served as the Early Career Representative on the Executive Council of the Screenwriting Research Network in

2019–2020 and has been a member of the editorial board of the *Journal of Screenwriting* since 2019. Besides screenwriting, her research interests include literary translation, theory of the novel, philosophies of time and Otherness, and narratology.

Rafael Leal is a screenwriter, executive producer and VR creator based in Rio de Janeiro, Brazil. Professor of Screenwriting at the Pontifical Catholic University of Rio de Janeiro and Ph.D. Candidate in Film at Fluminense Federal University, he researches the Poetics of interactive and immersive narratives. His creations include the feature film *Too Soon* (FOX) and TV shows *Queenpin* (CineBrasilTV) and *Jungle Pilot* (NBC Universal), whose development was subject of the chapter "Transcultural Collaboration in Screenwriting: Jungle Pilot's Case Study", published in the book *Transcultural Screenwriting: Telling Stories for a Global World* (Cambridge Scholars).

Ian W. Macdonald co-founded the Screenwriting Research Network in 2008. He was a founding co-editor of the *Journal of Screenwriting* and of the book series *Palgrave Studies in Screenwriting*. He has worked for the BBC, IBA and BFI Reference Libraries, as Associate Producer for London Weekend Television, as Director of Training for the North East Media Training Centre, Gateshead, as Head of the Northern Film School at Leeds Beckett University (where he was also Reader in Screen Studies) and as Associate Professor at the University of Leeds from 2006 to 2017. His book *Screenwriting Poetics and the Screen Idea* (2013) has been described as "enlightening" by Emeritus Professor David Bordwell. The chapter on Eliot Stannard demonstrates "exemplary scholarship" says Emeritus Professor Charles Barr, and the book is "required reading for ourselves and our students" according to Professor Jonathan Powell, the former Head of BBC Drama.

Margaret McVeigh is Head, Screenwriting and Contextual Studies, Griffith Film School, Griffith University, Australia. She is Chair of the SRN (Screenwriting Research Network) 2021–2022. Margaret has extensive national and international industry experience in Public Relations and Post-Production and has worked as Commissioning Editor for Wiley publishers and as a Writer of *ABC Splash,* for the Australian National Broadcaster. She is co-editor of *Transcultural Screenwriting: Telling Stories for a Global World* (2017). Her chapter, "Work in Progress: The Writing of Shortchanged" in *The Palgrave Handbook of Screen Production* (2019), explores her creative process writing a feature film, development-funded by Screen Queensland. She is co-writer of the award-winning feature documentary, *Love Opera* (2019), which premiered at the Brisbane International Film Festival 2019, won Best Documentary at the Australian Screen Industry Network Awards, was released in Australian and New Zealand cinemas in 2020, and screened at Cannes Cinephiles in the Cannes Film Festival 2021.

Caryn Murphy is a professor in the Department of Radio-TV-Film at the University of Wisconsin Oshkosh, where she teaches courses in film and television history and criticism. She earned her Ph.D. in Media and Cultural Studies from the Department of Communication Arts at the University of Wisconsin-Madison. Her research on the politics of race and gender in media representations has appeared in *Media History*, the *Journal of Screenwriting*, the *Historical Journal of Film, Radio, and Television*, and many edited volumes. She is currently at work on a book about television writers and producers in the early network era of the 1960s.

Díóg O'Connell lectures in Film & Media Studies specializing in Irish Cinema, Television Drama and Scriptwriting at National Film School, IADT, and is Programme Chair of BA in New Media Studies. She is the author of *New Irish Storytellers: Narrative Strategies in Film* (Intellect, 2010) and co-editor of *Documentary in a Changing State* (Cork University Press, 2012). She has written extensively on Irish Film and Media for academic books, journals and magazines and has presented her research at academic conferences in Ireland, Europe and America. She has worked in film and television drama production and as part of the Writers' Team for Irish television drama productions. She is part of Film EU (a collaboration between Film Schools in Ireland, Portugal, Belgium and Estonia) and is an Academic Leads in Creative Futures Academy (a collaboration between IADT, UCD and NCAD).

Funke Oyebanjo is a script consultant, trainer and screenwriter. Her script *The Window* was produced for Channel Four, and *The Land* was selected for development at the Berlin festival's talent campus. She has written episodes of Netflix's *The Governor* and joined the writers' team of Archery's upcoming drama *Lagos*. A Ph.D. candidate at Middlesex University, she was recently appointed a Royal Literary Fellow and a lecturer at the University of Greenwich. Previously, she has worked at University of the Arts London, Queen Mary University of London, Arts University Bournemouth, BBC Writer's Room, BBC World service, the UK Film Council and Creative England. She was a juror for Skillset's Creative and Innovative Award for Women in Television and Film, as well as for I Will Tell Women Over Fifty film festivals. She was also a development consultant with the Arena Majicka in Norway and is the webfeet programmer for Raindance.

Chris Pallant is Professor of Animation and Screen Studies at Canterbury Christ Church University. He is the author of *Demystifying Disney: A History of Disney Feature Animation* (Bloomsbury, 2011), *Animated Landscapes: History, Form and Function* (Bloomsbury, 2015), *Beyond Bagpuss: A History of Smallfilms Animation Studio* (BFI, 2022), editor of *Animation: Critical and Primary Sources* (Bloomsbury, 2021), and co-author of *Storyboarding: A Critical History* (Palgrave, 2015) and *Snow White and the Seven Dwarfs: New Perspectives on Production, Reception, Legacy* (Bloomsbury, 2021). He is the founding editor of Bloomsbury's "Animation: Key Films/Filmmakers" book series. He currently serves as President for the Society for Animation Studies.

Steven Price is Professor Emeritus of English Literature at Bangor University. He is the author of *The Screenplay: Authorship, Theory and Criticism* and *A History of the Screenplay*, co-author of *Storyboarding: A Critical History* and *Robert De Niro at Work: From Screenplay to Screen Performance*, and former principal editor of the *Journal of Screenwriting*.

Eva Novrup Redvall is Associate Professor at the University of Copenhagen where she heads the Section for Film Studies and Creative Media Industries. She has published widely on screenwriting and production, e.g. the monograph *Writing and Producing Television Drama in Denmark: From* The Kingdom *to* The Killing (2013) and the co-edited collections *European Film and Television Co-production: Policy and Practice* (2018) and *Danish Television Drama: Global Lessons from a Small Nation* (2020). She has been a member of the Screenwriting Research Network since its founding, serves on the editorial board of *The Journal of Screenwriting* and is one of the three book series editors for Palgrave Studies in Screenwriting. She is the Principal Investigator of the research project "Reaching Young Audiences: Serial Fiction and Cross-Media Storyworlds for Children and Young Audiences" (2019–2024, supported by Independent Research Fund Denmark and based at the University of Copenhagen, grant 9037-00145B).

Rakesh Sengupta teaches film and media at the University of Toronto. He has previously taught at the University of Amsterdam and holds a Ph.D. from SOAS University of London. His research interests include film history, screenwriting, media archaeology, South Asian cinemas and media cultures in the Global South. His academic and public writing have appeared in *BioScope: South Asian Screen Studies*, *Theory, Culture & Society*, and *The Wire*, among other journals and edited volumes.

Mpumelelo Skosana graduated from the University of the Witwatersrand with an advanced degree in Economic Development and now works as a Senior Communication Director with FTI Consulting in Johannesburg. He has always been a keen observer and analyst of society. In recent years, he has grown passionate about the art of telling stories and hopes to turn his commercial skills to finding international distribution and marketing solutions for African audio-visual content.

Murray Smith is Professor of Philosophy, Art, and Film and Director of the Aesthetics Research Centre at the University of Kent. He was President of the Society for Cognitive Studies of the Moving Image (2014–2017) and a Laurance S. Rockefeller Fellow at Princeton University's Center for Human Values (2017–2018). He has published widely on film, art and aesthetics. His publications include *Film, Art, and the Third Culture: A Naturalized Aesthetics of Film* (Oxford University Press, 2017; revised paperback 2020),

Trainspotting (BFI, revised edition 2021) and *Engaging Characters: Fiction, Emotion, and the Cinema* (Oxford University Press, revised edition 2022).

Tom Stempel grew up in Bloomington, Indiana, watching movies at the Indiana, Princess, Harris Grande, Von Lee and Roxy theatres. He graduated from Yale in 1963 and then received an MFA in Screenwriting in 1970 from the University of California at Los Angeles (UCLA). While at UCLA, he conducted an oral history interview with Nunnally Johnson, the screenwriter of *The Grapes of Wrath* and many other films. He returned to UCLA in 1971. He wrote his Ph.D. dissertation on Johnson, and it was published as a book in 1980 under the title of *Screenwriter: The Life and Times of Nunnally Johnson*. It was the first biography of a screenwriter to focus on his contributions to the films he wrote. He followed that book up in 1988 with *FrameWork: A History of Screenwriting in the American Film*, the first history of American screenwriting. In 1992 with the book *Storytellers to the Nation: A History of American Television Writing*, he has written three other books and many articles. From 1971 to 2011, he taught film history and screenwriting at Los Angeles City College, where he is a professor emeritus.

Kerstin Stutterheim is Professor in Creative Practice and Director of Research at the School of Arts and Creative Industries at Edinburgh Napier University. Before, she was the Rektor (principal) of the Academy of Media Arts KHM Cologne, Professor at Bournemouth University and Professor for dramaturgy and Aesthetics of audio-visual media at Film University Babelsberg Konrad Wolf. She has been a filmmaker and dramaturg for film since 1990, and a member of the German Film Academy. Her most recent monograph is *Modern Film Dramaturgy—An Introduction*, published by Peter Lang in 2019.

Petr Szczepanik is an associate professor at Charles University (Prague, Czech Republic), and his research focuses on East-Central European screen industries. He co-edited *Behind the Screen: Inside European Production Culture* (Palgrave, 2013) and *Digital Peripheries: The Online Circulation of Audiovisual Content from the Small Market Perspective* (Springer, 2020). His latest book is *Screen Industries in East-Central Europe* (Bloomsbury, 2021). He is currently leading the Screen Industries in Central and Eastern Europe Research Group (Charles University) and a joint research project with Czech public service television, focusing on its online strategy.

Kristin Thompson is an Honorary Fellow in the Department of Communication Arts, the University of Wisconsin-Madison, where she received her Ph.D. in cinema studies. She is the author or co-author of eleven books, including *Breaking the Glass Armor: Neoformalist Film Analysis* (Princeton, 1988), *Storytelling in the New Hollywood: Understanding Classical Narrative Technique* (Harvard, 1999) and *The Frodo Franchise: The Lord of the Rings and Modern Hollywood*. Since 2006, she has, with David Bordwell, maintained a blog, *Observations on Film Art*, and contributes video essays to a series of the same name on The Criterion Channel.

Dorota Vašíčková currently works at Česká televize (ČT)—the Czech public service broadcaster—where she is responsible for online-only content commissioning, while also participating in the formulation of ČT's new online-only production strategy. Since her undergraduate studies in the Department of Film Studies at Charles University in Prague, she has been focusing on web series and digital platforms. She is now working on her master's thesis, in which she uses ethnographic observations to analyse the development of ČT's first slate of online-only productions.

S. Louisa Wei is a professor at the City University of Hong Kong, a documentary director, a screenwriter and a member of the Hong Kong Director's Guild. She writes extensively on Chinese female directors and women's cinema, having published many articles, book chapters, encyclopaedia entries and two books on the topic. Her two feature documentaries, *Golden Gate Girls* (2014) and *Havana Divas* (2018), respectively focus on how Chinese language films and Cantonese operas travelled in North and Latin America from the 1920s to the 1960s. Both films have received positive reviews and reportage from major media like *The Hollywood Reporter* and BBC. She also worked as a screenplay writer and translator, with two feature films under her name.

Rosanne Welch serves as Executive Director of Stephens College MFA in TV and Screenwriting where she created History of Screenwriting courses and teaches One-Hour Drama. Her writing credits include *Beverly Hills 90210*, *Picket Fences*, *ABCNEWS: Nightline* and *Touched by an Angel*. She edited *When Women Wrote Hollywood* (2018), runner-up for the Susan Koppelman Award in feminist studies. She co-edited *Women in American History: A Social, Political, and Cultural Encyclopedia* (nominated as 2018 Outstanding References Sources List and Best Historical Materials by the American Library Association) and wrote *Why The Monkees Matter: Teenagers, Television and American Popular Culture*. She serves as Book Reviews editor for *Journal of Screenwriting*; and on the Editorial Board for both *Written By* and *California History Journal*. Since 2019, she is on the Executive Council of the Screenwriting Research Network. Welch's talk at TEDxCPP: https://www.youtube.com/watch?v=8JFNsqKBRnA.

Paul Wells has published widely in Animation and Film Studies, and written and directed numerous projects for theatre, radio, television and film. His publications include *Understanding Animation* (Routledge), *Animation and America* (Rutgers University Press), *The Fundamentals of Animation* (AVA), *The Animated Bestiary: Animals, Cartoons and Culture* (Rutgers University Press), *Drawing for Animation* (AVA, with master animator Joanna Quinn) and *Re-Imagining Animation* (AVA, with Johnny Hardstaff, leading graphic). His professional engagements include working with writers from *The Simpsons* and *Spongebob Squarepants*, and developing animated shorts, children's series, documentaries and features in Norway, Sweden, Belgium, The Netherlands and the US. He is Director of the Animation Academy, a consultant for the BBC's *Animation Nation* and Chair of the Association of British Animation Collections (ABAC), a collaborative initiative with the BFI, BAFTA and the National Media Museum.

Natalie Wreyford is Lecturer in Culture, Media and Creative Industries at King's College London. Her research focuses on inequality of opportunity in creative professions. She is author of *Gender Inequality in Screenwriting Work*. In 2021, she wrote "Creative Majority", a report for the All-Party Parliamentary Group for Creative Diversity on "what works" to improve equity, diversity and inclusion in creative jobs and is currently working on the next stage: pathways (and obstacles) from education into creative work. She was researcher on the AHRC-funded "Calling the Shots: Women and Contemporary Film Culture in the UK". Recent publications include the report "Locked Down and Locked Out: The impact of the COVID-19 pandemic on mothers working in the UK television industry", and (with Shelley Cobb) "'Could you hire someone female or from an ethnic minority?': Being both: Black, Asian and other minority women working in British film production" in *Black Film British Cinema II*.

Anna Zaluczkowska is a reader in film at Leeds Beckett University and teaches screenwriting and film production. She is an award-winning writer and filmmaker and her research is related to all forms of storytelling with a particular interest in participation and new media technologies. Her latest productions include *Red Branch Heroes* http://www.redbranchheroes.com/anna-red-branch-rev/ and *Secret Story Network* https://www.secretstorynetwork.com.

List of Figures

Fig. 3.1	SCAS modelling based on Hitchins' five-layer model	51
Fig. 3.2	Schematic illustration of cellular automata for *Westworld*, Season 1, Episode 1 (2016)	54
Fig. 3.3	Schematic illustration of cellular automata for *The Voorman Problem* (2011)	57
Fig. 3.4	Rules governing interactions between hosts and guests in *Westworld*	60
Fig. 3.5	Modularity of main communities of characters in *Bodyguard*	61
Fig. 3.6	Conflicted, push–pull dynamic relations with communities in *Bodyguard*	62
Fig. 3.7	Typical representation of a block universe	64
Fig. 3.8	Maeve's full attribute matrix as shown in *Westworld*, Season 1, Episode 6 "The Adversary" (2016)	65
Fig. 3.9	Primary attributes for Maeve in *Westworld* Season 1, Episode 6 "The Adversary" (2016) (author's re-elaboration)	66
Fig. 3.10	Likely projection of Maeve's modified primary attributes (author's elaboration)	67
Fig. 6.1	Levels of narration, character, and person in *Bye Bye Africa* (Haroun 1999)	126
Fig. 8.1	Bar graph of the numerical data in Table 8.1	159
Fig. 8.2	Ratio (logarithmic scale) between dialogue and scene text	159
Fig. 9.1	*Secret Story Network* logo (*Source* Bellyfeel Productions)	168
Fig. 9.2	IOU *Fulcrum* Set (fulcrum small)	174
Fig. 9.3	IOU *Fulcrum* (web-image)	175
Fig. 9.4	*Red Branch Heroes*—Who do you choose? (under Jpeg 3) (*Source* Bellyfeel Productions)	177
Fig. 9.5	*Red Branch Heroes*—Voting (under Negotiated Narrative) (*Source* Bellyfeel Productions)	179
Fig. 9.6	*Operation Black Antler*—Briefing (press) (*Source* Blast Theory)	181
Fig. 9.7	*Secret Story Network*—The app (Mock Up) (*Source* Bellyfeel Productions)	182

Fig. 9.8	*Secret Story Network*—Waiting for you (wfy) (*Source* Bellyfeel Productions)	184
Fig. 20.1	SWA office wall with images of illustrious Indian screenwriters (*Source* author's own photograph, courtesy of SWA)	366
Fig. 20.2	Unorganised archival records of the SWA office in Mumbai (*Source* author's own photograph, courtesy of SWA)	367
Fig. 20.3	Advertisement of poetry recital organised by FWA (*Source* author's own photograph of original, courtesy of SWA)	374
Fig. 20.4	Donations for Benevolent fund after an FWA meeting in 1971 (*Source* author's own photograph of original, courtesy of SWA)	379
Fig. 20.5	Inder Kumar Gujral (middle) and Krishan Chander (right) at the Film Writers' Convention in 1972 (*Source* author's own photograph of original, courtesy of SWA)	380
Fig. 30.1	The Animation Spectrum (Wells 2018, 79–95)	564
Fig. 35.1	Galadriel presents the Fellowship members with brooches that will become important in the second film (*Source* Screenshot from *The Fellowship of the Ring* DVD edition, 2002, EiV)	668
Fig. 35.2	Legolas holds up a piece of *lembas* and explains: "Lembas! Elvish waybread. One small bite is enough to fill the stomach of a grown man" (*Source* Screenshot from *The Fellowship of the Ring* DVD edition, 2002, EiV)	669
Fig. 35.3	A new shot of Saruman declaring his goal to defeat Rohan (*Source* Screenshot from *The Two Towers* DVD edition, 2003, EiV)	671
Fig. 35.4	A new flashback with Denethor interrupting a happy scene between Boromir and Faramir and berating the latter (*Source* Screenshot from *The Two Towers* DVD edition, 2003, EiV)	672
Fig. 35.5	An added scene as Gandalf explains to Pippin: "There's no leaving this city. Help must come to us" (*Source* Screenshot from *The Return of the King* DVD edition, 2004, EiV)	674
Fig. 35.6	A brief romantic scene between Éowyn and Faramir establishes them as a couple. In the theatrical version, there is no hint of this until they are together during the coronation scene (*Source* Screenshot from *The Return of the King* DVD edition, 2004, EiV)	676
Fig. 35.7	Balian's examination of a model siege tower has different implications in the shorter and longer versions (*Source* Screenshot from *Kingdom of Heaven* DVD edition, 2006, 20th Century Fox Home Entertainment)	678
Fig. 35.8	In an added subplot, Sibylla's son is crowned Baldwin V (*Source* Screenshot from *Kingdom of Heaven* DVD edition, 2006, 20th Century Fox Home Entertainment)	679

Fig. 35.9	In both versions of *Dances with Wolves*, a row of bridles signals Dunbar's mystification at the deserted fort, but the audience's reaction is different in each case (*Source* Screenshot from *Dances with Wolves* DVD edition, 1991, Pathé)	681
Fig. 35.10	The extended version shows the commander of the fort explaining the reasons for leading his men to desert (*Source* Screenshot from *Dances with Wolves* DVD edition, 1991, Pathé)	682

List of Tables

Table 2.1	Synthesis of the orthodoxy, based on a sample survey of 103 US texts/fragments 2015–2016 (Macdonald 2021a, 21–22)	31
Table 3.1	Quantitative analysis of components for a CA model comparing various screenwriting formats	58
Table 8.1	A selection of linguistic categories in *Citizen Kane*'s dialogue and scene text (organized according to ratio)	158
Table 8.2	The relativity category in *Citizen Kane*'s dialogue and scene text (organized according to ratio)	163
Table 16.1	The trajectory of above-the-line women filmmakers in early sinophone cinemas (1916–1949)	299
Table 26.1	Series included in the case study	493
Table 26.2	National character schema grid	494
Table 35.1	Added footage and act structure: *The Fellowship of the Ring*	667
Table 35.2	Added footage and act structure: *The Two Towers*	670
Table 35.3	Added footage and act structure: *The Return of the King*	673
Table 35.4	Added footage and act structure: *Kingdom of Heaven*	677
Table 35.5	Added footage and act structure: *Dances with Wolves*	680

CHAPTER 1

Introduction

Rosamund Davies, Paolo Russo, and Claus Tieber

Screenwriting research is a relatively young arena of enquiry in its own right. It has emerged in the last couple of decades at the intersection of disciplines such as film studies, film philosophy, media studies, literary and adaptation studies, drama studies, performance studies, game studies, communication studies, production studies, production culture research, reception studies, and revisionist histories. A growing number of researchers have developed this scholarship, adopting a range of methodological approaches: from more traditional ones, such as philology, dramaturgy, narratology, genre theory, aesthetic criticism, and textual and cultural analysis; to others such as cognitive film theory and other perspectives that draw on psychology and neuroscience, genetic criticism, practice-led and practice-based research, data visualisation, and other forms of software-assisted analysis.

R. Davies (✉)
School of Stage and Screen, University of Greenwich, London, UK
e-mail: r.davies@greenwich.ac.uk

P. Russo (✉)
School of Arts, Oxford Brookes University, Oxford, UK
e-mail: paolo.russo@brookes.ac.uk

C. Tieber (✉)
Institut für Theater-, Film- und Medienwissenschaft, University of Vienna, Vienna, Austria
e-mail: claus.tieber@univie.ac.at

© The Author(s), under exclusive license to Springer Nature Switzerland AG 2023
R. Davies et al. (eds), *The Palgrave Handbook of Screenwriting Studies*,
https://doi.org/10.1007/978-3-031-20769-3_1

Our aim, when we set out to design *The Palgrave Handbook of Screenwriting Studies*, was to represent both the range and the commonalities of such scholarship. Screenwriting studies, in our view, entail a specific approach, in the sense that they are concerned with studying the screenwriting process (understood as including all stages of development of a screen idea and all the people and professions involved in the related processes) and the screenplay text (in all its manifestations), as opposed to traditional analyses of finished screen products. However, this approach maintains an openness to and acknowledges the influences of the multi- and cross-disciplinary traditions mentioned above. Its composite, evolving parameters mean that screenwriting studies shape and keep their own distinctiveness as a constant work in progress, defined *as we go* by scholars and practitioners through their research and works.

1.1 Scholarship and Directions in Screenwriting Studies

Influential works by, above all, Steven Maras (2009) and Steven Price (2010) have initiated a line of enquiry into the history of screenwriting research, from its beginnings in the 1910s and 1920s to infrequent and yet seminal forays in subsequent decades, that investigate the criticality of screenwriting within a variety of contexts. Historically, the attention of scholars has tended to focus on two main objects of enquiry: the role and profession of the screenwriter on the one hand, and the screenplay on the other.

Study of the former often straddles a perceived tension between issues of *authorship* and the industrial, assembly-line nature of filmmaking (and other media) practices (see, for example, Corliss 1974; Azlant 1980; Bordwell, Staiger, and Thompson 1985; Loughney 1984; Fine 1985; Schatz 1989; Stillinger 1991; Staiger 1979, 1983, and 1995; Thompson 1999; Stempel 2000).

With regard to the screenplay itself, as early as the 1920s and 1930s, Soviet practitioners/theorists such as Sergei Eisenstein (1988), Vsevolod Pudovkin (2006), Lev Kuleshov (1987), and Dziga Vertov (1984) started to dissect the technical, transitional, and transformational substance of the screenplay. A discourse about screenwriting also began to develop in the "how to" manuals, which from early in the twentieth century set out to teach aspiring screenwriters how to master the craft (see chapter 3 in Maras 2009; chapters 2–4 in Price 2013; Curran 2019).

Subsequent scholarship has both developed the notion of the screenplay as a blueprint (see, for example, Gassner and Nichols 1943; Winston 1973; the above-mentioned Staiger and Thompson; Sternberg 1997) and theorised it as a form of literature (Brik 1936; Balász 1952; Malkin 1980; Davis 1984; Korte and Schneider 2000; Boon 2008), while filmmaker and theorist Pier Paolo Pasolini attempted to negotiate between these two conceptions in his influential essay "The Screenplay as 'Structure that Wants to Be Another Structure'" (1984 [1966]).

More recently, Ian. W. Macdonald disentangled the notion of the *screen idea* coined by Philip Parker (1998) to signify screenwriting activity as a locus of convergence between textual/scripting practices, other written and non-written materials, and the complex processes of idea development (Macdonald 2004). The notion of the *screen idea* transcends the material existence of any specific stable object/text to acknowledge and embrace the complex nature of the screenplay as a fluid, transient object. It has proved significant in the development of screenwriting research, which has continued to explore and expand on the initial concerns outlined above, while widening both the scope of the discussion and the variety of methodological approaches.

Macdonald has identified three significant areas of work—namely, *creative writing*, perhaps best exemplified by manuals about screenwriting, but also by scholarly work on poetics and techniques of screenwriting; *critical practice*, typically ranging from qualitative to practice-led research aimed at conceptualising screenwriting; and more traditional *reflective* or *critical analysis* (Russo et al. 2022. See also Macdonald's chapter in this volume). Maras, meanwhile, has categorised approaches to screenwriting research as following seven dominant trajectories—formalist, narratological, stylistic, historical, industrial/institutional, conceptual, and practice-based (Maras 2011).

In the last two decades, screenwriting scholarship has investigated non-conventional textual/scripting practices, discussed serial/multistrand drama formats, and approached screenwriting for animation and newer media such as videogames and VR. The screenplay has been theorised as proof of concept, database, boundary, liminal, or transitional object. Scholars have carried out ethnographies; developed screenwriting pedagogies; studied particular national and political contexts; elaborated postcolonial, transcultural and transnational approaches; considered ethics and morality, and discussed screenplays and screenwriting with regard to gender, race, and sexual identities. They have also proposed a range of new research tools and methods.

The Screenwriting Research Network (SRN), co-founded by Macdonald, then at Leeds University, UK, and Kirsi Rinne from the University of Art and Design (TaiK, now part of Aalto University), Helsinki, Finland, has played a key role in encouraging and disseminating this work and in establishing screenwriting as distinct research area. Since its first conference in Leeds in 2008, it has provided a forum to bring together scholars and practitioners of screenwriting, distributed across disciplines and geographical locations.[1] To date (i.e. Summer 2022), the SRN has enlisted more than 700 members from all continents, and its annual conferences (which celebrate their thirteenth edition in 2022) have thus far attracted more than a thousand papers, which are

---

[1] See Macdonald (2021) for an account of the difficulties that initially hampered screenwriting research, the developments that facilitated its growth and recognition, and the role played by the SRN in this process.

undisputed testament to the critical mass reached by studies in screenwriting globally.[2]

The *Journal of Screenwriting* (Intellect), set up in 2010 by Jill Nelmes and Jule Selbo, has also been pivotal, publishing much of this research. So too has the "Palgrave Studies in Screenwriting" book series. Launched in 2012 by Palgrave Macmillan, it includes monographs and edited volumes by Macdonald (2013), Eva Novrup Redvall (2013), Kathryn Millard (2014), Steven Price and Chris Pallant (2015), Maras (2016), Alexandra Ksenofontova (2020), and Adam Ganz and Steven Price (2020).[3] Indeed, Palgrave Macmillan has established itself as something of a home for the publication of screenwriting research, publishing a range of work in addition to the above-mentioned series, including Nelmes and Selbo's first comprehensive international guide to women screenwriters (2015); a handbook of script development edited by Craig Batty and Stayci Taylor (2021); and of course this handbook.

A large amount of screenwriting research has, of course, also been published elsewhere. The journal *Adaptation* has hosted a few case studies (e.g. Roblin's account of Harold Pinter's screen work, 2014) that show renewed attention to the specific role of screenwriting and screenwriters in the adaptation process. *New Writing—The International Journal for the Practice and Theory of Creative Writing* dedicated a Special Section to "Screenwriting in the Academy" (2016) with contributions that address creative practice research, ethical issues, digital literacy, and more. Articles have also appeared in *Journal of Media Practice* (e.g. Macdonald 2004; Pitts 2013), *MedieKultur* (e.g. Redvall 2009), *South Asian Screen Studies* (e.g. Sengupta 2018), and *Communication & Society* (e.g. Chiarulli 2021), to name just a few examples.

Several academic publishers have also shown growing interest in adding monographs and edited collections on screenwriting to their catalogues. These include but are far from limited to Cari Beauchamp's (1997) and Rosanne Welch's (2018) reassessments of the crucial role played by women screenwriters in the early decades of Hollywood; Claus Tieber's study of screenwriting and screenwriters in the Hollywood Studio System (2008); J. J. Murphy's investigations of the underlying principles of screenplays within American independent cinema (2007, 2019); Silvio Alovisio's archival research into screenwriting practices in silent Italian cinema (2005); Maria Pia Comand (2006) and Paolo Russo's (2014) extensive overviews of screenwriting practices and screenwriters in Italy; Antonio Sánchez-Escalonilla's analysis and comparison of strategies and techniques adopted by screenwriters (2009); Ted Nannicelli's philosophical account of the screenplay (2013); Bridget Conor's work on screenwriting as creative labour (2014); Miranda J. Banks's history of American screenwriters and their guild (2015); Peter Bloore's insights into the

---

[2] Up-to-date information about the SRN is available at https://screenwritingresearch.com/2022/07/26/srn-2021-22-activities-report/, accessed 26 May 2023.

[3] See https://link.springer.com/series/14590.

business of script development (2016); Jule Selbo's (2016) and Kira-Ann Pelican's (2021) books on writing characters; Paul Joseph Gulino's collaboration with cognitive psychologist Connie Shears, regarding the brain processes activated by common storytelling strategies employed in screenwriting (2018); Kerstin Stutterheim's work on dramaturgy in its applicability to the script development process (2019); Isabelle Reynaud's exploration of how scripts can be written, read, and rewritten in both fiction films and documentaries (2019); Nelmes's early collection of approaches to the analysis of the screenplay (2010); and Carmen Sofia Brenes, Patrick Cattrysse, and Margaret McVeigh's edited collection on transcultural screenwriting (2017).

It is clear that the range of research and scholarship is far from exhausted. Research directions that seem likely to develop further include those concerning ethics, politics, and policy; discussions of representation and identity; interrogation of the aesthetic, cultural, and institutional shifts implicated by technological and organisational changes in production and distribution; perspectives and approaches drawing on psychology; and new insights gained through software-assisted analysis. If screenwriting research as a whole has so far tended to focus on Western cultures, this needs and is likely to change, as screenwriting scholars continue to open up regional, national, transcultural, and postcolonial perspectives.

1.2 About This Volume

Acknowledging all the lines of enquiry mentioned above, *The Palgrave Handbook of Screenwriting Studies* seeks to both reflect the current state of the art and stimulate the debate towards further developments. Our aim is to focus on what we consider to have been key questions for scholars in screenwriting, while also bearing witness to the multiplicity of perspectives, their breadth, vitality, and critical mass. To this end, we have organised the chapters in this volume into five parts, which respectively address the What, When/Where, Who, How, and How to of screenwriting studies, while adopting a range of methodologies and approaches. Amongst the authors gathered here are several of the scholars mentioned above, whose work has been foundational to the development and recognition of screenwriting research and whose contributions both reprise the key concerns of their work to date and present new directions. The volume also includes chapters from scholars whose work has more recently turned to screenwriting as a focus, whether they are established experts in a related discipline or early career researchers bringing new perspectives.

Although much of this handbook is itself limited to work written in the English language, we recognise that screenwriting studies include international research that is published in many other languages. Indeed, many of the authors who have contributed to this volume also publish their research in other languages and make reference in their chapters to a range of sources beyond those published in English.

The content of each part and chapter is outlined below.

1.2.1 PART I: What—Screenwriting Ontology: Defining the Screenplay and Screenwriting

Part I includes theoretical chapters as well as case studies that champion screenwriting research as a diverse field of enquiry capable of producing new—ontological and epistemological—insights and approaches to interrogate the creative, processual nature of screenwriting activities and the status, usefulness, and validity of the resulting *materials*.

As Ian W. Macdonald reminds us, researching and studying screenwriting involve much more than simply reading screenplays or discussing talented writers. In his opening chapter, "How to Think About Screenwriting", he elaborates on the three "clusters" of work discussed above. Borrowing from psychology and creativity theorists, Macdonald goes on to reflect on "how to think about screenwriting" through the notion of *domain*, that is, "a culturally defined symbolic system" (Sternberg and Lubart 1999, 10) including all created products and conventions as developed and "shared by the members of the field" (Sawyer 2006, 125). Crucially, the *field* consists of all the intermediaries and gatekeepers (including practitioners as well as scholars) who, in turn, inform opinions and practices, a received wisdom or doxa (after Bourdieu) that scholars of screenwriting studies set out to investigate, test, and question.

In "Screenplectics: Screenwriting as a Complex Adaptive System", Paolo Russo expands on and inscribes the notion of *scripting* within a novel pragmatic/processual epistemological framework informed by complex system thinking and by Critical Digital Humanities tools and methods. After outlining the constituent ontologies and relational properties and processes of the screenwriting system, Russo focuses on character creation and proposes original modelling options (e.g. Cellular Automata, networks analyses, 4-D manifolds and block universe theory) that are best suited to show the creative potential of core screenwriting activities.

In "Collaboration, Cooperation and Authorship in Screenwriting aka How Many People Does It Take to Create an Author", Rosamund Davies brings together different frames of reference from recent debates that have attempted to both champion and challenge the notion of the author. She considers authorship in relation to the collective and collaborative practices and structures of the screen industries, and the cultural values and political and economic realities in which they operate, discussing the role that these play in constructing authorship and producing authors.

Dealing with the unfinished nature of the written text, Rita Benis turns our attention to the "Acts of Reading: The Demands on Screenplay Reading". Drawing on Roland Barthes's (1977) notion of Text as an open, multidimensional space, Benis reflects on how the visual information inscribed in the screenplay always waits for and relies on subsequent interactive, collaborative experiences through different ways of reading it.

In "The Reality of (Screen) Characters", Murray Smith considers the creation and development of characters through various stages—conception, development, scripting, directing, performing, reception—and different practices, by foregrounding the status of the entity that these activities bring into being and by raising some crucial ontological questions: "Just what is a character, and what sort of reality can we ascribe to a character?" "In more philosophical terms, what kind of ontological status do these fictional creatures possess?" And since they are fictional, "is it a contradiction in terms to think of characters as (in some sense) real?" Like Russo, Smith draws on *theories of possible worlds* to contend that characters are at once imaginary and real.

In "'We Come to Realize': Screenwriting and Representations of Time", Adam Ganz looks at how screenplay texts deal with the representation of time and argues that the coming of the sound film introduced a kind of syncopation between what Hitchcock called "the rhythm and pace of action and the rhythm and pace of dialogue" (1939) in the screenplay. Ganz exemplifies this by analysing the literary techniques employed by three different screenwriters (James Agee, William Goldman and Wes Craven) to represent time in the screenplay compared to how it is subjectively experienced by the audience of the finished film.

Warren Buckland's chapter, "The Motion Picture Screenplay as Data", makes use of Digital Humanities tools (i.e. the Linguistic Inquiry and Word Count software, or LIWC, developed by James Pennebaker) to quantify the linguistic texture of screenplays, using *Citizen Kane* (1941) as a case study. Buckland then pairs the automated, LIWC-generated quantitative analysis of dialogue and scene text in Mankiewicz and Welles's screenplay, with his own qualitative interpretation of how the spatial vocabulary employed creates a coherent storyworld.

The last two chapters of Part I shift our attention to screenwriting for interactive and immersive media, reclaiming the need for new, better suited, more specific forms of writing. In "Writer/Reader as Performer: Creating a Negotiated Narrative", Anna Zaluczkowska explores performance in new forms of visual production by presenting examples from her own work in collaboration with other writers and performance makers. Zaluczkowska argues for improvisational techniques and negotiated forms of narratives to be important aspects of a writer's toolkit in this new media age, especially in relation to interactive, participative, or immersive forms of production.

Rafael Leal reflects on "An Ontology of the Interactive Script" and points out how most traditional definitions—even those that cover a wide range of audiovisual formats—generally apply to linear scripts. Leal therefore calls for the need for a new understanding of the interactive script—a broad category characterised by the interactor's increased agency that ranges from games to immersive Virtual Reality (VR)—by tackling three pragmatic perspectives: the fruition of the interactive experience, the use of the script in the production process, and the poetic specificities of the development process.

1.2.2 PART II: When/Where—Screenwriting Historiography

As with any other field of research, knowledge of the history of a given research object and the manifold contexts of its genesis is essential to understand how and why related practices emerged and established themselves. The search for historical documents—in this case screenplays in their various stages and other, often more ephemeral material—can be difficult and the screenwriting historian often becomes an archaeologist, who has to reconstruct the writing process, its conditions, and its results based only on a handful of found documents. The archival situation globally is very diverse, which is one of the reasons why most film and screenwriting histories focus on the "standard model" of filmmaking (see Bordwell 2006) that is, on Hollywood, because its history is the best documented. Adding case studies from around the globe is one of the aims of this handbook and will allow the contextualisation and comparison of the genesis and evolution of different modes of screenwriting and of the way they continue to influence diverse narrative structures.

Screenwriting historiography is able to revise film history by shifting the investigative perspective from the finished film to analysing the screenwriting and production process. One of the results of this change is the visibility of women in the film industry, starting with pioneering female screenwriters, who accounted for half of all screenplays written in the United States during Hollywood's early years. The surveys and case studies presented in this part will demonstrate the range and breadth of screenwriting historiography, from European and Asian silent cinema to contemporary histories like post-Apartheid film and television writing in South Africa.

In his chapter "Historiographies of Screenwriting", Steven Price offers a sophisticated survey of screenwriting historiography before exemplifying how archival research can generate new insights with a case study of writer and director David Mamet. Price shows how the microhistory of Mamet's work with director Bob Rafelson on *The Postman Always Rings Twice* (1981) communicates with the contexts of historiographical research.

One of the *founders* of screenwriting historiography, Tom Stempel, delivers a memoir of his time in the archives searching for screenplays from the silent era. "They Actually Had Scripts in Silent Films?" is a personal reminiscence and homage to the analogue age of research that includes invaluable advice for the practice of historical screenwriting research. Stempel demonstrates that the researcher's way through the archives can be a *hero's journey* of sorts.

In "Silent Screenwriting in Europe: Discourses on Authorship, Form, and Literature", Alexandra Ksenofontova examines the discourses about the screenplay as a popular literary form in the 1920s. She demonstrates how Russian, German, and French writers regarded screenplays as ideal for literary experimentation, which were not just written to be filmed, but also to be published in that exceptional period of screenwriting history.

Rosanne Welch pulls the focus on a period when female screenwriters were as sought after as their male counterparts—the silent film era—in her chapter "When Women Wrote Hollywood: How Early Female Screenwriters Disappeared from the History of the Industry They Created". Welch not only reminds us of Hollywood's seminal female screenwriters, but also of independent filmmakers of colour like Alice Burton Russell Micheaux and Marion E. Wong.

Claus Tieber then examines the use of music and the writing of musical numbers in historical screenplays in his contribution, "Narrating with Music: Screenwriting Musical Numbers". His analysis of screenplays for American film musicals of the 1930s illustrates various ways in which screenwriters created and integrated musical numbers and were therefore responsible for more than just plot and storyline.

S. Louisa Wei's chapter "Women Screenwriters of Early Sinophone Cinema: 1916–1949" sheds light on Chinese female screenwriters, both in and outside the nation-state. She introduces the reader to female screenwriters from the silent era until 1949 and thus writes a feminist overview of the history of Chinese screenwriting.

Moving on to a different national cinema, Lauri Kitsnik delivers "A Historiography of Japanese Screenwriting" in which he examines existing film and screenwriting historiographies. He thus argues for a novel approach that shows how a focus on screenwriting can lead to significant, revealing insights in the historiography of a national cinema.

In "Writing Social Relevance: U.S. Television Dramas in the Civil Rights Era", Caryn Murphy uses the US TV series *The Defenders* (1961–1965), *The Nurses* (1962–1965), and *Mr. Novak* (1963–1965) to show how screenwriters tried to negotiate race politics in the 1960s. Through her close analysis of the teleplays as well as the structure of the TV networks of the time, Murphy discusses both chances and limits for screenwriters to react to recent political issues.

Jerónimo Arellano chooses the *unfilmed* screenplays of Colombian writer Andrés Caicedo—adaptations of American horror and fantasy authors—as examples of "the weird" as an aesthetic concept in Latin America and beyond in his chapter "Horror Bubbles: Andrés Caicedo's Weird Screenplays".

In his contribution "Writers as Workers: The Making of a Film Trade Union in India", Rakesh Sengupta surveys the history of one of the world's largest screenwriters' guilds, the Screenwriters' Association of India, from the 1950s to the 1970s.

Closing Part II, "The Evolving Depictions of Black South Africans in the Post-Apartheid Screenwriting Tradition" by Ziphozake Hlobo and Mpumelelo Skosana, focuses on the depictions of Black South Africans in films and TV series before and after the Apartheid in order to highlight how South

African screenwriters engaged in the creation of a Black South African identity after the end of the segregationist regime.

1.2.3 PART III: Who—Screenwriting and the Screen Industries

Part III focuses on screenwriting as a profession, as creative labour, and as a production culture, which is impacted by wider cultural, political, economic, and legal frameworks. Inequalities within the workforce and current practices of screenwriting and script development persist, raising issues of access, authority, and power. Questions need also to be asked about who is writing, what and why they choose/are permitted to write, as well as who they are writing for. Such questions are linked closely to the study and analysis of representation, with regard to how characters and stories are and might be constructed according to notions of national and other identities and experiences.

Building on existing work in this area (e.g. Staiger 1983 and 1995; Redvall 2013; Conor 2014; Banks 2015; Wreyford 2018), the chapters in this part illuminate the cultural, political, economic, and legal frameworks in which screenwriters, other participants in the development process, and their intended audiences are situated. From a range of perspectives, they unpick the complex relationships between institutional and national cultures, priorities and power structures, providing both critical analysis and potential solutions.

In "The International Writers' Room: A Transnational Approach to Serial Drama Development from an Italian Perspective", Luisa and Laura Cotta Ramosino discuss the challenges of developing culturally relevant dramas through the lenses of different cultures. Through case studies of the creative processes of transnational writers' rooms, they suggest that multilingual and multinational writers' rooms both challenge the traditional Italian and European idea of authorship and present the opportunity to produce culturally rich and relevant dramas with international appeal.

In "Writing Online Drama for Public Service Media in the Era of Streaming Platforms", Petr Szczepanik and Dorota Vašíčková discuss a different meeting of cultures in the development of a web series commissioned by Czech public service broadcaster Česká televize, aimed at a youth audience. The chapter focusses on how the development process both shaped and was shaped by the institutional culture, power structures, and strategic goals of the broadcaster. (For a discussion of the poetics of short form serialised narrative, see also Debbie Danielpour in Part IV.)

Eva Novrup Redvall addresses the priorities and issues involved in writing for an even younger audience. In "Screenwriting for Children and Young Audiences", she outlines key topics to consider when writing *for*, *about*, and potentially *with* children, tweens and teens, pointing to both the opportunities and challenges for writers and producers, when developing projects for young audiences in the contemporary competitive digital media landscape.

In "Imitations of Life? A Challenge for Black Screenwriters", Julius Ayodeji begins with a problem: the fact that, within mainstream cinema, screenplays by black screenwriters are rarely taken up by white directors and producers. He discusses three challenging screenwriting strategies, which speak to the cultural experiences and strategies of *passing*, *assimilation*, and *mirroring*, suggesting that they might be one way to introduce, *trojan horse-like*, a greater diversity of storytellers into the film and television industries.

Fadi G. Haddad and Alexander Dhoest's chapter "Beauties and Beasts: The Representation of National Identity Through Characterization in Syrian-Lebanese Pan-Arab Dramas" discusses the way that characters are constructed in relation to notions of "Syrian-ness" and "Lebanese-ness" in television drama produced by mixed Syrian and Lebanese production teams and aimed at a pan-Arab audience. They consider how these representations might relate to Syrian and Lebanese national identities, ideologies, and political realities, providing insights into screenwriting in this hybrid production context.

Turning to the question of gender in screenwriting employment and work practices, in "'That's a Chick's Movie': How Women Are Excluded from Screenwriting Work", Natalie Wreyford draws on original interviews and the work of Pierre Bourdieu to consider the gendered construction of taste and its consequences for women screenwriters, suggesting that, despite the increased acknowledgement of inequalities in the workplace, the gendering of taste is one significant reason why they remain unaddressed.

The final chapter of Part III concerns "The Different American Legal Structures for Unionization of Writers for Stage and Screen". Catherine L. Fisk examines the history of the legal structures governing unionisation of writers for stage and screen. Comparing the retention of copyright ownership prioritised by the Dramatists' Guild with the collective bargaining rights and contract protections secured by the Writers Guild of America (WGA), she considers how these arrangements differently empower and constrain writers and producers in film, television, and theatre.

1.2.4 *Part IV: How—Approaches to Screen Storytelling*

Screenwriting techniques are perhaps the most often discussed aspect of screenwriting, in both the scholarly literature and practitioners' manuals. This area is far from being exhausted, however, since, beyond the established basic conventions of style and form, the actual practice of screenwriting entails an inexhaustible multitude of choices and decisions that are unique to each project. The totality of such decisions, with regard to aspects such as medium; genre; audience; story structure; character; and other dramatic and stylistic elements, constitutes a particular aesthetic strategy, relating both to the affordances of specific media and formats, and to wider thematic and representational concerns. While every screen narrative embodies a specific application and interpretation of general rules, some may also present a challenge, subversion, or reconfiguration of established assumptions and practices.

Each of the chapters in Part IV focuses on a particular approach to storytelling, with regard to medium, audience, and/or dramatic or stylistic elements, examining both the reasons for and the potential effects of such an approach.

In "Random Access Memories: Screenwriting for Games", Narrative designer Colin Harvey provides an overview of the elements involved in writing for contemporary videogames, highlighting the ways in which games both borrow and deviate from other media such as cinema and television. Drawing on case studies of videogames he has worked on, he examines the role of subjective and collective memory in the narrative design of videogames.

Chris Pallant and Paul Wells then consider the context of screenwriting for animation. In "Exploring the Visual Toolbox of Animation Story Design", they discuss the need for a fuller understanding of the particular narrative techniques and vocabularies required in animation story design, focusing in particular on the contents of the *animation toolbox*, the role of *micro-narratives* as fundamental building blocks, the centrality of storyboarding, and the significance of different production contexts.

Debbie Danielpour's chapter, "The Short-Form Scripted Serial Drama: The Novice Showrunner's New Opportunity", reviews the poetics of long-form and short-form serialised dramas in order to determine how and why the short-form requires a set of poetics different to those of long-form serialised television shows. She suggests that the poetics of short-form episodic narrative are a necessary part of the screenwriting curriculum, since they offer unique opportunities to new screenwriters and filmmakers.

Ronald Geerts discusses the construction of characters beyond a traditional psychological approach in his chapter "The Plural Protagonist. Or: How to Be Many and Why". Starting with the Brechtian anti-illusionistic way of acting, Geerts goes on to discuss alternative forms of fictional characters and their creation by screenwriters.

Meanwhile, in "The Haptic Encounter: Scripting Female Subjectivity", Funke Oyebanjo approaches the writing of character from an entirely different perspective. Drawing on her own work to refigure female subjectivity within Nigerian historical drama, she outlines specific techniques whereby a screenwriter might stage a "haptic encounter" between character and reader.

Margaret McVeigh examines storytelling in Australian co-productions in her contribution "Script Development from the Inside Looking Out". In her reconstruction of two development processes, she discusses the key storytelling imperatives involved in writing a transnational story.

In the final chapter of Part IV, "Extended How? Narrative Structure in the Short and Long Versions of *The Lord of the Rings*, *Kingdom of Heaven*, and *Dances with Wolves*", acclaimed film scholar Kristin Thompson discusses how editing and the recent tendency for director's cuts change the act structure of films or—to use the screenwriter's perspective—how re-editing a film can re-install its original act structure as represented in the screenplay.

1.2.5 PART V: How To—Researching and Teaching Screenwriting: Discourses and Methods

The above-mentioned works by Azlant (1980, 1997), Staiger (1979 and 1983), Stempel (2000), and, more recently, Maras (2009), Price (2010, 2013), and Curran (2019) have traced the origins of screenwriting teaching as far back as the early 1910s: subsequent waves of the so-called *scenario fever* and the introduction of law provisions to protect copyright instigated an explosion in publication of handbooks (or "how to" manuals).

By broadening the scope to non-American cultures as well, Part 5 adds new insights as well as teases out other stages in the evolution of the discourses about the pedagogy of screenwriting that have so far received less attention. These include the post-World War II shift back to freelancing in film as opposed to television writing; the institutionalisation of teaching the "craft" in universities (at least since the 1920s) and specialised schools; the foundation of state-funded national film schools that trained new generations of writers in many countries; and how courses have developed over the following decades. In doing so, the five chapters provide an assessment of screenwriting teaching in both past and contemporary eras and of how the international revival of manuals has seemingly led to a widespread adoption of a "doxa" (or doxas) in teaching practices around the globe. They also look at the use of short films and at practice-based research as alternative forms of screenwriting teaching.

Kerstin Stutterheim's chapter, "Film Dramaturgy: A Practice and a Tool for the Researcher", opens Part V with an overview of dramaturgy as practice and discipline: from its origins in antiquity to its establishment as a theoretical and analytical approach to understand and support time-based narrative-performative arts; and, subsequently, as academic discipline: first in Central Europe, then in several other countries around the world. It then discusses dramaturgy more specifically in its usefulness for the screenwriting process and professional practice.

Paul Joseph Gulino takes the reader on a "search for the missing pieces" throughout the history of "Screenwriting Pedagogy in the United States", reflecting on the loss of the "valuable feedback loop" that informed the training ground of screenwriters in the classical era of the Hollywood studio system. Gulino goes on to compare it with the novel educational landscape that emerged since the 1970s; film schools and screenwriting manuals arose to fill the gap in training, but these approaches—Gulino suggests—have significant blind spots and limitations.

Mariapia Comand embarks on a similar journey that examines the introduction, evolution, and application of "Screenwriting Manuals and Pedagogy in Italy from the 1930s to the End of the Twentieth Century". Beginning with the establishment of the National Film School in Rome (1935–1936), Comand focuses her investigation on two main areas: publishing (e.g. journals, series and manuals) and education (e.g. screenwriting academies, schools, and university courses).

In "Screenwriting, Short Film, and Pedagogy", Díóg O'Connell explores the short film itself as "a site of pedagogical practice for screenwriting". Drawing parallels between silent cinema and contemporary short film practices in Ireland, O'Connell highlights formal attributes, techniques, style, provenance and legacy of the short film format, and their relevance for teaching screenwriting.

Craig Batty's chapter "Screenwriters in the Academy" sheds light on "The Opportunities of Research-led Practice": first by mapping how the growing number "of doctoral candidates engaging with screenwriting increases internationally" and then by raising key questions regarding form, process, and purpose of connecting academic research with screenwriting practice. Batty's remarks on the reciprocity of theory and practice aptly close *The Palgrave Handbook of Screenwriting Studies* on an auspicious note for the future of screenwriting research.

REFERENCES

Alovisio, Silvio. 2005. *Voci del silenzio: La sceneggiatura nel cinema muto italiano* [The Voices of Silence: Screenwriting in Italian Silent Cinema]. Milan: Il Castoro.

Azlant, Edward. 1980. *The Theory, History, and Practice of Screenwriting, 1897–1920.* Madison, WI: University of Wisconsin.

Azlant, Edward. 1997. "Screenwriting for the Early Silent Film: Forgotten Pioneers, 1897–1911." *Film History* 9 (3): Special issue "Screenwriters and Screenwriting", 228–56.

Balász, Bela. 1952. *Theory of the Film.* London: Denis Dobson.

Banks, Miranda J. 2015. *The Writers: A History of American Screenwriters and Their Guild.* New Brunswick, NJ: Rutgers University Press.

Barthes, Roland. 1977. "The Death of the Author." In *Image – Music – Text*, trans. Stephen Hill. New York: Hill and Wang.

Batty, Craig, and Stayci Taylor, eds. 2021. *Script Development: Critical Approaches, Creative Practices, International Perspectives.* Cham, Switzerland: Palgrave Macmillan.

Beauchamp, Cari. 1997. *Without Lying Down: Frances Marion and the Powerful Women of Early Hollywood.* Berkeley, CA: University of California Press.

Bloore, Peter. 2016. *The Screenplay Business: Managing Creativity and Script Development in the Film Industry.* London: Routledge.

Boon, Kevin Alexander. 2008. *Script Culture and the American Screenplay.* Detroit: Wayne State University Press.

Bordwell, David, Janet Staiger, and Kristin Thompson. 1985. *Classical Hollywood Cinema: Film Style and Mode of Production to 1960.* London: Routledge & Kegan Paul.

Bordwell, David. 2006. *The Way Hollywood Tells It: Story and Style in Modern Movies.* Berkeley, CA: University of California Press.

Brenes, Carmen Sofia, Patrick Cattrysse, and Margaret McVeigh, eds. 2017. *Transcultural Screenwriting: Telling Stories for a Global World.* Newcastle upon Tyne: Cambridge Scholars.

Brik, Osip. 1974 [1936]. "From the Theory and Practice of a Script Writer." Trans. Diana Matias. *Screen* 15 (3): 95–103. https://doi.org/10.1093/screen/15.3.95.

Chiarulli, Raffaele. 2021. "'Strong Curtains' and 'Dramatic Punches': The Legacy of Playwriting in the Screenwriting Manuals of the Studio Era." *Communication & Society* 34 (1): 109–22. https://doi.org/10.15581/003.34.1.109-122.

Citizen Kane. 1941. Written by Herman J. Mankiewicz and Orson Welles. Directed by Orson Welles. USA: Mercury Productions, RKO Radio Pictures.

Comand, Mariapia, ed. 2006. *Sulla carta. Storia e storie della sceneggiatura in Italia* [On Paper. History and Stories of Screenwriting in Italy]. Turin: Lindau.

Conor, Bridget. 2014. *Screenwriting: Creative Labor and Professional Practice.* London and New York: Routledge.

Corliss, Richard N. 1974. *Talking Pictures:* Screenwriters in the American Cinema, 1927–1973. Woodstock, NY: Overlook Press.

Curran, Stephen C. 2019. *Early Screenwriting Teachers 1910–1922: Origins, Contribution and Legacy.* Feltham, UK: AE.

Davis, Gary. 1984. "Rejected Offspring: The Screenplay as a Literary Genre." *New Orleans Review* 11 (4): 90–94.

Eisenstein, Sergei M. 1988. "The Form of the Script." In *Selected Works. Vol. 1: Writings 1922–34.* Trans. Richard Taylor, 134–35. London. BFI.

Fine, Richard. 1985. *Hollywood and the Profession of Authorship, 1928–1940.* Ann Arbor, MI: UMI Research Press.

Ganz, Adam, and Steven Price. 2020. *Robert De Niro at Work. From Screenplay to Screen Performance.* Cham, Switzerland: Palgrave Macmillan.

Gassner, John, and Dudley Nichols. 1943. *Twenty Best Film Plays.* New York: Crown.

Gulino, Paul Joseph, and Connie Shears. 2018. *The Science of Screenwriting. The Neuroscience Behind Storytelling Strategies.* New York and London: Bloomsbury.

Hitchock, Alfred. 1939. "Lecture: Radio City Music Hall, New York City (30/Mar/1939)." MoMA. https://www.moma.org/interactives/exhibitions/1999/hitchcock/lecture/index.html. Accessed 12 December 2021.

Korte, Barbara, and Ralf Schneider. 2000. "The Published Screenplay: A New 'Literary' Genre?" *AAA: Arbeiten aus Anglistik und Amerikanistik* 25 (1): 89–105.

Ksenofontova, Aleksandra. 2020. *The Modernist Screenplay. Experimental Writing for Silent Film.* Cham, Switzerland: Palgrave Macmillan.

Kuleshov, Lev. 1987 [1920]. "The Banner of Cinematography." In *Selected Works: Fifty Years in Film*, edited by Ekaterina Khokhlova, trans. Dmitri Agachev and Nina Belenkaya, 37–55. Moscow: Raduga.

Loughney, Patrick G. 1984. "In the Beginning Was the Word: Six Pre-Griffith Motion Picture Scenarios." *Iris* 2 (1): 17–32.

Macdonald, Ian W. 2004. "Disentangling the Screen Idea." *Journal of Media Practice* 5 (2): 88–99. https://doi.org/10.1386/jmpr.5.2.89/0.

Macdonald, Ian W. 2013. *Screenwriting Poetics and the Screen Idea.* Basingstoke, UK: Palgrave Macmillan.

Macdonald, Ian W. 2021. "Meeting Old Friends for the First Time: A Personal Reflection on the Development of the Screenwriting Research Network." *Journal of Screenwriting* 12 (2): 203–04. https://doi.org/10.1386/josc_00060_1.

Malkin, Yaakov. 1980. "The Screenplay as a New Literary Form." Doctoral lecture, May, Tel-Aviv University. Israel Film Archive.

Maras, Steven. 2009. *Screenwriting: History, Theory and Practice.* London: Wallflower.

Maras, Steven. 2011. "Some Attitudes and Trajectories in Screenwriting Research." *Journal of Screenwriting* 2 (2): 275–86. https://doi.org/10.1386/josc.2.2.275_7.
Maras, Steven, ed. 2016. *Ethics in Screenwriting: New Perspectives*. Basingstoke, UK: Palgrave Macmillan.
Millard, Kathryn. 2014. *Screenwriting in a Digital Era*. Basingstoke, UK: Palgrave Macmillan.
Murphy, J. J. 2007. *Me and You and Memento and Fargo: How Independent Screenplays Work*. New York: Continuum.
Murphy, J. J. 2019. *Rewriting Indie Cinema: Improvisation, Psychodrama, and the Screenplay*. New York: Columbia University Press.
Nannicelli, Ted. 2013. *A Philosophy of the Screenplay*. New York: Routledge.
Nelmes, Jill, ed. 2010. *Analysing the Screenplay*. London: Routledge.
Nelmes, Jill, and Jule Selbo, eds. 2015. *Women Screenwriters: An International Guide*. Basingstoke, UK: Palgrave Macmillan.
Parker, Philip. 1998. *The Art and Science of Screenwriting*. Bristol: Intellect.
Pasolini, Pier Paolo. 1984 [1966]. "The Screenplay as 'Structure That Wants to Be Another Structure'." *The American Journal of Semiotics* 4 (1–2): 53–72. https://doi.org/10.5840/ajs198641/28.
Pelican, Kira-Anne. 2021. *The Science of Writing Characters: Using Psychology to Create Compelling Fictional Characters*. London: Bloomsbury.
Pitts, Virginia. 2013. "Writing from the Body: Kinesthetics and Entrainment in Collaborative Screenplay Development." *Journal of Media Practice* 14 (1): 61–78. https://doi.org/10.1386/jmpr.14.1.61_1.
Price, Steven. 2010. *The Screenplay: Authorship, Theory and Criticism*. Basingstoke, UK: Palgrave Macmillan.
Price, Steven. 2013. *A History of the Screenplay*. Basingstoke, UK: Palgrave Macmillan.
Price, Steven, and Chris Pallant. 2015. *Storyboarding: A Critical History*. London: Palgrave Macmillan.
Pudovkin, Vsevolod I. 2006. *Vsevolod Pudovkin: Selected Essays*. Translated by Richard Taylor and Evgeni Filippov. London, New York, and Calcutta: Seagull.
Redvall, Eva Novrup. 2009. "Scriptwriting as a Creative, Collaborative Learning Process of Problem Finding and Problem Solving." *MedieKultur: Journal of Media and Communication Research* 25 (46): 34–55. https://doi.org/10.7146/mediekultur.v25i46.1342.
Redvall, Eva Novrup. 2013. *Writing and Producing Television Drama in Denmark: From* The Kingdom *to* The Killing. Basingstoke, UK: Palgrave Macmillan.
Reynaud, Isabelle. 2019. *Reading and Writing a Screenplay: Fiction, Documentary and New Media*. London: Routledge.
Roblin, Isabelle. 2014. "The Visible/Invisible Screenwriter: The Strange Case of Harold Pinter." *Adaptation* 7 (2): 180–90. https://doi.org/10.1093/adaptation/apu006.
Russo, Paolo, ed. 2014. *Nero su Bianco: Sceneggiatura e Sceneggiatori in Italia* [Black on white: Screenwriting and screenwriters in Italy]. N.p.: Quaderni del CSCI.
Russo, Paolo, Rosamund Davies, Alexandra Ksenofontova, Rafael Leal, Ian W. Macdonald, Steven Maras, and Claus Tieber. 2022. "Roundtable: Pushing the Boundaries of the Screenwriting Research Network." *Journal of Screenwriting* 13 (1): 115–34. https://doi.org/10.1386/josc_00085_1.

Sánchez-Escalonilla, Antonio. 2009. *Estrategias de guion cinematográfico: El proceso de creación de una historia* [*Strategies for the film script: The creative process of story*]. Barcelona: Ariel.
Sawyer, R. Keith. 2006. *Explaining Creativity. The Science of Human Innovation*. Oxford: Oxford University Press.
Schatz, Thomas. 2010 [1989]. *The Genius of the System: Hollywood Filmmaking in the Studio Era*. 2nd ed. Ann Arbor, MI: University of Minnesota Press.
"Screenwriting in the Academy". 2016. *New Writing–The International Journal for the Practice and Theory of Creative Writing* 13 (1): Special section, 59–152. https://doi.org/10.1080/14790726.2015.1134579.
Selbo, Jule. 2016. *Screenplay. Building Story through Character*. London: Routledge.
Sengupta, Rakesh. 2018. "Writing from the Margins of Media: Screenwriting Practice and Discourse During the First Indian Talkies." *BioScope: South Asian Screen Studies* 9 (2): 117–36. https://doi.org/10.1177/0974927618813480.
Staiger, Janet. 1979. "Dividing Labor for Production Control: Thomas Ince and the Rise of the Studio System." *Cinema Journal* 18 (2): 16–25. https://doi.org/10.2307/1225439.
Staiger, Janet. 1983. "'Tame' Authors and the Corporate Laboratory: Stories, Writers, and Scenarios in Hollywood." *The Quarterly Review of Film Studies* 8 (4): 33–45. https://doi.org/10.1080/10509208309361178.
Staiger, Janet, ed. 1995. *The Studio System*. New Brunswick, NJ: Rutgers University Press.
Stempel, Tom. 2000. *Framework: A History of Screenwriting in the American Film*. Syracuse, NY: Syracuse University Press.
Sternberg, Claudia. 1997. *Written for the Screen: The American Motion-Picture Screenplay as Text*. Tübingen: Stauffenburg.
Sternberg, Robert J., and Todd I. Lubart. 1999. "The Concept of Creativity: Prospects and Paradigms." In *Handbook of Creativity*, edited by Robert J. Sternberg, 3–10. Cambridge: Cambridge University Press.
Stillinger, Jack. 1991. *Multiple Authorship and the Myth of Solitary Genius*. New York: Oxford University Press.
Stutterheim, Kerstin. 2019. *Modern Film Dramaturgy: An Introduction*. Berlin: Peter Lang.
The Defenders. 1961–1965 (4 seasons). Created by Reginald Rose. USA: Plautus Productions.
The Postman Always Rings Twice. 1981. Written by David Mamet. Directed by Bob Rafelson. USA: Lorimar Productions, Northstar International.
Thompson, Kristin. 1999. *Storytelling in the New Hollywood: Understanding Classical Narrative Technique*. Cambridge, MA: Harvard University Press.
Tieber, Claus. 2008. *Schreiben für Hollywood: Das Drehbuch im Studiosystem*. Münster, Germany: LIT Verlag.
Vertov, Dziga. 1984. *Kino-Eye: The Writings of Dziga Vertov*. Edited by Annette Michelson, trans. by Kevin O'Brien. Berkeley, CA : University of California Press.
Welch, Rosanne. 2018. *When Women Wrote Hollywood: Essays on Female Screenwriters in the Early Film Industry*. Jefferson, NC: McFarland.
Winston, Douglas Garrett. 1973. *The Screenplay as Literature*. Rutherford, NJ: Fairleigh Dickinson University Press.
Wreyford, Natalie. 2018. *Gender Inequality in Screenwriting Work*. Cham, Switzerland: Palgrave Macmillan.

PART I: WHAT

Screenwriting Ontology: Defining the Screenplay and Screenwriting

CHAPTER 2

How to Think About Screenwriting

Ian W. Macdonald

2.1 Introduction: What Are We Studying Here?

We might expect to study screenwriting by looking at a screenplay, but this is not as straightforward as it seems. For example, which draft script should we study?

Here is the beginning of a draft screenplay for *Alien³* (1992) dated 10/10/90 (and surely one of the most ambitious exterior scenes ever written!).

>   FADE IN:
>
>   1. EXT. THE VOID
>   Airless, eerie silence.
>   A patina of stars that crawl away forever.
>   But silent as death itself, something is near...
>   The Sulaco.
>
>   (Hill and Giler 1990, 1)

It follows the standard generic format for Hollywood master-scene screenplays. Master-scene is the common format for screenplays in orthodox film

---

I. W. Macdonald (✉)
Independent Researcher, Leeds, UK
e-mail: iw.macdonald@virgin.net

© The Author(s), under exclusive license to Springer Nature Switzerland AG 2023
R. Davies et al. (eds), *The Palgrave Handbook of Screenwriting Studies*,
https://doi.org/10.1007/978-3-031-20769-3_2

production. It is divided into scenes which have a standard heading (slugline) defining INT. (interior) or EXT. (exterior), followed by the location and then NIGHT or DAY (although in space, of course, it is neither day nor night). For example, the first scene of *A Clockwork Orange* (Kubrick 1970) is headed INT. KOROVA MILKBAR – NIGHT. When an element in the scene heading changes, that becomes a new scene, with a new heading. This is standard; in practice, there are many ways to be creative with format, which can be subtle on the page.[1]

By the end of page one of *Alien³*—approximately one minute, conventionally—the drama is already ramping up. By then, scene three specifies "something unearthly… crawling onto [Newt's] faceplate", while she sleeps inside her hypersleep cylinder.

This master-scene screenplay draft is a literary, atmospheric, even poetic document designed to excite the reader ("a patina of stars that crawl away forever"… "silent as death itself"). In fact, some of it is unfilmable as written. How do you film an "airless, eerie silence"? Or an unearthly "something"? This style of script is a document written with affect in mind rather than technical detail.[2]

So, what happens next? How does this script translate into film, specifically actual film shots? Answer: the script is revised into a different style. The focus changes from literary to cinematic, reflecting the needs, and practical vision, of the director. For example, in 1929 the Russian director Sergei Eisenstein offered his own visual, technical interpretation of the emotion inspired by "deathly silence" in the screenplay for *Battleship Potemkin* (1925), as a series of still close-ups, e.g. of "the dark and silent pitching of the battleship's bows… perhaps a dolphin's leap", etc. (Ganz and Price 2020, 13).

In fact, the *Alien³* script went through several long and difficult years of script development. Despite a tortuous journey from 12-page treatment by producers Walter Hill and David Giler through several drafts and writers, to reach the version above, the film nevertheless started shooting on 14 January 1991 with the script still unfinished (Thomson 2000, 119–24). Then, during shooting another draft is issued, on 26 January 1991, but it looks different from the October 1990 version. The script has changed, from master-scene screenplay format to a list of shots.

---

[1] Standard formatting advice is commonly available online, e.g. the guidance on the BBC Writers' Room website (https://www.bbc.co.uk/writersroom/resources/medium-and-format/, accessed 20 November 2021) or from manuals (e.g. Trottier 1998; Riley 2021), or as formatting software such as *Final Draft* (https://www.finaldraft.com/, accessed 18 May 2022), or *Trelby* (www.Trelby.com, accessed 4 November 2021).

[2] See also Russell Brickey's reading of the opening of *Aliens* (2021, 233–235).

FADE IN:

1. EXT. DEEP SPACE – CREDIT SEQUENCE
   The void, luxuriously veiled in a star field.
                                           BEGIN CREDITS:
   1a. quick – a facehugger finger - -
   2. quick – a face, under glass, out of focus - - the glass shatters...
   2a. quick – a monitor - - A colorful catscan of a tendril, down someone's throat.
   3. quick – acid blood hits the floor, sizzles, eats through insulationwires...
   3a. quick – smoke passes a sensor - -
   4a. quick – a panel of lights explode on, flashing, urgent, something is very wrong...

(Hill and Giler 1991, 1)

The action starts more quickly in this version, which is a montage of images (despite generalities like "something is very wrong"), and is more detailed about pacing and drama ("quick", and later on the page "then"). This is stylistically and visually dramatic. The page also looks different. It is less literary and more image-based, filmic, broken into shots. This is a script for shooting, or for editing. Somewhere between these two scripts, the function has changed from reflective to pragmatic, from emotional to visual, from master-scene to "continuity" style on the page. It has become more like a technical blueprint guiding the production process, even if it has not lost its dramatic tone.[3]

Which script should we study? In most disciplines, there is a singular tangible object we can focus on—the film, the novel, the poem—and textual questions are often limited to identifying an *ur-text*, one which is seen as definitive. Not here. We surely cannot ignore either script. Each seems to exist in their own right. There is overlap in the echoes of previous scripts, more like a palimpsest (Davies 2013; Macdonald 2013, 185–87).

It gets complex. The current script draft—even one marked Final—is always subject to change, for any reason from notes from various important people, to cast changes or budget problems, personality clashes, accidents, malfunctions, Acts of God and unexpected rain. The script can be re-read, re-thought, re-written and re-made at any point. Corrections will be inserted into the current script, on different coloured paper (the "rainbow script"), or with a different colour typeface (Riley 2021, 143). There might be several versions from different authors—*Alien*[3] had five separate versions from around 10 writers, and at least one version, by William Gibson, has enjoyed a new life as a comic strip. How do we make sense of all these documents?

---

[3] Throughout Hollywood's history, the term "continuity" is applied in various ways and inconsistently (Price 2013a, 10–19), most of which seem to refer to a functional list of shots offering the technical coherence of the project, usually for principal photography, or post-production. See also Bordwell, Staiger and Thompson (1985).

It is tempting to consider the master-scene screenplay as the key, literary document, following the emphasis in screenwriting manuals. It is the common template in software for screenwriters although historically there have been variations in form and use.[4] The problem is, however, that any script remains only a transitional snapshot, until ultimately it loses authority to the emerging screenwork. There is no single definitive screenplay because it is never actually finished, only superseded.[5] It is a moving target.

Scholars have recognised this problem. Claudia Sternberg acknowledged the US master-scene screenplay as "literature in flux" (1997), and Steven Price's hunt for a firm text (2010, Ch. 3) seems both elegant and doomed. Price later acknowledges the more provisional nature of the screenplay, observing that the screenplay is neither literature in flux, nor a blueprint, but a "modular text", a middle ground where *some* (his italics) elements of the screenplay have been re-written and others not (Price 2013a, 236). And of course, screenplay practice has changed over the twentieth century and varies between different cultures (e.g. Thompson 2004; Kitsnik 2016; Černik 2020).

How then do we study the text—or texts—in hand? Perhaps by re-thinking our understanding of the process of screenwriting. Steven Maras points out that to treat either the script or the film as the sole object of screenwriting is questionable (2009, 11). There is an "object problem"—which object do we study? And how do we understand their differences? Pier Paolo Pasolini famously wrote an article entitled "The scenario as a structure designed to become another structure" ([1966] 1977). Maras notes "the line between where the script stops and where the film starts can... be mysterious and blurry" (2009, 11). How do we resolve this?

Maras points instead to the discourse(s) of screenwriting which sets the conditions for its practice (2009, 10; 2011). That practice could then include oral discussion and negotiation as well as a series of transitional documents which include the screenplay (e.g. Tieber 2008, 2014; Giarrusso 2019). The script-text (in whatever form) is then seen in a context which will include a range of other informants, from notebook jottings to Writers Room conversations, to shooting schedule. The screenplay is still regarded as a key document, of course, so how can we reconcile that with this broader understanding of screenwriting practice?

Some screenwriting scholars have applied the concept of a "boundary object" to the screenplay (Davies 2019; Giarrusso 2019). "The boundary object is one which allows different individuals … to cooperate towards a common goal by creating a shared space" (Davies 2019, 150). This is a

---

[4] For example, Carl Mayer's screenplay for the silent *Sunrise* (1927) has two columns, showing technical detail alongside story information. See also Price (2013a, 105–11) and Macdonald (2007).

[5] Published versions, versions created for the consideration of Awards' juries, or legal versions, are usually transcripts made for specific purposes and are not infrequently re-formatted (see Cole and Haag 2000; see Ksenofontova 2020, 8–10).

broad concept covering multiple elements—"artefacts, templates, ideals, theories and beliefs can be considered boundary objects in their own right" (Davies 2019, 159)—but, applied to the screenplay document, we can see how this is used as a focus by those who work on it and as a source of information by those who study it. The screenplay/boundary object is what holds their work together—not rigidly but as a framework which evolves with the production. Even in different states (e.g. writer's draft, shooting script, etc.), it is said to be "sturdy enough to maintain this meaningful identity across different sites of use" (Giarrusso 2019, 57). Adam Ganz and Steven Price have used this concept to provide a close textual analysis of the relationship, in several of his films, between Robert De Niro's copies of his screenplays and his annotations, which in turn provides the basis for a new understanding of the work of the actor, "so that a critical understanding of the work… is enhanced or reoriented" (Ganz and Price 2020, 211).

But we also have to account for other documents used in this process, or indeed anything that represents or informs the idea being worked on—what we might term the "screen idea". Are the jottings on the back of a cigarette packet a screenplay too? Are they part of the boundary object? We must consider more than just the screenplay document, and perhaps a wider idea of what constitutes screenwriting. The whole domain of screenwriting includes more ways of imagining the screen idea than just using the "sovereign script" form (Maras 2009, 40). How can we grasp this broader vision of writing for an audio-visual narrative (i.e. meaning a text which can be understood by the viewer/reader as a connected series of audio-visual events)?

2.2 Scripting the Screen Idea

Taking a lead from film scholars such as Adrian Martin, Steven Maras introduced the term "scripting" (2009, 2–4 *passim*) to describe any development and expression of the screen idea, including the narrower, orthodox use of the term "screenwriting", but without being tied to a specific literary format. Maras also refers to "screen writing", which includes writing that is not solely page-based, "as in writing with a camera" (2009, vii).

Scripting accounts for "multiple forms of writing for the screen (with bodies, improvisation, machines, lights, storyboards, notes, scribbles, gestures) that can support production" (Maras 2009, 129). Kathryn Millard (2011) suggested using the term "prototype" to encompass anything that previsualises a screenwork, rather than reliance on a literary model, although this assumes the prototype is an early version and the screenwork is the definitive end-point, which it might not be. Traditionally, screenwriting has been assumed to be the composition and fine-tuning of a screenplay, but Millard points to oral ballad traditions (as, e.g., described by Ganz 2010) and improvisation in general writing practice, as methods which also count as the "writing" of the film (Millard 2011, 145). Claus Tieber and Christina Wintersteller have referred to Walter Reich's self-reflexivity in screenplays as "writing with music" (2020).

Redvall and Sabroe describe the use of production design as a story-telling tool (2016), and Welby Ings uses drawing as a method for narrative development (2021). Visualisation as a form of writing can involve preliminary sketches, narrative drawings, designs, storyboards or preliminary animatics, says Paul Wells (in Millard 2011, 148). Chris Pallant and Steven Price (2015) analyse storyboarding, and "pre-viz" software has developed since the early 2000s. Like animation, digitised images and their manipulation are part of the writing process, says filmmaker Keith Griffiths (in Millard 2011, 146), and Kathryn Millard herself provides a number of examples of other non-script techniques which preview the construction of the film (2011, 2013, 2014).

From the examples above, the process of composing ideas for realisation as a moving image narrative, and the manner of their appearance, is far more varied than the orthodox process of writing a screenplay would suggest. It can indeed be radically different. Writing about Indian life and culture, V. S. Naipaul quotes one film writer who claimed he learned that "films can be made from… scraps of conversation" between himself and the director, and that things change all the time, whether in pre-production, shooting or editing (1998, 89). There was no written script at all.

Naipaul's experience may be singular, but it does seem that some Indian practice did not conform to the industrialised formality of the Hollywood script. It depended on orality and handwritten record-keeping, partly as the result of a tradition of employing a scribe—the Munshi—as (broadly) dialogue writer, during the first half of the twentieth century (Sengupta 2021). Rakesh Sengupta argues we should recognise this more improvisatory, immediate practice for what it is, rather than searching for the Indian "bound script" as a central textual reference. He thus steps broadly in line with Naipaul's example, and at the same time strengthens the argument for understanding screenwriting as scripting. This raises the question—if scripting includes anything, from a standard Hollywood master-scene script to no document at all, what links these elements?

Common to all the above forms of scripting is the concept of the screen idea (Macdonald 2004a, b). This can be described as:

> Any notion held by one or more people of a singular concept (however complex) which may have conventional shape or not, intended to become a screenwork, whether or not it is possible to describe it in written form or by other means.
>
> (Macdonald 2004b, 5)

The term "screen idea" was taken from Philip Parker's use in connection with his "creative matrix" (1998, 57 *passim*), and the concept echoes Stanley J. Solomon's "film idea" (1972). Adrian Martin refers to "the cinematic idea" (2014), also in terms of a matrix, which in turn resonates with Ed Branigan's "narrative schema" (1992, 17).

The screen idea can be seen as a form of boundary object, but to avoid confusion it might be better understood as a separate entity from the screenplay-as-boundary-object, because the screen idea has no material existence itself, and no end to its development. Scripting the screen idea, then, brings together two conceptual tools which allow us to study more than the orthodox (standard) beliefs and conventions about screenwriting practice.

Where does the individual screenwriter figure here? As author (rather than *auteur*), they will rightly get credit, payment and kudos (cultural capital) for their work on the literary document, the screenplay. Their work is central and fundamental, and needs careful study, not least for the personal vision they bring to the screen idea (see, e.g., Nelmes 2014). But if we were to observe all the creative input throughout all the development of the screen idea, we'd see the process is more collaborative than that. There are always more people involved in screen idea development, from the producer who agrees the script to the actor who changes the lines. As film scholar and critic David Thomson observed, there are many authors of *Alien* (1979)—from writers Dan O'Bannon and Ronald Shusett, through Alien designer H. R. Giger and actor Sigourney Weaver, to art student Bolaji Badejo "who wore the Alien costume in many shots just because he happened to bump into an agent in a London pub" (Thomson 2000, 19).

Even an inner circle of those directly involved in writing often emphasises collaborative working, such as the *botteghe di scrittura* (screenwriting cottage industries) in Italy from the 1930s to 1950s (Russo 2014a, 2015; Romanelli 2019), and today's Story Conferences and Writers' Rooms (e.g. Macdonald 2013, 81–110; Tieber 2014). There may be a yet smaller creative triangle of writer, producer and director (Ross 1997, 2001; Bloore 2013), which functions as the lead group on ideas being developed. These groupings are all manifestations of what can be called a Screen Idea Work Group (SIWG).

The SIWG exists only to develop a singular idea, sharing that idea imperfectly among its members, and subject to the way power is distributed. This underlines the importance of the discourse within a SIWG, and what it tells us about this screen idea development in a particular context. We can also see that it is not only the SIWG which shapes and forms the screen idea, but also its external context, from local conventions to the field of power (e.g. Szczepanik et al. 2015; Černik 2020; Szczepanik 2021).

So, with a different perspective on what screenwriting is, and does, how do we approach the study of screenwriting?

2.3 The Domain of Screenwriting

If a university library could classify everything on screenwriting in one place, we would have the IRL visual equivalent of the virtual "domain" of screenwriting.[6] A domain is a "culturally defined symbolic system" (Sternberg and

---

[6] IRL = In Real Life.

Lubart 1999, 10) which includes "all the created products that have been accepted by the field in the past, and all the conventions shared by members of the field; the languages, symbols and notations" (Sawyer 2006, 125).

A "field" here is the collection of intermediaries and gatekeepers (such as practitioners, scholars or any others with power) who take positions on what enters the domain, says creativity theorist R. Keith Sawyer (2006, 123–25). Sawyer's use of field is broadly similar to that of the social anthropologist Pierre Bourdieu, who referred to the literary or artistic field as "a field of forces, but... also a field of struggles" between agents and their position-takings (1993, 30). In other words, the field is made up of people's opinions and practices, which together forms a common sense of limits, a sacred collection of beliefs—an experience termed "doxa" (Bourdieu 1977, 164 *passim*). The doxa is all the received wisdom about a specific practice, including the generally held tribal beliefs (and disagreements) about the right way to understand and take part in that practice—in this case, of screenwriting. Hollywood has a need to codify its practices (particularly as it is organised around freelance or short-term working), and so feels obliged to "transform the doxa into the orthodoxy, or into dogma" (cf. Bourdieu 1996, 185). So it is the Hollywood doxa, alongside the cultural system(s) which allows it to dominate screenwriting practice inside and outside its own industry, as organised and expressed as a system of poetics in the orthodox manuals and other advice, which informs and shapes the practice of much screenwriting. It tells us what is "good" and what is not.

And screenwriting studies? It is part of this domain and of the same field. Study and practice overlap. Screenwriting studies has expanded over the last twenty years, countering the difficulties that already established fields (film studies, TV studies, literary studies) had in grasping and understanding the practice (Millard 2015; Maras 2021; Macdonald 2021b). There is now a greater awareness of the centrality of screenwriting, where the script (as a statement) represents both a potential screenwork *and* its own tangible existence as a literary or artistic object.

The expanding field of screenwriting has been seeking new explanations for what belongs in this domain. There has been some sense of discovery of other disciplines and fields, in particular those theories which deal with group practice and creativity, reader-oriented interpretation and interpretive communities, and ideas of work, text and author. As a result, more viewpoints/positions have joined the field, and more scholarly publications have entered the domain, although the field is still some distance from establishing comprehensive school(s) of thought. As a result we now have a broader domain, and a larger field, to study.

For the purposes of this essay, however, I propose we draw together work that shares an apparent affinity of purpose, into three clusters:

1. Orthodox Creative Screenwriting, which attempts to understand it as a set of orthodox, industrially applicable skills and principles;

2. Critical Practice, which understands screenwriting as an opportunity for new, original expression, on the page or elsewhere; and
3. Critical Analysis, which seeks to understand the processes and meanings behind the creation of any work regarded as moving image narrative, from a range of perspectives.

These labels are used only because they each broadly describe a distinct, observable approach to screenwriting. They each take something of a theoretical position. The first cluster could be said to propose a hermetic set of principles with an internal logic to them. The second cluster seeks new practices and challenges to established orthodox practice. The third cluster resonates with critical theory as the common Western approach to research in the social sciences, in that its content seeks "the descriptive and normative bases for social inquiry aimed at decreasing domination and increasing freedom in all their forms" (Bohman 2021).

These clusters resemble Alexandra Ksenofontova's use of Stanley Fish's notion of "interpretive communities" (Ksenofontova 2020, 5–7; Fish 1982), but they should not be confused with analytical frames through which one might focus on particular aspects of screenwriting, e.g. "the practitioner frame, the story and structure frame, the business frame…[etc.]" (Maras 2009, 10–11) which are instead useful for specific studies.

The limited space of this essay prevents close analysis of this proposal, and there are questions, e.g., about what is meant by "communities" (which community? How should we view separation, or overlaps?), but we can recognise that each cluster attracts a particular part of the field which chooses to approach screenwriting in the same or similar way. Therefore, there is some merit in a comparison between these approaches in relation to a particular topic—for example, in the development of the screen idea.

2.4 Cluster 1: Orthodox Creative Screenwriting

Orthodox screenwriting is the dominant approach to screenwriting practice. Based mostly on US (Hollywood) practice and exported elsewhere (see, e.g., Joyce 2015), it is, however, not all one-way traffic, and other influences are observable. Paolo Russo, for example, notes that a significant branch of this US tradition was influenced by the import to the USA of so-called Russian methods (i.e. those of Vsevolod Pudovkin), published in the US in the 1950s and later taught by the Czech-American professor František "Frank" Daniel (note to author 09/12/21). Russo also notes Pudovkin was studied by Italian writers from the Neorealist generation onwards who graduated from the National Film School in Cinecittà, Rome (notes to author 09/12/21, 15/03/22). Whatever the origins, the orthodoxy is the standard, coherent, familiar story-telling system found today in screenwriting manuals and internet advice. Many, if not most, screenplays are likely to be developed according to orthodox principles.

The orthodoxy insists on the master-scene screenplay form as standard, the study of exemplars as key to successful writing and the acceptance of received wisdom about best practice. The student here is led to understand and apply the orthodoxy which, throughout, is presented as non-negotiable, as a fact of professional life. In this, screenwriting manuals are "securitising and legitimising mechanisms" (Conor 2014b, 133). Learn the rules before you break them! The principles of orthodox screenwriting are convenient for teaching prospective professional writers, and their study and application can help form a stable, coherent, educational programme.

This cluster tends to be reliant on screenwriting manuals and other how-to advice of a similar nature (Conor 2014a; Ashton and Conor 2016). Screenwriting manuals vary, of course, but their authors all claim experience and authority in various ways, as either creator (e.g. Smethurst 1998; Snyder 2005) or trainer (Hauge 1992; Seger 2010; Alessandra 2010) or both (Horton 2000; Yorke 2013; Harris 2014) or even as literary agent (Friedmann 1995).[7] Some re-discover older ideas (Egri 1960; Howard and Mabley 1993; Vogler 1996), including ancient Greek (McKee 1999, interpreting Aristotle). Some clearly describe industrial practice directly (Trottier 1998; Thompson 2011), and some bring new thinking into their work, such as Parker's creative matrix (1998), or specific ways of stimulating individual creativity (Potter 1990; Pelican 2021). They compete for attention, claiming authority or success sometimes to the point of total hype, such as "the last book on screenwriting you'll ever need" (Snyder 2005, cover).

The manuals' framework may not always be an exact match with mainstream industrial practice, but nevertheless it claims (strongly) to represent it. The coherence of this orthodoxy was tested in 2015–2016, in a survey of the discourse of 103 books published in the US and 52 in the UK, websites and university-level course information (Macdonald 2021a). This found a strong degree of consensus, not only between US and UK sources, but also about what constitutes screenwriting competencies, or what should make a screenplay "good" (2021a, 19–20). The general principles found in the US sources can be re-constructed as a list of 28 elements regarded as good or important, when developing a screenplay, and which cohere as a manifesto or framework (Table 2.1).

The orthodoxy is a structural approach to developing screen ideas—a "new structuralist vision" (Parker 2000, 66). Breaking down the process into components in this way stimulates debate within the field about how best to use and combine them, and encourages the screenwriter to correct and re-draft until it is both standardised and felt to be right.

Some see this as responsible for a perception of the screenplay as non-literature, [as] "little more than a mediating device" (Price 2010, 56). It is technically flexible and, with its openness to any content, implies that this

---

[7] See also Friedmann's book series https://makemoneyscreenwriting.com/books/, accessed 18 May 2022.

Table 2.1 Synthesis of the orthodoxy, based on a sample survey of 103 US texts/fragments 2015–2016 (Macdonald 2021a, 21–22)

What makes a writer's draft screenplay "good" is…
1. The 3-Act template, or variation, as the starting point for all narrative structure in moving image narrative
2. A main plot, plus sub-plots which support or "push" the plotline
3. A 2nd Act (middle) which develops/complicates the story, shows clear direction and will be resolved in Act 3
4. The presence of changing tension, rising and falling (sawtooth), and progressing in this fashion to a major climax towards the end
5. A story based on emotion (which could be linked to subtext)
6. A central narrative question, of a problem or situation to be (re-)solved, and to which everything relates
7. A structure and format (Master Scene) based on scenes, which individually advance the story and reveal character
8. A scene structure which includes dramatic "beats" as specific elements of action
9. Scenes which can be built into sequences and collected into Acts, each of which also has recognisable structure
10. A tendency towards action and pace
11. A tendency to "show not tell", despite a prohibition on specifying shots
12. The restriction of shot-based narrative structures to designated montage sequences
13. Dialogue which reveals character, engages attention, progresses the narrative (as "verbal action")
14. A sense of overall cohesion, or unity
15. A central character (protagonist) with a goal, i.e. a motivation for action towards a clear objective
16. A significant goal, with significant difficulty (stakes, obstacles) in achieving it
17. (An) active character(s)
18. Drama that has "punch"
19. The use of outward conflict, or relational conflict
20. A tendency towards clarity of purpose, and narrative simplicity
21. A main character with a flaw and a range of emotions ("3D"), and/or…
22. … A character with fewer emotions but significant personal characteristic(s) which create a "signature" or incite specific admiration
23. A main character who changes, transforms, grows over the narrative (character arc)
24. Characters who relate to (rather than only conform to) character archetypes or roles
25. A relationship to genre conventions
26. Accurate conventional presentation on the page
27. Awareness of commercial issues, particularly around structure, novelty and the current market
28. Novelty, originality, the writer's voice (in most circumstances)

framework is a neutral vehicle. However, we see from the synthesis above that the orthodoxy is a very specific vehicle, a framework for a particular development practice which prescribes—if not the choice of story—particular ways of story-telling. This of course has implications for other possible ways of story-telling, and ethical questions around diversity, for example, and around its general claim to be universally applicable (Maras 2016, 2017; Hambly 2021).

This claim impacts on the educational setting. Some scholars have worried that "the governing methodology of how we teach screenwriters—both in the Academy and through public and private workshops—is based upon the McKee/Field/Hollywood paradigm" (Tobin 2014, 205), or in other words, upon the orthodoxy. In Australia, others have more recently challenged this view (Hambly 2020), as well as the accuracy of the claims of this paradigm (Hambly 2021). There is little doubt, however, that the orthodoxy—which includes an ideal of the individual writer working on a specific screenplay in ways that conform—dominates discourse in the advisory literature on professional screenwriting (Macdonald 2021a, 19–23).

At university level, learning and teaching discourses around screenwriting tend to reflect the industrial model of filmmaking, shaping divisions of labour "on technological and procedural fault lines", as filmmaker and teacher Erik Knudsen has pointed out (2016, 110). The problem for Knudsen is that these divisions are limited or skewed, with the traditional screenplay being heavily designed towards performance rather than focusing on the formal elements of cinema practice. What Knudsen wants to see is information on, among other things, "the faces, the postures, the minute details of gesture and looks, the eyes, the sounds, the colours, the compositions, the mise-en-scéne, the juxtapositions, the rhythms, the textures" (Knudsen 2016, 111)—all elements which may be better described through visual rather than verbal means. In contrast, the manuals which support the orthodoxy only offer "a limited palette of tools related to character psychology and motivation or their subsequent story arcs" (Knudsen 2016, 111).

What happens when we attempt to go beyond the limitations of the orthodoxy?

2.5   Cluster 2: Critical Practice

The limitations of the orthodox approach to teaching screenwriting are even clearer with the newer, digital ways of filmmaking. Echoing Kathryn Millard (2014, 136–57), Knudsen points to the digital revolution as an opportunity for change. Not only are more films being made, but (he claims) they are being made more democratically, undermining the traditional roles, to our advantage in film education (Knudsen 2016, 112, 125–26). Andrew Kenneth Gay, in another example, pointed out the value of lean management theory in educating film students towards "flexibility and continuous improvement", rather than holding to the more rigid literary script practices associated with Hollywood (2014, 261). This pressure for change fits with the expanding nature of the field, the increasing engagement with image and narrative manipulation through apps like *Tik Tok* and free editing software, and the overlapping interaction between producer and user on-line.[8]

Screenwriting that challenges the orthodoxy has been called "alternative scripting" (Maras 2009; Murphy 2019), "breaking the rules" (Dancyger and Rush 2002), "the experimental screenplay" (Ksenofontova 2020, 10–14 *passim*) and other such terms. The community that produces such work could be called alternative, independent or experimental screenwriters (or screen writers), but the essential question is broadly similar; how does their practice critique, inform or reject conventional practice, and create new knowledge, new practice, new principles or new understandings? This may form the basis for Practice-as-Research (PAR), sometimes perhaps seen as a more individual and less collaborative form of creative writing than the orthodox (Baker 2016).[9]

Suddenly, how to develop a screen idea becomes an open question.

Siobhan Jackson's and Mischa Baka's film *You Can Say Vagina* (2017), for example, had no screenplay "in the traditional sense", being "fashioned more or less straight to camera" (Jackson 2021, 239), and consciously recognising its affiliation to film movements like Mumblecore.[10] Jakob Lass, a filmmaker whose work has been compared with Mumblecore (Lass 2017), calls his own philosophy "Fogma" after the Danish Dogme 95 movement, and he reportedly has only one rule—that "each Fogma film should select its own development rules with confidence" (in Jackson 2021, 240).[11] Lass's Fogma rules are designed to provide minimal script framework, with only a few sentences per scene—"like two or three, maximum four sentences"—and there is no dialogue (Lass 2017). He has reputedly invented scenes on the spot, adapting to the found situation. Jackson's account of her own production also underlines the importance of making the film in her own way rather than following the orthodoxy. Her method underlines her belief in screen idea

---

[8] *Tik Tok* (www.tiktok.com, accessed 17 May 2022). One news story reports the development of an app—*NewNew*—in which fans and followers pay to vote to decide anything the creator asks them, including even what food to choose as a takeaway. It can be used to decide the detailed elements in a story, such as genre, character names and plot developments, which could be being written on another app, like *Wattpad* (Smale 2021).

[9] Or Practice-Led-Research (PLR) in Australia. See also the resources listed at https://www.methods.manchester.ac.uk/themes/qualitative-methods/practice-as-research/, accessed 24 November 2021.

[10] The mumblecore movement is "a[n] eclectic group of young, media-savvy filmmakers who came into prominence at the SXSW Film Festival in 2005 by making lo-fi naturalistic films that dealt with the problems of their own generation, namely people in their twenties" (Murphy 2019, 187). They often rely on non-professional actors and improvisation. Siobhan Jackson also refers to a similar Berlin Flow movement (2021, 239).

[11] *Dogme 95*: the name of the manifesto called 'the vow of chastity' by a Danish group of filmmakers which included Lars von Trier and Thomas Vinterberg. Rejecting common artifice such as genre films, the manifesto has nevertheless become something of a genre itself, even though the rules were not always applied. See, for example, the tribute website http://www.dogme95.dk/the-vow-of-chastity/, accessed 11 September 2021.

development as a process which includes making the film. Using the example of a football coach pleading with his players to stop thinking about their moves and get on and *do* something, she says "we figured it was better to risk making a bad film than make no film at all" (Jackson 2021, 243). In the end, the result was not misshapen craft, says Jackson (2021, 246), even while the development was unorthodox.

Challenging the orthodoxy takes confidence. In the university setting, students run the risk of being called incompetent, because university programmes usually require learning the orthodox rules first. Educator Nils Lindahl Elliot pointed out the particular difficulty for his students (2000, 20). Their unselfconscious adoption of craft, working in a vocational variant of his programme, led to recognisably coherent work, while those students working from a critical perspective produced work that was thought incoherent—the result of a struggle to think about new principles of coherence.

Coherent or not, any such new work can create debate and innovation within the doxa, perhaps becoming accepted within the orthodoxy, such as the shifting protagonists in *Fargo* (Murphy 2007, 65 *passim*).

Despite Jackson's "just do it" mantra, the process of thinking and doing is joined together in an ongoing process. Her *You Can Say Vagina* (2017) had a shooting ratio of 8:1 leaving a tidy amount of thinking on the cutting room floor (Jackson 2021, 246). Thinking the screen idea and its components is still screenwriting, orthodox or not, and the thinking does not stop when the director turns up on set. Making the whole film is screen writing and, even more today, it is "writing with light" in cinematographer Vittorio Storaro's phrase (Maras 2009, 2).[12] Selecting your own development rules is still screenwriting. Writing down the screen idea in different ways is screenwriting. (Not writing it down is also screenwriting.)

Screenwriting, or screen writing, is *de facto* a way of trying things out, proposing new ways, asking questions about the nature of a singular screen narrative, implying the question "we can do it this way, can't we?" On that basis, a script is not just a singular film prototype, it is also a practice-based statement of film philosophy or an analytical commentary, important because it occurs before the film is made, before any hindsight is possible.

2.6 Cluster 3: Critical Analysis

Cluster 3 is where a diverse field attempts to ask "what is (or was) happening here, and how can we understand it?" But any apparent unity then appears to fracture, because there is a whole range of different topics and perspectives on screenwriting that have been tackled in different ways over the past decade or two. Since 2010, for example, research work in the peer-reviewed *Journal of*

---

[12] See also Millard's use of the phrase (2013; 2014, 136–37). Maras also quotes Friedrich Wilhelm Murnau's "sketching pencil" and Alexandre Astruc's "*caméra-stylo*" (Maras 2009, 2).

Screenwriting has ranged over subjects as diverse as authorship, genre, screenwriting as creative labour, historical contexts, geo-political contexts, industrial contexts, silent films, digital and virtual screenwriting, feminism, the screenplay text, the screenplay and photography, scripting, documentary screenwriting, adaptation, ethics, etc.

This wide-ranging richness, I suggest, reflects the centrality of screenwriting in the production process, and its stand-alone relevance to whole disciplines (such as film studies, media studies, literary studies, communications studies and cultural studies). This provokes the breadth and diversity of research work across the domain. But how do we conceptualise and study such a patchwork of viewpoints?

Steven Maras (2011) proposed four attitudes found in screenwriting research—restorative, exemplification, evangelical and descriptivist (2011, 276–77)—and offered seven "trajectories" (formalist, narratological, stylistic, historical, industrial/institutional, conceptual and practice-based), as an "attempt at definition and articulation" of the range of directions that we were taking, or might take (2011, 278). Steven Price (2013b) suggested four "frames" (discourses surrounding screenwriting, the practitioner's frame, research and scholarship, and criticism and interpretation). Both Maras and Price suggest the value of particular research methods—Maras with discourse analysis and Price with textual analysis—although not to the exclusion of other techniques. Genetic criticism, for example, was developed from the structuralist movement in France as a literary research tool focusing on detailed analysis of the discourse of a range of written texts, in order to produce an understanding of an *avant-texte* (Ferrer and Groden 2004, 5). Applied to film scripts, Francis Vanoye noted in 1991 it produced a "rich perspective, little explored so far" (Boillat 2020, 147).[13] The field appears, *de facto*, to have recognised and moved towards accepting the co-existence and value of various ways of approaching screenwriting research.

For example, scholars consider screen idea development as complex, a "wicked problem" for investigation across several angles (Batty et al. 2018; see also Batty and Taylor 2015, 2021). So much is in flux during development—the flexible membership of the work group (SIWG), the exercise and interchange of power, the interplay and understanding of ideologies, specific discourses and frameworks, and the stated reason for production (the brief), not to mention the opportunistic, reactive decisions made around this screen idea. In what ways could we research and understand this complex set of activities? By employing several specific perspectives, I suggest.

One such perspective is through the frame of creativity research, drawing on the work of, e.g., Howard Gardner, Mihalyi Csikzentmihalyi and Dean Simonton. This is a mix of psychological, sociological and anthropological research, described as an inter-disciplinary socio-cultural approach (Sawyer

---

[13] Orig. "Perspective très riche, qui n'a encore été que peut explorée" (author's translation).

2006, 3–4). Creative development in groups has been described by creativity researcher R. Keith Sawyer as "hybrid", incorporating properties of both individuals and groups, working within a framework of "collaborative emergence" (Sawyer 2010, 366). His research within groups has investigated improvisational performance such as jazz (see Sawyer 2006, 119–21), improv theatre (1999; Sawyer and DeZutter 2009) and children's play (2002) as a way of taking a systems approach to understanding group creativity, one that "combines individualist perspectives with analyses of the social organisation of creative fields" (Sawyer 2010, 378). We can adapt this approach to screenwriting studies, to understand firstly the process in each particular case (by using, e.g., interviews, ethnographic observation and written records including scripts) and also the contextual—the local view of an orthodoxy, perhaps a manifesto, and cultural and industrial conditions (Macdonald 2013, 113–16; 2021a; Redvall 2013).

Separately, and differently, J. J. Murphy's work on improvisatory performance focuses instead on what is done with the script (2019). Referring to a group therapy technique termed "psychodrama", Murphy explores the role of the screenplay in some American independent films and asks "what are the limits of the script? What are the limits of performance? What happens when a filmmaker chooses not to employ a traditional screenplay?" (2019, 2). Kathryn Millard has also explored the interest in improvising with performers, resulting from the rise in digital cinema (2014, 97–117 *passim*). Both Murphy and Millard point to the tension between the "primacy of the screenplay" (Murphy 2019, 2), seen as a controlling device, and "the degree to which the screenplay remains open to new material throughout production" (Millard 2014, 116).

Another perspective is to see development practice through the institutional frame; what Petr Szczepanik calls the context of particular "local industry eco-systems" (2021, 65). Szczepanik examines the task of scripting a new screen idea within the local structures, regulations and prohibitions which impact on the work of the SIWG. In his work on screenwriting in the post-socialist Czech Republic (now Czechia), Szczepanik identifies four different types of development practice: Mainstream Arthouse, Mainstream Commercial, Marginal Arthouse and Marginal Commercial (Szczepanik et al. 2015; Szczepanik 2021). These types are not prescribed in advance and yet can be seen as separated for managerial as well as creative reasons. In the twentieth century communist state of Czechoslovakia, the eco-system of production was different to that of Western states, with greater government involvement at specified stages and (fortunately for the historian) more paper records of the development process (Szczepanik 2013). It also follows that screenwriting practices may be different between centres of screen narrative production, or between different time periods, and for different reasons— and that there is considerable comparative work to do to understand these differences. Szczepanik's study (2021) concludes with a call for comparative research, based on a "Bourdieu-inspired analysis of the semi-autonomous field of cultural production", in the hope that this will allow for "more fine-grained comparisons of development practices" (2021, 66). Similar studies in the same edited volume range from Australia compared with Denmark, to Iceland, and to the USA in the classic big network era (Batty and Taylor 2021).

2.7 Screenwriting Studies

Studying screenwriting is not only about reading screenplays, discussing talented writers and learning how to write a story in master-scene script form. If you have just read this essay, you will know it is more complex than that. It is also about understanding that:

1. A film script can be written and read in (at least) two ways: as a literary document focused on telling the story and as a filmic document imagining the film.
2. The scriptwriter is not the only author involved in this process.
3. Those who develop the film share an understanding of what it is—the screen idea.
4. There is no definitive screenplay (though a particular draft might be designated as such).
5. Any method of sharing the screen idea—treatment, back of an envelope, chat, gestures—can be thought of as "scripting" the screen idea.
6. Within the domain, it can be helpful to consider three clusters of work, each asking a different basic question, and so representing different approaches to understanding screenwriting.
7. Screenwriting is not just a part of film production, it is the basis of it, and for it. It is the creative answer to the philosophical question "what is a film?", represented by the contained question "what is *this* film?".

There is much yet to discover about how moving image narrative has been, and will be, conceived, not least in places where practice has differed from the Hollywood orthodoxy, such as India (Yadav 2010; Tieber 2012; Sengupta 2018, 2021; etc.). Archives are yielding new information, e.g., in Italy (Russo 2014b) and Czechoslovakia/Czechia (Szczepanik 2013, 2021; Szczepanik et al. 2015; Černik 2020). Even where traditional documents like screenplays have been discarded—a frequent occurrence—or never even existed, scholars are rising to the challenge of the "absent archive" (Sengupta 2021). The value of screenwriting research also lies in what it can do as a tool for uncovering more about screen narrative in general, such as Lauri Kitsnik's study (2020) on social issue films in post-war Japan. And, there is no doubt that new practices are developing for new forms of screen media, so there is every reason to suppose the domain (and the field) will continue to expand, as long as we remain open to the range and diversity of screenwriting practices, and to how we might study them.

Acknowledgements I am very grateful for the insights and suggestions from colleagues who commented on earlier drafts, in particular Prof. Kristyn Gorton (University of Leeds), Dr. Steven Maras (University of Western Australia) and Dr. Paolo Russo (Oxford Brookes University).

References

Alessandra, Pilar. 2010. *The Coffee Break Screenwriter*. Studio City, CA: Michael Wiese.
Alien. 1979. Written by Dan O'Bannon, and Ronald Shusett. Directed by Ridley Scott. USA: Brandywine Productions, 20th Century Fox, 117 mins.
Aliens. 1986. Written by Walter Hill, David Giler, and James Cameron. Directed by James Cameron. USA: Brandywine Productions, 20th Century Fox, 137 mins.
Alien³. 1992. Written by Walter Hill, David Giler, and Larry Ferguson. Directed by David Fincher. USA: Brandywine Productions, 20th Century Fox, 114 mins [standard edition].
Ashton, Daniel, and Bridget Conor. 2016. "Screenwriting, Higher Education and Digital Ecologies of Expertise." *New Writing* 13 (1): 91–108.
Baker, Dallas J. 2016. "The Screenplay as Text: Academic Scriptwriting as Creative Research." *New Writing* 13 (1): 71–84.
Battleship Potemkin [Bronenosets Potyomkin]. 1925. Written by Nina Aghadzhanova. Directed by Sergei Eisenstein. USSR: Mosfilm, 75 mins.
Batty, Craig, and Stayci Taylor. 2015. "Script Development and the Hidden Practices of Screenwriting: Perspectives from Industry Professionals." *New Writing* 13 (2): 204–17.
Batty, Craig, Radha O'Meara, Stayci Taylor, Hester Joyce, Philippa Burne, Noel Malony, Mark Poole, and Marilyn Tofler. 2018. "Script Development as a 'Wicked Problem'." *Journal of Screenwriting* 9 (2): 153–74.
Batty, Craig, and Stayci Taylor, eds 2021. *Script Development. Critical Approaches, Creative Practices, International Perspectives*. London: Palgrave Macmillan.
Bloore, Peter. 2013. *The Screenplay Business. Managing Creativity and Script Development in the Film Industry*. London: Routledge.
Bohman, James. 2021. "Critical Theory." In *Stanford Encyclopedia of Philosophy*, edited by Edward N. Zalta. Stanford, CT: The Metaphysics Research Lab, Stanford University. http://plato.stanford.edu/entries/critical-theory/. Accessed 2 December 2021.
Boillat, Alain. 2020. En Cas de Malheur, *de Simenon à Autant-Lara (1956–1958)* [In case of Adversity, *from Simenon to Autant-Lara (1956–1958)*]. Geneva: Droz.
Bordwell, David, Janet Staiger, and Kristin Thompson. 1985. *The Classical Hollywood Cinema. Film Style and Mode of Production to 1960*. London: Routledge.
Bourdieu, Pierre. 1977. *Outline of a Theory of Practice*. Cambridge: Cambridge University Press.
Bourdieu, Pierre. 1993. *The Field of Cultural Production*. Cambridge: Polity Press.
Bourdieu, Pierre. 1996. *The Rules of Art*. Cambridge: Polity Press.
Branigan, Edward. 1992. *Narrative Comprehension and Film*. London: Routledge.
Brickey, Russell. 2021. "Art in the 'Big Print': An Examination and Exercises for Cinematic Prose Writing Style." *Journal of Screenwriting* 12 (2): 227–42.
Černik, Jan. 2020. "The Strange Case of the Three-Column Screenplay Format in 1950s Czechoslovakia." *Journal of Screenwriting* 11 (1): 7–26.

Cole, Hillis R., and Judith H. Haag. 2000. *The Complete Guide to Standard Script Formats. Part 1: Screenplays.* North Hollywood, CA: CMC.
Conor, Bridget. 2014a. *Screenwriting. Creative Labor and Professional Practice.* London: Routledge.
Conor, Bridget. 2014b. "Gurus and Oscar Winners. How-to Screenwriting Manuals in the New Cultural Economy." *TV and New Media* 15 (2): 121–38.
Dancyger, Ken, and Jeff Rush. 2002. *Alternative Scriptwriting. Successfully Breaking the Rules.* 3rd ed. Boston: Focal Press.
Davies, Rosamund. 2013. "*Don't Look Now*: The Screenwork as Palimpsest." *Journal of Screenwriting* 4 (2): 163–77.
Davies, Rosamund. 2019. "The Screenplay as Boundary Object." *Journal of Screenwriting* 10 (2): 149–64.
Egri, Lajos. 1960. *The Art of Dramatic Writing.* New York: Simon & Schuster.
Elliot, Nils Lindahl. 2000. "Pedagogic Discourse in Theory–Practice Courses in Media Studies." *Screen* 41 (1): 18–32.
Fargo. 1996. Written and directed by Joel Cohen and Ethan Cohen. USA: Polygram, Working Title, 98 mins.
Ferrer, Daniel, and Michael Groden. 2004. "Introduction: A Genesis of French Genetic Criticism." In *Genetic Criticism*, edited by Jed Deppman, Daniel Ferrer, and Michael Groden, 1–16. Philadelphia: University of Pennsylvania Press.
Fish, Stanley. 1982. *Is There a Text in This Class? The Authority of Interpretive Communities.* Cambridge, MA: Harvard University Press.
Friedmann, Julian. 1995. *How to Make Money Scriptwriting.* London: Boxtree.
Ganz, Adam. 2010. "Time, Space and Movement: Screenplay as Oral narrative." *Journal of Screenwriting* 1 (2): 225–36.
Ganz, Adam, and Steven Price. 2020. *Robert de Niro at Work. From Screenplay to Screen Performance.* London: Palgrave Macmillan.
Gay, Andrew Kenneth. 2014. "Start Me Up: Lean Screenwriting for American Entrepreneurial Cinema." *Journal of Screenwriting* 5 (2): 259–75.
Giarrusso, Vincenzo. 2019. "An Insider Perspective on the Script in Practice." *Journal of Screenwriting* 10 (1): 41–61.
Hambly, Glenda. 2020. "Cultural Influences in Screenwriting. Australia vs Hollywood." *Journal of Screenwriting* 11 (1): 45–63.
Hambly, Glenda. 2021. "The Not So Universal Hero's Journey." *Journal of Screenwriting* 12 (2): 135–50.
Harris, Charles. 2014. *Complete Screenwriting Course.* London: John Murray Learning.
Hauge, Michael. 1992. *Writing Screenplays That Sell.* British ed. [London]: Elm Tree Books.
Hill, Walter, and David Giler. 1990. *Alien III.* Draft screenplay. 10/10/90. USA: Brandywine Productions. British Film Institute script collection S15831. Accessed 8 December 2021.
Hill, Walter, and David Giler. 1991. *Alien III.* Draft screenplay. 26/01/91. USA: Brandywine Productions. http://www.horrorlair.com/scripts/alien3_hill.html. Accessed 1 October 2021.
Horton, Andrew. 2000. *Laughing Out Loud. Writing the Comedy-Centered Screenplay.* Berkeley, CA: University of California Press.
Howard, David, and Edward Mabley. 1993. *The Tools of Screenwriting.* New York: St. Martin's Press.

Ings, Welby. 2021. "Renegotiating the Screenplay. Drawing as a Method for Narrative Development in a Short Film." *Journal of Screenwriting* 12 (3): 151–63.
Jackson, Siobhan. 2021. "The Promiscuous Screenplay. A Tale of Wanton Development and Loose Authorship." In *Script Development. Critical Approaches, Creative Practices, International Perspectives*, edited by Craig Batty, and Stayci Taylor, 237–69. London: Palgrave Macmillan.
The Journal of Screenwriting. Bristol, UK: Intellect Press. 2010–present.
Joyce, Hester. 2015. "Cargo Cults. Key Moments in Establishing Screenwriting in the New Zealand Film Commission." *Journal of Screenwriting* 6 (1): 71–87.
Kitsnik, Lauri. 2016. "Scenario Writers and Scenario Readers in the Golden Age of Japanese Cinema." *Journal of Screenwriting* 7 (3): 285–97.
Kitsnik, Lauri. 2020. "Scouting for Scripts: Mitsuki Yōko and Social Issue Film in Post-war Japan." *Journal of Screenwriting* 11 (3): 265–85.
Knudsen, Erik. 2016. "The Total Filmmaker: Thinking of Screenwriting, Directing and Editing as One Role." *New Writing* 13 (1): 109–29.
Ksenofontova, Alexandra. 2020. *The Modernist Screenplay. Experimental Writing for Silent Film*. London: Palgrave Macmillan.
Kubrick, Stanley. 1970. *A Clockwork Orange*. 07/09/70. Screenplay. Available at the Stanley Kubrick Archive, University of the Arts London, SK/13/1/13.
Lass, Jakob. 2017. *CIFF 2017: Jakob Lass on* Tiger Girl. Indie Outlook. https://indie-outlook.com/2017/10/24/ciff-2017-jakob-lass-on-tiger-girl/. Accessed 7 July 2021.
Macdonald, Ian W. 2004a. "Disentangling the Screen Idea." *Journal of Media Practice* 5 (2): 89–99.
Macdonald, Ian W. 2004b. "The Presentation of the Screen Idea in Narrative Film-Making." PhD diss., Leeds Metropolitan University.
Macdonald, Ian W. 2007. "Struggle for the Silents: The British Screenwriter from 1910 to 1930." *Journal of Media Practice* 8 (2): 115–28.
Macdonald, Ian W. 2013. *Screenwriting Poetics and the Screen Idea*. Basingstoke, UK: Palgrave Macmillan.
Macdonald, Ian W. 2021a. "Originality and Authorship in the Development of the Screen Idea." In *Script Development. Critical Approaches, Creative Practices, International Perspectives*, edited by Craig Batty, and Stayci Taylor, 9–29. London: Palgrave Macmillan.
Macdonald, Ian W. 2021b. "Meeting Old Friends for the First Time. A Personal Reflection on the Development of the Screenwriting Research Network." *Journal of Screenwriting* 12 (2): 203–26.
Maras, Steven. 2009. *Screenwriting. History, Theory and Practice*. London: Wallflower.
Maras, Steven. 2011. "Some Attitudes and Trajectories in Screenwriting Research." *Journal of Screenwriting* 2 (2): 275–86.
Maras, Steven, ed. 2016. *Ethics in Screenwriting. New Perspectives*. London: Palgrave Macmillan.
Maras, Steven. 2017. "Towards a Critique of Universalism in Screenwriting Criticism." *Journal of Screenwriting* 8 (2): 177–96.
Maras, Steven. 2021. "Screenwriting Research in Australia. A Truncated (Pre-) history." *Journal of Screenwriting* 12 (2): 179–202.
Martin, Adrian. 2014. "Where Do Cinematic Ideas Come From?" *Journal of Screenwriting* 5 (1): 9–26.

Mayer, Carl. 1927. *Sunrise*. Screenplay. Los Angeles: Twentieth Century Fox. In *Sunrise* [1927] 2004, DVD Disc 2 *Special features*. Los Angeles: Fox Film Corporation.
McKee, Robert. 1999. *Story. Substance, Structure, Style and the Principles of Screenwriting*. London: Methuen.
Millard, Kathryn. 2011. "The Screenplay as Prototype." In *Analysing the Screenplay*, edited by Jill Nelmes, 142–57. Abingdon, UK: Routledge.
Millard, Kathryn. 2013. "Writing with Light: The Screenplay and Photography." *Journal of Screenwriting* 4 (2): 123–34.
Millard, Kathryn. 2014. *Screenwriting in a Digital Era*. Basingstoke: Palgrave Macmillan.
Millard, Kathryn. 2015. "The Universe Is Expanding." *Journal of Screenwriting* 7 (3): 271–84.
Murphy, J. J. 2007. *Me and You and Memento and Fargo*. New York: Continuum.
Murphy, J. J. 2019. *Rewriting Indie Cinema. Improvisation, Psychodrama, and the Screenplay*. New York: Columbia University Press.
Naipaul, Vidiadhar Surajprasad. 1998. *India. A Million Mutinies Now*. London: Vintage.
Nelmes, Jill. 2014. *The Screenwriter in British Cinema*. London: British Film Institute/Palgrave Macmillan.
Pallant, Chris, and Steven Price. 2015. *Storyboarding. A Critical History*. Basingstoke, UK: Palgrave Macmillan.
Parker, Philip. 1998. *The Art and Science of Screenwriting*. Exeter, UK: Intellect Books.
Parker, Philip. 2000. "Reconstructing Narrative." *Journal of Media Practice* 1 (2): 66–74.
Pasolini, Pier Paolo. [1966] 1977. "The Scenario as a Structure Designed to Become Another Structure." *Wide Angle* 2 (1): 40–47.
Pelican, Kira-Ann. 2021. *The Science of Writing Characters*. London: Bloomsbury.
Potter, Cherry. 1990. *Image, Sound and Story. The Art of Telling in Film*. London: Secker and Warburg.
Price, Steven. 2010. *The Screenplay. Authorship, Theory and Criticism*. Basingstoke, UK: Palgrave Macmillan.
Price, Steven. 2013a. *A History of the Screenplay*. Basingstoke, UK: Palgrave Macmillan.
Price, Steven. 2013b. "The Screenplay: An Accelerated Critical History." *Journal of Screenwriting* 4 (1): 87–97.
Redvall, Eva Novrup. 2013. *Writing and Producing Television Drama in Denmark. From* The Kingdom *to* The Killing. Basingstoke, UK: Palgrave Macmillan.
Redvall, Eva Novrup, and Iben Albinus Sabroe. 2016. "Production Design as a Storytelling Tool in the Writing of the Danish TV Drama Series *The Legacy*." *Journal of Screenwriting* 7 (3): 299–317.
Riley, Christopher. 2021. *The Hollywood Standard*. 3rd rev. ed. Seattle: Michael Wiese.
Romanelli, Claudia. 2019. "From Dialogue Writer to Screenwriter: Pier Paolo Pasolini at Work for Federico Fellini." *Journal of Screenwriting* 10 (3): 323–37.
Ross, Dick. 1997. *Triangle. Rome – December 1996. A conference examining professional models and teaching practice in relation to concepts of collaboration between writer, producer and director students in film and television education.* [Rome]: CILECT/GEECT/Ente Cinema/MEDIA II.

Ross, Dick. 2001. *Triangle 2. A conference for teachers and students demonstrating the principles of collaboration between writers, directors and producers in the development of feature screenplays. Terni, Italy. October 1998.* Terni, Italy: CILECT/GEECT/Centro Multimediale di Terni/Provincia di Terni/MEDIA II.
Russo, Paolo, ed. 2014a. *Nero su Bianco. Sceneggiatura e Sceneggiatori in Italia.* Barcelona: Quaderni del CSCI.
Russo, Paolo. 2014b. "The De Santis Case: Screenwriting, Political Boycott and Archival Research." *Journal of Screenwriting* 5 (1): 101–23.
Russo, Paolo. 2015. "Suso Cecchi d'Amico." In *Women Screenwriters. An International Guide*, edited by Jill Nelmes, and Jule Selbo. Basingstoke, UK: Palgrave Macmillan.
Sawyer, R. Keith. 1999. "The Emergence of Creativity." *Philosophical Psychology* 12 (4): 447–69.
Sawyer, R. Keith. 2002. "Improvisation and Narrative." *Narrative Enquiry* 12 (2): 319–49.
Sawyer, R. Keith. 2006. *Explaining Creativity. The Science of Human Innovation.* Oxford: Oxford University Press.
Sawyer, R. Keith. 2010. "Individual and Group Creativity." In *Cambridge Handbook of Creativity*, edited by James C. Kaufman, and Robert Sternberg, 366–80. Cambridge: Cambridge University Press.
Sawyer, R. Keith, and Stacy DeZutter. 2009. "Distributed Creativity: How Collective Creations Emerge from Collaboration." *Psychology of Aesthetics, Creativity and the Arts* 3 (2): 81–92.
Seger, Linda. 2010. *Making a Good Script Great.* 3rd ed. Los Angeles: Silman-James.
Sengupta, Rakesh. 2018. "Writing from The Margins of Media: Screenwriting Practice and Discourse During the First Indian Talkies." *BioScope* 92 (2): 117–36.
Sengupta, Rakesh. 2021. "Towards a Decolonial Media Archaeology: The Absent Archive of Screenwriting History and the Obsolete Munshi." *Theory, Culture and Society* 38 (1): 3–26.
Smale, Will. 2021. "The App That Lets You Pay to Control Another Person's Life." *BBC News*, 17 July. www.bbc.co.uk/news/business-57085557. Accessed 18 July 2021.
Smethurst, William. 1998. *Writing for Television.* 2nd ed. Oxford: How To Books.
Snyder, Blake. 2005. *Save the Cat! The Last Book on Screenwriting that You'll Ever Need.* Studio City, CA: Michael Wiese.
Solomon, Stanley J. 1972. *The Film Idea.* New York: Harcourt Brace Jovanovitch.
Sternberg, Claudia. 1997. *Written for the Screen.* Tübingen: Stauffenberg.
Sternberg, Robert, and Todd I. Lubart. 1999. "The Concept of Creativity: Prospects and Paradigms." In *Handbook of Creativity*, edited by Robert Sternberg, 3–10. Cambridge: Cambridge University Press.
Szczepanik, Petr. 2013. "How Many Steps to the Shooting Script?" *Iluminace* 25 (3): 73–98.
Szczepanik, Petr. 2021. "Script Development and the Post-Socialist Producer: Towards a Comparative Approach to Cultures of Development." In *Script Development. Critical Approaches, Creative Practices, International Perspectives*, edited by Craig Batty, and Stayci Taylor, 51–68. London: Palgrave Macmillan.
Szczepanik, Petr, Johana Kotišová, Jakub Macek, Jan Motal and Eva Pjajčikova. 2015. *A Study of Feature Film Development in The Czech Republic: Introduction.*

Prague: Czech Film Fund. https://fondkinematografie.cz/assets/media/files/H/EN/SFK_studie_2018_ENG_KOR2_2_3.pdf. Accessed 1 July 2021.

Thompson, Chris. 2011. *Writing Soap*. Abergele, UK: Aber Books.

Thompson, Kristin. 2004. "Early Alternatives to the Hollywood Mode of Production. Implications for Europe's Avant-gardes." In *The Silent Cinema Reader*, edited by Lee Grieveson, and Peter Kramer, 349–67. London: Routledge.

Thomson, David. 2000. *The alien quartet*. London: Bloomsbury.

Tieber, Claus. 2008. *Schreiben für Hollywood. Das Drehbuch im Studiosystem* [Writing for Hollywood. The screenplay in the studio system]. Vienna: Lit Verlag GmbH.

Tieber, Claus. 2012. "Aristotle Did Not Make It to India. Modes of Narration in Hindi Cinema." In *Storytelling in World Cinema. Vol. 1: Forms*, edited by Lina Khatib, 11–25. New York: Wallflower.

Tieber, Claus. 2014. "A Story Is Not a Story but a Conference. Story Conferences and the Classical Studio System." *Journal of Screenwriting* 5 (2): 225–37.

Tieber, Claus, and Christina Wintersteller. 2020. "Writing with Music: Self-Reflexivity in the Screenplays of Walter Reisch." *Arts* 9 (13). https://www.mdpi.com/2076-0752/9/1/13?type=check_update&version=2. Accessed 20 November 2021.

Tobin, Ann. 2014. "Life's Blood. The Writer, the Practice and the Pedagogy of Screenwriting." PhD diss., Leeds Metropolitan University.

Trottier, David. 1998. *The Screenwriter's Bible. A Complete Guide to Writing, Formatting and Selling Your Script*. 3rd ed. Los Angeles: Silman-James.

Vogler, Christopher. 1996. *The Writer's Journey. Mythic Structure for Storytellers and Screenwriters*. Revised ed. London: Boxtree.

Yadav, Anubha. 2010. "An Evolving Present Within a Past: A History of Screenwriting Practices in Popular Hindi Cinema." *Journal of Screenwriting* 2 (1): 41–59.

Yorke, John. 2013. *Into the Woods. How Stories Work and Why We Tell Them*. London: Penguin.

You Can Say Vagina. 2017. Written and directed by Mischa Baka, and Siobhan Jackson. Australia: Jack Baka Productions, 74 mins.

CHAPTER 3

Screenplectics: Screenwriting as a Complex Adaptive System

Paolo Russo

3.1 Introduction

A screenplectics approach implies thinking screenwriting as a complex adaptive system or, better (and more precisely), as a network of complex systems nested/embedded within other complex systems. This particular slant has been only tangentially present in screenwriting research, even in the cross/trans/multi-disciplinary studies that address the multiple domains in which screenwriting is ontologically, socially, and culturally immersed (e.g. production, culture, labour, etc.). A declared and consistent appropriation of complexity and of notions from Complex Systems Theory (CST) can be found in recent lines of research in literature, film, and other screen media (e.g. Poulaki 2011; Ryan and Thon 2014; Welsh and Stepney 2018a; Grishakova and Poulaki 2019a) although all are limited to or revolve around narrative. To my knowledge, no specific study has tackled the idea of screenwriting as a *complex system*, although more than a glimpse transpire from the very notion of the Screen Idea Work Group propounded by Ian W. Macdonald (2013, 72–80)—of which, to a certain extent, this essay can be seen as a further elaboration via systemic thinking—or from the notion of boundary object that Rosamund Davies (2019) attaches to the screenplay, which implies interaction with a larger environment.

P. Russo (✉)
School of Arts, Oxford Brookes University, Oxford, UK
e-mail: paolo.russo@brookes.ac.uk

This chapter is an attempt to broach the subject by way of a foray into how to understand screenwriting as a complex adaptive system (of complex systems). Narratologists and screenwriting scholars who have attempted a similar task thus far mainly did so by defaulting to analogies and metaphors, which often results in a degree of self-conscious lexical entrainment—a rather common quagmire that Rosser and Rosser describe as meta-complexity (2015), likely driven by a perceived need to justify terminological appropriation from other fields. It is the aim of this essay to move beyond existing models and challenge related paradigms by resorting to new technology and relatively novel approaches—e.g. text and data mining, data visualisation, 2-D and 3-D modelling/mapping, quantitative analyses, and more. Although originating outside of the humanities, these prove extremely useful in capturing the composite nature of screenwriting artefacts/materials—which are generated by and in several different sources, formats, and media—and re-mediate them (in this essay, mainly through modelling) when necessary. An approach that can be seen as informed by Critical Digital Humanities insofar as the use of digital technologies is not limited to the production of data and/or computational thinking, but leads to the analysis of their application through a processual mindset aimed at extrapolating how meaning is eventually produced as a result of human creative activity within a systemic framework.

Before venturing into the core of the chapter, it will be useful to justify the choice of the term *screenplectics* as a fit descriptor of the approach that informs this inquiry. I am adopting the neologism introduced by George Varotsis, which "entwines the meaning of the words complexity, screen, and symplectics" (2015, 2), with a key difference: for me, it is more simply an apt play on the words *screenplay*—which is specific to screenwriting as opposed to the rather generic *screen*—and *plectics*, the term coined by Murray Gell-Mann to describe "a broad transdisciplinary subject covering aspects of simplicity and complexity" alike (1996, 3). Unfortunately, Varotsis misreferences, misquotes, and slightly misinterprets Gell-Mann when summarising the etymology of *symplectics*. Gell-Mann goes into much detail to explain that:

> The Indo-European root **plek-* gives rise to the Latin verb *plicate,* to fold, which yields *simplex,* literally once folded, from which our English word "simple" derives. But **plek-* likewise gives the Latin past participle *plexus,* braided or entwined, from which is derived *complexus,* literally braided together, responsible for the English word "complex". The Greek equivalent to *plexus* is πλεκτός (*plektos*), yielding the mathematical term "symplectic", which also has the literal meaning braided together, but comes to English from Greek rather than Latin. (1996, 3)[1]

---

[1] In fact, the adjective *symplectic* refers to a whole branch of geometry and was introduced by Hermann Weyl (1997 [1939]) as a Greek calque (i.e. συμπλεκτικός, *symplekticos*) of the Latin *com-plexus*, and therefore, it is not to be confused with *simplex* (simple) despite the apparent, misleading similarity between the two prefixes—the Greek **sym-* (together) and the Latin **sem-* (one).

James E. Cutting contends that simplicity is the obverse of complexity (2019, 202). My take from a screenplectical perspective—in keeping with Gell-Mann's original intent—is that simple is the obverse of complicated and that both signal the available range of the degree of complexity itself, which thus implies some kind of order achieved on a higher level.[2] Put another way, and more specifically, I adopt screenplectics as an epistemological term of convenience that can lead to an understanding of screenwriting as a complex adaptive system (from here on, SCAS) whose elements entertain complex relationships with one another that might range from simple to complicated—the baseline assumption being that screenwriting is a complex system regardless of whether specific projects employ simple or puzzling narratives.

Rather than outlining a fully comprehensive ontology of SCAS, the scope and aim of this essay—which also informs the methodological approach—is to develop a pragmatic/constructivist epistemology of SCAS instead, which will provide an understanding of a few exemplary combinatorial ontologies of a limited number of subsystems of SCAS by applying a select choice of modelling methods in order to extricate their relational affordances. The chapter sets forth with a brief overview of how narratological and media studies have so far engaged in the debate around complexity and appropriated some of its key notions. After highlighting some limitations in the current literature, it will then propose a general model of SCAS in order to frame and introduce a few modelling options that will include cellular automata, networks and 4-D manifolds. These models will draw on practical examples from different formats for screen narrative fiction content—e.g. serial drama, short and feature film—with the declared purpose of foregrounding key aspects of the dynamic complexity of SCAS. Specific case studies include serial dramas *Westworld* (2016–2022) and *Bodyguard* (2018–present) as well as the short film *The Voorman Problem* (2011).

3.2 Complexity in Narratology and Media Studies

A detailed overview of the genesis and evolution of complexity theories and related fields of inquiry falls outside the scope of this study. However, even a cursory look at the most recent iteration of Castellani and Gerrits's map of the complexity sciences suffices to discern fairly identifiable historical trajectories despite all the intricacies and overlaps (2021). Sayama proposes an alternative map that forgoes the historical/genetic outlook to better capture the above-mentioned inter-/transdisciplinary nature by identifying seven topical clusters: three of these—nonlinear systems, systems theory, and game theory—as foundational paradigms followed by four more recent developments—pattern formation, networks, collective behaviour, and evolution and organisation (see

---

[2] As further noted by Israel (2005), the Latin for "complicate" is *com-plicare*, meaning "to entangle/to confuse".

Sayama 2015, chapter 1).[3] Notably, culture, arts, and media are absent from both maps. The absence is striking because these domains can in fact claim a rather relevant history of systemic approaches, at the very least on the theoretical narratological front, that dates back to Russian Formalism in the 1920s (see Yury Tynyanov's "The Literary Fact", 2019 [1924]) and the Prague School in the 1930s (in particular, the work of Jan Mukařovský), both of which precede the nominal foundation of Ludwig von Bartalanffy's General Systems Theory. Although Grishakova and Poulaki remark that "[t]he variety in philosophical and aesthetic thinking as well as in experimental research in complexity has not been sufficiently theorized or adopted by narratology" (2019b, 8–9), in the past few decades studies of literary theory have shown growing interest in matters of complexity, a strand of inquiry that has culminated in three seminal publications—the three-volume project "Future Narrative" coordinated by Christoph Bode (Bode and Dietrich 2013; Meifert-Menhard 2013; Schenk 2013)[4] and two substantial collections of essays (Walsh and Stepney 2018a; Grishakova and Poulaki 2019a)—all of which extend their analysis to film and media as well.

The percolations between narratology and film theory have engaged discussions around complexity: on the one hand, through a whole strand of cognitive film studies that is best represented by Torben Grodal's articulation of notions of linearity, narrative homeostasis, and holism (2022 [1997]) and, more recently, by Kiss and Willemsen (2016); on the other hand, by expanding the theoretical vocabulary to fractals (Everett 2005), modularity (Cameron 2008), puzzle (Buckland 2009, 2014) and mind-games (Elsaesser 2021), as well as through more in-depth studies of the broader connections between cinema, complexity and CST (Poulaki 2011; Hven 2017).[5] To date, the only published study that purports to tackle "the underlying dynamics and mechanics that allow a screenplay to function as a unified whole" is Varotsis' *Screenplay and Narrative Theory. The Screenplectics Model of Complex Narrative Systems* (2015). However, the screenplay—let alone screenwriting—is barely mentioned throughout the whole volume which therefore remains very much rooted in general narrative theory instead.

---

[3] I will make use of some of these four latter paradigms later on in this essay when modelling some typical SCAS ontologies.

[4] Game theory heavily informs Bode and Dietrich's approach in their analysis of behaviours and decision-making in so-called Future Narratives, as an alternative paradigm to (normative and descriptive) decision theory (see 2013, 31–42).

[5] In the introduction to their *Narrative Complexity* volume, Grishakova and Poulaki offer a much more comprehensive overview that extends to other narrative media as well (2019b, 1–26).

3.3 Core Features of Complex Systems

A system is a way of describing natural and social phenomena as consisting of elements connected through a network of relationships and exhibiting common properties, patterns, and behaviours. When changes occur within a system or with/in its environment, the (nature and rate of the) response/outcome/effects may be linear—and therefore predictable—if proportional to such changes/causes over time, or nonlinear—and therefore not so easily predictable—if nonproportional. For a generic system to be considered a complex one, the interaction between its elements should typically be nonlinear. Interestingly—and perhaps counterintuitively—Ladyman, Lambert, and Wiesner (2013) show that *nonlinearity*, although possible, is *not* a necessary feature for a complex system. Complex systems can be and often are nonlinear, and yet, in some cases, they are also subject to linear dynamics.

Taking their cue from a special issue of *Science* magazine entirely devoted to complexity (1999), Ladyman, Lambert, and Wiesner identify a core set of other features most commonly ascribed to a physical account of complex systems. These include:

- A structure, typically comprising a *hierarchical organization* of highly-interconnected *nested levels* of embedded subsystems and *numerous interacting elements* that store and exchange information in intricate ways and produce multiple possible behaviours.
- Recursion, i.e. *feedback* from neighbouring levels.
- *Emergence*—i.e. when the resulting behaviour of the system as a whole (that is, at macroscopic scale) is different from and/or cannot be predicted from the properties of the constituent parts (i.e. at microscopic scale).
- Robust spontaneous order (*self-organization*), which is never neither totally ordered/regular/linear nor chaotic or random, thus ensuring stability in spite of *high sensitivity* to initial conditions and/or perturbations. This is achieved through *distributed rather than central control* (feedback loops being themselves a form of self-correcting local control) and refers to behaviour over time as opposed (but concurrently) to scale.

The literature on film and media produced so far has appropriated and elaborated on some of these key features. Marie-Laure Ryan (2019) foregrounds decentralised control (and therefore, self-organisation) and emergence. While Abbott (2008) "contests the applicability of the complex-systemic approaches and the concept of emergence to narrative" due to an essentially "centralized controlling instance" (as quoted in Grishakova and Poulaki 2019b, 11) that runs contrary to the wisdom outlined above, Ryan concludes that while narrative is centrally controlled from the top down at the level of authorial design, "it must give the impression of an emergent, bottom-up system on the level of the plot" (2019, 34). Ryan unpacks the discrepancy between the expectancy of causal relations within the narrative and the potentially high nonlinearity of the temporal sequence that makes for plot complexity (2019, 42).[6] According to Poulaki, non-sequential temporal structures—which are typical of complex plots—are evidence of the system's self-referentiality (see Poulaki 2011, 54–67). Walsh and Stepney condense the issue in their definition of narrative as "semiotic articulation of linear temporal sequence" (2018b, 4): that is, the presentation of narrative events occurs in a sequential order but, as Pianzola points out, the semiotic articulation—i.e. any meaning-making interaction with said narrative sequential presentation—is nonlinear (Pianzola 2018, 102). Furthermore, in tune with Alex Ryan's dictum that emergence is coupled with scope rather than hierarchical level (Ryan 2007), Pianzola argues for expanding the scope of the narrative system to include its environment, that is the audience, and, consequently, discourse-audience interactions that, by nature, are nonlinear (see Pianzola 2018).

Albeit far from exhaustive, this quick excursus shows how current literature tends to focus mainly on plot and narrative structure(s), issues of narration and narrativity, and a shift in attention to the recipients' end that has prompted many scholars to resort to embodied cognition paradigms as ways of untangling the relations between the film/narrative system and the viewer system.[7]

Conceding all of these still represent primary concerns in story development and storytelling systems for the screen, one can legitimately ask: where does screenwriting stand in all this? Even though from the perspective of a physicist investigating systems dynamics, Yaneer Bar-Yam (2009 [2002]) advises that the study of complex systems focus on how behavioural patterns arise from systemic interactions and how they evolve over time, thus determining the space of possibilities of a system. What I set out to explore in the following sections is the *space of possibilities* of screenwriting as a complex system.

3.4 Screenwriting as a Complex Adaptive System (SCAS)

Screenwriting can be understood as a complex system nested within other complex systems. Figure 3.1 exemplifies such a systemic framework: although extremely simplified, it has the advantage of offering an intuitive grasp of the possible connections and interactions both between individual components and as a whole.

The SCAS model presented here is adapted from Derek Hitchins' five-layer model—its frequent applications ranging from complex engineering to

---

[6] One should imply that Ryan is referring to the temporal dimension of the diegesis.

[7] For a most convincing example that reconciles various theories into anchoring narrative cognition to the embodied ground, see the *neurocinematic* approach adopted by Pia Tikka and Mauri Kaipanen (2019).

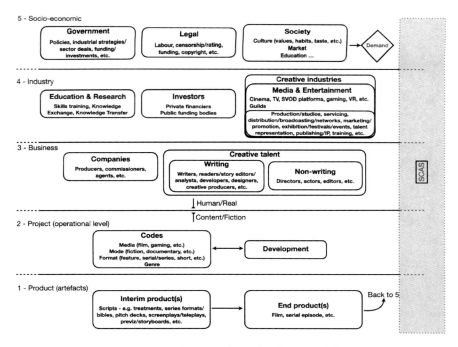

Fig. 3.1 SCAS modelling based on Hitchins' five-layer model

socio-economic and management systems frameworks (see Hitchins 2003)—to the specific purposes, processes, and dynamics of screenwriting, mainly by virtue of its ability to capture the scalar complexity of a system visually. This model differs from stack ontologies that have been popularised in the Digital Humanities in recent years in that its layering does not rely on sedimentation of increasing levels of abstraction (see Berry and Fagerjord 2017 after Benjamin Bratton's "theory of the Stack"); rather, they represent concrete human-driven agencies that enable creative intra- and inter-operability across a processual/generative framework.

The key take-home element of this model is that the system is open and SCAS spans across *all* five levels—although, from the designer's perspective, *core* SCAS activities tend to concentrate between Levels 3, 2, and 1. Most intra-level and inter-level connections are not shown in Fig. 3.1 for the sake of visual clarity. That said, one should consider that connections are typically more numerous and stronger between neighbouring levels and much more frequent at the lowest levels; nonetheless, they occur between non-neighbouring levels too (i.e. by skipping intermediate levels, if necessary or practical)—for instance, a contract with a producer (Level 3) is usually normed by laws established at Level 5 as negotiated, ideally, by a writers' guild (Level 4), and mediated through an agent (again Level 3). Overall, this results in a very complex network of ever-changing dynamical connections crowding the model at any given time as each layer constantly evolves, with upper layers tending to be pre-conditions (or, at least, working frameworks) for the lower levels. The structure is clearly hierarchical and recursive: decision-making exchanges tend to flow from the top down, and operational/creative exchanges tend to flow from the bottom up, but in many cases exchanges are bi-directional. As counterintuitive as it might seem at first, this is also true across the critical boundary between Levels 2 and 3, where exchanges/connections are not all limited to a top-down flow (i.e. from the designer/controller to the artefact in development)—a common view often derived from fallacious interpretations of the notion of agency in a complex system such as SCAS, or from useful but limited notions of the author as controller or regulator (see Tikka and Kaipanen 2019, 316; Varotsis 2015, 42, 46).[8]

The models and analyses presented in this essay concentrate on what can be considered *core activities* of SCAS insofar as they contribute to creative development. Such core activities usually entail distributed creative work by multiple individuals or groups. Hereon, I will mainly adopt the term *designer(s)* to refer to any creative role contributing to core SCAS activities—e.g. writers, story editors, creative producers, developers, and so forth. Sawyer defines this multiplicity as a "hybrid" framework of "collaborative emergence" (2010, 366; also quoted by Macdonald in this handbook)[9]; however, from a systemic perspective, SCAS can be better described as an *acknowledged* system of systems whose recognised objectives and designated resources are shared by components at all levels of the hierarchical organisation while, although reporting to higher levels, the participants in the core creative activities retain a substantial degree of independence. Rather than hybrid, this is a multimodal/performative framework.

Finally, Level 1 feeds its end product back to satisfy the demand originated up on Level 5, in a cyclical pattern. As a corollary to this, it must also be noted that systemic effects do not stop at completion of the processes inherent to Levels 2 and 1 (i.e. the project phase/scale). The reception of the end product—e.g. in terms of taste, commercial success, modes of fruition, or popularity—contributes to consolidate, adjust, or alter some of the systems' components in future projects and expectations. However, crucially, the end product can only be achieved as a result of the interim product, which is not an individual artefact but an often intricate combination of development materials of many different kinds—e.g. treatments, formats/bibles, breakdowns, screenplays/teleplays, and storyboards, to mention just the most commonly cited types of scripts—that usually require several iterations (e.g. drafts, revisions, etc.) and, perhaps counterintuitively, work together in both linear *and*

---

[8] For the more useful notion of multiagency, see Grishakova and Poulaki (2019b, 13).

[9] For an in-depth investigation of script development as collective practice, see also Rosamund Davies' chapter in this handbook.

nonlinear fashions. Therefore, rather than reasoning in terms of input/output dynamics, I contend that a systemic approach to the study of screenwriting is best justified by an analytical focus on the *dynamic throughput* of the core SCAS activities, as exemplified in the following sections. Furthermore, the manifest "highly processual" nature of this approach not only "resists" but de facto reconciles the "prising apart" of conception and execution lamented by Steven Maras (2009, 21–23).

In sum, to borrow another definition by Gell-Mann (1995), to really capture the *effective complexity* of the screenwriting system, one should assess the degree and depth of organisation of the ensemble wherein its components are embedded rather than just describe those components and/or their interactions.

3.5 Modelling SCAS

I will now adopt some of Sayama's topical clusters to propose a few examples of SCAS modelling, with particular emphasis on pattern formation (i.e. self-organisation), networks (i.e. graph theory), collective behaviour and evolution. Pattern formation refers to the self-organising processes entertained by a large number of components. In the models that follow, the components will be characters—a key element for screenwriters to develop creatively as discussed also by Murray Smith, Ronald Geerts, and Funke Oyebanjo in this handbook. Here, we look at how characters are organised/distributed over a spatial domain and how they act and/or interact over time so as to gain evidence and identify useful patterns at both local and global levels. As noted, the foundation of any model of complex system is to be able to describe and possibly predict how the system's behaviour evolves dynamically over time—which may or may not be due to changes occurring at local level to individual components.

3.5.1 Cellular Automata Models

A common (mathematical) and relatively simple model that can be used to carry out such an analysis in a rather intuitive way is cellular automata (CA). The components under scrutiny are typically arranged in a grid layout (technically, a lattice), each cell (called a lattice point) corresponding to a given finite state of that component at a given time.[10] Any change in any state variable (i.e. attributes) of any character will be reflected as a new value registered in the correspondent cell or lattice point. The ensemble of all the states associated with any character represents that particular character's time series. In this particular example (see Fig. 3.2), at a very basic level, the initial aim is to map out the *presence* of the main characters across the first three seasons

---

[10] Note that these models (i.e. CA arrays) represent time in discrete steps rather than as continuous.

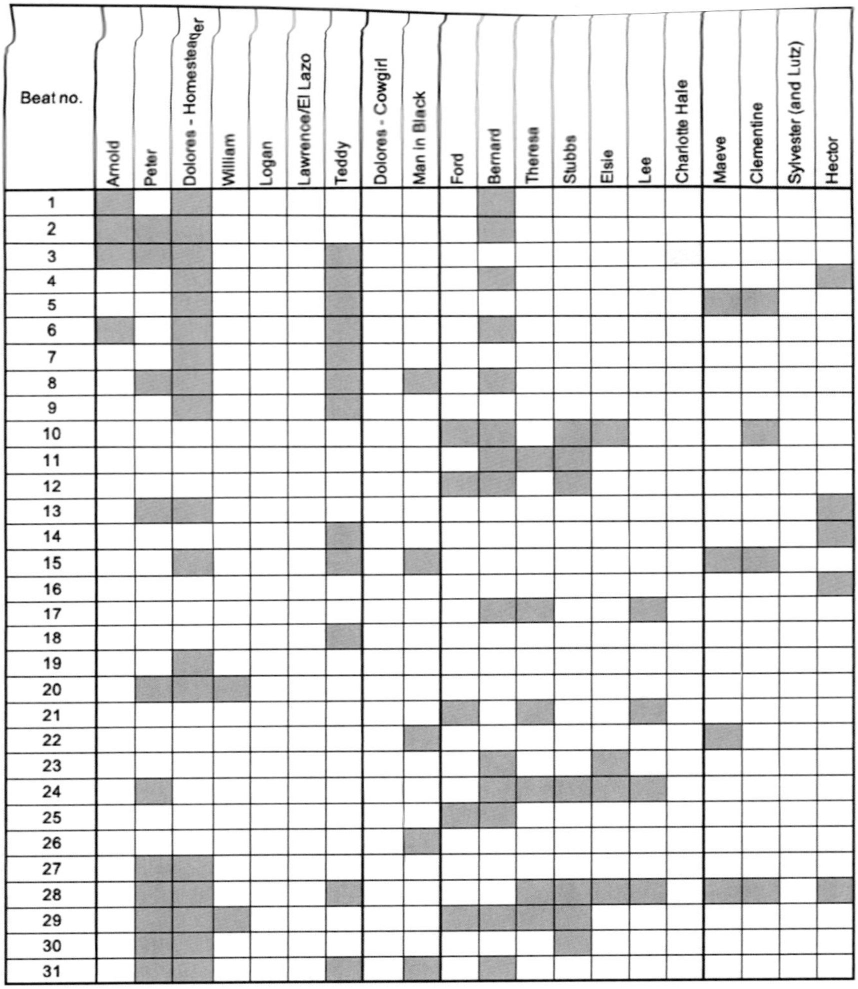

54   P. RUSSO

Fig. 3.2 Schematic illustration of cellular automata for *Westworld*, Season 1, Episode 1 (2016) (*Note* A grey [active] cell indicates the presence of a character in the correspondent beat. An empty [quiescent] cell indicates lack of presence)

of *Westworld* (2016–2022). The *presence*, or distribution, of characters in any narrative lends itself and is linked to a number of necessary authorial/design interventions, some of which will be examined later in this analysis. In this array, each column yields the storyline of one character in its sequential order of presentation. In them, time flows downwards vertically, but this is an arbitrary choice of the modeller, in this case justified simply for the purpose of readability. The metric unit in each timeline is one beat—conventionally considered the basic narrative unit in most story development practices as opposed to scene, which is not generally used until development reaches screenplay/teleplay stage.[11]

It must be noted that cellular automata do not normally work this way. A typical CA model is spatially (but not temporally) oriented: all cells in a whole array show their state at any one time, and as the model switches to the next discrete time unit, their state changes thus forming a new pattern altogether. Furthermore, cells interact with and influence the behaviour of neighbouring cells—i.e. the four ones at either side of each cell, resulting in a cross shape. The model in Fig. 3.2 differs in that it visualises the time units adopted (i.e. beats), thus orienting the model both spatially *and* temporally. The automata (i.e. characters) are arranged according to logical criteria derived from their narrative functions and/or the community they are assigned to, but such arrangement is nonetheless discretional (i.e. an arbitrary choice of the modeller). As a result, each individual row (instead of a cross shape) must be considered a neighbourhood wherein to check the state of the related cells, which may combine and interact in various ways regardless of their conventional placement in the row. Adapting the CA model to SCAS purposes this way has the advantage of allowing easy observation of pattern formation and evolution not just across the array as a whole, but also along rows (local spatial interaction) and any number of columns (evolution over time) within the same model iteration.

Based on the above configuration, the time series of *each* automaton/character across the first three seasons will be the sum total of the narrative beats—i.e. 263 in Season One + 296 in Season Two + 241 in Season Three = 778 beats. Before even attempting to assign any particular value to the state variables of characters, we can already draw some general quantitative considerations. Ryan observes that "the number of elements is far smaller in narrative than in most complex systems" (2019, 33), which sounds at odds with the numerosity requirement stated above. Other trivial constraints (e.g. the size of these pages) mean that Fig. 3.2 shows only a small fraction of what would be the resulting full grid if we were to include all characters (excluding extras and bits) that appear in the first three seasons of *Westworld*. More specifically, it shows the main (primary and secondary) characters of Season One—there are as many as twenty—and it maps their storylines in Episode One only. However, if we extended our analysis to include all characters through Seasons One to Three (28 one-hour episodes in total), we would obtain a total of 142, consisting of 39 humans—or, given the core philosophical implications of the serial, presumed humans—and

---

[11] Beats are a relative measure of time in that they chart the sequential progression of the action irrespective of the duration of each one of them in absolute terms. Absolute time can lead to interesting analytical insights too but is not a specific concern here.

103 hosts.[12] This means that the full CA grid for the three seasons would comprise a whopping 110,470 lattice points.[13] This might still be a small figure compared, for example, to many biological or even human population systems, but one must assess it based on the relative scale of the system under investigation—in this case, in relation to the sheer number of evaluations and decisions that the designers have to make when developing a project such as *Westworld*.

True it is that only a handful of active characters are usually on screen at any given time, and that several are killed off as the serial progresses while several others are introduced in later episodes or even seasons. However, this does not exempt the designers from having to identify all those characters as *inactive* whenever they are not directly involved or, better, visible. Furthermore, the storyline of any character (including any backstory) needs to be *known* (and therefore fully designed and developed) by the designer, regardless of their onscreen presence because (i) the entities perceived as human/humanoid characters do not stop existing in their own portion of the storyworld, even when they are not visible on screen or visibly interacting with other characters, and regardless of it; (ii) they still can, and usually do, influence other characters and the dramatic action indirectly when not visible on screen—even after their death—in which case their status should still be considered as active; and (iii) when they do join the dramatic action on screen (i.e. they are physically/visually present), their own actions will be justified also, often in substantial ways, by what their existence has been like while not visible. An interesting case in point is the feature film *Cast Away* (2000): because the protagonist Chuck (Tom Hanks) is cast ashore a deserted island, being the only survivor of a plane crash, most of the action concentrates on this one character, making it the only visibly active automaton in the potential CA grid of the film for the majority of screen time. One would wrongly assume that this makes the work of the designer any easier: although not visible, other characters who are related to Chuck would be looking for him and much of Chuck's efforts while on the island hinges on the hope that they do, thus being clearly influenced by such indirect interaction.

Surely, *Westworld* is an extreme example of complexity in screenwriting. So let us consider another example at the opposite end of the spectrum. *The Voorman Problem* (2011) is a 12-minute short film featuring just five characters interacting across eighteen beats. The CA model for it yields a grid

---

[12] My own manual count matches the tally found on the fandom wiki website https://westworld.fandom.com/wiki/ (accessed 25 July 2022).

[13] Figure 3.2 only shows 620, or about 1/178th of the full grid. Originally, this analysis was conducted by adapting a MIDI software, the results of which were presented at the 2019 SRN conference (Russo 2019). Here, page layout constraints were easily worked around by extrapolating the relevant portion of data and using a spreadsheet software instead. Cellular automata simulators might also prove useful but need ad hoc adapting to SCAS purposes.

Fig. 3.3 Schematic illustration of cellular automata for *The Voorman Problem* (2011)

Beat no.	Dr. Williams	Voorman	Gov. Bentley	Dr. Williams' Wife	Inmates
1	≈				
2	-				
3	+		≈		
4	≈		+		
5	+		-		
6	+	-			
7	-	+			
8	+	-			
9	≈	+			
10	+			≈	
11	≈			+	
12	-			≈	
13		≈			
14	≈	≈			
15	+	-			
16	-	+			
17	-	+			
18	-				

comprising a mere 90 lattice points (Fig. 3.3), thus showing how the possibilities can range from a few dozens to the hundreds of thousands.[14] Table 3.1 provides further comparison between different formats. The CA grid for the average feature film tends to range between 1,000 and 2,000 lattice points. Although Chuck is the only character on screen for a vast chunk of the narrative, *Cast Away* still features almost fifty characters and therefore is far from being a one-man show. A very simple, compact, and linear narrative with far fewer characters such as *The Full Monty* (1996) lies just below the one thousand threshold. Sit-coms tend to employ much more rigid parameters than

---

[14] Even more extreme cases are the one-minute shorts of the Filminute festival. As an example, Reza Moayedi's *The Last Performance* (2013) features just three characters and four clearly identifiable beats. Available online at: http://www.filminute.com/films/2013/the-last-performance/ (accessed 25 July 2022).

Table 3.1 Quantitative analysis of components for a CA model comparing various screenwriting formats

Title	Format	Characters	Beats	Totals (i.e. lattice points)
Westworld (Seasons 1–3)	One-hour drama	142	778	110,476
Friends (one episode)	Half-hour sit-com	6–10 (typical)	12–15 (typical)	72–150 (typical)
Fleabag (one episode)	Half-hour sit-com	4–8 (typical)	12–15 (typical)	48–120 (typical)
Cast Away	Feature film	49	35	1715
The Descendants	Feature film	34	34	1156
The Full Monty	Feature film	25	36	900
The Voorman Problem	Short film	5	18	90
The Last Performance	Short film	3	4	12

drama (e.g. limited number of recurrent characters, rather fixed format), a typical episode consisting of around 50–150 lattice points.

Because CA models work according to binary rules (e.g. active/quiescent cell), they are useful tools to analyse the dynamic behaviour of the system despite their apparent simplicity. Regardless of the extension of the CA array, an immediate result of mapping characters' presence via active or quiescent cells is the display of patterns of concentration. In Fig. 3.3, we can see how the action in *The Voorman Problem* is mostly driven by the two primary characters—Dr. Williams (Martin Freeman) and Voorman (Tom Hollander)—while the other characters' presence is rather sparse. This is typical behaviour in short and feature films, which tend to consist of one main plotline and one or more (but still limited in number) minor ones, if any. Some serial shows make use of similar configurations, but in the last two decades or so we have witnessed an increasing number of titles that rely on multi-strand narratives, combining horizontal and vertical developments. Figure 3.2 shows the most concentration along the storylines of Dolores (Evan Rachel Wood)—supported by Peter and Teddy—and Bernard (Jeffrey Wright), thus making them the central characters driving the dramatic action of Episode 1. Both will continue to be the protagonists of their own storylines through the whole season: however, one should not make the assumption, based on initial conditions, that they will be the only primary characters in *Westworld*. As evidence of the dynamic nature of the system, by conducting a similar analysis of further episodes one notices that at least four more characters take on as much relevant roles as the seasons progress: Ford, Maeve, William, and the Man in black.

Neither should one assume that less populated areas of the array shall carry less significant portions of the dramatic action. As an example, in *The Voorman Problem* (Fig. 3.3), the setup occurs between Dr. Williams and Governor Bentley (beats 3–5, one scene) and provides crucial background information that ensures adequate comprehension of the scenes that follow while at the same time priming the viewer with a first set of expectations. Likewise, the only exchange between Dr. Williams and his wife (beats 10–12, one scene) constitutes a pivotal moment that prepares the ground for the eventual reversal of those expectations. Without those scenes and the interactions with those two *minor* characters, the ensemble would lose most of its dramatic impact.

The observations made so far were based mostly on quantitative factors (e.g. presence). The CA model also allows to assign qualitative attributes and related values to the automata. One common type of interaction between characters is based on power dynamics. In Fig. 3.3, the cells in the first four columns are populated with the following symbols: a + sign indicates a character in control of a situation, having or gaining superiority (in psychological terms) over another one; a − sign indicates the opposite; a ≈ sign indicates a somewhat neutral situation or no relevant change for the character. If we follow the timeline for each character vertically, a pattern emerges: Dr. Williams tends to begin each new interaction seemingly in control (initial conditions) to then regularly lose the upper hand in the power game with his main antagonist, Voorman.

The CA model has some practical limitations regarding the number of ways in which we can visualise attributes—e.g. alphanumeric/symbolic/colour values per cell at any time. In smaller arrays, one could also link up interacting cells, but this becomes rather impractical and visually cumbersome in bigger arrays that are already grid-like and supposed to depict dynamically evolving systems. If we wish to analyse the type of connections and resulting specific behaviours between two or more characters in a CA neighbourhood, other models might prove more useful.

3.5.2 Network Models

Although they tend to be data-intensive, networks are an intuitive and highly effective tool to model dynamic interactions between system components. One of the simplest and most quoted examples is the *growth cycle* model popularised by Richard M. Goodwin, also known by the more colloquial moniker of "prey-predator" model (1967). The key assumption of Goodwin's model—that social properties couple with topological changes caused by the entry or the altered states of other members in a given community, thus leading to behavioural changes—lends itself perfectly to observing and describing typical interactions between characters. To exemplify this, I will apply one of the simplest network models—a causal loop diagram—to *Westworld*, an apt choice given that two of the main classes of characters that for the most part populate its storyworld are examples of preys (i.e. the hosts) and predators (i.e. the guests).

Figure 3.4 shows how the dynamic interactions between the two classes of characters analysed here are governed by so-called *Game of life* rules.

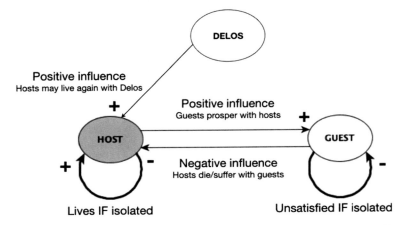

Fig. 3.4 Rules governing interactions between hosts and guests in *Westworld*

- A host remains alive *if not* interacting with guests;
- A host usually dies or, at the very least, suffers greatly *if* interacting with guests;
- A dead host can be resurrected *if* interacting with Delos' rescue team.

Once established, the rule model can then be extended as needed to all and any other characters who entertain analogous relationships. In fact, screen character interaction often tends to form multiple and much more intricate relational topologies, especially in serial formats. Networks are especially useful when trying to extricate the extent of modularity in recognisable communities of system components, that is, those elements that cluster together by means of particularly dense connections.

In Fig. 3.5, each coloured oval represents a recognisable community of characters in the BBC series *Bodyguard* (2018–present) based on their professional environment and main narrative function. Within each community, the structural arrangement of the actors tends to be hierarchical, the characters' authority and power expressed by the size of the corresponding actor.[15] The undisputed protagonist (David Budd, played by Richard Madden) lies right in the centre of the network and is connected via rather strong ties with all four communities. David's position relative to the particular modular topologies of the network as a whole and of its constituent communities is also

---

[15] In this essay, I use the terms *actor* and *tie* instead of, respectively, *node* and *edge* (or *link*), as per common usage in the social sciences (as opposed to physics and computer science) whose network theory models are more suited to analyse character relations in fictional storyworlds. Therefore, actor is not intended as performer. It must also be noted how, in possible network models that describe micro- or meso-systems pertaining specifically to development and scripting systems, ties can be directed or undirected based on the type of connection they represent.

revealing: taking David as its focal element, the network seems to spread out in a spectral layout, thus emphasising the pivotal role of David as a de facto, albeit willy nilly, mediator between all four communities. In Fig. 3.5, his ties with the main actors in each community are depicted as non-antagonistic relations. Figure 3.6 refines these further by assigning attributes to characterise the nature of those relations more specifically and resulting into strongly conflicted push–pull dynamics—i.e. sexual attraction and duty vs. beliefs with Julia, reciprocal trust vs. lack thereof with the police team, love vs. estrangement with family, and friendship and disillusion vs. duty with fellow Helmand veteran Andy.

Back to Fig. 3.5, if we isolate each individual community and its relation with David, its actors connect with one another in a relatively closed random layout that emphasises the internal hierarchies (size of actors) and relations (tie paths), which is dramaturgically justified by the level of secrecy and misgiven loyalties that pervade the plotlines.

By combining different layouts, rules and modular features associated with community clustering, these examples contradict Marie-Laure Ryan's claim that a "network diagram may tell you about the complexity of the system

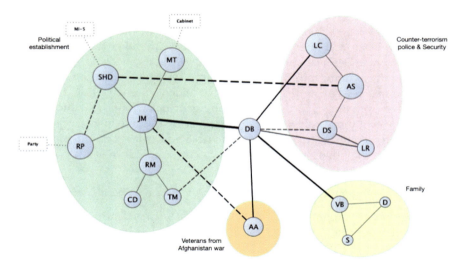

Fig. 3.5 Modularity of main communities of characters in *Bodyguard* (Key: DB [David Budd], JM [Julia Montague, Home Secretary], MT [Mike Travis, Minister for Counter Terrorism], SHD [Stephen Hunter-Dunn, MI-5 DG], RP [Roger Penaligon MP, Chief Whip, Julia's former husband], RM [Rob Macdonald, Special advisor], TM [Tahir Mahmood, advisor], CD [Chanel Dyson, advisor], LC [Lorraine Craddock, David's commanding officer], AS [Anne Simpson, Head of Counter Terrorism Command], DS [Deepak Sharma, DCI], LR [Louise Rayburn, DS], VB [Vicky Budd, David's wife], D [Daughter], S [Son], AA [Andy Apsted]; Solid tie: relation; Dashed tie: antagonistic relation; Tie weight: strength of relation)

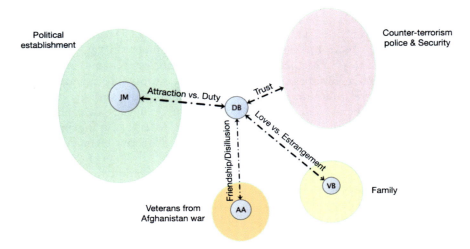

Fig. 3.6 Conflicted, push–pull dynamic relations with communities in *Bodyguard*

of human relations that underlie a narrative, but it does not tell anything about the nature of the interactions that constitute the plot" (2019, 37). In fact, networks lend themselves well to illustrate even much deeper levels of complexity. Their real limitations are the same as any other traditional model that relies on 2-D visual simplification: that is, they can equip the observer with enough accurate information about the system's conditions at a given point in time, thus giving them an intuitive understanding of how the system *may* evolve over time (i.e. the overall emergent behaviour), but they cannot show such evolution unless several iterations of the network are generated for sequential comparison, which seems viable and manageable if applied, for instance, to a short film, much less so in case of longer formats.

3.5.3   *4-D Topological Manifolds: Spacetime and the Block Universe Model*

A key notion mentioned earlier is the *space of possibilities*, which is intimately connected to theories of *possible worlds* (see Kripke 1972).[16] While here I will not engage in the philosophical debate these have sparked in the past few decades over whether *possibilities* are merely epistemic, it seems to me that the combinatorialism of the *space of possibilities* is particularly suited to describe the emergent modalities of SCAS as it adds a temporal dimension (i.e. possibilities) to a spatial framework of description (i.e. a coordinate system). The examples above should already provide an intuitive grasp of how a storyworld

---

[16] For further discussion of possible worlds theories, see Murray Smith's chapter in this handbook.

designed and developed in SCAS can itself be considered a space of possibilities.[17] For modelling purposes, the space of possibilities can be visualised as a *spacetime*, that is a collection of perduring events with a continuous coordinate system, which therefore implies an event ontology.[18] By definition, event ontologies imply that the observer of an object retain a *memory* of a past state and produce a visual image of the present state in order to generate a sense of a given trajectory over time. In a narrative system, this memory retention mechanism couples with the sequential presentation of events to generate an ongoing dynamic interaction between expectations (i.e. predictions about the future based on memory of past events up to the present state) and surprise (i.e. unexpected elements introduced at any present state that continuously reframe those expectations).

In practice, a spacetime translates into what mathematicians call a Minkovski diagram, that is a 2-D visual representation of a 3-D manifold that, in fact, stands for a 4-D topological manifold. While this sounds complicated or confusing, it can be understood by introducing the concept of *block universe*, a most trivial interpretation of which adds a fourth dimension (time) to traditional tridimensional spatial representations. Minkovski diagrams resolve the issue of having to represent four dimensions on a 2-D surface by dropping one space coordinate, thus assigning only two axes to space coordinates and reserving the third one for time (see Fig. 3.7).

As Kennedy explains, "*a block universe implies an event ontology*" (2003, 54; emphasis in original) and it relies on the assumption that all events (and related states of affairs) *already exist*, even future ones. Once again, what interests us here is the applicability of the block universe to SCAS rather than the debates around it. The block universe is a suitable and ideal model for generating storyworlds by SCAS because it can show how designers can navigate through the model back and forth and map how any state of affairs at any given point in time correlates dynamically to and influences other states of affairs at other given points in time. A few more examples are suggested below to elucidate some of the possibilities.

The key element to focus on in our ideal block universe is the slice of spacetime being observed at any given time (indicated by the label "Now" in Fig. 3.7)—technically called a *brane*. Each possible brane embeds the potential configuration of *all* the elements selected by the designer at that particular time in the storyworld. Therefore, one could extract, combine, and/or

---

[17] Informed by decision theory, Bode refines the notion as *space of consequences* (Bode and Dietrich 2013, 15).

[18] Quantum mechanics uses the term *phase space*: both are essentially a theoretical space that maps the degrees of freedom (i.e. all the states of all parameters) of a system over time at unique spatial locations. Other authors mentioned here use similar or altogether different terms: Varotsis (2015) opts for the more general *state space*; Tikka and Kaipanen (2019) for *ontospace*. Once again, although indirectly acknowledged by my arguments, I will not enter the philosophy of time fray around persistence/endurantism/exdurantism, A-time/B-time, or worm/stage theory as it falls outside the scope of this essay.

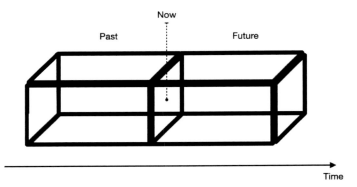

Fig. 3.7 Typical representation of a block universe (*Note* orientation of time axis is arbitrary as time does not have real space orientation; block edges are shown for the sake of visual representation but, being a theoretical space, the block itself does not have actual or fixed spatial boundaries, nor is to be considered to scale)

superimpose any of the models illustrated previously (e.g. cellular automata, networks) to any brane in the block universe of the respective storyworlds. For instance, one could use the CA model depicting power dynamics in *The Voorman Problem* (Fig. 3.3) by associating each discrete time unit (i.e. each row-based neighbourhood) to each corresponding brane in the related block universe—imagine a sequence of eighteen branes. Correlating them all along the time coordinates would yield a phase line (aka world line) per each concerned character that would resemble as many wave trajectories, whose combined patterns would render an immediate visual overview of the related dynamics.

But a block universe model is more useful when it reveals much finer and complex dynamics. I will resort to *Westworld* one last time as a way to illustrate one possible application. In Season 1, Episode 6 ("The Adversary", 2016), one of the hosts—Maeve (Thandiwe Newton)—finds it hard to accept that she is not human until one of the programmers shows her the tablet they use to control all the hosts' attributes. A fleeting shot shows the tablet screen displaying an impressive array of attributes organised around two concentrical rings (Fig. 3.8).

Only by freezing the frame and patiently counting them can one reckon that these represent a matrix comprising 120 configurable attributes, similar to those found in videogames. Leaving aside the meta-narrative aspects that are so crucial in *Westworld*, one could imagine the creators of the show— or of any other show or film, for that matter—applying the same such matrix to their own 142 characters and having to handle 17,040 qualitative attributes (see lattice points calculated above), every single one of which is then quantified scalarly with values between 0 and 20 (according to *Westworld*). Of course, in practice, designers operate much more selectively: in the first place, minor characters tend to be much less defined

Fig. 3.8 Maeve's full attribute matrix as shown in *Westworld*, Season 1, Episode 6 "The Adversary" (2016)

than primary characters. Kira-Ann Pelican draws on long-established research traditions in psychological studies to propose a more manageable model for developing characters based on five basic *personality dimensions*—i.e. extroversion/introversion, agreeableness/disagreeableness, neuroticism/emotional stability, conscientiousness/lack of conscientiousness, and openness/closeness to experience—each of which is then fine-tuned by six facets, for a total of thirty possible attributes (see Pelican 2020). Similarly, the same scene in *Westworld* goes on to show how the main matrix is organised in subsets of primary and secondary attributes. A subsequent shot shows a radial graph (or radar graph) displayed on the tablet that combines eighteen of them in the configuration shown in Fig. 3.9.[19]

Radial graphs are particularly useful as—by plotting together the relative strength of each variable/attribute—they visually shape the overall strength of any topology. When changes occur over time, the topology in the graph adapts in a continuous flow. Shortly after the scene mentioned earlier, Maeve begins to piece together the reality of her (and the other hosts') condition. The shock of such a realisation marks a pivotal change of tide in the dramatic action and will subsequently motivate Maeve in her vengeful intents—she herself will modify her own attributes by stealing the afore-mentioned tablet. One can reasonably hypothesise the resulting graph as similar to the one in Fig. 3.10. The difference in shape is remarkable: whereas previously (Fig. 3.9) Maeve

---

[19] Regardless of any criteria one applies, any selection of attributes is arbitrary and modifiable. In later episodes of *Westworld*, when the same type of radial graph is shown for Dolores, it includes twenty attributes—the same eighteen seen here plus "perception" and "emotional acuity".

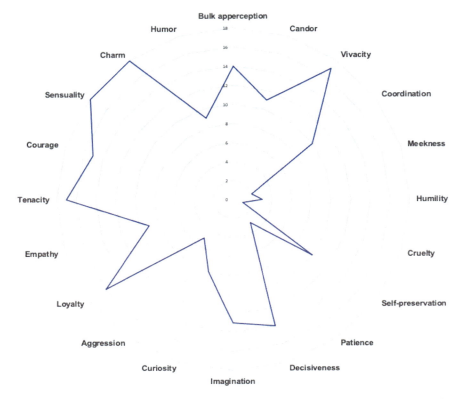

Fig. 3.9 Primary attributes for Maeve in *Westworld* Season 1, Episode 6 "The Adversary" (2016) (author's re-elaboration)

scored particularly high in attributes such as vivacity, loyalty, tenacity, courage, sensuality, and charm, with an overall configuration skewed towards the upper half and left side of the graph—let us say, her default settings—the new configuration has drastically shifted its focal attractors mostly towards the lower half, with a new outlook that maxes out on cruelty (previously barely on the radar), self-preservation, decisiveness, and aggression. It has maintained coordination, courage, and tenacity, but in this new configuration they take on a whole new meaning and function.

Looking beyond the individual example from *Westworld*, it can be easily argued that better grouping of primary attributes is possible (and even advisable) and that finer distinctions are required between actual personality traits and character disposition to particular emotional responses as a result of both ontological and cultural/nurturing traits. Compiling character dossiers (as suggested by various manuals) can be a useful starting point for the designer but remains a static reference set at best. Modelling the ways attribute matrices

Fig. 3.10 Likely projection of Maeve's modified primary attributes (author's elaboration)

evolve over time equips designers with the ability to test responses and consequences, and to evaluate the plausibility of any choice made at any stage of development.

3.6 Conclusions

This chapter is an initial attempt to break new ground in the study of screenwriting by introducing a *screenplectical*, that is, a pragmatic/processual epistemological take to the study of screenwriting as a complex adaptive system (SCAS) (i) by outlining its constituent functional ontologies as they express relational properties and processes of the core screenwriting system as nested hierarchically within higher-level complex systems with which it constantly interacts, and (ii) by proposing modelling options (e.g. cellular automata, networks, 4-D manifolds) that rely extensively on a Critical Digital Humanities approach.

The models proposed here are just examples, mere starting points to show the potential of SCAS for further elaboration. In a theoretical scenario, this could include the identification of all possible configurations, which may range from a few dozens (e.g. in short films) to literally billions (e.g. in very complex serial dramas such as *Westworld* or in videogames). In the real world, the main constraint faced by writers is time, in the sense of the actual time available to them to develop characters, stories, and plotlines, write all the relevant scripts and submit by stated deadlines. A pragmatic approach is therefore necessary: designers have to be highly selective in their creative choices and decision-making processes throughout the whole project. A long-term goal of SCAS should be to provide solutions aimed at aiding designers, and such a line of research has to be pursued by a partnership between academia and industry.

One must acknowledge some clear limitations that arise when having to commit the description of complex systems modelling to words and paper. For instance, to mention just the last modelling example presented above, it is easy to point out how the assessment of the dynamic evolution of the topologies shown in the radial graphs (Figs. 3.9 and 3.10) needed the comparison between two discrete iterations. Ideally, one could extrude similar configurations for any character from all or a selection of significant branes in any storyworld block universe—thus returning the respective elements (e.g. characters) to their fully tridimensional spatial orientation—and then correlate them in a point-to-point mapping that allows the designer to operate any creative decisions and changes at any time, and get an immediate dynamic response from the core system to show the emergent behaviour as ensemble. Only a few models have been shown here, all generated using easy-to-access software programmes: namely, *Microsoft Excel* and the free Java-based graph editor *yED*—with the mentioned exception of a MIDI editor (*ProTools*) that I have adapted specifically (albeit, admittedly, rather roughly) to the purposes of analysing storylining in serial dramas. More refined modelling tools could also be employed, especially ones capable of generating continuous time planar graphs and/or Agent-Based modelling, ideally with animation capabilities that are most suited to describe dynamic evolution over time. Furthermore, at present, a comprehensive simulation of SCAS in its entirety (i.e. all levels) would require a cumbersome combination of usually non-compatible software programmes—word processors (e.g. *Microsoft Word*, *Final Draft*), production management (e.g. *MovieMagic Scheduler*, *StudioBinder*, *Basecamp*, *Asana*), 2-D and 3-D vector-based and/or raster-based modellers and simulators (e.g. CAD, *yEd*, *NetworkX*)—as well as coding (e.g. Python). Most importantly, beyond its potential, the combination of theoretical framework, epistemological angle, analytical/modelling strategies, and available technologies presented here shows a need for much further inquiry.

Acknowledgment I am very grateful to Prof. Christian Bode for his insights and comments on an early draft of this chapter.

REFERENCES

Bar-Yam, Yaneer. 2009 [2002]. "General Features of Complex Systems." In *Knowledge Management, Organizational Intelligence and Learning, and Complexity – Volume 1*, edited by Lowell Douglas Kiel, 43–95. Oxford: EOLSS.

Berry, David M., and Anders Fagerjord. 2017. *Digital Humanities: Knowledge and Critique in a Digital Age*. Cambridge: Polity.

Bode, Christoph, and Rainer Dietrich. 2013. *Future Narratives. Theory, Poetics, and Media-Historical Moment*. Berlin and Boston: De Gruyter.

Bodyguard. 2018–present (1 season). Created by Jed Mercurio. UK: World Productions.

Buckland, Warren, ed. 2009. *Puzzle Films: Complex Storytelling in Contemporary Cinema*. Chichester, UK, and Malden, MA: Blackwell.

Buckland, Warren, ed. 2014. *Hollywood Puzzle Films*. London: Routledge.

Cameron, Allan. 2008. *Modular Narrative in Contemporary Cinema*. Basingstoke, UK, and New York: Palgrave Macmillan.

Cast Away. 2000. Written by William Broyles Jr. Directed by Robert Zemeckis. USA: ImageMovers, Playtone.

Castellani, Brian, and Lasse Gerrits. 2021. "2021 Map of the Complexity Sciences." *Art & Science Factory*. https://www.art-sciencefactory.com/complexity-map_feb09.html. Accessed 20 July 2022.

"Complex Systems." 1999. Special issue, *Science* 284 (5411). https://doi.org/10.1126/science.284.5411.

Cutting, James E. 2019. "Simplicity, Complexity, and Narration in Popular Movies." In *Narrative Complexity. Cognition, Embodiment, Evolution*, edited by Marina Grishakova and Maria Poulaki, 200–22. Lincoln, NE: University of Nebraska Press.

Davies, Rosamund. 2019. "The Screenplay as Boundary Object." *Journal of Screenwriting* 10 (2): 149–64. https://doi.org/10.1386/josc.10.2.149_1.

Elsaesser, Thomas. 2021. *The Mind-Game Film. Distributed Agency, Time Travel, and Productive Pathology*. London: Routledge.

Everett, Wendy. 2005. "Fractal Films and the Architecture of Complexity." *Studies in European Cinema* 2 (3): 159–71. https://doi.org/10.1386/seci.2.3.159/1.

Friends. 1994–2004 (10 seasons). Created by David Crane and Marta Kauffman. USA: Bright/Kauffman/Crane Productions, Warner Bros. Television.

Fleabag. 2016–2019 (2 seasons). Created by Phoebe Waller-Bridge. UK: Two Brothers Pictures.

Gell-Mann, Murray. 1995. "What Is Complexity: Remarks on Simplicity and Complexity by the Nobel Prize-Winning Author of *The Quark and the Jaguar*." *Complexity* 1 (1): 16–19. https://doi.org/10.1002/cplx.6130010105.

Gell-Mann, Murray. 1996. "Complexity at Large: Let's Call It Plectics." *Complexity* 1 (5): 3. https://doi.org/10.1002/cplx.6130010502.

Goodwin, Richard M. 1967. "A Growth Cycle." In *Socialism, Capitalism and Economic Growth*, edited by Charles Hilliard Feinstein, 54–58. Cambridge: Cambridge University Press.

Grishakova, Marina, and Maria Poulaki, eds. 2019a. *Narrative Complexity. Cognition, Embodiment, Evolution*. Lincoln, NE: University of Nebraska Press.

Grishakova, Marina, and Maria Poulaki. 2019b. "Introduction: Narrative Complexity." In *Narrative Complexity. Cognition, Embodiment, Evolution*, edited by Marina Grishakova and Maria Poulaki, 1–26. Lincoln, NE: University of Nebraska Press.

Grodal, Torben. 2022 [1997]. *Moving Pictures. A New Theory of Film Genres, Feelings, and Cognition*. 2nd ed. Oxford and New York: Oxford University Press.
Hitchins, Derek K. 2003. *Advanced Systems Thinking, Engineering and Management*. Norwood, MA: Artech House.
Hven, Steffen. 2017. *Cinema and Narrative Complexity: Embodying the Fabula*. Amsterdam: Amsterdam University Press.
Israel, Giorgio. 2005. "The Science of Complexity: Epistemological Implications and Perspectives." *Science in Context* 18 (3): 479–509. https://doi.org/10.1017/S0269889705000621.
Kennedy, J. B. 2003. *Space, Time and Einstein. An Introduction*. Chesham, UK: Acumen.
Kiss, Miklós, and Steven Willemsen. 2016. *Impossible Puzzle Films. A Cognitive Approach to Contemporary Complex Cinema*. Edinburgh: Edinburgh University Press.
Kripke, Saul A. 1972. *Naming and Necessity*. Cambridge, MA: Harvard University Press.
Ladyman, James, James Lambert, and Karoline Wiesner. 2013. "What Is a Complex System?" *European Journal for Philosophy of Science* 3 (1): 33–67. https://doi.org/10.1007/s13194-012-0056-8.
Macdonald, Ian W. 2013. *Screenwriting Poetics and the Screen Idea*. Basingstoke, UK, and New York: Palgrave Macmillan.
Maras, Steven. 2009. *Screenwriting. History, Theory and Practice*. London and New York: Wallflower.
Meifert-Menhard, Felicitas. 2013. *Playing the Text, Performing the Future. Future Narratives in Print and Digiture*. Berlin and Boston: De Gruyter.
Pelican, Kira-Ann. 2020. *The Science of Writing Characters*. London: Bloomsbury.
Pianzola, Federico. 2018. "Looking at Narrative as a Complex System: The Proteus Principle." In *Narrating Complexity*, edited by Richard Walsh and Susan Stepney, 101–22. Cham, Switzerland: Springer.
Poulaki, Maria. 2011. "Before or Beyond Narrative? Towards a Complex Systems Theory of Contemporary Films." PhD diss., University of Amsterdam.
Rosser, John Barkley Jr., and Marina V. Rosser. 2015. "Complexity and Behavioral Economics." *Nonlinear Dynamics, Psychology, and Life Sciences* 19 (2): 201–26.
Russo, Paolo. 2019. "The Maze and the Door: 'Hosted' Serial (Posthuman) Narratives as Turing Tests in *Westworld*." Paper presented at the 12th SRN Annual Conference, Universidade Catolica de Porto, 12–14 September.
Ryan, Alex. 2007. "Emergence Is Coupled to Scope, Not Level." *Complexity* 13 (2): 67–77. https://doi.org/10.1002/cplx.20203.
Ryan, Marie-Laure. 2019. "Narrative as/and Complex System." In *Narrative Complexity. Cognition, Embodiment, Evolution*, edited by Marina Grishakova and Maria Poulaki, 29–55. Lincoln, NE: University of Nebraska Press.
Ryan, Marie-Laure, and Jan-Noël Thon, eds. 2014. *Storyworlds Across Media: Towards a Media-Conscious Narratology*. Lincoln, NE: University of Nebraska Press.
Sawyer, R. Keith. 2010. "Individual and Group Creativity." In *Cambridge Handbook of Creativity*, edited by James C. Kaufman and Robert Sternberg, 366–80. Cambridge: Cambridge University Press.
Sayama, Hiroshi. 2015. *Introduction to the Modeling and Analysis of Complex Systems*. Geneseo, NY: Open SUNY Textbooks.

Schenk, Sabine. 2013. *Running and Clicking. Future Narratives in Film*. Berlin and Boston: De Gruyter.
"The Adversary." 2016. Written by Halley Gross and Jonathan Nolan. Directed by Frederick E. O. Toye. *Westworld*. Season 1, Episode 6. First aired: 6 November. USA: HBO Entertainment, Kilter Films, Bad Robot Productions, Jerry Weintraub Productions, Warner Bros. Television.
The Descendants. 2011. Written by Alexander Payne, Nat Faxon, and Jim Rash. Directed by Alexander Payne. USA: Ad Hominem.
The Full Monty. 1996. Written by Simon Beaufoy. Directed by Peter Cattaneo. UK: Redwave Films, Channel Four Films.
The Last Performance. 2013. Written and directed by Reza Moayedi. Iran: Reza Moayedi.
The Voorman Problem. 2011. Written by Mark Gill and Baldwin Li. Directed by Mark Gill. UK: Baldwin Li & Lee Thomas, in association with Actividéo Communications and Pipedream Pictures.
Tikka, Pia, and Mauri Kaipanen. 2019. "Intersubjectivity, Idiosyncrasy, and Narrative Deixis: A Neurocinematic Approach." In *Narrative Complexity. Cognition, Embodiment, Evolution*, edited by Marina Grishakova and Maria Poulaki, 314–37. Lincoln, NE: University of Nebraska Press.
Tynyanov, Yury. 2019 [1924]). "Literary Fact." In *Permanent Evolution: Selected Essays on Literature, Theory and Film*, edited by Ainsley Morse and Philip Redko, 267–82. Berlin: De Gruyter.
Varotsis, George. 2015. *Screenplay and Narrative Theory. The Screenplectics Model of Complex Narrative Systems*. London: Lexington.
Walsh, Richard, and Susan Stepney, eds. 2018a. *Narrating Complexity*. Cham, Switzerland: Springer.
Walsh, Richard, and Susan Stepney. 2018b. "Introduction and Overview: Who, What, Why." In *Narrating Complexity*, edited by Richard Walsh and Susan Stepney, 3–9. Cham, Switzerland: Springer.
Westworld. 2016–2022 (4 seasons). Created by Jonathan Nolan and Lisa Joy. USA: HBO Entertainment, Kilter Films, Bad Robot Productions, Jerry Weintraub Productions, Warner Bros. Television
Weyl, Hermann. 1997 [1939]. *The Classical Groups. Their Invariants and Representations*. Princeton, NJ: Princeton University Press.

CHAPTER 4

Collaboration, Cooperation and Authorship in Screenwriting aka How Many People Does It Take to Create an Author?

Rosamund Davies

4.1 Introduction

Drawing on the work of many scholars before me, this chapter will consider writing and authorship as two separate though closely related things, which are produced through "patterns of collective activity" (Becker 2008, 1) within film and television. I will consider each separately before bringing them together at the end to examine how notions of authorship intersect with the collective, cooperative and collaborative processes through which a screenplay is developed.

I will discuss authorship as it relates to the specific practice of screenwriting and the specific artefact of the screenplay, rather than to the question of who might or not be the ultimate author(s) of the final screen work (e.g. film, television programme, etc.), which has already been the subject of much debate and critique.

Furthermore, my primary interest in authorship is in relation to the processes and structures of the screen industries. I do not attempt a philosophical enquiry into what might or might not constitute authorship. Rather, I focus on how notions of authorship currently operate within the screen industries, with regard to considerations such as reputation, remuneration, control, organisation of labour and creative processes, as well as their relationship to cultural values and institutional norms.

R. Davies (✉)
School of Stage and Screen, University of Greenwich, London, UK
e-mail: r.davies@gre.ac.uk

© The Author(s), under exclusive license to Springer Nature Switzerland AG 2023
R. Davies et al. (eds), *The Palgrave Handbook of Screenwriting Studies*,
https://doi.org/10.1007/978-3-031-20769-3_4

4.2 Script Development as Collective Practice

Creative collaboration within screenwriting has been discussed from a range of perspectives. Some attention has been paid to collaboration between established writing partners (Johnson and Stevens 2016), although this relationship and working practice is not so frequently discussed as is that between writers, directors and producers (e.g. Bloore 2013; McAulay 2014; Milligan 2017; Murphy 2011; Price 2010; Tieber 2014).

The concept and practices of the writers' room have been subject to frequent analysis (e.g. Caldwell 2008; Henderson 2011; Maloney and Burne 2021; Phalen 2017; Redvall 2013), as have the corporate idea and script development processes of film studios and television companies (e.g. Bloore 2013; Redvall 2013; Ross 2011; Staiger 1985; Tieber 2014). Another focus has been on the role played by public institutions, for example, national film boards, who typically support script development by bringing in script professionals to work with writers on their scripts (e.g. Batty and Taylor 2021; Moore and O'Meara 2021; O'Connell 2012).

These various collective practices might be categorised according to Vera John-Steiner's three models of collaboration: *distributed*, *complementary* and *integrated*, wherein "distributed collaboration" (John-Steiner 2006, 114) is spread out in time and/or space rather than being a synchronous activity; "complementary collaboration" (John-Steiner 2006, 70) is characterised by a division of labour, in which collaborators draw on their individual strengths and skills to work simultaneously on a joint project; while "integrative collaboration", the rarest of the three, "requires a long process of committed activity… motivated by the desire to transform existing knowledge and paradigms into new visions" (John-Steiner 2006, 70).

According to John-Steiner, this latter form of collaboration, like the collaboration between Picasso and Braque (John-Steiner 2006, 63–96), is one which significantly impacts "both the field and the participants" (John-Steiner 2006, 70). In screenwriting, as in in other fields of creative practice, it is comparatively rare. When we think of collaborative screenwriting, it is perhaps complementary collaboration that most readily comes to mind. The work of writing partners/teams and writers' rooms, in particular, is frequently described by participants in terms of complementarity and division of labour. Writing partners Lee and Janet Batchler (writers of *Batman Forever* [1995]), for example, divide up the work so that she writes visuals and action, while he focuses more on "the emotional life of the character" (Johnson and Stevens 2016, 165). Andrew Reich and Ted Cohen divided up scenes between them when working on scripts for the television series *Friends* (1994–2004) (Johnson and Stevens 2016, 175). In addition to the division of labour that derives from the official hierarchies of the TV writers' room, writers in American and Australian writers' rooms also distinguish between writers who excel in verbal brainstorming and breaking of story and those whose strength is the actual writing of screenplays; between writers who are better at first drafts or at rewriting, and between story and joke writers in comedy (Maloney and Burne 2021; Phalen 2017).

Complementarity also features in accounts of writer/director collaborations. Isabelle Gourdin-Sangouard suggests a division of labour in the collaboration between director Lindsay Anderson and writer David Sherwin on the screenplay for *If…* (1968), in which Sherwin's strength was his imagination, while Anderson had a superior grasp of structure and "ability to push a dramatic situation to its logical conclusion" (Drazin 2008, cited in Gourdin-Sangouard 2010, 137). Writer Jon Raymond characterises the collaboration between himself and director Kelly Reichardt as that of writer and editor. While Raymond initially takes the role of writer, establishing the story structure, characters, tone, locations and dialogue in the form of a short story, in the writing of the screenplay the roles are reversed. At this point, Reichardt takes the lead as writer, concentrating on how to bring the story visually to the screen (Murphy 2011).

Claus Tieber (2014) identifies a division of labour in the relationship between writer/director and producer on the film *Grand Hotel* (1932), as represented in the script protocols from story conferences for the script. According to Tieber, the main focus for Irving Thalberg, head of production at MGM, was on whether the script would produce the right "emotional reactions and effects" (Tieber 2014, 233) in the audience, whereas writer/director Edmund Goulding's concern was with narrative structure and visual storytelling.

Forms of *distributed collaboration* are also common in the process of idea and script development. Episodes for television series may often be written by multiple writers who have minimum direct contact with each other, interacting principally with the writer-executive producer or head writer, and/or story or script editor, who oversee the continuity and coherence of the story across the series (Maloney and Burne 2021; Phalen 2017).

The practice of successively hiring writers to work on the same script might also be characterised as distributed collaboration. The contexts in which this take place are multiple, ranging from a "weekly mill" (Mazin 2015) that sees writers replaced in a relentless churn, to a situation in which it is the writer who takes the initiative to leave the project, either because of creative disagreement, or because they need to move on to follow through on other commitments. Adaptation is another common context, in which one writer undertakes to rework and rewrite story elements previously devised by another writer. Indeed, all rewrites might be considered a form of adaptation (Mazin 2015).

4.3 Collaboration Versus Cooperation

These last examples described above would seem to test the limits, however, of what modes of interaction we might appropriately term collaboration. As screenwriting scholar Ian W. Macdonald (2010) points out, there are many instances of collective idea and script development that might more accurately be described as cooperation. Since screenwriters are obliged to work with producers, directors, other screenwriters, script editors and other development personnel, if they want to see their script realised on screen (Bloore 2013; Sternberg 1997) they may often have to submit to demands that are imposed, rather than negotiated.

In his discussion of his own experience of rewriting and being rewritten, John August emphasises what he sees as the collaborative nature of the situation, suggesting that, wherever possible, the original writer should have some kind of continuing involvement with the project, commenting that "my relationship with some of my favorite writers came because I was being rewritten by them or I was rewriting them" (August 2015). Collaboration in this situation could potentially become rather one-sided, however. If one participant is collaborating full-heartedly and the other cooperating unwillingly or unknowingly, what do we call the process they are engaged in?

It is not only in the case of the distributed mode of interaction that this question arises. Writers working in writers' rooms, particularly newcomers at the beginning of their career and at the bottom of the hierarchy, might also feel that they are cooperating rather than collaborating, in the sense that they are contributing to a collective endeavour, but one whose rules of engagement and goals may not seem to be determined with much regard to their own interests.

The line between collaboration and cooperation is difficult to draw definitively. We might agree that *collaboration* is a particular instance of a wider set of possibilities that are comprised in the term *cooperation*. *Collaboration* implies a willingness on the part of the participant, a notion that is absent from the term *cooperation*, which can apply equally to interactions that are willing, reluctant or forced. This willingness derives from the existence of a shared goal between collaborators, which need not exist in the case of cooperation. Furthermore, although collaboration may take place within a hierarchical structure, it typically involves some choice and control over the nature and manner of the contribution made to the collective endeavour—something which is again not a necessary feature of cooperation. This is not to say, however, that collaboration is free of disagreement or conflict. The approach to resolving such issues, however, would derive from the circumstances described above.

The difference might well depend on perception, as suggested by John August's account above, in which he implies that it is largely his decision whether to make the situation of rewriting and being rewritten a collaborative one. At the same time, however, differing perceptions among participants as to the nature of a collective interaction often result from factors extrinsic to their own will or inclination. That is to say that their status within the group will affect the nature of their participation.

This is a particular concern for writers from marginalised groups (e.g. with regard to class, race, gender and so forth), who may feel that they need to modify their contributions and behaviour in order to be accepted by the dominant cultural cohort within the collective writing process (Coel 2018; Henderson 2011; Lawrence Taylor 2020; Maloney and Burne 2021; Phalen 2017).

African American writer and series creator Kenya Barris has stated that "the room doesn't care if you're Black, White, male or female. The best joke makes it into the script" (Barris quoted in Henderson 2011, 145). However, other writers state that sexualised, sexist and racist jokes and comments continue to be made in some writers' rooms, if not as frequently as they used to be (Caldwell 2008; Henderson 2011; Phalen 2017). Even when these are refrained from, where writers' rooms and development teams remain predominantly white male and middle class, people of colour, women and other marginalised groups may find their participation constrained. As one writer commented: "I don't want to be so abrasive that I get fired or ghettoized or silenced in some way. I want to stay in this mainstream room in mainstream culture and have my point of view be heard and taken seriously" (Phalen 2017, 91).

Such cultural differences and power imbalances between participants frequently remain unacknowledged, despite their significant impact on the experience and agency of all involved, since they tend to remain invisible to those who are dominant within the interaction. Thus, while one participant may feel they are involved in a close collaboration, another may feel they are cooperating under duress and find themselves sidelined and steamrollered (Caldwell 2008; Coel 2018; Lawrence Taylor 2020; Henderson 2011; Phalen 2017).

It is this potential mismatch of experience between participants that I want to attend to, as much as the difference between collaboration and cooperation per se. It is fair to say, however, that, once the screen idea work group (SIWG) (Macdonald 2010) expands beyond what Peter Bloore has called the "creative triangle" (Bloore 2013, 69–91) of writer(s), producer(s) and director(s) to include the many other people whose contributions shape idea and script development, the notion of cooperation becomes more apt to describe the wide range of relations and activities involved, as I will discuss below. It is as much an integral part of idea and screenplay development in the contemporary screen industries as is collaboration and neither is good or bad a priori. What I want to hold onto here, as indicated above, is that *cooperation* is a neutral term, while *collaboration* is inflected with particular values. It thus becomes important, when analysing or attempting to achieve the latter, to assess how these values might play out in practice. With regard to the former, meanwhile, the extent to which the cooperation might be willing, reluctant or forced, in what ways and for whom, becomes salient.

In the contemporary film and television industries, idea and script development participate in regional, national and global networks of organisations and individuals, which include production studios and companies; broadcasters; streamers; film finance companies and other investors; distributors and public institutions, such as screen agencies; along with the aforementioned writers, producers and directors; as well as agents, actors, production heads of department and so on. In an increasingly competitive environment, in which film and television compete in a digital economy with newer media and platforms, the commercial strategies of film and television companies employ tactics such as formatting, franchising and branding (Caldwell 2008; Hesmondhalgh 2019; Mann 2009; Saha 2018; Phalen 2017). Not only do these priorities inform decisions about what to commission, they also result in close supervision of projects in development to make sure they meet them.

Following sociologist Howard Becker's concept of "art worlds" (Becker 2008), to describe the extended networks of people and resources through which creative artefacts are produced, we might understand creative triangles, writers' rooms, other collective writing practices and larger institutions as all participating in a *development world*. Within this world, decisions, input and feedback are distributed across extensive networks of cooperation, regulated and controlled through different power dynamics, derived from the resources, reputations, skills and knowledge of those involved and how they employ them to protect and further their interests (Bloore 2013; Caldwell 2008).

As Becker points out, the organisation of such a complex, networked world relies on established conventions. When everyone is signed up to such conventions in advance, less negotiation and time is required than when attempting to break new ground regarding every aspect of a collective endeavour. This helps to streamline the process and minimise open conflict (Becker 2008). Adhering to existing orthodoxies as to what makes an idea or a screenplay good, for example, provides a readymade template for idea and script development (Macdonald 2021; Staiger 2021), helping to streamline a process stretched out across complex and extensive networks of cooperation.

However, adherence to established conventions also limits the range of contributions that will ever be recognised, or indeed put forward by members of the SIWG (Caldwell 2008; Macdonald 2021; Phalen 2017). Storytelling conventions and ideas about what audiences want are, moreover, informed by wider cultural norms and preoccupations, which promote some kinds of stories and suppress or disregard others (Caldwell 2008; Cattrysse 2017; Coel 2018; Hambly 2021; Lawrence Taylor 2020; Saha 2018; Wreyford 2018). While screenwriting scholar Díóg O'Connell has suggested that the Irish Film Board successfully brought together universalised Hollywood norms of story structure and script development with uniquely Irish cultural concerns and experiences, to help establish a distinctively Irish cinema (O'Connell 2012), Hambly suggests that Screen Australia's promotion of such norms are misguided. She argues that the dominant story model of "a driving cause-effect narrative, built around an empowered individual" (Hambly 2021, 81) actually runs counter to Australian cultural mythology, which valorises the community over the individual. She points out that narrative patterns associated with the community paradigm in fact characterise many of the Australian films that do well at the box office.

4.4 Prior Relationships and Group Identities

In addition to pre-established conventions, pre-established relationships provide another effective means of saving time and minimising negotiation in the complex and fast moving networks of cooperation that characterise the development world. The screen industries rely heavily on personal connections and prior relationships (Phalen 2017; Wreyford 2018). One such example is provided by Alison Peirse, who, in her study of the development of the television series *Bedlam* (2011–2013), points out that the executive producer's decision to settle on a series pitch from the production company RED was based not only on the quality and fit of the pitch and pilot script, but on her experience of working with the company and its founder on previous productions, meaning that "she absolutely trusted their ability to deliver" (Peirse 2022, 7).

As Natalie Wreyford discusses in her research into gender inequality in screenwriting, when people cannot work with people they know, they often opt to work with people who are like them (Wreyford 2018). What makes one person like another is not only about character types, but often has much to do with shared cultural background, experience and values. Bloore acknowledges the role of cultural background as a determining factor in facilitating collaboration, citing Duncan Kenworthy, producer of *Four Weddings and a Funeral* (1994), *Notting Hill* (1999) and *Love Actually* (2003), who comments "It was easy to get up a head of steam on Four Weddings, because Mike Newell (director), Richard Curtis (writer) and I all had similar backgrounds, reading English at Oxbridge" (Bloore 2013, 70–71).

Bloore does not, however, follow through on the implications of Kenworthy's statement, to point out the issues that can arise from the operation of homophily: "the tendency of individuals to associate and bond with similar others" (Wreyford 2018, 39). This inclination towards forming cooperative and collaborative groups between people who already share an established group identity frequently works within the screen industries to exclude writers due to their gender, race, class or other marginalised cultural identities (Caldwell 2008; Wreyford 2018), as indeed does the reliance on prior relationships and personal networks (Grugulis and Stoyanova 2012).

On the one hand, Peirse's example cited above suggests that personal relationships and homophily may also operate as a means of empowerment for non-dominant groups. Indeed Peirse's interest is in the largely hidden but "huge amount of power over screen storytelling" (Peirse 2022, 2) exerted by women working in commissioning and development. She argues that, although the series *Bedlam* was written, directed and shot by men, a network of five female executives were responsible for shaping key aspects of the story, including its main themes, story structure and format, and indeed for commissioning it in the first place (Peirse 2022). Although Peirse does not discuss homophily, one might infer that it played a part in the working relationships between these women, along with the prior working relationships she does discuss.

On the other hand, this case study also points to the limitations of what such networks of mutual empowerment can achieve, when operating within a dominant culture, given that the power that women may have in development roles does not equate to a similar prominence of women in the actual writing of television series. As Peirse states in her article, according to recent research undertaken by the Writers Guild of Great Britain, women were responsible for writing only 28% of UK television episodes (Kreager and Follows 2018 cited in Peirse 2022). I will return to this point in my discussion of authorship.

Apparently instant chemistry and spontaneously successful collaboration and cooperation between individuals often result in fact from tacit but common cultural histories, norms, assumptions and identities, as well as from the more obvious social and professional networks and experience that they share (Wreyford 2018). Where these are absent, established frameworks for collaboration and cooperation on idea development may not be fit for purpose, since they rarely acknowledge and therefore make no attempt to counter the forms of exclusion and coercion discussed above, which may not be deliberate, but are nevertheless real.

International co-productions provide a revelatory context for problems that may arise when such tacit shared understandings are absent, necessitating an alternative framework for collaboration (see Davies 2021; and the chapter by Laura and Luisa Cotta Ramosino in this volume). The same factors underpin national contexts of collective production, which bring together writers and other development workers of different genders, race, class and so on.

Conventions and orthodoxies are difficult to displace, however. As Becker points out, "the conventional way of doing things in any art utilizes an existing cooperative network, which rewards those who manipulate the existing conventions appropriately" (Becker 2008, 306). Since changes in conventions are likely to negatively affect those who are rewarded by the current arrangements, they will resist such changes (Becker 2008). Significant changes are therefore only effected through the mobilisation of enough members of the network, who "make them the basis of a new mode of cooperation" (Becker 2008, 309).

In the past half century, changes in the cooperative networks through which idea and script development happen and the conventions they follow have largely seemed to be driven by economic and technological developments. It is possible, however, that future changes may be provoked through a mobilisation of the network in pursuit of different interests and in response to different priorities.

This mobilisation can be effected most easily at the small-scale level of collective activity: within the writers' room, or between the members of the creative triangle. In such collaborations, where there is not already a sense of belonging to a shared culture to help shape and consolidate a successful group identity, participants need to work harder to create a shared space of collaboration (Davies 2021), in which a shared group identity can develop and be supported, but each individual participant's sense of self is not negated (Haslam et al. 2013).

As I will discuss below, the collaborative and cooperative nature of idea and script development and the power relations that play out within this process are integral to understandings of authorship and their material consequences within the screen industries.

4.5 Understandings of Authorship

Despite the extensive discussions of authorship and authors in the academic literature, and in contrast to the publishing industry, where the terms writer and author tend to be used interchangeably, the term *author* is not actually common in the film and television industries. It is nevertheless appropriate to consider authorship as something that concerns those involved in film and television development and production, in so far as the notion of authorship significantly affects matters such as the exploitation of treatments, screenplays, formats and other kinds of intellectual property; the value and number of income streams that individuals and organisations may derive from them; individual and corporate reputations and so on.

According to Foucault's influential theorisation of authorship, the notion of the author serves, among other things, to designate a text as property and to provide a "principle of unity" (Foucault 1995, 238), which explains both what the text is about and the form it takes, the author standing as a marker of both coherence and quality (Foucault 1995). The interpretation and evaluation of a text and its introduction into "the social order of property which governs our culture" (Foucault 1995, 236), are thus both organised around and operate to construct the "entity we call an author" (Foucault 1995, 236). The "author-function", as Foucault terms it:

> [...] is tied to the legal and institutional systems that circumscribe, determine, and articulate the realm of discourses; it does not operate in a uniform manner in all discourses, at all times, and in any given culture; it is not defined by the spontaneous attribution of a text to its creator, but through a series of precise and complex procedures. (Foucault 1995, 239–40)

In the discussion that follows, I want to examine how the notion of the author operates within the current legal and institutional systems of film and television. While drawing on Foucault's conception of the author as a function of discourse, my focus is on the implications of the operations of the "author-function" for people working within the cooperative networks of film and television worlds.

4.6 THE SCREENPLAY AND THE PRODUCTION OF AUTHORSHIP

As screenwriting scholar Steven Price points out, the screenplay and other development documents are tightly monitored by legal definitions and contractual requirements, overseen to a greater or lesser extent by professional trade bodies.[1] This is particularly true of the United States, where the Writers Guild of America (WGA) oversees them very closely and has articulated a nuanced hierarchy of terms to divide up the collective labour of writing into differentiated credits that may be awarded to individuals. In feature film, the most significant acknowledgement of authorship that a writer can obtain is usually the *written by* credit (as opposed to the *screenplay by* credit, where the authorship of story is allocated to another entity) (Price 2010). Other differentiated writer credits include *story by*; *adaptation by*; the use of & between writers' names to indicate a writing team; *and* between names to indicate successive contributions, and so on. The WGA rules also include detailed guidance as to how to determine such credits and also provisionally limit the number of writers or writer teams who can have screenplay credit to two (see Price 2010), although this may become more through arbitration.

Such differentiations between credits constitute "the most obvious way in which screenwriting differs from other kinds of textual authorship" (Price 2010, 13). Based on readings of the screenplay in its multiple instances across different drafts and other development documents, authorship is parsed and allocated across a number of individuals, producing a multiple, hierarchised definition of authorship. As Price (2010) points out, the allocation of authorship credits is an example of the way that the "author-function" is used to manage and avoid "the proliferation of meaning" (Foucault quoted in Price 2010, 20) within the film and television industry. This relates not only to the meaning of the text, but also to what the contribution of everyone involved means with regard to their legal, financial, moral and material claims over the text. It also has the important role of defining who does not have a meaningful claim.

Authorship is parsed slightly differently within television production, reflecting the higher status and level of creative control afforded to head writers on series. The production credit *created by,* and the frequent use of the term *creator* in relation to television series, perhaps come closest to the term *author*, as most commonly understood, identifying an individual as not only the writer but the origin of the work.

The creator of a series may often be involved in the production as well as the writing of the show, particularly in the USA. However, this is not necessarily the case. For example, Mann (2009) explains how Jeffrey Lieber has a

---

[1] The details of intellectual property rights and contractual agreements are complicated, differ from nation to nation and are not covered comprehensively by my brief reference to some of these complexities and their implications in this chapter.

creator credit on *Lost* (2004–2010) (as WGA rules require), having written the original pilot script, even though the script was rejected and J. J. Abrams and Damon Lindelof were then brought in to rewrite/replace it for the pilot that was actually shot. Meanwhile, in the public discourse around the series, it is Abrams, Lindenhof and Carlton Cuse, joint showrunner with Lindenhof, who are recognised and celebrated as the authorial voices of the show (Mann 2009), although Cuse does not have a creator credit. Abrams, meanwhile, did not continue with the day-to-day running of the show (Mann 2009) and only wrote a few episodes. The authorial recognition awarded to him with regard to the show, while it in part comes from the project itself, is likely also from his existing reputation.

Writer credits such as *story by*, *teleplay by* and *written by* for individual episodes of television series are again indicative but imperfect guides as to the precise individual contributions of writers participating in the collective process of television writing (Phalen 2017).

Another point to consider, particularly in the USA and within the writers' room hierarchy, is that producer credits are equally important to writers, since they provide access to further income streams, as well as more creative control (Johnson and Stevens 2016; Phalen 2017).

It is clear from the above that the legal construction of authorship within film and television can accommodate a broad recognition of collective authorship, not only through division of labour into *story by*, *screenplay by* and so forth, but also in shared credits between series creators, feature film and episode writers. At the same time, it is also apparent that legal definitions and contractual requirements do not necessarily reflect the realities of the creative process in any straightforward or consistent way.

Nor are they primarily concerned with matters of quality (Nesbit 1995). Thus, while it is vital to writers that they receive what they consider to be the correct credit and related intellectual property rights, along with their associated income streams, these legal and financial concerns are bound up with those relating to reputation, status and creative and practical control, as I will discuss further below.

4.7 Authorship and Voice

Commissioners, producers and development executives often say that what they are looking for in a script is a unique or distinctive voice. This concept of voice as authorship is familiar from other contexts of writing, such as fiction or journalism. In this context, the screenplay is not being read in order to divide up and limit legal claims to authorship between individuals, but to identify the "principle of unity" (Foucault 1995, 238) that marks it out from others and suggests the existence of an author.

Screenwriters strive to put this distinctive voice into their work in order to attract and hold the attention of script readers and others, on whose notice and interest they depend (Staiger 2021). As Robert Ramsey says, regarding his writing partnership with Matthew Stone, "our goal professionally has been to create a voice—that Ramsey & Stone voice" (Johnson and Stevens 2016, 60). Writers working on series need to write in the voice of the series and may indeed be rewritten by the head writer or other senior member of the writing team in order to achieve this (Phalen 2017).

The extent to which this voice is heard depends also on what the reader reads into it. We might see this voice as resonating through particular stylistic patterns and thematic concerns within the text that connect with the values of the reader. These may be personal values derived from personal experience, aesthetic values, commercial imperatives and so on. Producers and development executives seek and find particular voices according to such considerations.

Although voice is a textual effect, not the unmediated voice of a single individual, part of what makes the voice of a text resonate may also be its connection to the person or persons the reader understands to have produced it—to their identity as they present it and as the reader constructs it. The notion of the screenplay's distinctive voice constitutes a significant way in which authorship is produced. It functions as a ready shorthand, which facilitates the discussion, evaluation and exploitation of creative work and to conduct and manage professional relationships and interactions. It indicates features of a text that are important to writers, readers and audiences and integral to commercial branding strategies. It does, however, tend to elide the complexities, variations and discontinuities of process, through which ideas emerge, develop and are written.

4.8 Who Speaks as an Author?

If the way that a person or persons are heard to speak as authors is generally through the voice of the screenplay and other development documents, then, in order to speak as authors, individuals need, as discussed earlier, to engage with established aesthetic, commercial and technical conventions of screen storytelling in ways that are recognised as both valid and original within those conventions, and to produce a text that is recognised as both technically competent and distinctive and unified in its voice (Macdonald 2021; Staiger 2021).

These conventions are, moreover, part of a wider set of conventions that govern who has the authority to speak as an author, and, if they are awarded this authority, which kinds of texts they are allowed to author and for whom (Staiger 2003; Malik and Nwonka 2017).

Such authority derives in part from the authorial credits that an individual may already have and the reputational standing of the work associated with these credits. It also derives from cultural norms of authorial identity, which continue to conform largely to the Romantic conception of the author (see e.g. Burke 1995; Price 2010). This conception both understands the unique and subjective imagination of the writer to be the origin and primary determiner of meaning and value of literary works and sees the writer's individual consciousness as impersonalised through its articulation within the text, becoming a "transcendental subjectivity which holds in place all of a text's contradictions" (Burke 1995, xxvii). This conception has combined with dominant power relations to produce a particular model of authorship, in which the "transcendental subjectivity" that is the mark of the author and seen as universal, has been simultaneously grounded in a white, male experience of empowered subjectivity (Burke 1995, xxviii).

Not only has the "hegemonic identity and authority of the author" (Miller 1995, 195) historically worked to deny the authority to speak as authors to individuals who neither embody this identity in their persons, nor speak from this subject position; where they do gain the authority to speak as authors, they are often compelled to write through this hegemonic universalised subjectivity, rather than from their own positions as subjects (Burke 1995; Miller 1995; Staiger 2003).

These tacit assumptions underpin the cooperative networks within which ideas and screenplays are developed, giving rise to experiences such as that described by black British actor and writer Daniel Lawrence Taylor, in an article in *The Guardian* newspaper. According to Lawrence Taylor, the executive producer of the production company, with which he was working on a television series that he had created, was "so surprised at the quality of the writing that he assumed my white script editor was responsible for it. I was trusted so little that I found it easier to get a lot of my ideas through by pretending that they were either hers or co-signed by her" (Lawrence Taylor 2020). Overall, however, women are under-trusted as authors (Wreyford 2018), although white women are more numerous in this role in television than are writers of colour.

Meanwhile, Michaela Coel, a British writer, producer and actor of Ghanaian heritage, has questioned the practice of bringing in experienced co-writers to work with first-time television writers from marginalised groups—she prefers the term "misfits" (Coel 2018)—seeing it as a form of silencing. Coel suggests that, in guiding the work to fit into existing storytelling conventions, the co-writing process risks erasing the specific, situated subjectivities of "misfits"; despite the fact that the perceived cultural and commercial value of their "diverse" perspectives is the reason their work has been commissioned (Coel 2018).

In her own experience of the process, however, Coel cites the input of a script editor as having been very helpful to her as a first-time series creator and writer (Coel 2018, 2019), helping her structure the series according to the episodic conventions of television. In posting her screenplays for Episode 1 × 6 of *Chewing Gum* (2015–2017), her debut television series, on Twitter, Coel noted that she was doing so in order to help other writers, who may also have no prior knowledge of such conventions, saying "I wished I had read a script for a season of a show before I started writing one" (Coel 2019).

At one level, it seems odd that this might not have occurred either to Coel or the production company at the time as a suitable means of supporting her, but on another it is unsurprising. Since Coel was not aware of such conventions, she was unlikely to seek them out, while such rules are so internalised within television development that it might equally not have occurred to the producers that providing examples of TV scripts might be helpful. They focused instead on the perceived need to bring in co-writers.

Coel and Lawrence Taylor's discussions of what they found helpful and unhelpful suggest that there are no fixed rules for how to manage successful collaborations. They point, however, to the ways that assumptions about authorial authority may impact on the development process, producing the kinds of inequalities discussed earlier, and need to be taken careful account of in the organisation of collaborative work.

Limitations may also be enforced regarding the genres and modes of representation in which writers are allowed to be authors. Media scholars Sarita Malik and Clive Nwonka have discussed the way that television commissioning strategies linked to wider "political, legislative and cultural agendas" (Malik and Nwonka 2017, 423) privilege a type of urban crime drama characterised by "generic verisimilitude" (Malik and Nwonka 2017, 442), rather than social realism, which "compromises any socio-political imperatives that the practitioner may wish to communicate" (Malik and Nwonka 2017, 442). Wreyford has pointed to the way that women are commonly seen as having authorial authority only with regard to genres such as drama and others "concerned primarily with human relationships and the pursuit of romantic, heterosexual love" and not in relation to genres such as action, thriller, horror and so on (Wreyford 2018).

Moreover, departures from authorial conventions by women, people of colour and other marginalised groups often result in their being cast as "difficult" (Lawrence Taylor 2020), incompetent or otherwise problematic. In such instances, networks of collaboration and/or support may transform into more coercive mechanisms of control.

Conversely, departure from conventions of storytelling or behaviour on the part of even relatively inexperienced white middle class males is more likely to be interpreted positively, accommodated within established conventions of authorial rebelliousness, rather than understood as threatening behaviour or incompetence (Caldwell 2008).

One way that individuals seek to counter such issues is by maximising their control over the exploitation of their creative work in production and distribution (see e.g. O'Meara and Moore 2021). Michaela Coel, for example, has described how on the first day of shooting *Chewing Gum* (2015–17), which she wrote and starred in, she was horrified to find that all five main black actors had been put in a single trailer, whereas the main white actor had her own trailer. This and other instances during the production made her decide that she needed to exercise material control over the production of her work (Coel 2018). This affected the way she approached her next series,

I May Destroy You (2020), which she produced through her own production company, Falkna Productions (in partnership with Various Artists), signing a deal with the BBC and HBO. Coel stresses the importance of both the creative freedom and retention of rights she felt these arrangements offered, saying "I could have worked with Netflix on this show and I decided not to… it felt odd that a streaming service would demand 100% of my rights while I was directing, starring and writing the show, so I didn't do it" (Michaela Coel quoted in Ibekwe 2020). This strategy of authorship gives her more agency to work with others in "authoring practices" (Staiger 2003, 52) that may disrupt and resist dominant authorship conventions.

It is notable that Coel initially established her right to speak as an author through writing and performing a one-woman show for the stage, *Chewing Gum Dreams* (2013), from which her television series was adapted. Writer/performers Phoebe Waller-Bridge, creator of television series *Fleabag* (2016–2019) and *Killing Eve* (2018–2022) and Mindy Kaling, writer on the American version of *The Office* (2005–2012) and creator of *The Mindy Project* (2012–2017), also launched their careers through self-penned fringe theatre shows. Issa Rae (creator of television series *Insecure* (2016–2021) pursued a similar strategy through her web series *Mis-Adventures of Awkward Black Girl* (2011). While successfully inserting themselves into the cooperative networks of fringe theatre or online media was hardly easy, these women's self-creation as author-performers within these worlds necessitated the involvement and approval of fewer people and less money than in television. The worlds of fringe theatre and standup have indeed long been linked into that of television, as networks through which new talent can emerge, and online media now also participate in these. They constitute particularly important platforms for those marginalised as authors from other spaces. Online media may also be where they find a particularly appreciative audience, underserved by other media (Coel 2018).

4.9 Authorship, Collaboration and Cooperation

As John Caldwell (2008) points out, industry discourse acknowledges, promotes and celebrates collective and collaborative creativity while also working to construct, maintain and privilege the value of individual authors. The tendency, moreover, is to discount the extent to which both author and text are produced through the cooperative networks that constitute film and television worlds, as well as wider social worlds. Indeed, since these networks have developed around the convention of the transcendent, self-sufficient author, who is born not made, they tend to work to make their own author-producing functions invisible, rewarding those who adhere to this convention.

Although those who work in writing and script development have a lived understanding of the reality and importance of collaboration and cooperation in the creative process, they also have an interest in maintaining dominant conventions of authorship, since authorship constitutes a convenient currency, through which individuals and organisations can trade and accrue financial, symbolic, social and cultural capital.

These dominant conceptions of authorship have various effects on how the collaborative and cooperative processes of idea and script development are perceived, depending on an individual's prior reputation and credits as an author.

Where an individual's authorial identity has been established, with regard to both official credits and the reputational standing of their work, the rest of the cooperative network, which works to produce authorship, hitherto referred to for brevity as the network of authorship—including, for example, the role played by their personal relationships and connections, studios, production companies, development executives and other members of the writing team, financing, marketing and distribution arrangements—is likely to be rendered more or less invisible; except where a work is judged to be unsuccessful in one or more aspects, in which case other elements in the network may come into focus as potential agents of this failure.

On the other hand, where an individual's authorial identity is not so clearly established, the rest of the network of authorship tends to remain more visible, as Lawrence Taylor's experience suggests (Lawrence Taylor 2020). In the case of failure, however, this network is more likely to fade out of view, with the failure seen as directly attributable to them, delegitimising their claim to authorship with regard to this work and to future projects (Becker 2008; Wreyford 2018).

These operations are further impacted by the fact that the legitimacy of an individual's claim to authorship also depends on how the identity that this individual is seen to have matches cultural norms of authorial identity: still most readily recognised as incarnate in the person of a white, cis, heterosexual, non-disabled, middle class male. Where an individual fits cultural norms of identity, this may offset, to some extent, the disadvantage of lack of prior recognition; while the extent to which an individual departs from these norms is likely to both work against the impact of such prior recognition and to compound the disadvantage of the lack of it (Caldwell 2008; Lawrence Taylor 2020; Wreyford 2018).

These understandings of authorship also affect the levels of trust, moral authority and creative control that individuals are awarded within the collaborative teams and wider networks of cooperation in which they participate. Where their claim to authorship is less well established, trust, moral authority and creative control will be lower. This may be reflected in clear hierarchies or manifest in more informal and tacit ways. There are also likely to be limitations on what these individuals may be permitted to have authorship of, with regard to prestige, budget, etc., as well as with regard to subject matter, genre, etc. Where their contributions depart from established orthodoxies, they may be more likely to be judged as invalid and illegitimate rather than innovative.

4.10 Conclusions

Practices of writing and concepts of authorship are mutually constructive. They are subject to and determined by relations of power and interest, which tend towards the universalisation of dominant beliefs and behaviours through particular conventions governing how people in collaborative groups and cooperative networks work together; the work they produce, and to whom authorship is assigned.

The way that both small-scale collaborative processes and wider cooperative networks are organised impacts significantly on the experiences of those involved and on what they write. They can serve to both support and obstruct successful collective idea and script development, with regard to both the experience of participants in the process and the work it produces. The way that such processes are organised is influenced by prevailing models of authorship within film and television, which, simultaneously and somewhat paradoxically, understand authorship of the screenplay to be potentially shared and multiple, while also retaining a conception of the author as an autonomous creator. The latter notion frequently results in a failure to adequately acknowledge that authors are in fact created through the extensive cooperative networks of film and television worlds. These comprise, but are not limited to, personal networks, relations of homophily, commercial strategies, technologies and access to them, legal frameworks, aesthetic and business conventions and philosophies; the ways through which collective activity is organised; cultural values and beliefs; political and economic realities. Within these networks, orthodoxies of storytelling and other conventions of writing and authorship develop in tandem with dominant cultural norms that are closely aligned with dominant social groups. This makes it easier in several ways for individuals who belong to such groups to enter into and successfully negotiate the cooperative networks that produce authorship.

Taking such circumstances into account can provide a helpful starting point for developing effective approaches to managing networks of cooperation and processes of collaboration, while also offering a range of points of departure for scholars of screenwriting and screenwriting authorship.

References

August, John. 2015. "Transcript of Episode 216: Rewrites and Scheduling." *Scriptnotes* podcast. https://johnaugust.com/2015/scriptnotes-ep-216-rewrites-and-scheduling-transcript. Accessed 1 July 2022.

Batty, Craig, and Stayci Taylor. 2021. "Room for Improvement: Discourses of Quality and Betterment in Script Development." In *Script Development. Critical Approaches, Creative Practices, International Perspectives*, edited by Craig Batty and Stayci Taylor, 271–92. Basingstoke, UK: Palgrave Macmillan.

Becker, Howard S. 2008 [1982]. *Art Worlds*, 25th ed. Berkeley, CA and London: University of California Press.

Bloore, Peter. 2013. *The Screenplay Business. Managing Creativity and Script Development in the Film Industry*. London: Routledge.
Burke, Seán. 1995. "Introduction." In *Authorship. From Plato to the Postmodern: A Reader*, edited by Seán Burke, xv–xxx. Edinburgh: Edinburgh University Press.
Caldwell, John. 2008. *Production Culture: Industrial Reflexivity and Critical Practice in Film and Television*. Durham, NC: Duke University Press.
Cattrysse, Patrick. 2017. "Cultural Dimensions and an Intercultural Study of Screenwriting." In *Transcultural Screenwriting: Telling Stories for a Global World*, edited by Carmen Sofia Brenes, Patrick Cattrysse, and Margaret McVeigh, 8–27. Newcastle upon Tyne: Cambridge Scholars.
Chewing Gum. 2015–2017 (2 seasons). Created by Michaela Coel. UK: Retort.
Coel, Michaela. 2018. McTaggart Lecture. Edinburgh International Film Festival.
Coel, Michaela. 2019. *Twitter*. Annotated version of first episode of *Chewing Gum* "Pink Shooting Script 29.06.2015".
Davies, Rosamund. 2021. "Nordic Noir with an Icelandic Twist: Establishing a Shared Space for Collaboration Within European Coproduction." In *Script Development. Critical Approaches, Creative Practices, International Perspectives*, edited by Craig Batty and Stayci Taylor, 113–28. Basingstoke, UK: Palgrave Macmillan.
Foucault, Michel. 1995. "From 'What Is an Author?'." In *Authorship. From Plato to the Postmodern: A Reader*, edited by Seán Burke, 233–46. Edinburgh: Edinburgh University Press.
Gourdin-Sangouard, Isabelle. 2010. "Creating Authorship? Lindsay Anderson and David Sherwin's Collaboration on *If...* (1968)." *Journal of Screenwriting* 1 (1): 131–34.
Grugulis, Irena, and Dimitrinka Stoyanova. 2012. "Social Capital and Networks in Film and TV: Jobs for the Boys?" *Organisation Studies* 33 (10): 1311–31.
Hambly, Glenda. 2021. "Cultural Difference in Script Development: The Australian Example." In *Script Development. Critical Approaches, Creative Practices, International Perspectives*, edited by Craig Batty and Stayci Taylor, 113–28. Basingstoke, UK: Palgrave Macmillan.
Haslam, S. Alexander, Inmaculada Adarves-Yorno, Tom Postmes, and Lise Jans. 2013. "The Collective Origins of Valued Originality: A Social Identity Approach to Creativity." *Personality and Social Psychology Review* 17 (4): 384–401.
Henderson, Felicia D. 2011. "The Culture Behind Closed Doors: Issues of Gender and Race in the Writers' Room." *Cinema Journal* 50 (2): 145–52.
Hesmondhalgh, David. 2019. *The Cultural Industries*, 4th ed. London: Sage.
I May Destroy You 2020. Created by Michaela Cole. UK: Falkna, Various Artists.
Ibekwe, Desiree. 2020. "Michaela Coel: 'TV Is Unforgiving—But I'm Built for This'". *Screen International*, 3 June. https://www.screendaily.com/features/michaela-coel-tv-is-unforgiving-but-im-built-for-this/5150313.article. Accessed 1 July 2022.
Johnson, Claudia, and Matt Stevens. 2016. *Script Partners: How to Succeed at Co-writing for Film and TV*. Abingdon, UK: Routledge
John-Steiner, Vera. 2006 [2000]. *Creative Collaboration*. Oxford: Oxford University Press.
Lawrence Taylor, Daniel. 2020. "As a Black TV Writer in a White Industry, We Need Support—Not Doubt." *The Guardian*, 26 June. https://www.theguardian.com/tv-and-radio/2020/jun/26/trust-and-support-us-rather-than-doubting-us-tales-from-a-black-tv-writer. Accessed 7 July 2022.

Macdonald, Ian W. 2010. "'… So It'S Not Surprising I'm Neurotic': The Screenwriter and the Screen Idea Work Group." *Journal of Screenwriting* 1 (1): 45–58.

Macdonald, Ian W. 2021. "Originality and Authorship in the Development of the Screen Idea." In *Script Development. Critical Approaches, Creative Practices, International Perspectives*, edited by Craig Batty and Stayci Taylor, 9–29. Basingstoke, UK: Palgrave Macmillan.

Malik, Sarita, and Clive James Nwonka. 2017. "*Top Boy*: Cultural Verisimilitude and the Allure of Black Criminality for UK Public Service Broadcasting Drama." *Journal of British Cinema and Television* 14 (4): 423–44.

Maloney, Noel, and Philippa Burne. 2021 "So Much Drama, So Little Time: Writers' Rooms in Australian Television Drama Production." In *Script Development. Critical Approaches, Creative Practices, International Perspectives*, edited by Craig Batty and Stayci Taylor, 185–204. Basingstoke, UK: Palgrave Macmillan.

Mann, Denise. 2009. "It's Not TV, It's Brand Management TV. The Collective Authors of the *Lost* Franchise." In *Production Studies: Cultural Studies of Media Industries*, edited by Vicki Mayer, Miranda T. Banks, and John T. Caldwell, 99–114. Abingdon, UK: Routledge.

Mazin, Craig. 2015 "Transcript of Episode 216: Rewrites and Scheduling." *Scriptnotes* podcast. https://johnaugust.com/2015/scriptnotes-ep-216-rewrites-and-scheduling-transcript. Accessed 1 July 2022.

McAulay, Alec. 2014. "Based on a True Story: Negotiating Collaboration, Compromise and Authorship in the Script Development Process." In *Screenwriters and Screenwriting. Putting Practice into Context*, edited by Craig Batty, 189–206. Basingstoke: Palgrave Macmillan.

Miller, Nancy K. 1995 "Changing the Subject: Authorship, Writing and the Reader." In *Authorship. From Plato to the Postmodern: A Reader*, edited by Seán Burke, 193–212. Edinburgh: Edinburgh University Press.

Milligan, Christina. 2017. "Expanding the Dialogue: The Producer as Part of the Creative Triangle." *Journal of Screenwriting* 8 (1): 23–37.

Moore, Cath, and Radha O'Meara. 2021. "How Government Institutions Shape Script Development: Comparative Case Studies of Screen Australia and the Danish Film Institute." In *Script Development. Critical Approaches, Creative Practices, International Perspectives*, edited by Craig Batty and Stayci Taylor, 31–50. Basingstoke, UK: Palgrave Macmillan.

Murphy, J. J. 2011. "A Similar Sense of Time: The Collaboration Between Writer, Jon Raymond and Director Kelly Reichardt in *Old Joy* and *Wendy and Lucy*." In *Analysing the Screenplay*, edited by Jill Nelmes, 158–74. London: Routledge.

Nesbit, Molly. 1995. "What Was an Author?" In *Authorship. From Plato to the Postmodern: A Reader*, edited by Seán Burke, 247–62. Edinburgh: Edinburgh University Press.

O'Connell, Díóg. 2012. "Irish Cinema 1994–2009: The Trajectory of Script Development Policy at the Irish Film Board." *Journal of Screenwriting* 3 (1): 61–71.

O'Meara, Radha, and Cath Moore. 2021. "Negotiating Television Authorship and Gendering Creative Identity: Vicki Madden as Australian Showrunner." In *The Palgrave Handbook of Script Development*, edited by Stayci Taylor and Craig Batty, 9–32. Basingstoke, UK: Palgrave Macmillan.

Peirse, Alison. 2022. "The Hidden Work of Women: Commissioning and Development in British Television Drama." *Feminist Media Studies*. https://doi.org/10.1080/14680777.2022.2027804.

Phalen, Patricia. 2017. *Writing Hollywood. The Work and Professional Culture of Television Writers*. New York and London: Routledge.
Price, Steven. 2010. *The Screenplay. Authorship, Theory and Criticism*. Basingstoke, UK: Palgrave Macmillan.
Redvall, Eva Novrup. 2013. *Writing and Producing Television Drama in Denmark. From 'The Kingdom' to 'The Killing'*. Basingstoke, UK: Palgrave Macmillan.
Ross, Alexander. 2011. "Creative Decision Making Within the Contemporary Hollywood Studios." *Journal of Screenwriting* 2 (1): 99–116.
Saha, Anamik. 2018. *Race and the Cultural Industries*. Cambridge: Polity Press.
Staiger, Janet. 1985. "The Hollywood mode of production 1930–1960." In *The Classical Hollywood Cinema. Film Style and Mode of Production to 1960*, edited by David Bordwell, Janet Staiger and Kristin Thompson. London: Routledge
Staiger, Janet. 2003. "Authorship Approaches." In *Authorship and Film*, edited by David A. Gerstner and Janet Staiger, 27–57. New York and London: Routledge.
Staiger, Janet. 2021. "Scripting Protocols and Practices: Screenwriting in the Package-Unit Era." In *Resetting the Scene: Classical Hollywood Revisited*, edited by Philippa Gates and Katherine Spring, 254–66. Detroit: Wayne State University Press.
Sternberg, Claudia. 1997. *Written for the Screen. The American Motion-Picture Screenplay as Text*. Tübingen: Stauffen-Verlag.
Tieber, Claus. 2014. "'A Story Is Not a Story but a Conference': Story Conferences and the Classical Studio System." *Journal of Screenwriting* 5 (2): 225–37.
Wreyford, Natalie. 2018. *Gender Inequality in Screenwriting Work*. Basingstoke, UK: Palgrave Macmillan.

CHAPTER 5

Acts of Reading: The Demands on Screenplay Reading

Rita Benis

5.1 Introduction

Mainstream cinema built its hegemonic narrative paradigms upon an *ordo ab chaos* principle.[1] Nevertheless, the conception, development, and fruition of the moving image aesthetic experience never ceased to feed on chaos itself—from documentary to dreamy, hallucinatory, poetic films, including paradoxical, non-linear, space–time structures. Such is cinema: oneiric by the archetypal depths of its images,[2] and narrative by the statement of its movement. Chaos and order entangled on each other, image after image.

By addressing these principles, each script (e.g., outline, treatment, screenplay), developed prior to almost every film, gives shape to a form of writing characterized by the crossing of technical and poetic aspects, with elements of order tangled with the substance of chaos. In this light, the screenplay reader's competence is mainly defined by her/his ability to read the tension created by such a set of elements, dealing with the unfinished nature of the screenplay, its openness to the unfolding of meanings. Following on Roland

---

[1] *Ordo ab chaos* is a Latin expression whose literal meaning is *order out of chaos*.

[2] By archetypal images we mean ahistorical images. Images that have a charge and a timeless memory, rooted in the depths of our innermost being (such as images of maternity, innocence, or wisdom).

R. Benis (✉)
CEComp, Faculty of Letters, University of Lisbon, Lisbon, Portugal
e-mail: ritabenis@campus.ul.pt

Barthes's notion of Text as a plural, multidimensional space (1977), when a reader approaches the screenplay text as an open, "intermedial" (Maras 2009; Korte and Schneider 2000), "boundary" (Davies 2021; Star 2010) work, reading becomes an interactive, collaborative experience.[3] The *visual* information inscribed in the screenplay always waits for this type of collaboration. The use (reading) one grants to the screenplay gives life to its writing, such is the tension between the written text (screenplay) and the moving image (film to come).

In this sense and following previous works on the importance of the reader as a *coproducer* of the text, as well as on the intricate relationship between writing and reading (the screenplay)—including Pier Paolo Pasolini ([1972] 2005), Claudia Sternberg (1997), Steven Maras (2009), Steven Price (2010), Nadja Cohen (2013), Adrian Martin (2014), and Rose Ferrell (2017)—this chapter addresses the screenplay through the reader's experience. Namely, by exploring how a *screenplay* can be read as a text "closer to poetry than a plan, [in its] evoking rhythm and powerful images" (Maras 2009, 71).[4]

In recent years, screenwriting research has shown that script development can be "experienced in multiple ways depending on the scale and stage of the project and the production culture within which it is practiced" (Batty and Taylor 2021, 1). As such, there are diverse perspectives on screenplay models and on how they are developed. Kathryn Millard pointed out, for instance, that the critical difference between industrials models and those that value creative improvisation "is the degree to which the screenplay remains open to new material throughout production" (Millard 2016, 281). From another perspective, J. J. Murphy suggested that, when the industrial model of dialogue-driven screenplay became the standard convention, what happened was that "by emphasizing dialogue over action, written dialogue has become privileged over visual storytelling and improvisation" (Murphy 2010, 176). Facing that same issue, *avant-garde* writer-director Maya Deren declared: "the trouble with most films is that they are 'written', whereas cinematic thinking is another process altogether" (Deren 1965, 33). Today we could say that the trouble with some films (and other audio-visual products) is not so much that they are *written*, but that their *writing* (screenplay or film) lacks "visual storytelling" and "cinematic thinking," as highlighted by Murphy and Deren.

When characterizing the screenplay only by means of its writing, namely by conceptualizing a film primarily through its narrative techniques, we might risk leading the writing process away from its cinematic potential, thus not doing justice to the actual complexity and the full interplay of its elements in relation to the future film. When the reading of the screenplay is brought into the

---

[3] Here, the term *reader* is used to refer mainly to those who are involved in a film project and read the script/screenplay with a professional capacity: e.g. the director or the producer (but also the rest of the technical and artistic team) that will interpret the screenplay and then turn it into an audio-visual work.

[4] Throughout this chapter, the term *screenplay* is used mostly to refer to a *master-scene* screenplay format.

equation, the cinematic side of the text regains attention. Therefore, the act of reading should always be considered when we characterize the screenplay.

The elements of cinematographic thinking present in a screenplay are not only about technical cinematographic instructions, introduced in the text to complement a certain cinematic style, but also elements of a more literary or poetic realm, like the musical tensions created by the interplay of the scenes, phrases, and images. As André Bazin suggested, the cinematic style of the screenplay "becomes the inner dynamic principle of the narrative, somewhat like the relation of energy of its matter or the specific physics of the work" (Bazin 1971, 31). This is a dynamic that is not easy to describe or explain, but that can be perceived or felt while reading the screenplay text. We speak of images in tension, a sense of balance, a tone, and a rhythmic shape that are present in the text.

> A distinctive feature of the screenplay is that while it is open to technical forms of reading that break the script down, it also demands forms of reading that are literary in orientation, but which can more accurately be described as poetic. The "technical" and "poetic" aspects of the script cannot readily be placed in opposition or separated. A lighting director, for example, may find some evocative part of the poetry of the script crucial in the lighting of a scene. (Maras 2009, 73)

What is implied here is that a screenplay reflects not only the narrative and the technical expertise of its author(s), but also their poetic world, their stylistic vision: "the screenplay in cinema is constituted not only, or not even so much, by the progression of the plot but also by its 'stylistic' elements" (Eikhenbaum 1998, 200).[5] Elements of a musical order: rhythm and speed, fluidity, tension, cut and acceleration, alternations and bursts. A sense of balance that shapes the text, allowing the reader to ascend to its "cinematic ideas" (Martin 2014), its "screen ideas" (Macdonald 2013). That is, the singular pace/rhythm of the screenplay, its poetic aspects, could be as important as the very narrative content of the story.

5.2 Background

Before delving into the dynamics established between writing and reading the screenplay, it might be useful to recall that a screenplay is a written text drawn up (by one individual or a group of individuals) with the aim of serving as the basis to a cinematographic work; that is, a text that brings together a set of proposals for the audio-visualization of a particular vision, subject or narrative, in the form of moving images and sound. In addition, we would like to emphasize that the audio-visual moving image, not being solely fictional, can be presented in the form of a hallucinatory combination of images, like

---

[5] All translations from Portuguese, French, and Spanish are the author's own.

a dream: a cinema ruled by a logic of "attractions" (Gunning 1986) rather than driven by the common cause-and-effect continuity. Which is to say, the audio-visual moving image is not only temporal (narrative/fictional), but also (perhaps even more) functions by logical association (attractions): "the internal structures of non-narrative texts are not temporal but logical" (Chatman 1987, 161). That is, cinema can have narrative linearity or not.

In the adaptation/translation/passage from the idea to the written text (and later from written text to the film), the narrative aspect (the story) is certainly one of the main aspects to be considered (the most important, in most films), but not the only one. One mustn't forget, screenplays and films are linked by images: "You must return to photography to understand cinema" (Petzold 2021). That is, when we deal with the specificity of screenwriting, we should always bear in mind the *cinematographic image/moving image*.

Here, it is worth remembering Maria Filomena Molder's definition of *image*: "What is, then, an image? An intentional presentation that follows the light and is visible in the light: a shadow, a reflection in the water, dust, a dream, a story that we tell about our life" (Molder 1999, 154). Then, "cinema makes time enter into the images; as a movement" (Schefer 1997, 37). Equally revealing is the word *cinematographic* which, etymologically speaking, refers to a form of writing. The word *graph* derives from the Greek word $\gamma\rho\acute{\alpha}\varphi\omega$ (*gráphō*) whose meaning can be read as a way of drawing, marking, registering, recording (on a surface). The word *cinema* derives from the Greek word $\kappa\acute{\iota}\nu\eta\mu\alpha$ (*kínēma*), whose meaning is movement, motion. The combination of the two words *cinema+graph* can then be read as a "movement record." Thus, by *cinematographic image* we mean: the record of a moving representation (which follows the light/that is made in the light); the register of the movement of a dream, a shadow, a reflection, or, last but not least, a story.

The writings of Italian scholar Giambattista della Porta, dating back to the sixteenth century,[6] as well as *Ars Magna Lucis et Umbrae*, written by the Jesuit priest Athanasius Kircher in 1655 (with a depiction of a magic lantern), already theorized writing through moving images (cinematography).[7] We could say that since its early days, humanity has played with its shadows, waiting for cinematography to appear: "the search for animated shadows, the magic of the moving image [...] The dream of cinema, the magic of visions, is as old as humankind" (da Costa 1996, 23). It was only in 1895 that cinematography finally achieved the technical progress that allowed it to reveal itself in all its splendor. And accompanying this dream of cinema (closely attached to the

---

[6] Giambattista della Porta (1535–1615) addresses the notion of *cinematography* in his works on optical effects: *Magiae naturalis libri XX* (1589) and *De refractione optices parte libri novem* (1593).

[7] The work of Athanasius Kircher (1602–1680) on *cinematography* was made known by Henri Langlois three centuries later in 1955 (see Langlois 1955).

need of controlling film production risks), a complementary form of writing would soon be born: the writing of the screenplay.

The uniqueness of the screenplay text assumes that its configuration, when read, should awaken the imagery of the reader in order to stimulate their perception to the cinematic images engendered there, thus promoting the visualization of *cinematic ideas*. By "cinematic idea," we mean an idea about the very cinematic form. As Adrian Martin explained in his Keynote 2012 SRN lecture "Where do cinematic ideas come from?":

> Cinematic ideas are not necessarily, in the first place or ever, ideas about fully formed, psychological characters inside plot arcs or journeys […]. Cinematic ideas are ideas about *form* […] as the inspired conjunction of a certain kind of image with a certain sound or piece of music; as an idea of how to use or shoot a particular place or environment; as an anticipation of how to create or evoke a specific mood or feeling; as a concept for how to narrate, depict or present a piece of story information. (Martin 2014, 19)

The Italian director Rino Lupo, responsible for some of the most significant works of the Portuguese silent cinema era, defined the screenplay as follows: "The screenplay is not a novel, nor a romance, nor a play: it is a creation of ideas, translated into images. […] The screenplay, in film art, must have purely a visual form, synthesizing and analyzing the idea in successive images" (Lupo 1927 *in* Baptista 2008, 226). Likewise, in 1920, Frances Taylor Patterson, a famous instructor of "photoplay composition," wrote: "the story, from its primal inception, should be thought out in terms of pictures and not words" (Patterson 1921, 67). In the face of these characteristics, important questions arise: namely, how is the act of reading the screenplay capable of responding to its own iconography and, on the other hand, to what extent is the screenwriting work reflected in the cinematic ideas developed on the screen?

In cinema the irrational element is inalienable, as Pasolini told us ([1972] 2005, 172). The essence of life erupts in the moving image through archetypes, symbolic forms, mythological figures. As the Portuguese writer-director Marta Mateus explained in an interview to Jonathan Rosenbaum (about the characters/actors and the places that appear in *Farpões Baldios* [*Barbs Wastelands*], 2017): "These stories are in their hands, their eyes, in what binds us together, perhaps also in our blood and in our dreams. Landscapes also participates in it. It's the source, the roots, a matter of fertility, hope, grief, shadow, solitude, birth, rebirth, joy, struggle" (Mateus in Rosenbaum, 7 January 2021).

That is, the moving image is not only constituted by the narrative surface that we can decipher in a film, but also simultaneously by the mysterious *telluric current* that flows through it, "that mythical and infantile subtext which, because of the very nature of cinema, runs underneath every film" (Pasolini [1972] 2005, 172). This cinematic unconscious substrate, that every moving image carries with it, always emerges, whether or not it has been previously developed/worked. Sometimes it is devised, crafted, envisioned before the film—through sketches, notes, descriptions, lists, director's statement, outlines, treatments, screenplays, shooting scripts, storyboards. Other times it is ignored, left to itself. Ideally, it is during screenplay development that this cinematic substrate should begin to be crafted. Ignoring it would almost be like ignoring screenwriting's intrinsic nature. Paul Schrader's words, "I am not a writer. I am a screenwriter, which is half a film-maker" (as quoted in Hamilton 1990, ix), point out to this precise particularity of screenwriting.

All the same, even when we consider that this work is being done, even when the screenwriting performance is focused on its inner cinematic design, even then, the final result displayed in the screenplay—the verbal suggestion of images and its connections, the enunciation of moving images—is never definitely established. Every time a glance, a feeling, and a consciousness (a reader) deposit his/her attention on the screenplay, the images awake and become alive (in different ways, depending on the reader). It is the conscience/awareness (that reads the text) that gives life and sustains its images. The screenplay always waits for this attention, this imaginary reading, capable of articulating all the technical and poetic aspects of the text, translating them into moving images.

5.3 Reading the Screenplay Text

Claudia Sternberg highlights that "readers of screenplays thus have to develop a *cinematic competence* and look out for information that will materialise in acting, directing, cinematography, editing, set and production design, sound, image composition, and, last but not least, in plot and dialogue" (Sternberg 2000, 155). Yet, as argued, readers should also be able to capture the inner cinematic dynamic of the text. As Steven Maras recalls: "Different subtexts or ironic modes can be revealed through the language and the way the topic is treated. In this manner, the screenplay supports and engenders interpretation that will become the basis of collaboration [of writer and reader]" (Maras 2009, 74). The screenplay reader should be able to lend the screenplay "[a] 'visual' completeness which it does not have, but at which it hints. […] The technique of screenwriting is predicated above all on this collaboration of the reader: and it is understood that its perfection consists in fulfilling this function (of collaboration) perfectly" (Pasolini [1972] 2005, 189).

Consequently, the screenplay text needs a reader who knows how to deal with its unfinished nature. Ideally, someone who possesses the unique ability to make the gap between the two emanations of the text—writing and reading—disappear; the ability to turn a non-coincidence into a coincidence. In that sense, the screenplay text comes closer to Barthes' idea of Text: "The Text requires that one try to abolish (or at the very least to diminish) the distance between writing and reading, in no way by intensifying the projection of the reader into the work but by joining them [writing and reading] in a single signifying practice" (Barthes 1977, 162). According to Barthes, the very existence of the Text rests in the language itself, in the movement of its discourse (unlike the published written work, whose phenomenological existence occupies a space). The written work is definitive and concrete, while the Text is the meaning a reader takes from the written work, not being definitive. The nature of the Text "is the very infinity of language, itself structured without closure" (Barthes 1977, 126). While the finished written work is an object defined by a process of authorship, thus creating an affiliation with its author, a Text is open and carries a multitude of associations, a plurisignification of meanings, allowing a much more interactive, collaborative, reading experience. As Steven Price suggested, "this functions as an accurate summary of many accounts of the screenplay text, particularly those which tend to regard directing as an extension of writing" (Price 2010, 40). That is, the *textual* nature of the screenplay seems to meet the point of view that sees realization/directing as an extension of screenwriting (and vice versa) "in a single significant practice" (Barthes 1977, 62).

When looking at the screenplay through its *textual* dimension, we could say that, in the writing/reading approach, you either have the writer as the director/producer—and in this case the gap (writing/reading) is automatically closed—[8]or you have the writer (screenwriter) working with another collaborator (namely the director or the producer), sometimes knowing in advance that the reading of the screenplay will often overlap the written Text authorial voice, or even "erase it" (Price 2010, 32), thus imposing the reading of the Text as the principal authorial voice of the film work. The controversial adaptation of Bertolt Brecht's play *The Threepenny Opera* (1928) is just one of many cases in which this occurs.[9]

As stated above, the collaborative development of a screenplay can produce different results depending on the type of writing/reading tension involved. Again, there are different logics of writing/reading the screenplay and not all work the same way (Batty and Taylor 2021). For instance, in the case of US-based TV/streaming series productions the creative and executive work is often assumed by the emerging figure of the *showrunner*, who frequently oversees all the writing and production of the *show*. The word *showrunner* literally means the one *who runs the show*—most of the times an executive producer,

---

[8] If the gap between writing and reading can be resolved, the gap between reading and directing will hardly be. The space/time in which the active reading occurs—that is, when filming takes place—could impose unintended forms, gestures, sounds (that neither the screenplay nor the reading foretell): e.g. the unexpected expression of an actor, the wind in the tree, a ray of sun breaching through the sky.

[9] In 1930, the film company Nero-Film bought the rights to *The Threepenny Opera* (1928) from Bertolt Brecht, commissioning him to adapt it in the hope of capitalizing the play's success in Germany. Georg Wilhelm Pabst would direct the film. When the producers (i.e. the rights' holders) suggested changes in the screenplay, Brecht reacted badly. The production then contracted Bela Balász and László Vajda to re-write the script. Brecht took the case to court, where he lost against the rights holders (the producers). The film would premiere in 1931.

often also the head writer (less frequently a director). The *showrunner*, a typical figure in the American audio-visual industry (not yet as common in other countries), is usually the one who has the final say on the project and its concept. In this context, it is possible that the gap between writing and reading ends up being absorbed by the writing/reading interpretation of the *showrunner*, since it is him/her who controls the "Text." It can also be said that, in such circumstances, the screenplay reading might become more technical (given the control has become more executive). TV (and cinema) industrial productions tend to focus more on *formula* (narrative structure, genre, number of celebrities, soundtrack, and so on), and to be more pressured by results, being less improvised. In this context, the screenwriter's voice, or the director's voice, or any other artistic voice, tends to be absorbed by the imperative of the commercial formula (the true ruler of the show). In any case, regardless of the writing style, and of whether the reading of the screenplay is controlled by producers (TV/streaming productions) or by film directors (more common in arthouse cinema), the crucial role given to the reader, regarding the screenplay, will always be of the utmost importance, since it will be he/she/them who will scan the Text and master it into the future motion picture. In Carl Theodor Dreyer words:

> It is he who is the intermediary between script and screen. He has to visualize the writer's thought. It is he who has to "see" the images, not only "see" the individual images but "see" them in their changes and succession. It is he who creates the rhythm of the film through the selection and linking together of the motifs. [...] It is an artistic intuition and an immediate feeling for rhythmical balance of images that is necessary when the manuscript is scanned in images. (as quoted in Skoller 1973, 91–96)

In other words, the screenwriter (or group of screenwriters)'s genius and the artistic quality of the screenplay—narratively and beyond—are no guarantee for the artistic excellence of the future cinematographic work. We all know extraordinary films that start from a trivial, minor screenplay (and vice versa), or films that are based on the same screenplay with very different results. The screenplay reading style will always influence the artistic outcome of a film.

> Despite the possibility of a lack of consensus around what visualization means and how it works, recognizing that the script as screenplay is closely linked to an act of reading is important. [...] recognizing the screenplay as a format that makes specific demands on particular kind of readers enables us to affirm, in a non-reductive fashion, the importance of poetry to the technical processes of production. (Maras 2009, 65–66)

In short, the screenplay owes its textual/visual singularity, its cinematic vocation, not only to the style of its writing but also to the relationship established between the text and its reader. The screenplay text lives in this tension (writing/reading).

When we look at the screenplay, we realize that we are dealing with a series of floating fragments (a scene, an image, a sequence), that create symmetries, oppositions, patterns. It is in the aggregation (reading) of its constellation of meanings and patterns that a *tension/vision* arises, generating rhythms, images, intuitions of the film to come. The word *tension* is fundamental here. Since the inner tension of a screenplay does not always coincide with the tension of the film. The pace, the rhythm, and the unique cinematic tension each film achieves on screen, result from a complementary writing (to the screenplay): the cinematographic scripture, the film direction (writing with light, camera, sound, *mise-en-scène*, and so forth).[10] Such *writing* will always imprint its vision on the final result. Nevertheless, it is in the screenplay that the cinematic tension begins to be drawn. And for such tension to be achieved—between word and image, act of reading and perception of seeing, *stasis* and movement—the role of the reader is crucial. Portuguese writer-director Rita Azevedo Gomes reminds us that "there are many ways to read a text, as there are many interpretations of a song" (Gomes 2019). A screenplay can be formally precise but semantically vague (as music), generating innumerable interpretations. The reading of the screenplay will always shape the cinematic style of its future moving image.

5.4 Love Calls You by Your Name

When Johann Wolfgang Goethe discovered Luke Howard's studies on the various shapes and dispositions of clouds, he was so grateful for Howard's discovery (for him having given name to the formless), that not only he wrote a poem in Luke Howard's honor, but also he wrote a curious biographical note about Howard's life to serve as an introduction to his own studies on clouds.[11] In it, Goethe explains how he tried to get the most information about Luke Howard's life: "to better understand how a spirit like his is formed, what circumstances and abysses led him into such path of looking at nature in such a natural way, dedicating himself to it, studying its laws and applying them" (Goethe 2003, 30). Goethe would later receive a letter from Howard (who, in the meantime, had learned about Goethe's interest), containing a detailed personal biography of himself. This extraordinary story echoes a concern familiar to those wondering how a result of a given film is achieved, how it all begins: Goethe had to understand how Howard came up with his ideas about clouds in order to reach his own ideas on clouds, his own studies.

---

[10] After the concept of *caméra-stylo* [*camera-pen*] coined by Nouvelle Vague writer-director Alexandre Astruc in his essay *The Birth of a New Avant-Garde: La Caméra-Stylo* ([1948] 2009: 31–37).

[11] Luke Howard (1772–1864) is considered the father of modern meteorology and was the first to classify and appoint different types of clouds, dividing them in three essential groups: stratus, cumulus, and cirrus. Goethe also devoted a brief study to the composition of clouds (Goethe 2003).

Similarly, the Dutch director Joris Ivens, during the shooting of *Une Histoire de Vent* (1988), upon discovering the amazing *mask of wind*, which will help him overcome an essential challenge, declares without hesitation: "The man who made this mask: I want to meet him" (*Une Histoire de Vent* 1988). As if to say: I want to enter the intimate space of this precious work, understand its core and essential desire, discover how it took shape, how it was developed and metamorphosed into such result.

Likewise, we can learn about the diverse layers of the screenwriting's creative process by meeting first-hand testimonies that can provide us with vivid accounts of the screenwriting process, namely the ways that speak most to our hearts. In other words, it is possible that some of the most insightful reflections on writing and reading a screenplay could be found in the direct testimonies of those (whose works most interest us) who experienced and questioned the challenges brought by their screenwriting activity. Like the testimonials of screenwriters such as Jean-Claude Carrière, Suso Cecchi d'Amico, Carl Mayer, Frances Marion, or Dudley Nichols (to name a few), as well as those *about* screenwriting by writers-directors such as Pier Paolo Pasolini, Ingmar Bergman, or Chantal Akerman (among others).

All these examples reveal a screenwriting experience deeply rooted in a cinematic and poetic sensitivity (beyond the mere narrative talent). We speak of approaches to screenwriting that are often real individual systems, which manage to escape mainstream narrative conventions. Inspiring, immediate, and profound views of the living relationship between ideas, writing and image. For example, the *image* coined by Pasolini for the screenplay as "a structure that wants to be another structure" ([1972] 2005, 187–96). Or, again, the affinity between screenwriting and musical composition described by Bergman: on how the sequences of a film can trigger emotions close to those elicited by music, and how important it is to create such feeling of rhythm and melody reflected in the screenplay from the very beginning. Bergman considered that a "written dialogue is like a musical score, almost incomprehensible to the average person" (Bergman 1960, xvi). In fact, several screenwriters make this comparison with musical composition. Italian screenwriter Tonino Guerra often argued that "the structure [of the screenplay] is something musical. It is like an electrocardiogram that appears to me at a certain point and allows me, so to say, to feel whether the history has its own rhythm, homogeneity and sonority" (as quoted in Pelo 2010, 121). The German writer-director Werner Herzog, in his 2016 masterclass "Writing the script," provocatively declared: "Forget the three-acts screenwriting structure. Werner reveals how he draws on poetry and Beethoven to inspire scripts that capture his vision in words" (Herzog 2016). In the screenplays of Austrian screenwriter Carl Mayer, the poetic treatment of rhythm is a defining mark.[12]

---

[12] Carl Mayer worked, among others, with Robert Wiene, Leni Riefenstahl, Walter Ruttmann, Lupu Pick, but especially with Friedrich Wilhelm Murnau, for whom he wrote *Sunrise* (1927). According to Brigitte Mayr, the Austrian screenwriter was a perfectionist,

When reading a scene from his screenplay *Sylvestre* (1924), we can immediately visualize the succession of its images: a pattern is being built with carefully well-placed words. The visual intensity and the concision of his writing make us feel the scene cinematic composition:

> INTERIOR TEA SHOP
> WIDE SHOT: Small. Low. Filled with smoke.
> And!
> In flickering light: Tables! Already occupied densely.
> Men. Women. Yawning children, too.
> And!
> In a corner: A pianist. An old piano plonking.
> And!
> As many scream their orders. Noisily! Laughing! Impatiently! Drunk!
>
> (Mayer 1924, 20, in Ksenofontova 2020, 195)

The French screenwriter Jean-Claude Carrière, in his book *The Secret Language of Film* (1994), shares an interesting story about his first lesson in screenwriting (with Jacques Tati) which led him to develop his famous caterpillar/butterfly metaphor.

> First, he [Tati] asked what I knew about film. I said I loved it more than anything in the world, that I went to the Cinémathèque three times a week, that I... He raised a hand. "No, what I mean is, what exactly do you know about films? About how films are made?" I answered truthfully that I knew almost nothing. "You have never worked in films?" "No, sir." He, at once, called his editor, Suzanne Baron [...] "Suzanne, take this young man and show him what film is." [...] Tati had just given me my first great lesson: to handle film, from whatever angle—even if it is only to write a book based on a film—you must know how films are made; you must know, and preferably master, the techniques of film. You cannot assume, with literary aloofness, that you have no need to know about this. [...] That same day Suzanne Baron took me into the editing room. [...] She took the first reel of *Monsieur Hulot's Holiday* and fitted it into the machine. [...] Then, by manipulating a metal lever, Suzanne showed me how you could move the film forward, backward, stop it on a single frame, speed it up or slow it down. [...] [Then] Suzanne put the screenplay of the movie on the table beside me, and uttered a simple, unforgettable phrase, which was my second big lesson of the day [...] "The whole problem is to go from this [screenplay] to this [film]". [...] I have often compared this metamorphosis to the caterpillar's transformation into a butterfly. The caterpillar's body already

interested in every aspect of a film—in 1922 the magazine *Film-Kurier* recalled that "[a] pianist's presence is required in the editing room at all times, in case Carl Mayer—and the film—might lack the required rhythm" (Omasta et al. 2003, 58).

contains all the cells and all the colours of the butterfly. It is the potential butterfly. But it cannot fly. Yet the urge to fly is deeply buried in its most secret essence. (Carrière 1994, 149–51)

Through these brief examples, we can see how the screenplay text can be written not only on the narrative level, but also with rhythm, balance, concentration, and speed. Scenes and sequences flow, interconnect, cross rhymes in its motifs, actions, and descriptions, evolving like the melodic, harmonic lines of a piece of music. Fragments gain meaning as they follow one another, in their succession, in the choice and the connection of the motifs. And these fragments, themselves, are of the utmost importance for the overall balance: the well-polished sentence, the succinct, lean scene description, the precise dialogue line, all contribute to the power of the images evoked. Portuguese director Paulo Rocha, speaking of his screenwriting collaboration with poet António Reis, on the film *Mudar de Vida* [*Change of Life*] (1966)—for which Reis wrote the dialogues—unveils:

[António Reis] worked on the dialogues for six months, scratching and cutting away. Every day [he was] thinner, always in cold sweats, looking for the right comma, the exact pause, the secret and expressive assonance. The dialogues, pulled off at cost, reached the film set at the very last minute, and there was no time to ponder on them. It was not until years later, when the film debuted commercially in Tokyo, that I had the opportunity to study them. The work of translating them into Japanese was very slow, and only for that I could discover the musical concision, the secret richness of those phrases, written with an outstanding ear. (Rocha 1991, 6)

Commas, lines, voltages, rhythmic nodes, sounds, images attractions, pauses, energy. Something articulated, a *diction*. When reading a screenplay, the reader will focus not only on the dramatic structure but also on other less obvious aspects. Namely, the rhythmic and cinematic articulations of the screenplay. For each sentence and every movement are followed by a second movement and energy, and then by a third and so on, creating a tension that requires a special reading relationship: a tension that sustains the screenplay in a specular relationship with its reader, that invites us to read the Text not only through its fictional system, but also through its poetic quality, its deep-rooted rhythm, its vibration pattern, its music. That is, the screenplay is not only ruled by the dramaturgy's verisimilitude. Intensity is also its order. Many screenplays from the silent film period seem to follow this order, since, not infrequently, the assemblage of its scenes appears to be constructed according to an association of rhymes, or musical measures, rather than plot continuity. Claus Tieber argues that Frances Marion's screenplay *Daddy Long Legs* (1919) shows a narrative structure that does not quite reflect the Classical Hollywood Cinema paradigm, but rather offers Frances Marion's own personal writing style: an interweaving of scenes where "[t]here is no continuity in the plot in these scenes; one doesn't follow the other by cause and effect. Their "follow pattern," as Altman puts it, is related to opposites and symmetries, to ideas, not to plot development" (Tieber 2010, 97–98).

In short, the reader of a screenplay is required to be capable of reading its articulations and connections, synthesizing the disjunctions, the in-between of the fragments and the images, and, in this process, to be able to discover the balance, the tone of the set: a condensation, not only of plot, but more precisely of music. As Bergman observes:

> I have often wished for a kind of notation which would enable me to put on paper all the shades and tones of my vision, to record distinctly the inner structure of a film. [For when in the set of the film] I could remember how I originally saw and thought this or that sequence […], the relationship between the part and the whole, and put my finger on the rhythm. (Bergman 1960, xvi, xvii)

From this, we have a glimpse of how important rhythm is in a screenplay, and the effort it involves translating cinematic rhythm, movement, through the verbal images of a screenplay.

This effort is not evident in all screenplays. Still, most screenplays can reveal some sort of a *cinematic diction*, projecting a "voice" by which we can find "the authorial presence of the screenwriter(s) whose consciousness has shaped every aspect of the text" (Ferrell 2017, 161). We speak of an enunciation style, parallel to the cause-and-effect order of plot development, focused on rhythm, on organizing the geometry of the text by affinities, patterns, speed, tensions, and within it creating a singular screenplay's pace (or tone or mood). By *cinematic diction* we are referring to an aspect of the *voice* within the Text: *diction* is a characteristic of the author's voice (not necessarily of its discourse). A *diction* is something that goes beyond narratological concepts—like Gérard Genette's "narrative discourse" (1983) or Seymour Chatman's "double structured narratives," in which it is highlighted that: "All narratives, in whatever medium, combine the time sequence of plot events, the time of the histoire ('story-time'), with the time of the presentation of those events in the text, which we call 'discourse-time'. What is fundamental to narrative, regardless of the medium, is that these two-time orders are independent" (1987, 160). The idea of *diction* used here extends beyond the concept of "discourse-time" (Chatman 1987, 60); beyond Ken Dancyger and Jeff Rush's idea of "narrative voice" as "the agency that communicates the story" ([1995] 2007, 312); and beyond David Bordwell's "parametric narration" (1985, 279)—that is, a type of narration that plays more with stylistic parallelisms than narrative linearity. All these narrative concepts are related to how the story is presented and structured, but still closely linked to a rationalized perception of the text, while the idea of *diction* meets a much more biological, intuitive, unconscious perception, and development of the screenplay text. The term *diction* conveys an enunciative style, the intonation of a particular *voice*, something which relates more to the musicality involved in the individual personal discourse.

By *diction*, we understand the poetic musical links that are created by the geometry of the screenwriting discourse procedures.

5.5 Conclusion

When one is developing his/her singular screenwriting style, finding his/her *screenwriter's voice* (see Ferrell 2017), looking for ways to approach the right inner rhythm of a particular idea or story, it is always fruitful to follow the works/examples of those whose screenwriting creative process had impressed us, the works which had an impact and spoke to our heart (which made us say: I belong here!). Each singular writing experience, the way each screenwriter composes and decomposes, seeks, and builds (when trying to make a cinematic idea visible) his/her own screenwriting style, potentially offers a role model, a source of inspiration, unveiling that unique creative clue precious to a future screenwriter. Ultimately, screenwriting is not only about telling stories (which often end up repeating).[13] Is also about *voices* telling stories. It is about individuals (or group of individuals) who bring their unique, original, singular voice to give life to a visual story, who bring their personal style into the screenplay, who imprint their own cinematic-literary-poetic-musical diction into the script. In other words, the style of a screenplay is as much, if not more, a matter of individual vision than one of construction techniques. As the Count of Buffon put it: "The style is the man himself" (Leclerc 1753).[14] And therefore, discovering our own screenwriting affiliation (our own masters, our screenwriting *family*) is a fundamental step toward the encounter with one's own personal screenwriting style, one's own *inner voice* as a writer of moving images, as a visual storyteller. That each one seeks in his/her elected screenwriter his/her own *inner master*, this is perhaps the richest and the most vivid form of learning the craft.

Furthermore, understanding screenplay writing/reading dialectics helps us promote a dynamic dialogue between the written text and its cinematographic completion. As Rose Ferrell rightly observed, the screenwriter's "[v]oice is enmeshed in the relationships between writer, reader and text, and so is coloured not only by the context of its origins but also by the conditions and context of its destination" (Ferrell 2017, 162). Therefore, characterizing the screenplay also through its acts of reading can help us "to make room, within technical understandings of the script, for more artistic processes" (Maras

---

[13] As Paul Schrader explained: "Writers have always known there are a limited number of storylines. Christopher Booker's *Seven Basic Plots* popularised the number seven, but others have argued for three, 20 and 36 basic plots - Rudyard Kipling said 69. That's not new. We do tell variations of the same stories over and over" (Schrader 2009, 6).

[14] "Le style est l'homme même" were the words pronounced by Georges-Louis Leclerc, Count of Buffon, in his *Discours sur le Style* [*Discourse on Style*], given at the *Académie Français* [*French Academy*], on the day of his reception on 25 August 1753.

2009, 71). That is, when we ally screenplay writing to its reading perspective, we are opening space for a more evocative and poetic understanding of the text, thus doing justice to its singular form.

Acknowledgements Research for this essay was financed by Portuguese public funding through FCT–Fundação para a Ciência e a Tecnologia, I.P. [FCT–Foundation for Science and Technology, I.P.]—research project UIDB/00509/2020.

References

Astruc, Alexandre. 2009. "The Birth of a New Avant-Garde: La Caméra-Stylo." In *The French New Wave: Critical Landmarks*, edited by Peter Graham and Ginette Vincendeau, 31–37. Basingstoke, UK: Palgrave Macmillan.

Barthes, Roland. 1977. *Image, Music, Text*. Trans. Stephen Heath. London: Fontana Press.

Batty, Craig, and Stayci Taylor. 2021. *Script Development: Critical Approaches, Creative Practices, International Perspectives*. Cham, Switzerland: Palgrave Macmillan.

Bazin, André. 1971. *What Is Cinema? – Vol. II*. Trans. Hugh Gray. Berkeley, CA: University of California Press.

Bergman, Ingmar. 1960. *Four Screenplays of Ingmar Bergman*. New York: Simon and Schuster.

Bordwell, David. 1985. *Narration in the Fiction Film*. Madison, WI: University of Wisconsin Press.

Carrière, Jean Claude. 1994. *The Secret Language of Film*. Trans. Jeremy Leggatt. New York: Pantheon.

Chatman, Seymour. 1987. "What Novels Can Do That Films Can't (and Vice-Versa)." In *Literary Theories in Praxis*, edited by Shirley F. Staton, 159–70. Philadelphia: University of Pennsylvania Press.

Cohen, Nadja. 2013. *Les Poètes modernes et le cinéma (1910–1930)* [*Modern Poets and Cinema (1910–1930)*]. Paris: Classiques Garnier.

da Costa, João Bénard. 1996. "Como nos nossos sonhos" [As in our dreams]. In *A Magia da Imagem* [*The Magic of the Image*], 21–25. Lisbon: Fundação das Descobertas/Cinemateca Portuguesa/Museo Nazionale del Cinema di Torino.

Dancyger, Ken, and Jeff Rush. 2007 [1995]. *Alternative Scriptwriting: Successfully Breaking the Rules*, 4th edition. Burlington, MA: Focal Press.

Davis, Rosamund. 2021. "Nordic Noir with an Icelandic Twist: Establishing a Shared Space for Collaboration Within European Coproduction." In *Script Development: Critical Approaches, Creative Practices, International Perspectives*, edited by Craig Batty, and Stayci Taylor, 113–28. Cham, Switzerland: Palgrave Macmillan.

Della Porta, Giambattista. 1589. *Magiae naturalis libri XX*. Naples: Orazio Salviano.

Della Porta, Giambattista. 1593. *De refractione optices parte libri novem*. Naples: Orazio Salviano.

Deren, Maya. 1965. "Planning by Eye: Notes on 'Individual' and 'Industrial' Film." *Film Culture* 39 (Winter): 33–38.

Dreyer, Carl Theodor. 1973. *Dreyer in Double Reflection*, edited by Donald Skoller. New York: E.P. Dutton & Co.

Eikhenbaum, Boris. 1998. "Literature and Cine." In *Los formalistas russos y el cine* [*The Russian Formalists and the Cinema*], edited by François Albèra, 196–202. Barcelona: Paidós.
Ferrell, Rose. 2017. "An Introduction to Voice in Screenwriting." *Journal of Screenwriting* 8 (2): 161–75. https://doi.org/10.1386/jocs.8.2.161_1.
Genette, Gérard. 1983. *Narrative Discourse: An Essay in Method*. New York: Cornell University Press.
Goethe, Johann Wolfgang. 2003. *O Jogo das Núvens* [*The Cloud Game*]. Trans. João Barrento. Lisbon: Assírio & Alvim.
Gomes, Rita Azevedo. 2019. "No fundo estou a fazer um quadro com luz" [In the end, I am making a picture with light]. *À Pala de Walsh*. 17 March. https://www.apaladewalsh.com/2019/03/rita-azevedo-gomes-no-fundo-estou-a-fazer-um-quadro-com-luz/. Accessed 20 December 2021.
Gunning, Tom. 1986. "The Cinema of Attractions: Early Cinema, Its Spectator, and the Avant-Garde." *Wide Angle* 8 (3–4): 63–70.
Hamilton, Ian. 1990. *Writers in Hollywood, 1915–1951*. New York: Harper and Row.
Herzog, Werner. 2016. "Writing a Script." *MasterClass*. https://www.masterclass.com/classes/werner-herzog-teaches-filmmaking/chapters/writing-a-script. Accessed 15 December 2021.
Korte, Barbara and Ralf Schneider. 2000. "The Published Screenplay – A New Literary Genre?" *AAA—Arbeiten aus Anglistik und Amerikanistik* 25 (1): 89–105.
Ksenofontova, Alexandra. 2020. *The Modernist Screenplay*. Cham, Switzerland: Palgrave Macmillan.
Langlois, Henri. 1955. *300 années de cinématographie, 60 ans de cinéma* [*300 years of cinematography, 60 years of cinema*]. Paris: Cinémathèque française/Fédération des archives du film/Musée D'art Moderne.
Leclerc, Georges-Louis. 1753. "Sur le style – Discours de réception du comte de Buffon" [On style – Reception speech by the Comte de Buffon]. *Académie-Francaise*. 25 August. https://www.academie-francaise.fr/discours-de-reception-du-comte-de-buffon. Accessed 28 December 2021.
Lupo, Rino. 2008 [1927]. "Os elementos da cinematografia: o argumento" [The film elements: the screenplay]. In *As Cidades e os Filmes – uma biografia de Rino Lupo* [*The Cities and the Mountains: the biography of Rino Lupo*], by Tiago Baptista, 226–27. Lisbon: Cinemateca Portuguesa – Museu do Cinema.
Macdonald, Ian W. 2013. *Screenwriting Poetics and the Screen Idea*. Basingstoke, UK: Palgrave Macmillan.
Maras, Steven. 2009. *Screenwriting: History, Theory and Practice*. London: Wallflower.
Martin, Adrian. 2014. "Where the Cinematic Ideas Come From?" *Journal of Screenwriting* 5 (1): 9–26. https://doi.org/10.1386/josc.5.1.9/1.
Millard, Kathryn. 2016. "The Universe Is Expanding." *Journal of Screenwriting* 7 (3): 271–84. https://doi.org/10.1386/josc.7.3.271/3.
Molder, Maria Filomena. 1999. *Matérias Sensiveis* [*Sensitive Materials*]. Lisbon: Relógio d'Água.
Murphy, J. J. 2010. "No Room for the Fun Stuff: The Question of the Screenplay in American Indie Cinema." *Journal of Screenwriting* 1 (1): 175–96. https://doi.org/10.1386/josc.1.1.175/1.
Omasta, Michael, Brigitte Mayr, and Christian Cargnelli, eds. 2003. *Carl Mayer - Scenar[t]ist: Ein Script von Ihm War Schon ein Film*. [*A Script by Carl Mayer Was Already a Film*]. Vienna: Synema.

Pasolini, Pier Paolo. 2005 [1972]. *Heretical Empiricism*. Trans. Ben Lawton, and Louise K. Barnet. Washington, DC: New Academia Publishing.

Patterson, Frances Taylor. 1921. *Cinema Craftsmanship: A Book for Photoplaywrights*. New York: Harcourt Brace.

Pelo, Riikka. 2010. "Tonino Guerra: The Screenwriter as a Narrative Technician or as a Poet of Images? Authorship and Method in the Writer-Director Relationship." *Journal of Screenwriting* 1 (1): 113–29. https://doi.org/10.1386/josc.1.1.113/1.

Petzold, Christian. 2021. "Tens de regressar à fotografia para compreenderes algo sobre o cinema" [You must return to photography to understand something about cinema]. *À Pala de Walsh*. 19 April. http://www.apaladewalsh.com/2021/04/christian-petzold-tens-de-regressar-a-fotografia-para-compreenderes-algo-sobre-o-cinema/. Accessed 15 December 2021.

Price, Steven. 2010. *The Screenplay. Authorship, Theory and Criticism*. Basingstoke, UK and New York: Palgrave Macmillan.

Rocha, Paulo. 1991. "Uma figura luminosa" [A luminous figure]. *Jornal de Letras*, September 17: 6.

Rosenbaum, Jonathan. 2021. "Two Questions for Marta Mateus." *Jonathanrosenbaum.net*, 7 January. https://jonathanrosenbaum.net/2021/01/two-questions-for-marta-mateus/. Accessed 21 December 2021.

Schefer, Jean Louis. 1997. *Du monde et du mouvement des images* [*On the world and the movement of images*]. Paris: Cahiers du Cinéma–Éditions de L'Étoile.

Schrader, Paul. 2009. "Beyond the Silver Screen." *The Guardian*. 19 June. https://www.theguardian.com/film/2009/jun/19/paul-schrader-reality-tv-big-brother. Accessed 15 December 2021.

Star, Susan Leigh. 2010. "This Is Not a Boundary Object: Reflections on the Origin of a Concept." *Science, Technology, & Human Values* 35 (5): 601–17.

Sternberg, Claudia. 1997. *Written for the Screen: The American Motion-Picture Screenplay as Text*. Tübingen: Stauffenburg.

Sternberg, Claudia. 2000. "'Return, I Will, to Old Brazil' - Reading Screenplay Literature." In *Mediatized Drama/Drama Mediatized*, edited by Eckart Voigts-Virchow, 153–66. Trier: Wissen-schaftlicher.

Tieber, Claus. 2010. "The Narrative Structure of Frances Marion's Screenplays." In *Not so Silent: Women in Cinema Before Sound*, edited by Sofia Bull and Astrid Söderbergh Widding, 96–114. Stockholm: Acta Universitatis Stockholmiensis.

Une Histoire du Vent. 1988. Written and directed by Joris Ivens and Marceline Loridan. France: Capi Films, La Sept Cinéma.

CHAPTER 6

The Reality of (Screen) Characters

Murray Smith

6.1 Introduction

"What you've got to do is follow the characters, really", Danny Boyle remarks. "99% of people access the work through character", he continues. "And that's drawn from many different places. It's drawn from the writer's original version of that character, then it passes through a director's version of it, I suppose, and it certainly passes through the actor's version of it, which will always be different to somebody else's version of it" (Film4 2017). From the initial conception of character, through its elaboration at the various stages of film production, and onto the viewer's encounter with the work, characters are central to our engagement with and experience of narrative on the big screen, the small screen, and the mobile screen. Narratives in general, across media, are our principal vehicle for representing, exploring, and reflecting on human agency, via the actions, traits, and attitudes of the characters which partly constitute them.

In the context of film and television, character creation almost always begins with the writing of the screenplay—that act breaking down into various steps, such as writing a logline, outline, and treatment, and often dedicated character profiles, prior to the composition of the screenplay proper. Filmic characters are conceived in screenplays before they are incarnated by performers and born audiovisually in films. Of course there is variation on this

M. Smith (✉)
University of Kent, Canterbury, UK
e-mail: m.s.smith@kent.ac.uk

front: John Cassavetes and Mike Leigh are two well-known cases of writer-directors who develop their characters through workshops preparatory to the writing of a screenplay (and in Cassavetes' case, to some extent, through improvised performance before the camera), rather than on the basis of a pre-written screenplay. In the final section of this essay, I will turn to another unorthodox case, Mahamat-Saleh Haroun's *Bye Bye Africa* (1999), in which tightly-scripted scenes are interwoven with semi-scripted, improvised scenes and non-fictional *verité* footage. So, whatever the norm for character creation in film and television, practice varies around this norm.

The central issue that I will focus on in this essay, however, is one that bears on characters in any and all of these traditions. Rather than delving into whether a character is first given shape through words on a page, or through the improvised performances of actors, I will foreground the status of the entity that these activities bring into being—although we will see that the screenwriting process sheds particular light on this question. Just what is a character, and what sort of reality can we ascribe to a character? In more philosophical terms, what kind of ontological status do these fictional creatures possess? We certainly speak about characters and make reference to them, in many ways in just the same way that we speak about and refer to actual persons. "Begbie's a piece of work", we might say, of the *Trainspotting* (novel, 1993, film, 1996) character; "and so's my office manager". That suggests that we accord characters some kind of reality, even though characters are by definition fictional entities. Since they are fictional, is it a contradiction in terms to think of characters as (in some sense) real?

No. Characters are at once imaginary and real. Or so I will argue in this essay.

6.2 JUST WHAT IS A CHARACTER?

Let me approach the problem of the ontological status of characters by first saying something more general about what constitutes a character. To begin with what might seem obvious, a prototypical character is a fictional representation of a person—an individual human agent.[1] Granted, there are many characters—lions, tigers, bears, squirrels, goblins, dwarves, hobbits, dragons, ogres, boggarts, giants, talking trees, robots of various kinds, teapots, desk lamps, and so on and on—which do not take the outward form of fictional human agents. But in the vast majority of cases, these non-human characters are invested with many of the capacities of human agents, including speech

---

[1] Strictly speaking, the category *human agent* (roughly, a biological organism) is not quite co-extensive with the category *person* (roughly, an agent capable of conscious experience and reasoning and bearing moral rights and duties). Personal status is sometimes accorded to supra-individual entities, and some individual human agents are thought not to qualify as persons, or (in cases of multiple personality) to embody more than one person. But virtually all human agents are persons, and vice versa, and therefore I will treat them as identical here.

and facial expressions, gestures, and postures which are recognisably human. In short, many non-human characters are personified.

Not *all* such characters are thinly disguised humans, of course: the dinosaurs in the *Jurassic Park* (1993–) franchise are not human sheep in wolves' clothing, and neither are the aliens in the *Alien* series of films (1979–). Similarly, the extra-terrestrials who show up on earth in *Close Encounters of the Third Kind* (1977) and *Arrival* (2016), although benign, seem to be a radically different kind of species. And then there are those particularly unsettling characters who appear human, but are no longer human (zombies, the possessed, the body-snatched) or never were in the first place—consider Alicia Vikander's Ava in *Ex Machina* (2014), or Scarlett Johansson's alien character in *Under the Skin* (2013), who may be the apogee of such a figure. What all of these entities share is the capacity for intentional agency. So although characters are prototypically fictional human agents, they can be agents of a different kind.[2]

Note though that there is still a crucial distinction to be made between such intentional agents—typically but not necessarily human agents—and the other constituents of fictional worlds, such as the physical environment or setting of the action.[3] While certain questions can be raised about the fictionality of all the elements of fictional worlds, a cardinal point of the perspective on character elaborated here—as emphasised in the opening paragraph—is that characters are a uniquely salient aspect of fictional narratives. This is reflected in the practice of screenwriters, who commonly develop character profiles and backstories as fully as possible prior to and/or during the drafting of scripts. It is not an exaggeration to say that when we engage with a fiction, the first thing that we do is look for signs of agency. This is the first step in our search for the characters that will animate the narrative.

Whether straightforwardly human, or anthropomorphic, or actually not much like a human at all, characters are characterised by their actions, attitudes, and traits. Most obviously characters are characterised by what they do, or what they fail to do when they have the opportunity to, but don't: Rick Blaine declines to support the French Resistance, but ultimately commits to it. More subtly, characters are given substance by their attitudes, which we can think of as *virtual actions*—dispositions to act in certain ways, even if not yet realised in action. Rick's generosity is in his character, we might say, when we first encounter him, but it is buried beneath his bitterness and disappointment, and it takes the course of the narrative of *Casablanca* (1942) to release that

---

[2] Livingston and Sauchelli (2011, 353 and note 40), referring to Livingston (1996).

[3] Livingston and Sauchelli note one line of argument according to which "all objects, things, and events as well as persons" in a fiction count as "fictional characters" (2011, 352). They cite Friend (2007) as a theory that treats all the elements of fictional worlds on a par. Note, however, that although Friend states that her use of *character* is all-encompassing in this way, her discussion in fact focusses almost entirely on fictional characters in the more specific sense: fictional representations of intentional (typically human) agents.

attitude and give new life to this potential in his character. In screenwriting terms, this journey of growth and change represents the *arc* of the character. Actions and attitudes are at the heart of what makes characters matter, but they don't quite exhaust them, for we also need to take stock of the other traits giving shape to characters which don't straightforwardly express or imply attitudes: Rick is handsome, not very tall, and looks remarkably like Humphrey Bogart. All of these features can be activated and made relevant to the attitudes borne by a character, but not all traits will carry such a charge: some traits simply allow us to *recognise*—to individuate and reidentify—a character as that character across the narrative (see Smith 2022, especially chapters 3, 4, and the Afterword).

In the first edition of *Engaging Characters*, I held that "no humanist critic has ever argued that characters are real" (Smith 1995, 30). I still believe that to be the truth (the sentence is still there in the revised, second edition: Smith 2022, 35). But not the whole truth. It is important to emphasise the specific target of the claim: the "humanist critic". What I had in mind was the traditional critic working prior to or unaffected by the currents of High Theory, unself-consciously discussing the characters of films and novels in many ways as if they were real persons. Here's Pauline Kael, for example, on *Last Tango in Paris* (1972):

> When his wife commits suicide, Paul, an American living in Paris, tries to get away from his life. He goes to look at an empty flat and meets Jeanne, who is also looking at it. They have sex in an empty room, without knowing anything about each other—not even first names. He rents the flat, and for three days they meet there. She wants to know who he is, but he insists that sex is all that matters. (Kael 1972, 130)

And here is Manohla Dargis, on *Parasite* (2019): "Ki-taek doesn't have a lot obviously going for him. But he has a home and the affection of his wife and children, and together they squeeze out a meager living assembling pizza boxes for a delivery company" (Dargis 2019). And most interestingly, here are Ella Shohat and Robert Stam on *Barren Lives* (1963): "Fabiano and Vitoria complain constantly of being forced to live like animals" (Shohat and Stam 2014, 258). In all these cases, the critics adopt the kind of descriptive language we apply in the first instance to actual people. Each of these passages could very well be non-fictional accounts of real individuals—that is, individuals who actually do, or did, exist. Nothing in the form of the descriptions tells us whether we're reading a non-fictional account of a person, or a fictional account of a character.

But note the riders in my claim above: critics discuss characters *in many ways* as if they were real; in many ways *as if* they were real. Such traditional critics, I wanted to argue, were not so naïve as to confuse characters with real human agents; it is just that in parts of their critical discourse they sustain the *pretence* that the characters they discuss actually exist as persons, while in other parts of their discourse it is evident that they understand perfectly well that characters are fabrications, *person-like representations* but not persons.[4] In this they mirror the movements of screenwriters and other character creators, who must also shuttle between regarding their characters as artefacts—they are the ones making them, after all!—and pretending that their inventions exist as persons. After denying that traditional critics are subject to some sort of illusion, I went on: "Rather, [such critics] argue that characters can be successfully lifelike in so far as they give the impression of 'roundness', of a depth and complexity of motivation which is adumbrated but never exhausted by the fiction in which they appear" (Smith 2022, 35). Criticism in this tradition is certainly committed to a particular *aesthetic* of character, but not guilty of the kind of naïveté with which it is often charged.[5]

6.3 The (Ir)reality of Characters

So far, so good. But I said that my claim that "no humanist critic has ever argued that characters are real"—my defence of the traditional, humanist critic, and the argument that such critics are not prey to the illusion that characters are real, existent persons—was not the whole truth. In fact the reality or otherwise of fictional characters is a question that has been debated in the fields of metaphysics, possible world semantics, and philosophical aesthetics. That debate has been particularly busy and intense for the past twenty years—gaining momentum not long after the first edition of *Engaging Characters* in 1995—but its roots extend back through to the early twentieth century. Here I shall discuss three different positions on the ontological status of characters—the sense in which characters can be said to be real, or not.

One stance towards the ontology of characters draws on *possible world* theory and in particular on the version of that theory associated with David Lewis (1986).[6] Possible world theory arose in philosophy as a way of understanding our ability to contemplate the possible as well as the actual—the fact that humans think and talk about not just what is the case, but what could be the case. Within this body of theory, philosophers speak of *nearby* possible worlds (worlds very similar to ours, but differing in some contingent details); more *remote* possible worlds (worlds which remain possible, but differ substantially in contingent detail); and *impossible* worlds, which exhibit not merely contingent differences, but violate fundamental laws such that they can perhaps be conceived, but precisely not regarded as possible. Lewis' radical version of this theory, known as *modal realism*, holds that possible worlds—worlds ordinarily thought of as conjured up by us in order to consider how

---

[4] More on pretence later.

[5] See Shohat and Stam (2014). For responses, see Smith (2022), "Afterword", and Plantinga (2018).

[6] Possible worlds theories are also discussed in the chapter by Paolo Russo in this handbook.

the world might be otherwise than it is—in fact exist, parallel with the reality we inhabit (even though we can't interact with the individuals who exist in other possible worlds in the same way we can interact with those in the world we inhabit).

It is easy to see how fiction, and fictional characterisation, can be understood as bearing on cognition about what is possible: fictional stories can represent how things might have been in the past or could be in the present or the future, while fictional characters can represent possible persons—individuals we can imagine existing. If we follow this intuition and then give an account of fictional worlds in terms of possible worlds, and specifically possible worlds as understood in terms of Lewis' modal realism, we arrive at the conclusion that the fictional characters populating fictional worlds are real individuals (albeit individuals we can't interact with in the normal sense). Now, there are various problems with this proposal. But perhaps it is enough to record here the verdict of Michael Devitt and Kim Sterelny on Lewis' *actualist* version of possible world theory: "This is some elephant to swallow without blinking" (1987, 24).

At the other end of the spectrum of positions on the ontology of character, we have anti-realism or *irrealism*. On the anti-realist view, characters are strictly imaginary creatures. It is a mistake to think of characters as real in any sense; Mark Sainsbury characterises irrealists as "those who don't accept any form of realism about fictional characters" (2010, ix).[7] Thought and talk about characters as if they were real individuals is to be explained not by the existence (in any sense) of those characters, but by our adoption of the *pretence*, when we engage with fictions, that they exist. In Kendall Walton's terms, we *make*-believe that the fictional characters (and the fictional worlds of which they form a part) exist, rather than believing that these characters exist as actual individuals. Fictional works act as props in games of make-believe, prescribing and authorising what appreciators are to imagine (see Walton 1990).

A significant challenge faced by irrealism, however, comes from our pervasive recourse to *metafictional* language, where we speak of fictions as fictions—in statements such as "Humphrey Bogart plays Rick Blaine in the fiction film *Casablanca*", or "in *Trainspotting*, Begbie is Mark Renton's nemesis". In such cases, it looks as if we are straightforwardly referring to Rick, Begbie (played by Robert Carlyle), and Renton (Ewan McGregor) as real, existent entities, just as in the same sentences we refer to *Casablanca* (the film) and *Trainspotting* (the novel and the film) as real entities. Walton argues that, even in these cases, make-belief provides the explanation. When we use such metafictional language, while we "betray" or expose the fact that we are merely engaging in pretence in speaking and thinking of characters as persons, in doing so we nonetheless acknowledge only that such fictional works exist as to license the

---

[7] *Irreal* seems to have independent origins in Sartre (2010 [1940]) and in Goodman (1978).

pretence that these individuals exist (Walton 1990, 442). We do not acknowledge or imply that these characters really exist. But it is evident that this is a rather tortured and uneconomical explanation, given the availability of a more straightforward explanation—that in such sentences, we refer to characters, rather than persons, conceived as real entities. Begbie the character really exists, even if Begbie the person does not. The price of Walton's attempt to produce a tight, unified, and comprehensive explanation of fictional characters, appealing only to pretence and authorised games of make-believe, is actually rather high.

A third position beckons. According to this account, characters are *abstract artefacts* (Thomasson 1999, 2003). In order to grasp this idea, think of a character by analogy with a recipe or a notated musical composition: a set of instructions about how to imagine a certain (prototypically human) intentional agent. Recipes, notated compositions, and characters are all *artefacts* in the sense that they are items made by humans to serve certain purposes, but they are *abstract* in the sense that they are not to be identified with any particular concrete token: my recipe for spaghetti bolognese might be concretely recorded in a handwritten note and in a computer file, but the recipe itself is the information stored in these two notations rather than the physical notations themselves. We *imagine* characters as embodied agents, but characters *are* these abstract, artefactual entities.

If characters are real as abstract artefacts, they nonetheless come into being through the concrete acts of representation executed by creators—the writing of a treatment, character profile, or screenplay, the making of a film, the staging of a play, and so forth. Characters, on this view, are invented by authors at a certain moment, and are (arguably) capable of being transported between stories and between works.[8] When we say, "the protagonist of *Casablanca* is Rick Blaine", or simply speak of "the fictional character Rick Blaine", we are making reference to a character in this sense. And such characters are real; really really real, or at least as real as the works in which they appear. We just need to be clear about the sense in which characters are real: a real character is not a real person, any more than a real decoy is a real duck (see Austin 1962, 67–8). Certainly, characters are *mind-dependent*, not only in the sense that they are brought into existence by an author, but additionally in that their continued existence depends on the fictional work(s) of which they form a part, and on a community of appreciators who can access and imagine the character on the basis of these works.[9] But if we are prepared to grant that

---

[8] Enrico Terrone distinguishes between "an 'austere' artifactualism according to which fictional characters are nothing but functional components of works of fiction and a 'robust' artifactualism according to which fictional characters are self-standing entities that are embodied in works of fiction" (2021, 2). I am thus adopting a *robust* artifactualism in the current paper.

[9] Livingston and Sauchelli note: "Lord Jim is a contingent being like us. Should all of the instances of the text of Joseph Conrad's novel be destroyed and should there no longer be any agents capable of remembering or understanding the text, Lord Jim would

Casablanca is a feature film—a type of real object and part of the furniture of our world—then we should grant that Rick is real too.

This conception of character is particularly interesting in the present context. The theory of characters as real, abstract artefacts was formulated in relation to literary characters, but it might be regarded as problematic in the context of film. A screenplay is rather like a recipe or a notated composition; understood in terms of its standard function, a screenplay is a blueprint for the making of a film.[10] Insofar as characters are components of screenplays, the theory seems to fit. But as I implied in the opening paragraphs of this essay, film characters aren't fully realised until they are, well, filmed. Is it right then to think of *film* characters as abstract artefacts? Are they not rather concretely embodied in films? We need to be careful here not to confuse the concreteness of the medium through which a character's profile (the features constituting that character) is articulated with the profile that is so articulated. The words on the page of a screenplay are as concrete as the filmed performers in a film. But in both cases, the character itself—on the abstract artefact theory—is the informational profile *encoded* in the concrete vehicle of representation (the words or audiovisual display) rather than the vehicle itself.[11] It is true that film and language afford different possibilities for characterisation, and our perceptual engagement with fine-grained *kinoaudiovisual* depiction in film allows for a very rich and detailed encoding of the bodily appearance of characters. But that appearance is, nonetheless, a part of the encoded profile of a character, and language affords other kinds of precision and richness of representation (Livingston 2019). So in fact, contrary to initial appearances, the abstract artefact theory of character can accommodate the case of film characters.

It is important to underline, however, that when we say "Rick falls in love with Ilsa" and "Rick joins the Resistance", we are now using Rick-Blaine-the-abstract-artefact as a prop in the authorised imagining that Rick is a person, running a bar in occupied Casablanca in 1941, falling in love with Ilsa Lund, and becoming committed to the Resistance. When we speak and think in this way, as if Rick were an actual person just like you and me, we are engaged in a pretence. So we can mark a distinction between two stances we adopt towards characters: a stance internal to the fictional world, whereby we regard them, make-believedly, as persons, and a stance external to that world, whereby we

---

no longer exist" (2011, 343). Elsewhere (note 14, 357), they note that if only "mind-independent" objects are to count as real, then this third, artefactual perspective on the ontology of characters would not count as realist. But the criterion of mind-independence would rule out many objects and phenomena we standardly accept as real, and is thus unduly restrictive.

[10] But see Nannicelli (2013) for a defence of the view that screenplays can be, and in fact in certain contexts are, appreciated as artworks in their own right; consider the widespread publication of noted screenplays by prestigious publishers, commonly read as independent literary texts.

[11] It is this *profile* (or "source file", in Terrone's [2021] terms) that is the abstract item.

regard them as real abstract artefacts (Thomasson 2003; Friend 2007). To speak and think of a character as a character is to adopt the external stance; to speak and think of that character as a real agent is to adopt the internal stance. While the irrealist holds that the first stance, fully analysed, provides a comprehensive account of characters and our engagement with them, the realist holds that both stances are required and folds the first stance within the second stance (in the sense that we must have access to the character as an artefact in order to imagine that character as a real agent). On this view, then, our stance towards characters is *twofold*: characters (including screen characters) are artefacts designed to prompt acts of imagining, and when we engage with and appreciate characters, we recognise both their artefactual and representational facets, and we recognise them at once (Smith 2011, 2022, 240–45).[12]

6.4 Mimesis in Action

The mimetic dimension of character is inescapable, and that it is so should be obvious. But let us tease out this point more precisely. What is it to claim that a character is a fictional representation or imitation of a person? The first thing to note here is that what this claim describes is a part of a more general *mimetic hypothesis*, by means of which we make sense of a fictional representation by appealing to our understanding of the world itself (Smith 2022, 52–54, 240–45). That understanding is dynamic and not bound by these provisional mimetic assumptions: fictions may depart from the workings of the actual world in all manner of ways, large and small, as the genres of fantasy, horror, and science fiction perhaps most obviously demonstrate. But a mimetic stance is a necessary starting point.

There are really two claims at stake here. The most immediately evident claim, when the question is framed as it is in the paragraph above, is one about individual characters: any individual character—any specific representation that we are inclined to regard as a character—is a representation of a possible (rather than an actual) individual person (or more broadly, an individual intentional agent—see again Livingston, 1996). Begbie and Rick are representations of individual possible persons. As such, they surely also exemplify certain types of person; any individual will exemplify many different types—as originally invented by Irvine Welsh and adapted for the screen by John Hodge, Begbie is a man, a Scot, a thug, and a heavy drinker, among other things. But a prototypical character is not merely a representation of a type; even a *flat* character, lacking nuance and complexity and occupying only a background role, will nonetheless represent an individual within the fictional world. Even Christian, in John Bunyan's *The Pilgrim's Progress* (1678), is an individual, even if his function as a representative of a certain human type is much more salient than

---

[12] Note that the idea of the twofoldness of character depends on the special salience of character, and on the salience of the contrast between character-as-artefact and character-as-imagined-person.

it is in the kind of realist narration that became dominant in the West with the rise of the novel.

But behind the individual claim—the claim that any individual character is a mimetic representation of a possible individual person—lies a general claim: that the function of the phenomenon of characterisation is to represent possible human individuals (and through them, types). Put another way, this is the content or meaning of the concept *character*.[13] That is why voiding the concept of character of any mimetic component—as with structuralist attempts to reconceive *character* in narrowly linguistic terms, as *bundles of semes*—is incoherent (or at best amounts to the elimination of the concept of character as standardly understood, and its replacement with a new and quite different concept).[14]

We can anchor these claims by looking at some particular examples. Consider the following case from *Love Actually* (2003). At the audition of the singer and actress Lúcia Moniz, who plays the character Aurélia in the film, writer-director Richard Curtis noticed that Moniz sported a tattoo on her foot, and asked her if she had any other tattoos. Moniz replied that she had another tattoo on her back. "Maybe we can make that part of the character", suggested Curtis (Wark 2021). So here we have an example of mimesis in action: it's not merely the theoretical posit that a character is a mimetic representation of a human agent—or, still more abstractly, the representational counterpart of a human agent—but specifically the fact that (a feature of) this particular character, Y, was modelled on (a feature of) this particular person, X—who in this case happens to be a performer. As an example, the case of Moniz in *Love Actually* most obviously exemplifies the narrow claim that an individual character is a representation of a possible individual person, but indirectly exemplifies the more abstract and general claim, that the function of the phenomenon of characterisation is to represent possible human individuals.

Needless to say, modelling characters on actual individuals is not a new practice. To take one example from literary history: Betsey Trotwood, from Charles Dickens' *David Copperfield* (1850), was inspired by Mary Pearson Strong, from the town of Broadstairs in England.[15] But it is important to underline that not every character, or feature (action, attitude, trait) of a character, needs to have a specific, real-world model: Curtis might have had the idea of Aurélia possessing a tattoo on her back without any specific inspiration from an actual person, and it is surely the case that the majority of such details are invented by writers without reference to any specific actual model. All

---

[13] Note that the claim here bears on the meaning of the *concept* of a "fictional character". The *word* "character" is used in English to designate (at least) two distinct concepts: "fictional character" and "moral character" (that is, a moral disposition, good, bad, or mixed). These concepts are related in the sense that a fictional character will typically have a moral character, but they are not identical, since, in the first instance, it is real individuals who have moral characters.

[14] See the discussion in Chapter 1 of *Engaging Characters* (Smith 2022).

[15] Strong's former house in Broadstairs is now the Dickens House Museum.

the fictioneer requires is the knowledge that such features are possible—they could exist and be exemplified by real individuals. Moreover, once embedded in a fiction, the function of such details becomes quite different to their role in actuality or their function in a non-fiction—for they are to be imagined in fictions, rather than embodied (in actuality) or believed (in non-fictions). Cases involving the creation of characters inspired in whole or in part by actual persons, however, possess a heuristic value in making salient the mimetic dimension of character.

A more substantial example of this type is provided by Mike Leigh's working method—which begins with his actors listing real friends and acquaintances who might serve as models for the fictional characters they will create. In such cases, the creation of fictional characters is rooted in the most literal kind of mimesis (Leigh compares the practice with life drawing).[16] Here Curtis' strategy in modelling a specific feature of a character on a specific feature of a person is generalised, in a way that points to the underlying function of fictional characterisation, and the use fictional storytellers can and sometimes do make of actual individuals as models and reference points for their fictional characters. Once again, though, they are not required to do so: all that the fictional storyteller requires is the belief that a given feature of a character could exist and be exemplified by a real individual. In searching for such possible features and clusters of features, fictioneers are not restricted to actual persons as models, since they may also take inspiration from the vast and ever-growing population of existent fictional characters in creating new ones (as is particularly evident in genre fictions, where characters are as likely to be modelled on precursor characters in earlier instances of the genre in which they appear, as on actual individuals). The fictioneer, in sum, has recourse to the 'trait pools' of actual persons and the stock of social imaginings in the form of existing characters authorised by existing fictions, as well their own imaginings, in devising and creating new characters.

One might object here that the notion of mimesis occludes the inventive nature of character creation. Since characters are fictional entities rather than representations of actual individuals, and need involve no reference to or inspiration by specific actual individuals, in what sense can *imitation* be involved? As a fictional character, Rick is not an imitation of any one, specific, actual person. Even so, he might be taken to resemble various actual individuals. The act of mimesis at stake in the creation of characters, and fiction more generally, is at a remove from the direct imitative depiction involved in portraiture and non-fictional representation. The goal of the act of mimesis, in the context of fiction, is the creation and (in this indirect sense) representation of possible persons, where (the features of) actual individuals and the existing stock of characters function as resources in this creative act. Mimesis is more

---

[16] Leigh discusses his method in the episode of the BBC radio series *This Cultural Life* devoted to him, broadcast on 3 January 2022: https://www.bbc.co.uk/programmes/m0011bgr.

aptly conceived, in this context, as *inventive mimesis*, in order to underline that there is no tension between creative invention and imitation here.

6.5   The Artefact Strikes Back

Now that we've clarified what the mimetic dimension of individual characters, the concept of character, and the function of characterisation amount to, we need to return our attention to the other—artefactual—side of the character coin. For just as in the case of the mimetic dimension of character, complexities lie in wait here too.

Granted that characters are, in a fundamental sense, representations of possible persons, are there nonetheless ways in which the identity conditions of characters—the conditions that must be met if we are to say that this character is *the same as* that character—differ from those of actual persons? Consider the case of characters who recur across not just multiple stories, but multiple works, often created by different authors in different historical contexts, sometimes decades or more apart. Take James Bond as such a case. Is Daniel-Craig-as-James-Bond *the same* character as Sean-Connery-as-James-Bond? It may seem obvious that the answer is "no". But in asking this question, we need to be careful that we don't impose the standard of actual personhood automatically and inappropriately. Characters may admit of continuity and even identity in ways that are not possible for persons—this is one way in which it becomes apparent that characters are not wholly defined by the mimetic hypothesis, and are not *merely* fictional analogues of human agents. As I put it in *Engaging Characters*:

> Characters come into being initially through an imaginative, mimetic act—but they are not bound by this initial condition. In fantastic and experimental varieties of fiction, just about every constraint on human existence—physical, psychological, existential—can be stripped away: there are characters who can tell their stories from the grave, inhabit more than one place at the same time, be instantiated by more than one body, and even engage in dialogue with the authors who created them—thereby breaching the boundaries of the world in which they exist. (Smith 2022, 241)

James Bond might be a sustained, coherent character across the Bond films without this being in any way reflexive or postmodern—but simply part of the elasticity inherent to characters, where such elasticity is not a feature of actual persons. We need to be wary of a kind of mimetic fallacy, whereby characters are exhaustively understood against the backdrop of personhood. The ties that bind the various versions of James Bond the fictional character are not co-extensive with those would bind their real-world counterpart persons.

But exactly how can we make good on the idea that the James Bond written by Richard Maibaum, Johanna Harwood, and Berkely Mather for *Dr No* (1963) is, in some sense, the same character as the James Bond written by

Neal Purvis, Robert Jade, Cary Joji Fukunaga, and Phoebe Waller-Bridge for *No Time to Die* (2021)? And, indeed, the same James Bond invented by Ian Fleming in *Casino Royale* (1953)? Recall that from the *external* perspective of the artefactual fold, a character is an abstract artefact. Now we need to add the nuance that there are *gradations* of abstraction. At a certain level of abstraction, we can say that the James Bond of *Dr. No* is the same character as the James Bond of *No Time to Die*. But not at every level: once we are at the level of the incarnation of the character by an actor, the Bonds of these two films cannot really be seen as identical with one another. Daniel Craig-as-James-Bond is clearly discontinuous with Bond as incarnated by Sean Connery, George Lazenby, Roger Moore, and Pierce Brosnan in (at least) certain (highly salient) bodily ways; and these marked differences in appearance of course imply differences in attitude.

Peter Lamarque and Stein Holm Olsen make a closely related observation. Some characters appearing in different stories—such as the many versions of the character Faust, or Batman, or indeed Bond, in stories by authors working in disparate contexts—can be thought of as identical if thought of as *types*, they argue, but "character-*tokens* [are] individuated both by character-type and by a rootedness in some particular narrative" (Lamarque and Olsen 1994, 133; my emphases). So it makes sense to think of James-Bond-in-Dr-No as being the same character as James-Bond-in-No-Time-to-Die to the extent that we are thinking of the character somewhat abstractly, as something akin to a type. But the more we think of the character in terms of the specific features brought to the realisation of the character by a specific actor, the less plausible it is to think of these different incarnations of the character as strictly identical. When we get all the way to the most concrete end of the spectrum, perhaps it is no longer possible to identify characters independent of the specific stories and works in which they figure, as Lamarque and Olsen imply (see 1994, 132–33). Consider again the recipe analogy: while some recipes are very generic (like a type), some are very specific (like an individual): there's generic spaghetti bolognese, and then there's Marty's mother's spaghetti bolognese.

6.6 REAL IMAGININGS

Recall that the pretence theory of fictional engagement, which holds that a character is nothing more than "a figment of the human imagination" (Livingston and Sauchelli 2011, 338)—and not dependent on anything like an abstract artefact or actual agents existing in other possible worlds—is generally regarded as (implying) an anti-realist or *irrealist* theory of character. Earlier I noted that, on one traditional philosophical view, only what is mind-independent is real; it follows that mental states cannot be real. That conclusion is as absurd as it is impoverished—but perhaps partly explains why a philosopher like Lewis would find himself led to the conclusion that mere *possibilia* must actually exist in physical form. Imaginings—just like other states of mind such as beliefs, intentions, and emotions—are real enough; we just need to be careful not to confuse such mental states with the entities that they refer to or represent. As Livingston and Sauchelli put it: "what explains the illusory 'being' of nonexistent objects is human intentionality, which allows us to engage in thoughts and imaginings about what does not exist… While the act of imagining a particular train of thoughts is real, what those thoughts are about can, but need not, be anything actual or possible" (2011, 351–56). Imaginings are real, in the sense that they exist as mental states; but the contents of imaginings may include items which do not exist and have never existed, and in that sense are not real.

Moreover, we can give further substance to the idea that *merely imagined* phenomena are nonetheless real by taking note of the social character of imagining prompted by fictions, including centrally the imagining of characters. A crucial feature of a typical fictional character's presence in the world is the fact that communities of minds converge in the act of imagining the same entity, prompted and authorised in doing so by the fictional work. Catharine Abell puts such an emphasis on the social nature of the institution of fiction that, on her view, characters do not come into existence until they become social (are socially "sanctioned", as it were) (see Abell 2020, chapter 5). It must be the case that *something* comes into existence when an author begins to outline the profile of a character in the privacy of their own mind—including the various extensions of the mind in the form of diaries, notes, sketchbooks, rough cuts, demos, and so forth; so long as these remain unshared, they are *private* in the relevant sense. But such a creature of the individual imagination takes on a different ontological status once it enters the public sphere in the form of a fictional work, whether as a performance, a film, a novel, a cartoon, or whatnot. At this point, the character is, so to speak, socially baptised, becoming part of our social reality, and a shared object of attention, debate, and discussion.

A further extension of imaginative pretence as a real phenomenon concerns our *parasocial* relations with characters—that is, with those interactions with characters which in certain ways resemble or evoke our interactions with real persons. This may strike some readers as a much more obvious way in which we might think of characters as having a kind of reality for us, relative to the subtleties of abstract artefacts and actual agents existing in possible worlds separate from our world. Nonetheless, *this* kind of reality does depend on make-belief, on a willingness to regard fictional characters as persons. When we treat characters as friends or interlocutors—whether we imagine ourselves as inhabiting their world, or them inhabiting our world, or something altogether vaguer[17]—we engage in make-belief. But it is a form of make-belief that goes beyond Walton's authorised variety, for fictional works do not standardly invite us to imagine that we exist in the story world right alongside the characters,

---

[17] In exploring the nature of the film viewer's imaginative relationship with the world of the fiction—from a broadly Waltonian perspective—George Wilson (2011) argues that some features of this relationship are vague and indeterminate.

nor that characters can step into our world; comic or surreal exceptions, like *The Purple Rose of Cairo* (1985) and *Stranger than Fiction* (2006), derive their force from their violation of these norms. But note too that *unauthorised* does not imply irrational. Certainly, there are forms of parasocial interaction which verge on the pathological—one thinks of fictosexuality here, where sexual attachments are formed with fictional characters in place of real-world relations. But, such extremes aside, parasocial interaction with characters appears to be a well-established part of the world of popular art and media, and to that extent part of normal appreciative practice—at least on a broad understanding of such practice (see Blanchet and Vaage 2012).

An important part of my argument is that our stance towards characters is twofold, in that we are alert to both the mimetic and the artefactual dimensions of characters: characters are artefacts designed to represent intentional agents (prototypically, individual human agents). We have seen how this meshes with the idea that in engaging with fictional characters, we can regard them from the internal perspective (as persons we imagine existing in the fictional world) or from the external perspective (as abstract artefacts existing in the actual world). Note, though, that on my view both perspectives are integral to our appreciation of fictional characters. Indeed, "twofoldness" expresses the idea of a single appreciative stance with two facets; as Richard Wollheim puts it, "two aspects of a single experience that I have… two aspects [that are] distinguishable but also inseparable. They are two aspects of a single experience, they are not two experiences" (Wollheim 1987, 46). This contrasts with the view of some theorists. Enrico Terrone, for example, argues that awareness of the artefactual dimension is possible but not necessary in our engagement with fictional characters; such awareness is absent at a "basic level" of engagement, and only fully present at "the level at which sophisticated ('aesthetically-minded') appreciators such as critics or scholars engage with works of fiction" (Terrone 2021, 135). Lester Hunt's view contrasts still more strongly with mine. He holds, in effect, that the internal and external perspectives are mutually exclusive, and that only the internal perspective is relevant to our engagement with and appreciation of a character. To be imaginatively absorbed by a fiction film and experience, in imagination, a character as a real agent, is to be properly engaged with that fiction; to attend to the actor embodying the character is to lose that proper focus (Hunt 2021, 48, 50).

Both views are problematic. Artefactual awareness of character, as an aspect of twofoldness, is always present to some degree, and far from such awareness being problematic for the aesthetic appreciation of characters and fictions, it is essential to it. The origin of this fact lies in the design of works of fiction themselves, which may embed "metafictional" material drawing our attention to the artefactual dimension of character in an especially emphatic way. Consider the following kind of passage, from Henry Fielding's *Tom Jones* (1749): "As we have now brought Sophia into safe hands, the reader will, I apprehend, be contented to *deposit her awhile, and to look a little after other personages*, and particularly poor Jones, whom we have left long enough to do penance for his past offences" (quoted in Pelletier 2003, 199; his italics; quoted by Friend 2007, 152). Here Fielding adopts the external perspective on his character Sophia within the fabric of the fiction and invites the reader to do likewise. Note, then, that such metafictional discourse, embedded within the work itself, is distinct from the ordinary metafictional utterances we routinely make when adopting the external stance towards fictions, and which (as discussed earlier) provides the crucial challenge to irrealism. But embedded metafictional discourse is of a piece with ordinary metafictional discourse insofar as both point towards twofoldness and our artefactual awareness.

Bye Bye Africa, introduced at the outset of this chapter, features a much more elaborate and sustained example of metafictional play (Fig. 6.1). The film narrates, in quasi-autobiographical fashion, the story of Paris-based filmmaker Haroun, who is prompted to return to his native Chad by his mother's unexpected death. The film explores the (then) current state of Chadian society in general and filmmaking culture in particular, as well as Haroun's relationship with his homeland. In one stretch of the film, he rekindles a romantic relationship with Isabelle (Aïcha Yelena), an actress from one of his earlier films, made in Chad, before his departure for Paris. In this film, Isabelle plays a (fictional) woman who is HIV positive; in the wake of the film's release, she has been ostracised as if she herself—and not only the character she plays—carries HIV. Now in their re-encounter, Haroun seeks to woo her by playfully—but insensitively—reminding her of the role she played in the film. Isabelle berates Haroun: "I'm not a fictional character! I'm a real person!" Here the metafictional gesture goes a step beyond what we see in *Tom Jones*, for here it appears within the diegesis, in the speech of a character, rather than as part of the narration. In this way, *Bye Bye Africa* creates a double-deckered, bidirectional

• [PRESENT 1] Émigré Paris-based filmmaker Haroun (a fictionalized rendering of the director) returns to his native Chad following the unexpected death of his mother, exploring the state of the country and especially its moribund film culture; he sets about making a film called *Bye Bye Africa*.	
○ [PAST 1] Before emigrating to Paris, Haroun made another film featuring (his girlfriend at the time) Isabelle.	
▪ [EMBEDDED FICTION] In this film Isabelle plays a woman who is socially ostracised because she is HIV positive	
○ [PAST 2] Presumed to be HIV positive herself, Isabelle is then herself shunned: "Cinema is stronger than reality." >> *character treated as person*	
• [PRESENT 2] Upon his return, Haroun tries to woo Isabelle, reminding her of her role in this earlier film, but she retorts: "Reality scares you, so you cower behind your stupid dramas. I'm not a fictional character! I'm real!" [transliteration: I exist!] >> *person treated as character*	

Fig. 6.1 Levels of narration, character, and person in *Bye Bye Africa* (Haroun 1999)

metafictional scenario: through the film's scripted dialogue, Isabelle, a character in the fictional world, reminds us that she is a character, by denouncing Haroun, another character in that fictional world, for treating her as a character rather than as a person, knowing that he knows she has already endured the inverse—being taken as the real instantiation of a merely fictional character (within the *reality* of the film's fictional world).[18]

Now, clearly *Bye Bye Africa* is an innovative work, explicitly acknowledging the influence of Jean-Luc Godard (who is referenced within the action). But the ability of *Bye Bye Africa* to comment metafictionally on the idea of character within its fictional world builds on the twofold nature of our engagement with characters in general, evident even in the most conventional works. Haroun's approach to writing and directing his film is an elaboration of this norm rather than a radical departure from it. The twofold stance of appreciators begins in the twofold stance of fictioneers: both must move fluently between internal and external perspectives.

6.7 Conclusion

While products of the imagination prompted and authorised by the fictions created by screenwriters, filmmakers, and other fictioneers, characters are real enough. Literally speaking, characters are abstract artefacts, like recipes for possible persons—or more generally, possible intentional agents—created by authors at particular historical moments. In creating these recipes, as we saw in the cases of Richard Curtis and Mike Leigh, screenwriters and writer-directors may draw on real-world material, basing their characters to a greater or lesser degree on actual individuals or existing characters, building this or that actual feature or cluster of features drawn from these trait pools into their invented agents. But they need not do so: the naked imagination will suffice. Once invented, characters can break free of the context of the specific fictional work in which they were first given form, being developed by the same or other authors in new works. The practice of screenwriters in developing character profiles, separate from the outline, treatment, and other preparatory texts leading to the screenplay itself, is a particularly telling piece of evidence

---

[18] There is more: because the film plays on the boundary between fiction and non-fiction—incorporating a great deal of apparently documentary footage and testimony, and weaving together biographical with invented story elements—we remain uncertain about how much of this narrative is fictional. We might be confident that Isabelle's suicide within *Bye Bye Africa* is fictional, but perhaps she did play a character testing positive for HIV in an earlier film, and perhaps the actress playing the role was shunned in reality as a consequence, and perhaps she (the actress and/or the character) did have an affair with Haroun (the protagonist and/or the actual filmmaker).

in support of the (in Terrone's expression) *self-standing* (Terrone 2021, 2) nature of characters.

These abstract artefacts then become the basis for us to imagine that the possible persons they represent exist, within the fictional world projected by the fictional work of which they are a part. Our interactions with characters, authorised by the fiction or unauthorised, are real too, impacting not just on our immediate states of mind, but our evolving understanding of and attitudes towards the world. Our attention to these engaging creatures of the imagination is twofold in nature, characterised by fluid movement between the internal and external perspectives on them—as imagined agents and invented artefacts—and lies at the heart of our fascination with fiction.

Acknowledgments My thanks to Paolo Russo for helpful feedback and suggestions, and great patience, throughout.

REFERENCES

Abell, Catharine. 2020. *Fiction: A Philosophical Analysis*. Oxford: Oxford University Press.
Arrival. 2016. Written by Eric Heisserer. Directed by Denis Villeneuve. USA: FilmNation Entertainment, Lava Bear Films, 21 Laps Entertainment.
Austin, John Langshaw. 1962. *Sense and Sensibilia*. Reconstructed from the manuscript notes by Geoffrey James Warnock. Oxford: Oxford University Press.
Barren Lives. 1963. Written and directed by Nelson Pereira dos Santos. Brazil: Herbert Richers Sinofilmes.
Blanchet, Robert, and Margrethe Bruun Vaage. 2012. "Don, Peggy, and Other Fictional Friends? Engaging with Characters in Television Series." *Projections* 6 (2): 18–41. https://doi.org/10.3167/proj.2012.060203.
Bunyan, John. 1678. *The Pilgrim's Progress*.
Bye Bye Africa. 1999. Written and directed by Mahamat-Saleh Haroun. France-Chad: Image Plus, La Lanterne, Tele-Chad.
Casablanca. 1942. Written by Julius G. Epstein, Philip G. Epstein, and Howard Koch. Directed by Michael Curtiz. USA: Warner Bros.
Close Encounters of the Third Kind. 1977. Written and directed by Steven Spielberg. USA: EMI Films, Columbia Pictures.
Dargis, Manohla. "The Lower Depths Rise with a Vengeance." *New York Times*. 10 October 2019, updated 10 February 2020. https://www.nytimes.com/2019/10/10/movies/parasite-review.html?mc=adintl&ad-keywords=IntlAudDev&subid1=TAFI&fbclid=IwAR2_DhB-PdvdS8L6_Xgci8xDFZO7YtHsnk0OWUSBPVZxc3STCox7Ot19gLg&dclid=CjgKEAjw2rmWBhDA7K_4rMjr-SMSJACHi6dBK8flHLDhY4Ge0vNNjuaf_S2-bE87tOOj0SonAr1NgPD_BwE. Accessed 3 August 2022.
Devitt, Michael, and Kim Sterelny. 1987. *Language and Reality: An Introduction to the Philosophy of Language*. Cambridge, MA: MIT Press.
Dickens, Charles. 1850. *David Copperfield*.
Dr No. 1963. Written by Richard Maibaum, Johanna Harwood, and Berkely Mather. Directed by Terence Young. UK-USA: Eon Productions.

Ex Machina. 2014. Written and directed by Alex Garland. UK: Film4, DNA Films.
Fielding, Henry. 1749. *Tom Jones.*
Film4. 2017. "The Cast of Trainspotting Reunited: T2 Trainspotting—Film4 Interview Special." Film4. www.youtube.com/watch?v=9AdgBq2Mp2Q. Accessed 8 August 2022.
Fleming, Ian. 1953. *Casino Royale.* London: Jonathan Cape.
Friend, Stacie. 2007. "Fictional Characters." *Philosophy Compass* 2 (2): 141–56. https://doi.org/10.1111/j.1747-9991.2007.00059.x.
Goodman, Nelson. 1978. *Ways of Worldmaking.* New York: Hackett.
Hunt, Lester H. 2021. "Time to Revisit Classical Film Theory." *Journal of Aesthetics and Art Criticism* 79 (1): 42–51.
Kael, Pauline. "Last Tango in Paris." *New Yorker Magazine*, 28 October, 130. Available at https://www.criterion.com/current/posts/834-last-tango-in-paris. Accessed 8 August 2022.
Lamarque, Peter, and Stein Haugom Olsen. 1994. *Truth, Fiction, and Literature: A Philosophical Perspective.* Oxford: Clarendon Press.
Last Tango in Paris (Ultimo tango a Parigi / Le dernier tango à Paris). 1972. Written by Bernardo Bertolucci, Franco Arcalli, and Agnés Varda (dialogue). Directed by Bernardo Bertolucci. Italy-France: PEA (Produzioni Europee Associati), Les Productions Artistes Associés.
Leigh, Mike. 2022. *This Cultural Life.* BBC. https://www.bbc.co.uk/programmes/m0011bgr. Accessed 3 August 2022.
Lewis, David. 1986. *On the Plurality of Worlds.* Oxford: Blackwell.
Livingston, Paisley. 1996. "Characterization and Fictional Truth in the Cinema." In *Post-Theory: Reconstructing Film Studies*, edited by David Bordwell and Noël Carroll, 149–74. Madison, WI: University of Wisconsin Press.
Livingston, Paisley. 2019. "Impossible Characterizations." In *Screening Characters: Theories of Character in Film, Television, and Interactive Media*, edited by Johannes Riis and Aaron Taylor, 129–42. New York: Routledge.
Livingston, Paisley, and Andrea Sauchelli. 2011. "Philosophical Perspectives on Fictional Characters." *New Literary History* 42 (2): 337–60. http://www.jstor.org/stable/23012547.
Love Actually. 2003. Written and directed by Richard Curtis. UK: StudioCanal, Working Title Films, DNA Films.
Nannicelli, Ted. 2013. *A Philosophy of the Screenplay.* New York: Routledge.
No Time to Die. 2021. Written by Neal Purvis, Robert Jade, Cary Joji Fukunaga, and Phoebe Waller-Bridge. Directed by Cary Joji Fukunaga. UK-USA: Eon Productions, Metro-Goldwyn-Mayer.
Parasite. 2019. Written by Bong Joon-ho and Han Jin-won. Directed by Bong Joon-ho. South Korea: Barunson E&A.
Pelletier, Jérôme. 2003. "Vergil and Dido." *Dialectica* 57 (2): 191–203.
Plantinga, Carl. 2018. *Screen Stories: Emotion and the Ethics of Engagement.* New York: Oxford University Press.
Sainsbury, Richard Mark 2010. *Fiction and Fictionalism.* Abingdon, UK: Routledge.
Sartre, Jean-Paul. 2010 [1940]. *The Imaginary: A Phenomenological Psychology of the Imagination.* Trans. Jonathan Webber. New York: Routledge.
Shohat, Ella, and Robert Stam. 2014. *Unthinking Eurocentrism: Multiculturalism and the Media.* 2nd ed. New York: Routledge.

Smith, Murray. 1995. *Engaging Characters: Fiction, Emotion, and the Cinema.* 1st ed. Oxford: Clarendon Press.
Smith, Murray. 2011. "On the Twofoldness of Character." *New Literary History* 4 (2): 277–94.
Smith, Murray. 2022. *Engaging Characters: Fiction, Emotion, and the Cinema.* 2nd ed. Oxford: Oxford University Press.
Stranger than Fiction. 2006. Written by Zach Helm. Directed by Mark Forster. USA: Columbia Pictures, Mandate Pictures, Three Strange Angels.
Terrone, Enrico. 2021. "Twofileness. A Functionalist Approach to Fictional Characters and Mental Files." *Erkenntis* 86, 129–47. https://doi.org/10.1007/s10670-018-0097-2.
The Purple Rose of Cairo. 1985. Written and directed by Woody Allen. USA: Jack Rollins and Charles H. Joffe Productions, Orion Pictures.
Thomasson, Amie L. 1999. *Fiction and Metaphysics.* Cambridge: Cambridge University Press.
Thomasson, Amie L. 2003. "Speaking of Fictional Characters." *Dialectica* 57 (2): 205–23.
Trainspotting. 1996. Written by John Hodge. Directed by Danny Boyle. UK: Channel Four Films, Figment Films, Noel Gay Motion Picture Company.
Under the Skin. 2013. Written by Walter Campbell, and Jonathan Glazer. Directed by Jonathan Glazer. UK: BFI, Film4.
Walton, Kendall L. 1990. *Mimesis as Make-Believe: On the Foundations of the Representational Arts.* Cambridge, MA: Harvard University Press.
Wark, Kirsty. 2021. *The Reunion.* Episode "Love Actually". BBC Radio 4. 24 December. https://www.bbc.co.uk/programmes/m0012qfq. Accessed 8 August 2022.
Welsh, Irvine. 1993. *Trainspotting.* London: Secker and Warburg.
Wilson, George. 2011. *Seeing Fictions in Film.* Oxford: Oxford University Press.
Wollheim, Richard. 1987. *Painting as an Art.* London: Thames and Hudson.

CHAPTER 7

"We Come to Realize": Screenwriting and Representations of Time

Adam Ganz

"How long a film is it? How long is the script?" I thought this was a funny question.

I said "Twenty-two pages." And they said, "Okay, then, it's a twenty-two-minute picture."

I said, "Well, I think it's going to be a hair longer than twenty-two minutes. A hair."

—David Lynch on *Eraserhead*

7.1 Introduction

In this essay, I argue that a key task for the screenwriter is the representation of time. A screenplay describes the sounds and images we will see projected on the screen once the film is completed. What it doesn't do is directly record the duration of the script, or the tempo and pace with which the events described in writing will occur. And yet, time isn't just an aspect of the film narrative, it is the medium in which it comes to life. Time is essential to the cinema, not just to the duration of a scene, but also to the ways in which it is experienced subjectively. As Christian Metz observed:

A. Ganz (✉)
Royal Holloway-University of London, London, UK
e-mail: adam.ganz@rhul.ac.uk

There is the time of the thing told and the time of the narrative (the time of the signified and the time of the signifier). This duality not only renders possible all the temporal distortions that are commonplace in narratives (three years of the hero's life summed up in two sentences of a novel or in a few shots of a "frequentative" montage in film, etc.). More basically, it invites us to consider that one of the functions of narrative is to invent one time scheme in terms of another time scheme. (As quoted in Genette 1980, 33)

Paul Ricoeur considers that "narrative activity, in history and in fiction, provides privileged access to the way we articulate our experience of time" (1979, 17). "A plot," he writes, "establishes human action not only within time [...] but within memory. Memory, accordingly, *repeats* the course of events according to an order which is the counterpart of time as stretching along between a beginning and an end" (28). How does the screenplay register these different temporalities?

A screenplay differs from the writing of other forms of time-based media, like, say music or opera, where the expression of time is at the centre of the process of notation, with distinct methods for precisely recording all: the duration of a piece of work, its rhythm and tempo, and any particular requirements for its proper expression. Rhythmic notation and forms of relatively standardised instruction are generally absent from the screenplay, beyond the generally accepted suggestion that one page of a screenplay, when formatted in 12-point Courier, is equivalent to one minute of screen time[1]—a convention David Lynch responds to in the quote that opens this essay (from Stevens 2014, 833). In discussing his approach to filmmaking, Ingmar Bergman aptly captures some of the challenges faced by screenwriters: "[T]he transformation of rhythms, moods, atmosphere, tensions, sequences, tones and scents into words and sentences, into an understandable screenplay" (1960, 16), Bergman asserts, is a supremely difficult task, so that the script is but "a very imperfect *technical* basis for a film" (17; emphasis added). One of the more serious problems posed by the screenplay, for Bergman, concerns the inadequacy of the form for capturing that *vital third dimension* that is rhythm and the relationship of one picture, one moment, to another. "There is no art form," Bergman observes, "that has so much in common with film as music. Both affect our emotions directly, not via the intellect. And film is mainly rhythm; it is inhalation and exhalation in continuous sequence" (17–18). And yet, unlike musical notation, the screenplay is, as we have seen, an imperfect medium:

> I cannot clearly give a key, as in a musical score, nor a specific idea of the tempo which determines the relationship of the elements involved. It is quite impossible for me to indicate the way in which the film "breathes" and pulsates. I have often wished for a kind of notation which would enable me to put on paper all

---

[1] Consultant and analyst Stephen Follows has looked at this in some detail on his blog, and concludes that this is the least bad rule that we have (Follows 2020). For more on the rise of Courier as a convention see (Millard 2010).

the shades and tones of my vision, to record distinctly the inner structure of a film. (Bergman 1960, 16–17)

Reflecting on why that might be can help us to understand what a screenplay is and is not, as well as how it came to assume the form that it has. Given that time is at the heart of cinema, it is clearly important for the screenwriter to be able to convey the passage of time, and the more sophisticated the cinema became, the more techniques were developed to suggest how time comes to pass, and to represent how that time is subjectively experienced (Genette 1980, 33).

There is considerable debate about how screenplays came to assume the form they did, but what is clear is that the screenplay has never been a form of notation that directly addresses time. In the silent film that was perhaps unproblematic in that the notation was not necessary to create the work, and that the recorded work ultimately could act as its own notation. We can discern, in early cinema, an analogous process to how songs are often created.

> [T]here have always been musicians (today's rock bands, for example) who work out compositions without notation yet meticulously, in detail, and in advance. They fix their work in memory in the very act of creating it, so that it will be permanent. Every performance is expected to resemble every other one (which of course need not preclude retouching or improvement over time, or even spontaneously). Their work, while "oral," is not improvisatory. The creative and re-creative acts have been differentiated. (Taruskin 2005, 17)

This, Richard Taruskin notes, is how Gregorian chant appears to have evolved for no less than half a millennium. Had it been possible to record those songs, it might not have been necessary to develop musical notation, since all crucial parts of the expression of the music would have been present there in the recording—the recording could have served as its own notation. As Taruskin observes, "the nature of the early written sources" indeed "suggests that notation was at first not the primary means of transmission but only a mnemonic device (that is, a reference tool to refresh memory), or *an arbiter of disputes*, or even a status symbol" (2005, 17; emphasis added). If we look at film in the same way it's possible to argue that, as a film automatically generated a record of the script and its intended realisation there was no need for a separate script-only version (especially as there was little prospect of a different version of the same screenplay being recreated, as happens for example with sheet music). Once a film becomes its own record, there is no emphasis on the specific cinematic rendition of the story and events which are recounted in the screenplay. There was, then, no need for a record of the film separate from the film as the film itself offered a record of its own performance. Slavko Vorkapich described it thus:

> [T]he making of films was at the outset taken over either by people who were used to entertaining their audiences from the stage and who carried their habits

of theatrical thinking into the new field, or by people who thought the only worthwhile thing to do was to make a movie record of some short act, usually a bit of vaudeville, and to present it in such a manner as to give the audiences the illusion that they were watching the real show. (Vorkapich 1950, 144)

Techniques of representing time through writing, however, become transformed by the cinema, as it itself develops through time.[2] To employ Bertolt Brecht: "The filmgoer develops a different way of reading stories. But the man who writes the stories is a filmgoer too" (1964, 47). From the late 1920s, once the sound which accompanied the film was recorded directly onto the film rather than being provided by musicians or storytellers, the need for some form of representation of time passing became essential, because there were now two different modes of time present—"the rhythm and pace of action and the rhythm and pace of dialogue," as Alfred Hitchcock (1939) put it, and which, he observed, are two "entirely different things." As soon as the rhythm of dialogue enters the screenplay there is an implicit syncopation between the dialogue and the written description. Drawing on those who had knowledge of the rhythms of dialogue, both demotic and more sophisticated, screenwriters now began to develop literary strategies to capture time—to implicitly express not just duration, but rhythm, pace, tempo, and all the other qualities of lived time. Eisenstein, for example, draws on the poetry of John Milton: "*Paradise Lost* is itself a first-rate school in which to study montage and audio-visual relationships" (1943, 54)—a comparison also explored by Richard Wilbur in his essay "A Poet and the Movies" (1967). Others begin to employ the externalisation of the Imagists poets,[3] but also to respond to the many techniques which literature, often inspired by modernist responses to the cinema, had developed to convey the nature and passage of time. Screenwriting, indeed, now incorporates techniques that involve a different approach to punctuation and grammar, as seen in the demotic, journalistic narratives of Ben Hecht in the USA or Billy Wilder in Germany; and techniques of layout moving towards the word images which Apollinaire (whose own screenplays were sadly never made into films) had used in his *poèmes épistolaires*, or the collages of his contemporary Jacques Prévert, a poet who found the place in popular cinema which eluded Apollinaire,[4] quite possibly because his poetry

---

[2] Our understanding and experience of time itself, as Ronald Schleifer argues in *Modernism and Time: The Logic of Abundance in Literature, Science, and Culture 1880–1930* (2000), was transformed in the age of the cinema and to some extent as a result of it.

[3] A number of scholars have commented on the formal links between Modernism and screenwriting. In *Script Culture and the American Screenplay* (2008), Kevin Alexander Boon makes the point that "like the poetry of modernists such as William Carlos Williams and Robert Frost, screenplay descriptions often, if well-executed, present concentrated images. Their concision and economy share the poetics of Imagist poetry" (260).

[4] Prevert's screenplays for films such as *Le Crime de Monsieur Lange* (1936), *Le Jour Se Leve* (1939), and *Quai de Brumes* (1938), indeed, were enormously successful. *Quai des*

was already not only vivid, visual and popular, but also *rhythmic*, defined by a certain musicality.

In *The Modernist Screenplay* (2020), Aleksandra Ksenofontova comments on how screenwriters in Russia, Germany and France all find ways of simulating rhythm in their screenplays. With the coming of sound, the rhythmic, indeed, becomes more present and more defined. One example of this is Walter Reisch who, in Austria and later in Hollywood, can be found writing musical sequences which incorporate sound and image montages as a way of evoking the passing of time. As Claus Tieber points out:

> What becomes more important with sound film is the fine-tuning of sight and sound, which was now in control of the producing side and no longer in the hands of musicians and cinema owners. As a result of the closer and controllable connection of music, sound and moving images, new creative personnel were needed: the screenplay gained new functions (which can also be detected in the changing format), and screenwriters were faced with new tasks. (Tieber 2019, 301)

7.2 The Effect of Sound

As sound began to become a new feature of the cinema, Reisch and other screenwriters—in Austria and Germany especially—experimented with the new technical possibilities, and found innovative ways to combine speech, song, and music. Tieber also reveals that, for Reisch, the minor notational change involved in numbering paragraphs "makes a script out of a prosaic text, thus sharing his conception of the screen play format of his time and place […]. In other words: every sentence in a screenplay implies a camera angle or movement, even if it is not explicitly written on the page" (Tieber 2019, 296). It is pleasing that Tieber shows how Reisch's musical numbers, when combined with these paragraph numberings, contribute to changing the screenplay form. The numbers make notation.

Whilst early film didn't necessarily value screenwriters as writers, writers and especially modernist writers were fascinated with the cinema, and in particular the possibilities it offered to represent time. Laura Marcus' essay "Film and Modernist Literature" (2016) looks at how a number of twentieth-century writers, including Rudyard Kipling and Virginia Woolf, reacted to the invention of the cinema, and in particular how they, right from the beginning, understood the nature of the medium and what it meant for storytelling. The way in which Woolf represents simultaneity in *To the Lighthouse*, Marcus observes here:

> […] was almost certainly inflected by a familiarity with cinematic strategies. These include parallel editing (or cross-cutting) as a means to depict events

Brumes won the Prix Louis-Delluc, whilst *Les Enfants du Paradis* (1945) was nominated for an Oscar and regularly features in lists of greatest screenplays.

taking place at the same moment but in different spaces, as well as the shot-reverse-shot structure of continuity editing which has its literary correlative in the novel in the views from shore to sea, and back from sea to shore. (2016)

Samuel Beckett, too, Marcus reveals, was so taken with the possibilities of Soviet cinema that he wrote to Eisenstein asking to be considered for admission to the Moscow State School of Cinematography, stating that he was particularly interested in scenario and editing. Now, these techniques which were drawn from the cinema came back to the cinema via those writers who were Modernist or affected by modernism (Ksenofontova 2020; Jasmin Mirsal 2018). As a result of this interaction, the screenplay becomes, in effect, more literary. Whilst there was a greater literacy about the cinema from intellectuals, the literacy of filmmakers—by which I mean their knowledge of and ability to express themselves through audiovisual narratives (either as films or as screenplays which sought to tell a filmic story and summon it into existence)—drew on the processes of making narrative in many other disciplines, from journalism to theatre and vaudeville to oral narrative. As cinema matured, after the coming of sound, it drew increasingly on writers from all these and more, and they came to transform the screenplay, in how it represented time and how it induced different kinds of attention in the spectator. Cinema was not just what Walter Benjamin called an object or scene for "simultaneous collective reception" (2008, 36), but also involved an act of simultaneous collective witnessing, in which audiences were together in both space and time as they experienced the unfolding of the narrative and the placing of clues on the screen before them. The nature of the attention the narrative demanded changed as the story was collectively discovered together and in common. The visual prized what historian Carlo Ginzburg has called "venatic narratives"—which draw on the ability or, as Ginzburg puts it, *"permit the leap from apparently insignificant facts, which could be observed, to a complex reality which—directly at least—could not"* (1980, 13; emphasis added). The commodification of time in the cinema, driven by the desire of cinema owners to maximise the number of screenings each day, soon became one of the things which determined the nature of the film form. William Faulkner "both reshaped and was shaped by the alien territories of commercial film," as Ben Robbins has noted (2014, 241). He is just one of a generation of US writers who moved between various kind of writing, of which screenwriting is one manifestation. In the US and British traditions, we can think of Anita Loos, Ben Hecht, Billy Wilder and Emeric Pressburger, P. G. Wodehouse, Raymond Chandler or Scott Fitzgerald, all of whom were both shaped by and helped shape the screenplay form. Hecht in particular was, according to Jean Luc Godard, responsible for "80 per cent of what is used in Hollywood movies today" (1998, 23). Hecht came to the cinema from journalism. He was also part of the Chicago literary scene and was influenced by French writers like Prosper Merimée and Paul Verlaine. The lead writer on *Scarface* (1932) and Charles MacArthur's co-writer for *The Front Page* (1928), Hecht moved between genres—from *The Front Page* to Hitchcock's *Notorious* (1946)—as well as doing rewriting on films like *Gone With the Wind* (1939) and *The Shop Around the Corner* (1940). He also worked with Louis Armstrong and Kurt Weill. Hecht can be said to have invented the gangster film, the screwball, and the romantic comedy at large. As critic David Denby (2019) points out in a *New Yorker* article, what Hecht brought to the cinema, along with the new milieus and urban anti-heroes of the journalist and the gangster, was pace and rhythm. Hecht sensed, Denby argues, that the growing urban audience of the Depression wanted the fast life, and that he was able to give that pace in dialogue.

7.3 Individual Techniques

7.3.1 James Agee

I am now going to look at the way a number of other screenwriters have found ways to represent time in their screenplays. I am not suggesting that they are in any sense typical, but I think they offer a range of approaches which reveal the possibilities of the medium to both the scholar and the practitioner. I am particularly interested in the work of film critic and journalist-turned-screenwriter James Agee, whom theorist James Naremore describes as belonging "to the late phase of high modernism, when the scandalous and difficult art of the 1920s had achieved middlebrow respectability" (2014a, 250). Agee became a screenwriter via working as a film critic for *The Nation*, where his essays were praised by WH Auden, to writing *Let Us Now Praise Famous Men* (1941) with photographer Walker Evans and, later, screenplays for *The African Queen* (1951) and *Night of the Hunter* (1955). Agee also worked on documentaries *In the Street* (1948) and *The Quiet One* (1948) for which he wrote the commentary.

Naremore looks in some detail at Agee's writing about film in *The Nation*, noting that it "is highly adjectival or adverbial and attentive to the effects of rhythm. His sentences often have a bell-like quality achieved with triple or quadruple modifiers" (2014b, 102). More specifically, Naremore analyses Agee's description of a sequence in Buster Keaton's *Sherlock Jr* (1924) in *Life* magazine and highlights his use of a kind of para-notation, employing prose to evoke the pace of the film as well as describing what happened.

> Boiling along on the handlebars of a motorcycle quite unaware that he has lost his driver, Keaton whips through city traffic, breaks up a tug-of-war, gets a shovelful of dirt in the face from a long line of Rockette-timed ditch-diggers, approaches a log at high speed which is hinged open by dynamite precisely soon enough to let him through and, hitting an obstruction, leaves the handlebars like an arrow leaving a bow, whams through the window of a shack in which the heroine is about to be violated, and hits the heavy feet first, knocking him through the opposite wall. (Agee in Naremore 2014b, 102)

Naremore observes how Agee here deploys the techniques of prose rhythm including "punctuation, paragraph breaks, and the variation of short and long clauses or sentences, to create a variety of subtle or strong pauses," (202) so that the prose itself mirrors the film it describes. "[T]he extended string of verbs and participles punctuated by commas amusingly mimics the pace and cutting rhythm of the film. It is criticism of a high order in which description becomes meaning" (102).

It is an example of how Agee, combining his knowledge of writing and cinema, used prose to expand ekphrasis to incorporate not just the seen and the heard, but also the experience of time for the film audience, both subjective and objective. In his collaboration with Walker Evans, *Let Us Now Praise Famous Men*, Agee explores a different kind of relationship with image and text, which also influences his subsequent screenwriting and overall mode of writing. Walker Evans is particularly acute about the relationship between word and image: "There's no book but what's full of photography. James Joyce is. Henry James is. That's a pet subject of mine—how those men are unconscious photographers" (1971, n.p.). In the 2009 "The Case of the Inappropriate Alarm Clock (Part 4)," Errol Morris described the book as "an essay on the impossibility of translating the world into prose or even photographs." He continues: "What makes the prose of *Let Us Now Praise Famous Men* both poignant and peculiar is Agee's anguish about observing, as if Agee wishes to report on the limitations of his craft and at the same time provide an itemized inventory of everything…" (2009; online). Agee's screenplay for *Night of the Hunter* (Laughton) is extraordinarily distinctive. Jeffrey Couchman in *The Night of the Hunter: A Biography of a Film* compares Agee's original 300-page script with the published screenplay and shows how much of Agee's original work remains. It retains what Michael Sragow wrote of his criticism: "Agee always writes as a poet—as a maker, not a consumer of images" (2018; online).

```
CLOSE SHOT -- PREACHER
    He is the driver of the car. Pleasant river landscapes
(PROCESS) flow behind him. He is dressed in dark clothes, a
paper collar, a string tie. As he drives, he talks to himself.
(1955, 2)
```

The initial image of the Preacher villain, driving across the land whilst "pleasant river landscapes" flow behind him, introduces a symbolism present throughout the film, and Agee's prose combines visual description with its own rhythmical flow of passing time.

```
MEDIUM SHOT -- BART
    He approaches his children, across whose bed we SHOOT
without yet seeing them. He comes into MEDIUM CLOSE-UP. As he
leans and we TILT DOWN, he extends his large hands.
```

CLOSE DOWNWARD TWO-SHOT -- HIS CHILDREN

  Two rose-and-gold little GIRLS lie in sleep; BART's hands enter the SHOT and gently rearrange the covers so that their mouths and throats are free. We watch for a moment more, the two sleeping faces.

                                          LAP DISSOLVE TO

HEAD CLOSE-UP -- BART, HOVERING HIS CHILDREN

                     CHILDREN'S VOICES
                  (o.s., chanting)
     Hing, hang, hung. See what the Hangman done!

                                          LAP DISSOLVE TO

EXT. CRESAP'S LANDING -- DAY

  We are in Peacock Alley. The tree-shaded dirt street of a small, one-street river town; a picturesque, mid-19th century remnant of the old river civilization, which general Progress has left behind. Chiefly we see, in this order: A schoolhouse (on far side of street); Miz Cunningham's second-hand shop; a Grange House sporting a poster for a Western movie; Spoon's Ice Cream Parlor. At the end of the street, down the river-bank, is a brick wharf and Uncle Birdie's wharf-boat. In b.g. and in passing, suggestions of sleepy small-town life.

From the HEAD CLOSE-UP of BART the Hangman o.s. chanting, we

                                          LAP DISSOLVE TO

HEAD CLOSE-UP -- JOHN HARPER

  Chanting voices o.s. complete "see what the Hangman done!" (1955, 12–13)

[…]

PREACHER, WILLA and PEARL surround a little table. WALT stands by, puffing his pipe. ICEY, in BACKGROUND, stirs fudge at a little soda-fountain stove. WILLA looks both moved and pleased. PEARL, shyly flirting with PREACHER, all but hides in WILLA's skirts. PREACHER dandles PEARL's doll on his knee as he talks. All the grown-ups are avid for his words, which we don't hear through the glass. (1955, 19)

The writing evidences an acute awareness of the filmic possibilities of representing time. Here, for example, Agee shows a transition through space and time to discover the hangman putting his own children to bed, just as the children of the man he killed are now within reach of another killer, to the accompaniment of children singing "Hing hang hung." The various rhythms of song and Agee's poetic prose are combined with extraordinary ekphratic imagery; the phrase "two rose-and-gold little GIRLS lie in sleep" is both visually striking (though the film was ultimately shot in black and white) and also enjoys a peaceful quality in the choice of words through which the image is expressed. What is particularly interesting is the synthesis between the prose which replicates the image (which Naremore identified from, say, his review of *Sherlock Jr.* with his imaginative descriptions, often, of still images) with movement through the frame as, for example, when the body of the children's murdered mother is discovered in the water by Uncle Birdie fishing from his skiff.

```
DOWNSHOT -- FULL SHOT OF CAR AND WILLA; BIRDIE'S VIEWPOINT

CLOSE SHOT -- BIRDIE, HORROR-STRICKEN

MOVING UNDERWATER SHOT -- WILLA
   We hear PREACHER's voice o.s., singing:

               PREACHER (o.s.)
       Leaning! Leaning! Safe and secure from all
       alarms!

Meanwhile, we move vertically DOWNWARDS TOWARDS HER FACE,
serene in death. We may or may not glimpse the gashed throat,
through drifting hair. (1955, 53)
```

In his screenwriting Agee combines his skill, honed from his work with Evans, in invoking still pictures with his experience in describing pictures that move in his work at *The Nation*. He stresses the uncertainty of spectatorship: "we may or may not glimpse." As the children make their escape, the script contrasts the speed and violence in sound and action with the slowness of the narrative, and of the river down which they make their escape, which has powerful metaphorical resonances, as they are followed by the Preacher who is still determined to catch them.

```
They fly out of the house.
                    PREACHER'S VOICE
                 (bellowing, as they go)
       OPEN THAT DOOR, YOU SPAWN OF THE DEVIL'S OWN
```

> STRUMPET!
>
> FRAMING SHOT -- EXT. HARPER HOUSE
>   A pretty, pastoral shot of the house in light mist, as they run across and leave the shot. Before they disappear, we hear PREACHER's fists hammering against the door. We stay on the house at leisure; we hear him lunging, shoulder to door; we begin to hear squeaking of hinges and splintering of wood.
>
> FULL CIRCLE SHOT -- FRAMING BIRDIE'S WHARF-BOAT
>   An ultra-romantic image of shelter and peace. Frogs or river noises o.s., then the rattle of running footsteps. The CHILDREN enter, their backs to us,
>   sprinting towards the boat. (1955, 65)
>
> [...]
>
> FULL DOWN SHOT -- THE SKIFF, THEN PREACHER
>   The current catches it and spins it round like a leaf. JOHN's efforts with the oars are useless. PREACHER enters, wading fast. His hands are within an inch of reaching the helpless skiff; capriciously the current takes it downstream. (69)

The choice of the word "capriciously" is an example of a poetic use of language not generally associated with the screenplay, but which echoes and invokes the rhythms of the cinema. In his paean to the film in *Senses of Cinema*, Adrian Danks identifies the way Agee deals with time as at the very heart of what makes it so distinctive.

> At various points the film refers to domestic, pastoral, linear, gendered, narratological and generational conceptions of time and ranges across the varied experiences of "being in time" available to the cinema. This obsession with heterogeneous time, a time that also darts backwards and forwards across cinema history and memory, is visualised by Pearl and John's dreamy, timeless, ebbing-and-flowing free-fall journey downriver. The long scenes of the children's flight have a gentle and archaic rhythm and tempo, furthering the film's extraordinarily dynamic and poetic use of visual and aural motifs. But this is also a film that is out of time. It is both anachronistic and visionary; while fitting into neither the broader context of the mid-'50s or an earlier epoch. (2017; online)

Agee's understanding of cinematic time and how it can be represented in written form is what makes the film's treatment of time so spectacular. I could quote many more examples from the screenplay, which is a remarkable piece of poetic prose, despite its detailed visual descriptions of extraordinarily vivid scenes appearing directly in the completed film.

7.3.2 William Goldman

Gradually the forms of writing that had been developed to respond to the new understanding of time made possible by the cinema were adopted by those who were writing *for* the cinema, drawing on the many techniques from simultaneity of action and intercutting to a range of more experimental techniques for words to convey pictures. William Goldman, for example, in *Butch Cassidy and the Sundance Kid* (1969), uses blank spaces and punctuation as one of the methods in which he visually represents the image on screen. The film opens:

```
FADE IN
ON ALMOST THE ENTIRE SCREEN IN BLACK SHADOW
   The upper right corner is the only color, and that is a white
that almost stings to look at it -- it is the white heat of the
afternoon sun, and the shadow, we come to realize, is the side
of some building together with the shadow of that building on
the ground. If we don't know quite what it is that we're seeing
at this point, that's all right. (1968, 1)
```

Like Agee before him, Goldman foregrounds uncertainty and his script acknowledges time as one of the elements through which the audience perceives the image and assembles its meaning. "We come to realize" describes a process, not an act. Goldman makes use of several techniques which can be traced to modernist practice both in how he describes images and places them in succession. As in a poem, he uses prose to reproduce the succession of images. He not only uses words to represent images, but also employs prose to represent duration and to condense action. He also starts to develop his own form of notation around dialogue, where two indented dashes (--) mark the beginning of each line. This technique, which seems to be employed when Agee recognises that film an edited medium—a process that the writer needs to be aware of even if they are not in control of it—also serves to emphasise the role of other diacritic marks in making us aware of a special quality of the prose, reminiscent of Gerard Manley Hopkins' use of sprung rhythm.

Goldman, it is perhaps worth noting here, took his MA in Comparative Literature at Columbia (his thesis was on the comedy of manners in America), and one can even trace a direct lineage to Apollinaire through his lecturer Jacques Barzun, whose father was a member of the Abbaye de Creteil group, and whose childhood home was often visited by Apollinaire (see Goldman 1972, 37). Like Apollinaire, Goldman draws on the potential, well-analysed by W.J.T. Mitchell, for any text to move from word to image—how, for instance, making words be seen as *"black marks on a white background"* means that they now become objects of a different kind of attention (Mitchell as quoted in Nelson and Shiff 1996, 51). A screenplay that generates this kind of visual or aural attention becomes more effective in evoking its future state as an audiovisual text. And, in making that immediacy palpable, the script also underscores how time is experienced by the reader and will be present for a future audience. A script that draws attention to its own nature as an image is likely to make readers aware of the other images it is describing. The techniques that Mitchell refers to are increasingly present in Goldman's work. His screenplay is both avant-text and avant-image, constantly shifting from word to image, and from word to sound.

```
CUT TO:
BUTCH
    pushing off after Etta has hesitatingly gotten on the bike.
It's downhill but it's still precarious at first and they
almost tumble until he gets the hang of it, but once he's got
it, he never loses it, and as they begin to pick up speed we are
into:
```
<u>MUSICAL INTERLUDE NUMBER ONE</u>
    There are going to be three of them before the film is over. This, the first, is a song sung while Butch and Etta ride the bike. The song will be sung by male voices, and the feel of it is terribly contemporary, because in fact, the sound of the songs of this period are shockingly close in feel to the popular music of today.
    What we hear will <u>not</u> be a song like "Bicycle Built for Two." The song will be poignant and pretty as hell and [...] they will have an emotional connection with the scene, not a literal one. (1968, 51)

This is the sequence where, in the film, we hear Burt Bacharach's "Raindrops Keep Falling on My Head," composed specially for it. Goldman finds ways of breaking the fourth wall and exploring the meta-narrative. For example, when Butch Cassidy's leadership is challenged early in the film: "Butch delivers the most aesthetically exquisite kick in the balls in the history of the modern American cinema" (26). Goldman's mock-heroic tone here finds a way to use overblown prose for timing and shock value, slyly referring to the future film in a different, imagined context. In an essay for the *Los Angeles Times,* David Mamet is very critical of this kind of writing which he asserts turns the screenplay from "drama-in-schematic" to carnival amusement—into something that offers "not drama, but *thrills*" (1995; online). But the experience of the drama in the moment is something which distinguishes the cinema from the screenplay? and thrills, and being able to invoke the norm and the departure from it is precisely what made Goldman's reinvention of the Western so distinctive, and so successful. Goldman's knowing intertextuality is a feature of his writing. His 1974 novel *The Princess Bride* (which he subsequently adapted for the cinema in 1987) explores the process of time and the story, and how time within the narrative is both shorter and longer than in the world in which it exists. Director Rob Reiner explains:

> The film is about a little boy who is sick in bed and his grandfather comes over to read him a book. And the little boy is resistant to seeing his grandfather and to hearing the book read to him. And by the end of the film he's brought closer to his grandfather and he is now interested in books. [...] Even though the story of *The Princess Bride* is taking up 85–90 percent of the running time, the film is really about that wraparound 10–15 percent. (Reiner cited in Jacobson 1987; online)

The novel plays with the kinds of attention which belong to the cinema, both claiming and rejecting its populism, and to suggest (and reject) Goldman's own sophistication.

7.3.3 Wes Craven

Another literary writer who uses prose to explore the timing of horror is Wes Craven. Indeed, the ekphratic nature of Craven's action descriptions in the scripts of *Nightmare on Elm Street* (1984) draws on a very complex vocabulary and uses the complexity of that prose to reproduce the timings of horror.

```
TINA opens her mouth to scream but only a dry, yellow dust
pours out.! And at that precise moment a huge shadowy MAN
with a grimey red and yellow sweater and a weird hat pulled
over his scarred face lunges at her. And it's his fingers
that are tipped with the long blades of steel, glinting in the
boney light and giving the hulk the look of an otherworldly
predator. (1984, 3–4)
```

When asked what directors and authors have had the greatest impact on him, Craven replies: "The directors whose work I saw first: Buñuel—very influential; the Europeans such as Bergman, Fellini, Cocteau, Truffaut. Also, writers like Tolstoy, Dostoevsky, Kafka... the Theatre of the absurd" (as quoted in Skelton 2019, 52). Craven's literary influences are detectable in his screenplays. His first film *Last House on the Left* (1972) was adapted from Ingmar Bergman's *Virgin Spring* (1960), itself adapted from a sixteenth-century ballad of tragedy and revenge (see Laity 2007). I have already argued that the ballad in particular, and oral narrative more generally, is a useful model for looking at screenplay structure and exploring how texts can represent time (Ganz 2012). In Craven's screenplay for *Nightmare on Elm Street*, we find an extraordinary use of techniques both balladic and screen-writerly to evoke images and previsualise the narrative.

[W]e still haven't seen his face. We never will. We just SEE more metal being assembled with crude tools, into some sort of linkage -- a splayed, spidery sort of apparatus, against a background light of FIRE, and a deep rushing of STEAM and HEAVY, DARK ENERGY. (1984, 2)

Critic Isabel Pinedo has commented on the centrality of time in *Nightmare on Elm Street*

> In *A Nightmare on Elm Street,* there is a glaring discrepancy between the explicit focus on time—the radio announces it, characters set deadlines by the clock, and the alarm clock goes off at previously discussed times—and the implied duration of the narrative events taking place in those time frames. [...] Time is unhinged, and this adds to the dreamlike texture of the film. (1996, 23)

Pinedo goes on to make the point that:

> A film is not only a time-bound experience, it is also an imaginary one. The screen constitutes the spatial frame on which a film is projected. It marks off a bounded reality, one that need not conform strictly to lived experience. The borders of the screen establish parameters that free the viewer to engage in fantasy. (27)

Those parameters can be established in the screenplay, both in the way that the texts describe the events of the film, but also in the various other techniques for previsualisation which Mitchell describes. One intriguing technique employed by Craven is his application of a consciously literary language in this context. For example, when Tina attempts to escape Freddie when she encounters him in her dream for the first time, Craven uses the word "elephantine" to describe her inability to move in her nightmare: "TINA dodges away, her legs suddenly elephantine and slow. The MAN seizes the trailing hem of her nightgown and hauls her back!" (Craven 1984, 4). This use of language seems to directly contradict the generally accepted heuristics of screenwriting that the vocabulary should be as clear and unliterary as possible because the text itself will never be read. But here the very literary language is used to convey Tina's slowness compared to the speed of Freddie, who like the cinema lives in dreams, and of the ballad that helps to summon him up. The screenplay, indeed, refers to its future state in some fascinating ways and explores the difference between its current manifestation as prose and its future as cinema. At one point Craven describes Krueger stabbing Nancy "as if she were an optical illusion" before "falling down, down, down... And he's gone" (1984, 111). The screenplay is forever problematising the represented and showing it to be a representation, whilst at the same time continually finding diverse ways to represent in writing the question of who or what the illusion is, and where it can be found. Time, as Pinedo has noted, is at the centre of this disjuncture. The script of what was to be a franchise of nine films as well as a TV series ends with the triumph of Freddie Krueger and of dream over reality. In the film, this is mirrored by the victory of the oral over the written, with the conclusion of schoolchildren reciting a rhyme (which recalls the ballad that inspired Craven's first film, as it did Bergman who Craven drew so much from). But only those who have read the screenplay will know how Craven contrasts this orality with the polysyllabic literary language of "elephantine."

7.4 Conclusion

Another follower of Bergman, from a quite different filmic formation, also put time at the centre of his understanding of the cinema, and of the processes of writing the screenplay which will help to bring the future film into existence. In his book *Sculpting in Time,* Andrei Tarkovsky writes:

> If one compares cinema with such time-based arts as, say, ballet or music, cinema stands out as giving time visible, real form. Once recorded on film, the phenomenon is there, given and immutable, even when the time is intensely subjective [...] it is rhythm, and not editing, as people tend to think, that is the main formative element of cinema [...] Feeling the rhythmicality of a shot is rather like feeling a truthful word in literature. An inexact word in writing, like an inexact rhythm in film, destroys the veracity of the work. (Tarkovsky 1989, 118–20).

Tarkovsky is at pains to point out that the screenplay is not itself art:

> Anything in the scenario that has aspirations to literature, to prose, must as a matter of principle be consistently assimilated and adapted in the course of making the film. The literary element in a film is smelted; it ceases to be literature once the film has been made. Once the work is done, all that is left is the written transcript, the shooting script, which could not be called literature by any definition. It is more like an account of something seen related to a blind man [...] (134)

When something is smelted it has become something else, but it remains one of the initial elements that enabled that transformation to occur. Likewise, the literary elements which can be found in the screenplay are key in finding ways to suggest time and how it should be experienced before it is permanently recorded on film. The examples offered here are by no means representative but taken together they manifest the potential for the screenplay as a literary text which can and does draw on both classical and modernist literary techniques to previsualise and simulate the experience of time-as-narrative of the cinema. A text that is readable, syncopated, and constantly able to underline its own status as a story to be told in sound and moving image will be more compelling in helping readers imagine it, the script, as a movie. A successful screenplay is often referred to as a *page-turner*—and it is in turning the page that the materiality of paper and image is, as in a flicker book, transformed into the apparent movement of the cinema.

References

Agee, James, and Walker Evans. 1941. *Let Us Now Praise Famous Men*. Cambridge, Mass: The Riverside Press.

Benjamin, Walter. 2008 [1935]. *The Work of Art in the Age of Mechanical Reproduction*. Trans. J. A. Underwood. London: Penguin Books.

Bergman, Ingmar. 1960. *Four Screenplays of Ingmar Bergman*. Trans. Lars Malmstrom and David Kushner. New York: Simon and Schuster.

Boon, Kevin Alexander. 2008. *Script Culture and the American Screenplay*. Detroit: Wayne State University Press.

Brecht, Bertolt, and John Willett. 1964. *Brecht on Theatre: The Development of an Aesthetic*. New York: Hill and Wang.

Butch Cassidy and the Sundance Kid. 1969. Written by William Goldman. Directed by George Roy Hill. USA: Campanile Productions, George Roy Hill-Paul Monash Production, Newman-Foreman Company, Estudios Churubusco Azteca S.A.

Craven, Wes. 1984. *A Nightmare on Elm Street*. Screenplay. Available online at https://www.scriptslug.com/script/a-nightmare-on-elm-street-1984. Accessed 12 December 2021.

Danks, Adrian. 2017, March. "The Man in Black: The Night of the Hunter (1955)." *Senses of Cinema*. https://www.sensesofcinema.com/2017/cteq/night-of-the-hunter/. Accessed 15 June 2022.

Denby, David. 2019. "The Great Hollywood Screenwriter Who Hated Hollywood." *The New Yorker*, 4 February, https://www.newyorker.com/magazine/2019/02/11/the-great-hollywood-screenwriter-who-hated-hollywood. Accessed 25 January 2022.

Eisenstein, Sergei. 1943. *The Film Sense*. London: Faber and Faber.

Eraserhead. 1977. Written and directed by David Lynch. USA: American Film Institute, Libra Films.

Follows, Stephen. 2020. "Does One Page of a Film Script Really Equal One Minute of Screentime?" *Stephen Follows*, March 8. https://stephenfollows.com/is-the-page-per-minute-rule-correct/. Accessed 20 November 2021.

Ganz, Adam. 2012. "'Leaping Broken Narration': Ballads, Oral Storytelling and the Cinema." In *Storytelling in World Cinemas, 1: Forms*, edited by Lina Khatib, 71–88. New York: Wallflower Press/Columbia University Press.

Genette, Gerard. 1980. *Narrative Discourse: An Essay in Method*. Trans. Jane E. Lewin. Ithaca, NY: Cornell University Press.

Ginzburg, Carlo, and Anna Davin. 1980. "Morelli, Freud and Sherlock Holmes: Clues and Scientific Method." *History Workshop* 9 (Spring): 5–36.

Godard, Jean Luc. 1998. *Jean-Luc Godard: Interviews*. Jackson, MS: University Press of Mississippi.

Goldman, Richard Franco. 1972. "Portrait: Jacques Barzun." *The American Scholar* 42 (1): 15–17, 20, 22–25.

Goldman, William. 1968. *Butch Cassidy and the Sundance Kid*. Final (July 15). Screenplay. Available online at http://www.dailyscript.com/scripts/Butch_Cassidy_and_the_Sundance_Kid.pdf. Accessed 12 December 2021.
Gone With the Wind. 1939. Written by Sidney Howard. Directed by Victor Fleming. USA: Selznick International Pictures.
Hecht, Ben, and Charles MacArthur. 1928. *The Front Page*. New York: Covici Friede Publishers.
Hitchock, Alfred. 1939. "Lecture: Radio City Music Hall, New York City (30/Mar/1939)." *MoMA*. https://www.moma.org/interactives/exhibitions/1999/hitchcock/lecture/index.html. Accessed 12 December 2021.
In the Street. 1948. Directed by James Agee, Helen Levitt, and Janice Loeb. USA.
Jacobson, Harlan. 1987. "Prince Rob." *Film Comment*. https://www.filmcomment.com/article/rob-reiner-interview/. Accessed 12 December 2021.
Ksenofontova, Alexandra. 2018. "The Screenplay/Film Relationship Bifurcated: Reading Carl Mayer's *Sylvester* (1924)." *Journal of Screenwriting* 9 (1): 25–39. https://doi.org/10.1386/josc.9.1.25_1.
Ksenofontova, Alexandra. 2020. *The Modernist Screenplay: Experimental Writing for Silent Film*. Cham, Switzerland: Palgrave Macmillan.
Laity, K.A. 2007. "The Virgin Victim: Reimagining a Medieval Folk Ballad in *The Virgin Spring* and *The Last House on the Left*." In *Folklore/Cinema Book Subtitle: Popular Film as Vernacular Culture*, edited by Sharon R. Sherman and Mikel J. Koven, 180–96. Logan, UT: Utah State University Press.
Last House on the Left. 1972. Written and directed by Wes Craven. USA: Sean S. Cunningham Films, The Night Co., Lobster Enterprises.
Le Crime de Monsieur Lange [*The Crime of Monsieur Lange*]. 1936. Written by Jacques Prévert and Jean Renoir. Directed by Jean Renoir. France: Films Obéron.
Le Jour Se Lève [*Daybreak*]. 1939. Screenplay by Jacques Viot and Jacques Prévert. Directed by Marcel Carné. France: Production Sigma.
Les Enfants du Paradis [*Children of Paradise*]. 1945. Written by Jacques Prévert. Directed by Marcel Casrné. France: Pathé.
Mamet, David. 1995. "That's Entertainment. That's Too Bad." *Los Angeles Times*, 6 August. https://www.latimes.com/archives/la-xpm-1995-08-06-tm-31900-story.html. Accessed 15 June 2022.
Marcus, Laura. 2016. "Film and Modernist Literature." *Études britanniques contemporaines* [online] 50. https://doi.org/10.4000/ebc.3050.
Millard, Kathryn. 2010. "After the Typewriter: The Screenplay in a Digital Era." *Journal of Screenwriting* 1 (1): 11–25. https://doi.org/10.1386/josc.1.1.11/1.
Mirsal, Jasmin. 2018. *Writing Pictures: The Screenplay as a Form of Literary Modernism*. PhD diss., Royal Holloway–University of London. https://pure.royalholloway.ac.uk/portal/files/34056930/Jasmin_Mirsal_l_Writing_Pictures_The_Screenplay_as_a_Form_of_Literary_Modernism.pdf. Accessed 14 November 2021.
Morris, Errol. 2009. "The Case of the Inappropriate Alarm Clock (Part 4)." *Opinionator*. October 21. https://opinionator.blogs.nytimes.com/2009/10/21/the-case-of-the-inappropriate-alarm-clock-part-4/. Accessed 14 November 2021.
Naremore, James. 2014a. *An Invention Without a Future: Essays on Cinema*. Berkeley, CA: University of California Press.
Naremore, James. 2014b. "The Cinema According to James Agee." *New England Review* 35 (2): 100–15.

Nelson, Robert S., and Richard Shiff, eds. 1996. *Critical Terms for Art History*. Chicago and London: The University of Chicago Press.
Night of the Hunter. 1955. Written by James Agee. Directed by Charles Laughton. USA: Paul Gregory Productions.
Nightmare on Elm Street. 1984. Written and directed by Wes Craven. USA: New Line Cinema.
Notorious. 1946. Written by Ben Hecht. Directed by Alfred Hitchcock. USA: RKO Radio Pictures.
O'Malley, Sheila. 2019. "Present Tense: Frank O'Hara at the Movies." *Film Comment*, 2 May. https://www.filmcomment.com/blog/present-tense-frank-ohara-at-the-movies/. Accessed 18 December 2021.
Pinedo, Isabel. 1996. "Recreational Terror: Postmodern Elements of the Contemporary Horror Film." *Journal of Film and Video* 48 (1–2): 17–31.
Price, Steven. 2013. *A History of the Screenplay*. London: Palgrave Macmillan.
Quai de Brumes. 1938. Written by Jacques Prévert. Directed by Marcel Carné. France: Cine-Alliance.
Richard Taruskin. 2005. *The Oxford History of Western Music. Vol. 1: The Earliest Notations to the Sixteen Century*. Oxford: Oxford University Press.
Ricoeur, Paul. 1979. "The Human Experience of Time and Narrative." *Research in Phenomenology* 9: 17–34.
Robbins, Ben. 2014. "The Pragmatic Modernist: William Faulkner's Craft and Hollywood's Networks of Production." *Journal of Screenwriting* 5 (2): 239–57.
Scarface. 1932. Written by Ben Hecht. Directed by Howard Hawks. USA: The Caddo Company.
Schleifer, Ronald. 2000. *Modernism and Time: The Logic of Abundance in Literature, Science, and Culture 1880–1930*. Cambridge: Cambridge University Press.
Sherlock Jr. 1924. Written by Clyde Bruckman, Jean Havez, and Joseph A. Mitchell. Directed by Buster Keaton. USA: Buster Keaton Productions.
Skelton, Shannon Blake. 2019. *Wes Craven: Interviews*. Jackson, MS: University of Mississippi Press.
Stevens, George Jr. 2014. *Conversations at the American Film Institute with the Great Moviemakers: The Next Generation*. New York: Knopf.
Tarkovsky, Andrey. 1989. *Sculpting in Time*. Austin, TX: University of Texas Press.
The African Queen. 1951. Written by James Agee and John Huston. Directed by John Huston. USA: Romulus Films, Horizon Pictures.
The Front Page. 1931. Written by Ben Hecht. Directed by Lewis Milestone. USA: The Caddo Company.
The Princess Bride. 1987. Written by William Goldman. Directed by Rob Reiner. USA: Act III Communications, Buttercup Films, The Princess Bride Ltd.
The Quiet One. 1948. Written by James Agee. Directed by Sidney Meyers. USA: Film Documents.
The Shop Around the Corner. 1940. Written by Samuel Raphaelson. Directed by Ernst Lubitsch. USA: MGM.
Tieber, Claus. 2019. "Walter Reisch: The Musical Writer." *Journal of Screenwriting* 10 (3): 295–306.
Virgin Spring [Jungfrukällan]. 1960. Written by Ulla Isaksson. Directed by Ingmar Bergman. Sweden: Svensk Filmindustri.
Vorkapich, Slavko. 1950. "Creative Use of the Motion Picture." *Educational Theatre Journal*, 2 (2): 142–47.

Walker, Evans, and Paul Cummings. 1971. "Oral History Interview with Walker Evans, 1971, Oct. 13–Dec, 23." Smithsonian Institution Archives of American Art. https://www.aaa.si.edu/download_pdf_transcript/ajax?record_id=edanmdm-AAADCD_oh_212650. Accessed 8 August 2022.

Wilbur, Richard. 1967. "A Poet at the Movies." In *Man and the Movies*, edited by William R. Robinson, 223–26. Baton Rouge, LA: Louisiana State University Press.

CHAPTER 8

The Motion Picture Screenplay as Data: Quantifying the Stylistic Differences Between Dialogue and Scene Text

Warren Buckland

8.1 INTRODUCTION

The digital humanities employ statistics to facilitate the exact and rigorous study of linguistic features in all text types. Statistical methods reduce a text to data by quantifying its features, which are represented in numerical form in order to identify stylistic patterns and to generate new insights from those patterns. Unlike traditional qualitative analysis, a quantitative statistical analysis does not define the literary quality or general style of a text; nor does it focus on linguistic meaning or rhetorical effects or an author's worldview. Whereas a qualitative study is usually small scale and interpretive, a quantitative statistical analysis is large scale and systematic, reducing texts to data to discover stylistic patterns that are difficult for humans to perceive. A quantitative statistical analysis defines style numerically, in terms of frequencies and percentages, which can precisely measure a text's deviation from a norm. For N. E. Enkvist:

> Style is concerned with frequencies of linguistic items in a given context, and thus with *contextual* probabilities. To measure the style of a passage, the frequencies of its linguistic items of different levels must be compared with the corresponding features in another text or corpus which is regarded as a norm and which has a definite relationship with this passage. (Enkvist 1964, quoted in Culpeper 2014, 10; emphasis in the original)

W. Buckland (✉)
Oxford Brookes University, Oxford, UK
e-mail: wbuckland@brookes.ac.uk

A quantitative statistical analysis, therefore, defines style as a set of measurable patterns in linguistic features that deviate from a contextually defined norm—a context comprising either another text or a large reference corpus. Enkvist calls these numerically defined stylistic elements "style markers," and Jonathan Culpeper calls them "keywords." These style markers are, therefore, identified by their very low or very high frequency in relation to a predefined norm. But a statistical analysis can only measure linguistic features if they are quantifiable, computable, high rate, multiple, distinctive, and stable. The software program *LIWC* (Linguistic Inquiry and Word Count) developed by James Pennebaker, Ryan L. Boyd, Kayla Jordan, and Kate Blackburn is employed in this chapter to carry out these analytical tasks[1]; it measures and quantifies several linguistic features of texts, including grammatical categories such as pronouns, verbs, prepositions, and function words, together with punctuation, informal expressions, and words expressing positive or negative sentiment. The software also identifies different types of vocabulary related to social, cognitive, psychological, and biological processes, and personal concerns (such as work, home, leisure, and money). After quantifying the linguistic features of texts, Pennebaker and his colleagues carry out a qualitative—primarily psychological—interpretation of the numerical data. The *LIWC* program enables such qualitative interpretations to be more rigorous and in-depth.

Taking Claudia Sternberg's pioneering qualitative textual study of screenplays as its starting point (Sternberg 1997), this study isolates, measures, and quantifies a combination of relevant linguistic features from one of the most famous screenplays in the history of cinema—*Citizen Kane* (Herman J. Mankiewicz and Orson Welles, 1941)—to identify the linguistic differences between two of its major components, what Sternberg calls dialogue and scene text. In the following analysis, the relative frequency of the linguistic features of each component is generated in *LIWC*, and the two sets of results are compared to each other. These results are represented numerically as relative frequencies and ratio differences and are visualized in tables and graphs. Yet, qualitative analysis is not neglected in this study; toward the end a small-scale qualitative interpretation of the quantitative data generated by *LIWC* is carried out, an analysis that examines the way the specific spatial vocabulary (especially prepositions) in dialogue and scene text describes a coherent visual and aural storyworld.

8.2 Dialogue and Scene Text

The distinction between dialogue and scene text in screenplays is well-established and uncontentious. Claudia Sternberg distinguishes them in the following way: "dialogue text includes character speech (also off-screen and voice-over) and the scene text encompasses all other instructions, including all

---

[1] *LIWC* is available at http://liwc.wpengine.com/.

dialogue and character cues that are linked to passages of dialogue" (1997, 65–66). The two *Citizen Kane* components analyzed in this chapter are divided according to this distinction, although character cues (name of speaker) and dialogue continuity cues at the top and bottom of pages (*more* and *cont'd*) are excluded from the screenplay because they are standard formatting issues that do not constitute a stylistic choice.

Dialogue plays multiple roles in a screenplay. For example, Syd Field points out that, among other functions, it "moves the story forward," "reveals information about the characters," "establishes character relationships," and discloses "conflicts" as well as the "emotional states" of characters (Field 2005, 244). And in his comprehensive overview of dialogue, Robert McKee identifies three types, defined according to whom it is addressed (to others, to oneself, or to the reader) and spells out its three main functions (exposition, characterization, action) (McKee 2016, 12). What unites these forms of dialogue is that they constitute a speech act, "an action taken to satisfy a need or desire" (2016, 13)—an action that, moreover, is either dramatized (acted out) or narratized (addressed to the camera or spoken as a voice-over).

Within digital literary studies, Jonathan Culpeper (2014) employs statistical methods to quantify the dialogue of six characters in Shakespeare's *Romeo and Juliet* in order to discover if any style markers or keywords exist in their dialogue. He determines if the relative frequency of grammatical and lexical features in the speeches of the six characters deviate from one another and from a reference corpus (such as the 100-million-word British National Corpus).[2] Monika Bednarek employs Culpeper's keywords method (as well as concordances, which show the keywords in context) to study the linguistic characteristics of contemporary US television dialogue. She analyzes one episode from 66 different TV series (a corpus of 275,000 words) and classifies dialogue keywords into five categories (2018, 127):

1. Routine formulae (formulaic expressions such as greetings);
2. Interaction in the here-and-now (in which the dialogue is dominated by first- and second-person pronouns);
3. Formal and informal language;
4. Expressivity (emotional, evaluative, emphatic language);
5. Narrative concerns: words and phrases associated with the narrative.

She also raises the issue of the similarities and differences between television dialogue and spontaneous speech, as well as the difference between movie dialogue and dialogue on television.

The screenplay's scene text sections adhere to the thesis of physicalism developed by the logical empiricists (see Neurath 1983). In the physicalist thesis, sentences describe objects and events in terms of their spatio-temporal coordinates—that is, they are defined and verified perceptually, by observation

---

[2] See, for example, the British National Corpus online: http://www.natcorp.ox.ac.uk/.

of their external, public, physical properties. Like screenwriters, the logical empiricists reduced the unobservable (abstract entities or unverifiable personal inner states—such as the perceiver's own direct immediate experiences) to the language of the observable. Claudia Sternberg develops a nuanced analysis of scene text by dividing it into three components: description, report, and commentary. She defines description as "passages which describe the setting and objects to be visualized on the screen" (1997, 71). For example, the Prologue of *Citizen Kane* describes Xanadu from various distances, both from the exterior and from the interior:

```
Camera travels up what is now shown to be a gateway of gigantic
proportions and holds on the top of it - a huge initial "K"
showing darker and darker against the dawn sky. Through this
and beyond we see the fairy-tale mountaintop of Xanadu, the
great castle a silhouette at its summit, the little window a
distant accent in the darkness.
```
(In Kael, Mankiewicz, and Welles 1971, 91)

Description conveys the setting almost frozen in time. The report mode, instead, "is typified by events and their temporal sequence and generally centers on the actions of human beings" (1997, 72). In other words, the report mode uses verbs to convey actions and events unfolding in the story:

```
A hand - Kane's hand, which has been holding the ball, relaxes.
The ball falls out of his hand and bounds down two carpeted
steps leading to the bed...
```
(In Kael, Mankiewicz, and Welles 1971, 97)

Sternberg defines commentary in screenplays as "passages or parts of sentences which explain, interpret or add to the clearly visible and audible elements of the screenplay" (1997, 73). For example:

```
The dominating note is one of almost exaggerated tropical
lushness, hanging limp and despairing - Moss, moss, moss.
```
(In Kael, Mankiewicz, and Welles 1971, 95)

Such sentences do not describe physical settings or report on actions but instead convey an abstract mood. Commentaries are more literary and authorial than the standardized description and report sections, and screenwriters are not encouraged to adopt this mode of writing.

In solidarity with the logical empiricists' theory of language, Syd Field recommends that "the description paragraph should deal only with what *we see* [and hear]" (2005, 220; emphasis in the original). He elaborates, adding that "many times, the aspiring screenwriter will put various thoughts or feelings of the characters into the stage description, as if we, the reader, need to know what the character is thinking and feeling. If we can't see it through hand or facial gestures, or hear it through the dialogue, don't write it" (2005, 220). Mick Hurbis-Cherrier emphasizes that scene text is written in the present tense and follows the development of the action as it unfolds. Like Field's advice, his guidance on how to write scene text would not look out of place in a logical empiricist's research paper:

> There is no literary commentary in a film script and this necessitates two important practices:
>
> 1. The words on the page present each scene, action, image, character, and series of events to a reader as they would appear to the viewer of the film. […]
> 2. There should be nothing in the script that will not be seen or heard by the film's audience. (2007, 17)

The *Citizen Kane* prologue is written in the present tense, although for a classical Hollywood screenplay it is very long (three pages, with only one word of dialogue—"Rosebud!") and is unusual in that it contains commentary as well as description and report.

8.3 Method

The linguistic features in the written text must be measurable or countable, preferably automatically by a computer. The features need not only be countable but also unambiguous and computable. Features become unambiguous when the methods and finite series of procedures used to define them are spelled out and used consistently. A linguistic feature is computable when it can be subjected to a series of calculations that manipulate and transform it. If the features are countable and computable, they also need to score at a sufficiently high rate. Additionally, if these high-rate features are common elements of language, this means they are shared by many text types; different texts can, therefore, be compared according to the frequency of these shared features. No single feature distinguishes one text type from another; several features need to be analyzed to differentiate between text types. Furthermore, these distinctive features need to be linked to style rather than to random or general features of language. Finally, such a study needs to focus on those features that are stable and robust—that is, consistent and regular.

What aspects of a written text can be quantified or understood numerically? The following textual parameters are quantifiable: different word categories such as pronouns, function (grammatical) words, content (lexical) words, modal verbs, and intensifiers (*so, very, really, completely*, etc.); hedges (words such as *apparently, appears, likely, maybe, might, often,* and *partly* that express the speaker's uncertainty); synonymous word pairs (*on / upon, while / whilst,* etc.); word length, sentence length, punctuation, etc. In an analytical language such as English, function words (*on, to, in, of*, etc.) are important because they signal grammatical relations (unlike synthetic languages, which signal grammatical relations via inflection). In studying common function words, it is not simply their presence or absence that defines style, because they are present in all texts. Instead, it is their frequency. In more technical terms, it is not a matter of possessing or not possessing attributes but about identifying patterns of variability in the frequency of those attributes. This is one of the main goals of statistics: to study patterns of variability in data (which makes it pertinent to the study of style) and to reduce huge amounts of data to a manageable size. There is no fixed universal quantitative test for style; one needs to apply numerous tests to a text to determine the text's dominant and distinctive stylistic attributes.

The *LIWC* software measures and quantifies 92 linguistic categories (which Pennebaker and his colleagues call "specialized dictionaries"), including:

> 4 summary language variables (analytical thinking, clout, authenticity, and emotional tone), 3 general descriptor categories (words per sentence, percent of target words captured by the dictionary, and percent of words in the text that are longer than six letters), 21 standard linguistic dimensions (e.g., percentage of words in the text that are pronouns, articles, auxiliary verbs, etc.), 41 word categories tapping psychological constructs (e.g., affect, cognition, biological processes, drives), 6 personal concern categories (e.g., work, home, leisure activities), 5 informal language markers (assents, fillers, swear words, netspeak [and nonfluencies]), and 12 punctuation categories (periods, commas, etc). (Pennebaker et al. 2015, 2)

Pennebaker adds that the four summary variables "are the only nontransparent dimensions in the LIWC2015 output" (2015, 6), which is why I decided not to use them in this study. In its analysis of text, the LIWC software calculates the relative frequency of the linguistic features in each category, by dividing their observed frequency into the frequency of all the linguistic features in the text and then converting the sum into a percentage in order to standardize the results (enabling comparisons to be made between different-sized data sets). For example, the first-person plural pronoun category contains three words: *we, us,* and *our* (including *ourselves* and *let's*). In the *Citizen Kane* dialogue file, the observed frequency of first-person plural pronouns is 116 words; the dialogue file contains 13,988 words; the relative frequency of first-person plural pronouns in the dialogue file is therefore 116 / 13,988 × 100 = 0.83%.

LIWC is useful because it quickly generates the relative frequency of the 92 linguistic categories. In addition, Pennebaker and his colleagues interpret these categories in terms of personal and social psychology. Whereas the relative frequencies are descriptive, psychological dimension of their theory is more speculative (that is, inferential). For example, Pennebaker argues that the high frequency of articles (*a, an, the*), prepositions (*by, to, with, at, above*, etc.), and nouns is associated with concrete and analytical writing, for this group of words—which he calls the noun cluster (2011, 70–72)—creates formal and precise descriptions of objects, events, and plans in specific spatio-temporal coordinates. Furthermore, the related function words comprising prepositions and conjunctions (*and, but, whereas*, etc.) are associated with cognitive complexity, for several propositions are conjoined in the same sentence.

The opposite of this concrete and analytical writing style is an informal and personal type of writing, dominated by a high frequency of pronouns, verbs, auxiliary verbs (*is, have, do*, etc.), and hedges. For Pennebaker, this informal style—which he calls the pronoun-verb cluster (2011, 70–72)—reflects a dynamic storytelling mode of language. Pennebaker argues that, if first-person pronouns (*I, me, my*) are present at a high rate, this may signify greater focus on self-reporting—on conveying one's inner emotional states (such as depression).

These distinctions set up expectations, where one would predict dialogue to be more informal than scene text, with a higher rate of pronouns, verbs, and adverbs (pronoun-verb clusters), while scene text is expected to manifest a higher rate of articles, prepositions, and nouns (noun clusters). The remainder of this chapter tests these expectations by presenting a selection of results from *LIWC*, especially style markers or keywords that distinguish dialogue from scene text.

8.4 Results

Table 8.1 presents a selection from the 92 linguistic categories in the dialogue and scene text of the *Citizen Kane* screenplay. The *LIWC* software generates the relative frequency of each linguistic category, and the ratio between them is calculated by dividing one into the other (with dialogue on top, in the numerator position). Ratio identifies style by measuring the distinctiveness of each category. Table 8.1 is organized according to the size of the ratio, with the top and bottom of the table presenting the most distinctive categories, while the less distinctive categories are in the middle. Figure 8.1 visually presents the relative frequencies of the linguistic categories in the dialogue and scene text presented in Table 8.1 (minus word count, whose high value would skew the scale of the graph). The left side of the graph (from *second-person pronoun* to *third-person plural pronoun*) shows the values prominent in the dialogue and the right side reveals the values prominent in the scene text. Figure 8.2 presents the ratios between the dialogue and scene text using a logarithmic

Table 8.1 A selection of linguistic categories in *Citizen Kane*'s dialogue and scene text (organized according to ratio)

Linguistic category	LIWC mean (%)	Citizen Kane dialogue (%)	Citizen Kane scene text (%)	Ratio
2nd person	1.70	4.76	0.06	79.33
1st-person singular	4.99	5.29	0.16	33.06
Auxiliary verb	8.53	11.88	3.79	3.13
Personal pronouns	9.95	14.27	4.88	2.92
1st-person plural	0.72	0.83	0.29	2.86
Impersonal pronouns	5.26	6.84	2.78	2.46
Verb	16.44	21.36	10.05	2.13
3rd-person plural	0.66	0.69	0.35	1.97
Word count	–	53.9 (13,988)	46.1 (11,957)	1.17
Time	5.46	4.73	5.48	0.86
Preposition	12.93	11.75	16.22	0.72
3rd-person singular	1.88	2.70	4.01	0.67
Motion	2.15	1.91	3.06	0.62
Sentence length	17.40	9.04	14.83	0.61
Article	6.51	5.88	9.76	0.60
Space	6.89	5.25	12.99	0.40

scale (with word count reinstated).[3] A ratio value of one signifies no difference in the relative frequency of a linguistic feature in the dialogue and in the scene text (in which case that feature is not a marker of style), while a ratio of two signifies twice the relative frequency of a linguistic feature in the dialogue as in the scene text. A ratio value below one simply signifies the opposite: that the relative frequency of a linguistic feature is lower in dialogue than in scene text. For example, the ratio for *space*—0.40—signifies almost two-and-a-half times as much linguistic features relating to space (*down, in*, etc.) in the scene text than in the dialogue. Figure 8.2 shows that *second-person pronouns* and *first-person singular pronouns* are stylistic outliers, due to their very high frequency in dialogue relative to their low (almost non-existent) frequency in scene text.

The *LIWC mean* (in the second column of Table 8.1) derives from the report "The Development and Psychometric Properties of LIWC2015" (Pennebaker et al. 2015). It refers to the unweighted means of six genres of writing (blogs, expressive writing, novels, natural speech, *The New York Times*,

---

[3] Plotting ratios as histograms using a linear number scale creates problems because ratios below 1 appear asymmetrical. For example, the ratio for *space* is 0.4, for there are 2.5 times more spatial words in the scene text than in dialogue. But 0.4 is represented as a small magnitude on a linear number scale. To represent the magnitudes of the ratios below 1 correctly, the ratio values need to undergo log transformation—that is, must be converted to logarithms (and the baseline set at 1, which means ratio values below 1 appear underneath the baseline).

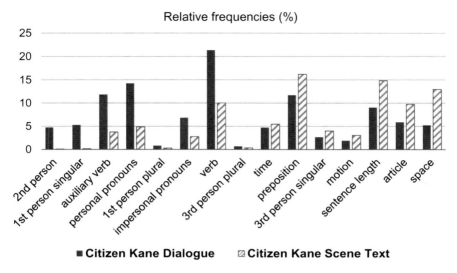

Fig. 8.1 Bar graph of the numerical data in Table 8.1

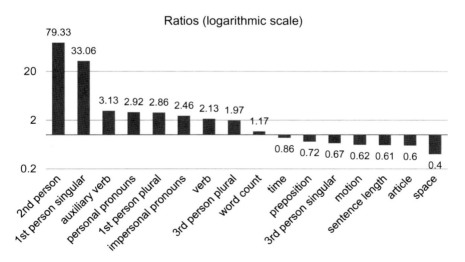

Fig. 8.2 Ratio (logarithmic scale) between dialogue and scene text

and Twitter) comprising a total of 231 million words, that Pennebaker and his colleagues used to test the 2015 version of the software. I have added the *LIWC mean* values to the table for comparative purposes, following Enkvist's advice quoted above ("To measure the style of a passage, the frequencies of its linguistic items of different levels must be compared with the corresponding features in another text or corpus which is regarded as a norm"). While it is possible to limit this study to a comparison of the results from the dialogue and scene text in *Citizen Kane*, the *LIWC mean* values represent the norm from a large reference corpus, a baseline presenting a broader context in which to understand the relative frequencies in *Citizen Kane*. On occasions I will also refer to the value of an individual genre of writing within this large reference corpus.

Word count occupies the middle of the table, with a small ratio of 1.17, which indicates that the volume of words in both dialogue and scene text is similar: dialogue comprises 13,988 words (53.9% of the screenplay total) and scene text comprises 11,957 words (46.1%). Finally, the length of sentences in the dialogue averages out at 9.04 words, and in scene text the average is 14.83 words. However, sentence-length analysis of screenplays can be problematic due to their layout, for different sections of text are marked by formatting rather than punctuation. Nonetheless, because it is the difference between dialogue and scene text that is most important rather than the actual numerical value of sentence length, comparison remains a viable option.

8.5   Discussion

In terms of relative frequency, *Citizen Kane*'s dialogue is dominated by *verbs* (21.36%), *personal pronouns* (14.27%), *auxiliary verbs* (11.88%), and *prepositions* (11.75%). Scene text is dominated by *prepositions* (16.22%), *sentence length* (14.83 words), *verbs* (10.05%), and *articles* (9.76%). Although *verbs* appear in both dialogue and scene text, the difference between them is still large (a ratio of 2.13 to 1 in favor of dialogue) and *auxiliary verbs* are also prominent in dialogue by a ratio of 3.13 to 1. In other words, both verb types distinguish dialogue from scene text. Prepositions also appear in both, with one-third more in scene text than in dialogue. It is not surprising that dialogue sentences are shorter than scene text sentences, for speech conventionally consists of a series of short statements, while descriptions of settings and objects and reports of actions and temporal events are usually much longer (conforming to the noun cluster, complete with prepositions specifying the spatio-temporal relations between the settings, objects, actions, and events).

Dialogue shares many features with the pronoun-verb cluster. The high percentage of verbs in the dialogue of *Citizen Kane* (over twice as many as in the scene text and 5% higher than the *LIWC* norm) points to dynamic storytelling moving the stories along—in the present (Thompson interviewing Kane's acquaintances) and in the past (accounts of Kane's multiple activities and ambitions). Both stories conclude in Thompson's summation of Kane's life at the end of the film, a typical example of narrative dialogue full of verbs and auxiliary verbs (which *LIWC* highlights):

> Charles Foster Kane **was** a man who **got** everything he **wanted**, and then **lost** it. Maybe Rosebud **was** something he **couldn't get** or something he **lost**, but it **wouldn't have explained** anything.

> I **don't think** any word **explains** a man's life. No – I **guess** Rosebud **is** just a piece in a jigsaw puzzle – a missing piece.
>
> (In Kael, Mankiewicz, and Welles 1971, 294)

The overall ratio of pronouns in the *Citizen Kane* dialogue compared to the *LIWC* norm is 1.5 to 1—that is, 50% higher in the *Citizen Kane* dialogue than in the *LIWC* 231-million-word sample. The LIWC norm is made up of six genres of writing—including Natural Speech, which scores 13.37% (Pennebaker et al. 2015, 10). The percentage of personal pronouns in the *Citizen Kane* dialogue (14.27%) is very close to natural speech. The exact same frequencies are also evident in auxiliary verbs: over three times as many in *Citizen Kane*'s dialogue than in scene text, and the dialogue percentage (11.88%) is higher than the *LIWC* norm (8.53%) but is close to natural speech (12.03%) (Pennebaker et al. 2015, 10). Thompson's speech about Kane's life is light on pronouns (three third-person and two first-person singular pronouns), because he is primarily talking to himself, although he is also indirectly offering a summation of the story to the reader. The dialogue between Kane and Susan on their first meeting is more interactive (the following extract contains the dialogue only):

> **You** poor kid, **you** are in pain, aren't **you**?
> Look at **me**.
> Why don't **you** laugh? **I**'m just as funny in here as **I** was on the street.
> **I** know, but **you** don't like **me** to laugh at **you**.
> **I** don't like **your** tooth to hurt, either.
> **I** can't help it.
> Come on, laugh at **me**.
> **I** can't – what are **you** doing?
> **I**'m wiggling both **my** ears at the same time.
>
> (In Kael, Mankiewicz, and Welles 1971, 204)

Every line in this exchange contains first- and second-person pronouns, with Kane referring to Susan (*you*) four times and to himself (*I, me*) three times in the first three lines alone, indicating strong personal engagement between the two characters. Closer inspection reveals that Kane dominates this exchange: he utters the first three lines, while Susan responds non-verbally to the first two (she sits down and looks at Kane) and when she does speak, she only responds to his questions (although other sections of their conversion are more evenly balanced).

Scene text shares many features of what Pennebaker calls the noun cluster: a low frequency of verbs, auxiliary verbs, and pronouns, and a high frequency of articles, prepositions, and nouns in long and more complex sentences that link several propositions to produce descriptions of specific locations, objects, events, and plans. It is no surprise that the relative frequencies of first-person singular and second-person pronouns are almost non-existent in scene text since this section of a screenplay does not describe the story from a personal perspective or in terms of the verbal interaction of characters. The corresponding ratio values for these pronouns are almost off the chart (Fig. 8.2). It is no surprise either that the ratio between articles in dialogue and in scene text in *Citizen Kane* is 0.6 to 1; in other words, scene text (9.74%) contains two-thirds more articles than dialogue (5.88%). The *LIWC* norm is 6.51%. But, again, it is more useful to examine the individual scores of each genre: the score for Novels is 8.35% and for Natural Speech it is 4.34% (Pennebaker et al. 2015, 10). The comparison of novels to scene text is only approximate, for it assumes that novels are dominated by narration and description rather than dialogue. Nonetheless, these *LIWC* percentages for articles mirror the percentages in *Citizen Kane*:

- *Citizen Kane* scene text: 9.74% / *LIWC* novels: 8.35%.
- *Citizen Kane* dialogue: 5.88% / *LIWC* natural speech: 4.34%.

Citizen Kane also mirrors the *LIWC* results in terms of prepositions. The ratio between the prepositions in dialogue and in scene text in *Citizen Kane* is 0.83 to 1, for *Citizen Kane*'s scene text (16.22%) contains one-third more prepositions than dialogue (11.75%). The *LIWC* norm for prepositions is 12.93%, while the score for Novels is 14.27% and Natural Speech is 10.29% (Pennebaker et al. 2015, 10):

- *Citizen Kane* scene text: 16.22% / *LIWC* novels: 14.27%.
- *Citizen Kane* dialogue: 11.75% / *LIWC* natural speech: 10.29%.

LIWC successfully quantifies the difference between scene text and dialogue in the *Citizen Kane* screenplay and shows the similar relative frequency of scene text and novels, on the one hand, and dialogue and natural speech, on the other.

The relativity category (space, time, motion) is also relevant because scene text conforms to the physicalist thesis of the logical empiricists, in that this section of a screenplay defines objects and events in terms of their physical appearance and their spatio-temporal coordinates. One would, therefore, expect space, time, and motion words to have a higher frequency in scene text than in dialogue. However, the time category is very similar in both, with a ratio of 0.86 to 1, suggesting that characters talk about time almost as much as the screenwriters write about it in the scene text. Motion is more distinctive, with a ratio of 0.60 to 1, or two-thirds more in scene text than in dialogue, while linguistic terms relating to space and spatial location are significantly higher in scene text than in dialogue—a ratio of 0.40 to 1, almost two-and-a-half times as much (see Table 8.2). Spatial words are also significantly higher

Table 8.2 The relativity category in *Citizen Kane*'s dialogue and scene text (organized according to ratio)

Linguistic category	LIWC mean	Citizen Kane *dialogue*	Citizen Kane *scene text*	Ratio
Space	6.89	5.25	12.99	0.40
Motion	2.15	1.91	3.06	0.62
Time	5.46	4.73	5.48	0.86

in *Citizen Kane*'s scene text than in the *LIWC* norm.[4] The following extract (dialogue omitted) is set in the Chicago office of the *Inquirer* after Susan's debut at the Chicago Opera House (*LIWC* highlights the spatial words in bold):

> Kane crosses the **length** of the **long city room** to the glass **door** indicated before by the hireling. The **city** editor looks **at** Bernstein. Kane **opens** the **door** and goes **into** the office, closing the **door behind** him
> (A **long** pause; finally …)
> (Starts **toward** the **door**)
> Dissolve **Out**
> Dissolve **In**
>
> (In Kael, Mankiewicz, and Welles 1971, 238)

This fragment of scene text is written primarily in what Claudia Sternberg calls the report mode, for it presents a temporal sequence focused on character actions. Yet, description is also evident. The spatial vocabulary includes prepositions that define the physical relation between two or more entities in space. For example, *at* links two points in space, the city editor to Bernstein, and *behind* links three points, Kane, the door, and the reader (and implies that the door blocks the spectator's vision, discussed below). Both prepositions define spatial relations statically. The preposition *toward* signifies movement along a line or surface in addition to spatial relation, and *into* signifies movement into a three-dimensional volumetric container. The fragment also contains descriptive spatial words (the noun *length,* the adjective *long*) that describe the city room as an extended horizontal space (compare with spatial words that describe an extended vertical space—such as *tall* building or *high* ceiling). It also names specific spaces (*city, room*) and objects that demarcate spatial boundaries (*door*). The syntactic configuration of this extract, therefore, links

---

[4] Story time and location are also stated in a screenplay's Scene Headings, which indicate whether the scene is an interior (INT.) or exterior (EXT.), and whether it takes place during the DAY or NIGHT. For example, the first scene heading in the *Citizen Kane* screenplay spells out the location, time of day, and the year: "EXT. XANADU – FAINT DAWN – 1940" (in Kael, Mankiewicz, and Welles 1971, 91).

a series of actions (*crossing, looking, opening, going, closing, starting*) to characters (*Kane, the city editor, Bernstein*) via prepositions (*at, behind, toward, into*), all taking place within a well-defined space (a long city room with a glass door at the far end).

The precise definition of spatial relations continues in the next scene, in Leland's office:

> Bernstein comes **in**. An **empty** bottle is standing **on** Leland's desk. He has fallen asleep **over** his typewriter, his face **on** the keys. A sheet of paper is **in** the machine. A paragraph has been typed. Kane is standing **at** the other **side** of the desk looking **down at** him. This is the first time we see murder **in** Kane's face. Bernstein looks **at** Kane, then crosses to Leland. He shakes him.
>
> (In Kael, Mankiewicz, and Welles 1971, 238)

Prepositions again situate the events in space: from *in* the office to *on* the desk to *over* the typewriter to *in* the machine, *at* the other side and down *at*. Once Bernstein enters the scene, the sentences become descriptive—the prepositions describe a static moment in time—but the description is also charged with narrative significance, for it juxtaposes a series of visual details (empty bottle, face on the keyboard, paper in the typewriter, a paragraph of text) to convey an implicit sequence of narrative events (that Leland has not written his review but has fallen asleep because he is drunk).

Like all screenplays, each scene is written to be visualized from a specific vantage point. This does not mean that technical terminology (camera placement, angle, etc.) should be used to define the scene; instead, it is the spatial vocabulary that creates this viewpoint. In the city room scene, Kane traverses the long room and enters the office. The reader is positioned in the city room, and Kane moves away from the spectator and *goes into* the office, disappearing from sight (compare to *Kane comes into the office*). The verb *to close* and the preposition *behind* collectively signify the spectator's lack of visual access to Kane. This is because Kane is in front of the door, and by closing it behind him, the door becomes a barrier that blocks the spectator's view of him (assuming, of course, that the glass door is made of frosted glass—which it is in the film). The description of the scene makes it evident that the city editor and Bernstein are also visible (and audible) to the spectator in the city room; they exchange a few words before Bernstein follows Kane by walking toward the office door.

In the following scene, the reader is already located in the office, for Bernstein is described as *entering into* the space. The vantage point could have remained in the city room (in which case the text would say that *Bernstein goes into the office*). Although the reader is already in the office, they do not know what is in there until Bernstein enters. Each sentence then presents one visual image mentioned previously (the bottle, Leland asleep on the typewriter, the typed paragraph on the sheet of paper), fragments that add up to create the scene. Kane is located on the *other side* of the desk—that is, opposite—to Leland, looking *down at* him. The spectator and Bernstein see Kane's facial expression, after which Bernstein acts. In this scene text, there is a rare pronoun, *we*, in a sentence that combines description of Kane's face with commentary, in which the narrator provides additional information that is not purely visual: *this is the first time …*

Within the scene text, the prepositions, verbs, and spatial vocabulary work together to evoke a visual and aural storyworld with a heightened sense of spatio-temporal order and coherence because it is described/seen from a distinct vantage point that orients the reader. However, *LIWC* categorizes a temporal use of the word *long* (*long pause*) as a spatial word. Furthermore, it does not highlight the preposition *to* in *to the glass door* and *to Leland*, even though it is a preposition that signifies spatial orientation (Kane's spatial relation to the door, Bernstein's spatial relation to Leland). In addition, *LIWC* does not highlight the word *office*, even though it is a specific space similar to the *city room* (which is, however, classified as two generic spaces—*a city*, and *a room*), and it highlights the verb *open* (Kane opening the door) but does not highlight the opposite action, of closing the door. And, although *LIWC* correctly categorizes the prepositions *in* and *out* in *dissolve in* and *dissolve out* as spatial, these prepositions are not describing space within the storyworld but space on the discursive level (the film transitions from one space to another via dissolves). Many screenplays simply use the words *dissolve to* (rather than *in* and *out*) to signify the same transition. *Citizen Kane* uses *dissolve in* and *dissolve out* 24 times apiece, which inflates the overall frequency of the spatial prepositions *in* and *out* by a few percent. Despite the anomalies generated by *LIWC*, it is evident that spatial terms are key characteristics of scene text in the *Citizen Kane* screenplay. (Studies of other screenplays will need to determine if the relative frequency of spatial words in *Citizen Kane*'s scene text is typical or an anomaly.)

8.6 Conclusions

This chapter has integrated quantitative research methods (relative frequencies and ratios) into the more traditional arts and humanities qualitative scholarship (analysis of dialogue and descriptive passages of text to determine how they create a storyworld). The quantitative framework is evidence based and complements rather than supplants the qualitative framework by making the qualitative analysis more precise and rigorous. Through this combined qualitative-quantitative methodology, we discover that dialogue conforms to the pronoun-verb cluster (an informal, dynamic writing style dominated by a high frequency of pronouns, verbs, auxiliary verbs, and hedges) and scene text conforms to the noun cluster (articles, prepositions, and nouns, which create descriptions of specific locations, objects, events, and plans), with relative frequencies and ratios precisely quantifying the differences between dialogue and scene text. While it is to be expected that dialogue matches the pronoun-verb cluster, the dominance of the noun cluster in scene text is unusual, considering the dynamic nature of the report mode of writing (which uses verbs to report actions). These results indicate that, at least in the scene text of the *Citizen Kane* screenplay, the report mode is subordinate to the descriptive mode (which describes settings and objects). Furthermore, scene text is written from a specific vantage point, evident in the spatial vocabulary that describes the visual dimension of the storyworld. The *LIWC* software systematically draws attention to all instances of this spatial vocabulary (and other word categories), whose high relative frequency (12.92%) in relation to dialogue (5.26%) in the *Citizen Kane* screenplay suggests it should be investigated further and subjected to a qualitative interpretation. Automated word counts carried out by computer software routinely make such discoveries possible.

References

Bednarek, Monika. 2018. *Language and Television Series: A Linguistic Approach to TV Dialogue*. Cambridge: Cambridge University Press.

Citizen Kane. 1941. Written by Herman J. Mankiewicz and Orson Welles. Directed by Orson Welles. USA: Mercury Productions, RKO Radio Pictures.

Culpeper, Jonathan. 2014. "Keywords and Characterization: An Analysis of Six Characters in *Romeo and Juliet*." In *Digital Literary Studies: Corpus Approaches to Poetry, Prose, and Drama*, edited by David L. Hoover, Jonathan Culpeper, and Kieran O'Halloran, 9–34. New York: Routledge.

Enkvist, Nils Erik 1964. "On Defining Style." In *Linguistics and Style*, edited by Nils Erik Enkvist, John Spencer, and Michael J. Gregory, 1–56. Oxford: Oxford University Press.

Field, Syd. 2005. *Screenplay: The Foundations of Screenwriting* Rev. ed. New York: Delta Trade Paperbacks.

Hurbis-Cherrier, Mick. 2007. *Voice and Vision: A Creative Approach to Narrative Film and DV Production*. Amsterdam: Focal Press.

Kael, Pauline, Herman Mankiewicz, and Orson Welles. 1971. *The Citizen Kane Book*. Boston: Little, Brown and Co.

McKee, Robert. 2016. *Dialogue: The Art of Verbal Action for Page, Stage and Screen*. Slingsby, NY: Methuen.

Neurath, Otto. 1983. *Philosophical Papers, 1913–1946*. Dordrecht, Netherlands: D. Reidel.

Pennebaker, James W. 2011. *The Secret Life of Pronouns: What Our Words Say About Us*. New York: Bloomsbury.

Pennebaker, James W., Ryan L. Boyd, Kayla Jordan, and Kate Blackburn. 2015. *The Development and Psychometric Properties of LIWC2015*. Austin: University of Texas at Austin: https://repositories.lib.utexas.edu/bitstream/handle/2152/31333/LIWC2015_LanguageManual.pdf. Accessed 24 May 2022.

Sternberg, Claudia. 1997. *Written for the Screen: The American Motion-Picture Screenplay as Text*. Tübingen: Stauffenburg.

CHAPTER 9

Writer/Reader as Performer: Creating a Negotiated Narrative

Anna Zaluczkowska

9.1 Introduction

There has always been a close relationship between writing for drama/performance and screenwriting, as evidenced by the continued and extensive studies of Aristotle (Laurel 2013; Kallay 2010) in the digital age. However, when we come to consider new forms of media, many suggest the need for new forms of writing (Millard 2014; Murray 2012; Riggs 2019). Kathryn Millard (2014) urges us to look back at past practices, particularly experimental forms, and mine them to discover potential current applications while Stephanie Riggs (2019) asserts that immersive/interactive forms mean the end of storytelling as we know it. These scholars question our understanding of what it is to write for the moving image, that writing for visual and immersive environments is shifting and changing, and that more interesting or pertinent ways can be found to express our ideas. However, even as they decry the end of more classical dramatic forms (Koenitz 2015), most scholars can agree that performative processes are at work in all writing endeavours for digital work. This chapter takes a closer look at dramatic forms and interactive media—asking what performance studies and processes are useful in this context and how. In particular, the chapter looks at the role of the writer and their relationship to the audience by discussing the participative elements which many (see, for instance, Jenkins 2006; Giaovagnoli 2011)

A. Zaluczkowska (✉)
Leeds Beckett University, Leeds, UK
e-mail: anna.zaluczkowska@leedsbeckett.ac.uk

© The Author(s), under exclusive license to Springer Nature Switzerland AG 2023
R. Davies et al. (eds), *The Palgrave Handbook of Screenwriting Studies*,
https://doi.org/10.1007/978-3-031-20769-3_9

say are crucial to most new media forms; it then suggests that we should expand the remit of the writer/creator in interactive work so that elements of performance are embedded in their practice.

Using examples from my own work and the work of other writers and performance makers (Robin MacNicholas, IOU and Blast Theory) engaged in immersive and interactive work, I suggest that writing that is informed/influenced by performance (and, therefore the writer/audience as performer) is an understudied and interesting addition to studies which have concentrated on the narrative, structure (Ryan 2012; Koenitz 2015; Knoller 2019) and systems evidenced in these new forms. Much has been written about the interaction between humans and technology and, while this chapter acknowledges such scholarship and its impact on the participative process, it is my intention to concentrate more fully on the performance processes at work in interactive digital narratives rather than the systems that they engage with. However, the work acknowledges Janet Murray's assertion that interactivity "refers to the combination of the procedural and participatory properties of the digital medium" (Murray 2012, 12). This chapter will therefore, explore performance and especially improvisational forms of performance to also suggest that these are important aspects of a writer's/creator's and

Fig. 9.1 *Secret Story Network* logo (*Source* Bellyfeel Productions)

reader's/user's toolkit in this digital age, especially in relation to interactive, participative or immersive forms of production.

9.2 Theoretical Overview

Brenda Laurel (2013) was one of the first to draw a parallel between the humanities and interactive systems. In fact, she went further than that and suggested a direct link between digital environments and theatrical representations. She argued for "computers as theatre" basing much of her work on performance studies but in particular on the theories of Aristotle. However, she very quickly moved from that position to suggest operational designs and criteria for the evaluations of such experiences. Her ideas have been challenged, tested and often marginalised in more contemporary debates about interactive digital narratives. As Koenitz points out there is a danger of "theoretical imperialism" (Aarseth 1997, 16) because once we focus on the similarities with the ancient Greek stage play, we can overlook the aspects that do not fit that particular frame of reference (2015, 91). And of course, performance studies is a wide-ranging area of concern that encompasses much more than the thinking of Aristotle and one that is as full of ideas as it is of practices. For the purposes of this chapter, it will be necessary to limit our investigations. As Richard Schechner points out: "because performance studies is so broad-ranging and open to new possibilities, no one can actually grasp its totality or press all its vastness and variety into a single book" (2020, 1). There is therefore little hope of doing so in this chapter: instead, I propose to investigate some of the ideas of Augusto Boal, Bertolt Brecht, Keith Johnson, Cecily O'Neill and Jerzy Grotowski, ideas that challenge the relationship between the audience and the author, to see how they can help us understand the writer/user relationship more fully and the processes that will help promote interactivity.

Grotowski suggests that theatre cannot exist without the actor-spectator relationship of perceptual, direct, "'live' communion" (2002, 19). Grotowski wanted to establish the primacy of the actor and actor's body where the audience is immersed in the performance through the liveness of the actors. The question in an interactive context becomes one of how we can replicate such a liveness in an online environment. Josephine Machon suggests that it is this liveness that characterises immersive theatre: "it is this awakening of the holistic sentience of the human body in immersive theatres that allows for an immediate and intimate connection with the ideas as much as with the artists and other participants in that immersive world" (2013, 279).

Where Brecht drew our attention to the artifice of drama and the dramatic production, Grotowski saw the play as an event that was an encounter with the actor as a human being. He suggested that theatre becomes "a place of provocation" (Grotowski 1969, 21). In his Theatre Laboratory, the audience was assigned a role to be judges and to support the actors. As a result, much of his practice and training was achieved through the use and application of improvisation. Brecht and Boal were perhaps more interested in the relationship between the theatre and the audience although for them this was also a political issue. Where Brecht was interested in analysing the product of production, Boal was interested in the process of making theatre to open up the possibilities of change. As such, he has much to offer the world of interactive production, regardless of whether its intention is political. Boal's work (1979) contains a compilation of *gamexercises* and improvisation work. For example, he uses the Joker system in both conventional play and his participative work as a way to disrupt roles of the audience and cast:

> The Joker has two main functions in a conventional play: Brechtian estrangement and intercontextual translation. In line with Brecht's theory, the Joker system destroys the individual actor's private ownership of a character. (McLaverty-Robinson 2017, n.p.)

The games aimed to help actors and what he later called "spectators" to engage together but, in the process, they would draw on improvisation in a way similar to that suggested by Johnstone in his seminal work *Impro* (1987), with games and techniques often made available to "non-actors" as an educational support and part of a development process. Such techniques have been used globally and are often known as process work or forum theatre, where participants are encouraged to articulate their concerns. This process theatre draws heavily on improvisational forms to achieve its ends.

Since Brenda Laurel's contribution, the debate has moved to explore structuralist and post-structuralist (Landow 1997; Bolter 2001) ideas of narrative and its relationship to digital media and authorship along with semiotic (Ferri 2015) and narratological (Ryan 2006) interpretations of interactive digital narratives and the adaptions and combinations that could be useful in applying these theories. Much criticism has been levelled at such ideas, suggesting that they are based on narrow definitions of *classical* or *traditional* storytelling that does not acknowledge many alternative models, such as cyclical African oral storytelling forms, Asian structures with different tension arcs and forms of participatory theatre as advocated by Boal. More recently, Koenitz (2015) challenges the adaptations of these classical theories, saying the "notion of what constitutes a well-formed plot… is in conflict with the concept of interaction" (96). Instead, he proposes that we change the artistic focus from product to process and in doing so concentrate on what he calls the "system, process and product" (Koenitz 2015, 96). The system being the interactive artefact which is made up of the software (programming code) and hardware (the computer, tablet, phone, plus keyboard, mice) that make up the digital interface and the process is what is created once the user starts to engage with the system (one walkthrough of the experience). This in turn creates the product/narrative of one instance of this process engagement. Therefore, different products can originate from the same system. He (among many others including Riggs) suggests a new vocabulary and terms (protostory, narrative design and narrative vectors) to describe what is happening in these narratives.

Riggs (2019) separates the ideas of story and narrative (as many have done from the Russian formalists and before) suggesting that "narrative involves the human capacity for creating meaning or forming an interpretation; 'story' is the events that are interpreted to create that meaning" (131). This is a particularly important distinction, she argues, in the interactive experience as, while story elements may remain the same, the resulting narratives are very different in each immersive or interactive experience. She therefore suggests that terms such as frame, director, audience, author, audio-visual, film and linear that are common to most theories relating to written and aural works be reimagined in interactive forms with terms such as worlds, creators, guests, agency, psychological experience and dynamic. She uses the concept of "storyplexing" and suggests storyplexing tools which she has distilled from observations of hundreds of projects (Riggs 2019) and which she believes should be adapted to the jobs at hand in immersive projects: "The Storyplex is a dynamic network that balances the traditions of storytelling, human psychology and the affordances of computational systems to create an immersive narrative" (151). Riggs's toolbox consists of three sections—technology, creators and participants—her work mirroring many of the concerns of performance studies. In this way her thinking is similar to that of Koenitz, who uses terms such as protostory, narrative design and narrative vectors as terms that capture the specifics of interactive digital narratives.

Janet Murray also defines interactive narratives through their affordances—the procedural, participative, spatial and encyclopaedic nature of such narratives. She talks further about agency, immersion and the transformation that the user experiences in such narratives, making an important distinction between interactivity and agency: "The appropriate design goal for interactive environments is not the degree of interactivity, but whether or not the system creates the satisfying experience of agency" (Murray 2011, 12). This, she suggests, is most effectively achieved when computer processing and human-directed participation fit together well (Murray 2011, 100) and result in the pleasure of making something happen in a responsive world. It is in this context that performance processes help us to understand what that responsive world needs to offer. Once again process and participation are crucial to Murray's understanding of the working of interactive digital narratives.

Koenitz further suggests that the processes of interactive environments have not yet been fully investigated and that more work is necessary: "In this particular area a look at performance studies should be productive" (Koenitz 2015, 102).

I develop some of Laurel's ideas by broadening the scope from drama to areas of performance studies such as the "liveness" of Grotowski, the questioning of the author/audience dynamic of Brecht and Boal and various improvisational forms from Johnstone and others to examine how useful they are in illuminating the process of interactive digital design. In looking at examples of interactive work, I consider how the storyworld or the storyplex impact on the creation of an idea and the design or writing of that idea to discover what that means for the writer.

9.3 Projects

Schechner suggests that a performance is more than the public performance we see when we go to see a play or dance, and consists of what happens both before and after that event—what he terms proto-performance, performance and aftermath. Indeed, the same notions can also be attributed to film where we see trailers, reviews and prepare ourselves for the cinematic experience. It is common to many other forms of public performance. Riggs (2019, 116) calls this the "Ritual of Story" which begins with "The Gathering" and starts when we first hear of a story, all elements that encourage us to physically or virtually come together. This is followed by "The Transition" where ritualistic signals prepare us for the performance—lights dimming, curtains opening; before "The Opening" which suggests what we may expect from the performance. Riggs says such traditions are as useful to interactive work which often features the pre-production and setting up of the world as much as the actual performance. The real world can be merged with the fictional world to prepare us to take part and, once we have taken part the performance, is followed up by a discussion, workshop or some distribution of by-products that is central to interactive endeavour. For example, in the Royal Shakespeare Company production *Dream* (2020), an online interactive playing of *Midsummer Night's Dream*, such theatrical and filmic traditions are fused so the audience/players are introduced to the making of the work as a prelude to the performance and then the actors enter the performance and are transformed into their characters. After the show we can visit the website, live and pre-recorded content to see details of construction and performance and ask questions in the live workshops about what we have just seen. The enjoyment and agency we experience is a direct result of being able to access all areas.

Schechner further asserts that performance is not only this time and space sequence but also a dynamic relationship between players; between what he calls *sourcers* (authors, composers, dramaturges), *producers* (directors, coaches, designers, technicians), *performers* and finally *partakers* (fans, spectators, the public). In his books, Schechner applies these concepts to a range of different theatre practices from linear to montage-based productions; but they could equally be applied to a range of interactive projects where the possible combinations of these processes by players are endless. For example, in *Dream* the relationship between the players and performers is marked by a direct link whereby players influence the direction of travel for the performers. Consequently, *sourcers* and *producers* have to work very closely in the design and production of the work to ensure the performer/partaker interface works both technologically and as a performance.

It is not just the "Ritual of the Story" that is in operation here, although that certainly exists in the production, but a mix of the behind-the-story, along with the unmasking of the performance elements and relationships in the performance that appears to provide the coherence for such interactive or immersive stories. In this context showing the mechanism of production while distancing the audience in a Brechtian sense seems to create a "liveness". This "liveness" does not detract from the performance as *The Guardian*'s chief theatre critic Arifa Akbar suggests. She maintains that the most exciting moment comes when the technology of the work is exposed to the audience and "seems more exciting than the film itself" (Akbar 2021) hitting home by giving us the impression of being let into the creation of the work. Of course, the actors in this piece are driven by the actions of the audience too. They light the way for Puck across the forest, involving some improvisation on behalf of the actors, who, clad in motion capture suits, perform a sort of human puppetry with one another in relation to a screen. Here, the connection between the audience and the performer that Grotowski was so concerned to develop is being explored to a degree.

That is why Schechner suggests that interactive installations and virtual performances develop the tradition of Grotowski (from 1957 to 1969; although it must be pointed out that Grotowski did not experiment with "audience participation"); the happenings and environmental theatre of Karpov and the performance/installation art of Marina Abramovic (among others) into the immersive tradition that is now being explored by companies such as *Blast Theory*. Steve Dixon (2007) defines "digital performance" as "performance works where computer technologies play a *key* role rather than a subsidiary one in content, techniques, aesthetics or delivery forms" (Dixon 2007, 3). In much the same way as Schechner, Dixon and Smith show even more clearly how such performances have grown out of avant-garde traditions and are a form that is both experimental and new. Although not specific about how these processes work, their study is a useful background to ideas of "liveness" and the role this plays in digital work. Auslander has written extensively on the concept of "liveness" (1999), detailing the complex relationships between concepts of "live" and "recorded" and in doing so places emphasis on the relationship between the spectator and the performer, rather than on whether the performer is live or recorded. As Dixon (2007, 70) points out, the emphasis is on the human contact rather than on the virtual or physical body. By showing us the work involved in construction through an online live performance, the actors in *Dream* are sharing with us the ways in which they have given their audiences agency to affect the production and somehow act as a form of contact. As Popat suggests, "performance has much to offer as a way of understanding and modelling the philosophies and practices of human/technological relationships" (2011, 141). Elements of "liveness" can therefore be seen to be crucial to our enjoyment and participation (Fig. 9.2).

A good example of how this can be achieved with minimal interaction is an IOU project known as *Fulcrum*, where an intricate diorama depicts a small

Fig. 9.2 IOU *Fulcrum* Set (fulcrum small)

town and a video camera on a long robotic arm swoops around zooming in and out picking out random scenes. The pictures from this robotic arm are projected live onto a cinema screen in a separate building. We see both the diorama and the cinema screen at different times and know that they are happening live and simultaneously. We can wander back and forth between both these places and witness a different response in each. The screen shows us recorded footage that focuses on the diorama while when we visit the diorama we can see the making of the film and the larger picture of the work. This live cinema experience, although involving only spectatorship, helps us create the hidden stories of the diorama, stories we would not have imagined if the cinema was not there. "Liveness" and the experience of construction invites us to create and add our own interpretations to the work (Fig. 9.3).

One can of course argue that audiences are never passive, as work only becomes a performance in the presence of an audience. As Popat suggests:

> If the communication between artist(s) and viewers is to be two-way with mutual effect, then the focus of the artwork shifts. Instead of a completed product, the interactive artist designs the framework that contains the potential for the creative experience of the participant. (2006, 34)

In the work of IOU, although there is little visible action on behalf of the audience, they have nonetheless been creating meaning that contributes to the work although such work remains private and is not included in the production.

Fig. 9.3 IOU *Fulcrum* (web-image)

Terms like immersion could be used here to describe the experience. However, as Murray points out, there is not "much agreement on what immersion is or how to achieve it" (23). Today it is often a term used to describe technology rather than process or to refer to the degree of sensory stimulation; but immersion is a key ingredient to most forms of cultural production. Ryan shows us that immersion works on a number of levels:

> If readers are caught up in a story, they turn the pages without paying too much attention to the letter of the text: what they want is to find out what happened next in the fictional world. (1999, 112)

Here Ryan is describing the immersion into the story rather than the immersion into the medium and this applies to a whole range of narratives and not just interactive ones. Digital formats can display the story in a variety of media but, as Ryan suggests, at times the more interactive the text, the less immersive it can be, because the story and the media format are in conflict with each other. Her solution is to combine immersion and interactivity so that language is turned into performance whereby readers are asked to play the role of a character. Frank Rose (2015) points out that having audiences lose themselves in a world is not the same as asking them to engage within it. Engagement happens when the audience is asked to take some form of action. Fan cultures, for example, show an increasing desire to step inside artificial worlds and deepen and broaden them—often acting them out in Comic Con public events or through their own parties or gatherings. Such activities mean that the writer/creator not only needs to build liveness into the production but also needs to provide performance opportunities for their audiences. Murray suggests that immersion "is the experience produced by the pleasurable exploration of a limitless, consistent, familiar yet surprising environment" (2011, 102). Here agency and immersion are "mutually reinforcing" (2011, 102): when we engage in the IOU world of the village, the robotic arm responds to us as we expect it to by showing us deeper levels of content and context as it zooms in and out, thus revealing greater detail so that we become more fully immersed.

Brian Boyd (2009) maintains that such behaviour is deeply rooted in the human psyche and our immersion in stories is an adaptive process that helps alter attitudes and beliefs. The link between the story and the process of engagement is clearly an element that warrants close attention in digital storytelling. As with Rose: "Storytelling is key, but as with any key it only gets you in the door. What people really want is to merge their identity with something larger. They want to enter the world the story lives in" (Rose 2015, n.p.).

Engaging in process theatre/drama is an active and collaborative practice where participants are asked to make and shape and control significant aspects of what is taking place. They both experience the drama and organise and contribute to it, while evaluating the experience. Initially, the leader/teacher is in control of what is happening, especially the growth of dramatic tension, so that the encounter raises expectations, but as the drama progresses the participants are equally central to the narrative drive. Although it is most commonly associated with the teaching of drama or the use of drama in education:

> Like theatre, it is possible for process drama at its best to provide a sustained, intensive, and profoundly satisfying encounter with the dramatic medium and for its participants to apprehend the world in a different way because of this encounter. (O'Neill 1995, 13)

In this process drama scenario O'Neill suggests starting with a pre-text—a provocation. Such techniques utilise the concept of liminality—a time and space between one meaning and another (Turner 1982). In this state, participants are on the threshold between what they have been and what they will become and are, by implication, in a process of transformation. In this state, O'Neill suggests people play with familiar situations and disarrange them (the basic activity of art) to force us to notice and to see anew. Bronwyn Patrickson (2011) has already designed a preliminary poetics for computer-mediated interactive process drama suggesting, when talking about Lance Weiler's *Sherlock Holmes & the Internet of Things*, that "the best practice principles imply

Fig. 9.4 *Red Branch Heroes*—Who do you choose? (under Jpeg 3) (*Source* Bellyfeel Productions)

this sort of event is not simply storytelling—but a social, playful, skilful drama with its own developing distinct poetics" (Patrickson 2016, n.p.).

However, often the only participation or interactivity that is available in current productions is the very basic opportunity to comment on, or react to, a set of variables that have been presented by the writer/author/producer. For example, while the *The Lizzie Bennet Diaries* (2013) offered the opportunity to comment on the material that was presented, there was no way that audiences could determine the direction that the drama would take. Even when the direction that the drama can take is encouraged, such as in *Black Mirror: Bandersnatch* (2018), in which the audience is actively urged to take on the role of director, all the variables are predetermined, thus limiting the audience's ability to influence the world of the drama. Of course, it is very useful to have this feedback loop in any production and from time to time the suggestions made by fans are incorporated into future storylines as was the case with BBC's *Sherlock* series (2010–2014) and the app that accompanied it *Sherlock: The Network* (2014). Such practices can promote greater contact and relationships between creators and players but are very distant from the work suggested by Schechner, Dixon and Popat, indicating that we are still in the early days of developing interactive work.

My work *Red Branch Heroes* (*RBH*), created in association with Bellyfeel Productions,[1] develops a prototype for a more extensive fictional interactive web series *The Eleven* that challenges author/audience relationships using Boal's performance techniques. A game-like scenario was developed where,

---

[1] Bellyfeel are an interactive production company and more information about them can be found at https://bellyfeel.co.uk/.

through their play, the audience influenced and built character and story elements. Acting as judges, the audience elect a new hero for Northern Ireland (the project was set there as it provided an interesting test ground set as it was across divided communities)[2]; in the larger research project, *The Eleven*, the hero would build a utopian community in the region and set the basis for an interactive collaborative soap. Through a feedback loop (judges could speak to producers of the programme, to each other, and to interview candidates live) that challenged the conventions of reality TV, judges had to examine and interrogate the artefacts of fictional applicants to understand who these people could be.

This interrogation through a feedback loop helped to build the characters for the story. The feedback loop goes one step further and offers an opportunity for the audience members to collaborate with the writer and producers to make real changes in the content of the storyworld on an ongoing basis and influence the direction that the drama takes. The aim was to give the participants a feeling of "liveness", of being there. Participation in *RBH* was in part promoted by adopting an unreliable narrator, Sky Bradford, as the central character in the story. Her lack of experience and lack of intervention left the audience unsure of their responsibilities and so they were forced to take action. As a result, they filled in the gaps and took control of the programme themselves. There is a theme and a small spine to the story that acts as an anchor to the narrative. But the research project also uses a further layer, the "inner level" of story generation—something Ryan calls "real time story generation" (Ryan 2012, n.p.). Here stories are not predetermined but "generated on the fly out of data that comes in part from the system, and in part from the user" (Ryan 2012, n.p.). The system, in this instance, is not a computer but an author or range of authors: me and the team at Bellyfeel. The challenge became one of how to produce a wide variety of stories in relation to audience actions—improvised storytelling. In *RBH*, we relied on several layers of improvisation. In the first instance I, as the author, would take the suggestions of the audiences and build those into character profiles for the performers who in turn would interpret these using their own improvisational techniques and feed these back to audiences through real live meetings. This promoted a strong communication between producers, judges and applicants but also created the impression that the judges (audience members) were involved in the programme production themselves (Fig. 9.5).

Ryan and others (Phillips 2012; Dowd 2016) ask how the interests of the user (the users' interest to create in this way) may be reconciled with the need to produce good stories. *Red Branch Heroes* used improvisatory techniques by actors, writers, producers, audiences and directors to attempt such

---

[2] RBH was keen to ensure that diverse communities were engaged with the project (including those from nationalist and loyalist communities) so that the hero and the larger project could be a representation of more than one view point. The project recognises the enduring legacy of the Northern Ireland conflict that was known as the Troubles but also reflects more recent community concerns in Northern Ireland.

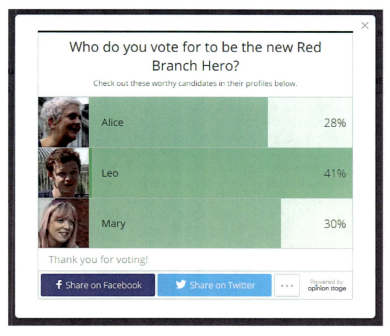

Fig. 9.5 *Red Branch Heroes*—Voting (under Negotiated Narrative) (*Source* Bellyfeel Productions)

a task and its success was in part due to the ability of the writers to understand the performance tasks needed and orchestrate these using performance processes already well developed in theatrical scenarios. The responsibility lay with the production team, who had to weave the ideas together in what I called *negotiated narratives* in such a way that would satisfy the audience and result in a good story: but the resultant story was itself open to critique by the audience and they could change the direction if they felt it was lacking in some way. The aesthetic rules for such a production are more akin to those found in television documentary, games and world-building games such as *The Sims*, or process theatre or montage, rather than in literature and film, as a wide range of views and actions can be built together to form the resultant narrative. Such narratives may not look like a piece of fiction, and indeed, this project resembled an activity or process with elements of gameplay taking place. Papaioannou suggests that "this potential of the audience is made possible by experimenting with, and sometimes blurring the boundaries between normality and irregularity, that is, between the safety of spectatorial distance and the unpredictability of proximity" (2014, 165). I would suggest that interactive productions require creators to think about a range of techniques which include how the making of the production can be combined with the production itself, how liveness can be achieved, the processes that invite participation but also how the audience can gain the confidence to perform in the activity themselves.

One company who have fused together such techniques in their work is Blast Theory. They seek to implicate audiences in the outcome by asking them to take action, make decisions and agree scenarios: as a result, flexibility and uncertainty are hallmarks of this approach. Their interest in new technologies stems from seeing the mobile phone as a social device and suggests that young people are interested in being more "active" in their engagement and that our culture needs to respond to that. However, they acknowledge that more recently there has been something of a backlash against such practices and so they wrestle with the boundaries of this work all the time. As a result, they insist that collaborative work is essential and gives them the strength to take the necessary risks associated with this form. Alice O'Grady identifies the common forms of interactive production at play in their work. She suggests that the artist is responsible for the framework or the structure and the environment. Within this she goes on to quote Steve Dixon's (2007, 536) four categories of interaction:

- *Navigation*, where users steer themselves through systems
- *Participation*, where they "join in"
- *Conversation*, where genuine dialogue is promoted and finally
- *Collaboration*, where things can be used or altered

Blast Theory attempts to incorporate all these four categories of interaction into their work but, as O'Grady points out, these are the areas that develop the risk factors. However, she suggests problems associated with inviting people to play and participate can be overcome by creating rules. Many role-playing games (RPGs) have such a setup, where everyone understands they will be led through the procedures of the game and that rules apply. However, while simple rules are useful, they don't necessarily ensure that the play is dynamic for the player or emphasise the meaning of the work.

Blast Theory uses gameplay and gaming models but, instead of seeking safety, they embrace the uncertainty and ask questions about those models. This results in a big difference between their work and that of role-playing, although both methods have much to offer the interactive world. This type of work, O'Grady suggests, "offer[s] open frameworks that allow for audience intervention and collaboration, performance itself becomes a vehicle for co-authorship" (2011, 108). Although light on technology, *Operation Black Antler* (2019) asks audiences to become undercover police officers investigating the emergence of a dangerous Fascist movement. I took part in this performance in Manchester 2019. The audience has to infiltrate the Fascist organisation by sympathising with this cause, encouraging us to reflect on our behaviour and decisions. A police briefing room sets the scene where the audience are asked to build a cover story for future undercover work. Then

Fig. 9.6 *Operation Black Antler*—Briefing (press) (*Source* Blast Theory)

we visit a pub where we meet with strangers to find out information. This involves agreeing to ideas that we do not uphold in order to gain trust and try to secure a way into the inner sanctum of the organisation. The final decision is whether to authorise an undercover operation against a Fascist group. There were no easy answers in this endeavour and slowly the audience began to cross their own moral boundaries. But what this project highlighted was that to engage fully as an audience member you had to quickly develop your performance skills using what you already knew of the world. Quick and easy solutions had been suggested in the briefing room about how to build trust and infiltrate groups but I suspect that further emphasis on this would have promoted a much fuller experience for those like myself who were inexperienced in performance techniques and nervous of such performance tasks.

My final point is that audiences may need to be given some form of performance preparation before being launched into new and challenging worlds if they are to participate effectively. A further project that I have co-developed though my research with Bellyfeel, *Secret Story Network* (*SSN*), tries to help audiences develop performance skills and utilises all these performance attributes described in an interactive storytelling scenario. This practice-research initiative produced a number of 60–90 minute online Role-Playing Games conducted on the social media platform *WhatsApp* (we are currently developing a dedicated app to play these on). These narratives involve some gameplay but they concentrate more on storytelling than gameplay and each playing produces a very different narrative. We worked with a simple system like *WhatsApp*, one a large number of people are familiar with, to identify and refine design strategies that incentivise engagement with the type of narrative collaboration that media scholars commonly call "collective storytelling" (Boje

Fig. 9.7 *Secret Story Network*—The app (Mock Up) (*Source* Bellyfeel Productions)

1991; McGonigal 2008; Woo 2010). Our study, however, explores an aspect of collective storytelling that is commonly overlooked. Rather than focus on activism, analysis or efficiency, we chose to examine the storytelling poetics that inspire participants to engage with such projects in the first place. Co-creators assume character roles and interact with one another in the manner of actors improvising a scene. Likavec et al. call this mode of digital creation "emergent storytelling" (2010, 94). They define it as "a style of participated narration in which the structure of the narrative emerges from the interaction between the characters instead of being defined by a predefined plot" (2010, 94). *SSN* uses Ryan's suggested way of avoiding narrative conflict inherent in interactive work by asking the reader to become a character in the story. As SSN projects centre on interfaces that are familiar and intuitive, participants were able to easily articulate diverse perspectives with minimal performance or technical skill. The storytelling was aided by a story conductor whose job it is to ensure narrative cohesion, fair play and equal involvement. This is similar to the "storymaster" role in role-playing games but differs insomuch as it relies much more on improvisation and therefore it approximates more fully to Boal's *Joker*. Thus, we were able to collaboratively generate stories negotiated ad hoc through the process of production. Based on behaviours observed and enacted throughout our study, we have identified four primary meta-roles:

1. Games
2. Drama
3. Simulation
4. Immersion

Such terms have been identified and used by other scholars in games and role-play studies such as John Kim (1997) who proposed the Threefold World Model for RPGs; games, drama and simulation. In 2003, Bøckman modified Kim's Threefold World Model by arguing that LARPs feature a different sort of role-playing where simulation is not really a significant factor because people are actually performing their narratives in real-world settings. In place of simulation, therefore, Bøckman proposes using the word "immersion" to define the more performative aspects of LARPing.

Our work with SSN suggests a similar revision of Kim's Threefold World Model to further explore the concepts of simulation and immersion in a "live" storytelling context. While we retain his original modes of gameplay, we further investigate the concept of "immersion" as part of our experiments. SSN utilises all the hallmarks of interactive theories, performance-based processes and RPGs to achieve the participative elements of such designs and develops a "fourfold model" as details above. The meta-roles are not so different from those identified by Dixon except that they describe the processes of performance more fully. In order to promote lively engagement, this type of collective storytelling had to strike an effective balance between

Fig. 9.8 *Secret Story Network*—Waiting for you (wfy) (*Source* Bellyfeel Productions)

narrative structure, theatrical presentation, world-building and gaming design, affording opportunities for participants to put their own unique mark on the narrative action. An example will elucidate this more fully. The story structure was relatively simple for *Mr Catty*. The participants gathered on *WhatsApp* to act as cat-sitters tasked with wrangling a particularly unruly feline. We followed the cat around a house trying to keep it happy and answer its often foolish questions. In this way we were drawn into the story through a variety of games (i.e. throwing dice and suggesting other mechanics) and acted as dramatists by advancing the plot in a step-by-step fashion creating action in each room. Suddenly when the cat decided to take a nap in the middle of the game, we were able to take over the narrative and *plot* an insurrection, getting our own back. We acted as performers by creating our own characters and were tasked with sketching drawings of ourselves and composing captions which put us into a showcasing role. We created simulations when the cat finally woke up and had to experience our collaboratively agreed punishments describing our surroundings and likely actions. In this way, the different meta-roles operated in conjunction to help construct different aspects of the evolving narrative. In a world where interactive practices are more commonly used across media, this practice/method has much to offer in terms of audience participation and interaction (Fig. 9.8).

9.4 Conclusion

Riggs sees participation as a central element to her storyplexing and urges us to use psychology and look within ourselves so that we are *inside* the experience. She suggests building a world rather than telling a story and to go beyond the frame and reach where the guest choses to interact. However, her solutions to how one does this involve new technological suggestions despite her insistence that we understand "*why* we do things, *what* constraints we have, and *how* we overcome them" (2019, 189). She is clear that we need new thinking and "that those who make the cognitive shift into immersive thinking... lead the charge in changing the world—and the craft of narrative—as we know it" (204). I would suggest that some of that thinking has already been expounded in a performance context and could be applied to emerging interactive narratives in new contexts. The goal of performance techniques used by Boal, Grotowski and others was indeed to transcend pre-existing assumptions and contribute to emancipation.

What implications does such thinking have for the creators and writers of such work? Screenplay writers, it could be argued, are as much improvisors as actors. As Leonard argues, "just as the actor must be his own playwright when he is improvising without a script, so the playwright must be his own actors when he is devising their language" (1963, 35). In screenwriting, I argue, it is as apposite to suggest that the screenwriter needs to be their own director too (possibly in some circumstances their own producer) given the visual nature of the endeavour. In that context the practice of improvisation is central to the task of writing. There are times when writers are in a state of "flow", where the characters seem to have a life of their own and tell the writer what their stories are (Bell and Magrs 2019). Improvisation is also a key tool in the teaching of writing and indeed in the process of script development. It has been extended to the collaborative or collective writing or devising of film scripts as in the work of Mike Leigh (Clements 1983). In such a group, a writer or director can take responsibility for supplying the basic information that can be improvised around and later written up by transcribing the actions and dialogue and polishing it into a final form. Collaborative writing techniques are also very much in evidence in forms of writing for television. Writers' rooms, series bible building and many forms of soap practices (storylining, etc.) involve large teams of writers and producers working closely together. Such processes open up the narrative, prising it open and offering an alternative to predictability and closure "thus offering the possibility of imaginative engagement in the production of a new story of the world" (Frost and Yarrow 2016, 240).

The chapter contends that the re-enactment or performative aspects of writing and more specifically the participatory practices, where writers work more closely with audiences, needs further development. Performance studies investigations into writer/reader and performer/spectator dynamics offer us some really useful tools in this respect. Writers could study performance as has been done to some success in many institutions that I have taught in, but some recognition of the broader concerns of author/reader dynamics are crucial to the process. This chapter therefore suggests that writing practices for interactive stories are best served by the concept of a negotiated narrative. The term implies that the work has been a negotiation between collaborators and makers and is a negotiation between audience and authors. The narrative produced as a result of such negotiations is multilayered and polymorphic and the stories produced shapeshift across different platforms. It also suggests that ethical considerations have been given due thought in the construction and development of the project and have been publicly debated. This is new territory for the screenwriter.

It goes without saying that such techniques and processes must work with the procedural nature of the systems they will work within. To date they have been tested outside conventional dramatic settings in relation to technological applications by theatre practitioners wanting to extend their practice in new areas. However, we are still very much influenced by silo thinking, calling this practice interactive theatre as if the origin of the makers is what is at issue here. Its true contribution is arguably towards interactive or immersive practices. This is perhaps an area of research that requires investment. How can such practices ensure diversity and be married into the design so that the build can address many audiences? This will necessitate much experimentation with rather than for audiences in the manner that has been suggested in the above examples relating to Blast Theory, IOU Theatre, The Royal Shakespeare Company, SSN and Red Branch Heroes and offers new challenges to writers of all formats.

References

Aarseth, Espen. 1997. *Cybertext-Experiments in Ergodic Literature*. Baltimore: The Johns Hopkins University Press.

Akbar, Arifa. 2021. "The RSC's Hi-Tech Dream Opens Up a World of Theatrical Possibility." *The Guardian*. 17 March. https://www.theguardian.com/stage/2021/mar/17/rsc-a-midsummer-nights-dream. Accessed 3 August 2022.

Auslander, Philip. 1999. *Liveness – Performance in a Mediatized Culture*. London and New York: Routledge.

Bell, Julia, and Paul Magrs. 2019. *The Creative Writing Coursebook*. London: Pan Macmillan.

Boal, Augusto. 1979. *Theatre of the Oppressed*. London: Pluto.

Boje, David. M. 1991. Consulting and change in the storytelling organisation. *Journal of Organisational Change Management*, 4 (3): 7–17.

Bolter, David, and Grusin, Richard. 2000. *Remediation*. Cambridge, MA: MIT press.

Black Mirror: Bandersnatch. 2018. Written by Charlie Brooker. Directed by David Slate. UK: Netflix.

Boyd, Brian. 2009. *On the Origin of Stories: Evolution, Cognition, and Fiction*, Harvard, MA: Belknap Press.

Clements, Paul. 1983. *The Improvised Play: Work of Mike Leigh*. London: Methuen.

Dixon, Steve. 2007. *Digital Performance*. Cambridge, MA: MIT Press.

Dowd, Tom. 2016. *Storytelling Across Worlds*. London: Routledge.

Ferri, Gabriele. 2015. Narrative Structures in IDN Authoring and Analysis, *Interactive Digital Narrative (ed)*. London: Routledge.

Frost, Anthony, and Ralph Yarrow. 2016. *Improvisation in Drama, Theatre and Performance*. London: Palgrave.

Sherlock. 2010–2017 (4 seasons). Created by Mark Gatiss and Steven Moffat. UK: Hartswood Films, BBC Wales, WGBH.

Giovagnoli, Max. 2011. *Transmedia Storytelling: Imagery, Shapes and Techniques*. n.p.: ETC Press.

Grotowski, Jerzy. 1969. "I Said Yes to the Past". Interview by Margaret Croyden. *Village Voice*, 41–42.
Grotowski, Jerzy. 2002. *Towards a Poor Theatre*. New York: Routledge.
Jenkins, Henry. 2006. *Convergence Culture: Where Old and New Media Collide*. New York: New York University Press.
Johnstone, Keith. 1987. *Impro: Improvisation and the Theatre*. London: Methuen.
Kim, John. 1997. "The rec.games.frp.advocacy FAQ: Part I: The Threefold Model." *Darkshire.net*. https://www.darkshire.net/jhkim/rpg/theory/rgfa/faq1.html. Accessed 10 November 2021.
Kallay, Jasmina. 2010. Cyber-Aristotle: Towards a poetics for interactive screenwriting. *Journal of Screenwriting* 1 (1): 99–112. https://doi.org/10.1386/josc.1.1.99/1
Knoller, Noam. 2019. Complexity and userly text, *Narrative Complexity:Cognition, Embodiment, Evolution (ed)*. Nebraska: University of Nebraska Press.
Koenitz, Hartmund. 2015. "Towards a Specific Theory of Interactive Digital Narrative." *Interactive Digital Narrative*, edited by Hartmut Koenitz et al., 91–105. Abingdon, UK: Routledge.
Laurel, Brenda. 2013. *Computers as Theatre*, 2nd edition. Indianapolis: Addison Wesley.
Landow, George. 1997. *The Convergence of Contemporary Critical Theory and Technology*. Baltimore: John Hopkins University Press.
Leonard, Charles. 1963. *Michael Chekov's "To the Director and Playwright"*. New York: Harper & Row.
Likavec, Silvia, et al. 2010. "Threading facts into a collective narrative world." In *Interactive Storytelling. ICIDS 2010. Lecture Notes in Computer Science*, edited by Ruth Aylett et al., 87–97. Cham, Switzerland: Springer.
McGonigal, Jane. 2008. Saving the world through game design:Stories from the near future. *Remotedevisce.net*, https://remotedevice.net/blog/saving-the-world-through-game-design/. Accessed April 2023.
McLaverty-Robinson, Andy. 2017. "An A to Z of Theory | Augusto Boal: Games and Techniques." *Ceasefire*. 19 January. https://ceasefiremagazine.co.uk/augusto-boal-games-techniques/. Accessed 15 June 2022.
Machon, Josephine. 2013. *Immersive Theatres*. London: Palgrave.
Millard, Kathryn. 2014. *Screenwriting in a Digital Era*. Basingstoke, UK: Palgrave Macmillan.
Murray, Janet. 2011. *Inventing the Medium: Principles of Interactive Design as a Cultural practice*. Cambridge MA: MIT Press.
Murray, Janet. 2012. *Inventing the Medium*. Cambridge, MA: MIT Press.
O'Grady, Alice. 2011. *Interactivity, Performance, Perspectives*. Basingstoke, UK and New York: Palgrave Macmillan.
O'Neill, Cecily. 1995 *Drama Worlds*. Portsmouth, NH: Heinemann.
Papaioannou, Spyros. 2014. "Immersion 'Smooth' Spaces and Critical Voyeurism in the Work of Punchdrunk." *Studies in Theatre and Performance* 34 (2): 16–34.
Partickson, Bronwyn. 2011. Mutli-user Interactive Drama: A Miro User Drama in Process. *Interactive Storytelling: 4th International Conference on Digital Storytelling*. 199–206. New York: Springer.
Patrickson, Bronwyn. 2016. "Playing the MOOC." *Storymaking*. https://storymakingblog.wordpress.com/abstracts/. Accessed 2 August 2022.
Phillips, Andrea. 2012. *Transmedia Storytelling, Fan Culture and the Future of Marketing*. Pennsylvania: Wharton Business Journal.

Pitches, Jonathan., and Popat, Sita. 2011. *Performance Perspectives. A Critical Introduction.* Basingstoke, UK and New York: Palgrave Macmillan.
Popat, Sita. 2006. *Invisible Connections: Dance, Choreography and Internet Communities.* London: Routledge.
Riggs, Stephanie. 2019. *The End of Storytelling.* New York: Beat Media Group.
Rose, Frank. 2015. "The power of Immersive Media." *Strategy and Business* 78 (Spring). https://www.strategy-business.com/article/00308?gko=92656. Accessed 22 June 2017.
Ryan, Marie-Laure. 1999. Immersion vs. Interactivity: Virtual Reality and Literary Theory. *SubStance.* 28 (2): 110–137. University of Wisconsin Press.
Ryan, Marie-Laure. 2006. *Avatars of Story: Narrative Modes in Old and New Media.* Minneapolis: Minnesota Press.
Ryan, Marie-Laure. 2012. "Peeling the Onion: Layers of Interactivity in Digital Narrative Texts." *Marie-Laure Ryan.* http://blogttn.info/dspace/rh/ba_r.pdf. Accessed 15 June 2022.
Schechner, Richard. 2020. *Performance Studies.* 4th edition. New York: Routledge.
Su, Bernie, and Green, Hank. 2012. *Lizzie Bennet Diaries.* Youtube.
The Project Factory. 2014. *Sherlock: The Network.*
Turner, Victor. 1982. *From Ritual to Theatre: The Human Seriousness of Play.* New York: Performing Arts Journals Publication.
Woo, Yen Yen Jocelyn. 2010. Voices from the Field—getting past our inner censor: Collective storytelling as pedagogy in a polarized media environment. *The National Association for Media Literacy Education's Journal of Media Literacy Education*, 1 (2): 132–136.

CHAPTER 10

An Ontology of the Interactive Script

Rafael Leal

10.1 Introduction

A script is an easily recognizable document, and has been for about a century. It is created in a particular style that preserves elements from the time of the typewriter, the influence of which is still present in the form. Screenwriting courses emphasize the importance of mastering this style as an essential condition for the understanding and validation of a script. In its most widespread and standard form within the context of the contemporary audiovisual industry, especially in the Brazilian case, in which I work professionally, the script can be defined as a document whose pages contain a linear sequence of written scenes that describe the sounds and images of the future screenwork.

Just as there is a fully established convention about how a script should look, a culture was also consolidated around the supposed correct way to read a script (when written in most Western languages): starting on page one, in the upper left corner, and proceeding linearly towards the right, word after word, line after line, page after page. This culture, inherited from the world of linear text, is a characteristic of written language in general, as taught by Vilém Flusser in *Video et Phénoménologie* (1973): "writing is a linear codification which forces the phenomenon to be a linear process".

Even though this definition and reading culture may be applicable in a myriad of audiovisual formats, it actually only applies to scripts that are

R. Leal (✉)
Pontifical University of Rio de Janeiro, Rio de Janeiro, Brazil
e-mail: laelleafar@gmail.com

themselves linear. When scripts for interactive narratives are taken into consideration, the limitations of such linear approaches are exposed, and the need for a new understanding of what a script is becomes evident.

In this vein, the objective of this chapter is to promote an ontological investigation into the nature of the script of an interactive screenwork, starting with the question: *what is an interactive script that a linear script is not?* This wide category of interactive media is characterized by the interactor's increased agency and includes from games, especially those privileging narrative over gameplay, to immersive Virtual Reality (VR) experiences competing in some of the most important film festivals. Considering the challenges brought by this broad scope, the answer to this complex question entails an approach that considers three pragmatic perspectives:

- the fruition, that is, the moment the script is read, film is viewed, or interactive experience is experienced;
- the production, of a teleological nature, which concerns the role and usage of the script in the audiovisual production process; and,
- finally, the poetics, which considers specificities applied to the script development process.

This chapter aims to understand what fundamental properties of the interactive screenplay are relevant to the screenwriter in the process of creation and development, and how they relate to the script itself. My goal is not to describe and classify all its properties—an inglorious task, considering that new interactive media, as well as the means to write for them, are undergoing intense development and transformation, but to bring our attention to the limitations of a linear code, such as writing, for expressing a non-linear phenomenon, such as the experience of an interactive audiovisual narrative.

I also wish to draw attention to the term *ontology*, which figures into the title of this chapter precisely because it reflects the intention to seek out the more general properties of the interactive script, isolating it whenever possible from the many distinct qualities that, by making it particular, cloud its integral nature. This goes hand in hand with my tendency of grounding the theory I propose in my practice as a screenwriter. On the one hand, I do not abandon my experience as a starting point for theoretical questioning, and on the other, I seek to promote reflection about the comprehensive meaning of the script, that is, what makes its multiple forms possible.

10.2   A Complex Definition

In Screenwriting Studies, most notably in the field of script development, the object of analysis has been increasingly shifting from the script as a document to the scripting process itself. The term *scripting* is defined by Steven Maras, for whom "one of the useful aspects of the concept of scripting […] is that it is highly procedural and thus resists the prising apart from a product (script) and the practices of composition supporting it (writing)" (2009, 21).

Further important evidence of this shift is the rising influence of the concept of *screen idea*, coined by Ian W. Macdonald to describe "any notion held by one or more people of a singular concept (however complex) which may have conventional shape or not, intended to become a screenwork, whether or not it is possible to describe it in written form or other means" (2016, 13).

However, although the focus on a procedural approach contributes to reviewing the creative dynamics involved in the script development, it adds little to the ontological analysis of the script. Thus, I propose a path that goes against the grain, momentarily setting aside the processual take on development, and returning the focus of my analysis to the script as a document, whether it is a material object or a digital file, and its circulation in the environments for which it is intended.

I acknowledge the difficulty of arriving at a solid definition for the screenplay, given its growing range of applications and forms of presentation, regardless of the consolidation of a mainstream form, which determines what is and what is not recognized as a screenplay. Nevertheless, the search for a sufficiently broad definition of the screenplay for linear screenworks will allow us to find, by contrast, a definition of what the script for an interactive screenwork can be.

From a complementary, and certainly more elegant, perspective, Macdonald (2004) presents a preliminary definition: the screenplay "is the record of an idea for a screenwork, written in a highly stylized form. It is constrained by the rules of its form on the page, and it is the subject of industrial norms and conventions" (81).

What these definitions and similar ones spread throughout the academy and in screenwriting manuals have in common is the use of written language as a code of expression. From this point of view, it is through writing that the information about the future screenwork will circulate among screenwriters, producers, executives, and other professionals, throughout the development and production of the screenwork. The same does not happen with the *screen idea*, which, as Macdonald explains, does not require its expression in writing, nor with *scripting*, which includes other modes of writing (as meant in the suffix -graphy) such as photography and choreography (Maras 2019).

The adoption of a procedural perspective favors the understanding of the logic of collaboration and the transformation of the screenwork project throughout its development and production. On the other hand, an approach that inextricably relates the script to the written text favors its understanding as a phenomenon, taking its creation or reading as material gestures, used to circulate ideas for whom they are intended. So who is the screenplay written for, and how does that influence its nature and form?

10.3 Servant of Two Masters

Like the linear script, the interactive script is situated within the scope of an audiovisual production, and even though it is often regarded as literature—a discussion I intend to avoid here, despite agreeing with this perspective—I see no purpose in analyzing it here as a literary text as opposed to as part of the production, read to be transformed in something else. This corroborates the thoughts of Vilém Flusser (2011), for whom "scripts are the swansong of texts: a melancholy farewell from literature and, with it, from history in the exact sense of the word. The essential thing about texts is that they are aimed at a reader. Scripts no longer are" (136).

I propose an analysis that takes as a phenomenon the gesture of reading made by the set of professionals involved in development and production of the screenwork. I refer specifically to artists involved in creation, mostly screenwriters and directors, producers and funding bodies' executives, but also to programmers, character and interaction designers, composers, sound and image editors, colorists, photographers, and, if any, the cast, among many possible readers. But it is important to note that I do not refer to those who read the script outside the context of production, nor to the interactors who will have access to the final screenwork.

In these cases, the script preserves its bigamous function: to communicate the proposal for a screenwork, which may or may not tell a story or contain a plot, and, at the same time, to offer technical instructions for its realization. Like Harlequin, the classic character by Carlo Goldoni, who simultaneously serves two different masters in pursuit of double rewards, the script lends itself to these two competing purposes in a delicate and dynamic balance. Favoring one over the other can result in a script unable to fulfill its dual function: if the script is overflowing with information that cannot be filmed, or that concerns only the narrative universe, its role as genetic instruction loses efficiency amid an abundance of expletive information. On the other hand, an excess of technical information in the script can compromise the fluidity of its reading and the ability to adequately understand the content of the projected screenwork.

If this seems evident when applied to linear scripts, it becomes even more evident when we examine the interactive script, a modality that preserves the future as a core trait, as teach Bode and Dietrich (2013), and therefore relies on possibilities that have not yet been realized, and which will not be realized before the moment when the script is read or played. Let us consider that the linear script describes the images and sounds that will appear on the screen, in an order previously defined by the scriptwriter. Similarly, the interactive script, in addition to images and sounds, contains the available interaction mechanisms, whatever they may be, defined by the characteristics of two media: the one in which this script is presented, and the one for which the screenwork is intended.

In this sense, beyond description, the interactive script can bring with it an architectural component, equivalent to a map, that covers all possibilities of interaction, meaning the navigation through narrative branches, all the virtual environments that the interactor can potentially visit and explore, and the prediction of reactions to all the interactor's gestures that may produce meaning or transform the diegetic world.

Furthermore, even if it is based on written text, the interactive script can take the form of a playable model, allowing its readers to experience a journey through the scene descriptions and the interaction options offered to them. In this case, the order of the scenes—that is, the plot itself—will be constructed with the participation of the interactor, who exercises their agency by making the decisions offered to them as they navigate through the branches of the screenwork.

Because of its similarity to documents from their area of work, programmers and other computer professionals are able to understand a script that consists of a navigational map, or that comes in a webpage format, more easily than producers or executives from the audiovisual industry, who are more accustomed to imagining linear screenworks from scripts written according to mainstream standards.

A personal story illustrates this phenomenon: in 2019, I submitted an immersive and interactive narrative project entitled *Whole Life Through* to a very important script development lab. The project consisted of taking the interactor through a handful of major life events: from the womb to early childhood, adolescence, adulthood, and old age up until death. In each event from infancy onward, the interactor was urged to choose between one path or another: either to obey his guardian and be raised by a family designated by the state, or rebel and live in direct conflict with security forces. Regardless of the path chosen by the interactor from the multiple possible combinations, all ultimately lead to the same outcome: death.

The script was submitted in two entwined formats: first, as a prose text—may I call it a treatment?—containing the description of the environments and media objects, and explaining the interactor's relative point of view in that space, and second, as a hypertext navigable through shortcuts (links), programmed as an HTML file, used mainly as internet pages, whose text has clickable links that lead to other web pages.

In the first form, the two narrative branches are described in a linear sequence, enabling an overview of the audiovisual work, even though the branches are parallel, mutually exclusive and in an undetermined order, as they will depend on decisions and physical actions of the interactor. In the second, the narrative branches are navigable just as in the screenwork, allowing the reader to have a glimpse of the path through the virtual world. Nevertheless, this form makes an overview impossible, because it excludes all the events belonging to the branches that the reader chose not to go through from the reading.

My project was not selected for the laboratory, which I attribute not only to the conceptual fragility of the project due to its beginning stage of development, but also to the way in which the script was presented. Despite the lack of specific feedback from the laboratory officials, creators and producers agreed that the binomial script, consisting of two complementary forms, proved to be ineffective in adequately communicating the future screenwork, preventing it from being evaluated in terms of content and production feasibility.

But this experience also highlights the persistence of great conservatism with regard to script form, as demonstrated by resistance to incorporation of formal innovations, however advantageous they may be to a given project. This reveals the difficulty of evolving or transforming a model in use since the 1940s. Furthermore, the mainstream form of the linear script presents itself as a defining element of what a script is, whether interactive or not, leaving out everything that does not fit into this category, as Kathryn Millard (2010) points out: "this message is exactly what many screenwriting manuals and funding guidelines have long been trying to drum into aspiring screenwriters. Present your scripts in the approved formatting, and you not only imbue your work with 'Dignity, Prestige and Stability' but announce your status as an insider in the film industry" (17).

In the future, though, as a specific form for this category is progressively developed and adopted, this will no longer apply to interactive scripts. This up-and-coming form has characteristics that will increase the script's capacity to transmit simultaneously and effectively both the projected story or experience and the technical instructions for its realization. Just like what happened with film in the first decades of the twentieth century, during its consolidation as a medium, interactive media will also see the rise of a specific culture of consumption, one that will make it easier for interactors to experience an interactive narrative and navigate through it, becoming progressively more accustomed to its codes. It is also possible to expect the development of a form for interactive scripts that allow the reader to adequately imagine the intended screenwork and its interactivity, as Janet H. Murray points out: "the challenge for the future is to invent scripts that are formulaic enough to be easily grasped and responded to but flexible enough to capture a wider range of human behavior" ([1997] 2016, 79).

At the same time, it is important to take into account the transformation of the screenworks that themselves result from these new modes of consumption. As smart televisions, computers, cell phones, and electronic game consoles, among other contemporary devices, become the dominant way to watch movies, play games, or experiment other interactive narratives, the same resources are made available to a wide spectrum of screenworks, a trend that was identified by Murray:

> Judging from the current landscape, we can expect a continued loosening of the traditional boundaries between games and stories, between films and rides, between broadcast media (like television and radio) and archival media (like

books or videotape), between narrative forms (like books) and dramatic forms (like theater or film), and even between the audience and the author. ([1997] 2016, 62)

We are witnessing a progressive blurring of the borders that delimit the different modes of interactive narratives, an interinfluence that occurs not only in the script form, but also in modes of creation and production. Thus, it is increasingly necessary to develop a common theoretical framework, applicable to all of them, as well as a script format capable of describing such interactive narratives regardless of the medium for which they are intended, preserving their harlequinesque quality of serving his two conflicting masters.

10.4 Interactivity and Film Production

In order to achieve greater specificity in defining the term interactivity in the context of this study, I identify three distinct modes of interaction that are available to the interactor, removing, for our purposes, other possible forms of interaction from under the broad umbrella of interactivity. It must be emphasized that they are not exclusive or hierarchical categories, but modes of interaction that, although distinct from each other, coexist in varying proportions in each screenwork, according to the characteristics of the medium for which they are intended and the use given to them by each creator.

- The *spatial exploration mode* accounts for the interactor's ability to move through the virtual space, whether starting from a fixed point at a time, limited to the 360 degrees characteristic of what Kath Dooley (2021) conventionally called Cinematic Virtual Reality, effectively moving their axis through the activation of controls, or effectively moving their physical body according to the equivalent movement of their point of view in the virtual world.
- I then give the name *manipulation of media objects* to the interactor's ability to interfere in the virtual environment, either through clicking on buttons or shortcuts, or picking up virtual objects, to name but a few virtual elements among a huge range that can be transformed through interaction.
- Finally, *nodal navigation*—which takes the notion of interactivity to its ultimate consequences—refers to the interactor's ability to navigate through the branches of the narrative, determining their own plot by choosing from the options available.

Generally speaking, these three modes of interaction describe the fundamental properties that are absent from a linear script. Furthermore, they describe what constitutes the basis of what is understood as an interactive script, in addition to that which is already part of what is understood as a linear script. Therefore, these are intrinsic characteristics of this type of screenwork, which need to be communicated between the parties involved in its conception and execution.

To this end, I propose a comparative analysis of linear and interactive scripts in two moments of their realization process, development/funding and production itself, in order to highlight their ontological differences from the context of their practical usage. Regarding the first moment, I understand script development as aligned with the definition of Craig Batty et al. (2018), who define it as "as a gradual, time-bound process of improving a 'screen idea': the object (idea) at the heart of a collaborative process of devising for the screen" (154). I take funding to mean the process by which the projected screenwork is presented to producers, story labs, public calls, and so forth, in the effort to secure the financial and human resources that will make its production viable. I take production to mean the steps related to the efforts of technical and artistic teams combined to build the screenwork within its intended medium.

Here lies one of the central differences between these two moments: during development and funding, the teams involved work on the script, improving it so that it gets to a place where it is capable of fulfilling its purpose, that is, to communicate a vision of a future screenwork to the teams that will produce it. The objective is to reach a common place that reflects the intended screenwork, a final version of the script that expresses (ideally) a consensus about the screenwork to be produced. On the other hand, during production, the teams move from the screenplay toward the final screenwork, transforming it in this process, producing secondary documents derived from the screenplay, and eventually discarding it as they continue the work within a new medium.

Observing the script as a phenomenon is in line with the view proposed by Rosamund Davies in her article *The screenplay as boundary object* (2019), which favors taking the script as an object of study in its practical use, as part of the script development process and not just as an autonomous univocal work with an internal coherence that is sufficient in itself: "the screenplay, in both conceptual and material form, provides a shared space at the boundaries between the habitual spheres of practice of all these different contributors, which can provide a 'means of translation' between them as they work towards the realization of the screen idea" (152).

The script presents itself as a starting point for technical teams, such as art, photography, and production, which "will produce more strongly structured boundary objects that relate to the screenplay but are more closely tailored to their needs" (Davies 2019, 154), such as financial spreadsheets, budgets, decoupages, storyboards, shooting scripts, props lists, among other possibilities. Davies (2019, 150) borrows the concept of "boundary objects" from sociologists Susan Leigh Star and James R. Griesemer: objects endowed with both enough plasticity, allowing them a high degree of flexibility, so that they can be adapted to each group member's specific needs, and that are robust enough to preserve their common identity throughout this adaptation process. Importing a sociological concept into Screenwriting Studies, Davies applies "the notion of the boundary object (…) to a wide range of scripting formats and approaches, not just to the standard industry screenplay format" (162). One of the characteristics of the script that leads Davies to consider it a boundary object is its ability to allow different groups to work together even in the absence of a definitive consensus about the writer's original intentions.

This means that while the development stage is centered on the screenwriter, whose vision for a future screenwork is taken into consideration by the various teams, the same does not traditionally happen during production and post-production, especially in the Brazilian context of linear screenworks. In this case, it is rare for the screenwriter to follow the shooting and post-production actively engaged in the construction of the screenwork. Throughout my professional career, in more than 15 years writing for flat linear media, I had few opportunities of this nature in productions where I did not have an additional role as a producer.

When creating a linear screenwork, the screenwriter engages in a speculative creative exercise to imagine the images and sounds that will be used to convey the narrative and describes them textually in the script. Someone reading that screenplay, whether a talent being prospected to join the project, or an executive being convinced to fund it, will be perfectly capable of reading the script and thus imagining the future screenwork according to the screenwriter's descriptions. In the same way, throughout the production of a linear screenwork, the creative teams frequently return to the script, and to other documents derived from it, as a source of the original vision that inspired the execution of that screenwork. In interactive narratives, however, the writer must also describe other elements that are not part of linear poetics: when conceiving an interactive narrative, the screenwriter needs to put himself in the interactor's place, imagining, in addition to the sounds and images they will see, the possibilities of interaction available to them. At the same time, the screenwriter needs to find a way to describe them in the script, communicating the project of the screenwork efficiently while preserving the fluidity of its reading.

In terms of the effort involved in the creative process, putting yourself in the place of the spectator of a linear screenwork seems a significantly less complex task than imagining them experiencing an interactive screenwork. Given our limited ability to imagine, combined with the absence of a consistent poetics for interactive media, we are faced with the need to test in practice the theoretical assumptions that traditionally ground the screenwriter's main creative tool: speculative imagination. This is due, in part, to the occurrence of greater interpenetration between development and production in interactive screenworks, stages that become less isolated than when compared to the process of developing linear screenworks. Millard (2010) notes that "pre-production, production and post-production tend to get collapsed into a single more fluid stage, in which images and sounds can be reworked to a much greater degree" (16). This is the equivalent of saying that you try, make mistakes, and get it right, going back and forth between script and production, testing propositions that may or may not work, selecting the ones that will be employed in the interactor's experience. This is a transdisciplinary process that includes those departments typically present in the process of linear film production, such as photography and editing, and others that are characteristic of the new interactive medium, such as the interaction designer.

As an unconsolidated medium, interactive screenworks can vary widely in terms of the composition of the teams that develop and produce them, a factor that also has a high degree of regional influence. This means that some teams will have interaction designers involved in the project from its beginning, as it often happens in the game industry, while on other teams the role of interaction design is performed by directors or screenwriters, or even delegated to post-production professionals.

Given the myriad possible functions to be described under the broad term interaction design, it is helpful to make use of the definition offered by Murray (2012), for whom this term is the most appropriate for describing "the many aspects of the system that have to be the subject of coordinated design decisions, including social and cultural elements as well as technical and visual components" (11). While interaction design is absolutely non-existent in the poetics of screenwriting for linear media, in the development of interactive narratives, it is a subject as important as the script itself. The professional who performs it is also a screenwriter in the broader sense of the word, and their craft, while still not standardized, is central to a poetics of screenwriting that encompasses the construction practices of non-linear screenworks, which are based above all on the interactor's experience. Because of this, through closely analyzing its role in the development and production of an interactive work, we can come to understand interaction design as an element that can be the key to understanding the nature of the interactive script, a subject at the core of this chapter.

10.5 The Poetics of Interactivity

In general terms, poetics is the study of a work as the result of a process of construction. It consists of an approach to the creative process that focuses on the systematic work undertaken by the authors of a given work over the course of its realization. As a direct consequence of this point of view, the process of creating the script is highly valued, such that a work's authors occupy a central place in such studies. The authorship of a screenwork, notably an interactive one, is a subject of increasing complexity, the in-depth discussion of which is beyond the scope of this chapter. The new division of creative functions brought about by the emergence of the current wave of interactive media challenges even the traditional delimitation between the functions of script, direction, photography, art, programming, and interaction design.

When entering a movie theater for a session, the only film available to the spectator is the one that will be shown, one whose form is already defined.

Inasmuch as different spectators may construct different meanings based on their own individual cultural, linguistic, and bodily experiences, the film to which all spectators are exposed is the same. The spectator does not have any agency over the linear film, and all authorship belongs to the creators, despite the meaning-making processes involved in active spectatorship.

In an interactive screenwork, however, the form of the interactor's experience is not yet defined, since they will be offered the possibility of choosing their own path among an array of possible options. This offer has impacted the way we tell stories due to the changes in the role of the spectator, whose transformation into an interactor, in the words of Felicitas Meifert-Menhard, "turns the spotlight away from the fictional world and onto us, and we suddenly find ourselves being granted constitutive power over story development, something that we usually think is reserved for the author of a tale" (2013, 8).

The authorship scenario in interactive screenworks becomes even more complex because the interactor exercises functions that traditionally have been reserved for the author. However, it is necessary to emphasize the distinction between playing a creative role within an environment proposed by the authors and being one of the authors responsible for creating that environment. These are not opposites, but two modes of interaction that mix together in different proportions according to the specifics of each medium and format. As Murray ponders, "certainly interactors can create aspects of digital stories in all these formats, with the greatest degree of creative authorship being over those environments that reflect the least amount of *prescripting*" ([1997] 2016, 142).

In other words, the more specific the script in its establishment of the possibilities offered to the interactor, the lower the interactor's degree of authorship. On the other hand, the more open the virtual world, and therefore more dependent on the interactor's actions, the more the interactor can be considered a co-author.

Furthermore, it can be argued that what constitutes an author is not merely the exercise of authorial functions, such as choosing between the possible trajectories within a nodal narrative. As Lev Manovich puts it: "to just create these trajectories is of course not sufficient; the author also has to control the semantics of the elements and the logic of their connection so that the resulting object will meet the criteria of narrative" (2001, 201).

Murray puts forth a similar argument, defining this procedural authorship and taking it as a characteristic of electronic (interactive) media:

> Authorship in electronic media is procedural. Procedural authorship means writing the rules by which the texts appear as well as writing the text themselves. It means writing the rules for the interactor's involvement, that is, the conditions under which things will happen in response to the participant's actions. It means establishing the properties of the objects and potential objects in the virtual world and the formulas for how they will relate to one another. The procedural author creates not just a set of scenes but a world of narrative possibilities. ([1997] 2016, 143)

"A world of narrative possibilities". This expression used by Murray illustrates the dimension of the creative challenge that awaits a screenwriter in the initial moments of an interactive script's creation, as opposed to the task of a screenwriter of a linear screenwork, who is expected to assemble "just a set of scenes", which sounds like an extreme simplification of an already complex creative task. What Murray tries to show, however, is that the linear scriptwriter can rely on a consolidated poetics of screenwriting that informs and guides his creative process, while the interactive scriptwriter deals with a double challenge: at the same time, there is more to consider in their creative process, and less theoretical support available. For the interactive scriptwriter, even the limits of their decision-making and creative power are unclear.

As a professional screenwriter with extensive experience in writing for linear media, it seems natural to look for the answer to these questions in the poetics of the linear screenplay. To create a feature film, for example, I divide the work into two consecutive stages: the development of the plot and the writing of the script itself. Both stages are well-known, so I know what to expect as a result of each stage. There is a known way of expressing both the plot, be it a synopsis, a treatment, or an outline, and the script itself, so that it is recognized as a script and fulfills its function in the production chain.

In creating an interactive screenwork, on the other hand, there are more questions than answers: how can a script contain all the possibilities of interaction offered to the interactor while simultaneously preserving its ability to efficiently convey the concept of a future screenwork? And, given the interactor's freedom to choose among the many options, how can it be possible to guarantee that the resulting order will provide any meaningful connections? Unable to answer such questions, the poetics of linear screenwriting starts to show large gaps, revealing that it is unsuitable when applied to interactive media.

However, many innovative interactive screenworks have been produced by creators with backgrounds other than film, who seek the poetic tools they need for the construction of their screenworks in their fields of origin, albeit with some adaptation. Electronic games stand out with theoretical and practical contributions to the process of developing interactive screenworks within the film industry, in part because of their technological similarity. This becomes clear, for example, in the adoption of computational systems known as engines, originally created for the construction of games, in the development of immersive and interactive films and aimed at circulation at film festivals. In the end, it is common for games and movies that fall under the umbrella of interactive media to end up being marketed to the consumer through the same devices, whether they are electronic game consoles or head-mounted devices specific for this kind of screenwork. For example, it is possible to find on the Oculus Quest Store or on Steam either *Beat Saber*, a VR game in which you fight with lightsabers, and *The Line* (2020), a Venice Film Festival winner fictional VR experience. In addition, one must consider the fact that the current wave of interactive media is relatively recent, to the point of not yet having acquired enough size to allow the division of its market into niches. Virtual Reality short films, immersive games and apps are sold and experienced with the same devices, blurring the boundaries of what is a game and what is a movie.

Unlike linear screenworks, whose production is script-centric and uses the widely adopted mainstream script form, in the electronic game development environment there is a new document rising in popularity: the GDD, game design document. Despite the existence of an industry that is strongly established, electronic games have a high degree of diversity in the way they are developed, so there is not, as of this writing, a standard consolidated form of GDD. In some cases, it will be a text document, while in others it will be a system of web pages linked by shortcuts, as if in a wiki format. In common, they have the fact that they will describe not only what Murray called "a world of narrative possibilities" but, most importantly, the concept of the future screenwork.

I understand that in linear screenwork, it is the script that fulfills the function of a boundary object, serving as a common link between the creative teams through the stages of production. In electronic games, it is the GDD that assumes this function: it is a document produced collectively by the development team, not necessarily centered on the scriptwriter, and it is this document that the teams turn to at all times, whether to consult it as the guide for the screenwork to be constructed, or to update it according to how the screen idea is transformed throughout the development and production processes.

To help acknowledge what the GDD is and shed light on some essential characteristics of the interactive script, one of the theoretical references that stands out in Game Studies is the methodological approach known as MDA—Mechanics, Dynamics and Aesthetics—developed by Hunicke, LeBlanc and Zubeck (2004) to facilitate the analysis of the iterative processes involved in the development of electronic games.

In general, the MDA approach allows us to categorize the interactor's experience within the context of a dynamic, temporal system, anticipating how creative decisions made by the authors will transform each element of the screen idea throughout development, influencing every aspect of the interactor's designed experience. For Hunicke, LeBlanc, and Zubeck, "understanding games as dynamic systems helps us develop techniques for iterative design and improvement allowing us to control for undesired outcomes, and tune for desired behavior" (2004, 5).

In short, Mechanics consists of the basic components of the game, the general rules of the virtual universe, and the way to interact with them, all at the level of data programming and system structure. Often delimited by the media and the technological format for which the screenwork is intended, the mechanics describe the nature of the actions that the interactor can perform in the game and the reactions to them, as well as the navigation structures and algorithms that are part of the engine. Dynamics, on the other hand, describes the behavior of game mechanics in motion, based on the actions of the interactor. Finally, Aesthetics refers to the set of reactions and emotional responses generated in the interactor from the sounds and images in the screenwork, which can be related to the interface to which the interactor is exposed. As per Murray, "interface is a convenient but imprecise term for the outward appearance, the visible control and feedback apparatus, for interactive devices. The interface is what the user sees and operates; it sits between the machine and the person" (2012, 10).

The MDA allows its authors to quantify and identify, in addition to the tasks of a linear scriptwriter of a linear work, everything that should be considered by the interactive scriptwriter in the scripting process, such as the interactor's point of view. Hunicke, LeBlanc, and Zubeck propose that "from the designer's perspective, the mechanics give rise to dynamic system behavior, which in turn leads to particular aesthetic experiences. From the player's perspective, aesthetics set the tone, which is born out in observable dynamics and eventually, operable mechanics" (2004, 2).

The excerpt above shows how MDA considers not only the author's—referred to as a designer—point of view but also the point of view of the interactor, whose incorporation into the creative process allows us to specifically address each and every objective reaction expected as result of the aesthetic experience. With this, it becomes possible to create appropriate dynamics for achieving such goals, and from that point forward to establish the mechanics that will sustain everything in the form of an interactive screenwork.

Nevertheless, it is impossible to ignore that, despite its wide use in Game Studies, as pointed out among others by Wolfgang Walk et al. (2017), MDA has been severely criticized. One core point is the implication that the relationship between mechanics and aesthetics is indirect and happens through dynamics, which leads to an excessive focus on mechanics to the detriment of the other two aspects. This criticism fosters a new generation of revised theoretical approaches. One of the best known among them is the Elementary Tetrad, proposed by Jesse Schell (2008), and adopted precisely in order to address this issue. It presents a different view of the central elements, including two elements in addition to Mechanics and Aesthetics: Story and Technology. While Technology refers to the underlying programming language and the computer device that processes it, Story accounts for the plot, the content of the interactor's experience. For Schell, all these elements are directly related, connected in an inseparable and interdependent way, even if they are barely perceptible by the interactor, contrary to what happens in MDA. These approaches share the common purpose of informing the creation and development of interactive screenwork beyond the assumptions of the poetics of linear screenwriting, therefore contributing to the construction of a new poetics of interactive screenwriting and even influencing the forms that interactive scripts will adopt in the future.

10.6 Conclusion

This chapter addresses questions that arise daily from my professional experience as a screenwriter. Not all of them have clear and definitive answers, and many of the practices described and analyzed here are at risk of rapid obsolescence, as interactive screenworks become more and more popular, and their production expands by incorporating practices originated from other contexts, favoring the creation of new screenworks that are natively immersive and interactive. In this sense, further research work considering the unstoppable evolution of these media will provide a more consolidated set of answers. However, as a means to conclusion, I evoke a final question, brought by visionary Janet H. Murray, by way of closing: "can we imagine a compelling narrative literature that builds on these game structures without being diminished by them, or are we merely talking about an expensive way to rewrite *Hamlet* for the pinball machine?" ([1997] 2016, 125).

This is one of the main challenges for creators of interactive scripts, and overcoming them requires understanding the nature of this specific mode of scripting and its essential ontological characteristics—the basis for a poetics of the interactive script leading to the creation and production of screenworks that can explore the full potential of the new media for which they are made.

Acknowledgements This study was supported by the DAAD's (Deutscher Akademischer Austauschdienst) Programme "Research Grants: One-Year Grants for Doctoral Candidates 20/21".

References

Batty, Craig, et al. 2018. "Script Development as a 'Wicked Problem'." *Journal of Screenwriting* 9 (2): 153–74.
Bode, Christoph, and Rainer Dietrich. 2013. *Future Narratives: Theory, Poetics, and Media-historical Moment*. Berlin and New York: De Gruyter.
Davies, Rosamund. 2019. "The Screenplay as Boundary Object". *Journal of Screenwriting* 10 (2): 149–64.
Dooley, Kath. 2021. *Cinematic Virtual Reality: A Critical Study of 21st Century Approaches and Practices*. London: Palgrave Macmillan.
Flusser, Vilém. 2011. *Writing: Is There a Future to Writing?* São Paulo: Annablume.
Flusser, Vilém, and Fred Forest. 1973. *Video et Phénoménologie* [Video and Phenomenology]. Video recording by Fred Forest, available at the Vilém Flusser Archive, Berlin. Accessed 17 July 2021.
Hunicke, Robin, Marc LeBlanc, and Robert Zubeck. 2004. "MDA: A Formal Approach to Game Design and Game Research." Proceedings of the AAAI Workshop on Challenges in Game AI 4 (1). https://www.aaai.org/Papers/Workshops/2004/WS-04-04/WS04-04-001.pdf. Accessed 8 August 2022.
Macdonald, Ian W. 2004. "Disentangling the Screen Idea." *Journal of Media Practice* 5 (2): 85–99.

Macdonald, Ian. W. 2013. *Screenwriting Poetics and the Screen Idea*. London: Palgrave Macmillan.

Macdonald, Ian W. 2016. "The Object that Is Not Yet an Object: The Screen Idea." In *Atas do VI Encontro Anual da AIM*, edited by Paulo Cunha, Susana Viegas, and Maria Guilhermina Castro, 10–26. Lisbon: AIM.

Manovich, Lev. 2001. *The Language of New Media*. Cambridge, MA: MIT Press.

Maras, Steven. 2019. *Screenwriting—History, Theory and Practice*. London: Wallflower Press.

Meifert-Menhard, Felicitas. 2013. *Playing the Text, Performing the Future*. Berlin and New York: De Gruyter.

Millard, Kathryn. 2010. "After the Typewriter: The Screenplay in a Digital Era." *Journal of Screenwriting* 1 (1): 11–25.

Murray, Janet H. 1997 [2016]. *Hamlet on the Holodeck: The Future of Narrative in Cyberspace*. New York: The Free Press.

Murray, Janet H. 2012. *Inventing the New Medium: Principles of Interaction Design as a Cultural Practice*. Cambridge, MA: MIT Press.

Schell, Jesse. 2008. *The Art of Game Design. A Book of Lenses*. Amsterdam and Boston: Elsevier/Morgan Kaufmann.

The Line. 2020. Directed by Ricardo Laganaro. VR Experience. São Paulo: Arvore Immersive.

Walk, Wolfgang, Daniel Görlich, and Mark Barrett. 2017. "Design, Dynamics, Experience (DDE): An Advancement of the MDA Framework for Game Design." In *Game Dynamics: Best Practices in Procedural and Dynamic Game Content Generation*, edited by Oliver Korn and Newton Lee, 27–46. Cham, Switzerland: Springer.

PART II: When/Where

Screenwriting Historiography

CHAPTER 11

Historiographies of Screenwriting

Steven Price

11.1 Introduction

Historiography is "[t]he writing of history; written history", but also "[t]he study of history-writing, esp. as an academic discipline" (OED). The aim of the present chapter is not to re-examine screenwriting history, but to consider some of the ways in which that history has been written about, why there has been so little substantial research in this area to date, and the enormous opportunities that lie ahead for future historians. The focus is on writing for fiction films: television history, which is quite another story partly because of differences in how studios were organized and how records were kept, will not be considered here.

To date, screenwriting historiography has had an Anglocentric bias, for a number of reasons: the predominant position of Hollywood as the focus of much of the earlier research in the field, the largely British and Anglophone origins of the Screenwriting Research Network and the *Journal of Screenwriting*—the main though certainly not exclusive drivers of screenwriting studies since 2008—and the relative paucity of English-language studies or translations of histories of screenwriting in non-Anglophone countries. Even the contrast between the resources available to British and American scholars is striking: while there have been significant archival studies of screenwriting in the UK (see, for instance, Macdonald 2011; Macdonald and Jacob 2011;

S. Price (✉)
Bangor University, Bangor, Wales, UK
e-mail: s.t.price@bangor.ac.uk

Nelmes 2014), they reveal a piecemeal set of industrial and archival habits, particularly in the earlier periods, quite at odds with contemporaneous record-keeping methods in Hollywood. Anyone who has attempted to research Alfred Hitchcock's career, for example, is immediately struck by the contrast between the sparse, fragmentary script materials pertaining to the British period and the voluminous, meticulously catalogued Hitchcock collection at the Margaret Herrick Library (MHL) in Los Angeles. European wars have also obliterated many records. There are significant surviving materials, of course, especially regarding particular eras in French, German and Russian cinema (see Thompson 2004, Ksenofontova 2020, and the sections pertaining to screenwriting in Crisp 1993), although several important monographs remain untranslated into English, especially from the German (see Schwarz 1982; Tieber 2008, 2011; Scholz 2016). Indeed, given the influence of Claudia Sternberg's English-language study of American screenplays (Sternberg 1997), which originated as a PhD in Germany, and studies in the related field of storyboarding (Henkel, Jaspers and Mänz 2012), a strong case could be made for German rather than English as the primary language of research into screenwriting history.

An important strength of the current Handbook is that it attempts to address these imbalances, with six of the ten chapters that follow in Part II examining histories of screenwriting beyond the United States. This may go some way towards excusing the largely Hollywood-centric focus of the present chapter, which is due partly to linguistic competence but also to the fact that from the 1910s onwards American studios provided an industrial structure for screenwriting while simultaneously developing meticulous record-keeping practices with few parallels elsewhere. The availability of many of these archives to the scholar makes it possible for the historian to situate a particular screenplay text within more clearly defined industrial contexts than is possible in many other industries and nations with more fragmentary historical records. Historiography is a matter not of the appreciation of individual texts or writers, but of exploring a significant corpus of texts and tracing their connections to wider historical, cultural or industrial contexts. That entails three things: a reasonably industrialized film-making culture, the retention of significant archival materials, and a large enough body of scholars on the ground willing and able to do the spadework. It is to be hoped that continuing research will make it possible to expand this paradigm for historiographical study into screenwriting in other countries.

11.2 Historiography and Academic Research

In histories of cinema, as in almost all writing about film, screenwriting has always come, at best, a distant second to the study of film texts themselves. Most of the reasons for this are obvious, but some of them are worth unpacking a little in the present context. One is teleological: the idea that the end product of any film project is the film itself. In this view, successive screenplay drafts are merely staging-posts on the journey to the final cut of the film, following which all such materials may be discarded. Just as one familiar trope holds that celluloid removed in the editing process ends up on the cutting-room floor, so another maintains that screenplays end up in "the wastepaper basket" (Brik 1974, 99). Similarly, while the film spectator may infer the prior existence of these discarded written and recorded elements, they are not materially present on the screen and therefore can logically form no part of the analysis of the film text itself. To the extent that the screenwriting historian is particularly interested in the processes through which script ideas are transformed, this lack of concern for the historical record becomes a matter to be addressed and rectified. This is why primary archival research is indispensable to the screenwriting historian, but is often less important to the student of film.

This teleological view is closely aligned with a second explanation for the marginalization of screenwriting. Early film theory, such as that of Rudolf Arnheim, was significantly indebted to the 'specificity thesis' that privileges what is unique to a particular art form (in cinema's case, the recorded moving image), and marginalizes connections to other art forms—in this case, not just literature generally, but the theatrical play script especially. In the silent era the specificity thesis was, perhaps, relatively easy to maintain, and helps to account for the contemporary hostility in some quarters to the coming of sound in the late 1920s, which threatened to reintroduce via dialogue and more static camera set-ups a theatrical quality that the montage editing of D. W. Griffith, Sergei Eisenstein and many others had promised to displace. Screenwriting historians might note, however, the delicious irony that due to the vagaries of U.S. copyright law, some of the earliest surviving film scripts in the Library of Congress, from 1904 to 1905, directly adopted the form of theatrical play scripts as a means of securing copyright on film works at a time of rampant piracy (see Loughney 1997; Price 2011).

A third explanation is practical, and especially important to the historian: in most cases it is simply easier to find a way to view a film than to read its screenplay, especially given the infrequent and unreliable publication of screenplay texts, often in edited forms that do not correspond directly to any iteration used during the production process; meanwhile, scripts that find their way onto the internet are generally unauthorized and lack any record of provenance. More promisingly, however, contrary to report many screenplays end their journeys not in the wastepaper basket but in painstakingly catalogued archives. (In some cases, indeed, lost films are survived by their script materials, providing a means of reconstructing otherwise missing films and television episodes.) The personal archives of major individual writers and directors are being sold or donated with increasing frequency to institutions such as the British Library (such as that of Harold Pinter), the Harry Ransom Center (HRC) at the University of Texas at Austin (Tom Stoppard, David Mamet), or in publicly accessible archives devoted to the work of an individual artist

(Stanley Kubrick in London, Ingmar Bergman in Stockholm). Meanwhile, the custom of the classical-era Hollywood studios of archiving script materials, for budgetary, ownership and legal reasons, means that the historian is able to examine virtually in their entirety the screenwriting practices of, for example, Warner Brothers (held at the University of Madison-Wisconsin) and MGM (at the MHL). To date, very little of this material has been digitized, and unless and until entire archives become fully digitized and remotely accessible, there will remain no adequate substitute for the on-site researcher. The combination of voluminous screenplay archives and the relative paucity of screenwriting scholars working within a still emerging field means that there are almost limitless opportunities for the augmentation and re-evaluation of screenwriting history.

11.3 Histories of Screenwriting

A distinction can be drawn between screenwriting as a set of practices—the creation and adaptation of story ideas, discussions between collaborators, the working lives of writers and so on—and screenplay texts as written, material artefacts. It might seem obvious that these are interrelated and need to be considered as such, but in practice it is remarkable how often the texts themselves remain marginal or even absent in otherwise substantial histories of screenwriting. Many scholars are legitimately interested less in textual analysis than in biographical information and the position of the screenwriter within the industry. Via oral histories and research into newspapers and trade journals, such studies often provide valuable information into the daily practices of writers. An important resource is Patrick McGilligan's *Backstory* series, currently amounting to five volumes and providing detailed interviews with Hollywood screenwriters from the 1930s through to the 1990s (McGilligan 1986, 1991, 1997, 2006, 2010). Within such narratives, the minutiae of the material documents writers were actually creating may be of only marginal interest compared to the preservation of oral records of the kinds of stories writers were creating, developing and adapting, and the opportunities and obstacles they encountered within the studio system.

The attempt to resist these institutional pressures and to identify a creative position for screenwriters within them informs Richard Corliss's *Talking Pictures* (Corliss 1974), one of the earliest sustained efforts to develop a systematic approach to a wide corpus of screenwriting within a historically and industrially circumscribed field, albeit within a book that is not specifically historicist in approach. In his introduction to a 1972 collection of essays on *The Hollywood Screenwriters* that sets the stage for his later study, Corliss challenges Andrew Sarris's affirmation of the primacy of the director (Sarris 1962, 1968) by proposing that "themes—as expressed through plot, characterization and dialogue—belong primarily to the writer" (Corliss 1972, 11), as do tone and "fugues": "the screenwriter as an auteur who, through detailed script indications of camera placement, cutting, and acting styles, virtually 'directs' his own films" (Corliss 1972, 19). In *Talking Pictures*, Corliss then constructs an evaluative pantheon of writers as a counter to the pantheon of directors previously compiled by Sarris, presenting a polemical, evaluative argument about the comparative status of screenwriters and directors, and what can be inferred about the writer's contribution across a corpus of cinematic films. Corliss's work represents a substantial intervention within the history of writing about screenwriters, while nonetheless marginalizing both screenwriting history and screenplay texts by merely inferring the presence of a script via the plot and dialogue of completed films. This presents an obvious methodological problem, because if we want to know what a screenwriter actually wrote we have to visit the archives: we do not have published versions of the scripts, and even if we did the status of that script is questionable due to practices of collaboration and re-writing. And we certainly cannot assume that the film itself is a reliable echo of what the credited screenwriter(s) actually wrote.

Corliss was attempting to address the perceived secondary status of screenwriters in relation to directors, and this is symptomatic of the primary motivations of more overtly historicized approaches. Probably the most widespread popular perception of the Hollywood screenwriter derives from the supposed travails of novelists and playwrights who made their way west, beginning with the migration stimulated by Sam Goldwyn's Eminent Authors programme in 1919. The origin story of artistic integrity thwarted by the compromise with commercial imperatives is particularly commonplace in the careers of novelists such as F. Scott Fitzgerald (in *The Last Tycoon*), Nathanael West (*The Day of the Locust*) and others who subsequently published autobiographical or fictional accounts of Hollywood as the supposed destroyer of talent. In *Hollywood and the Profession of Authorship*, Richard Fine studies 40 out of 138 writers he identifies as "Eastern" who arrived in Hollywood between 1927 and 1938, and scrutinizes the paradox that many of those who were most successful in Hollywood were also its harshest critics, while others who fared less well complained in far more muted tones. Fine concludes that Eastern writers were (mis)judging the culture of the Hollywood studio system in terms of another, that of literary New York: "a writer's talent was not under attack in Hollywood so much as the profession of authorship as he had known it" (Fine 1985, 14). Fine's book is a closely argued study of the frustrations such writers encountered: producers' preference for working from synopses and oral discussion rather than completed drafts, the re-writing of one writer's work by others, enforced collaboration, and even the practice of one producer who, according to scriptwriter Nunnally Johnson, assigned a different writer to each character: "The rationale behind this practice was that it promoted efficiency and used the special talents of each writer to enhance the total effect of a film—the whole being more than the sum of its parts" (Fine 1985, 118).

Practices that the sophisticated "Eastern" writer regarded, rightly or wrongly, as an affront to professional dignity also led to a gendered reading of the writer's role that has received extensive attention in screenwriting history.

As one screenwriter puts it, "[w]riters are the women of the film industry" (quoted in Francke 1994, 2), while according to another "[i]t is the writer's job to get screwed. Writers are the women of the movie business" (quoted in McCreadie 1994, 4). One might hesitate to repeat such comments were it not that they were uttered by female writers, Eleanor Perry and Nora Ephron, respectively. Marsha McCreadie asserts that in 1988 there were over 1500 men but only 33 women writing in Hollywood. Her contrasting estimate that in the period between 1900 and 1920, "women outnumbered men in the screenwriting trade ten to one" (McCreadie 1994, 4) is open to dispute: a more commonly cited figure, based on the 25,000 scripts deposited in the Library of Congress between 1911 and 1929, is that around fifty per cent of films to this date were written by women (Francke 1994, 5–28), while a more recent analysis puts the figure at between 20 and 25% (Slide 2012). In any case, the striking prevalence of women writers such as Anita Loos, Jeanie MacPherson, Gene Gauntier, Elinor Glyn, Frances Marion, Clara Beranger and Beulah Marie Dix in early American cinema—proposed explanations for which have included the non-specialized nature of family businesses in early cinema, and a greater career longevity for writers than female actors—and the equally extraordinary reversal thereafter, have naturally attracted the attention of historians. Such research was enormously assisted in the pre-internet era by the availability of a microfilm archive of women-authored scenarios between 1912 and 1929, with accompanying print commentary (Martin and Clark 1987). For further discussion of women writers in the silent era, see Rosanne Welch's and Louisa Wei's chapters in this Handbook.

Screenwriters' attempts to organize themselves professionally within an industry they often felt operated counter to their interest have also attracted the attention of historians of the Writers Guild of America (see Schwartz 1982; Banks 2015). Via oral histories and extensive original interviews, Banks investigates such matters as the effects of the introduction of sound, the Hollywood Ten and the McCarthyite blacklist, and the general struggle for rights, recognition and accreditation. In related vein, the opening chapter of Bridget Conor's *Screenwriting: Creative Labor and Professional Practice* (Conor 2014) re-examines some of the standard histories of Hollywood screenwriting with particular interest in how they represent the professionalization of working practices.

For present purposes, one of the most notable things about those histories—and, indeed, of most of the studies cited in this section—is that while it is not only legitimate but essential for the historian to explore such matters as oral histories, the conflict between the expectations of 'literary' authors and their actual working lives in Hollywood, the gendered construction of screenwriting roles, the experiences of women writers, and the ways in which screenwriters have organized themselves professionally, such investigations can be conducted with little or no direct engagement with the material texts the writers actually produced. Such areas of research are, to borrow Steven Maras's helpful phrase, some of the "discourses surrounding screenwriting" (Maras

2009, 1), and something can be surrounded without being inhabited. Maras's own ground-breaking and influential study comprises a minutely detailed, critically informed, and discriminating analysis of these discourses without quoting from any screenplays at all. Two interrelated elements help to account for this: a story is being told about biographies, organizations and practices rather than texts, and this story has tended to present those texts as unliterary and frustrating for the writers who crafted them—and therefore such screenplays need not be read, even if the films derived from them need to be seen.

11.4 HISTORIOGRAPHY OF SCREENPLAY TEXTS

Some of the assumptions embedded in the above proposition belong to different conversations, about the screenplay as literature for example, that need not detain us here. An alternative view is that regardless of 'literary' considerations, a detailed study of the kinds of text produced at different periods within the history of a film industry can tell us a great deal about how that industry was organized. As time has passed, the systematic attempt to write screenwriting history has tended to move from the abstract to the concrete: from discussions of screenwriters' themes and professional (and indeed private) lives, to detailed analysis of screenplays as material texts, for which archival research is mandatory. The latter can include localized attempts to clarify the historical record, for example by noting the role of a particular writer in the development of a film story, to more systemic attempts to demonstrate how and why film studios or national film industries made use of different text types.

Before considering this in more detail, it is worth observing the prematurely terminated analysis of screenplay texts within several histories that aim to study a larger span of screenwriting history. For example, two of the Hollywood histories on which Conor draws each incorporates a number of quotations from screenplay texts early in the narrative, but these largely disappear from view once the story moves into the sound era after the early 1930s. There is a methodological distinction between them: Marc Norman's account (Norman 2008) is informed almost entirely by books and articles in newspapers and magazines, eschewing scholarly journals and primary archival study altogether, and arguably is not therefore properly historiographical in the accepted sense. Tom Stempel (Stempel 1988), by contrast, conducts original archival research into the script materials used by directors such as J. Searle Dawley at Edison around 1910 and Mack Sennett at Triangle-Keystone around 1915–1916, developments in the writing of intertitles, and the often-studied role of the scripts written by C. Gardner Sullivan for Thomas Ince. Once again, however, as Stempel turns to the studio period from 1920 to 1950, the actual script materials rapidly fade from view.

Part of the explanation is that Stempel, like Norman (and indeed Maras), signals in his title that his is a book about screen*writing* rather than screen*plays*, and for both Norman and Stempel this largely though not exclusively entails accounts of individual screenwriters and their experiences at particular studios at particular times, resulting in a series of engaging stories about the lives of Hollywood writers of potential interest to the scholar and the general reader alike. Another reason, though, is that both Norman and Stempel appear to lose interest in screenplays themselves once they determine that screenplay format has become standardized, which for Stempel—as for Janet Staiger, as we shall see—seems to come shortly after the introduction of sound, and for Norman even earlier than that (for further discussion see Price 2013, 3–5).

As we shall see, more recent research has questioned assumptions about the homogeneity of screenplay form in the sound era, although it remains the case that, broadly speaking, screenwriting from the inception of cinema to the end of the silent era (c. 1895–1929) has been better served in historiographical studies. This is partly because the relative paucity of the surviving materials in the early years of silent cinema makes it possible to consider them in the round, partly because these materials *appear* to show a series of transitions from one form to another in tandem with industrial developments in cinema, and partly because of the proliferation of manuals and other "discourses surrounding screenwriting" that will be considered below. All of these resources inform a pioneering PhD thesis by Edward Azlant (1980) that regrettably was never published, although the broad thrust of its ideas, and some comparable scriptwriting materials, would be presented before long in Staiger's contributions to the ground-breaking and hugely influential work *The Classical Hollywood Cinema* (Bordwell, Staiger and Thompson 1985), while both of these studies inform my own *A History of the Screenplay* (Price 2013).

Briefly, these accounts tend to propose that changes in industrial conditions help to explain the emergence of different screenplay forms. To oversimplify, these forms initially included scripts modelled on the theatrical play text, which as noted earlier were required to secure copyright in the early 1900s; present-tense short stories and scene outlines, which could be constructed ad hoc according to the preferences of individual film-makers, prior to the feature era (beginning around 1913) that would usher in the longer *scenario* scripts that provided more detailed descriptions and tended to divide the action into scenes; and the fully industrialized *continuity* script from about 1917 to the end of the silent era, which provided a breakdown of the action into hundreds of individually numbered shots and catered to a professionalized division of labour by prescribing mise-en-scène, action and directions for specific shots, as well as spoken dialogue and, often in a later iteration, the wording of the intertitles.

The next phase, the classical sound era between 1930 and 1960, forms what can often seem to be the most familiar period of screenwriting history, partly because of the many autobiographical accounts of frustrated screenwriters, alongside memorable if fictionalized images of screenwriting practices in films such as *Sunset Blvd.* (1950). Yet as noted, researchers have tended to accept that, particularly in contrast to the marked script variations of the silent era, the "genius of the system" (Schatz 1988) imposed a standardized script format that remains overwhelmingly familiar today: the *master-scene* script, which subdivides action into scenes, rather than the numbered shots of the *continuity* script. The master-scene script removes specialized technical detail and thereby generates the minimalist look of a page with significant quantities of *white space* suitable for annotation.

Staiger suggests that the master-scene script was introduced following a 1932 conference of studio heads that was convened with the aim of regularizing an inter-studio format for screenplays (Staiger 1985, 322). Related assumptions perhaps account for the near-absence of script analyses after this date in the historical surveys of Stempel and Norman cited above. Other historians have modified or challenged aspects of this view, while tending to accept the interrelation between screenplay form and industrial organization: Sternberg, for example, proposes that it was not until the 1950s that the master-scene script became predominant (Sternberg 1997, 75). An explanation for the variations in the findings of different historians is that they are not always examining the same data. Staiger draws substantially on the Warner Brothers archives at the University of Madison-Wisconsin, but archives at the MHL indicate that MGM was using a related but noticeably different format (Price 2013, 148–49). A broad conclusion is that some form of standardization for the sound script did emerge in the 1930s, but that this varied in its detail between studios: there was intra-studio, rather than inter-studio, standardization, although the industrial imperatives behind the form remained similar across the studios. What this suggests, of course, is that broad principles established by earlier historians are subject to modification by later writers with the accumulation of data, while leaving room for disagreement about (for example) exactly what comprises a master-scene script, when and why certain practices became predominant, and the degree to which studios imposed standardized practices. Fine's chapter on how writers actually worked in different studios after the introduction of sound, for example (Fine 1985, 71–95), suggests that studios were less systematic in their practices than a Fordist reading of the mode of production might assume.

Following the anti-Trust Paramount case of 1948, in-house writing teams began to be phased out: screenplays would no longer routinely pass through stages prescribed by studio management but would instead become authored properties for sale to a studio, producer or actor, who could then use the script as one element within a "package" production (see Stempel 1988, 156). This has two momentous consequences for screenwriting historiography. The first is a fragmentation of the field: with less oversight from in-house writing departments, there was greater autonomy for writers to create scripts that differed from established norms, and fewer opportunities for the dissemination of those norms via studio-appointed mentors. The classical era was entering its closing stages by the end of the 1950s and would soon give way to the New Hollywood that ushered in younger, more unconventional talents. This new era tends to be associated with a new generation of directors, many of whom were influenced by the European art-house cinema of the 1950s and the opportunities afforded by the adoption of personal writing styles (such as Ingmar Bergman's) in shaping a directorial style. It starts to become axiomatic that deviations from established norms, especially in published and archived scripts, is a signifier of authorial status that permits the writer significant latitude. This is why the screenplays of some of the most lauded directors of the New Hollywood, such as Francis Ford Coppola, look so distinctive. Other figures such as William Goldman and Robert Towne became celebrated scriptwriters whose work could be analysed for a particular style (Goldman 1985; Lennon 2016). Studies of such figures tend to move away from historiography and towards literary or film criticism, because the bonds holding a system together have weakened or even disappeared, and instead the work of the writer can be considered in ways not wholly different from studies of more obviously *literary* authors.

In complete contrast, a second consequence of the fallout from the Paramount case is the standardization of the master-scene format and the elevation of the screenwriting manual. It is perhaps not entirely coincidental that John Howard Lawson's *Theory and Technique of Playwriting and Screenwriting* (Lawson 1949) was published the year after the Paramount Decree, following a long period in which a closed studio system meant that manuals had little value for outsiders. I have purposely avoided addressing manuals at length: partly because several chapters in the present Handbook will be doing just that, partly because manuals are overwhelmingly (and tediously) the most widely encountered form of writing about screenplays, and partly because they loom so large in the prior research that there is a danger of simple repetition. It would be remiss, however, not at least to note the consequences of their centrality to some of the key studies of screenwriting history (such as Azlant 1980; Staiger 1985; Maras 2009), which have used them to infer ways in which screenwriting was being conceptualized in early American cinema. At a minimum, the earliest manuals (for instance, Muddle 1911) can give us information about what the scenarios of the period might have looked like, at a time when extant examples from produced films are relatively few in number. More broadly, their descriptions of completed scripts (the scenario script in silent cinema between about 1907 and the early 1920s, and the master-scene script in the later) are broadly in line with industry practices of the time.

There are, however, several overriding problems with relying on manuals in the study of screenwriting history. The first is that they aim to guide the novice writer towards the completion of a *spec* script, but this overlooks the altogether messier processes of script development within film production as it was and is actually practised. Insiders were learning about screenwriting not from commercially circulated manuals or even necessarily from completed drafts, but from conversations with others at the studio, including ongoing and sometimes minutely detailed story conferences at which the producer's was often a powerful voice, both in the silent (Price 2013, 69–74) and sound

(Tieber 2014) eras. A second, corollary problem concerns the perhaps irresolvable question of the extent to which manuals actually influenced screenwriting itself. Were manuals genuinely in dialogue with professional screenwriting practice, or did these phenomena instead run in parallel without ever really meeting? The question arises, again, because such manuals have been explicitly targeted not at industry professionals but at amateurs hoping to gain entry via the *scenario fever* of the earlier period and the completed *spec script* of the later. And finally, manuals tend to take a profoundly a-historical view of screenwriting. In the silent era they frequently prescribed act structures derived from nineteenth-century sources (Curran 2019), while most later manuals have been heavily influenced by the three-act structure popularized by Syd Field (1979). There is some evidence that this later discourse has subsequently contributed to a tendency to describe films and screenplays in terms of act divisions, but historians of screenwriting manuals have yet to make a convincing case that dividing a story into acts was a significant part of the conversation at any point during the studio era. Meanwhile, manuals' preferred models—Aristotle (see Tierno 2002) and/or a version of the *hero's journey* ultimately derived from Joseph Campbell's *The Hero with a Thousand Faces* (Campbell 1949)—cast storytelling not in historical terms but in the universal structures of Aristotelian paradigms and the Campbellian *monomyth*.

11.5 Microhistories: Case Studies

If we want to know what screenwriters were thinking and doing, we would do much better to look in screenplay archives than in screenplay manuals. We should, however, be wary of finding ourselves in a hermeneutic circle whereby the individual script is comprehensible only in relation to the industrial structure, but that structure is validated only with reference to individual scripts. Structural surveys of studio systems can appear monolithic and prescriptive, arguably misrepresenting the ways in which the system accommodated the input of individual writers. Conversely, microhistories of script development within individual projects tend to look a good deal messier; scripts created outside the studio system and in the post-classical era can indicate such wide variations in individual practice that the field becomes atomized, and the wider implications of the research can become lost. Screenwriting historiography needs to be attentive to the dialogue between structure and microhistory, to the relationships between screenwriting practices and the forms of screenplay texts, and to the potential for each new piece of research to modify existing assumptions.

It is worth briefly recording one such investigation as an illustration. Back in 1988, as a PhD student, I had the opportunity to read my first unpublished screenplay: David Mamet's adaptation of James M. Cain's novella *The Postman Always Rings Twice*. Via his agent, Mamet generously gave me access to this script, which was dated September 1979. I duly read it and did the usual compare-and-contrast analysis to the source novel and the film. Some thirty years later a visit to Mamet's archive, deposited at the HRC in 2007, confirmed the naivete of that kind of approach.

Even in 1979, Mamet was far from a completely novice screenwriter: he had written several unproduced pilots for television series, and an unproduced adaptation of his 1974 play *Sexual Perversity in Chicago*. *Postman* was, however, his first opportunity to work alongside an established director in Bob Rafelson, with whom, Mamet stated in an interview, he worked on the script for almost a year (Kane 2001, 44). In another interview he recalled that Rafelson "showed me a lot of movies; we watched them together and talked about how a movie is made" (Katz 2000, 198). The archive gives additional information about how this conversation developed. Rafelson's influence was extensive: typed summaries of a story conference involving both the writer and the director show Rafelson shaping parts of the plot development, for instance. The archive also reveals other working practices, such as Mamet's creation of dialogue test scenes for the actors, that without the archive would have been entirely lost.

The creation of the screenplay itself was, of course, a far more complex affair than I had realized in 1988. Although the HRC's archive is meticulous in preserving the draft sequence in chronological order as far as possible, Mamet's methods both here and throughout his career could be confusing, with folders often containing undated notes jotted down on whatever scrap of paper might be to hand. As I became more familiar with different projects preserved in the archive, however, the general structure of his process became clearer. For *Postman*, as with many of his other screenplays, he used index cards to organize the story sequence and preserve dialogue notes; sometimes he would use step outlines or plot charts to organize a sequence or the entire story in more linear form. Once he was ready to transform his often handwritten preparatory work into a draft he would type it up; this would then be professionally re-typed by anonymous professionals into the familiar format of a master-scene script in Courier font. Mamet would then revise and annotate this new script by hand, and by inserting additional typewritten pages to replace or augment the existing text, until such time as the next professionally created typescript draft was created.

That September 1979 script, then, was one version of a story idea that underwent numerous changes; and while it post-dates a July 1979 draft, it is superseded by a December 1979 iteration in which Mamet has taken the September script and covered it with handwritten changes, with further dated script revisions thereafter, resulting in two further completed script iterations in January and May 1980. There is also a striking physical contrast between two of the later screenplay texts in the *Postman* sequence as archived in the HRC. One is a luxuriously bound copy presented to Mamet, containing script revisions through 12 May 1980, but cleanly edited and typed up to remove the material evidence of the far more chaotic story of its creation that is preserved instead in another hardbound version. This second screenplay contains essentially the same material but in the form of a compilation of coloured revision pages, thereby exhibiting the classic *rainbow* effect resulting from the process of colour-coding revised pages by date and then inserting these at the appropriate page number within the plot sequence.

What connections can we make between the *Postman* archive and screenwriting history more widely? It shows many continuities with established practice, such as the rainbow-coded script revisions, story conferences involving participants who would receive no screenwriting credit, and the employment of anonymous typists to produce the polished drafts of successive script iterations. Meanwhile, as an already successful playwright Mamet had always been interested in first principles, insisting in interviews and essays throughout the 1970s that the essence of playwriting is rooted in Aristotle. *Postman* shows him doing something similar with scriptwriting. It is remarkable to find him framing the first chapter of his paperback copy of Cain's novel with capitalized handwritten reminders to "TELL THE STORY WITH PICTURES". This is certainly a note to self; it also, possibly, preserves the voice of Rafelson as mentor. Mamet begins his screenwriting career in the same year that Field wrote the first of a new breed of screenwriting manual, and although there is no evidence that Mamet consulted such books, Rafelson was performing a similar function for him. Within a few years Mamet would be using the seventeen-stage *hero's journey*, drawing explicitly on Joseph Campbell, to create a mythic plot structure for an unproduced 1983 adaptation of *The Autobiography of Malcolm X*; it was not until 1992 that Christopher Vogler would popularize Campbell for screenwriters in another influential manual (Vogler 1992). Mamet, then, appears to have absorbed from his own reading and experience what have become the most familiar influences on contemporary screenwriters, without making use of the manuals that mediated such influences to subsequent generations of screenwriting students.

Postman also sees Mamet entering the profession at a time of acute change. By 1979 independent-minded directors like Rafelson were on the cusp of losing their influence due to the enormous losses sustained by Coppola's *Apocalypse Now* (1979) and Michael Cimino's *Heaven's Gate* (1980). With first the studio system and then the auteurist New Hollywood soon to be superseded by the producer-driven *comic-book* and *high concept* movies of the 1980s, the writer-for-hire would become a central figure, and Mamet would soon be lauded for the *Postman* script and those for *The Verdict* (1982), for which he was Oscar-nominated, and *The Untouchables* (1986); as the archives confirm, he also became one of the most highly sought-after script doctors of the 1980s and 1990s. In retrospect, the *Postman* experience shows Mamet anticipating how he would situate himself within this new system. There was mutual trust between writer and director, and although the conference notes show Rafelson proposing story changes, the writing itself was done by Mamet. The archives show that Mamet was a writer, and a re-writer of others' work; but he would not himself be re-written, a position that he consolidated in becoming a writer-director with *House of Games* (1987). This combination of uncompromising independence with a facility for rapid re-writing for hire and a seemingly instinctive and autonomous absorption of the dominant storytelling paradigms of the time helps to account for Mamet's reputation as the most celebrated American screenwriter of the 1980s.

11.6 Hidden and Future Histories

The historiography of screenwriting involves unearthing the hidden histories of materials stored in the archives, and these will not be exhausted any time soon. Future research in this area will inevitably at times seem like piecemeal investigation into the script development of individual projects, and not everything can be brought to light: prohibitions surrounding copyright and permissions can make it difficult for the researcher to disseminate information about such matters as credit attribution and the role of the *script doctor*, for example, even though these are central concerns historically and within contemporary screenwriting. Nevertheless, these microhistories can often provide granular detail about histories of screenwriting development more widely, and it is only though such work that existing assumptions about the shape of screenwriting history can be confirmed, augmented, challenged or overturned.

Although the present chapter has focused on Hollywood, future research is sure to reveal an increasing expansion of interest in other major filmproducing countries such as India and Japan, partly because of the developing interest in their screenwriting archives by researchers on the ground, and partly because of the increasing dissemination of their work within Anglophone and other research communities. Such studies should enable historiography to go beyond outlining the relationships between individual texts and national film industries, however, to investigate ways in which practices have been disseminated between film industries in different nations. An unresolved question from my own earlier research may help to indicate the potential for such developments. At different points during my research for *A History of the Screenplay* I encountered texts that deployed an unusual doublecolumn format, usually to separate dialogue and sound from action. The most puzzling cases concerned a number of scripts from around 1933–1934 that used an identical format but were produced for several different studios, at none of which was such a format in general usage. Something resembling it was, however, widely deployed in Czech studios in the 1950s, which Petr Szczepanik has attributed to the influence of the German *Drehbuch* (see Price 2013, 149–51). It is likely that answers to questions about whether or not there is a common German influence behind this phenomenon, and why these particular Hollywood screenplays adopted the format, can be supplied by further research into national archives and by a growing community of international historiographical scholars. The following chapters in Part II of this Handbook suggest that such a community is already being formed.

REFERENCES

Apocalypse Now. 1979. Written by John Milius and Francis Ford Coppola. Directed by Francis Ford Coppola. USA: Omni Zootrope.

Azlant, Edward. 1980. "The Theory, History, and Practice of Screenwriting, 1897–1920." PhD diss., University of Michigan–Ann Arbor.

Banks, Miranda. 2015. *The Writers: A History of American Screenwriters and Their Guild*. New Brunswick: Rutgers University Press.

Bordwell, David, Janet Staiger, and Kristin Thompson. 1985. *The Classical Hollywood Cinema. Film Style and Mode of Production to 1960*. London: Routledge.

Brik, Osip. 1974. "From the theory and practice of a script writer." Trans. Diana Matias. *Screen* 15 (3): 95–103.

Campbell, Joseph. 1949. *The Hero with a Thousand Faces*. Princeton, NJ: Princeton University Press.

Conor, Bridget. 2014. *Screenwriting: Creative Labor and Professional Practice*. London and New York: Routledge.

Corliss, Richard. 1972. "Introduction: Notes on a screenwriter's theory, 1973." In *The Hollywood Screenwriters*, edited by Richard Corliss, 9–27. New York: Avon.

Corliss, Richard. 1974. *Talking Pictures: Screenwriters in the American Cinema*. New York: Overlook.

Crisp, Colin. 1993. *The Classic French Cinema, 1930–1960*. Bloomington, IN: Indiana University Press.

Curran, Stephen. 2019. *Early Screenwriting Teachers 1910–1922. Origins, Contribution and Legacy*. London: Accelerated Learning Publications.

Field, Syd. 1979. *Screenplay. The Foundations of Screenwriting*. New York: Dell.

Fine, Richard. 1985. *Hollywood and the Profession of Authorship*. Ann Arbor, MI: UMI Research Press.

Fitzgerald, F. Scott. 1941. *The Last Tycoon* [unfinished]. New York: Scribner.

Francke, Lizzie. 1994. *Script Girls: Women Screenwriters in Hollywood*. London: BFI.

Goldman, William. 1985. *Adventures in the Screen Trade. A Personal View of Hollywood and Screenwriting*. London: Futura.

Heaven's Gate. 1980. Written and directed by Michael Cimino. USA: Partisan Productions.

Henkel, Katharina, Kristina Jaspers, and Peter Mänz. 2012. *Zwischen Film und Kunst: Storyboards von Hitchcock bis Spielberg* [Between Film and Art: Storyboard from Hitchcock to Spielberg]. Bielefeld, Germany: Kerber.

House of Games. 1987. Written by David Mamet. Directed by David Mamet. USA: Filmhaus.

Kane, Leslie, ed. 2001. *David Mamet in Conversation*. Ann Arbor, MI: University of Michigan Press.

Katz, Susan Bullington. 2000. *Conversations with Screenwriters*. Portsmouth, NH: Heinemann.

Ksenofontova, Alexandra. 2020. *The Modernist Screenplay: Experimental Writing for Silent Film*. London and New York: Palgrave Macmillan.

Lawson, John Howard. 1949. *Theory and Technique of Playwriting and Screenwriting*. New York: Putnam.

Lennon, Elaine. 2016. *ChinaTowne. The Screenplays of Robert Towne 1960–2000*. Self-published.

Loughney, Patrick. 1997. "From *Rip Van Winkle* to *Jesus of Nazareth*: Thoughts on the origins of the American screenplay." *Film History* 9 (3): 277–89.

Macdonald, Ian W. 2011. "Screenwriting in Britain 1895–1929." In *Analysing the Screenplay*, edited by Jill Nelmes, 44–67. London: Routledge.

Macdonald, Ian W., and Jacob U. U. Jacob. 2011. "Lost and Gone for Ever? The Search for Early British Screenplays." *Journal of Screenwriting* 2 (2): 161–77.

Mamet, David. 1974. *Sexual Perversity in Chicago*. Directed by Stuart Gordon. Chicago, Organic Theatre Company, June.

Maras, Steven. 2009. *Screenwriting: History, Theory and Practice*. London: Wallflower.

Martin, Ann, and Virginia M. Clark. 1987. *A Guide to the Microfilm Edition of* What Women Wrote: Scenarios 1912–1929. Frederick, MD: University Press of America.

McCreadie, Marsha. 1994. *The Women Who Write the Movies. From Frances Marion to Nora Ephron*. New York: Birch Lane Press.

McGilligan, Pat[rick]. 1986. *Backstory: Interviews with Screenwriters of Hollywood's Golden Age*. Berkeley, CA: University of California Press.

McGilligan, Pat[rick]. 1991. *Backstory 2: Interviews with Screenwriters of the 1940s and 1950s*. Berkeley, CA: University of California Press.

McGilligan, Pat[rick]. 1997. *Backstory 3: Interviews with Screenwriters of the 1960s*. Berkeley, CA: University of California Press.

McGilligan, Patrick. 2006. *Backstory 4: Interviews with Screenwriters of the 1970s and 1980s*. Berkeley, CA: University of California Press.

McGilligan, Patrick. 2010. *Backstory 5: Interviews with Screenwriters of the 1990s*. Berkeley, CA: University of California Press.

Muddle, E. J. 1911. *Picture Plays and How to Write Them*. London: Picture Play Agency.

Nelmes, Jill. 2014. *The Screenwriter in British Cinema*. London: British Film Institute.

Norman, Marc. 2008. *What Happens Next. A History of American Screenwriting*. London: Aurum.

Price, Steven. 2011. "The First Screenplays? American Mutoscope and Biograph scenarios revisited." *Journal of Screenwriting* 2 (2): 195–213.

Price, Steven. 2013. *A History of the Screenplay*. London and New York: Palgrave Macmillan.

Schatz, Thomas. 1988. *The Genius of the System. Hollywood Filmmaking in the Studio Era*. Minneapolis: University of Minnesota Press.

Scholz, Juliane. 2016. *Der Drehbuchautor. USA - Deutschland. Ein historischer Vergleich* [The screenplay author. USA – Germany. A historical comparison]. Bielefeld, Germany: Transcript Verlag.

Schwartz, Nancy Lynn. 1982. *The Hollywood Writers' Wars*. New York: Knopf.

Slide, Anthony. 2012. "Early women filmmakers: The real numbers." *Film History* 24 (1): 114–21.

Staiger, Janet. 1985. "The Hollywood Mode of Production to 1930." In *The Classical Hollywood Cinema. Film Style and Mode of Production to 1960*, by David Bordwell, Janet Staiger and Kristin Thompson, 85–153. London and New York: Routledge.

Stempel, Tom. 1988. *Framework: A History of Screenwriting in the American Film*. New York: Continuum.

Sternberg, Claudia. 1997. *Written for the Screen: The American Motion-Picture Screenplay as Text*. Tübingen: Stauffenburg.

Sunset Blvd. 1950. Written by Charles Brackett, Billy Wilder, and D. M. Marshman Jr. USA: Paramount Pictures.

The Postman Always Rings Twice. 1981. Written by David Mamet. Directed by Bob Rafelson. USA: Lorimar Productions, Northstar International.

The Untouchables. 1986. Written by David Mamet. Directed by Brian De Palma. USA: Paramount Pictures.

The Verdict. 1982. Written by David Mamet. Directed by Sidney Lumet. USA: 20th Century Fox.

Thompson, Kristin. 2004. "Early Alternatives to the Hollywood Mode of Production: Implications for Europe's Avant-Gardes." In *The Silent Cinema Reader*, edited by Lee Grieveson and Peter Krämer, 349–67. London: Routledge.

Tieber, Claus. 2008. *Schreiben für Hollywood: Das Drehbuch im Studiosystem* [Writing for Hollywood: The screenplay in the Studio System]. Munster, Germany: Lit Verlag.

Tieber, Claus. 2011. *Stummfilmdramaturgie: Erzählweisen des Amerikanischen Feature Films 1917–1927* [Dramaturgy of silent film: Storytelling in American feature films 1917–1927]. Munster, Germany: Lit Verlag.

Tieber, Claus. 2014. "'A Story Is Not a Story but a Conference': Story Conferences and the Classical Studio System." *Journal of Screenwriting* 5 (2): 225–37.

Tierno, Michael. 2002. *Aristotle's Poetics for Screenwriters. Storytelling Secrets from the Greatest Mind in Western Civilization*. New York: Hyperion.

Vogler, Christopher. 1992. *The Writer's Journey. Mythic Structure for Storytellers and Screenwriters*. Burbank, CA: Michael Wiese Productions.

West, Nathanael. 1939. *The Day of the Locust*. New York: Random House.

CHAPTER 12

They Actually Had Scripts in Silent Films? Researching Screenwriting in the Silent Era

Tom Stempel

12.1 Getting Started

What you are about to read is an account of my research on screenwriting in the American silent film. Because it involved so many twists and turns, I prefer to tell it in a narrative style, which means that you may well find it not only informative, which is the point of this volume, but entertaining as well.

When I was writing my first book (Stempel 1980), I was also writing it as the dissertation for my Ph.D. at UCLA. It was a biography of Nunnally Johnson, and it was to be the first biography of a screenwriter that focused on his work as a screenwriter. One member of my Ph.D. committee suggested that since it was the first such book, it might be helpful to write something to put Johnson in the context of screenwriting. So as the Introduction I wrote a mini-history, from all the obvious sources, of screenwriting. While I was doing that, the stray idea popped into my head that maybe it just might be possible to write a whole book on the history of screenwriting. By the time I finished the Johnson book, the idea had developed enough that I was ready to begin researching.

But where to start? Well, I had given myself one idea when I was writing in the introduction to the Johnson book about Frank E. Woods, listed on the credits of *The Birth of a Nation* (1915) as co-adaptor. I wrote: "Was Frank E. Woods to D. W. Griffith what Herman Mankiewicz was to Orson Welles?

T. Stempel (✉)
Los Angeles City College, Los Angeles, CA, USA
e-mail: kestrs@ca.rr.com

Without a doubt, this is a subject for further research" (Stempel 1980, 13). Well, that ought to be easy, I thought. Woods not only worked with Griffith, but was one of the founders of the Academy of Motion Picture Arts and Sciences in 1927. Obviously, he must have left his papers to the Margaret Herrick Library of the Academy. I went over to the library and let the people there know what I was doing (a useful way to help yourself: librarians all have a DNA that makes them want to help people). They looked in their files. No, they did not have any of Woods's papers. They looked in their files again and could find no record of any other library having them.

So what to do? I found out from an obituary that Woods had died in a small town up in the Eastern Sierras. I figured I could have a nice road trip and see if the local library had any boxes labeled "F. Woods". Before I did that, I checked the card catalogue (all this was done before the arrival of computers, which certainly can speed up the search process) at the Herrick. It only had two cards for Woods. One was for a speech he gave in 1931 to the Convention of Motion Picture Engineers on "The Improvement of Screen Entertainment". It was useless for my purposes. The second, however, was not. It was in an unpublished pamphlet "Introduction to the Photoplay", a collection of lectures given at the University of Southern California in 1929. Woods's lecture was titled "Growth and Development". It was a memoir of his life in the business, including working with Griffith. There was a section on the writing of *The Birth of a Nation*.

The section was pure gold: a first-hand account of how the film was created by its co-writer. It was well-observed (Woods had been a newspaperman before he got into movies), funny as hell, and incredibly modest. The last line was: "When the picture was produced Griffith had my name on the screen as co-author with himself in writing the adaptation, a credit to which I never felt that I was entirely entitled, although I had been in frequent consultation with him as production progressed" (Woods, unpublished pamphlet, 25). How many other screenwriters do you know would be that humble? In print, no less.

There were two other works that I especially wanted to consult as I started the project. The obvious one was Kevin Brownlow's *The Parade's Gone By* (1968). It was the book that revived public interest in silent film. I had read it when it came out and loved it, but I now only vaguely remembered what it had about screenwriting. I checked the table of contents and there is indeed a chapter called "Scenario". The chapter is only nine pages long, in a book that runs 577 pages. There are no oral history interviews with any screenwriters in a book that is full of interviews. The other material is not particularly impressive.

In the summer of 1982 I was in England and arranged to have lunch with Brownlow. I brought up rather delicately how disappointed I was in the "Scenario" chapter. Instead of taking offense, he agreed with me that it was the weakest part of the book. Then he told me why. He had set up an interview with a woman screenwriter, but discovered she was senile when he met her. Then he set up an interview with another woman screenwriter, who was very pleasant, but who insisted his tape recorder would not record her voice. He did a test, and it recorded it perfectly. She still insisted it wouldn't, but went along with the interview. When Kevin played back the tape later, there was nothing on it. He said to me: "About that time I decided screenwriters were crazy and not to try to do any more of them". Besides, he pointed out, everybody else was telling him they never used screenplays or else they just wrote notes on the backs of envelopes.

Kevin was interested in what I was finding out about screenwriting in the silent era. He suggested places where he knew there might be scripts. And when he came around to writing the last book in his trilogy of books on silent film—*Behind the Mask of Innocence: Sex, Violence, Prejudice, Crime: Films of Social Conscience in the Silent Era* (1990)—he made a particular effort to include the writers of the films he was writing about, something he had not done in earlier books. When I wrote to him thanking him for doing that, he replied: "I heard your voice in my ear".

The second source I wanted to check was a doctoral dissertation by Edward Azlant entitled *The Theory, History, and Practice of Screenwriting, 1897–1920* (1980). It is 331 pages of information about silent screenwriting. If I had not cared, I could have made up the whole silent film section in my book with just condensed bits from his dissertation. But that is not the best, let alone most honest, way to use source material of this kind. What I was looking for as I read the dissertation were the sources he found. Ones that looked particularly interesting to me I looked up and read myself. Sometimes I found information I already knew, and sometimes I did not. I was not particularly interested in his lengthy discussion of the screenwriting manuals of the 1910s, but I was about his writing on Thomas Ince and the way he ran his studio and the writing process there. The myth about Ince was that he insisted that scripts would be followed to the letter. Azlant showed that there were constant changes in the scripts. The one thing he had not done was to compare the scripts to the films, which would settle the questions once and for all. I found out that the Library of Congress in Washington, D.C. had both scripts and the films made from them. I eventually made a trip to Washington to look at them.

12.2 In the Belly of the Beast

I also read a number of other books about silent film that turned out to have a surprising amount of material about screenwriting that later film historians had ignored. For example, William C. De Mille's memoir *Hollywood Saga* (1939) has a lot of detail about being a writer in the early days of silents and being a director in the later days of silents. De Mille is very good on the conflicts between writers and directors, and is able to look at the conflicts from both sides.

There were not only published sources, but human sources. I had the good fortune to be researching at the Herrick Library when Anthony Slide was also doing research there. Slide had officially worked for the Herrick for several years, but then was in his freelance period. Slide has written or edited more books about film than anybody else, and they are all thoroughly researched. Fortunately for me, he has had a long-time interest in silent films, and many of his books are about various aspects of silent films. I read many of those, and whenever I had questions about them, I could usually count on seeing Tony at the Herrick within a day or two. He was a great backup who kept me headed in the right direction.

One reference to a manuscript that popped up in a book, probably one by Tony, was a memoir by Gene Gauntier. Gauntier was not only a screenwriter, but helped with costumes and props, did stunt work, and she acted in films, playing the Virgin Mary in *From the Manger to the Cross* (1912). Her manuscript had been published in 1928–1929 in *Women's Home Companion*, but the original manuscript was in the archives of the Museum of Modern Art in New York. Since I know what editors can do to a manuscript (there will be an interesting example of that later on), I wanted to look at the manuscript rather than the published version. So I added a stop in New York to my East Coast trip in the spring of 1983.

I was, however, warned by more than one historian, that Gauntier's memoir was *full* of errors. So I approached them with caution. I found exactly two errors, but they were both about points of general film history, not events that Gauntier was personally involved in. Early in the manuscript she mentions that in writing these memoirs, she relied on her diaries of the period. Well...

One of the problems with first-person accounts is that people's memories fade, or just change. But here she is not depending on her memory, but on what she had written down at the time. Part of what historians do is not only collect information, but analyze and evaluate it. What is the source of the information? Why are they telling this story? What motivations do they have for telling *this* story *this* way? My evaluation of Gauntier's memoirs is that they are a lot more honest and accurate than many memoirs of movie people. I have also found, after interviewing fifty-some screen and television writers, that writers tend to be more honest and accurate than other people, especially directors. There are exceptions of course, but as Billy Wilder and I. A. L. Diamond wrote, nobody's perfect.

All of this research on Gauntier led me to write in the book one of the snarkiest footnotes I have ever written. You can find it on page 265 of the third edition of *FrameWork: A History of Screenwriting in the American Film* (Stempel 2001, 265).

When you are researching not just silent film, but anything that leads you to writing it up as an article or a book, you are always at least partially aware of how you can use the material in your manuscript. Gauntier's manuscript was useful in two ways. First, it was a first-person account by somebody who was writing films in the first decade of the twentieth century. I had found copies of scripts, but often no context for them, and third- or fourth-hand accounts of what was happening. That is tricky when writing about silent films, since nearly everybody who worked in silent films is gone now, but one can look, as I did, for material that had been written earlier. There is more material out there than you may know.

The second way Gauntier's material was useful is that she was a woman screenwriter, so I could use her to establish there were women screenwriters in the early days. I wanted to avoid ghettoizing women screenwriters, but make clear they were a part of the real business of making film and not just a ladies' auxiliary.

So I had material from Gauntier for the first decade of the century and from Woods about drama in the second decade. The next element to work on was silent comedy. There were enough written in memoirs, interviews (including in Brownlow's *The Parade's Gone By*...), and biographies about Charlie Chaplin, Buster Keaton, and Harold Lloyd that I could put together sections on them. Mack Sennett, the founder of the Keystone Studios, was a more complicated case. The second film book I bought in my life was Sennett's memoir *The King of Comedy* (1954). I was twelve at the time and had seen a few silent films, which I loved. I had read James Agee's famous 1949 *Life Magazine* article "Comedy's Greatest Era" (Agee 1949), which provoked interest in silent comedy just as Brownlow's *The Parade's Gone By* did for silent film in general twenty years later. I found Sennett's book a rollicking good time, with stories about how they made up the movies as they went along and never had scripts or even notes on the backs of envelopes.

Over the years I learned there was an earlier book by Gene Fowler called *Father Goose* (1934), a biography of Sennett. I had not made any effort to locate a copy until I started working on this project. I then found and bought a copy of the paperback reissue from 1974. Fowler was a newspaper man best known for writing biographies, particularly of his friends during his Hollywood days. He was a fast writer and knocked out *Father Goose* in sixty days (Smith, 244). The book has a long and detailed section about the writing process at Sennett's studio. I opened up Sennett's book, and while the subtitle says "as told to Cameron Shipp", it appears that Shipp mostly took what Fowler had written in the third person and rewrote it in the first person.

With one notable exception. The chapters on the writing process at the Sennett studio are not there in any form. Instead we get the standard *no scripts* description. One of the problems with interviews and biographies of Hollywood people is that the older they get, the more they tend to believe their own publicity. It makes writing film history particularly difficult. And don't assume that if you find it in an archive, it is automatically true. Several *archive rats* colleagues of mine have fallen into that trap. Just as one should analyze and evaluate first person accounts, you should do the same for material you find in the archives.

So I had two different versions of working at the Sennett studio. My evaluation of the two books was that Fowler was the most accurate. He was writing earlier, before the legend of *no scripts* had been cast in bronze. He was also a writer and had a natural interest in what writers were up to. So I assumed I would go with that view.

Then one day when I was in the Herrick library, I happened to pass by one of the archivists who knew what I was doing. He said casually: "There are some scripts from the Sennett studios in the archives". WHAT? *SCRIPTS FROM THE SENNETT STUDIO?* I did manage to control myself and said, as casually as he had spoken, "Yes. I would like to see them".

Here is the difference between an archivist and a historian. An archivist is collecting stuff that he thinks will be valuable and then makes it available to scholars. The historian is evaluating the material and deciding if it is indeed valuable and important. In this case, it was extremely important.

In a couple of days, we had some of the boxes from the Sennett collection brought up to the main library and put on a desk for me to work on. I opened the first box and was instantly dazzled. Not by the papers, but by the smell. The boxes smelled like bubble gum. How that happened I have no idea. These were scripts from the 1910s, and bubble gum was not invented until 1928. I searched the boxes and could not find a trace of what was causing the smell, but it made for a pleasant time reading the material in the boxes.

There was a possible quibble about the material in the boxes. They were from a unit Sennett set up in 1916 to make one-reelers. He had moved on to making two-reelers, but his partner at Triangle wanted one-reelers as well. Sennett set up a unit under Hampton del Ruth, a former playwright and head of Sennett's story department. Technically the scripts were not from Sennett's main unit. But the scripts and the forms and documents in the boxes confirm the accounts that Fowler gives, showing us Fowler's version is a more accurate account of screenwriting at Sennett's studios. See what I mean about historians analyzing and evaluating what they find?

In fact, the material goes beyond what Fowler had written. Fowler makes no mention of rehearsals, but the files show several films had rehearsals, then notes on the rehearsals. As I wrote in *FrameWork*:

> In the folder for *Heart Strategy* there are, among other items several story synopses showing changes in the development of the story; sets of notes on character motivations, a working screenplay dated September 22,1916, a continuity dated October 5, 1916 (most likely prepared after the filming), and a printed Triangle-Keystone Production Report. (Stempel 1988, 29)

Very often there was more time spent on the writing of the film than on the filming of it.

The materials in the boxes also go beyond what Sennett said later. Fowler mentioned that there was a former stenographer hired to take down notes on gags. Sennett says he deliberately hired court stenographers to write down gags. But in the box are the stenographic rolls *and* the complete transcripts of the story conferences, not just the gags. The transcripts are not as funny as the meetings are reported to have been. The stenographer's job is to get down everything that was said, not necessarily to capture the tone of the meeting. Fowler was better at that. What you get from the stenographic transcripts is a sense of professionals at work. Sometimes their imagination gets them into trouble. At the end of the story conference on *Done in Oil* (1917), del Ruth tells Clarence Badger, the writer telling the story, "Simplify it". The next synopsis has simplified the story. (At the time I was looking at the material, the boxes were not numbered, so I cannot tell you what box this set of script materials was in.)

It rapidly became clear to me that there was more material in the archives than I could fit into a section of the chapter I planned on silent comedy for the book. But it was just such good stuff that I could not just not do something with it. So in 1985 I wrote what I would consider a long first draft of the section of the chapter and made that an article that I submitted to the British journal *Sight & Sound*. They published it until the title "The Sennett Screenplays" in their Winter 1985–1986 issue (Stempel 1985–1986, 58–60). That was three years before the book was published, but the article drew attention, and began to show up in film history books before my book came out. I was also approached to write an essay on Sennett for the *Encyclopedia of Urban America: The Cities and Suburbs* (Shumsky, 693). It discussed how Sennett shot his films on the streets of Los Angeles. Unfortunately, I was just learning to use a computer and hit the *change* key when I should have hit the *ignore* key, so there are a few errors in the essay.

Not every film historian was influenced by the material on Sennett in the article or the book. In 2003, Simon Louvish wrote *Keystone: The Life and Clowns of Mack Sennett* and did not include any material on the writing at the Sennett studios, although he had looked at the files in the Sennett collection at the Herrick Library.

And so I came to the Library of Congress in the spring of 1983. I had written to them and asked if I could see the Ince scripts and the Ince films. They said yes. When I got to the main desk of the reading room and told them I wanted to look at the scripts while I watched the films, the person at the desk said: "We can't do that".

Now there are two ways I could have responded to that. One would have been to have a fit and yell and scream. I have never found this to be effective. When someone tells me we can't do something, I lower my head slightly, lightly kick the ground with my shoe, and say: "Well, I guess then my question is: How can we do this?" This throws the other person off guard, which makes them easier to negotiate with. It also makes them begin to think about ways they can help.

The problem at the Library of Congress reading room seemed to be twofold. The first part, which I did not completely understand, seemed to be a bureaucratic battle between the reading room and the film vault people. I just had to wait for them to work that out among themselves. The other problem was that nobody but me wanted the scripts near the flatbeds where I was watching the movies, since the heat might set the scripts afire. Fortunately, the answer to that was easy and one I was agreeable to. The viewing room was right next door to the reading room. I could read the scripts in the reading room and then walk ten or so paces into the viewing room and watch the films. I could read the script, makes notes in my notebook, take my notebook into the viewing room (nobody but me cared if my notebook burned) and watch the film. I could stop watching, walk the ten or so steps, check something in the script, and walk the ten steps back. I just had to make sure I got to the reading room early enough each morning that I could get a reading table near the door and a flatbed near the other side of the door. It worked out fine and I got more exercise than I expected to in the five days I was there.

The point of the visit to the Library of Congress was to compare the Ince scripts to the Ince films to see how close the films follow the scripts. From that first day at Library of Congress, I was finding many changes from scripts to films. As I mentioned before the legend was that the directors were supposed to slavishly follow the script. I already knew from what Azlant had discovered that the script was undergoing constant changes. There are many changes done in handwritten notes, most of which appear to be in Ince's handwriting. He is often condensing the script, but sometimes adding details for the scene to make them emotionally richer, such as when Ince calls for close-ups in scenes.

There are some spectacular changes from the script to the films. In the 1921 adventure film *The Bronze Bell*, set in India, there is in the script an Indian who works as a spy for the British secret services. Many of his scenes are cut from the script to the film. The Indian is an Indian all the way through the script, but early in the film he is revealed to be a white man, Henry Knowlton of the British secret services. They may have done this because the actor's brown-face makeup is not very convincing, but it also makes the film more racist than the script by suggesting that only a white man can be the hero of the film.

In *Beau Revel* (1921), a sophisticated drama, the movie goes on about ten minutes after the script ends. Revel is an older man who seduces young women. He tries to seduce his son's girlfriend as a test of her loyalty to the son. He fails and the girl leaves both father and son. The script ends there, but in the film the son and girlfriend get back together, and the father jumps out of a window and has a nice death scene on the steps below. The ending is more moralistic than the rest of the film, which is more sophisticated.

Although there was a lot of material to be had from the Ince files and films at the Library of Congress, I decided not to do a separate article on Ince the way I had on Sennett. There was less to say about the Ince scripts than Sennett's approach. There was primarily one point to be made from the Ince material: the films did not always follow the scripts as religiously as had been thought. There were entertaining examples, such as those I mentioned above, but the issues were more nuanced than they were with Sennett. I could have done an article in a more academic manner, but I really wanted to get on with the book.

In the summer of 1983, a few months after I had been to the Library of Congress, my wife and I went to a family wedding in Sacramento. We added a side trip to Los Gatos, where we had lunch with Eddie Azlant and his wife. Eddie and I discussed what I had found in the Library of Congress, and we talked about what we still did not know about Ince and his studio. The discussion is repeated almost verbatim in *FrameWork* (Stempel 1988, 44–45).

When I completed the section on silent screenwriting for the book, I sent the manuscripts to Kevin Brownlow, Tony Slide, and Eddie Azlant for their comments and corrections. They made plenty of both. I had them read that section since I knew that I did not know as much about silent film as they did, and I wanted their expert eyes on it. Generally, with all my books I have at least three people (three so that if two disagree there is a tie-breaker) I know and whose judgment I trust read and evaluate the manuscript. It keeps you from making really stupid mistakes. Well, most really stupid mistakes.

12.3 Aftermath

So what happened then? Some I have already mentioned to you. Kevin Brownlow included mentions of screenwriters in *Behind the Mask of Innocence* but Simon Louvish in *Keystone: The Life and Clowns of Mack Sennett* does not have anything about writing at the studio. On the other hand, my material on Sennett has found its way into at least some film history books.

In 2012, Brian Taves of the Library of Congress published the first full-length biography of Thomas Ince, *Thomas Ince: Hollywood's Independent Pioneer*. It is a meticulously detailed look at Ince as a producer and businessman, but very little about screenwriting at the Ince studio.

There have been three other histories of screenwriting that have come out since *FrameWork*. The first, Ian Hamilton's *Writers in Hollywood: 1915–1951* (Hamilton 1990), has a short section on silent screenwriting, a good portion of which is material that first appeared in *FrameWork*. Hamilton is more interested in the literary figures who came out from New York after the introduction of sound. The second, Marc Norman's *What Happens Next: A History of American Screenwriting* (Norman 2007), has a longer section on silent screenwriting than Hamilton, but much of the Norman's material comes from the material in Hamilton's book that Hamilton got from *FrameWork*. When I was reading Norman's book, I was reminded of Yogi Berra's famous line that it was like *déjà vu* all over again.

The third and newest history is Miranda J. Banks's *The Writers: A History of American Screenwriters and Their Guild* (2015). It has almost nothing about silent screenwriting, hence the title and subtitle are misleading. The book is really a history of the Writers Guild of America (WGA), and aside from a mention of an early version of the Guild, it does not start until 1933, when the Guild was founded. In its defense, the book is first rate when it deals with the post-World War II period.

At the end of the introduction of the first edition (Stempel, xiv in the third edition), I encouraged more people to get into studying the history of screenwriting. As I noted in the end of the introduction of the third edition, (Stempel, xii), several people have, but only a few have done more work in the history of screenwriting in the silent film. I wrote a small bit about screenplay formatting in the silent era. Steven Price, in his *A History of Screenplay* (2013), expanded that research to nearly half his book.

The film historian who has made the most determined effort to go beyond what I have done in the history of silent screenwriting is Claus Tieber. I first talked to him when he was working on his first book, *Schreiben für Hollywood: Das Drehbuch im Studiosystem* (2008), and he told me specifically that wanted to expand on what I had done. Since I am always promoting that, I encouraged him. We have been emailing each other back and forth for years, and we always go to lunch or dinner when he is in Los Angeles doing research.

Unfortunately, I do not read or speak German, so I have been unable to read his books in detail. I have tried to help him get English translations published, but so far without success. However, I do know enough about what he is doing that I can get a sense of what is in his books. In *Schreiben Für Hollywood: Das Drehbuch im Studiosystem*, Tieber follows the pattern of *FrameWork*, but putting more emphasis on case studies. After a general discussion of screenwriting in the silent film, he focuses on Frances Marion, discussing in depth several of her films, both some of the silents and some of the early sound film. He stops in the mid-seventies, rather than going all the way up to the present.

Claus's next book, *Stummfilmdramaturgie: Erzählweisen des amerikanischen Feature Films 1917–1927* (Tieber 2011) is only about silent films and appears to be as much about theory as about history, judging by the books and articles in the bibliography. He focuses on patterns of narration in different genres.

I first covered the material in this essay in a presentation in January 2020 to a class from Stephens College, Missouri, who were in Los Angeles for a short field trip to Hollywood. Since Stephens College was originally an all-women's college, I knew that in their film history course they put an emphasis on women screenwriters (a collection of their essays on women screenwriters can be found in *When Women Wrote Hollywood: Essays on Female Screenwriters in the Early Film Industry* [Welch 2018]). I mentioned to one of the teaching assistants at the break in the class that I am sure that one of the students would raise the question of why I do not have more on Frances Marion, since I knew they were reading Cari Beauchamp's *Without Lying Down: Frances Marion and the Powerful Women of Early Hollywood* (1997).

The students did not. So I raised the question myself, which caused a certain amount of nodding heads in the class. The reason I did not have more on Marion is revealing about the historiography of screenwriting. I first learned about Frances Marion as more than just the name on the credits of some good movies when she brought out her memoir, *Off with Their Heads! A Seriocomic Tale of Hollywood* (1972). I read it and did not like it. She spent very little time writing about screenwriting and more about her social life. Later in 1972 she appeared as the first screenwriter in a series of tributes of screenwriters at the Los Angeles County Museum of Art. I figured I would give her another chance, so I went. I found her equally uninteresting in person. So ten years later when I started on *FrameWork*, my impression of her was not good.

Cari Beauchamp had another reaction when she picked up a copy of *Off with Their Heads!* in a used bookstore. She found Marion fascinating and set to work on what became *Without Lying Down* (1997). I first became aware of what she was doing when she submitted a couple of articles on Marion to *Creative Screenwriting*, where I was on the editorial board. When it came out in 1997, I was dazzled. It is one of the great screenwriting biographies. One thing that Cari found was that there was originally more about Marion's screenwriting work in the manuscript for *Off with Their Heads!* Her editor, in New York of course, where they don't like screenwriting much, insisted she cut a hundred pages out of the book (Beauchamp 1997, 369–70). What did I tell you about editors and manuscripts?

As you can see, there is still a lot more to be done. I have given you in this essay a look at how researching the history of screenwriting (and not just silent screenwriting) can be done. There are books, interviews, material in research libraries, and the films themselves. I have also given you ideas on how to deal with the people who can help you. Research is not just looking at old papers, scripts, and films. The process can be richer and more entertaining than you might have thought.

Acknowledgements Informal conversations with the following colleagues are referenced in this chapter: Edward Azlant, Kevin Brownlow, Steven Price, Anthony Slide, Claus Tieber, and Rosanne Welch.

References

Agee, James. 1949. "Comedy's Greatest Era." *Life Magazine*, 3 September. Reprinted in *Agee on Film: Reviews and Comments* [1964]. Boston: Beacon Press.
Azlant, Edward. 1980. *The Theory, History, and Practice of Screenwriting, 1897–1920*. Ann Arbor, MI: University Microfilms International.
Banks, Miranda. 2015. *The Writers: A History of American Screenwriters and Their Guild*. New Brunswick, NJ: Rutgers University Press.
Beau Revel. 1921. Written by Luther Reed and Louis Joseph Vance. Directed by John Griffith Wray. USA: Thomas H. Ince Corporation.
Beauchamp, Cari. 1997. *Without Lying Down: Frances Marion and the Powerful Women of Early Hollywood*. New York: Scribner.
Brownlow, Kevin. 1969. *The Parade's Gone By...* New York: Alfred Knopf.
Brownlow, Kevin. 1990. *Behind the Mask of Innocence: Sex, Violence, Prejudice, Crime: Films of Social Conscience in the Silent Era*. New York: Alfred Knopf.
De Mille, William C. 1939. *Hollywood Saga*. New York: E.P. Dutton.
Done in Oil. 1917. Written by Clarence G. Badger, Hampton Del Ruth, and John Grey. Directed by Charles Avery. USA: Triangle Film Corporation.
Fowler, Gene. 1934 [1974]. *Father Goose*. New York: Avon Books.
From the Manger to the Cross. 1912. Written by Gene Gauntier. Directed by Sidney Olcott. USA: Kalem Company.

Hamilton, Ian. 1990. *Writers in Hollywood: 1915–1951*. New York: Harper & Row.
Louvish, Simon. 2003. *Keystone: The Life and Clowns of Mack Sennett*. London: Faber and Faber.
Maras, Steven. 2009. *Screenwriting: History, Theory and Practice*. London: Wallflower.
Marion, Frances. 1972. *Off with Their Heads! A Serio-comic Tale of Hollywood*. New York: Macmillan.
McGilligan, Patrick. 1989. "Framework: A History of Screenwriting in the American Film." *Film Quarterly* 42 (4): 49–51.
Norman, Marc. 2007. *What Happens Next: A History of American Screenwriting*. New York: Harmony Books.
Price, Steven. 2013. *A History of the Screenplay*. London: Palgrave Macmillan.
Sennett, Mack, [as told to Cameron Shipp]. 1954. *The King of Comedy*. Garden City, NY: Doubleday.
Smith, H. A. 1977. *The Life and Legend of Gene Fowler*. New York: Morrow.
Staiger, Janet. 1979. "Dividing Labor for Production Control: Thomas Ince and the Rise of the Studio System." Reprinted in *Cinema Examined: Selections from* Cinema Journal. New York: E.P. Dutton [1982]: 144–53.
Stempel, Tom. 1980. *Screenwriter: The Life and Times of Nunnally Johnson*. San Diego: A. S. Barnes.
Stempel, Tom. 1985–1986. "The Sennett Screenplays." *Sight & Sound*, 55 (1): 58–60.
Stempel, Tom. 1988. *FrameWork: A History of Screenwriting in the American Film*. New York: Continuum. [2nd Edition: 1991; 3rd Edition: 2001]. Syracuse, NY: Syracuse University Press.
Stempel, Tom. 1998. "Mack Sennett". In *Encyclopedia of Urban America: The Cities and Suburbs*, edited by N. L. Shumsky. San Diego: ABC-CLIO.
Taves, Brian. 2012. *Thomas Ince: Hollywood's Independent Pioneer*. Lexington, KY: University Press of Kentucky.
The Birth of a Nation. 1915. Written by D.W. Griffith and Frank E. Woods. Directed by David W. Griffith. USA: David W. Griffith Corp.
The Bronze Bell. 1921. Written by Del Andrews and Louis Stevens. Directed by James W. Horne. USA: Thomas H. Ince Corporation.
Tieber, Claus. 2008. *Schreiben für Hollywood: Das Drehbuch im Studiosystem* [Writing for Hollywood: The screenplay in the Studio System]. Munster, Germany: Lit Verlag.
Tieber, Claus. 2011. *Stummfilmdramaturgie: Erzählweisen des Amerikanischen Feature Films 1917–1927* [Dramaturgy of silent film: Storytelling in American feature films 1917–1927]. Munster, Germany: Lit Verlag.
Welch, Rosanne, ed. 2018. *When Women Wrote Hollywood: Essays on Female Screenwriters in the Early Film Industry*. Jefferson, NC: McFarland.

CHAPTER 13

Silent Screenwriting in Europe: Discourses on Authorship, Form, and Literature

Alexandra Ksenofontova

13.1 Introduction

"We are all trying to write film-dramas",[1] declares Otto Pick (1957, 39), writer and a close friend of Franz Kafka in 1913. The journalist and writer Richard A. Bermann (1913) confirms: "young literary authors, among them some from the radical left. All these people are suddenly writing films" (1028). Starting from the early 1910s, screenwriting indeed received much attention from literary authors, film professionals, and the general public. Screenplays were published in trade press, in non-specialised journals, and as elegantly designed books; they were reviewed, discussed, and sometimes presented in public readings.[2] The interest in writing for the new medium among the European avant-gardes of the 1910s and 20s was remarkable, and so was the public awareness of screenwriting.

In this essay, I trace the major directions of the discourses on screenwriting throughout the silent film era in German, French, and Russian language. I take these discourses to be representative of the screenwriting discourse in Europe

[1] Unless indicated otherwise, all translations are my own—*A. K.*

[2] For instance, a public reading of the screenplay *The Blockhead* (*Der Dummkopf*, 1920) by the German screenwriter Carl Mayer took place in August 1920, entire six months before the premiere of the respective film (Kasten 1994, 26).

A. Ksenofontova (✉)
Freie University of Berlin, Berlin, Germany
e-mail: a.ksenofontova@fu-berlin.de

© The Author(s), under exclusive license to Springer Nature Switzerland AG 2023
R. Davies et al. (eds), *The Palgrave Handbook of Screenwriting Studies*,
https://doi.org/10.1007/978-3-031-20769-3_13

because of the prominence and influence of the respective film industries. This is not to negate the existence of other local discourses that might contrast the dominant ones; however, my aim here is to tease out a common, transcultural discourse.

I propose that in less than twenty years, from the early 1910s to the end of the 1920s, the screenwriting discourse in Europe passed through three main stages, each characterised by a different focal point. The pre-World War I screenwriting discourse focused primarily on the writing endeavours of famous literary authors; in the second half of the 1910s, the focus shifted to the emerging figure of the professional screenwriter, to their precarious position, and to their working relationship with the director; and in the 1920s, the discourse centred on the screenplay text and on the questions of genre and style. These thematic shifts heated up the public attention to screenwriting and ensured that it remained a matter of wide interest rather than a concern of a few professionals.

My exploration of historical screenwriting discourses follows the approach of Steven Maras: "Looking at screenwriting through a discourse frame involves exploring how the practice of screenwriting is constructed or constituted through statements that circulate through institutions, handbooks, trade magazines, academic studies, promotional materials and other writings" (2009, 13). This paper departs from the exclusive focus on the screenplay text—an approach I have previously taken elsewhere (Ksenofontova 2020b), and instead foregrounds the ways silent screenwriting was talked and thought about. To this end, I analyse multiple articles from mainstream and specialised press, screenwriting manuals, and other publications. Most of these articles have hitherto remained unknown to research. In bringing this evidence of early screenwriting discourse to light, I hope to demonstrate how it shaped the screenwriting practice, and conversely, how the writing practice manifested itself in the discourse. The history of silent screenwriting discourse outlined here should therefore be seen in direct connection to the history of screenplay texts rather than as a separate historical narrative.

The proposed three main stages in the development of screenwriting discourses are trends rather than axioms, and as any trends, they are not without exceptions. There are texts that anticipate certain trends years before they develop; there are also texts that fit into neither of the three subject matters I bring into focus. That said, I argue that these three topics reflect the major directions that the silent screenwriting discourse took across cultural and linguistic borders.

13.2 Pre-War Screenwriting Discourse: The Famous *Authors*

The beginnings of the European discourse on screenwriting lie in the press discussions of the French Film d'Art company and its productions. Film d'Art pioneered the collaboration between the film industry and eminent literary authors as early as 1908 by hiring the playwright Henri Lavedan as the company's literary director and by inviting multiple writers to contribute original scripts (Carou 2008, 11–19).[3] This endeavour provoked an immediate reaction in the press. The theatre journal *La Vedette* saw the willingness of famous authors to write for film as "treason" and "vulgar downfall", emphasising that film could not hope to provide "an even remotely correct translation of the thought" of the playwrights such as Lavedan, Henry Bataille, or Victorien Sardou (Hellem 1908, 299). The journal *La Nouvelle revue* was less dismissive, seeing the engagement of literary authors as a step in the aesthetic development of film: "Little by little scenario makers have been replaced by the best of our writers, the most famous of our playwrights" (Claris 1909, 546). The pejorative term "scenario makers" is symptomatic of how the author of the article regards the craft of screenwriting: "In reality the genre is simple. There is no need to have style. It suffices to group a few funny or tragic ideas around a quick piece of action" (546). He further holds that by contrast to "scenario makers", literary authors can offer proper "theatrical plays" to film, which are performed by renowned theatre actors and are shown in accordingly grand cinema theatres (546). From early on, the discourse on screenwriting is thus inextricably linked to the discourse on playwriting and famous playwrights by way of contrast or of analogy.

The opposition between "scenario makers" and playwrights further points to the difference between writing one-reel films (up to 350 metres or 15 minutes screen time) and multiple-reel films, or what later came to be known as *features*. One-reel films were either shot without any written plan or based on very rudimentary outlines, hence the pejorative attitude to those who composed these outlines. By contrast, eminent authors usually provided scripts for more prestigious multiple-reel films. The latter became established in Europe by the start of World War I (Sandberg 2005, 452); the tacit distinction between writing shorter or longer films therefore vanishes completely from the screenwriting discourse in the second half of the 1910s.

Two articles, both ironic in their tone and both published in 1913, provide an idea of the further development of the pre-war discourse in France. The first article appeared in the daily newspaper *Paris-Midi* and can be boiled down to the following thought: "It is almost as difficult to have a director of a film company read a film script, as a director of a Parisian theatre—to read a play manuscript" (Flagey 1913). The article is styled as a report of an aspiring screenwriter, contrasting his comical failures to the nonchalance of the famous authors who submit their scripts to the same film company. The moral of the essay is clear: Selling a script to a film studio is possible only by way of miracle or incredible persistence, unless one is an eminent literary author or a member of a prestigious academy.

---

[3] Other film companies, most notably Pathé, had employed literary authors before Film d'Art; however, the effort of Film d'Art was pioneering in regard to the authors' repute and the importance attached to their involvement.

The second article appeared in one of the largest daily newspapers, *Le Journal*. In recounting his failed attempt at screenwriting, the journalist juxtaposes the film's pretence of being a new art and the clichéd film repertoire of the time. He believes to have studied that repertoire to perfection after spending a week at the local cinemas: "Four formulas were offered to express all the modalities of universal thought. [...] I could compose a comic, a sentimental, a historical, or a dramatic scenario" (Choudens 1913, 7). Yet, all four scripts he writes are rejected, since they all present "ancient cinema", as the clerk of the film studio explains to him. In the words of the clerk, the screenwriter is expected to depart from everything that is typical of the films of the time: adapting literature, theatre, and history, and using intertitles and "tricks". What and how the screenwriter should write instead remains a mystery. Although the article does not discuss the screenwriting of literary celebrities directly, it exposes the consequences of the fashion for films written by famous authors: This fashion elevated the film's cultural status and ambitions, yet its artistic development fell behind.

In Germany, two interconnected sociocultural movements were also extremely interested in the figure of the prominent screenwriter: the so-called *Kinoreformbewegung* (literally: movement for cinema reforms) and the *Autorenfilm* (authors' film). Since around 1907, numerous educators, church workers, and morality activists had been voicing concerns with the corrupting effect of film, especially on children and the youth (Scholz 2016, 77–78). They demanded radical reforms in the film industry such as stricter censorship, cutbacks in the share of foreign films on the German market, and a promotion of educational films (78–79). When the German film industry began its transition to longer and high-budget feature films around 1912, the "cine-reformers" discovered the screenwriter as a possible "guarantor of the artistic [and moral—A. K.] quality of the film" (79).

An illustrative example of this situation is the 1913 article "Cinema poets" ("Kinodichter") by Fritz Müller. It starts with a complaint typical of cine-reformers, deploring the dominance of *Schundfilme* (literally: junk films), a term used to refer to "low-quality" and morally dubious films. The only solution to this problem, Müller (1913, 3) insists, is to invite established writers and poets to work for the film industry: only through them can the people express and exercise their will for "good films". Despite this nationalistic belief, Müller demonstrates a sober view on the obstacles preventing such development: First, the social prejudices against film, and second, the directors who believe that they can do without screenwriters (3).

These obstacles did not persist for long though. Already in 1913, two prominent Austrian authors broke with the prejudices against screenwriting: Hugo von Hofmannsthal wrote the pantomime *The Foreign Girl* (*Das fremde Mädchen*), realised by Mauritz Stiller in Sweden (*Den okända*, 1913), and Arthur Schnitzler adapted his own play *Flirtation* (*Liebelei*) into a script realised by August Blom and Holger-Madsen in Denmark (*Elskovsleg*, 1913). At the same time, the German playwright Gerhart Hauptmann who had just received the Nobel Prize in Literature sold the rights for the adaptation of his novella *Atlantis*, which resulted in a prestigious Danish production of the same name in 1913. These events made news. One of the most influential critics of the time, Alfred Kerr (1917, 132), even composed an ironic poem on this occasion: "Not some tiny nasty scribbler! / Gerhart Hauptmann; Arthur Schnitzler; / The hostility is dashed —/ Since the matter brings some cash!"[4] Kerr's assessment was correct: The hostility of literary circles towards film was broken, and German film companies followed the example set by their French, Italian, and Scandinavian colleagues, launching a wave of high-end *Autorenfilme* written by prominent literary personalities.[5]

The engagement of literary authors in the film industry was crucial in elevating the prestige of screenwriting and in establishing a discourse on authorship. For instance, the 1913 article "Problems of the Film Drama" ("Probleme der Kinodramatik") begins:

> We are standing at a turning point for the art of film. Outstanding playwrights and writers, including those who used to be outspoken opponents of film, have declared themselves ready to put their works in the service of the new art. (Schönfeldt 1913)

This outset gives the article's author reasons to argue against laconic scripts written in "telegram style". In his view, short scripts prevent the readers from fully comprehending the "intentions of the creator", and subsequently the cinematic "representation" of the script cannot "achieve the effect intended by the author" (Schönfeldt 1913). In this way, the article foreshadows the heated debates on the author/director relationship that unfolded in the second half of the 1910s.

At the same time, one of the earliest German handbooks on screenwriting, *Material for Film Writers* (*Material für Filmschriftsteller*), compiled by the editorial team of the literary journal *Die Feder*, reveals the downside of the "authors' cinema". Film companies are primarily interested in scripts by the "authors with a name", while for little-known authors sending in manuscripts often turns out to be a waste of time (Redaktion der Feder 1913, 6).[6] This

---

[4] Orig.: "Nicht nur winzig schofle Kritzler! / Gerhart Hauptmann; Arthur Schnitzler; / Widerstreben eingestellt — / Denn die Sache trägt a Geld!". Although the poem is dated 10.11.1912 in Kerr's collected works, it is possible that he actually wrote it in 1913, on the occasion of the premieres of *Atlantis* and *Elskovsleg*.

[5] The earliest examples of the German *Autorenfilm* are *The Other* (*Der Andere*, 1913) and *The Last Day* (*Der letzte Tag*, 1913), both written by the prominent playwright Paul Lindau and directed by the film pioneer Max Mack, as well as *The Student of Prague* (*Der Student von Prag*, 1913), written by the popular novelist Hanns Heinz Ewers.

[6] *Material for Film Writers* further demonstrates how little importance the industry attached to the format of the screenplay in the early 1910s. The editors of the volume organised a survey among nearly a dozen film companies, posing them six questions related to their practice of handling screenplay submissions. The first of these questions concerned the format, in which the scripts should be submitted to the respective company. Each company answered this question in a different way, e.g.: "A simple scenario is sufficient; the

judgement echoes the French article that exposes the difficulties of selling a script to a Parisian film studio (Flagey 1913), indicating that French and German novice screenwriters were facing similar obstacles. Moreover, around the same time German film companies developed the practice of crediting only those screenwriters whose names could be used for advertisement, while others mostly remained uncredited. The journalist, literary author, and screenwriter Hans Brennert[7] (1916, 22–23) still bemoaned this crediting practice three years later, in 1916.

The involvement of literary authors also initiated the screenwriting discourse in Russia. In 1912, the film *Anfisa* (1912) based on the screenplay by the prominent writer Leonid Andreyev attracted the attention of the press: "What used to be some kind of heresy has now come true. Leonid Andreyev is writing a special scenarium for the cinema, adapting his own play for it" (Lur'ye 1912, 14). In the same year, Andreyev published "A Letter on Theatre" ("Pis'mo o teatre") in the theatre journal *Maski*; this article gave such a significant push to the discourse on film and screenwriting that the largest film journal *Sine-Fono* republished it in 1913. In the article, Andreyev predicts the soon improvement of film technology and, subsequently:

> [the appearance of] the new cinema-playwrights, the yet unknown talents and geniuses. Cinema-Shakespeare, discarding the shy word, will deepen and expand the action, will find new and unexpected combinations for it, so that the [film] action will become as expressive as speech, and at the same time will become as incomparably convincing as only the visible and the tangible can be. (Andreyev 1913a, 13)

By contrast to his contemporaries, Andreyev seems to connect the future of film with the advent of professional film authors rather than with the famous literary names. However, this view did not prevent him from continuing his own screenwriting experiments as a layperson: his original comedy screenplay *Administrative Ecstasy* (*Administrativnyy vostorg*) was included into his collected works together with a reprint of "A Letter on Theatre" ("Iz 'Pisem o teatre'") in the same year (1913a and 1913b).[8] Until the appearance of the journal *Pegas* in 1915, Andreyev's writings remained among the most significant and widely discussed contributions to the Russian screenwriting discourse.

shorter the better"; "The best [format] is scene by scene, in the form of stage directions"; "Elaboration in dramatic form is desirable. Short but exhaustive manuscripts are preferred"; "My companies request that film ideas be written only in the form of theater plays, because our actors say their lines precisely" (Redaktion der Feder 1913, 26–28).

[7] In 1918, Brennert became the head of the screenwriting department in the newly founded professional union of film workers, "Bund der Film- und Kinoangehörigen" (Scholz 2016, 94).

[8] As I argue elsewhere (Ksenofontova 2020b, 55–58), Andreyev's *Administrative Ecstasy* aimed to compensate for the lack of speech in film through inventive use of ironic intertitles.

Still in 1912, both the Russian branch of Pathé and the key Russian film producer Khanzhonkov and Co. signed contracts with a whole series of prominent literary authors. As Alexander Khanzhonkov recalls in his memoirs:

> [. . .] several newspapers condemned the writers' transition to "cinematic" activities. [The newspaper] *Vecherneye vremya* directly called Russian writers "metres brewers". It looked down on this new type of creative work and reproached the writers who had forgotten "the interests of Russian literature" in favour of Pathé and Khanzhonkov. (Khanzhonkov 1937, 65)

The worries of the press were exaggerated, continues Khanzhonkov (1937, 65), since only very few contracted writers managed to submit original screenplays. Apart from a few exceptions such as Andreyev, attracting literary authors into the Russian film industry remained a largely unsolved task.

An article from 1914 in Khanzhonkov's trade journal *Vestnik Kinematografii* considers the possible reasons and solutions for this issue. It regards writing for film as a kind of literary work, and the screenplay—as a "novella divided into separate scenes according to the time and place of action" (Ulis 1914, 10). Yet unlike other literary works, "this novella is not offered to the reader's judgment"; it is at the full disposal of the director and the actors, who often "disfigure" it to the extent that the author is "unable to recognise his idea" (10). The article identifies this insipient writer/director struggle as the main reason why prominent writers are still reluctant to write for film in Russia and argues for a more thoughtful and attentive attitude to the screenplay on the part of directors and actors.

Overall, the pre-World War I discourse on screenwriting in Europe tends to spotlight the screenwriting efforts of famous literary authors, connecting them to the developing cultural status of film. Although writing for film is still often regarded as an unworthy activity, the endorsement by literary authors gradually contributes to legitimising film as a socially and culturally acceptable form of entertainment and art. Screenwriting of literary authors and its aesthetic potential are often contrasted to the *primitive* scripts of non-literary screenwriters on the one hand and to the crude treatment of scripts during shooting on the other. In this regard, the screenwriting discourse builds upon the tradition of theatre and drama. Film scripts are compared to theatrical plays, and the roles of the screenwriter and the film director—to those of the playwright and the theatre director. This is also the reason why the screenwriter is usually referred to as simply "the author": By analogy with theatre, the screenwriter is considered the author of the film, and the director's task is to "translate" (Hellem 1908, 299) or "represent" (Schönfeldt 1913) the author's ideas. However, this power structure privileging the screenwriter was radically revised before it could fully take shape. Unlike the prominent literary author, the professional screenwriter was powerless in the face of the director.

The active involvement of literary authors in screenwriting was largely responsible for the different directions screenwriting discourses took in Europe and in the USA. Film studios such as Universal, Famous Players-Lasky, and Samuel Goldwyn's studio attempted collaborations with literary authors only after professional screenwriting departments were established (see Maras 2009, 163–66). These largely unsuccessful attempts remained at the periphery of the screenwriting discourse. As a result, the screenwriter never became a figure prominent enough to challenge the privileged position of the director or producer; the screenwriter vs. director discourse didn't develop in the USA until the advent of the auteur theory around the 1960s (see Maras 2009, 97–116).

13.3 The Second Half of the 1910s: Screenwriter vs. Director

In Europe, the debates around the involvement of eminent authors in screenwriting were largely carried out in the non-specialised press, as the film trade press still had a limited circulation and could not yet offer a wide platform for discussion. However, this situation changed in the second half of the 1910s. The circulation of film press was increasing; the share of critical articles in the journals was growing compared to the share of advertisements; and at the same time, manuals and handbooks were gaining popularity and contributing to the development of the discourse. Throughout these expanding film press and book publications, two words appeared over and over again: scenario crisis.

Soon after the outbreak of the World War I, many countries limited the import of foreign films, while the general demand on the film market kept growing. Neither the quality nor the quantity of the scripts provided by literary authors could satisfy this demand. On the contrary, as Hans Brennert put it in one of the earliest specialised German books on the film industry, *The Flickering Screen* (*Die Zappelnde Leinwald (The Flickering Screen)* 1916), the industry now saw the literary author "as the somewhat eerie intruder, whose name and ideas one doesn't mind acquiring, but who leaves one wondering: how does he manage to write a film at all, *even though* he is a writer…" (Brennert 1916, 23, emphasis in original).

To meet the demands that neither the literary "intruders" nor the screenwriting competitions[9] could cover, film companies established screenwriting departments. The screenwriting discourse therefore focused on defining the place of the newly emerged professional screenwriter within the industry, their rights and responsibilities.

In 1919, the prestigious French film journal *Le Film* conducted a survey that provides the most versatile and exhaustive picture of the views on the new profession. Although the survey was published under the title "The Scenario:

---

[9] Screenwriting competitions were film companies' major means of acquiring new ideas until the mid-1910s (Scholz 2016, 103). The supposedly fraudulent nature of those competitions was a major issue in the screenwriting discourse of the time: Writers accused film companies of stealing the ideas of the rejected scripts (see, for example, Redaktion der Feder 1913, 8–9).

What It Should Be—Some Official Opinions" ("Le Scénario: Ce qu'il doit être—Quelques avis autorisés"), the absolute majority of respondents actually talk about the skills and position of the screenwriter rather than about the script. They identify the uncertain and precarious position of the screenwriter as the main cause of the scenario crisis.

In particular, the playwright and later screenwriter Francis de Croisset (*Le Film* 1919, 10) states that the key to improving the quality of films is attracting "good" writers into the industry. To this end, Croisset suggests banishing film "fabricators" who dream of abolishing the screenwriters altogether, and installing "conscientious" directors instead. Developing a similar line of thought, the theatre director, actor, and critic André Antoine (16) argues for a stricter separation of conception and execution in film production,[10] by analogy to that established in theatre. In his view, a detailed screenplay should have the status "ne varietur" (Latin: unchangeable), and the director should realise it without adding or changing anything. Another proponent of this view was the young founder of *Le Film*, screenwriter Henri Diamant-Berger. His 1919 book *Le Cinéma* articulates a most categorical standpoint on this matter:

> The scenario is the film itself. [. . .] It's wrong to believe that the film is a development of the scenario, that the scenario contains only the rough substance of the film [. . .]. The author of the scenario must bear responsibility for the film. [. . .] The author should be obeyed; accordingly, he should follow the execution of his scenario in order to make sure its production respects its intentions. (Diamant-Berger 1919, 35; trans. Diamant-Berger 1988, 183–84)

Further in the book, Diamant-Berger formulates almost the exact equivalent of Thomas H. Ince's legendary stamp "shoot as written": "The film should be written exactly as it will be shot" (1919, 145; trans. Diamant-Berger 1988, 185).[11] In the post-1914 Hollywood and the early Soviet film industry such a view developed from the need to optimise production, but for Diamant-Berger it is primarily a matter of honouring the screenwriter and their work.

Responding to *Le Film*'s survey, film director Louis Feuillade expresses an opposing opinion: In his view, the way out of the scenario crisis is for the screenwriters to learn directing and producing their scripts themselves (*Le Film* 1919, 18). As long as films are written and directed by different people, Feuillade holds the director rather than the writer responsible for the quality and success of the film. Elaborating on this view, Feuillade sets a milestone in the history of screenwriting discourse:

---

[10] On the separation of conception and execution and its significance for the historiography of screenwriting, see Maras (2009, 21–23).

[11] According to a historical myth, the US film pioneer Thomas H. Ince used to stamp the scripts he approved for production with the stamp "shoot as written" (see Azlant 1980, 166–67).

> The real author is, in my opinion, less the one who conceives the images in a dream than the one who brings them to light in reality. [. . .] And the author of a painting—let's not forget that we are talking about images—is not the one who found a motif but the one who realises it. (*Le Film* 1919, 19)

Without explicitly stating it, Feuillade clearly indicates that in his view, the director rather than the writer is the actual "author" of the film. In so doing, he becomes one of the first to use the term "author" not in the sense of *writer* or by analogy with theatre, but in relation to the person held responsible for the artwork as a whole. This early instance of film *auteurism* represents the opposite pole to the theatrical tradition as described by Antoine, which regards the director as a mere executor of the "author's", that is, the writer's idea.

Some industry professionals voice more moderate opinions on the writer/director question. In particular, the head of the second-largest film company of the time Léon Gaumont (*Le Film* 1919, 14) recognises the importance of both the screenwriter and the director for the success of the production. Gaumont envisages the improvement of collaboration between the two through the education of writers: ideally, they should study the art of filmmaking "to the point of being able to guide the directors, if necessary". Similarly, the actor René Navarre (best known for playing Fantômas in the film series of the same name, 1913–1914) recognises the importance of preserving the separation of conception and execution, as "it is [...] impossible for a director to write his own scripts" (19). However, in Navarre's view, the screenwriter should be up to date on the technical side of filmmaking and collaborate with both the director and the principal actor, so that the film's realisation can come as close as possible to the initial conception. Multiple respondents to *Le Film*'s survey thus identify the writer/director relationship as the key issue in the development of the industry and hope to resolve this issue primarily through the writer's training.

Such a view was also typical of the industry professionals in Germany and became the reason for the boom of screenwriting manuals on the German market. At least nine handbooks on screenwriting were published in the years 1917–1920. Schwarz (1994, 135) notes the contradictory nature of those manuals: Acknowledging the necessity of learning the screenwriting conventions, the handbooks provide only very scarce if any information on the specifics of these conventions. Instead, they refer to the exemplary manuscripts usually published at the end of the manual and proceed to discuss the questions of "film genres, authorship rights, censorship, and payment" (135). Schwarz's analysis confirms that the screenplay *text* and its conventions enter the screenwriting discourse only in the 1920s, while earlier publications focus largely on the figure of the screenwriter.

This emphasis on the screenwriter is evident not only in trade journals and industry books but also in the non-specialised press. An illustrative example is the "widely noted" (Schwarz 1994, 134) article by the screenwriter Julius Sternheim that appeared in the weekly journal *Das Tage-Buch*. Sternheim

(1920, 1142–44) reviews the entire historical development of the film industry through the lens of screenwriting. His verdict: To become the "ruler of the film stage" by analogy with the playwright in theatre, the screenwriter has to learn the production routine, the "film instinct", and the "graphic eye" (Ger. *plastischer Blick*, 1144); what exactly those mysterious skills are, remains unclear. Sternheim (1144) concedes that "some directors still regard the author as an evil and only necessary as a provider of the basic dramatic idea", yet he finds that such view should give the writers all the more motivation to prove those directors wrong. The patronising and categorical tone of Sternheim's article indicates how pressing the writer/director issue has become.

Besides the problematic relationship with the director many publications of the time note the poor remuneration of screenwriters. Brennert (1916, 28) and Diamant-Berger (1916, 7) raise this issue already in 1916; by the end of the decade, it becomes more and more critical. The main German trade journal, *Der Kinematograph*, dedicates an entire article to this problem in 1919. Comparing the fees for screenwriting in France, Germany, and the UK to those in the USA, Vera Bern (1919) deplores the European neglect for screenwriters. "The decisive factor for the high quality of the American film product is […] that the entrepreneurs ascribe the greatest importance to the film writers" and reward them accordingly, emphasises Bern (1919). Even the volume *Cinema* (*Kino*) by the journalist and writer Max Prels (1919, 28), which mentions screenwriters only in passing, notes their inadequate earnings and the subsequently low appeal of the profession.

Focusing on the figure of the screenwriter, the German discourse thus highlights not only the matter of technical know-how but primarily the screenwriter's extremely precarious position. Hence, the creation of the Association of German Film Authors (*Verband deutscher Filmautoren*) in 1919. As implied in the name of the association, screenwriters were still considered the film's principal authors, and they were determined to try and protect their rights as such.

The Russian screenwriting discourse of the time demonstrates similar concerns but a somewhat different chronology. The initial industry boom in the wake of the World War I was followed by the turmoil of the revolutions and the ensuing civil war of 1917–1922. These years mark a gap in the development of the industry and in publications, which resume only in the mid-1920s.

From the pre-revolutionary press, the most significant contribution to the screenwriting discourse undoubtedly belongs to the journal *Pegas*. As I elaborate elsewhere (Ksenofontova 2023a), the editorial policy of *Pegas* was to promote the screenwriter as a demotic authorial figure by contrast to the unapproachable literary genius. This screenwriter image was meant to appeal to middlebrow audiences, whom *Pegas* hoped to attract into the cinemas. At the same time, spotlighting the screenwriter as the main "author" of film was crucial to *Pegas*'s mission of stabilising the sociocultural status of film and legitimising it as a form of art. This editorial policy manifested itself in the structure and content of the journal, which published up to four original screenplays per issue, and in multiple articles by the journal's editor-in-chief Nikandr Turkin.

For instance, Turkin's editorial from 1916 analyses a conflict between the screenwriter Anna Mar and the director Yevgeni Bauer. Turkin starts by quoting the letter of Mar, addressed presumably to the editorial team of *Pegas*. In it, Mar details her impressions from a recent film based on her screenplay:

> It was a truly sad spectacle. The idea and the theme of the script are ridiculously distorted. Major intertitles are missing. Giving his due to Mr. Bauer as an artist, [. . .] I totally object to his interference with my authorial rights. (Mar quoted in Turkin 1916, 104)

Analysing the issue, Turkin acknowledges the disparity between Mar's script and Bauer's film, emphasising that the latter has had great success with the audience. For Turkin, the audience's approval means that Bauer managed to lend his film a visual appeal that Mar failed to capture in her script: "Jealously guarding the ideas of their work, the writers have not learned to think and speak in the language of cinema" (Turkin 1916, 105). The article concludes with a utopian hope for a new generation of screenwriters who are able to evoke the "picturesqueness" of film (106) and thereby perhaps eliminate the grounds for the screenwriter/director conflict.

Turkin's article is typical of the screenwriting discourse of the time insofar as it spotlights the issues of writer/director relationship, the lacking know-how of screenwriters, and the screenwriters' inability to provide satisfactory scripts. Like most of his colleagues throughout Europe, Turkin finds that the resolution of these issues requires radical innovation. Unlike most of his colleagues, Turkin guessed correctly the main subject and source of this innovation— the screenplay. The screenwriting discourse of the 1910s was still dominated by comparisons with theatre; consequently, many publications insisted on altering the organisation of film production, the screenwriters' status, and their payment to match the theatrical tradition. Rather than addressing these structural issues, the film industry attempted taking an easier way out of the scenario crisis by shifting attention from the screenwriter to screenwriting.

13.4 The 1920s: Enter the (Published) Screenplay

Whereas in the early 1910s, the film industry was chasing after famous authors, by the end of the 1910s the famous authors as well as the young avant-gardes started chasing after the film industry. There were many reasons for this explosion of interest in screenwriting. To begin with, film offered a rare opportunity of earnings among the post-war hardships. At the same time, the search for new means of expression and genres dominated the post-war literary scene, and on this search, the screenplay was a fortuitous find in many regards.

It broke with the nineteenth century ways of writing; it carried the excitement of the new medium and of the modern era; and it seemed to offer vast possibilities for experimentation. Or so the avant-gardes thought.

The poet and playwright Guillaume Apollinaire is often considered a pioneer of screenwriting discourse among the French avant-gardes because of his 1917 speech "The New Spirit and the Poets" ("L'Esprit nouveau et les poètes").[12] In it, Apollinaire (1971, 237) encouraged his fellow poets "to be the first to provide a totally new lyricism for these new means of expression [...] the phonograph and the cinema". Since Apollinaire was an incredibly influential figure in the literary scene, his encouragement produced an immediate response, and experimental scripts by young modernists started appearing in print, sometimes accompanied by short articles on film and screenwriting. By the mid-1920s, the amount of published scripts reached the point at which the screenplay became noticeable as a new literary genre. The 1925 special issue "Scénarios" of the journal *Les Cahiers du Mois* is indicative of this trend: With six experimental screenplays of young literary authors, it claimed to explore the screenplay as "a literary genre", "an expansion of the common literary technique", and as "literature set free by the cinema" (Berge and Berge 1925, 131, 134, and 135, respectively). The discourse on the "screenplay as literature" has emerged.

One of the most interesting contributions to it came from the literary critic and translator Benjamin Crémieux. Unlike the editors of *Les Cahiers du Mois*, Crémieux (1925, 2) held that the screenplay doesn't bring anything new into literature, since all textual features of the screenplay have already been tried out elsewhere: in the prose poems of the surrealists, in the interior monologue, and in the futurist and "simultaneous" lyric poetry. Moreover, he believed that the writers' efforts "should be judged based on the result obtained on the screen and not based on the scenario" (2). This view ran contrary not only to the common enthusiasm for the screenplay as a new literary genre but also to the professional screenwriting discourse. Journals such as *Le Film* (1918, 12) and *Pegas* (Turkin 1915, 52) were publishing screenplays to give the readers access to the "original intentions of the author", and the complaints about inadequate realisations of initially "good" scripts were piling up in film reviews and in trade press. Yet Crémieux (2) insisted: If the script is "shootable" (Fr. *filmable*), then its readers regret not being able to see the film instead of reading the script; and if the script is "unshootable", then the readers regret that the author hasn't chosen to tell the story in a different genre, e.g. as a novel.

---

[12] "The New Spirit" was first read by actor Pierre Bertin at the Théâtre de Vieux-Colombier on November 26, 1917, and published a year later in the literary magazine *Mercure de France* (Apollinaire 1918). The speech contains exactly two passages that refer to the cinema: one at the beginning and one at the end. Because of this conspicuous placement, and because these passages have been quoted in the research so often, the impression may arise that film is a central theme of "The New Spirit". Yet, these are only two passages in an essay of approximately 4,200 words; the rest of Apollinaire's speech is dedicated to poetry.

Crémieux was among the very few who opposed the idea of publishing scripts: An unparalleled number of experimental screenplays in French appeared in press and in book form during the 1920s.[13] The "screenplay as literature" discourse remained present in France throughout the entire 1920s (and beyond), highlighting in particular the conjunctions between screenwriting and poetry (see Wall-Romana 2013). However, this discourse was mostly limited to modernist writers and other industry "outsiders"; the professional discourse gravitated towards the question of screenwriting conventions. The appeal to establish such conventions came particularly from those familiar with the US film industry.

For instance, the only person to raise the question of screenwriting form among the respondents to *Le Film*'s survey was an employee of the US Famous Players-Lasky Corporation, scenario editor Mac Alaren. He expressed regrets that in France, there was "no particular requirement for the presentation of the scenarios. We receive them both in the form of an exhibit, a summary or narrated in detail" (*Le Film* 1919, 16). Four years later, the writer-director Louis Delluc (1923, 4) echoed this criticism in his article published in the established journal *Comoedia*: "In France, three quarters of films are based on a very good summary of twenty-five lines. Yet these twenty-five lines lack cinematographic writing". Delluc's own preferred screenwriting format was the American "continuity" or the French "découpage", as it allowed avoiding "the dangerous improvisation" during filming (4).

These and a few other critical voices notwithstanding, the French professional screenwriting discourse developed in full only after the advent of sound (see Török 1986, 48–49). As a result of World War I, the French film industry remained in deep crisis throughout most of the 1920s; the French film producers consequently had no need to debate screenwriting rules and conventions in order to streamline booming production, unlike their German, Russian, or US colleagues. In addition, several branches of French avant-garde filmmaking including abstract and Dada film were explicitly opposed to screenwriting (Ksenofontova 2020b, 83–87), and under their influence the French filmmakers of the time attached less and less importance to the screenplay.

By contrast, the need to establish screenwriting conventions was widely recognised in Germany and resulted in a proliferation of screenwriting handbooks. Compared to the handbooks from the late 1910s, those from the 1920s demonstrate more attention to the standards and techniques of writing. For instance, the manual by Urban Gad (1921, 37–46) and the second edition of the manual by Ewald André Dupont (1925, 37–44) both contain chapters on "The Form of the Film Manuscript". Even though these chapters are rather short, they establish a clear separation between different stages of script development. For instance, Gad (1921, 43–45) differentiates between a draft (*Entwurf*), a scenario (*Szenarium*), and an elaborated manuscript; Dupont

---

[13] For a bibliography of published silent screenplays in French, German, Russian, and other languages, see Ksenofontova (2020a).

(1925, 38; 41–42) mentions a draft (*Exposé*), a manuscript, and a director's script (*Regiebuch*). In this regard, the emerging conventions in Germany resemble those in Russia, where the publications differentiate between a "libretto" (i.e. a draft), a scenario or a "literary scenario", and a director's script (Cherkasov 1926a, 1926b; Shklovsky 1926; Sokolov 1926).

While the screenwriting manuals continued gaining popularity in Germany, the practice of screenplay publications remained practically non-existent. However, the idea of such a practice was being hailed with vigour. In his 1922 article "Film Drama as Book" ("Filmdrama als Buch"), journalist Paul Eller asserted that publishing screenplays would solve many if not most problems of the film industry in one blow. The writers would have their work presented to the public as they conceived it; prospective screenwriters would be able to learn from the published scripts; and the latter would attract the attention of critics, literary historians, and academics, whose criticism would improve the general quality of screenwriting (Eller 1922, 634). Furthermore, published scripts would allow both German and foreign film distributors to better estimate the value of films available for rent (635). Compared to the prize money film companies are willing to pay in screenwriting competitions, the expenses for publishing scripts would be insignificant, so "the film industry should cover the costs of publishing [film] dramas in book form", concludes Eller (635).[14]

One of the first attempts to start a regular publication of film scripts in Germany showed that Eller's expectations were premature. The Potsdam publishing house Gustav Kiepenheuer launched the book series "The Screenplay: A Collection of Selected Film Manuscripts" ("Das Drehbuch: Eine Sammlung ausgewählter Film-Manuskripte") in 1924. However, the series was discontinued right after the first publication, the script *New Year's Eve* (*Sylvester*, 1924) by Carl Mayer. Although Mayer was already an acclaimed screenwriter at the time, the publication did not attract much attention, save for a mention by the playwright and theatre critic Julius Bab. He condemns Mayer's script for working with "literary means" and for imitating the style of the expressionist poets, even though he finds that the script "also offers some curious new things" and "could be the beginning of a new literary genre" (Bab 1925, 192).

As German screenwriting practice and professional discourse grew increasingly complex and specialised with the rapid development of the industry, screenwriting was becoming more and more alien to literary outsiders. Rather than experimenting with the new genre, German-speaking writers and playwrights therefore preferred selling the rights for cinematic adaptation of their works. As a result, the number of published screenplays was significantly lower compared to France, and the "screenplay as literature" discourse was less present, even if remarkably enthusiastic.

---

[14] Erich Staude (1922) repeated Eller's ideas, some of them word for word, in his article in *Filmkurier*.

The discussion of the screenplay as a new kind of literature was also typical of the developing Soviet culture, but the tone of this discussion was almost diametrically opposed to that in France and in Germany. An early article by the literary critic Viktor Shklovsky, "New Literary Form" ("Novaya literaturnaya forma", 1923), shows some initial excitement about the emergence of a "literary-independent script". However, a few years and several completed screenplays later, Shklovsky's attitude changes to bitter-ironic:

> A person was once asked if they could play the piano. The person replied: "I don't know, I haven't tried". Those people who are now sending in scripts by the thousands to film factories are trying to see if they know how to play the piano. (Shklovsky 1926, 3)

The rest of the article emphasises the importance of basic knowledge of film production for screenwriters. Yet even with this knowledge, Shklovsky (1926, 3) stresses, prospective screenwriters should limit themselves to sending in a five-pages libretto instead of a hundred-page-long script: "such libretto will then be elaborated together with the director". Shklovsky does not expect literary authors or a "literary" manner of writing to improve the quality of scripts. In fact, he wishes for the exact opposite—that the strict, "rigid" form of the screenplay can "contribute to changing the outdated techniques of fiction" (1928, 102). In other words: instead of adapting the screenplay to match the features of the existing literary genres, Shklovsky hopes that the rest of literature can "catch up" with the screenplay.

The literary critic and writer Osip Brik occupied an even more uncompromising position. In his view, the fact that the screenplay came to be seen as a literary genre was one of the main reasons of the on-going scenario crisis. He argues that the specifics of screenwriting are neglected when screenplays are being judged based on the criteria applied to fiction and drama or compared to works by Leo Tolstoy and Nikolai Gogol (Brik 1927, 11). Just like Shklovsky (1926, 3), Brik believes that "a good script suitable for production can be made only at the [film] factory" (12).

Most Russian literary authors of the time seemed to share Shklovsky's and Brik's views. Hence, the observation by the poet Vladimir Mayakovsky:

> My previous experience of screenwriting [. . .] showed me that any script creation by "literary men" with no connection to the factory and production is a piece of hack work. Thus, starting from tomorrow, I plan to start hanging around the film factory, so that, having understood the cinema business, I can intervene in the realisation of my present screenplays. (Mayakovsky [1926] 1959, 125)

Unlike French and German discourse, Soviet screenwriting discourse showed no clear divide between the concerns of the industry workers and those of the literary avant-gardes. Both were invested in finding common ground. Literary authors strived to learn the craft of film production and collaborate with the directors; at the same time, more and more industry professionals realised that "the script cannot be separated from the *mise en scène* and vice versa. When producing a film, the drafting [...] by the scriptwriter and the director should be unified" (Sokolov 1926, 10). Both parties thus recognised the screenplay as a distinct genre (be it literary or not), and both strived to reduce the divide between conception and execution.

In this context, it may seem surprising that the discourse on the so-called iron screenplay—the exact opposite of the idea of joined conception and execution—developed at exactly the same time. The term *iron script* was probably introduced in an article by A. Cherkasov, published in the trade journal *Kino-Front* in January 1926, and further developed in his other article later the same year.[15] Cherkasov's (1926a, 6) primary concern is the financial ineffectiveness of Soviet film production: the amount of film stock and the costs of making a film always end up being much higher than initially estimated. He therefore suggests that the director write a detailed, technical "iron script" based on the "literary script" of the screenwriter, and follow it meticulously during shooting and post-production (Cherkasov 1926a, 6–7; 1926b, 3–4). Separated conception and execution would satisfy Cherkasov's strive for financial efficiency by restricting the creative freedom of the film crew. The famous position of Sergei Eisenstein according to which "a numbered script will bring as much animation to cinema as the numbers on the heels of the drowned men in the morgue" ([1929] 1988, 134), developed as a counter-reaction to this utilitarian approach.[16] The contrast between Cherkasov's ideas and the trend towards joined conception and execution thus translates into the tension between the economic and creative aspects of production. The Soviet screenwriting discourse focused on resolving or at least alleviating this tension by negotiating the specifics of the screenplay text.

13.5 Conclusion

Although the screenwriting discourse of the 1920s still concerns itself with the screenwriter and their position in the film industry (Scholz 2016, 134–50), it also shifts towards paying more attention to the screenplay. While the non-professional discourse raises the questions of script publications and their place in the literary system, the professionals focus on the issues of writing style, conventions, and the stages of script development. The screenplay is being explored as a literary and as a functional text, and the difference between the two perspectives gradually comes to light. At the same time, it becomes apparent that screenplays can be written in a variety of different ways, and

---

[15] The signature "A. Cherkasov" most likely belongs to Aleksandr Apollinar'yevich Cherkasov, head of the production department of the Association for Revolutionary Cinematography (Assotsiatsiya revolyutsionnoy kinematografii, ARK).

[16] For more on Eisenstein's screenwriting theory and practice, see Schwarz (1994, 315–44) and Ksenofontova (2020b, 206–13; 2023b).

that these various screenplay styles and formats offer different possibilities of working with the script in production.

This situation is fundamentally different from the USA, where screenwriting standards started developing already in the early 1910s. By 1915, there was a whole range of screenwriting manuals available on the US market (see Curran 2015; for a bibliography, see Ksenofontova 2020a, 38–43). Consequently, the textual particularities of screenwriting were never subject to much debate but rather to gradual normalisation. The US discourse therefore mainly revolved around screenwriting standards such as the formats of scenario, continuity, synopsis, etc. (Maras 2009, 89–92).

Unlike in the USA, in Europe the heterogeneous approaches to screenwriting and to filmmaking continued co-existing throughout the 1920s despite the first attempts at standardisation. Russian writer, literary critic, and screenwriter Yury Tynyanov summarised this situation in his 1926 article "On the screenplay" ("O stsenarii") as follows:

> One monumental director took offence at the literariness of the screenwriter's writing manner:
>
> —What do I need the style and the details for? Write simply: enters, sits down, fires a pistol. The rest is up to me.
>
> Another filmmaker, down-to-earth but also respectable, said:
>
> —The story? What do I need the story for? I can give you thirty stories on the spot myself. No, your task is to pull out every detail. The rest is up to me.
>
> Both were apparently right.
>
> (Tynyanov [1926] 1977, 323)

The purpose of my essay was to trace the major trajectories of the European discourse on silent screenwriting without downplaying its cultural and contextual diversity. I have shown that, on the one hand, this discourse follows some developments of silent film theory and criticism. In particular, screenwriting is considered key to improving the sociocultural reputation of film in the early 1910s, since both screenwriting and filmmaking are conceived by analogy with theatre. When the media, economic, and aesthetic specifics of film production come to light, the focus of the screenwriting discourse also changes. Screenwriting is gradually recognised as a distinct profession, and the screenplay—as a distinct genre.

At the same time, the screenwriting discourse does not simply reproduce the film discourse but also features its own specific focal points and contexts. It aims to delineate the rights and responsibilities of the screenwriter starting from at least the mid-1910s; it develops a concern for the place of the screenplay among other genres and publications; and it sensitises both professional and non-professional audiences to the questions of writing style and format. In this way, screenwriting could stay in the focus of public attention on par with filmmaking during the entire silent film era—a constellation that has so far remained an exception in film history.

References

Andreyev, Leonid. 1912. *Anfisa*, screenplay.
Andreyev, Leonid. 1913a. "Iz 'Pisem o teatre'." *Sine-Fono* 9 (19 January): 12–13.
Andreyev, Leonid. 1913b. *Administrativnyy vostorg (Administrative Ecstasy)*. In *Polnoye sobraniye sochineniy Leonida Andreyeva: S portretom avtora*, vol. 8, 317–22. St. Petersburg: Marks.
Apollinaire, Guillaume. 1918. "L'Esprit nouveau et les poètes." *Mercure de France* 491 (1 December): 385–96.
Apollinaire, Guillaume. 1971. *Selected Writings of Guillaume Apollinaire*. Trans. with a critical introduction by Roger Shattuck. New York: New Directions.
Atlantis. 1913. Written by Karl Ludwig Schröder and Axel Garde, based on Gerhart Hauptmann's novel. Directed by August Blom. Denmark: Nordisk Films Kompagni.
Azlant, Edward. 1980. "The Theory, History and Practice of Screenwriting, 1897–1920." PhD diss., University of Wisconsin, Madison.
Bab, Julius. 1925. "Film und Kunst." In "Zweiter Kongreß für Ästhethik und allgemeine Kunstwissenschaft Berlin, 16.-18. Oktober 1924." Special issue, *Zeitschrift für Ästhetik und allgemeine Kunstwissenschaft* 19: 181–93.
Berge, André, and François Berge. 1925. "Le cahier de la rédaction" [Editorial]. In "Scénarios." Special issue edited by André Berge and François Berge, *Cahiers du Mois* 12: 131–34.
Bermann, Richard A. 1913. "Gedrucktes Kino." *Die Schaubühne* 9/II (43): 1028–29.
Bern, Vera. 1919. "Film-Literaten und Honorare in aller Welt." *Der Kinematograph* 664 (24 September): n. p.
Brennert, Hans. 1916. "Kinometerdichter." In *Die zappelnde Leinwand*, edited by Max Mack, 19–28. Berlin: Eysler.
Brik, Osip. 1927. "Po sushchestvu stsenarnogo krizisa." *Sovetskoye kino* 8–9: 11–12.
Carou, Alain. 2008. "Le Film d'Art ou la difficile invention d'une littérature pour l'écran (1908–1909)." *1895. Mille huit cent quatre-vingt-quinze* 56: 9–38.
Cherkasov, A. 1926a. "Rezhisser kino dolzhen byt' inzhenerom." *Kino-zhurnal A.R.K.* [*Kino-front*] 1 (January): 6–7.
Cherkasov, A. 1926b. "Zheleznyy stsenariy." *Kino-front* 9–10: 3–4.
Choudens, Jacques de. 1913. "L'art et la manière d'écrire un Scénario." *Le Journal* 7754 (19 December): 7.
Claris, Edmond. 1909. "Le Théâtre cinématographique." *La Nouvelle revue, troisième série* VII (January–February): 544—51.
Crémieux, Benjamin. 1925. "Cinéma et littérature." *Les Nouvelles littéraires, artistiques et scientifiques: hebdomadaire d'information, de critique et de bibliographie* 147 (8 August): 2.
Curran, Stephen C. 2015. "Early Screenwriting Teachers 1910–1922: Origins, Contribution and Legacy." PhD dissertation, Brunel University.
Delluc, Louis. 1923. "Scénarii." *Comoedia* 3763 (6 April): 4.
Der Andere (The Other). 1913. Written by Paul Lindau. Directed by Max Mack. Germany: Vitascope.

Der letzte Tag (*The Last Day*). 1913. Written by Paul Lindau. Directed by Max Mack. Germany: Vitascope.

Der Student von Prag (*The Student of Prague*). 1913. Written by Hanns Heinz Ewers. Germany: Deutsche Bioscope GmbH.

Diamant-Berger, Henri. 1919. *Le cinéma*. Paris: La Renaissance du Livre.

Diamant-Berger, Henri. 1988. "The Scenario. The Decoupage." In *1907–1929*, edited by Richard Abel, vol. 1 of *French Film Theory and Criticism: A History / Anthology, 1907–1939*, 183–88. Princeton, NJ: Princeton University Press.

Dupont, Ewald André. 1925. *Wie ein Film geschrieben wird und wie man ihn verwertet*. 2nd edition, revised by F. Podehl. Berlin: Kühn.

"Editorial." 1918. *Le Film* 106–07 (2 April): 12.

Eisenstein, Sergei. [1929] 1988. "The Form of the Script." In *Writings: 1922–1934*, trans. by Richard Taylor, vol. 1 of *Selected Works*, 134–35. London: British Film Institute.

Eller, Paul. 1922. "Filmdrama als Buch." *Börsenblatt für den deutschen Buchhandel* 103 (4 May): 634–35.

Flagey, Etienne. 1913. "Les coulisses du Cinéma." *Paris-Midi* 916 (9 August): n. p.

Gad, Urban. 1921. *Der Film: Seine Mittel—seine Ziele*. Berlin: Schuster & Loeffler.

Hellem, Charles. 1908. "En Marge du Programme." *La Vedette* 1628 (18 June): 299–300.

Hofmannsthal, Hugo von. [1913] 2006. *Das fremde Mädchen* (*The Foreign Girl*). In *Ballette, Pantomimen, Filmszenarien*, vol. 27 of *Sämtliche Werke*, edited by Gisela Bärbel Schmid and Klaus-Dieter Krabiel, 181–86. Frankfurt am Main: S. Fischer Verlag.

Kasten, Jürgen. 1994. *Carl Mayer: Filmpoet: Ein Drehbuchautor schreibt Filmgeschichte*. Berlin: Vistas.

Kerr, Alfred. 1917. *Eintagsfliegen oder die Macht der Kritik*. Vol. 4 of *Gesammelte Schriften in zwei Reihen*. Berlin: Fischer.

Khanzhonkov, Aleksandr. 1937. *Pervye gody russkoy kinematografii: Vospominaniya*. Moscow: Iskusstvo.

Ksenofontova, Alexandra. 2020a. "Drehbuch im Stummfilm: Eine Bibliographie / Silent Film Screenplay: A Bibliography." *Medienwissenschaft: Berichte und Papiere* 188. http://berichte.derwulff.de/0188_20.pdf. Accessed 7 August 2022.

Ksenofontova, Alexandra. 2020b. *The Modernist Screenplay: Experimental Writing for Silent Film*. Cham, Switzerland: Palgrave Macmillan.

Ksenofontova, Alexandra. 2023a [forthcoming]. "Inventing Middlebrow Cinema: The Russian Film Journal *Pegasus* (1915–17)." In "Periodicals and Silent Cinema." Special issue, *Journal of Modern Periodical Studies*, edited by Jonathan Cranfield.

Ksenofontova, Alexandra. 2023b [forthcoming]. "Sergei Eisenstein's 'The Form of the Script': A New Translation." *Film History*.

"Le Scénario: Ce qu'il doit être—Quelques avis autorisés." 1919. *Le Film* 159 (15 April): 9–21.

L[ur'ye], S[amuil]. 1912. "Sredi novinok." *Sine-Fono* 7 (1 January): 13–16.

Maras, Steven. 2009. *Screenwriting: History, Theory and Practice*. London: Wallflower.

Mayakovsky, Vladimir. [1926] 1959. ["O kinorabote"]. In *Stat'i, zametki i vystupleniya. Noyabr' 1917–1930*, vol. 12 of *Polnoye sobraniye sochineniy v 13 tomakh*, 125. Moscow: Gosudarstvennoye Izdatel'stvo Khudozhestvennoy Literatury. First published in 1926. *Novyy zritel'* 35 (138).

Mayer, Carl. 1920. *Der Dummkopf* (*The Blockhead*), screenplay.

Mayer, Carl. 1924. *Sylvester: Ein Lichtspiel (The New Year's Eve)*. Potsdam, Germany: Kiepenheuer Verlag.
Müller, Fritz. 1912–13. "Kinodichter." *Bild&Film: Zeitschrift für Lichtbilderei und Kinematographie* 1: 2–3.
Pick, Otto. [1913] 1957. Otto Pick to Alfred Kubin, 1 February 1913. In *Alfred Kubin: Leben, Weg, Wirkung*, edited by Paul Raabe, 39. Hamburg: Rowohlt Verlag.
Prels, Max. 1919. *Kino*. Bielefeld: Velhagen & Klasing.
Redaktion der Feder. 1913. *Material für Filmschriftsteller*. Berlin: Federverlag.
Sandberg, Mark B. 2005. "Multiple-reel/feature films: Europe." In *Encyclopedia of Early Cinema*, edited by Richard Abel, 452–456. London: Routledge.
Schnitzler, Arthur. [1913] 2015. *Liebelei (Love's Devotee)*. In *Filmarbeiten: Drehbücher, Entwürfe, Skizzen*, edited by Achim Aurnhammer, Hans Peter Buohler, Philipp Gresser, Julia Ilgner, Carolin Maikler, and Lea Marquart, 29–64. Würzburg, Germany: Ergon Verlag.
Scholz, Juliane. 2016. *Der Drehbuchautor: USA—Deutschland. Ein historischer Vergleich*. Bielefeld, Germany: Transcript.
Schönfeldt, Max. 1913. "Probleme der Kinodramatik." *Der Kinematograph* 351 (17 September): n. p.
Schwarz, Alexander. 1994. *Der geschriebene Film: Drehbücher des deutschen und russischen Stummfilms*. Munich: Diskurs Film.
Shklovsky, Viktor. 1923. "Novaya literaturnaya forma." *Zhizn' iskusstva* 28: 8.
Shklovsky, Viktor. 1926. "Libretto i material." *Kino* 39 (159): 3.
Shklovsky, Viktor. 1928. "Dva bronevika." *Sibirskiye Ogni* 5: 102–16.
Sokolov, Ippolit. 1926. "Khoroshiy stsenariy." *Kino-front* 9–10: 8–12.
Staude, Erich. 1922. "Das Filmdrama als Buch." *Filmkurier* 118 (27 May) and 119 (29 May).
Sternheim, Julius. 1920. "Der Filmautor, gestern und morgen." *Das Tage-Buch* 35 (11 September): 1142–44.
Török, Jean-Paul. 1986. *Le scénario: Histoire, théorie, practique*. Paris: Veyrier.
Turkin, Nikandr. 1915. "O 'Pegase'" [Editorial]. *Pegas* 2 (December): 49–52.
Turkin, Nikandr. 1916. "Zapisnaya knizhka 'Pegasa'" [Editorial]. *Pegas* 4 (April): 102–07.
Tynyanov, Yury. [1926] 1977. "O stsenarii." In *Poetika. Istoriya literatury. Kino*, by Yury Tynyanov, 323–4. Moscow: Izdatel'stvo Nauka. First published in 1926. *Kino* 9 (2 March): 1.
Ulis. 1914. "Avtor i kinematograf." *Vestnik Kinematografii* 91 (11): 10–11.
Wall-Romana, Christophe. 2013. *Cinepoetry: Imaginary cinemas in French poetry*. New York: Fordham University Press.

CHAPTER 14

When Women Wrote Hollywood: How Early Female Screenwriters Disappeared from the History of the Industry They Created. A Case Study of Four Female Screenwriters

Rosanne Welch

14.1 INTRODUCTION

Over the last few decades Screenwriting Studies have grown exponentially in the United States. An Ivy League mainstay such as Yale did not even offer film and media studies as a discipline of study until 1985, and then screenwriting classes did not begin there until 1992 (Wray 2021). Many such universities felt such a discipline was not deserving of academic study. Yet even as it is taught today across the world, screenwriting courses tend to teach the scripts of male screenwriters more than females and film history courses include more male filmmakers in general than they do females. They tuck women safely away in separate elective courses focused solely on their gender which falls into the trope of preaching to the choir. Also, those courses tend to be titled "Women Filmmakers" and involve more analysis of the work of early directors like Lois Weber and Dorothy Arzner, not screenwriters, which marginalizes women writers still further, unless the artist utilized both skills in their storytelling. Over the last twenty years, the untold stories of early writing pioneers, many of them women and people of color, began to appear in books but still served as a sidebar to the full story. This chapter plans to bring their names back into the canon of screenwriting studies.

R. Welch (✉)
Stephens College, Columbia, MI, USA
e-mail: rwelch@stephens.edu

© The Author(s), under exclusive license to Springer Nature Switzerland AG 2023
R. Davies et al. (eds), *The Palgrave Handbook of Screenwriting Studies*,
https://doi.org/10.1007/978-3-031-20769-3_14

259

14.2 Act One: How They Entered the Fledgling Industry…

14.2.1 From the Theater

As films arrived, so did female writers and many quickly learned to produce, direct, and do many of the other crafts associated with this new art form. Copyright records offer proof that almost half of all films written before 1925 were written by women (Beauchamp 1997). Women came to the film business by several routes but most often these included the theater, the world of journalism, and by winning contests set up by the early studios (routes still used by many females today).

Women often came into writing through acting which suits a society that considered women as objects to be looked at, not to be in control of the view. For instance, Bess Meredyth studied piano as a child and performed on vaudeville stages in what were called *pianologues*, presentations that involved playing while singing or reciting. As with many of these early female screenwriters, she entered the industry as an extra, joining the Biograph Company in 1911. She soon realized that she could make more money if she wrote as well—so she did (Lucas 2004). By 1926, Meredyth's reputation as a screenwriter lead to quite a productive year. She wrote *Don Juan* (1926), the story of the infamous Great Lover, played by Hollywood's Great Lover, John Barrymore, and adapted Herman Melville's *Moby Dick* into *The Sea Beast* (1930). Meredyth co-founded the Academy of Motion Picture Arts and Sciences in 1928. When the first Academy Awards were held in 1929, Meredyth was nominated for the screenplay *Wonder of Women*.

Marion Fairfax found her way into the theater when she married Broadway actor Tully Marshall Phillips in 1899. She acted in *The Triumph of Love* in 1904, and *Bedford's Hope* in 1906 before she turned to writing a play that both she and Tully could appear in together. *The Builders*, played at the Astor Theatre in 1907 for 16 performances. After a few years of plays being produced (or not produced), a 1915 April edition of *Motion Picture News* printed: "The Lasky Feature Play company has entered into a contract with Marion Fairfax, the New York dramatist, who will leave for the studios in Hollywood, this week. The scenario department of the Lasky Feature Play company is completely in charge of William C. De Mille…" ("Marion Fairfax, Dramatist, Is with Lasky" 1915). She wrote a few films for William C. De Mille, then Marshall Neilan Productions signed Fairfax for their next four productions, which were to be distributed by First National. Also, a 1921 agreement reported that following those four productions, Marion Fairfax Productions was to be set up in "a working arrangement with Mr. Neilan" ("Marshall Neilan Again Signs Marion Fairfax" 1920). In April, she received a telegram from De Mille, welcoming her to the fray, and stating "I am glad and afraid to welcome you as a competitor. At least I will learn from your work and I wish you every success in the world. You don't need good luck only opportunity" (De Mille 1921).

While Fairfax was earning kudos from William C. De Mille, Jeanie MacPherson's career became entwined with his brother, Cecil. Like Fairfax and Meredyth, Macpherson too came from the stage. Having studied opera and dance at the Kenwood Institute in Chicago, she took on a string of small roles on Broadway in the early 1900s. By 1908 she had found acting in the movies more lucrative when a friend told her Biograph Studios was seeking actresses (Martin 1916). She eventually appeared in over 147 films and her personal scrapbook features photos from a slew of films made at Biograph and the Edison Company, many not named on IMDb (MacPherson, n.d.). Around 1912 she followed Jesse L. Lasky in his move to California and professionally moved into writing and directing. In 1913, she wrote, directed, helped produce, and starred in her own film, *Tarantula*, which was such a financial success; she was promoted to the head of her own department where she wrote, directed, acted, and oversaw an entire team of people, creating at least six films for Universal (Paramount press release 1913). Then she became a writer/director at Universal (writing 54 films) and began writing with Cecil B. DeMille, for whom she would write the bulk of his box office successes. It is not known exactly when her relationship with DeMille ended but they paused their working relationship in 1930 when Macpherson moved to MGM and wrote the comedy *Fra Diavolo* (1933) (*The Devil's Brother* in the United States) with Stan Laurel and Oliver Hardy. *Fra Diavolo*'s success buoyed the studio and she stayed at MGM for four more years, until DeMille needed her again for his planned production of *Cleopatra* (1934) this time not as a writer, but as a researcher. Despite the slight, with a team of twelve under her, she meticulously researched the point that "if Cleopatra herself had visited the set, she would have felt right at home" (Pawlek 2011, chapter 19).

Another way theater brought women into screenwriting was through play reading and eventually playwriting. This is true of writer-producer Eve Unsell who came to Broadway via Kansas City and a graduate degree at Boston's Emerson College for a year. After reading one of her short stories, theatrical agent Beatrice deMille (mother of Cecil and William) hired Unsell to work as what was then called a play reader and constructionist (Tibbets 1985). During her career, Unsell accumulated nearly 100 credits as a screenwriter. The work involved reading submitted plays which Unsell would restructure to suit deMille's tastes. Soon Beatrice's two sons saw the possibility of profits in the new medium of silent film and they began careers as directors and producers in collaboration with Jesse L. Lasky and his Famous Players Film Company. In 1914 they had Unsell adapt Anna Alice Chapin's novel *The Eagles Mate* into a film starring Mary Pickford. While other early screenwriters also worked as writer-directors, Unsell focused solely on the writing. She found her forte in the adaptation of short stories, novels, and plays—a hallmark of the era.

14.2.2 From Journalism

As the movies began to talk, producers began to court journalists, among them Dorothy Parker who moved to Hollywood with her second husband, actor Alan Campbell. They signed contracts with Paramount where she was paid four times as much as he was since the studio recognized Parker as the primary writer of the team (McDougall Jones 2020). Famous as an essayist, a critic, and a poet, Parker had held a seat at the largely male Algonquin Round Table matching wits with male writers of the day including critic Alexander Woolcott, playwright George S. Kaufman, and comedian Harpo Marx. She had attempted an entry into films alone a few years earlier when, fired from *Vanity Fair* magazine, Anita Loos and Frances Marion both suggested to actress and producer Lillian Gish that she hire Parker for a film she was currently supervising that starred her sister Dorothy. The experience proved unsatisfactory for all the women involved and Parker returned to newspaper work (Beauchamp 1997, 119). In her second attempt at screenwriting, with Campbell, their most successful film, *A Star is Born* (1937), involved an artistic couple undergoing a similar set of issues and a similar downward spiral based on the female's legendary fame. The 1938 Academy Awards nominated the film for seven awards, including Best Writing Screenplay, and it won two.

Frances Marion essentially blended both ways to enter screenwriting, theater, and journalism, having come to screenwriting from an early career where today she would be called a graphic artist. Marion moved from commercial artist to reporter to actress at Lois Weber Productions. She eventually chose writing over acting and is credited with writing more than 300 scripts covering every conceivable genre. Marion directed and produced half a dozen of those films. She was also the first Allied woman to cross the Rhine in World War I and served as Vice President and the only woman on the first Board of Directors of the Screen Writers Guild. From 1915 through 1935, Marion was the highest paid screenwriter—male or female—and remains the only woman to win two Academy Awards for Best Original Screenplay; one for *The Big House* (1930) and one for *The Champ* (1931) (see Beauchamp 1997).

14.2.3 From Contests

To earn her studio contract June Mathis entered a scenario contest. Though she did not win, her work attracted attention and in 1915, she was offered a position at Metro Pictures. Mathis climbed the ranks quickly, and after just two years was made head of the Scenario department, making her the first female film executive in history: "Unlike other women who were paid with a high salary, Mathis was strictly behind the scenes, and no such expectations were made of her to preserve some sort of image. Though Mathis never achieved the wealth and independence that Mary Pickford did, she was the highest achieving, ranking and paid female who did not appear on camera" (Rambova and Pickford 2015, 283). By 1918, Mathis found herself producing, casting, writing and editing, becoming one of the most powerful women in Hollywood. Her ability to adapt critically acclaimed novels and plays was quickly demonstrated in a string of revolutionary films: *The Four Horseman of the Apocalypse* (1921), *Blood and Sand* (1922), *The Saphead* (1920), and *Camille* (1921).

Mathis became known for her eye for talent which began with giving silent comedian star, Buster Keaton his feature length debut in the comedy *The Saphead* (1920), one of a handful of comedies she adapted (from the play *The Henrietta* by Bronson Howard and Victor Mapes). The next talent Mathis found, developed, and nurtured became film's first superstar—Rudolph Valentino, an Italian-American whom she cast in her anti-war sensation, *The Four Horseman of the Apocalypse*. To Mathis, Valentino became a canvas where she painted her philosophy for audiences to share. In *Horseman* she focused on the transgressive sexuality in all levels of society by character biographies that include the fact that the protagonist, Julio's beloved grandfather has a large number of illegitimate children among his servants and by incorporating a scene of German soldiers in drag at Marcello Desnoyers's castle. Mathis told The Los Angeles Times: "I had the German officers coming down the stairs with women's clothing on. To hundreds of people that meant no more than a masquerade party. To those who had lived and read, and who understood life, that scene stood out as one of the most terrific things in the movie" (Hallett 2013, 144). The film also popularized the Argentinian dance, the tango, and proved that a dark-skinned actor, given the chance, was more than capable of carrying the weight of an American film. Mathis was involved in everything from writing the script, to casting, to editing the final product.

14.3 Act Two: Why They Left the Now Mainstreamed Industry

In pre-1930s America, women made up 60–83% of the cinema audience (McDougall Jones 2020) and throughout the Silent Era women made up more than half the screenwriters (Welch 2018). As men gained positions in middle management, they made some decisions that sidelined female creatives. A few female screenwriters found themselves posted internationally but whether these posts were compliments to their creativity or creative ways to get them out of the way is not clear. Many of the female-led production companies from the silent era were lost by a powerful recession between 1920 and 1921, including The Eve Unsell Photoplay Staff, Ida May Park Productions, Margery Wilson Productions, Vera McCord, Lillian and George Randolph Chester, and Catherine Curtis Corporation (Mahar 2006). But later on, in the late 1920s, a more likely culprit was the industrialization of the film industry as more Wall Street investors were lured from the East once talkies insisted upon their adoption, and expensive sound stages were inevitable.

After years of research by a variety of academics, the general blame for how women left the profession of screenwriting lands with the rise of the studio system coupled with the early death of producer Irving Thalberg, the mismanagement of male partners, their own early deaths from illness, and the rise of censorship (also orchestrated by men). Whatever caused the women to exit, it left a void of mentors for whom new women could serve as apprentices in the way Lois Weber had mentored Frances Marion, thereby breaking an important cycle in a business built on professional relationships.

Once movies started turning larger and larger profits and studios began to be thought of as factories, male executives squeezed female creatives out of the way so that the ranks of female writers grew slimmer. The wild west of silent movie-making allowed for everyone to contribute in several creative areas but the factory-style compartmentalization did to Hollywood studios what it did to so many other arts. Job descriptions became more solidified, and contracts became a requirement of employment. Acting contracts stretched out seven years which made the sideways slide into screenwriting more difficult. Then as with most businesses, men were hired into middle and upper management and began making changes geared toward maximizing profits for the benefit of stockholders. Sometimes women entered business arrangements with men who mismanaged their careers and sometimes those men were their romantic partners, making disentangling their personal lives yet more difficult. Finally, the Hays Code played a small role in women leaving the business.

Historian Giuliana Muscio agrees that as the studios became larger machines and producers were given more power:

> This changed the nature of the collaborative relation of writer/producer into a power struggle. The construction of Writers' Buildings in the studio lots and the new schedules of work from eight to five probably were not too appealing to these writers, who were used to working at home. Most of all, their feminine quality was represented in their ability to cooperate in a team, to do a little bit of everything, and thus, they did not fit too well in a rigidly specialized schema of work. (Muscio 2010, 306–7)

Karen Ward Mahar argues that, when Wall Street investors arrived in Hollywood, "the presence of women in its ranks came under greater scrutiny. Women in the American film industry had thus far enjoyed more latitude and leverage than women in any other industry, including the stage. But women in powerful and visible positions were not the norm for most industries, particularly the financial industry" (Mahar 2006, 186). From the lives of a few of the women who built their own production companies, we will see some patterns emerge.

14.3.1 Studio Mismanagement (or Sabotage?) After Loss of Thalberg

As films became both more profitable and studios grew into corporate entities, women who had once run whole production units under their own names were asked to accept contracts as "junior writers" or did not receive new contracts at all. This happened to many prominent female screenwriters, especially after producer Irving Thalberg died in 1936.

The MGM studio exec had been known to support a slew of female screenwriters and filmmakers from Frances Marion to Bess Meredyth. With Thalberg producing their films they enjoyed greater control over choosing directors, casting and other creative aspects of the scripts they had written. Upon his death, Marion canceled her own contract rather than work under the new regime she found treating creatives in a way that today would be called toxic. Meredyth did not have the chance to quit first. Instead, the studio dropped her long-standing contract. In its place they offered one that would have her listed as a "junior writer" despite her having racked up over 140 credits dating back to 1913 (Beauchamp 1997, 340). Each woman handled that expected loss differently. Marion took a contract with Harry Cohn before returning to MGM. There, however, Cohn only offered the two-time Academy Award winner a week-to-week contract.

For Meredyth, the insult exacerbated anxiety attacks she had begun experiencing in the early 1930s so Meredyth announced her retirement in 1938. Yet she did not stop working. In 1929, while working as a writer at Warner Brothers, she had met and married the film's director, a Hungarian who changed his name from Mihály Kertész Kaminer to Michael Curtiz (Lucas 2004). Meredyth served as an unofficial and uncredited contributor on *Casablanca* (1942), which he directed, and which had been written by the brothers Julius and Philip Epstein with Howard Koch and Casey Robinson. In later reminiscences Julius remembered questioning some of Curtiz's directing choices: "Mike came in the next day and made criticisms or suggestions, we knew they were Bess Meredyth's ideas, not his, so it was easy to trip him up. We'd make a change and say, 'What do you think, Mike?'" (Harmetz 1992, 123). This indicates that Curtiz was secretive about Meredyth's input, but Lucas adds that when Curtiz would express displeasure, and the writers would ask him to elaborate, he would say: "I don't remember what the hell Bess tell me" (Lucas 2004).

14.3.2 *Mismanagement by Male Partners*

Marion Fairfax's career mirrors much of what happened to many other female filmmakers of her era in that they arrived, they thrived to the point of earning production companies that bore their own names, and then as the studios merged and moneymen entered the industry, they severed these female-led production arms seemingly in the name of economics. In the Fairfax case we can also add mismanagement by a male partner.

In March 1922, a contract between John (Jack) Jasper, Fairfax, and Edward Tanaka sets forth an agreement where Fairfax and Jasper would send scripts to Japan to be made by Tanaka. Those films would then be distributed by Jasper and Fairfax stateside. Written on the contract, in Marion's hand, is a sentence blaming Jasper, whom she calls Jack, for the ruination of their first project, *The*

Lying Truth: "He ruined by over cranking [the camera]" (Tanaka, Fairfax, and Jasper 1922). She then reiterates this in her hand at the bottom of a personal letter from Tanaka that says set design is going well, where she wrote: "Jack Jasper, by privately instructing Tanaka to grind at speed used in screen farces—caused Tanaka to ruin a beautiful picture—and leave me holding the bag! Jack is impossible" (Tanaka 1922).

For this (and unknown other reasons), they released the film a year later and it underperformed, which seemed to have harmed her company's reputation in that rather than producing more films under that banner, Fairfax began writing freelance scripts and worked as an editor for other production companies. Then Earl Hudson at First National contracted Fairfax to write an adaptation of Arthur Conan Doyle's *The Lost World* (1925). She became ill but rallied to finish that project and moved on to *The Desert Healer* (1926), which is referred to as a Marion Fairfax Productions project "in collaboration with Sam E. Rork" ("Algerian Village Erected for *Desert Healer*" 1926). Later First National released the film under the title *Old Loves and New*. After completing yet another film, *The Blonde Saint* (1926), Fairfax's recurring illness made her an invalid and therefore it became her last film.

Instead of screenplays, Fairfax wrote a column called "Marionettes" for Rob Wagner's *Script* magazine, which was upbeat and playful, though she did admit: "I haven't been inside of a studio for a couple of years"; and then: "I believe it's worse to be a semi-invalid than a whole one". In another column, she states: "The Doctors stabbed me with some of their new-fangled serums, determined to make me well at all costs (to me) and I took the count in the first round. After this last experience I've made up my mind to continue to enjoy ill health in my own little way instead of 'getting well' in theirs" (Fairfax, n.d.).

14.3.3 *Forced to Work Outside the Hollywood Factory System*

As noted, film history texts often neglect female screenwriters. This is doubly true for women of color such as Alice Burton Russell Micheaux and Marion E. Wong who are generally ignored altogether. When Alice Russell married silent film writer-director Oscar Micheaux, she joined his company and their work spanned from silents to sound films, all produced outside the growing Hollywood industry in their home base of Chicago. This also makes tracking her various contributions more difficult as their materials were not kept in any industry archives. Those films that still exist—among them *Murder in Harlem* (1935), *The Girl from Chicago* (1932), *Birthright* (1939)—carry his name as creator and her name as a member of the acting company (Regester 2020) yet their peers remember her as a co-writer. In interviews the lead actor in *God's Stepchildren* (1938), Carman Newsome, recalled how Alice wrote the film based on her own unpublished short story "Naomi, Negress" (Regester, 2020, 147). Another actor, Leroy Collins, remembered Alice acting as what he called a script supervisor but which sounded more like an editor and co-writer (McGilligan 2004, 332).

Many of their films also involve social justice issues of the day including in *Birthright* when an African American character's mother dies of food poisoning from an expired product sold by a white grocer. As she was the daughter of an African American newspaper editor, it is likely such issues had often been reported in her father's black press. Also, as an actress Russell Micheaux often played college-educated female characters representative of the black middle class she came into when she was born. Most often she appears as a good mother figure and matriarch and mentor to other characters. These characters served as role models to audiences who otherwise only saw African Americans mocked in mainstream films. It seems a clear mission of the Micheaux production company to provide better role models.

The other issue for many women is marital status. Even the new Academy Museum in Los Angeles, which has an exhibit on the work of her husband, Oscar Micheaux, does not treat Russell Micheaux equally, though she produced and acted in many of his films. As a married pair of filmmakers, patriarchy and the way society trained women not to outshine their husbands may have contributed to her own lack of acknowledging her work. In the 1930 New York census Alice listed herself as a "helper" in the motion-picture industry while her husband confidently wrote "motion-picture producer". Later, she referred to herself as a "presenter" of films because she worked on the distribution of them to theaters across the country (Regester 2020).

A native of San Francisco's Chinatown, Marion E. Wong took a trip to Hong Kong to meet a potential partner in an arranged marriage. She rejected the suitor, an act her mother supported, and Wong returned to working in her family's restaurant, Edvin's Café, in Oakland, California. Anecdotal stories say that in 1915, Wong met Charlie Chaplin and the crew she would later engage to make her own film in that way (Mark 2014). Another theory puts forward that Wong watched Chaplin film near the restaurant and met his crew that way, eventually hiring them for her film (Eagan 2010).

However it happened, in 1916, 21-year-old Wong formed the Mandarin Film Company of San Francisco. She wrote, directed, performed in, and produced *The Curse of Quon Gwon: When the Far East Mingles with the West* (1916). The story, focusing on a Chinese god who cursed his people because of the influence of western civilization, came to life thanks to a plethora of help from her Chinatown community and the use of nearby locations. First, she gained a loan from a well-to-do Chinese merchant and landowner (Eagan 2010). Then her family stepped in both financially and through their talents in marketing and distribution. Some also served as the actors for the piece including her sister-in-law, Violet Wong and close family friend Harvey Soo-Hoo (Mark 2014).

Once completed, Wong and her mother went to New York City to market the film but they came back home empty-handed (Mark 2014). The first female Chinese American filmmaker turned to a life singing on stage and later opened more restaurants, including the Singapore Hut where she would put on cabaret shows and perform for guests by singing in English and Italian (Mark 2014). Because the family considered the film a failure the relegated the reels to various basements until Violet's grandson, Gregory Yee Mark, found the 35-mm nitrate negative disintegrating, and transferred what he could to 16 mm for preservation (Mark 2014). In 2006, the National Film Preservation Board of the Library of Congress placed *The Curse of Quon Gwon* on the National Film Registry.

14.4 ACT THREE: WHY THESE FEMALE PIONEERS DISAPPEARED FROM HISTORY

Many of these women's memories were overshadowed by the directors they worked with who sometimes happened to be their husbands or lovers and who often outlived their female screenwriting partners. Some female writers became their own unreliable narrators, causing historians to dismiss them from larger collections.

14.4.1 Unreliable Male Narrators (Who Were Sometimes Partners)

Cecil B. DeMille downplayed the contributions of Jeanie MacPherson, though she wrote most of his most profitable movies. She died young so she could not refute his assertion in one 1957 interview: "She was not a good writer. She would bring in wonderful ideas but she could not carry a story all the way through in writing. Her name is on many things because she wrote with me. I carried the story and she would bring me many, many ideas. You'll find her name on a lot of scripts" (Gaines 2013). It is an odd quote considering that after Macpherson's death, DeMille wrote and directed just four films while MacPherson had written both *The Ten Commandments* (1927) and *The King of Kings* (1923), two films that essentially created DeMille's iconic status.

As a response to the DeMille quote about her work as a screenwriter, Daniel A. Lord, the official advisor for the Catholic Church during the production of *The King of Kings*, stated: "Jeanie MacPherson was the scenarist, swiftly killing herself with an intensity of work and a passion for precise detail that kept her on a sixteen-hour-a-day schedule during the long months of production ... she had no time for anything—friendship, correspondence, hobbies, or care for her health" (Birchard 2004).

It has been documented that MacPherson's understanding of the new art of screenwriting influenced many who came after her, including renowned Italian screenwriter Suso Cecchi d'Amico who studied a trade magazine article MacPherson had written and used those lessons when writing such films as *Ladri di biciclette" (Bycicle Thieves* 1948) and *I soliti ignoti (Big Deal on Madonna Street* 1958): "Cinema is inspired by theatrical technique. An essay by MacPherson from the early 1940s applies the three-act structure to the narrative arc of films, to be respected also in each individual scene" (Francione 2002, 12).[1] Yet even this female writer after many years forgot to name the female writer she credited for teaching her the most important lesson in writing. By the time these interviews were held later in life, even d'Amico had forgotten MacPherson's name and demoted her to being an assistant to Cecil B. DeMille:

> I've been working for so long that I have developed some laws, some rules that I work with but I never tell them to my pupils when I'm teaching. They would think I'm crazy. But I do remember a booklet I read many years ago. It was written by an assistant to Cecil B. DeMille. She wrote that every scene should contain three elements: the crucial moment of a situation, the beginning of new one and the end of the first one. I thought that was amusing. I have kept that in my head for many years. (Colville-Anderson 2016)

Similarly, Sarah Y. Mason's contributions to scripts she co-authored with husband Victor Heerman were downgraded in his 1976 oral history with Anthony Slide. In Heerman's own words he "told her what to write" (Slide 1976). Though she was still alive, Slide had chosen to interview only Heerman about his directing career and never went to Mason for corroboration about their joint writing process. This serves as another example of the continued power of the auteur theory despite the fact that Mason had collected more solo writing credits before their marriage and after as he turned mostly to directing (Slide 1976). As another example of the favoritism to directors, when each partner of this Oscar-winning writing team died, their obituaries showed a bias toward the male director, Heerman, who earned a nine-sentence obituary in *Variety*. It mentions his Oscar win for co-writing *Little Women* (1933) twice, and names several films he directed. It also names him as a "film industry pioneer" ("Film Pioneer Victor Heerman Dies" 1977). When Mason died only a few years later, she earned simply "Sarah Heerman 85, widow of writer-director, Victor Heerman, died Nov 28 at the Motion Picture & Television Country Home in Woodland Hills. She is survived by a son and a daughter. No services" ("Sarah Heerman" 1980). Note that the publication used her legal married last name, Heerman, not the maiden name under which she wrote. It also identifies her importance tied to having been married to a writer-director, but does not mention her part of the shared Oscar win for writing. Finally, for comparison, when their son Victor Heerman Jr. died in 2014 at the age of 89, he received nine sentences which mentioned he was the "Son of Oscar-winning screenwriters", his love of "good race horses… splendid cars, and well-bred dogs" (Obituary 2014).

For writer-director-producer Eve Unsell, who had her own unit at Universal Pictures, it was not an intimate partner who mis-narrated her importance. The

---

[1] Orig.: "E alla tecnica teatrale si ispira il cinema. Un saggio della Macpherson all'inizio degli anni Quaranta studia per il film l'arco narrativo in tre tempi da rispettare anche in ogni singola scena".

more she wrote and produced, the more company co-founder Adolph Zukor felt he needed her to take charge of scenarios for the newly formed British Lasky company. So in 1916 Unsell moved to London (Dick 2001). One of her first hires was a young Alfred Hitchcock and Unsell taught him "the ins and outs of story and screenplay mechanics as well as adapting novels for film" (Elliot 2010, as quoted in Welch 2018, 85). While in England she wrote and produced *The Great Day* (1921) and *The Call of Youth* (1921) for which she allowed Hitchcock to design the title cards (Dick 2001). Yet her name appears rarely or not at all in the many books covering his career.

14.4.2 Unreliable Female Narrators

Women often were their own unreliable narrators. They did not write their memoirs or they skipped the important parts. When historian Tom Stempel read Frances Marion's unpublished autobiography, he found more about her personal life and her interactions with the celebrities of the day such as Mary Pickford and Douglas Fairbanks. This led Stempel to downplay Marion in his *Framework* (1988). He later learned that Marion mistakenly thought celebrities would be more interesting to publishers and readers than a lengthy look at the professional part of her career. Stempel then offered to correct that mistake in a new edition of the book but his publishers did not think there would be enough audience for such an update to justify the costs or reprinting (Stempel 2016).

Though one of Silent Hollywood's most prolific and respected screenwriters when Bess Meredyth's own son John Meredyth Lucas wrote a memoir of his own screenwriting career, he never thought to interview his mother about her work as both a writer and producer in early Hollywood. In fact: "It, unfortunately, never seemed important that I learn Mother's early history. She never wrote it, only mentioned a few disconnected anecdotes. I never asked. By the time the questions were formed, the answers had died" (Lucas 2004). That's how easy it can be to be forgotten and why it is so important to highlight these stories today.

June Mathis died young, at the height of her career, and therefore earned a front-page obituary ("June Mathis Dies While at the Theater" 1927) yet she is most often noted because of discovering both Buster Keaton and Rudolph Valentino. In fact, no one has yet written her biography so she appears in those of others, mostly men, including *Rex Ingram: Master of the Silent Cinema* (O'Leary 1994). One could ask if anyone today remembers who Rex Ingram was, but if they would like to study him at least a complete book does exist.

Men more frequently left their papers to libraries or archives or if they were members of a male-female writing team, their papers can be grouped together, as is the case with the Victor Heerman papers at the Margaret Herrick Library which include the work he did with Mason. There is no separate collection in her name. If you did not know they were married at the start of a research trip about her, you would leave the library empty-handed (Heerman 1977).

Finally, as visual proof of that some women did not take their own legacies into consideration, Cecil B. DeMille and other early male producers and directors had large mausoleums, statues, or monuments erected to them upon their deaths. Yet women such as Lois Weber, Frances Marion, and many others were cremated with no stone edifices testifying to their prominence. Nor did their homes become tourist attractions such as Will Rogers Park or the William S. Hart Museum and Park, both of which can still be visited today by tourists.

14.4.3 Lack of Early Female Historians of Cinema

Though screenwriters participated fully in filmmaking from the start, histories dedicated to screenwriters did not arrive on bookshelves for over 70 years with Fred Lawrence Guiles' *Hanging on in Paradise* (1975), Tom Stempel's *Framework: A History of Screenwriting in the American Film* (1988), and Ian Hamilton's *Writers in Hollywood 1915–1951* (1990) to name a few of the early few. Those authors largely left women out of the story.

Then Cari Beauchamp researched and wrote *Without Lying Down: Frances Marion and the Powerful Women of Early Hollywood* (1997) which brought many early female screenwriters work back into broader recognition. Therefore, when Marc Norman's *What Happens Next: A History of American Screenwriting* appeared in 2007, it should have had plenty of new material to mine but instead Norman regurgitated most of the names that had come before: David W. Griffith, Thomas Ince, Herman Mankiewicz, Ben Hecht, the Epstein brothers. In fact, in his 2008 review for *The Guardian*, Philip French's major complaint was that Norman had failed to mention yet one more man, David Mamet (French, *Writers' Block*). On top of that, Norman relegated those many powerful women of early Hollywood to a short paragraph here or there accompanied by a quick dismissal of their importance. While he does admit Anita Loos' work on the first screenplay she sold, *The New York Hat* (1912) "discovered the key to all good movie writing, a story to be seen rather than told" he claims she made that discovery "naively" (Norman 2008, 19). Norman denigrates the contributions of early female screenwriters and misses the fact that Loos gave *The New York Hat* a particularly female perspective as a social satire highlighting the hypocrisy of how gossip destroys women's reputations but has no effect on the men who are equally involved in the potential assignation. Its a theme she returned to in her generation-defining novel *Gentlemen Prefer Blondes*.

14.5   Conclusion

Though these women all left the work of screenwriting for one reason or another, they did not stop being artists. Some turned to novels, some to sculpture or painting but they did turn away from the studios which meant that when the historians came calling to catalog the creation of the new medium, they interviewed men who talked mostly about other men and the history of Hollywood became the history of great men.

Much of the work of female screenwriters has been lost but attempts are being made to preserve what can be found among old reels of nitrate film or snippets of scripts that survived because they were included in memoirs. The work of some female screenwriters from Hollywood's earlier eras are becoming better known because mostly male historians of screenwriting have finally deemed them worthy enough to appear in their accounts of Hollywood. Powerhouse writers as Jeanie MacPherson, Bess Meredyth, June Mathis, Sarah Y. Mason, and others, left in the dustbin of history, are now making appearances in books and articles in print and on the web. For instance, in 2013 Columbia University launched the Women Film Pioneers Project under the principle that "What we assume never existed is what we invariably find" (https://wfpp.columbia.edu). Two years later Jill Nelmes and Jule Selbo published *Women Screenwriters: An International* Guide which engaged scholars from around the world in cataloging the female screenwriters of their individual cultures.

These and a series of newer books by current academics including Karen Ward Mahar, Charlene Regester, Shelley Stamp (and this author) document as much of this dissipating collection as possible. The next step is for someone to author a comprehensive history of screenwriting that includes writers of all genders and ethnicities and then the story will have fully been told.

References

"Algerian Village Erected for *Desert Healer*". 1926. *Motion Picture News*, 15 March: 1193.

A Star is Born. 1937. Written by Dorothy Parker & Alan Campbell, and Robert Carson. Directed by William A. Wellman. USA: Selznick International Pictures.

Beauchamp, Cari. 1997. *Without Lying Down: Frances Marion and the Powerful Women of Early Hollywood*. Los Angeles: University of California Press.

Bicycle Thieves (Ladri di biciclette). 1948. Written by Oreste Biancoli, Suso Cecchi D'Amico, Vittorio De Sica, Adolfo Franci, Gherardo Gherardi, Gerardo Guerrieri, and Cesare Zavattini. Directed by Vittorio De Sica. Italy: Produzioni De Sica.

Big Deal on Madonna Street (I soliti ignoti). 1958. Written by Agenore Incrocci & Furio Scarpelli, Suso Cecchi D'Amico, Mario Monicelli. Directed by Mario Monicelli. Italy: Cinecittà, Lux Film, Vides Cinematografica.

Birchard, Richard S. 2004. *Cecil B. DeMille's Hollywood*. Lexington, KY: University Press of Kentucky.

Birthright. 1939. Written by Oscar Micheaux. Directed by Oscar Micheaux. USA: Micheaux Film.

Blood and Sand. 1922. Written by June Mathis. Directed by Fred Niblo, Dorothy Arzner (additional footage). USA: Paramount Pictures.

Camille. 1921. Written by June Mathis. Directed by Ray C. Smallwood. USA: Nazimova Productions.

Casablanca. 1942. Written by Julius J. Epstein, Philip G. Epstein, and Howard Koch. Directed by Michael Curtiz. USA: Warner Bros.

Cleopatra. 1934. Written by Waldemar Young and Vincent Lawrence. Directed by Cecil B. DeMille. USA: Paramount Pictures.

Colville-Andersen, Mikael. 2016. "The Storytellers: Interview with Suso Cecchi d'Amico". https://colvilleandersen.medium.com/the-storytellers-interview-with-suso-cecchi-d-amico-c6ddee9f5642. Accessed 12 March 2022. *Curse of Quon Gwon: When the Far East Mingles with the West*. 1916. Written by Marian E. Wong. Directed by Marian E. Wong. USA: Mandarin Film Company.

De Mille, William C. 1921. Telegram. 16 April. The Marion Fairfax papers, held at the Margaret Herrick Library, Academy of Motion Picture Arts and Sciences, Los Angeles.

Dick, Bernard F. 2001. *Engulfed: The Death of Paramount Pictures and the Birth of Corporate Hollywood*. Lexington, KY: University Press of Kentucky.

Don Juan. 1926. Written by Bess Meredyth. Directed by Alan Crosland. USA: Warner Bros.

Eagan, Daniel. 2010. "The Curse of Quon Gwon." In *America's Film Legacy*, 55–56. London: Continuum.

Elliot, A. R. 2010. "The Scary Discipline of Alfred Hitchcok Wow 'em." *Investor's Business Daily*, 12 May.

Fairfax, Marion. n.d. Marionettes column (*Script* magazine). Held at the Margaret Herrick Library, Academy of Motion Picture Arts and Sciences, Los Angeles.

"Film Pioneer Victor Heerman Dies". 1977. *Variety*. Obituary, 7 November.

Fra Diavolo (aka *The Devil's Brother*). 1933. Written by Jeanie Macpherson and Eugène Scribe. Directed by Hal Roach and Charley Rogers. USA: Hal Roach Studios.

Francione, Fabio, ed. 2002. *Scrivere con gli occhi. Lo sceneggiatore come cineasta: Il cinema di Suso Cecchi d'Amico* [*Writing with your eyes. The screenwriter as filmmaker: The cinema of Suso Cecchi d'Amico*]. Alessandria, Italy: Falsopiano.

French, Phillip. 2008. "Inside the Writers' Block." *The Guardian*, 6 April. https://www.theguardian.com/books/2008/apr/06/film. Accessed 22 January 2022.

Gaines, Jane. 2013. "Jeanie Macpherson." *Women Film Pioneers Project*. https://wfpp.columbia.edu/pioneer/ccp-jeanie-macpherson/. Accessed 10 August 2022.

Girl from Chicago, The. 1932. Written by Oscar Micheaux. Directed by Oscar Micheaux. USA. Micheaux Film.

Hallett, Hilary A. 2013. *Go West, Young Women! The Rise of Early Hollywood*. Berkeley, CA: University of California Press.

Hamilton, Ian. 1990. *Writers in Hollywood, 1915–1951*. New York: Harper & Row.

Harmetz, Aljean. 1992. Round Up the Usual Suspects: The Making of "Casablanca" – Bogart, Bergman, and World War II. New York: Hyperion.

Heerman, Victor. 1977. "Heerman Papers", held at the Margaret Herrick Library Special Collections, Academy of Motion Picture Arts and Sciences, Los Angeles.

"June Mathis Dies While at the Theatre." 1927. *New York Times*, 27 June, 1.

Little Women. 1933. Written by Sarah Y. Mason and Victor Heerman. Directed by George Cukor. USA: RKO Radio Pictures.

Lucas, John Meredyth. 2004. Eighty Odd Years in Hollywood. Jefferson, NC: McFarland.

MacPherson, Jeanie. n.d. Personal photograph album, held at the Margaret Herrick Library Special Collections, Academy of Motion Picture Arts and Sciences, Los Angeles.

Mahar, Karen Ward. 2006. *Women Filmmakers in Early Hollywood.* Baltimore, MD: Johns Hopkins University Press.

"Marion Fairfax, Dramatist, Is with Lasky." 1915. *Motion Picture News*, April: 64.

Mark, Gregory Yee. 2014. "The Curse of Quon Gwon: Chinese American's Pioneering Film." In *Transcending Space and Time: Early Cinematic Experience of Hong Kong*, Book III, *Re-discovering Pioneering Females in Early Chinese Cinema & Grandview's Cross-border* Productions, edited by Winnie Fu and E. Chan, 208–33. Hong Kong: Hong Kong Film Archive.

"Marshall Neilan Again Signs Marion Fairfax." 1920. *Exhibitor's Herald.* 16 October: 41.

Martin, Alice. 1916. "From 'Wop' Parts to Bossing the Job." *Photoplay.* October: 95–97.

McCreadie, Marsha. 1994. *The Women Who Write the Movies: From Frances Marion to Nora Ephron.* New York: Carol.

McDougall Jones, Naomi. 2020. "When Hollywood's Power Players Were Women." *The Atlantic*, 9 February. https://www.theatlantic.com/culture/archive/2020/02/naomi-mcdougall-jones-wrong-kind-of-women-excerpt/606277/.

McGilligan, Patrick. 2004. "Me and Oscar: An Interview with LeRoy Collins." *Film Quarterly* 57 (4): 4.

Murder in Harlem. 1935. Written by Oscar Micheaux and Clarence Williams (cabaret sequence). Directed by Oscar Micheaux and Clarence Williams (cabaret sequence). USA: Micheaux Film.

Muscio, Giuliana. 2010. "Women Screenwriters in American Silent Cinema." In *Reclaiming the Archive: Feminism and Film History*, edited by Vicki Callahan, 289–308. Detroit: Wayne State University Press.

Nelmes, Jill, and Jule Selbo. 2015. *Women Screenwriters: An International Guide.* Basingstoke, UK: Palgrave Macmillan.

Norman, Marc. 2008. *What Happens Next: A History of American Screenwriting.* New York: Crown Books.

O'Leary, Liam. 1994. *Rex Ingram: Master of the Silent Cinema.* London: BFI.

Obituary. 2014. Heerman, Victor Eugene, Jr.. *Lexington Herald-Leader*, 2 November. https://www.legacy.com/us/obituaries/kentucky/name/victor-heerman-obituary?id=19273031. Accessed 20 January 2022.

Paramount press release. 1913. Held at the Margaret Herrick Library Special Collections, Academy of Motion Picture Arts and Sciences, Los Angeles.

Pawlek, Debra Ann. 2011. *Bringing Up Oscar: The Story of the Men and Women Who Founded the Academy.* New York: Pegasus.

Rambova, Natacha, and Hala Pickford. 2015. "June Mathis Biography." In *Rudolph Valentino: A Wife's Memories of an Icon*, 275–305. Hollywood, CA: 1921 PVG Publishing–The Rudolph Valentino Society.

Regester, Charlene. 2020. "Emerging from the Shadows: Alice Burton Russell—African American Film Producer, Actress, and Screenwriter." *Film History* 32 (1): 127–55. https://doi.org/10.2979/filmhistory.32.1.05.

"Sarah Heerman". 1980. *Variety.* Obituary, 2 December.

Slide, Anthony. 1976. "Unedited Transcript of an oral History with Victor Heerman." Heerman Papers, held at the Margaret Herrick Library Special Collections, Academy of Motion Picture Arts and Sciences, Los Angeles.

Stempel, Tom. 1998. *Framework: A History of Screenwriting in the American Film.* New York: Continuum.

Stempel, Tom. 2016. Interview with the author.

Tanaka, Edward, Marion Fairfax, and John Jasper. 1922. Production and distribution agreement. March. Marion Fairfax papers, held at the Margaret Herrick Library, Academy of Motion Picture Arts and Sciences, Los Angeles.

Tanaka, Edward. 1922. Letter to Mr John Jasper. Marion Fairfax papers, held at the Margaret Herrick Library, Academy of Motion Picture Arts and Sciences, Los Angeles.

Tarantula. 1913. Written by Jeanie Macpherson. Directed by Jeanie Macpherson. USA: Powers Picture Plays.

The Big House. 1930. Written by Frances Marion. Directed by George W. Hill. USA: Metro-Goldwyn-Mayer, Cosmopolitan Productions.

The Blonde Saint. 1926. Written by Marion Fairfax. Directed by Svend Gade. USA: Sam E. Rork Productions.

The Call of Youth. 1921. Written by Eve Unsell. Directed by Hugh Ford. UK: Paramount British Pictures.

The Champ. 1931. Written by Frances Marion. Directed by King Vidor. USA: Metro-Goldwyn-Mayer.

The Desert Healer (aka *Old Loves and New*). 1926. Written by Marion Fairfax. Directed by Maurice Tourneur. USA: Sam E. Rork Productions.

The Four Horseman of the Apocalypse. 1921. Written by June Mathis. Directed by Rex Ingram. USA: Metro Pictures Corporation.

The Great Day. 1921. Written by Eve Unsell. Directed by Hugh Ford. UK: Paramount British Pictures.

The King of Kings. 1923. Written by Jeanie Macpherson. Directed by Cecil B. DeMille. USA: DeMille Pictures Corporation.

The Lost World. 1925. Written by Marion Fairfax. Directed by Harry O. Hoyt. USA: Biograph Studios.

The Lying Truth. 1922. Written by Marion Fairfax. Directed by Marion Fairfax. USA: Eagle Producing Company, Marion Fairfax Productions.

The New York Hat. 1912. Written by Anita Loos. Directed by D.W. Griffith. USA: Biography Company.

The Saphead. 1920. Written by June Mathis. Directed by Herbert Blaché and Winchell Smith. USA: Metro Pictures Corporation.

The Sea Beast. 1930. Written by Bess Meredyth. Directed by Millard Webb. USA: Warner Bros.

The Ten Commandments. 1927. Written by Jeanie Macpherson. Directed by Cecil B. DeMille. USA: Paramount Pictures.

Tibbets, John C. 1985. *The American Theatrical Film: Stages in Development*. Madison, WI: The University of Wisconsin Press.

Welch, Rosanne, ed. 2018. *When Women Wrote Hollywood: Essays on Female Screenwriters in the Early Film Industry*. Jefferson, NC: McFarland.

Wonder of Women. 1929. Written by Marian Ainslee (titles), Bess Meredyth, and Hermann Sudermann. Directed by Clarence Brown. USA: Metro-Goldwyn-Mayer.

Wray, Caroline. 2021. "Screenwriting Grows Amidst Limited Resources." *Yale News*. 21 November. https://yaledailynews.com/blog/2014/11/21/screenwriting-grows-amidst-limited-resources/. Accessed 14 November 2021.

CHAPTER 15

Narrating with Music: Screenwriting Musical Numbers

Claus Tieber

15.1 INTRODUCTION

In an article about the Screen Idea Work Group (SIWG), Ian W. Macdonald quotes a British screenwriter who talks about the adaptations made to a TV series after a change of concept, aimed at making it more appealing to American audiences. Interestingly, the filmic element the screenwriter uses as his example for this process of cultural adaptation is the music (Macdonald 2010, 52). This anecdote serves to introduce the idea that a change in the members of a SIWG can lead to different creative decisions, both for the screenwriting as well as for the musical choices or more precisely: in the screenwriting *of* the music.

This chapter seeks to demonstrate that screenwriting and thus the work of the SIWG, is not restricted to plotting and dialogue. Drawing on the music in Hollywood screenplays of the 1930s, I focus on the writing of musical numbers, which is rarely discussed as a filmic device in screenwriting studies so far.

C. Tieber (✉)
Institut für Theater-, Film- und Medienwissenschaft, University of Vienna, Vienna, Austria
e-mail: claus.tieber@univie.ac.at

© The Author(s), under exclusive license to Springer Nature Switzerland AG 2023
R. Davies et al. (eds), *The Palgrave Handbook of Screenwriting Studies*,
https://doi.org/10.1007/978-3-031-20769-3_15

15.2 Screenwriting and Music

"The screenplay, as a system, is made up of specific elements: endings, beginnings, scenes, Plot Points, shots, special effects, locations, music, and sequences" (Field 2005 [1979] 183). Field mixes every filmic element that comes to mind in this quote. Interestingly, he does not add anything substantial in his books about music in screenplays. In the screenwriting manuals that appeared in the wake of Field's work, music, while not completely ignored, is still relegated to the margins of the tasks of a screenwriter. Most mentions of music in manuals are comparisons and metaphors, using musical terms to describe the functions of the plot, but not actually talking about how to use music in screenplays. For Robert McKee, "[t]he idea of story is like the idea of music" (McKee 1997, 19). He writes about "the orchestra of story" (10), whereas Lev Bauer uses the musical term aria when he is speaking about monologues, because "there is a musical aspect to dialogue" (Bauer 2017, 30).

The focus of screenwriting literature on plot, character, and dialogue leaves little place for anything else, so that the possibilities and variations of how to use music in a screenplay are generally not discussed in manuals, nor are they addressed in depth in scholarly literature so far. Nevertheless, music was and continues to be used by screenwriters as an effective filmic element, not just as diegetic music: so-called extra-diegetic music is specified in many screenplays. The distinction between the fictional world of the characters (diegetic) and its outside—the cinematic apparatus (extra-diegetic)—is not always clear-cut. Robyn Stilwell coined the appropriate and evocative notion of the "fantastical gap between the diegetic and the nondiegetic" (2007, 184–202), which is often bridged by music, especially in film musicals.

15.3 Story Conferences

If screenwriting is equal parts writing and discussion or negotiation within the SIWG, as has been established as one of the premises of screenwriting studies, then the various stages of a screenplay can be read as "documentations" of these discussions. The SIWG could take many forms throughout global cinema history, dependent on the mode of production, its members, and the given hierarchies. Take for example a SIWG within the classical studio system. Creative producers like Irving Thalberg or Darryl F. Zanuck headed the group which included the screenwriter and the secretary. At a later point also the director and in some rare cases an actor or actress joined. Listing the members of the SIWG by profession reflects the division of labor within a highly developed film industry like Hollywood in the 1930s and 1940s. But the profession of these film practitioners says little about their role during the script development process. If we take a brief look at the minutes of story conferences during the classical Hollywood era, it is easy to see that every aspect of filmmaking was being discussed (see Tieber 2014), leading to the members of the SIWG also taking over tasks they were not officially assigned.

In a story conference for *China Seas* (1935), an exotic adventure film starring Clark Gable, producer Irving Thalberg said: "I could see the thing open up on a beautiful shot of the ship at night steaming along—the piano playing in the saloon (…)" (N.N. 1932a, 7). Thalberg imagines a scene that includes music as an essential element in order to create a specific atmosphere. He explicitly mentions not just plot in his remark, but camera ("shot"), light ("night"), sound ("steaming"), and music ("piano playing"). In another story conference for the musical comedy *Blondie of the Follies* (1932), director Edmund Goulding discusses the screenplay by Anita Loos and Frances Marion (working title *Good Time Girl*). Goulding comments on setting and music: "This [i.e. a speakeasy; author's note] is where Snoozle sits down at the piano—it's developed so Blondie and Larry can have a theme song" (N.N. 1932b, p. 6). Goulding refers here to the construction of the scene within the plot that allows the theme song to be integrated into the narrative. By *integrated* I mean situating the song within the plot, regardless of the potential and plausibility of the characters to actually perform a given song. Goulding's remarks are based on the premise that a theme song is a useful convention in this type of movie. While the film is not a musical proper, it uses a setting that is closely connected with music. The task of integrating music into a film's plot, such as a theme song for example, is often taken over by screenwriters, director, and producer, even before a composer is chosen for the film.

These two examples from lesser-known films drawing on well-documented story conferences,[1] should suffice to support the argument stated at the beginning of this chapter: in classical Hollywood all aspects of filmmaking, including music, were discussed in story conferences.

15.4 Screenplays

If screenwriting is a collective endeavor and screenplays can also be read as documents of the collective development process, then decisions and suggestions about music can also be observed within screenplays, even if it is often impossible to trace back the person responsible for the creative decision. At the end of the day it is the screenwriter who delivers the script and finds a way to tell a story using filmic devices like camera positions, editing, and music. These devices might not always be explicitly mentioned in the screenplay, but every description of a scene implies a camera position as Walter Reisch said:

> The screenplay needs descriptions of situations. "A man is leaving a door, he rushes through a long corridor, the girl steps out into the corridor, her face expresses fear…" This is a purposeful description. What we actually read is: close-up, long shot, the camera moves, pans. (Krenn 2004, 62)[2]

---

[1] Verbatim minutes can be found at the Cinema Arts Library, Doheny Memorial Library at the University of Southern California, MGM collection.

[2] Orig.: "Das Drehbuch braucht Situationsbeschreibungen. 'Der Mann verlässt eine Tür, er eilt über einen langen Gang, das Mädchen tritt aus einer Tür auf den Gang, ihr Gesicht

Screenwriters have to translate the decisions of the SIWG on paper and thus help the film to come to life. As far as music in film is concerned, the screenplay works as a more or less detailed layout for the music, in which the manifold functions and intended effects of music are suggested and described.

In this chapter I want to demonstrate this approach by examining music in American screenplays from the 1930s, a time when the master-scene script was becoming the dominant screenplay format. My analysis also wants to show how music and sound influenced and undermined the formal development process of screenplays, and how they were finally integrated into the classic screenplay format that is still in use today.

15.5 WALTER REISCH: *THE GREAT WALTZ* (1938)

My first case study centers on Walter Reisch's screenplay for the Johann Strauss Jr. biopic *The Great Waltz* (1938). The screenplay will be compared with Reisch's work for various films and with other screenplays for American film musicals of the 1930s.

Austrian screenwriter Walter Reisch immigrated to the United States of America in 1936 to escape the National Socialist regime. He had worked as a screenwriter and sometimes as a director in Vienna since the silent film era. Music plays a crucial element in virtually all of his screenplays, even the ones he wrote for silent cinema. Based on Reisch's recurring themes and motifs, the characteristics of his screenwriting for his German language work can be summed up in the following paragraphs.

Self-reference and self-consciousness—Reisch wrote screenplays for a variety of genres but music always played an important role in his stories. His screenplays constantly reference the medium itself, drawing both the audiences' and the characters' attention to this fact. However, Reisch does not use self-reference in an avant-gardist way, but as a means for comedy and to bond the audience to the medium (see Tieber and Wintersteller 2020).

The Viennese film as subgenre of the music(al) film—Together with actor-director Willi Forst, Reisch invented the *Wiener Film*, Viennese Film, Austria's most popular film genre to date. *Wiener Film* are films that not only take place in a mostly historical Vienna, but they include music as a significant theme of the various plots and subplots, often dealing with the tensions of an artist's dedication to art (usually music) and the love of a *süßes Mädel* (sweet girl). Interestingly for such a popular genre, the story's resolution is not always a happy one in the conventional sense, as the great male artist often chooses his artistic passion over the girl. The genre was initiated with a biopic of composer Franz Schubert called *Leise flehen meine Lieder* (*Lover Divine*) (1933), that set the tone for the films to come. The particular musical and nostalgic Viennese setting of this subgenre of the music film became incredibly popular around the world and dominated foreign perceptions of Vienna and Austria

---

drückt Entsetzen aus...' Das ist Zweckbeschreibung. Da ist zu lesen: Nah, Totale, Kamera fährt, schwenkt." (author's translation).

for decades and to this day. *Leise flehen meine Lieder* was produced in Berlin due to better financial possibilities of the German film industry. After 1933, Reisch was no longer able to work in Germany, due to his Jewish background. Reisch himself had to flee to the United States in 1936, while Forst and others continued to produce similar films throughout the Nazi regime, both in Vienna and Berlin. The characteristics of the Viennese film, as described by Robert Dassanowsky, perfectly matched Hollywood conventions at the time:

> Despite its flirtations with eroticism and gender role destabilization, the Viennese Film genre and style were essentially moralistic, and with the added influence of the Catholic authoritarian Austrofascist regime starting in 1933, the Austrian formula played revealingly well to middle- American Puritanism, the Hays Production Code, and Hollywood's unique conservative liberalism. (Dassanowsky 2018, 362)

Cultural references—An essential part of Reisch's education was his musical knowledge, which penetrated his work throughout his life. His screenplays show a broad knowledge of various musical genres, from Viennese songs to operetta and opera, to classical music and contemporary *Schlager* (hit songs). In line with his traditional, bourgeois upbringing, also literary themes can be found in his screenplays. He recalled: "I knew all the plays from Molnár to Schnitzler … I still know *Peer Gynt* and *Faust* by heart…" (Krenn 2004, 23).[3]

Given the success of the Viennese Film in America, combined with the stereotypical view of Austrian immigrants, it is not surprising that Reisch was cast to write the screenplay for a biopic about Johann Strauss Jr., the King of Waltz, in 1938. The screenplay for *The Great Waltz* reveals how Reisch's treatment of music was adapted to Hollywood conditions and expectations and how the far more standardized mode of filmmaking (and thus screenwriting) within the studio system influenced and changed his writing. In addition, Reisch serves as an excellent case study to examine transnational aspects of the film industry and the cultural exchange of filmic and musical devices through the mobility of individuals.

This particular film and its screenplay constitute a paradigmatic example for a number of reasons: because of the musical content, the links to Reisch's homeland, and because in his later work in Hollywood, it becomes increasingly difficult to distill his specific contribution to scripts written by groups of writers. Among his collaborations are films such as *Ninotschka* (1939) and *Titanic* (1953) for which he received an Academy Award (together with Charles Brackett and Richard L. Breen). In *The Great Waltz*, Reisch's typical traits can easily be detected, although he shares screenwriting credits with Samuel Hoffenstein. The original story comes from Gottfried Reinhardt, son of famous Viennese theater director Max Reinhardt. The script version I refer to in this chapter also mentions John Meehan as co-writer, who is however

---

[3] "Ich kannte alle Stücke von Molnár bis Schnitzler … *Peer Gynt* und *Faust* kann ich heute noch auswendig vorsagen…" (author's translation).

not listed in the on-screen credits of the finished film. Hoffenstein is probably most famous for co-writing the screenplays of the musical comedies *Love Me Tonight* (1932) and *The Gay Divorcee* (1934).

15.6 THE SCREENWRITER AS MUSICAL ADVISER

One of the tasks screenwriters achieve at different levels of detail is the suggestion of pre-existing music to be heard either within the film's narrative (so-called diegetic music) or only by the audience (as extra-diegetic music). The use of pre-existing music gives insight into a screenwriter's musical education, their knowledge of different repertoires, and the connotations they try to evoke when suggesting a certain piece of music. Screenplays for American film musicals of the 1930s rarely contained extra-diegetic music and instead tended to feature a few diegetic musical numbers. For example, the Astaire/Rogers musical *Shall We Dance* (1937), made just one year before the Strauss biopic, uses the wedding march from Richard Wagner's *Lohengrin*. The use of the highly popular march is conventional, but the screenplay demands a special instrumentation:

> The Wedding March is being played on a portable organ, and also by a violinist. Next to them stands the old Flower Woman who tipped off the musicians. Several other people are also in the group – all smiling genially. Linda and Petrov walk into the scene as the March comes to an end. (Scott and Pagano 1936, 115)

Over time some musical pieces have been turned into tropes that are able to evoke specific associations and are thus being used with very explicit intentions and repeatedly. The screenplay for *The Great Waltz* includes several suggestions of specific pieces by Johann Strauss, Jr. that represent different stages in the composer's career and public reputation and that are mostly heard diegetically as I will show in the following section.

15.7 EXCURSION: MUSIC CHANGES FORMAT

I would be remiss not to address the screenplay format when talking about music in screenwriting, as musical numbers were the reason for significant changes in the format, particularly in comparison with European screenplays. In the early days of the sound film, screenplays often featured two columns, one for the visual elements (image-track) and another for the acoustic ones (soundtrack). The two-column format was more popular in Europe and persisted much longer than in Hollywood, where two-column formatted screenplays can be found in the early 1930s. A sort of hybrid version, the use of two columns only for the insertion of a musical number with the rest of the screenplay formatted in one column, can be detected in some cases until the 1940s.

The screenplay for *The Great Waltz* does in fact use this hybrid model and often changes the format from one column to two for the duration of a musical number. For example, a change from one to two columns appears at the beginning of the number "Vienna Woods", featuring a visualization of the composition process of Strauss' famous "Tales from the Vienna Woods". The left column represents the soundtrack and is smaller than in earlier two-column formatted screenplays where each column used to occupy equal space. I suggest reading this as a sign that the screenwriters considered what was an otherwise antiquated choice of formatting at this time—1938—necessary to clarify their intentions and to give the acoustic components, mostly the music, their place in the screenplay. Reisch was familiar with the two-column format, which he had used in most of his German-language screenplays, at least for musical numbers.

It is astonishing to see how sound and music found their way into this otherwise completely conventional screenplay in terms of formatting and in doing so subverted the formal layout of the screenplay. This can be detected within one and the same screenplay, where the inclusion of music becomes obvious without even reading the words on the page. The phenomenon can also be viewed from a historical perspective: the integration of music into the master-scene screenplay led from homogenously formatted screenplays (two columns) in the very first years to hybrid screenplays (change from one to two columns for musical numbers) and finally to the highly standardized, homogenous format we are familiar with today (one column).

Musical numbers, and especially so-called "musical moments", as Amy Herzog terms them, are scenes and sequences in which the conventional hierarchy of sound and image is reversed and the music "takes over". Herzog writes that musical moments appear "when music, typically a popular song, inverts the image-sound hierarchy to occupy a dominant position in a filmic work. The movements of the image, and hence the structuring of space and time, are dictated by song" (Herzog 2010, 7). Musical moments thus have the potential to undermine a film's structure. Examining the positioning of musical numbers in certain screenplays reinforces this argument: at a glance we notice that the music can change the screenplay's format. Sound and music materialize and claim their space on the pages of a film script—an extraordinary phenomenon that makes a strong case for paying attention to screenplays when examining music within film and filmmaking.

15.8 Musical Numbers

The topic of screenwriting musical numbers has not been paid any particular scholarly attention so far. With the notable exception of Steven Price in his monograph *A History of Screenwriting* (2013), I am not aware of any study that focuses on music in screenplays. Price analyzes early film musicals and, in his investigation of the films choreographed by Busby Berkeley, he finds that the elaborate song and dance numbers are not described in detail in the associated screenplays. Price thus concludes that *"the composite nature of the musical screenplay*, which draws together dialogue, scene text, song lyrics and separately-choreographed dance sequences, is in many ways representative of classical Hollywood screenplays in general" and that the screenplay for Berkeley's film *Gold Diggers of 1933* (1933) "typifies the nature of screenplays written for musicals" (Price 2013, 138–39). In the context of the highly structured division of labor within Hollywood's studio system of the 1930s and 1940s, the staging and choreographing of musical numbers therefore seems not to be the task of the screenwriters.

After studying Reisch's screenplays for Austrian-German as well as for Hollywood films and comparing them to other screenplays for film musicals and fictional films with more than one musical number, I come to the conclusion that the way musical numbers are described and integrated into screenplays in Europe and Hollywood are more diverse and more complex than previously accepted.

15.9 First the Song, then the Number

Before there can be a musical number in a film, there has to be a song, upon which the number is based. Screenwriters play a part in writing and integrating songs into the film's narrative. Film musicals are generally based on a certain amount of musical numbers, drawing either on pre-existing songs or based on songs composed specifically for a film. The Astaire/Rogers film musicals for RKO, for example, used a handful of songs by composers that feature heavily in the Great American Songbook such as Irving Berlin, Cole Porter, or Jerome Kern. It was the objective of the screenwriters to construct a plot around these songs. To add yet another example of films written by a German-speaking émigré such as Felix Jackson, the Deanna Durbin musicals at Universal are mostly based on pre-existing, lesser-known songs. Reisch did both during his career: he co-wrote songs for films, mostly with composer Robert Stolz, and he used pre-existing music for musical numbers as he did in *The Great Waltz*. Reisch describes his mode of collaboration with composers as follows: "Instead of action or dialogue I wrote lyrics, and the other men—composers like Robert Stolz (sic!), Willy Schmidt-Gentner, Werner Heymann, and Friedrich Holländer—took over and wrote the music to the lyrics" (McGilligan 1991, 216). Reisch just wrote the first line of a song and completed the lyrics after a composer had written the melody (McGilligan 1991, 216). Reisch had a clear intention when he was adding a song and he tried to integrate musical numbers into the narrative in a plausible and organic way: "I always wrote my own lyrics for every song. The songs were integral parts of the continuity of the shooting script. My songs were always so built-in that you couldn't take them out" (McGilligan 1991, 215). Allan Scott, screenwriter of several Astaire/Rogers film musicals for RKO, remembers a similar mode of cooperation with the composer of the film's songs: "(Jerome) Kern only lived a few blocks from me so instead of going to the studio, I would go up to Jerry's house. This way the songs were integrated in the script from the beginning" (McGilligan 1988, 323).

The *integrated musical* of the 1940s and 1950s is a prime example of a type of film musical wherein song and dance numbers are motivated by the story. Although breaking out in song and dance is a well-accepted genre convention, screenwriters nevertheless tried to integrate musical numbers in the plot from the start and in a plausible way. The question must therefore not be whether or not there is any motivation for a song, but how tight and acceptable this motivation is—it is a question of degree, not of either or. The only form in which no narrative motivation at all is needed for songs is the revue film, where one number after the other is displayed without any narration holding them together. Films like *The King of Jazz* (1930) were popular in the early days of the sound film but vanished quickly (at least as feature-length films).

15.10 Making the World a Stage for Music

The job of screenwriters for film musicals was to build a plot around a number of songs, which were in many cases already chosen before the proper screenwriting started. In a biopic of a famous composer, the film was naturally based on the music of its protagonist. *The Great Waltz* includes several numbers featuring Johann Strauss' music. The most famous scene is an extraordinary musical number: a coach ride into the Vienna woods, that Strauss takes with opera singer Carla Donner. As in some of his earlier German-language screenplays, Reisch uses the rhythmization of everyday sounds as a dissolve into a musical number. In this case, the noises are coming from the natural environment of the Vienna woods and they are described in the soundtrack column: singing of birds, horse's hooves, yodel. The "theme #1" is heard, played by flute and English horn. The trotting of the horse becomes not just louder but turns into "¾ temp" (Hoffenstein, Meehan, and Reisch 1938, 70). Bird sounds are leading to "theme #2" (Hoffenstein, Meehan, and Reisch 1938, 70). Strauss begins to whistle, Donner hums. The splitting of the page in two columns is neither continuous nor strict. The second, broader column now also mentions sound and music: "At first he hums with assurance then he becomes uncertain as to the melody and hums slowly, hesitatingly as if composing. Then he stops altogether" (Hoffenstein, Meehan, and Reisch 1938, 70). As Donner starts to sing, Strauss and the Coachmen join in. It is a singing without words: "with the sound of the last note, Strauss has jumped up, keeping his balance with difficulty in the jerking fiacre and ends the music like the conductor of an orchestra" (Hoffenstein, Meehan, and Reisch 1938, 71). The sounds of the environment are rhythmized, the world that surrounds the characters turns into music, and Strauss becomes creator and conductor at the same time. "The horse gives a long whinny, harmonizing with the chimes, if possible" (Hoffenstein, Meehan, and Reisch 1938, 72). As if this was not enough, the number continues: "In the background we see the Danube. A children's chorus is entering the monastery, singing the theme of the Vienna

Woods" (Hoffenstein, Meehan, and Reisch 1938, 73). The whole sequence ends with a dissolve to a garden restaurant where Strauss rehearses with his orchestra: they play "Vienna Woods", as it is called in the screenplay, which is short for Strauss's famous waltz "Tales from the Vienna Woods".

The sequence analyzed here is one of the many ways to visualize the process of composing. A conventional and often utilized way to do this would be to show the composer at this desk ruminating and a musical theme slowly and repeatedly appears until it dissolves into the finished, well-known piece of music. The music represents an acoustic point of view of the composer, the audience hears what is in the head of the composer. This is a highly popular way of filming "the act of composing", even though it is anything but realistic. The reason why this scene in *The Great Waltz* does revert to this convention is found elsewhere. Strauss is presented as a people's musician, not as a genius. His connection to the common man and to his environment makes him the celebrated and relatable composer he is portrayed as at the end of the film. The sequence in question therefore does not show the creative and extraordinary genius Strauss, but the grounded and folksy composer consistent with his natural and cultural surroundings.

In most other examples for musicalizing everyday sounds from the 1930s and 1940s, technological sounds are the basis for the start of musical numbers. In the Astaire/Rogers musical *Shall We Dance*, for example, the steaming engine of a ship forms the rhythmic background for Astaire's number as stated in the screenplay:

```
CAMERA FOLLOWS Petrov around the large boiler room as he
dances to the sound of the musical machinery. As he approaches
the various whirling parts of the machine, his feet rap out
a counterpart to the beat of that particular machine. Around
and around he goes - faster and faster up a landing and down
again, the ring of the iron steps changing pitch. The shafts
of one motor beat out a counter tempo to the other motors. All
these things Petrov takes advantage of as he leads up to the
spectacular climax.

FADE OUT
```
                                      (Scott and Pagano 1936, 33, emphasis added)

For a real musician—the sequence seems to claim—anything can become music: one just has to listen. This process of everyday noises being turned into music is a phenomenon that can be observed in Austrian, German, French, and American films in the early years of sound cinema (see Jacobs 2014). Screenwriter Hoffenstein has used this technique in the opening sequence of *Love Me Tonight*, when Paris awakens and the everyday sounds of the city develop into the musical basis for the opening song of the film.

Reisch himself has used this device in earlier films. In *Two Hearts in Waltz Time* (*Zwei Herzen im ¾ Takt*) (1930), the sequence is even called "Grosse Geräuscheffekte-Komposition" [Big Sound Effects Composition] in the screenplay (Reisch 1930, 72). In *A Gentleman to Order* (*Ein Herr auf Bestellung* a.k.a. *Der Liebling von Wien*) (1930) characters move to the rhythm of everyday props. The occurrence of this device in various national cinemas demonstrates that technological innovations like synchronized sound led to similar and simultaneous experiments in different places. The eventual collaboration of two screenwriters—Walter Reisch and Samuel Hoffenstein—who had experimented with the musicalization of ordinary sounds in most ambitious and successful ways, is one of the ironic twists of film and screenwriting history. As the screenplays for these films demonstrate, the idea of fusing sounds of the environment with music and rhythm was not added to the film during shooting or in post-production, but written on the pages of these screenplays in astonishing detail (see also Tieber 2014).

These two examples palpably show that the staging of a musical number could indeed be the task of the screenwriter. However, we can differentiate between elaborate descriptions of musical numbers and simple instructions *à la* "insert musical number". Numbers that rely on singing instead of elaborate (dance) choreographies are more likely to be described in detail. Finding precise choreography instructions in screenplays is indeed a rare case, and even more so if the choreographer is as renowned as were Busby Berkeley and Fred Astaire after their first films, which would guarantee the success of a film. Thus, the degree of detail regarding the description of a musical number also depends on the choreography, its assumed importance for the film's success and on the status of the choreographer.

If the choreography becomes as important and distinct from the rest of the film as in most Busby Berkeley films, then all that can be read on the pages of these screenplays is the simple term "number" referring to an additional artistic *text* external to the screenplay that has to be created by someone else. But even in screenplays for Busby Berkeley films, one can find descriptions of numbers like the following one from *Gold Diggers of* 1933.

```
67: A MUSICAL NUMBER
   This number is to cover the transition of Ann from the
school-girl type that has been heretofore, to an attractive
girl, beautifully groomed and gowned.
   It is suggested that Dick and Arline take Ann through all
the shops in the hotel—the lingerie shop, the beauty shop,
the shoe shop, the modiste's, the hats, until she emerges a
completely made-over person. These scenes will constitute a
series of DISSOLVES.
   There is a background of music and in each shop scene
thechorus girls appear as models, displaying the particular
wares, that the shop sells.
```

>   The rendition of the song should carry over in a DISSOLVE
>   from the final shop scene to some attractive exterior shot
>   on the grounds of the hotel. Ann, completely transformed, is
>   listening to Dick conclude the chorus.
>
>   (Milne and Seff 1935, 44)

Another criterion for a more or less detailed description of a musical number is its narrative integration. In *Top Hat*, the title song is placed at a point in the narrative where it produces additional meaning: "This song is delivered by Jerry as part of his regular routine but the lyrical implication is that he is really singing about his own situation" (Taylor and Scott 1935, 68).

The most famous number of the film, "Cheek to Cheek", is first mentioned in the screenplay simply as "cheek to cheek number" (Taylor and Scott 1935, 105). After Jerry (Astaire) starts singing and dancing, the screenplay describes the number as follows:

>   115 EXT. PAVILLION - NIGHT
>   Dale is affected in spite of herself by the romance of her
>   surroundings and the dance with Jerry. All during this dance
>   Jerry is in love with her and she, in the beginning of it,
>   tries hard to resist him, but after the song is sung and after
>   they are out on the patio, we have a few seconds of dramatic
>   pantomime when she suggests she wants to go away but he won't
>   let her and finally he puts his arms around her and this
>   time she yields to him completely so that the following dance
>   becomes a love scene between them.
>
>   (Taylor and Scott 1935, 105)

The line "cheek to cheek number", that introduces this scene in the screenplay, can be read as a placeholder for a more precise choreography to be added at a later point or for the well-known lyrics of the song, be it in the form of dance notation and/or created in rehearsal without recording it in writing or drawing. The narrative content of the number is described in detail, it includes all the necessary plot information and character's motivation that should be included in a screenplay. The essence of the scene is on the page. The insertion of the musical number does not interrupt or slow down the narrative, but it is a crucial part of it; one might even consider it a plot point. The dance is explicitly called "a love scene" (Taylor and Scott 1935, 105), a surrogate for a more intimate scene, emphasizing another convention of the film musical, which is "to dance means to love" (Altman 1987, 136).

The screenwriters do not put down any instructions for Astaire and Rogers as to how to dance, but they are constructing a narrative that makes the high points of this film—its musical numbers—seen as logical steps in the plot by integrating the song in the narrative. To put it differently, they are constructing a narrative around a number of songs. They are using these numbers as a way to tell their story, drawing on the conventions of the genre to create an elegant musical way of storytelling. The numbers as well as the film are of a "composite nature" (Price 2013, 135), but the overall layout for the composition is created by the screenwriters.

Musical numbers in film come in different shapes and forms, not all of them are elaborate song and dance sequences, in which every step is carefully choreographed in advance. However, the closer a song or number is integrated into the plot, the more details about it can be found in the screenplay. Screenwriters are not choreographers, but their task is to hold the different aspects of a film, its attractions and necessities, together. A screenplay might not even be the final blueprint of a film, but it is the basic document that everyone involved in the making of a film has to work with.

15.11 Music as Theme

Music is not just a crucial device for audiovisual storytelling, but it is also often the main theme of a film, especially in the film musical. To mention just one prominent example, the dualism between popular and elite art is a recurring topos of the genre (see Feuer 1978). In Reisch's Austrian films, especially in those that are considered Viennese Films, a similar dualism of modern (American) popular music and high art can be detected. In *The Great Waltz*, Reisch constructs a dualism between the wild, ecstatic, and popular waltz, and the boring and stiff baroque music of the aristocracy. It is a social and political dualism under the guise of a musical one: the sounds of the 1848 revolution as well as the revolutionaries themselves are seen and heard throughout the film. Reisch uses music and its staging to underline this point, siding clearly with the people's music, the frivolous waltz against the rituals of the court.

```
52 OVERHEAD SHOT – THE CROWD
   In the hall as they dance, wildly and extemporaneously
   waltzing.
   DISSOLVE TO

53 OVERHEAD SHOT OF A SMALLER GROUP
   Moving in the precise and decorous steps of the minuet. The
   music is mannered and dull.
```
(Hoffenstein, Meehan, and Reisch 1938, 23–24)

Wild and improvised music is pitted against the boring mannerism of the court dance. These two musical worlds collide when the famous opera singer Carla Donner tries to make music with the composer. The screenplay gives detailed musical instructions on how to represent this musical clash. Schani (short Viennese form for Johann and the name that Strauss Jr. is referred to throughout the screenplay) starts to accompany Donner, who suddenly "goes into an improvised cadenza" (Hoffenstein, Meehan, and Reisch 1938, 37). It is a battle of musical styles, representing different aesthetic as well as social worlds. Donner demonstrates the skills of an opera singer, much to Strauss' dismay. She "embroiders the melody with a brilliant coloratura obligato" (Hoffenstein, Meehan, and Reisch 1938, 38). After Strauss leaves the bandstand, she has to accompany herself: "…she walks quietly over to the piano and plays the concluding chord. The guests applaud madly" (Hoffenstein, Meehan, and Reisch 1938, 39).

The screenplay sets up this scene as a comic musical battle. The weapons of choice are unambiguous. On the one side the three-quarter time, the dance rhythm, the absence of virtuosity for the sake of popularity. On the other side highly artificial technique and devices like coloratura and cadenza, applied to demonstrate sheer technical brilliance. The screenplay uses music and musical details to construct a scene that in a different genre, for example, a screwball comedy, would be a quick, tongue-in-cheek dialogue—the couple is fighting, but they are obviously very much in love.

To erase any doubt about Strauss' ideological attitude and to underscore the narrative with a revolutionary fervor, the following dialogue between Strauss and representatives of the aristocracy emphasizes the dualism even further. The "barbaric" (Hoffenstein, Meehan, and Reisch 1938, 40) rhythm of the "lower classes" (Hoffenstein, Meehan, and Reisch 1938, 40) is juxtaposed to the "powdered, perfumed, unreal society" Strauss loathes: "your quadrilles, your minuets, your gavottes—will be out of date and ridiculous!" (Hoffenstein, Meehan, and Reisch 1938, 40).

The waltz is constructed as the people's music. Strauss comments about waltzes: "I love them because they're honest—like the people who dance them! Like the women we love—like the life we live in Vienna" (Hoffenstein, Meehan, and Reisch 1938, 41). The stereotypical "wine, women and song" mentality ("Wein, Weib und Gesang" is also a waltz by Johann Strauss) is the motto and mantra of Viennese *joie de vivre* as crystallized in the musical form of the waltz. Vienna is represented as a hedonistic utopia in which the most important elements for an enjoyable life are in balance. Waltz is the *solution to any problem* because it represents the easy-going life of the common people, an art form that is understood by them and is able to bridge the gap between high art and entertainment. This specific musical and aesthetic ideology is constituent of the Viennese Film, but also of most of the Viennese operetta on which many Austrian music films of the 1920s and 1930s are based. As the political revolution in Vienna begins, Strauss repeats the core argument of this film: "I am of the people. I belong to them … that's why I wrote for them. That's why they listened to me! I knew the tunes their feet would dance to because my own heart danced to them first" (Hoffenstein, Meehan, and Reisch 1938, 52).

The close emotional connection between an artist, often a musician, and the people is a fundamental characteristic of Austrian music films before the annexation to Nazi Germany in 1938. Biopics about Mozart, Beethoven or Schubert all include obligatory scenes highlighting this connection (see *Mozarts Leben*,

Lieben und Leiden, 1921, *Der Märtyrer seines Herzens*, 1918, and *Leise flehen meine Lieder*, 1933). People on the street or at the *Heurigen* (a typical Viennese wine tavern) singing or humming songs by Beethoven or Schubert are a convention of these films and stand in sharp contrast to the portrayal of the lonely genius that characterizes composer biopics during the Nazi era. The connection between composer and common people surfaces in many Austrian films, but it is left to Hollywood's "excessive obviousness" (Bordwell et al. 1985, 1) to display it explicitly and repeatedly in this screenplay about the King of waltz. The dualism between elite and popular art and the eventual prevalence of the latter, connects the Viennese film with the Hollywood musical.

15.12 Conclusion

In this chapter I have demonstrated some of the ways in which screenwriters co-create musical numbers and how they are dealing with music in screenplays. The case study of Reisch's screenplay for Julien Duvivier's *The Great Waltz* highlights how European traditions of writing film musicals perfectly suited the needs of Hollywood in the 1930s. The introduction of synchronized sound added new sensations to the medium and filmmakers with additional experience and knowledge in theater and/or music were in high demand. Reisch continued to write in his usual style, using his characteristic devices. The invention of sound and the popularity of the film musical led to similar experiments with sound and music throughout different national cinemas as we have seen with the example of the musicalization of everyday sounds.

The master-scene format, the new screenplay format necessitated by the sound film, was developed and widely adopted in an astonishingly short time (see Price 2013, 182–99). Music and musical numbers, however, subverted the screenplay format for the duration of a musical number and made music visible and distinct from the rest of the screenplay. On a broader level, the film musicals of the 1930s and the American film musical in general were trying to reconcile high art and entertainment in order to create a kind of folk art for the masses.

The questions and answers of this chapter can only be asked and answered by looking closely at these screenplays. The films themselves do not tell how they were created; they do not inform us about the intention of a scene. The final product erases almost all traces of the work, the collaboration, and the discussions that went into creating it. To further discuss questions about the construction and integration of musical numbers and about the role and function of screenwriters and screenwriting in the historiography of the film musical, a shift from the film to the screenplay as research object is essential. Screenwriting studies thus opens up old and hitherto neglected material to ask new questions about the role of music in film history.

The division of labor that is characteristic of the Hollywood studio system is not a fixed structure but a series of processes in which every filmic device and their creators get a chance to shine. But it is the screenplay that has to hold the production together. Screenwriting is thus also a crucial aspect of those elements of film production that are usually not brought into connection with it. The screenwriters of American film musicals of the 1930s constructed narratives around musical numbers and told their stories with the help of music. The degree to which they took over the professional tasks of others—composers, lyricists, and choreographers—depended on the form of the film musical (backstage, integrated, or something in between) and on the status of its stars and choreographers. Precise choreographies or visual breakdowns of musical numbers cannot be found in these screenplays. Instead, one can examine a growing degree of narrativization and integration of musical numbers, a discussion of music as an elite or popular art form, and a tendency to integrate the formal and formatting necessities of musical numbers within the master-scene script. Taken together, these aspects bear more than enough evidence to rethink and expand research on the role and function of screenplays and their writers.

References

Altman, Rick. 1987. *The American Film Musical*. Bloomington, IN: Indiana University Press.

Bauer, Lev. 2017. *Screenwriting Fundamentals. The Art and Craft of Visual Writing*. New York: Routledge.

Blondie of the Follies. 1932. Written by Anita Loos, and Frances Marion. Directed by William Goulding. USA: Metro-Goldwyn-Mayer, Marion Davies, Cosmopolitan Productions (uncredited).

Bordwell, David, Kristin Thompson, and Janet Staiger. 1985. *The Classical Hollywood Cinema: Film Style and Mode of Production to 1960*. New York: Columbia University Press.

China Seas. 1935. Written by James Kevin McGuinness, and Jules Furthman. Directed by Tay Garnett. USA: Metro-Goldwyn-Mayer.

Dassanowsky, Robert. 2018. *Screening Transcendence: Film under "Austrofascism" and the Hollywood Hope 1933–1938*. Bloomington, IN: Indiana University Press.

Der Märtyrer seines Herzens [*The Martyr of His Heart*]. 1918. Written by Emil Justitz, Emil Kolberg, and Fritz Kortner. Directed by Emil Justitz. Austria: Sascha-Meßter-Film.

Ein Herr auf Bestellung [*A Gentleman to Order*] (a.k.a *Der Liebling von Wien* [*The Darling from Vienna*]). 1930. Written by Walter Reisch. Directed by Géza von Bolváry. Austria: Super-Film GmbH.

Feuer, Jane. 1978. "The Theme of Popular vs. Elite Art in the Hollywood Musical." *Journal of Popular Culture* 12 (3): 491–99.

Field, Syd. 2005 [1979]. *Screenplay. The Foundations of Screenwriting*. New York: Dell.

Gold Diggers of 1933. 1933. Written by Erwin S. Gelsey, James Seymour, Ben Markson, and David Bohem. Directed by Mervin LeRoy, and Busby Berkeley. USA: Warner Bros.

Herzog, Amy. 2010. *Dreams of Difference, Songs of the Same. The Musical Moment in Film*. Minneapolis: University of Minnesota Press.
Hoffenstein, Samuel, John Meehan, and Walter Reisch. 1938. *The Great Waltz*. 4/13/38 draft, okayed by Mr. Hyman, screenplay. Available at Arts Library, Special Collections at UCLA.
Jacobs, Lea. 2014. *Film Rhythm after Sound. Technology, Music, and Performance*. Berkeley, CA: University of California Press.
Krenn, Günther, ed. 2004. *Walter Reisch: Film Schreiben*. Vienna: Verlag Filmarchiv Austria.
Leise flehen meine Lieder [Lover Divine]. 1933. Written by Willi Forst, and Walter Rausch. Directed by Willi Forst. Germany: Cine-Allianz Tonfilmproduktions GmbH.
Love Me Tonight. 1932. Written by Samuel Hoffenstein, George Marion Jr., and Waldemar Young. Directed by Rouben Mamoulina. USA: Paramount Pictures.
Macdonald, Ian W. 2010. "'… So It's Not Surprising I'm Neurotic' The Screenwriter and the Screen Idea Work Group." *Journal of Screenwriting* 1 (1): 45–58.
McGilligan, Patrick, ed. 1988. *Backstory 1. Interviews with Screenwriters of Hollywood's Golden Age*. Berkeley, CA: University of California Press.
McGilligan, Patrick, ed. 1991. *Backstory 2. Interviews with Screenwriters of the 1940s and 50s*. Berkeley, CA: University of California Press.
McKee, Robert. 1997. *Story: Style, Structure, Substance, and the Principles of Screenwriting*. New York: Regan Books.
Milne, Peter, and Manuel Seff. 1935. *Gold Diggers of 1935*. Screenplay. Available at the Public Library of Performing Arts, New York. Electronic Edition [2009] by Alexander Street Press.
Mozarts Leben, Lieben und Leiden [Mozart's Life, Love and Suffering]. 1921. Written by Heinrich Glücksmann, and Josef Teutscher. Directed by Otto Kreisler. Austria: Helios Filmproduktion.
Ninotschka. 1939. Written by Melchior Lengyel, Charles Brackett, Billy Wilder, and Walter Reisch. Directed by Ernst Lubitsch. USA: Metro-Goldwyn-Mayer.
N.N. 1932a. Story Conference for *China Seas*. February 20, 1932a, document. Available at Cinema Arts Library, Doheny Memorial Library at the University of Southern California, MGM collection.
N.N. 1932b. Story Conference for *Good Time Girl*, May 7, 1932b, document. Available at the Cinema Arts Library, Doheny Memorial Library at the University of Southern California, MGM collection.
Price, Steven. 2013. *A History of Screenwriting*. Basingstoke, UK: Palgrave Macmillan.
Reisch, Walter. 1930. *Zwei Herzen im ¾ Takt*. Screenplay. Available at Filmarchive Austria, Vienna, Reisch Collection, Box 3.
Scott, Allan, and Ernest S. Pagano. 1936. *Stepping Toes* (a.k.a. *Shall We Dance*) Final Script 12/23/36, screenplay. Available at the Film Studies Center, Museum of Modern Art, New York.
Shall We Dance. 1937. Written by Allan Scott, and Ernest Pagano. Directed by Mark Sandrich. USA: RKO Radio Pictures.
Stillwell, Robynn J. 2007. "The Fantastical Gap Between Diegetic and Nondiegetic. In *Beyond the Soundtrack: Representing Music in Cinema*, edited by Daniel Goldmark, Lawrence Kramer, and Richard Leppert, 184–202. Berkeley, CA: University of California Press.
Taylor, Dwight, and Allan Scott. 1935. *Top Hat*. Final script, May 8, 1935, screenplay. Available at the Public Library of the Performing Arts, New York.

Tieber, Claus. 2014. "A Story is Not a Story but a Conference. Story Conferences and the Classical Studio System." *Journal of Screenwriting* 5 (2): 225–37.

Tieber, Claus, and Christina Wintersteller. 2020. "Writing with Music: Self-Reflexivity in the Screenplays of Walter Reisch." *ARTS* 9 (1): 13. https://doi.org/10.3390/arts9010013.

The Gay Divorcee. 1934. Written by George Marion Jr., Dorothy Yost, and Edward Kaufman. Directed by Mark Sandrich. USA: RKO Radio Pictures.

The Great Waltz. 1938. Written by Samuel Hoffenstein, Walter Reisch, and John Meehan (uncredited). Directed by Juline Duvivier. USA: Metro-Goldwyn-Mayer.

The King of Jazz. 1930. Written by Charles MacArthur, and Harry Ruskin. Directed by John Murray Anderson. USA: Universal Pictures.

Titanic. 1953. Written by Charles Brackett, Richard L. Breene, and Walter Rausch. Directed by Jean Negulesco. USA: Twentieth Century-Fox.

Top Hat. 1935. Written by Allan Scott, Dwight Taylor, Ben Holmes, Ralph Spence, and Károly Nóti (uncredited). Directed by Mark Sandrich. USA: RKO Radio Pictures.

Zwei Herzen im ¾ Takt [Two Hearts in Waltz Time]. 1930. Written by Walter Rausch, Franz Schulz, and Joe Young. Directed by Géza von Bolváry. Germany: Deutsches Lichtspiel-Syndikat.

CHAPTER 16

Women Screenwriters of Early Sinophone Cinema: 1916–1949

S. Louisa Wei

16.1 Introduction

This chapter investigates female screenwriters of early Sinophone cinema from 1916 to 1949, covering both the silent and the early sound eras. In 1916, Marion E. Wong (黃女娣 1895–1969) wrote and directed *The Curse of Quon Gwon: When the Far East Mingles with the West* (關武帝, 1916) in Oakland, California, thus beginning the lineages of both Chinese women screenwriters and directors. The year 1949, as most film historians agree, marks the end of *early cinema* in greater China. By Sinophone cinema, include films produced by (ethnic) Chinese filmmakers, with dialogue in Chinese dialect(s) and/or dealing with Chinese subjects. This definition encompasses the concept's geo-cultural connotations as interpreted in recent studies (Yue and Khoo 2014; Pecic 2016; Lupke 2016; Peng and Raidel 2018; Tan 2021). Besides the twin centres of Shanghai and Hong Kong, cities like San Francisco and Singapore were also vital for early Sinophone film production. Research reveals that pioneer women filmmakers often worked on independent and transnational productions, moving from one location to another to sustain their careers. Thus, adopting a broad definition of Sinophone cinema is critical to reclaiming their contributions (Wei and Law 2018).

The following discussion consists of three parts. The first presents an overview of twelve women screenwriters (and directors) with confirmed

S. L. Wei (✉)
City University of Hong Kong, Hong Kong, China
e-mail: smlouisa@cityu.edu.hk

© The Author(s), under exclusive license to Springer Nature Switzerland AG 2023
R. Davies et al. (eds), *The Palgrave Handbook of Screenwriting Studies*,
https://doi.org/10.1007/978-3-031-20769-3_16

production and theatrical screening records. Three-fourths of them were barely or never mentioned in existing film histories. While constructing their obscured lineage in chronological order, their working conditions are inspected whenever possible. The second part looks into six original screenplays/films by five female writers working in both silent (1916–1934) and early sound (1933–1949) periods.[1] The concluding part summarizes the aesthetic and thematic conventions established by early screenwriting women still present in today's Sinophone films and women's cinema.

16.2 Early Women Screenwriters and Their Working Conditions

Within the larger context of Sinophone cinema, California diva Marion E. Wong was the first Chinese woman to write, direct, and produce a motion picture, even though such recognition was belated for nearly a century (Lau 2013; OT 1917). Wong's only film, *The Curse of Quon Gwon*, was made five years before any feature-length film had been made in China. In her time, Alice Guy-Blaché and Lois Weber—respectively the mother of world and American cinema—were prominent figures in the American film industry. As showcased by Women Film Pioneer Project profiles, over a hundred women had been writing and directing silent pictures. Under travelling and other restrictions enforced by the Chinese Exclusion Act (1882–1943), which was in effect for two-thirds of her life, Wong was unlikely to have a career in either the American or the Chinese film industry. *The Curse of Quon Gwon* was produced with family funds, but Wong inevitably failed to have it distributed. After generating headlines like "Chinese Have Joined the Ranks of Producers", Wong and her film were soon forgotten (OC 1917). Even Guy-Blaché and Weber, who both made several hundreds of films, were also forgotten for many years. Weber's biographer Anthony Slide "rediscovered" Wong a few years after her death (Tashman 1977; Slide 1996). Today, in both Sinophone and American cinema, Wong is regarded as a pioneer for writing, directing, and producing a feature-length film, casting mainly women in her crew and portraying Chinese women's living conditions, and incorporating themes of cross-cultural migration.

Pu Shunqing (濮舜卿, 1902–1998) was called China's first woman screenwriter as soon as she adapted her stage play *Cupid's Puppet* (愛神的玩偶, 1925) for Great Wall Motion Pictures—founded in Brooklyn in 1922 but relocated to Shanghai in 1924 (BLALIS 1928; Zhang Z. 2005). Pu was at the time a law student of Southeast University and the co-founder of the university's drama society—together with schoolmate and future husband, Hou Yao (Wei 2014b). In 1926, the couple joined China Sun Motion Picture—founded in Hong Kong in 1924 and relocated to Shanghai in 1926 (Law and Bren

---

[1] Names in this chapter are spelled as they are pronounced—Chinese names with surname first and English names with given name(s) first.

2004). Pu wrote at least six screenplays for China Sun, all directed by Hou. While heading the company's Script Department, she also worked as the editor or assistant director (Wei 2014b). Besides writing stage and screenplays, Pu published critical essays, translated western dramas, and edited the *Women's Monthly* magazine. She was a true advocate of women's rights, first as a screenwriter, then as a lawyer (Xu and Wu 2000; Xinleng 1932). Following her example, two women also made one-off efforts in writing. Cheng Xuemei (成雪梅, dates unknown) wrote a modern melodrama, *The Fox's Gratitude* (狐狸報恩, 1927), based on an ancient tale and acted in a supporting role. Her husband produced the film. Canada-born Florence Lim (林楚楚 a.k.a. Lam Cho-Cho, 1905–1979), lead actress of China Sun and wife of its director Lai Man-wai (黎民偉, 1893–1953), wrote *Retrieval* (再生因緣, 1928) and played both a male and a female role.

Even though many film actresses were educated women, the general attitude of the 1920s' Chinese media tended to consider them shallow. After Ai Xia (艾霞, 1912–1934) and Hu Ping (胡萍, 1910–unknown) joined Star Film in the early 1930s, they both published articles in newspapers and wrote screenplays. Ai Xia wrote *A Modern Girl* (現代一女性, 1933), and Hu Ping wrote *Sister's Tragedy* (姊姊的悲劇, 1934) around the same time (Mai 1932; Hu 1933; Cheng 1933). In her short acting career, Ai only played the female lead twice on screen and never made it onto a magazine cover. Even though *A Modern Girl* was a great commercial success and generated many reviews, Ai did not receive another leading role afterwards. Suffering from long-time depression, she committed suicide before Chinese New Year in 1934. A drawing of her made it to the cover of a film magazine because her death was shocking to all and widely reported by general news (not necessarily related to film). Ai Xia became a well-known celebrity posthumously and with lasting fame because of how her name was mentioned repeatedly whenever an actress committed suicide (Wang 1932). Her act of screenwriting has thus generated continued scholarly and public interest (Harris 1997; Zhang Z. 2005).

Hu Ping was a more successful actress, but *Sister's Tragedy* was a mediocre melodrama with much less enthusiastic reviews (Hu 1933; Qin 2021). Hu's most famous role was perhaps the female lead in Maxu Weibang's *Song at Midnight* (夜半歌聲 1937)—a loose adaptation of Gaston Leroux's novel *The Phantom of the Opera* (1909–1910). Even though the film was a great hit, Hu could not sustain her acting or writing career in the 1940s. Ai and Hu both contributed screenplays to Star Film, which needed original screenplays, but the company directors never encouraged them to write again. In 1935, Huang Hou (黃侯, dates unknown) wrote and produced *Under the E'mei Mountain* (峨眉山下, 1935) based on her life under the Sichuan warlords. As an outsider of the Shanghai film industry who lacked support in equipment and technical crew, her only film was funded by her mother and failed after the director quit the project before its completion (Huang 1936).

Both Shanghai and Hong Kong transitioned from silent to sound periods between 1930 and 1934, during which the silent film achieved great artistry while sound recording technology matured. Tong Sing-to (唐醒圖, dates unknown) was the first woman known to write and produce a film in Hong Kong—a partial talkie titled *Conscience* (良心, 1933). Tong joined the Hong Kong division of Lianhua Film just a year ago to pursue her film career. She co-founded the China Sound & Silent Film Production with her mentor Lai Pak-hoi (黎北海, 1889–1950), who directed *Conscience* and led Hong Kong into the talkie era (Law and Bren 2004). Next, Tong founded Big Time Film (*Dashidai*) with He Luo and wrote a thriller based on a real-life murder titled *House Number Sixty-six* (六十六號屋, 1936), which she also produced. Later she established Sing-to Film Company under her name and produced three more motion pictures, but she did not write them (DY 1939; Fu 1998).

Paralleling Tong's film adventure was that of an unexpected newcomer to Hong Kong. San Francisco-born Esther Eng (伍錦霞, 1914–1970) arrived in Hong Kong with a Cantonese talkie *Heartaches* (心恨, 1935) that she co-produced with Bruce Wong in Hollywood with a rare Chinese-American creative team (writer, director, and cast) and a Euro-American technical crew. Eng became Hong Kong's first woman director with *National Heroine* (民族女英雄, 1937), which premiered in Central Theatre in March 1937. After the Japanese military bombed and invaded Shanghai in August, refugees, including numerous filmmakers in Shanghai, travelled westward. Many also arrived in Hong Kong. By late 1937, Hong Kong replaced Shanghai as the centre of Sinophone film production. Between 1938 and 1939, Esther Eng directed another four Cantonese talkies for four different companies, with *Thirty-six Amazons* (a.k.a. *It's a Women's World* 女人世界, 1939) contributing to her writing credits (Wei 2014a, 2016).

Meanwhile, Hong Kong-born Wan Hoi-ling (尹海靈, ca. 1910–195?) began writing for and assisting director Hou Yao, who had relocated to Hong Kong with China Sun. Wan quickly became a full-fledged screenwriter and wrote fifteen films, half of which were adaptations of folklore or Cantonese opera episodes. She also co-directed more than ten of these between 1938 and 1939. After independently writing and directing *The Goddess* (觀音得道, 1940), Wan moved to Singapore in April 1940 with Hou Yao. They made six Malay language films, and Wan became the first female director in Singapore and Malay language cinema (Bren 2013; ST 1949). Both Eng and Wan were early examples of women sustaining their film careers by working on transnational and independent productions. After World War II broke out in Europe in 1939, Esther Eng returned to California and made four Cantonese films in the 1940s—three in California, one in Hawaii: *Golden Gate Girl* (金門女, 1941), *Lady from the Blue Lagoon* (藍湖碧玉, 1945), *Back Street* (虛度春宵, 1947), and *Mad Love Mad Fire* (怒火情焰, 1949). Two years after Japan surrendered, Wan Hoi-ling directed two Mandarin films in Singapore—*Spirit of the Overseas Chinese* (海外征魂, 1947) and *Honours and Sins* (南洋小姐, 1948). She wrote the latter concerning the theme of comfort women and was the first filmmaker to discuss the issue (MT 1946; Hee 2019).

In 1943, when Shanghai was still under Japanese occupation, writer-translator Sheng Qinxian (盛琴悇, 1921–2017) joined the script division of China Film Co. and wrote three screenplays over the next two years. The first was *The Honorable Beggar* (義丐, 1944), based on the real-life figure Wu Xun who begged for money to open schools for the poor (Meng 1945). She received a screenplay award, and the film had positive reviews. Her second film was a tragicomedy titled *Happy Reunion of a Troubled Couple* (歡喜冤家, 1945) that also performed well at the box office. Her third film was *Modern Women* (摩登女性, 1945), with stories inspired by the experiences of her friends, but she did not get a writer's credit on the film due to some conflict with the film's director. Sheng quit screenwriting and taught in secondary school till retirement. In 1947 and 1948, Shanghai's best-selling writer Eileen Chang (張愛玲, 1920–1995) wrote two screenplays for director Sang Hu and the newly established Wenhua Film Company with box office success: tragedy *Unending Love* (不了情, 1947) and comedy *Long Live the Mistress* (太太萬歲, 1948). While the former had mostly positive reviews, the latter was attacked by some Leftist critics. I will discuss these two films in more detail later (Table 16.1).

Table 16.1 The trajectory of above-the-line women filmmakers in early sinophone cinemas (1916–1949)

Women Screenwriters (Last Names Capitalized)	1916	1925	1926	1927	1928	1929	1933	1934	1935	1936	1937	1938	1939	1940	1941	1944	1945	1946	1947	1948	1949
黃女娣 Marion E. WONG	1																				
濮舜卿 PU Shunqing		1	1	3	1	1															
謝采貞 XIE Caizhen		1																			
成雪梅 CHENG Xuemei				1																	
林楚楚 Florence LIM					1																
王漢倫 Helen WANG						1															
楊耐梅 YANG Naimei						1															
艾 霞 AI Xia							1														
胡 萍 HU Ping							1														
黃 侯 HUANG Hou									1												
唐醒圓 TONG Sing-To							1			1	2										
伍錦霞 Esther ENG										1	1	3	1		1		1		1		1
尹海靈 WAN Hoi Ling												5	5	5	6			1	1		
盛琴傹 SGENG Qinxian																1	2				
張愛玲 Eileen CHANG																			1	1	

Legend: ■ written, directed, produced; ■ written & produced; ■ produced, written, acted; ■ written & acted; ■ produced & acted; ■ written; ■ directed; ■ written & directed; ■ directed & acted

The above chart summarizes women filmmakers who took up screenwriting (and directing). The year and the number of films they made are indicated. The silent period is marked in light orange, and the sound period in light blue. Due to the high demand for actresses in the silent era, nearly all women writers also acted in (their) films. We can see the trajectory is mostly intact since 1925, only with a gap between 1930 and 1932 and another one between 1942 to 1944—respectively caused by the transition from silent to talkie and the Pacific War. Most Chinese women who wrote for the screen were well-educated and greatly talented, but few could continue screenwriting for more than five years. Despite the impact of civil and world wars, these women managed to sustain other professions as literary writers, journalists, teachers, lawyers, and even entrepreneurs.

16.3 Cases of Chinese Women's Screenplays and Films

Due to wars and poor preservation after the wars, even some of the most celebrated films in early Sinophone cinema just exist in the form of long synopses, *film fiction* or, occasionally, *explanations* (i.e. the text of title cards) for silent films. The six films selected for closer reading here are high achievements of women's cinema in the 1910s, 1920s, 1930s, and 1940s. Unfortunately, no screenplays by the two Hong Kong writer-directors—Esther Eng and Wan Hoi-ling—are extant in either of the abovementioned forms, so I cannot examine their written works at this stage. I hope to capture the distinct aspects of writing in each of the chosen films.

16.3.1 Marion E. Wong and The Curse of Quon Gwon (1916)

In 1916, after Marion E. Wong's successful "debut as a prima donna with a musical comedy roadshow", she decided to make a film of her own (OT 1916). The *Oakland Tribune* followed her progress as she obtained financial support from her brother-in-law, "signed herself as president" of the Mandarin Film, and began working on the story and the sets for filming. She hired Charlie Chaplin's cameraman and a professional actor to play the male lead while drilling her sister-in-law Violet Wong and other women and girls in the family to play supporting roles (OT 1917). The completed film consisted of five reels (approximately 75 minutes), of which only 35 minutes survive today. The *Oakland Tribune* reports that Marion wrote a big part of the film referencing the mythology of Quon Gwon—a Chinese god worshipped in nearly every household in Canton.

> The first portion of the film pictures California scenes and the environment. It depicts life in American Chinese quarters, showing conspiracies being carried on by agents of the deposed Chinese emperor (since reinstated) and counter

measures working against them. A genuine love story proceeds through the picture. (OT 1917)

These establishing scenes are not visible in the 35 minutes extant today. The background of a reinstated emperor and the counterforce seems very intriguing, as such an event happened shortly after the film's completion. Did Marion hear any rumours from China? If yes, how? She wanted to show the American audience what real Chinese lives were like; all the reporters trusted Marion's take on customs, lifestyle, props, costumes, and settings to be authentically Chinese (OC 1917).

The main plot was a "love story" focusing on a nameless girl played by Violet, who was born and raised in America but fell in love with a Chinese merchant. They get married, and she follows him to China. Chinese men then could have more than one wife simultaneously. The merchant already has a wife (played by Marion), who is childless. Violet soon conceives a child, causing jealousy from Marion. The husband leaves home for business. When the baby is ill, Marion complains about Violet to their mother-in-law, who throws Violet out in rage. A sentimental sequence of the homeless Violet walking alone in wind and rain follows. After some days, she returns and falls on the stairs in front of her husband's home. The husband returns home and is furious with Marion, who later commits suicide. The film reflects on the fate, conflicts, and struggles of women. When Violet arrives at her husband's home, his mother and Marion give her jewellery as welcoming gifts. A shot of Violet wearing necklaces and bracelets dissolves into the imagery of chains restricting her. Are the chains a metaphor for marriage? When Marion stabs herself in guilt and shame, her bitterness is loud and clear: is a woman's worth only in her reproductive ability? A viewer might not feel catharsis at how the *villainess* died in such a spectacle. The tragic fate of women's place in the family comes forward forcefully. The thematic issues and scenarios of women's domestic life would appear again and again in later women's cinema.

16.3.2 *Pu Shunqing and* Cupid's Puppets *(1925)*

Pu Shunqing greatly admired Norwegian playwright Henrik Ibsen (1828–1906), who was first introduced by leading writer Lu Xun in 1907, very famous, with his *A Doll's House* being the most widely staged western play in China. Her stage play *Cupid's Puppet* displays influence from *A Doll's House*. Pu's adaptation of her four-act play for the screen demonstrates her understanding of the two forms. Comparing the stage script and the film's synopsis and *explanation* (or title-card text), we can see that the play has a rather linear plot suited for the stage, while the film utilizes parallel montages of different characters and spaces.

The play begins with a young woman Ming Guoying begging her father, Ming Qun, to reverse the arranged marriage to Yu Ren—the nephew of her stepmother, Madam Yu. Qun refuses, and Guoying leaves home. She supports herself by teaching in a primary school headed by her good friend and former schoolmate, Renda. On the other hand, the film begins with a small student asking Guoying whether she would go home for summer vacation. She sighs: "I have a home that I can't return to" (Pu 1996). What follows is a flashback to the conversation between Guoying and her father. Then the following intertitles appear on the screen.

Guoying:
My dear mother! If you didn't die, how could I...
[Title card] Principal of Minben Primary School, Luo Renda, Guoying's good friend (played by Zhai Yiyi)

Luo Renda:
Dear sister, I suggest you forget about your troubles!

Luo Renda:
You can have a home wherever you can settle. My home will be yours as well!
[Title card] Yu Ren, Guoying's fiancé (Liu Jinqun); Yu Xinzhi, Ren's father (Yi Yinqiao)

Yu Xinzhi:
Guoying left home for half a year. I want to find another wife for you, but why do you always refuse?

Yu Ren:
I want to find her back. I do not want anyone less pretty than she is.

(Pu 1996, 271)

These few lines suggest a montage from the school scene to Yu's family, and the next scene cuts to Luo Renda's home and introduces her mother and brother Renjun. The following sequence parallels Guoying's father spotting her fiancé wooing another woman while Renjun presents a small statue of Cupid to Guoying as a sign of affection. Guoying likes him but hesitates to accept the gift. The plot moves on with such montage sequences. Just as Qun releases Guoying from the arranged marriage, the father of Renjun's fiancée turns up at his home, demanding the fulfilment of another arranged marriage. Guoying is called to her father's sickbed, but Qun dies before he can tell Guoying about the reversal of the arranged marriage. Learning that Qun has left a large sum of money to Guoying, Madam Yu schemes with her nephew to push Guoying into a marriage so they can obtain her share of the inheritance. Guoying rejects fiercely. At the drama's climax, Yu Ren bribes a doctor to claim Guoying insane and gets locked up in an asylum. Her cohabitants are two women, both driven mad by broken hearts. Guoying sighs: "we are all Cupid's puppets! Either forced into marriages without love or unable to love the ones we truly desire". Renjun manages to infiltrate the asylum by pretending to be mad. In the end, they succeed in escaping. The last two intertitles are rather progressive statements for its time.

Guoying:
Where are we going now?

Renjun:
Let's find a life in a new society!

(Pu 1996, 271)

Pu began to work as a lawyer in 1932 in Tianjin, a city in Northern China. In an interview with critic/writer Xinleng, she said working as a lawyer made her realize women's reality was much worse than what she had learned from women around her. *Cupid's Puppets* remained her strongest film and continued to screen into the 1930s (Qian 1925).

16.3.3　*Ai Xia and* **A Modern Girl** *(1933)*

In 1933, Ai Xia played the leading role in a film penned by her: *A Modern Girl* (1933). The story focuses on a romantic young woman, Grape, who works in a real estate company where her manager Mr. Shi wants to make her his mistress. Grape seeks excitement and pleasure in life but is not attracted to the men wooing her. One evening, she rekindles a passion with an old flame—journalist Leng, who is now married to Yuru with two boys. Leng submits to Grape's desires and her constant demand to spend time together. He soon loses his job for neglecting work, while she loses hers due to her manager's jealousy. Worsening the situation, Yuru comes to Shanghai with the boys as one of them has fallen ill. The couple needs money for doctors. Grape spends a night with Mr. Shi in exchange for money to help Leng. Grape proposes an escape—a vacation outside Shanghai to save their faltering romance. She steals a check from Mr. Shi and gets caught after cashing out a large sum. Later, Leng is shocked by Grape's candid confession in the courtroom and leaves. Finding out about her husband's infidelity and suffering from the loss of her son, Yuru decides to divorce Leng and gain independence on her own.

In prison, a former friend Anlin—imprisoned for leftist activism—encourages Grape to think beyond romance and work for people's well-being. On the day of Grape's release from prison, she sees Leng being taken in for gambling and other crimes. Grape looks up at the blue sky, ready for a new beginning (Ai 2012).

Compared to other screenwriters, Ai Xia dared to inject an unapologetic subjectivity into every female character—Grape, Yuru, and Anlin, but Grape in particular. The theatrical screening of the film began in first-run cinemas like Central and Shanghai in mid-June of 1933 and went on to screen at a dozen other theatres for five months. The film company launched a series of making-of news and advertisements boasting about "the first kiss" on China's silver screen during production, and Ai Xia's bold embodiment of Grape's desire and despair was showered with praise by critics (Yu H. 1933; Yu J. 1933; Zhang W. 1934). *Eastern Times* published Ai Xia's novella *A Modern Girl*—a retelling of the film—in instalments. *Shenbao* published many reviews of the film, sometimes with more than one on the same page. While everyone in Star Film—from the producers to the directors and co-actors—seemed to ride on the film's success, Ai Xia alone took the blame for controversies. Her relationship with the married director Li Pingqian was made public (SB 1933). The media and the masses seemed to believe she had done everything Grape did in the film.

Ai Xia belonged to the Left-wing Drama Association under the secret leadership of the Chinese Communist Party, whose members were instructed to work in Shanghai's film industry for a leftist film movement. Leftist critics recognized the progressive message in the ending and applauded her acting, but few commented on the quality of the screenplay (Shi 1933, 21). While Yanzi finds the plot very "loose" throughout, Luyi finds Ai's acting "adds to the passion and tension in the plot" (Yanzi 1933, 19; Luyi 1933, 23). Yet, the truly unique aspects of the story were overlooked. Compared to two other films with three female characters—*Three Modern Women* (1933, written by Tian Han) and *New Women* (1934, written by Cai Chusheng)—Ai's three female characters have more agency and not simply after marriage/love, career, and pleasure (Basinger 1993). Grape is a unique presence who dares to pursue love and follow passion at any cost. No one else dared to make such a character the protagonist, even though she seems to have "changed" at the film's end. Yuru, the betrayed wife of Leng recognizes how much burden he has in raising a family and chooses to divorce him and earn financial independence rather than being a housewife. Anlin, a progressive young woman who wants to live her life for a good cause, is portrayed as an intelligent, disciplined, and optimistic person who offers emotional support to Grape in her despair and nurtures her back to good spirit. Anlin is the ideal woman for the future, but she has to face the harsh reality of her time. She is yet to be recognized as a prototype of a female martyr in later leftist films.

16.3.4 Sheng Qinxian's Modern Women (1945)

Sheng Qinxian, who had a B.A. degree in Chinese from St. John's University (Xiong and Zhou 2007, 504), was another woman screenwriter after Pu Shunqing with high education and saw film as an important educational tool. She joined the Screenplay Department of China Film Co. (or *Huaying*) in 1943, when Shanghai was still under Japanese occupation. Three of her screenplays were selected by Huaying's supervisory board to be made into films: a biopic titled *The Honorable Beggar* (1944), a tragic-comedy *Happy Reunion of a Troubled Couple* (1945), and a woman's film *Modern Women* (1945), which still exist. Even though the third film is based on Sheng and her friends' stories, the director Tu Guangqi credited himself as the writer. Had Sheng not published "Before *Modern Women* Is in Theatre", we would not know what happened (Sheng 1945b). *Modern Women* is still extant, so I can compare its plot to Sheng's original film fiction "Wives" (Sheng 1945a). "Wives" has two plotlines: one focusing on Yunfei—a spoiled young woman from a rich family, and a subplot revolving around her husband Zhiqi's troubles at work. The subplot was not included in the film.

The film begins with the university life of Yunfei and her cousin Meiying. Yunfei's university assignments are done by her eager suitors while she maintains a busy social life. Her schoolmate Zhiqi—also from a rich family—intends to propose to Yunfei, but his best friend Hanmin warns him that Yunfei would not make a good wife. Overhearing the two men's conversations, Yunfei invites the two men to her home for dinner and shows off her cooking skills, though the dishes were actually cooked by the family chef. Zhiqi marries Yufei, but she refuses to perform any housework or motherly duties after having a baby. In Sheng's story, the couple maintains a busy social life together; but in the film, she leaves him home alone and goes out to dancing and charity parties herself. When their baby girl has a high fever, Yunfei's cousin Meiying and her husband Hanmin pay her a visit and nurture the baby back to life. The main couple finally divorce, after which Yunfei feels emptiness gradually invade her heart and realizes that home is important to her. With the help of Meiying and Hanmin, the couple reunites on the night of the Moon Festival.

The film's director Tu Guangqi claimed that he made serious adaptations, but all the above plot was Sheng Qinxian's story (Sheng 1945a). The adaption simplified characters and exaggerated Yunfei's vanity and rejection of housework to the degree that it villainized her. However, Sheng's characterization principles stated that no character should be a complete villain, even if it adds drama to a story. In her mind, Yunfei and Meiying have different understandings of a woman's "freedom", and it is not difficult to see that Meiying is portrayed as the ideal modern woman (Sheng 1945c). After the success of her first two screenplays, the incidents surrounding her third film says a lot about the working condition of women in the film industry. Sheng quit after this film and carried out her ideals in education by working as a school teacher until her retirement (Yang 2003, 9).

16.3.5 *Eileen Chang's* Unending Love *(1947) and* Long Live the Mistress *(1948)*

Eileen Chang showed an extraordinary literary talent early in her life and became a best-selling writer in wartime Shanghai between 1943 and 1944. Her essays are witty, and her fiction is famous for satires of "the manners and affections of Shanghai's middle-class, especially their pettiness, hypocrisy, infidelity, and calculation" (Lin 2016, 101). Shortly after the foundation of Wenhua Film in 1947, writer-director Sang Hu invited Chang to collaborate on a new film. She wrote an original screenplay *Unending Love* (1947). The plot focuses on a young educated woman Jiazhen who finds work as a tutor for the daughter of Zongyu—an unhappily married 35-year-old company manager with a bed-ridden wife. Well-versed in Hollywood cinema, Chang knew exactly what she was doing. The film stars actress Chen Yanyan in her comeback film. Chang created details to hide Chen's chubby figure and limited the setting to three homes to save money for the production. With two main characters and six supporting ones, the plot has enough drama to keep the audience's attention. Many viewers were crying at the end. The film was so successful that it put Chen in high demand and pointed Wenhua in a new direction as Shanghai's film industry recuperated after World War II.

Wenhua, rumoured to pay Chang "six million yuan" for *Unending Love* and "seven million" for her second feature *Long Live the Mistress* (1948), made more money than other film companies in Shanghai in 1948 (Wen 1947; QQDY 1947). While *Unending Love* is a melodramatic tragedy, *Long Live the Mistress* is a comedy. A critic summarizes *Unending Love* as "selling emotions" and *Long Live the Mistress* as "selling sex"; another comments on *Unending Love* as being "sometimes a comedy and sometimes a tragedy" and not coherent or complete (DYZB 1948; Wu 1947). While writing weepies was not easy, writing a comedy was harder. As Esther Eng once commented to a *Seattle Times* columnist, Chinese audiences enjoyed comedies but *loved* tragedies (Lynch 1948). Chang was a big fan of Hollywood screwball comedies, which were very popular in Shanghai and Hong Kong. She most likely watched classics like *The Awful Truth* (1937), *Holiday* (1938), *His Girl Friday* (1940), and *My Favorite Wife* (1940), which were shown in Shanghai. *Mistress* has a screwball character setup with the wife's family wealthier than the husband's, and a plot dealing with marriage, second marriages, divorce, and re-marriage (Glitre 2006).

The film begins with a newlywed Sizhen, "who could be found on every block of Shanghai neighborhood" (Chang 2001). Sizhen lies to please everyone in her and her husband's family, from the parents to siblings and servants. Many comedic moments came from Sizhen's seemingly witty lies and her embarrassment when her lies were unravelled. She hides the romance between her brother and sister-in-law from her mother-in-law and then lies to her father that her mother-in-law has gold, so he finally agrees to lend money to her husband Zhiyuan to start a new business. Not long after her husband becomes rich, her world turns upside down as she discovers that her husband had a mistress called Mimi. Additionally, she finds he gave gifts initially bought for her to the other woman. Mimi's hooligan husband often pretended to be her brother and now attempts to blackmail Zhiyuan by claiming that Mimi was pregnant. Sizhen sees through their trickery and arrives in their apartment. She congratulates Mimi and invites her to live with her and her husband: "Our mother will be so happy about the baby!" This time, Sizhen's lie brings her triumph: Mimi breaks things off with Zhiyuan (Zhen 1947). In Hollywood screwball, equality between sexes was a basic rule, but in China at the time, the wife could not exact revenge on the husband by having another man (Glitre 2006). Chang arranged the story to make women more "proactive" in pushing the plot forward. For instance, after much suffering, Sizhen proposes a divorce to Zhiyuan for her much-beaten dignity. The story ends when the couple reconciles and celebrates with their lawyer in a high-class cafe, overhearing and witnessing Mimi seducing another man with the same lines she said to Zhiyuan. The last shot was of Mimi's seductive glare and a wink to the camera or the viewer (Rea 2021). As always, Chang "effortlessly leads the reader through a maze of deceits, lies, and threats that endeavours to pull the two apart" yet "never loses focus or suspense" (Swalwell 2016, 2F).

In 1948, after *Long Live the Mistress* sold out for two weeks straight. Many reviews praised Chang for being able to build dramatic tension with trivial details of daily life. Sha Yi says: "I admire Eileen Chang's writing techniques. I am truly surprised that she can turn a story lacking real drama, like *Long Live the Mistress*, into a script" (Sha 1947, 8). Dongfang Zhuodong compares Chang to that Hollywood writer-director Lillian Hellman (1905–1984), who adapted her stage plays for the screen, admiring their ability to use witty dialogues in configuring characters but still personally regarding Hellman as superior (Dongfang 1949). Most criticisms came from leftist critics who promoted nothing but proletarian film and art. Many "progressive" men did not identify with the male characters portrayed, while "liberated" women did not like the wife's endurance and hesitation to finalize a divorce. To them, even Eileen Chang's films were popular, but they did not provoke "thoughts" or lacked "the power of reality" (Bei 1948; Mao 1948). Such criticism could hardly do justice to Chang's works since the reality for Sizhen in the late 1940s Shanghai was portrayed with no exaggeration and, unfortunately, still broadly relevant for many Chinese women today.

16.4 Conclusion: Towards a Women's Cinema

The lack of early Sinophone screenplays and films in early cinema due to continuous wars and poor preservation creates a big challenge for this study. However, from published synopses, film fiction, reviews, reportages, and so forth, a trajectory of women filmmakers and a general outline of their working conditions can still be constructed. The impact these women had on later Sinophone cinema, and women's cinema is at least three-fold. Firstly, their presence in the early film industry encouraged other women to join the trade. Pu Shunqing's success, for instance, directly influenced Florence Lim and Cheng Xuemei, who were in similar circles. Ai Xia and Hu Ping's works also inspired other actresses to take up writing for the screen. Sheng Qinxian, Eileen Chang, Esther Eng, and Wan Hoi-ling made the general public of the late 1930s to 1940s aware of women's creative power. Chang's commercial success in 1947 and 1948 was vital to the demand for her scripts in the 1950s and 1960s, during which she came back for another period of screenwriting.

Secondly, women screenwriters have created many unforgettable female images, and their contribution to the genre of woman's film continued into later Sinophone films. In general, women writers mostly focused on female characters, who had more agency and subjectivity and refused to be reduced to symbols. Like their real-life models, these screen women's struggle with their desires and the harsh reality around them. In wartime and under nationalist currents, Esther Eng, Tong Sing-To, and Wan Hoi-ling all contributed images of women warriors and soldiers to the trend of National Defence Cinema, yet they never stopped portraying ordinary women. From Marion E. Wong's two wives, to Sheng Qinxian's two cousins, and Eileen Chang's duo of housewife and mistress, women writers never lost touch with women's living statuses and conditions.

Lastly, women often use "emotion" as narrative drive and build their plot around "trivial" scenes from daily life. Male critics thus often dismiss their story as "eventless" or not "thought-provoking" (Bei 1948). However, daily life's "trivial" scenes are more universal and timeless than ideological-ridden scenarios and characters, which lose relevance over time. This is why audiences can still resonate with the portrayal of women's life in *The Curse of Quon Kwon*, even though its *Chineseness* may feel strange to both American and Chinese audiences today. Women's universal status as the second sex results in women's cinema as a kind of world cinema, with aesthetic traits and thematic concerns that can overcome national and cultural barriers (White 2015).

To summarize, I hope this chapter has pointed out how women screenwriters (and directors) were largely forgotten in historiography because they did not always belong to recognized trends and movements, usually with ideological implications. They tackled different social issues from their own perspectives and engaged an alternate set of aesthetics: involving more fluid rather than fixed character relationships, relying on emotions rather than logic as narrative drives, and so forth. The digitization of old periodicals and emerging of early footage in recent years led to the rediscovery of pioneers like Marion E. Wong, Esther Eng, Wan Hoi-ling, and Sheng Qinxian. Their creative experiences make us revise our understanding of Sinophone cinema and women's cinema in a new light. For instance, we now know transnational and transcultural film history did not begin in the 1930s but in the 1910s. The paths of Esther Eng and Wan Hoi-ling remind us not only of the close ties between Hong Kong, American Chinatowns, and Southeast Asian countries—but also of how women's cinema, starting from its pioneers, has been continued by generations of female screenwriters and directors. When I began to focus my research on women screenwriters two decades ago, only Pu Shunqing, Ai Xia, and Eileen Chang were already written into film histories. While plugging the gaps in the history of women filmmakers' by discovering more female authors, we can get a better understanding of the work and careers of Pu, Ai, and Chang and how they and the other nine women screenwriters (and directors) discussed in this chapter relate to one another.

Acknowledgment This research is partially sponsored by the General Research Fund (project title: "Female Auteur in Early Sinophone Cinema: A Cultural History: 1916–1949"), Research Grant Council, Hong Kong.

References

A Modern Girl (现代一女性). 1933. Written by Ai Xia. Directed by Li Pingqian. China: Star Film.
Ai Xia. 2012. "Xiandai Yi Nvxing (Dingying Xiaoshuo)" [*A Modern Girl* (Film Fiction)]. In *Ai Xia: Xiandai yi Nvxing* [*Ai Xia: A Modern Girl*], ed. Chen Zishan and Zhang Keke, 1–72. Beijing: Dophin Press.
Back Street (虛度春宵). 1947. *Written and directed by Esther Eng.* USA: Silverlight Film.
Basinger, Jeanne. 1993. *A Woman's View: How Hollywood Spoke to Women 1930–1960.* New York: Knopf.
Bei, Ou. 1948. "Zhixiang Dianyingquan" ["Critique on Cinema"]. *Yingju Chunqiu* [*Drama and Film*] 1 (2): 53.
BLALIS. 1928. "Orientals Study Cinema Here." *Brooklyn Life and Activities of Long Island Society*, 21 April, 17.
Bren, Frank. 2013. Woman in White: The Unbelievable Wan Hoi-ling. *Hong Kong Film Archive Newsletter* 65: 10–15.
Chang, Eileen. 2001. *Complete Collection of Eileen Chang (Volume 7): Fiction after 1945*. Taipei: Crown Publishing.
Cheng, Da. 1933. "Zizi de Beiju Ping" [On *Sister's Tragedy*]. *Xinwenbao*, 15 September, 5.
Conscience (良心). 1933. Written by Tong Sin-to. Directed by Lai Bak-hoi. Hong Kong: Lianhua Film.
Cupid's Puppet (爱神的玩偶). 1925. Written by Pu Shunqing. Directed by Hou Yao and Mei Xuechou. China: Great Wall Motion Pictures.
Doane, Mary Ann. 1987. *The Desire to Desire: The Woman's Film of the 1940s*. Bloomington In: Indiana University Press.
Dongfang, Zhuodong. 1949. Ti Yin Deng. *Shuiyin Deng* [*Mercury Lamp*] 7: 2.
DY. 1939. "Cong beiguo lai de yige nanguo yingxing" ["A Southern China Film Star from Northern China"]. *Dianying* [*Cinema*] 47: 8.
DYZB. 1948. "Sang Hu zhaoli Aile Zhongnian" [Sang Hu Working on Middle Age Drama]. *Dianying Zhoubao* [*Film Weekly*] 1: n.p.
Fu, Winnie. 1998. Heroines of the Movie World—Tong Sing-To. *Hong Kong Film Archive Newsletter* 4: 10–11.

Glitre, Kathrina. 2006. *Hollywood Romantic Comedy: The States of Union, 1934–1965.* Manchester: Manchester University Press.
Golden Gate Girl (金門女). 1941. Written by Moon Kwan. Directed by Esther Eng. USA: Grandview Sound Pictures.
Happy Reunion of Troubled Friends (歡喜冤家). 1945. Written by Sheng Qinxian. Directed by Zheng Xiaoqiu. China: China Film.
Harris, Kristine. 1997. The New Woman Incident: Cinema, Scandal, and Spectacle in 1935 Shanghai. In *Transnational Chinese Cinema: Identity, Nationhood, Gender*, ed. Sheldon H. Lu, 277–302. Honolulu: University of Hawaii Press.
Heartaches (心恨). 1935. *Written and directed by Frank Tang, produced by Esther Eng and Bruce Wong*. USA: Cathay Pictures.
Hee, Wai-Siam. 2019. *Remapping the Sinophone: The Cultural Production of Chinese-Language Cinema in Singapore and Malaya before and during the Cold War*. Hong Kong: Hong Kong University Press.
His Girl Friday. 1940. Written by Charles Lederer. Directed by Howard Hawks. USA: Columbia Pictures.
Holiday. 1938. Written by Donald Ogden Stewart and Sidney Buchman. Directed by George Cukor. USA: Columbia Pictures.
House Number Sixty-six (六十六號屋). 1936. Written by Tong Sin-to. Directed by Lai Pak-hoi. Hong Kong: Big Time Film.
Honour and Sin (南洋小姐). 1948. Written and directed by Wan Hoi-ling. Singapore: China Motion Picture Studio.
Hu, Ping. 1933. "Zizi de Beiju (Benshi)" [*Sister's Tragedy* (Synopsis)]. *Mingxing* [*Star*] 1 (3): 3–4.
Huang, Hou. 1936. "Cong E'meishan Xia Tanqi" [From *Under the E'mei Mountain*]. *Yisheng* 2 (2): n.p.
Jian, Ren. 1948. "Jisuan 37 nian zui … de mingxing" [The Most … Stars of 1948]. *Qing Qing Dianying [Qing Qing Cinema]* 16 (2): 48.
Jun, Yun. 1925. "Recent News from Great Wall Film Company." *Shenbao*, 28 September, 14.
Lady from the Blue Lagoon (藍湖碧玉). 1945. *Directed by Esther Eng*. USA: Grandview Sound Pictures.
Lau, Jenny Kwok Wah. 2013. "Marion E. Wong." In *Women Film Pioneers Project*, edited by Jane Gaines, Radha Vatsal, and Monica Dall'Asta. New York: Columbia University Libraries. https://doi.org/10.7916/d8-s9yz-e287.
Law, Kar, and Frank Bren. 2004. *Hong Kong Cinema: A Transcultural View*. Lanham md: Scarecrow Press.
Leroux, Gaston. 1909–1910. *The Phantom of the Opera* (*Le Fantôme de l'Opéra*). Paris: Le Gaulois.
Lin, Pei-yin. 2016. "Comicality in *Long Live the Mistress* and the Making of a Chinese Comedy of Manners." *Tamkang Review* 47 (1): 97–119.
Long Live the Mistress (太太萬歲). 1948. Written by Eileen Chang. Directed by Sang Hu. China: Wenhua Film.
Lu, Mengshu. 1927. "Cong Huli Baoen shuoqi" ["Begin with The Fox's Gratitude"]. *Yinxing* [*Silver Star*]. No. 11: 37–41.
Lupke, Christopher. 2016. *The Sinophone Cinema of Hou Hsiao-Hsien: Cutlre, Style, Voice and Motion*. Amherst, NY: Cambria Press.
Luyi. 1933. "*Xiandai yi Nvxing* Guanhougan" ["After Watching *A Modern Girls*"]. *Shenbao*, 11 July, 23.

Lynch, Frank. 1948. "Seattle Scene Column." In *Seattle Post-Intelligencer*, 2 July, n.p.
Mad Love Mad Fire (怒火情焰). 1949. Written and directed by Esther Eng. USA: Silverlight Film.
Mai. 1932. "Nv mingxing de bianju" ["Female Stars Writing Screenplays"]. *Shenbao*, 2 November, 29.
Mao, Li. 1948. "Wo suo renshi de Shi Hui" [Shi Hui as I Know Him]. *Qingqing Dianying* [*Qingqing Film*], 16.22: n.p.
Meng, Yu. 1945. "Yi Gai yu fendou" ["An Honorable Beggar and His Struggles"]. *Shanghai Film Circle* 2 (4): 34–35.
Modern Women (摩登女性). 1945. Written by Sheng Qinxian. Directed by Tu Guangqi. China: China Film.
MT. 1946. "S'pore Film Industry Has Big Chinese Following." *Malaya Tribune*, 15 November, 3.
My Favorite Wife. 1940. Written by Leo McCarey, Samuel Spewack, Bella Spewack, Garson Kanin, and John McClain. Directed by Garson Kanin. USA: RKO Radio Pictures.
National Heroine (民族女英雄). 1937. Written by Yu Jiping. Directed by Esther Eng. Hong Kong: Kwong Ngai Talking Pictures.
OC. 1917. "Chinese Have Joined Ranks of Producers." *The Ottawa Citizen*, 11 August.
OT. 1916. "Dainty Maid from China Is Actress Now—Pretty Marion Wong Is Annexed by the Columbia Theatre." *Oakland Tribune*, 19 November, 5.
OT. 1917. "Chinese Girl Is Film Star in Own Dramas—Marion Wong of Oakland Is the Directress of New 'Movie' Company." *Oakland Tribune*, 22 July, 15.
Pecic, Zoran Lee. 2016. *New Queer Sinophone Cinema: Local Histories, Transnational Connections*. London: Palgrave Macmillan.
Peng, Hsiao-yen, and Ella Raidel, eds. 2018. *The Politics of Memory in Sinophone Cinemas and Image Culture: Altering Archives*. New York: Routledge.
Pu, Shunqing. 1927. *Renjian de Leyuan* [*Paradise on Earth*]. Shanghai: Commercial Press.
Pu, Shunqing. 1996. "Aishen de Wanou" [Cupid's Puppets]. In *Chinese Silent Screenplays*, vol. 1, ed. Zheng Peiwei and Liu Guiqing, 268–277. Beijing: China Film Press.
Qian, Ou. 1925. "Cupid's Puppet." *Shenbao*, 22 October: 12.
Qin, Xiqing. 2021. "Hu Ping." In *Women Film Pioneers Project*, edited by Jane Gaines, Radha Vatsal, and Monica Dall'Asta. New York: Columbia University Libraries. https://doi.org/10.7916/d8-5csf-xh71.
Qing, Miao. 1948. "Liangfeng xin: Zhi Zhang Junxiang Wu Yonggang" ["Two Letters: To Zhang Junxiang and Wu Yonggang"]. *Juying Chunqiu* [*Drama and Cinema*] 1 (3): 99–100.
QQDY. 1947. "Zhang Ailing Sang Hu zaidu hezuo Taitai Wansui kaipai" ["Eileen Chang and Sang Hu Collaborate Again, *Long Live the Mistress* in Production"]. *Qingqing Dianying* [*Qingqing Film*], Post-War restored issue 4, n.p.
Rea, Christopher. 2021. *Chinese Film Classics 1922–1949*. Vancouver: University of Columbia Press.
Retrieval (再生因緣). 1928. Written by Florence Lim. Directed by Lai Man-wai. China: China Sun Film.
SB. 1933. "Li Pingqian's Putao ran jiao piaopiaoran geng jinyibu" [Li Pingqian's Grape Is More than a Flare]. *Shenbao*, 21 July, 23.

Sha, Li. 1947. "Taitai Wansui guangan" [On *Long Live the Mistress*]. *Peace Daily*, December 13, 8.

Sheng, Qinxian. 1944a. "Yi Gai" ["The Honorable Beggar"]. *Xin Yingtan* [*New Cinema*] 3 (5): 39–40.

Sheng, Qinxian. 1944b. "Ge You Qian Qiu" ["Each Has Its Own Merit"]. *Hanlin Magazine* 1: 19–21.

Sheng, Qinxian. 1945a. "Qizi jijiang paishe, bianju Sheng Qianxian" ["Wives Will Begin Shooting: Screenplay by Sheng Qinxian"]. *Xin Yingtan* [*New Cinema*] 3 (5): 39–40.

Sheng, Qinxian. 1945b. "Fanpai zuofeng" ["The Way of Anti-heros"]. *Xin Yingtan* [*New Cinema*] 3 (6): 14.

Sheng, Qinxian. 1945c. "Xie zai Modeng Nvxing shangying zhi qian" ["Written before Modern Women Is in Theatre"]. *Shanghai Cinema* 2 (7): 18–19.

Shi, Zeyong. 1933. "Ping *Xiandai yi Nvxing*" [On *A Modern Girl*]. *Shenbao*, 21 June, 21.

Sister's Tragedy (姊姊的悲劇). 1934. Written by Hu Ping. Directed by Zhang Shichuan. China: Star Film.

Slide, Anthony. 1996. *Lois Weber: The Director Who Lost Her Way in History*. Westport ct: Greenwood Press.

Song at Midnight (夜半歌聲). 1937. Written by Tian Han. Directed by Maxu Weibang. China: Xinhua Film.

Spirit of the Overseas Chinese (海外征魂). 1947. Written by Zhu Jun. Directed by Wan Hoi-ling. Singapore: China Motion Picture Studio.

ST. 1949. "Malaya's Only Woman Film Director." *Sunday Tribune* (Singapore), 20 February, 8.

Swalwell, Ian. 2016. "Love and Loss in China of the 1930s." *The Harald Sun*, 3 April, 2F.

Tan, See Kam. 2021. *Hong Kong Cinema and Sinophone Transnationalisms*. Edinburgh: Edinburgh University Press.

Tashman, George. 1977. "Women in the Film Industry." *Berkeley Gazette*, 24 June: 18–19.

The Awful Truth. 1937. Written by Viña Delmar. Directed by Leo McCarey. USA: Columbia Pictures.

The Curse of Quon Gwon (關武帝). 1916. Written and directed by Marion E. Wong. USA: Cathay Film.

The Fox's Gratitude (狐狸報恩). 1927. Written by Cheng Xuemei. Directed by Liao Xueqin. China: Zhenhua Film.

The Goddess (觀音得道). 1940. Written and directed by Wan Hoi-ling. Hong Kong: Nanyang Film.

The Honorable Beggar (義丐). 1944. Written by Sheng Qinxian. Directed by Yue Feng. China: China Film.

Thirty-six Amazons (三十六女天罡 a.k.a. It's a Woman's World 女人世界). 1939. Written and directed by Esther Eng and Lu Si. Hong Kong: Wode Film.

Under the E'mei Mountain (峨眉山下). 1935. Written by Huang Hou. Directed by Wan Laitian. China: Star Film.

Unending Love (不了情). 1947. Written by Eileen Chang. Directed by Sang Hu. China: Wenhua Film.

Wang, Lian. 1932. "Dao Ai Xia bing yi zimian" ["Mourning Ai Xia and Self Encouragement"]. *Shanghai Weekly* 3 (13): 245.

Wei, S. Louisa. 2014a. "Esther Eng." In *Women Film Pioneers Project*, edited by Jane Gaines, Radha Vatsal, and Monica Dall'Asta. New York: Columbia University Libraries. https://doi.org/10.7916/d8-rhpq-0f69.

Wei, S. Louisa. 2014b. "Pu Shunqing." In *Women Film Pioneers Project*, edited by Jane Gaines, Radha Vatsal, and Monica Dall'Asta. New York: Columbia University Libraries. https://doi.org/10.7916/d8-fp66-k424.

Wei, S. Louisa. 2016. Finding Her Voices through Her Images: *Golden Gate Girls* as an Attempt in Writing Women Filmmakers' History. *Feminist Media History* 2 (2): 32–46.

Wei, S. Louisa., and Kar Law. 2018. *Can ruo Jinxia: Diyidai Kuayang Yingren yu Jindai Zhongguo* [*Bright as Esther Eng: Transnational Filmmaking Pioneers and Modern China*]. Beijing: Beijing Times Chinese Press.

Wen, Hai. 1947. "Zhang Ailing maitou bianju, 'Bu liao qing" juben baochou liubaiwan" ["Eileen Chang Buried Herself in Writing *Unending Love* and Getting Paid Six Million for the Screenplay"]. *Xin Shanghai* [*New Shanghai*] 64: 2.

White, Patricia. 2015. *Women's Cinema, World Cinema: Projecting Contemporary Feminism*. Durham NC: Duke University Press.

Wu, Bian. 1947. "Bu liao qing" ["Unending Love"]. *Shenbao*, 14 April, 9.

Xinleng. 1932. "An Interview with Woman Lawyer Pu Shunqing" ("女律師濮舜卿訪問記"). *Ta Kung Po*, 30 April, 2.

Xiong, Yuezhi, and Zhou Wu. 2007. Eds. *History of St. John's University*. Shanghai: Shanghai People's Press.

Xu, Jiali, Wu., and Yunhao. 2000. *Zhongguo Lvshi Zhidu Shi* [*A History of Chinese Lawyer's System*]. Beijing: China University of Political Science and Law Press.

Yang, Jie. 2003. "Xianfeng nvsheng: Zhonghua Minguo zaoqi Shanghai nvzi jiaoyu" [Pioneer Girls: Early Women's Education in Shanghai Schools of the Republican Period] in Li, Xiaojiang ed. *Rang nvren ziji shuohua: duli de licheng* [*Let Women Speak for Themselves: the Path to Independence*]. Beijing: Joint Publisher, 9–22.

Yanzi. 1933. "Guanba Ai Xia Bianyan de *Xiandai yi Nvxing* Hou" ["After Viewing *A Modern Girl* Starring Ai Xia"]. *Frontiers of Art and Literature* 2 (18–19): 37–38.

YC. 1934. "Yinmu shang de shige re nvlang" ["Ten Hot Ladies on Screen"]. *Young Companion* 84: 33.

Yu, Hua. 1933. "Wen" ["Kiss"]. *Mingxing* [*Star*] 1 (2): 4.

Yu, Jiaqing. 1933. "Guan Xiandai yi Nvxing" [Watching *A Modern Girl*]. *Shenbao*, 21 June, 21.

Yue, Audrey, and Olivia Khoo, eds. 2014. *Sinophone Cinemas*. Basingstoke UK: Palgrave Macmillan.

Zhang, Wen. 1934. "Dao Ai Xia—Jidian Ganxiang" ["Remember Ai Xia—A Few Thoughts"]. *Qianqiu* 19: 6–7.

Zhang, Zhen. 2005. *An Amorous History of the Silver Screen: Shanghai Cinema, 1896–1937*. Chicago: University of Chicago Press.

Zhen, Xin. 1947. Viva la Mistress, Rebel the Husband. *Saturday* 106: 10.

CHAPTER 17

A Historiography of Japanese Screenwriting

Lauri Kitsnik

17.1 Introduction

Steven Price has astutely suggested that the "screenplay is a kind of doppelgänger of the film, seemingly physically separate and yet operating as a second, parallel form that can never wholly be repressed" (Price 2010, 53). Taking cue from here, one could also ask whether the screenplay and screenwriting can serve as such an alternative lens for examining the entire course of film history. Richard Corliss in his *Talking Pictures* (1974) has shown that the core of classical Hollywood can indeed be rearranged based on screenwriting rather than the far more common options of genre, actors or directors. In Japan, which for a long time was the world's second largest film industry, interventions with precisely the aim of putting screenwriting at the very center of cinema have been surfacing at least since the late 1950s. This chapter explores the organizing structures adopted by several histories of Japanese screenwriting and the implications of these historiographical strategies. In order to do this, I will

---

An earlier version of this chapter was part of my PhD dissertation "Scenario Culture: Reconsidering Historiography and Readership in Japanese Cinema" (University of Cambridge, 2015).

L. Kitsnik (✉)
Graduate School of Humanities and Social Sciences, Hiroshima University, Higashihiroshima, Japan
e-mail: lauri@hiroshima-u.ac.jp

© The Author(s), under exclusive license to Springer Nature Switzerland AG 2023
R. Davies et al. (eds), *The Palgrave Handbook of Screenwriting Studies*,
https://doi.org/10.1007/978-3-031-20769-3_17

introduce both cursory and comprehensive attempts at historicizing screenwriting in order to examine their capacity to confirm or contest the focus of general film histories.

17.2 Screenwriting in Japanese Film Histories

Screenwriting is rarely dealt with in general film histories; this also remains the case with English language scholarship on Japanese cinema. Joseph L. Anderson and Donald Richie's *The Japanese Film: Art and Industry* (1959, revised 1982), despite its age still considered an authoritative work, is attentive to the industrial process behind filmmaking which makes its failure to address screenwriting all the more baffling. While Staiger (1985) regarded screenwriting as an integral part of successive developments in Hollywood production mode, in *The Japanese Film*, although a great deal of attention is paid to everything from studio mergers to actor profiles, Noda Kōgo (1893–1968) and Susukita Rokuhei (1899–1960) are the only two writers mentioned by name in the main body of the book, while the role of screenwriting goes unassessed.[1] Anderson and Richie's work, however groundbreaking in its other aspects, seems to be symptomatic in its neglect of the place of screenwriting in Japanese film.

Eric Cazdyn (2002) has provided a typology of Japanese film histories by introducing six works produced between 1931 and 1995, aligning these against each other based on their ideological underpinnings and particular socio-political backgrounds. He also makes a distinction between teleological and chronological types of histories. The latter—wherein Cazdyn has placed both Anderson and Richie, and Tanaka Jun'ichirō's *Developmental History of Japanese Film* (*Nihon eiga hattatsushi*, 1957, revised 1968 and 1976)—is characterized by a forward-moving timeline, inclusivity, the use of larger history as ballast, being bottom-heavy in contrast to the top-heavy teleological history, and unconsciously diachronic by grouping "products together by their stylistic or generic similarities" (Cazdyn 2002, 68). Cazdyn argues that the third major history, Satō Tadao's *History of Japanese Film* (*Nihon eigashi*, 1995, revised 2006–2007), also adheres to this model while also spreading out horizontally, exceeding the borders of national film history by including the foreign reception of Japanese cinema (Ibid., 85).

What both teleological and chronological histories have in common is the way they are embedded in the notion of development which remains instrumental to organizing historical narrative. For instance, Janet Staiger (1985) describes the development of screenwriting from an industrial point of view,

---

[1] Susukita, misspelled Susukida (and once again in the appendix as Kokuhei Susukita), is noted as responsible "for the style and structure of present-day period drama" (Anderson and Richie 1959 [1982], 59). Noda Kōgo appears twice: as the origin of a quote on the workload of Shōchiku screenwriters (Ibid., 53–54) and as a man "who has done many of [Ozu's] scripts" (Ibid., 362). A few relatively obscure names of writers are thrown in for the charts section (Ibid., 495–500).

seen as tied to certain practices in production; shifts in these bring about stylistic changes in the format of the script. However, Price justly notes that Staiger's otherwise influential model becomes less effective when looking at screenwriting beyond the emergence of the master-scene screenplay (Price 2013, 8). Could it be argued, then, that screenwriting as such ceased to be part of cinema's development once its exact role and boundaries had been fixed? Could this be one of the reasons behind the paucity of historical accounts of screenwriting? Could it be that to a certain extent screenwriting is even resistant to historiography?

Ostensibly, it might be for some of the reasons stated above that an early attempt, conspicuously titled "History of Japanese Screenwriting" (*Nihon shinarioshi*) by Kishi Matsuo (1906–1985) and serialized in the journal *Eiga hyōron* (*Film Criticism*) from January 1962 to August 1964, ends up being something of an aborted effort. In its 27 installments it fails to get any further than the early 1920s, focusing as it does on various episodes and anecdotes from the life of several writers. While undoubtedly making for a pleasurable reading and valuable as a source for screenwriting minutiae, Kishi's history clearly adheres to the chronological type but is cut short way before it can begin to make a substantial contribution to considering Japanese screenwriting along a sufficiently long timeline.

Joanne Bernardi's *Writing in Light* (2001), a rare book-length study focusing on Japanese screenwriting, shows that it can indeed be approached from a teleological point of view. She echoes general film histories in placing screenwriting as part of the discursive constellation called the Pure Film Movement that advocated a number of innovations including the abolishment of male actors in female roles, and arguably helped to bring about change in Japanese cinema that was considered at the time to be relying too heavily on practices of traditional theater and the presence of silent film narrator (*benshi*). But once again, when this goal had been attained, screenwriting seems to have lost its former role; this is also where Bernardi's account leaves off without addressing developments in film script beyond the early 1920s. In a way, Bernardi's can be placed in the long list of studies that have sought to trace certain *firsts* in film history, which in this case happens to be screenwriting. This has a parallel in the way some histories such as Tanaka's *Developmental History of Japanese Film* shift focus to other aspects of filmmaking once the script's industrial function is consolidated. While recognizing the crucial role of the script at certain turning points for cinema, such as the adoption of sound, this is where these studies commonly come to a halt, with no further effort made toward addressing subsequent developments of the script form or the contribution of writers.

While there seem to be benefits to providing an alternative film history from the point of view of screenwriting, there are also possible pitfalls to such endeavors. Cazdyn has warned that.

[i]nstead of undermining the dominant history, including the hitherto underrepresented material may serve only to reinforce the dominant history's authority ... the assumptions of writing and organizing history are usually left unchanged and are legitimized ... Failing to inquire into the methods of writing history and the social situation out of which the underrepresentation of certain content emerged in the first place risks merely filling in the absences in the existing dominant histories and participating in the self-marginalization of its own content. (2002, 86–87)

Is there, then, a meaningful way to discuss screenwriting without falling prey to the same chronological and teleological approaches discussed above that have left it out from general histories in the first place? Of course, this question cannot be easily answered. The least that can be done while examining histories of Japanese screenwriting is to keep this possibility in mind and to be attentive to what extent these texts subscribe to certain received models. Next, I will proceed to introduce a number of such accounts in order to reveal their historiographical strategies and the implication they hold for setting the history of Japanese screenwriting against general film histories.

17.2.1 A Cursory History: "Sketches on Developmental History of Screenwriting" (1959)

The first attempts to provide a systematic account of the history of screenwriting from the silent era to the present day can be found in *Scenario Reader* (*Shinario tokuhon*), published as a special edition of the journal *Kinema junpō* in 1959. This volume opens with introductory remarks about the importance of the script by none other than Kido Shirō (1894–1977), the legendary head of Shōchiku Studios, and includes both practical and theoretical essays on screenwriting. Falling into the latter category is the two-part essay "Sketches on Developmental History of Screenwriting" (*Shinario hattatsushishō*), authored by Iida Shinbi and Kobayashi Masaru, respectively. Divided roughly into dealing with prewar and postwar cinema, the two parts occasionally overlap by going over the same texts and developments. While unified under the same title, the differences in their structuring principles and emphases are worth examining.

Iida Shinbi (1900–1984), a prominent film critic, was a regular collaborator (since 1927) to *Kinema junpō*, the quintessential Japanese film journal, writing extensively on screenwriting while also pursuing a career in documentary filmmaking. Iida structures his essay by following a certain evolutionary logic and vocabulary: the birth (*tanjō*) of the scenario, the establishment (*kakuritsu*) of the format, the completion (*kansei*) of the silent scenario, the maturation (*seijuku*) of the form and content, the transition (*ikō*) to talkie and the perfection (*kansei*) of dialogue (Iida 1959, 14–19). In order to underline the development in the script format, Iida inserts extensive quotations from seminal silent films such as *The Glory of Life* (*Sei no kagayaki*, written by the director Kaeriyama Norimasa under the pen name Mizusawa Takehiko, 1919), *Kyōya Collar Shop* (*Kyōya erimise*, written and directed by Tanaka Eizō, 1922) and the three-part *Samurai Town* (*Rōningai*, Yamagami Itarō, 1928–1929, dir. Makino Masahiro). Iida's account stops around the time of the complete adoption of sound in the mid-1930s and concludes by introducing excerpts from Yoda Yoshikata's (1909–1991) early work for Mizoguchi Kenji, *Sisters of Gion* (*Gion kyōdai*) and *Ōsaka Elegy* (*Naniwa erejii*, both 1936), and Ozu Yasujirō's first talkie, *The Only Son* (*Hitori musuko*, Ikeda Tadao and Arata Masao, 1936) (Ibid., 18–21). With its teleological buildup and protracted script passages, it is the development of the format that clearly remains in the focus of Iida's historiographical sketch.

The second part of "Sketches on Developmental History of Screenwriting" is authored by Kobayashi Masaru (1902–1982). After graduating from Tokyo Imperial University, Kobayashi entered the P. C. L. Studios (the precursor of Tōhō) where he found acclaim for writing a string of scripts for films directed by Yamamoto Kajirō, notably the adaptations of Natsume Sōseki's novels *Young Master* (*Botchan*, 1935) and *I Am a Cat* (*Wagahai wa neko de aru*, 1936). After the war, Kobayashi focused on other roles in the film world, which included membership in Eiga Rinri Kanri Iinkai (Film Classification and Rating Committee, abbreviated as Eirin) from 1950 to 1970. At the time of writing his historiographical sketch, Kobayashi was also very active in teaching screenwriting: *Scenario Reader* even displays a photo of him standing in front of a blackboard with the word "scenario" written on it in Latin letters. Subsequently, he was as a major contributor to script anthologies such as *Complete Classical Scenarios of Japanese Film* (*Nihon eiga shinario koten zenshū*, 1965–1966).

Kobayashi leads in with a discussion on the position of *shinario sakka* (scenario author) and the changes in the film industry's recruitment practices that had shifted from the prewar *senzokusei* (exclusive contract system under which each writer worked for only one company) to a more flexible model (Kobayashi 1959, 21). Compared to Iida, Kobayashi was more of an industry insider, a fact well reflected in his concern for the issue of labor relations. His account is also completely devoid of quotations from scripts, and instead focuses on the industrial and interpersonal aspects of the screenwriting process. Rather than structuring his essay by evolutionary terms, Kobayashi keeps inserting pivotal historical events such as the Marco Polo Bridge Incident (1937) that signaled both the start of the Second Sino-Japanese War and the tightening grip of state control on the film world. Kobayashi goes into lengths to emphasize the ideologically strained atmosphere of wartime filmmaking: he refers to an incident from 1938 when the screenwriters' representatives from each studio were summoned by the Minister of Internal Affairs. This, in turn, leads to an account on how the film industry was increasingly collaborating with the military regime (Ibid., 24–25). All in all, while Iida presents the film world as relatively isolated from the currents of history, Kobayashi's account is decidedly related to contemporary events.

Kobayashi makes a considerable effort to make screenwriting appear as a focal point in film history by charting a number of seminal works according to their writers rather than directors. For instance, he emphasizes the individual contributions of writers such as Yagi Yasutarō (1903–1987) and Hatta Naoyuki (1905–1964) to late-1930s literary adaptations (*bungei eiga*) (Kobayashi 1959, 23). Kobayashi draws another notable example from the immediate postwar period of confusion and uncertainty.

> The change reached the organisation of the studios. With the exclusive affiliation system [*senzokusei*] gone, everything became contractual [*keiyakusei*]. Unions were formed. The conflicts of labor and management began. Strikes broke out. There had been no such phenomenon before the war. There was shortage of staff and materials; the facilities had not been repaired but amidst the burnt-out ruins films continued to be made. Most people had not yet woken from their stupor. In such times, it is the script that takes the lead. This is because it determines the ideas behind a film. The year 1945 ended with musicals and trivial entertainment but already 1946 saw the emergence of scripts with a backbone. (Kobayashi 1959, 26)

According to Kobayashi, this moment when screenwriters rose to the occasion was best manifested by an unprecedented ratio of original scripts; postwar screenwriting was also characterized by contributions from four distinctive types of writers: novices (*shinjin*),[2] women (*joryū*),[3] those continuing with equal strength from the prewar[4] and veteran writers such as Noda Kōgo and Yasumi Toshio (1903–1991) who had emerged to the front line after the war. Kobayashi states his personal top five postwar Japanese screenwriters as Shindō Kaneto (1912–2012), Kikushima Ryūzō (1914–1989), Mizuki Yōko (1910–2003), Kinoshita Keisuke (1912–1998) and Yasumi (Kobayashi 1959, 26–27). In addition, Kobayashi posits that the postwar has brought new working practices such as "script scouting" (*shinario hantingu*) which he also calls "writing by feet" (*ashi de kaku*). Kobayashi signs off with expressing his dream of further international acclaim for Japanese cinema and suggests that screenwriting's role in its recent success should not be overlooked (Ibid., 27).

Ending on such a high note speaks volumes of the era *Scenario Reader* was published in. At the height of the Golden Age, in 1959, the studio system was at its most prosperous, with Japanese films performing strongly at the domestic box office. Reportedly, over a billion tickets were sold that year with the domestic film production steadily coming to over 500 films per year. Screenwriters, too, were allegedly in the best position they would

---

[2] Shindō Kaneto, Uekusa Keinosuke, Ide Toshirō, Kikushima Ryūzō, Hashimoto Shinobu, Tanada Gorō, Funahashi Kazuo, Matsuyama Zenzō, Susaki Katsuya et al.

[3] Mizuki Yōko, Tanaka Sumie, Kusuda Yoshiko, Wada Natto et al. For more of the contribution of female writers, see Kitsnik, Selbo, and Smith 2015 and Kitsnik 2020.

[4] Yagi Yasutarō, Yoda Yoshikata, Oguni Hideo, Inomata Katsuhito, Ikeda Tadao, Yanai Takao, Saitō Ryōsuke et al.

ever be, most of them employed by studios with generous monthly salaries but free to work elsewhere on a contractual basis.[5] *Scenario Reader*, where Iida's and Kobayashi's histories appeared, concludes with the script of *Odd Obsession* (*Kagi*, Wada Natto, 1959, dir. Ichikawa Kon), a film that had considerable international exposure, winning the Jury Prize at the 1960 Cannes Film Festival.

17.2.2 General Film Histories: Tanaka Jun'ichirō (1957) and Satō Tadao (1995)

The title of the joint effort by Iida and Kobayashi, "Sketches on Developmental History of Screenwriting", and the inclusion of the diminutive *shō* (sketch) is hardly chosen by accident. This is an obvious allusion to a major work in historiography published only two years earlier, Tanaka Jun'ichirō's *Developmental History of Japanese Film*. This groundbreaking work, initially published in three volumes (1957) and eventually in five volumes (1976), has arguably not been surpassed in scope and breadth, and is rivaled only by Satō Tadao's *History of Japanese Film* (1995, revised 2005–2006). Tanaka (1902–1989), who belonged to the same generation as Iida and Kobayashi, was a formidable presence in the world of Japanese film criticism, not least for holding the position of chief editor of *Kinema junpō* for many years. Much like Anderson and Richie's *The Japanese Film: Art and Industry* in the English-speaking world, Tanaka's history has been an overwhelming influence on subsequent Japanese film scholars. Cazdyn even suggests that Satō waited long to publish his own history, both out of deference and anxiety, and only did it when Tanaka had passed away (2002, 85).

Inasmuch as Tanaka influenced attempts of writing a history of screenwriting, it is also important to examine to what extent he includes the topic in his own work. If one peruses through the five volumes of *Developmental History of Japanese Film*, it seems to be all but absent. One of the few instances when Tanaka mentions the script is when he discusses the innovations by Kaeriyama Norimasa (1893–1964) in the late 1910s, one of which was "importing" the scenario from Hollywood; he also provides a quotation about the value of the film being decided in equal parts by the script and shooting (Tanaka 1976, vol. I, 282–84). Elsewhere, Tanaka point out how young Japanese writers learned their skills from Bluebird films (Ibid., 375), and the work of the screenwriter Susukita Rokuhei (1899–1960) during the late silent era (Ibid., 380–381). In the second volume of the book, an account of the Shōchiku studio's script department (*kyakuhonbu*) employs a prominent position as an introduction to the chapter on sound film (Tanaka 1976, vol. II, 58). Subsequently, Tanaka rarely returns to the topic of screenwriting; this takes place only in tiny insertions, mostly in the lists of studio employees. It is characteristic of Tanaka's history, then, that the discussion on screenwriting

---

[5] See Kitsnik 2016 on writing practices of the 1950s Golden Age of the studio system.

remains limited to the prewar years. An overall impression from Tanaka (and indeed most other general histories) is that the film script disappears at some point from the historian's radar: once completed and perfected, it ceases to be part of the development of cinema.

An oddity that permeates Tanaka's history is the way he consistently uses the term "adaptation" (*kyakushoku*) rather than script (*kyakuhon*) to refer to screenwriting credits, regardless of the script being an original or an adaptation. While the reason for this usage is not explained by Tanaka himself, it is clearly not general practice and above all extremely confusing. Although Tanaka should be given credit for always carefully adding the names of the writers alongside directors and actors, there seems to be an underlying patronizing element to this approach. One might wonder whether Tanaka did not regard screenwriting highly enough to elevate it to the level of *hon* (book), but relegated it to *shoku* (color), as if all screenwriting merely consisted of adding some shades to the already complete work. Together with only brief mentions of screenwriters in his magnum opus, Tanaka appears to display his disregard to the topic also on a terminological level.

In clear contrast to his older colleague, Satō Tadao's four-volume *History of Japanese Film* allocates more space and gravitas to screenwriting, and to the contributions of individual screenwriters. Satō (1930–2022), was without any doubt Japan's foremost film scholar, effortlessly bridging the gap between the roles of critic, historian and theorist. His bibliography comprises well over one hundred single-authored volumes and encompasses everything from Japanese film to Asian, European and Hollywood cinemas. In his *History of Japanese Film*, screenwriting is no longer considered as a function ascribed to a nameless mass once the first few pioneers have set the standard. Like Tanaka, Satō emphasizes the importance of Shōchiku's script department by pointing out the term "scenario system" which refers to the way the studio head Kido saw the script's role as central within the film production process (Satō 2006, vol. I, 211–25).

However, Satō goes much further and dedicates several subchapters solely to screenwriters to whom he consistently refers as *shinario sakka* (scenario author).[6] Within the overall structure of his history, these sections are part of larger sequences dealing with successive decades of Japanese cinema from the 1930s through the 1970s, follow respective passages on studios and directors, and precede those on actors. In effect, Satō is (re)structuring film history around the contributions of screenwriters; among general film histories

---

[6] Writers discussed in length in these subchapters include Shindō Kaneto. Uekusa Keinosuke, Hisaita Eijirō, Yagi Yasutarō, Hashimoto Shinobu, Kikushima Ryūzō, Ide Toshirō, Mizuki Yōko, Tanaka Sumie, Yasumi Toshi, Noda Kōgo (Satō 2006, vol. II, 328–35), Shirasaka Yoshio, Ishidō Toshirō, Tamura Tsutomu. Ide Masato, Matsuyama Zenzō, Wada Natto, Narusawa Masashige, Abe Kōbō, Hasebe Keiji, Suzuki Naoyuki, Yamada Nobuo, Yamanouchi Hisashi, Terayama Shūji, Yoda Yoshikata (Satō 2006, vol. III, 86–91), Nakajima Takehiro, Kasahara Kazuo, Kuramoto Sō, Baba Ataru, Saji Susumu, Tanaka Yōzō, Ido Akio, Katsura Chiho, Matsuda Shōzō and Arai Haruhiko (Ibid., 190–95).

this certainly amounts to a radical gesture that questions dominant historiographical methods. The exclusive use of the term "scenario author"[7] is complemented by the recurring pointing out of the themes and motifs that permeate (*ikkan suru*) the work of writers in question, emanating from what Satō calls authorial capacity (*sakkateki shishitsu*) (Satō 2006, vol. II, 100, 331). By doing so, Satō also challenges the notion of directors as sovereign auteurs, as in his example of the collaboration between Noda and the director Ozu whose late-career shift to depicting the life of middle high class he locates in the preferences of the writer (Ibid., 335).

Eric Cazdyn has noted how Satō's history departs from a simple chronological model by not only moving ahead vertically but also spreading out horizontally to exceed the borders of Japan and including various aspects of film culture hitherto unaddressed by studies of similar scope and aims (Cazdyn 2002, 85). This inclusivity has a clear parallel in the extent to which Satō has included the topic of screenwriting within his history, and particularly in discussing the work of several dozens of screenwriters in order to provide an alternative model for thinking about film authorship.

17.3 A Comprehensive History of Screenwriting

While Satō's work has done much to bring attention to screenwriting as a crucial part of cinema, Shindō Kaneto's *History of Japanese Screenwriting* (*Nihon shinarioshi*, 1989)[8] arguably remains the only historiographical work that gives it real gravitas. At the end of this magisterial work, Shindō, in a moment of introspection, admits that he has unwittingly ended up writing a history of people (*jinbutsushi*) rather than texts (Shindō 1989, vol. II, 247). Shindō also remains markedly personal on another level, smuggling in his own relationship to Japanese film as well as dealing with historical traumas experienced by the entire nation. *History of Japanese Screenwriting* is so far the only comprehensive history of Japanese screenwriting, covering the work of major screenwriters from early cinema to the 1980s when it first appeared. Besides locating these contributions within developments in film industry, Shindō also remains attentive to the major historical events of twentieth-century Japan and displays a considerable debt to earlier histories. However, it is the way Shindō includes frame stories to his history that sets it clearly apart from its more modest antecedents.

17.3.1 Structuring Principles

On the several hundred pages of *History of Japanese Screenwriting*, Shindō makes a singular contribution to the historiography of screenwriting, arguably

---

[7] The ideological implications of this term are discussed further in Kitsnik 2016.

[8] The title could as well be translated as *History of Japanese Scenario*, as the word *shinario* is used both for the writing process activity and its result.

on a global scale. Numerous passages quoted from the scripts, often preceded with detailed synopses, accompany a narrative that links together major developments in screenwriting since the silent era. Shindō carefully adds brief passages on the lives and selected works by nearly a hundred writers he considers important. The overall seven-chapter structure reveals both a debt to earlier general film histories as well as the context in which it was first published. Taking cue from Tanaka and Iida, Shindō employs evolutionary terminology in marking the successive phases of unfolding history. This preference can also be traced to the fact that *History of Japanese Screenwriting* initially appeared as installments in the eight-volume *Lectures on Japanese Film* (*Kōza Nihon eiga*, 1985–1988), thus making Shindō dependent on the overall timeline and thematic emphases of this important multi-authored anthology. The role of Shindō's entries on screenwriting in this collection conspicuously resembles that of Staiger's contribution to *The Classical Hollywood Cinema*, published around the same time on the other side of the Pacific Ocean.

Located temporally between the final edition of Tanaka's *Developmental History of Japanese Film* (1976) and the first edition of Satō's *History of Japanese Film* (1995), *Lectures on Japanese Film* more or less neatly subscribes to the dominant developmental model of Japanese film history present in these works. Likewise, Shindō has the film script pass through various changes in Japanese cinema: perfected during the silent era, then replaced by the talkie, going through wartime and arriving at the Golden Age of the studio system, followed by decline and further diversification. In the account on the earliest stages of screenwriting, Shindō puts particular emphasis on the contribution of Kaeriyama and other proponents of the Pure Film Movement such as Osanai Kaoru (1881–1928) and Tanizaki Jun'ichirō (1886–1965) (Shindō 1989, vol. I, 12–42).

In Shindō's opinion, it was period film (*jidaigeki*) of the late 1920s and its revisionist trend in the 1930s that was crucial for the development of screenwriting in general. This prompts him to discuss the work of Itō Daisuke (1898–1981), Susukita Rokuhei, Yamagami Itarō (1903–1945), Itami Mansaku (1900–1946), Yamanaka Sadao (1909–1938) and Mimura Shintarō (1895–1970) in separate entries.[9] These passages are intercepted by accounts on the developments in writing for films dealing with contemporary matter (*gendaimono*), notably those produced at Shōchiku Studios (Ibid., 93–104, 147–57). Placing the prewar period film in such a prominent place is characteristic of the first volume of *History of Japanese Screenwriting*, while the second volume on postwar films seems less partial by focusing on a wider array of genres. This also means, however, that the contributions of individual writers are no longer discussed in vivid detail comparable to the ones above.

---

[9] See Shindō 1989, vol. I, 52–55, 71–75, 125–32; 60–64; 64–71, 204–11; 107–25; 13–44; 175–87, respectively.

As a result, the second volume is clearly built around film studios even when focusing on the work of individual screenwriters, coming precariously close to becoming a studio history, at least to the extent of how Shindō has structured it.

History of Japanese Screenwriting is permeated by an effort to treat screenwriters as individuals by providing biographical information and often tracing thematic preoccupations of their work back to their familial, educational and professional background. It might seem a contradiction, then, that Shindō's accounts of individual writers are often organized according to their industry affiliation. By doing so, Shindō indeed subscribes to the familiar model of structuring history around studios with only a handful of prewar screenwriters presented purely on their own terms. Arguably, this might have been done out of necessity in order to anchor his chapters on screenwriting in the overall framework of *Lectures on Japanese Film*. The same tendency is underlined by starting each chapter with an outline of the current situation in studio filmmaking.

As the large part of Shindō's history engages with the period commonly considered as the flourishing of the studio system, this approach might seem well justified. However, in many ways, aligning screenwriters with the studios where they were (first) employed can be misleading because, as mentioned, since at least the early 1950s, it became a common practice that the more prolific screenwriters (as was the case with certain directors and actors) contributed elsewhere beyond their main affiliation. In short, the focus on the studios might be a convenient and easy-to-follow principle but is certainly at odds with Shindō's general attempt to make the contributions of screenwriters more visible. However, one advantage of this approach is that it at least avoids structuring the work of screenwriters around the director(s) they most often collaborated with, and thus eliminates the biggest anxiety for any study treating the authorial scope of screenwriters.

Judging from its structure, Shindō is writing parallel to general film history and filling in the gaps about screenwriting as he proceeds, without any discernible attempt to break away from the model established by Tanaka. This influence is further underlined by Shindō placing corresponding trends in foreign cinema at the end of each chapter. Regarding Tanaka's case, Cazdyn has argued:

> [T]he inclusion of this material is without doubt the principal controlling device of the work. Of course, foreign films have much to do with the development of Japanese film, so the inclusion of these works is not surprising. But the way in which these pages are left suspended at the end of each chapter, almost in note form, illustrates how chronological histories use *other* histories as a timeline, or as a ballast, without delving into what the relation between the histories might be. (2002, 69)

While I disagree with Cazdyn on whether this could be seen as *the* principal device of organizing history (this understanding would play into the hands of geopolitical interpretations that reduces everything about Japan to its submissive relationship with the West), the repetition of this pattern in Japanese film histories that are temporally so apart from each other as Tanaka and Shindō certainly attests to an anxiety that foreign cinema imposed in relation to the domestic product. As a result, the foreign films cannot be hidden from view, but neither can they be discussed in length. However, Shindō goes a bit further than Tanaka by making brief remarks on the influence on Japanese screenwriting by works such as *La Roue* (1923, dir. Abel Gance) for its innovative cross-cutting techniques and *Grand Hotel* (1932, dir. Edmund Goulding) for its overall dramatic structure.

Nevertheless, there are certain (albeit rare and scattered) moments where Shindō seems to depart from an evolutionary model of film history. For instance, toward the end of the book, he suggests that the form of the Japanese scenario has remained essentially the same from the 1930s to the 1980s. In order to illustrate his point, Shindō makes a tongue-in-cheek comparison to show how an early sound script, *The Village Bride* (*Mura no hanayome*, Fushimi Akira, 1928, dir. Gosho Heinosuke)[10] comes surprisingly close in its depiction of intimacy to a recent soft porn (*roman porno*) film, *Wet Straits* (*Nureta kaikyō*, Tanaka Yōzō, 1980, dir. Takeda Kazunari) (Shindō 1989, vol. II, 228--0). A pressing issue that follows from here is that as screenwriting does not seem to have undergone much change over time, it would not make for a very compelling story. This might be another reason behind Shindō's choice to focus on writers rather than their texts and historical development of the script format. Much like Corliss (1974), Shindō seems to have realized that advocacy of screenwriting works better when approached from its human, rather than chronological or teleological aspects.

Along with declaring that he is writing a history of screenwriters rather than screenwriting, Shindō notes that having known most of the people he is writing about made it easier for him to see behind their personal motives, thematic and stylistic preoccupations. In contrast, he admits to having considerable difficulties discussing foreign writers because he has never met them in person (Shindō 1989 vol. II, 144). By these remarks, Shindō is hinting at an intimate dimension that he brings to this history that also touches upon his own agency as a writer.

17.3.2 Personalized Time Frames and National History

Among comparable histories of Japanese film, Shindō's comes somewhat close to Ōshima Nagisa's (1932–2013) documentary film *100 Years of Japanese Cinema* (1995) where the director made an effort to include most of his own films within the survey, at times appearing to structure the entire history

---

[10] For an analysis of the script of *The Village Bride*, see Kitsnik 2022.

around them. This comparison with Ōshima leads to the issue of film histories being sometimes written by active participants in the industry. As we saw, both Iida and Kobayashi had been involved in film production earlier in their careers. One can speculate about the extent to which the roles of a practitioner and a critic can be successfully merged. Despite being one of the most prolific Japanese screenwriters of all time, Shindō appears surprisingly modest about including his own sizable contribution in his history. He does, however, frequently insert personal recollections of the surrounding events he is discussing. In this capacity, Shindō's role might be better described as a witness than a historian.

In comparison to such prominent writers on cinema as Iida and Kobayashi, or even Tanaka and Satō, Shindō's position in the Japanese film world is quite unique. As an acclaimed screenwriter, and later as director and essayist, he has covered most roles in that field of cultural production. Given that one of these was that being the president of the Japan Writers Guild (Nihon shinario sakka kyōkai, 1972–1982, 1997–2001), it seems suitable and even conceivable that it was Shindō who produced the most comprehensive history of Japanese screenwriting. His book, then, is also a contribution toward the visibility of the status of screenwriters, coming from the head of their professional union.

In the case of a bulky work of nearly five hundred pages in two volumes, it is crucial to note how its structure is held together, and particularly how it begins and ends. Shindō commences his history with the infamous Zigomar Incident in 1912 when the eponymous French film (1911, Victorin Jasset) about a criminal mastermind was banned by the Japanese authorities allegedly due to a string of real-life crimes that followed certain patterns introduced in the film. Aaron Gerow has shown how this incident prompted new laws which anchored the meaning of cinema to the films' verbal synopses which became the object of censorship (Gerow 2010, 52–65). Shindō, however, introduces this emblematic film for a completely different reason. He argues that while earlier, simpler stories might have been filmed without the help of a well-prepared script, the makers of *Zigomar* with its intricate plotline clearly must have had one at their disposal (Shindō 1989, vol. I, 3).

This claim allows Shindō to throw in a rhetorical question about whether Makino Shōzō, commonly regarded as the father of Japanese cinema and its first major director, saw *Zigomar* and by association, fathomed the future of narrative cinema with the script as its central planning document (Shindō 1989, vol. I, 8). In other words, Shindō is asking when exactly a proper script came to replace earlier practices exemplified by rudimentary devices such as *oboegaki* (memorandum) or Makino's infamous *kuchidate* (improvisation) that meant shouting out directions to the actors before letting the camera roll. While the first screenwriting credits in Japan can be traced to 1908 (Kishi 1973, 813), Shindō has preferred to disregard this fact, apparently for the sake of a good story with a proper start and ending.

While remaining rather modest about his own contribution to Japanese screenwriting, Shindō still organizes his history by imposing time frames that seem to overlap conspicuously with that of his own life and involvement in the film industry: each chapter begins with a photo of Shindō that corresponds to the period under scrutiny. By presenting an infant in a family photo to finally a middle-aged man staring into the lens of a camera, both autobiographical and authorial (now a director not merely a writer) roles of Shindō are emphasized. In this way, the human history also points at Shindō himself who at least implicitly equates the span of his life with that of Japanese cinema. After all, Shindō was born in 1912, the year of the Zigomar incident. A "belt paper" (*obi*) of *History of Japanese Screenwriting* describing it as "Nihon eiga no hajimete no jijoden" (the first autobiography of Japanese film) makes this semi-auto-historio-biographical aspect even more explicit. At the same time, however, Shindō enhances this personal timeline with national history.

At the beginning of the second volume of *History of Japanese Screenwriting* the biggest trauma of Shindō's generation, the Second World War, is introduced as an additional organizing principle. Besides upbringing and employment history, Shindō adds details about each writer's wartime and immediate postwar experiences. Indeed, a sharp sense of postwar permeates the whole second volume of the book; Shindō even divides screenwriters into a series of waves of the postwar generation regardless of their initial industry affiliation. Even the end of the first volume hints at the importance of the war experience: a subchapter that stands stylistically apart from the rest of the work, tells the story of Yamagami Itarō, a seminal silent era screenwriter, who failed to keep writing after the advent of sound, turned into a full-blown nationalist during wartime, and perished in the Philippines (Shindō 1989, vol. I, 204–11).

Both the war and the postwar condition were something that had to be dealt with and along these lines, Shindō refers to screenwriter Ide Masato (1920–1989) who claimed that the postwar (*sengo*) was something that could only start after war experiences were written about (Shindō 1989, vol. II, 48). Shindō's uses his own to begin the second volume in a rather lyrical mode: he returns to the Shōchiku studio in October 1945 only to witness it overgrown with summer grasses. Shortly after that, he wrote his first scripts, notably *A Woman Kept Waiting* (*Machibōke no onna*, 1946, dir. Makino Masahiro), based on observations about the immediate postwar milieu (Ibid., 3–4). This effectively started his long and celebrated writing and directing career which spanned to the beginning of this century. Shindō's last feature, *A Postcard* (*Ichimai no hagaki* 2011), took as its premise his own real-life experience of spending the last days of the war in cleaning duty while the rest of his unit was killed in combat.

At the very end of the book, in contrast to his initial speculations on how and when exactly the screenings of foreign films might have incited Japanese filmmakers to first consider introducing the script into film production, Shindō comes up with a decidedly Japan-centered utopia.

How many writers have appeared and disappeared since Susukita Rokuhei? Each of them invested their whole talent and passion in film. It is their glory and dead bodies that we are now standing upon. They have erected an enormous mountain of manuscript papers [*genkō yōshi*] and one by one filled their slots [*masume*].

Let us make an experiment. Assume that a script is written on 250 sheets of *genkō yōshi* (200 characters, 27 cm long, 18 cm wide). Now let us say that each year about 500 films of all kinds were made. (In the silent era, each company produced about 150 films.) What would this make in sixty years?

If we placed the sheets on the railway tracks sideways, they cover the distance between Aomori and Himeji. If done lengthwise, Aomori and Nagasaki. All sheets densely filled with characters. (Shindō, 1989, vol. II, 242–43)

In what amounts to an idiosyncratic cine-geographical fantasy, Shindō has the archipelago and its main railway line from the north of Honshū to the western shores of Kyūshū covered with the scripts of all films ever produced in Japan. This visualization underlines the enormous work screenwriters have done for the success of Japanese cinema by providing the script a status and visibility that has been hitherto held back by the dominance of the final product on the screen. Within this image, particularly worth of attention is *genkō yōshi*, a variety of slotted manuscript paper and a uniquely Japanese writing device. In parallel to the Courier typeface that evokes typewriter even in the digital age and features in/on most books on Hollywood screenwriting, *genkō yōshi* is very much the metaphor for screenwriting in Japan. These literally handwritten manuscripts readily allude to both the individuality and craftsmanship behind the writing, suggesting that the script should be considered as much more than merely a disposable technical document.[11]

Although Shindō's *History of Japanese Screenwriting* remains without a rival as an attempt to comprehensively cover its topic, it occupies an uneasy position between being a reference book (which it cannot be due to the uneven way the material is organized) and a truly engaging narrative (due to the general sketchiness and many list-like insertions). However, Shindō clearly surpasses the early cursory efforts not only in scope but by connecting the history of screenwriting to his own life story and on a larger scale to the history of the twentieth-century Japan.

17.4 Conclusion

In this chapter, I introduced a variety of attempts at writing a history of Japanese cinema with screenwriting as its focus. I examined how the texts that make up this corpus have been structured around certain concerns ranging from technological developments to key moments in national history. It

[11] An earlier version of this passage appears in Kitsnik 2017.

became clear that rather than focusing on the *universal rules* of screenwriting which remain the domain of how-to-do-books, such histories tend to delineate the script's development toward the master-scene format. At the same time, by the virtue of meticulous attention paid to the contributions of individual *scenario authors*, these accounts often effectively become histories of writers. It is also notable that the roles of the authors of these histories within Japanese film culture, whether as critics or active filmmakers, tend to inform their respective emphases and historiographical strategies. Admittedly, most of the histories presented here are either cursory or possess a narrow temporal focus; the only work coming close to a comprehensive treatment is Shindō Kaneto's *History of Japanese Screenwriting* that ultimately prompts broader questions about how histories of cinema can become entangled with those of a nation.

Acknowledgements This research was funded by the Japan Society for the Promotion of Science (JSPS KAKENHI Grant Number JP21K12900).

References

100 Years of Japanese Cinema. 1995. Directed by Ōshima Nagisa. UK: British Film Institute.
Anderson, Joseph L., and Donald Richie. 1959 [1982]. *The Japanese Film. Art and Industry*. Princeton NJ: Princeton University Press.
Bernardi, Joanne. 2001. *Writing in Light. The Silent Scenario and the Japanese Pure Film Movement*. Detroit: Wayne State University Press.
Cazdyn, Eric. 2002. *The Flash of Capital. Film and Geopolitics in Japan*. Durham NC: Duke University Press.
Corliss, Richard. 1974. *Talking Pictures: Screenwriters in the American Cinema*. New York and Baltimore: Penguin Books.
Gerow, Aaron. 2010. *Visions of Japanese Modernity: Articulations of Cinema, Nation, and Spectatorship, 1895–1925*. Berkeley CA: University of California Press.
Gion kyōdai [*Sisters of Gion*]. 1936. Written by Yoda Yoshikata. Directed by Mizoguchi Kenji. Japan: Daiichi Eiga.
Grand Hotel. 1932. Written by William A. Drake. Directed by Edmund Goulding. USA: Metro-Goldwyn-Mayer.
Hitori musuko [*The Only Son*]. 1936. Written by Ikeda Tadao and Arata Masao. Directed by Ozu Yasujirō. Japan: Shochiku.
Ichimai no hagaki [*A Postcard*]. 2011. Written and directed by Shindō Kaneto. Japan: Kindai Eiga Kyōkai.
Iida Shinbi. 1959. "Shinario hattatsushishō: sono ichi [Sketches on Developmental History of Screenwriting: Part One]." In *Kinema junpō bessatsu: Shinario tokuhon* [Scenario Reader], edited by Kinema Junpōsha, 14–21, Tokyo: Kinema Junpōsha.
Imamura Shōhei, et al., eds. 1985–1988. *Kōza Nihon eiga* [Lectures on Japanese Film]. 8 vols. Tokyo: Iwanami Shoten.
Kaeriyama Norimasa. 1917 [2006]. *Katsudō shashingeki no sōsaku to satsueihō* [The Production and Photography of Moving Picture Drama]. Tokyo: Yumani Shobō.

Kagi [*Odd Obsession*]. 1959. Written by Wada Natto. Directed by Ichikawa Kon. Japan: Daiei.
Kinema Junpōsha, ed. 1959. *Kinema junpō bessatsu: Shinario tokuhon* [Scenario Reader]. Tokyo: Kinema Junpōsha.
Kinema Junpōsha, ed. 1965–1966. *Nihon eiga shinario koten zenshū* [Complete Classical Scenarios of Japanese Film]. 6 vol. Tokyo: Kinema Junpōsha.
Kishi Matsuo. 1973. "Kaisetsu [Commentary]." In *Nihon shinario taikei* [Collection of Japanese Scenarios], Vol. 1., edited by Shinario Sakka Kyōkai, 794–812. Tokyo: Maruyon Purodakushon.
Kishi Matsuo. 1962–1964. "Nihon shinarioshi" [History of Japanese Screenwriting]. 27 installments. *Eiga hyōron* 19 (1)–21 (8).
Kitsnik, Lauri. 2016. "Scenario writers and scenario readers in the Golden Age of Japanese cinema." *Journal of Screenwriting* 7 (3): 285–297.
Kitsnik, Lauri. 2017. "From Page to Screen to Page Again: Writing and Reading Japanese Film Scripts." *Proceedings of the Japan Society* 154: 105–121.
Kitsnik, Lauri. 2020. "Scouting for Scripts: Mizuki Yōko and Social Issue Film in Post-War Japan." *Journal of Screenwriting* 11 (3): 265–285.
Kitsnik, Lauri. 2022. "Gosho and the Gagman: Scriptwriting at the Time of the Talkie Crisis." In *A Companion to Japanese Cinema*, ed. David Desser, 493–509. Oxford: Wiley-Blackwell.
Kitsnik, Lauri, Jule Selbo, and Michael Smith. 2015. "Japan." In *Women Screenwriters: An International Guide*, ed. Jill Nelmes and Jule Selbo, 108–130. Basingstoke UK: Palgrave Macmillan.
Kobayashi Masaru. 1959. "Shinario hattatsushishō: sono ni [Sketches on Developmental History of Screenwriting: Part Two]." In *Kinema junpō bessatsu: Shinario tokuhon* [Scenario Reader], edited by Kinema Junpōsha, 21–27. Tokyo: Kinema Junpōsha.
Kyōya erimise [*Kyōya Collar Shop*]. 1922. Written and directed by Tanaka Eizō. Japan: Nikkatsu.
La Roue. 1923. Written and directed by Abel Gance. France.
Machibōke no onna [*A Woman Kept Waiting*]. 1946. Written by Shindō Kaneto. Directed by Makino Masahiro. Japan: Shōchiku.
Mura no hanayome [*The Village Bride*]. 1928. Written by Fushimi Akira. Directed by Gosho Heinosuke. Japan: Shochiku.
Nureta kaikyō [*Wet Straits*]. 1980. Written by Tanaka Yōzō. Directed by Takeda Kazunari. Japan: Nikkatsu.
Ōsaka Elegy [*Naniwa erejii*]. 1936. Written by Yoda Yoshikata. Directed by Mizoguchi Kenji. Japan: Daiichi Eiga.
Price, Steven. 2010. *The Screenplay. Authorship, Theory and Criticism*. Basingstoke UK and New York: Palgrave Macmillan.
Price, Steven. 2013. *A History of the Screenplay*. Basingstoke UK and New York: Palgrave Macmillan.
Rōningai [*Samurai Town*]. 1928–1929. Written by Yamagami Itarō. Directed by Makino Masahiro. Japan: Makino Production.
Satō Tadao. 1995 [2006–2007]. *Nihon eigashi* [History of Japanese Film]. 4 vols. Tokyo: Iwanami Shoten.
Sei no kagayaki [*The Glory of Life*]. 1919. Written and directed by Kaeriyama Norimasa. Japan: Tenkatsu.

Shindō Kaneto. 1989. *Nihon shinarioshi* [History of Japanese Screenwriting]. 2 vols. Tokyo: Iwanami Shoten.

Staiger, Janet. 1985. "Blueprints for Feature Films: Hollywood's Continuity Scripts'." In *The American Film Industry*, 2nd ed., ed. Tino Balio, 173–192. Madison: University of Wisconsin Press.

Tanaka Jun'ichirō. 1957 [1968, 1976]. *Nihon eiga hattatsushi* [History of the Development of Japanese Film]. 5 vols. Tokyo: Chūō Kōronsha.

Tanaka Jun'ichirō. 1970. *Nihon eigashi hakkutsu* [Excavations from Japanese Film History]. Tokyo: Tōjusha.

Zigomar. 1911. Directed by Victorin Jasset. France.

CHAPTER 18

Writing Social Relevance: US Television Dramas in the Civil Rights Era

Caryn Murphy

18.1 Introduction

When *The Defenders* (1961–1965) was halfway through its first successful season on the CBS network, producer Herb Brodkin told the press that the courtroom drama series about a father-son legal team could tackle any topic, except racial segregation (Woodstone 1962). As an experienced television producer who trained as a set designer before becoming a producer of acclaimed dramatic programming, Brodkin spoke with an insider's knowledge of the industry. He had produced live anthology dramas in the "golden age" of the 1950s, when most television programs were owned by single sponsors. As the era of network control dawned in the late 1950s, Brodkin transitioned to a new phase of his career as a producer of telefilm series, launching Plautus Productions, a program supplier that originated a number of social issues dramas. His career moves were indicative of the shifts taking place in the television business as a whole; the three national networks were taking control of television schedules and programming from sponsors, and their dominance would continue through the 1980s. The network system rapidly evolved into a complex web of interrelated interests, each of which had the ability to wield some authority over television representations. This chapter uses the archived papers of television writers and producers to explore the structure of the network system, focusing on how its component parts

C. Murphy (✉)
University of Wisconsin–Oshkosh, Oshkosh, WI, USA
e-mail: murphyc@uwosh.edu

© The Author(s), under exclusive license to Springer Nature Switzerland AG 2023
R. Davies et al. (eds.), *The Palgrave Handbook of Screenwriting Studies*, https://doi.org/10.1007/978-3-031-20769-3_18

exercised influence over depictions of race and racial politics in a genre cycle of social issues dramas about idealistic professionals. Taken together, the case studies in this chapter create a functional picture of how the television writer's authority was limited within the network system.

Media historians refer to the network era that began in the 1960s as the "classic network era" or "classic network system." Michele Hilmes writes about the basic characteristics of the system in her history of NBC, calling it a period characterized by "highly centralized network control over all phases of the industry: production, distribution, and exhibition" (2007, 171). Media scholar Jason Mittell further explains that this era "[s]aw the full transformation of its radio ancestry to the television medium, the establishment of stable and fruitful relationships with the film industry and advertisers, and the creation of efficient mechanisms to fill out television schedules to minimize financial risk and maximize network profits" (2008, 44). In the late 1940s and early 1950s, television was an experimental medium that showcased live programming that originated from New York. These programs were typically owned by sponsors and produced by advertising agencies, who purchased time from the national networks in order to reach the available audience. As more Americans bought television sets and it became clear that the new technology would compete with Hollywood films, the industry began to take shape. Live television production was inefficient and expensive, and the resulting programs had limited profit potential; they could only be re-aired if they were filmed as inferior quality kinescopes. Hollywood studios and independent program suppliers like Plautus increasingly sought to produce on film. For the most part, filmed programs were too expensive for a single sponsor to own. By the late 1950s, the networks had wrested control away from sponsors (MacDonald 1990, 139–40). CBS, NBC, and ABC became national networks, made up of affiliate stations located across the nation. Producers like Brodkin brought their program pitches to the networks, and negotiated with the creative input and feedback that executives would provide continually throughout a series' development and execution. The networks selected and scheduled programs and sold advertising minutes to sponsors. The networks theoretically wielded the most authority over programming and were allowed to hold this role because they were charged with serving the public interest. Network control was touted as a way to limit the profit motivations of sponsors and maintain an emphasis on serving the needs of the public.

As filmed programming proliferated and the era in which television presented a version of the New York theater in living rooms across the country faded into the past, concerns about program content increased. Government subcommittees regularly held hearings in the 1960s, investigating television programming and systems of oversight. In her history of the early network era, Mary Ann Watson argues that a cycle of dramas about professionals, which she refers to as "New Frontier character dramas" found network support because of this pressure (1994, 43). Herb Brodkin had been developing *The Defenders* for CBS since 1960, working with Reginald Rose, one of the most acclaimed television "playwrights" associated with the live anthology drama. *The Defenders* was an adaptation of Rose's *Playhouse 90* (CBS, 1956–1960) entry "The Defender." Brodkin and Rose aimed to turn the father-son legal team from the anthology into appealing continuing characters, hoping that viewers would tune in regularly to see these capable professionals wrestling with social issues and the legal system. CBS invested in the series' development, but did not place it on the schedule until the network was faced with government scrutiny over their lack of "quality" programming (Watson 1994, 43). The success of *The Defenders*, alongside the issues-oriented medical series *Ben Casey* (ABC, 1961–1966) and *Dr. Kildare* (NBC, 1961–1966), launched a genre cycle of filmed dramas that often wrestled with socially relevant topics. These series share a relatively clear formula; a young professional develops skills and acumen under the guidance of an older, experienced professional. They are set in professional and institutional environments including the courts, hospitals, schools, and government agencies. Within the genre cycle, there is an emphasis on realism. Problems are not always solvable, and the series' everyday heroes are fallible. This relatively open story structure is one that allowed these series to take on social issues of all stripes. As Brodkin told the trade press however, there was one topic that seemed to be impossible to approach: the politics of racial integration.

What forces discouraged television writers from scripting dramas about racial politics? Network control provides a simple explanation, but in practice, the network system was more complicated. Many sponsors believed that the subject of racial integration was divisive, and that a substantial proportion of viewers would reject programming that took a stance on the issues involved. Even though networks controlled the programming, they did so in the interests of sponsors; they discouraged producers from developing story ideas in controversial areas, because ad buyers might object. Writers, aware of the preferences of producers and sponsors, also censored themselves, believing that "controversial" work would be rejected (Barnouw 1962, 27). Writers who did engage with social issues related to race received heightened scrutiny from network Standards and Practices departments, and might tune in to a broadcast to find their work had been revised without their input. A writer's intention could be substantially altered by this kind of official censorship, which was motivated by a desire to protect the mass-market appeal of the network and the sponsor. Producers, while espousing the goal of making quality programs that would benefit the viewer, had a first responsibility to meet the demands of the network that sought to serve the sponsor. Writers and producers sometimes reached out to professional organizations and public interest groups, seeking approval or seals of authenticity to help support a case for important scripts about "difficult" issues. Writers, producers, sponsors, censors, and public interest groups all played a role in the network system, operating with varying degrees of influence. The remainder of this chapter focuses on several case studies that illuminate the exercise of influence in the network system and therefore the operations of the system as a whole.

18.2 Integration Without Identification: *The Defenders*, "A Man Against Himself"

NBC introduced a policy in the early 1950s that they referred to as "integration without identification" (NBC's "Talent" 1953). This was posited as a non-confrontational way to present racially integrated television shows. Black actors could appear alongside white performers, as long as the scripts made no mention of race or racial issues. This policy continued into the early 1960s. In 1962, NBC representatives met with program producers to share basic guidelines, including, "Producers should cast Negroes as people, not as Negroes" (as quoted in "NBC Programmers" 1962). CBS did not publicize a similar policy, but in practice, the networks essentially shared the same approach. Broadcast historian William Boddy quotes Herbert A. Carlborg, who was in charge of censorship for CBS in the late 1950s, explaining: "In the matter of segregation, it would be difficult to present a dramatization dealing with some aspects of this problem on a sponsored program, particularly at a time when the subject is considered highly inflammatory... It would be impossible to maintain any balance of dramatizations highlighting one side of such a currently explosive issue..." (1993, 202).[1] As discussed above, Herb Brodkin expressed the intention of dealing with social issues in *The Defenders*, but was aware of the limitations that would be imposed by the network. In the series' second season, the episode "A Man Against Himself" navigated these boundaries by using a strategy of non-identification. The script by Raphael Hayes offers no racial designations for any characters, and none of the dialogue makes reference to racial identity.

"A Man Against Himself" tells the story of Danny Ross, a man who seeks to represent himself in court when he is charged with manslaughter. Danny and his girlfriend, Janet Lamb, were walking in a city park one night when they crossed paths with an inebriated group of people, celebrating after a football game. Two drunk men from the group began to scrimmage with each other, and one of them grabbed Danny's hat from his head to use as a mock football. Their playful game quickly got out of hand, and one of the drunk men tossed Danny's hat into a puddle. Danny asked the offender to retrieve it, and instead the man offered him cash. This interaction escalated into a physical conflict when Danny took offense and punched the man. The man fell to the ground and struck his head, dying as a result. On the page, this altercation takes place in the street instead of a park, and the story does not seem to have a racial dynamic.[2] However, when Black actors Ivan Dixon and Ellen Holly were cast

---

[1] Boddy cites this censor as "Harold" A. Carlborg.

[2] The episode stages this action in a park, rather than on a sidewalk. The drunken revelers are taking a buggy ride around the park, and they disembark to play football. They grab Danny's hat as he attempts to pass. As in the script, the interaction escalates into a physical altercation; Danny pushes one of the men, who hits his head on the base of a fountain and dies.

to play the roles of Danny and Janet, racial signification became a component of the story.

Danny and Janet are introduced in the script as, "A boy and girl walking down the sidewalk." Danny is "in his early twenties ... He moves with a certain wariness, silent, moving past people with an arrogance ... and pride." Socioeconomic status is implicated in Hayes' descriptions of both characters. Danny "wears a cheap poplin jacket" and Janet is "thin, big-eyed and poorly dressed." The intoxicated couples who arrive in a taxicab are not described as white. They are "obviously well-to-do and in their thirties" (Hayes 1962, 1). The fraught dynamic that emerges between the two drunk men and Danny could be read as a combination of their scripted points of contrast; they are older, wealthy, and drunk, and Danny is not.

Danny, as played by a Black actor, is disrespected by the drunk white men who grab his hat for their sport and then toss it into the gutter. When he asks for his hat back, he is seeking to be treated with human decency. The episode's focus on humanity and respect is made overt later in the script, when Danny cross-examines the dead man's widow in a courtroom scene. Mrs. Palmer testifies that she thinks Danny is an "animal," and he questions her on the specifics. Danny serves as his own attorney, but he receives guidance from series' lead Lawrence Preston (E. G. Marshall). With Preston's help, Danny uses his questions for Mrs. Palmer to establish that he and his girlfriend had reason to fear the loud, drunk group of people that approached them in the night. The group had no similar reason, and no mention is made of racial animus, to fear the unassuming couple or view them as a physical threat. In a key moment, Danny asks Mrs. Palmer, "Who frightened whom?" (Hayes 1962, 48).

There is no indication in the script that its central conflict will involve a Black man who is on trial. Network executives from CBS or advertising agency representatives of the show's multiple sponsors would not have flagged that "A Man Against Himself" was going to become an episode that might be viewed as a commentary on the social dynamics of racial inequality, until it was cast. The episode was praised by critics for this reason. A review in the *New York Amsterdam News*, an African-American newspaper, suggested: "A bouquet should be tossed to the scriptwriter Raphael Hayes, who has depicted a man as a man and a girl as a girl without any reference to color" (White 1963, 11). As a character, Danny's pleas for human dignity and the right of every person to be treated with respect certainly resonated because the role was inhabited by a Black actor. This resonance may have been the writer's intention, but it is not directly expressed on the page. Hayes' script makes evident that he sought to write about human dignity through the lens of class difference. He may have undertaken this approach strategically, to avoid the difficulties that would attend producing a script that utilized a racial lens. Donald Bogle writes about *The Defenders* in his history of African-American representations on television, noting that some of its episodes with Black characters "(...) chose not to focus on racial tensions. Rather it acknowledged the presence of the American Negro in national life" (2001, 100).

Hayes' script does not suggest that there may be racial prejudice at work in the legal system. Danny insists on representing himself, and Lawrence Preston gains his trust by providing input that helps him to do so effectively. Danny pleads "not guilty," but the viewer knows that he has committed manslaughter; the episode opens with the scene on the street described above. The jury finds Danny guilty, but stipulates that they would like the judge to be lenient; the judge agrees that this is warranted. As the episode closes, Danny and Lawrence talk about the possibility of appealing the verdict. The legal system is thus presented as just and fair. It is a system that can work in Danny's favor, offering him the opportunity to be heard and be respected. This episode of *The Defenders* does not acknowledge the possibility of racial inequality in the legal system and thus supports a worldview in which justice is blind.

18.3   A Writer's Intent: *The Nurses*, "Express Stop from Lenox Ave"

The Nurses (CBS, 1962–1965), another series Herb Brodkin produced at Plautus, followed in *The Defenders* model.[3] It made a young nurse-in-training and her experienced mentor the continuing characters in an open-format drama that could tackle any issue that would reasonably occur within a hospital. "The Prisoner," an episode in the first season, adhered to the integration without identification edict. In the episode, a man shoots a pharmacist during an attempted robbery and is then shot by a police officer. The nurse who treats the wounded gunman is aware that if he recovers, he will probably be convicted in a criminal court and receive a death sentence. William Taylor, the doomed man, was portrayed by Black actor Louis Gossett, Jr. Gossett's presence in the mostly white milieu of the hospital would have invited viewers to consider the story's racial implications, but George Bellak's script focuses on the issue of capital punishment and makes no reference to race. The character of William Taylor is described simply as a "man in his late thirties" whose typically rough features have been slackened by "a tapped vein of suffering" (1962, 3).

A more developed meditation on racial identity aired later in the first season of *The Nurses*. Adrian Spies scripted "Express Stop from Lenox Avenue," the story of Jenny Bishop (Ruby Dee), a Black nurse who takes pride in her skills and seeks to advance in a white world. Jenny is introduced as a competent nurse who has a close relationship with a patient who is suffering from cirrhosis. Jenny is disconcerted when her aunt and cousin Lonnie (Carl Lee) appear at the hospital. Mrs. Hill (Claudia McNeil) wants Lonnie to get a hospital job, so that he can start to enjoy a better life, in the same way that

---

[3] For its third and final prime-time season in 1964, the series was retitled *The Doctors and the Nurses*. It is referred to as *The Nurses* in this chapter, because the episodes discussed are from the series' first season.

Jenny has done. Jenny is hesitant to recommend Lonnie, and when he is hired at the hospital, her attitude at work changes. Her supervisor, Liz Thorpe (Shirl Conway), worries that Jenny is overly aggressive with other staff, particularly Black co-workers. The tension that Jenny is feeling is evident. Her favorite patient becomes seriously ill when someone sneaks him a bottle of alcohol. Jenny explodes at Lonnie, certain that he is responsible. She believes that the patient offered Lonnie money in exchange for the liquor, and that Lonnie is so ill-suited to hospital work that he fulfilled the request. Lonnie denies this, but he leaves the hospital in shame. The patient reveals that Lonnie was not responsible, and Jenny is forced to reckon with her own prejudice. Her actions have been based in bigotry, and specifically the fear that the behavior of other Black people will damage her own upward mobility. She goes to her aunt's house in Harlem to beg Lonnie to return to the hospital with her; the hospital is a symbol of a promising future for both of them. In the episode that aired on CBS in the spring of 1963, Jenny and Lonnie walk into the hospital together in the last act, ready to strive for a better life together.

Spies was a talented television playwright with a background in live anthology dramas who had previously created *Saints and Sinners* (NBC, 1962–1963), a social issues drama set in the newspaper milieu. Spies' papers include handwritten notes on the script of "Express Stop," indicating that "[p]arts of the last act … were rewritten against the author's wishes" (Spies n.d.). The note names Harriet Van Horne as a television critic who responded negatively to the changes, a specificity that suggests that his lack of creative control was painful for the writer. Van Horne's review praised it as a "bold, imaginative well-made" episode, but sounded a single sour note. The critic felt that Jenny's final dramatic scene with her aunt should have provided a conclusion, "[b]ut author Adrian Spies foolishly tacked on some hysterical scenes in the Harlem flat that were simply too much" (1963).

A comparison of the complete script in Spies' papers, dated January 25, with the shooting script held in Brodkin's archive, dated two weeks later, reveals the extent of the changes that were made. Spies' final act is far bleaker than the version which was filmed. Jenny begs Lonnie for forgiveness and asks him to return to work with her. He refuses, indicating that he will pursue a low-paying job opportunity instead. Jenny has caused him to realize "his place" and this means that he will no longer picture a better possible future for himself than the rundown neighborhood in which he currently lives, and the short-term jobs to which he has become accustomed. Jenny returns to the hospital alone and prepares to begin her shift (Spies 1963, 69–70). In the revised version, Lonnie angrily confronts Jenny, accusing her of trying to act white. He grabs her arm and tells her to, "Look at it! It's black!" Lonnie has far more dialogue in this version and is revealed as an angry young man who feels powerless in a white-dominated society. At the end of their exchange, Jenny views him with "an admiring look" as he agrees to return to the hospital with her (Brodkin 1963, 72). This finale scene suggests that both Jenny and Lonnie might move on from their Harlem upbringing, and that Lonnie has forced Jenny to realize her status as an outsider in a white world.

Most critics, including Harriet Van Horne, praised "Express Stop." It was recognized as a significant achievement in television drama at the time. Lee and McNeil were both nominated for supporting performance Emmy awards, and Dee was nominated for her leading role. In the years that followed the broadcast, CBS granted permission for the script to be included in short fiction collections. Scholastic Book Services marketed *Prejudice: The Invisible Wall* to educators; it included a truncated version of "Lenox Ave" alongside other contemporary pieces about racial identity. Hunter College included the script in a reader called *Striving*. Both of these publications featured the revised ending that was scripted over Spies' objections.[4]

"Express Stop" was considered a dramatic success, but it points to the lack of authority that writers had in the network era. As a freelance writer for *The Nurses*, Spies signed a contract to submit a script. Once the production had the script, it belonged to the production, and not Spies. At some point, a decision was made to change act four, and no one contacted Spies to ask him to handle the rewrite. Instead, a different writer was brought in to do uncredited work on the script. Spies was left with no recourse. CBS shared the script with published anthologies who wished to include it, and the network's version matched the story that was broadcast. In other words, once Spies submitted the script to fulfill his contract, it no longer belonged to him. There were writers in the network era who maintained pseudonyms, so that when changes were made to their scripts that they could not control, they could ask to be credited under their professional alias.[5] This practice allowed writers to maintain a distance from scripts that had been revised in ways that altered the original intent and vision. The necessity of this practice indicates that television writers were frustrated by the lack of control they had over the production of their work.

18.4 Standards and Practices: *Mr. Novak*

Mr. Novak (NBC, 1963–1965), a social issues drama starring James Franciscus as a high school English teacher, also staged an acclaimed episode about racial prejudice and integration in the fall of 1963. "A Single Isolated Incident" was considered a standout episode by the show's production team, as well as television critics. In it, a Black student reports that a dozen white

---

[4] *Prejudice: The Invisible Wall* and *Striving* are both archived in Spies' papers at the Wisconsin Historical Society.

[5] The writer David Davidson explained this process in a note he included in the papers related to his script for the social issues drama *Breaking Point* (ABC, 1963–1964), "Whatsoever Things I Hear ..." Davidson wrote the script, and when the production brought in another writer to alter his work, he contacted the Writers Guild for arbitration, requesting to use the name "Albert Sanders" (Davidson n.d.).

students attacked her as she was walking to school. The school administration investigates, discovering that the white students involved had conducted an orchestrated campaign against the school's many Black students. In the episode's climax, Principal Vane (Dean Jagger) gathers the entire student body together in the auditorium and encourages them to reject this kind of racial prejudice en masse, demonstrating a unified front in opposition to the presumed handful of prejudiced students at Jefferson High. The script was revised during pre-production and the episode's title was changed from "The Incident" to "A Single Isolated Incident" (Stambler 1963). As the revised title indicates, *Mr. Novak* presents racism as a non-issue for the series' public high school. The incident in the episode is shocking to both students and administrators, because it is so far outside their community norms.

"A Single Isolated Incident" was written and directed by E. Jack Neuman, who created *Mr. Novak* and served as its executive producer. Neuman was an experienced writer for both radio and television before he began creating his own series. He originated several social issues dramas, including *Mr. Novak*, the television version of *Dr. Kildare*, and the legal series *Sam Benedict* (NBC, 1962–1963). Neuman was devoted to observational and interview-based research, which not only contributed to the realism of his scripts, but also created a promotable story around the production of his television shows. Newspapers reported that he traveled for months, visiting American high schools to seek out stories for *Mr. Novak* (Laurent 1964).

The depiction of racial prejudice in this episode's script was shaped by input from the National Education Association (NEA), a professional group that offered oversight to *Mr. Novak*. Neuman contacted the NEA during the series' development process, and the professional organization established a media relations arm to consult on his show, as well as other film and television projects. The *NEA Journal* reported that a panel of working educators reviewed first draft scripts for the series and submitted their feedback ("Meet Mr. Novak" 1963). As with Neuman's research visits to high schools, the series' consultation with the NEA contributed to its aura of realism in a way that could be widely promoted. As a television producer, Neuman realized how difficult it was for dramatic series to generate significant viewer attention. His relationship with the NEA was certainly also intended to encourage the professional organization to promote the series to its membership of educators, who might in turn promote *Mr. Novak* in their classrooms.

Henry Noerdlinger, the NEA liaison to *Mr. Novak*, sent line-by-line feedback on the script to "A Single Isolated Incident" in August of 1963. The panel of educators who reviewed the initial draft asked Neuman to clarify that even though its school administrators acknowledged that racial integration had caused tensions elsewhere, "(a)t Jefferson High, the situation had always been so well in hand that it never caused any problem until now" (1963). The panel requested that the word "ignorant" be used to describe the perpetrators of racial prejudice in multiple scenes. They noted that little was said about what motivated the culprits, and suggested that when questioned, one of the white students might voice their resentment with a phrase like: "Give them an inch, and they'll take a yard" (1963). Neuman incorporated this suggestion, changing "yard" to "mile" to put his own spin on the line. The panel suggested Principal Vane's climactic speech to the student body be augmented and proposed the line: "We are against you because we are still proud of our American tradition here, and we still feel that any student can walk with dignity on this campus" (1963). Neuman appreciated this suggestion so much that he handwrote it onto his copy of the episode's outline; it provides the conclusion to Vane's address to the student body in the episode.

The feedback that Neuman received from NBC's Broadcast Standards department was more general and seems designed to alter how the episode would present prejudice and discrimination as a social problem. Neuman's original version specified that a troublesome reporter character would indicate his own racial prejudice and also comment that Jefferson High seemed to have an "integration problem" on its hands. Network censors stipulated that it was a "race" problem and not an "integration" problem (Bushnell 1963). They further suggested that the reporter's worldview was an unnecessary addition to the story; instead of being a racist, he should just be an opportunist in pursuit of a headline. The censors objected to a line from an investigating police officer, who would explain that he understood prejudice because he was Jewish. They requested that this be excised, and Neuman complied. Broadcast Standards also objected to exposition indicating that there had been racial tensions over school integration in the recent past. They stipulated that the episode should specify that nothing similar had ever occurred before. Finally, the network asked for a change from the original ending, in which some students who participated in the assault were still unidentified. They wanted a more rousing, clear solution to the problem (Bushnell 1963). Neuman's outline and original script painted a picture of institutional racism, in which Black and Jewish people were well aware of the presence and effects of prejudice and discrimination. NBC asked for changes that suggested instead that indeed the events that transpired in the episode would be discussed as, and responded to as the episode's title indicated, "A Single Isolated Incident."

Neuman's revisions indicate that he was grateful for the input of the NEA, and compliant with the suggestions of network standards and practices. From an early point, it was clear that the episode would be promotable. Based on the story outline, an MGM studio executive instructed the director of publicity that "[w]e certainly will proceed with plans to give it all the exploitation and publicity possible, aiming at its airdate when this is known" (Weitman 1963). The nationally syndicated columnist Hal Humphrey extolled the research that Neuman put into the episode, spending "many hours interviewing the principal" of a school where a similar incident had taken place. He praised the episode as "[o]ne of Neuman's nobler achievements in the TV realm" (1963). Other write-ups in local newspapers noted that it was a socially relevant and necessary topic. *Mr. Novak* won a Peabody Award for its first season, a recognition of the show's effort to address subjects of social importance.

"A Single Isolated Incident" was not a confrontational or controversial episode of television drama. It did not take a stand on the issue of school integration; in fact, it was carefully designed to clarify for the audience that it was not attempting to do so. As a result, it traveled a relatively smooth path from script to screen. In contrast, a Stirling Silliphant script about race consciousness and drug addiction that he submitted for the series' second season was roundly rejected by both Standards and Practices and NBC's program department. By 1964, Silliphant was well known in the television industry as a prolific television writer who had created the successful dramas *Naked City* (ABC, 1958–1959, 1960–1963) and *Route 66* (CBS, 1960–1964). Just a few years later, he would win the Academy Award for his screenplay, *In the Heat of the Night* (1967). Leonard Freeman produced the second season of *Mr. Novak* and contracted with Silliphant for a script about race and drug addiction. The basic pitch involved the teacher intervening to help a young Black man going through heroin withdrawal. In a memo to Freeman confirming their agreement, Silliphant described his intent to write a moving story that would hinge on "the spoken and unspoken conflict between Novak and the Negro boy" (1964b). Although "He Grabs a Train and Rides" progressed past the outline stage to a full script, the episode was never filmed.

Silliphant outlined the episode in April of 1964, committing most of his attention to the development of the first act. Pete Butler (Vince Howard), a Black history teacher, appeared frequently in season one of *Mr. Novak*, in accordance with the policy of representation without identification. Silliphant's outline suggested that Novak and Butler could agree to take a weekend off from their school-related responsibilities, and plan a Saturday of activities that would include Novak's girlfriend and Butler's wife. When Novak and his girlfriend arrive at the Butlers' on Saturday morning, they learn that Pete's younger brother is paying a surprise visit. Ricky Butler is nineteen years old and wants to drop out of college. Novak recognizes the signs of drug addiction and tells Pete that Ricky is about to go through withdrawal. After some difficult conversations, Novak convinces Pete to let him step in to help. Silliphant elided the rest of the specifics by summarizing as follows:

> This confrontation of teacher and student—of white and black—of a man who has found himself and a boy who has lost himself now becomes for three acts our tour-de-force story during which I intend to explore the deepest levels of humanity, dig into prejudice, uncover the problem of young people in an automated society where anyone less than a college graduate seems forever doomed. (1964a, 5)

It is difficult to imagine how an hour-long episode could meaningfully delve into these areas, especially considering the amount of exposition it would require to put the series' white protagonist into a one-on-one counseling session with a Black drug addict, going through withdrawal.

After receiving the outline, John Bushnell, NBC's manager of film programming, sent a memo to the production, suggesting caution. He praised Silliphant's talent, but warned that the focus on withdrawal might doom the idea and noted: "It must be clearly understood that the ultimate acceptance of this property by the network is quite doubtful, and time and talent could possibly be expended to no avail" (1964). The network's Broadcast Standards division also weighed in, suggesting that based on the "somewhat sketchy" outline, there were "serious questions regarding the proposed extent and handling of narcotics withdrawal as well as the involvement of racial representations and issues" (Dewey 1964a). The memo does not offer further specifics on the latter half of the caution, but seems to imply that the episode's intention to discuss racial issues at length would make it unacceptable for broadcast. Despite these warnings, Neuman moved forward with the episode; Silliphant submitted a complete draft of the script the next month.

The draft script for "He Grabs a Train and Rides" contains a number of elements that Silliphant must have known would lessen its chances for broadcast. It includes a scene where two vagrants attempt to rob Ricky as he jumps off a train, but they lose interest when they discover the track marks (implying heroin use) on his arm (1964c, 11). A later scene has Novak and Pete breaking down a bathroom door and finding Ricky with a needle in his arm. Ricky's experience of withdrawal is protracted and continues through most of acts two through four. He contorts in pain from spasms that wrack his body, and he begs for a fix. At one point, Ricky grabs and uses a fireplace poker to threaten Novak's life (1964c, 55).

The episode also includes the content that Silliphant referenced briefly in his initial outline. As their conversation develops, Ricky tells Novak that he has been pressured to go to college, and told that he has to work harder to succeed, because of his race. He longs to work with his hands, but has found that automation has eliminated these opportunities. After Ricky and Novak make it through the long night together, the episode concludes in a moment of uplift; the teacher returns to the classroom. His students congratulate him, believing that took the weekend off from his professional responsibilities to enjoy some much-needed rest and relaxation (1964c, 67).

Neuman's records on "He Grabs a Train and Rides" indicate that Broadcast Standards immediately rejected the script, and that some effort was made to push past that rejection. In May of 1964, an NBC administrator reviewed the script and notified production that it was "unacceptable in its present form." The memo explained that the issues included the drug-related subject matter which was inappropriate for the series' early evening "family" timeslot, and that "[s]evere dialogue editing would be necessary to avoid an objectionable stereotype on the part of Ricky" (Dewey 1964b). Unlike typical content reports, this memo from Broadcast Standards did not include specific suggestions for revision. This might indicate that there were too many issues to enumerate, or that the department assumed that the script would not move forward. Despite this, it continued to progress toward production. MGM had their own legal research department clear the names and references in the script in June, and they expedited a legal check to clear the episode's title (a reference to an old Blues song, famously recorded by Jimmie Rodgers) in July (Larkin 1964; Stambler 1964). Feedback from the NEA was supportive, noting: "The tensely dramatic play carries an important but difficult message which should create the desired psychological impact upon the audience" (1964). The advisory panel suggested that the production should seek medical input on the details of withdrawal depicted in the episode, but did not indicate any awareness that the subject matter as a whole might be deemed unsuitable for broadcast. The production of season two was already underway when NBC sent a final determination. In a memo updating the status of a number of potentially controversial episodes, Broadcast Standards confirmed that "He Grabs a Train and Rides" was rejected (Jones 1964).[6]

Cecil Smith, a syndicated columnist, wrote about the *Mr. Novak*'s battles with network censorship in the fall of 1964. He claimed to have read "He Grabs a Train and Rides" and described it as a "skillful and sensitive study of a young Negro who turns to drugs out of the frustrations of his own existence in a white world" (1964). The write-up also quoted the series' producer Leonard Freeman, who claimed that if the episode had been produced correctly, it would have been a significant television achievement.

18.5 Conclusion

Television writers had a limited amount of authority in the early years of the US network system, which formed in the late 1950s. Writers who wanted to use their talents to confront the issues of the day faced interference from network executives, censors, sponsors, and sometimes-unsupportive producers. Under the freelance writing contracts that were the norm for television dramas in this era, producers held more creative control than did writers. Producers of social issues dramas like Herb Brodkin and E. Jack Neuman recognized that it was worthwhile to pursue subject matter that was considered "difficult"; strong dramatic episodes could draw significant attention to a series, potentially from both critics and viewers. The case studies in this chapter touch on the major components of influence in the network system. The obstacles involved in writing about race relations and the politics of civil rights certainly discouraged television writers from approaching these areas, or from making their messages overt. The writers who chose to tackle these topics faced network censorship, producer interference, problems with affiliate clearance, and a lack of sponsor support. The network system did not completely prevent writers from addressing topics of social importance. It functioned as a set of impediments that had to be navigated, for those who were willing to try.

---

[6] The word "rejected" is underlined on Neuman's copy of this memo.

Acknowledgements Research for this chapter was supported by the Faculty Development Program at the University of Wisconsin Oshkosh.

References

Barnouw, Erik. 1962. *The Television Writer*. New York: Hill and Wang.
Bellak, George. 1962. *The Nurses*, ep. "The Prisoner," shooting script dated July 11, unpublished screenplay. Box 18. Herbert Brodkin papers, available at Yale University, New Haven CT.
Ben Casey. 1961–1966 (5 seasons). Created by James Moser. USA: Bing Crosby Productions.
Boddy, William. 1993. *Fifties Television: The Industry and Its Critics*. Chicago: University of Illinois Press.
Bogle, Donald. 2001. *Primetime Blues: African Americans on Network Television*. New York: Farrar, Straus and Giroux.
Breaking Point. 1963–1964 (1 season). Created by Meta Rosenberg. USA: Bing Crosby Productions.
Brodkin, Herbert. 1963. *The Nurses*, "Express Stop from Lenox Ave," shooting script dated February 11, unpublished screenplay credited to Adrian Spies. Box 19. Herbert Brodkin papers, available at Yale University, New Haven CT.
Bushnell, John. 1963. Broadcast Standards memo to E. Jack Neuman regarding "A Single Isolated Incident." July 26. Box 13, Folder 2. E. Jack Neuman papers, available at the Wisconsin Historical Society (WHS).
Bushnell, John. 1964. Broadcast Standards memo to Leonard Freeman regarding "He Grabs a Train and Rides." April 29. Box 26, Folder 9. E. Jack Neuman papers, available at the Wisconsin Historical Society (WHS).
Davidson, David. n.d. Author's note regarding *Breaking Point*, "Whatsoever Things I Hear …" Box 16, Folder 1. David Davidson papers, available at the Wisconsin Historical Society (WHS).
Dewey, Ray. 1964a. Broadcast Standards memo to Leonard Freeman regarding "He Grabs a Train and Rides." April 23. Box 26, Folder 9. E. Jack Neuman papers, available at the Wisconsin Historical Society (WHS).
Dewey, Ray. 1964b. Broadcast Standards memo to Leonard Freeman regarding "He Grabs a Train and Rides." May 27. Box 26, Folder 9. E. Jack Neuman papers, available at the Wisconsin Historical Society (WHS).
Dr. Kildare. 1961–1966 (5 seasons). Created by E. Jack Neuman. USA: Arena Productions, MGM.
Hayes, Raphael. 1962. "A Man Against Himself," unpublished screenplay. Box 31, Folder 2. Reginald Rose papers, available at the Wisconsin Historical Society (WHS).
Hilmes, Michele, ed. 2007. *NBC: America's Network*. Los Angeles: University of California Press.
Humphrey, Hal. 1963. "'Mr. Novak' Episode Strikes New Tone." *Victoria Advocate*, 20 October. https://newscomwc.newspapers.com/image/440082626. Accessed 7 August 2022.
Jones, Bob. 1964. Broadcast Standards memo to Leonard Freeman. August 11. Box 26, Folder 9. E. Jack Neuman papers, available at the Wisconsin Historical Society (WHS).

Larkin, Ruth. 1964. Inter-office Communication at MGM regarding legal research and clearances for "He Grabs a Train and Rides." June 23. Box 26, Folder 9. E. Jack Neuman Papers, available at the Wisconsin Historical Society (WHS).

Laurent, Lawrence. 1964. "Producer of 'Novak' Off for School." *Los Angeles Times*, 20 April. https://www.proquest.com/historical-newspapers/producer-novak-off-school/docview/168577408/. Accessed 7 August 2022.

MacDonald, J. Fred. 1990. *One Nation Under Television: The Rise and Decline of Network TV*. Belmont CA: Wadsworth Publishing.

"Meet Mr. Novak" 1963. *NEA Journal* 52 (6): 32.

Mittell, Jason. 2008. "The 'Classic Network System' in the U.S." In *The Television History Book*, edited by Michele Hilmes, 44–49. London, BFI.

Mr. Novak. 1963–1965 (2 seasons). Created by E. Jack Neuman. USA: MGM.

Naked City. 1958–1959, 1960–1963 (4 seasons). Created by Herbert Leonard and Stirling Silliphant. USA: Screen Gems.

"NBC Programmers Get 'Guidelines' on 'Do's' and 'Don'ts' for '62-'63 Schedule." 1962. *Variety*, 18 April. www.proquest.com/magazines/radio-television-nbc-programmers-get-guidelines/docview/962760028/. Accessed 7 August 2022.

"NBC's 'Talent Has No Color' Projects Negro Contribs to New High in 1952." 1953. *Variety*, 18 March. https://www.proquest.com/magazines/nbcs-talent-has-no-color-projects-negro-contribs/docview/963280823/. Accessed 7 August 2022.

Neuman, E. Jack. 1963. "A Single Isolated Incident," unpublished screenplay. September 20. Box 13, Folder 2. E. Jack Neuman papers, available at the Wisconsin Historical Society (WHS).

Noerdlinger, Henry. 1963. NEA Panel Review of "A Single Isolated Incident." August 27. Box 13, Folder 2. E. Jack Neuman papers, available at the Wisconsin Historical Society (WHS).

Noerdlinger, Henry. 1964. NEA Panel Review of "He Grabs a Train and Rides." May 22. Box 26, Folder 9. E. Jack Neuman papers, available at the Wisconsin Historical Society (WHS).

Playhouse 90. 1956–1960 (4 seasons). USA: CBS Productions and Screen Gems.

Route 66. 1960–1964 (4 seasons). Created by Herbert Leonard and Stirling Silliphant. USA: Screen Gems.

Saints and Sinners. 1962–1963 (1 season). Created by Adrian Spies. USA: Four Star.

Sam Benedict. 1962–1963 (1 season). Created by E. Jack Neuman. USA: MGM.

Silliphant, Stirling. 1964a. "He Grabs a Train and Rides" script outline. April 15. Box 26, Folder 9. E. Jack Neuman papers, available at the Wisconsin Historical Society (WHS).

Silliphant, Stirling. 1964b. Memo to Leonard Freeman (producer). April 13. Box 1. Stirling Silliphant papers, available at the Special Collections, University of California, Los Angeles.

Silliphant, Stirling. 1964c. "He Grabs a Train and Rides" draft script. May 8. Box 26, Folder 9. E. Jack Neuman papers, available at the Wisconsin Historical Society (WHS).

Smith, Cecil. 1964. "Video Sharpens Its Blue Pencil." *Los Angeles Times*, 10 November. https://www.proquest.com/historical-newspapers/tv-scene/docview/155046084/. Accessed 7 August 2022.

Spies, Adrian. 1963. "Express Stop from Lenox Ave," unpublished screenplay (January 25). Box 5. Adrian Spies papers, available at the Wisconsin Historical Society (WHS).

Spies, Adrian. n.d. Personal note regarding "Express Stop from Lenox Avenue." Box 5. Adrian Spies papers, available at the Wisconsin Historical Society (WHS).

Stambler, Bob. 1963. Memo to Milton Beecher regarding "The Incident." August 27. Box 13, Folder 2. E. Jack Neuman papers, available at the Wisconsin Historical Society (WHS).

Stambler, Bob. 1964. Memo to Milton Beecher on title clearance for "He Grabs a Train and Rides." July 1. Box 26, Folder 9. E. Jack Neuman papers, available at the Wisconsin Historical Society (WHS).

Studio One. 1948–1958 (10 seasons). USA: CBS Productions.

The Defenders. 1961–1965 (4 seasons). Created by Reginald Rose. USA: Plautus Productions.

The Nurses. 1962–1965 (3 seasons). USA: Plautus Productions.

Van Horne, Harriet. 1963. "Two Fine Plays—For a Change." *Knoxville News-Sentinel*, 10 May. https://newscomwc.newspapers.com/image/596539338. Accessed 7 August 2022.

Watson, Mary Ann. 1994. *The Expanding Vista: American Television in the Kennedy Years*. Durham NC: Duke University Press.

Weitman, Robert. 1963. Memo to John Rothwell, MGM Director of Publicity. Box 13, Folder 2. August 1. E. Jack Neuman papers, available at the Wisconsin Historical Society (WHS).

White, Poppy Cannon. 1963. "Polish the Emmys." *New York Amsterdam News*, 26 January. https://www.proquest.com/historical-newspapers/polish-emmys/docview/226700774/. Accessed 7 August 2022.

Woodstone, Art. 1962. "Brodkin's Formula on How to Get Rich and Stay Happy in Television." *Variety*, 20 June. https://www.proquest.com/magazines/radio-television-brodkin-s-formula-on-how-get/docview/1017085638/. Accessed 7 August 2022.

Horror Bubbles: Andrés Caicedo's Weird Screenplays

Jerónimo Arellano

19.1 Introduction

In the summer of 1973, Andrés Caicedo travels to the United States with a head full of films he never made.[1] His older sister Rosario had left Cali and relocated to Houston, Texas, where her husband was a resident at Baylor College of Medicine. Caicedo was a consummate cinephile. In Cali, he spearheaded the film journal *Ojo al cine* [*Cinema View*] and cofounded the first film club of the city, the Cine Club de Cali, alongside future film directors Carlos Mayolo and Luis Ospina. In both *Ojo al cine* and Cali's Cine Club Caicedo's omnivorous film appetite went on full display. Caicedo conceived of this film-viewing frenzy as a disease: *cinesífilis* [film syphilis], he liked to call it, punning on the Spanish *cinefilia* [cinephillia]. Caicedo's *cinesífilis* did not distinguish between high and lowbrow, embracing classical Hollywood and international art-house cinema with the same fervor with which it consumed American B-movies saturated with horror and pulp. In Caicedo's private film pantheon, George Romero and Roger Corman rubbed elbows with Godard and Cassavetes. *The Last Picture Show* (1971), he writes in one of his letters, "is better than any film by Bob Rafelson, Paul Mazursky, Stuart Rosenberg, Mike Nichols... and other New Hollywood directors"; in another letter, he

[1] Unless otherwise noted, all translations from Spanish into English are mine.

J. Arellano (✉)
Brandeis University, Waltham, MA, USA
e-mail: jarellano279@g.ucla.edu

refers to a family viewing of Tod Browning's *Dracula* (1931) as the founding moment of his film addiction (Caicedo 2008, 75).

At the height of this movie affliction that consumed much of his life, Caicedo embarks on an adventure that to contemporary eyes reads as part gothic horror, part screwball comedy. Arriving in Texas, Caicedo writes two feature-length film scripts and a film treatment in Spanish. He then recruits his sister to translate them, precariously, into English, with a little help from a Spanish–English dictionary that Rosario still keeps in her personal archive, alongside other mementos from her brother. The physical copy appears in Jorge Nava's recent documentary *Balada para niños muertos* (2020): "So, this is the dictionary I used to translate the scripts," she says, and shows it to camera, yellowing pages falling off the book's spine. "The poor thing ended up like this. And I told Andrés, I'm going to keep this forever as a memory of the hell I went through translating your screenplays, and [Andrés] burst out laughing."[2]

Caicedo planned to take these scripts to Los Angeles and sell them to B-movie uber-producer Roger Corman. In Caicedo's fantasies, the sale of these screenplays would allow him to go back to Cali with enough funds to secure financial independence from his family and purchase in the States an Arriflex camera and a Nagra recorder, which he planned to use in film shoots with his friends back in Cali. But like the films he wrote for Corman, these youthful dreams never materialized.[3]

19.2 Between Hollywood and McOndo

In Los Angeles, Caicedo rooms in a motel on Alvarado Street. He spends his days watching movies that would have been hard to find in Cali and frequenting the film department at UCLA. Eventually, with the help of Flora Mock—a graduate student in the animation department at UCLA—Caicedo manages to get his script in the hands of Joel B. Michaels, a film producer in Roger Corman's inner circle. But he soon meets rejection. "This letter will not come with the good news you expect", he writes to Rosario on July 23, 1973 (Caicedo 2008, 87). Caicedo's letter transcribes passages from the letter he received from Michaels, after he struggled to read one Caicedo's screenplays:

---

[2] Orig.: "Bueno, y este fue el diccionario con el que yo traduje los guiones…Así quedo después de la traducida de los guiones. Y yo le dije a Andrés, estoy lo voy a guardar de por vida, como un recuerdo del martirio por el que pasé traduciendo estos guiones, y se atacó de la risa".

[3] Sandro Romero Rey alludes to the range and depth of Corman's influence on Caicedo's work, starting with its titles: "Roger Corman había rodado un film con Vincent Prince llamado *Tales of Terror*, cuya traducción en español fue cosas del destino, *Destino fatal*" (Trans.: "Roger Corman had shot a film with Vincent Price called *Tales of Terror*, the title of which was translated into Spanish as *Destino fatal*") (Romero Rey 2015, 69).

Dear Andres: Thank you for letting me see your script. I tried very hard to read it, but in its present condition (grammar, spelling, and format), I found it very difficult to grasp its content. I hope you will accept as a suggestion that you review the script with a writer that is more familiar with idiomatic English and the conventional screenplay form. Thank you again. I wish you the very best of luck. (Caicedo 2008, 87)

It does not take long for Caicedo to realize that his plan to sell his scripts to Corman was nothing short of a fever dream: "I've become aware that it was sheer madness to try to sell a script without having the faintest idea of how to write in English, and I worry that this lunacy has now poisoned every one of my actions)" (Caicedo 2008, 87).[4] Wrestling with these impossible odds and worried by the expiration of his tourist visa, Caicedo posts ads throughout UCLA, seeking "a spanish–english [sic] writer to translate screenplays" (Caicedo 2008, 87). He spends his days holed up in his room, haunted by panic attacks. In *Balada para niños muertos*, Rosario describes her brother's time in Los Angeles as an inflection point in his life. When he returns to Houston, Caicedo is not the same person that had left.

A decade after Caicedo's untimely suicide at the age of twenty-five, his friend Luis Ospina stands in a corner of a plaza in Cali, interviewing passersby for his documentary *Andrés Caicedo: Unos buenos pocos amigos* [Andrés Caicedo: A Few Good Friends] (1986). "Does the name Andrés Caicedo ring a bell?", he asks them as they go by. Most of his interviewees return blank stares. A few mistake Andrés Caicedo for the name of a guerrilla fighter or perhaps a soccer player? Fast-forward to the 2020s, Caicedo's legacy looks strikingly different. Felipe Gómez, one of the leading scholars of Caicedo's work, writes about when he began his research more than a decade ago:

Few people outside Colombia had heard of them. Since that time, the three most visible leaders of this group, writer and film critic Andrés Caicedo Estela and filmmakers Carlos Mayolo and Luis Ospina, have gained momentum in terms of critical reception, leading to the publication of edited volumes, dozens of articles in Colombian and international magazines, new or translated editions of their works intended for broader audiences, as well as to significant local and international awards and recognitions. (Gómez 2019, 51)

Andrés Caicedo's posthumous rise to fame is due in large part to the efforts of family and friends who doggedly recovered, edited, and published the manuscripts he left behind—neatly ordered and cataloged in file folders, as if awaiting publication. But time after time scholars and critics of Caicedo's body of work also point out the *timeliness* and *ultracontemporaneity* of his writing as a key reason for his growing popularity in the new millennium. In his literary

---

[4] Orig.: "He sido consciente de que fue una especie de locura pretender vender un guión sin tener idea de cómo se escribe en inglés, y temo que ahora esta locura esté contaminando todo mi comportamiento" (Caicedo 2008, 87).

fiction and film scripts, Caicedo breaks ranks with dominant trends in Latin American literature and cinema of the 1960s and 1970s, particularly what has been codified, in the cultural history of the region, as the "Latin American boom"—a hyperbolic moment in Latin American literary history where a group of writers including Gabriel García Márquez, Carlos Fuentes, Mario Vargas Llosa, and Julio Cortázar, attain worldwide critical acclaim for their ambitious, ground-breaking literary work. One of the epicenters of the Latin American boom is the fiction Colombian writer Gabriel García Márquez, celebrated for his sweeping magical realistic tales, where wondrous, extraordinary events infiltrate mundane, quotidian reality. Caicedo is often portrayed as a writer that labored in the shadows of the boom, a dark counterpoint to García Márquez's wondrous universes. "To see and read of cannibals, vampires, and zombies roaming the homes, streets, and haciendas in the Colombian city of Cali in the 1970s allows us to visualize parts of contemporary Latin America as tropical gothic spaces", writes Gómez (2019, 52). Caicedo's interest in young protagonists drifting through media-saturated and drug-fueled undergrounds, the neogothic underworlds and necrotic settings of his narratives, and his exploration of nonnormative sexualities, for Gómez, darken the tone and texture of Latin American narratives that were most consumed in Colombia during his lifetime (2014, 223–24).

Emblematic of this reception as a dissident, counter-boom writer is Alberto Fuguet's encounter with Caicedo's work at La Casa Verde, a now-defunct bookstore in the San Isidro neighborhood in Lima. The year is 2008 and Fuguet is already well-known around Latin America as one of the leading voices of a new generation of Latin American writers. Back in 1996, Fuguet had co-edited with Sergio Gómez a literary anthology entitled *McOndo*. *McOndo* highlights a schism between the literature of Latin American boom writers and a new sensibility rising in Latin American fiction—wary of marvelous tales or sweeping sagas exploring Latin American identity; minimalist in style and infused with global pop culture and new media. *McOndo* sets out to encapsulate Latin American urban cultures at the turn of the millennium: the term "McOndo" is both a pun García Márquez's Macondo, the fictional town he devised as a setting for his fiction, and a nod to a brave new world filled with "McDonalds, Mac computers, and condos".[5] Upon finding *¡Qué viva la música!* [*Liveforever*] and *Ojo al cine* [*Cinema View*]—a volume collecting Caicedo's film reviews—Fuguet experiences a revelation:

> I set aside the other texts I was holding to pick up this unknown volume. I exaggerate if I say that my hands were shaking, but not quite. At least I wish they were (close-up to hands picking up a book). I sensed that more than encountering a book, I was facing a person. The person that years later would

---

[5] "The thing is, I get suffocated by thick, sweet, humid air that smells like mangos, and I get the munchies when I begin to fly among thousands of colorful butterflies. I can't help it; I'm an urban dweller through and through. The closest I'll ever get to *Like Water for Chocolate* is cruising the titles at my local Blockbuster" (Fuguet 1997, n.p.).

transform into a part of me and, for better and for worse, I suppose, into part of my family. (Fuguet 2014, 42)

Fuguet's embrace of "Planet Caicedo," as he calls it, hinges on a recognition of artistic kinship across the decades. The Chilean writer sees himself—and the literature of his generation—in Caicedo's *!Qué viva la música!* and *Ojo al cine*: Caicedo's Cali in the 1970s in his eyes shows up as a prelude to Latin American culture in the new millennium. "I like to imagine him embodying the idea of the movie buff as martyr", Fuguet writes, "the postadolescent Latin American crazed for Hollywood. He was the solitary person that committed himself to the big screen while others were supporting the cause, the older brother of McOndo, the missing link to the twenty first century" (Fuguet 2014, 42).

Fuguet's reading of Caicedo as "McOndo's older brother" is a sticky idea. It appears and reappears, in different guises, throughout the critical literature on Caicedo's work. And yet major discrepancies between Caicedo and his McOndian cousins come to light if you take a closer look. *There are no zombies in McOndo.* Or cannibals, or vampires. The neogothic atmospheres Caicedo cultivated are in fact entirely at odds with the aesthetics of cool, urban realism that the McOndo writers cultivated. Caicedo was not a McOndian writer avant la lettre, and neither was he solely a practitioner of what scholars of the Grupo de Cali label the "tropical gothic"—the assimilation and transfiguration of gothic horror in Southern and subtropical regions, where the gothic genre is repurposed as a tool for the exploration of structural inequalities, racial capitalism, and the afterlives of colonialism (see, e.g., Edwards and Vasconcelos 2016). Caicedo was, rather, *a weird* writer, a label that is at times applied to him casually when describing the marginality or eccentricity of his work.

When compared to García Márquez's conquest of the world-literary mainstream, Caicedo's work certainly seems strange, obscure, off the beaten track. But the term *weird* as it is employed in contemporary aesthetics applies to him beyond these casual remarks. When taken seriously as an *aesthetic category* gaining traction in the present, the weird allows us to highlight dimensions of Caicedo's literary and screen narratives that escape the discussion of their tropical-gothic leanings or their foreshadowing of McOndo. The weird as an artistic form worthy of scrutiny in its own right focalizes Caicedo's concern with the inappropriate, with *that which does not belong*, highlighted by Marc Fisher as a central element of his theory of the weird in contemporary culture (Fisher 2016, 10). It also throws into relief the Lovecraftian atmospheres Caicedo constructed—horror bubbles infused with the "breathless and unexplainable dread of outer, unknown forces" (Lovecraft 1973, 15).

The two screenplays Caicedo wrote in Houston are a key element in this rereading of Caicedo as a weird writer and avid Lovecraft reader. They constitute one of the clearest articulations of the weird mode in his work. Caicedo's Texan screenplays thus reset the artistic genealogy of his work as a prelude not to the McOndo movement, but to a still inchoate movement toward the

New Weird currently rising in postmillennial Latin American literary fiction and film. But Caicedo's screenplays are also as a microcosm of Latin American screenwriting a field of creative practice uniquely positioned as speculative media generated at the juncture of literature and cinema. I have previously argued that Latin American screenwriting is an artistic tradition with its own cultural history, aesthetic principles, and industrial culture. One of the distinguishing characteristics of this tradition is the strong relationship screenwriting practices developed throughout their history with the literary fiction of the region (see Arellano 2016b and 2016a). Lacking the "normative poetics" of screenwriting identified by Ian W. Macdonald in Hollywood screenwriting (Macdonald 2013, 46–47), Latin American screenwriting turns time and again to the literary fiction of the region as playground and toolbox where Latin American screenwriters transform forms of aesthetic innovation first developed as literary forms into cinematic potentiality. They establish in this way a transmedia corridor where new tendencies forming within literary movements cross-pollinate defined shifts in Latin American audiovisual culture (Arellano 2016b, 128). Once they leave the literary field and enter the arena of screenwriting, these creative seeds gleaned from literary fiction come to guide the creation of film narratives and screen ideas—imaginary films that in some instances reach the big screen and in other cases, as it happened with Caicedo's weird scripts, remain unproduced.

19.3 Caicedo's Screenplays

According to Romero Rey, Andrés travels to the United States, "the country of Alphaville", with three movie ideas (2015, 69). Two of these, Caicedo writes out as feature-film screenplays—*La sombra sobre Innsmouth* [*The Shadow over Innsmouth*] and *La estirpe sin nombre* [*The Nameless Offspring*]; the third one he puts down as a film treatment for a Western film, *Los amantes de Suzie Bloom* [*Suzie Bloom's Lovers*].

La sombra sobre Innsmouth [*The Shadow Over Innsmouth*] is based partly on Lovecraft's story of the same title and partly on August Derleth's weird tale *The Seal of R'lyeh*. In true Lovecraftian fashion, *La sombra* follows the descent of Adam Hopkins—an introverted young man described by Caicedo as "... not at all confident in himself, unsympathetic and haunted by internal contradictions" (Caicedo 1973a, 2)[6]—into a world of weird horror. In the first act of the script, Hopkins, an architecture student interested in old relics and graveyards, travels to Dunwich, Massachusetts, hoping to visit the town's antiquaries. In Dunwich, Hopkins finds a strange tiara collected from Innsmouth, an old town nearby wrapped in mystery and legend. Once prosperous, Innsmouth had fallen on hard times a few years after the Civil War, when the bounty of fish near its shores dwindled. One night, Obed Marsh, one of the town's fishermen, runs into the Devil at the "Arrecife del Diablo", or Devil's

---

[6] Orig.: "nada seguro de sí mismo... contradictorio y antipático".

Reef, and strikes a bargain with him. In exchange for the company of Marsh's beautiful young daughter, Estella, the Devil agrees to fill Obed's vessels with fish night after night.

The second and third acts of *La sombra* narrate Adam's visit to Innsmouth and his discovery of a monstrous race, redolent of Lovecraft's racial prejudices and his obsessions with genealogical "contaminations", product of Estella Marsh's union with the Devil. Caicedo describes their offspring as similar to "those drawings, very much in vogue these days, that show a man turning into a reptile, inspired by drug-fueled hallucinations" (Caicedo 1973a, 3)[7]—introducing a psychedelic twist into Lovecraft's teratology. As Adam finds himself unable to escape this miserable town, with row upon row of boarded-up windows and decrepit houses, he also begins to discover that the origins of his own bloodline may be traced back to the nights Estella Marsh spent with the Devil.

La estirpe sin nombre [*La estirpe*]—based on Clark Ashton Smith's weird tale *The Nameless Offspring* (1947)—is guided by a similar aesthetics. In this script, Caicedo writes, "horror will seep through slowly among seemingly ordinary events and refined yet mundane characters... audiences will first be introduced to a frivolous and comfortable atmosphere, and once they start feeling at home in it, they will be thrust into supernatural and inordinate occurrences" (Caicedo 1973b, 2).[8] Set in Tremont Hall, an old, gothic estate in England, *La estirpe* tells the story of John Tremont, the owner of the property, and his young wife, Madeline. Tremont is introduced to Madeline by his friend Arthur Jameson during one of Jameson's visits to Tremont Hall. At the center of John's estate rises an old family mausoleum. When setting up this graveyard, John tells Arthur one night, a group of laborers found a strange white boulder. When they moved it aside to continue their work, they found a hole in the ground so deep it seemed to reach the bowels of the earth. "The smell of hell", says John, wafted through this orifice to greet them (Caicedo 1973b, 22). John and Madeline marry during Arthur's visit. But, during their wedding night, after Arthur has left, Madeline falls into a catatonic state. Believing she is dead, and worried about potential repercussions, John promptly buries her in the family's graveyard, where Madeline is a visited by a white-haired creature that has been seen at times lurking around the mausoleum. Hearing the news, Arthur returns to Tremont Hall and warns John that Madeline has suffered from cataleptic attacks since childhood; they find her alive in the crypt where she was interred, her hair grayed overnight. Months later Madeline dies giving birth to the "nameless offspring" to which

---

[7] Orig.: "esos dibujos, muy en boga actualmente, que muestran al hombre volviéndose reptil, basados en la experiencia de la droga".

[8] Orig.: "el horror irá aflorando en medio de unos acontecimientos cotidianos y unos personajes de costumbres refinadamente mundanas... [s]e introducirá al público en un ambiente frívolo y agradable, y cuando ya empiece a sentirse a gusto, se lo sacará violentamente, pasando a ocuparse de los hechos extranormales y desproporcionados".

the script's title refers. John raises him as a son under lock and key, in a dark corner of his mansion.

Common themes and narrative forms run through both of Caicedo's screenplays. The idea of sex as a strange act with potentially ominous ramifications—unfolding into monstrous anatomies and family curses—appears as a connecting thread, as does the idea of dark family secrets, bubbling up underneath a seemingly mundane world. Caicedo's predilection for neogothic settings articulated in his fiction reemerges here as well, in the little towns Adam Hopkins visits in his journeys and in the imaginary architecture of Tremont Hall, transposed this time into a potential mise-en-scène. Both scripts are written in a screenplay format that flaunts the conventions of a Hollywood screenplay—the "conventional format" Michaels refers to in his rejection letter—and set out to create their own cinematic language. Caicedo's screenplays use sluglines only rarely and avoid the architectures of dialogue and action description observed by the standard Hollywood screenplay. Instead, Caicedo breaks up his scenes into detailed, individual shots, forming sequences, interspersed by lines of dialogue and evocative prose as in the following example:

Close-up a John

JOHN: Verdad?

Plano medio del grupo.

MADELINE: He estado leyendo sus libros. Quisiera poder plantearme mi amor hacia Dios tal como usted lo hace. Pero es tan difícil.

Long shot. A la distancia, una especie de animal cuadrúpedo se interna en el bosque. Tiene pelo blanco y miró a cámara.

MADELINE (Voice over): Dios demanda un amor más profundo del que yo …

Close-up a Colin, que ha visto el plano anterior. Se levanta de su asiento.

Trans. (Close-up on John.

JOHN: Is it true?

Medium angle on the group.

MADELINE: I have been reading your books. I'd like to look at my own love for God the way you do. But it's hard.

Long shot. In the distance, a strange kind of four-legged animal enters the forest. His fur is white, and he looks at camera.

MADELINE [Voice-over]: God demands a love that is deeper than the one I
…

Close up on Colin, who has seen the previous frame. He rises from his seat.)

(Caicedo 1973a, 13)

While it might be tempting to think of *La sombra* and *La estirpe* as fumbling transpositions of Caicedo's literary fiction into a new medium, his screenplays also introduce a number of notable dissonances within his corpus and the critical reception of his work. As we have seen, one of the main frameworks invoked when discussing Caicedo's fiction is the notion of the "tropical gothic" where the iconic motifs of the Anglophone gothic are adapted to and transfigured in Southern latitudes. The screenplays Caicedo writes in Texas, however, sidestep the creative transformation at the heart of the tropical gothic, a process critical to much of his fiction as well as to the films of Caicedo's friends and collaborators Ospina and Mayolo. Caicedo's American screenplays are neither gothic nor tropical—not only because they are set in the English countryside or in small New England towns, far from the tropics, but also because they never filter gothic motifs through the landscapes, textures, and (sub)cultures of Cali in the 1970s, as happens in the stories of Caicedo's *Angelitos empantanados o historias para jovencitos* [*Angels in the Mud, Or Stories for Young Readers*] (1977), in Ospina's *Pura sangre* [*Pure Blood*] (2008), and in Ospina and Mayolo's cult mockumentary short film *Agarrando pueblo* [*The Vampires of Poverty*] (1978), a vampire tale that satirizes the Western appetite for "misery porn" hailing from Latin American countries. *La sombra* and *La estirpe* gravitate, rather, toward other locations and cultural referents, creating atmospheres of dread and horror that lean heavily on Lovecraft but reimagine his fiction for the big screen, infusing it with cinematic flair. As Adam approaches Innsmouth on a bus, the view outside the window splinters into an evocative and decidedly weird sequence:

Interior Del Bus.

Medium shot a la nuca horrible de Jose Sargeant. Plano, subjetiva de Adam, hacia la calle. Se ven algunas personas, pero es como si evitaran mirar el autobús que pasa. De allí llegan a "High Street" y a uno zona de edificios majestuosos de los primeros años de la República …

Plano a Adam, que mira de un lado a otro.

Luego vemos que la vegetación comienza a escasear, y las casas, y así que empieza la arena y el pasto seco, signos de la cercanía del mar.

Plano a unos postes de teléfono, ennegrecidos y descascarados por la brisa y el sol.

Trans. (Bus Interior

Medium angle on the back of Jose Sargeant's horrifying head. POV shot, Adam looking at the street. A few people walk by but look away from the bus. They arrived at "High Street," an area with majestic buildings from the first years of the Union …

Angle on Adam, looking from side to side.

Then we see the greenery of the land become more and more sparse, and the houses giving way to sand and scorched grass, signs of the ocean nearby.

Angle on a few telephone poles, blackened and eaten in by the sea breeze and the sun.)

(Caicedo 1973a, 76)

19.4 CAICEDO AND THE WEIRD

In the introduction to the edited collection *The American Weird*, Julian Greve and Florian Zappe draw on Sianne Ngai's discussion of the zany, cute, and interesting as three alternative categories in contemporary aesthetics to propose the weird "as yet another foundational category of not merely, or predominantly, twentieth-century American culture but in particular that of the new millennium" (Greve and Zappe 2020, 2–3). Like the concepts discussed by Ngai in *Our Aesthetic Categories* (Ngai 2015), Zappe and Greve note that the contemporary Weird is an intermedial phenomenon found across "a broad spectrum of artistic practices" (2020, 3), which for them includes the films of David Lynch, Jordan Peele, and Ana Lily Amirpour, Alan Moore's graphic novels, Charles Burns's comics, and the videogame *The Secret World* (Greve and Zappe 2020, 5). We could add to this ever-expanding list a wide range of Latin American films, including Amat Escalante's *La región salvaje* [*The Untamed*] (2016), Cristóbal León and Joaquín Cociña's *La casa lobo* [*The Wolf House*] (2018), and Issa López's *Vuelven* [*Return*] (2017), as well as the literary fiction of Mariana Enríquez, Bernardo Esquinca, and Samanta Schweblin.

Johnny Murray (2020) defines *the weird* as stories that articulate encounters "with outlandish things hopelessly beyond human comprehension, bringing us into contact with the radically alien, the utterly inconceivable, or, as Arthur Machen puts it,… 'that for which we have no name'" (28–29). Murray recognizes that the weird presents a challenge to critical analysis precisely because of its unnamable qualities and its propensity to live in what he calls "fuzzy sets" that recombine features of gothic, horror, science fiction, and fantasy narratives into new, unfamiliar hybrids. And yet for Murray it is still possible to distinguish certain central features of the weird from the genres it draws from by focusing on its morphological qualities. The weird, Murray argues, distinguishes itself from gothic fiction, for example, in that it does not feature haunting-yet-recognizable presences—such as ghosts or vampires—but deals with "a radically new other, another that is unprecedented rather than haunting"—unearthly, unfamiliar, and often times impossible to describe (2020, 31).

This is a useful distinction to keep in mind when reading Caicedo's screenplays. The creaturely horrors of *La estirpe* and *La sombra* do not feature gothic others—tropical or otherwise—but deal, rather, with weird presences and atmospheres. True to their origins in American Weird tales, the monstrous offspring of Estella Marsh and the Devil recombine human and amphibian species. To bring them to life, Caicedo imagines cinematic details that draw on animation and VFX: hands covered in reptile or fish scales, insert shots of "shape-shifting gray cells bubbling up before our eyes" (Caicedo 1973a, 51).[9] The creatures featured in *La estirpe* are similarly intractable. The monster that visits Madeline's grave is an unnamable presence—as is her son, a cannibalistic creature that toward the end of the narrative feeds on his father's corpse.

Looming over Tremont Hall and Caicedo's re-creation of Lovecraft's Innsmouth hangs a thick and heavy atmosphere of weird dread. On the back cover of Caicedo's unfinished novel *Noche sin fortuna* (2009), Romero Rey describes the narrative procedure at the heart of Caicedo's work as a journey in which "middle-class youths leave home, and, gradually, the world around them becomes a horror bubble" (Romero Rey in Caicedo 2009, back cover).[10] Caicedo anchors his screenplays in a similar process of gradual disintegration into horror. Yet in *La estirpe* and *La sombra* Caicedo also steps out of his own fictional universe—by then already well developed, with the precociousness that characterizes his literary output—in the process of adapting stories by weird American writers for the screen. In the process, the fictional mechanism by which an ordinary, middle-class environment becomes a horror bubble acquires new dimensions. Merely ten years ago, when the current surge in New Weird fiction in Latin American was barely starting, these two screenplays might have simply looked like outliers in the Caicedo corpus—strange tentacles veering away from the aesthetics of the tropical gothic and reaching Northern territories. Read now, however, in the context of what Gerry Canavan and Andrew Hageman call "global weirding" (2016)—the convergence of weird ecological patterns or events and the growing popularity of weird speculative fiction, unfolding on a planetary scale—Caicedo's screenplays appear as more timely and visionary narratives in his body of work, never mind their subversion of Hollywood screenwriting norms and their invention of sui generis film grammar. Set against this background, these screenplays urge a revision of Caicedo's position in the Latin American canon

---

[9] Orig.: "un conjunto de células grises burbujeando".

[10] Orig.: "jovencitos burgueses salen de sus casas y, poco a poco, el mundo se va convirtiendo en una burbuja de horror".

as a proto-McOndian writer—a reading that glosses over the aesthetic specificity of Caicedo's literature and its wide-ranging experimentation with various horror subgenres. As it turns out, Caicedo's *grandchildren* in Latin American fiction and cinema are not Gen Xers like Fuguet but, rather, a new, postmillennial generation that—not unlike their obscure predecessor—suffers from Lovecraft fever and drinks from the reservoir of the weird across cultures.

But while Caicedo's screenplays suggest a recasting of his figure as a writer of the weird, it remains unclear whether or not his work anticipates The Weird—capital T, capital W—as a sociohistorical threshold precipitated by widespread, structural crisis. Tim Lazendörfer (2020) usefully distinguishes between one and the other: while the "merely weird" is a specific genre or form that is not bound to any specific location or time period, "The Weird" is the supercharged appearance of that same form at moments when it becomes invested with widespread significance, acquiring cultural prominence. In this second instance, The Weird unfolds as an artistic language, expressive of "moments of crisis because of its capacity to think nonsupernatural apparent outsides to socioeconomic systems that appear to be failing" (72–73). For Lazendörfer, writing from and about American culture during the 1930s and post-2010s, the times of the Great Depression and the Great Recession constitute these crisis moments where the weird becomes The Weird (2020, 73).

Caicedo's penchant for the weird and his voracious reading of American weird writers from the early twentieth century reveal an idiosyncratic and intuitively forward-looking sensibility. Yet his narratives stop short of reflecting the deep generational apprehension of a world gone awry that characterizes The Weird as a cultural moment. Indeed, one of the reasons why it might have taken several decades for his fiction to acquire the following it enjoys now is that Caicedo's stories, at the time of writing, failed to gain the cultural traction they would gain when the weird forms he cultivated begin to find stronger resonances in the age of The Weird. During his lifetime, however, Caicedo's weird aesthetics remained emblematic only of his own luminous eccentricity as a Latin American who preferred Lovecraft to the writers of the Latin American boom and Hollywood B-movies to the quest for Latin American identity that weighed heavily upon his contemporaries.

As noted above, one of the distinguishing features of Latin American screenwriting is that it is often developed as a "born literary practice" wherein developments in literary fiction become laboratories where "screen ideas" and images of audiovisual potentiality—imaginary films and television series that in some cases reach the screen but not always—are incubated.[11] Belinda Barnet and Darren Tofts's observation that "scientists and technologists are often guided by 'images as potentiality'—the untested theories, unanswered

---

[11] For a discussion of the notion of "screen ideas", the creative kernels of film and television projects and where they come from, see Novrup Redvall 2013 and Macdonald 2013.

questions, and unbuilt devices that they view as their agenda for five years, ten years, and longer" (Barnet and Tofts 2008, 283)—is useful here. When adapted to the domain of (Latin American) screenwriting in general and Caicedo's weird screenplays in particular, the notion of "images as potentiality" plants the seeds for an alternative ontology of the *unproduced screenplay* as a creative playground and womb. The creative architecture of an unproduced screenplay rests upon a weave of untested aesthetic theories, unanswered formal questions, and the spectral image of an unbuilt artistic object—the hypothetical, phantasmic film a screenplay gives shape to. I like to refer to these never-made or yet-to-be-made films, such as Caicedo's *La sombra* and *La estirpe*, as "speculative media", keeping in mind the uses of the term *speculative* in literary studies to define works that color outside the lines of what is found in material reality. Like their literary counterpart, speculative media are forms that push these boundaries, dreaming up future possibilities that may or may not ever be realized. As Allyson Nadia Field reminds us in a recent call for papers, "the field of cinema and media studies has been organized around extant material, with histories closely tethered to surviving evidence… the result has been a conspicuous bias, one that has overlooked the overwhelming percentage of moving image media that does not survive, is fragmentary, is in danger of obsolescence, or whose survival is contingent on specialized preservation practices" (Field 2020). Rescuing the unproduced screenplay from oblivion and treating it as an object of study in its own right helps correct this bias, opening (Latin American) film history and screenwriting studies to a number of untested possibilities.

19.5 Conclusion

In previous work, I have suggested that in the history of Latin American screenwriting, canonical literary movements—such as the literature of the so-called *boom* period in the 1960s and 1970s—are often taken as reference points for the development of a regionally specific poetics of screenwriting (Arellano 2016b). In this context, aesthetic theories and formal or thematic concerns that beat at the heart of regional literary movements are transformed into images of audiovisual potentiality, guiding specific screenplays and/or pedagogical principles grounding screenwriting instruction at Latin American film conservatories. What is notable about Caicedo's work as a screenwriter is that his screenplays sidestep these canonical reference points yet still look toward literature as a creative matrix. Caicedo's screenplays are still *born literary* works, only in his case the images of potentiality they cultivate are incubated in the womb of weird Anglophone writing rather than in the aesthetic of Latin American boom writing. In method and process *La sombra* and *La estirpe* thus uphold the cross-pollination between literature and cinema as a structural principle in Latin American screenwriting. But by opening up the form of the screenplay to sources and reservoirs largely untapped by both Caicedo's contemporaries and writers of succeeding generations—postboom writers such as the McOndo collective—his screenplays also introduce a swerve into the weird, the importance of which might not have become fully legible until recently. It is only on the heels of an aesthetic of weirdness currently surging across Latin American literature and cinema that images of audiovisual potentiality circulated by Caicedo's screenplays can be assessed as a watershed event in Latin American film and literary history—a prelude to The Weird in Latin American cultural history. It is also not without consequence that Caicedo wrote his first published novel, *!Que viva la música!* [*Liveforever*] (2015), while writing and trying to sell these weird scripts. The way Caicedo's experimentation with the atmospheres and otherness of the weird influenced his novel—and, more broadly, the development of the aesthetics of the tropical gothic—is yet another story that might one day be told by further work on Caicedo's unproduced screenplays.

Acknowledgements My thanks to Rosario Caicedo, whose boundless generosity made this chapter possible.

References

Agarrando pueblo [*The Vampires of Poverty*]. 1978. Written by Carlos Mayolo. Directed by Luis Ospina and Carlos Mayolo. Colombia: Satuple.

Andrés Caicedo: Unos pocos buenos amigos [*Andrés Caicedo: A Few Good Friends*]. 1986. Written and directed by Luis Ospina. Colombia: Instituto Colombiano de Cultura, Compañía de Fomento Cinematográfico.

Arellano, Jerónimo. 2016a. "Gabriel García Márquez's Scriptwriting Workshop: Screenwriting Pedagogy and Collective Screenwriting in Latin America." *Journal of Screenwriting* 7 (2): 191–205.

Arellano, Jerónimo. 2016b. "The Screenplay in the Archive: Screenwriting, New Cinemas, and the Latin American Boom." *Revista Hispánica Moderna* 69 (2) (December): 113–32. https://www.academia.edu/30894116/The_Screenplay_in_the_Archive_Screenwriting_New_Cinemas_and_the_Latin_American_Boom. Accessed 8 August 2022.

Balada para niños muertos [*Ballad for Dead Children*]. 2020. Written by Jorge Navas and Sebastián Hernández. Directed by Jorge Navas. Colombia: Telepacífico, Desert Hotel Films.

Barnet, Belinda, and Darren Tofts. 2008. "Too Dimensional: Literary and Technical Images of Potentiality in the History of Hypertext." In *A Companion to Digital Literary Studies*, ed. Ray Siemens and Susan Schreibman, 283–381. Oxford: Blackwell.

Caicedo, Andrés. [1973a]. *La sombra sobre Innsmouth* [*The shadow over Innsmouth*], 1st draft, Unpublished screenplay. Andrés Caicedo's papers/Rosario Caicedo's personal archive.

Caicedo, Andrés. [1973b]. *La estirpe sin nombre* [*The nameless offspring*], 1st draft, unpublished screenplay. Andrés Caicedo's papers/Rosario Caicedo's personal archive.

Caicedo, Andrés. 1977. *Angelitos empantanados, o historias para jovencitos* [*Angels In the Mud, or Stories for Young Readers*]. Medellín: La Carreta.
Caicedo, Andrés. 2008. *Mi cuerpo es una celda: Una autobiografía* [*This Cell I Call My Body: An Autobiography*]. Edited by Alberto Fuguet. Bogotá: Grupo Editorial Norma.
Caicedo, Andrés. 2009. *Noche sin fortuna* [*Nights Without Fortune*]. Bogotá: Grupo Editorial Norma.
Caicedo, Andrés. 2015. *!Qué viva la música!* [*Liveforever*]. Barcelona: Alfaguara.
Canavan, Gerry, and Andrew Hageman. 2016. "Introduction: 'Global Weirding'." In "Global Weirding," edited by Gerry Canavan and Andrew Hageman, special issue, *Paradoxa* 28: 7–13. https://paradoxa.com/wp-content/uploads/2020/06/1-Intro-Global-Weirding-Canavan-Hageman-pp-7-14.pdf. Accessed 19 May 2022.
Dracula. 1931. Screenplay by Garrett Fort. Directed by Tod Browning. USA: Universal Pictures.
Edwards, Justin D., and Sandra Guardini Teixeira Vasconcelos. 2016. "Introduction: Tropicalizing the Tropics." In *Tropical Gothic in Literature and Culture: The Americas*, edited by Justin D. Edwards and Sandra Guardini Teixeira Vasconcelos, 1–10. New York: Routledge.
Field, Allyson Nadia. 2020. "CFP: Speculative Approaches to Media Histories." *H-Film*, 15 December. https://networks.h-net.org/cfp-speculative-approaches-media-histories. Accessed 14 December 2021.
Fisher, Marc. 2016. *The Weird and the Eerie*. London: Repeater.
Fuguet, Alberto. 1997. "I Am Not a Magic Realist." Introduction by Rob Spillman. *Salon*, 11 June. https://www.salon.com/1997/06/11/magicalintro/. Accessed 19 May 2022.
Fuguet, Alberto. 2014. "Planet Caicedo." Trans. Christina Miller. *World Literature Today* 88 (3–4): 38–42.
Gómez G[utiérrez], Felipe. 2014. "Andrés Caicedo: 'Rareza, belleza y sabor,' o un pozo que no quiso llamarse Macondo." In *Fuera del canon: Escrituras excéntricas en América Latina*, edited by Carina González, 223–50. Pittsburgh: Instituto Internacional de Literatura Iberoamericana–University of Pittsburgh Press.
Gómez G[utiérrez], Felipe. 2019. "The Tropical Gothic and Beyond: *El Grupo de Cali*'s Legacies for Contemporary Latin American Literature, Cinema, and Culture." *eTropic* 18 (1): 50–69.
Greve, Julius, and Florian Zappe. 2020. "Introduction: Conceptualizations, Mediations, and Remediations of the American Weird." In *The American Weird: Concept and Medium*, edited by Julius Greve and Florian Zappe, 1–11. London: Bloomsbury.
La casa lobo [*The Wolf House*]. 2018. Written by Cristóbal León, Joaquín Cociña, and Alejandra Moffat. Directed by Cristóbal León and Joaquín Cociña. Chile: Diluvio and Globo Rojo Films.
La región salvaje [*The Untamed*]. 2016. Written and directed by Amat Escalante. Mexico: Mantarraya Producciones.
Lazendörfer, Tim. 2020. "The Weird in/of Crisis, 1930/2010." In *The American Weird: Concept and Medium*, edited by Julius Greve and Florian Zappe, 72–87. London: Bloomsbury.
Lovecraft, H. P. 1973. *Supernatural Horror in Literature*. New York: Dover.
Macdonald, Ian W. 2013. *Screenwriting Poetics and the Screen Idea*. Basingstoke UK: Palgrave Macmillan.

Murray, Jonny. 2020. "The Oozy Set: Toward a Weird (ed) Taxonomy." In *The American Weird: Concept and Medium*, edited by Julius Greve and Florian Zappe, 28–39. London: Bloomsbury.

Ngai, Sianne. 2015. *Our Aesthetic Categories: Zany, Cute, Interesting*. Cambridge MA: Harvard University Press.

Novrup Redvall, Eva. 2013. *Writing and Producing Television Drama in Denmark: From the Kingdom to the Killing*. Basingstoke UK: Palgrave Macmillan.

Pura sangre [*Pure Blood*]. 2008. Written by Luis Ospina and Alberto Quiroga. Directed by Luis Ospina. Colombia: Proimágenes.

Romero Rey, Sandro. 2015. *Memorias de una cinefilia (Andrés Caicedo, Carlos Mayolo, Luis Ospina)* [*Cinephillia Memories: Andrés Caicedo, Carlos Mayolo, Luis Ospina*]. Bogotá: Siglo del Hombre Editores/Universidad del Valle.

Smith, Clark Ashton. 1947. "The Nameless Offspring." In *Strange Tales: Second Selection*, 16–27. London: Utopian.

The Last Picture Show. 1971. Written by Larry McMurtry and Peter Bogdanovich. Directed by Peter Bogdanovich. USA: Columbia Pictures.

Vuelven. [*Tigers Are Not Afraid*]. 2017. Written and directed by Issa López. Mexico: Filmadora Nacional and Peligrosa.

CHAPTER 20

Writers as Workers: The Making of a Film Trade Union in India

Rakesh Sengupta

20.1 Introduction

In his well-known essay, "The Author as Producer", Walter Benjamin (1998) argued that writers must dialectically reflect on their position within the material processes of production instead of glorifying themselves as *men of mind*. The writer must, therefore, be an *intellectual worker* who addresses the class struggle through technical innovations that mediate new forms of solidarity with the proletariat.[1] In other words, Benjamin positioned the writer within the production relations of cultural work when technology and mass culture in the early twentieth century rapidly reconfigured modes of aesthetic engagement.

In this chapter, I draw upon Walter Benjamin's socialist emphasis on writers as *intellectual workers*, not vis-à-vis the apparatus of cultural production, but in relation to labour institutions that safeguard workers' rights. I attempt to insert the idea of the screenwriter as the worker within material histories of trade unionism and labour movements by studying the formation of the Film

---

[1] Benjamin upheld Bertolt Brecht's *epic theatre* as an exemplary form of such technical innovation. Brecht's reworking of the bourgeois theatrical conventions of tragedies and operas of the time demonstrated his political commitment to class struggle: "Epic theatre does not reproduce conditions; rather, it discloses, it uncovers them" (Benjamin 1998, 100).

R. Sengupta (✉)
University of Toronto, Toronto, ON, Canada
e-mail: rakesh.sengupta@utoronto.ca

© The Author(s), under exclusive license to Springer Nature Switzerland AG 2023
R. Davies et al. (eds), *The Palgrave Handbook of Screenwriting Studies*,
https://doi.org/10.1007/978-3-031-20769-3_20

Fig. 20.1 SWA office wall with images of illustrious Indian screenwriters (*Source* author's own photograph, courtesy of SWA)

Writers' Association (FWA) in India during the 1950s–1970s. Recently, in 2016, the trade union was renamed as the Screenwriters' Association (SWA). It is one of the largest screenwriters' unions in the world today with over 30,000 members (see Fig. 20.1).

During my fieldwork in Mumbai in 2018–2019, the Screenwriters' Association office became one of my regular haunts. I searched their dusty cartons for old photographs and carefully looked through torn scrapbooks for important newspaper clippings about the organisation (see Fig. 20.2). I also spoke with members and employees about the past and present activities of the trade union, and frequently observed aspiring and established screenwriters registering their scripts at the union office before meeting prospective producers. The SWA office in Andheri, therefore, doubled up as an archival and a quasi-ethnographic site. In this chapter, I will try to reconstitute the largely unknown history of this film trade union through their fragmentary archival records.[2] By focusing on one-film trade union, I attempt to trace the forgotten futures of creative labour in the Bombay film industry during the period of 1950s–1970s when postcolonial efforts of nation-building intersected with Fordist models of work and welfarism.

---

[2] The screenwriter Kamlesh Pandey has also put together a brief historical account of the organisation on the SWA website using some of the same source materials (see Pandey n.d.).

Fig. 20.2 Unorganised archival records of the SWA office in Mumbai (*Source* author's own photograph, courtesy of SWA)

20.2 Precarity and Unionisation

The history of trade unions is inextricably linked with the development of capitalism in the nineteenth century.[3] In the twentieth century, welfare-oriented labour regulations and steady economic growth of post-war Fordist capitalism from the period of early 1940s to early 1970s intensified the economic and political power of trade unions in developed countries.[4] While trade unions continue to be associated with traditional models of action that emerged in the Fordist era, unions worldwide are now facing epochal changes with the rise in casualisation of work and the erosion of welfare models in the neoliberal era.[5] Recent efforts to revitalise trade unions within shifting paradigms of work and welfare have been examined in relation to the disintegration of the old working class (Doellgast et al 2018). The *precariat* is a new social

---

[3] Trade unions emerged in the first factories in England during the first half of the nineteenth century and gradually consolidated with the expansion of large corporations by the beginning of the twentieth century. Labour unions were organised by specific trades and then grouped together to form large national and international unions over the nineteenth and twentieth centuries.

[4] With the rise of trade unions, labour activism took on a progressive political dimension, demanding not only economic improvements in factories but also increased participation of workers in the running of corporations, industries and nations. The institutional power of employees and trade unions burgeoned with the expansion of the welfare state and the regulation of conditions of work. Provisions for collective bargaining, health care, minimum wage and protection against dismissal gradually improved the position of employees in the workplace as well in the society within the framework of the welfare state.

[5] Since the 1970s, neoliberal policies have corresponded to ruling class strategies designed to exploit local and global labour through new political expressions, social subjectivities and legal mechanisms (see Harvey 2005).

class that represents vulnerable forms of life and employment (Standing 2011). With no prospect for stable employment, precarious workers now navigate the uneven aspirational terrain of gig economy and freelance work, typically with little social benefits—a cultural condition Lauren Berlant (2011) appropriately called *cruel optimism*.

20.2.1 Creativity and Precarity

Such casualisation of work in the neoliberal order of things has impacted cultural and creative workers as well. Angela McRobbie has analysed creativity as a mode of governmentality whose ideological sway over young people makes them embrace precarious entrepreneurial work and forego "mainstream employment with its trade unions and its tranches of welfare and protection" (2016, 16). In the context of American and British screenwriters, Bridget Conor (2014) has argued that although their profession shares many features with the freelancing and flexible nature of creative labour in neoliberal markets, screenwriting work cannot be studied through post-Fordist lenses of atomised labour because it has historically been an individualised profession (47–48). Additionally, screenwriters' long histories of unionisation, especially in Hollywood, depart from McRobbie's conceptualisation of creative labour as inherently non-unionised. However, neoliberalism has also generated an amnesia of the long history of organised labour and welfare rights in media industries. As McRobbie rightly warns us:

> Being expected to work without workplace entitlements severs a connection with past generations who not only had such protection (in the form of sick pay, pensions, maternity leave etc.) but also fought hard to get them. And once these go, if indeed they do, it becomes difficult to imagine them being reinstated, especially since they took almost a century of struggle to win. (2016, 16)

This intensified precarisation of creative work through a cultural amnesia of unionisation makes histories of film trade unions important as they reveal forgotten futures of creative labour and welfare activism. In their study of the Writers Guild of America (WGA), Banks and Hesmondhalgh have pointed out that "in the recent 'turn to labor' in media and cultural studies, there has been little sustained consideration of unions" (2016, 267). There is, however, some dedicated scholarship on trade unions in Hollywood (Prindle 1988, Horne 2001, McKercher and Mosco 2006–2007), labour movements in the British film industry (Chanan 1976, Burrows 2018; Galt 2020), the role of different collectives and unions in combating precarious work in Indian film industries (Mazumdar 2015; Kaur 2020; Mannil 2020; Mini 2020), and trade unionism in Turkish cinema (Yüksel 2020). This chapter contributes empirically and conceptually to this body of scholarship on creative labour and unionisation through a history of the Film Writers' Association, which was founded in

Bombay in 1954 and formally registered as a trade union in 1960. The case study of FWA retraces an under-researched history of film trade unions in India whose labour activism coincided with broader national and international trade union movements of the postcolonial and post-war period.

20.2.2 Trade Unions in India

As Rohini Hensman (2011) has argued, the precarisation of work in India has a longer colonial history and therefore cannot be studied exclusively as a consequence of post-Fordist neoliberalism and globalisation. In the Indian context, the history of trade unions needs to be understood within their colonial and postcolonial contexts. After the establishment of textile and jute mills as well as the coming of railways in the 1850s, Indian labourers endured atrocious working conditions under colonial rule. As precursors to trade unions, workers' welfare associations were established in these industries in Bombay (now Mumbai), Madras (now Chennai), Ahmedabad and Calcutta (now Kolkata).[6] The trade union movement in India is said to have begun with the formation of the Bombay Mill Hands Association under the leadership of N.K. Lokhands in 1890. In the following decades, with the rapid increase in the population of wage workers and a rise in living costs during World War I, an evident working-class consciousness grew in different parts of the country. Around 1919–1920, workers' strikes and other forms of labour agitation were witnessed all over colonial India, which led to the formation of many trade unions and eventually an integration of these unions into a federation. The All India Trade Union Congress (AITUC) was constituted in 1920 in Bombay which represented around 140,000 members from 64 affiliated unions (Bardhan, 1995, 5). The increased agitation of Indian workers and the rapid proliferation of unions eventually forced the colonial government to enact the Trade Union Act in 1926.

The labour movement gained momentum again after India's independence from British rule in 1947, particularly in Bombay (see Hensman and Banaji 1998; Sherlock 2001). The Indian government's new industrialisation policies during the 1950s–1970s were designed to regulate imports, encourage the growth of public enterprises and generate large-scale employment.[7] The mushrooming of public enterprises went hand in hand with the formation of

---

[6] These were the Bombay Millhands Association (1890), the Servants of India Society (1905), the Amalgamated Society of Railway Servants (1907), the Kamgar Hitwardhak Sabha (1909) and the Social Service League (1910).

[7] After India's independence in 1947, a series of laws were enacted to improve the conditions of work and employment. These included the Industrial Employment Act (1946), the Industrial Disputes Act (1947), the Indian Factories Act (1948), the Minimum Wages Act (1948), the Plantation Labour Act (1951), the Employees' Provident Fund and Miscellaneous Provisions Act (1952), the Companies Act (1956) and the Maternity Benefit Act (1961).

trade unions within them.[8] The number of workers' organisations registered under the Trade Union Act increased considerably from 3,766 in 1950 to 29,438 in 1975 (Sinha et al 2006, 86). It is within this broader context of postcolonial labour activism that the film trade union movement emerged in India.

20.2.3 Film Trade Union Movement in India

In Hollywood, the stranglehold of an exploitative studio system as well as the Roosevelt administration's pro-union policies during the Great Depression motivated the formation of several film trade unions by the 1930s. Similarly, in the Indian context, a range of political and industrial factors spurred the film trade union movement in the 1950s. The Indian film studios' fortunes had declined over the 1940s due to limited raw stock available during the war as well as the entry of wartime profiteers who unscrupulously invested their untaxed *black money* in film production. These industrialists and businessmen gradually lured the stars away from the studios by paying them exorbitant fees. Consequently, the Indian studio system collapsed and gave way to a freelancing star system wherein anticolonial attitudes rationalised tax evasion during late colonial rule. Barnouw and Krishnaswamy have discussed how anticolonial sentiments fuelled practices of tax evasion in the new star system during the 1940s:

> A problem for the black marketeer was that his profits could not be openly reinvested. Therefore offers made to film stars in the early 1940s included a device that was apparently new to the film world. The star would receive a one-film contract calling for payment of Rs. 20,000. In actuality he would receive Rs. 50,000, but the additional Rs. 30,000 would be in cash, without any written record. To the star this extra sum, this payment 'in black' was of course tax free. This not only made it especially attractive but gave it a patriotic tinge. For years the withholding of taxes from the British Empire had been held a service to freedom. Now, when taxes were going into an 'imperialist war' denounced and boycotted by the National Congress, evasion of taxes was all the more easily rationalized—if need for rationalization was ever felt. The star's delight, personal and patriotic, in a partly tax-free salary coincided neatly with the investor's interest in off-the-record investment". (1963, 121)

While organisations such as the Motion Picture Society of India (MPSI) and the Indian Motion Picture Producers' Association (IMPPA) safeguarded producers' interests since the 1930s, crafts unions came into existence only in

---

[8] The four major trade union conglomerates that emerged during this period were the Indian National Trade Union Congress (INTUC), Hind Mazdoor Sabha (HMS), All India Trade Union Congress (AITUC) and United Trade Union Congress (UTUC). These bodies were powerful enough to pressurise the Indian government to nationalise different industrial sectors.

the 1950s with the rise of precarious forms of employment in this new star system.

> Until the early fifties most of the craftsmen and technicians worked with studios. There were no freelancers. In fact, they were considered as permanent employees of the studios. The need to have a trade union body was never felt. (Chanana 2011, 118)

A range of historical factors such as global currents of Fordist welfarism, national trade union movements in the backdrop of postcolonial industrialisation and precarious reconfigurations of creative work in the film industry informed the formation of multiple film trade unions in India during the 1950s. Apart from the Film Writers Association, several other craft unions—Assistant Film Directors' Association, Association of Film Editors, Cine Costume and Make up Artists' Association, Cine Dance Directors' Association, Western India Cinematographers Association, Western India Sound Engineers' Association, Indian Motion Picture Employees' Association, Character Artists' Association, Cine Production Association and Art Directors' Association—were founded during this decade. In 1956, the elected and executive members of these craft unions came together to establish the Federation of Western India Cine Employees (FWICE), the apex organisation of film workers in Bombay.

20.3 The Formation of FWA

The following sections will explore the early years of the FWA from its informal establishment in 1954 as a social club of screenwriters, directors and film to its registration under the Trade Union Act later in 1960. The conflict between studio proprietors and screenwriters is often studied in relation to the detailed division of labour in Hollywood film studios that operated along an intensely divisive and exploitative assembly line model (see Bordwell, Staiger and Thompson 1985). In the Indian context, however, the origins of a screenwriters' union must address the rich history of writer-director partnerships formed under studios that operated like "family units" (Vasudevan 1991, 183–184, Prasad 1998, 39–40).[9] In contrast to the emergence of Hollywood unions within the highly organised studio system, the creation of the Film Writers' Association was informed by a desire for stable structures of work in the Indian studio system.

---

[9] Some of these successful writer-director partnerships included Niranjan Pal and Franz Osten, Kamal Amrohi and Sohrab Modi, Nabendu Ghosh and Bimal Roy, K.A. Abbas and Raj Kapoor, Abrar Alvi and Guru Dutt, Pandit Mukhram Sharma and B. R. Chopra.

20.3.1 The Early years

Threatened by the contract system introduced by Chimanlal Trivedi in the early 1950s, the Film Writers' Association was forged out of the need to re-establish the secure partnerships between writers and directors under the old studio system. Mahesh Kaul got involved in the formation of a directors' association, while Safdar Aah took charge of forming a writers' association.

> Till 1950, in every film production company, a director and writer were permanent employees. That is why till 1950 there did not rise any need for an association of either directors or writers. When after 1950 producer Chimanlal Trivedi started the contract system in his production company, the old relationships between producers and directors began to crack. The director could no longer work with the writer of his choice nor could a writer offer his creation to the director of his liking. That was the reason why both of them felt it necessary to form independent associations and organisations of their own. (Girish 1980, 35)

Initially, the screenwriters' group functioned without an office. The music director Anil Biswas used to host *open house* meetings at his Matunga residence in Bombay where writers, screenwriters and other artistes would gather. The prominent attendees would include Mahesh Kaul, Narendra Sharma, Ramanand Sagar, Safdar Aah, Pt. Chandrashekhar, K. A. Abbas and Madhusudan. Discussions and deliberations at these gatherings made the screenwriters increasingly aware of their unsatisfactory working conditions in the new freelancing system.

> Talk over a cup of tea is said to be very creative. Sometimes, someone would read out something he had composed or written. Sometimes, the talk was general—about life and death, about politics, about the insecurities and indignities that sensitive people (writers especially) used to suffer in the film industry. (Abbas 1980, 27)

K. A. Abbas recalled how these informal meetings motivated some of the screenwriters to organise an association "with an office, elected office-bearers and members" (1980, 27). In 1950, a meeting of 150 screenwriters was organised in Shree Sound Studios in Dadar in central Bombay (Shimpi 1980, 69). It was decided that an association of screenwriters should be formed for collective bargaining with producers. A president, two vice-presidents, a general secretary and a treasurer were appointed, a constitution was drafted, and an executive committee was also formed. The Film Writers' Association first executive committee included Kamal Amrohi, Safdar Aah, Narendra Sharma, Inder Raj Anand, Arjun Dev Rashk and Ramanand Sagar. However, after the initial period of enthusiasm, the organisation quickly became inactive within one year due to the lack of office space and adequate funds.

20.3.2 The Revival of FWA

A few years later, the association was revived through the initiative of Ramanand Sagar. In 1954, a meeting was held in Bombay to reconstitute an association of screenwriters where K. A. Abbas, Ramanand Sagar, Krishan Chander, Hasrat Jaipuri, Shailendra, Indivar and C. L. Kavish were present. Lessons had been learned from previous efforts, and fundraising was now put high on the new association's agenda. Committees were appointed to conduct *mushaira* and *kavi sammelan* (Urdu and Hindi poetry recitals) for fund collections (see Fig. 20.3) and to organise awards for screenwriters. After multiple meetings, a new constitution was adopted, which stated that FWA membership would be open to all Bombay-based writers of film stories, screenplays, dialogue and lyrics "whose names have appeared on the screen or in a booklet of a picture at least once" (Shimpi 1980, 75). Film credits, therefore, became a pre-requisite for membership eligibility.

During the initial period of revival, the FWA meetings were sometimes held at Famous Studios in Mahalaxmi in south Bombay. However, without a fixed office space, FWA functioned mostly as an itinerant group. Mahendra Saral recalled how some members had once secretly held a meeting in a tutorial classroom near the Dadar railway station in central Bombay: "It was possible to hold the meeting only because the students of the tutorial class were given a holiday on Sunday" (1980, 59). Later the meeting place was moved to "a small room adjoining the *masjid*" next to Roop Tara Studios in Dadar (Saral 1980, 59). During the early years, the makeshift office was moved multiple times within Dadar, from Shree Sound Studios to Ranjit Studios.[10]

The pioneering and painstaking efforts of the first active members resulted in quickly increasing the membership of the organisation. Ramanand Sagar and Qamar Jalalabadi were at the forefront of this membership drive. Sagar's managerial efforts in bringing together "disparate elements, temperaments and egos" (Abbas 1980, 27) eventually led to his appointment as the first General Secretary of the organisation. Jalalabadi went from studio to studio with printed and cyclostyled membership forms in his *thaila* (bag) to register screenwriters: "The entire office of the Association was in a bag which I used to carry from studio to studio in an enrolment drive" (Jalalabadi 1980, 29).

The Bombay screenwriters' success in forming an association was not reported widely in Indian film magazines. *Filmindia* mostly reported any news about FWA in acerbic terms: "… the quality of our stories has not improved even 1%, notwithstanding so many 'progressives' in the (executive) committee" ("Film Writers" 1957). Only the periodical *Screen* covered the development of FWA during the 1950s in an unprejudiced manner. In an interview with *Screen*, the first General Secretary of FWA, Ramanand Sagar, discussed the difficult experiences of screenwriters whose stories would often be misleadingly rejected by producers and later plagiarised entirely or with

---

[10] As mentioned earlier, now the Screenwriters' Association office is in Andheri West.

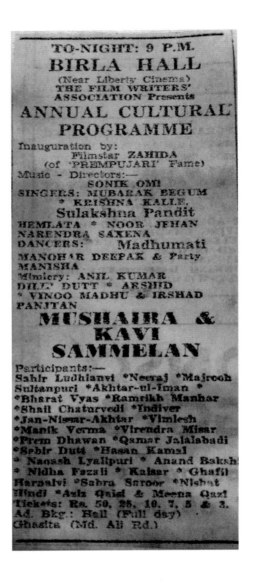

Fig. 20.3 Advertisement of poetry recital organised by FWA (*Source* author's own photograph of original, courtesy of SWA)

some modifications. Such malpractices necessitated sufficient legislative protection for screenwriters, especially when writers themselves perceived copyright laws to be vague. It was decided that FWA would maintain an official register in which copies of all stories, scripts and songs could be deposited to deter the plagiarist tendencies of fraudulent producers. Sagar also informed the readers how exploitative working conditions affected the quality of films, referring to how irregular payment of screenwriters lowered the quality of their stories and screenplays.

An average writer… 'chases' a producer for five months in a year to get work and six months to get his money. Thus there is only a month at his disposal for doing the script… If producers give writers ample time and all other facilities, India can easily look forward to better quality films. (Ramanand Sagar quoted in Shimpi 1980, 3)

FWA's tasks were difficult because of widespread precarity and corruption in the film industry under the freelancing star system. Elections were held regularly at FWA to institute different committees to protect the rights of vulnerable members. Funds were arranged by frequently organising poetry recitals by star lyricists. The activities of FWA were aimed at creating a democratic consciousness of both screenwriting craft and community under precarious and atomised conditions of work. Recreational events, such as a Christmas day picnic at the Jogeshwari caves in 1954, were also regularly organised.

Within a few years of its founding, FWA fought and won a number of cases against defaulting film producers. Film credits constituted a major bone of contention between screenwriters and producers as the latter would refuse to name screenwriters in publicity materials. Printed forms were regularly sent to producers pressing them to credit writers in film advertisements.

A long correspondence was started to persuade producers (many of them had to be forced) to recognize the individuality and importance of the Writer. Once that was established, the next step was to make the Government realize that a film had to be *written* before it was produced and directed. (Abbas 1980, 27–29)

FWA persistently lobbied for state support. The central government was approached to make state-sponsored cultural delegations, censor boards and award committees more inclusive of screenwriters. K. A. Abbas lobbied for screenwriters to be nominated for national awards, specifically for the story writer of the President's Gold Medal winning film to be honoured. FWA members declared their collective decision to not co-operate with producers who insisted on plagiarism and planned to institute scholarships for promising screenwriters to attend film schools abroad. As the pressure for state support mounted, FWA was reportedly assured "due help and cooperation by the Ministry of Information and Broadcasting" in the implementation of their plans ("Editorial Notes" 1954).

20.3.3   *Differences and Disagreements*

Although FWA members were largely committed to collective goals, archival records suggest that they also had strong disagreements on certain issues. In a multilingual context like the Bombay film industry, screenwriters would often specialise in different languages like Hindi, Urdu, English, Bengali and Punjabi. Linguistic competency became an issue of debate when K. A. Abbas proposed during a meeting that the FWA secretary ought to be proficient in English. The then secretary, Qamar Jalalabadi, felt rather insulted by this suggestion.

> The remark caused a storm in a tea cup. It evoked an angry rejoinder from the usually quiet and serious-minded Qamar Saheb, who said, "Is it being implied that I do not know English? And, please enlighten me as to why is it necessary to know English to carry out the work of the Film Writers' Association? Do we make films in English?" (Saral 1980, 59)

A screenwriters' union in a multilingual context was bound to harbour differences over language. One such conflict surfaced in 1970 when Sahir Ludhianvi, the then FWA President, was accused by Vrajendra Gaur of trying to impose the Urdu language[11] and the Nastaliq script[12] on other members of the organisation. A motion of no confidence was then passed against Ludhianvi, predominantly by the Hindi-language screenwriters of FWA ("Sahir Ludhianvi" 1970).

Like language, the political ideology of the organisation was also a contested subject. During the early years, FWA members had decided that prominent technicians, such as photographers, directors and recordists would be regularly invited to speak and discuss common issues. Eminent members of the association as well as distinguished public figures would also be invited to give talks at FWA. There were strong disagreements, however, on the issue of one such invitation. When some members proposed an invited talk by an American political writer who was visiting Bombay at the time, Mohinder Nath vehemently argued that FWA should not offer a platform to Americans. Pandit Sudarshan responded sharply: "Is ours an association of communists? Are we so brittle and impressionable as to be swept away by merely listening to a speech?" (Pandit Sudarshan as quoted in Saral 1980, 59). After much debate and discussion, the American writer was eventually invited to deliver a speech at FWA. The political differences of the Cold War in a non-aligned India were, however, evident in such ideologically inflected disagreements over the organisation's quotidian affairs.

---

[11] The subject of Bombay film industry's lingua franca has generated polarising debates since the coming of talkies in India in the early 1930s. Films made in Bombay (now Mumbai) have historically popularised the syncretic usage of Urdu and Hindi vocabularies and promoted secular cultural attitudes. However, Hindu majoritarians in India continue to deride Urdu as the language of Muslim minorities, often exaggerating the *national* dominance and superiority of the Hindi language in mainstream Indian cinema.

[12] The Urdu language is conventionally written in a Perso-Arabic script called *Nastaliq*, a cursive script that is read from right to left.

20.4 Writers as Workers

Most of the founding members of FWA were associated with anticolonial and Marxist cultural organisations such as the PWA (Progressive Writers' Association) and the IPTA (Indian People's Theatre Association). Despite the socialist writer Premchand's[13] disillusionment with the commercial constraints of screenwriting, the work of later Progressive writers such as K. A. Abbas and Sahir Ludhianvi in the film industry gradually aided in an extension of the radical literary sphere of the PWA and the IPTA through a conscious exploration of the possibilities of syncretic and socialist nation-building through film story (see Abbas 1955b) and dialogue (see Abbas 1955a). With their creative work in the film industry, the radical literary activism of several prominent FWA members was purposefully channelled into the mass attractions of commercial cinema. However, despite their progressive creative work across media, their cultural politics remained separated from labour politics. Drawing on Premchand's unsatisfactory screenwriting stint in Bombay, Debashree Mukherjee has briefly discussed how Progressive writers distanced their cultural work from conventional forms of labour: "The *mazdoor* (labourer) could only be the worker in the factory" (2020, 256).

It would be helpful to re-examine Premchand's insightful distinction between writers and labourers through the lens of creative labour and welfare activism. Scholars of creative industries have tried to bridge the divide between creativity and labour, and demystify different forms of cultural work from their romantic conceptions (Banks 2007; Caldwell 2008; Mayer 2011; Brouillette 2014). The focus on screenwriting as creative labour (Conor 2014) has further contested the binaries of the traditional understanding of writers as mental creators and workers as manual labourers.[14] However, the privileges of caste and class as well as the prejudices of literary erudition would often prevent Indian screenwriters from identifying themselves as workers. Even though screenwriters had officially come together as an association with collective interests, FWA members were long divided on the issue of registering as a labour union. The minutes of a meeting of the Organising Committee in 1955 state that "though the discussion was quite exhaustive, no final decision could be arrived at" (Shimpi 1980, 87). Like Premchand, for some FWA members, the writer could still not be a worker. It was, however, only a matter of time before the inevitable happened.

---

[13] Premchand (1880–1936) was an eminent writer of Hindi and Urdu novels and short stories. As a socialist intellectual and a pioneering literary figure, he was also the first president of the Progressive Writers' Association.

[14] As Bridget Conor has argued, "[f]ocusing on the particularities of this profession, a theory of screenwriting as creative labor requires a particular and malleable vocabulary. This vocabulary consists of a number of terms and traits that highlight contestations and contradictions—old and new, craft and creative, individualized and collaborative, industrial and invisible, marginal and standardized, atomized and unequal" (2014, 56).

> There are of course some writers who feel that a writer is too much an individual to be a member of a trade union. But in these days of collective bargaining and collective security, a writer cannot remain isolated. He has to join not only other writers to be in a position to have a code of conduct but also other workers in their struggle for better wages and other service conditions. (Sathe 1980, 55)

V. P. Sathe's clarion call for screenwriters to join the workers' struggle in trade union movements across post-Independent India resonates with Walter Benjamin's appeal to writers to join the class struggle as *intellectual workers*. Finally, in February 1960, the decision to run the association on trade union lines was taken in a general body meeting. In June of the same year, FWA was registered under the Trade Union Act of 1926. Unionisation was an important point of solidarity among Indian workers in different industries, whether it was an organised sector like the railways or an informal one such as the Bombay film industry. Screenwriters in Bombay, like other workers, were also concerned about precarious work, poverty, disability, health and housing problems, collective bargaining, minimum wage and so on. As the following sections will show, with the registration of FWA as a trade union, screenwriters established their solidarity with other workers through their demands for similar work and welfare rights.

20.4.1 *Supporting Precarious Writers*

The Finance Committee of FWA, first headed by Agha Jani Kashmiri, initially proposed the creation of a trust fund for disabled and indigent screenwriters. Some years later, a proposal was also made to set up a separate Benevolent Fund to support writers during hardship and distress. After a general body meeting in 1971, the fund was finally established with a target of Rs. 50,000, and Rs 1647 was collected on the meeting day itself ("Benevolent fund for writers" 1971) (see Fig. 20.4). The then General Secretary, Mohinder Nath, appealed to the more prosperous screenwriters to contribute generously to the Benevolent Fund, invoking the socialist vision of Prime Minister Indira Gandhi.

> We are quite aware and also happy to know that a few writers are well off. But the plight of the majority of writers is aweful (sic). For us, there is no pension, no gratuity, no provident fund, no medical aid, nothing to sustain us, when we are old, or without work or even disabled... We are waiting for the day, when the dream of our Prime Minister Smt. Indira Gandhi will become a reality and the capitalist era is transformed to socialist era. We know, the change will come. But it will take time. Till this change is ushered, we have to help ourselves. (Nath 1971, n.p.)

Fig. 20.4 Donations for Benevolent fund after an FWA meeting in 1971 (*Source* author's own photograph of original, courtesy of SWA)

20.4.2 Housing for Screenwriters

During the early 1970s, FWA approached the Government of Maharashtra for providing housing solutions to screenwriters belonging to a lower income group. In 1972, a Film Writers' Convention was organised where Inder Kumar Gujral, the then Union Minister for Housing, was invited as the chief guest (see Fig. 20.5). In his presidential address, Krishan Chander referred to screenwriters as "intellectual workers" who, like other film workers, did not have basic workers' rights because the Indian film industry did not fall under the jurisdiction of the Factories Act of 1948. Chander informed the chief guest and the audience that film writers did not belong to a fixed income group and, therefore, faced major housing problems:

> Many are forced to live in slums and shanty towns. I know of one writer who sleeps on a pavement. There was another one many years back who lived in a grave-yard because he had no other place to live. That writer died in the same grave-yard and his picture was published in many news-papers. (Krishan Chander, quoted in "Film writers demand" 1972)

Chander also revealed that the Government of Maharashtra had made housing provisions for Marathi writers in Kala Nagar, near Bandra, a coastal suburb in Bombay. However, the state officials discriminated against screenwriters for their choice of medium: "… they generally admit those writers who write books—not those who write films" ("Film writers demand" 1972). Chander demanded "a cheap but decent housing plan for our film writers not miles

Fig. 20.5 Inder Kumar Gujral (middle) and Krishan Chander (right) at the Film Writers' Convention in 1972 (*Source* author's own photograph of original, courtesy of SWA)

away from the City but in the nearing suburbs where Kala Nagar is placed" ("Film writers demand" 1972). Eventually, Maharashtra housing state officials allotted tenements for destitute screenwriters near Borivali in north-western Bombay. The Managing Committee of FWA formed the Film Writers' Cooperative Housing Society in the mid-1970s to facilitate the housing process (Fig. 20.5).

20.4.3 Settling Disputes

The Dispute Settlement Committee began functioning in July 1954, headed by Mahesh Kaul as its convener. Its main objective was to resolve creative and commercial conflicts between producers and screenwriters as well as among screenwriters. It was rare for a disagreement between two parties to arise in cases where a written agreement would exist. However, even though screenwriters were duly encouraged by FWA to formalise their oral agreement in writing, it was often the case that work on a film would start before a written contract had been drawn. If FWA's Dispute Settlement Committee could not resolve the issue, the case would be escalated to the Joint Dispute Settlement Committee of the Federation of Western India Cine Employees. In case a film producer decided to fight the dispute in court, FWA would defend its members through legal means. On several occasions, the courts eventually upheld decisions made by the Dispute Settlement Committee (see Mehrotra 1980).

20.4.4 Minimum Wage

From the mid-1950s, the Drafting Committee of FWA, under the leadership of Arjun Dev Rashk, began formulating standard contracts after discussions with the Indian Motion Picture Producers' Association (IMPPA) and the Film Producers' Guild of India (now the Producers Guild of India). FWA created four types of contracts in keeping with the different forms of screenwriting work in Indian cinema: (1) sole writer of the story, screenplay and dialogue, (2) screenplay writer, (3) dialogue writer and (4) lyricist. Their respective minimum wages were also included in these contracts after several meetings and discussions on the issue. Film producers, represented by the IMPPA, were initially opposed to the proposal of fixing minimum wages and argued that "it was purely a matter of contract between the parties concerned" (Shimpi 1980, 89). FWA, however, kept pressing the issue. In 1961, K. A. Abbas wrote to the IMPPA as well as individual producers about the minimum wages fixed by FWA—Rs. 2000 for story, Rs. 2500 for screenplay, Rs. 3000 for dialogues and Rs. 500 per song. These wages were ultimately accepted by the producers.

20.4.5 Copyright Activism

A decade after India's independence, the Copyright Act of 1957 was implemented.[15] The coming of the new copyright laws had coincided with the early years of FWA's formation. However, as the film composer and trade unionist M. B. Srinivasan recalled, most Indian screenwriters were "not aware even vaguely about the minimum rights that are assured for them under Indian Copyright Act, 1957" (1980, 37). Inevitably, FWA founders had to devise ways of educating fellow members about their rights. The existing copyright laws also presented a different set of challenges for screenwriters in India, especially film lyricists whose works generated significant revenue beyond the exhibition of films:

> What about all the subsequent exploitation of our works? What do we gain from such utilisation? What do we gain from gramophone discs issued of performances all over the world, of works into the creation of which we have spent our days and nights? (Srinivasan 1980, 37)

FWA members organised several meetings to negotiate with film producers in their fight against disc manufacturers to seize the rights of mechanical reproduction of their film music. Due to their persistent efforts, the Indian Performing Right Society (IPRS) was constituted in 1969, which continues

---

[15] The first copyright laws in India were enacted in 1847 during the colonial rule of the British East India Company. They were subsequently replaced by the Copyright Act of 1914, which was modelled on the Imperial Copyright Act of 1911 and included works of art and literature. The Copyright Act of 1957 constituted the first copyright laws passed in independent India. The Act has been amended six times till date, most recently in 2012.

to issue licences to music users and collects royalties from them on behalf of music directors and lyricists.

20.4.6 The Foundations for a Federation

The Liaison Committee of FWA, first convened by C. L. Kavish, was created to coordinate the functions of different FWA committees. Soon this committee went above and beyond its responsibilities and facilitated a dialogue among different film workers' associations in Bombay. In August 1954, C. L. Kavish wrote a letter to the presidents of other craft associations and invited them for a meeting to build solidarity and cooperation among the organisations. The letter was received positively, and a meeting was soon held at FWA's makeshift office in Famous Studios in Mahalaxmi. The idea for a joint Film Workers Federation was supported unanimously by different associations, such as Cine Junior Artistes Association, Society of Film Editors, Cine Dancers' Union, Association of Art Directors, Cine Musicians' Association, Western India Society of Cinematographers and Society of Audio Visual Engineers. Soon an appointed committee drafted a joint constitution that integrated the common goals and objectives enshrined in the respective constitutions of these organisations. It is worth mentioning that the Film Workers Federation was a precursor to the Federation of Western India Cine Employees (FWICE), which today includes 31 affiliate organisations and over 500,000 film workers in India. The seeds of this federation were arguably sown by members of the Film Writers' Association.

20.5 Conclusion

The COVID-19 pandemic has highlighted the casualisation of film work in Mumbai where thousands of daily-wage workers were left jobless when film production was discontinued over several months (see Srivastava 2020). Despite the individual contributions of stars and the collective efforts of producers and unions, such deplorable circumstances of insufficient income and aid forced a painful exodus of migrant film workers to their hometowns and villages. This chapter will hopefully serve as a reminder that media industries in India are not driven by their hyper-visible stars but their "invisible" workers (Mazumdar 2015).[16]

Histories of film trade unions constitute an invaluable archive of creative labour against the growing amnesia of welfare politics in the neoliberal era. This chapter has retraced the formation of the Film Writers' Association (now the Screenwriters' Association) in the immediate post-independence period of

---

[16] The relentless attacks on Bollywood by Hindutva right-wing forces as well as the determined disdain of cultural elites towards Hindi cinema overlook the fact that the film industry employs millions of cultural workers whose wages "generally compared favourably with those that could be earned by the same people doing similar kinds of work outside the film industry" (Thomas 2015, 200).

trade unionism in India, bringing to light an important history of creative labour and class struggle from the Global South. It contextualised the emergence of film trade unions in Bombay within global and local networks of labour activism. Further, it provided an account of the pioneering endeavours of screenwriters in instituting and sustaining the organisation. Finally, it detailed FWA's activities on issues of housing, poverty, disability, minimum wage and piracy. As writers increasingly imagined themselves as workers through a collective desire for stable and satisfactory conditions of work, unionisation helped in bridging the socio-cultural divide between creativity and labour. The history of FWA during the first decades of India's independence represents forgotten futures of work and welfare that ought to be remembered as an institutional refusal of precarious cultural work.

References

Abbas, Khwaja Ahmad. 1955a. "Dialogue and Dialogue Writers." In *Film Seminar Report*, 252–56. New Delhi: Sangeet Natak Akadami.

Abbas, Khwaja Ahmad. 1955b. "The Importance and Significance of a Good Film Story—Its Power with the Masses." In *Film Seminar Report*, 241–47. New Delhi: Sangeet Natak Akadami.

Abbas, Khwaja Ahmad. 1980. "The 'cat' came out of the bag." In *Silver Jubilee Commemorative Volume*, edited by Pandit Shimpi, 27–28. Bombay: The Film Writers' Association.

Banks, Mark. 2007. *The Politics of Cultural Work*. Basingstoke UK: Palgrave Macmillan.

Banks, Miranda J. 2015. *The Writers: A History of American Screenwriters and Their Guild*. New Brunswick NJ: Rutgers University Press.

Banks, Miranda J., and David Hesmondhalgh. 2016. Internationalizing Labor Activism: Building Solidarity among Writers' Guilds. In *Precarious Creativity: Global Media, Local Labor*, ed. M. Curtin and K. Sanson, 267–280. Berkeley CA: University of California Press.

Bardhan, A. B. 1995. *Outline history of All Indian Trade Union Congress*. New Delhi: AITUC.

Barnouw, Erik, and Subrahmanyam Krishnaswamy. 1963. *Indian Film*. New York: Columbia University Press.

"Benevolent fund for writers." 1971. *Film Industry*, n. p., 9 August.

Benjamin, Walter. 1998 [1966]. "The Author as Producer." In *Understanding Brecht*. Trans. A. Bostock. 85–103. London: Verso.

Berlant, Lauren. 2011. *Cruel Optimism*. Durham nc: Duke University Press.

Bordwell, David, Janet Staiger, and Kristin Thompson. 1985. *The Classical Hollywood Cinema: Film Style and Mode of Production to 1960*. New York: Columbia University Press.

Brouillette, Sarah. 2014. *Literature and the Creative Economy*. Stanford ca: Stanford University Press.

Burrows, Jon. 2018. "'Certificated Operators' versus 'Handle-Turners': The British Film Industry's First Trade Union." *Journal of British Cinema and Television* 1 (1): 73–93.

Caldwell, John T. 2008. *Production Culture: Industrial Reflexivity and Critical Practice in Film and Television*. Durham NC: Duke University Press.
Chanan, Michael. 1976. *Labour Power in the British Film Industry*. London: BFI.
Chanana, Opender. 2011. *The Missing 3 in Bollywood: Safety, Security, Shelter*. Nyon, Switzerland: UNI Global Union.
Conor, Bridget. 2014. *Screenwriting: Creative Labor and Professional Practice*. London: Routledge.
Doellgast, Virginia L., Nathan Lillie, and Valeria Pulignano, eds. 2018. *Reconstructing Solidarity: Labour Unions, Precarious Work, and the Politics of Institutional Change in Europe*. New York: Oxford University Press.
"Editorial Notes." 1954. *Filmfare*, 9 March, 3.
Elsaesser, Thomas. 2019. "The (Re-)Turn to Non-Linear Storytelling: Time Travel and Looped Narratives." Keynote address presented at the annual conference of the Screenwriting Research Network, Porto, Portugal, 12–14 September.
"Film writers demand formation of Film Council." 1972. *Film Industry*, 23 March, 6.
"Film Writers." 1957. *Filmindia*, 1 February, 56.
Galt, Frances. 2020. *Women's Activism Behind the Screens: Trade Unions and Gender Inequality in the British Film and Television Industries*. Bristol: Bristol University Press.
Girish, Pandit. 1980. "FWA—Growth and development." In *Silver Jubilee Commemorative Volume*, edited by Pandit Shimpi, 35–36. Bombay: The Film Writers' Association.
Harvey, David. 2005. *A Brief History of Neoliberalism*. Oxford: Oxford University Press.
Hensman, Rohini. 2011. *Workers, Unions, and Global Capitalism: Lessons from India*. New York: Columbia University Press.
Hensman, Rohini, and Jairus Banaji. 1998. "A short history of the employees' unions in Bombay, 1947–1991." Paper presented at the 1st conference of the Association of Indian Labour Historians (AILH), New Delhi. https://eprints.soas.ac.uk/17056/1/Employees%20unions.pdf. Accessed 5 August 2022.
Horne, Gerald. 2001. *Class Struggle in Hollywood, 1930–1950: Moguls, Mobsters, Stars, Reds, and Trade Unionists*. Austin: University of Texas Press.
Jalalabadi, Qamar. 1980. "Our Association." In *Silver Jubilee Commemorative Volume*, edited by Pandit Shimpi, 29–30. Bombay: The Film Writers' Association.
Kaur, Pawanpreet. 2020. "'If Globalization Is Happening, It Should Work Both Ways': Race, Labor, and Resistance among Bollywood's Stunt Workers." *Media Industries* 7 (1): 111–125.
Mannil, Bindu M. 2020. "The Gendered Film Worker: Women on Cinema Collective, Intimate Publics and the Politics of Labour." *Studies in South Asian Film & Media* 11 (2): 191–207.
Mayer, Vicki. 2011. *Below the Line: Producers and Production Studies in the New Television Economy*. Durham NC: Duke University Press.
Mazumdar, Ranjani. 2015. "'Invisible Work' in the Indian Media Industries." *Media Industries* 1 (3): 26–31.
McKercher, Catherine, and Vincent Mosco. 2006–2007. "Divided They Stand: Hollywood Unions in the Onformation Age." *Work Organisation, Labour & Globalisation* 11: 130–43.

McRobbie, Angela. 2016. *Be Creative: Making a Living in the New Culture Industries*. Cambridge: Polity.
Mehrotra, Vishnu. 1980. "Pattern of dispute settlement." In *Silver Jubilee Commemorative Volume*, edited by Pandit Shimpi, 41–46. Bombay: The Film Writers' Association.
Mini, Darshana S. 2020. "Cinema and the Mask of Capital: Labour debates in the Malayalam Film Industry." *Studies in South Asian Film & Media* 11 (2): 173–189.
Mukherjee, Debashree. 2020. *Bombay Hustle: Making Movies in a Colonial City*. New York: Columbia University Press.
Nath, Mohinder. 1971. *An Appeal: Writer's Benevolent Fund*. Bombay: n. p.
Pandey, Kamlesh. n. d. *Film Writers Association: The Diamond Years*. SWA India. https://www.swaindia.org/history.php#1. Accessed 5 August 2022.
Prasad, Madhava M. 1998. *Ideology of the Hindi Film*. New Delhi: Oxford University Press.
Prindle, David F. 1988. *The Politics of Glamour: Ideology and Democracy in the Screen Actors Guild*. Madison wi: The University of Wisconsin Press.
"Sahir Ludhianvi ke virudh avishwas prastav." 1970. *Madhuri*, 10 July, 27.
Saral, Mahendra. 1980. "Down memory lane." In *Silver Jubilee Commemorative Volume*, edited by Pandit Shimpi, 59–60. Bombay: The Film Writers' Association.
Sathe, V. P. 1980. "FWA should provide legal aid in copyright disputes." In *Silver Jubilee Commemorative Volume*, edited by Pandit Shimpi, 55–58. Bombay: The Film Writers' Association.
Sherlock, Stephen. 2001. "Labour and the remaking of Bombay." In *Organising Labour in Globalising Asia*, ed. Jane Hutchison and Andrew Brown, 152–172. New York: Routledge.
Shimpi, Pandit. 1980. FWA—Surveying The Silver Years. In *Silver Jubilee Commemorative Volume*, edited by Pandit Shimpi, 69–94. Bombay: The Film Writers' Association.
Sinha, P. R. N., Indu Balha Sinha, and Seema Priyadarshini Shekhar. 2006. *Industrial Relations, Trade Unions, and Labour Legislation*. New Delhi: Pearson Education.
Srinivasan, Manamadurai Balakrishnan. 1980. "Copyright." In *Silver Jubilee Commemorative Volume*, edited by Pandit Shimpi, 37–40. Bombay: The Film Writers' Association.
Srivastava, Roli. 2020. "Coronavirus Halts Bollywood Filming, Puts Spotlight on Casual Workers." *Reuters*, 23 March. https://www.reuters.com/article/health-coronavirus-bollywood-idUKL8N2BD00E. Accessed 5 June 2023.
Standing, Guy. 2011. *The Precariat: The New Dangerous Class*. London: Bloomsbury.
Thomas, Rosie. 2015. *Bombay Before Bollywood: Film City Fantasies*. Delhi: Orient BlackSwan.
Vasudevan, Ravi. 1991. "The Cultural Space of a Film Narrative: Interpreting *Kismet* (Bombay Talkies, 1943)." *The Indian Economic and Social History Review* 28 (2): 171–185.
Yüksel, Hasan. 2020. "The Urbanization of Labor and Its Struggle for Unionism in Turkish Cinema." *Cinej Cinema Journal* 8 (2): 151–194.

CHAPTER 21

The Evolving Depictions of Black South Africans in the Post-Apartheid Screenwriting Tradition

Ziphozakhe Hlobo and Mpumelelo Skosana

21.1 Introduction

The on-screen depictions of Black South Africans have come a long way since the days of Apartheid. An analysis of how they have gradually evolved, as South African society has, is long overdue. Unlike in some other regions of the globe, cinema is only a small part of the South African screenwriting story. Hence, a project of analysing these depictions is incomplete without a keen focus on television. Television has always been a powerful communication medium, both globally and in South Africa. In South Africa's recent past, the medium occupied an important space in society because of the nature of the Apartheid system, as a form of capitalism premised on the super-exploitation of black labour and the exclusion of black South Africans from the country's public life. As a de facto authoritarian regime, social control was a significant component of the Apartheid strategy. Media, in general, and television, in particular, were useful platforms to achieve this end (Evans 2012, 294). Not only did South Africa receive television late, but it was characterised by the near monopoly of the South African Broadcasting Corporation (SABC) (Cowell 1984). Before 1993, the SABC operated primarily as a state broadcaster that overwhelmingly

---

Z. Hlobo (✉) · M. Skosana
Kwa-Zulu Natal Film Commission, Durban, South Africa
e-mail: ziphozakhe.hlobo@gmail.com

M. Skosana (✉)
FTI Consulting, Johannesburg, South Africa
e-mail: lelo.skosana@gmail.com

served the interests of the Apartheid government, not South African society's interests (Bevan 2009, 18). This dominance of the Apartheid government on the South African media landscape meant that their views, as expressed on SABC television, played a significant role in determining how black people ultimately perceived themselves.

After enduring years of legalised and state-sponsored racism throughout Apartheid, black South Africans finally emerged from the shadows of public life as they began the journey from second-class citizens to full members of South Africa's fledgling democracy. Corresponding with this transition, the way that screenwriters wrote black people for television kept pace with the changing national character, resulting in ever-evolving depictions of black South Africans.

During Apartheid, television depictions of black people could generally be described as keeping in line with the official status of black South Africans as marginalised people that were not citizens of South Africa but rather citizens of their respective homelands or Bantustans. However, as the political pressure mounted on the Apartheid government and the morally reprehensible system began to subside, the growing black voice slowly started taking shape, in the form of more progressive depictions of black people in television screenwriting.

Before discussing the evolution of the depictions, it is essential to briefly outline the audio-visual industry's racialised nature in South Africa. Production companies were almost exclusively white, with all the critical roles performed by white South Africans to the exclusion of all other races. So, the story of the evolving depictions of black South Africans is also a story of the emergence of black production companies, staffed with black writers, directors and producers and their increasing prominence, in line with more textured and nuanced depictions as these new companies came to the fore.

The evolution of the depictions can be informally placed in various phases, differentiated from each other by the distinct character of the characterisations and their close relationship with the corresponding journey that black people were on from marginalised to recognised and equal to their compatriots. The dying days of Apartheid, a period that corresponds with the era of democratic negotiations for a new constitutional order, was characterised by black people finally being incorporated in the national South African conversation and black characters taking more responsibility on screen. While not prominent, their roles began showing their presence as people in the national dialogue and set a platform for the following eras.

In addition to seeing more black people on screen, the dying days' phase of South Africa progressively moved more black South Africans from the prior invisibility to a more prominent role. All the while, these black characters appeared on screen with Apartheid in the background—their real-life marginalisation being ignored in almost all their depictions. While the marginalisation was not an issue directly tackled in screenwriting, the context in which these characters appeared and the languages the screenplays were written in very much illustrated the Apartheid social relations. A key example is S'dumo from *S'gudi S'naysi* (*It's Good, It's Nice*) (1986–1993), an unemployed black South African overwhelmed with debt and attempting to make ends meet in a Gauteng township with limited economic opportunities. This depiction is underscored by the problematic reality it depicts both on and off screen.

As it became increasingly clear that majority rule was to replace the oppressive Apartheid regime, screenwriting depictions of black people began to reflect the overwhelmingly hopeful disposition of the anticipated change. These sets of depictions are characterised as hope. The African National Congress (ANC), led by their charismatic President at the time, Nelson Mandela, ushered in the *Rainbow Nation*. However, much of what the new society was set to look like was undetermined, leaving enormous scope for anticipation and interpretation. Partly to fill this void, black characters were urban and affluent, like the Moroka family in *Generations* (1993–2014). Depictions of successful black people were not entirely new to South Africa,[1] as some American television shows like *The Cosby Show* (1984–1992) had begun to purposefully depict black people in a more prosperous and *normal* manner, yet the depiction of black South African people as being anything more than subservient to white people was novel. In this way, these depictions played an essential role in anticipating and seeking to influence the new role of black people in South Africa.

Following on from the nation's formative years, the optimistic depictions gradually gave way to depictions that understood that as much as South African society was changing, a large amount remained the same—including the continued disadvantage of black people. Screenwriting in this phase turned its focus to more youthful depictions of children and young adult black South Africans, acknowledging that outcomes were not likely to change for the larger older adult cohort of black people. In this phase, young black characters are given a sense of agency and seek to do the hard work of changing the character of their environment and social relations.

These youthful depictions included showcasing the experience of young adults dealing with the complex issues that define their identity, be it their cultural backgrounds like Ndoda from *Umthunzi Wentaba* (*The Mountain's Shadow*, 2007) or sexual orientation as in the case of Beth from *Society* (2007–2010). Another key feature of this period is that it takes place with the HIV/AIDS pandemic raging in the backdrop, and this crisis for South Africa finds its way into screenplays of the era, often with the intent to positively influence behaviour with "socially desirable behaviours from models—in this case, fictional characters—depicted in a television series" (Dlamini 2012, 27).

---

[1] Using the *Generations* soapie as her particular focus, Tager (2010) explores how the socio-political change in South Africa contributed to reshaping representations of collective and individual aspirations of social mobility in popular media discourses, and also among the consumers of that media.

As black South Africans increasingly felt a sense of dissatisfaction with their continued poverty and underdevelopment under the democratic dispensation, significant changes were seen in screenwriting. The hopeful tone, which was already in decline, gets wholly replaced with a more sombre and realistic style.

This dissatisfaction necessarily called for a re-emergence of agency, seen in how South African screenwriters have claimed their place in the world through shows like *The Republic* (2019–2021), *Queen Sono* (2020) and other international hits. As reflective as they are, the characters in these shows are not resigned to the status quo, as can be seen in the dangerous adventures of *Queen Sono*, who is adamant about finding her mother's killer(s). The commentary made by these shows is that black South Africans certainly have a place in the world and do not have to give in to their external limitations.

The objectives of this chapter are to describe and provide an understanding of the features of South African television screenplays as well as to facilitate a discussion on how the on-screen roles of black people have evolved and continue to do so. It is valuable to progress sequentially through the various periods and examine the prevailing characteristics of each period as a critical building block to developing an understanding of the mutual interdependence of how black South Africans have been depicted and how these depictions influenced both their cultural identity and political reality.

21.2 Depictions

In assessing the extent of the role screenwriting had in determining South African national development, a useful starting point is to get an appropriate sense of the character of the South African television and film culture. Specifically, it is helpful to ask whether South Africa does, in fact, have a national on-screen (TV and film) tradition, and if so, what is it? The answer to this question helps us situate the evolving depictions of black South Africans in the broader context of the national film and television industry, as an interdependent understanding of both the depictions—as brought to the screen by the screenwriters—and the general development of the South African audio-visual industry is required.[2] Jacqueline Maingard argues that "since cinema is a medium that has the ability both to shape and reflect our perceptions, how it visualizes identities has crucial significance for our citizenship and nationhood" (2007, 3).

Addressing the issue of a potential national cinema, Maingard (2007) further argues that a [South African] national cinema and television tradition does not currently exist. She argues that the biggest obstacle in developing a national cinema is the need to transcend the singularised categorisations of identity enforced by Apartheid, noting that the development of a national film

---

[2] For more on the existence and/or usefulness of a national film culture in South Africa, with a distinct focus on cinema, see Ebrahim and Ellapen (2018). This paper also has the post-apartheid period as its focus. Also useful is Botha (2007). Flanery (2009) gives a helpful overview of the work done in trying to determine this. Saks's contribution (2001) is also extremely valuable.

tradition was impeded by the nature of the oppressive system that determined social relations in the country. So, the conclusion drawn is that a national television or cinema doesn't exist or, if it does, is only of limited use because of the compartmentalised nature of the South African national identity.[3]

In a rigorous attempt to transcend the singularised categorisations that dominated the country and the national cinema tradition, the SABC started contemplating a path to see scripts about black people written and influenced by black creatives taking more prominence over the previously dominant white screenwriters, thereby incorporating more textured depictions of black South Africans. Under the influence of Head of Drama Kethiwe Ngcobo (2004–2011), the SABC, in partnership with the National Film and Video Foundation, adopted an explicit mandate of underwriting a screenwriting tradition that centred the black experience in a more nuanced and complex manner, and not through a linear, pedagogical white gaze as it had been done before. Despite these attempts, the fractured nature of South African screenwriting persisted. The lack of success in developing a unified national television culture is an essential feature in understanding how on-screen depictions of black South Africans have evolved in the post-Apartheid era.

21.3 The Dying Days of Apartheid

The screenwriting during the final phase of Apartheid, which roughly corresponds with the years 1985–1993, can be understood as a period initially dominated by the adaptations of books and existing written material into television content for black South African audiences, then later, the appearance of original screenplays focused on the lives of black South Africans. Throughout Apartheid, black characters appeared on South African screens as essentially background figures in the white parts of South Africa.

While this was generally the case, a possible exception could be the films produced under the so-called B Scheme. These films constituted an emergent *black film industry* in Apartheid South Africa—one that emerged entirely due to a differential state subsidy for film production introduced in 1972–1973. Even though these films were ostensibly black, in that they had majority African casts, were primarily in African languages and were intended for a mass African audience, white South Africans nonetheless produced these films with Africans playing minor roles as actors and in some instances as crew, and rare examples of Africans directing these films as employees of white-owned production companies (Paleker 2010, 93). Furthermore, despite the apartheid government playing no direct role in the writing or producing these films, Gairoonisa Paleker argues that "white individuals assumed surrogate roles in the articulation and perpetuation of apartheid ideology" (2010, 102). So, even within this supposed Black film industry, Africans had minimal opportunity or

---

[3] For more on the representation of this difficult identity especially as it relates to the production of post-apartheid, South African cinema. See Treffry-Goatley (2010).

power to represent themselves.[4] Where this had been possible, it was within the ideological and political boundaries set by the apartheid government (Paleker 2010, 2), albeit enforced by private citizens. Petr Szczepanik points out that authoritarian governments have the option of censoring produced output or dominating the production process to manipulate its outcomes (2013, 73): the Apartheid government clearly preferred the latter.

The shows that will be spotlighted in the first phase of black South African depictions in the post-apartheid era are illustrative of these general trends. These shows include *S'gudi S'naysi* (*It's Good, It's Nice*), written by Roberta Durrant, and *Ingqumbo yeminyaya* (*The Wrath of the Ancestors*, 1991) written by Harry Hofmeyer and Joyce Ndamase.

S'gudi S'naysi—whose title means "It's good, it's nice", a colloquial way of responding positively to the question of how are you—was a television sitcom created by Roberta Durrant, produced by her production company Penguin Films; and was made up of 78 half-hour episodes in six seasons running from 1986 to 1993.

The show chronicles the adventures of an unemployed township man (S'dumo) renting a room from a widowed woman landlord (Sis' May) who enjoys a rich social life. The show is set in an entirely township setting. Townships in South Africa are defined as the peri-urban areas designated under apartheid legislation for exclusive occupation by people classified as blacks, coloureds and Indians. Importantly to note, townships have a unique and distinct history, which has had a direct impact on the socioeconomic status of these areas and how people perceive and operate within them (Donaldson 2014, 1).

The humour in the sitcom is created by Sdumo's attempts to get money to pay for his lodging and debts. The show was incredibly popular and consistently achieved high ratings. While ground-breaking in its complete focus on a township context, the depiction of black South Africans in the *S'gudi S'naysi* universe is primarily one that aligns with their social positioning in Apartheid. Almost all the characters have their entire lives in the township and don't have the desire to be part of the broader South African society or economy. The humour is also premised on the characters' identities as Africans in the Apartheid system—a key example of this is the trouble S'dumo has in finding a job and a legitimate place to stay—in line with the employment and residential restrictions of the Apartheid system.

The main contribution to *S'gudi S'naysi* made by the Penguin Films team led by Roberta Durrant was sensitising and familiarising South African audiences to life in the township by showcasing life in it for the first time on television. Despite reinforcing some potentially problematic stereotypes

---

[4] Of interest, Punyanunt-Carter (2008) examines the feedback loop between on-screen representations and real-life perceptions of audiences, outside of the media portrayals. Her study focuses on African American representations but provides great insight on how the interplay between reality and media portrayals.

about township dwellers, the show was pivotal for South African screenwriting because it took an in-depth look at people who had been previously marginalised and vastly underrepresented on screen, validating the yet untested question of whether the township (as a predominantly black setting) is a suitable setting for a television show and worth depicting to a South African audience. In this regard, the show was a significant step forward in the journey of black people taking on more of a presence on South African screens and influencing how black people understood their experience in South Africa.

Despite the positive role that showcasing the township had in contributing to the South African national screenwriting tradition, there were considerable limitations to the screenwriting team's depictions of black South Africans in *S'gudi S'naysi*. While the writing credit goes to Roberta Durrant, the entire series is shot and recorded in isiZulu, a language that Ms Durrant cannot speak or write in. The problem of a head writer that cannot speak the language of the production has persisted for a long time in the South African screenwriting context, where there are eleven official languages. These head writers have mostly been white people who do not speak the African languages and that presents some significant concerns about the scriptwriting process. Writing involves understanding the relationship between language and culture, something Frantz Fanon best theorises in the first chapter of his book, *Black Skin, White Masks* (1970). According to Fanon, language is the home in which cultural identity resides, so, to speak any language is to assume its culture (1970, 17). Unfortunately, Durrant does not speak or write in IsiZulu even though *S'gudi S'naysi* is about people of the Zulu culture, meaning, the black story she is telling in her native tongue (which is translated for the production) is diluted by her cultural nuances. The conception of the character bible is questionable because their indigenous language is missing. In essence what Durrant and others alike did was conceive characters as seen from their white gaze, consequently telling black actors what it looks, and sounds like to be black.

Moving to a very different set of depictions contained in the *Ingqumbo Yeminyanya* (*The Wrath of the Ancestors*), first aired on SABC in 1991, a screen adaptation of A.C. Jordan's classic novel in isiXhosa, originally published in 1940 by Lovedale Press. The show showcases the isiXhosa culture of the Mpondomise tribe. The story is set in the outskirts of the Eastern Cape Province and focuses on Zwelinzima, a young missionary-educated Mpondomise prince who reluctantly and prematurely leaves the University of Fort Hare to go back to the land of his ancestors to take his place as king of the Mpondomise. The story's central conflict comes from the explosive clash between the Western-educated Prince's ideas and the traditional viewpoints held by the people he has come back to lead. Tension mounts in the story because neither group yields, each wanting to exert their will on the other. This leads to the tragic end of Zwelinzima's reign.

As a primarily rural story, this depiction of black South Africans differed from the peri-urban or township context of *S'gudi S'naysi*. The source material for the show was a literary novel, which, much like other post-colonial novels, tells the story of the coming together of Western culture and African traditional beliefs.[5] Narratives like these focused on the *outcast* who had to assimilate to missionary or Western ways, but when they were back to their ancestral home or original context, they had to rid themselves of missionary influence. Thus, A.C. Jordan was curious about this negotiation or dual existence the black person experienced in these two very different worlds, with the only outcome foreseeable being a collision. Harry Hofmeyer and Joyce Ndamase, the screenwriters of the dramatisation, downplay the internal conflict and emphasise and foreground the external conflict between Zwelinzima and the Amapondomise people.

There are two types of conflict in the story and the first one appears in Linda Kwatsha's (1995) psychoanalysis of the characters. She finds that Zwelinzima's inner conflict stems from separation anxiety, abandonment, and neglect. She argues that being separated from Amampondomise at such a young age "results in an inner conflict which develops to a change of personality. He loses his identity and drifts into a state of uncertainty" (Kwatsha 1995, 66). The second conflict is one that comes from a culture that is rejecting missionary schools. Zwelinzima, who has a stake in both institutions, is at the centre of the conflict and the deeper he goes into Western education, the more the traditional ways seem irrelevant. These two conflicts lead to the question of which medium of the two stories offers a deeper dive into the characters. Thomas Leitch (2003) argues that it is not necessarily true that novels create more complex characters than movies and offer more immediate and complete access to characters' psychological state. Instead, in each medium, readers/audiences are encouraged to fill in different gaps, where novels offer a deeper access into a character's thoughts, films focus on dialogue and behaviour to shed light into a character's psychology. For instance, "…few moviegoers read screenplays for pleasure—not because screenplays have no gaps (they specify many fewer details than either the literary text they are based on or the movies that are based on them), but because their gaps are designed to be filled once and for all by the cast and crew" (Leitch 2003, 159). Using this perspective, we see that in the *Ingqumbo Yeminyanya* novel we can devour the complexity of the story's central conflict from the author's description of Zwelinzima's inner conflict, whereas how we appreciate this conflict in the series through all the actions of all the characters as well as the visual representations of the world of the story.

Therefore, from both mediums, the ultimate message was clear; traditional beliefs could not coexist with Western ways; one would have to choose. This

---

[5] For a complete review of A.C. Jordan's Xhosa novel *Ingqumbo Yeminyanya* (1940), see Opland (1990). He draws out themes that are fairly widespread in contemporaneous works of African writers.

identity crisis or tension between the *traditional* and *Western* is a theme that repeats itself in the screenwriting of the post-apartheid period, as black South Africans negotiate their reality of integrating in the broader society and away from their isolated Apartheid identities. Consequently, this depiction suggests that Africans would find it difficult not to stay in their traditional mindsets foreshadowing a conflict, as they increasingly experienced the Western world.

Therefore, the two essential features of screenwriting in this era are the dominant role played by white head writers and their limited ability to understand the depth of the black experience as well as the introduction of the tension between the traditional and Western worlds for black South Africans as a narrative device.[6] Illustratively, the two shows analysed in this era highlight the various contexts in which black people lived in South Africa and showcased them on South African screens for the first time. These depictions, however, suffered the limitation of being descriptions of black people within their Apartheid identities, a stark contrast to the new era of hope which was glimmering in the horizon of screenwriting.

21.4 A Hopeful Nation

South African democracy was ushered in through the 1993 Interim Constitution, drawn up through negotiations among various political parties, culminating in the country's first non-racial election in 1994. All South Africans above the age of 18 were able to cast their vote for the first time on 27 April 1994 to mark the end of apartheid rule and establish a new Constitutional order. The South African government had a massive task to educate black people—because they had not been allowed to vote and were left to experience many social ills in their communities without much intervention. It must be noted that such a task was mammoth because educational programming at the SABC had been geared to a younger audience, as is the case even today. Considering this, shows like *Khululeka* (*Be Free*, 1994–2008) and *Soul City* (1994–2015) emerged as pioneer educational programmes for the SABC targeting the adult black audiences. Situational comedies like *Suburban Bliss* (1996) as well as shows like *Generations* and *Isidingo: The Need* (1998–2020) pioneered the soap opera (soapie) genre even though a screenwriting culture was not systematised yet. There had been no school specifically dedicated to training aspiring practitioners in this industry until in 1994 when the Africa Film Drama Art (AFDA), a technical private Higher Education institution that offers courses in film, television and performance, was founded by Garth Holmes, Bata Passchier and Deon Opperman.

A defining feature of this era, which roughly corresponds with the years 1994–1999, was the number of new black shows broadcasted. There were significantly more shows with black characters in black worlds than the dying

---

[6] This tension, between the tradition African experience and the increasingly westernising world, is something that becomes a feature of all subsequent eras, albeit in varying forms.

days' phase. However, the era is also characterised by excessively optimistic depictions of the kind of place South Africa was becoming, whether it was the educational shows that overestimated the impact they could achieve or the soapies that represented their black characters with almost vulgar expressions of wealth or the unrealistically harmonious race relations in the situational comedies.

To better understand where film and television were in South Africa around this era, we can look at two significant reports: "The White Paper on Arts, Culture and Heritage: All Our Legacies, Our Common future" by The Department of Arts, Culture, Science And Technology (1996) and "A Strategy for Realising the Potential of the Cultural Industries" (1998). Both were prepared by Creative South Africa for the Department of Arts, Culture, Science and Technology. Although one was submitted and published a few years after South Africa's transition to democracy, it remains a critical document of findings collected when the atmosphere was hopeful. For example, under the Film and Television section, it was found that the industry still experienced a lack of audience development for cinema but that television programmes had a large domestic audience (Creative South Africa 1998). This sheds light on why the South African government saw it fit to use television as the primary medium to prepare the masses for the huge change that was to come politically from the dawn of democracy.

Focusing on the *Soul City* television series, whose screenwriting is uncredited but was created by Soul City Institute for Justice, whose "vision is for a just society in which young women and girls and the communities they live in have the health and wellbeing to grow, flourish, and reach their full potential" (Soul City Institute for Social Justice). So, to play their envisaged role of educating adult black audiences, the writers created a fictitious township called Soul City. Most of the action took place in the characters' homes and at the Soul City Hospital. The key theme from *Soul City* was the suggestion that black people have the agency to address their social ills. Each episode focused on a single topic, usually a social ill that dovetailed with the rest of the work of the Soul City Institute for Justice, which included pamphlets and radio dramas and other educational media channels. In particular, the television shows built characters that interacted with problems and used their agency to solve them.

When we look at the *Soul City* narrative through Joseph Campbell's theory of the hero's journey (described in 1949 in his book, *The Hero with a Thousand Faces*) which "describes the stages of the transformation that heroes share" (Sonnenburg and Runco 2017, 3), we can understand the narrative structure employed by the educational dramas of the time. *Soul City* season 1 takes the hero through a circular journey of learning about infant health and then applying the knowledge. Nonceba, our hero, in this instance, tragically loses her child to dehydration but takes the necessary steps to learn about infant health from the soul city hospital and raises awareness of challenges raising infants to the broader community. The season ends with her applying these lessons to her new-born child. This structure is repeated in educational shows like *Khululeka*, where a character undergoes the transformation of being uninformed, to be the informed "hero" of their community.

In contrast, the soapies were more of an escape from the harsh reality that black people were still enduring, as they attempted to showcase black South Africans advancing in society, depicting black people who were owners of businesses, with luxurious houses and significant amounts of money. The Moroka family in *Generations, a show written by various screenwriters but created by Mfundi Vundla,* was the epitome of this. The show's visual language was flashy and glossy, replicating the exaggerated opulence of American Soapies such as *Days of Our Lives,* where the gigantic houses, wardrobes and offices were as much characters as any of the cast were. However, the central *Generations* storyline sought to bring blacks, coloureds, whites and Indians together—imagining a world where these people lived in harmony and where the business owners and company executives were black people (in contrast to the *actual* situation in South Africa at the time). As an example, early in the show, a prominent black advertising professional hires a white assistant, a dynamic that is still rare in South Africa, even in the 2020s. Additionally, the show's aesthetic look and feel demonstrate the importance of the location, colourful costume, make-up, set, music, colour pallets and shooting style to the writing team. The aesthetic is its own character throughout the show, and the ad agency industry profiled in the soapie was a life-changing aspirational depiction for black people who had been previously allowed limited professions in Apartheid South Africa.

However, after the euphoric high that came about with the change in society and the introduction of democracy, the mood in the country slowly started to sour. Political freedom did not coincide with the *Generations* economic equality that was the ultimate aspiration of the economically excluded majority. Important to note that the soapie over the years moved away from its initial visual treatment and storyline to contain more discontent and township depictions of black characters. This discontent would come to characterise a new era of screenplay depictions of black South Africans led by a stronger focus on the black South African youth. Shows like *Yizo Yizo (It Is the Way It Is,* 1999–2004), with various writers but created by Teboho Mahlatsi and Angus Gibson and *Soul Buddiez* (2000–2011) again with various writers but created by the Soul City Institute for Health and Development Communication and SABC Education in collaboration with the Department of Education, both placed children's characters in the spotlight. Even though the dying days and the hopeful era had an increasing number of black characters on screen, a significant limitation was the fact that the screenwriting teams were still predominantly white, limiting the depth of portrayals of black South Africans; this was set to change in the next era of the youthful renaissance. Another element of the hopeful era's screenwriting was the setting of stories in a South Africa that was incredibly idealistic in its racial integration and harmony and depicting a level of economic prosperity for black South Africans that is yet to be achieved in contemporary South Africa.

21.5 A Youthful Renaissance

Representation in the industry started coming into sharper focus at the end of the 1990s, with the lack of black people behind the scenes becoming a pressing concern. The Department of Arts, Culture, Science and Technology's report found "[…] poor representativity in the industry: the production industry is still predominantly white and male-dominated" (Creative South Africa 1998, 22). This concern was also highlighted by Ngcobo (2021), who emphasised the shortage of skilled black South African filmmakers who could write, direct and produce for the SABC (and the broader industry) when she joined the broadcaster. Ngcobo notes that SABC at that time was at a similar place to where the BBC was in the 1970s, and as a person who grew up in exile in the UK, she applied some of the strategies she thought worked in BBC's mission to hone a cultural identity (see Ngcobo 2021).

The Youthful Renaissance era was characterised by changes in the types of screenplays developed for the SABC. While sitcoms, soapies and, to a lesser extent, educational programming were still present, they played a more minor role, and there was a marked shift towards dramas. Another feature was the overt attempts to remedy the injustice behind the scenes. SABC partnered with the National Film and Video Foundation (NFVF)[7] and under the Sediba Spark Program 2005 created a structured approach towards developing black screenwriters. In tracking the Hollywoodisation of the South African screenwriting culture in his paper, "Blackening the Silver Screen: A Cinema of Black Consciousness in South Africa?", Kealeboga Aiseng observes:

> The programme had sub-programmes for offering training to experienced and emerging filmmakers, particularly in the areas of screenwriting and production. The sub-programmes were as follows: SEDIBA Spark Programme, SEDIBA Masters Scriptwriting Training Programme, and SEDIBA International Financing Programme for Producers as well as a SEDIBA Spark Document programme. (Aiseng 2017)

Therefore, a structured tradition of writing and editing was in motion, pioneered by the NFVF and the SABC resulting in the Major Turning Points document [a widely used industry guide to narrative structure] a rework of Campbell's hero's journey. The plot points in this document were inciting incident, refusal to call, Act one climax, false victory, mid-point, Act two climax, crisis, Act three climax and finally, resolution. With this guide, drama series like *Shakespeare in Mzansi* (a collection of series that adapted select Shakespeare's works into then-contemporary South African society) were created. These titles dealt with the urban black identity and sexual emancipation, two

---

[7] More on the National Film and Video Foundation and its origins can be found in Creative South Africa (1998) and Department of Arts, Culture, Science and Technology (1996).

crucial aspirational themes that were not just about grandiose houses and luxurious lives (see Ngcobo 2021).

A useful example of this was *Umthunzi Wentaba (The Mountain's Shadow)*, written by Mntunzima Nkwinti, one of the Shakespeare in Mzansi adaptations, and produced by Seipati Bulane-Hopa and Baleka Hopa, a black South African writer and producer duo. The show depicted the Xhosa ulwaluko ceremony (also known as traditional male initiation), which marks how Xhosa boys transition into manhood, controversial subject matter to cover due to the cultural sensitivities involved in sharing the details of the ritual. This depiction occurred against the backdrop of a raging debate about how the ritual puts young men at risk of contracting STDs, HIV/AIDS and other blood-based diseases. In many instances, the young men's unattended injuries during this ritual have led to death. This depiction represented how young South Africans were attempting to make sense of their experience in the country.

Umthunzi Wentaba depicted a reluctant *mkwetha* (initiate) who fears dying or contracting a disease in the mountains (where the ritual takes place) and rebels against his forefathers' customs, which dictate a young man's fate into manhood. This story highlighted the *man–vs.–society* type of conflict, leading to a dramatic question that asked "will Ndoda complete initiation school?" The central conflict of the story was so strong that it shook the custodians of this culture in the story and outside of it, leading to the show's discontinuation after only two of four episodes being aired and complaints from the National Heritage Council and traditional leaders (Hawker and Makoba 2007).

Interestingly, the situation around the show displayed that South African audiences were not yet ready to receive screenplays with the unfiltered and textured perspectives that come with black experiences translated onto the screen. Talking to TVSA after the conflict arose, Mntunzima Nkwinti describes how he did not receive any support from SASWA (The South African Screenwriters Association) and that his "main objective was to revive the conscience of my people, AmaXhosa" (Tagg 2007).

What followed *Umthunzi Wentaba's* controversy was caution around the *man-vs.-tradition* type of central conflict, an interesting way in which screenplays were being silenced by society's lack of appetite for such scripts. This was until the critically acclaimed film *Inxeba (The Wound* 2017) explored the same topic. The film looked at the sexual relationship of homosexual caregivers in the circumcision ritual school. Again, a large section of society led by traditional leaders was up in arms about such a depiction, an exposition of what is considered a sacred tradition and explicit sexual scenes at an initiation school. In the Eastern Cape, the home of Xhosa people, the depiction was dubbed disrespectful to the culture and movie theatres in the province cancelled the film screenings as several groups had threatened to protest, picket and boycott its screening (News24 2018). The lead actor, Nakhane Toure's life was in danger as he received threats from Xhosa men for his supposedly shameful depiction of the ritual that is central to their very existence.

If contemporary South Africa is still not ready to disrupt the single narrative of unreserved pride associated with the ritual, it is easy to imagine what the atmosphere was like in 2007 after the release of *Umthunzi Wentaba*. Some sections of the intended audience were beginning to be misaligned with the creation of the dramas, and perhaps boundaries were being pushed too far. Moreover, the depictions made those it represented uncomfortable.

Another aspect of the Youthful Renaissance era was that the SABC dramas began depicting the sexual emancipation of black women in a way they had never done before. One of the vital narrative tools used in *Society* was character agency. Written by Makgano Mamabolo and Lodi Matsetela and produced by black-owned Puo Pha Productions, the show took us through Beth's metamorphosis that was at once an identity crisis and self-actualisation. It was the first of its kind on South African TV, led by successful black females under 30. It was very much a visualisation of the complete emancipation of black women as agents of their destiny.

The character of Beth Mazibuko is depicted as a confident, homosexual teacher teaching in a prestigious private school in Johannesburg. Throughout the show, Beth transforms from an unremarkable teacher at a private girls' school to a proudly homosexual woman that is no longer in the closet. She goes from being fearful at the expense of her relationship to being fearless and proud despite what this does to her social positioning in a conservative society. A notable consideration is the intentionality displayed by Mamabolo and Matsetela (the *Society* screenwriting team) on the detailed and refined portrayal of a black homosexual woman being part of a *normal* loving relationship, in stark contrast to other depictions of lesbian relationships. Thomas Cruz (2019) notes in the "Stigmatization of Queer Black Women in Television" that many problems persist with the portrayals of queer black women in US television. He notes that they are often punished or made out to look like criminals or sexual deviants simply because of their sexuality. Beth's characterisation was vital because it not only broke from this established mould—but also did a significant amount to bring the plight of black lesbians to the forefront of the South African mainstream.

Along with *Umthunzi Wentaba* and *Society*, shows like *Home Affairs* (2005–2010), written by various writers but created by Roberta Durrant, and *Intersexions* (2010–2013), the writers are uncredited but the show is created by Johns Hopkins Health and Education in South Africa (JHHESA) and SABC Education, start showing the multidimensional character of black South Africans through character bibles that show character complexity by adding flaws and intrapersonal conflicts. The depictions of earlier eras were less dynamic and more stereotypical to a large extent, whereas the depictions of this era started portraying better-rounded black characters who were in the driver's seat of their own lives.

While the inclusion of black filmmakers and black female stories was on the rise, during the 2008 global recession, the SABC's audited financial statements reflected a loss of nine hundred and ten million rand for the 2008/2009 financial year, signalling the beginning of the collapse of SABC, and South Africa continued to shift as Jacob Zuma became President as of May 2009 (Mail and Guardian 2018). Ngcobo (2021) notes the role of the escalation of corruption and "increasingly more preposterous bureaucratic processes" as having been the beginning of SABC's downfall, which led to many who worked for the corporation to leave, including herself. South African television's decentralisation and fragmentation continued as competitor pay—TV provider MultiChoice (who had traditionally been more for affluent (read white) audiences) started to launch *black* channels pioneered by the very staff that left SABC.

In July 2010, MultiChoice launched Mzansi Magic, which presented a new platform for black depictions in South Africa. The channel's first telenovela, *Isibaya* (*The Kraal*, 2014–2021), was created by BOMB Shelter (various writers), who had created for SABC as well previously. In the years that followed, Mzansi Magic became a household channel in black homes and housed the country's hit telenovelas. The depictions in the telenovelas were different from *Generations* in that they were more balanced in showing the reality of black people still living in the townships. So, this era's screenwriting starts to feature more textured, nuanced and rounded black characters as well as new platforms for black depictions to be showcased.

21.6 Finding a Place in the World

With Mzansi Magic's newly dominant position as the home of black South African stories, new shows appeared that ushered in the current era of screenwriting, where there are legitimate questions posed about the usefulness or accuracy of the "Rainbow Nation" concept, but where the quality of scripts has been deteriorating. A show that captures the character of this new era is *The Republic*, written by international Emmy Award-nominated duo of Phathutshedzo Makwarela and Gwydion Beynon, who were nominated in 2019 for their Mzansi Magic's telenovela *The River* (2018–2022). *The Republic* is a reality-inspired political drama that closely tracks the details of the decline in the quality of South Africa's political leadership and its impacts on the broader society. Paralleling the ruinous presidency of Jacob Zuma, the show documents the decay that characterises the South African political landscape, highlighting the travails of a well-intentioned President that is trying to restore ethical political leadership (see Mbonambi 2022).

Setting up what will be the main characteristic of the screenwriting of this era, *The Republic* explores the discontent that comes with having a hopeful past with unfulfilled promises in the present. President Zondo (a character based largely on Jacob Zuma) is overthrown by a discontent public, and President Mulaudzi (a character inspired by Cyril Ramaphosa) is appointed as the anti-corruption leader who will clean up the country. But the damage caused by Zondo's pervasive and enduring corruption means that the entire cabinet is in moral decay, highlighting the limitations of even the most well-intentioned leader. The disillusionment characterised by Moss and the dogs of Soshanguve is an on-screen translation of the frustration experienced by black South Africans as expressed in the countless service delivery protests across townships in the 2010s. These protests are primarily driven by extreme government incompetence and the failure to deliver "basic municipal services such as clean running water, electricity, and toilets…" (Mamokhere 2019, 374) as well as the astonishingly high levels of unemployment in South Africa—highlighting the inability of the once-promising government to transform society as promised. So, at the heart of this screenwriting perspective is ethical leadership vs corruption as the central dramatic issue, and what the story does well is to present the complexity of these two binary ideas when President Mulaudzi experiences the same backlash as the country is not transforming fast enough under her rule. While trying to transform the country, the general public do not see her as ethical because in her cabinet corrupt politicians still find a way to maintain significant political influence.

However, the series suffers from this era's technical shortcomings that are present in the overall depiction of the world that is created in *The Republic*. The character motivations are not plausible enough to be compelling, and the script feels as if it has not been given enough editing. One glaring example of this is the character of Thabang (portrayed by Warren Masemola), who is conceived as a reformed character that used to serve the corrupt cabinet but has changed after falling from grace. This is an important depiction that has the potential to inspire change from politicians whose morality has decayed. But this reluctant hero's journey is not developed enough to be a tool powerful enough to inspire change. The failure to create a compelling motivation with all of the complexity required for plausibility is a key feature of the screenwriting in this era.

Like in the rest of the world, the single most significant industry change to South African television has been the arrival of online streaming platforms, such as Netflix, Amazon Prime Video and the local MultiChoice-owned streaming platform Showmax (Singh 2021). The biggest change is the investment by the subscription video on demand platforms in the commissioning of local content for their platforms as they began to enter the South African market to compete with traditional South African television platforms.

In this era, an interesting example of screenwriting is the Netflix South African original *Queen Sono*, which represented a landmark moment for on-screen depictions of black South Africans, due to the centrality of a powerful black female character. Starring Pearl Thusi, the show is a South African crime drama television series created and written by Kagiso Lediga that premiered on February 28, 2020. *Queen Sono* is an African female spy, assisted by her cohorts from a secretive African peacekeeping organisation. She uses her lethal skills to keep the continent's people safe from transnational terror threats. She is a dynamic hero, but she battles with continual post-traumatic stress disorder of having witnessed her mother's assassination during South Africa's Apartheid era.

A key screenwriting technique that is carefully used in the series is flashbacks, only to repeat one particular scene where Queen witnesses her mother being assassinated. The past (through flashbacks) is still present in her life, distracting her from her present adventures as a spy. In a crucial scene, she attends an event, and her life is in danger; seeing bubbles being blown takes her back to being at the park with her mother, blowing bubbles and then hearing a gunshot. These flashbacks always shake her to the core because the memories are invasive and undermine her competence. This suggestion is a powerful comment on how present-day South Africa's past still looms large today, its invasiveness and how it still threatens progress even for the most competent. Lediga and his team seem to be making the point that to go forward, South African black people need to fix what is holding them back and take their power back. Perhaps this is why he imagines a black woman character who is not disempowered but holds the gun, gives orders, has the lethal skills, and can affect change.

Queen Sono's visual language is colourful, glossy and lively, and the music is vibrant and distinctly African. It gives Africa a different character beyond the usual international depictions of poverty and misery. The show represents Lediga's way of educating a global audience that there is more to Africa; he offers an exciting and hopeful way of writing about Africa. A potential shortcoming is that there is more focus on the look and feel of the visuals that seem to come at the expense of the depth of characters (Fienberg 2020).

A reflective tone has characterised the current era of screenwriting and the desire to situate black experiences in their appropriate global and historical contexts. There is deep thought on how the past has influenced the present, and this stands out as a feature of South African screenplays of recent years. This reflection of a complex society is a unique element that South Africa can continue to nurture to help audiences make sense of what has been a turbulent ride from a closed, autocratic society to the open, globalised country that South Africa now is. No one has had a bumpier ride on this journey than Black South Africans. Another essential feature of the latest era is the presence of open, global platforms that exist for showcasing South African audio-visual products. This means that there is a change of psychology required to understand that the depictions of South Africa, including those of black South African people, are now in open competition with content from the rest of the globe. Therefore, the technical execution of screenwriting needs to be on par with, or better than, our global counterparts to compete meaningfully in the global battle for eyeballs.

21.7 Conclusion

It is then clear that the depictions of black South Africans have come a long way since the dying days of Apartheid to the present quest for finding a place in the world. The portrayals of black South Africans have evolved in line with thematic eras that have been outlined in the above analysis. Screenwriting in South Africa has not existed in isolation; it has been heavily influenced by the evolution of a fast-evolving society, recovering from the traumatic dehumanisation of Apartheid. Black people have undergone a massive transformation from being marginalised, exploited second-class citizens to full members of society that have the agency to affect change in their situations, whether it is through violent service delivery protests to the simple act of voting for change, options that previously were not available to them. Drama screenplays for mass media have, therefore, been a strong cultural tool used to grapple with and influence South Africa's political reality and very complex cultural identity. It seems inevitable, then, that the future of South African screenwriting is in the acknowledgement that representation alone has run its course, now, the focus should be on making South African black-produced screenplays synonymous with world-class excellence.

References

Aiseng, Kealeboga. 2017. *Blackening the silver screen: A cinema of Black Consciousness in South Africa?* Johannesburg: University of Witwatersrand Press. https://core.ac.uk/download/pdf/188775967.pdf. Accessed 10 November 2021.

Bevan, Carin. 2009. "Putting Up Screens: A History of Television in South Africa, 1929–1976." Ph.D. diss., University of Pretoria. https://repository.up.ac.za/bitstream/handle/2263/24845/Complete.pdf. Accessed 4 February 2020.

Botha, Martin, ed. 2007. *Marginal Lives & Painful Pasts: South African Cinema after Apartheid*. Parklands, South Africa: Genugtig!

Campbell, Joseph. 2020 [1949]. *The Hero with a Thousand Faces*. eBook, n.p: Joseph Campbell Foundation.

Cowell, Alan. 1984 "South Africa Whites Seek Black TV." *New York Times*, 1 August, https://www.nytimes.com/1984/08/01/arts/south-africa-whites-seek-black-tv.html. Accessed 12 November 2021.

Creative South Africa. 1998. "A Strategy for Realising the Potential of the Cultural Industries. A Report to the Department of Arts, Culture, Science and Technology." https://www.gov.za/sites/default/files/gcis_document/201409/mso1ba0.pdf. Accessed 22 October 2021.

Cruz, Thomas. 2019. "The Stigmatization of Queer Black Women in Television." *Film Matters* 10 (1) 26–36.

Department of Arts, Culture, Science and Technology. 1996. "White Paper on Arts, Culture and Heritage: All Our Legacies, Our Common Future." https://www.southafricanculturalobservatory.org.za/download/90. Accessed 21 October 2021.

Dlamini, Lungelo. 2012. "Spotlight on Aids." Ph.D. diss., University of Kwa-Zulu Natal. https://ccms.ukzn.ac.za/Files/articles/MA_dissertations/lungelo%20dlamini%20-%20masters%20thesis%20(2012).pdf. Accessed 12 October 2021.

Donaldson, Ronnie. 2014. "South African Township Transformation". In *Encyclopedia of Quality of Life and Well-Being Research*, edited by Alex C. Michalos, 623–28. Dordrecht, Heidelberg, New York and London: Springer. https://doi.org/10.1007/978-94-007-0753-5_4186.

Ebrahim, Haseenah Ebrahim, and Abner Jordache Ellapen. 2018. "Close-Up: South African Cinema: Cinema in Postapartheid South Africa: New Perspectives." *Black Camera: An International Film Journal* 9 (2): 169–76. https://doi.org/10.2979/blackcamera.9.2.12.

Evans, Martha. 2012. "Transmitting the Transition Media Events and Post-Apartheid South African National Identity." Ph.D. diss., University of Cape Town. https://open.uct.ac.za/handle/11427/10475. Accessed 9 October 2021.

Fanon, Frantz, 1970. *Black Skin, White Masks*. London: Paladin.

Fienberg, Daniel. 2020. "'Queen Sono': TV Review." *The Hollywood Reporter*, 28 February. https://www.hollywoodreporter.com/tv/tv-reviews/queen-sono-review-1281706/. Accessed 18 May 2021.

Flanery, Patrick Denman. 2009. "What national Cinema? South African Film Cultures and the Transnational." *Safundi: The Journal of South African and American Studies* 10 (2): 239–53.

Generations. 1993–2014 (21 seasons). Created by Mfundi Vundla. South Africa: Morula Pictures.

Hawker, Dianne, and Ntomboxolo Makoba. 2007. "SABC pulls contentious drama on circumcision." *Independent Online (IOL)*, 2 April. https://www.iol.co.za/news/south-africa/sabc-pulls-contentious-drama-on-circumcision-321363. Accessed 12 October 2021.

Home Affairs. 2005–2010 (4 seasons). Created by Roberta Durrant. South Africa: Penguin Films.

Ingqumbo Yeminyanya (The Wrath of the Ancestors). 1991 (1 season). Created by Harry Hofmeyr and Joyce Ndamase, based on work by Archibald Campbell Jordan. South Africa: Seventh Street Productions.

Intersexions. 2010–2013 (2 seasons). Created by Johns Hopkins Health and Education in South Africa (JHHESA) and SABC Education. South Africa: Quizzical Pictures and AntS Multimedia.

Inxeba (The Wound). 2017. Written by John Trengove, Thando Mgqolozana, and Malusi Bengu, based on a story by John Trengove and Batana Vundla. Directed by John Trengove. South Africa: Urucu Media.

Isibaya (The Kraal). 2014–2021 (8 seasons). Created by Angus Gibson, Desiree Markgraaff, Teboho Mahlatsi, and Catherine Stewart. South Africa: The Bomb Shelter

Isidingo: The Need. 1998–2020 (22 seasons). Created by Gray Hofmeyr. South Africa: Endemol Shine Africa, Pomegranate Media.

Jordan, Archibald Campbell. 1980. *The Wrath of the Ancestors*. Alice, South Africa: Lovedale Press.

Khululeka (Be Free). 1994–2008 (3 seasons). Created by Roberta Durrant. South Africa: Penguin Films.

Kwatsha, Linda Loretta. 1995. "A Psychoanalytical Evaluation of Ingqumbo Yeminyanya by AC Jordan." MA diss, Vista University, Johannesburg (South Africa). file:///Users/p0075215/Downloads/PDF%20Document.pdf. Accessed 5 August 2022.

Leitch, Thomas. (2003). "Twelve Fallacies in Contemporary Adaptation Theory." *Criticism* 45 (2): 149–71.

Mail and Guardian. 2009. "SABC Loses R910-million in 2008/09 Financial Year." *Mail and Guardian*, 18 December. https://mg.co.za/article/2009-12-18-sabc-loses-r910million-in-200809-financial-year/. Accessed 18 November 2021.

Maingard, Jacqueline. 2007. *South African National Cinema*. London and New York: Routledge.

Mamokhere, John. 2019. "An exploration of reasons behind service delivery protests in South Africa: A case of Bolobedu South at the Greater Tzaneen Municipality." Paper presented at the International Conference on Public Administration and Development Alternatives (IPADA), Johannesburg, South Africa, 3–5 July.

Mbonambi, Buhle. 2022. "'The Republic' Is A Biting Critique of the State of South Africa." *Independent Online (IOL)*, 23 January. https://www.iol.co.za/entertainment/tv/local/the-republic-is-a-biting-critique-of-the-state-of-south-africa-93bcaaaf-dc26-4c7d-8e8a-a6364f77d37a. Accessed 20 February 2022.

News24. 2018. "Screening of Inxeba (The Wound) Suspended Due to Protests." *News24*, 2 February. https://www.news24.com/News24/screening-of-inxeba-the-wound-suspended-due-to-protests-20180202. Accessed 2 December 2021.

Ngcobo, Kethiwe. 2021. Interview by Ziphozakhe Hlobo. Sandton, Johannesburg, South Africa, 13 September.

Opland, Jeff. 1990. "The Publication of AC Jordan's Xhosa Novel, Ingqumbo yeminyanya (1940)." *Research in African Literatures* 21 (4): 135–47.

Paleker, Gairoonisa. 2010. "The B-Scheme Subsidy and the 'Black Film Industry' in Apartheid South Africa, 1972–1990." *Journal of African Cultural Studies* 22 (1): 91–104.

Punyanunt-Carter, Narissra Maria. 2008. "The Perceived Realism of African American Portrayals on Television." *The Howard Journal of Communications* 19 (3): 241–57.

Queen Sono. 2020 (1 season). Created by Kagiso Lediga. South Africa: Diprente Films, Netflix.

Saks, Lucia Ann. 2001. "The Race for Representation: Reconstructing National Identity in South African Cinema." Ph.D. diss., University of Southern California.https://www.proquest.com/openview/0f0e1c16fe80a6962acf519153c76ace/1?pq-origsite=gscholar&cbl=18750&diss=y. Accessed 2 December 2021.

S'gudi S'naysi (It's Good, It's Nice). 1986–1993 (6 seasons). Created by Roberta Durrant. South Africa: Penguin Films.

Singh, Nirvana. 2021. "TBI Spotlight on Africa: SABC's Nirvana Singh." *Television Business International*, 27 October. https://tbivision.com/2021/10/27/tbi-spotlight-on-africa-sabcs-nirvana-singh/. Accessed 22 February 2022.

Society. 2007–2010 (2 seasons). Created by Makgano Mamabolo and Lodi Matsetela. South Africa: Puo Pha Productions.

Sonnenburg, Stephan, and Mark Runco. 2017. "Pathways to the Hero's Journey: A Tribute to Joseph Campbell and the 30th Anniversary of His Death." *Journal of Genius and Eminence* 2 (2): 1–8.

Soul Buddiez. 2000–2011 (5 seasons). Created by Soul City Institute for Health and Development Communication and SABC Education in collaboration with the Department of Education. South Africa: Bobby Heaney Productions.

Soul City Institute for Social Justice. "About Us." Soul City Institute for Social Justice. https://www.soulcity.org.za/about-us. Accessed 20 December 2020.

Soul City. 1994–2015 (12 seasons). Created by The Soul City Institute for Health and Development Communication. South Africa: T.O.M. Pictures.

Suburban Bliss. 1996 (1 season). Created by Craig Gardner and Gray Hofmeyr. South Africa: Dapple Films, Endemol Entertainment.

Szczepanik, Petr. 2013. "How Many Steps to the Shooting Script? A Political History of Screenwriting." *Iluminace* 25 (3): 73–98.

Tager, Michele. 2010. "The Black and the Beautiful: Perceptions of (a) New Generation (s)." *Critical Arts: A Journal of South-North Cultural Studies* 24 (1): 99–127.

Tagg, Tashi. 2007. "uMthunzi we Nthaba's Writer Speaks Out." *TVSA*, 24 April. https://www.tvsa.co.za/user/blogs/viewblogpost.aspx?blogpostid=11639. Accessed 22 October 2021.

The Cosby Show. 1984–1992 (8 seasons). Created by Michael Leeson. USA: Carsey-Werner Productions.

The Republic. 2020–2021 (2 seasons). Created by Phathutshedzo Makwarela and Gwydion Beynon. South Africa: Tshedza Pictures.

The River. 2018–2022 (5 seasons). Created by Phathutshedzo Makwarela and Gwydion Beynon. South Africa: Tshedza Pictures.

Treffry-Goatley, Astrid. 2010. "The Representation and Mediation of National Identity in the Production of Post-Apartheid, South African Cinema." Ph.D. diss., University of Cape Town. https://open.uct.ac.za/bitstream/handle/11427/11290/thesis_hum_2010_treffry_goatly_a.pdf?sequence=1&isAllowed=y. Accessed 13 June 2021.

Umthunzi Wentaba (The Mountain's Shadow). 2007 (1 season). Created by Mntunzima Nkwinti. South Africa: Ochre Moving Pictures.

Yizo Yizo (It Is the Way It Is). 1999–2004 (3 seasons). Created by Teboho Mahlatsi and Angus Gibson. South Africa: Laduma Film Factory, Bomb Productions.

PART III: Who

Screenwriting and the Screen Industries

The International Writers' Room: A Transnational Approach to Serial Drama Development from an Italian Perspective

Luisa Cotta Ramosino and Laura Cotta Ramosino

22.1 Introduction

The writers' room is a development system that originated in the United States, within the production system of the large networks that needed to efficiently produce a large number of episodes in a limited period of time (22 or 24 per season). It revolves around a professional figure, the showrunner, now known within—although in reality never fully imported to—the European television system, as well (Bennet 2014; Phalen 2017; Guarnaccia 2013). This same model, in its most sophisticated form, is at the basis of the so-called golden age of television seriality, well outlined by Mittel in his study *Complex TV*. Mittel contextualises the practice of writing within a production system that evolves in parallel with changes in viewership of television narratives, which the US anticipated, but which have now become a global reality (Mittel 2015; Lotz 2009).

The European-style writers' room, moreover, was created in the first instance for projects with a relatively short format (prestige international products tend to have ten or fewer episodes)—whose model is actually that of American cable and premium cable products, and not of the long seriality of

Luisa Cotta Ramosino (✉) · Laura Cotta Ramosino
Netflix Italia, Catholic University of Milan, Milan, Italy
e-mail: luisactt@hotmail.com

Laura Cotta Ramosino (✉)
Cattleya, Catholic University of Milan, Milan, Italy

the networks—and this has implications in terms of the selection of the writers' profile, the size of the writing team, but also the available budget (Barra and Scaglioni 2020).

In fact, for a long time, European producers, when building a project with international ambitions, to be filmed in English, have chosen to hire American showrunners to lead European projects at a distance, involving local authors only in certain cases (this is the case with the series *Borgia* (2011–2014)[1] created by American showrunner Tom Fontana for Canal Plus), before trying the path of totally autonomous writers' rooms based in Europe.

These are the first instances of international writers' rooms, which, however, present significant imbalance on the showrunner's side, at least regarding the writing, since the "production" side remains anchored to the European perspective (for resources and budget management), thus profoundly differing from the American method, where the showrunner is almost always also the "manager" of the budget, as well.

Moreover, each country has developed the system in a different way, hybridising it with already existing processes, which are centred on more or less strong authorial figures (writers, but also directors or non-writing producers) or more closely linked to a strong and hands-on producer. That development has also been linked to the specificity of the audience and to the presence of commissioners able to focus on productions conceived and designed from the beginning, not only for the domestic market, but also for the international one (Guarnaccia 2018).[2]

The last ten years have witnessed a further evolution of the international writers' room model, which is based on a decade of experience with "transnational" projects, linked to the opening of global markets to European productions, driven also, but not only, by the growth of platforms and their "hunger" for products intended for transnational circulation (Barra and Scaglioni 2020).

Meanwhile, as we will show through our case studies, a new generation of European authors is emerging, trained through programmes aimed at the diffusion of the writers' room system and used to collaborating (almost always in English) with colleagues from other countries, first as students and then as professionals, on projects commissioned by production companies interested in European co-productions.

In this contribution, we will briefly go over the issues related to the distribution of authorship in European writers' rooms (comparing it with the American one) in order to identify the key figures in these processes. Then, through some case studies, we will try to show the opportunities, challenges and difficulties encountered in different situations, suggesting working paths and perspectives regarding writing and production practices in continuous

---

[1] Not to be confused with the similar series *The Borgias*, created by Neil Jordan.

[2] On this issue for Italy, compare the interviews with Tinny Andreatta (RAI Fiction) and Nils Hartmann (Sky Italia) in Guarnaccia 2018.

evolution with respect to the market demands and the expectations of the creatives involved.

Through the examination of transnational projects born in the Italian context with different identities, commissioners and outcomes, we will try to highlight the challenges, opportunities and adaptive processes that the model of a writers' room has had to face, highlighting the limits and opportunities of "collective" creative work under the challenge of an ever-changing production horizon. Starting from the testimonies of scriptwriters and producers and retracing the trajectories of some projects, we will try to identify constant elements and points of reflection on issues related to the sharing of authorship and the comparison between different professional cultures.

We believe the birth of training programmes specifically focused on the work in international writers' rooms is a fundamental part of this evolution, and therefore, in order to clarify the context, we will refer to the most famous and long-lived of these programmes, Serial Eyes based in Berlin, thanks to the testimonies collected both from a teacher and from some course alumni.

22.2 Writers, Showrunners and Producers: Differences Between the US and Europe

Even in the variety of declinations of the writers' room model in the American context (linked first of all to the length of the series, to the commissioner, but also to the experience of the creator of the series itself, sometimes too junior to be able to take on the role of showrunner),[3] one element remains constant, and that is the centrality of the writing process with respect to the general creative process. The scriptwriter/showrunner is the project's leader, responsible for both its dramaturgical development and budget management, with competencies involving both the articulation of the initial idea and its practical realisation, in compliance with a vision that has to be included in all the project's practical aspects (cast, locations, costumes, photographic choices, editing, etc.), to be negotiated with commissioners and producers. It is not for nothing that the writers' room admits only writers and that interfacing with producers is managed by the showrunner (Phalen 2017).

In Europe, on the contrary, writers have always represented only one of the poles of production, and, at least until now, they have certainly not been the decisive factor except in a few cases. Before the arrival of American professionals (but on closer inspection even afterwards), the figure of a pure showrunner is not present, and this role is normally shared between a head writer and a non-writing producer (executive/creative).[4] The dynamics

---

[3] In these cases, it is not uncommon to find a showrunner/manager next to the series creator to assist him in managing those aspects of the production in which the writer is not yet trained.

[4] As creative producer at Lux Vide, Luisa Cotta Ramosino worked on a few series, such as *Un passo dal Cielo* (2011–2021) and *Viola come il mare* (2022). This is a similar role

of this collaboration may be more or less positive, but they certainly have an impact on the nature of the work within the writers' rooms, which are normally focused solely on development work and very little on the practical aspects of production.

Moreover, whereas in the American model writers are hired (almost always exclusively) on a project for a given number of weeks, and therefore, their commitment in the writers' room is constant and total, in Europe the writers' rooms do not meet for more than two or three days a week, sometimes in non-consecutive weeks, with a commitment that must also take into account the extended timeframe of feedback from producers and clients. This certainly has an impact on the compactness of the writing work, which, as we shall see, becomes even more complicated when it involves individuals of different national origins.

In an interview given to the authors of this contribution, showrunner Frank Spotnitz stated that the different extent of the commitment of the writers constitutes one of the discriminating factors in the quality of the work of the writers' rooms, a commitment that is also linked to a different remuneration:

> The economics of a writers' room is an issue. In the American system you are paid to work full time in a writers' room and your script is on top of that and it is just the reverse here in Europe, where is a nominal fee to be in a writers' room and the writers' room are shorter. It is my feeling that a writers' room should be two weeks per episode, at least, and it is almost never the case [in Europe]. And in a lot of countries, certainly in the UK, it is very rare to have a writers' room five days a week, because the writers are involved in other projects. (Spotnitz 2021)

In order to better understand the logic of what we have analysed so far, it is essential to consider some specific cases that in different ways have led to the creation of different types of transnational writers' rooms.

22.3   MEDICI—MASTERS OF FLORENCE

The case of *Medici* (2016) is particularly interesting because it is the first real Italian example of a serial drama conceived from the outset as an international project, commissioned by the Italian broadcaster, RAI, but destined for a global market. For this reason, the series was developed and written in English with British and American writers who worked in concert with the Italian producer (Lux Vide) in the form of a writers' room based in London (in the headquarters of the company that owned by showrunner Frank Spotnitz, Big Light). However, it was preceded by in-depth discussions held in Rome on the concept, themes and characters, a need that emerged after an

---

to Gina Gardini's in many series produced by Cattleya. For Gardini's view of roles and duties on a series see her interview with the Writers Guild Italia website on *Suburra – La serie* (2017–2020): https://www.writersguilditalia.it/speciale-suburra-gina-gardini/.

initial attempt to develop the series with English screenwriter Michael Hirst (*The Tudors*), who was less willing to negotiate a development project in which the producers would be more involved.[5]

The decision to work with an American writer and showrunner such as Frank Spotnitz, who has been living in Europe for some time (and it is no coincidence that he is, as we'll see, actively involved in the Serial Eyes programme), arose from the desire to create a product capable of going beyond the formula of the traditional European co-production of a miniseries (with which Lux Vide had experimented many times in the past, also with great success). The concept was to create a drama with an international pedigree, but which was able to capture the specificity of Italian identity and meet the needs of a commissioner like Rai 1 with precise public service obligations.

This meant that the project was part of a highly specific agenda dedicated to promoting national artistic and cultural heritage.[6] Such a point of departure obviously required a choice closer to the notion of highly "factual" and "historically correct" in its presentation (Cotta Ramosino 2017, 2018).

This was especially the case since the historical period considered in the series was none other than the Florentine Renaissance, one of the foundational moments of Italian identity, with ramifications in art, politics and overwhelmingly in the feeling of commonality that remains powerful even to this day.

However, the need to address an international audience applied certain pressures and created the impetus for a more "casual" approach to the historic material, in line with the Anglo-Saxon approach. The nature of that approach is twofold: it tends to seek to emphasise the immediacy of characters and situations, and at the same time, it tends to lose sight of the relative unfamiliarity of the period in question, in terms of its values and behaviour models (Cotta Ramosino 2018; Cotta Ramosino, Cotta Ramosino, and Dognini 2004).

The balance between the general direction and the operational choices in the definition of the concept, the characters and the plot were, therefore, the object of negotiation within a writers' room that was made international, at least in the first season, above all by the presence (not continuous, but constant) of non-writing producers (in the person of Sara Melodia and one of the authors of this chapter, Luisa Cotta Ramosino).

From this point of view, the writers' room of the first season of *Medici* is certainly an interesting example of how professionals from different countries (in this case the US showrunner, British scriptwriters and Italian producers) were able to create a common working method capable of mediating between the consolidated structure of American serial work, the hybridised version that exists in Great Britain and Europe, and the needs of a client interested in

---

[5] For a detailed reconstruction of the various stages of the project, see Fumagalli in Fumagalli, Albani and Braga 2021, 226.

[6] As expressed in the guidelines for Rai Fiction call for projects: https://www.rai.it/portale/Nessuno-escluso-86dc82f3-3f7a-4f7a-9b06-bf21e4185832.html.

finding a positive compromise between more modern and efficient writing and the objectives of a project conceived as a tribute to Italian culture.

In addition to the already mentioned comparison between the different ways of approaching a period product, it is also worth mentioning the need to agree between authors and producers on the typology of documents coming from the writers' room. We should not underestimate, in fact, the difference between American and Anglo-Saxon outlines (documents of 8–10 pages that rarely contain dialogue, but focus on narrative articulations) compared to an Italian treatment, a document normally much longer, which includes pieces of dialogue and often also details related to settings, a story that seeks to evoke the episode's atmosphere and tone. In the Italian serial production, there is also a shorter preliminary document, called "soggetto", which has a literary form and does not yet provide for many of the plot points contained in the English outlines. From this document one passes directly to the scripts or through an intermediate step consisting of a treatment or scene by scene.

Without understanding the differences between the two document types, communication between the creatives and the executives (the production company and the client) would have been very difficult, and so for that, the possibility for a Lux Vide executive to attend the writers' room was crucial. It was necessary to make the writing process homogeneous and shared, and above all to mediate with respect to the Italian broadcaster's expectations, which, though not directly involved in the work of the writers' room, proved decisive in defining the project.

Therefore, while normally the producer and the broadcast executive would come into play only after receiving the materials produced by the writers' room, in the case of *Medici* a system of exchange of information and feedback was created even concerning intermediate phases of the work (not stable in the first season, but more codified, with weekly meetings and reports, in the following seasons), which sometimes included having the Italian creative producer view the daily reports of the writers' room work, an informal but very interesting document for following the flow of the writers' thinking, the reasons for some choices, and the deepening of the characters.[7] The opportunity to provide historical insights was often the cue to delve into dramaturgical junctures, both in terms of greater or lesser historical accuracy and in the comparison of "national" narrative codes, in order to find a happy compromise between the different styles of storytelling. The writers' room of the first season of *Medici* covered much more than the traditional twenty weeks expected for this kind of project (from September 2014 well into the months

---

[7] Note from Luisa Cotta Ramosino: "As the creative producer of the series, I found it generous of the writers to share this kind of material, which has always helped me to evaluate the official materials more carefully, and get a better understanding of the reasons for certain choices, thus being able to discuss them with the writers of the individual episodes more effectively. This kind of collaboration obviously requires a deep respect of the roles and sensibilities of others, as well as an understanding of the layered processes of working on materials in different contexts".

of principal photography starting September 2015) but that is certainly understandable given the language barrier (each document had to be translated into Italian before it could be shared with the commissioner) and the fact that for Lux Vide it was the first experiment in this kind of production context, as well as the Italian broadcaster's unfamiliarity with this way of working, which necessitated much longer feedback times than those with American networks.

However, it is also interesting to consider an even more "internal" perspective, namely that of an Italian writer who participated in the writers' room for the second and third seasons of the series, Francesco Arlanch. He is a scriptwriter who in Italy had had wide experience as author of miniseries and episodes of successful series, but also as head writer of series he created himself (*Doc—Nelle tue mani*, *La strada di casa* and *Blanca* among others) and who, therefore, knew the system of collaborative writing in the Italian writers' rooms, but who nevertheless grasped important differences in the work of a transnational writers' room, first of all in the articulation of the work.

> Compared to the Italian writers' rooms, in the *Medici* writers' room the confrontation and discussion took place in a much more oral way. In *Medici* we shared with the entire creative team (all the authors of all the episodes) what was to be the horizontal development of the series. While in Italy, there tends to be a headwriter or headwriters who develop the Bible of the series (with the character arcs), in *Medici* all these lines were defined collectively through a rather open discussion, in which even the author of a single episode could propose twists or changes to the arcs that concerned the series as a whole. Even though there was a headwriter [who in Italy would have presented his work already well articulated at that point], the whole series was on the table in the writers' room. It is a more collective form of authorship. After this first phase, once the macro-movements of the eight episodes (our series treatment) had been agreed upon, each author concentrated on developing his own episode. The first thing to be presented, however, was not a written text, a treatment, but a very specific oral pitch, starting with a certain number of cards on which a story beat to be told in one sentence was marked. Starting from the cards, the author had to narrate the episode by sticking the beats on a corkboard, already divided into four acts. Each author could then offer objections or give suggestions on the others' episodes. The author must first of all win the interest of the other authors with his story. This oral system is in some ways stimulating, because you have no room for bluffing, for writing by taking refuge in "literature" to cover plot holes. It starts with the bare and crude structure of twists and turns, which is a very healthy approach from certain points of view, because it forces you to think of a solid and rich plot right from the start, but it also has a bit of a limitation in that the anxiety to construct these plots and surprise your audience means that you end up focusing mainly on that. It's good for us Italians to think deeply about the plot, but the risk is forgetting the characters. (Arlanch 2021)[8]

---

[8] Note from Luisa Cotta Ramosino: "In my capacity as creative producer of the three seasons of *Medici*, I feel I can say that the encounter between the different working

For an Italian scriptwriter, therefore, it was a new experience to share so deeply the creative work on the episode he was going to write, to be accountable not only to the showrunner/head writer, but also, in a way, to his fellow episode writers.

Finally, *Medici*'s experience allows us to reflect on another element highlighted at the beginning of this chapter and related to the different weight given to the writers in defining the final identity of a series in Italy, as compared to the United States. Broadcasters (and sometimes producers) in Europe in general, and in Italy specifically, believe they have the last word even in elements of detail, something that could never happen in the American context, where the writing "guides" the creative process, and the showrunner (in that case also with managerial weight with respect to the management of production resources) is decisive in the decision-making process (Pahlen 2017; Priggé 2005). This difference of context has certainly required, in this specific case, a form of negotiation in order to find a compromise that would respect the work of the creatives, and, at the same time, meet the needs of the other interlocutors, engaged in an operation of considerable financial weight.

The result, in terms of ratings, was extremely satisfactory (29.9% share for the first episode with over 7.5 million viewers, with a final season average of over 6.5 million and 26% share) and worldwide sales in over 120 countries constituted a springboard for Lux Vide's international productions, including *Devils*, for which, however, a different development model would be attempted, reshuffling the elements of the creative process.

22.4 *Devils*

The case of the series *Devils* (2020) presents some points in common with the previous one (starting from the production company and therefore the figures belonging to it who participated in the writers' room), but also numerous differences linked to the origin of the project (based on a novel by trader turned novelist Guido Maria Brera) and to the phases of elaboration of the various materials (from the concept to the Bible, up to outlines and scripts). In this case, in fact, the concept of the series was elaborated in Italy by Italian authors (in distinct phases, first Daniele Cesarano, Barbara Petronio, Fabrizio Abbate and then Alessandro Sermoneta, Elena Bucaccio and Mario Ruggeri were involved), who worked with Guido Maria Brera to re-elaborate the narrative material in the service of an industrial serial form.

In this case, the challenge of the scriptwriting work was, on the one hand, to find a way of translating complex financial concepts and procedures into dramaturgical form (creating comprehensible and relevant stakes), and on the other hand, to create a serial structure that intertwined the serial arc that

---

methods has made it possible to yield the best of both worlds to the writing of the series. It has led to process a gradual *maturation* from one season to the next that has made it possible to explore characters and storylines with increasing complexity and originality".

formed the backbone of the novel with a strong episodic structure, as well as working deeply on the characters. The fact that most of the story takes place in London, and the decision to produce the series in English, made it possible from the outset to involve English writers at a certain point in the development process, in order to give the story greater authenticity (in terms of setting, but also of specific slang) and to make the project more attractive to potential international partners.[9] This was an anomalous choice and in retrospect, not without problems, because the absence of a showrunner implied that the responsibility of maintaining the identity of the project was entrusted not to one or more writers or to a director, but to executives of Lux Vide production company (non-writing producers, in the person of two executive producers, Sara Melodia and one the authors of this contribution, Luisa Cotta Ramosino). This was perhaps an inevitable anomaly due to the origin of the project but resulted in a complex workflow, not without missteps, which lengthened the writing time and made it more expensive.

From the point of view of the dramaturgical elaboration, the Italian authors worked above all on the definition of the characters and their narrative arcs, and then on the elaboration of the outlines of the episodes, while in a second phase two British authors (Chris Lunt and Michael A. Walker) took over, working for a fortnight together with the Italian authors to deepen the materials in view of a re-elaboration of the outlines and the elaboration of the scripts. Ruggeri comments on the different phases of the collaboration with the foreign authors:

> The biggest difference remains the cultural difference in the approach to the story (and perhaps also to life…). Italians are more used to working from the characters, starting from a more philosophical approach, sometimes even apparently dispersive, while English authors have always had a more pragmatic approach, more linked to the plot of the story. There was also a difference in sensibility on the type of personal stories to attribute to the specific characters. There is no doubt that we Italians had a sensitivity defined by the authors across the Channel as more *melodramatic*, a tendency to enter more forcefully into the personal feelings of the protagonists, while the English authors were more inclined to much drier choices, much more British, in fact. These are profound cultural differences, which are difficult to manage, but differences that nonetheless brought richness to the series, albeit in a sometimes somewhat chaotic development. (Ruggeri 2021)

It was, in fact, a rather anomalous collaboration, a writers' room that was perhaps much too short-lived to allow the creation of an effective long-distance collaboration, in part because it involved an advanced phase of the work and not the initial elaboration of the project. In this phase, the work on the materials was concentrated on re-examining the characters, plot junctions and staging, with the aim of giving a credible and effective identity to

---

[9] On this, see also the interview with Nils Hartman in Guarnaccia 2018.

a story set in the City. Writers were able to observe the difference in style and approach in the elaboration of the materials indicated as "outline", which in the original Italian version were instead "soggetti/treatments", documents designed to deepen the psychology of the characters and the context (in this regard it is worth remembering what Francesco Arlanch said about his experience in the British writers' room of *Medici*).

The intention was to entrust the British authors with the development of 8 out of a total 10 episodes, while the three Italian authors (Sermoneta, Bucaccio and Ruggeri) would develop two scripts for "special" episodes (one almost entirely dedicated to exploring the characters in a previous timeline and shot 70% in Italy, and therefore in Italian). To complete the work, two other English authors (Ben Harris and Peter Jukes) were then involved, who again worked with the Italian authors and Lux Vide executive producers in an informal writers' room for two weeks. All the episodes of the series, however, underwent numerous rewrites and the interaction between the authors of different nationalities was articulated in different phases in the writing work, not without some slowdowns and difficulties.

Specifically, the fragmentation of the work phases in writers' rooms involving authors of different nationalities is probably to be considered the most problematic aspect because it made it more difficult to find a common language in the elaboration of both plot and characters.

The final scripts, therefore, are the result of stratifications, which, on the one hand, allowed the development of what would become the dramaturgical and visual style of the series (also linked to a very recognisable directing and editing contribution)[10] while, on the other, do not represent a fully satisfactory example (both for the writers and for the producers) of collaborative work between professionals from different countries. In this case, the lack of clarity in defining who had ultimate responsibility for the series (and here we return to the lack of a recognised showrunner) sometimes caused frustration among the creatives involved, but also the multiplication of certain steps first in the elaboration of the scripts and then in the definition of the final version of the episodes shot.

Moreover, considering the additional difficulties faced in establishing a common working method capable of taking into account divergent working practices to create communication channels and shared processes, this case study suggests that a transnational writers' room needs, especially in the initial phases, extended periods of common work (at least four weeks full-time to set up the series) either in person or through sharing platforms. In addition, with regard to the subsequent phases of articulation of the episodes (the "breaking" of the stories), as Spotnitz suggested, it would be useful to foresee two weeks per episode.

---

[10] A dramaturgical style made of a mix of fictional and non-fictional elements (underlined with the use of original news footage and "fictional" news materials).

Only by taking the time to work together on the premise of the story (and by doing so while also discovering national differences in the approach to serial writing) can we really create an efficient and rewarding working methodology for everyone.

The series was very well received in its first airing on Sky (over 600,000 viewers for the first episode, the third-best debut for the channel dedicated to series) and was then distributed in over 160 territories.

22.5 DJANGO

A different path is taken by *Django* (2022), a western series which is the most recent international challenge of Italian production company Cattleya, after the success of the continental epic on cocaine trafficking *Zerozerozero* (2020), already characterised by an international and multilingual creative team (production, writing and direction).

The project, from the outset conceived as an international serial to be filmed in English, was actually born in France, because the rights to Sergio Corbucci's 1966 film *Django* starring Franco Nero were owned by French production company Atlantique (which from 2011 to 2014 had produced the three seasons of *Borgia* for Canal + and Sky, and more recently *The Eddy* for Netflix). It was Atlantique who approached Cattleya, who had many years of experience in premium series and was a stable partner for Canal + and Sky, entrusting from the beginning the Italian partner with the search for writers who had in-depth knowledge and the right taste to develop a western in the best tradition of *spaghetti western*.[11]

From that moment on, the development process was coordinated between France and Italy, with a unified production of notes and feedback for the writing work, and then later for the other aspects of production (Di Benedetto 2021).

Even in an experience like this, which initially combines an Italian and a French production, the *lingua franca* of communication and also of the writing remains English, and this, understandably, considerably lengthens the time taken to develop and circulate the material. In this context, the synergy and affinity between producers of different nationalities are a fundamental element for the production to proceed smoothly and effectively (Di Benedetto 2021), but it also has an inevitable impact on the composition of the writing group and on the internal dynamics of the writers' room.

While starting from the undoubted appeal of Corbucci's title, the intention was immediately to find an original take on the intellectual property, and for that Cattleya turned to a select group of Italian writers, within which a real

---

[11] This choice was influenced as much by Cattleya's experience in the field of large-scale international co-productions as by Sky Italia's entry as a commissioner.

contest took place, and out of which arose the winning idea of Michele Pellegrini and Francesco Cenni, who worked throughout the initial development phase until the production of the series treatment.

At a certain point of the development, however, it was practical to expand the writing team to adapt it to the needs and timescales of the project and the choice of Cattleya fell naturally on the screenwriters of *Gomorra: La serie* (Leonardo Fasoli and Maddalena Ravagli), fresh from their international experience with *Zerozerozero*. They brought to the project not only their many years of know-how, but also the international prestige of their previous productions.

In the phase of transition to the actual writers' room, this Italian core was joined by American scriptwriters, who would give the material authenticity, especially as regards the historical setting and delicate themes such as those linked to the representation of racial conflicts. It was also essential at this stage to have someone on the creative team who could write in English and who could eventually take charge of the final version of the scripts.

The choice fell on Max Hurwitz, with whom Fasoli had already collaborated on *Zerozerozero*, who already entered the series treatment phase and was in charge of the final polish for all the episodes. Hurwitz, with a long career in American serial television (among his credits figures the post-Civil War western *Hell on Wheels*), had the right experience to consolidate American cultural aspects and participated in the writers' room, which took place in various stages, first in the United States and then in Italy.

From this phase emerged the episode treatment, signed collectively, which has been the basis of the scripts written and signed by the individual scriptwriters. Fasoli and Ravagli, as headwriters, were responsible for the final version of the scripts, while, as mentioned, the shooting drafts in English were produced by Max Hurwitz.

This was a necessary, but obviously complicated procedure to manage, both from an organisational point of view (considering that scriptwriting continued even after principal photography had begun) and in terms of authorship, which worked best thanks to the strong and clear presence of the producer and a pre-existing relationship between the members of the writers' room.[12]

The relationship between writers of different languages and cultures, including professional ones, was at least partly mediated by the presence of co-executive producer/creative producer figures belonging to the two production realities involved in the project, and the complementarity and coherence of both formal and content objectives between these different realities are fundamental for a harmonious development of the writing phase first and then the production phase (Di Benedetto 2021).

The same figures were in fact present for the whole duration of principal photography, playing a similar role for the three directors (Italian directors

---

[12] On this internal dynamics of the multilingual writers' room, see also the interesting interview with Leonardo Fasoli and Gina Gardini in Guarnaccia 2018.

Francesca Comencini, also artistic director for the series, and Enrico Maria Artale, and the English director David Evans) who succeeded each other at the helm of the series.

At the time of the closing of this chapter, the production of *Django* is not yet finished, and it will be interesting to see how the multinational and multilingual triangulation that has worked so far will translate into the last phase of the series.

22.6 Serial Eyes: Training New Authors for a New International Production Horizon

If initially the adaptation of the writers' room model to individual national contexts was implemented in a more or less unconscious and approximate way,[13] the multiplication of international projects and productions involving actors from different countries has at least partially changed the traditional power relations between writing and production (Barra and Scaglioni 2020).

In this new perspective, the case studies discussed so far also show how increasingly necessary it is to build structured pathways to train writers able to perform at their best in the writers' room system both nationally and transnationally, ensuring levels of excellence both in writing and in the ability to meet the production challenges of a global market. The development of international writers' rooms is also linked to the formation of a common basic professional culture that allows a fruitful exchange of ideas and is not limited to an effective compromise between substantially divergent dramaturgical and production requirements.

It was precisely with this in mind that Serial Eyes was founded in Berlin in 2013,[14] a post-graduate residential programme open to young European and non-European writers,[15] which now has a number of alumni approaching one hundred, half of whom have been involved in the past years in a more or less continuous way in international writers' rooms experiments.

The twelve yearly participants, young scriptwriters, but also producers, coming from different European countries, develop personal and collective projects and learn to work as a team with the aim of developing a European model of showrunning, working not only on the writing system, importing American best practices into Europe, but also exposing scriptwriters to the world of budgeting and production scheduling, an element that is rightly considered a priority in order to give the writer an adequate weight within the

---

[13] A first exploration of the adaptation of this working method in some Italian realities can be found in Cotta Ramosino 2007.

[14] For a general presentation of the programme see: https://serial-eyes.com.

[15] As one might assume, a significant number of Serial Eyes' students is of German nationality, and the German market is also the one that most decisively and systematically imported the writers' room model into its own production reality (see Krauss 2018). However, in almost a decade of existence, Serial Eyes has also had Americans, British, Italians, French and many Eastern European writers as students.

production system. One of the strengths of the programme is the involvement in the faculty of professionals of various nationalities, who also act as tutors in the development of the projects.[16] Frank Spotnitz, one of the teachers of the programme since its inception, underlines the importance of this aspect in the preparation of the new generation of European scriptwriters:

> Writers need to be given the opportunity to learn about production, they need to be exposed to budgeting, scheduling and beyond the set, and understand what a production designer does, cinematographer, costume designer and so on. Because this makes them better writers. A writer without an understanding of production is limited. The flip side is that there are many writers in Europe who want to be a showrunner, they even negotiate to have it in their contract, but they don't know what it means to be a showrunner, it is not automatic, you have to learn it.[17] (Spotnitz 2021)

The writers' room experience is the heart of the Berlin programme, which includes seminars, workshops and participation in the most important meetings of the European television industry, but where the practice of the model with professionals and colleagues of various nationalities remains the most important element. Working inside a "real" writers' room, in the role of showrunner or collaborator for other projects, is an essential training step according to the testimony of the Italian scriptwriters who took part in it (Pellegrini and Serino 2021) and allows building a shared method of idea development with which to dialogue with interlocutors of different nationalities.

The *lingua franca* of communication in taught modules is English, and the series projects developed during the course are written in English, which will then eventually be translated into the language of the show.

For its alumni, Serial Eyes offers the possibility of direct contact with foreign productions, which used to be naturally mediated by local producers (Serino is developing two different serials that should be shot in German and French) and which also opens up interesting questions regarding the distribution of roles within the writing groups, where the author-showrunner can supervise most of the writing project but not be the one who signs the shooting draft of the script (as already seen in the case of *Django*).

It remains problematic, at least in Italy, to systematically transplant this method of serial development to an industrial and writing culture which, on the one hand, has a strong concept of authorship, which is not compatible with the collective creation typical of the writers' room (Pellegrini 2021), and on the other hand, besides being unbalanced in favour of the producer,

---

[16] Among them British Ben Harris (one of the writers of the first season of *Devils*), Luke Franklin, Italian Nicola Lusuardi (Sky Italia's executive in the development of *Devils*), French Olivier Bibas (one of the producers of *Django*), Spanish Maria Cervera.

[17] Interesting reflections on the same theme can be found in the interviews with Stefano Bises and Gina Gardini in Guarnaccia 2018.

does not contemplate certain development timeframes compatible with the total commitment of a traditional writers' room (Serino and Pellegrini 2021). The passage from the German training programme to Italian reality might be complicated for young writers willing to profit from their experience:

> At Serial Eyes they concentrate a lot on the conception and the scaling of the pilot in a very Anglo-Saxon way. (...) From my point of view it's an excellent experience because it trains you to a rigour that is very rare to find in our environment, especially in Italy. If you stay in Germany later, you can find that method in the real world. It's a consolidated method. I came back to Italy with that training, which I was partly starting from because I had worked on *Non uccidere* with Claudio Corbucci, who was an all-round showrunner there, from writing to editing. When I returned to Italy, it was challenging to return to a context where almost no one worked in that way. (Pellegrini 2021)[18]

On the other hand, from this point of view, it would seem more promising to give rise to a seriality that from its conception is an expression of different cultures, not only professional, favoured by the early cohabitation of writers from different countries who experiment with working together, experiments that seem to be increasingly favoured by the presence of new international players in the European field (Serino 2021).

The linguistic element remains a fundamental critical issue in the prospect of transnational European creative and productive collaborations, as is also the time each group is able to devote to the shared work and the way the work is divided between the members of the room.

> The international writers' room works if at the end everyone writes their own episode. You work together for weeks, exchange ideas and make notes but then everyone is in charge of their own instalment. (Serino 2021)

Europe is witnessing the growth of new commissioners (Disney, Netflix, Amazon and soon HBO Max, Paramount+ and more), with increasing investments and their specific internal culture (Barra and Scaglioni 2020), and this reinforces English as a transnational lingua franca. On the other hand, the search for increasingly global production and the unexpected success of original language serials in the US market, as well, have opened the way for productions in other languages.

---

[18] The writing and producing model for *Non uccidere* (*Thou Shalt Not Kill*) originates in the soap opera model, where Corbucci worked extensively, and where scripts must have specific characteristics in terms of length and structure to be produced on time and within budget.

22.7 Conclusions

The analysis of the case studies highlights common problems, but also many opportunities, which require reflection on methods of collaboration, starting from the internal practices of the writers' rooms (the prevalence of the oral element compared to the written one, which "surprised" but also stimulated the Italian authors), but also with respect to the contiguity between the sphere of writing and that of actual production, which implies a different type of training, the latter normally outside the competence of writers in all European countries, but instead usual in the homeland of the writers' room system.

Talking to the Italian scriptwriters involved in the different projects, we encountered a great openness to the possibility of testing themselves in different systems, integrating their own perspectives and professional history into a different working method. For that, the passage through common training courses seems very useful to establish the basis of this confrontation at an early stage and in a "protected environment", creating the premises to build new projects with even higher ambitions, such as, for instance, those bypassing the use of English as a *lingua franca*, by working on the specificity of the starting concept connecting non-Anglophone countries or authors.

This is something that hasn't happened yet. The writers' room model has been imported from the United States and has travelled, also from the terminological point of view, in English thanks to professionals hired to lead local work groups. English, on the other hand, until recently, was a guarantee of a greater possibility of exporting the product, a reality that is changing, thanks also to the expansion of international players who also make content in different languages travel.

In this sense, a greater awareness of the opportunities offered by a type of writing practice that foresees a sharing of authorship in project elaboration is a challenge that Italian authors are starting to face more and more, often finding themselves working with foreign colleagues in international writers' rooms.

Moreover, it seems evident that the challenge of harmonising different production systems, but especially the quality of writing, is linked to the time devoted to *tailor-made* collaborations between professionals coming from different professional traditions, with training paths probably more compatible among the younger generations (who normally have a better knowledge of English and are more willing to engage in the production side of their work, as Serino and Pellegrini confirmed in their interviews) and less among professionals with more experience and deeper curriculums. Paradoxically, it may happen that scriptwriters with decades of writing experience and a recognised prestige (therefore theoretically more authority to deal with the other components of the production system, directors, executives and commissioners) are the ones least interested in taking on the responsibilities related to the realisation of their texts, consuming time to discuss with production companies about budgets, schedules and other daily problems of serial production.

It must be kept in mind that this part of the work, at least in Italy, is rarely requested by the producers (who prefer to keep control over the budget) and if requested, it is not paid after the approval of the shooting scripts (as is not paid the participation in the writers' rooms). In this sense, the negotiation on the creative leadership of a TV show is partly linked to a further economic negotiation between creatives and producers.

Programming a minimum number of weeks of writers' rooms, possibly foreseeing an almost total commitment of the authors involved, clearly also implies a financial investment (for the payment of the authors involved), which is not part of the production tradition of all countries (and in particular the Italian one, to which the case studies considered are linked) and implies, as well, a paradigm shift in the general context.

The openness of the big international commissioners who landed in Europe to promote in the Old Continent a system more centred on screenwriters/creators should be acknowledged and communicated, as screenwriters will have to prove their willingness to train in a different field (budget, schedule, cast, etc.) as well as to invest more of their time to claim and support an idea of authorship that goes beyond the writing process.

In order to claim the title and the role of showrunner, in fact, European and Italian scriptwriters, in particular, need long and varied training, corresponding to the years of experience that American writers have in writers' rooms, gradually acquiring skills that go beyond purely dramaturgical ones. Due to their greater familiarity with the writers' room system, international commissioners have shown greater interest in offering these professional training opportunities.[19]

Lastly, it will be interesting to see in the next few years whether the progressive formation of a shared professional practice will somehow be reflected in a deeper capacity of communication and sharing from the point of view of themes and content, i.e. whether television seriality (we continue to call it that for the sake of simplicity, beyond the increasingly diversified models of realisation) will be able to become part and driver, from the point of view of both production and achievement, of a common transnational and European culture that goes beyond the media world.

This is a mission that the authors we met seem willing to take on, with curiosity and competence, in the spirit of a practical and pragmatic creativity fully consistent with the logic of the writers' rooms.

---

[19] See the training programmes designed by Netflix in collaboration with Anica (Italy's Association of Audiovisual and Multimedia Industry) through the newly created Anica Academy (www.anicaacademy.org).

References

Arlanch, Francesco. 2021. Interview with one of the screenwriters of *Medici* for Lux Vide, 12 December. Translation from Italian by the authors.

Barra, Luca, and Massimo Scaglioni 2020. *A European Television Fiction Renaissance. Premium Production Models and Transnational Circulation*. London: Routledge.

Bennet, Tara. 2014. *Showrunners. The Art of Running a TV Show*. London: Titan Books.

Blanca. 2021– (1 season). Created by Francesco Arlanch, Luisa Cotta Ramosino, Mario Ruggeri, and Lea Tafuri. Italy: Lux Vide, Rai Fiction.

Borgia. 2011–2014 (3 seasons). Created by Tom Fontana. France, Germany, Czech Republic, Italy: Canal+, Sky Italia, Netflix et al.

Cotta Ramosino, Luisa. 2007. "I modelli organizzativi della serialità in Italia. Dieci anni di sperimentazione" [The organization models of serialized television in Italy. Ten years of experimentation]. In *La bella stagione. La fiction italiana, l'Italia nella fiction* [The beautiful season. Italian fiction, Italy in fiction], edited by Milly Buonanno, 131–54. Turin: RAI/Eri.

Cotta Ramosino, Luisa. 2017. "Medici, Masters of Florence: From Facts to Fiction." Paper presented at the annual conference of the Screenwriting Research Network, Dunedin, New Zealand, 28 August–3 September.

Cotta Ramosino, Luisa. 2018. "Medici, Masters of Florence. Challenges and Compromises of an International Coproduction: Characters, Storytelling and Production Issues." Keynote address at the annual conference of the Screenwriting Research Network, Milan, Italy, 13–15 September.

Cotta Ramosino, Luisa, Laura Cotta Ramosino, and Cristiano Dognini. 2004. *Tutto quello che sappiamo su Roma l'abbiamo imparato a Hollywood* [Everything we know about Rome we learned in Hollywood]. Turin: Bruno Mondadori.

Di Benedetto, Donatella. 2021. Interview with the executive producer of *Django* for Cattleya. December. Translation from Italian by the authors.

Devils 2020–2022 (2 seasons). Created by Ezio Abbate, Guido Maria Brera, Elena Bucaccio, Daniele Cesarano, Barbara Petronio, Mario Ruggeri, and Alessandro Sermoneta. Italy: Lux Vide, Sky Italia, Orange Studio, Sky Studios, Orange Cinéma Séries.

Doc – Nelle tue mani [*Doc – In Your Hands*]. 2020– (2 seasons). Created by Francesco Arlanch and Viola Rispoli. Italy: Lux Vide, Rai Fiction.

Django. 1966. Written by Sergio Corbucci, Franco Rossetti, Piero Vivarelli, José Gutiérrez Maesso, Bruno Corbucci, and Fernando Di Leo (uncredited). Directed by Sergio Corbucci. Italy, Spain: B.R.C. Produzione Film, Tecisa Film.

Django. 2022 (1 season). Created by Leonardo Fasoli and Maddalena Ravagli. Italy, France: Atlantique Productions, Cattleya, Canal Plus, Sky.

Fumagalli, Armando. 2013. *Creatività al potere. Da Hollywood alla Pixar, passando per l'Italia* [Creativity in power. From Hollywood to Pixar via Italy]. Turin: Lindau.

Fumagalli, Armando. 2021. "L'Italia nelle grandi coproduzioni internazionali" [Italy in major international co-productions]. In *Storia delle serie TV Volume II* [History of Tv Series. Volume II], edited by Armando Fumagalli, Cassandra Albani, and Paolo Braga, 226–48. Rome: Dino Audino.

Gomorra: La serie (*Gomorrah – The Series*). 2014–2021 (5 seasons). Created by Stefano Bises, Leonardo Fasoli and Roberto Saviano. Italy: Sky, Cattleya, Fandango, Beta Film.

Guarnaccia, Fabio. 2013. *Serial Writers, Link. Idee per la televisione vol. 15* [Serial Writers, Link. Ideas for television, vol. 15]. Cologno Monzese, Italy: Rti.
Guarnaccia, Fabio. 2018. *Autori Seriali, Link. Idee per la televisione vol 23* [Serial Authors, Link. Ideas for Television, vol. 23]. Cologno Monzese, Italy: Rti.
Hell on Wheels. 2011–2016 (5 seasons). Created by Tony Gayton and Joe Gayton. USA: Entertainment One, Nomadic Pictures, (gayton)^2, Endemol, AMC, Endemol Entertainment UK, H.O.W. Productions.
Krauss, Florian. 2018. "'Quality Series' and Their Production Cultures: Transnational Discourses Within the German Television Industry". *Series* IV (2): 47–60.
La strada di casa [*The Way Home*]. 2017–2019 (2 seasons). Created by Francesco Arlanch and Andrea Valagussa. Italy: RAI.
Lotz, Amanda D. 2009. "What Is U.S. Television Now?" Annals of the American Academy of Political and Social Science: End of Television: Its Impact on the World (So Far), 625: 49–59.
Medici. Masters of Florence 2016–2019 (3 seasons). Created by Frank Spotnitz and Nicholas Meyer. Italy: Lux Vide, Big Light Productions, Altice Studios, Wild Bunch TV, Rai Fiction.
Mittel, Jason. 2015. *Complex TV. The Poetics of contemporary Television Storytelling.* New York: NYU Press.
Non uccidere (Thou Shalt Not Kill). 2015–2018 (2 seasons). Created by Claudio Corbucci. Italy: Rai Fiction, Freemantle Media Italia.
Pellegrini, Bernardo. 2021. Interview with the screenwriter and Serial Eyes alumnus, writer for series both for Amazon and Sky. 17 December. Translation from Italian by the authors.
Phalen, Patricia F. 2017. *Writing Hollywood: The Work and Professional Culture of Television Writers.* London: Routledge.
Priggé, Steven. 2005. *Created by... Inside the Minds of Tv's Top Show Creators.* Los Angeles: Silman-James.
Ruggeri, Mario. 2021. Interview with one of the screenwriters of *Devils* for Lux Vide. 5 December. Translation from Italian by the authors.
Serino, Davide. 2021. Interview with the Serial Eyes alumnus and screenwriter of series for both for Amazon and Sky. December 2021. Translation from Italian by the authors.
Spotnitz, Frank. 2021. Interview with the screenwriter and showrunner of *Medici*, *Leonardo* and *Devils* 2 for Lux Vide. 24 November.
Suburra – La serie (Suburra: Blood on Rome). 2017–2020 (3 seasons). Series bible by Daniele Cesarano and Barbara Petronio. Italy: Cattleya, Rai Fiction, Netflix.
The Eddy. 2020 (1 season). Created by Jack Thorne. France, USA: Augury. One Shoe Films, Boku Films, Fifty Fathoms, Atlantique Productions, Endeavor Content.
The Tudors. 2007–2010 (4 seasons). Created by Michael Hirst. UK, Canada, Ireland, USA: Working Title Television, Octagon Entertainment, Peach Arch Entertainment, Reveille Eire, Showtime Networks.
Un passo dal Cielo (One Step from Heaven). 2011–2021 (6 seasons). Series bible by Mario Ruggeri, Enrico Oldoini, Andrea Valagussa, Francesca De Michelis and Salvatore Basile. Italy: Lux Vide, Rai Fiction.
Viola come il mare [*Purple Like the Sea*]. 2022 (1 season). Created by Elena Bucaccio and Silvia Leuzzi. Italy: Lux Vide, RTI.

WGI (Writers Guild Italia). 2017. "Suburra, la serie" [Suburra, the series]. *Writers Guild Italia*. https://www.writersguilditalia.it/speciale-suburra-gina-gardini/. Accessed 20 February 2022.

Zerozerozero. 2020 (1 season). Created by Leonardo Fasoli, Mauricio Katz, and Stefano Sollima. Italy: Cattleya and Bartleby Film.

CHAPTER 23

Writing Online Drama for Public Service Media in the Era of Streaming Platforms

Petr Szczepanik and Dorota Vašíčková

23.1 Introduction

The chapter analyses the development process of the first public service fiction web series in the Czech Republic and virtually the whole of East-Central Europe, where, in the same way as its Western counterparts, public service media (PSM) has been undergoing a transformation to adapt to the online platform-dominated markets, while also facing existential threats from anti-liberal political opponents. The short-form, ten-part queer love story titled *TBH* (an internet acronym for To Be Honest) about a group of troubled teenagers involved in a shooting incident at their high school focuses on bullying and identity struggles in the high-school community. It was co-written and directed in 2020–2021 by queer auteur filmmaker Lucia Kajánková, who also involved a group of film academy students to form a writers' room, an atypical move in the local industry. Inspired by the trend of using extensive research into audience needs to build relatable characters (Redvall 2018) and by what has been labelled an "ethnographic shift" (Andersen and Sundet 2019, 3) in Scandinavian youth-oriented online series development, the team conducted research among local high-school students

P. Szczepanik (✉)
Charles University, Prague, Czech Republic
e-mail: petr.szczepanik@ff.cuni.cz

D. Vašíčková (✉)
Česká Televize, Prague, Czech Republic
e-mail: dorota.vasickova@ceskatelevize.cz

© The Author(s), under exclusive license to Springer Nature Switzerland AG 2023
R. Davies et al. (eds), *The Palgrave Handbook of Screenwriting Studies*,
https://doi.org/10.1007/978-3-031-20769-3_23

to map out their lifestyles, needs, and communication practices. The chapter follows the transformations of the authorial vision, the collaborative process of the project's development, while focusing on its embeddedness in and conditioning by the institutional culture, power structures, and strategic goals of the national public service broadcaster Česká televize (ČT), which has been undergoing a key stage of its digital transformation. What appears to be a progressive struggle in the field of identity politics and auteur filmmaking on the representational level thus plays out as the manifestation of a larger struggle for the future of public service media in the era of streaming platforms and antiliberal movements. The PSM web series development thus appears as a testing ground for implementing a new PSM online strategy.

We assert that *TBH*'s development contributed to or accelerated ČT's transformation along the lines of creative innovation, youthification, and platformization. However, this transformation was not caused by *TBH* per se: it is far from over, and its outcome remains unclear. From a future perspective, *TBH* may appear a mere ripple on a wave of more radical institutional change driven by far more disruptive forces, or, on the contrary, it may appear a small deviation on the route of using online content for cementing ČT's traditional mode of practice in the evolving market. Instead of predicting *TBH*'s future significance, we aim to show how the ongoing, top-down-initiated institutional transformation plays out on the ground when seen from within the development process, thus showing how studying script development contributes to critical media industry studies.

Methodologically, the chapter combines ethnographically informed screenwriting studies with platform studies and an industry analysis of public service media. It does not focus on the script as text, nor on its individual mutations, but rather on the key stakeholders' subjective depictions of the development process and reads them against the context of ČT's ongoing transformation. By doing this, we propose an industry analysis of the development process, of what one of us elsewhere called the "development culture" (Szczepanik 2021), whereby an innovative, platform-specific, youth-oriented project in development acts upon and is simultaneously shaped by the production system and institutional culture of a small-nation public service broadcaster.

23.2 Online-Only Content Development as a Site of Creative Innovation, "Youthification", and "Platformization" of Public Service Media

There are roughly three main bodies of literature offering conceptual frameworks to understand the specificity of public service media's online-only content production and indicating lines of public service media's transformation: one on independent web series, the second on PSM online content strategies, and the last one on the "platformization" of cultural production and circulation. Independent web series have been academically discussed mostly outside Europe, with regard to North America (Zboralska 2017; Christian 2018), Australia (Monaghan 2017; Leder 2021), and Asia (Kang 2017; Cunningham and Craig 2019), both in terms of their alternative business models and innovative creative practices.

Independent web series have enjoyed special attention as "change-making efforts that directly respond to […] the dominant norms, paradigms and patterns embedded" in the current television industries (Zboralska 2017, 30). More specifically, web series development has been praised for the way it is subverting the dominant practices of pitching, greenlighting, casting, and piloting (whose aim is to estimate a show's potential to attract large audiences before it is fully made) and upfront financing through advertisement sales by relying heavily on undiscovered talent, unpaid labour compensated by the promise of self-realization, creative freedom and IP ownership, long-term fan engagement as proof of the show's value, and various minority themes and communities (Christian 2014). According to Aymar Jean Christian, independent web series production cultures have been characterized by horizontal, informal, community-based organization, with individual members (including actors) combining different job roles beyond their credit and merging production work proper with fundraising, marketing, and reaching out to audiences. The flipside of creative freedom has always been highly precarious work conditions, and vulnerability to corporate value extraction when initial resources dry up and the creators seek partnerships with brands or more prestigious and financially sustainable models in legacy TV networks (Christian 2018, 68–100). Although PSM web series do not rely on unpaid labour and are not prone to corporate takeover, they tend—similarly to their independent counterparts—to significantly diverge from institutionalized development practices.

In a series of studies, Stayci Taylor has argued that web series potentially challenge traditional notions of script development and story paradigms by operating without fixed budgets, schedules, episode length, and script formats, often deploying deeply personal, character- and improvisation-driven stories with loose narrative structures, and looking beyond traditional demographic categories when interacting with fan communities. Various extratextual factors may take up the role of the mainstream plotting, which is based on a map of plot points: pop-culture references, platform-specific methods of communication between characters and with the audiences, amateur actors shaping their characters through improvisation, etc. The web invites more niche-oriented, discovery-led, audience-facing development approaches than legacy TV networks with their conservative executives, standardized programming slots, and highly selective approval mechanisms: by allowing creators to reach online audiences quickly, while the story is still being developed, with just a vague idea that may be tested and adjusted according to audience response and that may evolve in reaction to topical issues (Ellingsen and Taylor 2019; Taylor 2021).

The second body of literature, focusing on European PSM online-only content, has been inspired by the global success of the NRK's web series *Skam*. It concentrates mainly on new methods of researching, representing, and communicating the lived realities of narrowly defined, mostly young target groups, and studies PSM web series as part of a broader strategy of *youthification* (per se drawing on a longer tradition of youth television, not limited to online-only content). Youthification in the context of PSM online strategies refers to the broadcasters' attempts at winning back the teenage, social media savvy audiences that have mostly abandoned linear television, with the aim of *building* them as citizens, and thus preserving the core public value of universality. Youthification's most distinct manifestation to date might be the transmedia, multi-perspective storytelling of *Skam*, whereby the strongly relatable teenage characters communicate about their inner lives via social media apps, both among themselves and directly with audiences in *real-time* chats and *stories*. While *Skam* and similar PSM web series tackle socially relevant issues such as sexual identity politics or racism, thus clearly manifesting their public service mission, they strive to remain true to and non-judgmental about the teenage life worlds and systematically avoid an adult's moral perspective (Andersen and Sundet 2019; Lindtner and Dahl 2019; Krauß and Stock 2021).

As a way of generalizing her findings on Nordic PSM web series production, Vilde Schanke Sundet distinguished between two innovative tendencies that PSM institutions use to adapt to the changes in the market: what she termed the "going small" production model (as opposed to the "going big" model of exportable "quality television") employs low budgets, small multi-functional production teams, and tight schedules, while prioritizing the effects of authenticity, liveness, social relevance, and audience insight over more conventional notions of "quality" (see Sundet 2021, 57–65). More importantly for the theme of this chapter, the development processes corresponding to the "going small" model and the *Skam*-style transmedia storytelling require changes in the existing institutional culture by shifting or blurring the borderlines between writing, directing, and publishing, between different job roles, different formats of programming, different divisions and channels, and even between the designated PSM space and commercial online platforms used to reach the digital-native audiences (Andersen and Sundet 2019). When given strategic priority, online-only content thus functions as an internal vehicle or accelerator of a broader institutional change that might be termed the platformization of public service media.

Platformization in the context of PSM, the focus of the third body of literature providing a theoretical framework for this chapter, refers to the ongoing penetration of the "social media logics" (van Dijck and Poell 2013, 2015), of "contingent commodities" that are "modular in design and informed by datafied user feedback" (Nieborg and Poell 2018, 4276), or digital platform principles more generally into the legacy media's modes of operation (Stollfuß 2021). While a certain level of platformization, including collaboration with commercial platforms, seems inevitable for PSM for it to keep in touch with the changing consumer behaviour, critics point to the danger that it might also affect their ability to fulfil the public mission (e.g. by relying overly on algorithmic recommendation, thus creating so-called *filter bubbles*, eventually compromising the core public value of universality) (Sørensen and Hutchinson 2018). However, first empirical studies of the subject indicate that PSMs' strategic responses to the growths of transnational SVOD services and platforms proceed in stages and vary contextually (D'Arma, Raats, and Steemers 2021). The adoption of specific platform principles such as personalization is being implemented with caution and is running up not only against technological limits, but also resistance within the institutions traditionally centred around linear programming, channel brands and older demographics, with the likely outcome being a balanced, path-dependent mix of free-choice online and editorial on-air programming approaches (Lassen and Sørensen 2021).

When looking at online-only content's overall production volume and budget allocation, it must be clear that in the present and near future, web series remain just a marginal supplement to mainstream linear TV programming, far from constituting any kind of dominant trend for PSM either in Scandinavia or—even less so—in East-Central Europe.[1] Although not able per se to initiate a paradigmatic change in the cultural or organizational functioning of the respective PSM, they still seem to be, as this case study shows, a powerful magnet for both public and professional imaginations of what PSM institutions might look like in the online platform era. Furthermore, divisions between online and on-air programming are likely to blur, because PSM incline towards a close interplay rather than separation between linear scheduling and online curating (Bruun 2020), distributing their catalogues across multiple devices and platforms, wherever target audiences reside. Therefore, online-only (or rather online-first) content will probably be *infiltrating* other types of programming, including primetime, with the principles of creative innovation, youthification, and platformization.

To understand how PSM institutions and professional communities make sense of the challenges and opportunities brought to them by online-only formats, it might be useful to employ Karin van Es and Thomas Poell's concept of *platform imaginaries*, referring to "the ways in which social actors understand and organize their activities in relation to platform algorithms, interfaces, data infrastructures, moderation procedures, business models, user practices, and audiences" (van Es and Poell 2020, 3). In our case study, various stakeholders involved in pitching, approving, producing, and publishing the first ČT's fiction web series *TBH* projected specific ideas about what a public service web series should involve and how its audiences might respond, and

---

[1] This assessment is based on a work-in-progress comparative research into PSM online strategies conducted by our team of a research project "Strategies for Public Service Television's Sustainability in the Internet Era: Best Practices Based on International Comparison" (Technology Agency of the Czech Republic, TL03000251).

oriented their actions according to them. Faced with the radical uncertainty of the possible outcome and of the youth audience response, they delved into extensive speculation, research, and testing, including programmatic vision statements, formal and informal interviewing, a questionnaire survey, focus groups, and self-observation or introspection.

An industry analysis of a development process requires a conceptualization of the interdependencies between a (collective or distributed) creative agency, a (potentially disruptive) project in development and an (changing) organizational environment. Janet Staiger's study of the Hollywood mode of production explained its gradual systemic changes as a circular interplay between industrial conditions and signifying practices (Bordwell, Staiger, and Thompson 1985, 90): while the textual features of films are certainly conditioned by the existing production system, the system also evolves (e.g. by establishing a new department or by refining the division of labour) to accommodate the requirements of textual innovations (such as new trends in sound design or digital effects). From a micro-level perspective of individual productions, project development appears to be the most risky and uncertain stage of production, where an evolving cultural product, not yet materialized, requires the intense but fragile and open-ended collaboration of various actors with often diverging interests and creative visions of the screen idea being developed (Bloore 2013; Macdonald 2013). In her *sociomaterial* study of film development, the art sociologist Sara Malou Strandvad proposed considering the "organizing consequences" of the evolving product itself: to investigate the "two-way relation between the product and the social relations around it. [... how] the organizing of cultural projects and the progression of the product are co-produced; mutually constitutive processes" (Strandvad 2009, 158). Although not fully adopting the sociomaterial perspective, this case study similarly assigns the project-in-development its own agency, however circumscribed by the institutional conditions. It elaborates on two levels of the *mutually constitutive* processes: on the organizational level, the development of ČT's first fiction web series established or rather redrew the collaborative and power links between different institutional divisions, teams, and freelancers; on the institutional-cultural level, it exposed and rearticulated the *platform imaginaries* of all agents involved in developing it.

23.3 Czech Public Service Television on a Journey Towards a VOD Platform

The director general of ČT until mid-2023, Petr Dvořák, announced an ambitious plan for the next step of ČT's digitalization in his 2017 re-election vision statement, where he promised to ramp up investment in online activities from 1 to 5% of ČT's overall budget. Despite being vague about the actual form of its online services and stressing rather the educational and archival functions than a fully fledged VOD portal, he also mentioned a personalized recommendation system and "new online formats responding to the expectations of young online viewers" (Dvořák 2017, 17). Two years later, he was more explicit about the strategic goal of competing with Netflix and HBO Go in the national market by offering local original content (Straková 2019), and in 2021, he speculated about a joint streaming platform with the two leading local commercial broadcasters, while referring to the examples of the UK-based Britbox and French Salto (Aust 2021).

But on the ground inside ČT, something slightly different was going on, and it took several years before the top management decided what exactly it wanted and from whom. In 2018, ČT management formally decided to create a new video platform—labelling it "the most important change in ČT's online activities in terms of following new trends" in a later internal report (Maxa 2020, 14)—and a provisional team was initiated within the Marketing division. It eventually prevailed over other, internally competing video platform ideas and was finally given an official mandate in 2019 to develop a new VOD portal, and a provisional organizational place outside ČT divisions, under the direct supervision of the Director General (in a newly created Managing Committee for Digital Projects, made up of several ČT division heads). A larger team gradually came together under the dual leadership of the veteran UX designer and front-end developer Zdeněk Lanc and a young sociologist Josef Zukal, populated mostly by new-coming, partly freelance back-end and front-end developers and UX designers. Speaking retrospectively, Zukal acknowledged that the original assignment his team had received from the top management—epitomized by the misleading label of "ČT Netflix" that had for a time circulated within ČT—was disturbingly vague, and it took him and his colleagues many months to brainstorm, specify and negotiate not just the objectives, methods, timelines, and technological form of the platform, but also its uncertain position within ČT, among two older *new media* teams with partially overlapping agendas.[2] The co-existence of the contradictory approaches to what ČT should do online, with the *old new media* personnel used to producing mainly metadata and bonus materials supporting on-air programming in the online rather than thinking in terms of autonomous online curation and online-only content, required the new platform team, especially in the early stages, to engage in an overwhelming work of self-explanation and translation between different institutional cultures and professional groups. This manifested in various strategic plans, vision statements, consumer analyses, and other conceptual material that the platform team prepared for both the top management and their future collaborators in other divisions. When Zukal's team finally found its permanent institutional home in the Development division in 2020, the shift from Marketing to Development marked, according to him, the increasing recognition of the importance of online curation and online-only content as opposed to merely servicing linear programming: "Development is the place where project

[2] Josef Zukal interviewed by Klára Smejkal and Lukáš Slavík, 15 April 2021.

ideas are solicited from the outside world, where the incubator of what gets approved or rejected is situated, where content experience accumulates. […] There is a more experimental way of thinking encoded in the genes of this division compared to others".[3]

The head of the Development division, Jan Maxa (whose responsibilities since January 2021 included also what was termed New Media), decided to bring together ČT's online activities, dispersed across several channels and organizational divisions and standing somewhat outside the ČT programming system, by introducing a product-based management model with a product manager at the top of each online *product*, overseen by the newly created Digital Board approving annual product plans and new products in terms of technical functionality, UX design, and content (see also Maxa 2020). The new platform product team, headed by Zukal, gained a central position within ČT's five-member online product *family* due to its vital horizontal links with other products and divisions, and became better integrated within the institution, which has been traditionally organized hierarchically and around programming projects rather than around products. Maxa saw the main objective of the new platform in "active curation and autonomous online programming"[4] as opposed to ČT's previous catch-up service launched in 2008, which was strictly subordinated to the scheduling logic of linear broadcasting. The online-only content initiative was, for him as a development executive, a way of introducing more narrowly targeted and innovative programming cheaply, which is crucial especially at a time of the stagnating licence-fee revenues and austerity measures imposed on the ever-more expensive linear programming. But he also saw his role as diplomatic: finding a balance between ČT's heritage and professional culture, on the one hand, and the demands of the new online strategy, on the other.

A small and the most junior group within the approximately 50-member platform team has been responsible for the content strategy, meaning online curation and online-only content.[5] While most of the platform team's workforce and internal discussions concentrated on the technical functioning and design of the portal, plans to launch online-only production, initially a marginal addition to the new product, paradoxically became its publicly most visible part, and—as will be shown in the following part of this chapter—also a way to communicate the vision of the platform to fellow ČT workers. In the fall of 2019, ČT management announced the first public call for online-only projects, which was the first occasion when the new online strategy was

[3] Josef Zukal interviewed by Klára Smejkal and Lukáš Slavík, 15 April 2021.
[4] Jan Maxa interviewed by Petr Szczepanik, 2 December 2021.
[5] Dorota Vašíčková, the co-author of this chapter, has been part of this group, starting as an intern in 2019 and later moving to a regular position of online-only content editor.

introduced to the professional community and film students. The call specified that the projects should have 10–20 episodes of 15 minutes or less and should explain why they are suitable for online or mobile viewing and what extratextual ways of addressing their target audience they will employ. A surprisingly high number of over 130 applications arrived, of which an ad hoc committee[6] selected thirty for a pitching session which ended with a slate of about ten winners approved for development, six of them finally produced and released in late 2021 or early 2022. The large number and wide scope of the proposals, coming both from in-house and external producers or authors, reflected the professional community's interest in and understanding of the public service online mission and formats. Although a significant portion were just re-purposed linear projects (hoping to get a speedier green light in the less-crowded new online service as opposed to the tight on-air schedule), several tropes emerged in the presentations that revealed a relatively wide awareness of online-only formats' specificity, including the importance of the short form, social media aesthetics, authenticity over spectacle, narrower target audiences and low entry barriers for talent, as well as their public service potential: sexual identity politics, motherhood, social satire, YouTubers as educators, mockery of fake news production, home childcare, generation Z's housing issues, and so forth.[7] A second open call for online-only projects targeting the 14–34 age groups followed in December 2020, this time with several pre-defined themes such as climate change or communication barriers during the COVID-19 pandemic; it was even more successful, attracting over 200 proposals, fifteen of which were approved for development. When considered in the context of the virtual absence of such openness in the field of on-air programme commissioning, these unexpected turnouts indicated the intensity and diversity of imagination inspired by ČT's launch of the online-only production.

While nonfiction formats slightly dominated in the first call, there was a smaller portion of youth-oriented short-form drama, too. At the time, the global success story of the NRK web series *Skam* had already circulated among local professionals, partly due to the recent screenings of *Skam* at the international TV series festival Serial Killer (based in the Czech town of Brno), which runs a web series section.[8] It was not surprising that several projects explicitly mentioned *Skam*, and the most positively assessed of the story ideas, *TBH*, resembled *Skam* most closely in its youth focus, the emphasis on authenticity and identity politics as well as social media aesthetics. Since then, *TBH* has become a centrepiece of ČT's publicity for the new platform, whose launch had been repeatedly shifted towards the end of 2021 for technical and organizational reasons. It was the only fiction in the first slate of ČT's online-only

---

[6] Both authors of this chapter were part of the committee, together with one of the two VOD portal heads and two senior executives, the heads of development and marketing.

[7] Based on the authors' notes from the selection session.

[8] See https://www.serialkiller.tv/en/.

titles approved for production; it won the best web series award at the Serial Killer festival 2021, was screened at the Tallinn Black Nights 2021 and the Séries Mania 2022 festivals and selected as a finalist of the 2022 Prix Jeunesse International television festival.

23.4 *TBH*'s Development

TBH's creator Lucia Kajánková (1987) is a Slovak-born, openly bisexual screenwriter-director, who graduated in philosophy and film studies at Charles University in Prague, as well as screenwriting and dramaturgy at the FAMU film school, where she has since been teaching and working on her PhD thesis. At the time of ČT's 2019 open call, she had already been an acclaimed author of a short arthouse film, a recognized script advisor, and a festival selector (e.g. programme director of Mezipatra Queer Film Festival till 2015), but not established as a TV writer or director. Her initial story idea responded to the ČT call and its emphasis on specific features of public service online-only content. The proposal included a PowerPoint presentation with a logline stating: "A failed shooting attack on a high school turns the lives of a group of teenagers upside down". After quoting a real-life incident report from local news, it referred to four high-school dramas dealing with students' sex lives, three of them Nordic PSM series: *Skam* (NRK), *Nudes* (NRK), *Manners* (RÚV) and *13 Reasons Why* (Netflix). In her pitch book, Kajánková specified the format (10 episodes of 8–12 minutes each) and the educational mission targeting the audience of 13–18 years; she also sketched out a plan to employ social media in the visual style and the promotional cross-platform campaign, and to involve her FAMU students in an improvised writers' room, capitalizing on their recent high-school experiences. She elaborated on the main narrative line revolving around bullying that preceded the prank shooting incident, and the emotional impact on a group of characters which followed. But she hinted only vaguely at the sexual identities of the characters that would eventually define the second narrative line, coming forth in the later stages of development. In general, the *TBH* pitch demonstrated the most specific knowledge of the web series format and the clearest focus on youth audiences among all competing projects, which immediately resonated with the selection committee.

After the successful pitch, Kajánková's project got pre-greenlit and had to be assigned an in-house producer. In ČT, all projects (apart from news, current affairs and sports programmes, and a few other exceptions) need to be developed by one of the in-house *creative producer units*, who act as protectors accompanying projects in all their stages, mediating between the authors and other ČT divisions. However, they do not have the decision-making power or control over a programming slot that would make them comparable to the West-European commissioning editors (see Szczepanik 2021, 188–89). Since Kajánková had no pre-established collaboration with any of the units, and none of the units had had any experience with youth-oriented web series,

TBH (together with other winners of the pitching session) was offered in an internal tender to whomever might be interested, ending up in the unit of Alena Müllerová, a seasoned expert in documentary, educational and hybrid or cross-genre programmes (such as docufiction or docureality). Müllerová was interested in working with a debuting female author and the student writers' room, attracted by the theme of bullying and eager to pick up the challenge of the online format.[9] She then assigned her close collaborator, a former film critic, and Hollywood connoisseur Alena Prokopová, as the in-house script editor to work closely with Kajánková on developing the scripts for the individual episodes. At the same time, the ČT platform team started talking to the unit heads about their online-only production plans and put together a manifesto-style vision statement, inspired by the online programming of Western European public service media such as NRK or ZDF and ARD's funk.net, that was circulated among ČT employees in early 2020 and eventually went public.[10] The new platform team believed that *TBH* is an ideal embodiment of their vision for online-only content, but apart from such an indirect contact, it had little influence on its early development.

Kajánková and her six-member student team (mostly in their early 20s) largely worked on their own, brainstorming, watching reference series, and digging into their personal teenage experiences to increase the authenticity of the high-school characters. The improvised writers' room originated from a FAMU screenwriting workshop, for which Kajánková, already preparing for her ČT pitch, designed an assignment of writing the outline for a new season of the Netflix teenage series *Sex Education*. When interviewed together with her group in July 2020, she stressed the public service value of the story, in which the prank shooting plays the part of a narrative instigator to reveal and accelerate the internal struggles of the characters. Avoiding representation of the actual physical violence and not focusing on the shooter was also a way for her to be true to the Czech social reality where gun violence at schools remains rare, but where bullied students might still resort to imagining shooting as a desperate last resort.[11] At the same time, a school shooting allowed the writers to playfully draw on tropes from American high-school films and series, in a similar way as they derived the social hierarchy of characters from their positions within or around the school floorball team, choosing the locally popular, but low-profile sport to mark a difference from the typical masculine sports of choice at US high schools.[12] Starting from this premise

---

[9] Alena Müllerová interviewed by Petr Szczepanik, 17 December 2021.

[10] The document, drafted by one of this chapter's authors, Dorota Vašíčková, consists of five key points: A variety of smaller publics; authenticity as a key quality; open (experimental) forms; relevant message over production values; liveness (ČT 2020).

[11] Kajánková mentioned this repeatedly in public interviews as an autobiographical fact.

[12] Gus Van Sant's *Elephant* (2003) was specifically mentioned in an interview with the writing team, among other references. Lucia Kajánková and her writing team interviewed by Petr Szczepanik and Dorota Vašíčková, 20 July 2020.

and loglines of individual episodes from the pitch book, the group spent the spring of 2020 drafting episode outlines together, debating the social world of the high school, and elaborating on characters' backstories, including their style of social media use.

Although Kajánková defined her role as a showrunner, acted as the group's moderator, and took up the task of speaking for the project and negotiating with ČT, the student writers described the inner workings of the group as democratic and egalitarian at this stage of development. At the time of the first COVID-19 lockdown, the writers' room switched from face-to-face meetings at ČT offices to *Zoom*, complemented by other online tools, such as *Google Jamboard*. This created a peculiar *safe space* in a sense of a protected work environment, but also isolated the group from any physical contact with the institution and delayed official feedback. At the time of moving online, the group started experimenting with so-called chat stories and role plays, using *WhatsApp* as a platform for fictional chats with each member speaking for one of the characters, thus building deeper emotional ties between them. As one of the student writers put it: "Identifying with my character was extremely intense, having to think for them, chat for them, while somehow functioning in my real life at the same time. [...] It actually generated the content of individual narrative lines; the authenticity of the characters generated the story itself". When they felt they were ready, Kajánková divided episodes among them and asked them to write drafts with dialogues simultaneously in just twenty-four hours, to "give it a sense of almost automatic writing [...] a pure, instinctive draft zero".[13] Next, they moved to structuring and editing the whole together again, processing notes from an in-house and an external script editor (a ČT employee, Alena Prokopová, and an accomplished screenwriter, Miro Šifra, commissioned on behalf of Kajánková), shortening the episodes to fit the agreed 12–14 min and the budget cap. In June, two sample episodes were ready for the Program Board meeting, ČT's key institutional greenlighting ritual attended by top executives, which went uncharacteristically smoothly, because all parties involved backed it as a model for the new online-only content strategy, agreeing that the new platform needs a youth fiction to be properly promoted.[14]

The group's sense of working for ČT as a public service institution remained rather vague, marked by the lack of prior professional experience in TV production: they perceived it as a place protected from commercial pressures that give them more creative freedom than local private networks or internet portals producing web series, but also as a traditionalist broadcaster that had so far entirely missed the opportunity to address young audiences. The short online format played a role in the development, according to Kajánková, but not necessarily as an explicit reference framework. Rather, it shaped the writing

---

[13] Lucia Kajánková and her writing team interviewed by Petr Szczepanik and Dorota Vašíčková, 20 July 2020.

[14] Alena Müllerová interviewed by Petr Szczepanik, 17 December 2021.

process via the groups' imaginaries of their teenage target audience as largely overlapping with their own life experiences, including the social media logics governing their communication styles and relationships:

> I think it [our awareness of the web series format] is mainly a question of the target group, it comes organically, because we knew what format it is from the very beginning. It also results from the fact that we write on WhatsApp, but also from how old we are, characters chatting and social messages inserted in the image appeared to us as absolutely natural.[15]

The short form and continuing narrative pushed them to condense and intensify the narration to the maximum level for each episode, and structurally to use efficient, quick opening scenes as well as cliffhangers. The cliffhangers are not story-based, but rather character-based: they leave, Kajánková said, a question of "what the characters do next, what does this mean for them", rather than simply "what happens next".[16] The character-driven approach typical for web series was also manifested, according to her, in the way the whole episodes are narrated from a specific character's point of view. The flexible length of the 12–14-minute episodes, as opposed to the strict timing of traditional TV production, proved to be extremely important in the shooting stage. While all the episode scripts had 13 pages, the freedom of length gave Kajánková an option to preserve the internal rhythm and length of individual scenes.

Inspired by the above-mentioned ethnographic shift in youth series production, the group designed, with the help of ČT's research department, an anonymous questionnaire to collect data about high-school students' lived realities, covering themes such as bullying, sex and relationships, friends, visions of the future, and more. Instead of using questionnaire data as a starting point for writing, the team employed them ex post as a "reality check" on the authenticity of their characters. To the series producer Alena Müllerová, the research proved that sexual identity is a crucial issue for the target group, which played a role in her willingness to accept the LGBT narrative line introduced later in the development process but missing in the original pitch (see more on this below).[17] The questionnaire was not the only external data feeding into the development process, and the script kept changing up until the shooting (and even the postproduction). Kajánková wanted to make sure she had an opportunity to implement late changes in the scripts based on her experience of casting young actors and non-actors:

---

[15] Lucia Kajánková and her writing team interviewed by Petr Szczepanik and Dorota Vašíčková, 20 July 2020.

[16] Lucia Kajánková and her writer team interviewed by Petr Szczepanik and Dorota Vašíčková, 20 July 2020.

[17] Alena Müllerová interviewed by Petr Szczepanik, 17 December 2021.

Being a showrunner as well as the director and doing a teenage, ensemble-based project, I said from the beginning that the last version of the shooting script must be allowed to be fine-tuned depending on who gets cast, which is a director approach [to development]. The characters, their relationships and the dynamics were supposed to get completed together with the actors. […] I wanted the young people I'd select to bring in a lot of their own personalities, their life experiences, so that I can fine-tune the characters based on that. […] From a certain stage they had to take the responsibility for their characters […] to make them their own. […] Together, collaboratively, we were then building the dynamics of their relationships.[18]

For the sake of authenticity, Kajánková wanted to cast unknown young faces that would overshadow professional actors playing their parents or teachers. Together with a young production manager based in a ČT-affiliated studio in the town of Brno, they prepared an open call, and since the lockdown was still ongoing, they first collected video recordings with the candidates responding to prescribed personal questions, performing a monologue and a dialogue; this was followed by a second in-person round, based on improvisation assignments (without a prior knowledge of the scripts) centring on the shooting incident. Kajánková explained that casting—which she managed to keep under her full creative control by avoiding traditional ČT procedures—was, similarly to the questionnaire data, "a test of the script, of the characters […] to see how they react".[19] At the same time, casting and rehearsing were a truly collaborative process for her: she debated personal life experiences with the candidates that corresponded with the key story themes (including coming outs as perceived by both hetero and non-hetero actors), incorporated concrete lines from the improvisations into the scripts, asked the selected actors to create playlists for their characters (some of which ended up in the soundtrack), and discussed costumes (some pieces owned by the actors appeared on screen). She remained flexible about who would play whom until the end of the casting process, experimenting with switching the roles, to allow for the interpersonal dynamics to take shape more naturally.

Such an open-ended creative process, where casting feeds back into the scripts, was radically different from the traditional way casting is done in ČT's serial production, where a casting director typically presents a pre-selection, the rating potential of well-known actors makes the main difference, and the borderline between development and production or between scriptwriting and directing remains very clear. With *TBH*, the scripts kept changing until the start of shooting, and casting was repeatedly reconsidered, while the approval process got delayed, partly due to the broken communication between the creative team based in Brno, 200 km from Prague, and the ČT producer, who thus missed the moment when she could still efficiently intervene in casting. It resulted in short-term misunderstandings and conflicts between Kajánková

[18] Lucia Kajánková interviewed by Petr Szczepanik and Dorota Vašíčková, 14 July 2021.
[19] Lucia Kajánková interviewed by Petr Szczepanik and Dorota Vašíčková, 14 July 2021.

and ČT executives. As Kajánková admitted: "the status of the project changed shortly before the physical production started […] people who had not been involved so far started sending notes. Those responsible for approving the scripts felt they had not been sufficiently informed about all the changes".[20] One of the main issues was the queer romantic line (revolving around a relationship between a bisexual and a gay character) that came to the foreground from the third episode on during the later stage of development, but was not featured in the pitch as a dominant component. The ČT producer and the script editor were not critical of the LGBT theme per se, but felt frustrated seeing their preferred theme of high-school bullying, structurally a key element as a cause of the shooting, eclipsed by extensive, relationship-centred dialogues of the queer couple. As the script editor Alena Prokopová noted:

> According to the original agreement, *TBH*'s main theme was supposed to be bullying. Lucia [Kajánková] escaped from that, and I saw my role as correcting this diversion towards gay and lesbian relationships. Since Lucia is a very strong personality, I had to consistently protect the theme of bullying, because that's what ČT approved: that *TBH* is about bullying, not about high school kids discovering their sexual identity. […] The writers' team developed deeply personal relationships with their characters, and eventually got carried away by this new team from the main storyline as writing proceeded.[21]

Although she made clear that their objections to the LGBT theme were not ideological, but procedural and structural, she still expressed a frustration with the representation of the youth lifestyle and strong language: "I felt there was an absence of a borderline for what moral behaviour is; even though the generation clearly has a different view of morality, there still should have been a character embodying a moral standard from which other characters may diverge".[22] Kajánková's reasoning that bullying and LGBT identities are not separate but rather internally connected themes (with bullying directly targeted at and disrupting queer relationships) did not seem to work within ČT.[23] Nevertheless, despite accepting some of Prokopová's and Müllerová's critical notes related to the distinctly strong language and the structure of scripts, Kajánková eventually defended most of her creative choices, including the prominence of the queer-relationship line in the second part of the series and what was perceived as casting *against type*, by energetically asserting, as the respondents reported, the autonomy of her authorial vision. However, our analysis of the process proves that the institutionally ambiguous and uncertain status of the online-only project also played a role: the untypical pitching and approval procedures (with the powerful Programming division's voice missing

---

[20] Lucia Kajánková interviewed by Petr Szczepanik and Dorota Vašíčková, 14 July 2021.
[21] Alena Prokopová interviewed by Petr Szczepanik, 7 January 2022.
[22] Alena Prokopová interviewed by Petr Szczepanik, 7 January 2022.
[23] E-mail communication with Lucia Kajánková, 14 March 2022.

and replaced by the insecure platform team), the spatial distance (online meetings of the writers' room, casting and shooting managed by the regional studio outside Prague, the anti-pandemic protective measures), the short timeline, and above all, the *platform imaginaries* that shaped expectations of individual stakeholders.

While there is no space here to analyse *TBH*'s publishing and audience response, it suffices to say that they further support the claim that the project had intense "organizing consequences" (Strandvad 2009, 154). In a podcast issued immediately after *TBH*'s release in late February 2022, Kajánková elaborated on her insistence on the showrunner credit, which has otherwise not been standardized in ČT or the Czech TV industry more generally (in ČT's official terminology, her role would be called *project leader*), by pointing to her deep engagement in all stages and aspects of the project, including in postproduction, the publishing and online marketing strategy. By assuming the executive task of approving the visuals and other elements of the promotional campaign, she effectively crossed the established organizational borderline between the in-house *creative producer unit* and the external author. Kajánková also stressed how her editor Michal Reich acted as a script advisor by helping her find the final shape of the story in the editing room, or how writing Instagram stories for actors to speak about their characters in what she called "mini-therapeutic monologues" was an integral part of her work (Zabloudilová 2022). In Autumn 2021, shortly before *TBH*'s official release, the platform team commissioned a special focus-group/questionnaire research of youth audience responses (perception of authenticity, relevance, consumer habits), whose results were used to adjust *TBH*'s publishing and marketing strategy, including bonus materials. Here again, the experimental approach to development as an open-ended creative process, informed by audience feedback and blurring of the borderlines between screenwriting, production, and marketing, was manifested clearly.

23.5 Online-Only Content Development as an Accelerator of ČT's Institutional Change

When seen from the institutional rather than personal perspective, the initial mismatch between different visions of the project, resolved by the willingness of the key decision-makers to eventually make concessions and to an extent back down from their standards and routines, indicated something other than just a strength of Kajánková's authorial voice: a broader transformation of ČT was underway, and *TBH* (as the most visible title of ČT's first online-only slate) apparently speeded it up. The new online format—associated in key stakeholders' expectations or *imaginaries* with new values, norms, audience groups, and modes of practice—contributed to the ongoing change of the institutionalized production mode and culture by mediating the change as a concrete material practice or re-alignment of various decision-making centres and organizational divisions within ČT. The online platform team, the main institutional locus of the change, did not have much contact with the producer unit or the creative team. They did not raise serious objections throughout the whole development and production process, because they considered *TBH* to be an ideal embodiment of its content strategy, mainly due to its youth focus and the emphasis on authenticity. Nevertheless, the unit head Alena Müllerová insisted that the most important difference for her between producing *TBH* and linear TV programmes was that she was dealing with the young and eager online platform team instead of the powerful, but hands-off on-air Programming division: "Our collaboration with the platform team was more intense [compared to the Programming division] and at the same time more open in the sense of them giving us more space to shape the project as we wanted".[24] The Programming division acts primarily as a final gatekeeper, through its loud voice in the Program Board's greenlighting meetings, notorious for justifying its decisions by referring to the supposedly majority public tastes, with an implicit inclination to the conservative demographics of 55 + and to safe, widely recognizable genre labels and actor names. In contrast with this, the inexperienced online platform representatives proved to be less authoritative in terms of approval, but more involved throughout the development and production process, and specifically interested in new talent and the narrow (younger) audience groups that were to be addressed in their own language, in a way they would recognize as distinctly authentic.[25] By replacing the Programming division in its approval and scheduling role and by participating simultaneously in commissioning and development, the online platform virtually adopted the role of the commissioning editor, which is otherwise absent from ČT's organizational system, characterized by the organizational split between Development and Programming. For the online-only projects following *TBH*, a new board, called Digital, was created by ČT top management as the main greenlighting body—unlike *TBH*, subsequent web series are thus to be approved by a group of executives in which the Programming division head is effectively replaced by the online platform representatives.

The co-author of this chapter Dorota Vašíčková, the online platform team member responsible for online-only content commissioning, was acting as an occasional liaison with *TBH*'s creative team and took a field note from a casting meeting stating: "I reminded myself again that for us, *TBH* is a precedent for all the future ČT web series, absolutely crucial for online-only production in general. It is better to make it twice as expensive, just do not let it be embarrassing".[26] Although the online platform team tried to communicate their content strategy in the form of the vision statement to all ČT's producer units, it was only after *TBH* demonstrated key features of the web series format in the material practice of development that senior ČT

---

[24] Alena Müllerová interviewed by Petr Szczepanik, 17 December 2021.

[25] See also the platform team's public presentation of their first slate of online-only projects at a local summer film festival (LFŠ 2021).

[26] Dorota Vašíčková's field notes, 11 February 2021.

personnel realized and accepted the necessity to partially change their standards and work methods. This did not happen due to differences in the aesthetics or physical production (which were not that many), but rather through the speedy, open-ended, low-threshold, group-based, social media savvy, and boundary-breaking development process.

Kajánková, conscious of the online-only content's specificity, and having a good knowledge of Scandinavian web and TV series production (mediated to her, as she admitted, partly by her partner at the time, a selector of Scandinavian content for ČT), effectively played the role of a cultural intermediary, translating and infiltrating the format into ČT's institutional culture, and thus helped to facilitate the institutional change on the level of development that had not materialized through top-down organizational and administrative measures, despite attempts at it. The change established a direct link between the online platform team and producer units as the traditional centres of development, thus giving the former a commissioning legitimacy it had acutely lacked. It made divisions responsible for audience research and marketing involved with *TBH*'s development and with Kajánková as a showrunner. It also potentially changed ČT employees' perception of online content and online audiences, making them recognize that authenticity is the key value and youth audiences are not just to be educated, that more radical themes and language might be acceptable, that openness of the creative process and last-minute flexible changes are not necessarily wrong. As Müllerová noted, *TBH* has resonated very well among ČT employees after internal screenings: "They now can imagine what [a web series] looks like [...] and how it can function within ČT".[27] While online-only content production was not a key part in the early strategic debates about the new ČT platform, it gradually came to the foreground and proved to be an efficient vehicle of institutional change in terms of both organizational structure and the institutional culture.

Acknowledgements This chapter is a result of the research funded by the Technology Agency of the Czech Republic as the project TL03000251 "Strategies for Public Service Television's Sustainability in the Internet Era: Best Practices Based on International Comparison". This work was also supported by the European Regional Development Fund project "Creativity and Adaptability as Conditions of the Success of Europe in an Interrelated World" (reg. no.: CZ.02.1.01/0.0/0.0/16_019/0000734).

References

13 Reasons Why. 2017–2020 (4 seasons). Created by Brian Yorkey. USA: Produced by Paramount Television and Anonymous Content for Netflix.

Andersen, Mads Møller T., and Vilde Schanke Sundet. 2019. "Producing Online Youth Fiction in a Nordic Public Service Context." *View* 8 (16): 1–16.

[27] Alena Müllerová interviewed by Petr Szczepanik, 17 December 2021.

Aust, Ondřej. 2021. "Moje vize? Czechflix. Ještě máme čas vytvořit protiváhu globálním videotékám, říká Petr Dvořák" [My vision? Czechflix. We still have time to create a counterweight to global VOD services, says Petr Dvořák]. *Euro*, 22 March. https://www.tydenikeuro.cz/moje-vize-czechflix-petr-dvorak/. Accessed 16 June 2022.

Bloore, Peter. 2013. *The Screenplay Business: Managing Creativity and Script Development in the Film Industry*. London: Routledge.

Bordwell, David, Janet Staiger, and Kristin Thompson. 1985. *The Classical Hollywood Cinema. Film Style and Mode of Production to 1960*. London and New York: Routledge.

Bruun, Hanne. 2020. *Re-Scheduling Television in the Digital Era*. London: Routledge.

Cunningham, Stuart, and David Craig. 2019. *Social Media Entertainment: The New Industry at the Intersection of Hollywood and Silicon Valley*. New York: New York University Press.

Christian, Aymar Jean. 2014. "Indie TV: Innovation in Series Development." In *Media Independence: Working with Freedom or Working for Free?*, edited by James Bennett and Niki Strange, 159–81. New York: Routledge.

Christian, Aymar Jean. 2018. *Open TV: Innovation beyond Hollywood and the Rise of Web Television*. New York: New York University.

ČT. 2020. "Základní principy vývoje originálního online obsahu v ČT" [Basic Principles of developing original online content in ČT]. https://img.ceskatelevize.cz/boss/image/contents/vyber-projektu/zakladni-principy-online.pdf. Accessed 16 June 2022.

D'Arma, Alessandro, Tim Raats, and Jeanette Steemers. 2021. "Public Service Media in the age of SVoDs: A Comparative Study of PSM Strategic Responses in Flanders, Italy and the UK." *Media, Culture & Society* 43 (4): 682–700.

Dvořák, Petr. 2017. "Koncepce dalšího rozvoje České televize jako televize veřejné služby" [A vision of Czech Television' further development as a public service broadcaster]. https://img.ceskatelevize.cz/boss/document/996.pdf?v=1&_ga=2.155181691.292854941.1643191562-1181038139.1464633631. Accessed 16 June 2022.

Elephant. 2003. Written and directed by Gus van Sant. USA: Meno Film Company.

Ellingsen, Steinar, and Stayci Taylor. 2019. "Writers, Producers and Creative Entrepreneurship in Web Series Development." In *The Palgrave Handbook of Screen Production*, edited by Craig Batty et al., 181–92. Cham, Switzerland: Palgrave Macmillan.

Kang, Jennifer M. 2017. "Just Another Platform for Television? The Emerging Web Dramas as Digital Culture in South Korea." *Media, Culture & Society* 39 (5): 762–72.

Krauß, Florian, and Moritz Stock. 2021. "Youthification of Television Through Online Media: Production Strategies and Narrative Choices in DRUCK/SKAM Germany." *Critical Studies in Television* 16 (4): 412–32.

Lassen, Julie Münter, and Jannick Kirk Sørensen. 2021. "Curation of a Personalized Video on Demand Service. A Longitudinal Study of the Danish Public Service Broadcaster DR." *Iluminace* 33 (1): 5–33.

Leder, Marilyn. 2021. "The Web Series Empowering Diversity on the Australian Screen." *Continuum* 35 (4): 585–99.

LFŠ. 2021. "Nové online-only pořady České televize" [New online programs of Czech Television]. *iVysílání*. https://www.ceskatelevize.cz/porady/10000000479-letni-filmova-skola-uherske-hradiste-2021-stan-ct/221254003100006/. Accessed 16 June 2022.

Lindtner, Synnøve Skarsbø, and John Magnus Dahl. 2019. "Aligning Adolescents to the Public Sphere: The Teen Serial Skam and Democratic Aesthetic." *Javnost – The Public* 26 (1): 54–69.

Macdonald, Ian W. 2013. *Screenwriting Poetics and the Screen Idea*. Basingstoke, UK: Palgrave Macmillan.

Manners (Mannasiðir). 2018 (1 season). Written and directed by María Reyndal. Iceland: Produced by Glassriver for RÚV.

Monaghan, Whitney. 2017. "Starting From … Now and the Web Series to Television Crossover: An Online Revolution." *Media International Australia* 64 (1): 82–91.

Maxa, Jan. 2020. "Informace o činnost ČT v oblasti nových médií za rok 2020 pro Radu České televize." [A report on ČT's activities in the field of new media in 2020 for the Board of Czech Television]. https://img.ceskatelevize.cz/boss/document/1738.pdf?v=1&_ga=2.64923695.1400815028.1646237661-1181038139.1464633631. Accessed 16 June 2022.

Nieborg, David B., and Thomas Poell. 2018. "The Platformization of Cultural Production: Theorizing the Contingent Cultural Commodity." *New Media & Society* 20 (11): 4275–92.

Nudes. 2019 (1 season). Created by Nina Barbosa Blad, Jørgen Færøy Flasnes, Liv Barbosa Blad, and Erika Calmeyer. Norway: Produced by Barbosa Film for NRK P3.

Redvall, Eva Novrup. 2018. "Reaching Young Audiences through Research: Using the NABC Method to Create the Norwegian Web Teenage Drama SKAM/Shame." In *True Event Adaptation: Scripting Real Lives*, edited by Davinia Thornley, 143–61. New York: Palgrave Macmillan.

Sex Education. 2019–present (4 seasons). Created by Laurie Nunn. UK: Produced by Eleven Films for Netflix.

Skam. 2015–2017 (4 seasons). Created by Julie Andem. Norway: NRK.

Sørensen, Kirk Jannick, and Jonathon Hutchinson. 2018. "Algorithms and Public Service Media." In *Public Service Media in the Networked Society*, edited by Gregory Ferrell Lowe, Hilde Van den Bulck, and Karen Donders, 91–106. Gothenburg: Nordicom.

Stollfuß, Sven. 2021. "The Platformisation of Public Service Broadcasting in Germany: The Network 'funk' and the Case of Druck/Skam Germany." *Critical Studies of Television* 16 (2): 126–44.

Straková, Kateřina. 2019. "Dvořák: ČT se snaží tvorbou vyrovnat HBO nebo Netflixu" [Dvořák: ČT aims to match HBO or Netflix with its production]. *Mediaguru*, 18 July. https://www.mediaguru.cz/clanky/2019/07/dvorak-ct-se-snazi-tvorbou-vyrovnat-hbo-nebo-netflixu/. Accessed 16 June 2022.

Strandvad, Sara Malou. 2009. "Inspirations for a New Sociology of Art: A Sociomaterial Study of Development Processes in the Danish Film Industry." PhD diss., Copenhagen Business School. https://research.cbs.dk/en/publications/inspirations-for-a-new-sociology-of-art-a-sociomaterial-study-of-. Accessed 16 June 2022.

Sundet, Vilde Schanke. 2021. *Television Drama in the Age of Streaming: Transnational Strategies and Digital Production Cultures at the NRK*. Cham, Switzerland: Palgrave Macmillan.

Szczepanik, Petr. 2021. *Screen Industries in East-Central Europe*. London: Bloomsbury – BFI.

Taylor, Stayci. 2021. "Just Ask what if and Go from There: The Role of Mainstream Story Structures in Women's Web Series Script Development." *Studies in Australasian Cinema* 15 (1–2): 48–64.

van Dijck, José, and Thomas Poell. 2013. "Understanding Social Media Logic." *Media and Communication* 1 (1): 2–14.

van Dijck, José, and Thomas Poell. 2015. "Making Public Television Social: Public Service Broadcasting and the Challenges of Social Media." *Television & New Media* 16 (2): 148–64.

van Es, Karin, and Thomas Poell. 2020. "Platform Imaginaries and Dutch Public Service Media." *Social Media + Society* 6 (2): 1–10.

Zabloudilová, Táňa. 2022. "Teenageři jsou taky lidi, říkají Kajánková a Müllerová, tvůrkyně webseriálu TBH" [Teenagers are also people, say Kajánková and Müllerová, the creators of the TBH web series]. https://a2larm.cz/2022/02/teenageri-jsou-taky-lidi-rikaji-kajankova-a-mullerova-tvurkyne-webserialu-tbh/. Accessed 16 June 2022.

Zboralska, Emilia. 2017. "No More Status Quo! Canadian Web Series Creators' Entrepreneurial Motives Through a Contextualized 'Entrepreneuring As Emancipation' Framework." *International Journal on Media Management* 19 (1): 29–53.

CHAPTER 24

Screenwriting for Children and Young Audiences

Eva Novrup Redvall

24.1 Introduction

Many screenwriters agree that there is no one recipe for how to write a good screenplay. There are many useful manuals or *how-to* books with tips and tricks from people with experience in the field, but approaching new stories for the screen is always marked by having to find the best strategy for the particular storylines, characters or moods that one wants to write about, which is never an easy task. This is also the case when trying to write for a specific audience, such as children and young audiences.

As this chapter will outline, there are definitely traditions and trends in creating content for the youngest segments of the population, and approaches that seem conducive when targeting human beings that are on their way to becoming adults. However, even if one is aiming for writing for a very specific age group, one has to consider how children, tweens and teenagers come in many shapes and sizes and are in fact as diverse as adults, not only in terms of questions of gender, race, socio-economic background or geography, but also in their personalities, tastes and interests, even if they are at a certain stage in their life development.

Accordingly, while this chapter addresses issues to consider when writing for children and young audiences, it also stresses the fact that one can write in most genres, for many different film and television cultures or for old and new media, all of which will create a certain framework for how to approach

E. N. Redvall (✉)
University of Copenhagen, Copenhagen, Denmark
e-mail: eva@hum.ku.dk

© The Author(s), under exclusive license to Springer Nature
Switzerland AG 2023
R. Davies et al. (eds), *The Palgrave Handbook of Screenwriting Studies*,
https://doi.org/10.1007/978-3-031-20769-3_24

a screenwriting task. The shared element across all of this is how one thinks about children and young audiences in this process.

This chapter suggests to always consider three main issues: screenwriting *for* children and young audiences, referring to how one thinks of the intended audience; screenwriting *about* children and young audiences, referring to writing stories about young protagonists and dealing with their life worlds and concerns, for instance in coming-of-age stories; and screenwriting *with* children and young audiences, referring to recent trends of involving the intended young audience still more in the writing and production processes to try to ensure that what is being created is in fact of interest to them.

The focus here is on live action scripted fiction, even though animated content is highly popular with young audiences and deserves a chapter of its own. Moreover, many of the examples used in the chapter come from a joint research project entitled "Reaching Young Audiences: Serial fiction and cross-media storyworlds for children and young audiences" at the University of Copenhagen 2019–2024 (supported by Independent Research Fund Denmark, RYA 2022), focusing on how to create quality content and remain relevant to young audiences in times of remarkable change in the media landscape and children's media use. This means that there is a focus on film and series from the Scandinavian countries which have a long tradition for prioritizing and funding content for children and young audiences. However, most of the main points and considerations should be transferable to other film and television contexts where writers are trying to create content that can be fun and silly, dark and scary, historical or contemporary, wondrous fairytales or social realist dramas, adaptations or original stories for the screen—or something completely different that we might not even have seen yet among all the amazing content that is produced for children and young audiences around the world today. As argued by Alan Brown in his chapter on writing children's literature, creating stories for children and young audiences can be "as diverse as all adult writing put together, and then some" (Brown 2014, 162).

24.2 Books on Writing for Children and Young Audiences

While there are many manuals on writing film and television for grownups, few books on screenwriting specifically address the topic of writing for children and young audiences. There are scholarly studies of the films and series produced for them, and handbooks which offer useful analysis and discussions of how to think of film and television for children and inspiring case studies of existing productions (e.g., Hermansson and Zepernick 2019), but little on the process of writing as such.

In the foreword to the *Palgrave Handbook of Children's Film and Television*, Karen Lury points out how much has been written about "interactions between actual children, texts produced for children, and the represented child" in what can be regarded as a vast field of study where we can all argue to be some kind of expert since *children*, *childhood* and *the child* are universalizing categories, children are everywhere and we were all children once (2019, v–vi). However, one needs to nuance the widespread understanding of *the universal child* and acknowledge the many potential differences among children growing up in different places, as well as the fact that "adults easily and inevitably forget what it meant and how it felt to be the child they once were" (2019, vii). Moreover, while certain elements of being a child and growing up are shared across generations, childhoods at a particular point in time are also marked by specific conditions and challenges, making it hard to directly channel one's own experience of childhood as an adult to that of younger generations.

When it comes to the topic of *writing* for children, there are several books from the field of literature studies, often written by acclaimed writers of children's literature. An early example is George J. H. Northcroft's manual *Writing for children*, dating back to 1935 and offering advice on creating good content for young readers at the time. More recent books, with the very same title, widen the scope by addressing everything from picture books, fiction, poetry, plays, non-fiction or educational books while also offering advice on the children's book market, even on matters of publicity, setting up a website or tax and accounting (e.g. Clark 1993; Strachan 2008). Some books consider issues of memory and moral passion (Harrison 1999) or honesty (Fritz and Zinsser 1989) when writing for children, while others focus on specific genres such as writing utopian and dystopian stories (Hintz and Ostry 2003). There is even a *Writing Children's Books for Dummies* manual (Buccieri and Economy 2012) offering advice for the unpublished writer with, as the authors' state in the book's promotional text, a good story idea and love of kids.

While there are thus many different kinds of books on writing children's literature that can offer general advice on how to think of children as a particular audience and storytelling for them, there is little on writing specifically for audio-visual media. One exception is the screenwriting guide by Motti Aviram (published in Hebrew in 2010 and translated into English in 2015) which has chapters on the cognitive abilities of young viewers, transferable techniques from children's literature (such as rhyming, accumulation, repetition and rhythmic patterns) or children's humor while also including chapters on using puppets which indicates its focus on smaller children. Another exception is Christina Hamlett's *Screenwriting for Teens* (2006) which stands out by encouraging teenagers to write their own content.

A major reason for the lack of literature on writing film and television for children and young audiences is the challenge of trying to boil this highly complex topic with an intended audience as the main defining trait into a useful manual for writing in many different genres and styles. At the outset of the RYA research project, we conducted a small survey with screenwriting members of the Danish Writers Guild with experience in writing for children on how to best go about it. Their answers illustrated how most writers find their own way, both in developing the content that they are attracted to and the way to best make this content come alive in a strong screenplay. Yet, when writing for children, all writers must consider the fact that they are writing for and/or about a certain age group and whether this age group should be involved in the research, writing for development or not. This is the reason why, rather than trying to offer specific advice on writing particular kinds of children's content, the rest of this chapter addresses the questions of *for whom?*, *about what?* and *in a co-creative process or not?* that are hopefully of relevance across different genres, media and countries.

24.3 SCREENWRITING *for* CHILDREN AND YOUNG AUDIENCES

Children's film and television can be defined in various ways depending on whether one thinks of this as productions that follow young protagonists or deal with representations of childhood, or whether one more pragmatically regards the main defining trait to be film and television produced for and widely received as targeting children (see, for instance, Bazalgette and Staples 1995; Parry 2013; or Brown 2017 that has a chapter on these discussions over time). Most definitions focus on productions deliberately intended for children, but these can have different modes of address. In his book on genre, nation and narrative in the children's film, film scholar Noel Brown emphasizes how "child-oriented" productions can have *a single address* (where the target audience is restricted to children), a *double* or *dual address* (where both children and adults are addressed as separate entities with differentiated forms of engagement) or an *undifferentiated address* (where children and adults are addressed as a single entity) (Brown 2017, 21). As a writer, it is conducive to consider the mode of address from the outset since the strategy chosen can have major consequences for the story and storytelling.

Moreover, thinking about children as well as young audiences (in this chapter understood as tweens and teens) means thinking about a very broad age span marked by remarkably different cognitive competencies, concerns and interests. There have always been certain understandings of what content is suited for smaller or older children, something which is also reflected in the approach to film and television censorship in most countries. However, the past years have seen still more segmentation of the individual age groups, particularly in the television industry.

As an example, after many years of producing children's television as programming for the regular main channel DR1, the Danish public service broadcaster DR launched the children's channel DR Ramasjang in 2009, targeting 3-to-6-year-olds, which was supplemented with the DR Ultra channel in 2013, focusing on content for 7-to-12-year-olds. In 2020, this was changed to DR Ramasjang focusing on 4–8-year-olds and DR Ultra on 9-to-14-year-olds based on an analysis that while a defining moment in the media use of Danish children used to be when they started school, the defining moment in their media in the 2020s was the age of getting their first smart phone around the age of 8 or 9 (Hansen 2019).

Following several years of deliberately not producing content for children under the age of 3—partly based on the notion that they shouldn't be looking at screens—the changes in the DR Ramasjang and Ultra target audiences were accompanied by the introduction of a third children's brand in 2021, Minisjang, targeting 1-to-3-year-olds, since Scandinavian public service broadcasters had to address the fact that even "viewers in diapers" were now watching content on multiple screens, pointing to a need for national public service media to also produce quality content for them (Christensen 2020). If one is aiming to write television fiction for children in the Danish context, one must thus be keenly aware of whether one is trying to address the 4-to-8-year-olds, the 9-to-14-year-olds or the older teenagers which in 2021 became part of the very wide target audience of the DR youth/young adult brand P3.

The increased segmentation in thinking about young audiences points to the fact that screenwriters wanting to write *for children* are also very much writing *for commissioners* with a very specific view of what kind of content is suitable and appropriate for children and young audiences. Screenwriters always have to convince potential producers or funders of the quality of their work and win acceptance for their ideas, but this is even more the case when writing for what scholars such as David Buckingham (2005) or Anna Potter and Jeanette Steemers (2022) have discussed as "a special audience." Screenwriters of children's fiction often have to navigate tensions between "pedagogy and pleasure" (Brown 2017, 19) based on ideas of what children should learn from watching fiction, ambitions of educational takeaways or certain notions of how to best promote media literacy. As an example, the website for BBC Children's Commissioning clearly states that the ambition of BBC Children is to "aim to model good behaviours, show kindness and active citizenship, be aspirational and informative—and we believe kids have a right to be carefree and laugh their socks off too" (BBC 2021). The commissioning of children's content is often based on quite particular ideas of what signifies *good content*, particularly when it comes to the youngest viewers.

The increased competition for the youngest viewers and still more segmentation has also led to still more reports on how to create popular content for this special audience as well as detailed analysis of not only their media use, but also their general opinions and preferences on small as well as big matters in life. Based on interviewing Danish children, the DR Media researchers have thus defined the "main ingredients" for a DR Ultra streaming hit, highlighting the importance of (1) a great cast; (2) a personal mission; (3) something at stake; (4) recognizable situations from the daily life of the target audience; (5) elements of fascination; (6) human relations; and (7) serial format (in Redvall and Christensen 2021, 169–70). Many of these ingredients clearly mirror suggested strategies for writing fiction for adults, but the last point on the age group appreciating serialized storytelling also illustrates how the changes in the media use of the audience have consequences for the stories and formats commissioned.

In contrast to writing most other kinds of content, writers of children's screen content thus have to be keenly aware of exactly which age group and which platform they are targeting and of the specific ideas of *good content* for them in particular "screen idea systems" (see Redvall 2018a). While crafting children's screen stories can in principle be as diverse and imaginative as crafting children's literature, there are most often quite concrete institutional and industrial constraints to negotiate when writing audio-visual fiction for children that demands an awareness of why and how writing for this audience is particular and how one's story engages with this in a specific context. This is the case whether trying to write a new public service *affordable fiction* television serial, creating an ambitious magical storyworld with Harry Potter franchise potential or making a personal short film about growing up and feeling different.

24.4 Screenwriting *about* Children and Young Audiences

Even if one works with a definition that children's film and television fiction is first and foremost content created *for* the young audience, children's film and television are also most likely *about* members of this audience. This facilitates the possibility for recognition, alignment and allegiance with characters (Smith 1995) and for addressing issues of relevance in their life worlds.

There are many wonderful films with young protagonists that might be interesting for young audiences but are not necessarily written specifically with them in mind. A film such as Taika Waititi's adventure comedy drama *Hunt for the Wilderpeople* (2016, with a 12-year advisory parental guidance certificate) about a boy and his foster uncle who go missing in the New Zealand bush ought to appeal to teenagers and adults alike as an example of Brown's definition of undifferentiated address. However, a beautiful coming-of-age film such as Sean Baker's *The Florida Project* (2017, with a 15-year certificate) with the 6-year-old Mooney and her playmates in the lead is—as the censorship classification suggests—not intended for Mooney's peers but for the rest of us who are offered an opportunity to experience a poignant portrait of growing up at a motel in the shadows of Disney World (see Murphy 2021 for an excellent analysis of the film and its production story). The age of main characters is thus in no way indicative of the age of the intended core viewer, and in general there is a lot of "viewing up the age-range" (Brown 2014, 163) where children and young audiences watch content with protagonists who are older than them or content that is not in any way created with them in mind in the first place.

There can be many reasons why writers want to tell stories about children, tweens and teens, but this chapter only focus on the stories which are *about* them and also primarily *for* them. The literature on writing for children and young audiences emphasizes that while children's stories can be incredibly diverse, there are certain traditions and recurring storylines. In the following, I will focus on three main strands in stories about children and young audiences: first of all the rather natural approach of focusing on the theme of growing up and coming-of-age, secondly, the many stories focusing on fantastic or magical elements targeting this audience, and finally, stories about the everyday life and dilemmas of children and young audiences, which have been particularly prominent in television fiction formats in the 2020s.

As highlighted by Alan Brown in his chapter on creative writing for children, the theme of growing up can be addressed in many different ways while writers try to give children "what is thought to be appropriate to their age and development" and tell stories matching their cognitive abilities (Brown 2014, 163). In his book on children's films, Noel Brown also highlights the prominence of coming-of-age stories in cinematic content for children and discusses how they are marked by themes, narratives and conflicts that often:

- reaffirm family, friendship and community
- foreground real or symbolic children
- marginalise disruptive social elements, or engage with them in order to defeat them
- downplay 'adult' themes and situations
- have narratives that are relatively straightforward, easily grasped and negate ambiguity
- and work to uphold social norms, create emotional uplift and engender kinship. (Brown 2017, 19)

These characteristics illustrate how children's film and television fiction often stresses reaffirming and uplifting elements. There can be tensions in the storylines and possibilities of unpleasant outcomes, but these productions predominately have happy endings that are "supportive of the status quo" (Brown 2017, 15). Again, there are great differences between writing for small children or older teenagers (who might, for instance, appreciate a sad love story), and several teenage television series have storylines with both upbeat and more depressing side stories. However, for most content targeting children and young audiences, the main stories support the existing norms and end on a positive note, even if they might have been rather hard stories about troubles with feeling different and fitting in or bullying. As argued by Natalie Krikowa in an article on ABC Australia's television serial *First Day* (2020) about a young transgender girl's troubled transition to high school, fiction for children and youth can be a site of negotiation, where coming-of-age stories explore questions of possible identities and life choices (Krikowa 2021).

Even if mainstream storytelling most often leaves the main character with a happy ending, many short films about children and young audiences end on a more ambiguous note, making them a good *conversation starter* in educational settings. In Denmark, 25% of the state film funding allocated by The

Danish Film Institute is targeting films for children and youth, which has led to many both fiction films and documentaries targeting them in long as well as short formats. Several of these are included in teaching material and screening programs for schools, not the least the stories focusing on some of the many potential challenges of growing up and finding your way in the world.

Again, depending on genre and context, coming-of-age stories can take many different forms and appeal across the age group portrayed, as illustrated by a classic such as Rob Reiner's *Stand by Me* from 1986 (based on a novella by Stephen King) or the Norwegian web series *SKAM* (2015–2017) which ended up having a large adult audience despite the deliberate intention of particularly addressing the life concerns of 16-year-old girls (Redvall 2018b). Many of the coming-of-age themes are universal, and they naturally appeal to writers who often want to share and build on experiences from when they were growing up.

While coming-of-age stories can be regarded as an indigenous genre in the realm of children's fiction, the strong focus on fantastic and magical story-lines in screen content about children often has more potential to cross-over and have a wider appeal. Alan Brown highlights how humor and the fantastic or super-natural world are often important elements in children's fiction, partly since children are more willing to suspend disbelief than adults (2014, 163). Brown encourages writers to invite children "to identify with characters in situations both strange and familiar, allowing them to imagine how they themselves might act in such situations" (2014, 168), mirroring the appeal of a blend of recognition/identification and fascination in the streaming hit ingredients from DR and in many screenwriting manuals.

In the RYA screenwriters' survey, many of the Danish writers expressed how they found great freedom in writing for children and consistently argued that creating content for this special audience allows writers to experiment more than when writing for adults (Redvall and Christensen 2020). As one screenwriter put it, most children are imaginative and might wonder "what if this ice cream could last forever?" or "what would happen if this fruit could talk?" Children are more easily invested in unconventional or fantastic narratives and the storytelling is not limited by the fact that the narrative has to "mean something" or have an ambition to change aspects of society; in children's content, the world can simply be poetic, adventurous or nutty (as discussed in Redvall and Christensen 2021).

While silliness or nuttiness is often a feature in animated content where everything is visually possible, it has also been a prominent feature in much of the Danish public service television content which has deliberately tried to rebel against the "boring" world of the adults (e.g., Christensen 2013; Jensen 2017). Hollywood studios can convincingly create magical wizard worlds, make ET aliens come to earth or revamp popular franchises such as *Ghostbusters* with young protagonists and amazing CGI, but writers from small nation film and television cultures have traditionally had to aim for cheaper concepts or more simple magical realism.

A particular genre targeting children and young audiences in this realm in Scandinavia is the highly popular format of the television Christmas calendar which tells a serialized story through 24 episodes running from 1 to 24 December (Agger 2013). These stories often involve elves and/or a parallel world with dangers that must be defeated before Christmas Eve. The 2021 installment on Danish screens, *Christmas of the Comets,* had four children going to an "astro camp" and accidentally ending up on the hypothetical Planet 9, trying to combine an adventurous, fantastic story with a science communication agenda, through the storylines in the television serial as well as a transmedia universe around it (Redvall and Christensen 2021).

While writers of children's literature have created many wondrous, magical worlds, budgetary restraints for making these worlds come alive on screen create certain obstructions for writers of audio-visual media, particularly in small nation contexts. There are, however, many innovative ways to work with everyday magic or the fantastic in realist settings, as many screenwriters of fiction from outside of Hollywood have demonstrated over the years, and children are attracted to the *what if?* playful and imaginative views of the world in the hands of talented writers.

However, the 2020s have also seen a strong realist strand of particularly television fiction for children and young audiences emerge, partly based on wanting to produce more content on limited budgets and partly on mirroring the content that many tweens and teens appreciate on YouTube or social media. In the Danish context, this content clearly builds on the need to produce many episodes (as emphasized in the streaming hit guidelines by the DR media researchers) in an *affordable fiction* framework (Redvall and Christensen 2021). A broadcaster such as DR wants to be present in the everyday life of Danish children in a similar way to the YouTubers, vloggers and influencers that they follow on a regular, sometimes daily, basis. This has led to a remarkable increase in the number of fictional episodes produced, with DR Ultra offering 23 episodes of scripted fiction in 2015 and 257 in 2020 (DR 2020).

An example of the new realist affordable fiction strategy is the serial *Klassen* ("The Class," 2016-now, with episodes around 10 minutes, based on a Dutch scripted fiction format) following the life in a regular sixth grade at an ordinary Danish public school. In 2021, the series was in its twelfth season with altogether 649 episodes, making it the serial with the most number of episodes produced in Danish television history. The content of *Klassen* focuses on everyday conflicts around friendships, schoolwork and whatever might be on the radar of children around the age of 12. The writing process is intense, with eight scripts produced per week when production is up and running. This requires writers who are close to the world of children and their everyday lives and able to produce at a high speed where they get notes from not only producers and commissioners, but also children (as will be discussed in the next section on writing *with* children).

The writing framework of *Klassen* is comparable to the industrial set-up of working on a soap opera (as analyzed in Macdonald 2009), and yet a quite particular framework since the content covered has to reflect what is currently going on in Danish classrooms, e.g., when everyone is suddenly interested in playing *Fortnite* or having an overnight popular gadget such as a fidget spinner. Writing this kind of television fiction is not about expressing one's personal, artistic vision, but about taking an interest in making fun and engaging content as part of a large collaborative team.

In the 2020s, more of this serialized content for children emerged—for instance with *Klassen* also being adapted in Norway and Sweden—but the attempt to stay close to the everyday reality of the young audience has also led to productions outside of the established institutions and broadcasters as various forms of low-budget/no-budget productions. A Danish example is Jonas Risvig's streaming serial *CENTRUM* (2000) which he made in close collaboration with a large group of teenagers during the COVID-19 lockdown in the spring of 2020 (Christensen and Redvall 2020). The ambition of *CENTRUM* was to capture the life of teenagers during the pandemic, while also inspiring young people to make productions of their own (based on sharing screenplays, technical details and other production material as part of the serial's YouTube channel). While Danish cinema has a long and proud tradition of social realist youth dramas since the 1970s (Langkjær 2012), and there are still beautiful international and Scandinavian shorts and feature films with a social realist focus, television fiction emerged as a particular window for this approach in the late 2010s, offering several new writers the opportunity to get their first credits and try their hands at writing fiction for children.

This new line of writing is also the one that currently seems the closest to portraying the life and concerns of children, tweens and teens today, through working with various forms of user participation or co-creation. While coming-of-age stories and magical and fantastic genre fare productions stand strong and have a more transnational appeal, the current approach and turnaround time of national television production in the local languages offer an opportunity to stay close to children of today and involve them in the writing processes for them to a larger extent than ever before. This is also related to the issue of mode of address, since new feature films traditionally have to be selected for viewing by parents who buy the expensive cinema tickets—encouraging a mode of address in popular family films for both children and adults—while new television fiction and web series are likely to be consumed on other screens, often smartphone screens, by the children themselves. Adults might watch *Klassen* to try to keep up with what is going on among 12-year-olds, but the writing of the series and its portrayal of everyday life is targeting children. As argued by Becky Parry in her book on *Children, Film and Literacy*, "films for children can be seen to offer both a site of negotiation about children, childhood and parenting and yet are also spaces in which children can distance themselves from adults, developing their own playful, imaginative and transgressive responses" (2013, 14). In the 2020s, this tension was visible in the way that more content focused on the single mode of address—and on involving children to take part in these content negotiations.

24.5 Screenwriting *with* Children and Young Audiences in an On-Demand Age

As emphasized by Casie Hermansson and Janet Zepernick in their *Handbook of Children's Film and Television*, both children's film and television "are for youth and frequently about youth but are seldom produced and often not procured by youth" (Hermansson and Zepernick 2019, 1). As discussed in the above, this started to change in the 2020s where there was still more focus on how to remain relevant to young audiences when facing increased competition from numerous widely available digital platforms and different media, such as TikTok and various forms of games and social media.

In the worlds of both film and television, writers and producers were asking themselves how one can help counter the *nobody knows* element of creating new fiction by increasingly analyzing and involving the intended audience. This was not least the case with regard to the young audience members who are first movers in finding new content and platforms and can be regarded, in the words of Danish children's television legend Mogens Vemmer, as "the world's worst viewers," since they are unfaithful and will quickly discard your content if they find it uninteresting (Vemmer 2006).

The European Broadcasting Union was one of the many institutions looking for answers in terms of how to best create appealing public service television content for children and young audiences in a rapidly changing media landscape, for instance in an EBU youth report entitled "What works?" (2020) that, for instance, contains the advice that European public service youth fiction should be "local and relatable—something that Netflix and YouTube cannot do" (EBU 2020). In the report, the Head of the Norwegian public service broadcaster NRK's youth department P3 explains that NRK aims "to create content that is authentic, genuine and real, while also aiming to produce a 'wow' effect" (EBU 2020). The question of course is how one does that when there are no simple recipes?

One way to attempt this is to work with young talent and involve the young audience, something which the EBU report also recommends. In the early 2020s, this became an integrated part of many writing and producing strategies at the Scandinavian public service broadcasters, for instance when not only conducting extensive research into the target audience, but also involving representatives from the targeted age group as *experts*, hiring them as *junior editors* to take part in the development and writing framework of *Klassen* (see Redvall and Christensen 2021 for more on this). This strategy was also encouraged by The Danish Film Institute, which launched a new audience research website in 2021 (DFI 2021a) after establishing an Audience Focus initiative where screenwriters could apply for money to conduct substantial research into their intended audience, for instance through observation studies or focus groups (DFI 2021b).

While the writing manuals on children's literature have traditionally built on a conviction that adults know what stories to tell and how to tell them, the early 2020 was marked by a sense that grownup writers do not necessarily know what children and young audiences are in fact interested in and how to best tell stories about this. At least, there seemed to be widespread agreement in both the film and television industries that it was conducive to find out more about this audience before deciding to pursue a certain direction and spend substantial time and money on a specific project.

This belief was also visible in new initiatives for educating talent in writing for children and young audiences in the Scandinavian countries. As an example, The National Film School of Denmark has historically not focused on specifically teaching screenwriting for children and youth as part of their writing program and there have been no other educational initiatives with this particular focus until the establishment of the independent Cross-Media School of Children's Fiction in 2020 which teaches storytelling for children across media and with an emphasis on writers learning to collaborate with children in their writing processes (see Redvall 2021).

Moreover, there seemed to be a change in the prestige allocated to children's content, which has traditionally been regarded as less prestigious content than for instance primetime drama. Accordingly, as analyzed by Beth Johnson and Alison Peirse in an article on genre, gender and television writing, there has been a tendency of pigeonholing, making it hard for writers, not the least female writers, to move from children's programming to other genres (Johnson and Peirse 2021). In the Scandinavian context, the public service broadcasters were historically the only producers of children's programming, but this has changed in the on-demand media landscape, where having children's content as part of a content catalog can be crucial for selling subscriptions to parents who would like content for themselves as well as their children. This has helped make, at least certain kinds of, children's programming more attractive and visible, and there seems to be better pay and opportunities for writers of children's content in the 2020s than in previous decades even if, as often discussed by for instance the Children's Media Foundation (2021), public service television programming is—as much of public service broadcasting—also under pressure.

24.6 Concluding Remarks and Cliffhangers

This chapter has outlined some of the many things to consider when thinking about screenwriting for children and young audiences in the film and media industries of the 2020s. Rather than trying to present how to-advice on writing content across many different genres and platforms, the chapter has tried to raise awareness of some of the many different aspects to always consider when writing *for* and *about* this special audience. Moreover, the chapter has highlighted new developments in this field, such as the increased focus on actually involving children and young audiences in the writing process in various ways.

Technological, industrial and political changes naturally have an impact on writing processes as well as the commissioning of content. Moreover, what might have been an engaging story for a child at the time when a middle-aged screenwriter was young, might not present the same appeal to young digital natives who are incredibly story savvy and have high expectations for their media diet in an age of content abundance.

While some points about writing stories for children from manuals such as the one by Northcroft from 1935 are still valid and some aspects of growing up and coming-of-age can be thought of as universal, the process of writing audio-visual stories for children and young audiences is, as most work in the media industries, a constant process of balancing continuity and change and being sensitive to how one might best structure what one is hopefully passionate about telling to the young audiences at a particular point in time (see Brown 2019 for a discussion of this in analysis of contemporary children's cinema).

An interesting question is whether the years to come will see still more children and young audiences writing and producing their own content without supervision by adults rather than mostly co-creating alongside grownup writers and producers. It has been many years since Francis Ford Coppola announced, in *Hearts of Darkness: A Filmmaker's Apocalypse* (1991), that the coming of new technology, such as 8-mm video recorders in the 1990s, could lead to "some little fat girl in Ohio" becoming "the new Mozart," thereby destroying "the so-called professionalism about movies" and, according to him, making cinema "a real art form." It would not the least be interesting to see a wonderkid screenwriting Shakespeare emerge in the world of film and television, and in the 2020s the means of both production and distribution ought to now be in the hands of the young generation.

Acknowledgements This chapter was written as part of the research project "Reaching Young Audiences: Serial Fiction and Cross-Media Storyworlds for Children and Young Audiences" based at the University of Copenhagen (https://comm.ku.dk/research/film-science-and-creative-media-industries/reaching-young-audiences-serial-fiction-and-cross-media-storyworlds-for-children-and-young-audiences-rya/) and supported by Independent Research Fund Denmark, grant: 9037-00145B. Eva Novrup Redvall is a board member of The Danish Film Institute, but is not involved in initiatives such as "Viden om publikum" or "PublikumsFokus."

REFERENCES

Agger, Gunhild. 2013. "Danish TV Christmas calendars: Folklore, myth and cultural history." *Journal of Scandinavian cinema* 3 (3): 267–80.

Aviram, Motti. 2015. *The Complete Guide to Screenwriting for Children's Film and Television*. Kindle edition.

Bazalgette, Cary, and Terry Staples. 1995. "Unshrinking the Kids: Children's Cinema and the Family Film." In *Front of the Children: Screen Entertainment and Young Audiences*, edited by Cary Balzagette and David Buckingham, 92–108. London: British Film Institute.

BBC. 2021. "BBC Children's Commissioning." https://www.bbc.co.uk/commissioning/childrens/. Accessed 15 April 2021.

Brown, Alan. 2014. "Writing for Children." In *The Handbook of Creative Writing*, edited by Steven Earnshaw, 162–68. Edinburgh: Edinburgh University Press.

Brown, Noel. 2017. *The Children's Film: Genre, Nation, and Narrative*. London and New York: Wallflower.

Brown, Noel. 2019. "Change and Continuity in Contemporary Children's Cinema." In *The Palgrave Handbook of Children's Film and Television*, edited by Casie Hermansson and Janet Zepernick, 225–43. Basingstoke, UK: Palgrave Macmillan.

Buccieri, Lisa Rojany, and Peter Economy. 2012. *Writing Children's Books for Dummies*. London: Wiley.

Buckingham, David. 2005. "A Special Audience? Children and Television." In *A Companion to Television*, edited by Janet Wasko, 468–86 London: Blackwell.

Children's Media Foundation, The (CMF). 2021. *Our Children's Future. Does Public Service Media Matter?* Report by The Children's Media Foundation. https://www.thechildrensmediafoundation.org/wp-content/uploads/2021/11/PSMR-REPORT-WEB.pdf. Accessed 15 December 2021.

Christensen, Christa Lykke. 2013. "Engaging, Critical, Entertaining: Transforming public Service Television for Children in Denmark." *Interactions: Studies in Communication & Culture* 4 (3): 271–87. https://doi.org/10.1386/iscc.4.3.271_1.

Christensen, Christa Lykke. 2020. "Danish Children's Content for 1–3-Year and the Importance of National Broadcasting Platforms Like the Danish Broadcasting Corporation, DR." *CSTonline*, 16 October. https://cstonline.net/danish-childrens-content-for-1-3-year-olds-and-the-importance-of-national-platforms-like-the-danish-broadcasting-corporation-dr/. Accessed 15 December 2021.

Christensen, Katrine Bouschinger, and Eva Novrup Redvall. 2020. "COVID-19 From a Teenage Web Series Perspective." *CSTonline*, 12 Jun. https://cstonline.net/covid-19-from-a-teenage-web-series-perspective/. Accessed 15 December 2021.

Christensen, Katrine Bouschinger, and Eva Novrup Redvall. 2021. "Trying to Make Natural Sciences Exciting Through Television Fiction: The Case of *Christmas of the Comets*." *CSTonline*, 17 December. https://cstonline.net/trying-to-make-natural-sciences-exciting-through-television-fiction-the-case-of-christmas-of-the-comets-by-katrine-bouschinger-christensen-and-eva-novrup-redvall/#comments. Accessed 20 December 2021.

Christmas of the Comets/Kometernes jul. 2021 (1 season). Created by Jenny Lund Madsen. Denmark: Nordisk Film *for* TV 2.

Clark, Margaret M. 1993. *Writing for Children*. London: A & C Black.

DFI. 2021a. "Viden om publikum" ["Knowledge about audiences"]. https://www.dfi.dk/branchen/viden-om-publikum. Accessed 15 December 2021.

DFI. 2021b. "PublikumsFokus" ["Audience focus"]. https://www.dfi.dk/search?query=publikumsfokus. Accessed 15 December 2021.
DR. 2020. "Børneproducenternes dag". DR industry event for independent producers of children's content. DR Byen, 18 August, Copenhagen.
EBU (European Broadcasting Union). 2020. "Youth report: 'What works?' Strategic guide." 24 November. https://www.ebu.ch/publications/youth-report. Accessed 15 December 2021.
First Day. 2020–2022 (2 seasons). Created by Julie Kalceff. Australia: Epic Films *for* ABC Australia.
The Florida Project. 2017. Written and directed by Sean Baker. USA: Cre Film, Freestyle Picture Company and June Pictures.
Fritz, Jean, and William Knowlton Zinsser. 1989. *Worlds of Childhood: The Art and Craft of Writing for Children*. Boston: Houghton Mifflin.
Jensen, Helle Strandgaard. 2017. *From Superman to Social Realism: Children's Media and Scandinavian Childhood*. Amsterdam-Philadelphia: John Benjamins Publishing Company.
Hamlett, Christina. 2006. *Screenwriting for Teens: The 100 Principles of Screenwriting Every Budding Screenwriter Must Know*. Burbank, CA: Michael Wiese Productions.
Hansen, Sarah Cecilie Simone. 2019. "DR skifter børnemålgrupper fra 2020." ["DR changes children target audience groups from 2020"]. *dr.dk*, 4 September. https://www.dr.dk/om-dr/nyheder/dr-skifter-boernemaalgrupper-fra-2020. Accessed 15 December 2021.
Harrison, Barbara. 1999. *Origins of Story: On Writing for Children*. New York: McElderry Books.
Hearts of Darkness: A Filmmaker's Apocalypse. 1991. Written by Fax Bahr and George Hickenlooper. Directed by Fax Bahr, George Hickenlooper, and Eleanor Coppola. USA: Zaloom Mayfield Productions and Zoetrope Studios.
Hermansson, Casie, and Janet Zepernick, eds. 2019. *The Palgrave Handbook of Children's Film and Television*. Cham, Switzerland: Palgrave Macmillan.
Hintz, Carrie, and Elaine Ostry, eds. 2003. *Utopian and Dystopian Writing for Children and Young Adults*. New York: Routledge.
Hunt for the Wilderpeople. 2016. Written and directed by Taika Waititi. New Zealand: Defender Films, Piki Films and Curious.
Johnson, Beth, and Alison Peirse. 2021. "Genre, gender and television screenwriting: The problem of pigeonholing." *European Journal of Cultural Studies* 24 (3): 658–672. https://doi.org/10.1177/13675494211006089.
Klassen. 2016–present. Created by various at DR Ultra. Denmark: DR Ultra.
Krikowa, Natalie. 2021. "Writing Inclusive and Diverse Children's Television: Transgender Representation in ABC Australia's *First Day*." *Journal of Screenwriting* 12 (3): 325–43.
Langkjær, Birger. 2012. *Realismen i dansk film*. ["Realism in Danish cinema"]. Frederiksberg, Denmark: Samfundslitteratur.
Lury, Karen. 2019. "Foreword." In *The Palgrave Handbook of Children's Film and Television*, edited by Casie Hermansson and Janet Zepernick, v–vii. Cham, Switzerland: Palgrave Macmillan.
Macdonald, Ian W. 2009. *Screenwriting Poetics and the Screen Idea*. Basingstoke, UK: Palgrave Macmillan.
Murphy, J. J. 2021. *The Florida Project*. Austin: The University of Texas Press.
Northcroft, George J. H. 1935. *Writing for Children*. London: A & C Black.

Parry, Becky. 2013. *Children, Film and Literacy*. Basingstoke: Palgrave Macmillan.
Potter, Anna, and Jeanette Steemers. 2022. "Children and the Media Industries: An Overlooked but Very Special 'Television' Audience." In *The Routledge Companion to Media Industries*, edited by Paul Macdonald, 247–56. London: Routledge.
Redvall, Eva Novrup. 2018a. "Film and Media Production as a Screen Idea System." In *The Creative System in Action*, edited by Phillip McIntyre, Janet Fulton, and Elizabeth Patton, 139–54. Basingstoke, UK: Palgrave Macmillan.
Redvall, Eva Novrup. 2018b. "Reaching Young Audiences Through Research: Using the NABC Method to Create the Norwegian Web Teenage Drama SKAM." In *True Event Adaptation: Scripting Real Lives*, edited by Davinia Thornley, 143–61. Basingstoke, UK: Palgrave Macmillan.
Redvall, Eva Novrup. 2021. "Cross-media, Co-creative and Current: New Strategies for Educating Talent for Danish Children's Film and Television in the 2020's." *Film Education Journal* 4 (2): 184–94.
Redvall, Eva Novrup, and Katrine Bouschinger Christensen, eds. 2020. *Replikker*, 32, Special Issue "Writing for children and young audiences". https://www.dramatiker.dk/wp-content/uploads/2020/replikker32_indhold_web.pdf. Accessed 15 December 2021.
Redvall, Eva Novrup, and Katrine Bouschinger Christensen. 2021. "Editorial: Screenwriting for children and young audiences." *Journal of Screenwriting* 12 (3): 259–68.
RYA. 2022. "Reaching Young Audiences: Serial Fiction and Cross-Media Storyworlds for Children and Young Audiences (RYA)." https://comm.ku.dk/research/film-science-and-creative-media-industries/reaching-young-audiences-serial-fiction-and-cross-media-storyworlds-for-children-and-young-audiences-rya/. Accessed 15 December 2021.
SKAM. 2015–2017 (4 seasons). Created by Julie Andem. Norway: NRK.
Smith, Murray. 1995. *Engaging Characters: Fiction, Emotion and the Cinema*. Oxford: Oxford University Press.
Stand by Me. 1986. Written by Raynold Gideon and Bruce A. Evans. Directed by Rob Reiner. USA: Columbia Pictures and Act III.
Strachan, Linda. 2008. *Writing for Children*. London: A & C Black.
Vemmer, Mogens. 2006. *Fjernsyn for dig: 50 år med verdens værste seere*. [Television for you: 50 years with the world's worst viewers]. Copenhagen: Gyldendal.

CHAPTER 25

Imitations of Life? A Challenge for Black Screenwriters

Julius Ayodeji

25.1 Introduction

Imitation of Life, Douglas Sirk's 1959 film adaptation of 1933 novel *Imitation of Life*, written by Fannie Hurst, is a story of African-American integration and assimilation where a light-skinned daughter rejects her dark-skinned mother as she tries to pass as white. These themes offer an opportunity to discuss how black screenwriters might strategically respond to using the unique perspective that one has when working as a minority in a dominant culture. There are any number of ways of depicting black faces, stories and concerns on the screen. This chapter proposes three differing but connected strategies—*passing*, *assimilation* and *mirroring*—whereby black screenwriters might go on to create work for non-black filmmakers to make.

These three strategies are not meant as *either/or*. *Black Panther* (2018), incredibly well-reviewed worldwide and the highest-ever grossing film by a black director, means that black films that have predominantly black characters can still play worldwide. Instead, these strategies should be seen as being responsive in acknowledging that there is a richness possible that perhaps is not being fully, *deliberately*, exploited by black writers, or indeed by development executives. As a minority black writer, one has a foot in at least two cultures and crucially, this affords the ability to write with authenticity from multiple positions that others cannot. Screenwriter Dwayne Johnson-Cochran

J. Ayodeji (✉)
Leeds Beckett University, Leeds, England
e-mail: j.ayodeji@leedsbeckett.ac.uk

had this to say: "If you are interested in cinema, you'll write what you like.... a writer writes, just because he's a black person is a misnomer and a disservice to a writer's rights" (Harris 1996, 17).

This chapter examines the context of the UK and North American film industries from the 1930s to the modern day. It feeds into a wider discussion of representation and how one might increase and develop inclusive strategies for those who are under-represented and/or disenfranchised. From Oscar Micheaux's silent era films to the present, writing and directing your own work have often been seen by under-represented filmmakers as the strategy for ensuring some diversity of storytelling. However, this paper focuses on the screenwriter, rather than the writer/director. Throughout, the term Black screenwriter is used to describe screenwriters of the African diaspora who are working predominantly as screenwriters and not writers/directors.

25.2 Diversity Through the Screen

Social movements such as Black Lives Matter and #MeToo have afforded sustained conversations around diversity since the 2015 #OscarsSoWhite hashtag debate provoked by media strategist April Reign. Increasing the diversity of storytelling through providing better access to industry levers for those other than white, middle-aged men has become a prominent agenda in recent years. This requires addressing several interlocking mechanisms of preferment and exclusion.

Susan Rogers' (2007) survey of the UK film industry mentions that "a very high proportion of screenwriters (24 of out 26) believed they were hired as a result of their previous work and that the work was known to the employer in advance of contact being made" (Rogers 2007, 27). Fifty per cent of them also had a prior working relationship with this employer and forty-two per cent of these writers had a prior personal relationship with them (Rogers 2007). Whilst this is unsurprising, it underlines the difficulty of disrupting an established hegemony. It also points to related issues. In her research into gender equality in screenwriting, based on interviews with a range of screenwriters and their employers, Natalie Wreyford (2018) found that writers' prior work tended to be conflated with their demographic characteristics, so that female screenwriters were seen as only good at writing about certain subjects (e.g. women) and in certain genres (e.g. drama), whilst male screenwriters were seen as having a broader range. Wreyford further argues that it is not only prior work but personal connections and the operation of homophily, i.e. "the tendency of individuals to associate and bond with similar others" (2018, 39), that leads producers and other decision-makers to employ particular writers. This constitutes another way in which writers from minority and marginalised groups can be excluded.

Getting definitive figures on the numbers of black screenwriters currently working in the United States and the UK is very difficult. Diversity data typically looks at generally unrepresented sections of society and in the UK reports issued around diversity tend to group gender and sexual orientation industry representation alongside ethnicity data, or do not even seek to collect ethnicity data. In a recent report into diversity in television by Ofcom—the UK's regulator for communications—the broadcasters surveyed did not collect racial group data for 20 per cent of their employees (2017). For freelancers working with the five main UK broadcasters—i.e. BBC, ITV, Channel 4, Sky and Viacom (owners of Channel 5)—no racial data was provided for 42 per cent of them.

In the United States, the 2017 study titled "Colour of Change: Hollywood Race in the Writers Room" puts the percentage of black writers working across network American television at 4.8 per cent. Contrast this with the likely future makeup of the American population. Referring to a bill passed in the 1960s, which ended preferential immigration quotas for Europeans into the United States, Halter points out: "Here was legislation that in the years since its approval has led to the kaleidoscopic demographic change and to so complete a shake-up of the country's racial and ethnic composition that by 2050 there will be no white majority, every American will belong to a minority group" (Halter 2000, 3–4). So, the ability to write stories through *a culture* but not necessarily depicted through *that culture* is potentially a useful skill for the black screenwriter.

25.3 Subtext, Dual Task Thinking and Double Consciousness

The three screenwriting strategies this chapter will go on to propose are essentially bound up in identity and each one of them is deeply reliant on subtext. Control of subtext is what allows narrative connection between the ideas developed by the screenwriter and carried by the screenplay, and how well these ideas are transmitted to its audience. The contention of this chapter is that, for an author's work to have any meaning, the energy that underpins the author's process of creation must be transferred into a document, the screenplay, that forces the reader to attempt interpretation or translation. The ideas become words become images and sounds. In order to interpret these ideas—deliberate, structured stories represented by the screenplay—this narrative translation is required. It involves agency on the part of author and audience. The work is a promissory note that says come along with me on this journey and see if we might learn, enjoy, distract, reflect and thus connect.

The screenplay inhabits a transitory, liminal space existing as it does as both prosaic, technical production document and a creative, semi-literary, creative writing text. Whilst film is often described as a director's medium, the majority of professionally produced screen works originate with the word. Screenwriter John August describes writing as "carefully shaping a thought for its desired impact" (Brodnitz 2007) and for the professional screenwriter the primary first reader of the work is not the audience at point of broadcast but in fact the producer, director or lead actor. These first readers are the audience that the screenwriter needs to engage.

Stories that are situated in the black experience for the first readers of the screenwriter's work that are not black might require an extra layer of translation. The three strategies proposed by this paper are translation aids for the non-black audience. Writing from the black experience, but not exclusively about the black experience, can perhaps allow these initial first readers for that screenplay to more easily empathise, thus resulting in more work being commissioned from black screenwriters and therefore in a more diverse pool of screenwriters being able to impact the stories that we tell. Easing the translation process speaks to what Mark Torrance and David Galbraith describe as the likely degradation of performance when undertaking simultaneous tasks; the simultaneous task here being the additional imaginative effort potentially required if the reader does not see themselves or people they know in the screenplay. Torrance and Galbraith assert that cognitive capacity should be "thought of as a single resource that is shared across all currently running" (Torrance and Galbraith 2006, 69). This additional layer required for white first readers reading black-focused work could be problematic as regards getting work commissioned, since, as I have argued above and elsewhere, recruitment practices in the industry are still predominantly one of recommendation or a reliance on prior knowledge (Ayodeji 2017) and therefore strategies that might *profile raise* become increasingly significant.

In a prior work, "The Screenplay as Research Palimpsest" (Ayodeji 2012), I have argued that the screenplay should be seen not only as a collection of words building to literal and metaphorical representation at the later production stage of filmmaking, but also as a document that emphasises the meta-fiction, the screenwriting techniques and conventions used to write it, and which also reflects the role of the screenwriter as author of the piece. The paper goes on to describe how Torrance and Galbraith (2006) discuss the cognitive processes required when writing involves dual tasks, which is relevant to the fact that the screenplay is both literary and technical document. Examination of this idea of the dual task writing process is also relevant in this discussion. The adoption of any of the three strategies proposed here requires this kind of cognitive dual task thinking. To this purpose, I will also link this *dual task* idea to Du Bois' notion of double consciousness. W. E. B. Du Bois is generally acknowledged as one of the most significant African-American writers on racial politics. His *The Soul of Black Folks* (1903) in particular is seen as a seminal work. Hine (as quoted in Early 1993) argues that for Du Bois "[…] race was the master key to understanding America reality and the most potent factor shaping identity" (Hine, as quoted in Early, 338). Double consciousness was coined by Du Bois as a way of describing what he saw as the internal conflict that any colonised or oppressed group suffer as oppressed people living in a racist society. More recently, the term has been used to describe other societal inequalities: for instance, regarding gender and sexual identity.

Double consciousness necessitates *code switching*. Code switching, the broad meaning of which linguists originally described as switching languages, in conversation now includes cultural expression. It indicates a way of changing speech, dress, social interaction in order to fit into the majority culture of a particular place. Andrew Molinsky describes cross-cultural code switching as "the act of purposefully modifying one's behaviour in an interaction to accommodate different cultural norms for appropriate behaviour" (2007, 624). Whilst Molinsky's paper is focused on the psychological challenges of code switching when living in a different country, I am seeing it through Du Bois's double consciousness framework. Molinsky discusses the performative aspect of code switching, and it is in this context I propose the three strategies:

1. *Passing*—where a person of one ethnic minority attempts to pass themselves off as being from the dominant culture. In black culture this manifests itself as light-skinned black people passing themselves off as white. As Peter Bradbury describes a revival in films about passing (Bradbury 2018), the contention of this author is that any black writer who is living as a minority in a majority culture and switching between cultures, can write passing stories that are not about race. Racial imposter syndrome (Yun 2017) describes how children of immigrant parents can often operate in a fluid racial identity context and this context underpins the passing strategy proposed. Identity is a key to this strategy. When writing inside this strategy, specific attention should be drawn to the cross-cultural movement. This chapter shows how these stories do not have to be about race.
2. *Assimilation*—where the black screenwriter absorbs the dominant culture and writes from that perspective. Assimilation is traditionally used as a counter-point to multiculturalism. In his review of assimilation and multiculturalism, *Incorporating Diversity: Rethinking Assimilation in a Multicultural Age*, sociologist Peter Kivisto cites Glazer's claim that assimilation is "still the most powerful force affecting the ethnic and racial elements of the United States" (Kivisto 2015, 113). Kivisto also cites Ewa Morawska's discussion of what she describes as three "more advanced" (Kivisto 2015, 129) stages of assimilation: integration into social relations with the dominant group, the disappearance of a collective ethnic identity and the extinction of individual or subjective ethnic identification. Kivisto contrasts Morawska's position to the one taken by Herbert Gans in his essay "Towards a Reconciliation of 'Assimilation' and 'Pluralism': The Interplay of Acculturation and Ethnic Retention", which redefines assimilation as acculturation, that is becoming American culturally but not necessarily socially (Kivisto 2015, 139). This latter position constitutes my speculative strategy.
3. *Mirroring*—perhaps the most ambitious strategy of the three, mirroring assigns particular stories to minority cultures but then seeks to tell those stories through white characters. In the context of this chapter, mirroring

is described as writing a film where the black screenwriter might write a screenplay whose subject matter draws on his or her personal experience and then places or uses that experience in a majority culture setting, in a story that is designed, by allusion, to throw a mirror up for the viewer to that specific black experience.

Whilst these three strategies are distinct and do differ, the connection between the three approaches is identity with agency, as their aim is to get a more diverse pool of storytellers working consistently in the industry through the adoption of these strategies as storytelling approaches.

The screenwriter's initial first readers, due to their specific industry knowledge and understanding, have memory retrieval. Memory retrieval is the ability to find remote associations and to use that to correlate their insight into the performance or the work. Code switching, double consciousness and being a minority in majority culture afford the black screenwriter a unique place to potentially achieve deeper insight through allusion. The challenge is how to write enough into the work that the first readers see themselves in it. Black screenwriters have a lived experience that will allow emotional access that can translate to their first readers, which the majority white culture writer cannot have in the same way.

25.4 THE SCREENPLAY AND THE CAPTIVATED AUDIENCE

As discussed above, for the professional screenwriter the primary audience is not the audience at point of broadcast but in fact the producer, director or very rarely the imagined lead actor. What is an audience? When considering the discipline of audience studies, Magnifico (2010) describes the idea of the audience as a necessary abstraction that must occur as, and indeed if, the author considers their audience during the creation of the work. What each audience member brings to a work is unquantifiable. The audience can only ever be re-structurer or re-constructor of work as they apply their own phenomenological interpretation of that work (Schooler and Melcher 1995, 123). The screenwriter working in genre—for example, thriller, horror, biography—might usefully assume that the producer, director, actor first readers have some understanding of the tropes and conventions of that form/genre. As those tropes and conventions can then be manipulated for affect and effect, there is a well-established relationship in place as both screenwriter and first readers work with their understanding of the conventions of the screenplay. This relationship has been described as "analytical mutuality" (Tulloch 1990, 24).

Language utilised by the screenwriter either visually through stage directions or spoken dialogue is at the heart of the screenplay. Language, either embodied or verbal, provides some sense of agency for the characters that then define the script thematically. Screen works that resonate are recognised as truthful in some form or another. These works demonstrate writing to find the truth of a situation, however specific this truth might be, because this allows access to the universal truths of life: hope, family, ambition, disappointment, frustration, love and loss, and so forth. Narratology, the phenomenology of the narrative experience, modern hermeneutics and intentionality is all tied into this idea of agency.

These ideas of agency and contextual awareness that the audience performs in order to translate the text might not conform to the first law of thermodynamics, which states that energy is transformed and never lost, as not everything can be captured in a translation. This *loss* can usefully be utilised by the screenwriter as a space to create, if connected with the idea of activating memory retrieval and remote associations in the initial readers of the screenplay work.

The three strategies explored are designed to speak to the first readers, in order that the screenplay form, cognitive dual thinking and understanding of genre can be exploited by the black screenwriter to help engage that primary audience.

25.5 The Preservation of Self in Everyday Life: The Place of the Screenplay

In *The Picture of Dorian Gray*, Dorian Gray retains his youthful beauty as all around him age. A special portrait of him ages and reveals his inner ugliness. This is the *shock reveal* at the end of the film, his physical beautiful form is contrasted with the painting's decay, we see the psychic cost of this deal, Goffman's (1956) invisible costs are made visible. This, making invisible costs visible, is often a rhetorical device of black movies that have race as a theme. *Boyz n The Hood* (1991), *The Hate U Give* (2018) and *Green Book* (2018) are examples where the struggles against pervasive racism are made visible after some period of stoic acceptance, but "the problem of dramatizing one's work involved more than making invisible costs visible" (Goffman 1956, 21).

The three strategies are an attempt to introduce a less literal, more allusive attempt to speak to invisible costs. I also have proposed practical examples of story themes, genres or ideas. I aim to consider each strategy in three ways:

1. What each term is taken to mean generally in the literature/culture?
2. How each term describes the subject position taken by the screenwriter?
3. How each term might be explored thematically in the screenplays the black screenwriter writes?

25.5.1 Strategy One: Passing—Denial

As Kroeger describes it, "passing means that other people actually see or experience the identity that the passer is projecting, whether the passer is telegraphing that identity by intention or by chance" (2003, 7–8). Passing stories are stories where the protagonist sublimates an aspect of themselves in order to better integrate into a society they wish or need to be a part of. Passing is when people can't be who they are. Passing stories are compassionate stories.

In the two adaptations of *Imitation of Life* (Stahl 1934; Sirk 1959), one of the major themes of the story is how the black daughter of the black housemaid wishes she were white. In her concerted attempts to pass as white and after multiple rejections of her mother, on the mother's death the daughter is full of remorse. Here we have a white author Hurst writing about a black person trying to pass as white.

In *Boys Don't Cry* (1999) female Teena Brandon attempts to pass as male Brandon Teena. In *Gentleman's Agreement* (1947) a reporter passes as Jewish to expose bigotry. In the comedy *Stir Crazy* (1980), after being mistakenly jailed in a case of mistaken identity, Richard Pryor and Gene Wilder attempt to pass as tough guys in order to survive in jail. In the student film *Identity* (2017)[1] a young sportsman whose identity is tied up with basketball wrestles with the constriction he feels and struggles to pass himself off as someone who loves the game that he actually hates. In *The Escape* (2017), Tara restarts her life after realising she's passing as someone happy in her life as a wife and mother.

The cultural switching that the black screenwriter will have experience of can easily be translated into a variety of identity stories through this framework of passing, so that stories that might initially be seen as racial stories can instead be stories about gender, religion, gangster comedies or self-identity.

25.5.2 Strategy Two: Assimilation—Enveloped

> Belonging is the innate human desire to be part of something larger than us. Because this yearning is so primal, we often try to acquire it by fitting in and be seeking approval, which are not only hollow substitutes for belonging, but often barriers to it. Because true belonging only happens when we present our authentic, imperfect selves to the world, our sense of belonging can never be greater than our level of self-acceptance. (Brown 2022)

Echoing Gans's definition of assimilation as acculturation discussed above, Rumbaut defines assimilation as denoting "the cumulative changes that make individuals of one ethnic group more acculturated, integrated and identified with the members of another" (as cited in Kivisto 2015, 158). In adopting assimilation as a strategy, the black screenwriter adopts the national characteristics of the majority and firmly anchors stories in that context.

---

[1] Link to this short film can be found here https://www.intofilm.org/news-and-views/articles/fotm-identity?fbclid=IwAR2mkQyyVuxbR3w_ESvPvD4gNfZFNPEK4z8uSzn0zaNCYM066VjD3BOR68s.

The Hate U Give is a story set in this world of assimilation, with the main character literally telling us her struggles to live in two worlds. With the unwarranted killing of a young black man at its heart, this story treads somewhat familiar worlds but arguably is a story about assimilation, cultural appropriation and acculturation, as the main character Starr is forced to choose between the distinct and separate black and white worlds that she lives in. This might easily have been retold as a story about class rather than racial divisions.

Migration, either into or out of a culture or country, is tied up with ideas of assimilation. *Brooklyn* (2015) is an immigration/assimilation story as Irishwoman Eilis Lacey emigrates to Brooklyn, United States, from County Wexford, Ireland, to find work. There she struggles to determine whether to return to her familiar hometown or stay in this unfamiliar new world. Black screenwriters can write stories about migration but this migration might be class rather than race and culture. The multi-award-winning *Roma* (2018) subtly looks at class divisions in Mexico, so how about a black screenwriter writing a modern-day retelling of Thomas Hardy's *Jude the Obscure*? Black screenwriters will have access to imposter syndrome and the burden of representations as useful emotional resonances.

The gangster movie is often a story about disenfranchisement *A Most Violent Year* (2014) can be seen as an update of the classic immigrant story. Although not a gangster film it has some of the tropes of gangster movies, with some similar themes to *Once Upon a Time in America* (1984) or *The Godfather* series of three films (1972, 1974, 1979) with the immigrant outsider attempting to fully partake in the American dream of social progression and this immigrant status challenging the status quo with violent results. *Mean Girls* (2004), where white teenager, Cady Heron, after years being home-schooled in Africa attempts to make friends when enrolled in a high school upon the family's return to America, can be read as a story of assimilation.

Other types of stories that can allow a reframing of some of the ideas outlined in this section are disaster movies where *entire humanity!!!!!!*, hyperbole intended, is at stake. Joe Robert Cole, the first writer of colour to be a part of the Marvel writing programme and the co-screenwriter of *Black Panther* (2018), is incredibly well-placed to write these stories where race can be integrated as part of the story tapestry in ways that could question ideas of assimilation or acculturation, such as stories of migration. Portmanteau movies, of which *Crash* (2004) is an example, might also be another avenue. Or again, when writing movies aimed at young audiences, bullying, adolescence and the vulnerability of first love, a deep passion for a thing that separates a person from another, are all themes for which a black screenwriter from a minority culture will be able to draw on personal experience of dislocation, apartness, migration or the longing for a type of simplicity of social relations that a mono-culture might seem to offer. These themes, all with obvious connections to ideas of assimilation and integration, can be written in ways designed to immediately engage with that screenwriter's audience. If Caucasian writer/director Joel Schumacher when talking about his work on

Car Wash (1976) and *The Wiz* (1978) can state that he was "a black writer" when interviewed by Spike Lee (*Michael Jackson's Journey from Motown to Off the Wall*, 2016) then the reverse can happen.

25.5.3 Strategy Three: Mirroring—To See Oneself Through Others

As screenwriter Carol Munday Lawrence has said: "Somebody writes these things: somebody who is not necessarily just like the people featured in them" (Harris 1996, 80). How do minority black people see themselves? What cultural references and/or associations can be defined as black? This strategy relies on utilising the lived experience as an ethnic minority and then applying a narrative framework to the particular experience to create a film where the subject matter, character and setting or world of the story gently persuade, force or suggest that the screenwriter's experience is being reflected, but at one remove. An example of how the idea of racial prejudice might be mirrored is the gender swap movies. Instead of racial differences this would be about gender prejudice. *Orlando* (1992), *Freaky Friday* (2003), *Mrs. Doubtfire* (1993) are films where the gender swap results in significantly different treatment for the affected character/s. Age prejudice films where the character is aged up or down, *Big* (1988), *Shazam!* (2019), also allow the audience to mirror the central dilemma at the heart of the piece often by subtly questioning what decisions they themselves might make.

Movies about aliens are also potentially rich sources for mirroring. *The Day the Earth Stood Still* (1951, 2008) uses the idea of the alien to force us to look at ourselves. Multi-Oscar-winner *The Shape of Water* (2017) was often talked about as a film about tolerance, acceptance and discrimination (Lambie 2018; Bradshaw 2018). Allegorical films are by definition designed to provoke mirroring and so stories in situated here might afford opportunity for the black screenwriter. Stories of persistence, for example, might be great for mirroring. There is great scope for stories where a character has to work twice as hard to catch a break, so many a sporting Biopic could be written with real insight by a black writer. Scenes that surprise because the writer has minority culture experience can lead to an emotional richness that the white majority culture writer will find difficult if at all even possible to access. As mentioned earlier, stories about class barriers or underdog stories or stories about trying to break out from a reputational shadow are all stories that minority black screenwriters can write from a position of some transferable knowledge and/or experience.

The outsider trope is potentially another area rich for exploration. The *Elephant Man* (1980), *Untouchable* (2011) recently remade as *The Upside* (2017), all feature one or two outsiders as main characters—with that particular outsiderness in these three films being discrimination based on impairment, disability and race.

Clever adaption can also usefully provoke mirroring reflection in the audience. The 2018 Publishers Association report (The Publishers Association 2019) on publishing's contribution to the wider creative industries through its analysis of box office returns from 2007 to 2016 concluded that adaptations are the original source for 43 per cent of the top UK films, so adaptation of material continues to be almost industry policy—what books can black screenwriters find that might exploit mirroring?

The recent film adaptation of James Baldwin's *If Beale Street Could Talk* (2018) is very much set in the black African-American experience of the time, compare that to Baldwin's *Giovanni's Room*. Although this book features white characters exclusively, I would be amazed if readers did not see it as part of a black African-American experience given its author and subject matter, tales of outsider, dislocation and identity struggles, it is written through the filter of Baldwin as a black man but Baldwin made the deliberate decision to write his main characters as white.

Stories of desirability, sex, deceit, authority, infidelity and superstition abound, so the black screenwriter might then bring their multi-culturally specific embodied knowledge to telling that story. For example, a Charles Dickens's biography could be a great mirroring example. His writings about his travels through Italy, particularly his description of his time in Naples, might result in a great alternative biography as a story of disillusionment, the disenfranchised, discrimination and wasted potential through the eyes of the one who made it out. There will be many black screenwriters who might be able to bring their own personal insight and experience to this story. As screenwriter Dwayne Johnson-Cochran put it:

> My words of encouragement to black writers who are writing film for the American or the world market is to watch as many films about the world, including your world, as you can. That will give you the language you need. (Harris 1996, 17)

25.6 Conclusions

Filmmaker Robert Townsend noted that "when I write, I think there's a universal message to all my films. The thing that I deal with is the human side of people. Anyone who wants to come along for the ride is welcome" (Harris 1996, 145). This proposal for black screenwriters to consider adopting these strategies is an unashamed way to get more work commissioned: "The link between economic self-interest and cultural dynamics has always been the basis of immigrant and ethnic entrepreneurship in this country" (Halter 2000, 137). All writers bring more to their work than their gender, colour or sexual orientation. Perhaps the writing of a spec script that adopts one of the above strategies will show range and might additionally more readily resonate with a broader range of industry gatekeepers, those being agents, producers, actors, directors, and because each strategy is a translation of a cultural experience, these works should and could still be infused with the creative and cultural life of that writer. Equally, these first readers need also to be alive to the range of experience that Black screenwriters are uniquely placed to write about.

It is worth considering, however, what might be some potential objections to this approach. Whilst in the 1970s a white screenwriter, Joel Schumacher, could write film after film for the black community so much that he described considering himself a black writer (Lee 2013), such a statement today would be highly controversial and understood as a form of cultural appropriation. So, how might these three strategies sit within this frame? Might adopting any one of them lead to a continuance of the current system's lack of visibility for Black screenwriters? As Kroeger has suggested: "Passing is commonly regarded as a way of perpetuating a problematic status quo because the passer, by slipping through an oppressive system, helps keep that system in place" (2003, 212) and, fundamentally, all three strategies are about assimilation. Does this negate the cultural pluralism paradigm?

No. It looks to redefine cultural appropriation. The strategies I am proposing should be seen as being situated as potential strategies for subverting and disrupting dominant cultures. When he posited a reconceptualisation of cultural appropriation, Richard A. Rogers (2006) defined transculturation as "cultural elements created from and/or by multiple cultures such that the identification of a single originating culture is problematic" (477). This last strategy has transculturation at its heart. The black screenwriter has the ability to bring any specific cultural insights to their work and yet present it in a way where this specific cultural identification is deliberately difficult to identify.

So, black screenwriters, the challenge is out there: use metaphor, allusion and imagery, couple this with your imagination to help embed your voice— "there are joys and benefits in bilingualism" (Jones 2018).

References

A Prophet (Un prophète). 2009. Written by Jacques Audiard, Thomas Bidegain, Abdel Raouf Dafri, and Nicolas Peufaillit. France, Italy: Why Not Productions et al.

Ayodeji, Julius. 2012. "The Screenplay as Research Palimpsest." In *The Visual and Performing Arts: An International Anthology: Vol II*, edited by Stephen Andrew Arbury, 7–18. Athens (Greece): Atiner.

Ayodeji, Julius. 2017. "To Genre or Not To Genre: Typecasting the Screenwriter." In *Avanca/Cine 2017*, edited by António Costa Valente and Rita Capucho, 250–55. Avanca, Portugal: Edições Cine-Clube be Avanca.

Big. 1988. Written by Gary Ross and Anne Spielberg. Directed by Penny Marshall. USA: Gracie Films.

Black Like Me. 1964. Written by Carl Lerner and Gerda Lerner. Directed by Carl Lerner. USA. The Hilltop Company.

Black Panther. 2018. Written by Ryan Coogler and Joe Robert Cole. Directed by Ryan Coogler. USA: Marvel Studios.

Boys Don't Cry. 1999. Written by Kimberley Peirce and Andy Bienen. Directed by Kimberley Peirce. USA: Hart-Sharp Entertainment, Independent Film Channel, Killer Films.

Bradbury, Janine. 2018. "Passing for White: How a Taboo Film Genre Is Being Revived to Expose Racial Privilege." *The Guardian*, 20 August. https://www.theguardian.com/film/2018/aug/20/passing-film-rebecca-hall-black-white-us-rac. Accessed 28 June 2022.

Bradshaw, Peter. 2018. "The Shape of Water Review—An Operative Plunge into Guillermo Del Toro's Immersive Cinema." The Guardian, 15 February. https://www.theguardian.com/film/2018/feb/15/the-shape-of-water-review-guillermo-del-toro. Accessed 28 March 2022.

Brodnitz, Dan. 2007. "An Interview with John August." *About Creativity*, 7 July. http://about-creativity.com/?s=John+august. Accessed 9 March 2022.

Brown, Brené. 2022. *The Gifts of Imperfection*. 10th ed. Center City, MN. Hazelden.

Brooklyn. 2015. Written by Nick Hornby. Directed by John Crowley. UK, Ireland, Canada: BBC Films, Wildgaze Films, Telefilm Cnada, Irish Film Board, BFI, Sodec Quebec, Parallel Films, Finola Dwyer Productions, Ingenious Media, BAI, RTÉ, HanWay Films.

Crash. 2004. Written by Paul Haggis and Bobby Moresco. Directed by Paul Haggis. USA, Germany: Bob Yari Productions, DEJ Productions, Blackfriars Bridge, Harris Company, ApolloProScreen Productions, Bull's Eye Entertainment.

Du Bois, W.E.B. 1996. *The Souls of Black Folk*. Project Gutenberg (eBook). https://www.gutenberg.org/files/408/408-h/408-h.htm. Accessed 25 June 2022

Early, Gerald, ed. 1993. *Lure and Loathing. Essays on Race, Identity and the Ambivalence of Assimilation*. New York: Allen Lane/Penguin.

Ellis-Petersen, Hannah. 2017. "Lenny Henry: OFCOM Is Practising 'Fake Diversity' with On-Screen Targets." *The Guardian*, 19 July. https://www.theguardian.com/media/2017/jul/19/lenny-henry-ofcom-practising-fake-diversity-on-screen-tv-targets. Accessed 1 February 2022.

Freaky Friday. 2003. Written by Heather Hach and Leslie Dixon. Directed by Mark Waters. USA: Walt Disney Pictures, Gunn Films.

Frontier Economics. 2018. "Publishing's contribution to the wider creative industries. A report prepared for the Publishers Association." https://www.publishers.org.uk/wp-content/uploads/2020/02/Publishings-Contribution-to-the-Wider-Creative-Industries-2018.pdf. Accessed 1 August 2022.

Gentleman's Agreement. 1947. Written Moss Hart. Directed by Elia Kazan. USA: Twentieth Century Fox.

Goffman, Erving. 1956. *The Preservation of Self in Everyday Life*. Edinburgh: University of Edinburgh Social Sciences Research Centre. https://monoskop.org/images/1/19/Goffman_Erving_The_Presentation_of_Self_in_Everyday_Life.pdf. Accessed 21 February 2022

Halter. Marilyn. 2000. *Shopping for Identity. The Marketing of Ethnicity*. New York: Shocken.

Harris. Erich. 1996. *African-American Screenwriters Now: Conversations with Hollywood's Black Pack*. Los Angeles: Silman-James.

Imitation of Life. 1959. Written by Eleanor Griffin and Allan Scott. Directed by Douglas Sirk. USA: Universal International Pictures.

Imitation of Life. 1934. Written by William J. Hurlbut. Directed by John Stahl. USA: Universal Pictures.

Jones, Tobias. 2018. "The Joys and Benefits of Bilingualism." *The Guardian*, 21 January. https://www.theguardian.com/commentisfree/2018b/jan/21/the-joys-and-benefits-of-bilingualism. Accessed 21 February 2022.

Kivisto, Peter. 2015. *Incorporating Diversity: Rethinking Assimilation in a Multicultural Age*. 2nd ed. London: Routledge.
Kroeger, Brooke. 2003. *Passing. When People Can't Be Who They Are*. New York: Public Affairs.
Lambie, Ryan. 2018. "Guillermo Del Toro Interview: The Shape of Water, Shame and Perversity." Den of Geek, 12 February. https://www.denofgeek.com/UnitedKingdom/movies/guillermo-del-toro/55247/guillermo-del-toro-interview-the-shape-of-water-shame-and-perversity. Accessed 8 March 2022.
Lee, Jason. 2013. *The Psychology of Screenwriting: Theory and Practice*. London: Bloomsbury.
Magnifico, Alecia. 2010. "Writing for Whom? Cognition, Motivation, and a Writer's Audience." *Educational Psychologist* 45 (3): 167–84.
Michael Jackson's Journey from Motown to Off the Wall. 2016. Written by Spike Lee, John Branca, and John McClain. Directed by Spike Lee. USA: Optimum Productions, Sony Legacy, 40 Acres & A Mule Filmworks.
Molinsky, Andrew. 2007. "Cross-cultural Code Switching: The Psychological Challenges of Adapting Behavior in Foreign Cultural Interactions." *The Academy of Management Review* 32 (2): 622–40.
Mrs. Doubtfire. 1994. Written by Randi Mayem Singer and Leslie Dixon. Directed by Chris Columbus. USA. Twentieth Century Fox, Blue Wolf Productions.
Office of Communications (Ofcom). 2017. "Diversity and equal opportunities in television. Monitoring report on the UK-based broadcasting industry." Ofcom. https://www.ofcom.org.uk/__data/assets/pdf_file/0028/166807/Diversity-in-TV-2019.pdf. Accessed 2 March 2022.
Orlando. 1992. Written and directed by Sally Potter. UK, France, Italy, Netherlands, Russia: Adventure Pictures, LENFILM, Mikado Fil, Rio, Sigma Film Productions, British Screen Productions.
Randle, Keith, and Nigel Culkin. 2009. "Getting In and Getting On in Hollywood: Freelance Careers in an Uncertain Industry." In *Creative Labour: Working in the Creative Industries*, edited by Alan McKinlay and Chris Smith, 93–115. Basingstoke, UK: Palgrave Macmillan.
Rock, Lucy. 2018. "'This is the Movie I Wish I'd Had Look Up to'. Joe Robert-Cole on co-writing Black Panther." *The Guardian*, 13 February. https://www.theguardian.com/film/2018/feb/13/black-panther-joe-robert-cole-black-superhero-interview. Accessed 13 February 2022.
Rogers, Richard A. 2006. "From Cultural Exchange to Transculturation: A Review and Reconceptualization of Cultural Appropriation." *Communication Theory* 16: 474–503.
Rogers, Susan. 2007. "Writing British Films - who writes British films and how are they recruited?" Report for the UK Film Council. University of London: Royal Holloway College. https://www2.bfi.org.uk/sites/bfi.org.uk/files/downloads/uk-film-council-writing-british-films-who-writes-british-films-and-how-they-are-recruited.pdf. Accessed 13 March 2022.
Roma. 2018. Written and directed by Alfonso Cuarón. Mexico, USA: Espectáculos Fílmicos El Coyúl, Pimienta Films, Participant Media, Esperanto Filmoj.
Schooler, Jonathan W., and Joseph Melcher. 1995. "The Ineffability of Insight." In *The Creative Cognition Approach*, edited by Steven M. Smith, Thomas B.

Shadow and Act Staff. 2014. "The Art of Lighting Dark Skin for Film and HD." *Shadow and Act*, February 4. https://shadowandact.com/the-art-of-lighting-dark-skin-for-film-and-hd/. Accessed 12 June 2022.

Shazam!. 2019. Written by Henry Gayden. Directed by David F. Sandberg. USA, Canada: New Line Cinema, DC Films, The Safran Company.

Stir Crazy. 1980. Written by Bruce J. Friedmann and Charles Blackwell (uncredited). Directed by Sidney Poitier. USA: Columbia Pictures.

The Day the Earth Stood Still. 1951. Written by Edmund H. North. Directed by Robert Wise. USA: Twentieth Century Fox.

The Day the Earth Stood Still. 2008. Written by David Scarpa. Directed by Scott Derrickson. USA: 3 Arts Entertainment, Dune Entertainment.

The Elephant Man. 1980. Written by Christopher De Vore, Eric Bergen, and David Lynch. Directed by David Lynch. USA: Brooksfilms.

The Escape. 2017. Written and directed by Dominic Savage. UK: Lorton Entertainment, Shoebox Films.

The Picture of Dorian Gray. 1945. Written and directed by Albert Lewin. USA: Metro-Goldwyn-Mayer.

The Searchers. 1956. Written by Frank S. Nugent. Directed by John Ford. USA: Warner Bros.

The Shape of Water. 2017. Written by Guillermo Del Toro and Vanessa Taylor. Directed by Guillermo Del Toro. USA: Fox Searchlight Pictures, TSG Entertainment, Double Dare You Productions.

The Upside. 2017. Written by John Hartmere. Directed by Neil Burger. USA: Escape Artists.

Torrance, Mark, and David Galbraith. 2006. *The Processing Demands of Writing*. Handbook of Writing Research. New York: Guildford.

Tulloch, John. 1990. *Television Drama: Agency, Audience and Myth*. London: Routledge.

Untouchable (Intouchables). 2011. Written and directed by Olivier Nakache and Éric Toledano. France: Gaumont, TF1 Films Production, Chaocorp, Quad Productions, Ten Films.

Ward, and Ronald A. Finke, 97–134. New York: Guilford.

Wreyford, Natalie. 2018. *Gender Inequality in Screenwriting Work*. Basingstoke, UK: Palgrave Macmillan.

Yun, Arden. 2017. "Racial Imposter Syndrome: When you're made to feel like a fake." *BBC News*, 3 February. https://www.bbc.co.uk/news/stories-55909105. Accessed 13 March 2022.

CHAPTER 26

Beauties and Beasts: The Representation of National Identity Through Characterisation in Syrian-Lebanese Pan-Arab Dramas

Fadi G. Haddad and Alexander Dhoest

26.1 Introduction

Since the civil war in Syria erupted in 2011, over 1.5 million refugees have fled from Syria to Lebanon (Karasapan and Shah 2021), thus complicating an already historically delicate relationship between the two neighbouring countries. Simultaneously, an artistic migration from Syria to Lebanon also took place. As the once-thriving Syrian drama industry, which had its golden age with a "drama outpouring" (Salamandra 2011) between 2000 and 2010, faced a backlash due to the war as well as a boycott by the major transnational Arab Gulf-based networks, many Syrian talents moved to Lebanon and joined the local drama industry, producing television series with mixed cast and crew as well as hybrid plotlines, which will be known as Syrian-Lebanese

F. G. Haddad (✉)
American University in Dubai, Dubai, UAE
e-mail: ffadigeorgehaddad@gmail.com

F. G. Haddad · A. Dhoest (✉)
University of Antwerp, Antwerp, Belgium
e-mail: alexander.dhoest@uantwerpen.be

pan-Arab dramas (Arabic: *Al-drama al-mushtaraka al-sooriya al-lubnaniya*).[1] This is thought to have revived the industry on both sides of the border, combining the Syrian experience in screenwriting, acting, and directing with the Lebanese production capabilities and "pretty faces" (Behna 2019; El-Hajj 2019).[2] Opinions vary as to who took the most advantage from this collaboration. Nevertheless, more and more Syrian-Lebanese dramas are being made and broadcasted every Ramadan,[3] achieving very high viewership ratings in both countries and across the Arab World, and promising high-end drama (Goodfellow 2017). As characters drive plots through their actions, and thus activate social and personal discourses becoming embodiments of ideological values (Fiske 1987), this paper aims to investigate these Syrian-Lebanese pan-Arab dramas, particularly the four series produced and broadcasted in the season of Ramadan of 2020, focusing on the way they represent Syrian and Lebanese national characters. In this way, we hope to better understand how the Syrian and Lebanese characters are constructed in these shows and to what extent their characterisation aligns with or departs from the general knowledge of both countries' national cultures. It is important to understand how *Syrian-ness* and *Lebanese-ness* are represented in these series, as they can influence viewers' perceptions, cultural values, and identities (Lita and Cho 2012). Moreover, since these series are developed by mixed teams of creators from Syria, Lebanon, and other Arab countries, commissioned by transnational pan-Arab broadcasters and platforms, they present a particularly interesting case of mediated identity construction, which also gives insight into the nature of the screenplays produced in the culturally hybrid pan-Arab drama industry.

26.2 Characterisation: Schemata, Cognition, and Development

In television, characters are "the point of connection" (Wickham 2007, 91). Therefore, characters and their plots are often anchored in everyday beliefs, values, and cultural awareness, providing points of reference for their viewers (Schweinitz 2010), and screenwriters are thought to "model their characters on their culture's conceptions of people, making them person-like" (Pearson 2007, 41). In this study, we are interested in how the identity construction of characters may reflect certain *schemata*, which are "chunks of knowledge about the world, events, people, and actions" (Eysenck and Keane 2000, 352), particularly the ones related to national character and stereotypes, and

---

[1] Pan-Arab dramas (Arabic: *al-drama al-arabiyya al-mushtaraka*) are serialised dramas that present an ensemble of characters from various Arab nationalities in a transnational narrative setting (Haddad and Dhoest 2020).

[2] Generally, the plotlines of most Syrian-Lebanese dramas revolve around a love story between a Syrian actor and a Lebanese actress. These actresses are often former beauty pageant winners or models.

[3] Ramadan, the holy month of fasting for Muslims, is considered the high season of television programming in the Arab world.

how fictional characters appear as members of a certain nation when they correspond with the constructed cognition of its national character. For this purpose, we consider those schemata as "modes of characterisation" (Dyer 2013), and therefore, we explore how they function within the process of character development.

Culpeper (2001) discusses the topic of character construction and interpretation in fiction storytelling, introducing a mixed approach in which meanings are constructed through the interaction between a top-down process projecting the interpreter's background "knowledge of real life" (87) onto the text and a bottom-up process triggered by "textual cues" (163) embedded in the text itself such as dialog or speech form and character propositions (e.g. appearances). Culpeper explains that the first impressions of characters are guided by social schemata or "cognitive stereotypes" (2009, 128), in which characters are perceived as members of social groups or social categories. He presents these categories in three broad groupings:

1. Personal categories, which include interests, traits, and goals.
2. Social-role categories, which include kinship roles, occupational roles, and relational roles.
3. Group membership categories, which include gender, race, class, age, nationality, and religion.

He affirms that this cognitive process of categorisation can also lead to further links and assumptions between the different categories. Moreover, he distinguishes between textual cues that are explicit, either in self-presentation or in other-presentation; implicit (e.g. accent or dialect and setting); or authorial (e.g. proper names).

Therefore, classifying characters by associating them with the traits of some social, geographical, and historical type or archetype facilitates their "anchorage and stability within the narration" (Brenes 2012). Culpeper also evaluates fictional characters in terms of their depth, distinguishing *round characters* from *category-based* or *flat characters* that "tend to exhibit the same behaviour regardless of context" (2001, 259). Indeed, in many cases, a character only develops full-fledged character traits over the course of the narration, which is reminiscent of the concept of stereotypes that helps drama achieve a sense of universality (McIlrath 1955). Moreover, Dyer (2013) differentiates between a *type*, a character constructed through a few immediately recognisable and defining traits that do not develop through the course of the narrative, and a *novelistic* character, which is defined by a multiplicity of traits that are only gradually revealed to us through the course of a narrative that is hinged on the growth or development of the character.

In that sense, characters in fiction are not limited to their initial characterisation but are developed over their trajectory throughout the conflict (see

McKee 1999). The greater the agreement between the character's initial characteristics and its final ones, the more the character appears as one-dimensional and not as a complex character with individual traits (see Florack 2010). Building on this, Brenes (2012) explores a definition of a "good character" which serves the world of fiction it is in, and argues it is detectable through two aspects: the transformation arc, which is the change the character undergoes between the beginning and the end of the story, and emotional coherence of the character within that transformation. Similarly, Hogan (2010) distinguishes two sorts of development principles: *alteration principles*, which serve to alter the basic prototype or its representation, and *specification principles*, which make the abstract prototypes rather concrete. This, in addition to the concepts explored earlier, provides us with useful tools to assess how much the characters in the Syrian-Lebanese dramas we study confirm or contrast with the *chunks of knowledge* the creators and the assumed target audience may have of Syria, Lebanon, and their people, which we will explore in the following section.

26.3 National Culture in Representation: Syria and Lebanon

Before delving into Syria and Lebanon's cultural production, it is necessary to contextualise this discussion within their intertwined *story of creation*, to sense how this may have spilled into the consequent development of their distinct-yet-overlapping national identities. When the two nation-states were established in the aftermath of World War I and the fall of the Ottoman Empire to colonial powers, the populations of both countries were so heterogeneous and factionalised that they struggled to construct a unanimous national identity (Salibi 1988). Although both countries gained their independence in the 1940s, only in 2008 did Syria recognise Lebanon's sovereignty, and were diplomatic relations officially established. This postcolonial complexity is further enhanced by the twenty-nine-year-long Syrian military presence in Lebanon (1976–2005) and the Syrian intervention in Lebanese politics before and after the withdrawal of Syrian troops. Consequently, Lebanon is often claimed as a part of a *Greater Syria* by pan-Syrian and pan-Arab nationalists on both sides of the borders. Those borders have never been officially demarcated, so up to this day Syrian and Lebanese maps often show considerable discrepancies (Mouawad 2018; Picard and Ramsbotham 2012).

Against this backdrop, we will explore the opposite directions both countries have taken with the construction of their national identity, by looking into a variety of their cultural products. This will help us map out the schemata shaping *Syrian-ness* and *Lebanese-ness*, from which we will deduce a set of thematic identifiers used to analyse characterisation in our case study. In doing so, we emphasise that national identities are constructed representations of "imagined communities" (Anderson [1983] 2006). This imagination is a collective phenomenon that is discursively embedded in people's daily lives through *common points* (Kelman 1997) such as folk stories, common histories, and popular culture (Hall, Held, and McGrew 1992). Therefore, our approach is in line with the field of imagology, which studies the mechanism of national othering (Hoenselaars and Leerssen 2009) in the images of national character in cultural artefacts, and their resulted *perceptual schemata* of normalised emotional dispositions and attitudes that are reproduced and incorporated through socialisation, education, politics, and the media (Wodak, De Cillia, and Reisigl 1999). Our interest is in national character stereotypes, which have been proven to be irreflective of nations' true personality traits and behavioural dispositions (Terracciano et al. 2005; Beller and Leerssen 2007). We focus on their representation-value as a "process of giving meaning" (Hall 1997, 5) rather than their truth-value.

26.3.1 Lebanon: A "Bridge Between the East and the West"

In his book "Inside the Lebanese Confessional Mind", Hilal Khashan (1992) comes to the pessimistic conclusion that the Lebanese are merely a plurality of people who "lack consensus on fundamentals" (3). It is no surprise that Lebanon is often referred to as a "country of contradictions" (Hudson 1997). Evidently, as a result of a brutal sectarian war—a main theme in Lebanese post-war cinema (Haugbolle 2010)—that ended with a fragile peace and a growing number of unresolved grievances, Lebanon has long struggled to create a unifying narrative for such a traumatised society divided by a history of mutual violence amongst its confessional groups. Consequently, different educational systems following different denominations still teach their own textbooks, each telling their own version of the history of Lebanon, resulting in constructing competing memories (Medawar 2007; Blaik-Hourani 2017).

While Lebanon's socio-geographic complexity can be considered a matter of historical coincidence, the construction of a Lebanese national identity that plays on the notions of contradiction is not. It is a result of the articulation of a Lebanese subjectivity premised on separatism from the Arab context, which at the time had a predominant pan-Arab nationalist discourse, branding Lebanon as a "bridge between the East and the West" (Al-Khazin 1991), and a *merchant republic* that represents complete social and economic liberties (Reinkowski 1997). For instance, exploring the promotional prints issued by the National Council for Tourism in the 1960s, Maasri (2016) detects an antagonistic stance towards politics of Arab nationalism and the visual endorsement of a Euro-Mediterranean character. On a similar note, in his study of popular culture and nationalism in Lebanon, Stone (2007) examines how the Baalbeck International Festival established in the mid-1950s transformed the ancient Roman ruins into a symbolic representation that stands for modern Lebanon, disclosing a strong connection between the festival founders, the Lebanese state, and associated Christian national elite. With highbrow international performances, it intended to project "a westward looking nation that is a cultivator of culture and civilization" (Stone 2007, 32). At this festival, the musicals and concerts of the Rahbani Brothers, a composer and songwriter duo, along with their lead singer Fairouz, became an icon of what would become "typical Lebanese" music (Kraidy 2003, 281). The Rahbanis are thought to have employed "idealized and nostalgic versions of the Christian Mount Lebanon to stand for Lebanon as a whole" (Stone 2003, 11), establishing an image of the Lebanese people as freedom-loving (Stone 2007). Despite the years of civil atrocity throughout the 1970s and 1980s, the resonance of this image has maintained Lebanon's reputation in Arab popular culture of quintessentially beautiful and charming country, with indulgence and light-heartedness as "Lebanese qualities" (Haugbolle 2013, 73).

In the 1990s, as the civil war officially ended, Lebanon promoted a carefully engineered postcard picture of a modern, well-educated, recovering nation (Haugbolle 2013). With the rise of Gulf-funded transnational Arabic satellite broadcasting, where the Lebanese creative class with its provocative demeanour and fashionable allure occupied the social-liberal extreme of the Arab spectrum, a "Lebanese element" in television programming became a major contributor to any programme's success (Kraidy 2009). This *element* clearly capitalised on the sexiness and exoticness that sells in other more conservative Arab countries (Dabbous-Sensenig 2000; Haugbolle 2013). Similarly, post-war Lebanese television drama tends to portray an exaggerated Lebanese reality by presenting westernised and extravagant characters and plots (Chamieh 2016), and therefore contributes to obscuring the highly nuanced Lebanese society through characters with generic names and plots that avoid socio-political divisiveness (Kraidy 2003). This explains why Lebanese drama has had a poor reputation in the Arab popular media discourse compared to the thriving industries of Syria and Egypt. Nevertheless, Lebanese drama established a character that distinguished itself by being *risqué*, discussing themes that are generally avoided in family-friendly Arabic drama such as prostitution, drug use, and premarital and extramarital relations. This resonated with the Lebanese industry and audience as a reflection of the Lebanese open-mindedness and special character that entangles the *East* with the *West* (Akiki 2011; Kraidy 2003).

26.3.2 Syria: The "Den of Arabism"

While it is unfair to reduce a country's culture to a single political regime, it is impossible in the case of Syria to underrate the effect of the Ba'athist regime that has ruled the country continuously and single-handedly since 1963, and within which most of what constitutes Syria's national character today—for better or worse—has been shaped through a controlled media system and a guarded culture of communication. The Ba'ath regime promoted Syrian identity through its government-controlled agents, the media, and the educational system (Zisser 2006). Even in the few decades of political pluralism before the Ba'ath regime, when Syrian national identity was still in question, Syria was branded as the "Den of Arabism[4]" as per the national anthem adopted in 1936 and still in use till today. However, it is during Hafiz al-Asad's rule (1970–2000) that the Ba'ath took it upon itself to build an *Arab Syrian Nation*, returning to Syria's ancient roots and basing the state's identity on its cumulative ancient history: the regional Arab experience as well as the pre-Arab and pre-Islamic past of the Syrian lands (Zisser 2006). In contrast to Lebanon's system that acknowledged sects, in Syria, sectarianism and tribalism were supposed to cease to exist and all Syrians, irrespective of sect, religion, or ethnicity, were represented as Syrian Arab nationals through strategic communication on diverse cultural platforms and across different genres: television, film, music, novels, and poetry (Matar 2019). Wedeen (1999) terms this culture of communication as the *Asad cult*, in which the state is omnipresent in the media and the public sphere through the character of its leader, al-Asad, depicted as the father of Syrian citizens. Furthermore, Wedeen (2019) explains how such tropes promote understandings of the community through "a chain of filial piety and paternal authority that promotes family and gender values on the basis of obedience" (49).

These national self-presentation motifs were further advanced with state support to the drama industry, intended to create an alternative political and cultural authority (Al-Ghazzi 2013). In addition to the rise of pan-Arab satellite television channels, this contributed to what has come to be known as the Syrian *drama outpouring* (Arabic: *al-fawra al-dramiya*), Syria becoming a leading producer of Arabic television drama (Salamandra 2015). Moreover, state patronage reinforced the rise of specific genres, most obviously historical series inspired by ancient non-Islamic and Islamic Arabic and Syrian history, or series set in the late Ottoman and French mandate which promoted an anti-colonial Syrian identity (Salamandra 2008). Another genre that contributed to certain imaginations and stereotypes of the Syrian identity rooted in *authenticity* is the *Damascene milieu* (Arabic: *Al-bi'a al-shamiyah*), which presents stories set in an imaginary or existing neighbourhood (Arabic: *hara*) in the old city of Damascus, typically at an unidentified point during the late nineteenth or early twentieth centuries when Syria was ruled by either the Ottoman Empire or the French mandate authority (Al-Ghazzi 2013). Zaatari (2014) states that this genre strategically contributed to dramatise a Syrian national identity pillared on nostalgia for a nationalist desirable *antimodern* masculinity, depicting family relations where youths are portrayed as obedient to their elders and women to men, which in her view enforces patriarchy and submissive femininity. In a different approach to control opposition, the regime also adopted a *safety valve* strategy allowing socially and politically engaged Syrian series (Della Ratta 2015). As a result, more television dramas commented

---

[4] While the official English translation of the Syrian national anthem uses the term den of Arabism, which is a literal translation, it is necessary to clarify here that the term *den* in Arabic (*areen*) does not have the negative connotation it generally conveys in English (e.g. den of thieves). In this context, the term can be translated as *throne*.

on social, political, and economic conditions, reflecting a secular and socialist tradition in a social realist *dark aesthetic* that correlated with Syrian drama's character since the early 2000s (Salamandra 2015). This might explain why, from a Syrian perspective, Syrian-Lebanese dramas' tendency to avoid sociopolitical specificity makes them "more Lebanese than Syrian" (El-Hajj 2020) and even a suspicious "conspiracy" by the Gulf and Lebanon to "transport the Syrian drama outside Syria" (Joubin 2013, 27).

As shown throughout this section, by drawing on memory and history, popular culture plays an important role in "the process of constructing the boundaries of social identity" (Armbrust 2000, 1). Television drama, in particular, is a dominant cultural product that resonates with local attitudes or beliefs (Gerbner and Gross, 1976). Obviously, this relatively new phenomenon of Syrian-Lebanese dramas comes at a critical time in Syrian-Lebanese relations. With the influx of Syrian refugees into Lebanon since 2011, Lebanese media have often fed racist stereotypes, by which Syrian refugees are often presented as a reason for crimes and economic hardships (Sadaka, Nader, and Mikhael 2015). While reality television shows with contestants from the two countries competing had previously provided an arena for waging political battles becoming *idioms of contention* (Kraidy 2006, 2010), the fact that there has been no academic literature studying Syrian-Lebanese pan-Arab dramas in specific makes this study even more timely.

26.4 Case Study: Syrian-Lebanese Dramas of Ramadan 2020

In this section, we discuss the data used for our study and our methods of analysis. Building on the theoretical and conceptual framework developed above, the aim of this study was to answer the following questions: How are characters constructed as *Syrian* or *Lebanese* in Syrian-Lebanese pan-Arab dramas? To what extent does this distinction play a role in these characters' development arcs? And how do these representations relate to schema-based knowledge of the national character of both countries?

To answer these questions, we conducted a qualitative analysis of all four Syrian-Lebanese dramas produced and released in the 2020 Ramadan season (Table 26.1).[5] We selected shows from the Ramadan period because it is considered the Arab World's *Super Bowl for adverts* (Langton 2018), attracting the highest viewership and taking up the biggest share of annual advertisements on Arab television. Together, these four series constitute a comprehensive and rich case study. In addition to the diversity in themes and characters, they also offer an insight into the changing television drama

---

[5] It is worth mentioning that while the four series are set in Lebanon, they were developed, produced, and released before the Beirut Port explosion, hence the absence of this event or its repercussions from their plots.

industry between traditional broadcasters and emerging digital streaming services.

Considering that it is a challenge to trace something as "malleable, fragile […] ambivalent and diffuse" as national identity (Wodak, De Cillia, and Reisigl 1999, 4), a thematic analysis is best suited to our study as it helps to identify, analyse, and report patterns within data (Braun and Clarke 2006). In line with Culpeper (2001), we decided to focus on the text rather than the performance, given that "nonverbal features—the features that constitute a performance—are specified, to a degree, within the text" which "lays down parameters which guide performance" (41). In that sense, we define the text as the characters' dialog and dramatic actions that advance the story and not the audio-visual narrative and *mise-en-scène*.

To prepare the analysis, the first author watched all four series entirely to better familiarise himself with them. This process allowed identifying the protagonists of each series and the major turning points of their plot, the key scenes in terms of the characterisation or *Syrian-ness* or *Lebanese-ness*, as well as aspects of the world of the story or the setting that might reflect a certain perception of Lebanon or Syria. As the series vary in number of episodes, and to make the analytical process more manageable, we drew a purposive sample by selecting an equivalent number of scenes from each show, distributed over the beginning, middle, and end of each series. The selected scenes were fully transcribed, to facilitate the analysis.

Table 26.1 Series included in the case study

Series	Screenwriter	Director	Production company	Channel/Platform
Hawas [*Obsession*]	Nadia al-Ahmar (Syria)	Mohammad Lotfi (Jordan)	Jawwy TV (Saudi Arabia) Golden Line (Syria) I See Media (Jordan)	Jawwy TV (Saudi Arabia)
Al-Saher [*The mentalist*]	Salam Ksiri (Syria)	Mohamad Lotfi (Jordan) Amer Fahed (Syria)	Abu Dhabi Media (UAE) I See Media (Jordan)	Abu Dhabi TV (UAE)
Al-Nahhat (*The Sculptor*)	Butheina Awad (Syria)	Majdi Smairi (Tunisia)	Abu Dhabi Media (UAE) I See Media (Jordan)	Abu Dhabi TV (UAE)
Awlad Adam [*Children of Adam*]	Rami Kousa (Syria)	Al-Laith Hajjo (Syria)	Eagle Films (Lebanon)	MTV (Lebanon) MBC4 (Saudi Arabia)

The analytical process was implemented in two phases. In the first phase, we used a coding grid to systematically chart the portrayal of the protagonists in each show. For each main character, we took note of their name, nationality, and key relationships. We also used Culpeper's model of social schemata to analyse three aspects of the characters: group membership (such as gender, race, class, and age); personality (preferences, interests, traits, goals, and abilities); and social role (e.g. kinship and occupational and relational roles). Besides taking note of elements of relevance in the transcripts, we also looked for textual cues, whether explicit, implicit, or authorial (Culpeper and Fernandez-Quintanilla 2017). Finally, in this stage, we also identified each main character's transformational arc.

After this first, rather descriptive phase, the second phase was more analytical as we started looking for characteristics, patterns, or trends which resonated with the schematic knowledge of Syrian and Lebanese national character as explored above. Based on the assumption that national identity is viewed as "an awareness of difference" and a "feeling and recognition of we and they" (Lee 2012), and that identities can only be defined by referring to the differences with "others" (Dhoest 2004), we extracted a set of thematic identifiers from the literature, presenting *Syrian-ness* and *Lebanese-ness* through contrasting binaries to be used as an analytical tool (Table 26.2).

For the sake of clarity and coherence, in what follows we will first present our findings for each series separately. After presenting a brief plot description that focuses on the plot structure and the protagonists' character arc, we will explore the presence of nationality and national character stereotypes in the characters and plot construction. In the conclusion, we will bring together insights from the four series to systematically discuss the three contrasting binaries defining the relationship between Syria and Lebanon, also reflecting on the screenwriting practices used for national character construction.

Table 26.2 National character schema grid

Syria	*Lebanon*
Constraint	**Disorder**
• Autocracy	• Civil unrest
• Patriarchy	• Competing memories
Rootedness	**Hybridity**
• Authenticity	• Multiculturalism
• Anticolonialism	• Pluralism
• Connection to Arab and Islamic civilisation	• Bridging East and West
• Traditional family values	
Social Reform	**Indulgence**
• Social and political commentary	• Social and economic liberalism
• Social realism	• Extravaganza

26.4.1 Hawas [Obsession]

Hawas (2019) tells the story of the Syrian Ziad, an eccentric yet famous cosmetic surgeon, whose adored wife falls into a coma after a car accident. When he is approached by an obsessed fan, the Lebanese Lana, a neurotic young woman with a burnt face who would do anything for him to "make her pretty", he fakes his wife's death and hides her in his basement, then turns Lana—who knows nothing about the hidden wife—into a replica. Soon enough, Lana discovers she is just a replacement and pledges to make Ziad fall for her and forget about his wife while secretly plotting to kill her. As she starts to play along, Ziad finds himself falling in love with Lana, which puts him in a dilemma of guilt for betraying his beloved wife. Lana's scheme is eventually exposed, and just before his wife gets murdered, Ziad kills Lana after admitting to her that he has "created a monster".

By all appearances, it does not seem that the distinction between who is Syrian and who is Lebanese plays a significant role, if any, in the plot and character development. In fact, there is no referral to anyone's nationality throughout the series. Nevertheless, one could observe that the series adheres to the general genre conventions of Syrian-Lebanese pan-Arab dramas with the dominant Syrian male protagonist and the beautiful Lebanese female love interest, a particular representation that promptly connects to a common criticism of Lebanese women for their "unhealthy attraction to plastic surgery" (Mckay 2013). In more than one scene at their early encounters, Ziad tells Lana off for wanting to change her looks just to look like a specific film star or beauty queen. He also expresses his frustration in how women (assumedly Lebanese) have become identical copies of each other. In fact, cosmetic surgeries in Lebanon, the country that has been dubbed the middle east's "Mecca for cosmetic surgeries" (Neiled 2010), are considered a social phenomenon, pressuring Lebanese women to what can be called as the "beauty regime in the country" (Doherty 2008). In this light, the premise of the show—even though rooted in an extensive cinematic legacy ranging from Georges Franju's *Eyes Without a Face* (1960) and Pedro Almodóvar's *The Skin I Live In* (2011)—must be seen within this specific Syrian-Lebanese context, as the choice of the protagonists' nationalities can only suggest a *male gaze* towards Lebanese women, even if the Syrian screenwriter of the series is a female.

26.4.2 Al-Saher [The Mentalist]

Al-Saher is the story of Mina, a Syrian man who lives illegally in Lebanon struggling with work and life, and Carmen, a wealthy Lebanese socialite who is desperately trying to expose the infidelity of her husband, whom she had regretfully allowed to control her family's legacy to launch a career in politics. One day, she meets Mina who is instantly charmed by her and pretends to be a fortune teller. Later on, she discovers that he is a bluffer, but is still fascinated by his ability to read minds. She then offers him a partnership with which she would give him access to the high society of Lebanese businessmen and politicians' wives who are thirsty for certainty, if in return he tricks her husbands to make choices that would expose his infidelity to her. At first, Mina accepts the offer hesitantly but only to solve some personal financial matters. However, as he quickly gains fame and media attention, he starts enjoying the taste of it, especially as he and Carmen start developing feelings for one another. Only when he realises that he has become a puppet of corrupt people in power who use him to sell hope to the poor, he regrets it all and eventually exposes himself and those behind him on live television.

With Mina being an illegal refugee and Carmen's status and privilege, it is evident that nationality and class distinction play a significant role in constructing contrasting characters and setting up a dramatic contrast. Mina's illegal status also plays a role, to some extent, in advancing the conflict through indirectly limiting his options and influencing his actions. Moreover, while Carmen's developmental arc is limited to her personal family drama, we see Mina transform more drastically as he climbs the social ladder, adopting a new persona that dresses and speaks differently. However, despite the occasional plot points where Mina is threatened by his illegal status, he is not explicitly confronted with xenophobia or racism, which could be expected in such circumstances. This kind of *vigilance* is notable throughout the different series analysed, which we will address at a later stage.

On another note, while the series conforms to the typical *charming Syrian man versus beautiful Lebanese woman* formula, the relational dynamic between Carmen and Mina is not entirely male-dominated but rather alternating between both. That said, Carmen is almost entirely driven by a single motivation, connected to her husband's infidelity. This, in addition to her lack of any professional or political role and the recurring interest in vanity and social gatherings, reinforces a typical female social role. As almost all other Lebanese female characters seem to fall into the same "housewife" category and share the same preoccupancy, a specific *cliché* of Lebanese womanhood seems to be suggested in which—as Mina protests in one scene—all the women "look identical". Moreover, the overarching setting of the series against the backdrop of Lebanon's political corruption and the role of media therein corresponds to a recurrent mediated representation of the country. It is almost as if, the more Mina gets immersed in this Lebanon with its indulgences and turmoil, the more he becomes *Lebanonized*, but only for a little while before eventually rebounding to his elemental commitment to higher values.

26.4.3 Al-Nahhat (The Sculptor)

Al-Nahhat (2020) is the story of a renowned sculptor, the Lebanese-Syrian Yaman, who moves back to Beirut from Paris to teach sculpture. Residing in the old family house that had been locked down since his father got murdered over 30 years ago, he quickly embarks on a quest to solve the mystery of this silenced crime, relying on hints that seem to be planted around the house in addition to *apparitions* by his dead father, which lead him to discover that his father had an identical twin who was abducted at birth by a mob boss and grew up involved in organised crime. As Yaman pursues his goal, he struggles with the increasing mistrust in the person closest to him, his mother, whom he suspects has deliberately kept secrets from him, and puts his own life at risk as this unfolding seems to upset those who wanted to bury this mystery.

Yaman presents an interesting case in terms of nationality. He is Lebanese by citizenship, but he speaks with a Syrian dialect due to having been raised by his Syrian mother after the death of his father. In fact, since an Arabic-speaking viewer would normally identify a character's nationality by its dialect, Yaman could have passed as Syrian had he not explained his situation in one scene. Aside from this nuance, which does not affect the conflict in any way and suggests this choice of nationalities might have been due to a casting preference rather than a characterisation necessity, the characters' nationalities do not seem to play a role in the plot development. While Yaman obviously struggles with all sorts of physical and personal obstacles trying to solve his family drama, his mixed national background does not seem to affect his quest and he fits seamlessly into his predominantly upper-middle-class entourage. However, on a deeper level, his character does share a lot with the Syrian male protagonist schema in Syrian-Lebanese dramas in being poised, chivalrous, and dominant, so he comes across more as a Syrian than anything else.

On another note, while the series alternates between modern-day Lebanon and an unspecified time in the past, assumingly over 30 years ago, the setting feels rather generic and universal. There are no identifiable references to contemporary circumstances or even the Lebanese Civil War (1975–1990), a period the flashback scenes could be expected to take place in. This generic character has been typical of Lebanese post-war dramas that avoided any specificity in socio-political or cultural backgrounds of stories and characters (Al-Hajj 2020). Nevertheless, this *generalized Lebanon* is also marked by turmoil and disorder where organised crime and weaponry rule, particularly as most of the events happen in nightclubs and entertainment venues where characters exhibit an indulgent lifestyle, all of which comply with the schematic media representation of Lebanon.

26.4.4 Awlad Adam [Children of Adam][6]

Awlad Adam tells the story of two couples at opposite ends of the social scale. On the one side, there is the Syrian Ghassan, a famous TV host who hides his narcissistic psychopath character behind the mask of a reformist, and his Lebanese wife Deema, an idealistic judge (later minister of justice) striving to fight corruption despite having her share of hidden mistakes. On the other

---

[6] Children of Adam is the literal translation of the Arabic term *Awlad Adam*, which is used to suggest that all humans come from one root, Adam.

side, we have the Syrian Saad, a playboy pickpocket, and his Lebanese girlfriend Maya, a bold low-ranking belly dancer. When Saad and Maya steal Ghassan's mobile, they discover he secretly recorded all the women he has slept with and they see an opportunity to blackmail Deema and Ghassan to help Saad's mother who is terminally ill, and Maya's sister who is unjustly serving a life sentence. Despite being shaken by the revelation, Deema must help Ghassan both to protect her public image and because he blackmails her as well. The conflict takes a more aggressive turn as Ghassan kidnaps Saad and Maya and threatens to kill them. Realising there is no point to invest in a wrecked marriage, Deema intervenes and makes a deal with Saad and Maya behind the scenes, which ruins Ghassan's image and as a result he ends his life on a social media live-streaming. Deema manages to salvage her reputation but only through readjusting her moral compass. As for Maya and Saad, the crisis brings them closer and reveals aspects of their character showing they are essentially good people who have been pushed into some wrong directions by life.

With an ensemble of characters, *Awlad Adam* has the chance to present a more diverse and nuanced representation than the other series in this study. Moreover, in this series, the characters from both nationalities exhibit consciousness about their nationalities and often address this diversity explicitly by saying things like "in Syria we do this..." or "in Lebanon we say that". As in the *Al-Saher* series, they avoid putting these differences in contexts that are too divisive, but we do notice more explicit expressions that conform to familiar clichés about Lebanon and Syria. These presentations introduce Lebanon as a playground for media and corrupt politics, broken justice, and the culture of *turning a blind e*ye, and Syria as a *police state* where everyone is under surveillance.

There are several ways to understand the characters: as an upper-class couple versus a lower-class couple, or as Syrian male characters versus Lebanese female characters. As to class, we find that the lower-class couple (Maya and Saad) sets out with a more stereotypical characterisation than the upper-class couple (Deema and Ghassan). Maya seems to match the common Arab media stereotype of Lebanese women with her liberal and even promiscuous character and lifestyle. Similarly, Saad's character as an illegal migrant and a thief aligns with a common stereotype of Syrian refugees in Lebanese media. However, their developmental arcs reveal a departure from those stereotypes as they grow and change as a result of their relationship and the conflict, in addition to the uncovering of more nuanced relationships with other friends and family members that justifies how these characters became who they are.

If we compare the Syrian men (Ghassan and Saad) to the Lebanese women (Deema and Maya), we notice some correspondence to the typical genre conventions, both men being dominant and pursued by women while the women are beautiful and permissive. Nevertheless, we also find some departures from typical representations, especially looking at characterisation as a whole. First, the two men and the two women show contrasting characterisations and transformations, not conforming to a single male or female stereotype. Second, Deema in particular is characterised in an atypical way as she is presented as a career-driven and politically active woman, in opposition to the female protagonist in *Al-Saher*.

The series also occasionally suggests, directly as expressed by characters or indirectly through the events, a different set of social borders which are not drawn around nationalities but around social classes, where the *us* and *them* concern the rich and powerful versus the poor and insignificant. National borders are even questioned more fundamentally towards the end of the series when Ghassan states that evilness is inevitable in "this part of the world", which may be understood as both Syria and Lebanon or even the broader Arab World, that "breathes wars, corruption, ignorance and tyranny" and whose inhabitants as a result have become a group of "loose maniacs". Such a proclamation is particularly intriguing, as it proposes a totally different definition of the *us*, as a big melting pot unified by turmoil and anguish.

26.5 Discussion and Conclusion

It is evident that these four Syrian-Lebanese pan-Arab dramas do rely on presenting identifiably distinct Syrian and Lebanese characters in regard to nationality in the general sense. Presenting characters with different national backgrounds is a selling point for any transnational co-production, to appeal to audiences from both markets. It is important to note that Arabic-speaking viewers can immediately identify characters' nationalities by their dialect—in this case, Syrian or Lebanese. Significantly, in the series, we analysed Syrian characters always spoke in the Damascene Arabic Dialect, while Lebanese characters spoke in Lebanese Arabic, the standard spoken dialect also known as the "White Dialect" (Stone 2007, 134). This shows some sort of uniformisation in the representation of national characters. Therefore, this distinction through language is the cornerstone of establishing national distinction. Nevertheless, these national distinctions are hardly an explicit theme. While characters are introduced as having different national backgrounds, these discrepancies do not directly steer the conflict. Even in the two series that showed more references to the characters' national background, *al-Saher* and *Awlad Adam*, nationality-related issues such as racism or xenophobia, are *erased* rather than emphasised. This may be partly related to the genre of *musalsalat*, which most Arabic series fall under, and is generally known to be social "domestic drama" (Abu-Lughod 2008, 112). Although we can see some thematic and subgenre diversity in the studied cases, with hints of thriller or crime, the four series contained a romantic theme that mostly leads the characters' arcs. After all, these series were produced for Ramadan, the holy month of fasting for Muslims, and supposedly aimed at a general audience, which explains why such *complexities* are avoided.

Nevertheless, all four series still comprised more implicit yet recognisable schemas of Lebanon and the Lebanese, and to a lesser degree, of Syria and the Syrians, at least in the primary character and story set-up. To describe this, we will reflect back on the thematic identifiers of national character presented in Table 26.2, connecting *Syrian-ness* to constraint, rootedness, and social reform and *Lebanese-ness* to disorder, hybridity, and indulgence.

Constraint versus disorder is most present in *Hawas* through the contrast between Ziad's patriarchal struggle to tame Lana and similarly in *Awlad Adam* in the relationship of Saad and Maya but with a different dynamic as the two characters eventually reach a middle ground. Moreover, in *Awlad Adam*, the two Syrian protagonists have suffered a suppressive past in Syria, which serves as a justification for how they came to be as adults. In fact, across the four series, all Syrian protagonists, including *al-Nahhat*'s, are constructed as rather controlling in their mannerism and relational attitude. Moreover, in the four series, Lebanon is presented as a backdrop of disorder, moral and political corruption, and consequently, Lebanese characters are all willingly or unwillingly entangled in this.

Rootedness versus hybridity is present in *Hawas*, *al-Saher*, and *Awlad Adam* in almost the same way. Syrians are more connected to traditionalist values or lifestyle choices while Lebanese characters tend to be more malleable in terms of identity, with foreign names that might suggest religious diversity and multilingualism, and also in terms of their expressions of music and fashion choices, as well as relational roles. Significantly, the upper-class Syrian character (Ghassan) in *Awlad Adam* presents many elements of hybridity through his mannerism and speech patterns, and so does Mina in *al-Saher* as he gets acquainted with the upper class, which suggests that while hybridity is a Lebanese quality regardless of social class, Syrians only get hybrid when they move upwards the social scale or attempt to do so. Only *al-Nahhat* does not seem to play on this contrast.

Social reform versus indulgence is present in *al-Saher* and *Awlad Adam*, in which social and political critique is an explicit theme against a backdrop of an indulgent society (i.e. Lebanon, where the stories are set). However, while in both series we see the characters invested in a moral crusade against an unjust system, *vis-à-vis* other characters whose goals and most prominent characteristics are rather individualistic, only in *al-Saher* are Syrian and Lebanese characters constructed to match their presumed reformist or indulgent stereotypes. This association is less clear-cut in *Awlad Adam*, where there is more overlapping. At various points of the story, we also see Syrian characters immersed in self-centred desires, and Lebanese characters pursuing societal goals. Moreover, this binary is less present in *Hawas* and *al-Nahhat* where on the one hand indulgence is strongly present but only as a general vibe of the Lebanese setting, and on the other hand, reformist themes are more diluted in the personal drama and not particularly highlighted as a part of a bigger societal dysfunctionality. Nevertheless, indulgence in itself is rather present in all four series, as a Lebanese *couleur locale* of liberalism that both Lebanese characters and Syrian characters (who happen to live in Lebanon) are influenced by to various degrees.

Reflecting on these findings, it is safe to state that the mentioned thematic identifiers of national character are generally present yet in various and uneven ways, and that the portrayal of Lebanon and the Lebanese conforms more to their schematic stereotypes than that of Syria and the Syrians. Moreover, connecting this back to screenwriting as a craft and as a production process, we can conclude that Lebanese characters are less prone to diverge from their initial character traits over their transformational arcs than Syrian characters who move more freely in the spectrum, often adopting some *Lebanese-ness* over the span of the plot. This may explain why Syrian-Lebanese dramas are often seen more as an extension of Lebanese drama than of Syrian drama, as Lebanon and Lebanese-ness are more conspicuous.

On a relevant note, it is evident in the studied cases that the *Lebanese female versus Syrian male protagonists* formula remains prevalent. There are two aspects that may explain this, and both have to do with industrial considerations. As the Syrian drama industry and its stars are more established in the market, and arguably better trained, it is possible that production companies prefer going with a *safer* venture. While these series are promoted by their Syrian-Lebanese hero couple, analysis of their screenwriting shows that the Syrian character mostly drives the plot. Consequently, these Syrian characters are generally more *round* than their Lebanese peers who rather present a love interest or a supporting role with less *roundness* and more linkage to national stereotypes. From a marketing perspective, it makes sense to create a set-up where the production can capitalise on the acting capabilities of Syrian male stars and the attractiveness of Lebanese female stars, two components that have been proven to be commercially successful. Moreover, in a previous study on screenplay development practices in Arabic drama (Haddad 2019), we have shown that producers and broadcasters are not very keen on taking risks, and that production companies often tailor series to stars. Furthermore, it was found that screenwriters often make creative decisions based on personal influences. This, in particular, is thought-provoking in the light of this study, considering that the four screenwriters who wrote these shows are actually Syrian, which might suggest a process of *othering* in the construction of Lebanese characters, specifically women, and could also highlight a certain aspect of exoticism in the representation of Lebanon and the Lebanese might reflect an attitude of *us* (Syrians) versus *them* (Lebanese). Nevertheless, it is important not to jump to hasty conclusions regarding cultural hegemony in which a Syrian upper hand is assumed. While Syrian-Lebanese pan-Arab dramas are often written and directed by Syrian screenwriters and directors, they are also often produced by Lebanese teams and commissioned by pan-Arab broadcasters based in the Gulf. Therefore, from a production point of view, it is fair to conclude that these series are equally Syrian and Lebanese, as well as pan-Arab.

References

Abu-Lughod, Lila. 2008. *Dramas of Nationhood*. Chicago: University of Chicago Press.

Akiki, Viviane. 2011. "Al-drama al-lubnaniya...bayna naql al-waqe' wa i'timad al jor'a ka nahj." [Lebanese drama: between representing reality and addressing boldness as a style]. *Elaph Online*, 28 March. https://elaph.com/Web/arts/2011/3/642268.html. Accessed 25 June 2021.

Al-Ghazzi, Omar. 2013. Nation as Neighborhood: How Bab al-Hara Dramatized Syrian Identity. *Media, Culture & Society* 35 (5): 586–601.

Al-Khazin, Farid. 1991. *The Communal Pact of National Identities: The Making and Politics of the 1943 National Pact*. Beirut: Centre for Lebanese studies.

Al-Nahhat (The Sculptor). 2020 (1 season). Written by Butheina Awad. UAE, Jordan: Abu Dhabi Media Company, I See Media.

Al-Saher [The Mentalist]. 2020 (1 season). Written by Salam Ksiri. UAE, Jordan: I See Media, Abu Dhabi Media Company, Abu Dhabi Television.

Anderson, Benedict. 2006. *Imagined Communities*. London: Verso.

Armbrust, Walter. 2000. "Introduction: Anxieties of Scale." In *Mass mediations: New Approaches to Popular Culture in the Middle East and Beyond*, 1–31.

Awlad Adam [Children of Adam]. 2020 (1 season). Written by Rami Kousa. Lebanon: Eagle Films.

Behna, Collette. 2019. "Surat lubnan al-nasi'a fil drama al-lubnaniya" [Lebanon's Spotless Image in Lebanese drama]. *al-Hurra*, 18 May. https://www.alhurra.com/different-angle/2019/05/18/%D8%B5%D9%88%D8%B1%D8%A9-%D9%84%D8%A8%D9%86%D8%A7%D9%86-%D8%A7%D9%84%D9%86%D8%A7%D8%B5%D8%B9%D8%A9-%D9%81%D9%8A-%D8%A7%D9%84%D8%AF%D8%B1%D8%A7%D9%85%D8%A7-%D8%A7%D9%84%D9%84%D8%A8%D9%86%D8%A7%D9%86%D9%8A%D8%A9. Accessed 12 June 2021.

Beller, Manfred and Joep Leerssen. 2007. *Imagology: The Cultural Construction and Literary Representation of National Characters. A Critical Survey*. Amsterdam: Rodopi.

Blaik-Hourani, Rida. 2017. A Call for Unitary History Textbook Design in a Post-Conflict Era: The Case of Lebanon. *The History Teacher* 50 (2): 16–36.

Braun, Virginia, and Victoria Clarke. 2006. Using Thematic Analysis in Psychology. *Qualitative Research in Psychology* 3 (2): 77–101.

Brenes, Carmen Sofia. 2012. Good and Bad Characters: A Poetic Difference. *Revista de Comunicación* 12: 7–23.

Carelli, Paolo. 2015. Pan-Arabism Through Television: Arab TV Series Between National Identities and Transnational Media. *Comunicazioni Sociali* 2: 218–229.

Chamberlain, Jill. 2016. *The Nutshell Technique: Crack The Secret Of Successful Screenwriting*. Austin: University of Texas Press.

Chamieh, Joelle. 2016. Arab Drama Series Content Analysis from a Transnational Arab Identity Perspective. *Journal of Arts and Humanities* 5: 22–38.

Culpeper, Jonathan. 2001. *Language and Characterisation: People in Plays and Other Texts*. New York: Routledge.

Culpeper, Jonathan. 2009. Reflections on a Cognitive Stylistic Approach to Characterisation. In *Cognitive Poetics*, ed. Jeroen Vandaele and Geert Brone, 125–168. Berlin: Mouton De Gruyter.

Culpeper, Jonathan, and Caroline Fernandez-Quintanilla. 2017. Fictional Characterisation. In *Pragmatics of Fiction*, ed. Miriam A. Locher and Andreas H. Jucker, 93–128. Berlin: De Gruyter.
Dabbous-Sensenig, Dima. 2000. Portrayal of Women in the Media. *Al-Raida Journal* 88: 26–28.
Della Ratta, Donatella. 2015. "The Whisper Strategy: How Syrian Drama Makers Shape Television Fiction in the Context of Authoritarianism and Commodification." In *Syria from Reform to Revolt, vol. 2: Culture, Society, and Religion*, edited by Christa Salamandra, and Leif Stenberg, 53–76. Syracuse, NY: Syracuse University Press.
Dhoest, Alexander. 2004. *De verbeelde gemeenschap: 50 jaar Vlaamse tv-fictie en de constructie van een nationale identiteit*, vol. 8. Leuven University Press.
Doherty, Sandra B. 2008. Cosmetic Surgery and the Beauty Regime in Lebanon. *Middle East Report* 249: 28–31.
Dyer, Richard. 2013. *The Matter of Images: Essays on Representations*. NY: Routledge.
El-Hajj, Maya. 2019. "An al-batala al-lubnaniya wal batal al Suri: Duo Drami Ghayr Motakafe'" [On Lebanese Heroine and Syria Hero: an unbalanced Drama Duo]. *Daraj Media*, 5 May. https://daraj.com/17243/. Accessed 20 May 2021.
El-Hajj, Maya. 2020 "Al-drama al-mushtaraka bila hawiyya" [Pan-arab productions lack identity]. *Independent Arabia*, 12 May. https://www.independentarabia.com/node/119076/%D9%81%D9%86%D9%88%D9%86/%D8%A7%D9%84%D8%AF%D8%B1%D8%A7%D9%85%D8%A7-%D8%A7%D9%84%D9%85%D8%B4%D8%AA%D8%B1%D9%83%D8%A9-%D8%A8%D9%84%D8%A7-%D9%87%D9%88%D9%8A%D8%A9-%D9%88%D8%A3%D9%88%D9%84%D8%A7%D8%AF-%D8%A2%D8%AF%D9%85-%D9%8A%D8%B9%D9%83%D8%B3-%D8%A7%D9%86%D9%87%D9%8A%D8%A7%D8%B1%D8%A7%D9%8A-%D8%AC%D9%85%D8%A7%D8%B9%D9%8A%D8%A7%D9%8B. Accessed 1 June 2021.
Eyes Without a Face (*Les yeux sans visage*). 1960. Written by Georges Franju, Jean Redon, Pierre Boileau, Thomas Narcejac, Clause Sautet, and Pierre Gascar. Directed by Georges Franju. France, Italy: Champs Élysées Production, Lux Film.
Eysenck, Michael W., and Mark T. Keane. 2000. *Cognitive Psychology: A Student's Handbook*. London: Taylor & Francis.
Fiske, John. 1987. Cagney and Lacey: Reading Character Structurally and Politically. *Communication* 9 (3–4): 399–426.
Florack, Ruth. 2010. Ethnic Stereotypes as Elements of Character Formation. In *Characters in Fictional Worlds: Understanding Imaginary Beings in Literature, Film, and Other Media*, eds. Jens Eder, Fotis Jannidis, and Ralf Schneider, 478–505. Berlin: De Gruyter.
Gerbner, George, and Larry Gross. 1976. Living with Television: The Violence Profile. *The Journal of Communication* 26 (2): 173–199.
Goodfellow, Melanie. 2017. "How the High-End TV Boom Has Reached the Middle East." *Screen Daily*, 10 December. https://www.screendaily.com/features/how-the-high-end-tv-boom-has-reached-the-middle-east/5124882.article. Accessed 1 Sept 2020.
Haddad, Fadi. 2019. Influences on Story Development in Transnational Pan-Arab Dramas: A Case Study of the Series *04*. *Journal of Screenwriting* 10 (2): 179–194.
Haddad, Fadi, and Alexander Dhoest. 2020. Cosmopolitanism in Dubai's Pan-Arab Drama: Case Study of the '04' TV Series. *Middle East Journal of Culture and Communication* 13: 190–209. https://doi.org/10.1163/18739865-01302002.

Hall, Stuart. 1997. *Representation: Cultural Representations and Signifying Practices*. London: Sage.
Hall, Stuart, David Held, and Anthony McGrew. 1992. *Modernity and Its Futures*. Cambridge: Polity Press, in association with the Open University.
Haugbolle, Sune. 2010. *War and Memory in Lebanon*. New York: Cambridge University Press.
Haugbolle, Sune. 2013. Pop Culture and Class Distinction in Lebanon. In *Muslims and the New Information and Communication Technologies: Notes from an Emerging and Infinite Field*, ed. Thomas Hoffmann and Goran Larsson, 73–86. New York: Springer.
Hawas [*Obsession*]. 2019 (1 season). Written by Nadia al-Ahmar. Saudi Arabia, Syria, Jordan: Jawwy TV, Golden Line, I See Media.
Hoenselaars, Ton, and Joep Leerssen. 2009. The Rhetoric of National Character: Introduction. *European Journal of English Studies* 13 (3): 251–255. https://doi.org/10.1080/13825570903223467.
Hogan, Patrick Colm. 2010. Characters and Their Plots. In *Characters in Fictional Worlds: Understanding Imaginary Beings in Literature, Film, and Other Media*, eds. Jens Eder, Fotis Jannidis, and Ralf Schneider, 134–154. Berlin: De Gruyter.
Hudson, Michael C. 1997. Trying Again: Power-sharing in Post-Civil War Lebanon. *International Negotiation* 2 (1): 103–122.
Joubin, Rebecca. 2013. Syrian Drama and the Politics of Dignity. *Middle East Report* 268: 26–29.
Karasapan, Omer, and Shah Sajjad. 2021. "Why Syrian Refugees in Lebanon Are a Crisis within a Crisis." *Brookings Institution*, 15 April. https://www.brookings.edu/blog/future-development/2021/04/15/why-syrian-refugees-in-lebanon-are-a-crisis-within-a-crisis/. Accessed 5 August 2021.
Kelman, Herbert C. 1997. Nationalism, Patriotism, and National Identity: Social-Psychological Dimensions. In *Patriotism: In the Lives of Individuals and Nations*, ed. Daniel Bar-Tal and Ervin Staub, 165–189. Chicago: Nelson-Hall Publishers.
Khashan, Hial. 1992. *Inside the Lebanese Confessional Mind*. Boston: University Press of America.
Kraidy, Marwan M. 2003. Globalization Avant la Lettre? Cultural hybridity and Media Power in Lebanon. In *Global Media Studies: Ethnographic Perspectives*, ed. Patrick D. Murphy and Marwan M. Kraidy, 276–295. London: Routledge.
Kraidy, Marwan M. 2006 (Spring). Popular Culture as a Political Barometer: Lebanese-Syrian Relations and Superstar. *Transnational Broadcasting Studies* 16.
Kraidy, Marwan M. 2009. *Reality Television and Arab Politics: Contention in Public Life*. Cambridge: Cambridge University Press.
Langton, James. 2018. "How Middle East Advertisers are Making Ramadan their Super Bowl." *The National*, 24 May. https://www.thenational.ae/uae/how-middle-eastadvertisers-are-making-ramadantheir-super-bowl-1.733761. Accessed 5 April 2018.
Lee, Yoonmi. 2012. *Modern Education, Textbooks, and the Image of the Nation: Politics and Modernization and Nationalism in Korean Education: 1880–1910*. New York: Garland.
Lita, Rahmiati, and Yoon Cho. 2012. The Influence of Media on Attitudinal and Behavioral Changes: Acceptance of Culture and Products. *The International Business & Economics Research Journal* 11 (12): 14–33.

Maasri, Zeina. 2016. "Troubled Geography: Imagining Lebanon in 1960s Tourist Promotion." In *Designing Worlds: National Design Histories in the Age of Globalization*, edited by Kjetil Fallan and Grace Lees-Maffei, 125–41. New York and Oxford: Berghahn.

Matar, Dina. 2019. The Syrian Regime's Strategic Communication: Practices and Ideology. *International Journal of Communication* 13 (1): 2398–2416.

Mckay, Hollie. 2013. "Real Housewives of Beirut? Filmmaker Says Plastic Surgery an 'Epidemic' in Lebanon." *Fox News*, 13 May. https://www.foxnews.com/entertainment/real-housewives-of-beirut-filmmaker-says-plastic-surgery-an-epidemic-in-lebanon. Accessed 5 July 2021.

McKee, Robert. 1999. *Story: Structure, Substance, Style, and the Principle of Screenwriting*. NY: Regan Books.

McIlrath, Patricia. 1955. Stereotypes, Types and Characterization in Drama. *Educational Theatre Journal*, 1–10.

Medawar, Eric. 2007. *Lebanese Historical Memory and the Perception of National Identity through School Textbooks*. (Unpublished Paper). https://www.academia.edu/16846254/History_Textbooks_and_the_Construction_of_National_Identity_in_Lebanon. Accessed 1 April 2020.

Mouawad, Jamil. 2018. *Lebanon's Border Areas in Light of the Syrian war: New Actors, Old Marginalisation*. Florence: European University Institute.

Neiled, Barry. 2010. "Lebanon Emerges as Mideast's 'Mecca' for Cosmetic Surgery." *CNN*, 19 November. https://edition.cnn.com/2010/WORLD/meast/11/19/Lebanon.plastic.surgery/index.html. Accessed 15 April 2020.

Pearson, Roberta. 2007. "Anatomising Gilbert Grissom: The Structure and Function of the Televisual Character." In *Reading CSI: Crime TV Under the Microscope*, edited by Michael Allen, 39–56. London and New York: I. B. Tauris.

Picard, Elizabeth, and Alexander Ramsbotham, eds. 2012. "Reconciliation, Reform and Resilience: Positive Peace for Lebanon." *Accord: An International Review of Peace Initiatives* 24: 64–66. https://halshs.archives-ouvertes.fr/halshs-00741581/document. Accessed 30 May 2020.

Reinkowski, Maurus. 1997. National Identity In Lebanon Since 1990. *Orient* 38 (3): 493–515.

Sadaka, George, Jocelyne Nader, and Tony Mikhael. 2015. "Monitoring Racism in the Lebanese Media: The Representation of the 'Syrian' and the 'Palestinian' in the News Coverage." *Maharat News*. https://www.maharat-news.com/Temp/Attachments/6e546361-c10b-448c-b019-19490547bc99.pdf. Accessed 8 August 2022.

Salamandra, Christa. 2008. "Through the Back Door: Syrian Television Makers Between Secularism and Islamization." *Arab media: Power and weakness*, 252–262.

Salamandra, Christa. 2011. Spotlight on the Bashar al-Asad era: The Television Drama Outpouring. *Middle East Critique* 20 (2): 157–167.

Salamandra, Christa. 2015. Syria's Drama Outpouring: Between Complicity and Critique. In *Syria from Reform to Revolt: Culture, Society, and Religion*, ed. Christa Salamandra, et al., 36–52. Syracuse ny: Syracuse University Press.

Salibi, Kamal. 1988. *A House of Many Mansions: The History of Lebanon Reconsidered*. University of California Press.

Schweinitz, Jörg. 2010. Stereotypes and the Narratological Analysis of Film Characters. In *Characters in Fictional Worlds: Understanding Imaginary Beings in Literature, Film, and Other Media*, ed. Johanna Eder, Fotis Jannidis, and Ralf Schneider, 276–289. Berlin and New York: De Gruyter.

Stone, Christopher. 2003. The Ba'albakk Festival and the Rahbanis: Folklore, Ancient History, Musical Theater, and Nationalism in Lebanon. *The Arab Studies Journal* 11 (2/1): 10–39.

Stone, Christopher. 2007. *Popular Culture and Nationalism in Lebanon: The Fairouz and Rahbani Nation*. London and New York: Routledge.

Terracciano, Antonio, et al. 2005. National Character Does Not Reflect Mean Personality Trait Levels in 49 Cultures. *Science* 310 (5745): 96–100.

The Skin, I., Live In, and (La piel que habito). 2011. Written and directed by Pedro Almodóvar. Spain: El Deseo, Blue Haze Entertainment, FilmNation Entertainment.

Wedeen, Lisa. 1999. *Ambiguities of Domination: Politics, Rhetoric, and Symbols in Contemporary Syria*. Chicago: University of Chicago Press.

Wedeen, Lisa. 2019. *Authoritarian Apprehensions*. Chicago: University of Chicago Press.

Wickham, Phil. 2007. *Understanding Television Texts*. London: BFI.

Wodak, Ruth, Rudoloph De Cillia, and Martin Reisigl. 1999. The Discursive Construction of National Identities. *Discourse and Society* 10 (2): 149–173.

Zaatari, Zeina. 2014. Desirable Masculinity/Femininity and Nostalgia of the 'Anti-Modern': Bab el-Hara Television Series as a Site of Production. *Sexuality & Culture* 19: 16–36. https://doi.org/10.1007/s12119-014-9242-5.

Zisser, Eyal. 2006. Who's Afraid Of Syrian Nationalism? National and State Identity in Syria. *Middle Eastern Studies* 42: 179–198. https://doi.org/10.1080/00263200500417512.

CHAPTER 27

"That's a Chick's Movie!": How Women Are Excluded from Screenwriting Work

Natalie Wreyford

27.1 Context

In 2005, I commissioned two of the first ever reports into gender inequality in screenwriting work whilst employed at the UK Film Council (Sinclair et al. 2006, Rogers 2007). These reports confirmed what I already felt to be true from my experience working with screenwriters—that men were writing the majority of screenplays in the UK film industry. I hoped that drawing attention to this would begin a process of redress—and the UK Film Council did launch the reports at an event with many invited guests from the British film industry—but by the time I was made redundant whilst pregnant at the end of 2007, nothing had really changed. There was, however, a growing awareness of gendered and other inequalities in film work worldwide. This was spearheaded through the work of people like Martha M. Lauzen at the Centre for the Study of Women in Television and Film at the University of San Diego and her annual Celluloid Ceiling reports;[1] Melissa Silverstein in her *Women and Hollywood* blog;[2] actress Geena Davis's Institute on Gender in Media;[3] as well as high-profile speeches by actors at awards ceremonies. Frustrated at

[1] https://womenintvfilm.sdsu.edu/research/.
[2] https://womenandhollywood.com/.
[3] https://seejane.org/.

N. Wreyford (✉)
Kings College London, London, UK
e-mail: natalie.2.wreyford@kcl.ac.uk

the lack of change in the UK, I decided that I wanted to dig deeper to try to understand what was happening and what could be done. Having worked for many years in the UK film industry, I was in a good position to talk to both screenwriters and their employers and my results were published by Palgrave Macmillan in 2018 as *Gender Inequality in Screenwriting Work* (Wreyford 2018). This chapter is drawn largely from my book and in particular from the culmination of my research and thinking: understanding the way that taste is constructed along gendered lines and used to both exclude women and then excuse that exclusion. I am grateful to Palgrave Macmillan for allowing me to reproduce parts of my book here, and hope (as they do) that it will lead readers to seek out the rest of the book for a deeper understanding of the gendered contexts of screenwriting work.

Screenwriting work was repeatedly discussed in traditionally masculine terms by the workers that I spoke to. For example, screenwriting was likened to being a prop forward in rugby, a good carpenter, or an architect. The screenwriter was *king* but never *queen* and compared to historical artists who were men—Leonardo da Vinci and Henry Moore. Screenwriters, according to my participants, needed to be *tough*, have *muscle*, and be able to cope with the *brutality* of the filmmaking world which was also compared to the military and prison. It is perhaps not surprising then that most British feature films are written by white men (Rogers 2007). Only 13% of UK-qualifying films have a woman screenwriter (Cobb, Williams and Wreyford 2016),[4] 28% of television episodes and 14% of prime-time television episodes (Kreager and Follows 2018). Women from a minoritized racial background are less than 2% of the screenwriters of British films (Cobb and Wreyford 2021). Furthermore, just 11% of films were written solely or predominantly by women, and men were nearly 40% more likely than women to be the screenwriter of more than one film (Kreager and Follows 2018).

However, despite high-profile campaigns and conversations about the dominance of men in screen industries globally, the numbers of women in key filmmaking roles have not improved significantly since 2003 (the earliest year that the British Film Institute has records of filmmaking roles) (Cobb, Williams, and Wreyford 2019). In 2003, 18% of the screenwriters on British films were women; in 2005, it was 15%; and in 2015, it was 20% (ibid). Research in the UK and in the USA has shown that women's involvement in key filmmaking roles can go up or down a few percentage points each year but rarely is there any definite upward trajectory or notable improvement (ibid, Lauzen 2021). It is also difficult to remain optimistic about the chances of improvement for women screenwriters when the data on those most influential in their employment similarly show entrenched gender inequality, with women making up just 13% of directors on British films, 27% of producers, and 18% of executive producers (Cobb, Williams, and Wreyford 2016; see also Lauzen 2021 for an equivalent picture in the USA).

[4] Including co-productions and inward investment films that originate outside the UK.

The data included in this chapter were gathered as part of a wider research project where I conducted forty interviews with screenwriters and employers of screenwriters between 2015 and 2017. The *employers* range from individual producers working as sole traders, to the senior personnel of large production companies, distribution companies, public financiers, and broadcasters, all of whom have some authority in the hiring of screenwriters. The screenwriters had, at the time of our conversations, experience ranging from no produced features to more than 12 feature film credits. My participants included 34 white British or British-resident individuals, three of South Asian background, two describing themselves as African black British, and one who was brought up in England, having been born in Jamaica. My sample was deliberately weighted to include a higher percentage of women than is found in the UK film industry generally, as I really wanted to hear their stories and opinions. The men screenwriters were included to make gendered comparison possible. I was not able to include any non-binary individuals as they are not visible in the UK film workforce, possibly a sign that it is still difficult to present yourself as such in UK film industry culture. All the participants' identities are protected by the use of pseudonyms, and I have not provided any demographic information when quoting from the interview transcripts. However, if a particular feature of someone's identity is relevant, I highlight it in the text.

Pierre Bourdieu's theories (1977, 1984, and Bourdieu and Wacquant 1992) make visible—and therefore, discussable—how characteristics of individuals that are widely understood to be naturally occurring and inevitable have actually been socially constructed. His dissection of scholastic measurements, judgements of taste and aesthetics, and the way that the dominant classes are able to position their own achievements and dispositions as having more value than those of the dominated, are extremely useful in understanding how, in the film industry, subjective choices are able to be positioned as market-driven or meritocratic.

For Bourdieu, an individual's social, economic, and cultural capital, along with their dispositions, taste, preferences, and interests can be understood as socially constituted capacities that operate at a subconscious level and are embodied in a person in a way that makes them appear natural. Whilst Bourdieu's work focuses predominantly on class difference, this chapter will follow feminist arguments that his ideas are nevertheless extremely useful for analysing gender. In particular, his concept of the habitus enables an understanding of how an individual's interests and skills are both socially constructed and how (as a result) different genders may experience the world differently.

Bourdieu has rightly received much criticism for his lack of consideration of gender. It has been shown that he positions sexuality and gender (and race) as secondary to class (Lovell 2000), and that he appropriated the work of French feminist thinkers without acknowledging them or citing them (Bilge 2006). However, feminist scholars have also recognized the usefulness of his thinking for understanding gender inequality and have sought to extend and build on his theories through a feminist lens (see Adkins and Skeggs 2004 for a critical discussion of the possibilities here). In this chapter, I will draw extensively on a 1991 article by Toril Moi: *Appropriating Bourdieu: Feminist theory and Pierre Bourdieu's sociology of culture*. Coming from a background in both literature and philosophy, much of Moi's work has explored the interplay of the embodied social, cultural, and psychological aspects of gender with women's writing. In the article, Moi outlines a way to use a conception of the gender habitus to explain how symbolic violence is used to suppress the discourse of the experience of women and non-binary individuals:

> The right to speak, legitimacy, is invested in those agents recognized by the field as powerful possessors of capital. Such individuals become spokespersons for the doxa and struggle to relegate challengers to their positions as heterodox, as lacking in capital, as individuals whom one cannot credit with the right to speak.[5] (Moi 1991, 1022)

27.2 Women's Interests

One of the most persistent debates around women screenwriters is whether women write differently from men, have different preoccupations, styles, and points of view, and whether women as viewers have different interests, needs, and tastes to men (see for example Francke 1994; McCreadie 2006; Seger 2003). Revered script doctor Linda Seger claims that "women's films change the focus, often emphasising the character's emotions, behaviour, and psychology above the character's actions" (2003, 118). However, Seger also demonstrates that women have successfully written "male" action films and argues that denying that there is such a thing as a "woman's voice" may simply contribute to the devaluing of women's interests and stories. Taste, as inscribed in the habitus, offers a way to theorize the contradiction that Seger's arguments illustrate so succinctly. Women have for too long been perceived as a special interest group by film producers and distributors (Christopherson 2009). They have been stereotyped as consumers and practitioners concerned primarily with human relationships and the pursuit of romantic heterosexual love as the root to happiness (Smith and Cook 2008). Even when they were aware of these clichés, film workers I spoke to found themselves discursively relying on them when talking about film projects, suggesting that these beliefs have become taken for granted. For example, Nicola described a book that she had recently optioned and for which she was currently looking for a screenwriter to work on the screen adaptation:

> (…) this period adaptation that we've got; there's a long list of female writers because it's that sensibility, it's a romantic story. I sound like such a cliché saying out loud but I think it's true that a woman writing stories about a woman and she has an affair with someone and then she goes back to her husband. There

---

[5] For Bourdieu, "doxa" is the term used to denote what is taken for granted in any particular society (Bourdieu 1977).

are men that could write that and write it brilliantly, but you sort of think maybe a woman can write it slightly better? (Nicola, employer)

Nicola realizes that she is problematically relying on stereotypes as soon as she says it, and tries to justify her position by flattering the imagined women screenwriters and acknowledging that men can (and of course, do) write these types of stories.

In Nora Ephron's 1993 film, *Sleepless in Seattle*, the character Suzy, played by Rita Wilson, describes in some detail the climactic scenes of *An Affair to Remember* (1957). Suzy's emotional description is accompanied by the men characters in the scene rolling their eyes. The film's protagonist, Sam Baldwin, played by Tom Hanks, famously concludes her performance by declaring: "That's a chick's movie". The term "chick's movie" or "chick flick" suggests that some films are aimed towards, and enjoyed by, women viewers. These films are usually emotional and focus on love and relationships, but there is also a clear sense of them being more lightweight or frivolous—a theme also seen in publishing's similarly termed "chick lit" label. In *Sleepless in Seattle*, Sam goes on to parody Suzy's emotional description whilst talking about *The Dirty Dozen* (1967), a film about a mass assassination mission of German officers in World War II. *The Dirty Dozen* is being held up as a contrast to *An Affair to Remember*: an example of a "guy's film", full of action and conflict and heroics.

Sam's little boy, Jonah, is depicted as not being able to comprehend Suzy's behaviour, but later on in the film, his young female friend instinctively has the same tearful, emotional reaction to the film as Suzy, as if this reaction to a story type is innately gendered and can't be helped. Ephron herself has said Suzy's scene "had cutting room floor written all over it", because it serves no purpose in the film in terms of moving the plot forward (American Film Institute Archives 2002). She also called it her *favourite scene* in the same interview. Ephron acknowledged that with *Sleepless in Seattle*, she was "trying to have our cake and eat it, too" (Frascella 2012) by trying to be "smart, sophisticated and funny" about romantic films as well as wanting to be one of those films at the same time. She admits that *An Affair to Remember* left her "awash in salt" when she first saw it and would likely have the same effect if she watched it now. However, in an echo of the Rita Wilson scene, Ephron says to Lawrence Frascella, the *man* interviewing her, that "maybe you wouldn't be crying".

Despite her cynical, feminist sensibility, Ephron seems to be suggesting that preferences for certain types of films emerge according to one's gender. This becomes a commercial consideration for the film industry because of the distaste that boys and men come to have for anything identifying as "female" taste. Linda Obst, who produced *Sleepless in Seattle*, explains:

> Girls will go to a guy movie if it's good, but guys will not go to a movie if it appears to cater to girls.… In other words, if a movie is supposed to be for

everyone—and that's always the goal these days—you target it toward men. (Barnes 2013)

The Brooks Barnes *New York Times* article, from which Obst's quote is taken, is about pitching a movie idea to "industry insiders" to get feedback on the idea's viability. Obst's remarks as a successful producer demonstrate how men's concerns and interests dominate the filmmaking process from the very beginning. It also goes a long way to explaining film's apparent obsession with young men as the prime cinemagoers, even though they are no longer the biggest section of the audience (BFI Statistical Yearbook 2020, Sinclair et al. 2006). The audience for *Downton Abbey*, the UK's highest performing film in 2019 (the last year for which figures are currently available), was 78% women (BFI Statistical Yearbook 2020). According to the Motion Picture Association of America (MPAA), 51% of cinema goers were women in 2018 (MPAA 2019) and 50% in 2019 (MPAA 2020). It is not the predominance of young men that makes them so key to film financiers, but it is their unwillingness to compromise and watch a film that isn't centred on "a guy".

27.3 Constructing Gender, Constructing Taste

Gender is one of the first identity labels that babies are assigned, before they even have a name, as this will most likely be predicated on the decisive binary announcement "It's a boy/it's a girl!" as they arrive into the world, or even many weeks earlier due to antenatal screening programmes. From this point, it is very difficult for this new human to avoid the socializing process of gender. It's not hard these days to find social media campaigns run by parents objecting to the narrow roles subscribed to their children through clothing, toys, books, colours, adverts, television, and even bedding and tableware. The Let Toys Be Toys campaign group (www.lettoysbetoys.org.uk) grew out of a thread on parenting site *Mumsnet* (www.mumsnet.com/), which brought together parents frustrated by the increase in marketing and promotion to children that pushed narrow gendered stereotypes. They have successfully campaigned to have gendered signs removed from toy stores, children's clothing websites, book covers, and more. However, the reality for most parents is that their children remain policed by advertisers, the media, the world around them, their peers, and other adults, picking up clues and controls on what they are "supposed" to be interested in, and more importantly, what they must avoid for fear of judgement and ridicule.

Unusually, it is boys who have more to fear in this process. It is still far more acceptable for a girl to play football or own a train set than it is for a boy to take ballet lesson or own dolls. Not letting boys associate with anything that's been socially assigned to girls is an indication of how little girls and women are valued. Boys who steer away from the assigned masculine interests and pursuits risk losing their social status. It is not difficult to see why Toril Moi (1991) argues that gender actually has much in common with Bourdieu's concept of class: it is perceived as natural and self-evident, and it is socially and historically reproduced, embodied, and renders an individual open to judgement. She argues that the habitus is at least partly constructed by a socialized process of inscribing gender onto the individual:

> (...) to produce gender habitus requires an extremely elaborate social process of education and inscription of social power relations on the body, so even such basic activities as teaching children how to move, dress and eat are thoroughly political. (Moi 1991, 1030)

Bourdieu's theory of taste as socially constructed and then naturalized in an individual's habitus is particularly relevant to understanding why girls might steer away from STEM[6] careers (O'Mara 2014), or why they might choose to write with a pink pen (Furness 2012). The habitus internalizes the structure in which it grows up. Individuals do not act entirely freely in their choices.

In film labour markets, men and women certainly appear to be regarded as very different. Patterns of employment often follow gender stereotypes, a segregation which has been shown to uphold inequality (Hesmondhalgh and Baker 2015). Hair and Make Up departments, for example, are dominated by women, whilst jobs that use technical machinery such as camera operators and cinematographers are still workforces predominantly made up of men (Cobb, Williams, and Wreyford 2018). In this section, I consider how gender is constructed as part of an individual's habitus, and how this has serious consequence for women screenwriters. For example, the labour women in general are expected to undertake on their own physical appearance (see Elias et al. 2017, for a thorough exploration of this issue) may make them more disposed than men to a career in film and television Hair and Make Up departments, and also gives them the appropriate habitus and superior capital to be recognized as skilled in that particular field. This may indicate that women have a fair chance of employment in film and other creative careers, but hierarchies of reward and recognition within creative professions often mean women are found in roles that have less status. So that, whilst it is possible to claim that women make up half the film workforce (Creative Skillset 2012, 33), they are still scarce in senior and key creative roles such as CEOs (4%) and directors (13%), whilst they have a higher representation in cleaning (63%), HR (73%), and administration (80%).

Bourdieu proposed that the dominant powers of a society define aesthetics, and by means of that definition, social class determines a person's interests, tastes, and likes and dislikes. Using everyday examples such as food and music, he demonstrated that preferences were shared among socio-economic groupings. This variance in aesthetic tastes reinforces inequalities by making "difference" appear natural and apparently legitimating social differences. In

---

[6] STEM is an acronym which stands for Science, Technology, Engineering, and Mathematics.

particular, it is important for the dominant class to make a "distinction" between their own tastes and those of the lower classes, in order to mark themselves as "better": in matters of taste, more than anywhere else, all determination is negation, and tastes are perhaps first and foremost distastes, disgust provoked by horror or visceral intolerance ("sick-making") of the tastes of others (49).

This essentializing and polarizing of taste and aesthetics was described in my interviews, but in relation to gender:

> [I]t's definitely "oh there's a woman in the room". And they'll say that. "Gillian what do you think?" you know, as if like, but then other times slightly sort of a different species, "oh you don't like action, this isn't for you anyway". "You're not really the audience". (Gillian, employer)

> I had every rom-com known to man, *27 Dresses 2*, *Bride Wars 3*; it all came to my door. (Hannah, screenwriter)

> It was very clear that women are not supposed to do genre, they're not supposed to action, or thrillers, maybe we can do comedy but a certain kind of comedy but really what we're supposed to do is drama and if we can do gritty, heartfelt drama that's good. (Usma, screenwriter)

Bourdieu does touch upon gender in relation to taste and food in *Distinction*, but he seems to have less awareness or insight into this as a socially constructed difference as he does in his that analysis of taste and class. For example, he reports that:

> Meat, the nourishing food par excellence, strong and strong-making, giving vigour, blood, and health, is the dish for the men, who take a second helping, whereas women are satisfied with a small portion. It is not that they are stinting themselves, they really don't want what others might need, especially the men, the natural meat-eaters. (1984, 190)

Bourdieu links men with signs of dominance, for example, "par excellence", "strong", "vigour", but rather than viewing this through the same social lens he views class, he perceives the differences he describes in women and men as "natural" and calls them "strictly biological differences". Indeed, Bourdieu seems only interested in women when they can further illustrate his claims about class and taste, showing an incredible lack of insight on occasion, for example, suggesting that upper-class women know "the intrinsic, natural beauty of their bodies" (204) and don't suffer from the same body issues of women from lower classes. I argue that feminist scholars should not allow Bourdieu's own shortcomings—and perhaps ironically, his own inability as a man to recognize the lived experience of women—to prevent us from thinking about gender *with* Bourdieu's concepts, as Toril Moi (1991) has done.

Moi describes the usefulness of seeing gender in terms of the dominant and the dominated just as Bourdieu describes class. She understands the dominators as those in possession of significant capital in the field, which enables them to set the rules and speak with legitimacy, whilst silencing and excluding those that they dominate. Most importantly for my research, she shows how an understanding of taste as part of a gendered habitus can help to explain why men's success in the field of screenwriting is experienced as merited, rather than a simple recognition of dominant tastes:

> Legitimacy (or distinction) is only truly achieved when it is no longer possible to tell whether dominance has been achieved as a result of distinction or whether in fact the dominant agent simply appears to be distinguished because he (more rarely she) is dominant. (Moi 1991, 1023)

Moi pinpoints the value of Bourdieu's concepts of habitus, capital and distinction, and how they function within a given field to both enable suppression of one section of society by another and disguise the processes by which this happens. Although subordinate social classes may appear to have equally strong views about what constitutes good taste, merit, or value, there is an imbalance of power: "The working-class 'aesthetic' is a dominated aesthetic, which is constantly obliged to define itself in terms of the dominant aesthetics" (Bourdieu 1984, 41). This observation echoes feminist criticisms of women as the "other" (de Beauvoir 1949) and post-structuralist attentions to the notion of "female" as defined by what is "not male" (Butler 1990; Irigaray 1985) and highlights the similarity between the dynamics.

Feminists have long highlighted how men's lives, work, and concerns have been deemed more interesting and valuable than women's (Friedan 1963). In post-feminist cultures (Gill 2007b), men don't often consider themselves intrinsically more interesting, but through history, education, and culture, white, upper-class men's tastes, concerns, preoccupations, and preferences are positioned as superior, and of greater worth and merit. Creative women of all classes, backgrounds, and ethnicities have been marginalized by the educational and cultural establishment. Making these hidden naturalized hierarchies visible offers a way to potentially challenge their dominance:

> Bourdieu's highlighting of [the] ultimately arbitrary character of social distinctions (so that, for example, what counts as 'tasteful' is an effect, not of intrinsic properties, but of social relations) gives us a way to challenge the taken-for-granted. (Lawler 2004, 113)

Bourdieu recognized that taste is not simply an expression of individuality, nor is it a harmless preference for one thing over another: "aesthetic intolerance can be terribly violent. Aversion to different lifestyles is perhaps one of the strongest barriers between the classes" (Bourdieu 1984, 56). Indeed, it is one of the most effective ways that those with power hold onto it. "Good" taste is displayed through symbolic violence as a natural quality of an individual, making it appear innate and objective rather than learnt and highly subjective. This is particularly clear in the creative industries, where "taste" is one of the principal ways that individuals are judged, relationships are formed, and products are chosen and promoted over others: "taste [is] one of the most vital stakes in the struggles fought in the field of the dominant class and the field of cultural production" (11).

In the next section, I will look at how the workers in the UK film industry that I spoke to discursively position women's taste and how this discourse is used to account for the lack of women screenwriters.

27.4 The Currency of Taste in the UK Film Labour Market

In analysing my interviews with screenwriters and their employers, I observed frequent references my participants made to "taste", and the associations made between gender and taste, for example:

> (…) you have to feel in some way confident in your taste and creative instinct. (Nick, employer)
>
> I learnt and I know my taste, my skills, my taste as a producer was very much formed there. (Jo, employer)
>
> I wasn't terribly taken with the script, and she took it very personally, thought I was challenging all of her taste. (Frank, employer)
>
> And it isn't really my taste either. (Frankie, screenwriter)
>
> My own taste isn't like that. (Laura, employer)
>
> If you look at the BBC, or Film 4 or the BFI. It's the same people with the same taste. (Jay, employer)

Often taste was closely associated with power and money, such as in one employer's comment that "if the tastemaker, the financier, disagrees, it's irrelevant" (Eloise, employer). Here, being a film financier appears to be synonymous with having the power of making judgements based on taste. In fact, her use of the term "tastemaker" echoes Bourdieu's own use of the word in reference to museum curators, whom he described as artistic guides to the elite. Eloise used the term in reference to powerful people who head up organizations that financially support film development and production, giving them the power to endorse their own tastes. These are still predominantly men. Men have the dominant habitus in the film industry and are therefore perceived to have more worthwhile ideas and more valuable stories than women.

And he to this day can go in, even—amazing—two massive flops in a row and still walk into the studios and convince them. You show me a woman who could do that! (Colin, employer)

Many of my participants talked about taste in gendered terms, a discourse in which men and women were positioned as having different interests and instinctive understandings. For example:

I think there's a perception that women are more interested in relationships and emotions and the hidden depths and complexities of human drama, human life, quite rightly, okay. (Rob, employer)

(…) instinctively when you meet a male writer you think he has a better understanding of genre and therefore of audience than a female writer does (Kate, employer)

A dominant discursive pattern can be identified in which women are seen as interested in relationship dramas, whilst men are viewed as naturally inclined to write genre films full of action and special effects. This discourse has an effect in limiting employment prospects for women screenwriters whether they want to write these films or not. Gendered taste was clearly linked to employment opportunities for screenwriters by the employers:

From my point of view I know that there are female screenwriters that I'll go to for drama, male screenwriters I'll go to for genre (Frank, employer)

So, there's a book that we've optioned recently which is absolutely a woman's story. It's about a female friendship and mothers and daughters and relationships, so I'm looking for a writer now and I'd ideally like to find a woman to write it. (Vanessa, employer)

More worryingly, and without any reference to data or evidence, several of my participants made a connection between women screenwriters' association with drama and the reasons why they may have trouble getting their films made. For example, here are some of the answers I received to the question "Why do you think there are so few women screenwriters?".

(…) because the female screenwriter is writing drama (Frank, employer)

Um—so it's what's perhaps left on the shelf are the more character-driven pieces written by more intuitive, character-interested female writers (Nick, employer)

(…) things that one might imagine women would write, more drama-led, might be tougher to get made (Vanessa, employer)

In this discourse, taste is presented as conforming to very stereotypical gendered roles that echo the public/private dichotomy. Women are positioned as being interested in people and relationships whereas men are all about action and adventure. These types of stories are then in turn given different economic values, without taking into account other influencing factors, such as production and marketing budgets. Indeed, the one genre recognized to be both "for women" and commercial—the romantic comedy—was often described in disparaging terms. Romantic comedies were described as "sappy", "soppy", and "half-baked" in my discussions.

In this extract from my conversation with Nick, it is clear that he is having to do discursive work in order to explain to me his understanding of gendered differences in taste without sounding sexist. He gets himself into uncomfortable corners and is not very successful in navigating his way out:

> (…) teenage boys who grow up to be young adolescents they want—again, generally speaking—they want the brash loud thriller things, they want *The Fast and the Furious* and the superhero movies and um—loads of explosions and car chases. You know I'm sure there have been countless studies exploring the relationship between violent movies and testosterone levels and pre-adolescent and men and what can you do about that? So it's no surprise that those young boys who do turn out to be writers, who pursue that as a career, grow up to be writers who write the sort of thing that they were drawn to when they were younger, you know. It's certainly not the reverse that girls grow up to be female writers who only write sappy romantic comedies or *Tinkerbell* movies, you know. I think, generally speaking, female writers can be more versatile in the market place as much as anything because you know the big tent pole movies or the mainstream films their first point of access for the audience tends to be male-skewed. (Nick, employer)

Nick starts by trying to establish a natural link between boys and men and action-packed films. He even uses the discursive technique of drawing on "experts", although the "studies" he refers to are most likely ones trying to judge whether violent films and video games *increase* aggression in boys' behaviour (Anderson and Bushman 2001). These studies are looking for causality and influence on behaviour, but Nick's comment "and what can you do about that?" seems designed instead to make the association appear inevitable and rooted in biology. However, once he moves to extend his argument to why men screenwriters are drawn to write this type of material, he quickly realizes that he is potentially limiting what women screenwriters are allowed to write and so then contradicts himself whilst at the same time reinforcing the sexist idea that young girls prefer to watch romantic comedies and films about fairies. It ends with a suggestion that women potentially have more opportunities as they "can be more versatile", an extraordinary reversal of what actually happens in the film labour market.

What is missing from this discourse of gendered preferences is some awareness that screenwriters do not often get to choose the projects that they work on (McCreadie 2006).

> The reason I was commissioned was because they thought I would be able to write the women, the relationships between the four women at the centre. (Catherine, screenwriter)
>
> But they're like, "you're a woman, you don't know about fighting". (Emily, screenwriter)
>
> People don't give me war movies or Sci-Fi's but I'm not interested so it's not that surprising. And certainly I do get sent "oh this is supposed to have a strong female character in it" etc. etc. so I suppose there is that. (Rachel, screenwriter)

Certainly, in my conversations with women screenwriters, few of them felt that their skills or interests were limited to women characters and romantic relationships. I asked all the screenwriters whether there were any subjects or genres of film that they felt they either could not or would not be interested in writing. Very few expressed any kind of limit on their abilities or interests, and many who did then added a caveat that they probably could depending on the story within the broader genre. Overall, the genres that were specified as uninteresting were very similar for men and women. The women screenwriters mentioned horror (four writers) and crime (two writers) but also kitchen sink dramas (one writer), children's films (one writer) and "chick flicks" (one writer). The men screenwriters also mentioned horror (two writers) but also science fiction (three writers), romantic comedy (two writers), drama (one writer) and "women's issues" films (one writer). Sometimes the same people who didn't limit themselves had no problem suggesting limits on others. Most notably Jack, who answered my question as to why he thought there are fewer women screenwriters thus:

> Well, I can see how the traditional genres, things like thrillers, superhero movies, horror are boys natural comfort zone, um—so many films do lean towards teenage boys, you know action, all that stuff, that's got to be part of it.

Then, *my very next question* was about his own tastes and abilities and he answered without any apparent awareness of the parallels:

> Yes. Horror. I have absolutely no interest in writing that. Um—big action movies, you know I don't have the experience for that. I'm more interested in character relationship movies compelled by a strong narrative.

However, Catherine echoed the gendered perceptions of her employer suggesting she has taken on these gendered associations in her own habitus:

> But what I thought I can't do is, I thought I can't do the action, the car chases, I can't do the heist bit. I can do the plotting; I can't do the crime. I can't do all the technical things. Oh but yes I'm a woman and I can do all that emotional stuff.

Although she also went on to contradict herself:

I suddenly just got completely carried away with all the action and I was really excited about shooters and people were going to be hanging off hooks in the— and everybody just suddenly stopped and looked at me and I suddenly realized that I had assimilated, completely, the world that I thought was actually not my domain. So I suppose what I'm trying to say by that, I'm not sure that, there may be gender perceptions of what we're good at but I don't think they actually hold true.

Catherine's initial comment may also imply that many of the women screenwriters who have found some success in the UK may be those who conform to the expectations of commissioners about what women can write, as Rachel's comment earlier also suggests.

Some of the biggest box office successes of all time illustrate clearly that women can and *do* write films that are full of action and heroics and appeal to broad audiences. For example, *The Lord of the Rings* (2001), written by Fran Walsh and Philippa Boyens; *The Hunger Games* (2012), co-written by Suzanne Collins based on her own novel—the fastest-selling non-sequel ever; *The Empire Strikes Back* (1980) co-written by Leigh Brackett—voted the best film ever by the British public (Daily Mail Reporter 2014). Brackett died of cancer before the film was made and revisions to the script were made by Lawrence Kasdan, but Brackett was responsible for most of the iconic scenes such as "the Battle of Hoth, the wise words of an old Jedi Master, the excitement of zooming through a deadly asteroid field, a love triangle, a majestic city in the clouds, unexpected betrayals, and the climactic duel between Luke Skywalker and Darth Vader" (Saavedra 2021) as well as the creation of the character of Yoda. These sorts of examples are not the majority, but they do trouble the notion that women's tastes and talents are limited. Indeed, the success of women screenwriters was also repeatedly framed as being due to their ability to write like men, or to write so that their gender is not obvious, much the way American director Kathryn Bigelow has had success:

I mean the point, in fact the celebration, of her by audiences, by critics, is that you wouldn't know she was a woman, because she can direct a war film. (Yvonne, employer)

There were repeated references by my participants during our conversations to Jane Goldman writing *Kick Ass* and *X-Men: First Class* (2010, 2011), Kelly Marcel writing *Terra Nova* (2011) and *Mad Max: Fury Road* (2015), and Lucinda Coxon writing *Crimson Peak* for Guillermo del Toro (2015) as signs that women screenwriters were becoming more successful. Little or no mention was made of Laura Wade writing *The Riot Club* (2014), Misan Sagay writing *Belle* (2013), Abi Morgan's screenplay *Suffragette* (2015), or even another of Kelly Marcel's scripts, *Saving Mr. Banks* (2013), which was being released at the time of my interviews. It is worth noting that three of these four screenplays were made into films with women directors and also that Kelly Marcel is uncredited on *Mad Max: Fury Road* as is Lucinda Coxon on

Crimson Peak, both seemingly replaced by men screenwriters and the men directors.

Women's screenwriting success then is often defined by the UK industry as women writing films that men like. This clearly conflicts with the sort of films that the employers believe women want to write and indeed frequently commission them to write. If we are going to be able to include stories by and about women on the big screen, decision-makers and powerful financiers need to understand that their taste is subjective, constructed, and not necessarily shared by significant portions of the audience. Currently, in the UK film industry, white, heterosexual, able-bodied men's taste is dominant and anyone who does not share these tastes risks having their creative preferences judged as less valuable and even distasteful by those with the power to finance films, most of whom are still rich white men. Women screenwriters are associated with less commercial stories simply because of their gender and can find themselves restricted to writing films that predominantly revolve around relationships and the pursuit of love, despite evidence that they can successfully write big, funny, action-packed box office hits. Indeed, it may only be when they find a way to write such films that they are seen as having real talent enough to compete for jobs alongside men screenwriters.

I wish to argue here that women should not be restricted to writing certain *types* of stories or genres, but their approach to any story or genre may offer a different perspective because of their lived experience. In this, I do not mean to overgeneralize or treat women as a homogeneous group; indeed, we need to hear all sorts of women's and non-binary voices and perspectives on all kinds of stories as well as a wider variety of men's voices in terms of class, race, sexuality, and other forms of embodied subjectivities. In this way, we can start to offer new ways of looking at the world, and new ways of understanding those we perhaps view as not so much like ourselves. At the very least, we can find some new approaches to telling stories, which perhaps even some white men might appreciate, such as Ed, who described his experience running a team of men writers on a show he originated:

> So it's like four men which is slightly predictable in itself, but because it's four men the first week all the ideas were hookers and strippers, hookers and strippers, and I was literally screaming at them by the end "there are no hookers and strippers in this thing!" not because I'm banging the table for some feminist agenda, but because it's corny, we've seen it before. Until the point where they were going "what about fat hookers?" (Ed, screenwriter)

27.5 Conclusion

A feminist appropriation of Pierre Bourdieu's study of the social construction of taste provides a way to understand why those with power fail to recognize the value of women's stories. Just as the dominant *class* constructs its tastes and preferences as naturally superior (Bourdieu 1984), the dominant *gender* (men) is considered to have superior and more universal tastes and preferences than the dominated (women and non-binary people). This point of view can of course be taken on and accepted by anyone, not just men, as they are likely to have been socialized to reproduce accepted discourses to survive in the field of film production. However, it is possible that the embodied and lived experiences of gender can allow women critics to see value in women's stories where men critics cannot. When women have written films about women's experiences that do well at the box office, they are most often chalked up by journalists and producers alike as an anomaly or side-lined into a specialist "for women" category. Rarely is the success followed up with copycat films or sequels. I have argued that the construction of gendered taste plays a significant role in this as men critics, financiers, and audiences often judge women's tastes as frivolous and distasteful. This distaste has very real consequences in upholding the lack of opportunities for women screenwriters, as these judgements of taste appear natural and meritocratic rather than constructed and contentious. Women screenwriters are disadvantaged in a way that is self-fulfilling and difficult to circumnavigate. They are perceived as having innate gendered taste, which is considered less commercial and resulting in films that only women will watch. They are shut out from the biggest budgets and the most action-packed genres. These films are then made by and targeted at men and boys and often do not show a nuanced understanding of women as characters or include their views of the world. Indeed, this can mean women are more likely to want to watch films that *do* contain women characters and women's perspectives. If women wish to pursue a career in screenwriting, they are likely to be influenced by the films they grew up watching. However, these films are not valued by the industry, even when they succeed, making it difficult for women screenwriters to sustain a career. Conversely, should they wish to shrug off the shackles of stereotyped gendered taste, or break new boundaries, they are likely to be considered less knowledgeable and therefore less trustworthy than their men colleagues.

Habitus allows an understanding of how different genders may indeed write about the same subject in a different way, as may Africans or Europeans, heterosexual and lesbian writers, cisgender or transgender individuals, and so on. Habitus is a way to understand experience as both constructed and lived so that the individual cannot help but bring a unique perspective to creative work. This is a strong argument for why it matters that the majority of screenwriters are white, rich, CIS-gender, heterosexual men. Even if they do create stories *about* poor, minoritized, lesbian, disabled women, they will most likely be unable to provide the same perspective on those experiences as a diverse range of women and non-binary screenwriters would. As one black woman employer clearly understood:

> (…) it's about having been on the receiving end of something and how when you're telling a story the different nuances that say being a Muslim woman writing, or being a Muslim man writing, as opposed to being a white man writing. (Esther, employer)

Stephanie Taylor and Karen Littleton have argued that identities are socially constructed "because they are resourced and constrained by larger understanding which prevail in the speaker's social and cultural context" (2006, 23). Like screenwriting, these are all professions that are theoretically open to all genders, but, also like screenwriting, they are dominated by and more frequently associated with men.

In this chapter, I have argued that the world is divided up through a socialized process of gendering through which certain interests, traits, preferences and *tastes* become associated with different genders. This process has significant consequences for women screenwriters because they are expected—and commissioned—to write certain types of stories, but only judged as good screenwriters when they write other (men-associated) stories. Gender, whilst understood as plural, non-binary, and constructed, is also a lived experience and Toril Moi has convincingly argued that viewing gender through the lens of Pierre Bourdieu's concept of habitus allows us to understand both of these things as simultaneously true. It also explains why women's writing is routinely undervalued and how different genders may not view the world—or the same story, or even the same character—in the same way. This chapter contributes to the arguments for a diverse range of decision-makers of all backgrounds and genders in senior decision-making roles in creative industries like the UK film industry, but also for a more nuanced understanding of the complexities of gender. Without this, we are likely to continue to see a narrow world view on our movie screens and limited opportunities for women and non-binary screenwriters.

REFERENCES

Adkins, Lisa, and Beverley Skeggs, eds. 2004. *Feminism after Bourdieu*. Oxford: Blackwell.

American Film Institute Archives. 2002. "Nora Ephron's Favourite Scene in Sleepless in Seattle". Cheideo.com. https://www.chideo.com/chideo/afinora-ephron-favorite-sleepless-in-seattle-scene. Accessed 21 April 2022.

An Affair to Remember. 1957. Written by Delmer Daves, Leo McCarey, Mildred Cram (story), and Donald Ogden Stewart. Directed by Leo McCarey. USA. Twentieth Century Fox.

Anderson, Craig A., and Brad J. Bushman. 2001. Effects of Violent Video Games On Aggressive Behavior, Aggressive Cognition, Aggressive Affect, Physiological Arousal, and Prosocial Behavior: A Meta-Analytic Review of the Scientific Literature. *Psychological Science* 12 (5): 353–359.

Barnes, Brooks. 2013. "Save my blockbuster!" *New York Times*. https://archive.nytimes.com/www.nytimes.com/interactive/2013/06/28/movies/BLOCKBUSTER.html. Accessed 21 Apr 2022.

Belle. 2013. Written by Misan Sagay and Amma Asante (uncredited). Directed by Amma Asante. UK. British Film Institute.

BFI Statistical Yearbook. 2020. https://www.bfi.org.uk/industry-data-insights/statistical-yearbook. Accessed 16 May 2023.

Bilge, Sirma. 2006. Behind the 'Culture' Lens: Judicial Representations of Violence Against Minority Women. *Canadian Woman Studies* 25 (1): 173–180.

Bride Wars. 2009. Written by Greg DePaul, Casey Wilson, and June Diane Raphael. Directed by Gary Winick. USA. Fox 2000 Pictures.

Bourdieu, Pierre. 1977. *Outline of a theory of practice*. Cambridge: Cambridge University Press.

Bourdieu, Pierre. 1984. *Distinction: A Social Critique of the Judgment of Taste*. Cambridge ma: Harvard University Press.

Bourdieu, Pierre, and Loïc. Wacquant. 1992. *An Invitation to Reflexive Sociology*. Chicago: University of Chicago Press.

Butler, Judith. 1990. *Gender Trouble: Feminism and the Subversion of Identity*. New York: Routledge.

Creative Skillset. 2012. "Employment census of the creative media industries." http://creativeskillset.org/assets/0000/5070/2012_Employment_Census_of_the_Creative_Media_Industries.pdf. Accessed 24 Apr 2018.

Crimson Peak. 2015. Written by Guillermo del Toro, Matthew Robbins, and Lucinda Coxon (uncredited). Directed by Guillermo del Toro. USA. Double Dare You.

Christopherson, Susan. 2009. Working in the Creative Economy: Risk, Adaptation, and the Persistence of Exclusionary Networks. In *Creative labour: Working in the creative industries*, ed. Alan McKinlay and Chris Smith, 72–90. Basingstoke uk: Palgrave Macmillan.

Cobb, Shelley, Linda Ruth Williams, and Natalie Wreyford. 2016. "Calling the Shots: Women Working in Key Roles on UK Films in Production During 2015." https://womencallingtheshots.com/reports-and-publications/. Accessed 17 December 2021.

Cobb, Shelley, Linda Ruth Williams, and Natalie Wreyford. 2018. "Calling the Shots: Women Directors and Cinematographers on British Films Since 2003." https://womencallingtheshots.com/reports-and-publications/. Accessed 17 December 2021.

Cobb, Shelley, Linda Ruth Williams and Natalie Wreyford. 2019. "Calling the Shots: Comparing the Numbers of Women Directors, Editors and Cinematographers on UK-Qualifying Films 2003–2015." https://womencallingtheshots.com/reports-and-publications/. Accessed 17 December 2021.

Cobb, Shelley, and Natalie Wreyford. 2021. "'Could You Hire Someone Female or from an Ethnic Minority?' *Being Both: Black, Asian and other Minority Women Working in British Film Production*. In Black Film British Cinema II, eds. Clive Nwonka and Anami Saha, 165–84. London: Goldsmiths, MIT Press.

Daily Mail Reporter. 2014. "Empire Strikes Back Is Number One Film: Star Wars Beats The Godfather to Be Named Greatest Movie of All Time. *The Daily Mail*. http://www.dailymail.co.uk/tvshowbiz/article-2643379/Empire-Strikes-Back-number-one-film-Star-Wars-beats-The-Godfather-named-greatestmovie-time.html. Accessed 21 Apr 2018.

de Beauvoir, Simone. 1949. *The Second Sex*. New York: HM Parshley.

Dresses. 2008. Written by Aline Brosh McKenna. Directed by Anne Fletcher. USA. Fox 2000 Pictures.

Downton Abbey. 2019. Written by Julian Fellowes. Directed by Michael Engler. UK: Focus Features.

Elias, Ana Sofia, Rosalind Gill, and Christina Scharff, eds. 2017. *Aesthetic labour: Rethinking beauty politics in neoliberalism*. Basingstoke uk: Palgrave Macmillan.

Francke, Lizzie. 1994. *Script girls: Women Screenwriters in Hollywood*. London: British Film Institute.
Frascella, Lawrence. 2012. "On the Front Lines with Nora Ephron." *Rolling Stone*. https://www.rollingstone.com/movies/news/on-the-front-lines-with-noraephron-20120626. Accessed 21 Apr 2018.
Friedan, Betty. 1963. *The Feminine Mystique*. New York: Dell.
Furness, Hannah. 2012. "BIC Ridiculed over 'Comfortable' Pink Pens for Women." *The Telegraph*. https://www.telegraph.co.uk/news/newstopics/howaboutthat/9503359/BIC-ridiculed-over-comfortable-pink-pens-for-women.html. Accessed 19 Apr 2018.
Gill, Rosalind. 2007. Postfeminist Media Culture: Elements of a Sensibility. *European Journal of Cultural Studies* 10 (2): 147–166.
Gill, Rosalind. 2014. Unspeakable Inequalities: Post Feminism, Entrepreneurial Subjectivity, and the Repudiation of Sexism Among Cultural Workers. *Social Politics* 21 (4): 509–528.
Hesmondhalgh, David, and Sarah Baker. 2015. Sex, Gender and Work Segregation in the Cultural Industries. *The Sociological Review* 63 (1): 23–36.
Irigaray, Luce. 1985. *This Sex Which Is Not One*. New York: Cornell University Press.
Kick-Ass. 2010. Written by Jane Goldman and Matthew Vaughan. Directed by Matthew Vaughan. UK: Lionsgate.
Kreager, Alexis, and Stephen Follows. 2018. "Gender Inequality and Screenwriters. A Study of the Impact of Gender on Equality of Opportunity for Screenwriters and Key Creatives in the UK Film and Television Industries." The Writers Guild of Great Britain. https://writersguild.org.uk/wp-content/uploads/2018/05/Gender-Inequality-and-Screenwriters.pdf. Accessed 17 December 2021.
Lauzen, Martha M. 2021. "The Celluloid Ceiling: Behind-the-Scenes Employment of Women on the Top U.S. Films of 2020." https://womenintvfilm.sdsu.edu/wp-content/uploads/2021/01/2020_Celluloid_Ceiling_Report.pdf. Accessed 6 June 2022.
Lawler, Steph. 2004. Rules of Engagement: Habitus, Power and Resistance. *The Sociological Review* 52 (2): 110–128.
Lovell, Terry. 2000. "Thinking Feminism With and Against Bourdieu. *Feminist Theory* 1 (1): 11–32.
Mad Max: Fury Road. 2015. Written by George Miller, Brendan McCArthym Nick Lathouris, Byron Kennedy (uncredited), and Kelly Marcel (uncredited). Directed by George Miller. USA: Warner Bros Pictures.
McCreadie, Marsha. 2006. *Women Screenwriters Today: Their Lives and Words*. Connecticut: Praeger Publishing.
Moi, Toril. 1991. Appropriating Bourdieu: Feminist Theory and Pierre Bourdieu's Sociology of Culture. *New Literary History* 22 (4): 1017–1049.
MPAA 2018 Theme Report. 2019. https://www.motionpictures.org/wp-content/uploads/2019/03/MPAA-THEME-Report-2018.pdf. Accessed 4 June 2022.
MPAA 2019 Theme Report. 2020. https://www.motionpictures.org/wp-content/uploads/2020/03/MPA-THEME-2019.pdf. Accessed 4 June 2022.
O'Mara, Eileen. 2014. "How Can We Better Tackle the Gender Imbalance in Technology Careers?" *Huffington post*. https://www.huffingtonpost.co.uk/eileenomara/how-can-we-better-tackle-_b_6179346.html. Accessed 19 Apr 2018.
Rogers, Susan. 2007. Writing British Films: Who Writes British Films and How They Are Recruited. *A report produced for the UK Film Council*. Royal Holloway

University of London. https://www2.bfi.org.uk/sites/bfi.org.uk/files/downlo ads/uk-film-council-writing-british-films-who-writes-british-films-and-how-they-are-recruited.pdf. Accessed 18 April 2023.

Saavedra, John. 2021. "Star Wars: Leigh Brackett and The Empire Strikes Back You Never Saw." *Den of Geek.* https://www.denofgeek.com/movies/star-wars-the-emp ire-strikes-back-leigh-brackett/. Accessed 3 June 2022.

Saving Mr. Banks. 2013. Written by Kelly Marcel and Sue Smith. Directed by John Lee Hancock. USA: Walt Disney Pictures.

Seger, Linda. 2003 [1996]. *When Women Call the Shots: The Developing Power and Influence of Women on Television and Film.* Lincoln, NE: iUniverse.

Sinclair, Alice, Emma Pollard, and Helen Wolfe. 2006. "Scoping Study into the Lack of Women Screenwriters in the UK. A Report Presented to the UK Film Council." UK Film Council. http://www.bfi.org.uk/sites/bfi.org.uk/files/downlo ads/uk-film-council-women-screenwriters-scoping-study.pdf. Accessed 17 December 2021.

Sleepless in Seattle. 1993. Written by Nora Ephron, David S. Ward, and Jeff Arch. Directed by Nora Ephron. USA: Columbia Tristar.

Smith, Stacy L., and Chrystal Allene Cook. 2008. "Gender Stereotypes: An Analysis of Popular Films and TV." Annenberg School for Communication and The Geena Davis Institute on Gender in Media. https://seejane.org/wpcontent/upl oads/GDIGM_Gender_Stereotypes.pdf. Accessed 17 December 2021.

Suffragette. 2015. Written by Abi Morgan. Directed by Sarah Gavron. UK: Pathé.

Taylor, Stephanie, and Karen Littleton. 2006. Biographies in Talk: A Narrative-Discursive Research Approach. *Qualitative Sociology Review* 2 (1): 22–38.

Terra Nova. 2011. Created by Kelly Marcel and Craig Silverstein. USA: 20th Century Television.

The Dirty Dozen. 1967. Written by Nunnally Johnson and Lukas Heller. Directed by Robert Aldrich. USA. Metro-Goldwyn-Mayer.

The Lord of the Rings. 2001. Written by Fran Walsh, Philippa Boyens, and Peter Jackson. Directed by Peter Jackson. New Zealand: New Line Cinema.

The Hunger Games. 2012. Written by Gary Ross, Suzanne Collins, and Billy Ray. Directed by Gary Ross. USA: Lionsgate.

The Riot Club. 2014. Written by Laura Wade. Directed by Lone Scherfig. UK: Blueprint Pictures, Film4, HanWay Films, Pinewood Films.

The Empire Strikes Back. 1980. Written by Leigh Brackett and Lawrence Kasdan. Directed by Irvin Kershner. USA: Twentieth Century Fox.

Wonder Woman. 2017. Written by Allan Heinbeerg, Zack Synder, and Jason Fucks. Directed by Patty Jenkins. USA: Warner Bros.

Wreyford, Natalie. 2015. Birds of a Feather: Informal Recruitment Practices and Gendered Outcomes for Screenwriting Work in the UK Film Industry. *The Sociological Review* 63: 84–96.

Wreyford, Natalie. 2018. *Gender Inequality in Screenwriting Work.* Cham, Switzerland: Palgrave Macmillan.

Wreyford, Natalie, and Shelley Cobb. 2017. Data and Responsibility: Toward a Feminist Methodology for Producing Historical Data on Women in the Contemporary Film Industry. *Feminist Media Histories* 3 (3): 107–132.

X-Men: First Class. 2011. Written by Ashley Miller, Zack Stentz, Jane Goldman, Matthew Vaughan, Sheldon Turner, and Bryan Singer. Directed by Matthew Vaughan. USA: 20th Century Fox.

The Different American Legal Structures for Unionization of Writers for Stage and Screen

Catherine L. Fisk

28.1 Introduction

Writers for the screen are among the few highly-educated, well-paid workers in the United States who are also relatively committed unionists with the legal right to bargain collectively. Their union, the Writers Guild of America (WGA), protects their interests as creative professionals (Fisk 2016) (the WGA actually consists of two related organizations that divide jurisdiction over writers geographically: the Writers Guild of America East and the Writers Guild of America West). Although some film and TV writers express ambivalence about its role in protecting their interests as paid labor when they have had to go on strike, most writers most of the time recognize the value the WGA provides in advancing writer interests in negotiations, in training, in addressing systemic issues in the industry, and in administering a portable system of health and pension benefits that cover writers as they move from job to job. The collectively bargained system governing compensation and the allocation of rights in creative work has endured since it was established (circa 1940). It survived the end of the studio system in the late 1940s and the growth of independent film production. It expanded to cover new media (TV in the 1950s, cable in the 1970s, and streaming in the 2010s). And it expanded to cover new production companies and studios, including Netflix, Amazon, Hulu, and others (Fisk and Szalay 2016).

C. L. Fisk (✉)
University of California-Berkeley, Berkeley, CA, USA
e-mail: cfisk@law.berkeley.edu

Writers for the stage, in contrast, have no legal right to bargain collectively because they are deemed in law to be *independent contractors* rather than *employees*. The entity that represents them collectively, the Dramatists Guild, is therefore thought by writers and producers to be a professional association rather than a union, and because it is not a union it is barred by antitrust law (known as competition law outside the United States) from negotiating collectively on their behalf (Fisk and Salter 2022). Stage writers believe that sacrificing the legal right to unionize is necessary to keep the copyright in their work, and they think copyright ownership is essential to creative autonomy.

The Dramatists Guild has nevertheless negotiated a series of collective agreements since 1926, and the agreements are widely honored except when a producer believes it is not in its interest to abide by it (Salter 2022). But the Dramatists Guild's collective agreement (currently known as the Approved Production Contract) is not legally binding on either writers or producers. The APC outlines the standard minimum terms on which theatre producers are expected to agree when retaining the services of, or licensing works from, playwrights and dramaturgs, but unlike the Minimum Basic Agreements negotiated by the WGA, there is no enforceable contractual mechanism to compel compliance. The complex intersection of antitrust law (which prohibits collective action by independent contractors), labor law (which carves out an antitrust exemption only for employees), and copyright law (which treats employees less favorably than independent contractors when it comes to authorship of creative works) has left the Dramatists Guild and its APC under a cloud of legal uncertainty.

Dramatists are alone among the major talent working on both stage and screen to be excluded from the protections of labor law and prohibited by antitrust law from unionization and collective bargaining. All others—writers for the screen, actors, directors, choreographers, set designers, musicians—are deemed by law to be *employees* for purposes of federal labor law and therefore not prohibited by antitrust law from engaging in collective negotiation. The legal uncertainty has meant that the Dramatists Guild and theatre producers have largely failed to negotiate a new APC since 1985, which has made it hard for them to adapt the minimum terms to changes in the economics and business practices of theatre. And, when the coronavirus pandemic shuttered theatres for most of 2020 and halted film and TV production, unions representing other entertainment industry participants negotiated for cushions for the impact on out-of-work performers and craft and technical workers, while the Dramatists Guild was excluded from the negotiations. In a few cases, playwrights were even asked to bail out struggling theatres by returning money they had already been paid for productions that were canceled (Fisk and Salter 2022).

The contrast between the largely successful century of collective bargaining for film and TV writers and the more legally uncertain but nevertheless functional century of negotiation for stage writers illustrates the significance of collective solutions to collective problems in the two tightly-knit industries.

The success of the film and TV writers' strike in 2007–2008, the negotiation of a new WGA contract in 2020, and the WGA's leading role in forcing talent agents in 2021 to change practices regarding packaging of shows that harmed writer interests all show the continuing value that film and TV writers see in unionization to address the dramatic changes in the industry. In contrast, the precarious situation of writers for the stage and the relatively weak position of the Dramatists Guild are, as explained by Brent Salter, a product of the legal and business history of American theatre (Salter 2022). There is no principled basis for the anomalous treatment of these two unions of writers. After exploring the reasons for, and the consequences of, the different unionization rights for writers in Hollywood and on Broadway, this chapter notes some paths for future development.

28.2 Origins and Evolution of the Guilds of Writers for Stage and Screen

Film and stage writers began seriously exploring unionization in the late 1910s and early 1920s as each group saw the success that the craft and technical workers in their respective industries had in improving working conditions through unionization. Both groups of writers were initially skeptical of unionization, believing that unions were for blue-collar workers, not autonomous creative professionals such as writers. On Broadway, after scenic artists established the United Scenic Artists union in 1918, and a fierce Actors' Equity strike shut down Broadway production for a month in August of 1919, dramatists formed a new organization they dubbed the Dramatists Guild (Salter 2022, Middleton 1947). When the Guild negotiated a collective bargaining agreement with the association of Broadway producers in 1926, however, a few influential producers filed suit challenging the contract as unlawful and unenforceable on the ground that it violated state and federal law prohibiting restraints on competition. The challenge was based on the way the 1926 Minimum Basic Agreement (MBA) restricted both who producers could hire and the terms on which playwrights could agree to work. By prohibiting producers from hiring non-Guild writers or work for less than the minimum conditions that all Guild members voted to insist upon, the contract ensured that writers would not undersell each other in their desperation to get a job. The litigation was eventually withdrawn without a definitive resolution of whether the MBA was lawful, but the antitrust threat has loomed over the Dramatists Guild ever since (Fisk and Salter 2022).

In Hollywood, writers were initially skeptical of unionizing, preferring to describe themselves as creative professionals and their organization as a *guild*. They had a change of heart about forming an independent union a decade after the dramatists, when writers saw that the union contract covering the craft workers saved set builders, electricians, and camera operators from the fifty percent pay cut that the studios imposed on everyone else (except the studio executives) in depths of the Depression (Fisk 2016). Writers formed the

Screen Writers Guild in 1933, sought and won recognition for the union from the National Labor Relations Board in 1938, and negotiated the first writers' collective bargaining agreement between 1940 and 1942 (Banks 2014; Fisk 2016).

Negotiating a first contract in the late Gilded Age rather than at the height of the New Deal made a significant difference. In 1926, when the Dramatists Guild negotiated the first MBA, unions were illegal. Courts regarded most union contract goals and negotiating tactics (including strikes) as conspiracies in restraint of trade, prohibited by both federal and state antitrust or unfair competition law. By the late 1930s, when the Screen Writers Guild negotiated its first contract, the right to unionize and bargain collectively was protected by the National Labor Relations Act of 1935, and the United States Supreme Court (whose membership had changed since the 1920s) had abandoned the old view of antitrust law as prohibiting unions and union contracts. But if the different years of origin of the two Guilds were the only thing that explained the undisputed legality of the WGA and the questioned legality of the Dramatists Guild, the anomaly between them would be easy to address. The problem, however, goes deeper.

28.3 Independent Contractors and Copyright Law

The different legal histories of the origins of the two guilds result from a constellation of slight factual differences between the two sectors of the entertainment industry. The National Labor Relations Act protects the rights of *employees* to unionize. In 1938, the movie studios argued that screenwriters weren't employees because some of them worked autonomously, at the time and place of their choosing, and delivered completed scripts to the studio (NLRB 1938). The National Labor Relations Board had little trouble rejecting this argument, pointing out that many writers worked in bungalows on the studio lots, at the hours dictated by studio management, on the projects assigned by the studio. The fact that some writers had the market power to work without studio control did not mean most did, and all were therefore included in the union contract (NLRB 1938, MBA 1942, Fisk 2016).

When the Dramatists Guild in the 1940s sought to take advantage of the favorable ruling that writers are employees eligible to unionize even if they work autonomously, the producers' lawyers had crafted a new argument to thwart them: If writers are employees for purposes of labor law, they must be employees for purposes of copyright law. And if a writer is an employee, everything he or she writes is a work made for hire under copyright law, which means the employer is the legal author and the legal owner of the work. Stage writers thus faced what they thought was a choice: either they could relinquish their copyrights and become employees with the right to unionize, or they could insist on being independent contractors for purposes of both copyright and labor law. Playwrights chose their copyrights.

The copyright problem arose because of a provision first introduced into the copyright statute as part of the major 1909 revision, now codified in Sects. 101 and 201 of the 1976 Copyright Act, which declare that the employer is the author, for copyright purposes, of a work prepared by an employee within the scope of his or her employment (17 U.S.C. §§ 101, 201, *Community for Creative Non-Violence v. Reid*, 490 U.S. 730 (1989)). An independent contractor, by contrast, is the author and owner of their copyrighted work unless the creator and the person or entity that commissioned it agree in writing that the commissioning party will be the owner.

The work for hire provision seemed (at least in the early years) less galling for film writers than it did for playwrights because of the differences in writing in the two sectors. Writing did not become a significant part of the creative work of filmmaking until after the advent of sound. By then, norms about collaborative writing and serial rewriting had been established. Moreover, studio ownership of the copyright in the constituent parts of a film—the script and the music—was crucial to studio ownership of the copyright of the film. And the market value of a script was not imagined to be significant after the sale to the studio because it was a single-use form of writing, unlike the script to a play, which would be used and re-used every night of a play's run in New York and around the world.

As the years went by, copyright protections expanded to include as copyrightable contributions made by others involved in theatrical production and who were employees with union rights protected by federal labor law, including stage directions and choreography. In 1975, a federal court ruled that stage directors are employees, not independent contractors, and therefore that the Society of Stage Directors and Choreographers (which had signed a collective bargaining agreement with Broadway producers in 1962 in exchange for not pursuing copyright protection for stage directions) was exempt from antitrust liability. And then, the 1976 Copyright Act created opportunities to claim a copyright for any creator who "fixed" their work "in any tangible medium of expression". In the 1990s and 2000s, high profile cases begin to appear in the courts involving copyright claims of a range of theatre collaborators, including directors, designers, choreographers, and dramaturgs (*Thomson v. Larson*, 147 F.3d 195 (2d Cir. 1998)). Most settled, with non-writer collaborators negotiating a greater stake in the future of works. The anomalous position of playwrights thus became even more anomalous, as others gained both the benefits of unionization and the benefits of possible copyright ownership.

28.4 Independent Contractors and Labor and Antitrust Law

Theatre producers had one final blow to land, and in 1947, it proved to be the coup de grace that the producers had been seeking since the 1920s. In 1927, the producers had withdrawn their suit asserting that the Dramatists Guild and the 1926 Minimum Basic Agreement were illegal restraints of trade. The producers had signed new Minimum Basic Agreements with the Dramatists Guild in 1931, 1936, and 1941. The latter two rounds of negotiations were especially testy on the subject of how producers and playwrights would share the profits from the sale of film rights, which created the context in which producers sought in the late 1940s to gain the upper hand in negotiations by challenging the legality of the Dramatists Guild and the whole process of collective negotiation.

When theatre producers went on the offense in the late 1940s, they were part of a larger effort by business groups and employer organizations to rein in the power of unions. Across industry, but especially in creative, white collar, or technical work, lawyers for business launched a legal campaign to exclude certain categories of workers from the protections of the NLRA. At the same time, they also argued that collective action by them was not only unprotected by labor law but affirmatively prohibited by antitrust law. Creative and professional workers in New York, including musicians, insurance agents, artists, architects, engineers, and radio writers who unionized in significant numbers in the 1940s, were a major target of that campaign. The Supreme Court had ruled in 1944 that Hearst newspaper vendors were employees, and the business community's outrage at the holding and reasoning in that case provided additional traction in Congress to include in the 1947 anti-labor Taft-Hartley Act a provision stripping independent contractors of their rights under labor law (*NLRB v. Hearst Publications*, 322 U.S. 111 (1944); 29 U.S.C. § 152(3)).

With independent contractors removed from the protection of labor law, employers saw a new opportunity to use antitrust law to quell unionization among them. This was a strategy employed both by the league of Broadway theatre owners and producers and by advertising agencies confronted with a major unionization effort among the freelance writers who wrote and produced radio programs under contract with ad agencies (Fisk 2016). But the paths of the antitrust strategy embraced by lawyers for theatre owners and producers and the strategy embraced by lawyers for radio and TV writers diverged.

The ad agencies' effort to use antitrust law to prevent unionization of freelance radio and TV writers ultimately failed because the agencies and producers insisted on the power to require writers to make revisions to scripts. The ad agencies hired and supervised radio and TV writers on behalf of their clients, the radio/TV program sponsors. The agencies and sponsors alike considered the power to control content to be essential to their work. As the president of the Radio Writers Guild later reflected, the power of ad agencies and producers to require a writer to make revisions—the right of control that galled many radio, film, and TV writers—proved to be key to their ability to bargain collectively (Barnouw 1996). To this day, employees under the MBA for television (which is the successor to the radio writers' contract) covers those who "write literary material ... where the Company has the right by contract to direct the performance of personal services in writing or preparing such material or in making revisions, modifications, or changes therein" regardless of whether the person is designated an employee or contractor for purposes of federal or state tax or other laws (WGAW 2020 MBA).

But dramatists insisted on creative control, which (ironically) gave the theatre producers leverage. A lawyer named Carl Ring decided to produce (and invested a large sum in) a play about Abraham Lincoln. Ring got into a dispute with the playwrights over Ring making unauthorized changes to the play, known as *Stovepipe Hat*. The playwrights invoked the arbitration provision of the MBA and terminated the production contract. Ring, the producer, sued the play's three authors, their agent, the Dramatists Guild, and the Authors League (an umbrella organization of all professional writers), alleging that the MBA was void because collective action by the Dramatists Guild violated federal antitrust law.

Ring's antitrust suit against Spina and others revived the effort that the producers had dropped in 1927. Ring lost in the trial court, but appealed to the influential federal court of appeals in New York, which expressed considerable doubt over the legality of the Minimum Basic Agreement, but did not definitively decide the issue. Noting that the Basic Agreement prohibited different actions over subsidiary streams of revenue, the Court held that the Agreement appeared to be "an attempt to control the industry", and to fix prices that "is not saved by the high purpose for which it is conceived". Reasoning that the relationship between writer and producer is relatively short, the writer is not paid salary or a wage but instead license fees for the play, and the producer does not control the writer's working conditions or the creation of the play, the Court held that the labor exemption to antitrust law did not apply (*Ring v. Spina*, 148 F.2d 647 (2d Cir. 1945)). The ruling, however, was on a preliminary issue (whether the dispute was subject to an enforceable agreement to arbitration) and not on whether the Dramatists Guild was an illegal conspiracy or on whether the Minimum Basic Agreement was entirely unlawful as a restraint of trade. The court of appeals sent the case back for trial.

While the *Ring v. Spina* litigation dragged on for several more years, the Dramatists Guild and the organization of producers agreed to another MBA in 1946. When, after a partial victory at trial, Ring's suit went back to the federal court of appeals, the judges again declined to address the question whether the Dramatists Guild was an illegal conspiracy in restraint of trade. The jury verdict that the writers had violated antitrust law was the only direct pronouncement on the antitrust issue at any stage of the case, and the court of appeals vacated it because there was insufficient evidence that Ring had suffered any damage (*Ring v. Spina*, 186 F.2d 637 (2d Cir. 1949)). The Guild and the producers were left in the same position they had been in before Ring began the litigation. The producers could contest the Guild's ability to negotiate and the MBA's enforceability whenever it suited them, and the Guild could continue to insist that it and its MBA were entirely lawful. The uncertainty about the legality of the Guild and the contract made it extraordinarily difficult for the parties to negotiate any changes to the MBA, so the terms negotiated in 1961 remained largely unchanged until the 1980s.

As the economics of theatre and the nature of play production changed in the 1970s and thereafter, an independent producer and the president of the New York League of Theatres, Richard Barr, sued the Dramatists Guild alleging again that the MBA was unenforceable and the Guild was unlawful. This time, the dramatists counterclaimed, arguing that the producers themselves had been involved in an antitrust conspiracy against authors. The dramatists' theory was that 70% of theatres were controlled by a single organization, which conspired to fix the compensation paid to playwrights and to insist upon other unfavorable contract terms. After lengthy pretrial proceedings, the parties settled the litigation when they entered a new industry-wide agreement known as the Approved Production Contract in 1985. It significantly changed the terms of the MBA, particularly in reducing how much writers would be paid before investors recouped their initial investment and how royalties were calculated (see Salter 2022).

Meanwhile, the way that plays made their way from the page to the stage changed significantly. Regional theatres, through an organization known as the League of Regional Theatres (LORT), became a significant aspect of the development of commercial theatre. Plays developed in these regional theatres, which are usually operated as tax-exempt non-profits, often are transferred to Broadway, where a few become quite lucrative. LORT sought contractual flexibility in how a work moved from the original author to the regional stage and into subsidiary streams of exploitation, which inclined them to circumvent the cumbersome APC. The Dramatists Guild tried to protect writers by negotiating a uniform agreement with LORT. But LORT resisted (Walsh 2016). As commercial producers had long done, LORT threatened antitrust litigation. The Guild's effort to negotiate a uniform contract with LORT was even resisted by some playwrights who had built long-term relationships with particular theatres and were resistant to a uniform agreement. By late 1992, the protracted negotiations over a uniform agreement had ended. Although the regional theatres declared that collective bargaining would "undermine the steady, positive, productive process that exists between [nonprofit] theatres and playwrights", it was also clear that the regionals had gateway access to the industry and thus considerable influence over negotiations with emerging writers (Fisk and Salter 2022).

By 1990, it was clear to the Dramatists Guild, and to some scholars, that the compromises that playwrights had long tolerated were no longer working (Bassin 1995). The APC had reduced the money playwrights could earn, even on successful New York plays. The royalties some collected for successful plays overshadowed the absence of any guaranteed income for unsuccessful writers. Movie studios were ever more deeply enmeshed in creating Broadway plays; whereas once successful plays became movies, increasingly successful movies became Broadway plays or musicals. Economic changes in the theatre meant many playwrights could not negotiate as individuals from a position of strength. Playwrights had tolerated doubt about their legal rights to negotiate collectively when their economic and cultural power in the industry had enabled some to negotiate effectively and when the power of the Guild was not significantly undermined by legal doubts about the basic agreement and the Guild. But those days were gone. The artistic control playwrights secured through copyright ownership meant more to some than to others, but increasingly copyright ownership seemed unable to deliver financial security.

In Hollywood, by contrast, most writers did not see copyright ownership as a source of creative control or financial security. For young writers, the collectively bargained WGA minimums provided some financial security, and a fair Guild-controlled system for allocating screen credit enabled writers to build the reputation that—along with having a good agent—was the only way to gain whatever degree of financial security that successful writers get. A reputation, in turn, was the leverage that writers had to assert creative control (Fisk and Szalay 2016).

In sum, for much of the history of writing for the stage and screen, antitrust and copyright were the dominating legal regimes for playwrights. Labor law and the work for hire rule of copyright dominated the prospects of screenwriters. (And, of course, in both sectors writers, producers, agents, and others involved in creating works negotiated complex arrangements for compensation, credit, and rights in derivative works.)

But lawyers in the movie business have embraced antitrust law when they considered it in their clients' interest. In 1979, writer Victor Miller signed a brief contract with Manny Company under which Manny employed Miller to write a screenplay that became *Friday the 13th* (1980). In 2016, Miller invoked the rights available to authors under Sect. 203(a) of the Copyright Act to terminate the transfer of his copyright to the production company Manny and its successor, Horror Inc. The companies opposed the effort, asserting that because Miller was a member of the Writers Guild of America when he wrote the script, the work was made for hire under copyright law, and therefore, Miller was not an author with termination of transfer rights. In the companies' view, any writer who is a member of the WGA must be an employee within the meaning of federal labor law and, therefore, must be an employee within the meaning of federal copyright law. The Second Circuit Court of Appeals rejected the contention, concluding that the term employee under copyright law "serves different purposes than do the labor law concepts regarding employment relationships, there is no sound basis for using labor law to override copyright law goals". Rather, the court explained: "That labor law was determined to offer labor protections to independent writers does not have to reduce the protections provided to authors under the Copyright Act" (*Horror Inc. v. Miller*, 15 F.4th 232 (2d Cir. 2021)).

One significance of the ruling in the *Friday the 13th* case is that the same influential federal court of appeals that in *Ring v. Spina* in the 1940s cast doubt on the legality of playwrights bargaining collectively if they are independent contractors who own the copyright in their work has now determined that there is no necessary reason why employee status for purposes of labor law should affect copyright ownership. The court's reasoning signals that henceforward it is possible to argue that writers for stage and screen can, if their working conditions fit the legal test, simultaneously be employees with the legal right to unionize and to enforce collectively bargained agreements, and therefore with the labor exemption to antitrust law, and be independent contractors for purposes of copyright law who own their copyrights. If writers are independent contractors, they own the copyright unless or until they sign an agreement stating that the work is specially commissioned for use as part of a motion picture under Sect. 101(2), or an agreement transferring the copyright (in the case of a play).

As a practical matter, the case gives the screenwriter who sold a script for a sum that turns out to have been small relative to the later success of the movie a chance to negotiate for back-end payments. The company that owns the copyright to *Friday the 13th* will have to decide whether to pay Miller for the continued use of his contribution to the movie, which would be necessary to allow continued distribution of the film, or whether they will decline to pay and allow him to block further distribution based on unauthorized continued use of his script.

28.5 Authors, Owners, and the Role of Mediating Institutions in Collaborative Creation

In both theatre and film and TV, the most significant feature of the creator-producer relationship is that it is not a dyad. Rather, as Salter has shown, mediating institutions play a crucial role (Salter 2022). In Hollywood, talent agents are the essential broker between writers and production companies. Research showed that writers represented by the dominant agencies "had substantially higher levels of career success than did writers with comparable track records who were not represented by such agencies" (Bielby and Bielby 1993). The dominant agencies had transcended the traditional role of broker between talent and producer, and instead had begun initiating projects by *packaging* talent (including writer, director, and actors) and became investors in the project. By 2014, according to a study commissioned by the WGA, the consolidation of agencies into four behemoths (William Morris Entertainment (WME), Creative Artists Agency (CAA), United Talent Agency (UTA), and International Creative Management (ICM)), the disappearance of mid-sized agencies, the rise of packaging, and the studios' preference for film franchises and sequels and for making fewer movies overall adversely affected the careers of film writers, especially those not represented by the dominant agencies. Moreover, women and people of color were substantially underrepresented in film and TV writing as compared to the population as a whole (Bielby 2015).

Talent agencies fundamentally changed their structure and business model since the 1970s. Traditionally, agents worked on commissions paid by clients; the amount was capped at 10% by state law and by regulation of the WGA and the Screen Actors Guild (now SAG-AFTRA) (Smith 2020). Packaging, however, led to fees paid directly from the producers to the agents. As revenues from packaging fees led to growth in the largest agencies' wealth and influence, they diversified their business model, creating affiliate production companies to produce and own movies and shows themselves, which in turn attracted outside investment. "The result is that the most powerful talent agencies now operate more as divisions of vertically-integrated corporate conglomerates than as independent firms in the business of individual artist representation" (Smith 2020). That led to a conflict of interest between the agency and the client, as the agency was no longer an independent broker between the writer and the producer, but was instead in the role of producer itself (Smith 2020; Emerson 2021). Recently, one of the significant functions that the WGA has played in Hollywood is to enable writers to assert collective strength in the face of the countervailing power of their agents.

The talent guilds have long sought to use the collective power of their members to force agencies to avoid practices that compromised their loyalty to their clients. They adopted regulations enforced by an arrangement by which the Guilds would recognize only those agents that adhered to the Guild regulation prohibiting conflicts of interest. As the big agencies moved from packaging into production and their outside investors exerted ever more control over the agency's business, the WGA's 1976 Artists' Manager Basic Agreement (AMBA) came up for renewal in 2019, setting the stage for a showdown between writers and their agents. Writers had witnessed what happened since 2001 when the Association of Talent Agencies refused to adhere to the SAG rule limiting agency conflicts of interest and the SAG board suspended the Guild rule forbidding members from signing with non-franchised agents: outside investment in the large agencies exploded, with several coming under majority control of outside investors, and SAG lost any leverage it had to prevent agency conflicts of interest (Smith 2020). In 2018, therefore, WGA announced its intent to renegotiate the 1976 AMBA for the first time in 43 years and proposed eliminating agency packaging and affiliate producing and returning to a traditional commission system. In April 2019, after the WGA membership voted overwhelmingly in favor of a new Code of Conduct that prohibited writers from signing with agents that engaged in packaging and producing, and the ATA and the big agencies refused to agree, over 7,000 of the WGA's 8,800 active members fired their agents (Emerson 2021).

Then, the WGA and several big-name TV writers sued the big four agencies for breach of fiduciary duty (Smith 2020). The ATA and the agencies responded with their own suit charging that the WGA and writers' plan—the mass firing of agents, concerted refusal to deal with noncompliant agencies, and guidance to use individual lawyers rather than the agencies to negotiate contracts—violated federal antitrust law, state unfair competition law, and the California Talent Agencies Act (Emerson 2021). Just as the producers have long done in theatre, the agents asserted that the writers' collective action was unlawful combination, conveniently overlooking their own threat to blacklist all writers who fired their agents, their own argument that only licensed talent agents, not licensed lawyers, were authorized to represent talent, and the fact that their own vertical integration and domination of the market for talent and the production and distribution of films and TV were highly concentrated. While the litigation continued in court, writers and producers met directly—through WGA-supported internet submission boards and Twitter boosts, and at in-person mixers around Los Angeles—to pitch projects and discuss employment (Emerson 2021). In the summer of 2019, smaller agencies began capitulating and signed the WGA's new Code of Conduct. The first of the big agencies, UTA, signed in July 2020. In December 2020, the same day that the federal judge presiding over the antitrust litigation denied a preliminary injunction that would have ended the WGA's boycott of the agencies, the executive director of the Directors Guild of America (DGA) weighed in on the side of the WGA, asserting that agencies' continued conflicts of interest is "exceedingly important to the DGA and our members" and "not acceptable to the DGA. Absent prompt resolution, we intend to take all necessary and appropriate steps to protect our members" (Robb 2021). Finally, by early February 2021, all of the major talent agencies had signed. Both the WGA and the agencies dropped their litigation against each other without resolving whether the writers or the agencies had engaged in unlawfully anticompetitive practices (Robb 2021).

The settlement of the dispute with the agents gives the WGA an ongoing role in ensuring that agencies comply with the Code of Conduct. The agencies are required to provide information to the WGA to enable it to address issues about timeliness of payment to writers and requests to perform uncompensated work and to ensure that the WGA can monitor financing of agency ownership transactions to protect against a conflict of interest. And they reserved the right of the WGA to suspend the agencies' ability to represent writers if the agencies failed to adhere to the agreement. Acknowledging its status as a labor union, the WGA negotiating committee email to WGA members explaining the settlement closed: "In solidarity" (Robb 2021).

28.6 Conclusion

Theatre, film, and television are highly concentrated industries on the production side. In theatre, for well over a century a few major companies have controlled first-run commercial theatres in New York and around the United States (Salter 2022). In screen entertainment, although companies have come and gone over the years, from the Classic Hollywood days when there were five major studios and three slightly less dominant ones, through the days of the three major television networks, and down to today, production and distribution have tended to be concentrated. Even in today's landscape of a huge number of streaming platforms distributing an unprecedented number of scripted television programs, the move to concentration continues as the four dominant talent agencies sought to control the hiring, production, and distribution of content. For a century, writers for the stage and screen have sought to match the concentration on the employment side with collective action on their side.

But the legal constraints on writer collective action have been quite different in theatre than in film and TV. Theatre production companies have effectively wielded federal antitrust law to curtail the Dramatists Guild's power to represent the interests of playwrights and dramaturgs. In film and TV, by contrast, all writers have a federally protected right to unionize and bargain collectively which gives them an exemption from antitrust restrictions on collective action. Theatre producers have successfully threatened playwrights that to unionize would jeopardize their continued ability to own the copyrights in their work, and have long pointed to Hollywood, where most scripts are written as works made for hire under federal copyright law, which makes the production company or studio the author and owner of the script. Copyright's work for hire doctrine, it is said, is what enables the serial rewriting and loss of artistic control and creative autonomy that playwrights have long prized.

Two recent developments reveal tensions in these legal and institutional arrangements. First, the Second Circuit Court of Appeals, one of the two most influential federal appellate courts in matters of copyright law, ruled in 2021 that a film writer's membership in the WGA is irrelevant to whether a script was a work made for hire. This means that a writer could be an independent contractor (and thus an author and owner) for copyright purposes even while being an employee for labor and, therefore, antitrust purposes. That could create an opening for stage writers to join all other talent and craft workers in theatre and seek the benefits of unionization and secure the legal certainty that the Directors Guild's 1985 APC is legally valid and enforceable.

On the other side, the powerful corporations that hire writers proved willing during the 2018–2021 dispute between writers and talent agencies to invoke antitrust law to limit the ability of the WGA and writers to act collectively in any circumstance except the traditional triennial negotiation of the Minimum Basic Agreements governing film and TV writing. Although the talent agencies dispute ended with a victory for the writers because of their solidarity in refusing to deal with agents who had egregious conflicts of interest, and because the judge presiding over the litigation refused to order the writers to end their boycott, lawyers for business groups have filed antitrust suits against worker collective action outside of the creative industries and have had some success in persuading courts to limit the antitrust exemption to traditional employees.

Although the complex web of copyright, labor, and antitrust law both empowers and constrains writers and producers in film, TV, and theatre, the settlements of both recent and long-running disputes reveal at least one thing. Whatever the law may be, writers and the companies that hire them share an interest in developing a framework that allows the continued production and distribution of entertainment. They have long been motivated to put aside their wrangling so they can put on a show.

References

Banks, Miranda. 2014. *The Writers: A History of American Screenwriters and Their Guild*. New Brunswick NJ: Rutgers University Press.

Barnouw, Erik. 1996. *Media Marathon: A Twentieth-Century Memoir*. Durham NC: Duke University Press.

Bassin, Joel. 1995. "The Minimum Basic Agreement of the Dramatists' Guild: A History of Inadequate Protection." *Journal of Arts Management Law & Society* 25: 157.

Bielby, Denise. 2015. "Talent Agencies and the Market for Screenwriters: From the Origins of Packaging to Today's Transformations." In *Brokerage and Production in the American and French Entertainment Industries: Invisible Hands in Cultural Markets*, edited by Violaine Roussel and Denise Bielby, 23–54. Lanham MD: Lexington Books.

Bielby, William, and Denise Bielby. 1999. "Organizational Mediation of Project-Based Labor Markets: Talent Agencies and the Careers of Screenwriters." *American Sociological Review* 64: 64–85.

Emerson, Tyler. 2021. "Litigators and Dealmakers: A Comprehensive Critique of the California Labor Commission's *Solis* Decision and the Talent Agencies Act in the Context of the 2018–2019 WGA-ATA Packaging Dispute." *Hastings Communications and Entertainment Law Journal* 43: 1–58.

Fisk, Catherine L., and Michael Szalay. 2017 [2016]. "Story Work: Nonproprietary Autonomy and Contemporary Television Writing." *Television and New Media* (*TVNM*) 18 (7): 605–20. https://doi.org/10.1177/1527476416652693.

Fisk, Catherine L. 2016. *Writing for Hire: Unions, Hollywood, and Madison Avenue*. Cambridge MA: Harvard University Press.

Fisk, Catherine L., and Brent Salter. 2022. "Assumptions About Antitrust and Freelance Work and the Fragility of Labor Relations in American Theatre." *Ohio State Law Journal* 83 (2): 217–82.

Friday the 13th. 1980. Written by Victor Miller. Directed by Sean S. Cunningham. USA: Georgetown Productions Inc.

Maxwell, J. 2008. "Making a Federal Case for Copyrighting Stage Directions: *Einhorn v. Mergatroyd*." *John Marshall Review of Intellectual Property Law* 7: 393.

Middleton, George. 2021 [1947]. *These Things Are Mine: The Autobiography of a Journeyman Playwright*. Stoke-on-Trent, UK: Hassel Street Press.

Robb, David. 2021. "WME Signs WGA Franchise Agreement, Giving Guild Historic Win in Campaign to Reshape Talent Agency Business." *Deadline*. 5 February. https://deadline.com/2021/02/wme-signs-writers-guild-deal-WGA-reshapes-talent-agency-business-1234688833/. Accessed 14 December 2021.

Salter, Brent. 2022. *Negotiating Copyright in the American Theatre: 1856–1951*. New York: Cambridge University Press.

Smith, Brian T. 2020. "Sending Agents to the Principal's Office: How Talent Agency Packaging and Producing Breach the Fiduciary Duties Agents Owe Their Artist-Clients." *UCLA Entertainment Law Review* 27: 173–225.

Walsh, Thomas. 2016. *Playwrights and Power: The Making of the Dramatists Guild*. Hanover NH: Smith & Krauss.

PART IV: How

Approaches to Screen Storytelling

CHAPTER 29

Random Access Memories: Screenwriting for Games

Colin Harvey

29.1 Introduction

In this chapter, I will explore the theory and practice surrounding the creation of screenplays for video game media, with a particular emphasis on the manifold ways in which both collective memory and subjective memory inform the creation of video game stories. I'll draw on my ongoing interest in memory as a creative and analytical tool to discuss how games both embrace and resist storytelling approaches from other media, particularly cinema. I'll discuss this at both a representational level and in terms of the production processes game development *remembers* and adapts from other storytelling media.

As a professional video game screenwriter and researcher studying the relationship of storytelling and play in video games, I'll take an autoethnographic approach throughout, weaving in my own biography as a creator, consumer and analyst of video game stories and related transmedia narratives. I'll outline some of the components utilized in the communicating of game stories and explore the narrative processes involved in implementing those elements, as well as discussing the intimately related practices of game writing and narrative design. I'll then move on to discuss two case studies of games that I've written and narrative designed: *Sniper Elite 4* (Rebellion Developments 2017) and *Blood and Truth* (Sony Interactive Entertainment 2019).

C. Harvey (✉)
Videogame Writer, London, UK
e-mail: colinharvey@colinharvey.net

29.2 Memory Games

The intersections between subjective and collective memory were of concern to French sociologist Maurice Halbwachs, a key figure for the contemporary field of Cultural Memory (Erll 2011, 14–18). As Astrid Erll explains, Halbwachs saw individual memory as dependent on social structures; advocated the importance of intergenerational memory; and gave prominence to the role of cultural transmission and tradition. Much more recently, Anna Reading has explored how digital connectivity has complicated such discussions still further by allowing individuals to easily and rapidly transform subjective experience *into* collective experience (2016, 106–107).

As a writer working in the field of games, my memory and understanding of the codes and conventions of screenwriting for this medium are constantly interpolated by my personal experience of the medium and vice versa, as well as the wider network of relations of which we are all a part. Such relations might be cultural, social, energetic and/or material in their nature. As I will show, my prior experience of playing games and of other media, together with my own autobiography, constantly feed and interpolate my creation of video game stories.

I won my first home computer in a competition organized by the *Daily Express* newspaper and the electronics chain Laskys. It was 1983 and I was eleven years old. At that stage, no-one I knew owned a home computer. My prize—an Atari 800—sat on the floor in the corner of our family sitting room, underneath our rented DER television set. After school each evening I would kneel (and often lie down), typing in programs from the manual that came with the computer and from magazines. My dad would look on, cigarette in hand, while I entered programs from the Atari manual intended to generate a stars-and-stripes American flag or a simple *blues* musical score.

This was the era of the text adventure. I would routinely go to my friend Michael Halford's house to play the computer game adaptation of *The Hobbit* (Melbourne House 1983) on his Commodore 64, which would offer up some crude graphics along with text descriptions and the ability to make simple choices that would affect the unfolding of the narrative, along the lines of "LOOK" and "GO NORTH". The text adventure genre was very similar to the *Choose Your Own Adventure* books that were also popular at this time, supplying the player/reader a branching narrative to explore. Though my coding abilities were extremely limited, I began experimenting with creating my own text adventures. Very quickly I discovered the challenge of the branching form, in that paths would quickly proliferate, necessitating a huge amount of writing on the part of the author.

On the plus side, I also noticed that the assignment of variables meant it was possible to make the game *remember* a player's choice which could then be called upon at a later point. For instance, if the player chooses to pick up a sword early in the adventure, then because "SWORD = 1" they can then use this to defeat the dragon at a subsequent juncture in the game. If they instead chose not to pick up the sword so that "SWORD = 0", then the encounter with the dragon would play out very differently.

A few years later, while studying screenwriting as part of my undergraduate degree, I would notice the similarity between the process of assigning and recalling variables with the *setup* and *payoff* mechanic indicated by theorist Robert McKee in relation to movie screenplays:

> To express our vision scene by scene we crack open the surface of our fictional reality and send the audience back to gain insight. These insights, therefore, must be shaped into *Setups* and *Payoffs*. To set up means to layer in knowledge; to pay off means to close the gap by delivering that knowledge to the audience. When the gap between expectation and result propels the audience back through the story seeking answers, it can only find them if the writer has prepared or planted these insights in the work. (1999, 238–39, emphasis in original)

Like McKee, I see the importance of setups and payoffs in ensuring that the story possesses the requisite emotional and ironic charge. However, the spatial, non-linear nature of many interactive environments can make the deployment of setups and payoffs challenging for game writers and interactive fiction writers, since the player may not necessarily encounter these elements in a predefined order as they would in a more conventionally organized sequential story (and this of course includes novels, films and theatre productions that play with the chronology of their stories). The particular challenge of non-linear setups and payoffs in interactive contexts would become—and continues to be—an ongoing fascination for me. In the context of games, the success of a setup/payoff arrangement relies on the memory of both player and game to succeed. As a result, the relationship between setup and payoff will differ from player to player.

Beyond this example, my memories of the structural formation of these early games continue to inform my approach to game writing and narrative design. As I'll show in the course of my case studies, structural formation plays a key role in framing narrative experience and in helping a player inhabit the role of a specific character as well as shaping the development of memory throughout the game. Memories of other factors, like genre and use of time and space, also exert considerable influence over my creative process, whether I'm consciously aware of them or not.

29.3 Terminology and Technology

Prior to exploring further some of the considerations I've touched upon in the preceding Memory Games section, I'll outline some key contextual information concerning narrative design and writing for games. Many contemporary video games constitute highly complex narrative ecologies. Different game studios take different approaches to the implementation of narrative, partly driven by the role of narrative in the project they are making and partly driven by other concerns, including the studio's existing approach to implementing narrative. A key factor in this is undoubtedly the element that differentiates video games from other screen-based, storytelling media: the technological nature of games, particularly the interface and the manifold ways in which this interface can be used to control the game.

This adds a layer of complexity to storytelling discussions that is absent from other screen media. For instance, genre is doubly articulated in relation to games—we might talk about a science fiction game, but it is important to know whether the science fiction game in question is an Action Role-Playing Game or a futuristic racing game or some other variation (Wolf 2001, 113–34). Unlike other storytelling media like novels or films where codes and conventions remain much more fixed, the ever-changing nature of gaming technology means that the medium and how we talk about aspects of the medium are always to some extent in flux. As Kline, Dyer-Witheford and De Peuter note, video games exist at the intersection between "technology", "marketing" and "culture" (2003, 58).

The sheer diversity of game types, and studios' approaches to making games, means that processes often differ considerably as well. There is, famously, no standard screenplay format for games in the way we might expect from film, television or radio. This is not to say that commonalities in approach don't exist—rather that each project is liable to force those involved in creating the project to constantly rethink their approaches, and tailor them accordingly.

Related to this, a key part of my discussion in this chapter will examine the ways in which games emulate production processes undertaken in other media (notably cinema) and the points at which such processes cease to be applicable. It is also worth bearing in mind that many games are not driven by narrative at all, and that for a lot of games story is very much a secondary consideration. Indeed, lots of critically and commercially successful games have only a glancing relationship with storytelling as we conventionally understand it, and some none at all.

29.4 STORYTELLING IN VIDEO GAMES

As indicated above, interactivity is an obvious, key differentiating factor between games and other storytelling media like films. I've written elsewhere that this should not be taken to suggest that other media are somehow *passive*, since there's a substantial body of research indicating that this is very much not the case. Indeed, to suggest otherwise is to engage in a reader-text binarism that has been heavily challenged since the so-called *affective turn*.[1] The interface and means by which a player interacts with a game render the medium

---

[1] This refers to the point in recent history at which theorists working in multiple disciplines embraced the concept of "affect" to describe the drives, motivations, feelings and emotions which constitute human experience (Damasio 2003, 8). Key figures in this field include Gilles Deleuze and Felix Guattari, whose work responds to that of the seventeenth-century philosopher Baruch Spinoza.

explicitly and obviously experiential—but other storytelling media such as films, theatre plays and novels are also experiential, just in different ways (Harvey 2015, 117–19).

As a background to this conversation, it's worth mentioning that the interrelationship between storytelling and playing in video games was the dominant debate within the nascent field of Game Studies since its inception at the beginning of the new century. Indeed, my own PhD—conferred in 2009—explores exactly this tension, using a theoretical approach embedded in affect and memory. The first PhD to be awarded in this area was, however, much earlier. Mary Ann Buckles's 1985 doctoral thesis applied Vladimir Propp's morphology of folktales to the sword and sorcery themed text game *Adventure* from 1976. Buckles concludes that Propp's approach is of only very limited assistance in helping understand the game (1985, 125).

The debate around storytelling in games and how it should be understood was forcefully articulated at the seminal Game Cultures Conference at the University of the West of England in 2001. This event saw a clash between those propounding a more narrative-focussed understanding of games—the *narratology* or *narrativist* camp—and those who preferred to see games from more of an experiential, rule-based perspective, the so-called *ludologists*. Subsequent coverage by the gaming magazine *Edge* helped crystallize the debate around this supposed ludology-narratology dichotomy. However, Gonzalo Frasca, a key figure identified with the ludology camp, rejected this binary, suggesting this was a phantom debate engineered by the media (2003).

Norwegian scholar Espen Aarseth's ground-breaking work provided one of the most important keys to understanding the role of storytelling in games and other interactive media. Aarseth's concept of the "ergodic" identifies interactive stories in terms of the "non-trivial effort" required to engage with them (1997, 1). It's possible—as Aarseth does—to identify other kinds of storytelling as ergodic, beyond story-driven video games, such as experimental novels and theatre. The ergodic remains an invaluable tool within the field of game studies and cognate fields.

Even if the narrativist-ludology debate was initially exaggerated by the media, it's also true that subsequent theorists tended to identify around these two tendencies or sought to offer compromise approaches synthesizing both positions. In the context of professional games development, the tensions between gameplay and story remain ongoing, live issues, articulated in all kinds of ways and which I encounter routinely in my day-to-day work.

Clint Hocking, former Creative Director at LucasArts and subsequently Ubisoft, identified the term "ludonarrative dissonance" to describe situations where story and gameplay function in opposition with one another, and these terms continue to be actively discussed within the field (2007). In fact, I would argue that such issues are not to be shied away from, but rather enthusiastically embraced. The challenge of fusing story and gameplay is integral to the medium—bringing to it richness and complexity—and a key motivating factor for writers and narrative designers who choose to work in games.

29.5 The Complexity of Games

As already indicated, contemporary video games are often highly complex narrative ecologies, containing multiple strands of storytelling and multiple methods by which these strands are communicated. In the contemporary field of game studies and the industry itself, there's an increased understanding that this complexity makes a simple bifurcation between story and play difficult to sustain.

In some areas, however, this complexity is less understood. Game reviewers will often alight on those elements which fit a definition of *story* remembered from other visual media like television or cinema. Cut scenes, sequences in which story is dramatized and which often look most readily like cinema sequences, are the most obvious examples. Indeed, such sequences do tend to be used for the most significant narrative beats. Historically, these sequences have been non-interactive, although increasingly developers have sought to introduce some level of interactivity, perhaps as a means of tutorializing the game's controls, or as a way of keeping the player active and engaged.

Cut sequences are the most expensive elements of narrative within games. Depending on the kind of game, they are often given prominence in story-led trailers. The complexity and expense of cut scenes means that once the scenes in question have been captured, it's extremely unlikely they'll be *reshot* and possibilities for amending the content after the fact tend to be limited. This can be an issue because, unlike the film and television industries' hierarchical approach in which the screenplay comes before everything else, the games industry tends to favour what we might call *parallel development*.

In other words, while the story is being developed, the script being written and actors' performances captured, other disciplines might be prototyping and exploring possibilities which if successful will dictate the direction of the project. So for instance, the art team might be building characters, while design might be constructing levels and the coding team might be experimenting with new approaches to NPC behaviour (that is, Non-Playable Characters, which I'll talk about in more depth below). From a narrative perspective, this means that the story and aspects of the worldbuilding might need to be changed to accommodate input from these other disciplines. If the more *front and centre* material has already been captured, the rest of the story will have to flex and adapt to incorporate these changes.

Cut scenes, then, are expensive and impressive and often used to promote games to potential audiences. However, as I've alluded to, contemporary games are complex and often use a wide range of other mechanisms to deliver story content. These include in-game interactive sequences in which players are able to converse with characters, perhaps using dialogue trees to select their responses; *discoverable* documents that the player might come across in their explorations, and which give might give background information about the world, the characters or the plot; and User Interface (UI) content, on screen text or illustrations that might provide diegetic or non-diegetic story information. As Ross Berger observes, unlike cut scenes which are "expensive and rigid", devices such as dialogue trees and collectible items are far easier to change, and so much more *likely* to be changed if they're not sufficiently appealing to players (2020, 28–29). It's worth saying, though, that this kind of flexibility has benefits for the writer as well, allowing them to modify or completely alter story beats for creative reasons.

29.6 CHARACTERS

Functionally speaking, there are two kinds of character in a video game—those you control and those that you don't. The player-character or avatar is the focal point for the player in the game space, allowing them to interact with the world around them. This character might be a representation of a human being, but it might equally be a robot or dog or a car, a plane or a spaceship. In the case of Virtual Reality games, the avatar frequently takes the form of a pair of disembodied hands. In games where story is non-existent or barely exists, this focal point might be something altogether more abstract, and it might constantly change, like the tessellating blocks in the original *Tetris* (Pazhnitov 1989).

As the player's key point of focus, one of the primary purposes of the avatar is to "stitch" together cut scenes, the non-interactive elements of the game, with the interactive, gameplay elements. For instance, *The Last of Us Part 2* begins with one of the main characters, Joel, explaining the climactic events of the previous game to his brother Tommy in a non-interactive sequence. The player then takes control of Joel as he rides his horse through the environment with Tommy while the opening credits play. Julian Holland Oliver describes the avatar as a kind of "dynamic suture", a focal point for making the movement from non-interactive to interactive and vice versa as seamless as possible (2001).

Another lively debate within narrative development for games centres around the idea of the protagonist, and whether theories drawn from conventionally sequential, superficially non-interactive media like film and theatre can be mapped onto the avatar. A protagonist in a film or theatre play will do what the writer, director and cast have decreed the protagonist should do. The same does not necessarily hold true for an avatar in an explicitly interactive story. A player-character may have a stated objective for a level or mission, but the player's ability to control this character means they don't necessarily need to adhere to these objectives (though the game may punish them if they don't).

As with so many of these debates, the answer is almost certainly driven by context. Some games allow a player much more agency than others. So-called *sandbox* games like the *Grand Theft Auto* series (1997–present) or *Cyberpunk 2077* give players the ability to explore massive worlds and to encounter and create multiple situations. Other games like the branching science fiction adventure *Detroit: Become Human* carefully circumscribe the choices available to the player.

For game writers and narrative designers, aligning the objectives and super-objective of the protagonist with the needs of moment-to-moment gameplay represents a major, ongoing challenge. The skill of the game writer or narrative designer often obtains in this ability to *wrap* gameplay objectives up in such a way that they make sense in terms of the wider story—although ideally the writer/narrative designer will have played a part in shaping these objectives in the first place. Despite these efforts, some degree of ludonarrative dissonance is sometimes inevitable and certainly commonplace within many games featuring story elements.

As the name suggests, Non-Playable Characters are not controlled by the player but rather by the game's AI or scripts (Ince 2006, 170). NPCs can often, however, be interacted with by the player, although the nature of this interaction can differ markedly depending on the character and the game. In the crudest sense, this might mean killing the NPC, as is the case with many varieties of game, notably first-person shooters. Once again, context is vital: many games offer the ability to interact with NPCs in other ways than just combat. These might include the ability to talk to an NPC by cycling through a menu of dialogue choices, as in *Deus Ex* or *Disco Elysium*. Often a player-character is required to carry out a task for an NPC, as is the case with the *Fable* games.

A key challenge for the writer and narrative designer is that interactions with NPCs might have to be systematized in some way. The most obvious example of these are "barks", short lines that play when a player-character has alerted enemy NPCs to their presence (Berger 2020, 16–17). These will invariably differ depending on whether an NPC is only mildly aware of the player-character's presence and is hunting them, or whether the player-character is in full-throated battle with the NPC(s) in question. Game writers will be tasked with writing multiple barks based on these distinctions, e.g. a *cautious* bark to indicate the NPC is becoming aware of the player's presence, or a *combat* bark to indicate that the NPC and the player are fighting.

Hearing the same bark over and over again is a particular problem, since it can grate upon the player and thus ruin their immersion in the game world. There are a number of ways of dealing with this. The most obvious is for the writer(s) to generate multiple versions of a dialogue line conveying the same essential meaning. Further variety can be afforded by employing a range of actors with distinct voices. The sound design team, in collaboration with Quality Assurance, can work to identify when a particular bark is triggering too often or not enough, and then seek to mitigate the problem.

Though barks are often considered the least glamorous aspect of game writing and narrative design, as C. J. Kershner points out, in open world games the player is liable to be exposed to more of this kind of writing than any other, and certainly more than that provided by expensive cut scenes constituting a relatively minor component of the overall game experience (2016).

29.7 Game Writers and Narrative Designers

This complexity means in turn that the roles associated with the creation of story material for games are multiple and often attuned to the nature of the specific project. Screenwriting for games is therefore a broad category. It might include creating a screenplay akin to that of a film or television script in which the story is told primarily through cut scenes. Additionally, it might include supplying written material for branching sequences in which the player can choose which action or path to take, or the creation of dialogue for interactive conversations in which the player can converse with characters in the game.

Clearly, though, story development for games isn't just concerned with the generation of written material. As well as the many disciplines involved in the creation and development of story, the specific role of *narrative designer* has emerged across the industry. The American writer, artist and academic Stephen Dinehart originated the job title and concept of the *Narrative Designer* in 2006 on behalf of game developer THQ and was subsequently offered the role. As related on his website, the job description Dinehart originally wrote indicates that "The Narrative Designer will focus on ensuring that the key elements of the player experience associated with story and story telling [sic] devices, script and speech are dynamic, exciting and compelling" (2021). As with game writing, the role of narrative designer can differ markedly from project to project, and studio to studio.

There's a great deal of crossover between the role of game writer and narrative designer, but it's possible to differentiate the two jobs around particular emphasizes. We might see game writing as primarily temporally-based, involving the creation of story material that travels forwards in a sequential manner. The creation of the story's plot, the structuring of that plot and the resulting screenplay might be understood as mainly temporal in their conception and execution. As previously discussed, cut scenes are largely and sometimes wholly non-interactive, and can be written in screenplay format, following a sequential structure familiar from cinema and television. Such sequences unfold in a temporal fashion, moving from beginning to end with little or no opportunity for exploration on the part of the player.

Conversely, some of the other forms of narrative delivery I've already described might be better understood as primarily spatial in their execution, since they rely on the player's exploration of the environment—these days often a three-dimensional environment operating on the Z-axis—such as collectible documents. Often these might be unrelated to game progression, perhaps adding flavour to the game world or embellishing character relationships.

Alternatively, the acquisition of secret plans, for instance, might be a major objective that the player has to fulfil in order to progress the game. The design and execution of these elements might be understood as spatial and therefore fall more under the remit of the narrative designer. Written content for collectible documents, in-game dialogue and barks might equally be created by the narrative designer as the game writer, though the act of *placing* these elements within a spatial environment falls more obviously under the category of narrative design.

29.8   CASE STUDY 1: *SNIPER ELITE 4*

Developed by Rebellion and published in 2017, *Sniper Elite 4* is the fourth instalment in a first-person shooter game series set in World War II and which began in 2005. It's an open world game taking place in Italy in 1943. The player assumes the role of Karl Fairburne, a British sniper working for the Special Operations Executive. Since the first game in the saga is set during the Allied sweep through Germany at the conclusion of the war, both *Sniper Elite 3* and *Sniper Elite 4* function as prequels in Fairburne's timeline.

As is common in video game development, I joined the project as Narrative Designer part way through the development process, when the levels and many of the key art assets had already been created. The *Sniper Elite* franchise is marked by an emphasis on historical accuracy, particularly with regard to the uniforms, equipment and weaponry depicted. This emphasis exists in tension with the primary need for fun and satisfying gameplay, and the necessity to tell a dramatically engaging story.

Early in the development process, a number of key elements were decided upon. Since the setting was Italy, it was important that the game should reflect—as far as possible—the real-life narrative of the Italian campaign. Prior to my joining the project, it had been decided that Southern Italy would provide a more visually interesting setting to explore and more gameplay opportunities. Unfortunately, this didn't quite reconcile with the history of the Partisan movement, which was another key element we wanted to include, since resistance to the Fascists was primarily restricted to the north of the country, following the Allied invasion.

The notable exception to this was Naples, and I ended up drawing extensively on the book *Four Days of Naples* (1979) by Aubrey Menen in the narrative design for the game. Menen's book recounts how the homeless youth of Naples played a pivotal role in assisting the overthrow of Nazi and Fascist forces during the invasion of Italy by Allied forces in 1943. While the story of *Sniper Elite 4* doesn't attempt to retell these real-world events, the game does use them as a starting point for explaining Partisan resistance in the south of the country, when in reality that was primarily focussed in the north of the country later in the timeline. In many ways, Menen's book might be seen as a corrective to the dominant collective memory of resistance in Italy during World War II, providing some evidence of an important counter-narrative.

My creative approach to *Sniper Elite 4* was heavily informed by famed screenwriter William Goldman's account in *Adventures in the Screen Trade* (1990) of his challenges adapting the book version of *A Bridge Too Far* to the screen for the 1977 film version. Goldman talks extensively about his approach to reconciling the facts of the Allies' unsuccessful Operation Market Garden military operation in World War II with the requirements of telling a gripping, pacy Hollywood narrative.

Sniper Elite 4's open world nature means it is not a branching narrative in the sense I have already described and which we would understand from a Choose Your Own Adventure book, or a recent branching game like *Detroit: Become Human*. In *Sniper Elite 4*, a player can choose which route they take across an island, for instance, or through a town. Such decisions might mean the player alerts enemy combatants—triggering appropriate barks of course—or conversely that they manage to slip past unnoticed. Equally, it might mean the player stumbles across useful resources like weapons that can be used in other contexts.

The game provides the narrative context through the audiovisual environment, including dialogue spoken by the player-character Karl Fairburne and by other characters the player encounters including barks but also *overheard* conversations. Some elements the player meets might carry more narrative weight than others. For instance, in one level, the player comes across a crashed aircraft being guarded by Nazi soldiers. The player has a series of connected objectives that they need to carry out to complete this part of the mission successfully. Since the order in which the player undertakes these tasks is to some extent up to them, they might be perceived as *ergodically* creating their own story, or at least unpacking the story in their own way.

Along the way, the player can find collectible documents. It's not necessary to read these documents to either understand gameplay or the main narrative thread—the one told through interactive or non-interactive cut sequences—and many players choose not to. Some documents are primarily gameplay-led, giving details about patrol routes which might be of use to more strategic players. In contrast, a huge number of documents are letters. "Last Letters", for instance, are inspired by the real-life letters that soldiers would write to their loved ones in the event of their deaths. These can be collected from NPCs upon their death, and as with other documents, the player can choose whether to read these or not.

Many Last Letters are self-contained, telling a complete mini story within the space of the document. In writing these, I researched real-world examples as much as possible. Through these letters, I attempted to explore some of the complexities of war by provoking different emotional responses from players. Some attempt to move players by highlighting the age—either very young or very old—of the dead individual or by suggesting a bereaved husband or wife, son, daughter, mother or father. Others are valedictory and defiant, indicative of the expansionist, imperialist and genocidal objectives of the Nazis, and the associated propaganda. Other letters tend towards the humorous.

Unsurprisingly, amongst those players who chose to engage with these documents, responses were many and varied. Some players were irked that they were made to feel guilty for killing an enemy combatant, while others appreciated the *fleshing out* of characters who would otherwise simply have been target-fodder. Intriguingly, a *YouTube* video put together by fans of the game presents the letters against an orchestral soundtrack, framing them as though they're real documents, and beginning with a title caption "Dedicated to All Soldiers, Past Present and Future" (Chadtopia 2017).

Respondents to the video seem to be articulating their subjective memory of playing the game with the collective memory of the battlefield drawn from the wider culture. A number of respondents discuss their emotional responses to the documents, including one respondent who talks about feeling "guilty killing them" (Matt M 2019). Unlike other documents, Last Letters are only available to be collected and read if the player does indeed kill the NPC carrying them. Players' ergodic understanding of the story is therefore predicated on whether they *choose* to read the document or simply ignore its content.

Collectible documents highlight the particular challenges of shaping memory in a non-linear environment. Some documents are linked and designed to be engaged with in any order. This meant that I had to pay careful attention to my construction of setups and payoffs, understanding that the non-linear way in which some players might engage with them might invert their function. Many of these connected documents provide background details that flesh out the main storyline, creating a much more complex narrative ecology than is necessarily apparent from the cut sequences alone. These documents also provide connecting tissue between this game and other games in the series, anticipating future events, as well as connecting to the prequel comic *Andartes*, which I also wrote and which tells Karl's story immediately prior to *Sniper Elite 4*.

In one instance, the player encounters a Partisan soldier called Lucio in a number of interactive cut sequences. For reasons of cost, Lucio had to be cut from the main storyline, leaving me with no means of resolving his character arc. However, later in the development cycle, designers created a side mission in which a group of Partisans are attempting to defend a watermill against attack by Nazis and Italian Fascists. Without the player's help, the Partisans will undoubtedly be wiped out. Since the heads of the Partisans were stock art assets, I requested that Lucio's head be swapped onto one of the bodies, in order to activate the player's memory of this character in the game.

I then set about making sure that discoverable collectible documents told the story of this character, with the intention that if the player engages fully with his story, this will affect their relationship with the character (and potentially influence the player's decision as to whether to aid him and his fellow Partisans in defending the watermill when they later recall this relationship). Additionally, I made sure that Karl's dialogue in this encounter reinforced the identity of the lead Partisan but also offers the player a choice: "Lucio—maybe I should stay and help him fight". The player can help Lucio or use the firefight as a distraction, concentrating instead on the main mission.

This is not branching narrative in the commonly understood sense, because there is no distinct outcome resting on the decision as to whether to help Lucio or not beyond the battle at the watermill. For the encounter to succeed as intended, however, the player will need to recall the character from cut sequences earlier in the game and probably to have engaged with and remembered the breadcrumb trail of collectible documents. Once again, the player's subjective experience and memory of the game may or may not contribute to their decision and understanding of the unfolding narrative. Whether or not a memory is activated, and how the player chooses to respond, will influence how the player interprets this element of the story.

29.9   CASE STUDY 2: *BLOOD AND TRUTH*

Following the release of their Virtual Reality anthology *VR Worlds* in 2016, Sony's London Studio (now PlayStation London Studio) decided to build on the stand-out success of the *London Heist*, a short narrative-led, gangster-themed VR experience featuring a missing diamond, a car chase and a shoot-out. The result was *Blood and Truth*, a similarly gangster-oriented thriller, also VR, but this time a full-length game in its own right.

The released game tells the story of Ryan Marks, voiced throughout by Felix Scott. When the game begins, we're inhabiting the role of Ryan, sitting alone in a broken down warehouse, a table in front of us. We can see and move our Caucasian, young male hands—even clenching and unclenching them. We can look at the environment around us, picking up on details like the broken window or graffiti etched into the table, an example of what Henry Jenkins terms "Embedded Narrative" (2004, 126–28). The player can pick up a clipboard which shows a photograph of Ryan and some biographical details. A mysterious figure enters who we quickly learn is Agent Carson, played by Colin Salmon. It's quickly clear that this is an interrogation and that Ryan is very hostile towards Carson.

We flashback to a mission in an unidentified foreign country to rescue his fellow soldier Mike Deacon (Bryan Larkin). During this pre-credits sequence, Ryan and Deacon have to shoot their way out, stealing a battered car and making their way to the helicopter rendezvous point. As the credits play out over black, we learn that Ryan has been recalled home to London because of the death of his father. Once we reach London, we discover that Ryan is actually part of a gangster family and that a rival criminal outfit headed by Tony Sharp (played by Steven Hartley) has seized on the death of Ryan's father to take over the Marks family business.

As with *Sniper Elite 4*, I again joined the project part way through the development process. Although they weren't at this stage fleshed out, the game's primary characters had been decided upon, the majority of the actors had been cast and their faces and bodies had been scanned. Similarly, levels—known as missions—had been decided upon. One mission in particular, set in a lavish casino with attached hotel, had been developed to a high level of polish and used to demonstrate the game at the Paris Games Week in 2017. This sequence featured gameplay, placeholder voices for the characters and a spectacular *on-the-rails* chase sequence in which the player is automatically propelled in pursuit of a villainous character.

Henry Jenkins identifies "enacting stories" as another model of storytelling in games, in which the player effectively roleplays a familiar story (2004, 124–26). In this instance, the sequence culminates in a confrontation between the player and the villain, with the player able to elicit responses by shooting the air around the character, shooting at the character with an intention to wound or simply shooting the character dead. The player-character is once more sent on-the-rails to leap through a window, replaying a classic action movie motif in first-person perspective. In enacting this familiar story, the game is once again activating collective memory of an action movie trope and then reframing it via interactivity as a subjective experience for the player.

When I joined the project, although there was a broad understanding of the functional role of the characters—the hero, the brother of the hero, the villain, etc.—specifics had yet to be decided upon. One of my first tasks was to work closely with the Design Director to flesh out these characters. We were, however, able to use the fact that the actors had been cast to help inform how the characters could be developed. (The exception was the role of Carson, who at that stage hadn't been cast.). Later in the process our performance directors worked extensively with the actors to help hone these characters, a process which in turn informed the development of the screenplay.

At the same time, at this stage there was no structure or plot to speak of. As with *Sniper Elite 4*, missions existed, meaning that while they were far from finished, sufficient work had been carried out that they would necessarily have to be incorporated into the story. This meant that any plot would have to utilize a desert sequence, the casino/hotel sequence, as well as missions in an art gallery, a London tower block that's about to be demolished, an airport hangar, the villain's headquarters, a penthouse block, a chase sequence through London and a climax aboard a plane. Along the way, we wanted to include a planning session for an infiltration and a *death slide* over the Thames. The Carson sequences would provide "breathing space" between the missions, reasserting plot points as necessary and locating us chronologically within the narrative. In addition, sequences between the family helped establish what the next mission would be.

Both the resulting plot and structure were heavily dictated by these elements, since they already existed in some form. Flexibility obtained in how these elements were presented narratively, either through dialogue or other storytelling mechanisms like art assets or visual or auditory effects, and in how the chain of these missions were presented to the player.

We were keen to retain the non-sequential structure which had worked so well in the team's previous project the *London Heist*, but the structure of *Blood and Truth* is actually much more complex. Up until the midway point, when Ryan's mother (played by Natasha Little) is killed by Tony Sharp's henchwoman Kayla (Amy Bailey), the story is being told in flashback. This is the point at which we discover Ryan has been arrested and come into Carson's custody. It's also a key turning point for Ryan, in which he teams up with Carson to bring down Tony and try to find out more about the sinister organization seemingly pulling Tony's strings.

From this halfway point, the story flows forwards in time. In fact, the subsequent sequence in which Ryan and Deacon plan the infiltration into Tony's shell company headquarters actually includes a series of *flashforwards*, as the player controls a drone to recon the site and eventually searches a workman's apartment for a key-card. Once again, this can be seen as an example of an Enacted Story, whereby we replay a sequence familiar from multiple heist and spy movies.

As with other storytelling media like film and television, making the story's structure sufficiently robust was a fundamental challenge and formed a major aspect of my role as a both screenwriter and narrative designer. This then underpinned the eventual screenplay and afforded the creative team the required flexibility for sequences which were heavily interactive. A good example of this is the sequence in which Ryan and his brother break into Tony's modernist art gallery. To achieve the necessarily realism, the performers were given free rein to riff off the script. In the finished game play sequence, the player can interact with and indeed sabotage many of the exhibits, eliciting naturalistic responses from the brother character.

A further challenge for Virtual Reality is the necessity to tell the story from the player's viewpoint throughout. Unlike a more conventional game, there's no recourse to editing as a way of conveying meaning, moving the narrative along or providing transitions. Instead, the player's POV remains consistent. As a result, for the most part *Blood and Truth* uses fades from and to black as a method of ending a scene and beginning a new one so as not to disorientate the player. Ultimately, players accepted this transitional approach, presumably as it's once again "remembered" from other familiar media like television and film.

As the medium of VR develops it's possible to imagine multiple other approaches to relocating a player in time and space which enhance the story and experience. For instance, the VR adaptation of Neil Gaiman and Dave McKean's book *The Wolves in the Walls* (2018) borrows transitional approaches from other media and but also invents its own techniques specific to the VR medium. Inevitably, the grammar of VR will become more sophisticated as the medium evolves.

29.10 Conclusions

Clearly, screenwriting for games is not the same as screenwriting for other sequential storytelling media such as cinema or television. This is not to deny that there are similarities, most obviously in terms of creating character and worldbuilding, act structures, plotting and, at a more granular level, the ways in which cut sequences mimic the approaches of these other media. As a result, some elements of the screenwriting process are "remembered" across in terms of the screenplay and associated documentation.

However, these expectations of games as a storytelling medium are often challenged by the spatial, exploratory nature of contemporary games. These elements of interactivity make games very different to sequential storytelling media. As a result, we might see the emergence of the narrative designer role in more recent years as an admission on the part of the games industry that conventional approaches to storytelling will only go so far. Extremely complex narrative ecologies require a multitude of storytelling techniques.

Memory, then, operates in multiple ways in relation to video game storytelling. My subjective experience of games and other media from an early age informs my approach to creativity, as does my understanding of players' collective memory of games and their resulting expectations, which I might choose to reinforce or subvert. Games similarly exist as elements in a network of relations, informed by the memories and expectations of those creating them and those playing them, but also by their dialogical relationship with other media, notably film and television. Players are often asked to re-enact tropes familiar from these other media, the interactive component transforming these experiences from the realm of collective to subjective memory.

The game writer role might be seen as primarily temporal, while the narrative designer role is primarily spatial. Understanding the operation of memory in these contexts is vital for both roles, though the game screenwriter can draw more readily on precedents from other sequential media, notably cinema and television. The narrative designer, conversely, must seek to exploit the unique characteristics of the game medium in terms of its spatial, non-sequential characteristics. There is, of course, huge overlap between these two related disciplines, though the aim of synthesizing gameplay and story—of minimizing ludonarrative dissonance or even reframing it to the story's advantage—remains the same.

Acknowledgements I'd like to thank PlayStation London Studio and Rebellion Developments for their support in the creation of this chapter.

References

Aarseth, Espen. 1997. *Cybertext: Perspectives on Ergodic Literature*. Baltimore MD: The John Hopkins University Press.
Beam Software. 1983. *The Hobbit*. Melbourne House. Commodore 64.
Berger, Ross. 2020. *Dramatic Storytelling and Narrative Design: A Writer's Guide to Video Games and Transmedia*. London: CRC Press.
Big Blue Box, Lionhead Studios, Flaming Fowl Studios, Playground Games. 2004–present. *Fable* series. Xbox Game Studios. Xbox/Microsoft Windows/macOS/Xbox 360/Xbox One/Xbox Series X/S.

Buckles, Mary Ann. 1985. "Interactive Fiction: The Computer Storygame 'Adventure'." PhD diss., University of California, San Diego. https://archive.org/details/maryannbuckles/page/n137/mode/2up?q=Propp. Accessed 10 May 2022.
CD Projekt Red. 2020–2021. *Cyberpunk 2077*. CD Projekt. Microsoft Windows/Playstation 4/Stadia/Xbox One/Playstation 5/Xbox Series X/S.
Chadtopia. 2017. "Sniper Elite 4 – Last Letters Home." https://www.youtube.com/watch?v=-llm7hAfEDM. Accessed 28 August 2021.
Crowther, William. 1976. *Adventure*. Crowther. DEC PDP-10.
Damasio, Antonio. 2003. *Looking for Spinoza: Joy, Sorrow and the Feeling Brain*. London: William Heinemann.
Dinehart, Stephen. 2021. [2006] "What is a Narrative Designer?" *The Narrative Designer*. https://narrativedesigner.com/narrative-designer%3F. Accessed 28 August 2021.
Erll, Astrid. 2011. *Memory in Culture*. Basingstoke UK: Palgrave Macmillan.
Frasca, Gonzalo. 2003. "Ludologists Love Stories Too – Notes from a Debate That Never Took Place." http://www.digra.org/digital-library/publications/ludologists-love-stories-too-notes-from-a-debate-that-never-took-place/. Accessed 15 June 2021.
Fable Studios. 2018. *The Wolves in the Walls*. Oculus Rift/Oculus Rift S.
Goldman, William. 1990. *Adventures in the Screen Trade*. London: Futura.
Halbwachs, Maurice. 1992. [1925] *On Collective Memory*. Chicago: University of Chicago Press.
Harvey, Colin B. 2015. *Fantastic Transmedia: Narrative, Play and Memory Across Science Fiction and Fantasy Storyworlds*. Basingstoke, UK: Palgrave Macmillan.
Hocking, Clive. 2007. "Ludonarrative Dissonance in Bioshock." In *Click Nothing – Design from a Long Time Ago*. https://clicknothing.typepad.com/click_nothing/2007/10/ludonarrative-d.html. Accessed 4 September 2021.
Ion Storm. 2000. *Deus Ex*. Eidos Interactive. Microsoft Windows/Mac OS/Playstation 2.
Ince, Steve. 2006. *Writing for Video Games*. London: A&C Black.
Jenkins, Henry. 2004. "Game Design as Narrative Architecture." In *First Person: New Media as Story, Performance and Game*, edited by Noah Wardrip-Fruin and Pat Harrigan, 118. Cambridge, MA and London: The MIT Press.
Kershner, C. J. 2018. "The Lives of Others: How NPCs Can Increase Player Empathy." GDC Talk, https://www.youtube.com/watch?v=Ew9aLIp0Evc. Accessed 28 August 2021.
Kline, Stephen, Nick Dyer-Witheford, and Greig De Peuter. 2003. *Digital Play: The Interaction of Technology, Culture, and Marketing*. Montreal & Kingston, London and Ithaca: McGill-Queen's University Press.
London Studio. 2019. *Blood and Truth*. Sony Interactive Entertainment. Playstation 4.
Matt M. 2019. "Response to 'Sniper Elite 4 – Last Letters Home'." https://www.youtube.com/watch?v=-llm7hAfEDM. Accessed 30 August 2021.
McKee, Robert. 1999. *Story: Substance, Structure, Style, and the Principles of Screenwriting*. London: Methuen.
Menen, Aubrey. 1979. *Four Days of Naples*. New York: Seaview.
Naughty Dog. 2020. *The Last of Us Part II*. Sony Interactive Entertainment. Playstation 4.

Oliver, Julian Holland. 2001. "Polygon Destinies: The Production of Place in the Digital Roleplaying Game." In *COSIGN 2001 Conference Proceedings*. http://www.cosignconference.org/cosign2001/papers/Oliver.pdf. Accessed 18 August 2022.

Pajitnov, Alexey, and Vladimir Pokhilko. 1989. *Tetris*. Nintendo. Game Boy.

Quantic Dream. 2018–2019. *Detroit: Become Human*. Sony Interactive Entertainment/Quantic Dream. Playstation 4/Microsoft Windows.

Rockstar North, Digital Eclipse, Rockstar Leeds, Rockstar Canada. 1997–2013. *Grand Theft Auto* series. Rockstar Games. Android/Dreamcast/Fire OS/Gameboy Advance/Gameboy Color/iOS/Mac OS/Microsoft Windows/MS-DOS/Nintendo DS/Playstation 1–5/PSP/Windows Phone/Xbox/Xbox 360/Xbox One/Xbox Series X/S.

Rebellion Developments. 2005–2021. *Sniper Elite* series. MC2 France/Namco Hometek/Reef Entertainment/MC2-Microids/505 Games/Rebellion Developments. Microsoft Windows/Playstation 2, 3, 4/Wii/Wii U/Xbox/Xbox 360/Xbox One/Nintendo Switch/Oculus Quest.

Reading, Anna. 2016. *Gender and Memory in the Globital Age*. Basingstoke UK: Palgrave Macmillan.

Wolf, Mark J. P. 2001. *The Medium of the Video Game*. Austin: University of Texas Press.

ZA/UM. 2019. *Disco Elysium*. ZA/UM. Microsoft Windows/Mac OS/Playstation 4/Playstation 5/Stadia/Nintendo Switch/Xbox One/Xbox Series X/S.

CHAPTER 30

"Everybody Chips in Ten Cents, and Somehow It Seems to Add up to a Dollar": Exploring the Visual Toolbox of Animation Story Design

Chris Pallant and Paul Wells

30.1 Introduction

As in many aspects of research and publication about animation, the specific endeavour of identifying a particular approach to writing for the animated form is a comparatively new area of enquiry and theoretical development. Fortunately, animation now has a burgeoning literature re-claiming its history worldwide (see: Bendazzi 1994, 2016; Crafton 1993; Cavalier and Chomet 2011; Furniss 2016), a clear engagement with its various techniques and applications (see Beck 2004; Holliday 2018; Harris, Husbands, and Taberham, 2019; Purves, 2014; Ruddell and Ward 2019), and a variety of methods adopted for its analysis and critique (see Beckman 2014; Cholodenko 1995 and 2007; Pallant 2015; Pallant and Price 2015; Pickov 2010; Wells 1998; Wells and Hardstaff 2008a, b, Wells and Moore 2017). Long thought of as merely *the history of the American animated cartoon*, animation is now embraced as a truly international art-form of long-standing in many nations and is recognised as constituting a considerable body of work in the articulation of visual culture and social identity. It has been created by auteurs

C. Pallant (✉)
School of Creative Arts and Industries, Canterbury Christ Church University, Canterbury, UK
e-mail: chris.pallant@canterbury.ac.uk

P. Wells (✉)
School of Creative Arts and Design, Loughborough University, Loughborough, UK
e-mail: p.wells@lboro.ac.uk

and studios and is omnipresent as a vehicle of communication and expression across a variety of technologies and points of exhibition.

This creates as many problems and issues in defining what writing for animation actually is as it does in recognising the contexts in which animation resides and has been long present. Arguably, for every animation project there is a distinctive method and approach. This is related to the view that *writing* for animation is bound up with its production context and its eventual outcome. For example, in the list below we identify multiple contexts in which writing for animation takes place.

- Feature/Animated film (70 + mins)
- TV episodes (2 × 11 / 15 / 24 mins)
- Independent short
- Visual effects/Games
- GIFs/Memes/Banners, etc.
- VR/AR/UXD
- Commercial/Public information film/Music video

This is correspondent to a concept that Wells has also developed, termed the Animation Spectrum (Fig. 30.1), in which animation as a form may be identified, and in which particular kinds of *writing* might take place.

In essence, both the above list and Fig. 30.1 acknowledge production contexts and applied technologies as key arenas where animation is a specific

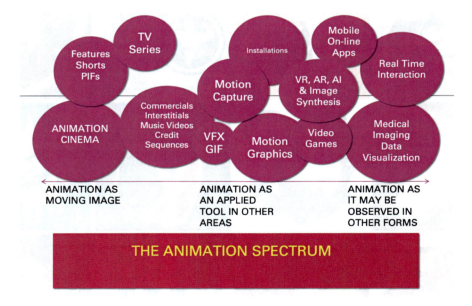

Fig. 30.1 The Animation Spectrum (Wells 2018, 79–95)

tool of expression, with some being readily obvious as places where known and particular approaches to writing are taking place, and others where *animation* itself might not even be identified, let alone the methods by which it might be written for.

When animation occurs in moving image forms it is most obviously seen in feature films, documentaries, TV sit-coms and dramas, public information films, commercials, interstitials, credit sequences, music videos, and so forth. Where it is also present, however, is as a significant agent of narrative in the use of motion capture, visual effects, gifs, motion graphics, video games and apps. Further, and increasingly significantly in (A)rtificial (I)ntelligence applications, (A)ugmented (R)eality, (V)irtual (R)eality and Image Synthesis, as well as in real-time interaction and models of Data Visualisation. The latter models—animation as it may be seen in other forms—may be viewed as problematic in some senses because there may be the case that algorithmic interventions and the interface of software marginalises or even removes individualised and/or collaborative artistic craft from the production process (Wells 2018, 79–95). Equally, although the artist might not be present, this does not necessarily absent a creative or writerly intervention, and it becomes important, therefore, to identify what kinds of writing may be required related to what application, context, outcome and audience addressed. It is this that will be the subject of the following discussion.

There has been the emergence of an extensive screenwriting literature, per se, in recent years (see Dunnigan 2019; Vogler 2007; Yorke 2013), all of which may be pertinent to writing for animation to some degree, in that dependent on the nature of both the moving image and technical forms cited above, there may be an appropriate text to engage with concerning story structure, generic tropes, writing dialogue and so forth, that is just as relevant to animated forms as to traditional live action models. This begs the question, however, of what constitutes the specificity of animation as a form of expression, especially in the digital era where the creation and construction of film using computers is much closer to the long-determined condition of making animation than making orthodox camera-led, character-led cinema. The pro-filmic and pre-filmic premise of making animation now characterises much film-making practice—especially in its use of storyboarding (see later in this discussion)—stressing the significance of editorial decisions *before* making the film, rather than in post-production. To make effective decisions in this regard, it is crucial to know the core vocabulary available in animation—what Wells has elsewhere stressed is the Animation Toolbox (2011b, 18–27)—and how this informs screenwriting practice for each context of production and its outcome.

30.2 The Animation Toolbox

These are the core characteristics of animation that underpin the development of any animation script and are essentially the *tools* that any one writer must be aware of when thinking about creating animated narratives, and importantly, the *world building* in which the context for the narrative possesses its own logic, laws and models of self-conscious fabrication and illusionism. These include aspects that directly relate to conventional film-making practice.

- *Transitions*: these are usually traditional elements in film grammar—crucially, the specificity of the single shot—in order to enhance the methods of storytelling by using multiple screen conventions that stress the *motion* in image transition (e.g. ellipses, wipes, moving text, substitution, rapid cut, layer change, scrolling, mobile split screens or zoom in/out). This sometimes uses the movement of a rostrum camera itself across layouts to suggest motion or the implied camera in most CG environments.
- *Metamorphoses*: a fundamental aspect of animation in which imagery can change from one thing and flow seamlessly into another without edit *in the shot*. Viewers literally see the *flow* of this transition as one thing breaks down and reforms as another. Usually this is best achieved in 3-D/2-D line drawing, clay and malleable materials, and more, but may be executed in all forms with digital interventions. As master Russian animator, Yuri Norstein, insists, "our advantage lies in the fact that we can control the flow of time at any point within a single frame, in contrast to live action where time flows at a constant rate throughout each shot" (Quoted in Sharman 1994, 20). This is a key element to recall and keep in mind for the screenwriter, but more importantly for practitioners working in other aspects of visualisation, for example, illustration and graphic design, because there is no need to be preoccupied with complex variations of movement and motion that might be created by the most skilled animators, but a concentration on what *needs* to move in any one shot to prompt narrative progress and meaning.
- *Condensation*: in essence, the maximum of suggestion in the minimum of imagery, and potentially focusing on using icons and symbols, developing single concept scenes, and sometimes using compositional conventions from graphic narrative and illustrative forms e.g. *emanata* from comics and children's picture books.
- *Visual metaphor*: a familiar and simple visual concept, which better reveals and explains a more complex idea. Normally, this involves the use of signs and symbols as representations of a person, object or environment so that the signs and symbols express an idea or concept rather than a literal meaning. Much animation encourages this shift from literal to figurative or symbolic thinking, in order that such visual motifs help reveal or explain a complex concept that may be difficult to comprehend. Approaches include sometimes taking two ideas that may seem initially un-alike, but which ultimately reveal their relationship or meaning, in turn provoking further creative thought in the viewer about a topic or subject.

These aspects are usually mediated through two modes of address. Firstly, *Aesthetic codes*: the creation and composition of visual elements using the functional and associative characteristics of colour, size, shape, form, etc. *As all* components of the animated image—e.g. foreground and background, character, objects, environments—are specifically *chosen* for their particular affect and meaning, all such visual elements become aesthetic codes with implied but overt intention. This may initially seem contradictory but is a key condition in animation screenwriting—the choice of a colour, shape, scale, texture, prop, etc., is deliberate in the overt construction of scenography, since these aspects must be *wholly* created, but their overall meaning is implied. Though live action cinema makes similar selections they are often determined by Directors and Art Directors rather than being specifically included in the script. In feature film production, this is often made manifest, for example, in *colour scripts*, but in all cases by the writer's implied art direction in the script and storyboarding, which simultaneously functions as narrative and conceptual design. This is further made explicit, too, in *series bibles* for television series, where characters, objects and environments are visualised and fixed.

And secondly, *Characters*: animation essentially defines character in three ways, and this may manifest as a human, an animal, a mythical or imagined creature, an object, or an environmental element that is either natural or manufactured:

a. as the embodiment of a *type*—sometimes a stereotype—but normally a figure who personifies a dominant trope or characteristic, e.g. frustration, ignorance or confusion (the dwarves in *Snow White and the Seven Dwarfs* are the most obvious exemplar of this phenomenon);
b. as the embodiment of a social role or symbolic function; and
c. as a vehicle, which is revealed and defined by interior states of mind, such as dream, fantasy, memory, solipsistic thought and acts of the conscious/unconscious mind.

In the latter aspects, again, the address of scenography may be especially pertinent. Character will be addressed further later in this discussion, in relation to specific contexts of production and storytelling. Fundamentally, though, character needs to take into account two dominant factors:

- *Performance and Choreography*: the conscious execution of an acted gesture in the service of (emotive) expression, practical function or typical human actions, for instance, giving a direction, playing an instrument or washing hands. It is the particular choreography and blocking attached to this performance though that remains the specific characteristic of the animated form in that *every* choice of movement is the driver of what is seen and communicated to the viewer. The conscious construction of motivated motion in any one gesture, shot or scene is therefore

the determining factor in the creation of animation, but crucially, in its assemblage of *micro-narratives*, which will be addressed later in the discussion. The understanding of micro-narratives in animation is necessary for the screenwriter in ensuring that script *descriptors* are informed by an increased degree of visual detail than in most conventional live action scripts, as it needs to prompt design idioms and intrinsic motion.
- *Anthropomorphism*: objects, animals, imaginary creatures, machines, elements, environments, or else, that are imbued with human characteristics. This often enables visual representation beyond that determined by conventional identity politics and cultural/national orthodoxies. It also permits and enables reconfigurations of *the body*; the performance of gender, age, sexuality, race and ethnicity; and all aspects of otherwise physically or materially coded norms. It is also important to note that even in the construction of the humanoid figure, the *selection* of human characteristics is vital because the complete performance of the live action actor is not available, and therefore, recognisable physical, behavioural and motion-based actions must be chosen and made specific to narrative, metaphoric and emotive purpose.

All the above aspects link animation to filmic, theatrical and illustrative codings, but it is also important to deploy key technical and graphic elements. These include:

- *Data visualisation*: this is normally the animation of infographic elements like charts, maps, mathematical concepts and more.
- *Diagrammatic flow*: a moving infographic interpretation of a process, system or mechanism, often showing cyclic models, interrelated components in a complex model of production or revealing internal or infrastructural movement.
- *Text*: the choice and particularity of words, phrases, slogans, figures and other symbolic insignia deliberately used in a visual composition.
- *Sound*: the specific and necessary sound design—e.g. voice-over, dialogue, song, music and effects—for a form that does not have the immediate diegetic sound in the conventional way that orthodox notions of live action film might have. Voiceover performances often inform visual performances when animators use actors not merely for their vocal work but as inspiration for visual interpretation. Sound is often also significant in offering narrative suggestion and association, which may ultimately mean that less animation is required as the work of creating the story world through resonant contextual sound motifs may be enough.

30.3 Micro-Narratives

One of the key differences in approaches to devising, developing and creating animated texts is the use of micro-narrative. The micro-narrative is the fundamental building block of constructing animated narratives in the sense that it is the smallest device in starting and developing animated stories, from the single animated gesture, right through to the complete accumulation of micro-narratives as a feature-length story. The core initial micro-narratives that the writer/deviser/animator can explore are:

- The single movement (one gesture or action).
- The icon or symbol (one signifying element or sign).
- The single object (one associative artefact).
- The generic motif (one defining aspect of a genre).
- A sequence of metamorphosis (one thing changing into another without edit).
- An incremental element of design (Colour, shape, line, form).
- A spot gag (one sequence revealing a joke).
- A single-subject exchange (a scene focused on one topic).
- A focus incident (one event which is the subject of all story elements).

All these micro-narratives are informed in the first instance by attention to the shot, itself a micro-arc in the narrative, and each is both a possible beginning or an end in itself. A character can be defined by a single movement (e.g. a salute) or as an environmental element (e.g. a wave, the falling of rain); by operating as an icon or symbol (e.g. a bureaucrat, a priest); by becoming a single object (e.g. a chair, a clock); by embodying a generic motif (e.g. a gun, a superhero cape); by metamorphosing (e.g. changing from young to old; by turning into a werewolf); by being identified through a design element (e.g. simply being a shape, colour or form); by being revealed through humour, one subject or a moment of dramatic conflict.

As such, those writing for animation are less interested in the notion of three acts (Field 2005), five acts (Freytag 1897, Campbell 1949; Murdock 1990), six stages (Hauge 1992), eight sequences (Daniel in Howard and Marbley 1993, and in Gulino 2004; Aronson 2010) or twenty-two steps (Truby 2007) structures—though these may be of use later as writers develop and revise work—than in the *strategic* possibilities of what is available in animation in relation to how visual images may be created. In essence, instead of starting with the standard principles of character or plot—which again may become important later in the development process—most animation screenwriters start with a visual concept, and extend the visual elements of the potential narrative from these core visual kernels and compositions.

One way of immediately understanding this point is to recall that many animation devisers work first in sketchbooks, drawing characters, scenes they have observed, landscapes and buildings, machines, objects and similar. At the outset, such devisers are considering a *narrative strategy* about these images rather than seeking out a narrative structure that can accommodate them, though again, this is something that may be necessary later, especially as the *animation toolbox* becomes related to conventional aspects of conventional cinematic practice.

Take for example, Pete Docter's now iconic drawing that stimulated his film, *Up*—written by Bob Peterson and Pete Docter (2009). A seemingly grumpy old man holds a big bunch of colourful balloons. Why does such a drawing operate in such a resonant way? At this point, it is useful to go back to a core principles of theatre. An empty stage, like an empty page, is essentially a context in which something is expected to happen. As soon as a character, prop or object emerges on the stage, or a dot, a line, a coloured shape, or a figure, or an object emerges on the page, the stage or the page is effectively *dramatised*. The image itself starts to invite questions about why something is there, what is going to happen and what might be the ongoing implications of this. Crucially, whatever the presence of these forms may be—however small—they also invite the audience to deduce any possible narrative or meaning from these forms that they already possess or know, from what the forms have been previously associated with.

This is where the concept of the *micro-narrative* begins. Docter's drawing—what traditional screenwriters might call an *inciting incident*—begs any number of questions. Why is an old man holding a bunch of balloons? Why is he seemingly unhappy? Where did the old man get these balloons and what is he doing with them, or more to the point, what is he going to do with them? Broader questions might emerge. What is the old man actually like? Is he physically fit or incapacitated in some way? Why is his skin a pallid green? Does green indicate envy, jealousy, decay? Is he a part-time balloon seller in retirement just trying to earn a little more money? Is he holding the balloons for someone else? Will that person come back soon? Notice that it is almost inevitable that the more questions that might be asked of an initial situation the greater the tendency is to begin to narrativise or start the process of promoting a story that *makes sense* of a situation. Though many written fictions may be prompted by visual stimulus and continue to employ visual reference, the animation screenwriter must necessarily sustain the visual parameters emerging from such initial images into extended pictorial schemes and art direction—it is this notion of sustaining the visual codes across sketches, scripts, storyboards and other visualisation materials that ultimately constitutes story design.

The creators of an animated narrative, then, begin their development of a piece *not* from the potential of arcs and structural mechanisms but from the principle of using micro-narrative both in and of itself, and thereafter as the accumulation of minimum units in the development or apprehension of an extended text or story. In this, they speak to Yorke's notion of opposites assimilated and conflict resolved, but on both the most *minimal* and *extended* terms and conditions.

Fundamental to this principle is that any one form has embedded associative and symbolic characteristics—its embedded micro-narrative. At one and the same time, an animation screenwriter will necessarily develop a narrative or story, but also potentially *apprehend* one from within the embedded characteristics of the form. This is why micro-narrative is an important and fundamental idea in animation because it can facilitate more experimental and abstract works as well as more traditional notions of storytelling.

To give this idea flesh, and to help understand how micro-narrative might be specifically defined it is useful to see that even if an animation screenwriter is making an abstract piece, lines, shapes, colours and forms in their own right *narrate* a space but don't (necessarily) tell a *story*. What this draws into relief or *calls forth* though is the status of lines, shapes, colour and forms as potential storytelling devices, and ultimately, as fundamental aspects of story design in animation per se. As such *art direction* in animation operates as a fundamental aspect of *story design*.

Essentially, every aspect of choreographed motion in animation is a micro-narrative, simply because no piece of movement is accidental, and is a particular choice. Every movement essentially narrates its own purpose and meaning. Every line drawn, every grain of sand moved, piece of clay manipulated, brush of colour painted, vector line adjusted or puppet manipulated has a particular narrative and as such becomes what Norstein calls *a gesture* (Quoted in Sharman 1994, 20) It is this idea of the gesture and the fact that it calls attention to itself in the way that live action motion does not, which amplifies the difference in animated images, stressing the intensity imbued in the deliberately constructed particularity of a piece of choreography, rather than the sheer totality of action apprehended and recorded by the camera in any one live action shot. One way of thinking about this is to consider it as the *hyper-perception* of objects, materials and elements, and as such minor details and singular forms take a pre-eminent place. The gesture then is the very first building block in understanding micro-narrative, since small movements constituted within the frame carry with them embedded meaning and affect. A blink, a tear, a pointed finger, a kick of a ball, etc., all narrate in animation because they are chosen and not merely included as part of a bigger picture the camera voraciously includes.

If a live action script can be written in isolation, and precede production, animation screenwriting is usually and inherently bound up with its production process. The accumulation of micro-narratives may prompt everything from a thirty second commercial to a full-length feature animation, but these written components rarely operate without simultaneous and ongoing visualisation. Art direction, prompted by these conceptual units of action, becomes story design, often informed by developmental character and environmental sketching, model sheets, layout drawings, and most notably, storyboards and animatics (an edited assembly of storyboard shots with a basic soundtrack). The storyboard, and thereafter, an augmented shooting script, is a core aspect of most animation production, and crucially, is not an *illustration* of script but an *iteration* of script. The storyboard is literally screenwriting underpinned by animation film-making.

30.4 Frames of Reference

If the process and presentation of screenwriting has resisted standardisation within the arena of animation production, then its companion, the storyboard, arguably has an even greater tradition of defying convention. This might seem like an unlikely proposition at face value, considering how the history of storyboarding for animation has been popularly portrayed across countless "Art of"/ "Making of" books, where the standard narrative is dominated by the large, cork-board format storyboards popularised by Disney in the 1930s–1940s; or the A4/Legal sheets of paper with four or six panels pre-printed to support storyboard activity; or the recent proliferation and domination of digital platforms such as *Toon Boom*, *Previs Pro*, and *Photoshop*, to name but a few, that provide various layers of computer assistance to the storyboard artist. Yet, the act of animating stories has repeatedly encouraged—and necessitated—highly flexible approaches to the craft of storyboarding that do not always align with the popular conceptions noted above.

A good example of storyboard versatility can be found in the work of animator Ray Harryhausen. To develop his iconic Dynamation sequences, Harryhausen used a wide array of storyboard aesthetics when working with directors such as Don Chaffey on *Jason and the Argonauts* (1963) and *One Million Years B.C.* (1966), Desmond Davies on *Clash of the Titans* (1981), or Jim O'Connolly on *The Valley of Gwangi* (1969), dozens of on-screen performers, and producers such as Charles H. Schneer and Michael Carreras, to present his planned animation ahead of production. While not strictly storyboards, Harryhausen's fine artistry is visible in his concept art, where his frequently used charcoal and pencil to visualise, in a highly detailed manner, a dramatic set piece (Pallant and Price 2015, 99–100). These were a good starting point, since these images were often crafted very early in the process to help the producer, predominantly Schneer, to secure studio funding for the planned production. While these images evolved into more functional storyboards once production commenced, the ability of concept art to condense narrative information into a singular image, as well as evoking a sense of filmic tone, establishes them as significant—and developmental—bridging points between the script and storyboard. Again, such concept art readily reveals the micro-narrative and a significant indication of accented motion.

As indicated, when working on a specific film in a concentrated manner, Harryhausen would take his large-format, highly detailed concept art as a starting point for the development of smaller scale, hand-drawn storyboards. Often maintaining a degree of illustrative detail not necessary in storyboard work, Harryhausen's storyboards range in size and shape across his numerous film projects, with some storyboard pages presenting nine panels per page while others offer eight, six and four per page, yet varying in terms of portrait/landscape orientation. For *One Million Years B.C.*, Harryhausen used four-panel pages of highly detailed storyboarded key frames presented in landscape orientation, alongside eight-panel pages of rougher (but still very clear) storyboards, presented in portrait orientation, that give greater coverage of the action being portrayed. Tony Dalton, long-time biographer of Harryhausen, writes of the finely detailed four-panel pages: "Although Ray executed a storyboard for most of the major animation scenes *in his movies*, he occasionally produced a small set of drawings *as an initial aid* for the screenwriters" (Harryhausen and Dalton 2011, 55—italics added). Although Dalton chooses not to label the four-panel page as a storyboard, reserving the term for his rougher eight-panel pages, the fact that he implicitly suggests that *One Million Years B.C.* is Harryhausen's movie and not that of the director or the producer, and that the four-panel page was intended to shape the work of the screenwriters, it is hard not to view the pages in question as storyboards given their significant role in plotting and managing the visual—and narrative—development of the film.

Another important observation to make of Harryhausen's storyboards, beyond their varied formatting, is how he uses them to precisely map out his preferred choreography—see definition above. While a storyboard for an action sequence not involving stop motion model animation and analogue image compositing techniques might seek to provide a good approximation of how the action is to be filmed or computer animated, there is still considerable room for creative adjustment either by the director, the on-screen performer or the visual effects team working on the image in post-production. However, for Harryhausen, establishing accurate expectations—if not parameters—regarding the on-screen blocking of the live action performers was essential to support his stop motion model-based animation that would be produced separately and be integrated via rear projection into the final film edit. Across Harryhausen's storyboards, they frequently adopt an approximate rule of thirds across the horizontal axis, whereby the left-hand third of the screen and the right-hand third of the screen provide the oppositional spaces in which either live action or stop motion characters are to be situated. Such staging helped to contribute to the believability of the Dynamation sequences by allowing clear margins for the rear projection. Of course, Harryhausen's virtuosity meant that he often transgressed this boundary and constructed sequences where the stop motion and live action characters overlap or interact in the central third of the screen—think, for example, of the cowboys and cave folk facing down Harryhausen's allosauruses in *The Valley of Gwangi* and *One Million Years B.C.*, respectively.

While the storyboard approaches discussed above reveal Harryhausen's flexible approach to the visual development of story, they share the common thread of being entirely hand-drawn. Within The Ray and Diana Harryhausen Foundation's archive there are also surviving storyboard materials that demonstrate photographs being used as the material platform for storyboard work. For example, as seen in the "Ray Harryhausen: Titan of Cinema" exhibition that ran at the Scottish National Gallery of Modern Art (2020–2022), for the films *Earth vs The Flying Saucers* (1956) and *One Million Years B.C.*, Harryhausen adopted the same mixed-media approach, by photographing the actual location where the scene would be set, and then drawing and painting on top of the photographic reference. Harryhausen's practice affords the opportunity to note the significant difference between the requirements of live action shooting and the parameters for animated sequences. At any one time, Harryhausen embraces the absolute motion of the live action story arcs and the accented motion of the set-piece animated narratives, which are the scenes both working literally and figuratively, authentically fabricating and dramatising a mythic world, informed by visual metaphors and symbolic concepts.

While scrutiny of Harryhausen's storyboarding versatility reveals the range of styles employed when crafting animated stories from an individualistic perspective, we now turn our attention to an example from the opposite end of the spectrum by considering how storyboarding has evolved within a studio context. At the time of writing, Pixar has released twenty-four computer animated feature films and what is remarkable from a storyboarding perspective is the sheer range of storyboarding styles that have been employed over the years to support the production of these films. For example, the storyboards created by Max Brace and Peter Sohn, for the sequence in *WALL-E* (2008) where Eve is shown WALL-E's lighter, are produced digitally, but in a crisp style that seeks to evoke pencil and charcoal drawings, and they feature selective use of colour to help convey the emotive warmth of the lighter when it is first revealed (Hauser 2008, 28–29). Whereas Michael Yates's storyboards for *Soul* (2020) showcase a rougher sketchier style, with a greater emphasis on black and white shading. In one sequence, which depicts the character Joe Gardiner in motion, it is clear to see how Yates's style amplifies the character's energetic disposition (Disney 2021). While looking at Joe Ranft's storyboard's for Pixar's second feature *A Bug's Life* (1998), we see a completely different aesthetic *on display*, with a full colour palette used across highly detailed and polished panels (Pixar Central, 2020). Giving the volume of work that Pixar has now produced, it is surely to be expected that storyboard styles will have pushed and pulled in various directions over the decades as a multitude of different storyboard artists have faced the challenge of pitching their work-in-progress boards to the story department team.

Beyond these celebrated examples of Pixar's pre-production work, what must not be overlooked is the vast amount of storyboard work that may never be made public. For example, for the Pixar films cited above, the total number of logged storyboards (thereby excluding those efforts that were discarded) produced across each films' entire production cycle were: *A Bug's Life*: 27,565,

WALL-E: 98,173,[1] and *Soul*: 73,611 (T. J. 2020).Given the restricted access to Pixar's studio archives, and the likelihood that many of these storyboards will have been shredded after production wrapped, there is evidently an additional, unknowable level of storyboard variety that sits silently alongside those storyboards that are in the public domain. The scale of work here readily signals two key aspects of the production process: first, the way in which storyboard visualisation is used as a system of script *notation* (See Wells 2008a, b, 86), where micro-narrative concepts are visualised and subject to a number of drafts; and second, the way in which formal script and storyboard development oscillate, bouncing back and forth as the emerging story advances, and gradually becomes fixed, and the animation is put into production.

This readily reflects veteran Disney director's Ben Sharpsteen's observation that "Everybody chips in ten cents, and somehow it seems to add up to a dollar" (quoted in Peri 2010, 57), but there is a clear resonance here regarding the popular impression that Pixar has cultivated regarding their industrialised story savvy. There is a long tradition of popular interventions by Pixar when it comes to (re)presenting their story craft as seen through the prism of the storyboard. Take the examples addressed in this chapter so far: there is the staged story review session from *A Bug's Life*, which was originally offered by Pixar as a DVD special feature, where several aesthetic, contextual and narrative revisions are executed in a brisk, uncomplicated manner; then there is the "Side-by-Side" video, hosted on Disney's main YouTube channel, which shows several sequences from *Soul* closely corresponding to storyboard work; and there are the *WALL-E* storyboard images, which are presented in a luxuriously glossy manner in Disney's official *The Art of WALL-E* book (2008). The "somehow it seems to add up" portion of Sharpsteen's remark above about twentieth century Disney practices takes on added weight here. Clearly, Disney and Pixar have been actively seeking to control the studio narrative by concealing the protracted, often bumpy, marathon that is feature animation production and the central role played by storyboards as ever evolving roadmaps within this journey since the production's first sprint. "Somehow" serves to euphemistically imbue Pixar's—and Disney's—creative activity with an aura of steady predictability, which, given the financial exposure of animated feature production, is a popular narrative that likely appeals to the shareholders just as much as the fanbase.

We reached out to former Pixar animator Steve Segal, who worked at the studio during its formative years, to gather his views on how storyboard use and utility has evolved at Pixar. Reflecting on the shift within film-making practice more broadly, from analogue production practices to digital alternatives, Segal suggests that the storyboard has "a fluid flexibility now because of the computer, you're not necessarily looking at a page or a bunch of papers, you're

---

[1] Data for *A Bug's Life* and *WALL-E* sourced from: Pixar Studio Exhibit, "Fun Facts: Storyboards Delivered for Each Pixar Feature Film (Since We Started Counting)", Emeryville, CA. Viewed by Chris Pallant, 23 June 2013.

looking at text and images on a screen, so you can move stuff around pretty easily". Yet, he highlights how this increased fluidity holds true to how storyboards were originally formalised at the Disney studio in the 1930s: "that's the nature of the storyboard technique that Disney devised, which was pinning them on the board, then you could take one down and replace it with something else, move things around, so it was very fluid" (Segal 2022). Drawing a connection with the work of Walter Murch, Segal recounts: "I remember Murch talked about how in the days of film, he would hang his film strips on little hooks, so you'd have streams of film, and he could glance at it and get an overall feeling for, 'ok, this is happening, and then this is a dark scene and this is a light scene', and I think the same way about storyboards" (Segal 2022). Despite the profound digitality of Pixar, Segal notes how this type of analogue overview/review is still valued at the studio, confirming that they "still do that at Pixar to this day… they still pin the drawings up on the wall" (Segal 2022).

The emergent art direction, framed in storyboards, and manipulated both in analogue and digital technologies, fundamentally determines story design, but this of, and in itself, permits the ongoing engagement with the concepts in the animation toolkit and the constant enhancement of micro-narratives. It remains then to briefly discuss how these models work within some different production contexts drawn from the Animation Spectrum (see Fig. 30.1).

30.5　Production Contexts

30.5.1　The Feature Film

Though production of animated features has increased significantly in recent years, within the body of cinematic production in general, there are still comparatively few (see Osmond 2010, and Edera 1977). Inevitably, this is dominated by production in the United States, and much of the screenwriting for animation literature addresses these American features. These texts largely draw on the established canon of screenwriting books for live action and modify it in relation to animation practice—Vogler, for example, discusses his interventions in Disney's The Lion King (1994) (Vogler 2007, 264). There remains a focus on structure, production processes, and some emphasis on comedy writing in line with the expectation that most production will be related to the freedoms of the cartoon, and the tradition of American slapstick and Vaudevillian humour. The focus remains on character first, story second and design last, in the overall schema suggested by most texts speaking to writing Hollywood screenplays.

Hayao Miyazaki, and a number of Japanese directors, like Makoto Shinkai, however, are not in the first instance especially preoccupied with story and characters, but move their narratives through design, thinking about the nature of story through possible environments, situation-based action, unusual visual idioms, emotional imperatives and so forth. This is not surprising given the pre-eminence of manga as a literary form in Japan. Not confined by the sometimes limited structures and script formulas in the Western context, and by the ready understanding that Japanese culture is responsive to the spiritual and supernatural as well as material worlds (and therefore, three arenas of action that are ontologically equivalent) Japanese artists are liberated to embrace different approaches to narrative. Miyazaki's remarks are instructive here:

- The animator must fabricate a lie that seems so real viewers will think the world depicted might possibly exist.
- You speak about the sunset by drawing on the many sunsets stored inside you.
- Draw many pictures, as many as you can. Eventually, a world is created.
- The scenario is a process of elimination.
- One must have the clear core of what one wants to convey. This is the trunk of the story that penetrates through in a strong and simple way. What catches the audience's eye is the treetop, the shimmer of the leaves. What is most required of a scenario are roots that spread deep into the earth and a strong trunk hidden by a mass of shimmering leaves. As long as there is a trunk strong enough to support branches and leaves—the rest, hanging decorations, letting flowers bloom, and adding accessories—can be best accomplished by everyone sharing their ideas. The best scenario might be one that includes the mass of leaves and even the insects that crawl among those leaves (Miyazaki 2009, xx).

This more visually-directed, quasi-metaphoric approach, speaks more obviously to the accumulation of micro-narratives, with the focus on producing material that enables a story to emerge, which is informed by association, selection, detailed representation, collaboration, and crucially, the attention to *hidden worlds* that might not be readily visible, or offering a view of the world from a different point of view.

30.5.2 *The TV Episode*

The animated TV episode for many series is based on a traditional script, though some series move directly from short treatments to storyboarding (see Wells 2011a). All are regulated quite strictly by their length, which requires an approach that can tell clear complete stories in the short form.

Crucially, most live action and animated series in the UK and USA use a *bible* providing background material about the series, including profiles of the characters, detailing key overall storylines and narrative arcs for the characters, sample episode summaries and provisional episode titles and suggestions and other technical and production information. What is distinctive about the animated series bible, though, is that it includes character, prop and environment designs, model sheets and layouts, and significantly, the *rules* of the series that are dictated by the practical requirements of the technique and the animation itself.

Writing characters, for example, under these conditions is partly about the capacity for performance that the technique and production budget may permit. A 2-D drawn character, for example, may have a greater capacity for dynamic movement and malleable form than a 3-D puppet character, and physical sets for 3-D puppet animation may have certain limits that permit only a certain number of characters and scenery. Further, the writing of such characters is often about repetition and reinforcement of core traits and behaviour determined at the outset, and working within the generic or established imperatives of the episodes—comic, educational, mystery-led and so forth—in relation to the intended audience, e.g. pre-school children, students and adults between 25 and 35 years old. The approach to television animation is normally about creating a set of assets and core material created by an origination team, which can then be used and extended by a team of writers thereafter.

30.5.3 *The Independent Short Film*

This is the most diverse category in that it accommodates all independent approaches to developing and making an animated film. The independent short is normally the most obviously authorial and usually reflects the most personal and complex concerns, as well as being produced in a wide range of innovative techniques of production. Almost, for each individual film, there is a distinctive method of animation screenwriting, devising and creating, often combining written, drawn, material and technical experimentation. Many countries have a rich tradition of independent animated film-making, and the major figures in the animated short form have served to define animation outside the dominant orthodoxy of the American animated cartoon—these include Norstein noted above, Priit Parn (Estonia), Paul Driessen (The Netherlands), Jan Svankmajer (Czech Republic), Caroline Leaf (Canada), Suzan Pitt (USA), Norman McLaren (Scotland), Lotte Reiniger (Germany), Igor Kovalyov (Russia), Walerian Borowczck (Poland), Satoshi Kon (Japan) and Joanna Quinn (UK) to name but a few. For every approach to an independent short is probably a different model of writing, but arguably such films reflect a greater and more specific engagement with exploiting the distinctive characteristics animation as a form offers.

Inevitably, the nature of *character* operates very differently under these circumstances, but might be broadly understood in two ways. First, most characters in independent short films will look, act and behave in ways that are different from characters in mainstream films and television series, foregrounding their alternative perspectives, indigenous cultures and personal and social pre-occupations. *Deadsy* (1990), created by David Anderson, and written by novelist and poet, Russell Hoban, for example, features a skeletal character in a flux of gender positions, speaking a corrupted post-apocalyptic language, and in Shaun Tan and Andrew Ruhemann's *The Lost Thing* (2011), the eponymous character is a giant teapot-style urn with crab and octopus limbs. Second, many characters will be presented through their *interior states*—animation is especially good at showing dreams, fantasies, thought processes, and most particularly, memories, with many independent animated shorts concerned with depicting these states as a closer representation of the human condition. Suzan Pitt's film, *Asparagus* (1979), for example, explores the inner pre-occupations of an artist and the complex engagement with polymorphous sexuality, while Alison De Vere's *The Black Dog* (1987) engages with dream states.

Throughout the whole history of animation, there have been many independent short films, and usually they are defined through the distinctiveness of their authorial voice or through the national cultures in which they are made and may be read often as responses to particular historical contexts and conditions. This is not to say, however, that there are not significant trends in independent production, which both define approaches to animation screenwriting and devising, but also become influential in how these aspects may formalise a generic outcome particular to animation. This may be seen in the rise of the animated documentary, successfully combining the pre-occupations and stylings of the documentary with the freedoms of animation in representing subjective voices, events and situations not recorded by live action, and taboo subjects that cannot be easily depicted. Provocative examples include *Carlotta's Face* (2018) concerning a young girl overcoming a brain disorder through art, *The Driver is Red* (2017), about the pursuit of Nazi War criminals, and *Flee* (2021) concerning a refugee escaping from Afghanistan.

Estonian master animator, Pritt Parn, who has essentially re-defined the cartoon through his own style of caricature, and thematic pre-occupations, has offered an interesting perspective on the ways he develops his own story narratives. They may be summarised as follows:

- It is useful to pair A (one unusual character/situation) with B (a different unusual character/situation) to evolve C (a consequence emerging from apparent incongruity) and to keep testing pairs and possible consequences until an idea finds form. This is both pertinent to *joke-making* and to advancing an abstract narrative.
- The narrative must happen in time, so it is helpful to have a timeline to place an event on, and to see what might come before it and after it. Events can also be shifted around the timeline as they evolve to create an unorthodox narrative structure.
- The characters should be kept as *unfixed* and as abstract as possible for as long as possible. They should represent an idea or an emotion or a situation or an event, and this will help to explore the field of possibilities available.

- Characters should operate in ways in which they can seamlessly shift between the interior world and the exterior world, so that thought and experience can be seen to be the same thing.
- When the characters have evolved, there should always be tested with another problem.
- The film should try to aspire to the condition of the novel in that the audience should be able to read the film on their own terms and conditions and not be hampered by generic structures or formulas that enable them to easily anticipate what will happen or the end. (Parn 2011)

30.5.4 Metamedia Writing

Manovich suggested that the ongoing hybridity and shifting interfaces of media technologies and applications were both revising old media models and creating new ones (Manovich 2013, 161–95). Inevitably, this has resulted in the necessity for animation screenwriters to be mobile and adaptive in applying their skills and approaches to what might now be termed *transdisciplinary* media contexts. This has meant that the animation screenwriter has necessarily had to address how *script* is now functioning in each of the models of practice as it relates to the previous—if unorthodox—ways of creating animated texts. This is often an engagement with how technology has modified a point of exhibition and requires a re-address of how micro-narratives might be used or applied as tools in each context—again, this is related to a strategic rather than structural approach to narrative pertinent to the content and. output.

Briefs that determine the requirements for a commercial, interstitial, credit sequence or public information film can be responded to in a range of strategies drawn from those that oscillate between script, storyboard and pre-visualisation cited above. Each can be responsive to the technology used, but crucially, must be increasingly cognisant of the kinds of imagery that can be created digitally in lateral, layered and 360-degree environments where not merely uniplanar and cross-planar movement within a known depth of field is possible, but in which considerations of different aspects of parallax, planes of action, simulated space, etc., may inform narrative choices. This idea is not new in animation per se, and indeed, may already be a taken-for-granted aspect of conventional screenwriting. Such screenwriters might just merely assume that whatever can be imagined can be executed using contemporary technologies, but animation screenwriters speak to a wider context of creative opportunity beyond conventional notions of film, TV or online broadcast.

Metamedia—essentially the potential for digital and analogue forms to mix, and for new contexts in which form and content can be revised and re-developed from its previous codes, conventions and conditions—provides an apt context for animation screenwriters to work. This is simply because animation screenwriters (however defined as auteurs, devisers, visualisers, animators or else) have always taken into account the transdisciplinary context of animation production, and therefore, its relationship to other established production contexts in theatre and performance, art and design (e.g. drawing, sculpture, painting), song and dance, radio, film and video-making, public display and exhibition. As such, writing for the use of visual effects, games, VR, AR and real-time interaction echoes this model, where the micro-narrative can be an effect, a POV context in a game or VR model, an intervention in a *real world* context, a vehicle for image-synthesis, or simulated environments where real-time participation is required. These units of action are normally predicated on a range of potential narrative choices that might be available to the creator *and* participant, but instead of a traditional idea that they can be just be accumulated and enhanced through *linear* models of storytelling (even if moving backwards and forwards in time), this model of writing permits *lateral* interventions, but most importantly, *rhizomic* development which requires multiple outcomes and a plurality of narrative strategies and constructions. The animation screenwriter is especially grounded therefore in the more openended potential of the imaginative contexts of animated film *because* of its relationship to other disciplinary possibilities, which may be applied in these metamedia contexts. At one and same time, for example, VR can be used both within a narrative context, and as a narrative context, while AR can be used within a physical or virtual context, creating multiple touchpoints of visual communication, and potential units of action for stories and other models of information exchange. It is clear, therefore, that the animation screenwriter might also be creatively adaptable in using the animation toolbox, micro-narrative strategies, storyboarding, etc., in both fiction and non-fiction vehicles using these technologies. Baobab Studios have already demonstrated considerable ingenuity in their VR interactive scenarios like *Paper* Birds (2020) and *Baba* Yaga (2020) which more fully take into account not merely potential *viewer* experience but *user* experience in providing a range of narrative and interactive outcomes.

30.6 CONCLUSIONS

Marcel O'Gorman has suggested that media theory needs to be re-thought by creatively engaging with technology, often playfully and radically mixing analogue crafts and digital applications to re-determine their value and purpose—sometimes literally and metaphorically "writing with a soldering iron" (O'Gorman 2018, 48–57). This is partly in an attempt to challenge some of the seemingly canonical models of production, applications of software, and embedded methodologies that reinforce contemporary social orthodoxies and an established ideologically normative political economy—this is particularly evidenced in the ways that Disney/Pixar have quickly established a new *classicism* in its contemporary CG aesthetics and storytelling that echoes the dominance of the original Disney Studio in the 1930s and 1940s when it first developed the Classical styling that was to remain the state-of-the-art not merely for the studio but for animation worldwide for many years per se. In this analysis, the stress is placed on the ways in which animation screenwriters can be more conscious of the specific creative tools available to them in their chosen medium and form of practice, in that they might be freely applied not merely in further progressive applications to film and media practice, but also as animation appears in, and helps reveal other media technologies. It is clear that after many years of marginalisation as a form, the digital shift has enabled animation to become a more recognised model of screenwriting since the practice of creating contemporary film, television, theatre productions, public display, web and phone material, theme park experiences, etc., is now much closer to the traditional practice of writing and assembling animated productions than ever before. As such the continued use of the animation toolbox, the micro-narrative script development strategy, and the advanced use of storyboarding and pre-visualisation in immersive and interactive models of communication and exchange, can extend the recognition of the form itself. Inevitably, this will re-invent the ways in which *screenwriting* might be thought about, existing in many forms across a range of transdisciplinary contexts. It may be singly and multiply realised within complex collaborative creative networks in which applied technologies play an increasingly prominent role. Crucially, it will also prompt the consistent review of design practice to trace and continually enhance its most innovative and socially inclusive outcomes. In a world often seen in a highly dystopian light, *animated writing* may offer hope for the most utopian considerations and applications, offering the opportunity to *bring life to* fresh contexts and newly emerging cultures. Animation culture has in many senses, always promoted a Utopian outlook in this way, framing its Festivals as truly international gatherings of like-minded progressives since the first, Annecy Festival in 1960, and in the worldwide ASIFA organisation supporting animation practitioners. By viewing animation writers, creatives, and artists as a global community, there remains a collective spirit of engagement in embracing the form as future directed and future proof.

References

A Bug's Life. 1998. Written by Andrew Stanton, Donald McEnery, and Bob Shaw. Storyboards by Joe Ranft. Directed by John Lasseter. USA: Walt Disney Pictures, Pixar Animation Studios.

Aronson, Linda. 2010. *21st Century Screenplay: A Comprehensive Guide to Writing Tomorrow's Films*. Crows Nest, Australia: Allen & Unwin.

Asparagus. 1979. Written and directed by Suzan Pitt. USA.

Baba Yaga. 2020. Written by Eric Darnell. Directed by Mathias Chelebourg. USA: Baobab Studios.

Beck, Jerry, ed. 2004. *Animation Art: From Pencil to Pixel, the History of Cartoon, Anime & CGI*. London: Flame tree.

Beckman, Karen R. 2014. *Animating Film Theory*. Durham, NC: Duke University Press.

Bendazzi, Giannalberto. 1994. *Cartoons: One Hundred Years of Cinema Animation*. Bloomington, IN: Indiana University Press.

Campbell, Joseph. 1949. *The Hero with a Thousand Faces*. Princeton NJ: Princeton University Press.

Carlotta's Face. 2018. Written and directed by Valentin Riedl and Frédéric Schuld. Germany: Fabian and Fred.

Cavalier, Steven, and Sylvain Chomet. 2011. *The World History of Animation*. Berkeley, CA: University of California Press.

Cholodenko, Alan. 1995. *The Illusion of Life: Essays on Animation*. Sydney: Power Publications.

Cholodenko, Alan. 2007. *The Illusion of Life II: More Essays on Animation*. Sydney: Power Publications.

Clash of the Titans. 1981. Written by Beverley Cross. Storyboards by Ray Harryhausen. Directed by Desmond Davies. UK, USA: Metro-Goldwyn-Mayer.

Crafton, Donald. 1993. *Before Mickey: The Animated Film, 1898–1928*. Chicago: University of Chicago Press.

Deadsy. 1990. Written by Russell Hoban. Created by David Anderson.

Dunnigan, Brian. 2019. *Screenwriting Is Filmmaking: The Theory and Practice of Writing for the Screen*. Marlborough, UK: The Crowood Press.

Earth vs The Flying Saucers (aka *Invasion of the Flying Saucers* and *Flying Saucers from Outer Space*). 1956. Written by Curt Siodmak, George Worthing Yates, Raymond T. Marcus (aka Bernard Gordon). Storyboards by Ray Harryhausen. Directed by Fred F. Sears. USA: Clover Productions.

Edera, Bruno. 1977. *Full Length Animated Feature Films*. Waltham Abbey, UK: Focal Press.

Field, Syd. 2005. *Screenplay: The Foundations of Screenwriting* Rev. ed. New York: Delta Trade Paperbacks.

Flee. 2021. Written by Jonas Poher Rasmussen. Directed by Jonas Poher Rasmussen. Denmark: Final Cut for Real, Sun Creature Studio, Vivement Lundi.

Freytag, Gustav. 1895. *Freytag's Technique of the Drama: An Exposition of Dramatic Composition and Art*. Chicago: Griggs.

Furniss, Maureen. 2016. *A New History of Animation*. New York: Thames & Hudson.

Gulino, Paul Joseph. 2004. *Screenwriting: The Sequence Approach. The Hidden Structure of Successful Screenplays*. New York and London: Continuum.

Harris, Miriam, Lilly Husbands, and Paul Taberham. 2019. *Experimental Animation: From Analogue to Digital*. London and New York: Routledge.

Harryhausen, Ray, and Tony Dalton. 2011. *Ray Harryhausen's Fantasy Scrapbook: Models, Artwork and Memories from 65 Years of Filmmaking*. London: Aurum.

Hauge, Michael. [1992]. *Writing Screenplays that Sell*. British ed. [London]: Elm Tree Books.

Hauser, Tim. 2008. *The Art of WALL-E*. San Francisco: Chronicle Books.

Holliday, Christopher. 2018. *The Computer-Animated Film: Industry, Style and Genre*. Edinburgh: Edinburgh University Press.

Howard, David, and Edward Marbley. 1993. *The Tools of Screenwriting: A Writer's Guide to the Craft and Elements of a Screenplay*. New York: St Martin's Press.

Jason and the Argonauts. 1963. Written by Apollonius Rhodios. Storyboards by Ray Harryhausen. Directed by Don Chaffey. USA: Morningside Productions.

Manovich, Lev. 2013. *Software Takes Command*. New York: Bloomsbury.

Miyazaki, Hayao, 2009. *Starting Point: 1979–1996*. Trans. Beth Cary and Frederik L. Schodt. San Francisco: Viz Media.

Murdock, Maureen. 1990. *The Heroine's Journey: Woman's Quest for Wholeness*. Boston: Shambala.

One Million Years B.C. 1966. Written by Michael Carreras. Storyboards by Ray Harryhausen. Directed by Don Chaffey. UK: Hammer Film Productions, Seven Arts.

O'Gorman, Marcel. 2018. "Writing with a Soldering Iron: On the Art of Making Attention." In *The Routledge Handbook of Digital Writing and Rhetoric*, edited by Jonathan Alexander and Jacqueline Rhodes, 48–57. New York: Routledge.

Osmond, Andrew. 2010. *100 Animated Feature Films*. London: BFI.

Pallant, Chris, and Steven Price. 2015. *Storyboarding. A Critical History*. Basingstoke, UK and New York: Palgrave Macmillan.

Pallant, Chris. 2015. *Animated Landscapes: History, Form and Function*. New York: Bloomsbury.

Paper Birds. 2020. Written by German Heller. Directed by Federico Carlini German Heller. Argentina: 3DAR.

Parn, Prit, 2011. Interview by Paul Wells.

Peri, Don. 2010. *Working with Walt: Interviews with Disney artists*. Jackson, US: Univ. Press of Mississippi.

Pikkov, Ülo. 2010. *Animasophy: Theoretical Writings on the Animated Film*. Tallinn: Estonian Academy of Arts.

Pixar Central. 2020. "A Bug's Life: 'Storyboard Pitch' Documentary." *YouTube*, 4 January. https://www.youtube.com/watch?v=DlRWqK3gFAc. Accessed 7 March 2022.

Purves, Barry. 2014. *Stop-Motion Animation*. London: Fairchild.

Ruddell, Caroline, and Paul Ward, eds. 2019. *The Crafty Animator: Handmade, Craft-based Animation and Cultural Value*. Cham, Switzerland: Springer.

Segal, Steve. 2022. Interview by Chris Pallant.

Sharman, Leslie. 1994. "Down the White Road: The Animator Yuri Norstein Talks with Leslie Felperin Sharman." *Sight and Sound* 5: 20.

Soul. 2020. Written by Pete Docter, Mike Jones, and Kemp Powers. Storyboards by Michael Yates. Directed by Pete Docter. USA: Walt Disney Pictures, Pixar Animation Studios.

T. J. 2020. "Our First Impressions of Pixar's 'Soul' After Screening 35 Minutes – It's a Living Art Piece." *Pixar Post*, 9 October. https://www.pixarpost.com/2020/10/pixar-soul-first-impressions.html. Accessed 7 March 2022.

The Valley of Gwangi. 1969. Written by William Bast, Julian More, and Willis H. Brien. Storyboards by Ray Harryhausen. Directed by Jim O'Connolly. USA: Charles H. Scheer Productions.

The Black Dog. 1987. Written and directed by Alison De Vere. UK: Black Dog, Malinka Films.

The Lion King. 1994. Written by Irene Mecchi, Jonathan Roberts, and Linda Woolverton. Directed by Roger Allers and Rob Minkoff. USA: Walt Disney Pictures, Walt Disney Feature Animation.

The Lost Thing. 2011. Written by Shaun Tan. Directed by Shaun Tan and Andrew Ruhemann. Australia: Passion Pictures Australia.

The Driver is Red. 2017. Written and directed by Randall Christopher. USA: People People Media, RSC Creative.

Truby, John. 2007. *The Anatomy of Story: 22 Steps to Becoming a Master Storyteller*. New York: Faber and Faber.

Up. 2009. Written by Bob Peterson and Pete Docter.

Vogler, Christopher, 2007. *The Writer's Journey: Mythic Structure For Writers*. Studio City, CA: Michael Wiese Productions.

Wells, Paul. 1998. *Understanding Animation*. London: Routledge.

WALL-E. 2008. Written by Andrew Stanton and Jim Reardon. Storyboards by Max Brace and Peter Sohn. Directed by Andrew Stanton. USA: Walt Disney Pictures, Pixar Animation Studios.

Wells, Paul, and Johnny Hardstaff. 2008a. *Re-imagining Animation: The Changing Face of the Moving Image*. Bloomsbury.

Wells, Paul. 2008b. *Basics Animation 03: Drawing for Animation* (Vol. 3). Bloomsbury.

Wells, Paul. 2011a. "Boards, Beats, Binaries and Bricolage: Approaches to the Animated Script." In *Analysing the Screenplay*, edited by Jill Nelmes, 89–105. New York: Routledge.

Wells, Paul. 2011b. "The Toolbox of Technology and Technique: Animation in 100 Objects." In *Watch Me Move: The Animation Show*, edited by Greg Hilty and Alona Pardo. London and New York: Merrill.

Wells, Paul, and Samantha Moore. 2017. *The Fundamentals of Animation*. London: Bloomsbury.

Wells, Paul. 2018. "Playing on the Animation Spectrum: Sport and Visualisation." *Imago: Studi di cinema e media* 16: 79–95.

Yorke, John, 2013. *Into the Woods: How Stories Work and Why We Tell Them*. London: Penguin.

CHAPTER 31

The Short-Form Scripted Serial Drama: The Novice Showrunner's New Opportunity

Debbie Danielpour

31.1 Introduction

For the past two years, I have been teaching a course at Boston University on developing the short-form series for the web. Each year the course was over-subscribed. The department approved the course with no pushback. The seasoned editors of this volume deemed the subject a worthy idea. Why?

A simple answer: the short-form web series is surfacing in many platforms. In 2020, Quibi launched a well-financed platform dedicated to streaming the short-form for viewing on mobile devices. Quibi shut down six months after its launch (Mullen and Rizzo 2020), and its properties were picked up by Roku, which leads many to believe that the commercial future of short-form shows is indeterminate. YouTube, however, continues to host many popular short-form series and streamers are producing and hosting short-form narrative dramatic and comedy series.[1]

For years, executives, managers, and talent scouts have been scouring TikTok and YouTube for independently produced series (Secret Agent Man 2020). In November 2020, The Canadian Independent Production Fund

---

[1] Short form series include *State of the Union, The Guild, The Lizzie Bennet Diaries, High Maintenance, The Misadventures of Awkward Black Girl, Special, The Other F Word, Her Story.*

D. Danielpour (✉)
Boston University, Boston, MA, USA
e-mail: ddc@bu.edu

announced that it was dedicating $1.7 million to finance six scripted short-form series (Independent Production Fund 2021).

What has interested me most, however, is the fact that the short-form series provides an ideal opportunity for student writers and filmmakers to produce their material inexpensively and to publish their series without having to push through the infernal industry gates. Without the time constraints of network or cable television, the short-form streaming series has become an arena for experimentation and emerging talent (Johnson 2019, 89). This means screenwriters, critics, and professors must be versed in this format's content, types of characters and structures—essentially, we must understand a new set of poetics.

This chapter will briefly review the conventions or poetics—content, characters, and season and episode structure—of serialized prestige television drama and dramedy in *Breaking Bad* (2008–2013), *The Chi* (2018–) and *The Marvelous Mrs. Maisel* (2017–) and then demonstrate, with an analysis of Quibi's *The Stranger* (2020), Amazon's *The Other F-Word* (2016), and Netflix's *Special* (2019–2021), how those conventions inform but must also be altered for the short-form series. The exploration will culminate in a poetics for the short-form prestige series.

Why use serialized, premium prestige one-hour serialized narrative dramas and a dramedy as a standard? The scripts of prestige series that are serialized present the greatest challenges for this new short-form, and therefore offer the most to learn. Serialized narrative television can be defined as a series wherein each episode is a part of a progressive, larger story, both in terms of events and characters (Landau 2018, 31), whether that be part of an infinite or finite storytelling mode (Ianniello and Batty 2021). This chapter's focus is on serialized rather than episodic or procedural shows also because over the last 10–20 years, scripted television is increasingly dominated by serialized series. Viewers now have the technology to watch or re-watch a highly serialized show at their own pace as well as engage in platforms to discuss their chosen series (Mittell 2015), which has increased the popularity of serialized television.

If most short-form shows are either anthologies or sitcoms, why bother analyzing the minority of shows that aspire to prestige television? Is it ludicrous to assume that a short-form series can reach the standards of long-form prestige series? Not at all. Netflix's *Special* can claim prestige status. Katzenberg and Whitman's mobile-only platform Quibi funneled $1.75 billion into its operations, attracting prestige talent and crew for its productions (Horton 2020). With higher narrative and production standards for television and the groundwork already laid for short-form to aspire to prestige-TV, a showrunner has good reasons to aim above the fray.

31.2 Television Poetics

In his 2006 essay, "Toward a Poetics of Television Narrative", Michael Z. Newman wrote "a poetics can help explain why so many people take so much pleasure in television's stories" (16). Newman's television poetics aim to demonstrate how a show develops clear, ongoing stories about compelling characters facing difficult obstacles, how a show satisfies a viewer's desires for knowledge about these characters, forges an emotional connection, and secures a viewer's commitment to continued viewing of the show. Essentially, these poetics define what a writer needs to achieve in order to write a successful show, be it a one-hour drama, half-hour comedy, or fifteen-minute episodes (Newman 2006).

In my years of analyzing and teaching serial television dramas, I have found that the following characteristics are common in successful cable or streaming prestige shows. These attributes are consistent with widely cited television writing theory and manuals (see Jacobs and Peacock 2013; Cook 2007; Douglas 2011; Landau 2014, 2018; Rabkin 2017).

1. Themes/organizing principles that connect episodes and seasons.
2. Relatable characters with enough complexity to unpack over multiple seasons, i.e. they change, sustain relationships that test allegiances and generate story lines.
3. Freedom in terms of format and content, often with graphic content.
4. High production values.
5. Weighty or universal subjects.
6. Ongoing conflicts and questions, the solutions of which give way to extended story lines and character arcs until the series ends.
7. Setting or world is well-suited to premise and stakes.
8. Some level of episodic integrity via plot, character, or theme.
9. Effective episodic structure, sometimes a recurring pattern or blueprint.

31.3 Premium Prestige Long-Form Television Series

31.3.1 Content

Esquire's critic Eric Thurm writes that "any set of rules you can string together to define a prestige TV series is designed to signal one thing: That the show is meant to be taken seriously"(Thurm 2017). Shows typically considered prestige—*Breaking Bad*, *The Wire* (2002–2008), *Mad Men* (2007–2015), *The Chi*, *The Marvelous Mrs. Maisel*—explore weighty themes and criticize social structures, even if delivered in the skin of comedy.

In *Breaking Bad*, Walter White struggles with his own hubris in deciding to amass money from his meth empire. The show ultimately explores how a good man turns "bad", the elixir of power, the detachment necessary to make inhumane choices, the grip of the drug trade on lower class populations and the irreversible path of an illegal, high-stakes enterprise. Serious and ripe for a promising franchise? Indeed.

Unlike *Breaking Bad*, *The Chi* does not focus on one character's struggle to take us through all five of its seasons, but instead focuses on how the murder-retaliation cycle plagues a *group* of characters who live on the south side of Chicago. Their stories expose the unreliability of Chicago's criminal justice system, demonstrate the seeming inevitability of violence in the face of hopelessness, and show many ways in which love can shape each character's story.

The Marvelous Mrs. Maisel, categorized as comedy by the Academy, explores the sexism of late 1950s America and the struggle of a recently divorced young mother to find her identity and voice through stand-up comedy. The protagonist's journey, as well as those of recurring characters, cover themes of marital politics, censorship, income insecurity, and the cancer of the capitalist dream.

31.3.2 Characters

The characters of prestige series make us care enough to commit to watching each episode of the season, in part because these characters are psychologically complex. This complexity allows viewers to develop an intimate relationship with the characters as they grow and change (Hilmes et al. 2014). Character complexity is an implicit advantage of the television series (versus the 90-minute film) and an absolute necessity in a multi-season drama because the layers and resulting changes in key characters allow for ongoing story branches.

Walter White is a loving father and husband, a teacher with an understanding of chemistry that exceeds his pay grade, a dedicated provider who works two jobs and a victim of his partners' betrayal. Mrs. Maisel is torn between her drive to succeed in comedy, her conformity to 1950s feminine standards, and her sympathy for her ex-husband who failed at the same endeavor.

Relationships provide our protagonists' stakes (something our characters fear losing)—a romantic partner, friend, family member, colleague, teacher, or business partner—and also function as an antagonistic force or enabler. This is why the settings for *Breaking Bad* or *The Chi*, replete with characters *necessarily connected*, either by location or family, are well-suited for a multi-season show.

31.3.3 Structure

Any structural analysis of a serialized, scripted television show must consider:

1. the thematic integrity, arc and structure of *the entire franchise,*
2. the integrity and structure of *each season,* and
3. the structure of *each episode.*

It is important to first make the distinction between a show that is essentially *a film broken into parts* versus a true serialized television show. Several of the short-form series produced by Quibi—*Most Dangerous Game* (2020), *When the Streetlights Go On* (2020)—are just that—a film broken into parts. A series that satisfies viewers who are not bingeing but rather consuming episodes one at a time, as well as producers with commercial interests provides story structure *within* each episode, that is, some sort of *episodic integrity*, either via theme or story or character arc, and sets up the last act of the episode as a cliffhanger or a lure to watch the next episode.

This distinction is important for several reasons: first, most serialized shows are designed for an infinite future. For writers, this challenging and yet lucrative "infinite model" storytelling means their show is a success only as long as it continues. Feature films have a beginning, a middle and an end—so if you split a feature into, let's say, ten 12-minute episodes, the episodes will likely *not* have episodic integrity, nor will they end each episode with a cliffhangeresque ending. Essentially, cutting up a feature film can't support the "infinite model" (Rabkin 2017, 42).

In sum, despite the vast changes in how audiences consume television narratives, "the idea of the television episode as always containing a potential to exist as a whole, individual unit, is still alive and well" (VanArendonk 2019, 79).

31.3.4 Thematic Integrity of a Franchise

Given that character arcs are the anchor of many prestige shows, a character's development will generally be woven into the series franchise's central question and become a component of the series' organizing principle.

For example, the structure of most of *Breaking Bad*'s episodes are organized by Walter's character arc—how long before a good man's intentions turn him into the evil he's fighting against? The organizing principle of *The Marvelous Mrs. Maisel* is whether or not our protagonist can succeed in her effort during the late 1950s without losing her family and community's respect.

31.3.5 Arc or Integrity of a Season

Each season of a successful series possesses its own unity with a central theme, narrative drive, and/or character arc acting as the season's *glue*. For example, the pilot episode of *Breaking Bad* works because it's a complete story in its own right but also sets up the series' critical story lines and lures us into a season that has its *own* unity: the season is about whether or not Walter will succeed at making meth and empowering himself.

31.3.6 Structure of Episodes

Despite the increased elasticity of streaming episode formats, many prestige one-hour cable dramas like *Breaking Bad* or *The Chi* employ the once-codified five-act structure, owing partly to what writers and readers have grown accustomed to from its progenitors with commercial breaks. Most episodes of long-form one-hour streaming series also have A, B, C, and/or D storylines as well as *runners* which could be considered less significant story lines that start and end within a season. Some prescriptions suggest that each act should begin and end on the A story (Cook 2007, 50).

The *Mrs. Maisel* pilot introduces almost all the primary and secondary characters of the first season, a rule of thumb for a long-form series. The A story of the pilot is about whether or not Midge will move on via stand-up comedy. This supports the franchise's larger theme or organizing principle. The B story is her relationship with Joel, which is fueled by questions of love, loyalty, jealousy (because of her talent), and humility. The C story covers the budding partnership between Midge and Suzie, Midge's connection to the Gaslight Café and ultimately her agent. And the D story is occupied by Midge's parents, Abe and Rose, and the pressures they exert on her now that she's divorced, has been arrested and will be "a lost cause". Lenny Bruce's story functions as a runner.

The bones of the Aristotelian paradigm, Pity-Fear-Catharsis, work here to secure our allegiance with this show's protagonist despite her initial unlikability. The pilot promises multiple ongoing conflicts, leaves us with several unanswered questions, and takes place in New York City, the perfect setting for a series about getting a start in stand-up comedy. By the end of season one, Midge's character changes significantly.

The Showtime series *The Chi* spreads its stories across several characters, rather than organize its arc around one protagonist as is the case with *Breaking Bad* or *The Marvelous Mrs. Maisel*. Lena Waithe has set the story in Chicago's south side and focuses on the entwined lives of four African-American males. This structure is a deliberate storytelling choice: without a reliable criminal justice system, people often take matters into their own hands, creating a wide and messy web of individuals affected by violence (Hale 2019).

The pilot is structured around five acts, with a teaser that functions as an inciting incident, act one establishing the key characters "normal lives", and act two establishing the motivation for one character to seek retribution for a murder. Every future beat of the story casually relates to the previous—as we shall see below, a seemingly obvious point in screen storytelling but even more critical for the shorter form. The cliffhanger leaves us wondering if Brandon, a young man aspiring to launch his own restaurant, will avenge his little brother's death—which supports the franchise's essential organizing principle.

31.4 The Short-Form Series

In 2016, the Television Academy expanded its classifications to include short-form programs "defined as program epicodes averaging 15 minutes or less". The Emmy category is defined as "Outstanding Short Form Series—Comedy or Drama" (Television Academy, 2016).

31.4.1 Content and Characters

The first season of Netflix's *Special*, released in April of 2019, runs eight episodes with each no longer than 15 minutes. The series earned four Emmy nominations for its first season, including best short-form series and best actor in a short-form series. It also won the Short-Form New Media–Original award in the 2020 Writers Guild of America Awards. The show has received mostly positive reviews from critics, holding a 96% approval rating on Rotten Tomatoes. It was renewed for a second season.

Starring, written and created by Ryan O'Connell, *Special* is a coming-of-age dramedy series about a young gay man with mild cerebral palsy who, over the first season, rewrites his identity based on the lie that he's the victim of an accident. The season focuses on whether or not the protagonist will gain the courage to tell his truth and live independently. The series contains several components of a prestige show: high production values, graphic content (gay sex), serious subjects such as the biases toward the disabled and coming into one's identity, story lines that can extend beyond the first season, characters who change over the season and a modicum of seasoned actors such as Jessica Hecht (*Breaking Bad, Red Oaks, Dan in Real Life*) and Patrick Fabian (*Better Call Saul, 24, Veronica Mars*).

The show's target audience addresses a niche of 20-somethings, LGBTQ communities, people with disabilities and those interested in the podcast or online magazine universe. *Niche shows* are common among scripted and non-scripted short series such as *The Guild* (2007, 2012–2013), a comedy series about the lives of a guild of online gamers, which premiered on YouTube and is now hosted on Netflix. Similarly, *The Misadventures of Awkward Black Girl* is a comedic confessional-style series about the struggles of a 20-something black woman. *High Maintenance* appeals to those interested in cannabis culture, and *Broad City* (2014–2019) to 30-something women trying to make it in New York City.

Much like the pilots of our aforementioned long-form series, the *setup of Special* establishes essentials, but is *more* efficient than the setups in the pilots of long-form shows: the locations are archetypical—a Los Angeles neighborhood, a middle-class home, a hipster start-up company EggWoke that publishes confessional essays, and a high-end pool party—so there is *little need to world-build* as would be the case in a period drama like *Mrs. Maisel* or a fantasy or science fiction show. The protagonist's relationships are initially with one family member (Ryan's mother) and one work friend (Kim) and only expand into a few more characters *after* the first couple episodes—very different from the vast number of characters introduced in the pilot of *Mrs. Maisel* or *The Chi*.

The success of *Special*'s first season, as a short-form show, is partly due to the fact that *the world is small*—a story about Ryan's personal goals with a small cast of characters—again, very different from the multi-character, large neighborhood in *The Chi*, or from the spread of New York neighborhoods and characters in *Mrs. Maisel*. As with *Mrs. Maisel* and *The Chi*, all the characters are *necessarily connected*, but the cast of primary characters is smaller and the story takes place *within a much more confined* world. Further, these characters' connections—at work, within family, or in relationships—are *not* all established in the pilot episode.

The short-form pilot, then must *introduce primary characters over the course of several first season shows*, rather than in the pilot episode. This allows enough time to focus on Ryan, which permits the *unfurling of Ryan's complexity* without requiring 45-minute-long episodes.

As comedic as many of the series' situations might seem, our protagonist's character can still develop complexity within the short-form for several reasons:

1. Each of the short episodes focuses primarily on *one of Ryan's specific challenges* or choices. For example, the pilot establishes why Ryan lies about his cerebral palsy, claiming his disabilities are due to a car accident. Another episode focuses on his first sexual experience.
2. Each of the characters with whom Ryan is in relationship responds to him or affects him with their choices. For example, his mother starts a relationship with the next-door-neighbor, something his mother tries to hide from her son, triggering later tension between mother and son.
3. Ryan has conflicting traits, skills, and weaknesses in his quest to become independent and to honestly identify himself. He is smart, articulate and self-aware, but also timid, and mute when ridiculed. Add to this, he desperately wants to belong, be known, and connect with others, but lacks the social skills. These contradictions within a character—achievable in both long and short-form—guarantee character complexity and material for ongoing episodes.

The Stranger was created by filmmaker, writer, director, and EP Verna Sud. The thriller stars Maika Monroe (*It Follows*) as Clare, a young rideshare driver who picks up a passenger Carl E. (Dane DeHaan) from a posh Hollywood Hills address and soon learns that he is a sociopathic murderer. The show is a harrowing 13-hour cat and mouse pursuit through the Los Angeles area with each episode titled by the hour and averaging nine minutes. The cast is limited to three primary characters, which serves the short-form well: Clare, Carl E, and a convenience store clerk JJ (Avan Jogia), who becomes Clare's only ally.

Locations are many and varied, which increases the series budget but is necessary for the premise. The cast and production values resemble that of a prestige show, however the genre (thriller verging on horror), quality of acting and the story's resolution call into question the quality of the series as a whole.

The thriller genre need not be a liability of the short-form, but this series' DNA did not motivate story beats based on character complexity. To portray more about Clare's character beyond her stamina, trifling writerly aspirations and previous tendency to lie (which causes the police to doubt her), the nonstop pursuit would need to pause to dedicate one or two of the short episodes to deepening an aspect of her character. Similarly, the antagonist's motivation about the ruinous effects of social media is hidden until the season's end.

In contrast, *Special*'s Ryan is given a choice at EggWoke to write about his lie or to tell his truth, a choice grounded in the series' theme. *The Stranger*'s Clare never writes a blog or tells Carl a Scheherazade-like story to save her life. She can only choose how to evade her pursuer, which has little to do with the show's alleged theme—how social media intrudes on individuals' privacy.

The *Other F-Word*, created by filmmaker Caytha Jentis, is described by Renee Kemper in her April 2020 blog *That's Just Life* as "an edgy comedy about a group [of 40- or 50-something female] friends who find that the angst of raising kids may be nothing compared to the angst of starting over after they are grown". The eight episodes of the first season range in length from four minutes to 13 minutes. The episodes of season two run longer, up to 19 minutes. The series seems to be angling for prestige status based on its graphic content, high production values, and some actors of note: Steve Guttenberg (*Police Academy*), Michael Boatman (*The Good Wife*), Reiko Aylesworth (*24*), and Judy Gold (*The Jim Gaffigan Show*).

Use of archetypical locations—primarily houses, apartments, offices, and parks—keeps the budget low and reduces the script's responsibility to worldbuild, which suits a low-budget short-form show. The series aims to appeal to a niche, another attribute of the short-form: privileged women in their 50s who resemble the women in the show. The four primary characters plus these characters' spouses or boyfriends, children, and colleagues—many of whom are introduced in the pilot episode—enable future story lines but dangerously expand the cast of characters beyond the short-form series' capacity to develop them deeply. Part of what helps a short-form series cohere, is *an ever-present theme*, and yet that is hard to detect in this show other than the myriad struggles the women face.

31.4.2 Season Structure and Integrity

As was stated earlier, the integrity of a season depends on the presence of the series' theme or organizing principle in all episodes as well as the degree of seriality between each episode.

31.4.3 Special

Like *Breaking Bad* and *The Marvelous Mrs. Maisel*, *Special* is a protagonist-centered series. The stakes—whether or not Ryan will be accepted for who he is—fit the world that the series has created. His is not a world where people die by gunshot—as is the case with *The Chi*, or where drug lords threaten one's safety as we see in *Breaking Bad*. What is at stake is not his very life, but rather his identity and happiness.

The first season is securely held together by the tension of his lie and by the protagonist learning to love himself and claim his identity: he enters the professional world as an intern and falsely attributes his disability to a car accident, befriends his colleague Kim, fails at having sex, hires a sex worker, develops the courage to move out of his mother's home, suffers the indignity of no one attending his housewarming party and by the first "act" *of the season* (after three episodes) gathers the courage to admit to Kim that he just moved out of his home and is "a loser who's been masquerading as a non-loser".

The first season of *Special* builds this tension in a fashion *similar to that of the three-act structure in a feature film*. The first three episodes could be considered act one of the series, as they establish almost all the key characters, the central conflict, and the few subplots. The season is definitely not a film broken into parts, but rather comprised of episodes that are causally connected to each other. This stands in contrast to long-form serialized dramas with their sequential introduction of new antagonistic forces and inclusion of many more subplots.

As is detailed in the structural analysis below, *Special's* pilot, episodes two and three all maintain some level of episodic integrity in that *they focus on one or two central conflicts per episode*. Further, the season carries are a few plants (or setups) for later payoffs (Mom's new boyfriend's jacket, Ryan's inability to tie his shoes, love-interest Carey), which serve multiple functions. They establish the storyteller's authority because the viewer is ultimately gratified in seeing how these small plants later payoff. They create mystery, conflict, test and deepen characters and stand as critical tools in connecting serialized episodes.

Episode four begins to complicate all that has been established, much as is the case in act two of a feature film. The episode maintains episodic integrity via the theme of "being real", in that it focuses on two subplot characters who act honestly: Ryan's mother finally sleeps with the next-door neighbor and Kim admits to her pennilessness, demonstrating that she had also lied and now demands honesty from Ryan going forward. Both of these subplots contribute to the ongoing A plot and season's thematic integrity. The episode also establishes a plant: Ryan is besotted with Carey, a friend of Kim's.

Episode five is nearly a stand-alone episode in that it focuses on Karen's dissatisfaction with being her son and mother's caregiver. By maintaining this tight focus, the episode can delve deeply into one storyline, character, or theme, enabling a level of character complexity. This episode spotlights

Karen's loneliness which motivates her to intensify her intimacy with the neighbor, Phil. This ties into a larger story arc of the season—can Mom and Ryan discontinue their codependency?

It logically follows that episode six centers around Ryan's and Karen's respective romantic relationships and how this challenges their codependency. Complications arise around the discovery and attempt to hide the meaning of Phil's jean jacket (planted earlier). As Ryan continues his lie about the car accident and grows smitten with Carey, Mom's relationship with Phil strengthens. Ryan's hopes are then dashed: Carey has a boyfriend. This episode is held together by mother and son's blooming relationships and the lies they maintain to keep the truth from each other.

Episode seven examines Karen's inability to separate from Ryan: Ryan is upset to discover that his mom and Phil are in a relationship and that she lied to him. Karen feels she cannot "abandon" Ryan to take a weekend away with Phil, which leads to their break up. Ultimately, both mother and son question their ability to sustain a romantic relationship—a short episode elegantly glued together by a theme.

The last episode maintains episodic integrity about truth-telling while bringing together all the series' key characters—a convention of season finales. If the season had not been renewed, this episode could have closed the entire series—with a few tweaks. Ryan finally tells everyone the truth about his condition and while much is gained, his relationship with his mother seems lost—herein the reason why the series can continue. Further, Phil rejects Karen's attempt to renew their relationship because he "doesn't want to be in a relationship with someone else's kid". Ryan writes a blog post: "Why lying about who you are is not fucking awesome, AKA Why I owe everyone a big apology".

This signals resolution of the conflict introduced in the inciting incident of episode one. Ryan now stands in front of his co-workers to admit he has Cerebral Palsy, which makes Olivia offer Ryan a "freelance "job". Ryan works to regain his trust with Kim, gets kissed by Carey and returns home to his mother without the birthday cake she'd asked for. Karen feels unseen and underappreciated and blames her son. Ryan walks home.

The season grants the viewer *a story that progresses from the first episode to the last*, sustains tension as it deepens the characters of mother and son, introduces universal questions, and leaves us with open-ended questions about each primary character's future.

In order to deeply develop characters within such short episodes, this analysis demonstrates that each episode must limit the number of story lines it hosts while setting up story lines for future episodes. In contrast to the long-form shows that contain up to five story lines in one episode, in *Special*, there are usually no more than two narrative lines per episode. Each beat in each episode hones close to that episode's central question or theme and never veers into territory outside the limited world of the show.

31.4.4 The Stranger

Designed as a limited series, *The Stranger's* story resolves in its last episode. It mirrors the Scheherazade mythology in that the protagonist, who aspires to be a writer, must tell the killer a story in order to save her life. It is a shame that this conceit dissipates after the first episode because it would have provided a sensible way to structure each short episode and simultaneously deepen Clare's character.

Instead, the season's narrative drive shifts around the questions: will Clare escape from this sociopathic stalker? Is the stalker, Carl, all in her head? This question is supported by the fact that the story is primarily told from Clare's POV; the viewer rarely sees Carl after the first episode and the viewer understands that Clare has a history of fabricating stories and false accusations. Limiting POV is a clever tool in developing a short-form series because the array of events is necessarily curbed.

Episodes have some measure of integrity in that each reveals at least one new way in which Carl manages (story logic be damned) to have superior knowledge that enables him to track Clare and eventually her ally, JJ. Each episode successfully leaves the viewer at a cliffhanger.

The season fails to cohere as a whole, however, because the last episodes upend our genre/tonal expectations by turning the show into a social commentary. We believed this show was about how Clare will figure out Carl's *modus operandi* and save her life, not about indicting the world of social media and its resulting algorithms.

31.4.5 The Other F-Word

The series tells multiple stories based on the lives of the four featured female characters who are smartly different from each other and longtime friends. The series attempts to connect the other women's stories around that of one character, Amy. However each woman's story runs parallel to the other, rarely impacting Amy's story or raising tension through the season. In contrast, in *The Chi*, any big decision made by one character, for example Ronnie killing Coogie, affects at least one other character. The only coherence in season one of *The Other F-Word* stems the fact that the four women are friends and are responding to how one of the women's husbands dies at the start of the series. In short, the seriality of the show is weakened by the fact that each woman's journey does not complicate the others and that the episodes rarely dedicate enough time, per episode, to delve deeply into any of the women's conflicts.

The episodes could have developed integrity and seasonal coherence if single episodes limited their focus—in terms of character and conflict—and causally connected story events throughout the season.

31.4.6 Episode Structure

Because part of the attraction of the short-form episode is the assumption that viewers will watch the episodes on their mobile devices in situations where they might only have available the seven minutes of the episode, effective episodic structure is a critical goal for writers of the short-form. Writers could greet the short episode as an opportunity to focus on one theme, storyline, or character arc, which would ultimately result in more memorable and meaningful episodes. Therefore, *both* the coherence of a season as well as the structure of an episode are essential in formulating the poetics of the short-form series.

With the first season's eight episodes at 13–15 minutes per episode, *Special*, has 120 minutes to develop not only the protagonist, Ryan, but also the other primary characters: his mother, his friend Kim, his mother' boyfriend, and Ryan's boss and the show's antagonist Olivia. Analysis of the show's pilot demonstrates Ryan's complexity, its structure, how it maintains episodic coherence and contributes to the season's thematic unity.

In the *teaser*, Ryan walks in a suburban Southern California neighborhood and explains to an annoying kid the vagaries of Cerebral Palsy. In a mere minute, the script has established the setting, revealed some of Ryan's physical limitations, and demonstrated his mature attitude toward his condition. We are instantly sympathetic.

Act one starts in a gym, where Ryan expresses his desires and fears to his trainer: he is attracted to another man, he got a bum deal by being gay and disabled and his mild case renders him not able-enough, too in-between and therefore he doesn't know where he belongs. Here, we have the franchise's central theme: Where do I belong and how do I claim my identity? Critical to any starting point for a complex protagonist, we hear about his key desires and struggles. Critical to the short-form, these desires and the central theme are established in the pilot's first minutes.

At 2'35", Ryan is hit by a car, which stands as the episode's inciting incident because it fuels his pivotal decisions going forward. Three months later, Ryan's overprotective mother Karen infantilizes him as she advises him for his first day of his internship. Here, we are introduced to the B story and the most influential relationship of the season—can Karen allow her son to grow up? Similar to the long-form, this protagonist's relationship with his mother acts as both a stake and, as we see later, an antagonistic force but far different from the long-form, the relationship is established three minutes into the pilot.

At the offices of EggWoke, a website that posts over-the-top confessional blogs, Ryan—the new intern—is demeaned by the self-absorbed, insensitive boss Olivia—the overt antagonistic force—and befriended by the bossy but kind co-worker, Kim. As with *The Chi* and *Mrs. Maisel,* act one of *Special* has introduced the inciting incident and established the world of our protagonist, but the inciting incident surfaces far sooner and the "world" is much smaller.

Act two could be said to begin when Ryan enters EggWoke (4'52") and is demoted to opening mail, or after Ryan has lunch with Kim, who assumes his physical condition is caused by his car accident and he chooses to let her believe this ruse. At 9′11″, we wonder if Ryan will tell the truth. The tension of Act two, then, is whether or not Ryan will tell the outer world he has CP. This returns us to the series' organizing principle—who am I? How will I identify to the outer world?

In contrast, in a long-form show with more characters and subplots, it is not until act two (page 20 of the screenplay) that we see, for example, the inciting incident of Walter White's cancer in *Breaking Bad*. It takes until the third act of the 58-page pilot for the organizing principle to become clear. In long-form shows like *Breaking Bad,* average scenes run 2–3 minutes. Each scene in *Special runs about a minute* with important scenes running two minutes. Almost all primary characters of the first seasons of the long-form shows are introduced in Act one, but only four are smartly introduced in *Special*: Ryan, his mother, Olivia and Kim.

The second act returns to EggWoke where Ryan is ridiculed for not being able to open mail. At home, his mother encourages him to tell his colleagues about his CP. Back at EggWoke, Ryan is about to pitch the truth to his boss. Here, we enter what could be called *the third act*—wherein the protagonist and antagonist come together, or where the protagonist must make the most pivotal choice or take the most significant action of the episode. Much like the pivotal choice Mrs. Maisel makes to step on stage (but on page 55 of the 67-page pilot script), Ryan is about to come clean and then his boss says she heard about his car accident and he *must* write about this. This scene runs from 11′10″ to 13′00″, one of the longest in the pilot and builds to the climax moment of truth—will Ryan tell her he actually has CP and that his disability is *not* due to a car accident? In a scene at Ryan's desk (13′00″–13′30″), he deletes the title of a previous document "Journey to Healing" and replaces it with "Getting Hit by a Car", the last image of the episode, essentially conveying his choice to continue the lie, which guarantees more complications in the next episode.

The pilot of *Special* follows *a three-act structure:* the teaser runs about one minute, act one ends at 4′50″, act two ends at 11′00″, and act three runs from approximately 11′00″ to 13′30″. The economy of the pilot is well served by the limited settings: the neighborhood street, the gym, EggWoke offices, and Ryan's home. Each act does, in fact, begin and end on the A story.

Within the structure of the pilot, the A story is about whether or not Ryan will tell the truth about his situation, the B story focuses on his mother's influence and the C story touches upon his budding friendship with Kim. This three-act structure, with similar proportions, is used in every future episode of the season—generally focusing most of the time on the A story—with a few episodes granting the B stories almost as much heft as the A story. With the entire pilot episode running only 13 and a half minutes, the writers smartly chose to limit each episodes' foci on the journey of one, sometimes two characters and to make sure every scene contributed to mounting complications of Ryan's response to the inciting incident.

Scenes in *Special* are tightly and *causally connected by consequence and therefore build a story with beats that test characters, raise tension, pose important questions via action (rather than dialogue), and *rise to a climax or moment of truth that's connected to the franchise's organizing principle*. While *The Other F-Word* does connect the four primary characters by their friendship, those connections never test the very bonds that bring the characters together, as is the case in *The Marvelous Mrs. Maisel, Breaking Bad,* or *The Chi*.

The structure of the pilot of *The Stranger* does connect each significant beat by consequence, as must be the case in the thriller genre. The entire series is also fueled by mystery, as is the case with *The Chi*. As with *Special*, *The Stranger's* pilot follows a three-act structure, the inciting incident being when Clare allows Carl to sit in the front seat with her and thereby trusts a man she does not know, the issue of distrust and fear central to the episode. The first act ends at the 6-minute mark, when Carl claims he killed the people in the house they just left. At 8′48″, the episode hits a climax of sorts, where Carl proposes his bargain: "if you tell me a really good story, I will let you live…" and the episode ends. This genre supports a structure different from that of *Special*, dismissing the need for a typical act three denouement. This structure is repeated in the next few episodes, two acts that leave us at a cliffhanger at the end of act two.

The structure of the pilot of *The Other F-Word* is far less clear and therefore never establishes the show's episode template or pattern. The A story purports to be about Amy, as it ends with Amy's questioning her "reason for being", but the entire episode is actually dedicated to introducing us to each of the four primary characters. Were this not a short-form series, time could be allotted to credibly develop each character, as is the case with *The Chi*, but with 15-minute episodes, the series is both overpopulated and poorly structured because it cannot achieve engagement based on interest in character or story. Other episodes demonstrate a varying structure, sometimes ending the episode in the middle of the exposition of the episode's central subject, thereby failing to create a mini-story or ending with a cliffhanger that would vault the viewer to the next episode. Further, it is difficult to connect viewers to our characters via pity, fear, and catharsis, an emotional pattern useful when compressing character development, a paradigm that works to hook us into the characters of *Special* and *The Stranger*.

31.5 Summary: Poetics of the Short-Form, Serialized Drama and Dramedy

The poetics of short-form series, based on the aforementioned analyses, can be distilled as follows:

31.5.1 Content

1. Subject addresses a niche, based on topic or demographic. As long as the series maintains universal appeal, it can endure once streamed on a platform with larger distribution.
2. Settings are archetypical with little need to world-build, therefore easy to identify, and contained, forcing characters in relationship with one another.
3. Stakes fit the size of the story world.

31.5.2 Character

1. Cast of characters introduced in pilot episode is limited, remainder of small cast is introduced in successive episodes.
2. All characters are connected via family, work, friendships, history, enmity, actions. or location, allowing for causal consequences to characters' actions.
3. Protagonist's character development is woven into the A plot which generally starts and ends each episode, his/her/their complexity allows for future story branches.

31.5.3 Structure

1. Episodes are limited in focus—either in terms of plot or character. Story is limited to one or two plot lines per episode, each causally connected to inciting incident in pilot or previous story beat.
2. The entire season, as well as each episode, is often structured into three acts and hones close to theme and central story question.
3. Structure of episode is often based on three actions, though genre requires varying length of each act and potentially dismissing act three, with scenes for a 15-minute show running approximately one minute each and more pivotal scenes running two minutes.
4. Episodes are linked via causal connections or consequences, leaving us with a cliffhanger at the end of each and a clear sense of the episode's subject.
5. Series theme is evident in each episode and well defined, rather than ambiguous and broad.

Graduate and undergraduate students in my short-form web series course wrote many excellent, viable pilots and series bibles. Production students in our film and television department are preparing to produce their episodes as their capstone projects. Unlike the traditional route of screening a student short film at festivals and eventually, if one is lucky, snaring distribution, these short-form shows can be distributed on YouTube or other web platforms. The screenwriters, directors, and crew can directly *show* their work rather than beg interested parties to read it. The students will have accelerated their entry into the industry—all from their independent efforts.

In the interests of artistic freedom and emancipating ourselves from the titanic forces in the entertainment industry, it is important to understand the poetics of this interloper—the short-form narrative web series—and how it might be clearing the way for new showrunners' voices to be seen and heard.

Acknowledgements Many thanks to my talented, dedicated, and generous students in our course, "Developing the Short-Form Web Series". Your scripts and series bibles have taught me more than I could ever glean from years of research.

References

24. 2001–2010. Created by Robert Cochran and Joel Surnow. USA: Imagine Entertainment, 20th Century Fox Television, Real Time Productions, Teakwood Lane Productions.

Better Call Saul. 2015–present. Created by Vince Gilligan and Peter Gould. USA: High Bridge Productions, Crystal Diner Productions, Gran Via Productions, Sony Pictures Television American Movie Classics (AMC).

Breaking Bad. 2008–2013. Created by Vince Gilligan. USA: AMC.

Broad City. 2014–2019. Created by Ilana Glazer and Abbi Jacobson. USA: Paper Kite Productions/Comedy Central.

Cook, Marti. 2007. *Write to TV: Out of Your Head and Onto the Screen*, 2nd ed. Burlington ma and Oxford: Focal Press-Elsevier.

Dan in Real Life. 2007. Written by Peter Gardner and Peter Hedges. Directed by Peter Hedges. USA: Touchstone Pictures, Focus Features, Jon Shestack Productions.

Douglas, Pamela. 2011. *Writing the TV Drama Series*, 3rd ed. Studio City ca: Michael Wiese Productions.

Hale, Mike. 2019. "Review: 'The Chi' Returns to the South Side of Chicago." *The New York Times*, 5 April.

Story, Her. 2015. *Created by Jen Richards*. USA: YouTube.

High Maintenance. 2012–2020. Created by Katja Blichfeld and Ben Sinclair. USA: Janky Clown Productions, Vimeo, HBO.

Hilmes, Michele, et al. 2014. Rethinking Television: A Critical Symposium on the New Age of Episodic Narrative Storytelling. *Cinéaste* 39 (4): 26–38.

Horton, Adrian. 2020. "The Fall of Quibi: How Did a Starry $1.75bn Netflix Rival Crash So Fast?" *The Guardian*. 29 June. https://www.theguardian.com/tv-and-radio/2020/jun/28/quibi-netflix-jeffrey-katzenberg-crash. Accessed 26 January 2020.

Ianniello, Marco, and Craig Batty. 2021. Serial offenders? Defining the boundaries of series and serial TV for screenwriting practice and theory. *Journal of Screenwriting* 12 (1): 55–74. https://doi.org/10.1386/josc_00048_1.

Independent Production Fund. 2021. "Development Packaging Program: Short Form Scripted Series." https://ipf.ca/guidelines/development-packaging-program/. Accessed 13 December 2021.

It Follows. 2014. *Written and directed by David Robert Mitchell*. USA: Northern Lights Films, Animal Kingdom, Two Flints.

Jacobs, Jason, and Steven Peacock, eds. 2013. *Television Aesthetics and Style*. New York and London: Bloomsbury.
Johnson, Catherine. 2019. *Online TV*. Abingdon uk and New York: Routledge.
Landau, Neil. 2014. *The TV Showrunner's Roadmap*. Burlington ma: Focal Press.
Landau, Neil. 2018. *TV Writing on Demand: Creating Great Content in the Digital Era*. Abingdon uk New York: Routledge.
Mad Men. 2007–2015. Created by Matthew Weiner. USA: Lionsgate Television, AMC.
Mittell, Jason. 2015. "Why Has TV Storytelling Become So Complex?" *The Conversation*, 27 March. https://theconversation.com/why-has-tv-storytelling-become-so-complex-37442. Accessed 20 January 2021.
Most Dangerous Game. 2020. Created by Nick Santora. USA: Blackjack Films, Quibi.
Mullen, Benjamin, and Lillian Rizzo. 2020. "Quibi Was Supposed to Revolutionize Hollywood. Here's Why It Failed." *The Wall Street Journal*, 2 November.
Newman, Michael Z. 2006. From Beats to Arcs: Toward a Poetics of Television Narrative. *Velvet Light Trap* 58 (Fall): 16–28.
Police Academy. 1984. Written by Neal Israel, Pat Proft, and Hugh Wilson. Directed by Hugh Wilson. USA: The Ladd Company, Warner Bros.
Rabkin, William. 2017. *Writing the Pilot: Creating the Series*, Vol. 2. CreateSpace Independent Publishing Platform.
Red Oaks. 2014–2017. Created by Jo Gangemi and Gregory Jacobs. USA: Amazon Studios, Picrow.
Secret Agent Man. 2020. "Agent's Tips on How to Get Signed Through Social Media Platforms Like TikTok." *Backstage*, 9 November. https://www.backstage.com/magazine/article/how-to-get-an-agent-through-social-media-and-tiktok-72013/. Accessed 1 January 2021.
Special. 2019–2021. Created by Ryan O'Connell. USA: Netflix.
State of the Union. 2019. Created by Nick Hornby. USA: Sundance.
The Chi. 2018–present. Created by Lena Waithe. USA: Showtime.
The Good Wife. 2009–2016. Created by Michelle King and Robert King. USA: Scott Free Productions, King Size Productions, Small Wishes, CBS Productions.
The Guild. 2007, 2007–2013. Created by Felicia Day. US: YouTube.
The Jim Gaffigan Show. 2015–2016. Created by Jim Garrigan and Peter Tolan. USA: Jax Media.
The Lizzie Bennet Diaries. 2012– (5 seasons). Created by Bernie Su. USA: Pemberley Digital, YouTube.
The Marvelous Mrs. Maisel. 2017–present. Created by Amy Sherman-Palladino. USA: Amazon Studios, Dorothy Parker Drank Here Productions, Picrow.
The Misadventures of Awkward Black Girl. 2011–2013. Created by Issa Rae. USA: Issa Rae Productions, YouTube.
The Other F Word. 2016. *Created by Caytha Jentis*. USA: Fox Meadow Films.
The Stranger. 2020. Created by Veena Sud. US: Touchstone Television, Quibi.
The Wire. 2002–2008. Created by David Simon. USA: Blown Deadline Productions, HBO Entertainment/Warner Bros. Television Distribution.
Television Academy Emmys. 2016. "Television Academy Expands Short-Form Categories and Increases Directing and Writing Nominees." https://www.emmys.com/news/press-releases/television-academy-expands-short-form-categories-and-increases-directing-and. Accessed 22 June 2021.

Thurm, Eric. 2017. "It's Not Prestige, It's Just TV." *Esquire*, 27 April. https://www.esquire.com/entertainment/tv/a54762/the-flaws-of-prestige-tv/. Accessed 27 January 2021.

VanArendonk, Kathryn. 2019. Theorizing the Television Episode. *Narrative* 27 (1): 65–72. https://doi.org/10.1353/nar.2019.0004.

Veronica Mars. 2004–2019. Created by Rob Thomas. USA: Silver Pictures Television, Stu Segall Productions, Rob Thomas Productions, Warner Bros. Television.

When the Streetlights Go On. 2020. Created by Hutton, Chris O'Keefe, and Eddie O'Keefe. USA: Paramount Television Studios, Quibi.

CHAPTER 32

The Plural Protagonist. Or: How to Be Many and Why

Ronald Geerts

32.1 Introduction

In screenwriting theory and research and narratology alike, the interest in the construction and functioning of characters in narratives has grown in the last twenty years (Jannidis 2021).[1] The development of complex TV (series) also seems to favour more complex protagonists. In this chapter, I want to challenge the still prevailing doxa that represents the dramaturgy of a character purely in terms of psychology. A character then resembles and will be interpreted—our willing suspension of disbelief permitting—as a "human being", albeit an "imaginary" one (Eder et al. 2010, 8). I want to examine the dramaturgical construction of screen characters not in their relationship to the narrative story world, but to historical reality. I will move from the more common psychological character as an individual to what I will call the "plural protagonist", who surpasses the boundaries of a single character. This plural protagonist is the construction of a character as a plural, not merely individually portrayed, but as part of a group in which his/her individual worries and concerns and individual psychological motivations all merge into a theme that surpasses (his/her) individuality. I will illustrate this strategy of character

---

[1] Jannidis (2021) also provides a concise, general introduction to the concept of *character*.

R. Geerts (✉)
Vrije Universiteit Brussel, Brussels, Belgium
e-mail: ronald.geerts@vub.be

© The Author(s), under exclusive license to Springer Nature
Switzerland AG 2023
R. Davies et al. (eds), *The Palgrave Handbook of Screenwriting Studies*,
https://doi.org/10.1007/978-3-031-20769-3_32

construction through a corpus of cases, premising on what literary theory, dramaturgy and performance, and screenwriting studies can tell us about character construction.

Let's start with the state of play of views on character construction and from there expand the existing views in screenwriting theory and studies so that they can include other types of characters. Definitions of *character* almost without exception represent the more intuitive approach, which considers a character as *realistically* or, should I say, *mimetically* portrayed, approximating a real-life human.

32.2 The Doxa as the Heritage of Realism

Isn't it strange that screenwriting manuals never give a clear definition of the all-central concept of *character*? As if we would all know very clearly what a character would be. Syd Field ponders: "What is Character? That's a question that has haunted literary theorists from the beginning of the written word. The challenge of *creating real people in real situations* is so varied, so multifaceted, so unique, so individually challenging, that trying to define how you do it is like trying to hold a bundle of water in your hands" (Field 1984, 60, emphasis added).

Field's quote is typical in that he asks the question but answers primarily that "it is complicated" (69). He then diplomatically shifts to how to create "real people", to conclude that he does not know how to proceed. A bit further, he seems to know the answer: "action is character and character, action; what a person does is who he is, not what he says" (Field, 69). Robert McKee follows roughly the same line of reasoning. Although he distinguishes between "true character" and the "putting to action of characterization", in both cases, it is about human beings: "Characterization is the sum of all observable qualities of a human being" (McKee 1997, 127) and "TRUE CHARACTER is revealed in the choices a human being makes under pressure" (127, emphasis in original). These practice-oriented descriptions do not start with the question "what is a character?" but with the question "how are they presented?" We almost must conclude that they make no distinction at all between a human being in reality and a human being in fiction.

Thus, unlike Smith (2011) in his introductory paragraphs, these approaches do not take into account the confusion that can arise between reality and fiction when we do not get enough context to make that distinction clear.

Considering characters as merely "imaginary human beings" (Eder 2010, 18) is by no means unique. It is often the foundation on which character theory is built, as for example by Varotsi: "[A] character is the textual construct of a hypothetical human being" (Varotsi 2019, 12). Effortlessly, this conception is complemented by elements of psychological theory, as in Indick (2004a, 2004b) and Pelican (2021). Cognitively oriented views should be added here because they often link an individualised psychology with character construction, as in the "mimetic hypothesis" by Smith (2010, 235). Even when a character is also determined by the story world (Margolin 1990), it retains a certain autonomy. This implies that "the most prominent characteristic of a 'person' is her individuality, or else, what distinguishes her from the rest of her species through a number of criteria" (Varotsi 2019, 6). No wonder these mimetic-realist characters easily get attributed autonomy, even an aspiring rebellious autonomy against the author (Hamon 1983, 12). Although it should be added that recent studies such as those presented in Ryan (2018) or Riis and Taylor (2019) almost jealously try to avoid considering characters as too individual, even though "[t]o this day, the model of the individual main character has prevailed in literature, the theatre, and film throughout the various historical paradigms in both theory and practice" (Tröhler 2010, 459).

Culpeper and Fernandez-Quintanilla amend the "mimetic/hypothetic" model by claiming that interpreting the behaviour of fictional characters doesn't happen in the same way as interpreting the behaviour of real people. Notably, two differences are important: the behaviour of fictional characters is complete because it exists only in and through how they appear and behave in a narrative and—importantly for our argument—"character behaviours have greater significance" (2017, 96). Actually, any aspect of a character's behaviour can and will be interpreted as meaningful. So, how do we understand characters who get involved in socially inspired plots? Most screenwriting manuals will argue that two dimensions of a character must be developed by the scriptwriter: an individual and a social one, which are not mutually exclusive: the social dimension complements the individual one. Primarily, this happens because human beings are also social beings. This social dimension might on occasion include a Brechtian, even Marxist interpretation of character: as an individual who is first and foremost at the crossroads of social relations (Koutsourakis 2018, 70). According to Hans-Thies Lehmann, the latter is by no means in contradiction with the individually oriented character construction. Rather, Brechtian drama should be interpreted as the antithesis of Aristotelian drama. It implies a "renewal and completion of classical dramaturgy" (Lehmann 1999, 33). Unwittingly, Plantinga (2019) accomplishes exactly such a reading when he combines "Brecht, Emotion and the Reflective Spectator" in his essay on Spike Lee's *BlacKkKlansman* (2018).

In the traditional doxa form of the scenario, then, the two dimensions are more likely to be in sync than out of sync. They are communicating vessels, giving a character a psychologically individualised motivation, often a traumatic experience in the past that leads the protagonist to act in a social context. In *Dirty Harry* (1971), Harry's motivation stems from the fact that his wife has been killed. Even, if the actions are situated in a social context (a killer threatening a whole city), the motivation will still not be altruistic, but personal. The main character in *Under Fire* (1983), a news photographer, only acts when he is personally and emotionally touched when witnessing an assassination attempt. Although it is described as "an existential film about the necessity for personal engagement in the moral struggle of our times", that necessity can only arise from an individual emotional trauma (Palmer 1995,

137). The psychological evolution of a character in this context often implies an individual *Bildung*. As Tröhler observes: "Although embedded in the entire network of figures, as a main protagonist such a character centres the narrative dynamics through his activities or inner conflicts. He also subjects the interaction with the other characters in a given constellation to his development" (Tröhler 2010, 460).

32.3   Universals and Archetypes

Although the psychologically constructed character is presented as a complete individual (think about all the actors who create role biographies for the characters they have to incarnate), the viewer/reader also needs some leads and handles that allow him/her to adhere to the characters. Cognitive narratological approaches aim to understand how this exactly works and often rely on the character as a "hypothetical human being" that evolves in a story world. The screenwriting manuals usually apply more outdated versions of this when they refer to universals and archetypes to explain why we adhere to and empathise with fictional characters. Brecht would call this "identification", the viewer who "recognises" by "being immersed" in something (Brecht 2014, 65). In practice, it involves an universalisation of emotions, (social) situations that in the story are represented in an individualised form by psychological characters. On the other hand, characters will often be extended to archetypes. In both cases, the universalisation and even the de-historicising of what is told reflect a common definition of storytelling as *normalising* and *explaining* the world and imply a conforming to the (social, ideological) norm, often through the psychological evolution of the protagonist.

Sometimes both psychology and archetyping are used as narrative strategies, which implies a radical change in the character's narrative construction. A glaring example can be found in the final sequence (the third act or resolution) of the Schwarzenegger vehicle *Commando* (1985). The liberation of his kidnapped daughter leads the protagonist, aptly called Matrix, to a confrontation with the kidnapper that turns into a battle between good and evil. The setting also changes to a dark, hell-like (fire and heat included) underground. For the time of this archetypal confrontation, the individually driven motivations of the protagonist disappear. His dramatic goal diverts from rescuing his daughter to destroying Evil. Once, he finishes the job, the girl reappears, and the nuclear family is reinstated and completed when the protagonist leaves with his daughter and the woman whom he met during his adventure and who will substitute for the deceased mother of the little girl. The narrative takes the viewer from an individualised but recognisable adventure to an archetypal confrontation between good and evil, and when good triumphs, the individualised problems and obstacles are also overcome, and order re-established—to use Todorov's description of a narrative as a movement from order to disorder and back to order (see Todorov 1971).

32.4 Thwarting the Doxa (From the Inside Out)

In theatre as well as in literature studies, the "crisis of character as a critical concept" (Murphet 2011; Abirached 1994) questions the individualised mimetic character, or, in other words, the ontological relationship between the character and reality.

A first element that plays an important role in this juxtaposition can be described as the "twofoldness" (Smith 2011) or the Stanislavskian *as if character* of the character. An actor will interpret and incarnate the character described in a script (in drama and film alike). According to Schechner's definition, "while performing, actors are not themselves, nor are they the characters". For an actor performing a character situates him/herself between "not me [and] not not me", between being the character ("not me") and being oneself ("not not me") (Schechner 2020, 72). Characters are also constructed with acting in mind; they are embedded in the script, and actors will study and analyse the character as it appears in the screenplay to shape it (Petitjean 2003; Nannicelli 2019; and for an interesting case study, Ganz and Price 2020). As viewers, we are aware of this, but our cognitive attitude of denegation—or *willing suspension of disbelief*—ensures that the reality, that *an actor is playing a character*, is ignored. Unless, of course, an actor *lets it be known* that she/he is playing a character. This can be the deployment of Brechtian *Verfremdungseffekte*, although in contemporary theatre an actor often interprets characters in a more hybrid way. These performers aim to combine the actor and the character in a complementary practice. Willem Dafoe explains that while he is acting "there's a double thing happening. I'm saying the text, but I'm always wondering what my relationship to the text is" (Dafoe as quoted in Auslander 1997, 309).

On the other hand, since we are aware of the twofoldness, we recognise the identity of the actor through the character she/he is playing. This becomes even part of the set of codes used when watching a *star vehicle* or those acting performances considered as being *Oscar-worthy*, when an actor invests all his/her skills to apparently disappear into the character, which contradictorily enough makes him/her visible again as a great actor (Glitre 2019). The twofoldness can also be used as a Brechtian alienation strategy. In Bertolucci's Novecento (1976), the characters that represent their social class are played by well-known actors: Robert De Niro is Alfredo, representing the capitalist social class, and Gerard Depardieu incarnates Olmo, who represents the oppressed peasant's class. Their familiar faces contrast with those of the characters performed by unknown actors, playing the anonymous members of a social class.

The twofoldness Smith describes concerns the relationship between character and actor. Another type of twofoldness of the character could be added here based on Eder's well-known "clock of character", which represents the character construction as a "clock" with four quadrants, which he calls "aspects" (Eder 2010, 21). The first aspect of characters is "[a]s artifacts, shaped by audiovisual information", which leads to the second aspect, which describes them as fictional beings with "certain bodily, mental, and social features" (Eder 2010, 21). From there we move to the character as a "symbol" (third aspect), imparting higher-level meanings, and finally as a "symptom" pointing to socio-cultural causes in their production and to effects in their reception. Aspects one and two are inherent to the fictional character, whereas aspects three and four are more ambiguous because they point to external meanings linked to the character, which can create a form of twofoldness: the more a character expresses aspects three and four, the more it will become (socially) stereotyped or universalised to an archetype (as a symbol). Interpretation tends to become more ambiguous when individual traits (aspect two) and symbolic or social meanings in a character (aspects three and four) become the heart—and thus the motor—of the dramatic conflict, therefore creating an internal tension in the character that itself becomes the arena of conflict. The result is a duality, a seemingly unsolvable internal schism in the characters. Let's look at a striking illustration. In *Novecento*, the two protagonists, Olmo and Alfredo, respectively, symbolising the proletariat and the capitalist landowner, as young adults visit a prostitute who suffers an epileptic seizure in their presence. At that crisis moment, the friction between the individual/social duality in their character construction is clearly highlighted. When Alfredo flees, should that act be interpreted as evidence of his psychologically justifiable cowardice, or is his attitude a trait of the social class that he belongs to, merely giving proof that the padrone shows no empathy? And does Olmo out of class consciousness express solidarity with the situation of the woman or does he also only act on a psychological motivation?

This (deliberate) confusion or duality about a character's drive appears in Brechtian-inspired character constructs. However, this dramaturgical strategy is much older: in medieval European theatre and literature, it created conflict and suspense. Conflict arose within the character as an internal tension between all-too-human basic urges (usually of a sexual nature) that clashed with the divine predestination (of becoming a saint). The suspense it creates doesn't originate in the conflict itself, since the narrative and its outcome were familiar to the medieval spectator. The question is not *if* but *how* the character will succeed in getting back on the right divine track laid out by God (Duvignaud 1965, 75–147). In Duvignaud's view, as in that of others such as Dario Fo, this duality in the character creates the possibility of introducing (social or political) criticism.[2] A contemporary case that took inspiration from this medieval narrative strategy can be found in *The Last Temptation of Christ* (1988), adapted by scriptwriter Paul Schrader from Nicolas Kazantzakis' eponymous novel, and directed by Martin Scorsese. The *last temptation* itself is created by Satan by exploiting the internal conflict in the Jesus Christ character: the choice between his (human) individuality and

---

[2] As Duvignaud points out, the dual character functions in conjunction with an episodic plot construction. On Brecht and Fo's use of episodic dramaturgy, see Russo (1998).

his (divine) mission as the son of God. The crucified Jesus chooses to live the life of a man and with the help of what he believes to be his guardian angel (actually Satan in disguise) descends from the cross. The internal conflict leads to the blasphemous final sequence and resolution of the conflict. Jesus expresses his (individual and human) free will when he screams "I want to be the Messiah!" whereupon we return to Christ on the cross. The decision to accomplish his divine mission is his own, not God's. The story ends as foreseen and expected by the audience, but with a humanist twist that infuriated a number of fundamentalist Christians, especially Catholics. It is interesting to note that the construction of a dual character has implications for the narrative composition: narrative loops are inserted into a well-known history that deviates from the narrative development that the viewer knows, although she/he is aware that eventually, the plot will move back to the known and expected outcome.

Another variation of thwarting the doxa can be found in characters that are designed in a hyper-realist way, meaning that they are individualised to the extreme so that the viewer cannot easily identify with them, nor understand their motivations (Murphy 2007, 27–29). Such characters are described from the outside only, making it virtually impossible to fathom their inner feelings, emotions, or even thoughts. As Murphy suggests, these characters often are confused and lack motivation, but that is not a *conditio sine qua non*, as proven by many of the characters in Luc and Jean-Pierre Dardenne's films. Characters such as Rosetta in *Rosetta* (1999) or the protagonists in *Le fils* (2002), *L'enfant* (2005), and others clearly do not lack motivation, but the way they are narratively constructed, closed as an oyster, does not allow us to catch a glimpse of what happens *inside* these characters, their psychological motivations. This approach is reflected in the audiovisual narrative strategy of having the camera constantly and literally *running behind* the protagonists and the lack of a musical score underlining emotions (Geerts 2007).

This leads us to the question of whether it is possible to deal with social themes and issues in narratives while at the same time avoiding the reduction to individual problems or avoiding the confusion between the psychological and the social. The obstacles seem to lie in traditional narrative composition (the doxa) and the creation of individualised, psychological characters that go along with that (or the other way around, if you wish). The answer will not be a theoretical or hypothetical one. Let us look for narrative strategies that have been set out and tried by screenwriters who expand the concept of character to include aspects that transcend individuality.

32.5 Beyond the Individual Character: The Plural Protagonist

Maybe I should first define what a plural protagonist is not. It is not a "multiple protagonist" as described by (Aronson 2010) and (del Mar Azcona 2010). In ensemble films, as they are sometimes labelled, the story is not really about the group, but about "how an individual is limited or in some way affected by a group", or "how an individual affects a group", or even "the group as being versions of the same protagonist" (Aronson 2010, 208–09). It is not about what characters have in common or how they form a group, but about how they are "different versions" of a type of character (209). Moreover, it is often about conflict within the group, often about how they are "running the adventure" (215). The group is populated by individualised characters, and the development of the narrative is motivated by how several individuals function in the given situation. The distinction lies in the "plural" versus the "multiple", in "the group" versus "a collection of individuals". I will argue that several individual characters can combine as a group to form a "plural protagonist". They do not function individually as characters but as a group that drives the story. Although Tröhler seems to suggest as much in the definition of the first of her three "heuristic dramaturgical patterns", she doesn't develop the concept of the "group character" any further than "as a collective entity, this integrates the individual via a central idea more or less stringently into a large and sometimes differentiated assembled character and structures the narrative through a dynamics tending towards argumentation or demonstration" (Tröhler 2010, 462).

I propose to distinguish between *character* and *protagonist*, whereby a character, as a psycho-social mimetic representation of an individual human being, is only one part of the protagonist. Theoretically, the reverse is also conceivable: one character consists of several protagonists—e.g. a character that suffers from dissociative identity disorder like Norman Bates in Hitchcock's *Psycho* (1960) or the Narrator (or was it Tyler?) in Fincher's *Fight Club* (1999). The definition of *character* may follow Frow's as he describes the evolution of the word and concept of character from a "letter of the alphabet" to "finally, *quite late in this sequence*, to the sense of 'a personality invested with distinctive attributes and qualities'" (Frow 2014, 7–8, emphasis added). Triau joins Frow's historicising approach when he concludes that from the twentieth century onwards, the character is either manipulable (as in Brecht's case) or inscrutable, so that it often loses its individual identity and becomes anonymous (Triau 2019, 649–50).

A description of the character as an artefact can also be described in terms of "actants" (Greimas 1987), the constituent elements of a narrative. This structuralist approach avoids defining characters as hypothetical human beings because "[d]efined in this way, the actor is not to be confused with the established but intuitive notion of character. It is not necessarily human, anthropomorphic, or animated. It does not necessarily correspond to a naive ontological entity: a process like 'the fall of the dollar' can be a very presentable, indeed all too real, actor" (Rastier 1997, 45). "Actor" is understood here as *actant* and not as *thespian*. A character can include several actors, or several characters can make up the same actor. Characters can also appear on/as objects (Wilde 2019). A landscape can be a character if it has autonomy and agency, without falling into the symbolic, such as the landscape of the mind (see Melbye 2010). In films by Peter Weir, such as *Picnic at Hanging Rock* (1975) or *The Mosquito Coast* (1986), nature appears as a protagonist, albeit inscrutable and not personified and therefore also devoid of (human) motivations. This can lead to atypical narrative structures, as in Picnic at Hanging Rock, where no answer can be formulated to the seemingly whodunnit question: what happened to the missing girls? Since there is no clear solution to the intrigue, the concluding third act is missing.

The definition of *protagonist* then is a type of *actant* (or *actor*) which can consist of one or more characters. In the case of a plural protagonist, i.e. with several characters, the individualities merge into a larger whole, a group, and it is that group that expresses the meaning, not one individual member. In other words, the analysis of one character does not shed light on the meaning or theme of the entire narrative. It will only be by considering all the characters together that the true meaning will emerge. As a result, these characters are often anonymised, losing their individual identity to become the voice and speak on behalf of an entire group. The definition of the group can be broad but is always in relation to a social context. This group is often founded in a vision du monde (Goldmann [1964] 2016), a concept that refers to a worldview as a collective consciousness, shared by a (social) group of individuals, and which finds its expression in an artistic work. Goldmann observes that "[a]lmost no human actions are performed by isolated individuals for the subject performing the action is a group, a 'We', and not an 'I', even though, by the phenomenon of reification, the present structure of society tends to hide the 'We' and transform it into a collection of different individuals isolated from one another" (1964, 16). The idea of a protagonist who becomes a "we" can also be found in Augusto Boal's approach to the function of theatre. He claims that if theatre wants to have an impact on social reality, it should move beyond the character from the "individual" to "we", "a theatre of the first-person plural" (Boal 2013, 45).

Let's take this idea of the "I" as a "we" and discuss a number of plural protagonist cases in a film context: Chantal Akerman's *Histoires d'Amérique: Food, Family and Philosophy* (1989), Bernardo Bertolucci's *Novecento* (1976), Chloé Zhao's *Nomadland* (2020), but also *The Last Wave* (1977) or *Witness* (1985) by Peter Weir, Zack Godshall's post-Katrina film *Low and Behold* (2007), *Portrait de la jeune fille en feu* (2019) by Céline Sciamma, and *C'mon C'mon* (2021) by Mike Mills.

Histoires d'Amérique is one of the most extreme examples of the use of a plural protagonist. The film starts with several testimonials of anonymous women and men. They are filmed in a documentary style: in a non-staged environment, close to the New York Harbour—we can see how the water reflects on the brick walls—the characters address a fixed camera directly. The stories have in common that they are told by Polish Jews who left their home country because of persecution by the Nazi regime. They also testify about the difficulties they have had adjusting to culture and life in the United States.

Although the stories are very personal, detailed, and anecdotal, their narrators remain anonymous. They are interspersed with funny sketches that also bear witness to the adjustment problems when arriving in a foreign environment. There is no hierarchy in the characters, nor is there between the testimonials and the skits. All these characters, all these stories come together in one plural protagonist, expressing the *vision du monde* they share. The film is introduced by an off-screen narrator's voice that tells a story about passing on a prayer from one generation to the next. Each time something is lost from the prayer, but—she tells us—still God heard them. The story ends with: "My own story is full of missing links, full of blanks and I do not even have a child" (to pass on the story to; my addition). Some viewers might recognise the narrator's voice as belonging to the author herself, Chantal Akerman, by the French accent, but she never introduces herself as such.

Nomadland, adapted for the screen by Chloé Zhao from a nonfiction book by Jessica Bruder, seems to close to Augusto Boal's idea of a protagonist in the first-person plural: each individual story is immediately *pluralised* by blending it in the group of *nomads*. Unlike in *Histoires d'Amérique*, the characters are real people with real stories who sometimes even appear as themselves in the film. The Facebook page of the film uses as a cover photo a composite licence plate, which besides referring to the nomadic existence of the plural protagonist creates an image of a group with several different members—but all are American, as the fragments of the licence plates indicate. As a narrator, Fern mediates between the viewer and the narrative world, and she holds together the fragmented episodic structure as a binding agent. At the same time, she is part of the plural protagonist because she lives the same situation as the others. She continuously asserts this position, for instance, when explaining to old acquaintances her current situation as a nomadic worker, not a homeless woman. Fern as a mediating narrator facilitates the viewer's empathy for the plural character. In *Histoires d'Amérique*, the narrative lacks such an instance, and the plural protagonist literally looks us straight in the eyes. It confronts rather than immerses the viewer as *Nomadland* attempts to do through Fern.

In *C'mon C'mon* (2021), written and directed by Mike Mills, the interviews with the youngsters about how they experience reality and envision the future multiply the story of young Jesse, broadening the predicaments of one individual dysfunctional family into a sociological study of America today. In the words of critic Brian Eggert, the film, "despite its specific subject matter, feels like it's about everything" (2021). The script describes mainly actions and dialogues by the characters and in the didascaly often leaves blanks, suggestions like "improv" (e.g. scenes 26–27, 36, 38, 51b…), or formulates questions:

JESSE
And she got an abortion.
Oops. How did we get here? What to say?

(*C'mon C'mon*, 31)

Or:

> **JOHNNY**
> What if I don't? She'd crack?
>
> **VIV**
> OK, so you thought you were the hero and now it's rough and so you're gonna bail?
>
> **JOHNNY**
> I came to see *you*. She can't even really talk to him if he's gonna pull that?
>
> (*C'mon C'mon*, 53)

The quotes from children's books, feminist essays on motherhood, philosophical tractates, or how-to-film books (mentioned by title and author in the script and on screen) also serve as an echo chamber for the thoughts and actions of the characters. The chosen narrative strategies all work together: the characters need to be created in a collaboration between the writer, actors, and possibly other members of the crew (one of the books mentioned is "*An incomplete list of what the cameraperson enables* by Kristen Johnson") and secondly creating openings toward historical reality in what basically is a fictional story.

The final sequence of *Novecento* consists of a people's tribunal organised immediately after the end of World War II by Italian peasants who have taken over power from the landowner, Alfredo. It must pass judgement on the *padrone*. In a continuous flow, several anonymous people, one after the other, pronounce their accusations and as such operate as a plural protagonist. The scene is not about the individual injustices done to these peasants, but the accumulation of the various individual accusations. This is clearly illustrated when the peasant-prosecutors cannot remember whether it was the accused Alfredo, or his father, or his grandfather who committed the crimes against them. Their conclusion is: "Who cares! A padrone remains a padrone!", which immediately transforms Alfredo from an individual character into one of the many members of a social class. The people's court turns into the finale of the (Marxist) class struggle when the plural protagonist, the proletariat, sentences the padrone and declares Alfredo symbolically dead. As one of the peasant characters concludes: "He is the living proof that the padrone is dead!" The film designates this act as a utopian moment. It didn't happen, but in Bertolucci's view, the end of the war was a privileged window in Italian history that could have allowed a revolution.

Zack Godshall's post-Katrina film *Low and Behold* (2007) confronts an insurance claims adjustor with a plural protagonist consisting of the group of people who not only have lost their homes but also feel abandoned by the authorities. The plural protagonist is constructed in a similar way as in the tribunal sequence in *Novecento*: an accumulation of close-up after close-up of faces of anonymous witnesses, embodying post-Katrina New Orleans, testifying to the inexperienced and initially uninterested insurance claims adjuster about how unfairly they were treated in the aftermath of the floods. In the narrative, none of them can be identified as a *singular character* advancing the plot.

A last case uses the plural protagonist in a feminist context. The *Portrait de la jeune fille en feu* (2019), written and directed by Céline Sciamma, turns out to be not the portrait of one girl on fire, but of a sorority of (socially) very different female characters who act as a plural protagonist. Individually, they are very different characters with very different social backgrounds. What transcends these differences and brings them together in a plural protagonist is womanhood. The film accomplishes this in its dramaturgical construction as well as in its visual composition. The women's growth into a plural character is illustrated in the two abortion scenes that punctuate the narrative. The first abortion scene marks the initiating step towards a certain autonomy as a woman. It is a complex multi-layered scene in which contradictory feelings come together in the presence of a baby and Sophie tenderly holding hands while she is undergoing the operation. The second abortion scene is a re-enactment of the first one, by Heloise and Sophie. Marianne then paints the re-enactment as a representation of what has become a symbolic act. From that moment on, the women will also visually be represented as a group, continuously looking and moving in the same direction. As in the other cases I discussed, there is a specific moment in which the plural protagonist materialises in a group in which people lose their individuality, in which they blend into a larger whole. In *Portrait de la jeune fille en feu*, this happens in the scene in which the three women join a group of women singing together. The choir literally expresses these characters as a group, singing with different voices, tonalities, but in harmony, in togetherness. At that point in the film, the plural protagonist evolves from a party of three characters that still might be identified individually to one community full of characters. Or as Iris Bray describes it: "The portrait of a woman is conjugated in the plural" (2020, 69).[3]

These scenes of togetherness, of blending traits or problems that might be recognised as being individually defined into a larger whole, appear to be a typical narrative strategy. In *Novecento* it takes the form of a tribunal, in *Histoires d'Amérique* it is a party, in *Nomadland* the stories told round the campfire, in *C'mon C'mon* the second line parade in New Orleans, and in

---

[3] Orig.: "Le portrait de femme se conjugue au pluriel" (author's translation).

Portrait in the singing scene. In each case, the issues dealt with will be taken on by a larger group. As it says in the script of *Nomadland*:

```
We all got the same fucking
problems. The same shit to deal
with. Isn't that nice to know?
```
(*Nomadland*, 54)

But why and when would it be "nice to know" that we have the same problems? Only when this knowledge might lead to a resolution, or at least point to one. It might be a utopian one, in the sense of Ernst Bloch, but it must be imaginable, at least in stories. So let us conclude with a beginning, the first words of Bloch's *The Spirit of Utopia*: "I am. We are. That is enough. Now we have to start" (Bloch 2000, 1).

References

Abirached, Richard. 1994. *La crise du personnage dans le théâtre moderne* [The Crisis of Character in Modern Theatre]. Paris: Gallimard.
Aronson, Linda. 2010. *21st Century Screenplay: A Comprehensive Guide to Writing Tomorrow's Films*. Crows Nest, Australia: Allen and Unwin.
Auslander, Philip. 1997. "Task and Vision: Willem Dafoe in L.S.D." Chapter 4 in *From Acting to Performance*. New York and London: Routledge.
BlacKkKlansman. 2018. Written by Charlie Wachtel, David Rabinowitz, and Kevin Willmott. Directed by Spike Lee. USA: 40 Acres and a Mule.
Bloch, Ernst. 2000 [1923]. *The Spirit of Utopia*. Trans. Anthony A. Nasser. Stanford, CA: Stanford University Press.
Boal, Augusto. 2013. *The Rainbow of Desire: The Boal Method of Theatre and Therapy*. New York and London: Routledge.
Bray, Iris. 2020. *Le regard féminin. Une révolution à l'écran* [The Female Gaze. A Revolution on the Screen]. Paris: Editions de l'olivier.
Brecht, Bertolt. 2014. *Brecht on Theatre*. London: Bloomsbury.
C'mon C'mon. 2021. Written and directed by Mike Mills. USA: A24. Screenplay available online: https://deadline.com/wp-content/uploads/2022/01/CMon-CMon-Read-The-Screenplay.pdf. Accessed 10 August 2022.
Culpeper, Jonathan, and Carolina Fernandez-Quintanilla. 2017. Fictional Characterisation. In *Pragmatics of Fiction*, ed. Miriam A. Locher and Andreas H. Jucker, 93–128. Berlin: De Gruyter Mouton.
del Mar Azcona, Maria. 2010. *The Multi-Protagonist Film*. Chichester, UK: Blackwell-Wiley.
Dirty Harry. 1971. Written by Harry Julian Fink, Rita M. Fink, and Dean Riesner. Directed by Don Siegel. USA: Malpaso.
Duvignaud, Jean. 1965. *Sociologie du théâtre. Essai sur les ombres collectives* [Sociology of Theatre. Essays on Collective Shadows]. Paris: P.U.F.
Eder, Jens. 2010. Understanding Characters. *Projections* 4 (1): 16–40.
Eder, Jens, Jannidis Fotis, and Ralf Schneider. 2010. *Characters in Fictional Worlds*. Berlin: De Gruyter.

Eggert, Brian. 2021. "Review of *C'mon C'mon*, by Mike Mills." *Deep Focus Review*, 8 December. https://deepfocusreview.com/reviews/cmon-cmon/. Accessed 10 August 2022.
Field, Syd. 1984. *Screenplay*. New York: Dell.
Fight Club. 1999. Written by Jim Uhls, based on the novel by Chuck Palahniuk. Directed by David Fincher. USA: Fox 2000 Pictures.
Frow, John. 2014. *Character and Person*. Oxford: Oxford University Press.
Ganz, Adam, and Steven Price. 2020. *Robert De Niro at Work: From Screenplay to Screen Performance*. Cham, Switzerland: Palgrave Macmillan.
Geerts, Ronald. 2007. "Realism in the Films of the Dardenne Brothers: Post-Neorealism?" *Excavatio* XVII: 272–86.
Glitre, Kathrina. 2019. "Character and the Star Vehicle: The Impact of Casting Cary Grant." In *Screening Characters. Theories of Character in Film, Television, and Interactive Media*, edited by Johannes Riis and Aaron Taylor, 37–54. New York, London, and Los Angeles: Routledge and American Film Institute.
Goldmann, Lucien. 2016 [1964]. *The Hidden God. A Study of Tragic Vision in the Pensées of Pascal and the Tragedies of Racine*. Trans. Philip Thody. New York, London: Routledge.
Greimas, Algirdas Julien. 1987. Actants, actors and figures. In *Selected Writings in Semiotic Theory*, ed. On. and Meaning, 106–120. Minneapolis mn: University of Minnesota Press.
Hamon, Philippe. 1983. *Le personnel du roman: Le système des personnages dans les Rougon-Macquart d'Émile Zola [The System of Characters in Emile Zola's Rougon-Macquart]*. Geneva: Droz.
Histoires d'Amérique. 1989. Written and directed by Chantal Akerman. Belgium, France: Paradise Films, Arte.
Indick, William. 2004a. *Movies and the Mind: Theories of the Great Psychoanalysts Applied to Film*. Jefferson, NC and London: McFarland.
Indick, William. 2004b. *Psychology for Screenwriters: Building Conflict in Your Script*. Burbank, CA: Michael Wiese.
Jannidis, Fotis. "Character." In *The Living Handbook of Narratology*. https://www.lhn.uni-hamburg.de/node/41.html. Accessed 12 December 2021.
Koutsourakis, Angelos. 2018. *Rethinking Brechtian Film Theory and Cinema*. Edinburgh: Edinburgh University Press.
L'enfant (The Child). 2005. Written and directed by Luc and Jean-Pierre Dardenne. Belgium: Les films du fleuve.
Le fils. 2002. Written and directed by Luc and Jean-Pierre Dardenne. Belgium: Les films du fleuve.
Lehmann, Hans-Thies. 1999. *Postdramatisches Theater*. Frankfurt: Verlag der Autoren. English edition: Lehmann, H.-T. 2006. *Postdramatic Theatre* (trans. Karen-Jürs Munby). New York and London: Routledge.
Low and Behold. 2007. Written by Zack Godshall and Barlow Jacobs. Directed by Zack Godshall. USA: Mama Bear Studios, Blindwall Pictures, Sidetrack Films.
Margolin, Uri. 1990. Individuals in Narrative Worlds: An Ontological Perspective. *Poetics Today* 11 (4): 843–871.
McKee, Robert. 1997. *Story*. New York: Harper-Collins.
Melbye, David. 2010. *Landscape Allegory in Cinema: From Wilderness to Wasteland*. New York: Palgrave Macmillan.

Mills, Mike. n.d. *C'mon C'mon*. Screenplay. Available online: https://8flix.com/screenplays/ cmon-cmon-2021-screenplay-written-by-mike-mills/. Accessed 10 August 2022.
Murphet, Julian. 2011 (Spring). "The Mole and the Multiple. A Chiasmus of Character." *New Literary History* 42 (n°2): 255–276.
Murphy, J.J. 2007. *Me and You and Memento and Fargo: How Independent Screenplays Work*. New York and London: Continuum.
Nannicelli, Ted. 2019. "Seeing and Hearing Screen Characters: Stars, Twofoldness and the Imagination." In *Screening Characters. Theories of Character in Film, Television, and Interactive Media*, edited by Johannes Riis and Aaron Taylor, 19–36. New York and London: Routledge and American Film Institute.
Nomadland. 2020. *Written and directed by Chloé Zhao, based on the book by Jessica Bruder*. USA: Cordium Productions, Hear/Say Productions, Highwayman Films.
Novecento. 1976. Written by Franco Arcalli, Giuseppe Bertolucci, and Bernardo Bertolucci. Directed by Bernardo Bertolucci. Italy: Produzioni Europee Associati.
Palmer, William J. 1995. *The Films of the Eighties: A Social History*. Carbondale il: Southern Illinois University Press.
Pelican, Kira-Anne. 2021. *The Science of Writing Characters. Using Psychology to Create Compelling Fictional Characters*. London: Bloomsbury Academic.
Petitjean, André. 2003. "Problématisation du personnage dramatique" ["Problématising Dramatic Characters"]. *Pratiques: Linguistique, Littérature, Didactique* 119/120: 67–90.
Picnic at Hanging Rock. 1975. Written by Cliff Green, based on the novel by Joan Lindsay. Directed by Peter Weir. Australia: McElroy & McElroy, Picnic Productions.
Plantinga, Carl. 2019. Brecht, Emotion, and the Reflective Spectator: The Case of 'BlacKkKlansman.' *NECSUS* 1: 151–169.
Portrait de la jeune fille en feu [Portrait of a Lady on Fire]. 2019. Written and directed by Céline Sciamma. France: Lilies Films.
Psycho. 1960. Written by Joseph Stefano, based on the novel by Robert Bloch. Directed by Alfred Hitchcock. USA: Shamley Productions.
Rastier, François. 1997. *Meaning and Textuality*. Trans. Frank Collins and Paul Perron. Toronto: University of Toronto Press.
Riis, Johannes, and Aaron Taylor, eds. 2019. *Screening Characters: Theories of Character in Film, Television, and Interactive Media*. New York, London, and Los Angeles: Routledge and American Film Institute.
Rosetta. 1999. Written and directed by Jean-Pierre and Luc Dardenne. Belgium: Les films du fleuve.
Russo, Anna. 1998. *Bertolt Brecht und Dario Fo: Wege des epischen Theaters* [Bertolt Brecht and Dario Fo: Ways of the Epic Theatre]. Stuttgart: Springer.
Ryan, Marie-Laure. 2018. What Are Characters Made of? Textual, Philosophical and 'World' Approaches to Character Ontology. *Neohelicon* 45: 415–429.
Schechner, Richard. 2020. *Performance Studies: An Introduction*. New York & London: Routledge.
Smith, Murray. 2010. "*Engaging Characters*. Further Reflections." In *Characters in Fictional Worlds. Understanding Imaginary Beings in Literature, Film, and Other Media*, edited by Jens Eder, Fotis Jannidis, and Ralf Schneider, 232–58. Berlin, New York: De Gruyter.
Smith, Murray. 2011. On the Twofoldness of Character. *New Literary History* 42 (2): 277–294.

The Last Temptation of Christ. 1988. Written by Paul Schrader, based on the novel by Nikos Kazantzakis. Directed by Martin Scorsese. USA: Universal.

The Last Wave. 1977. Written by Peter Weir, Tony Morphett, and Petru Popescu. Directed by Peter Weir. Australia: McElroy & McElroy, Last Wave.

The Mosquito Coast. 1986. Written by Paul Schrader, based on the novel by Paul Theroux. Directed by Peter Weir. USA: The Saul Zaentz Company, Jerome Hellman Productions.

Todorov, Tzvetan. 1971. The 2 Principles of Narrative. *Diacritics* 1 (1): 37–44.

Triau, Christophe. 2019. "Personnage" ["Character"]. In *Dictionnaire des idées et notions en littérature et en théâtre* [*Dictionary of Ideas and Concepts in Literature and Theatre*] 646–50. Paris: Encyclopaedia Universalis France.

Tröhler, Margit. 2010. "Multiple Protagonist Films. A Transcultural Everyday Practice." In *Characters in Fictional Worlds. Understanding Imaginary Beings in Literature, Film, and Other Media*, edited by Jens Eder, Fotis Jannidis, and Ralf Schneider, 459–77. Berlin, New York: De Gruyter.

Under Fire. 1983. Written by Ron Shelton and Clayton Frohman. Directed by Roger Spottiswoode. USA: Cinema '84, Lion's Gate Film, Under Fire Associates.

Varotsi, Lina. 2019. *Conceptualisation and Exposition: A Theory of Character Construction*. New York and London: Routledge.

Wilde, Lukas R. A. 2019. Recontextualizing Characters. Media Convergence and Pre-Meta-Narrative Character Circulation. *Image* 29: 3–21.

Witness. Written by William Kelley and Earl W. Wallace. Directed by Peter Weir. USA: Paramount, Edward S. Feldman.

Zhao, Chloé. 2020. *Nomadland*. Written and directed by Chloé Zhao. Based on the book by Jessica Bruder. Screenplay. Screenplay available online: https://deadline.com/wp-content/uploads/2021/02/Nomadland-Screenplay.pdf. Accessed 10 August 2022.

CHAPTER 33

The Haptic Encounter: Scripting Female Subjectivity

Funke Oyebanjo

33.1 Introduction

The haptic encounter is a screenwriting method which emerged in my attempt to disrupt gendered practices inherent in the conception of the screenplay (see Taylor 2017). I devised this method of screenplay writing by interrogating traditional historical drama forms, by reimagining the female protagonist as a subject and not an object limited by patriarchal conventions in the historical drama. I investigated how the haptic can bring its *corporeal* quality to character subjectivity by answering the question, how might a haptic approach to screenwriting facilitate a rescripting of female subjectivity within Nigerian historical drama? This chapter discusses the hegemonic bias found within several Nigerian historical dramas, where it impacts on representations of Nigerian women, and reduces the female protagonist into a passive object. I will discuss how the writer of the historical drama can use the haptic encounter to reframe female subjectivity.

In my discussion of the haptic encounter, I refer to the screenplays I wrote for a three-part Yoruba (Western Nigerian) historical drama titled *Efunsetan's Story*, *Bodunrin* and *Adire Girl,* comprising nine webisode screenplays (three webisodes in each part). The screenplays were part of research inquiry into the haptic. I choose the web series as the context of my research following the proposition of screenwriting theorist Anna Zaluczkowska (2011, 98) who

---

F. Oyebanjo (✉)
University of Greenwich, London, England
e-mail: a.oyebanjo@gre.ac.uk

suggests that the internet offers the screenwriter new opportunities, specifically referring to transmedia storytelling. She explains, "if these opportunities are pursued, they must be willing to become more adaptable in their approach to writing" (Zaluczkowska 2011, 99). The main character of these screenplays, Efunsetan Aniwura is a prominent figure in Nigerian history and drama. She lived in Ibadan (Western Nigeria) during the nineteenth century and was an eminent aristocrat. She has been written into dramas by Akinwunmi Isola (1970, 1981, 2005).

I explain how I use the haptic encounter in the screenplay *Efunsetan's Story*, to bestow Efunsetan Aniwura with a more sensuous subjectivity and how the employment of the haptic may inform the reader's understanding of pre-colonial Nigerian history and more intimate perception of the characters located within that time. I aim to help the reader form an alternative bond with Efunsetan by sensing what she senses and perceives. The haptic makes the character's body extend beyond the screenplay page to the reader's body, as their senses connect and intertwine.

I propose that embedding the haptic into the screenplay provides the screenwriter with an enriching framework to rethink her approach in developing the character's subjectivity. By focusing on the sensual, the writer can evoke the senses and thus can produce new knowledge.

From this perspective, the meaning of the screenplay can be extended from the cognitive and emotional to a possible, intimate and experiential intersubjectivity within the relationship between the reader and the character's lived experience. I would suggest that the senses play a meaningful role in reconfiguring the character's interaction with the reader, thus providing recourse for writers creating characters from marginalized and excluded groups. For example, the African American screenwriter James L. White, screenwriter on the American feature film *Ray* (2004), elaborates on how his lived experience underscores his process in addressing the audience by "[i]nviting them in and allowing them to spend two hours inside the skin of a black man or a woman, to see what the world is about" (White, in Hanson and Herman 2010, 125). White's invitation reminds us that the screenwriter, through scripting (Maras 2009, 2), can harness the powers of the haptic to create sensory and thereby more relational characters in their screenplays.

33.2 Audiovisual Image: Viewership and Haptic Visuality

The haptic concern with cinematic spectatorship is an evolution within a long line of sensuous scholarship that foregrounds the tactile, material and the corporeal dimension of cinematic expression, in its consideration of the bodily response and sensations elicited by the aspect of the cinema viewing experience that does not necessarily make itself visible to sight. Laura Mulvey contends that passive psychoanalytic meaning is framed by the camera's voyeuristic and essentially phallocentric gaze steeped in power and control (Mulvey 1999,

833). Vivian Sobchack counters Mulvey, stating: "we do not see the movies through our eyes, we feel film with our own whole bodily being" (Sobchack 2004, 63). She succinctly sums up the sensuous interaction between spectator and film by highlighting how these viewings create a new spectatorial relationship with the image. In line with Sobchack's argument, Laura Marks' notion of haptic visuality actively erodes the subject/object division between the film and spectator, insisting that "an image is not visual but multi-sensory, comprising all the information that one's senses perceive about an object" (2000, 146), and therefore "it is common for cinema to evoke sense experience through intersensory links: sounds may evoke textures" (2000, 213). For example, the effect of a cold breeze on a sweaty damp brow and the cacophony of sounds on a busy street. Marks asserts that the viewing experience oscillates between visual (optic) visuality and haptic visuality (2000, 162). Optic visuality is a viewing experience which relies on distance and separation and "depends on a separation between the viewing subject and the object" (Marks 2000, 162); it is fuelled by control in the observational and analytical viewer.

Haptic visuality, on the other hand, brings the spectator closer to the image and is concerned with what lies beyond the controlling gaze of the optic look by *grazing* the indiscernible object: the emphasis here lies in discerning the texture of the object by scanning the surface of the image, a viewing experience where the eyes of the viewer act like "organs of touch" (Marks 2000, 162). In this instance, it is the interaction between the eyes and the image that reveals the intimate tactility of the image and brings the spectator close to the object in a process akin to *touching*. Marks' concept establishes a link that implies the spectator can have an "intersubjective relationship" (Sobchack 2004, 314) with the characters in the film, thus encouraging a space for the spectator to consider other sensory elements, forging collaboration and empathy, and problematizing the hegemonic control of the visual. In addition, the haptic explores a form of embodied subjectivity in which, by "discern(ing) texture" (Marks 2000, 162), the viewer's visual attention is directed towards a viewing that privileges sensory, tactile and corporeal elements that shape the physical experiences of the characters' interaction with individual subjective spectators' bodily sensations.

It is the haptic which makes the viewer's body engage with an empathetic relationship triggered by bodily sensation, for example, a shiver from watching a character in a dangerous situation in a scene in a horror film. The quiver infuses the body and encourages her sympathy and empathy for the protagonist. By fostering a sensory interplay between the viewer and the haptic image in cinema, Marks posits that haptic visuality's persistent refusal of "visual plenitude" (Marks 2000, 177) and abundant "change in (lens) focus" (Marks 1998, 343) empathizes the film's formal process in its suggestion that the spectator "yields to the thing seen" (Marks 2000, 191).

The screenplay, however, has mainly been overlooked in the discussion around haptic visuality. The haptic is not only located in the film's image.

The screenplay can be perceived as providing a more complex haptic engagement, where the eyes can function as "organs of touch" (Marks 2000, 162), as they slide across the words on the page and "enter the reader's body, to produce meaning" (Cohen 2009, 23). Cohen here refers to the reader's experience regarding the novel. Similarly, the scene description in the screenplay employs syntax structure often found in the novel (Sculley 2017). But most importantly, as Adam Ganz observes, the script is a form where "the camera is inevitably at its centre" (Ganz 2012, 8).

For Ganz, the camera lens is the primary consideration the screenwriter makes when writing. Furthermore, the screenplay is employed as part of the film's production process in generating, conceptualizing and presenting these images to the reader.

Indeed, it is the sense of relation between the lens, and the possibility of foreshadowing and suggestion of the film's images by implying shots and their effect on the reader's perception of the screenplay's depiction of action, emotion and cognition that makes Ganz's lens-based concept so apt for the screenwriter engaging with the haptic. I would also like to suggest that the reader's engagement with the screenplay informs and provides the initial engagement with the story world, character, genre and narrative, which makes the sensory engagement complex. This means that that haptic visuality can be deployed in the conception of the screenplay and perception of the character and by extension the material and corporeal aesthetic of the film's visual style. Ganz's lens-centred concept provides the basis for the writer to produce and situate haptic encounters within the screenplay's story world through the perception of the characters.

33.3 The Haptic Encounter

The haptic encounter as a screen writing method is predicated on the fact that the image activates an embodied engagement from the viewer (Marks 2000, 163), which emanates from the screenplay as a lens-based practice as proposed by Ganz (Ganz 2012). From this perspective it is possible for the writer to privilege the sensory over the phallocentric gaze and decentre the distance, power and control which would render the female protagonist passive. The writer does this by creating situations in the narrative where the viewer encounters the sensory perception of the character. The female protagonist therefore avoids the typical cultural framing. This offers the viewer a basis for engaging with the character from an intimate, unfamiliar and sensory perspective. The haptic encounter reframes the reader's relationship to the character in several ways. The haptic in the screenplay text may create a "connective tissue" (Marks 2002, xiv) between character subjectivity and the reader's body to evoke an intersubjective relationship (Sobchack 2004, 182). It calls attention to sensuous and tactile qualities in the screenplay, it emphasizes the character's sensory perception of the story events, other characters, character action and story world and the relationship to cultural representation.

33.4 THE HISTORICAL DRAMA

Historical dramas are an established and very popular genre (Julius-Adeoye 2013). These dramas initially developed and cultivated their audience via the traditional travelling Yoruba theatre. Whilst many film and television genres are consumed by African and diasporic audiences, such dramas have produced recognizable forms of cultural representation. It is interesting to note that most of the material that informs the Nigerian historical drama dwells on Nigeria's pre-colonial era. The representation of and connection to Nigeria's past, resplendent with kingdoms, kings and nobles, resonates deeply with audiences on the African continent and the diaspora. The Nigerian Historical drama has been explored and presented in quite a few stage, cinematic and televisual productions; examples are *Oba ko so* (*The King Did Not Hang*) (1964); *Moremi* (1961); *Moremi Ajasoro* (2009); *Kurunmi* (1969); *Women of Owu* (2006); *Ijaye War* (1970); *Kiriji* (*The Kiriji War*) (1971) and *Madam Tinubu: The Terror of Lagos* (1964).[1] Historical dramas employed classic tropes and symbols such as singing, dancing and rich praise poetry. The genre evolved into the televisual historical drama during the introduction of television to Nigeria in 1959, allowing itself to formulate and adapt to new visual formal strategies. For example, scenes driven by naturalistic dialogue, conveying character motivation, and recognizable naturalistic, panoramic mise-en-scène style shots were used as a background for huge set pieces fuelled by oral incantation. There was also a focus on plots driven by well-known predominantly male historical figures amid political upheaval (Julius-Adeoye 2013, Adeleye-Fayemi 1997, 127, Bryce 2012, 72).

These historical stories, spaces and characters were framed to foreground important cultural considerations and pursue the construction of a post-independent, national identity. Ola Rotimi a playwright and scholar, suggests that historical drama is a nation-building tool as "Nigerian artists are critically probing into the past to make our historical experience and cultural heritage positively relevant to the present and future" (Coker, 2003, 90). The genre thereby allowed for a space to construct a shared vision of a collective ethnic identity in response to the aftereffects of British colonialism. The construction of the genre's narratives also served as a space for the negotiation of contemporary socio-political and cultural anxieties through the "prism of the past" (Pidduck 2012, 103), which has significant implications for the depiction of female characters in the historical drama. In an attempt to approach these troubling concerns, the genre produced and promoted an iconic image of a pre-colonial utopia, complete with pastoral landscapes and gendered roles (Adeboye 2018, 667; Adeleye-Fayemi 1997, 126). These images were actively tied to an authentic Nigerian past, affirming faith in Nigerian cultural identity.

---

[1] It is important to note that the production dates of certain texts may not match their publication dates. Also, some texts are originally released on *YouTube* and later translated into English.

However, a number of female critics have argued that these iconic images have several fundamental problems. Ajayi, for one, is certainly correct when she observes the past is created in the creative consciousness of male writers (Ajayi, cited in Ogunleye 2004, 305) in the construction of female roles such as *Segi,* the alluring temptress. Similarly, Adeleye-Fayemi echoes Ajayi's views by acknowledging that male-defined values shape female characters (Adeleye-Fayemi 1997, 128) hence are they depicted as "powerful and dangerous", "longsuffering" (Adeleye-Fayemi 1997, 126) or as an *Omo oluwabi* (a decent, good human being) who lacks a complex female self. Female characters are generally conceptualized and written by male dramatists working under the assumption that women's status in society is subordinate and, as such, female characters are *othered* in relation to men. Busia argues she is not permitted her version of the story (Busia 1989, 86). Although Busia's comments speak to colonial literature, these tools still persist in post-colonial literature and resonate with African women's televisual and cinematic representation. African male authors use inherited tools to render her still "a[n] [inert]subject" (Busia 1989, 86). As a result, the historical dramas articulate a historical interpretation of the past where female characters collude or are usually oblivious and impotent against the larger forces of patriarchy. These gendered constructions are grounded within what Adeleye-Fayemi would call "conservative cultural nationalism"; this is where culture is created under the guise of restoring a cultural identity eroded by colonialism and imperialism (Adeleye-Fayemi 1997, 127).

Whilst cultural identity is important, Adeleye-Fayemi argues cultural nationalism enforces compliance with dominant stories privileging patriarchy. In this way, cultural nationalism parallels the British "post-heritage" film, which not only offers a conservative view of the past but dwells on an "over-concern with sexuality and gender" (Monk 2001). Even though Monk's observation refers to British period films produced during the 1980s to 2000s, I see useful parallels with Adeleye-Fayemi's conservative nationalist concerns and Ogunleye's arguments regarding female agency (Adeleye-Fayemi 1997; Ogunleye 2004, 306). *Efunsetan Aniwura, Iyalode of Ibadan,* (Isola 1981, 2005) and *Madam Tinubu* (Isola 1998) are examples of historical dramas which demonstrate the lack of female agency in the celebratory vision of a Nigerian historical, cultural utopia. Even more important, these dramas present a vision of the past which explore gender but are compelled to uphold the male construct of femininity, to create a soothing visual style of an uncomplicated Nigerian past where women know their place as the *other,* creating and reinforcing objectified female constructs in "the way society perceives them but also expects them to be" (Adeleye Fayemi 1997, 128).

Consequently, despite their explicit intention of visualizing gender on screen, these historical films pursue and frame a dominant visual style that complements a hegemonic narrative of the past where women maintain a passive presence, limiting the possibility of an alternative female subject on the screenplay page.

Addressing the issue of passive Nigerian female subjectivity in the historical drama brings me to the role of the screenwriter in the construction of character. This may not only affect the genre, which serves as a "touchstone for audience recognition" (Selbo 2014, 23) but can possibly dictate the overall style of the screenwork. Because the haptic image calls upon the spectator's bodily consciousness to gain its awareness from the visual tools utilized in the creation of the tactile image, for example, camera shot sizes, character point of view, sound and editing, the haptic has the possibility of creating a far stronger connection with images linked with the past. With regard to presenting a historical drama with a haptic image, the screenwriter, as Parker believes, can approach genre by connecting the screenplay's character, setting and visual aesthetics to create the screenplay's style (Parker 1999, 159).

In this way, it becomes clear that the screenwriter can skillfully manipulate character development and reframe the historical genre's visual style to create a new kind of meaning, sensation and empathy by ordering the character's subjectivity within the fictional storied world.

What is of particular interest to me is potentially employing a fresh way of constructing and experiencing Efunsetan from a tactile perspective. In effect, I aimed to assign Efunsetan, the protagonist of *Efunsetan's Story*, a subjectivity where she is "an active participant of both perception and expression" (Barker 2009, 8). What can emerge from the haptic experience, Alison Landsberg points out, is that the "body [viewer/reader's] is activated, brought into proximity to the conditions of existence for the person [Efunsetan] in the historical past" (Landsberg 2015, 35). From Landsberg's perspective, the historical genre offers the screenwriter the opportunity to craft a screenplay which speaks from the characters' bodily subjectivity and material surroundings to create new aesthetic possibilities. At the same time, I intend to shift the audience's attention from the *familiar* gendered protagonist, *mise en scene*, songs and dances to the *unfamiliar* intimate spaces in Efunsetan's life, by drawing on her corporeality and the materiality of the space she inhabits in the pursuit of creating new meanings from Efunsetan's embodied experience. It is the relationship between Efunsetan's subjectivity and the material intimate spaces she inhabits that interests me.

Furthermore, the small intimate space is not caught up in male-driven events and intrigues. Nor is it foregrounded by a male protagonist operating within the panoramic vistas of social and political change. It is a space which can explore a female bodily experience created not out of male expectations, but a subjectivity which explores the female tactile experience "circumscribed by laws, customs, values, social mores, political and economic circumstances" (Landsberg 2015, 37). The haptic encounter utilizes sound and textures to convey a personal history comprising of intimate Yoruba gestures of interaction, giving a fleeting miniature of everyday life and may even lead to "the quickening of a new historical sense and perhaps a more active and reflective historical subject" (Sobchack 1996, 38). In this way, a textured approach to character subjectivity opens up Efunsetan's perspective and experience of patriarchy in nineteenth-century Ibadan.

33.5 THE *IYALODE* CHARACTER: WHY EXPLORE *EFUNSETAN'S STORY*?

The background to the screen idea for *Efunsetan's Story* started in 2013 with my fascination with Efunsetan Aniwura, the Iyalode of Ibadan (an Iyalode is a high-ranking female), a renowned Yoruba aristocrat who lived in the nineteenth century. Female leaders were not a novelty during Nigeria's precolonial history, according to Onayemi (2007, 298). Some female aristocrats and queens served in royal courts like the *iyeoba* (Onayemi 2007, 303). There were also aristocrats who emerged from heading political pressure groups, *Egbe Iyalode* (Fadipe, cited in Afigbo 2011, 8). In some Yoruba towns, like Ibadan, the president, *Iyalode*, represented the pressure group in the state council. It is around the subject of finance that the blurring of roles was most acutely played out in the predominantly patriarchal, pre-imperialist Yoruba society. A woman bestowed the title of *Iyalode* mainly relied on acquiring capital, status, power and civic responsibilities (Afigbo 2011, 8). Although a woman's finances could be independently acquired, her assets as a defining symbol of influence still related to her marital status, in so far as they were usually inextricably linked to her husband. Very little is known and documented, however, about Efunsetan's marital life and whether she was unique in acquiring her vast wealth. As Awe notes, most accounts of women before the colonial era are based on oral tradition, legend and eyewitness accounts (Awe 1992, 57). However, what is known from oral praise songs explored by Awe is that Efunsetan was a very successful businesswoman, whose trade in gun, slaves, horses and bullets made her net worth "surpass those of the Aare" (i.e. the commander-in-chief) (Awe 1992, 57). Thus, I was provided with an opportunity to develop the unknown gaps of Efunsetan's earlier life with the perception of Efunsetan through a tactile aesthetic which drove my choice of Efunsetan as the main character in the screenplay.

Historically, Efunsetan is remembered and characterized as a strong-willed character and an icon of radical evil (Isola 1970; Smith 2005) who conflicted with societal expectations of a maternal and benevolent female chief (Awe 1992, 65). What is even more striking about Efunsetan, as dramatized by Isola, are the allegations of brutal beheadings of her pregnant slaves. This implies a sexist prejudice and enacts a cautionary tale to all potential female leaders (Akinyele, Cited in Adeboye 2018, 668). Many commentators have cited this aspect of Efunsetan's character, and many of them point to her gender as a female oddity as a reason for her behaviour, resulting in moral judgements; for example, when a statue was commissioned in her honour, the "rank and file of Ibadan seem to view the memorial more as a reminder model of 'evil personified'" (Smith 2005, 26) in response to the *Efunsetan Aniwura* (Isola 1981) adaptation. A senior chief refused to comment on Efunsetan's role as an

Iyalode, insisting he "had no desire comment on an evil woman" (quoted in Adeboye 2018, 671). I decided to re-present and reposition her as a character with agency and power, operating within the confines of patriarchy. Hence, I believe emphasizing her subjective bodily response to her situation, marked by societal values, would create, as Marks submits, a subject (who) comes into being not through abstraction from the world but (elicit from the reader) a compassionate involvement with it (Marks 2000, 141). By countering the unsympathetic portrayal of her by male dramatists such as Akinwunmi Isola's *Efunsetan Aniwura, Iyalode Ibadan* (Isola 1970), I set out to disrupt and encourage a different and sensuous encounter with Efunsetan. I wanted to displace the inherited representation of Efunsetan in the nostalgic historical hegemonic story by repositioning her to the *ordinary*; focusing on her *intimate* and tiny bodily details in the writing of the story and providing her with a sensuous perception of her bodily state.

33.6 The Haptic Encounter and *Efunsetan's Story*

In an attempt to reconfigure the relationship between the reader and the screenplay text through the haptic (Marks 2000; Barker 2009; Bruno 2002), the haptic encounter allows for a reimagining of the characters' subjective relationship with the reader and eventual viewer. As I mentioned earlier, embedding of the haptic in the screenplay necessitates the marshalling of the screenwork's dominant visual style (Parker 1999,159) or the screenplay's stylistic visual expression in a particular way. For the purpose of this discussion, the stylistic visual expression refers to the interplay of filmic devices suggested in the screenplay, for example, the positioning of characters, implied shots, editing and the use of sound; all engaged in the design of an aesthetic in anticipation of its realization on the screen. In order for the stylistic visual expression of the screenplay to emphasize tactility and highlight Efunsetan's corporeal subjectivity and the materiality of the story world, the visual style has to evoke the screenplay's sensory mode, through the scene description. I was determined that, through this exploration, the reader and eventual viewer would have a tactile and embodied experience of the character and the story. I relied on this approach to explore a sensory form of storytelling that challenges the familiar engagement. By familiar engagement, I mean the prior appropriative cultural knowledge possessed by the reader when reading a screenplay, which facilitates a form of interaction for the reader and eventual viewer that transforms the character into the passive object.

For example, as a character development tool, the mother archetype draws on a Jungian theory and alternative archetypal theory (Jung 1953; Vogler 1998; Jacey 2010), based on characteristics founded upon familiar psychological and culturally learned knowledge. This cultural entanglement maps the character and socially inscribes her body. In this case, the mother archetype reinforces the passive distance between the reader and the character whilst upholding her as the *other*. Furthermore, the screenplay's visual expression may stress and tie both the character and reader to culturally laden societal norms, for example, Annie Johnson, the black maid and loving mother, is othered from her mixed-race daughter Sarah Jane, in *Imitation of Life* (1959).

Although archetypes can function as a character development tool, they can also serve to enforce the hegemonic principle of othering characters through objectification. However, by employing the haptic, the interchange between the reader/eventual viewer and the character is achieved because of a re-mapping of character development. Based on exploring the sensual, it may initiate a defamiliarization process where the reader actively deciphers the character with little or no prior knowledge of the viewed character.

Then a refamiliarization occurs when the reader's body actively connects *to* or *touches* the character's body because the reader brings in her sensory skills and sense memory into the interaction. In return, the character's body reciprocates this way of tactile engagement. In adopting this approach, I wanted to disturb and provoke the reader's familiar interaction with the character, which fuels a distant and controlling look, by separating "viewing subject and object" (Marks 2000, 163). Therefore, the haptic encounter presents a repositioning of character and creates an embodied knowledge, providing the space and understanding for the marginalized, subjective character experience.

For example, in an early draft (2) of webisode 1 of *Efunsetan's Story* (2018) below, Efunsetan's sensory perception of breath is evident in the webisode where Efunsetan is making a decision regarding Bodunrin's fate. The assignment of Efunsetan's sensory perception of breath is evident when the reader sees how:

```
Her palm gently brushes against Tinu's strangely smooth but
scarred face, her breathing falters, it's shallow! Suddenly,
she inhales deeply.
```
   (Oyebanjo 2018, draft 2, 1)

Efunsetan, the Iyalode of Ibadan, is now presented as a vulnerable character; by this, I mean her irregular breathing reveals her discomfort, and it is possible to see how the viewer is able to connect with Efunsetan sensorially. It is the revelation of and connection to Efunsetan's irregular breathing which expresses her private subjectivity and yet creates a sensed intersubjectivity with the reader (Marks 2000, 153; Quinlivan 2012, 163). The haptic stylistic expression in the screenplay is made possible by opening up the character's subjective corporeal sensuality, in the process, shaping and revealing the sensuous experience of the character's world. This intersubjective relationship between the character and the reader is facilitated by two main strategies: the internal and external haptic encounters.

33.6.1 Internal *Haptic Encounter* Through *the Frame*

The internal haptic encounter is encouraged by a focus on the character's sensorial subjectivity, looking *through* the frame; that is, the reader (and implied audience) *sees* or *experiences* as if she is *within* the character. The screenplay implies and frames the shot, to shape the materiality of the storied world according to a specific character's *interior sensory perception*—objects of their gaze, movement, gestures. To elaborate further, the character's corporeal entity is captured by drawing attention to their bodily presence. For example, the excerpt from draft 3, of webisode 1 of *Efunsetan's Story* (2019) below, contains moments where Efunsetan's corporeality is indicated through our awareness of her body parts: her hands grasping at objects; her breathing; her gaze.

```
INT. EFUNSETAN'S PARLOUR. DUSK.
A bejewelled, elegant middle-aged hand caresses, fondles,
and pats down stiff glistening gold-coloured Aso-Oke Ipele
(shawl) slowly, deliberately in time with her considered slow
breathing like that of a hunter...
```
   (Oyebanjo 2019, draft 3, 1)

The relationship between Efunsetan's hands and her breathing structures foregrounds her corporeality: by turning the attention to Efunsetan's corporeal expression, the description allows the reader and eventual viewer to apprehend her desire, namely, to control her breathing as conveyed by the corporeal expression of her hands. The screenplay attempts to represent the interiority of the character by placing the reader and eventual viewer within the frame—as a representation of not only what the character, in this instance Efunsetan, is seeing but *how* she sees—or specifically *in,* how she sensorially perceives and experiences her world through the frame. The focus on the interior processes of the character positions the reader *inside* her bodily experience.

Within the conceptualization of the internal haptic encounter, not only is the *how* in terms of the stylistic visual expression of the screenplay's story manifested, but also the *what* in terms of the content of the story, which enables the writer to reposition the character within the story by destabilizing the hegemonic and contained visual objectification between the reader and Efunsetan, where she was grounded in the socio-cultural look of control. Instead, through the haptic encounter, her subjectivity is expressed and hopeful experienced in a more intimate and tactile way. Her embodied metaphorical scars are placed under the "caressing gaze" (Marks 2000, 169). For Marks, the caress cannot be appropriated, objectified or sensationalized (Marks 2000). Instead, it is my intention as a writer that a process occurs where there is a connection between the reader's interior and Efunsetan's body, evoking "a kind of empathy between our body and the film's body" (Barker 2009, 75).

At times this process elicits an intersubjective empathy, where the reader and Efunsetan are "reversibly enfolded in each other" (Sobchack 2004, 287). For Sobchack, the connection between the film and the spectator can be blurred. In *Efunsetan's Story*, Efunsetan's breath hopefully reaches out to the reader and forms a connection with her. In doing so, the reader actively *touches* Efunsetan facilitating the *enfolded* interchange rather than the distant passive frame of control from the reader.

Barker, Sobchack and Marks, are united in their observation of the reverberation between subject and object as "dynamic subjectivity between looker and image" (Marks 2000, 164). In this instance, the reverberation is created by the screenwriter's skill in encouraging the reader and potential viewer to experience Efunsetan's bodily experience, her positioning and the object she handles. Therefore, I suggest, the internal haptic encounter between the reader of the text and the eventual web series creates a heightened or intense intimacy which may enable the reader to experience the tactility of Efunsetan's story world, and the corporeality of her subjectivity. Efunsetan's sensory perception drives and facilitates this tactile engagement.

33.6.2 External *Haptic Encounter* With *the Frame*

Just as the internal haptic encounter is invaluable in calling attention to the sensory elements present in the haptic web series screenplay, the external haptic encounter is another strategy that facilitates the haptic in the screenplay. In the *external* haptic encounter, the writing brings into focus the materiality of objects and the corporeality of the character in the way the camera sees them. This encounter involves the screenplay implying the characters' subjectivity through an external or seemingly objective viewpoint. For example, the camera might focus on the character's breathing as viewed from outside (rather than implied from within, as in the *internal* haptic encounter). This is encouraged by a focus on the character's experience, linking her appearance to what she sees, by looking *with* the frame; the reader and subsequent viewer observes the character looking: in this case, the frame is outside the subjective body of the character. The framing here concentrates on the external performance of the characters' objective bodily and facial expressions—i.e. the encounter is manifested objectively. For example, in the excerpt below from a draft 3 of webisode 2, of *Efunsetan's Story* (2019), the scene is written as follows:

```
INT. EFUNSETAN'S FATHER'S COMPOUND - PAST.

Efunsetan's toes wiggle helplessly; a warm, rich bloody
globule trickles down her youthful shin towards her bony
ankle; Efunsetan wipes the red ball with her thumb, it
breaks, red smeared across her hand. Muffled groaning. Her
blood-encrusted nails clench into a fist.

    Her eyelids wrinkle, her mouth opens, gulping vast breaths
of air followed by shallow, rapid breaths; her hands cup her
```

soft rolled *iro* to absorb the blood from her upper thigh.
Muffled strained breaths envelop her.

(Oyebanjo 2019, draft 3, 9)

In the examples the *external haptic encounter* is orchestrated where the script creates the experience of being invited to watch Efunsetan, *with* the framed camera shot as opposed to *through* the camera shot. What should begin to emerge for the reader is an approximation of experiencing the sensation of blood smeared across her fingers and the anguish that spreads across Efunsetan's face as she takes in the enormity of her situation. Here, Efunsetan's "eyelids wrinkle and her mouth open, gulping vast breaths of air" is specifically framed with the camera, conveying her terror, fear and distress. Notably in "gulping vast breaths of air", followed by "shallow, rapid breaths" this framing unfolds as we watch Efunsetan's breathing express her bodily activity whilst we sense her despair. In contrast to the *internal haptic encounter*, where the encounter is framed by the sensory perception of the character, Efunsetan's face is not seen *through*—the frame of her subjective, sensorial POV perception but framed *with* the camera, which opens up such perception by inviting the reader and eventual viewer to watch her bodily behaviour, Efunsetan's mouth and facial features are framed, her "shallow, rapid breaths" are made tangible. When viewing films, Marks asserts that we call upon remembered sensory experiences (Marks 2000, 213): here we are invited to recall inhaling oxygen and exhaling carbon dioxide as gasps triggered by our bodily response to terror. We summon our experience of the feeling of troubled breathing with Efunsetan. The persistence of the ribcage expanding, the rush of oxygen through the mouth, into the larynx and, when captured, the lungs, coupled with the dizzying release as we exhale carbon dioxide connects us *with* Efunsetan's sensory perception to an unsettling experience. I deliberately employed *fleshy* and material adjectives, verbs and nouns in the sentence, "rapid breaths, then her hands cup her soft rolled *iro*[2] to absorb the blood from her upper thigh" to watch Efunsetan's corporeal expression and her response to the beginnings of miscarriage and to underscore what she feels and does—the materiality of *iro* acts as a container for her disappointment, as it absorbs her blood. Furthermore, recalling the stickiness and warmth of blood as it oozes out of her vulnerable body prompts the reader to sense Efunsetan's intense emotional loss but, more importantly, her corporeal response to trauma. For the Yoruba, children represent continuity and secure a women's position in her family and her stakes in the wider community as she transitions from patriarchal social markers such as her father's daughter to her husband's wife and motherhood.

In developing this aspect of Efunsetan's character, I wanted to make her body's most intimate state visible through tactility as it breaks down, revealing the fragility of a circumscribed body, which evokes the reader's visceral, tactile

---

[2] Large piece of woven, printed or patterned cloth, worn wrapped around the waist.

response to Efunsetan's body. Now made vulnerable without the patriarchal status attached to motherhood to protect her. In this way, Efunsetan is denied an important social marker of Yoruba womanhood—i.e. pregnancy and childbirth—potentially casting Efunsetan into the realms of social exclusion.

33.6.3   Internal *and* External *Haptic Encounters*

There are moments in the screenplay where the external haptic encounter and the internal haptic encounter participate simultaneously in the screenplay. In their co-presence, both these haptic strategies create an enhanced focus on the character's subjective state. An overlap of the *external encounter* of the character with the *internal encounter* can determine how the character sees herself in the action of the scene as linked to her internal bodily processes. How the encounters work together in order to elicit a tactile response can be seen from the following example, taken from draft 3 of *Efunsetan's Story* (2019), act two in webisode 1.

```
EFUNSETAN'S PARLOUR. DUSK - 40 YEARS AGO.
A large, speckled fly whisk dances on the back of a
man's shoulders - EFUNSETAN'S FATHER 50's. A TEN-YEAR-OLD
EFUNSETAN's voice squeals and giggle as she yanks it from him
and hits him with it, he attempts to grab it from her, but she
won't let go.
    Finally, he grabs it from her. The fly whisk sways and blurs
as he punctuates his words with it.
```
   (Oyebanjo 2019, draft 1, 3)

The screenplay implies an internal haptic encounter—from Efunsetan's POV where her gaze is fixed on the shot of the fly whisk and on her father's back. The internal haptic encounter is suggested by the materiality of the flywhisk made present by the description, "large, speckled flywhisk dancing on the back"—the screenplay here is emphasizing Efunsetan's POV and externalizes her state of mind—i.e. recollection of her naivete and playfulness. The corporeality of a ten-year-old Efunsetan's hands yank it from him, and her breath is voiced in "squeals and giggle" as she "hits him with it". The frame is determined by her fixed subjective gaze on the flywhisk, her sensory perception of the texture of the flywhisk hitting her father's back. Framed by the internal haptic encounter—the reader experiences the event from Efunsetan's subjectivity—her gaze, gestures and breath. The internal haptic encounter in this scene coincides with a childhood memory triggered by the "flapping" sound of a flywhisk from the previous scene.

In the same scene, the reader's attention is directed to Efunsetan's father as he faces her. Here, an external haptic encounter is evoked when "he attempts to grab it from her, and she won't let go". The implication here is that a frame is created *with* the camera and not *through* Efunsetan's point of view.

The reader is guided by her father's gestures when rising and tussles with her. The frame this time is *with* the camera—framing what Efunsetan's father can see: a ten-year-old Efunsetan from an objective point of view. Despite the change in point of view, corporeality and materiality simultaneously dominate Efunsetan's perception, raising the reader's awareness of Efunsetan's bodily and material consciousness. Thus, the process creates a heightened intimacy and facilitates identification with Efunsetan.

As the scene progresses, an additional internal haptic encounter is instigated through movement in which "the flywhisk sways and blurs as he punctuates his words with it". The very blurry nature of the flywhisk is determined by Efunsetan's sensory perception and rearranges the external haptic encounter to the internal haptic encounter. Efunsetan's concentration on the moving flywhisk not only underscores its materiality but deemphasizes the visual focus on her father.

In this scene, both internal and external haptic encounters give shape and direction to Efunsetan's sensory perception and the reader's understanding of her interiority, not only through the tried and tested aspects of experiencing Efunsetan's emotional identification or by following her cognitive action; but also through a more layered manifestation of Efunsetan's character as negotiated between her body, emotions and actions by evoking a connection informed by her sensory subjectivity.

Crucially, the example illustrates the advantage for the screenwriter in using internal and external haptic encounters. They complement each other as they both reposition the viewer's relationship with the character, not only by conveying, the corporeality and intimate proximity of the character with the materiality of the story world, but also, by acknowledging and capturing how the haptic disables the distance and power and control of the viewer/reader over Efunsetan, and her relationship to her environment. Directing attention to an intersubjective *sensory* moment between Efunsetan, her space, the objects, other characters, encourages the viewer/reader to a more complex tactile, *fleshy* relationship (see Baker 2009), where Efunsetan is given agency: she is not a passive object to be observed or captured through the reader's distance. The haptic encounters have a direct impact that heightens the importance of the reader's direct engagement with Efunsetan's inner frustrations at the dynamics of her gendered daily realities.

To sum up, the simultaneity of internal and external haptic encounters extends the bodily presence of a character into the screenplay and aims to elicit corporeal and material awareness in the reader and eventual viewer through the awareness of the character's sensorial perception *in* the storied world. In the negotiation and interrelationship between these two concepts, the haptic screenplay attempts to represent the subjectivity of the character by placing the reader and eventual viewer *inside* their experience sensorially.

33.7 THE HAPTIC ENCOUNTER AS COMPASSIONATE INVOLVEMENT WITH EFUNSETAN

In *Efunsetan's Story*, the haptic encounter validates Efunsetan's personal and intimate encounters and the everyday. When trying to maintain control of Ibadan, whilst most of her body is stilled, the implied close-up of her physical activity of *breathing, gesticulating* and *looking* all become tactile extensions of the reader's body. Through the act of reading the scene description, the bodily responses of the reader are, hopefully, actively summoned as she *touches* Efunsetan. The dense scene description allows for a gradual unfolding. It conveys the impression of Efunsetan's body, which enables the reader to pay close attention to and simultaneously sense Efunsetan, resulting in an intertwining which creates a meeting sensation. This process repositions Efunsetan's body from the notoriously cruel Iyalode of Ibadan to a vulnerable and relational being, thus disrupting the reader's conventionally passive, yet organizational gaze of power and control. Furthermore, employing the "compassionate involvement" (Marks 2000, 141) ensured by the haptic deepens the development and interpretation of the character and enables a further sensory knowing that complements the emotional, psychological and cognitive. Hence, I interweave the character's cognition and emotion with the bodily into a narrative that facilitates repositioning the character by defamiliarization. In *Efunsetan's Story*, Efunsetan's character is not presented in an easy, familiar or superficial manner, like a character who gives the "illusion of completeness that lends itself to the narrative" (Marks 2000, 163), as illustrated by the following excerpt from the final draft of webisode 1 *Efunsetan's Story* (2021):

> INT. EFUNSETAN'S PARLOUR. DUSK
>
> A formidable middle-aged woman, who always considers herself with pleasure, sits on an ornately carved chair. A shadow from the window obscures her face; her mind is hazy.
>
> Considering ODETOLA. Her green-veined hands slide calmly down her *iro* as they smooth down the veins of her ornate peacock feathered fan.
>
> She deliberately raises the fan towards the nape of her neck. The peacock feathers sway gently as she enjoys the cool air, goosebumps form along her curved neck.
>
> Her delicate pale-yellow lace Buba is crisp and dry despite the hot air. This is EFUNSETAN ANIWURA.
>
> (Oyebanjo 2021, draft 3, 1)

Instead, Efunsetan's introduction as a character resonates with Elsaessar and Haganer's take on the haptic, which "calls forth memories which were virtually present and needed [for] the film[screenplay] to be actualised" (Elsaessar and Hagener 2010, 124). I do not give the reader full power of interpretation. A reconfiguration occurs through this process of decentring the reader, producing defamiliarization. It is by decentring and repositioning the reader to sense Efunsetan's physicality and as her body engages with Efunsetan. I hope that the subject/object distinction is blurred to provide new meaning and to reposition the relationship between Efunsetan and the reader, giving Efunsetan more agency in her personal history than a hegemonically situated retelling of Efunsetan's narrative would achieve.

33.8 Conclusion

To conclude, this chapter discussed a haptic approach to developing Efunsetan's subjectivity through the haptic encounter in the historical drama. In addition to repositioning characters, the haptic also makes it possible for the screenwriter to employ her cultural, embodied experience to *unfreeze* (Marks 2000, 85), *reframe* and *reposition* objects as well as bodies as they emerge "re-endowed with history" (Marks 2000, 99). For Marks, this means the screenwriter can draw attention to and reclaim the optical framing of the object infused with control, and possibly racist representation, by positioning the reader to engage with the object in more depth, thus serving as a means of producing and accessing knowledge about the character and the story world. For example, Efunsetan's flywhisk in the screenplay is an object which has been fetishized as primitive and decorative by the dominant western frame in films such as *Coming to America* (1988); *Mister Johnson* (1990) and *Beasts of No Nation* (2015). On the other hand, the haptic encounter allowed me to restore and charge the object with "reactivity" (Marks 2000, 78) by imbuing it with its historical, cultural and spiritual function and significance. This is because, in re-presenting the character, the screenwriter also repositions the objects she handles by enabling the reader to *touch* the object, which is then no longer subject to conventional norms of *mastery* and, as such, creates a new connection through contact to *represent* the framed object conveyed in a way which protects it from the dominance of the familiar "commodifying gaze" (Marks 2000, 79) that reduces and *others* the object to the clichéd *trifle* and *fetish*. In *Efunsetan's Story*, thanks to the haptic, the flywhisk belongs to the story world where it is valued as an item of royal insignia and not confined by cultural restraints.

Returning to the question of *how a haptic approach to screenwriting facilitates a rescripting of female subjectivity within Nigerian historical drama*, I am convinced that the construction and conveying of compelling female characters in the screenplay is still open to creative ambition (Taylor 2017; Jacey 2010). I believe that my research offers some valuable reflections on critical concerns for exploring female subjectivity via the sensory within the screenplay. By drawing upon the concept of haptic visuality, the discussion identifies several factors involved in creating sensory imagery. As a form of screenplay practice, the screenplay stands as an example of writing undertaken with the intent of vividly presenting a sensory experience for the reader by repositioning character subjectivity. It could be argued that there may be moments where character-embodied experiences that are socio-culturally situated may still be found in Efunsetan, but the relationship with Efunsetan can be and has been repositioned within *Efunsetan's Story*. The haptic encounter is an approach offered to screenwriters who are prepared to rethink character agency or even consider employing their own *embodied experience* in conceptualizing traditionally marginalized characters. It is my hope that the haptic encounter would suggest an approach to subjectivity that may create more relational characters in the screenplay.

References

Adeboye, Olufunke. 2018. "Framing Female Leadership on Stage and Screen in Yorubaland: Efunsetan Aniwura Revisited." *Gender & History*, 30 (3): 666–81.

Adeleye-Fayemi, Bisi. 1997. "Either One or the Other, Images of Women in Nigerian Television." In *Readings in African Popular Culture*, edited by Karin Barber, 125–31. Bloomington in, London and Oxford: Indiana University Press, in association with The International African Institute and James Currey.

Afigbo, Adiele. 2011. "Women in Nigerian History." In *Shaping Our Struggles: Nigerian Women in History, Culture and Social Change*, edited by Obioma Nnaemeka, and Chima Korieh, 3–22. Trenton nj: Africa World Press.

Awe, Bolanle. 1992. "Iyalode Efunsetan Aniwura" ["Owner of Gold"]. In *Nigerian Women in Historical Perspective*, edited by Awe Bolanle, 167. Lagos and Ibadan: Sankore and Bookcraft.

Barker, Jennifer M. 2009. *The Tactile Eye: Touch and the Cinematic Experience*. Berkeley, Los Angeles CA: University of California Press.

Beast of No Nation. 2015. Written and directed by Cary Joji Fukunaga. USA: Participant Media, Red Crown Productions, New Balloon, Primary Productions and Parliament of Owls.

Bruno, Giuliana. 2008. "Yes, It's about Time: A Virtual Letter to Sally Potter from Giuliana Bruno." *Journal of Visual Culture* 7 (1): 27–40.

Bryce, Jane. 2012. Signs of Femininity, Symptoms of Malaise: Contextualizing Figurations of 'Woman' in Nollywood. *Research in African Literatures* 43 (4): 71–87. https://doi.org/10.2979/reseafrilite.43.4.71.

Busia, Abena. 1989. Silencing Sycorax: On African Colonial Discourse and the Unvoiced Female. *Cultural Critique* 14 (2): 81–104.

Bruno, Giuliana. 2002. *Atlas of Emotion: Journeys in Art, Architecture, and Film*. London: Verso.

Coker, Adeniyi. 2003. "A Director's Vision for Theater in Africa: Adeniyi Coker Interviews Ola Rotimi—One of Nigeria's Foremost Playwrights and Directors." *The Free Library*. https://www.thefreelibrary.com/A+director%27s+vision+for+theater+in+Africa%3a+Adeniyi+Coker+interviews...-a0113562799. Accessed 6 August. 2022.

Cohen, William. 2009. *Embodied: Victorian Literature and the Senses*. Minneapolis mn: University of Minnesota Press.

Coming to America. 1988. Written by David Sheffield and Barry W. Blaustein. Directed by John Landis. USA: Eddie Murphy Productions.

Efunsetan Aniwura. 1981. Written by Akinwunmi Isola. Directed by Bankole Bello. Nigeria: Isola Ogunshola Theatre Productions.

Efunsetan Aniwura. 2005. Written by Akinwunmi Isola. Directed by Tunde Kelani. Nigeria: Aloy Productions.

Elsaessar, Thomas, and Malte Hagener. 2010. *Film Theory: An Introduction through the Senses*. Abingdon uk: Routledge.

Ferrell, Rose. 2017. *Voice in Screenwriting: Discovering/Recovering an Australian Voice*. PhD diss., Edith Cowan University. Available at: http://ro.ecu.edu.au/theses/ Accessed 5 August 2022.

Ganz, Adam. 2012. To Make You See: 'Screenwriting, Description and the 'Lens-based' Tradition. *Journal of Screenwriting* 4 (1): 7–24.

Hanson, Peter, and Paul Robert Herman. 2010. *Tales from the Script: 50 Hollywood Screenwriters Share their Stories*. New York: HarperCollins.

Imitation of Life. 1959. Written by Eleanore Griffin and Allan Scott. Directed by Douglas Sirk. USA: Universal-International.

Ìṣọ́lá, Akínwùmí. 1970. *Efunsetan Aniwura, Iyalode Ibadan*. Ibadan: Ibadan University Press.

Ìṣọ́lá, Akínwùmí. 1998. *Madam Tinubu: The Terror in Lagos*. Ibadan, Nigeria: Heinemann Education Books.

Ìṣọ́lá, Akínwùmí. 2005. *Efunsetan Aniwura: Iyalode Ibadan, and Tinuubu Iyalode Egba (The Yoruba Historical Dramas of Akinwunmi Isola)*. Trans. Pamela. J Olubunmi Smith, Eritrea: Africa World Press.

Ìṣọ́lá, Akínwùmí. 2009. *Ẹfúnróyè Tinubu: Ìyálóde Ẹ̀gbá*. Ibadan, Nigeria: DB Martoy Books.

Jacey, Helen. 2010. *The Woman in the Story: Writing Memorable Female Characters*. Studio City ca: Michael Wiese Productions.

Julius-Adeoye, Rantimi. 2013. *The Drama of Ahmed Yerima: Studies in Nigerian Theatre*. [Doctoral dissertation, submitted to Leiden University] Leiden, Netherlands.

Jung, Carl G., Herbert Read, Michael Fordham, and Gerhard Adler. 1953. *The Collected Works of C.G. Jung*. New York: Pantheon Books

Kurunmi. 1969. Written by Ola Rotimi. Directed by Vanessa Harte Nigeria: Lagos state University Theatre.

Ladipọ, Duro, and Ulli Beier. 1964. *Three Yoruba Plays: Ọba Koso, Ọba Mọro, Ọba Waja*. Ibadan: Mbari Publications.

Landsberg, Alison. 2015. *Engaging the Past*. New York: Columbia University Press.

Maras, Steven. 2009. *Screenwriting: History, Theory and Practice*. New York: Wallflower.

Marks, Laura U. 1998. "Video Haptics and Erotics." *Screen* 39 (4): 331–348.

Marks, Laura U. 2000. *The Skin of the Film*. Durham nc: Duke University Press.

Marks, Laura U. 2002. *Touch: Sensuous Theory and Multisensory Media*. Minnesota: University of Minnesota Press.

Marks, Laura U. 2009. Information, Secrets and Enigmas: An Enfolding-unfolding Aesthetics for Cinema. *Screen* 50 (1): 86–98.

Mister Johnson. 1990. Written by William Boyd. Directed by Bruce Beresford. USA: Avenue Pictures.

Monk, Claire. 2001. "Sexuality and heritage." In *Film/Literature/Heritage: A Sight and Sound Reader*, edited by Ginette Vincendeau, 6–11. London: British Film Institute.

Moremi Ajasoro. 2009. Written by Duro Ladipo. Directed by Abiodun Olanrewaju. Nigeria: 1st Eye Pictures and Duro Ladipo Theatre INT'L.

Mulvey, Laura. 1999. "Visual Pleasure and Narrative Cinema." In *Film Theory and Criticism: Introductory Readings*, edited by Leo Braudy, and Marshall Cohen, 833–44. New York: Oxford University Press.

Oba ko so (The king did not hang). 2022. Written by Duro Ladipo. Directed by Adeyemi A. Usman. Nigeria: University of Ibadan–Theatre Arts Production.

Ogunleye, Foluke. 2004. A Male-Centric Modification of History; Efunsetan Aniwura Revisited. *History in Africa* 31: 303–318.

Ogunyẹmi, Wale. 1970. *Ijaye War in the Nineteenth Century: A Historical Drama*. Ibadan: Orisun Acting Editions.

Ogunyẹmi, Wale. 1976. *Kíriji: An Historic Drama on Ekiti Parapo War in the Nineteenth Century*. Ibadan: African Universities Press.

Onayemi, Folake. 2007. Finding a Place: Women's Struggle for Political Authority in Classical and Nigerian Societies. *Women's History Review* 16 (3): 297–309. https://doi.org/10.1080/09612020601022071.

Osofisan, Femi. 2006. *Women of Owu*. Ibadan: Ibadan University Press.

Parker, Philip. 1999. *The Art and Science of Screenwriting*. Bristol: Intellect.

Pidduck, Julianne. 2012. The Body as Gendered Discourse in British and French Costume and Heritage Fictions. *Cinémas* 22 (2–3): 101–125.

Quinlivan, Davinia. 2012. *Place of Breath in Cinema*. Edinburgh: Edinburgh University Press.

Ray. 2004. Written by James L. White. Directed by Taylor Hackford. USA: Bristol Bay Productions, Anvil Films, Baldwin Entertainment Group.

Selbo, Jule. 2014. *Film Genre for the Screenwriter*. New York: Routledge.

Sculley, Stephen. 2017. *The Screen Novel*: A Creative Practice Approach to Developing a Screen Idea for the Television Crime Thriller. PhD diss.: RMIT University.

Smith, Pamela. J. Olubunmi. 2005. Introduction. In *Isola, Akinwunmi. 2005. Efunsetan Aniwura: Iyalode Ibadan, and Tinuubu Iyalode Egba (The Yoruba Historical Dramas of Akinwunmi Isola)*. Trans. by Pamela. J Olubunmi Smith, Eritrea: Africa World Press.

Sobchack, Vivian. 1996. History Happens. In *The Persistence of History: Cinema, Television and the Modern Event*, ed. Vivian Sobchack, 1–17. New York: Routledge.

Sobchack, Vivian. 2004. *Carnal Thoughts*. Berkeley ca: University of California Press.

Taylor, Stayci. 2017. Hidden A-gender? Questions of Gender in Screenwriting Practic. *Networking Knowledge: Journal of the MeCCSA Postgraduate Network* 10 (2): 4–13.

Vogler, Christopher. 1998. *The Writer's Journey: Mythic Structure for Writers*. Studio City ca: Michael Wiese Productions.

Women of Owu. 2004. Written by Ola Rotimi. Directed by Chuck Mike. UK: National Video Archive of Performance.

Zaluczkowska, Anna. 2011. Storyworld: The Bigger Picture. Investigating the World of Multiplatform/Transmedia Production and its Affect on Storytelling Processes. *Journal of Screenwriting* 3 (1): 83–101.

CHAPTER 34

Script Development from the Inside Looking Out: Telling a Transnational Story in the Australian Films *33 Postcards* (Chan, 2011) and *Strange Colours* (Lodkina, 2017)

Margaret McVeigh

34.1 Introduction

> The single most important gift you must bring to your screenplay is writing what you feel deeply about. Very likely what you are about is what every human being on this planet is about … (Froug 1996, 197–98)

The telling of stories that aim to connect with audiences across national and international borders is a defining characteristic of screenwriting and script development in international film co-productions and collaborations. As the Chinese-Australian writer-director Pauline Chan says of writing and developing *33 Postcards* (2011), the second official China-Australia feature film co-production, she set out to make a film that was "many voiced", seeking "[t]o meld two cultures, two storytelling traditions, two talent pools… two very different business environments" (Chan 2012).

But how do screenwriters partner up to tell stories that are "many voiced"—transnational stories that meld cultures and storytelling traditions to cross borders and reach multiple audiences? This chapter contributes to the field of screenwriting research by applying and interweaving theories from the emerging academic fields of Script Development and Transnational Film theory, to understand what is important in telling a transnational story in the

---

M. McVeigh (✉)
Griffith Film School, Griffith University, Brisbane, QLD, Australia
e-mail: m.mcveigh@griffith.edu.au

© The Author(s), under exclusive license to Springer Nature Switzerland AG 2023
R. Davies et al. (eds), *The Palgrave Handbook of Screenwriting Studies*,
https://doi.org/10.1007/978-3-031-20769-3_34

script development of two Australian international collaborations. The first case study is of the aforementioned official Australia-China co-production, *33 Postcards* by Pauline Chan; and the second case study is of the Venice Biennale College-funded *Strange Colours* (2017) by Russian-born Australian writer-director Alena Lodkina.

Transnational Film Theory as it informs Script Development is characterized by an investigation of the connections between the *local* and the *global*, and is "less concerned about film stories being representative of a particular country but rather representative of issues and themes that may be regarded as transnational" (McVeigh 2017, 51). Therefore, to specifically explore the creative decisions Chan and Lodkina make in the script development of the co-production, *33 Postcards* and the international collaboration, *Strange Colours*, I consider "what are the practitioner approaches, preferences and storylines that enable the screen story to resonate across borders?" (Moore 2015, 369). In this exploration I consider how "issues and themes" that resonate transnationally may be addressed by narrative scenarios, characters, genres and key story metaphors deployed in the context of a universal story—in this case the family story at the heart of *33 Postcards* and *Strange Colours*, as well as the coming-of-age genre which provides the story envelope of both films.

34.2 What Does Script Development Mean?

Research into the individual and their writing processes during script development is an emerging field as noted above. In their key article, "Script Development: Defining the Field", script development researchers Craig Batty, Staci Taylor, Louise Sawtell and Bridget Conor, interrogate the definition of script development and underline this point:

> The literature on script development … is wide, varied and multi-faceted; and … arguably fragile and still emerging … this comprehensive overview… points to the potential for further research. (Batty et al. 2017, 240)

Batty et al. suggest that considerations of plot, character, story, theme and emotional impact are paramount in script development, and they question: "What development actually entails: which aspects of screenwriting craft beyond plot are used in/by/for script development, and what tools are used to achieve this?" (2017, 228). The practice of script development may take many guises including personal journaling, readers' reports, improvisations with actors and intensive workshops which highlight "constant negotiations … made between the self (ideas, visions, feedback) and the commercial product" (Kerrigan and Batty 2016, 136). Elsewhere, Batty, in his discussion of theme as a tool for use in screenplay development, underlines the importance of the individual writer in the process (2013, 4).

Following Batty and his emphasis on the individual writer in the project, in this chapter I investigate the issues and themes relevant to transnational storytelling by research into the screenwriter's individual and unique negotiations between self and others as part of script development (McVeigh et al. 2019, 158). I conduct this investigation via evidence from interviews with the Writer/Directors, supported by a textual and poetic analysis of the films in order to understand the creative and craft decisions Chan and Lodkina make in telling these transnational stories that reach international audiences via co-production or collaboration.

34.3 Transnational Film Theory and Telling Stories for the Screen

However, first to understand what transnational screenwriting means and how "the universal dimensions behind genres and story formats" interact with "more specific social and cultural contexts" (Bondebjerg et al. 2017, 2), it is useful to understand how Transnational Film Studies has informed the term.

Theories of Transnational Film are useful to a consideration of script development because they investigate the continuities between the *local* and the *global* and they enable us "to better understand the changing ways in which the contemporary world is being imagined by an increasing number of filmmakers" (Ezra and Rowden in Yeates, McVeigh and Van Hemert 2011, 82). In particular, they focus on what "connects" people from across the globe rather than what divides them (McVeigh 2017, 49).

As filmmakers, film academics and screenwriters, we understand and study the power and ability of cinema to capture and project the *universal* in the *local*. We know that cinema can reach out to people across geographical, social, economic, gender and ethnic boundaries to crystallize the essential meanings of life and the imperatives of global citizenship, as well as the sovereignty of the individual in his or her landscape. Cinema can also bring about enlightenment and changes in knowledge about, attitudes to, and behaviours towards our neighbours near and far. We know that cinema can play a vital role in showcasing cultural diversity, forging links across national borders and providing a working arena for filmmakers. We understand how the local can have global resonance, as Elena Oliete-Aldea, Beatriz Oria and Juan. A. Tarancon argue in their discussion of the transnational dimensions of Spanish cinema, the National and Transnational are "both part of the same political, social and cultural environment and thus interdependent, where the one cannot function without the other" (Oliete-Aldea et al. 2015, xix).

Therefore, in this context if films are to travel to international audiences, they must address the imperative that their stories can connect across languages and cultures, in essence they must tell what is termed in Transnational Film theory, a "transcultural" story, one that in its "transcultural properties, may have a particular capacity to represent continuities across apparently radically dissimilar global settings" (McDougal 1998, 261).

Here it is also relevant to consider the various terms that are associated with the often interchangeable term "transcultural" storytelling, so as to inform script development. The study of *transculturality* relates to "commonalities and connections, without intending to homogenize cultures or establish monocultures" (Gesche and Makim 2008, 243). Therefore, of use to the study of screenwriting for transnational storytelling, are the craft-based elements of creating a cinematic story and how these elements are created to *connect* with audiences across cultures. We must remember that cinematic story is an artistic and cultural exchange between people—whether they be from Asia, Europe or Australia. It must address universal themes that people from all parts of the globe may relate to (Dancyger 2001, 218). Contemporary transcultural film theorists have tended to focus on both the *micro* and *macro* dimensions of the field, investigating the forces that link films, filmmakers, audiences and film industries across nations and borders in transnational films. They "are not so concerned about the 'national' lurking within the term 'transnational'; they further define transnational cinema itself as that which 'transcends the national as autonomous cultural particularity while respecting it as a powerful symbolic force'" (Ezra and Rowden in Yeates, McVeigh and Van Hemert 2011, 80).

If we are to translate these film theory ideas into scriptwriting terminology, we can read the *micro* as the local and the *macro* as the universal, or a universal *truth* about life understood by people across cultures as at one stage in their lives, they experience this truth. This leads to the key storytelling conceit of finding the universal in the local. But finding universality and maintaining the local is both a blessing and a challenge. While a film may tell a local story, the scriptwriter must be mindful of exploring story scenarios that have a universal resonance, so that people no matter where they live in the world, can relate to them. These story scenarios may include for example, stories about relationships, and the interrelationship between the individual, the family and their society (Dancyger 2001, 218). But it is not enough to explore a scenario that is relatable across cultures, to really connect with an audience the screenwriter must explore a *truth* as noted above. To crystallize the notion of truth in this chapter, I consider the work of Milcho Manchevski in the extended essay *Truth and Fiction: Notes on (Exceptional) Faith in Art (2012)* where he proposes an excellent notion of what storytelling can reveal about the truths of life and how audiences universally can relate to these truths.

> Every piece of art has to contain the truth. But, not the truth of what happened. It needs to contain the truth of how things are—and the difference between what happened and how things are is what is important. Is it the events (and by extension the facts) of what happened, or is it the emotional and conceptual underpinning and thus understanding of how things are? (Manchevski 2012, xx)

Manchevski ruminates the ways in which both filmmakers and audiences create, experience and absorb the cinematic narrative with a certain trust and faith in the artwork to render, not the factual truth, per se, but the importantly shared experience of trusting what artist and audience can see and feel together, what feels real becomes the truth of the world we inhabit, "how things are", wherever we live, and thus is universally relatable.

To build on Manchevski's notion of truth from a storytelling perspective, the search for how to find *universal truths* in the local and tell transnational stories, the long and deep tradition of global cinema theory may be considered in more detail. Transnational film theory has emerged out of National or World Cinema Theory which had been used to "describe a series of industrial and artistic practices that are seen as confined to a particular territory" whereas Transnational Film Theory is "structured around the notion of flows ... movements across borders" and "seeks to illuminate the processes of exchange and interpenetration ... often obscured under the national paradigm" (DiLuog and Dapena 2001, 16, quoted in Oliete-Aldea et al. 2015: xviii). As Yeates, McVeigh and Van Hemert contend, it is of note that transnational cinema theory and its development out of National or World Cinema Theory (Ezra and Rowden 2006; Yeates, McVeigh and Van Hemert 2011) has impacted on storytelling by creating less of a focus on films that were grounded in local issues that explored themes and ideas that became more or less homogenized and regarding as being typical of Third Cinema, to a more universal Transnational Cinema which:

> [...] directs the focus away from clearly delineated national cinemas toward a more expansive system of cinema, in which locally specific stories can cross national borders, and distinct national cinemas become increasingly hard to grasp and define. (Yeates, McVeigh and Van Hemert 2011, 80–81)

As Oliete-Aldea, Oria and Tarancón argue, while national cinemas are aesthetically, culturally and historically unique, the determinants on which "the meaning of actual films ultimately rest are inextricably global *and* local" (Oliete-Aldea et al. 2015, 2).

So if we are mindful of the development of Transnational Cinema theory and apply it to screenwriting theory, the question is: How do screenwriters write stories that are both locally specific yet can travel across international borders? How does a screenwriter know what story scenarios have been successful in crossing borders, given that a story may be specific to a particular landscape and culture—particularly in international collaborations and co-productions?

34.4 Transnational Script Development

The study of transnational storytelling for the screen from the screenwriter's perspective is an emerging one and has been variously addressed from the field of Cultural Studies, Screen Studies and Critical Television Studies, as well as Script Development.

Key work in the field includes Lina Khatib's edited volumes: *Storytelling in World Cinema Volume 1—Forms* (2012) and *Storytelling in World*

Cinema Volume 2—Contexts (2013), which explore the cultural, structural and aesthetic traditions of cinematic storytelling in various world cinemas via a formal and contextual lens. In the field of television and screenwriting studies, there are a number of significant works including Eva Novrup Redvall's seminal text *Writing and Producing Television Drama in Denmark from the Kingdom to the Killing* (2013), which traces the development and impact of Nordic Noir on the world stage. Ib Bondebjerg, Eva Novrup Redvall, Rasmus Helles, Signe Sophus Lai, Henrik Søndergaard and Cecilie Astrup-gaard's 2017 volume, *Transnational European Television Drama: Production, Genres and Audiences* (part of the Palgrave European Film and Media Studies series) also provides a comprehensive account and insight into the development of television drama for European audiences by considering issues driving "drama production, distribution and reception at the national, European and global levels" and the cultural negotiations involved in the production and reception of European television drama (Bondebjerg et al. 2017, 2).

Likewise, Rosamund Davies' chapter, "*Trapped*: A Case Study of International Co-Production", in *The Palgrave Handbook of Screen Production* provides key insights into the collaborative development from script to screen for the television crime drama *Trapped*. This television series was set in Iceland and developed by Iceland, Germany, France and the UK and was based on "the premise that internationally successful TV series offer audiences familiar ingredients in different settings, a kind of armchair travel experience" (Kjartansson, personal communication, September 2016 in Davies 2018, 282). There are also a number of key articles in recent volumes of *the Journal of Screenwriting*, including Cath Moore's 2005 article "Riding the Wave – Creative Preferences, Spatial Tension and Transnational Story Components in the Collaborations of Susanne Bier and Anders Thomas Jensen" which explores "the creative dimensions of the screen story as a transnationalizing tool" (2015, 368). Moore posits the use of the "trans-prefix paradigm"—"transition", "translation" and transformation"—as a means of considering ways in which researchers may consider "how elements of the story such as plot, character arc, film genre and theme may contribute towards the narrative as a whole moving through, beyond and across to international screens and audiences" (2015, 373–74). Moore also explores via case study how "cultural familiarity and tone impacts on international reach" (2015, 368).

Finally, a major work in the field of transnational script development itself in writing for both television and film is the 2017 volume, *Transcultural Screenwriting: Telling Stories for a Global World* (edited by Brenes, Cattrysse, and McVeigh), which sets out to provide an "interdisciplinary approach to the study of screenwriting as a creative process by integrating the fields of film and TV production studies, screenwriting studies, narrative studies, rhetoric, transnational cinema studies, and intercultural communication studies…to open new perspectives in the debate around notions of transnationalism, imperialism and globalisation, particularly in the screenwriting context" (2017, back cover).

34.5 It's All in the Family: Script Development and the Transnational

While it has been noted that there is little literature in script development theory about the transnational (McVeigh 2017, 51–52), in his book *Global Scriptwriting*, renowned screenwriting theorist Ken Dancyger does provide us with some important insights which will form the basis of the analysis of the case studies in this chapter. Dancyger suggests that in exploring the means by which national films may be understood in a transnational context, family and relationship narratives serve as a sound starting point. He notes that "there are basic universal elements that transcend national boundaries: relationships, the individual in society, the influence of politics on the individual, and the family" (2001, 218). Likewise, in her work on transnational script development, Moore underlines the importance of "the use of film genre as a strong narrative frame. Another narrative preference, one that lends itself to melodrama in particular, is the deconstruction of family as a thematic trope" (2015, 368).

Equally, Dancyger proposes that genre is a means for stories to travel across borders globally by broadly aligning particular national cinemas with particular genres. He posits that "in order to speak to and reach their national audiences, national cinemas have favoured particular genres" (Dancyger 2001, 197). However, while Dancyger investigates the use of genre in specific case studies, he does not aim to address transnational story scenarios beyond a broadly categorized "national model" (Dancyger 2001, 126). For example, he aligns the western and gangster film with the US as an exploration of national mythologies, and melodrama with Germany as a means of exploring the past (Dancyger 2001, 197).

However whatever the genre a writer may use—with its recognized narrative thematic and visual tropes such as that of the Western—as Oliete-Aldea, Oria and Tarancón note, "for all their transnational, formulaic nature, these [genres] are not to be approached simply as imitative products" (2015, 3). Instead they suggest that filmmakers build upon and transform genre as a means of telling a story. They tellingly note that genre is both local and global:

> Besides, the relationships actual films establish with the traditions from which they derive their lexis are complex and unpredictable. What is more important, films, regardless of their generic resemblances, engage in a context that is always changing as a consequence of concrete political, social and cultural forces, and genre conventions—although developed in a supranational sphere—always derive their meanings from these forces as much as from the histories and traditions they carry with them. (Oliete-Aldea et al. 2015, 3).

Overall, what is of most importance for this study is an understanding by screenwriters that storytelling genres can be understood globally (Dancyger 2001, 197–98). Following Dancyger, this chapter therefore will use the family story scenario as a key means of considering the script development of *33 Postcards* and *Strange Colours* as transnational stories. It also uses Oliete-Aldea, Oria and Tarancón's observation that genre, and in the case of my discussion below, the coming-of-age genre, may be used as an envelope which draws upon generic story scenarios but is in effect shaped by local factors which ultimately investigate themes and issues which have universal resonance.

34.6 Telling Transnational Stories and the Co-Production Model: *33 Postcards*

Writer-director Pauline Chan's *33 Postcards* provides an example of a transnational story that is both locally specific and globally relevant. *33 Postcards* was the second film to be completed under the 2008 Australia-China Co-Production Treaty. Co-productions are particularly important for the survival of the Australian film industry. Since co-productions with Australia commenced in 1986, in that time over 132 co-productions have been made with the longest agreements being between running France, UK and Canada and the most recent being between China (2006), Singapore (2007) and South Africa (2010) (Screen Australia 2012, 13) and Korea (2014). But while Australia is viewed as an important partner by countries like China, South Korea and Malaysia, there are challenges as well as benefits in working with partners across cultures (Dalton, 2012). Australia has particularly recognized the importance of the script in the co-production scenario, Screen Australia notes "the patterns of Australia's co-production activity with partner countries are affected by several factors, including the availability of suitable stories and partner producers" (Screen Australia 2012, 13).

Interestingly, the script development of *33 Postcards* did not commence as a story that deliberately set out to be transnational. It developed organically with a focus on character development and theme. When director and then co-writer, Chan, first read the script titled *Mei Mei*, it was the story of a Vietnamese girl who had been abandoned at an orphanage (Edmond 2005 in Dillon 2012, 95). However, the Australia-China co-production treaty was signed during the script development process and aligned with Chan's desire to develop and explore the sub textual layers of character and theme (Chan in Dillon 2012, 95). Chan's script also received international workshop development, including the Tribeca Film Institute workshop which helps international filmmakers with interesting projects (Nemiroff 2013, np). The Melbourne International Film Festival promoted the film as one that "explores identity, belonging and redemption in *33 Postcards*, a tale of two mismatched people from across the world swept into each other's lives, to find that their paths are very much the same" (2011). Chan started the development of the script with a very strong premise of two different worlds coming together. She notes:

> The film has been inspired by real life stories. They provided the shape of the key characters, whose paths were interwoven to explore the main themes of

family connections, self-redemption and growth. Through telling their stories, I wanted to show that hopes and dreams can possibly become a reality ... By Mei Mei turning up and shattering the illusion, both their dreams, and ultimately their lives, are turned upside down. Through their two worlds colliding, I wanted to emphasize the vast cultural and personal disconnection experienced by the two key characters. (Chan 2012)

33 Postcards' narrative scenario is Dancyger's universal one of the family. Mei Mei (Little Sister, a girl with no name and no family) is abandoned in a Chinese orphanage. She finds meaning in her life as part of the Orphanage Choir and the postcards she receives from her sponsor in Australia who tells her about his wonderful family life as a park ranger, living by the beach with his wife and two children. Mei Mei dreams of meeting him one day as she sees him as a father figure whose support has meant that she can get an education and aim for a better life. However, her sponsor, Dean Randall (played by well-known Australian actor Guy Pearce) is in fact a criminal. During the ten-year period he has been sponsoring and sending postcards to Mei Mei, he has spun a fantasy life to her while he has in fact lived behind bars in jail. He, like Mei Mei, is without a family. His brother who is a criminal, never visits him nor supports him, even though Dean is in jail "taking the rap" for a crime they were both involved in. One day Mei Mei's Orphanage Choir travels to Australia to perform in the Australian Choir Festival. Mei Mei manages to sneak away from her minders and make her way to effect her dream to visit Dean, only to eventually find him in jail. Despite this, she continues to visit him while hiding from her Choir mistress. She experiences a series of fateful events while unknowingly living with Dean's former criminal contacts, under the care of Carl, the young man who genuinely looks out for her. However unbeknown to Mei Mei, her new "family" operate an extortion racket and they will involve her in their criminal work as an innocent bystander. Eventually, Dean comes to see Mei Mei as someone who is important in his life and works with his parole officer to find a family who will adopt her (he cannot do so because of his criminal convictions). Pauline Chan notes:

> The girl being sponsored is a common factor, but the girl never gets to meet the sponsor. All the things in the film, the elements, are based on research and things we did, but we just created the characters to represent that life. So the extortion scheme in prison, that is real. I met the character during the research time, but of course the name is not such. And also, the father and son story in the garage, there were also stories like that. (Nemiroff 2013)

In this story we can see elements of the family story in the protagonist, Mei-Mei's, search for an imagined father as well as the disconnect that ultimately will be solved by changes in the character, most notably in terms of the coming-of-age genre which is the story envelope of this film.

Chan also notes that the character of Dean is very complex and is also transformed by learning essential truths of life as befits the coming-of-age genre.

> His character goes through such a growth and Guy Pearce is multidimensional and so talented. He basically can transform himself from the beginning of the journey to the end of the journey where he actually risks his life to try to save someone [after having been] someone who's skeptical and withdrawn. (Nemiroff 2013)

The climactic moment of the story comes when both Dean and Mei Mei face the greatest jeopardy—Dean is released on parole only to find Mei Mei will be involved in a car stealing crime through her involvement with Carl. Dean sacrifices his freedom to try to free her from the criminal associates who lock her up when she pleads with them not to send Carl to steal a car. Dean finds himself back in jail the very day he gets out. Here his life descends into even more hell. He is stabbed by a stand-over gang member in jail as his brother has not paid protection money for him. The final sequences reveal Mei Mei at Dean's hospital bedside as we wonder whether he will survive and whether she will stay in Australia, now that she has the chance to live with a foster family. Ultimately however Mei Mei decides to return to China to follow her dream to become a Choir Conductor. In the final scenes we see Dean and his parole officer in the audience as Mei Mei conducts the Choir for the first time in their final Australian performance. As Chan says of this film, "it ends with hope" (SBS 2011). In the resolution we know that both these key characters have come of age and have learnt valuable life lessons. While both Mei Mei and Dean do not have a natural family to support them, they become a family of sorts.

In the development of the script, Chan encapsulates the unique vision of any filmmaker who seeks to tell a universal story about family and the search for identity via the coming-of-age genre identified above as a powerful method for creating transnational stories.

> For me, the making of this film has been a personal journey on many levels—not least the wonderful opportunity to work in my mother tongue, the Chinese language, but also to collaborate with the most talented cast and crew from East and West ... Like Randall's gift for Mei Mei in the film, I fantasize about living in a spiritual space where cultural and physical boundaries do not exist ... *33 Postcards* looks at two social misfits whose lives come together despite their different cultures, ages and circumstances. Peeling away the layers of their differences, I hope to explore the similarity of what lies in the depth of the human heart. (Chan 2012)

The script development of *33 Postcards* involved extensive research and was based on real-life scenarios. As Chan says:

> It's inspired by real life stories. The girl is kind of an inspiration I had from three different documentaries about homeless children in different countries. And the Australian man, the fake character, Mr. Randall, was inspired by an article that my co-writer and myself read in the Australian newspaper one day. And so we felt that even though they're from two worlds apart and two totally different stories—in real life, these two characters never met—but we decided that there's enough of a connection in the internal world and the themes of these peoples' lives, so we decided to go about it. (Chan 2012)

As Moore notes one of the important factors ensuring the success of transnational storytelling are the strong human emotions explored at the core of a film that successfully connects with international audiences (2015, 366). Chan strongly focused on this aspect of the story during the script development and pre-production phase. She notes: "The most inspiring things I keep hearing people say is that it is an emotional story that has a strong narrative, but a very delicate internal world" (Nemiroff 2013).

In the development of the character of Mei Mei, this was a very important factor.

> So she didn't speak any English and through the auditions, the script was in English and she didn't do well. But I detected something really interesting about her spirit. There's a quality about her that fit my imagination of the girl, so I told her about the essence of the scene in Chinese and I said, "I want you to audition the scene in Chinese. Throw away the script and come back tomorrow to play the scene again". And she did and it really moved me to tears because the emotion was real. She drew from herself the feelings of longing and the sense of family and identity and love. It was all there for me. (Nemiroff 2013)

The script development and production of *33 Postcards* showcases a successful cultural exchange between two countries via the coproduction model as well as evidencing the power of universal storytelling as a means of finding the global in the local. Pauline Chan says in an interview that she:

> Remains convinced that such co-productions "can be done" as long as the right team of people—among them "strong and very independent" producers … is in place… What I found is that people are fine bridging or forming a cultural and creative bridge with the right team of people. It means finding the right solutions and the right connections to bridge the gap … China is unique like France is unique. There is the script challenge—to meet cultural sensitivities. (Dillon 2012, 95)

The making of *33 Postcards* is an excellent example of the successful development of a transnational film in a co-production scenario because ultimately Chan made the movie she wanted to make. Of additional interest, the film's marketing serves as an illustration of what may be important to highlight at pitch or synopsis stage of script development. For example, in China, *33*

Postcards, in order to make it stand out from the over 500 feature films produced every year, was marketed as a co-production with Australia. The *exotic* Australian locations were highlighted as a part of this strategy. The producers also played up the role of the lead hero character, Dean Randall, played by Guy Pearce, whose Hollywood career gives him some recognition in China. In Australia the story was pitched in direct contrast. Rather than the story of the male hero, it was the story of Mei, Mei, the Chinese orphan:

> The story for the Chinese was, here is this Australian, a hero, a kind hearted man with a hard facade who has a hard time in jail because he wants to take care of a Chinese girl [...] For the Chinese market the hero's journey is very important. It promises action and suspense. The Australian angle is the opposite. Our distributors and producers are interested in the little girl coming to look for her sponsor. They're interested in a warm hearted story about a little girl looking for a father. (Dillon 2012, 96)

34.7 Transnational Story Script Development: *Strange Colours*

Strange Colours is a break-out feature film by Russian-Australian writer-director Alena Lodkina where "nothing much happens at all". Based on Lodkina's work with *outsiders*—that is, opal miners in Australia's remote outback—the film is an elliptical and contemplative coming-of-age story whose script was informed by Lodkina's documentary research, love of the character in the landscape, transnational funding and cinematic inspirations. Lodkina, with her rich personal experience as a Russian Australian, combined with a communications degree and a love of classic literature and film, was deeply inspired by other films and film forms including the Australian outback film *Wake in Fright* (1971) and Italian Neorealist films including *Stromboli* (1950) (see McVeigh 2018).

The narrative scenario of *Strange Colours* is also the universal one of the family which as noted above, Dancyger advises as important for a transnational story. Like *33 Postcards,* it focuses on the father/daughter relationship in an envelope of the coming-of-age genre as the key driver of the story. Milena is a young psychology student who travels on a bus to a remote opal mining community to see her estranged and terminally ill father. Here she meets a world of men who live a rugged and bare-bones existence as they live in hope to strike it rich with a lucrative opal find. The symbol of the opal and its iridescent multi-coloured beauty are the *Strange Colours* of the title. Like *33 Postcards* where the postcards represent joy, beauty and hope in an otherwise barren world of the orphanage or the jail, so these opals represent beauty, and hope for a richer life in the shanty towns and settlements where the opal miners live. This is a story of the last frontier a world of criminals, outcasts and loners who are brought together because they all dream of striking it lucky on precious gems in their desire to escape the reality of their past.

Like *33 Postcards*, *Strange Colours* it is a family story involving a fish-out-of-water narrative scenario which involves elements of the road and coming of age genres. The fish-out-of-water scenario was also one lived by Lodkina herself, who she draw from her experience for the development of the story: "I wanted to create tension with a fish-out-of-water story" (Eeles 2018, np).

> As an outsider, I could see that Lightning Ridge is a refuge for misfits ... What that meant, of course, was leaving things behind. Lots of people in Lightning Ridge have stories of broken relationships and criminal pasts, or all kinds of paths that have led to that place. (Carroll Harris 2018, np)

Also like the main character of Mei Mei in *33 Postcards*, Milena, the protagonist in *Strange Colours*, goes on a journey to find her father and ultimately learns where she will find meaning in her life. Like *33 Postcards*, *Strange Colours* also benefited from international funding and development, in this case rather than through an official Australian co-production treaty, via the 2017 Venice Biennale College Cinema, a prestigious low-budget development programme that selects three outstanding young filmmakers from outside Italy each year. Lodkina reflects that the lack of local development support proved to be a bonus as she found this enabled her to look at Australia and Lightning Ridge "with an outsider's eye" (Carroll Harris 2018, np). Film critic Adrian Martin notes in the film's 2017 premiere at the Cinema College of the Venice Biennale, that the eminent film scholar David Bordwell commented on the film's lack of artifice:

> Comparing the film to an Anton Chekhov play, he rightly stressed its eschewal of the "plotty propulsion of a conventional family-problems movie". The script "avoids those traumatic flashbacks that often supply backstory", and the deliberately parsimonious narrative intrigue "never creates conventional suspense". (Martin 2018)

Strange Colours also involved extensive research. Initially Lodkina made a documentary, *Lightning Ridge: The Land of Black Opals* (2016) about her fascination with the Outback world of Lightning Ridge. This eventually gave birth to the feature film which as Lodkina says, in its emotional resonance provided a strong entry point for audiences which as Moore proposes, is a key feature of successful transnational storytelling (Moore 2015, 371). Lodkina notes that she:

> [w]as inspired by the kinds of stories that I kept hearing when I was interviewing people. They would tell stories about not seeing their families for a long time ... There were all kinds of stories of estranged lives and characters. I thought that would be the perfect entry point into the community from this outsider who has a strong connection to the community without being a part of it directly. (Eeles 2018 np)

The development of this elliptical film was both scripted and improvised with ethnographic slices-of-life, enacted by the actors playing themselves inside the fictional story as the narrative emerged. For example: "I haven't seen my son or my daughter in 20 years … I had a broken relationship and she took the kids away" (Carroll Harris 2018, np). Lodkina says of this process which was built on the memories and contemporary reality, "That [idea of the] grand three-act plot feels generic and patriarchal". Instead, "[i]t's inspiring when film-makers are able to connect to the bigger world beyond the film-making machine" (Carroll Harris 2018, np). Of the improvisations that fed the script, and of her iterative work with the untrained local characters who acted in her film, Lodkina comments on the way their work seemed to come from a place of truth, based in the reality of who they were as people: "With some of the guys from Lightning Ridge, they were best if I could just chuck them in front of a camera and let them do their thing. It was all very experimental" (Eeles 2018, np).

The stand-out sequence that evidences the success of Lodkina's ability to capture the nuances of character in this environment is one of the early scenes where Milena's father's friends, Rat and Martin, come to visit her at his shanty to see if she is ok, as he has asked them to do. Lodkina points to the veracity of this scene during script development where she improvised the script with untrained actors:

> We had scripted a scene. A month prior to filming we had a recce and I had gone to Martin and Rat who are people who play the guys in that scene… We sat down and read through (the scenes) and they said: "Aw, I'd never say that"… I made notes… put in more swear words. I rewrote the scenes. I came back to them with things that they said and they said: "Aw, I'd never say that!" So we rewrote the scene together. (McVeigh 2018)

As the story of *Strange Colours* unfolds, we see through Milena's eyes as she experiences her father's world and we come to understand with her that the fabric of existence for these men is not their past which they have left behind—but their community and the goal of striking it rich. They want for nothing emotionally. In the final sequences of the film, Milena advises her father she will move on. He tries to make her feel guilty by letting her know he has kept her baby tooth with him always. Alena Lodkina observes that in her film, the characters are unable to connect with each other. Essentially this is the essence, the truth, of the film:

> None of the characters need each other; they can't deliver what the other needs. That's the next layer of the film. It's just these characters floating around, unable to satisfy those desires. The father and daughter don't resolve their relationship; nobody finds money; no one falls in love… And I know that's kind of sad—and yeah, anti-narrative—but somehow there's still hope. (Brady-Brown 2018, np)

This hope can be observed by Milena's final actions in the film. Before she leaves she senses her father needs her and she borrows a car from his friend Frank to visit him at his opal mining selection. She finds him collapsed in the very underground tunnels we see first see men working in the Neo-Realist inspired opening sequences from films, like *Stromboli* and *Casa de Lava*, which Lodkina referenced so that she could work out how to combine non-professional actors within a fiction narrative as in the mode of Italian Neo-Realism. Lodkina discusses how she combines inspiration from these films and the people and landscape of her story in a way that is guided by tension and mood and atmosphere, rather than traditional plot.

> I looked to these films because mine was born out of this interest in a place, its geography, and the ways people live. My primary objective was to record how people live … And then the script was basically constructed around settings: we need a scene at Brett's camp, we need a scene at the mines. It was a strange puzzle in which the pieces kept being rearranged. Like *Stromboli* and like *Casa de Lava*, the film is a mosaic of these faces and places. I was guided by mood and atmosphere, and that's probably my strongest thing—I get confused with narratives and script, it doesn't come naturally to me, but the Venice Biennale College was really helpful because it got me and Isaac [Wall, her co-writer] to kind of respect the narrative, to think about what tension is in film and how it works. I know *Strange Colours* isn't classic tension in the sense it doesn't really go anywhere, but there's the *feeling* of tension. (Brady-Brown 2018, np)

Ultimately, *Strange Colours* like *33 Postcards*, does not set out to provide any answers other than to present life as it is in all its ambiguity, using the universal family scenario. However, it is a scenario which may provide hope as symbolized by the titular metaphors of the regular postcards and the glory of the opals. This universal truth is perhaps best summed up by Lodkina as she observes how the metaphor of the opal reflecting its beautiful and ever-changing colours which are essentially not stable, just like the characters of both movies are not stable in their relationships:

> There's also the curious juxtaposition between this rugged, masculine community and the fragile nature of opals—it's not a stable mineral like a diamond, it's got water in it, and it has this really strange nature …The idea's that because an opal is unstable it changes over time, but the change is so slow that it's imperceptible to the human eye. It's meant to be a meditation on the warp of time. So I was putting these kinds of contradictory ideas together. I saw so much genuine beauty and melancholy in the place, and then these men who have nothing, whom you don't expect such things from. I learned that a film should have a provocation inside it, but it shouldn't figure things out. It should be a process of figuring out, but not an answer. (Brady-Brown 2018, np)

34.8 Transnational Transformations

This chapter has discussed ways in which two Australian filmmakers have developed transnational stories where characters and viewers truly cross borders and connect with each other (Yeates, McVeigh, and Van Hemert 2011) via the exploration of the global in the local, and issues and themes that have universal resonance across cultures.

These coming-of-age genre narratives show the main characters Mei Mei in *33 Postcards*, and Milena in *Strange Colours*, transitioning through the landscapes of the story "until a commitment to one place and relationships within has been made" (Moore 2015, 373). Mei Mei returns to China to live her true purpose and we know this is where Dean will write to and visit her. Milena returns to her father's holding to save him even though she has told him she will leave and she makes peace with who he is as he returns to hospital and she sits by his bedside. Both films embrace genre with their clean lines of narrative intent understood by transnational audiences and illustrate Moore's concept of "translation" as a "key creative strategy and key element to reaching an international audience" (2015, 373).

Both *33 Postcards* and *Strange Colours* are coming-of-age films where, as is the premise in this genre: "heroes undergo their own particular transition toward maturity" (Oliete-Aldea et al. 2015, 219–20).

In the narrative scenario of the family and as the young fish out of water, protagonists Mei Mei and Milena learn key lessons about life as the story unfolds. Finally, both films evidence Moore's concept of *transformation* as a transnational storytelling precept. This is a theoretical concept which alludes to the fact that "the characters remain in a world that is still compromising and challenging despite any personal insights garnered along the way. There is an absence of absolutes, a certain restraint that acknowledges the limitations of transition in life" (2015, 374). This is the real world after all and we can all relate to this as do Mei Mei and Milena. But as both writer-directors acknowledge, the key message of both films is *hope*.

Alena Lodkina on her inspirations for the film notes in her Director's Statement, what she hoped to achieve in developing *Strange Colours*. Her goals echo many of those of Pauline Chan in her vision for *33 Postcards*—goals that include finding the global in the local, anchoring the narrative in the family story scenario, using recognizable genres appropriate to the issues and themes of the story and focusing on familiar emotions that connect with people no matter where they may be.

> I wanted to tell a story of three lonely people floating in this unique microcosm with its own ideals and rules, surrounded by vast stretches of bush [...] The characters seek connection with one another, but are torn apart by themselves and the world around them. They struggle to find what to say... The film tells a fictional story, but is also a record of place [...] I worked towards images that would carry the languid magic, the melancholia I myself felt in my travels. (Lodkina 2017)

In her 2018 interview with me, Lodkina discussed the joy and power of this script development process. She observed the personal accomplishment that a screenwriter feels when they discover what I consider *universal truths*—Manchevski's notion of the way things are, not the plot points of what happened. These are the themes and issues, the emotional and intellectual concepts generated at the local level which have global resonance. They underpin the "understanding of how things are" (2012, xx), a universal truth that the screenwriter engenders beyond the narrative and aesthetics of the story. For Lodkina, this is that "something else":

> The joy of film for me is observation. These details are poetry. Sometimes you walk around on a particular day and something pops out. Some interaction between two people. Something not relevant to you but that's what you remember from that day and you don't know why you remember it or what you were thinking. It's moments in cinema that have nothing to do with plot that express something inexplicable about the everyday experience … I think a lot about this because to get a film funded you have to present a really strong story but then for your ambition in terms of form and doing something interesting with form, it really is about something else, it's not just about storytelling. (McVeigh 2018)

In conclusion, the transnational cinematic stories *33 Postcards* and *Strange Colours* evidence Moore's trans-prefix paradigm—transition, translation and transformation—in the ways in which their story elements "contribute towards the narrative as a whole moving through, beyond and across to international screens and audiences" (Moore 2015, 373–74). In using the transnational film theory lens, we may understand the similarities between these two films and the connections that may be made between Chan and Lodkina's script development to explore issues via the story thematic of the family and conventions of the coming-of-age genre, to explore a *universal truth* that connects with audiences across the world.

References

Batty, Craig. 2013. "Creative Interventions in Screenwriting: Embracing Theme to Unify and Improve the Collaborative Development Process." *Creative Manoeuvres: Making, Saying, Being*. Refereed proceedings of the 18th Conference of the Australasian Association of Writing Programs, 1–11.

Batty, Craig, Staci Taylor, Louise Sawtell, and Bridget Conor. 2017. Script Development: Defining the Field. *Journal of Screenwriting* 8 (3): 225–247. https://doi.org/10.1386/jocs.8.3.225_1.

Bondebjerg, Ib, et al. (eds.). 2017. *Transnational European Television Drama: Production, Genres and Audiences*. Cham, Switzerland: Palgrave Macmillan.

Brady Brown, Annabel. 2018. "Dancing on the Volcano: Alena Lodkina Discusses 'Strange Colours'." MUBI, 4 September. https://mubi.com/notebook/posts/dancing-on-the-volcano-alena-lodkina-discusses-strange-colours. Accessed 18 August 2022.

Brenes, Carmen Sofia, Patrick Cattrysse, and Margaret McVeigh, eds. 2017. *Transcultural Screenwriting: Telling Stories for a Global World*. Newcastle upon Tyne: Cambridge Scholars.
Carroll Harris, Lauren. 2018. "Alena Lodkina's Strange Colours: A Bold New Australian Voice Takes on Lightning Ridge." *The Guardian*, 5 June. https://www.theguardian.com/film/2018/jun/06/alena-lodkinas-strange-colours-a-bold-new-australian-voice-takes-on-lightning-ridge. Accessed 18 August 2022.
Chan, Pauline. 2012. "Director's Notes." http://33postcardsthemovie.com. Accessed 22 November 2021.
Dalton, K. 2012. Local TV must connect with Asia on production projects, says ABC head. *Media Supplement*, The Australian, 29 November.
Dancyger, K. 2001. *Global Scriptwriting. Imprint Boston*. Oxford: Focal Press.
Davies, Rosamund. 2018. Trapped: A Case Study of International Co-Production In *The Palgrave Handbook of Screen Production*, ed. Batty Craig, Marsha Berr, Kath Dooley,Bettina Frankham, and Susan Kerrigan, 281–291. Springer International Publishing.
Dillon, Jo. 2012. "Letter to a Neighbour: Pauline Chan on Crossing Cultural Lines through Film." *Metro* 173 (Winter). Victoria: ATOM (Australian Teachers of Media).
Eeles, Matthew. 2018. "Interview: Alena Lodkina." *Cinema Australia*, 17 July. https://cinemaaustralia.com.au/2018/07/17/interview-alena-lodkina/. Accessed 22 November 2021.
Elena, Alberto, and Ana Martín Morán. 2015. Transnational Contours and Representation Models in Recent Films about Immigration in Spain. In *Global Genres, Local Films: The Transnational Dimension of Spanish Cinema*, ed. Elena Oliete-Aldea, Beatriz Oria, and Juan T. Tarancon, 215–230. London: Bloomsbury.
Ezra, Elizabeth, and Terry Rowden. 2006. General Introduction: What Is Transnational Cinema? In *Transnational Cinema, The Film Reader*, ed. Elizabeth Ezra and Terry Rowden, 1–12. London and New York: Routledge.
Froug, William. 1996. *Zen and the Art of Screenwriting——Insights and Interviews*. Los Angeles: Sillman-James.
Gesche, Asrid, and Paul Makeham. 2008. Creating Conditions for Intercultural and International Learning and Teaching. In *Researching International Pedagogies: Sustainable Practice for Teaching and Learning in Higher Education*, ed. Meeri Hellstén and Anna Reid, 241–253. Dordrecht, Netherlands: Springer.
Halle, Randall. 2010. Offering Tales They Want to Hear: Transnational European Film Funding as Neo-Orientalism. In *Global Art Cinema*, ed. Rosalind Galt and Karl Schoonover, 303–319. Oxford: Oxford University Press.
Harper, Graeme. 2013. "A Version of Beauty and Terror: Australian Cinematic Landscapes." In *Cinema and Landscape*, edited by Graeme Harper and Jonathon Rayner, 245–54. Bristol: Intellect.
Kerrigan, Susan, and Craig Batty, eds. 2016. *Re-conceptualizing Screenwriting for the Academy: The Social, Cultural and Creative Practice of Developing a Screenplay* 13 (1): 130–144. https://doi.org/10.1080/14790726.2015.1134580.
Manchevski, Milcho. 2012. *Truth and Fiction: Notes on (Exceptional) Faith in Art*. Brooklyn, NY: Punctum.
Martin, Adrian. 2018. "Anyway Here We Are. *Strange Colours* Australia/Italy 2017." *Film Critic*. http://www.filmcritic.com.au/reviews/s/strange_colours.html. Accessed 22 November 2021.

Lightning Ridge: The Land of Black Opals. 2017. Directed by Alena Lodkina. Australia: Fountain Vista.
Lodkina, Alena. 2017. "*Strange Colours* Director's Statement." La Biennale di Venezia. https://www.labiennale.org/en/cinema/2017/program-cinema-2017/alena-lodkina-strange-colours. Accessed 22 November 2021.
McDougal, David. 1998. *Transcultural Cinema*. Princeton nj: Princeton University Press.
McVeigh, Margaret. 2017. "*Screenwriting Sans Frontières*: The Writing of a Transnational Film and the Key Factors Impacting on the Creation of Story in the Film Co-Production Scenario." In *Transcultural Screenwriting: Telling Stories for a Global World*, edited by Carmen Sofia Brenes, Patrick Cattrysse, and Margaret McVeigh, 47–68. Newcastle upon Tyne: Cambridge Scholars.
McVeigh, Margaret. 2018. Alena Lodkina. Interview with Margaret McVeigh. 22 November 2018. Melbourne.
McVeigh, Margaret. 2019. Work-in-progress: The Writing of *Shortchanged*. In *A Companion to Screen Production*, ed. Craig Batty, et al., 157–168. Cham, Switzerland: Palgrave Macmillan.
MIFF (Melbourne International Film Festival). 2011. "*33 Postcards* MIFF 2011 Australian Showcase." https://miff.com.au/festival-archive/films/id/24370. Accessed 22 November 2021.
Moore, Cath. 2015. Riding the Wave——Creative Preferences, Spatial Tension and Transnational Story Components in the Collaborations of Susanne Bier and Anders Thomas Jensen. *Journal of Screenwriting* 6 (3): 363–378.
Nemiroff, Perri. 2013. "Interview: 33 Postcards Pauline Chan." *Shockya*. 16 May. https://www.shockya.com/news/2013/05/16/interview-33-postcards-pauline-chan/. Accessed 22 November 2021.
Oliete-Aldea, Elena, Beatriz Oria, A. Juan, and Tarancon, eds. 2015. *Global Genres, Local Films: The Transnational Dimension of Spanish Cinema*. London: Bloomsbury.
33 Postcards. 2011. Written by Martin Edmond, Philip Dalkin, and Pauline Chan. Directed by Pauline Chan. Australia, China: Portal Pictures Pty.
Redvall, Eva Novrup. 2013. *Writing and Producing Television Drama in Denmark from* The Kingdom *to* The Killing. Basingstoke uk: Palgrave Macmillan.
SBS (Special Broadcasting Service). 2011. Interview with Pauline Chan. https://www.sbs.com.au/ondemand/video/11770947527/33-postcards-pauline-chan-interview?/?cx_cid=od:search:sem:convert:alwayson::prog&gclid=EAIaIQobChMI5sik6trI8wIVwg5yCh0WJwUmEAMYASAAEgL8l_D_BwE&gclsrc=aw.ds. Accessed 22 November 2021.
Screen Australia. 2012. "Friends with Benefits: A Report on Australia's International Co-Production Program 2012." http://www.screenaustralia.gov.au/getmedia/f243d30d-b24b-4a25-a525-d582c16dc47e/Rpt_CoPro_2012.pdf. Accessed 12 August 2021.
Strange Colours. 2017. Written by Alena Lodkina and Isaac Wall. Directed by: Alena Lodkina. Australia, Italy: Strange Colours Productions.
Stromboli. 1950. Written by Sergio Amidei, Gian Paolo Callegari, Art Cohn, and Renzo Cesana. Directed by Roberto Rossellini. Italy, USA: Berit Films, RKO Radio Pictures.

Wake in Fright. 1971. Written by Evan Jones and Ted Kotcheff. Directed by Ted Kotcheff. Australia, UK, USA: NLT Productions, Group W Films.

Yeates, Helen, Margaret McVeigh, and Tess Van Hemert. 2011. From Ethnocentrism to Transculturalism: A Globalised Pedagogical Journey. *Cultural Studies Review* 17 (2): 71–99.

CHAPTER 35

Extended How? Narrative Structure in the Short and Long Versions of *The Lord of the Rings*, *Kingdom of Heaven*, and *Dances with Wolves*

Kristin Thompson

35.1 Models of Act Structure

This essay began as a keynote address to the Screenwriting Research Network's conference "Screenwriting in a Global & Digital World", held at the University of Wisconsin—Madison in August 2013. Years earlier I had published *Storytelling in the New Hollywood: Understanding Classical Narrative Technique* (Thompson 1999), which laid out some basic principles used in modern, mainstream Hollywood narratives. As the word "classical" suggests, I argued that those principles were much the same ones that had been used since being formulated in the mid- to the late 1910s.

One aspect of standard classical storytelling that I dealt with extensively is the act structure of narratives, perhaps the most basic element that aspiring screenwriters learn. My approach was descriptive of the traits of existing films rather than prescriptive for as yet unwritten films. Nevertheless, *Storytelling in the New Hollywood* seems to have had as much, if not more attention as an unintended screenplay manual than as a demonstration of how a knowledge of classical narrative techniques can be useful for the analysis of films. That may help explain why, to my surprise, the book is still in print twenty-three years after its publication.

I did not wish to question the usefulness of the concept of filmic acts, either for the screenwriter or the scholarly critic. Quite the contrary, I think

K. Thompson (✉)
University of Wisconsin-Madison, Madison, WI, USA
e-mail: kmthomps@wisc.edu

that acts do exist in classical films and have done so since roughly the mid-1910s. Indeed, the identification of the turning points that separate them in a screenplay or a film is one of the screenwriting researcher's basic tactics of analysis.

I did, however, question one widely held assumption about filmic acts, one which I believe is misleading for both screenwriter and critic. That is the widely held opinion, popularized by screenwriting guru Syd Field, that all fiction features have three acts. His model has been highly influential with aspiring screenwriters and within the industry ever since it appeared in 1979. Field's basic claims are:

- All fiction features have three acts.
- The acts have strict proportions: first act, ¼ of the film; second act ½; third act, ¼.
- In a two-hour feature, this means acts of 30 minutes, 60 minutes, and 30 minutes.
- Each act ends in a "turning point", an event "that hooks into the story and spins it around into another direction".
- All features, whatever their length, have these three acts.
- All films, whatever their narrative approach, contain these three acts (including such films as *Last Year at Marienbad*).
- More recently Field has conceded that films may have a "midpoint" halfway through, but it is not a Turning Point.

This model is entirely prescriptive. Any film that does not have three acts in these proportions is simply bad. One wonders what he would have made of Béla Tarr's 430-minute *Sátántangó*.

My model is instead inductive, based on close analyses of ten films from the New Hollywood era that are widely considered to have excellent narrative structure, as well as an appendix providing act timings of 100 films by decade starting in the 1910s, when features became the norm. My basic claims are:

- Classical feature films tend to have four large-scale parts or acts.
- These acts tend to fall into equal lengths, typically about 25–30 minutes long, but the range is flexible.
- Acts are divided by Turning Points, usually significant changes in protagonist's goals, revelations of crucial new information, or significant stages in the accomplishment of a long-term goal.
- Longer films often contain additional ones, usually in the same 25- to 30-minute range.
- The classical model applies mainly to Hollywood films and those that imitate Hollywood's approach.
- Hollywood's approach. Independent films, films made abroad in different production circumstances, and those made with an eye to conforming

to other norms typical of festival and art-cinema fare. (see Chapter 1 in Thompson 1999)

Note the terms "tend to", "typically", and "usually". All sorts of variants and departures from these observed act structures are possible. They are norms that have developed over the course of Hollywood's history, and as I emphasize in my book, the norms that define numbers and lengths of acts are flexible.

In *Storytelling*, I also do something that Field did not attempt, which is to suggest how the different acts typically function, giving each a name indicative of its function:

> **Setup:** "An initial situation is thoroughly established. Often the protagonist conceives one or more goals".
> **Complicating action:** Typically "serves as a sort of counter-setup, building a whole new situation with which the protagonist must cope".
> **Development**: "This is where the protagonist's struggle toward his or her goals typically occurs, often involving many incidents that create action, suspense, and delay".
> **Climax**: Once "all the premises regarding the goals and the lines of action have been introduced [...] The action shifts into a straightforward progress toward the final resolution, typically building steadily toward a concentrated sequence of high action". (Thompson 1999, 28–29)

Field never talks about unusually long films and how their length would affect act structure. My book includes a chapter on *Amadeus* (160 minutes) as a five-act film. In long films with more than four acts, one or more of these acts will be doubled. There might be two development portions, as in *Amadeus* and *Heat* (Thompson 1999, 37–38) or even two climaxes, as in *Titanic*.

Versions of films that have substantial amounts of footage added present a puzzle for these generalizations about norms of act-length. Theatrical films are made with a certain act structure based on the original screenplay. What happens if parts of that screenplay are eliminated to make the theatrical version conform to a studio's desired length and later the filmmakers add considerable footage to create a new version? Often, they create a version that utilizes material cut from the shooting script.

How do such changes affect the act structure of the film? What happens if the filmmakers add more than 30 minutes, the average length of a classical act? Where does that footage get added and how does it affect the act structure? Do the existing acts get longer? Are extra acts, and hence Turning Points (hereafter TPs), added?

To address these questions, I chose from the list of films below, all of which added 30 minutes or more. One would expect that in some cases putting in that much footage would lead the filmmakers to add one or more acts. Some extended films receive at least a limited theatrical run, but most have appeared on Laserdisc or VHS or DVD or Blu-ray. They may be described with different terms, as in the examples below (from their DVD/Blu-ray cases):

- *The Fellowship of the Ring* (2001) + 31 minutes "Special Extended DVD Edition" (2002)
- *The Two Towers* (2002) + 41 "Special Extended DVD Edition" (2003)
- *The Return of the King* (2003) + 48 "Special Extended DVD Edition" (2004)
- *Dances with Wolves* (1990) + 53 "Special Edition" (1991)
- *Kingdom of Heaven* (2005) + 50 "Director's Cut" (2006)
- *That Thing You Do!* (1996) + 41 "Tom Hanks' [sic] Extended Cut" (2007)
- *Troy* (2004) + 34 "Director's Cut" (2007)
- *The New World* (2005) + 37 "The Extended Cut" (2008)
- *Gods and Generals* (2003) + 60 "Extended Director's Cut" (2011)
- *Margaret* (2011) + 36 "Extended Cut" (2012)
- *Alexander* (2004) + 31 "Ultimate Cut" (2014)

I am focusing on the first five Extended Editions in the above list, in part because they fall into three different popular genres: fantasy, historical epic, and western.

As it turned out, only two have an extra act: *The Two Towers* and *The Return of the King*. Adding an act is rare, presumably because it is difficult to restructure a film so radically. Sprinkling short bits of new footage in sections across the film is easier.

Is a study of decades-old Extended Editions relevant in an era of shrinking DVD/Blu-ray sales and the concomitant decline in the number of director's cuts? The films listed above are still watched in these longer versions. The Extended Editions of all five films I analyze here are currently available on DVD and Blu-ray. Streaming services also offer extended versions. As of November, 2021, the three such versions of *The Lord of the Rings* are streaming on HBO Max. All eight of the other extended titles listed above are streaming on Amazon Prime.

35.2 Added Footage and Act Structure: *The Fellowship of the Ring*

There is a great deal that can be said about how added footage affects the narratives of films, but I shall focus primarily on act lengths and balances among acts. (Total running times are rounded off to the nearest minute. See Table 35.1)

Table 35.1 Added footage and act structure: *The Fellowship of the Ring*

Version	Length without credits	# of acts	Average act length
Theatrical	171 minutes	Six	28'40"
Extended	201 minutes	Six	33'30"

Act 1, the Setup, deals with the revelation of the Ring's powers and dangers. The decision for Frodo to take the Ring to Bree establishes the first goal (Table 35.1).

The most striking thing about Act 1 of *Fellowship* is that it is considerably longer than the average, especially in the extended version. The length stems largely from the presence of a prologue outlining the Ring's history, a leisurely introduction to hobbits and the Shire, and a surprisingly full treatment of Bilbo's birthday party. There is Gandalf's exposition about the Ring.

The TP that ends the act comes when Gandalf parts from Frodo and Sam, cautioning them, "Remember, it *wants* to be found". Because the plot involves so much traveling, the goals are often short-term and involve getting to a certain place, in this case, Bree. There is no suggestion that Frodo's ultimate goal will be to destroy the Ring.

The two versions of Act 1 last 37'25" and 44'15".

Act 2, the first Complicating Action, takes the hobbits to Bree, where they meet Aragorn. Saruman, Merry, and Pippin are also introduced, and Gandalf is imprisoned. The TP comes when Aragorn announces that he will take the hobbits to Rivendell, creating a new short-term goal. In both versions we have a shorter than average act, to balance out the length of the first.

The theatrical Act 2 lasts 19'44"; the extended one, 23'22".

Act 3 provides another Complicating Action. At Rivendell, the Council of Elrond introduces numerous new premises. This scene alone runs about seven minutes in the Theatrical Version and eight in the extended one. Important new characters appear, including three of the nine Fellowship members. Two long-term goals are set in place: the destruction of the Ring for the quest line of action and the military defeat of Sauron for the war line of action.

The two versions of Act 3 last 34'57" and 40'22".

Act 4 moves into the Development, where the characters meet obstacles and delays. The Fellowship's short-term goal involves crossing the Misty Mountains. A blizzard blocks them on the mountain pass, they meet checks and dangers in the Mines of Moria, and ultimately, they lose their leader. They are in desperate straits once they escape the Mines, having made only slight progress toward the long-term goals.

Again the act is quite long. The Moria section is long in the novel, but the filmmakers have added the cave-troll fight and the giant collapsing staircase. To be fair, this is an action film that so far has not had much action, apart from some skirmishes with the Black Riders and a Saruman's battle with Gandalf.

The two versions of Act 4 last 36′44″ and 44′17″.

With Act 5 we encounter one notable phenomenon of these Theatrical Versions: the strikingly short act. All five films discussed here have one short act, probably resulting from the removal of a large chunk of the narrative from the screenplay. The Extended *Fellowship*'s Act 5 doubles that of the Theatrical Version. This big excision is typical in that it comes during the development portion, which tends to consist of obstacles and delays. Thus it is the obvious place to remove footage without damaging the essentials of the causal flow too greatly.

Such eliminations, however, often remove moments that set up for actions later in the film, creating minor confusion. This happens in the Lothlórien episode, of which about half is missing from the theatrical version, including the important farewell gift-giving scene.

To those who have not read the book, the function of the Lothlórien episode in the Theatrical Version may be unclear, since it seems to accomplish little. At the end of the Mirror scene, Galadriel convinces Frodo that the Ring will corrupt the other Fellowship members. He says he knows what to do—the TP that ends the act—and yet he does not say what his new short-term goal is. We find out only later that he has decided to leave the Fellowship and go on alone.

The absence of the gift-giving scene creates unexplained events later on. In that scene, the Fellowship members receive Elvish cloaks fastened with a leaf-shaped brooch (Fig. 35.1), and Celeborn suggests that they can camouflage the wearer.

In *The Two Towers*, Pippin manages to drop his brooch as a sign to Aragorn, who is tracking the band of Uruk-hai that has kidnapped him and Merry. Aragorn finds it, saying "Not idly do the leaves of Lórien fall". Only to readers of the book would Aragorn's line be meaningful. Similarly, the camouflaging

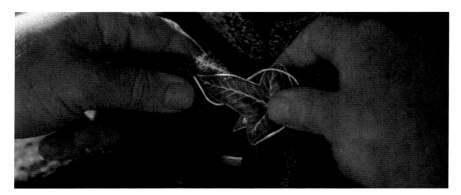

Fig. 35.1 Galadriel presents the Fellowship members with brooches that will become important in the second film (*Source* Screenshot from *The Fellowship of the Ring* DVD edition, 2002, EiV)

Fig. 35.2 Legolas holds up a piece of *lembas* and explains: "Lembas! Elvish waybread. One small bite is enough to fill the stomach of a grown man" (*Source* Screenshot from *The Fellowship of the Ring* DVD edition, 2002, EiV)

power of the cloaks, which becomes important later, is never set up. Finally, the special properties of *lembas* are explained, helping to motivate Frodo and Sam's ability to keep going for so long without carrying any other food (Fig. 35.2). The extended version inserts the gift-giving and hence explains these later events.

The two versions of Act 5 run 13′30″ and 26′12″.

Act 6, the Climax, resolves neither of the long-term goals. The only plotline that gets resolved is Boromir's gradual succumbing to the Ring's temptation, with his redemptive heroism and death during the battle with the Uruk-hai. Aragorn declares that he, Gimli, and Legolas will try to rescue Merry and Pippin, creating their specific short-term goal for the next film. Frodo and Sam set out toward Mordor to pursue the long-term goal of destroying the Ring. Both versions end with dangling causes, as serials tend to do.

The two versions of Act 6 last 29′02″ and 35′58″.

35.3 Added Footage and Act Structure: *The Two Towers*

Act 1, the Setup, introduces two major new locales and their inhabitants: Rohan and the Rohirrim and Fangorn Forest and the Ents. A crucial character, Gollum, is also introduced here. The same goals continue to the end of the act: for Frodo and Sam, now guided by Gollum, reaching Mount Doom, and for the remaining Fellowship members, rescuing Merry and Pippin. The TP that ends the act is the slaughter of the Uurk-hai by the Rohirrim, setting in motion the active pursuit of the war plotline (Table 35.2).

In the Theatrical Version, this act is considerably shorter than that of the Setup of *Fellowship*, largely because the primary exposition concerning Rohan is delayed until Act 3, when the characters arrive at Edoras. The transformation

Table 35.2 Added footage and act structure: *The Two Towers*

Version	Length without credits	# of acts	Average act length
Theatrical	172 minutes	Six	28'40"
Extended	214 minutes	Seven	30'28"

of Gollum from threat to guide is quickly accomplished. No new goals are introduced. This is also true of the Extended Edition's Setup.

The two versions of Act 1 last 24'00" and 30'02".

Act 2, the Complicating Action introduced important new premises. Treebeard appears and ends the rescue-Merry-and-Pippin goal. Gandalf returns, resurrected as "the White", meaning that the war plotline regains its main strategist. He proposes a new short-term goal: going to Rohan to defend it from Saruman. Frodo gets another short-term goal when he agrees to Gollum's offer to reveal a secret way into Mordor: the pass of Cirith Ungol. The TP that ends the act in both versions is Frodo's announcement of this agreement: "Lead the way, Sméagol!".

The two versions of Act 2 last 29'08" and 46'43".

With Act 3, we encounter for the first time an added act, giving the Extended Edition seven. The Theatrical Version's third act is quite long at 39'14", over ten minutes beyond the average. The extended version adds 15'29" to this section, which would make for a total of 54'43", or about twice the length of a typical classical act. Instead, the filmmakers broke it into two acts, both Developments, of 26'38" minutes for Act 3 and 28'05" for Act 4—nicely proportioned lengths. This structural change suggests that the acts in Extended Editions are returning to the well-balanced act structure of the original screenplays.

Two major obstacles are confronting the main characters: Frodo and Sam are captured by the Gondorian army, and Aragorn seemingly dies. This gives Frodo and Sam a new short-term goal, to escape from Faramir; Legolas and Gimli continue to try and defend Rohan, but they're obviously much less likely to succeed. A new ally is gained with Gandalf's curing of Théoden, but he immediately faces an attack by Saruman's army. The TP that ends the theatrical Act 3 comes at the end of the *warg*-army attack on the refugees headed for Helm's Deep, when Aragorn falls over a cliff and is assumed to be dead. This same moment will serve as the end of the Extended Edition's Act 4.

The two versions of Act 3 last 39'14" and 26'38".

In the extended version's Acts 3 and 4, both Development sections, several new scenes are added and others are expanded. Important new scenes in this version of Act 3 (which ends before the departure from Edoras for Helm's Deep) include Théodred's funeral and Aragorn meeting his horse Brego. In the new Act 4, there are scenes of Éowyn recognizing that Aragorn is one of the Dúnedain and flashbacks of Faramir remembering celebrating a victory

Fig. 35.3 A new shot of Saruman declaring his goal to defeat Rohan (*Source* Screenshot from *The Two Towers* DVD edition, 2003, EiV)

with Boromir in Osgiliath. The scenes of Gríma with Saruman at Isengard are also added.

The splitting of the original Development into two acts involves the addition of a new TP. In a new shot of Saruman and Gríma, with the Wizard declaring his new short-term goal: "The world of Men shall fall. It will begin at Edoras" (Fig. 35.3).

This ends the extended Act 3. Much of what happens thereafter in *Towers* revolves around his army's battles with the Rohirrim and the Ents (The TP of the Theatrical Version has him shouting "To war!").

The extended Act 4 covers the departure from Edoras to Helm's Deep and, as with the Theatrical Version's Act 3, this new act ends with Aragorn's apparent death as the TP.

With the two versions back in sync, the numbering of the Extended Edition's acts will be one ahead. There will be a total of three Development sections in the Theatrical Version and four such sections in the expanded one. This is certainly unusual, but the characters have split up, and the action moves among them as they face increasingly significant obstacles.

The extended version of Act 4 lasts 28′05″.

Act 4 (theatrical)/Act 5 (extended) deals with the arrival of the Rohirrim at Helm's Deep, Saruman's army departing Isengard toward Helm's Deep, Arwen's decision to leave Middle-earth, and Faramir's belligerent questioning of Frodo and Sam. In general, the act functions to suggest that the forces of good face overwhelming odds.

We have seen how Theatrical Versions often have one or two particularly short acts. Act 4 of the Theatrical Version of *Towers* lasts 20′15″ minutes. Again, a single sequence has been cut out. This is a four-and-a-half-minute flashback of Faramir remembering a happy scene where he and his brother Boromir, celebrated a victory (Fig. 35.4).

Fig. 35.4 A new flashback with Denethor interrupting a happy scene between Boromir and Faramir and berating the latter (*Source* Screenshot from *The Two Towers* DVD edition, 2003, EiV)

Their father Denethor arrives and hints that Elrond's summons to a council at Rivendell means that the One Ring has been found. We also see Denethor harshly belittling Faramir. This provides considerably more motivation for Faramir's decision that "The Ring will go to Gondor," which forms the TP that ends this act. It also makes Faramir a more sympathetic character, which is consistent with his behavior in *The Return of the King*. So again, restored material strengthens the characterizations and the cause-effect chain.

The two versions of Act 4/Act 5 last 20'15" and 27'21".

Act 5 (theatrical)/Act 6 (extended) is very short in both versions. It is the end of the long build-up to the two battles, at Helm's Deep and Isengard. In terms of the timing, essentially about 15 minutes has been borrowed from these acts and added to the lengthy climax. The Theatrical Version lasts 14'08" and the extended one little longer at 16'46". The main function is to counter the hopelessness of the previous act and suggest that some help might bolster the Rohirrim. It begins with Aragorn riding toward Helm's Deep, initiates the Ents' consideration of what to do about Saruman, and ends with a troop of Elvish warriors' arrival to participate in the battle. The next shot opens the Helm's Deep battle.

Act 6 (theatrical)/Act 7 (extended) forms the climax of *Towers*.

The unusually long final act of *Towers* consists almost entirely of battles intercut: the Helm's Deep conflict, the Ent's decimation of Orthanc and defeat of Saruman, and the fighting at Osgiliath during which Faramir frees Frodo and Sam. Unlike in *Fellowship*, this final act genuinely wraps up the three main short-term plotlines that dominated the action.

The two versions of Act 6/Act 7 last 45'09" and 47'20".

An epilogue reasserts the long-term goals established at the Council of Elrond. Gandalf announces that the Battle of Helm's Deep is over and the battle for Middle-earth looms. The two hobbits travel on toward Mordor, with Gollum setting up a new threat by revealing that he has an ally ("she") who can kill the hobbits. With this potent dangling cause established, a crane upward reveals the first clear view of Mt. Doom, the long-term goal of their journey.

35.4 Added Footage and Act Structure: *The Return of the King*

As the first act of a new film, the opening of the Theatrical Version of *The Return of the King* is technically a Setup. Were someone to join all three of the films together with no interruption, it would act as yet another Development section, since little progress is made toward the long-term goals and new obstacles are thrown into the characters' paths (Table 35.3).

Act 1 begins, however, with an unexpected digression: a sort of prologue flashback to the finding of the Ring by the hobbit Déagol and his murder by Sméagol, who immediately is corrupted by the Ring and steals it. A brief montage sequence shows Sméagol degenerating into the creature named Gollum. This scene explains how the Ring got to Gollum and then to Bilbo; in the book, Gandalf relates this information at the Council of Elrond. After this filling-in exposition, Frodo and Sam move further toward Mordor, the other Fellowship members retrieve Merry and Pippin from Isengard, a celebration of the Helm's Deep battle is held at Edoras, Pippin is caught stealing the Palantír, and Gandalf takes Pippin to Minas Tirith. There the wizard urges the Steward, Denethor, to call for Rohan's help in the impending attack from Mordor. The TP is yet a new obstacle for the war plotline, Denethor's refusal to call for help or cede the throne to Aragorn, the rightful heir. Gandalf's new short-term goal becomes forcing Denethor to cooperate.

The theatrical Act 1 lasts 36′00″.

The Extended Edition is quite different. It creates a new structure by splitting the theatrical edition's Act 1 in two, largely by inserting a six-and-a-half-minute scene at Isengard involving Saruman. It replaces the simpler scene in the theatrical edition where Merry and Pippin are fetched from Isengard but Saruman does not appear. In a sense this scene accomplishes little, but the death of the main visible villain in *Towers* provides closure for that plotline.

Surprisingly, the new act reverses one of the major premises in the Theatrical Version. There Gandalf says that Saruman remains dangerous and simply bids Treebeard to keep him locked in his tower. In the extended version, however,

Table 35.3 Added footage and act structure: *The Return of the King*

Version	Length without credits	# of acts	Average act length
Theatrical	192 minutes	Six	32′00″
Extended	241 minutes	Seven	32′43″

Gandalf says, "Be careful. Even in defeat Saruman is dangerous ... We need him alive. We need him to talk!" They need to know where Sauron will attack first. It is a weak premise, since everything has suggested that the attack will target Minas Tirith, as indeed it does. (In the book, Gandalf visits the tower to magnanimously give Saruman a last chance to renounce evil and join the fight against Sauron.) Gandalf twice asks Saruman to reveal where Sauron will attack, but as he seems about to answer, Gríma kills him.

The expanded scene explains how the *palantír* got into the water, where Pippin finds it. Since the *palantír* provides the means for finding out where Sauron will attack, I take its discovery to provide a new first-act TP, as Pippin hands it to Gandalf.

The expanded Act 1 lasts 20′16″.

Act 2 of the extended version covers the rest of the story from the theatrical Act 1: the celebration and Pippin's theft of the *palantír*. The stone's revelation that Minas Tirith will be attacked first explains why Gandalf rushes to Minas Tirith. The scene with Denethor that ended the theatrical Act 1 is extended, as Gandalf takes Pippin outside and explains the situation (Fig. 35.5). He's disturbed by Theoden's reluctance to aid Gondor. This forms the TP that ends Act 2. From this point on, as with *Towers*, the extended version is one act ahead.

Act 2 (theatrical)/Act 3 (extended) constitutes the Complicating Action section, where new premises are introduced. Frodo, Sam, and Gollum reach their short-term goal, the pass of Cirith Ungol and see Sauron's troops marching out. Gandalf and Pippin achieve their short-term goal by defying Denethor and lighting the beacons, which in turn causes Théoden to decide to ride in aid of Gondor. Thus he, Aragorn, and the others gain the new short-term goal of helping to win the Battle of the Pelennor. Faramir's men retreat from Osgiliath, but Denethor again shows bad judgment by sending

Fig. 35.5 An added scene as Gandalf explains to Pippin: "There's no leaving this city. Help must come to us" (*Source* Screenshot from *The Return of the King* DVD edition, 2004, EiV)

them back. Gollum poisons Frodo's mind against Sam. The TP that ends the act is Frodo's rejection of his friend: "Go home!".

The two versions of Act 2 (theatrical)/Act 3 (extended) last 29′30″ and 34′32″.

Act 3 (theatrical)/Act 4 (extended) provides a classic Development, with obstacles cropping up before the big battle. Major characters are seemingly lost. Faramir is presumed to have been killed and Aragorn's party takes the dangerous Paths of the Dead rather than riding with the Rohirrim. Finally, with the forces of Sauron attacking Minas Tirith, Denethor despairs and orders his troops to flee. The TP comes as Gandalf assumes command: "Send these foul beasts into the abyss!".

The two versions of this act last 27′39″ and 31′42″.

Act 3 (theatrical)/Act 4 (extended) is again a classic development portion, with major obstacles creating delays in the forward action. After a suspenseful scene in Shelob's cave, Frodo is stung by the giant spider and captured by Sauron's orcs, necessitating a long digression in the next act as Sam rescues him. The defense of Minas Tirith is going badly, and yet Denethor's madness and decision to kill himself and Faramir draws Gandalf away from the battle. The TP comes when the Rohirrim appearing over a ridge. Gandalf's premise from the previous TP is being fulfilled with help coming from outside.

The two versions of this act last 25′48″ and 32′56″.

Act 5 (theatrical)/Act 6 (extended) is arguably the first of two climaxes, one for the war plotline and one for the quest. Much of the footage deals with the battle at Minas Tirith: the Rohirrim engage the enemy, Gandalf and Pippin save Faramir, Merry and Éowyn kill the Witch King, the ships with the Army of the Dead, led by Aragorn, arrive, all leading to the victory and its aftermath. Intercut with all this is Sam's rescue of Frodo from captivity, which constitutes the TP, as Sam suggests: "We'd better find you some clothes. You can't go walking through Mordor in naught but your skin".

The two versions of this act last 27′12″ and 33′31″.

Act 6 (theatrical)/Act 7 (extended), the second climax begins with a battle before the Black Gate. This battle is a diversionary tactic—a short-term goal—not to win but to draw Sauron's eye away from Mount Doom. Frodo and Sam's quest is accomplished as Gollum seizes the Ring and accidentally falls into the Cracks of Doom holding it. The TP comes with the shot of Frodo and Sam marooned on a rock surrounded by lava and Gandalf and the eagles arriving to save them.

The Extended Edition adds several new scenes, including one between Éowyn and Faramir (Fig. 35.6) setting up their romance—thus explaining why they are apparently a couple in the coronation scene.

The new scene of "The Mouth of Sauron" taunting the Aragorn, Gandalf, and the others before the Black Gate adds suspense and pathos to their sacrifice, for it appears that Frodo has been captured and their cause lost.

The two versions of this act last 27′11″ and 35′11″.

Fig. 35.6 A brief romantic scene between Éowyn and Faramir establishes them as a couple. In the theatrical version, there is no hint of this until they are together during the coronation scene (*Source* Screenshot from *The Return of the King* DVD edition, 2004, EiV)

The sense of balance among large-scale parts of a classical narrative film, whether achieved consciously or through instinct, is demonstrated by these two versions of *Return*. Though the difference in overall lengths between them is 48 minutes, the average lengths of the acts differ by less than a minute: 32'00" and 32'43".

The lengthy epilogue (18'22" in both versions) could almost be treated as an act in itself. Reviewers and some moviegoers complained about the film's many endings, and this portion is much longer than most epilogues. (Tolkien's novel contains just over four chapters after the coronation of Aragorn.) Still, if one considers the three parts as one film, having a nearly twenty-minute epilogue for a twenty-act film might be justifiable.

Without the final credits, the Theatrical Version lasts 8 hours, 58 minutes, and the Extended Version 11 hours. The average length of the 18 acts of the Theatrical Version is 30 minutes; that of the 20 acts of the Extended Edition is 33 minutes.

35.5 Added Footage and Act Structure: *Kingdom of Heaven*

Kingdom of Heaven has five acts in both versions, and since it adds about 50 minutes, the result is that the average act length is expanded by ten minutes. Still, 37 minutes is still not all that far off from Field's 30-minute ideal. It is long enough for an extra act, but Scott did not take that option (Table 35.4).[1]

---

[1] For a detailed account of additions and changes to the Director's Cut, timed down to the second, see Doc Idaho's "Kingdom of Heaven" on Movie-Censorship.com: https://www.movie-censorship.com/report.php?ID=3097 (c. 2010). Accessed 10 December 2021.

Table 35.4 Added footage and act structure: *Kingdom of Heaven*

Version	Length without credits	# of acts	Average act length
Theatrical	136 minutes	Five	27′15″
Extended	186 minutes	Five	37′20″

Act 1, the Setup, deals with Balian, a French blacksmith, mourning his wife's suicide. A nobleman, Godfrey of Ibelin, reveals that Balian is his illegitimate son. The two set out for the Kingdom of Jerusalem to serve its king, Baldwin IV, and help to keep the current peace between the king and the Sultan, Saladin. Balian's goal is to atone for his sin of killing a priest and his wife's sin in committing suicide. Late in both versions of Act 1, Godfrey, who has been wounded during an attack on the road, is on his deathbed and gives a speech which I've taken as the TP. It is a privileged moment, since the title is explained: "A kingdom of Heaven. There is peace between Christian and Muslim, all. Between Saladin and the King, we try".

The extended first act has a lot of additional footage, including more information about the family of Godfrey and his estate at Ibelin, in Jerusalem. The priest is revealed as Balian's half-brother. He turns out to have beheaded Balian's wife for killing herself—providing motivation for the otherwise strange act of Balian's killing him.

This extended act also restores a crucial piece of exposition which had inexplicably been cut out. During Balian's journey to Jerusalem and after he reaches it, he performs feats of military and engineering prowess. In the climax he skillfully leads the defense of Jerusalem against the Muslim forces. Throughout one wonders how a blacksmith could do such things.

In the extended version, Balian says that he has fought in several battles, and his brother mentions that he has built military devices like siege towers. In both versions, after his arrival in Jerusalem in Act 2, Balian notices a model fort and siege towers. He examines one of the towers (Fig. 35.7).

In the Theatrical Version, we will probably assume he is curious about it, being inexperienced in war. In the Extended Edition we know that he is assessing the tower with an expert eye. Saladin's army uses similar siege towers in the final battle, and Balian's tactics ultimately destroy them.

The two versions of Act 1 last 24′42″ and 40′26″.

Act 2, the Complicating Action, sees Balian passing a series of tests as he travels to and arrives in Jerusalem. He survives a shipwreck and other dangers along the way. He takes up his father's title, restores his father's unproductive estate at Ibelin, and gains the trust of King Baldwin, who is gradually succumbing to leprosy. In addition, important characters are introduced: the villainous Guy de Lusignan, whose Templar knights are fanatically devoted to killing Muslims. He is the primary obstacle to the king's desire to keep Jerusalem a peaceful and diverse city. His wife Sibylla, who is also the king's

Fig. 35.7 Balian's examination of a model siege tower has different implications in the shorter and longer versions (*Source* Screenshot from *Kingdom of Heaven* DVD edition, 2006, 20th Century Fox Home Entertainment)

sister, hates her husband and soon becomes Balian's lover. Balian's goals of redemption and promoting the peace that the king has struggled to maintain remain unchanged. The TP threatens that peace: Lusignan and his knights massacre a peaceful Saracen caravan.

The scenes of Balian and his companions traveling have been extended, including a battle in the forest. More time is spent on characterization.

The two versions of Act 2 last 28′42″ and 41′12″.

Act 3, the first Development section of two, is this film's unusually short act I mentioned, just under 19 minutes in the Theatrical Version. Its main action in the Theatrical Version includes Saladin's army marching toward the castle of Reynauld, Lusignan's accomplice in killing Muslims; Sibylla and Balian falling in love; and Baldwin convincing Saladin not to attack the castle.

The act's brevity results from the elimination of an important subplot. In the Theatrical Version Sibylla inherits the throne when her brother dies and passes it on to Lusignan. In the extended version, she has a small son who, as the king's nephew, is the actual heir to the throne. We see the boy and his growing friendship with Balian. The son will become king briefly in Act 4 when Baldwin dies of leprosy. He turns out to have the disease as well, and Sibylla poisons him to prevent his suffering. The boy's disease embitters her and thus causes a change in her character that is not adequately explained in the Theatrical Version. Restoring this plotline makes her a more prominent and sympathetic character. It also lengthens both Acts 3 and 4.

Other additions include Saladin's doctors treating the dying Baldwin while Lusignan angrily practices swordplay nearby. Sibylla and Balian discuss what will happen once her son becomes king. A long scene between Sibylla and Lusignan has them discussing the same thing.

The TP of Act 3 comes when Balian refuses to take command of the army and marry Sibylla, because if he does so, Baldwin will have Lusignan killed. Sibylla's resulting break with him forms the TP as she angrily declares, "There'll be a day when you will wish you had done little evil to do greater good".

The two versions of Act 3 last 18'46" and 30'02".

Act 4, the second Development, begins in the Theatrical Version with Baldwin's death, followed by the coronation of Sibylla and then Lusignan. Lusignan's Templars start a war against Saladin's army, guaranteeing that Jerusalem will be attacked. Balian agrees to lead the defense of the city. Throughout, he continues to follow his goal of protecting the poor and preserving Jerusalem as Baldwin had left it, a city of tolerance for all sects.

The extension of the act consists mainly of scenes involving Sibylla's son: his coronation (Fig. 35.8); three scenes which suggest that he, like his uncle, suffers from leprosy; and a final one where she poisons him. Another new scene has Balian, disillusioned, discussing the existence of God with the Hospitaler.

The two versions of Act 4 last 28'26" and 40'26".

Act 5, the climax consists mainly of the lengthy battle for Jerusalem and Balian's unexpected surrender of the city to Saladin. This act is only a few minutes longer in the extended version than in the theatrical. This is typical, especially in epics like this and *The Lord of the Rings*: the big, expensive action scenes tend to come here. Shots of violence and gore are added, and Balian gives his estate to Marek, his faithful servant. Lusignan gains more screen time when he is shown as Saladin's captive being handed over to Balian. Later the two have a duel; Balian wins but refuses to kill Lusignan.

The climax ends with Balian joining Sibylla among the crowd leaving Jerusalem under Saladin's promised safe-conduct.

Fig. 35.8 In an added subplot, Sibylla's son is crowned Baldwin V (*Source* Screenshot from *Kingdom of Heaven* DVD edition, 2006, 20th Century Fox Home Entertainment)

A brief epilogue shows Balian and Sibylla visiting his old blacksmith shop in England. They are visited by Richard the Lionhearted, on a crusade to recapture Jerusalem. He is seeking Balian, who claims to be just a blacksmith. The couple ride off on a different road to an unknown destination. They pass the grave of Balian's wife, suggesting that he has achieved his goal of expiating his and her sins.

The two versions of Act 5 last 35'26" and 37'50" (including the epilogue in both timings).

35.6 ADDED FOOTAGE AND ACT STRUCTURE: *DANCES WITH WOLVES*

Dances with Wolves adds 53 minutes, the most of any film under consideration here. *The Return of the King*, second at 48 minutes, adds an act. *Dances* does not. The Theatrical Version contains six acts, which is what one would expect for a three-hour film. Unlike in the other four films, however, no major scene or plotline had been cut, so no significant structural changes were necessary in restoring the extra 53 minutes. Instead *Dances* simply extends the actions within each act (Table 35.5).

Unlike for the other four films, reaction to the longer version was generally unfavorable. A perceptive summary of the problems was given in a review on the *DVD talk* site:

> What exactly does the additional 52 minutes of new footage give us? Largely, more of everything that we already have. Instead of one well-chosen image or scene, we get several of the same; instead of a scene trimmed to its essentials, we get insignificant material before and afterwards. It's clear right from the beginning that this additional material disrupts the pacing and dilutes the impact of the film. (Ordway 2003)

There were a few deleted scenes whose re-insertion seemed to me to enhance the story, but on the whole, *Dances* is the only case where the longer version provides nothing essential to the cause-effect chain or the characterization.

The story is quite simple, focusing on one character, rather than the large casts of the four other films. John Dunbar is a Civil War soldier who requests a transfer to a posting on the Western frontier. Once there, he becomes increasingly fascinated by the Indians in a Lakota village nearby, whom he has been

Table 35.5 Added footage and act structure: *Dances with Wolves*

Version	Length without credits	# of acts	Average act length
Theatrical	176 minutes	Six	29'26"
Extended	229 minutes	Six	38'10"

assigned to surveil. Gradually he learns and adopts their customs, eventually becoming part of the tribe. The entire arc of the action up to the crisis follows his progress in renouncing the military life and joining the Indians.

Act 1, the Setup, shows Dunbar seeking to commit suicide by attacking Confederate troops. Gravely wounded, he survives and is decorated. An insane officer sends him to the isolated, crudely constructed Fort Sedgewick. Although a small garrison of soldiers has been stationed there, Dunbar finds it unaccountably deserted.

The extended version of Act 1 contains a scene that exemplifies how adding material can vitiate the effects of the original.

In the Theatrical Version, there is an eerie quality to Dunbar's exploration of the deserted fort. There are no horses, yet a row of bridles hangs in the crude stable (Fig. 35.9).

Dunbar finds caves dug into a hillside where the soldiers were apparently living. The river is full of dead deer. The mystery of what happened to the garrison is never explained. There's a lingering, slightly ominous sense that at any point Dunbar might find the men's bodies or that they might return with a horrible tale to tell.

In the extended version, however, a scene is inserted before Dunbar's arrival. Nearly three minutes long, it explains the garrison's disappearance. The officer in charge addresses his surly men (Fig. 35.10).

He mentions that "they" have stolen their horses—presumably referring to one of the local Indian tribes—and that the supply wagon (which is transporting Dunbar) is days late. The men desert and are never seen again. Thus we, though not Dunbar, know what has happened to the garrison. As a result the sense of eeriness that enhances the subsequent scenes at the fort disappears, to the detriment of the drama. Other additions are less problematic,

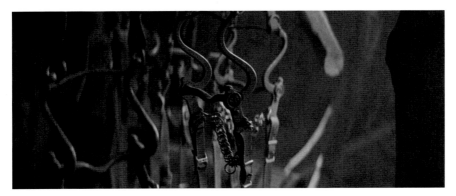

Fig. 35.9 In both versions of *Dances with Wolves*, a row of bridles signals Dunbar's mystification at the deserted fort, but the audience's reaction is different in each case (*Source* Screenshot from *Dances with Wolves* DVD edition, 1991, Pathé)

Fig. 35.10 The extended version shows the commander of the fort explaining the reasons for leading his men to desert (*Source* Screenshot from *Dances with Wolves* DVD edition, 1991, Pathé)

but there are many that make plot points much more explicit, if not downright heavy-handed. The studio-enforced cuts to the film gave it an evocative, almost poetic tone that is diminished in the longer version.

The TP that ends Act 1 is the departure of the supply wagon, leaving Dunbar alone at the fort. His goal has been established as being a good soldier, enjoying the pristine prairie, and gathering information about the local Indian tribes. He keeps a journal, which motivates lengthy voiceover speeches by Dunbar, aiding our comprehension of the narrative.

The two versions of Act 1 last 26′32″ and 36′12″.

Most of the subsequent TPs mark major stages in Dunbar's increasing fascination with his Lakota neighbors. These do not exactly swing the action into "another direction", as Field claims all TPs do. His acceptance as a member of the tribe is accomplished by Act 5. The TP ending that act launches the climax; it is the only one that introduces a new direction for the action.

Act 2 is the first of two Complicating Action sections. Dunbar cleans the fort and explores the prairie. A wolf starts visiting him. Pawnee warriors kill the supply-wagon driver. An Indian tries to steal Dunbar's horse. He buries the fort's supply of rifles. He tries to visit the Lakota village but finds an injured white woman in Indian garb. He takes her to the Lakota village and is chased away. The TP comes when Ten Bears, the leader of the tribe, holds a council and appoints two delegates to peacefully visit Dunbar. Their initial purpose is to gather information about the possible encroachment of white men into their territory—much as Dunbar is trying to gather intelligence on them. Dunbar's initial goals do not change.

The two versions of Act 2 last 29′13″ and 43′38″.

Act 3, the second Complicating Action, is very long in both versions. It lingers over Dunbar's steady progression toward admiring and wanting to be with the Lakota tribe. This major change of goals must be motivated thoroughly and not seem sudden. The Lakota delegation is mystified but charmed by Dunbar; they ask for news on white encroachment. Stands with a Fist, a white woman raised by the Lakota, translates. Dunbar joins the tribe for a buffalo hunt. The TP occurs as he watches the hunting party leave him at the fort. In voiceover he says, "Many times I've felt alone, but until this afternoon, I'd never felt completely lonely". Earlier we've seen him living happily alone at the fort, so this confession seems a culminating moment.

The two versions of Act 3 last 40'44" and a remarkable 52'39".

Act 4, the first of two Developments, continues to follow Dunbar's progress toward joining the Lakota. He is given a teepee in the village and the name "Dances with Wolves". Nevertheless, he is forbidden to join the war party attacking a Pawnee village (the Pawnees being the villainous Indians in this drama). Dunbar's romance with Stands with a Fist develops. By this point he has been almost entirely integrated into the tribe, with few of the obstacles typical of a Development portion. To ramp up the drama, news comes that the Pawnee will launch a revenge attack on the village.

The TP consists of Dunbar offering to give the rifles hidden at the fort to the Lakota. His gesture signals his complete abandonment of any lingering loyalty to the military and of his goal to provide information on the Indians.

The two versions of Act 4 last 27'13" and 31'06".

In Act 5, the second Development, the gift of the rifles has earned Dunbar the right to fight alongside the Lakota braves against the attacking Pawnee. Dunbar marries Stands with a Fist. At this point, he also reveals that many whites will soon be coming into the area. He has been keeping this information secret, but presumably as a member of the tribe he feels obliged to warn the others. The chief decides to move the village to the tribe's winter camp. Dunbar realizes that he has left his journal, which could reveal the tribe's location, behind at Fort Sedgewick. The TP arrives when he rushes off to retrieve it.

The two versions of Act 5 last 21'21" and 31'13".

Act 6, the Climax, is surprisingly short in both versions, which are almost the same length. Clearly Costner and the screenplay writer were far more interested in the Indians than the soldiers. The climax provides some military action but mainly serves to confirm that Dunbar was wise to desert and join the Lakota. When Dunbar finds soldiers at Fort Sedgewick, they kill his horse and beat him. They set out for his execution at the main fort, taking the journal along. Lakota warriors attack and easily defeat the escort. One of them throws Dunbar's journal into the river, and the final TP shows it being carried away, no longer a danger to the tribe.

The two versions of Act 6, not counting the Epilogue, last 20'57" and 20'50".

In contrast to Act 6, the Epilogue is somewhat long. Dunbar has a new goal, to avoid endangering the tribe and to plead the Indians' case with the authorities. The Indians all object, but Stands with a Fist agrees to go with him and they leave. Before he goes, a young warrior gives Dunbar the journal, which he has retrieved from the river. A band of soldiers arrives and finds that the camp has been moved. The last shot shows Dunbar and Stands with a Fist riding away into the snowy wilderness.

The Epilogue lasts 14′12″ and 13′24″.

35.7 Conclusion

The variety of changes and timings in act structure that we have seen across these five films upholds the point I made about the flexibility of Hollywood norms. The acts examined here have been as short as fifteen minutes and as long as 52. In general, extended scenes can add comedy, motivation for actions to come, characterization, and any number of other devices. Norms are not rules, and the claim that all films have three acts occupying one quarter/one half/and one quarter of their length is a rigid structures that the imaginations of filmmakers have blithely ignored.

The flexibility of Hollywood's storytelling norms helps to explain why the classical cinema has lasted for over a century now. They allow for originality and variety in screenplays and in the films made from them. For the screenwriting researcher, the malleability of classical norms should foster a willingness to encounter deviations from those norms. If one approaches a script or a film with a preconceived and invariable assumption of how its narrative is structured, it usually will be possible to segment that narrative into the requisite three acts. As I have tried to show here, act structures can vary even within the same film if different versions are offered to the public as equally valid iterations of the original script.

References

Alexander. 2004. Written by Oliver Stone, Christopher Kyle, and Laeta Kalogridis. Directed by Oliver Stone. Germany, France, Italy, Netherlands, UK, USA: Intermedia Films, Ixtlan Productions, France 3 Cinéma, Pacific Film, Egmond Film & Television, IMF Intertionale Medien und Film GmbH & Co. 3, Produktions KG.

Alexander. 2014. "The Ultimate Cut." Blu-ray. USA: Warner Bros

Amadeus. 1984. Written by Peter Shaffer. Directed by Miloš Forman. USA: The Saul Zaentz Company.

Dances with Wolves. 1990. Written by Michael Blake. Directed by Kevin Costner. USA: Tig Productions.

Dances with Wolves. 1991. "3 Disc Special Edition." DVD. USA: Pathé.

Field, Syd. 2005. *Screenplay: The Foundations of Screenwriting*. Rev. ed. New York: Delta.

Gods and Generals. 2003. Written and directed by Ronald F. Maxwell. USA: Ted Turner Pictures.

Gods and Generals. 2011. "Extended Director's Cut." Blu-ray. USA: Warner Home Video.

Heat. 1995. Written and directed by Michael Mann. USA: Warner Bros, Regency Enterprises, Forward Pass.
Kingdom of Heaven. 2005. Written by William Monahan. Directed by Ridley Scott. USA: Scott Free Productions, Inside Track, Studio Babelsberg Motion Pictures GmbH.
Kingdom of Heaven. 2006. "4 Disc Special Director's Cut." DVD. USA: 20th Century Fox Home Entertainment.
Last Year at Marienbad. 1961. Written by Alain Robbe-Grillet. Directed by Alain Resnais. France, Italy: Terra Film, Société Nouvelles des Films Cormoran, Precitel, Como Films, Argos Films, Les Films Tamara, Cinétel, Silver Films, Cineriz.
Margaret. 2011. Written and directed by Kenneth Lonergan. USA: Camelot Pictures, Gilbert Films, Mirage Enterprises, Scott Rudin Productions.
Margaret. 2012. "Extended Cut." Blu-ray and DVD. USA: Fox Searchlight.
Ordway, Holly E. 2003. "Dances with Wolves—Special Edition." *DVD talk*. https://www.dvdtalk.com/reviews/6464/dances-with-wolves-special-edition/. Accessed 10 December 2021.
That Thing You Do! 1996. Written and directed by Tom Hanks. USA: Clavius Base.
That Thing You Do! 2007. "Tom Hanks' [sic] Extended Cut." DVD. USA: 20th Century Studios.
The Lord of the Rings: The Fellowship of the Ring. 2001. Written by Fran Walsh, Philippa Boyens, and Peter Jackson. Directed by Peter Jackson. New Zealand, USA: New Line Cinema, WingNut Films.
The Lord of the Rings: The Fellowship of the Ring. 2002. "Special Extended DVD Edition." DVD. USA: EiV.
The Lord of the Rings: The Return of the King. 2003. Written by Fran Walsh, Philippa Boyens, and Peter Jackson. Directed by Peter Jackson. New Zealand, Germany, USA: New Line Cinema, WingNut Films.
The Lord of the Rings: The Return of the King. 2004. "Special Extended DVD Edition." DVD. USA: EiV.
The Lord of the Rings: The Two Towers. 2002. Written by Fran Walsh, Philippa Boyens, Stephen Sinclair, and Peter Jackson. Directed by Peter Jackson. New Zealand, Germany, USA: New Line Cinema, WingNut Films.
The Lord of the Rings: The Two Towers. 2003. "Special Extended DVD Edition." DVD: USA: EiV.
The New World. 2005. Written and directed by Terrence Malick. USA: New Line Cinema, Sunflower Productions, Sarah Green Film, First Foot Films, The Virginia Company LLC.
The New World. 2008. 7 "The Extended Cut." USA: EiV.
Thompson, Kristin. 1999. *Storytelling in the New Hollywood: Understanding Classical Narrative Technique*. Cambridge MA: Harvard University Press.
Titanic. 1997. Written and directed by James Cameron. USA: Paramount Pictures, 20th Century Fox, Lightstorm Entertainment.
Troy. 2004. Written by David Benioff. Directed by Wolfgang Petersen. USA, UK, Mexico, Malta: Warner Bros. Pictures, Helena Productions, Latina Pictures, Radiant Productions, Plan B Entertainment, Nimar Studios.
Troy. 2007. "Director's Cut." DVD. USA: Warner Home Video.
Sátántangó. 1994. Written by Béla Tarr and László Krasznahorkai. Directed by Béla Tarr. Hungary, Germany, Switzerland: Mozgókép Innovációs Társulás és Alapitvány, VVF, Vega Film, Magyar Televizió, TSR.

PART V: How To

Researching and Teaching Screenwriting: Discourses and Methods

CHAPTER 36

Film Dramaturgy: A Practice and a Tool for the Researcher

Kerstin Stutterheim

36.1 Introduction

Dramaturgy is a practice and also an academic discipline. As the latter, it is a sub-discipline of aesthetics, which "is a particular historical regime of thinking about art and an idea of thought according to which things of art are things of thinking" (Rancière 2011, 5). Etymologically, dramaturgy is defined as the "science of the composition and production of plays", or more simply, as "making drama work" (Hay 1983, 75). Dramaturgical knowledge forms the conceptual basis for the organisation of structure, the design of the *sujet* [*suzhet*], the development of the *story* [*fabula*], as well as the corresponding character design—particularly the relation of character(s) in space and time in a narrative-performative artwork—and the design of the audio-visual narrative, among other aspects. One can describe dramaturgy as the art of thoughtful comprehension and logical abstraction of pattern passed on through time. It reflects on and presents models and correspondent possibilities for action, expressing an embedded, implied meaning, implicit theme, or aim. In the sense of being a regime of thinking, and thus a philosophical approach, dramaturgy applies to all elements of the aesthetic composition of a narrative-performative work in all its complexity—and more specifically to screenwriting, not only but starting from a concept, treatment, or screenplay. It can be characterised as a "practice-theory" and, as such, also as a "a reflective

K. Stutterheim (✉)
Edinburgh Napier University, Edinburgh, Scotland, UK
e-mail: k.stutterheim@napier.ac.uk

theory [...] as production of and reflection on communication of communications to society about society" (Szatkowski 2019, 6). Thus, a dramaturg's work ideally provides knowledge, experience, and support at all levels of a production, is not restricted to one stage or department, and does not end with the finished script.

Consequently, this chapter argues that dramaturgical knowledge is core to screenwriting. Dramaturgy has been established as an academic discipline that can support the study of screenwriting, given the importance of screenwriting as the basis for the production of a film, providing the backbone of any screenplay for any film or TV series, no matter what length, and indeed in any time-based media production. This is true independently of whether the screenwriter's dramaturgical choices are made consciously or unconsciously. From experience, tradition, and academic reflection, as explored more in detail below, dramaturgy can serve as an analytical method of film analysis as well as an investigative tool for any other narrative or performative artwork.

Dramaturgical knowledge enables the researcher to investigate and recognise aesthetic means and artistic approaches that help give an artwork or film its affective quality. At the same time, this knowledge can be utilised to identify reasons for a work failing to captivate its audience. And while aesthetic analysis and philosophical reflection in dramaturgy are inseparable, it should be emphasised that the philosophical reflection derives from the analysis of the work and consideration of the production practice. It is not a free improvisation around the theme developed in the dramatic work. As with Rancière, "what aesthetics refers to is not the sensible. Rather, it is a certain modality, a certain distribution of the sensible" (2009, 1). Dramaturgical knowledge enables us to gain insights into creative and artistic decision-making. It also helps us analyse what might have inspired an artistic decision as well as understand the overall effect of a work or even the limits of the creative work in question. Dramaturgical knowledge provides recognition of the immanent processes inscribed in a work having a particular impact on the audience. Within a dramaturgical analysis one also reflects on cultural, moral, religious, and social traditions, regional peculiarities, and the Zeitgeist reflected on or mirrored in the work under discussion.

36.2 Roots and Tradition

Dramaturgy has a long tradition in the theatre, the performing arts, and in musical performance. Various key texts laid the foundation for dramaturgy as practice and theoretical reflection. Dating back to a period that spans between 500 BCE and 500 CE, the *Nāṭyaśāstra* [*Science of Drama*] "is the earliest and most authoritative Indian text on the performing arts" consisting of "a series of accounts on various aspects of theatrical arts" (Lidova 2014). Greek author, satirist, philosopher Lucian of Samosa, (c. 125–after 180) wrote an influential text on the art of dance that focuses on the spiritual diffusion of the narrated action, rhythm, the aesthetic realisation as a whole, and the understanding of the performed story (see Franz 2014, 38; Lada-Richards 2007). Lucian's work had a wide-ranging impact on Western literature and theatre. Horace's *Ars Poetica* [*The Art of Poetry*] (19 BCE) (Horatius Flaccus and Schäfer 2002) too engages with all forms of artistic storytelling, broadening the approach beyond the tragedy of fate. Dating back to the tenth century CE, *Dasarupa* [*A Treatise on Hindu Dramaturgy*, also known as *Treatise on the Ten Forms of Drama*] is one of the most important works on Hindu dramaturgy: composed by Dhanamjaya, it is a brief manual presenting the basic rules of composition as derived from tradition (see Haas 1912).

Although Aristotle's *Poetics* is often regarded as the most influential text within the tradition of playwriting, it "was treated by playwrights as prescriptive guidebook for hundreds of years after its rediscovery and translation into Latin" (Potolsky 2006, 32). It discusses only the texts of the imitative form of tragedy. As Aristotle himself emphasises, the "myth-based tragedy" is only one out of four different style types of tragedy which he summarises in short but does not discuss further (Aristoteles 2008, Chapter 18). Therefore, his treatise is relevant to only one tradition among a broad variety of narrative styles although already he discusses *epos* and *epic narration* in comparison with the myth-based tragedy (Aristoteles 2008, Chapter 5 b10–b20). In order to get a better understanding of the complexity of the traditions of narration, it might help to bring to mind here that the *Poetics* was originally written as pedagogical material with references to the texts, the plays, not the performance. This is why one can define the *Poetics* as the origin of drama theory, or as "the single most influential work of literary criticism" (Potolsky 2006, 32). It was part of a broader collection of texts, Aristotle did not intend it to be published, and it was almost forgotten for many centuries (Schmitt 2008a, 47; Busch 2008, xxvii; Gellrich 1988, 163–242; Potolsky 2006, 32). In the first century BCE, long after Aristotle had passed away, Andronikos of Rhodos edited and published a complete edition of Aristotle's lecture notes that included the *Poetics* (see Busch 2008, xvii). It was not until after 900 CE that the first known Arabic translations and commentaries were written: among others, by Ishaq ibn Hunain (see Arnzen 2021; Filius 1999), Abū Bishr Mattā ibn Yūnus (see Aristotle et al. 1911; Matta Ibn Yūnus), Yahya ibn Adi (see Busch 2008, xix; Jahjā Ibn-ʿAdī al-Mantiqī 1982), Ibn Sina, also known as Avicenna (see Kemal 2007), and Averroes [aka Averroës] (Averroës and Butterworth 2000). Later, in the Middle Ages, the *Poetics* was first translated into Latin and commented on, followed by an intensive study of the text from the sixteenth century onwards—including new translations, new interpretations, and further commentaries (see Busch 2008; Gellrich 1988, 161–242; Frietsch 2009; Huss et al. 2012). As Schmitt emphasises, the *Poetics* is one of Aristotle's late texts within a broad corpus on rhetoric and philosophy (Schmitt 2008a, 48; 2008b). Referring to the rediscovery and corresponding reinterpretation of Aristotle's *Poetics* in the Italian Renaissance, Schmitt points out that this was fundamental for the establishment of the "Aristotelian Canonisation" (Schmitt 2008a, 46), established within drama theory as *Regelpoesie* [*Canonisation*], a rule system derived from formalism as presented in the *Poetics* (see Gellrich 1988, 166), and *Nachahmungspoesie* [*Imitation*] (see Armstrong 1941; Potolsky 2006, 50–54).

> Aristotle initiated a theoretical tradition that has persistently sought to approach drama as a system of patterns, which response [sic] to expectations of order. The systematic view of tragedy, beginning with the *Poetics*, has typically subscribed to the fundamental assumption that plays submit to reason. Within such an approach, indeterminacies and wonders that provoke irresolvable *aporia* are relegated to the margins of study or regarded as unfortunate anomalies. (Gellrich 1988, 5)

The rediscovery and interpretation of the *Poetics* established during the sixteenth century led to the dogma of the closed form in the tradition of the Western world—that is the linear-causal drama defined by strict rules as known from the Aristotelian canon, as e.g. the time frame of 24 hours, being hero driven, caused by a conflict to be solved through the *catarsis*—which became standard in Italy and Central Europe (Fiebach 2015, 106–10; see also Klotz 1980, Asmuth 2004, Stutterheim 2015). "Renaissance literary, one could say, performs a kind covert policing service, by bringing the works over which it assumes authority into line with established and general acceptable norms", thus reacting to the broad variety of themes and practices within literature and performative arts, which often were provocative and not meeting Christian norms of moral and behaviour, as, for instance, Rabelais' *Gargantua and Pantagruel* (1532) (Rabelais 2016). Renaissance dramatic theory can be described "a Christian-humanists synthesis" (see Gellrich 1988, 173) derived from the that time rediscovery and new interpretation of Aristotle's *Poetic* "that renders moral coherence and instruction in virtue fundamental conditions of literary usefulness" (Gellrich 1988, 172). As Gellrich points out, "beginning with their colonization in the Renaissance, Aristotle's principles have assumed a kind of institutional power over the centuries" (1988, 5). *Imitation* [Nachahmungspoesie], associated with "moral coherence", contains until today two levels of definition. One is "the phenomenon of rhetorical imitation, the imitation of artistic role models, which for the long stretch of Western history between the height of the Roman Empire und the end of the eighteenth century was a central principle of literary production. In addition to imitating nature and human action, poets also actively sought to imitate exemplary forerunners and the artistic conventions they made authoritative" (Potolsky 2006, 50). This development in the field of dramatic narration has its counterpart in the visual arts, following the introduction of the linear perspective (see Goldstein 1988), and the "new image of the individual" and "clearly the beginning of a process that will culminate in the identification of the individual subject as the locus and source of meaning" (Tally 2013, 19).

In more recent times, the *Poetics* became most influential for screenwriting through Gustav Freytag's *Technique of the Drama* (published in 1897), which was translated and published in the United States: much later, Syd Field would refer to the *Poetics* as presented by Freytag (see Field 1979). In the United States, this initiated a new scholarly enthusiasm for the linear-causal and hero-driven principle as derived from the reception of Aristotle's poetic. Consequently, the *Poetics* became dogmatised as the most relevant reference source for screenwriting, although mostly in countries primed by Christian religion, thus mirroring its rediscovery in the sixteenth century. However, the *Nyatasastra* and the *Dasarupa* are still influential in India (see Datta 2016; Bharata 2010; Muni 2016). And influence from the traditions derived from the other forms mentioned by Aristotle but not discussed in detail, is also evident in East European or Asian Cinema.

36.3 Influential Dramaturgs

To be aware of and possibly be educated about these various traditions, their context and practicalities, is a core background for any dramaturg, as it enables them to apply their knowledge in analysis and practice. The practice of working as a dramaturg within a theatre and as part of a creative team began with Gotthold Ephraim Lessing. Lessing was a successful author of several plays—e.g. *Minna von Barnhelm* (1763–1767), *Emilia Galotti* (1772), and *Nathan der Weise* (*Nathan the Wise*) (1779)—but also a critic and a philosopher. Between 1767 and 1770, he served at Hamburg's *National Theatre*, Europe's first permanent national theatre. Lessing was appointed to advise the theatre management as well as the creative team which productions might interest and excite an audience. In addition, Lessing analysed all performances produced at this theatre during his period there. He focused on the relationship between the qualities of the playwright's work, the staging, the actors' performance, and the audience's reaction to the production in question (see Lessing 2011). The dramaturgical approach of combining aesthetic theory and knowledge derived from his own practical experience enabled Lessing to analyse and discuss the causes behind any failure of these performances. As a result, he published a series of texts, known as *Hamburgische Dramaturgie* [*Hamburg Dramaturgy*] (1767–1769). This collection of writings laid the foundation of theory and practice of dramaturgy as it is still known today.

Inspired by the concept of dramaturgy introduced by Lessing and propagated through his publications, a broad discourse about dramaturgical issues was initiated (see Hammer 1968, 1987; Szatkowski 2019; Börne 1987; Friedrich Hölderlin 1987; Wöhrmann 1967), which reflects on both Aristotle's principles and Lessing's writings. In his *Vorlesungen zur Ästehtik* [*Lectures on Aesthetics*]—held between 1818 and 1829, and later compiled in a volume in 1835—Georg Friedrich Wilhelm Hegel analyses practices of storytelling and particularities of epic narration (see Hegel 1971, 2003). Other influential authors and philosophers of the eighteenth and nineteenth centuries—such as Johann Wolfgang von Goethe, Friedrich Hölderlin, Arthur Schopenhauer, Heinrich Heine, Georg Büchner—and of twentieth century such as Bertolt Brecht, Thornton Wilder, Heiner Müller), to name a few, analysed their own work as well as the work of others employing dramaturgical analysis resulting from Lessing's methodology and Hegel's theoretic reflection (see Börne 1987; Hammer 1968, 1987).

To this day, all theatres in Germany as well as many theatres and/or companies in Central Europe, the UK, Scandinavia, and around the world employ dramaturgs (see Romanska 2016b). Famous dramaturgs include Heiner Müller at the Berliner Ensemble, Ken Cerniglia in New York, Marco Paolini in Italy, Kentarō Kobayashi (小林 賢太郎, Kobayashi Kentarō) in Japan, Gideon Lester and Oskar Eustis in the United States, and Sami Parkkinen in Finland, to me.

36.4 Dramaturgy as Academic Discipline and Education

Dramaturgy became part of production considerations from the early establishment of national cinemas. To support the new art form, dramaturgy was either adapted from theatre to film production or taught in newly established film schools and film academies as well as through formative approaches within film companies. The first film school, founded as early as 1919 in the former Soviet Union, was the Gerasimov Institute of Cinematography (VGIK, now the Russian State University of Cinematography) where dramaturgy was taught since its inception. Vladimir Turkin, one of the professors at the department of Dramaturgy and Screenplay, provided the foundation with a series of lectures titled *искуство экрана* [*Screen Art*] (Marievskaya 2019, 138) and, in 1938, he published *Драматургия Кино* [*Dramaturgy of the Cinema*] (Turkin 2007). Boris Michajlovič Ėjchenbaum, Yury Tynyanov, and Viktor Shklovski among others have also been influential in the development of dramaturgy for film (see Ėjchenbaum et al. 2016; Beilenhoff 2005). The aim was to teach and discuss cinematic dramaturgy (see Hennig 2013, 147). In 1929, Sergei Eisenstein, who also taught at the VGIK, published his seminal text about the *Dramaturgy of Film Form* as a study of the dialectics of the style of film, introducing the concept of *visual counterpoint* as a cinematic form of conflict (Eisenstein 2010). One of the students was Frank Daniel who, decades later, would introduce the knowledge he acquired at VGIK to the United States of America (see Marievskaya 2019, 137) thus becoming a key reference for contemporary screenwriters.

36.5 The Merging of Dramaturgy for Theatre and for Film

During the 1910s, film established itself as the new form of entertainment in several countries—e.g. Denmark, Sweden, France, Germany, and United States. Max Reinhardt and his theatres played a key role in applying dramaturgy, as it was well established within theatre practice, into the new medium, not only in Germany. Deutsches Theater, like all of Reinhardt's theatres, permanently employed dramaturgs such as, for example, Carl Zuckmayer (known for *Der Hauptmann von Köpenick* [*The Capitain of Koepenick*]) and at that time little-known but promising young author Bertolt Brecht.

Reinhardt established his own academy to educate talents for his theatres and film productions: authors, directors, and actresses worked for stage and film productions alike. One production worth mentioning is *Sumurûn* [*One Arabian Night*] (Freksa 1909). Reinhardt directed the first performance based on Freksa's play in 1910 at Deutsches Theater, with Ernst Lubitsch starring among others.

> Sumurun, a wordless play in nine scenes directed by Max Reinhardt, was conceived as an experiment. It opened at Reinhardt's 300-seat Kammerspiele Theatre on April 22, 1910. Because of its opening night success it was moved to the1000-seat house next door, the Deutsches Theatre, where it entered the repertory in May 1910. In 1911 the pantomime was presented in Vienna and twice in London. On January 16, 1912, it opened in New York. After 62 performances at the Casino Theatre it toured Chicago in March and Boston in April, again in Shubert houses, and left for a Paris engagement. In 1913 Sumurun returned to the London Coliseum for another short run, less enthusiastically received, and was presented, not to Reinhardt's satisfaction, on the relief stage of the Munich Art Theatre. (Kueppers 1980, 75)

Short after the opening in 1910, Reinhardt directed and produced *Sumurûn* as film too, of which Lubitsch directed a new version in 1920.

Another significant figure of the Modern Theatre of the Weimar Republic was Erwin Piscator, mainly known for epic and multi-perspective shows. Piscator, Brecht, and Friedrich Wolf are regarded as the most influential representatives of Berlin Dramaturgy (Haarmann 1991).

Simultaneously, with the establishment of the Universum Film Aktiengesellschaft, better known as UFA, in 1918, dramaturgy gained even more prominence in German film productions. The early 1920s are described as the era of the "theatrification of cinema" and of the "cinemafication of theatre" (Fiebach 2015, 346–52). In fact, "[d]espite a few later successes, the German Cinema was never to know another flowering like this one, stimulated, as it was, on the one hand, by the theatre of Max Reinhardt, and on the other, by the Expressionist Art (it is essential not to confuse these opposing styles)" (Eisner 1994, 7–8). A few years later, Reinhardt, as well as some of his former students who were then famous actors such as Lubitsch, and Piscator too, would migrate to the United States and work for Hollywood studios, where they applied modern dramaturgy successfully in their work: for example, by presenting a female lead protagonist (*Ninotschka*, 1939); by organising the plot over more than one storyline and perspective (*A Midsummer Night's*

Dream 1935); by applying the alienation effect by introducing a narrator (*The Shop around the Corner*, 1940; *To Be or Not To Be*, 1942).[1]

The cross-enrichment between theatre and film dramaturgy was mirrored by one of the most influential academics in terms of establishing dramaturgy for theatre, film, and performative arts as an academic discipline: Max Herrmann. A professor at Humboldt University since 1902, in 1923 he founded the Theaterwissenschaftliches Institut [Theatrical-Scientific Institute], which focussed on dramaturgy as fundamental to understanding theatre history and practice, in order to educate dramaturgs for practice and academic analysis. Herrmann's outstanding achievement was the result of his change in the approach to narrative-performative arts within the academia striving for more "philological exactitude: the facts must be ascertained before synthesis can be made or even a pragmatic nexus established. Max Herrmann insisted that a method must be developed that would allow for a scientific approach to theatrical facts" (Nagler 1959, 22). Herrmann's approach can be understood as a response to the context of his time and it led to the integration of the tradition of dramaturgy as practice derived from philosophical reflection to the curriculum. His academic approach reflected the influence that modern urbanism, the merging of theatre and film, a vibrant cultural explosion reacting to World War I, and the flowering of capitalism and consumerism had on the practices and the interrelationship of theatre, political performance, and cinema productions. The core of Herrmann's pedagogical approach drew on the sensual aspect and on a new understanding of the relation between space and performance in the narrative-performative artwork. His theoretical fundament to German theatre—inspired by the work of Reinhardt, Wolf, Piscator, and Brecht among others—was to have substantial influence on American theatre theory too, others (see Corssen 1998; Herrmann 1998; Heuner 1999).

Before Herrmann established theatre theory as a discipline in its own right, teaching theatre and performative arts postulated that every aspect of a narrative-performative work depended on written and spoken dialogue as shaped by *naturalism* and resulting from the concept of *imitation* as described above. As Nagler observes, with Herrmann "[...] the meaning of the verbal text is unchanged, but it ceases to be the only one. The theatrical performance is the played version of the text of a play" (Nagler 1959, xxi). Both dramaturgy and the practice of a dramaturg support such an understanding of performative arts as well as of the relation between the text and the complexity of the performance.

Consequent to the developments summarised here, one can recognise the nature of theatre and its central aspect of *symbolic action* [*symbolisches Handeln*] in today's audio-visual works—as, for example, feature films. Performative presentation results from communicative practice and human creativity, defined as *mimesis* [imitation] (see Aristoteles 2008, 1451b8–10; Plato 2021,

---

[1] For more detail on these examples, see Stutterheim (2019, 21–27).

book 10; Schmitt 2008a, 118–20; Weimann 1988; Gebauer and Wulf 1995; Foucault 1970; Fischer-Lichte et al. 2005, 201–08; Potolsky 2006). Therefore, dramatic art is always a symbolic act, be it on a stage, observed in public, in politics, or in a media production: using technological tools to produce images and sounds does not take the dramatic moment away from any representation of human beings. What is defined as *theatrical* can be recognised in human culture of all times all around the world (see Schechner 2010; Fischer-Lichte and Wihstutz 2013; Fiebach 2015) and, in particular, in contemporary media productions as well as political or ideological performances of any kind.

In this sense, via Herrmann and his successors, the experience of practice became an integral part of the concept of teaching dramaturgy as an essential part of the studies of performative arts globally. Early cinema productions, not only in Germany but in other countries of continental Europe, the United States, the Soviet Union, Latin America, and other regions, drew on this tradition of applying dramaturgy. Early film theorists, such as Ricciotto Canudo, also referred to dramaturgy as a relevant aspect of cinema (2017). Although film dramaturgy had already been taught in Moscow and Berlin, the (most likely) first book on dramaturgy for film was published in Budapest in 1925: *A filmjáték esztétikája és dramaturgiája* [*Aesthetics and Dramaturgy of the Film Play*] by Iván Hevesy (1925). Hevesy was a film critic and playwright who taught film dramaturgy at Bela Gaal's private school in Budapest.

> Hevesy's approach is an original mix of theory and practice: he applies to the new art form the theoretical apparatus he acquired during his studies and that he had already applied in writing on art history, literary and art criticism, and music. As to practice, Hevesy had a keen sense for the technical aspects of filmmaking of the day. (Szekfü 2018, 56–57)

Although this book got never translated into any other language, one can suppose it has influenced Hungary-born Bela Balázs and his writings, since he published a book on film dramaturgy as well (Balázs ca. 1926). As screenwriter (see Balázs 2019; Bartók and Balázs 2018; Grosz and Balász 2006; Balázs 1936; *Das blaue Licht* [*The Blue Light*] 2010), dramaturg (e.g. for *The Threepenny Opera*), and film scholar (see Balázs ca. 1926, 1966, 1970, 2001, 2013a, 2013b, 2021), Balázs' creative as well as theoretical work (e.g. *Theory of the Film*, 1970) is still considered of fundamental importance nowadays.

In light of these examples, it seems obvious that film dramaturgy was broadly discussed in Europe throughout the 1920s. Dramaturgy was then exploited and perverted by dictatorial regimes for their film propaganda, in Germany, Italy, the Soviet Union, and beyond. As a result of its political instrumentalisation in the 1930s and 1940s, dramaturgy fell into disrepute. Herrmann's institute, closed by the Nazi regime, was re-opened no earlier than 1961. However, film dramaturgy became part of academic education at most film schools in Eastern Europe in the 1950s and 1960s—at FAMU Prague (Czechoslovakia), Łódź (Poland), HFF *Konrad Wolf* and Humboldt University Berlin (both in the former GDR)—as well as at other academic institutions around the world, including Aalto University Helsinki (Finland), La Fémis in Paris (France), Filmakademie Vienna (Austria), ZhdK Zuerich (Switzerland), Middlesex University London, Southbank University London (UK), Academy of Arts Banska Bystricha and Academy of Performing Arts Bratislava (Slovakia), Saint Petersburg State University of Film and TV (Russia), Kampala Film School (Uganda), ERAM—Universidad de Girona (Spain).

36.6 Dramaturgy and Screenwriting

As argued above, dramaturgy supports screenwriters in their work. Dramaturgical knowledge provides a range of established principles and models that screenwriters can rely on and apply to their writing, thus anticipating a film: "Dramaturgy [...] is a process of making sense for the production and the audience. A good dramaturg helps to articulate that sense" (Hay 1983, 67). As mentioned, the dramaturg's unique skill is to support the artistic–practical activity of the entire creative team, not just the writer, combining scholarly knowledge and experience derived from professional practice and practice-based research. It is the combination of practice-based and scholarly knowledge, on the whole aesthetic complexity of the performative work that distinguishes dramaturgy from narratology, among other disciplines. Narratology focusses on written or verbally performed texts, literature mostly, rather than the full and varied aesthetic range of performative arts; and, to my knowledge, there is no such profession as a *narratolog* within the practice of performative arts.

> Meaning is central to human existence and art. Every artist must seek meaning for himself. In the performing arts, the quest is more complicated because some kind of consensus has to be reached first with the group of artists and then with the larger tribe represented by the audience. The drama does not work, and cannot be made to work, if the artists and audiences that are involved do not seek a meaning of their own work and of the work itself. I am not suggesting that there are always answers when the questions are asked, only that there can be no meaning to play-making without a serious quest for that meaning. Every good production is the quest itself. (Hay 1983, 75)

This is especially true for film productions of any kind (feature films of any length, TV series, and so forth), where the production process is even more specialised and separated than in theatre, because "the dramaturg, inasmuch as he is concerned with the text, must have a more lasting perspective both backwards and forwards in time than the director who is in charge of the momentary performance and meaning" (Hay 1983, 15). Hence, the work of a dramaturg is dedicated support for everyone involved in achieving the best possible overall aesthetic realisation of a production, supported by knowledge derived from tradition and sense of the Zeitgeist: "The dramaturgical skills of analysis, critical and structural thinking, and interconnectivity also become tools that gain applicability in a world outside of theatre" (Romanska 2016a, 8).

Ideally, a collaboration of the screenwriter (and the director and/or producer) with the dramaturg starts the moment the idea evolves, continues throughout the development of the screenplay and the production until its release. A dramaturg can support any of the creative team with dramaturgical advice, sometimes also interpreted as artistic advice. The work of a dramaturg—or of a writer/director applying dramaturgical knowledge that derives not only from drama theory—results from the long-standing tradition that predates the establishment of film as outlined above. However, it must be acknowledged that the role of a dramaturg is not common—or known under the same term—everywhere. Sometimes, their position gets split into different roles—as script editor, script doctor, artistic advisor, and editor—or is understood as one of the responsibilities of the director, which reduces the impact that dramaturgical support can have on a film production. This is because a dramaturg can give an additional view and knowledge to a production by combining professional reflections on practice and academic theory derived from aesthetics and philosophy to support a production of a narrative-performative work (see Romanska 2016a, b; Gindl-Tatárová 2008; Reichel 2000). As Brustein put it: "The dramaturg is potentially the artistic director's Good Angel" (1997, 36).

> Dramaturgy is a concept with expanding borders, functionally, theoretically, and geographically. Dramaturgy today provides us with important knowledge on how values are at work in theatre, film, television, the internet, and other performative media practices where human body-to-body communication is communicated to society. (Szatkowski 2019, 32)

For screenwriters, dramaturgy is relevant to design a solid and entertaining plot structure. Dramaturgical knowledge also facilitates the organisation of explicit and implicit levels of the story, which is central in contemporary and especially in poetic and postmodern media productions. Dramaturgical knowledge can support the screenwriter and their story when reflecting on society and human interaction to address and attract an audience. Screenwriters create the basic dramaturgical structure and can anticipate or inspire the implicit level of a film, its cinematic narrative. To reiterate, this is true even if screenwriters do not consciously think about dramaturgy or interact with a dramaturg, when studying structures and contexts of cinematic storytelling, traditional as well as contemporary. Screenwriters decide on a structure that they think works best to present their story. Nonetheless, a good screenplay requires more than a perfect structure. Shklovski wrote in this regard that, when focussing only on the story, one could compare the work of the screenwriter to shaking a kaleidoscope to get new variants of the fabula/story (Shklovski n.d., 68). Dramaturgy affords the search for those variants.

When trying to challenge given expectations about the formatting of a story to be presented, the choice comes back to dramaturgical basics, which offer a unique approach while, at the same time, respecting the basic elements of storytelling. Jean-Claude Carriere describes such a situation from his own experience when, early on in his career, he wrote the screenplay for *The Milky Way* (*La Voie lactée*, 1969) with Luis Buñuel trying to ignore all known rules. As they were outlining their screenplay it became obvious that a few rules cannot in fact be ignored; that there is a "secret order" that has to be respected (Carrière and Bonitzer 1999, 207). Dramaturgy offers the key to that secret order. Especially in film, a few basic rules form the basis to the "secret of cinematic storytelling" (Carrière and Bonitzer 1999, 143 and 207): most importantly, all elements of a movie or TV production should be non-replaceable and immovable (Aristoteles and Schmitt 2008, Chapter 8, A30–A35). If one can omit or rearrange a word, gesture, sound, or image without it affecting the narrative that element is superfluous and breaks the attention flow (see Carrière and Bonitzer 1999): one should respect the importance of being in the moment.

Another aspect of dramaturgy that I wish to emphasise here is that one cannot postulate a strict formula (such as the three-act or the five-act structure) as the best and most efficient for all themes, stories, and specific cultural traditions within different regions. Consequent to the context described above, there are very different structures from the tradition and the range of possibilities. From this spectrum, one can choose a form that best supports the story to be told. One element relevant to the organisation of the explicit structure is the act. We know from theatre and film history that the term *act* describes a particular section of the plot. In it, a subplot might take place—either in a place that does not change or in the context of a certain group of people. If something happens that permanently changes the quality and course of the action, one act ends and the next one begins. Thus, a film can have one, three, four, five, or more acts. In the 1920s, films usually consisted of six or eight acts, whereby an act coincided with the length of one reel of film (i.e. 10 to 15 minutes). The writers were advised to consider the running time of a reel when designing the dramatic action, since there was often a break when the reels got changed. More recently, *North by Northwest* (Hitchcock USA 1959) can be interpreted as either a three-act, five-act, or nine-act structure; *The Shining* (Kubrick UK/USA 1980) was developed according to the structure of a symphony and consequently comprised of four acts. The key point is to decide on a structure that best helps structure the story being told, not the other way around, and to use a specific descriptor, as *anagnorisis*, *peripetia*, *tragic moment* to name a few, and definition for each of the so-called turning points. Thus, the first turning point is either called the establishment of the *conflict* in a linear-causal structure or the impetus to action or *collision* in a work that applies modern dramaturgy. These terms include corresponding derivations that have grown out of tradition and a screenwriter and/or a director can apply them to the respective media realisation. The impetus to action, for example, differs from conflict in that the main character(s) have not themselves contributed to the creation of the challenging situation, nor has someone from their family or social group. Such an impetus may result from a natural disaster, a war situation or simply a relevant change that has a significant impact on the situation of the main character (see Carrière and Bonitzer 1999, 216).

Dramaturgy offers a broad range of possible combinations of constant and variable elements to develop a screenplay (see Stutterheim 2015, 2019, 35; Klotz 1980). *Constant elements*—e.g. beginning, *recognition* (*anagnorisis*) and *reversion* (*peripeteia*), resolution and end—provide stability and are recognisable for creators and audience alike. Many Anglo-American publications mention the so-called midpoint, which is known in dramaturgy as a combination of two constant elements: the interaction of *anagnorisis* and *peripeteia*. One can intensify or supplement these with the variable element of the *tragic moment*. These dramaturgically significant aspects of a plot occur one after the other and interact.

Anagnorisis contains the change from unknowing to knowing, through (re)recognition of a person or situation, by means of a relevant conclusion resulting from the plot, which gives a new meaning to the whole event—either of the main character(s) or of the audience (Aristoteles 2008, Chapter 11; Stutterheim and Kaiser 2011, 369, Stutterheim 2019, 43–47). Aristotle (2008, Chapter 16) defines six different kinds of possible recognition: through signs or icons; invented by the poet/writer; triggered by memory; by conclusion, or by fallacy of the audience caused by a false messenger or such; and the one he likes most—one that results from the sequence of actions when, according to probability, an affect action occurs.

Anagnorisis leads into *peripetia*, which defines the moment in the action marking the reversal of the action activity of the main character and/or of the hierarchy of power between protagonist and antagonist in the plot (Aristoteles 2008, Chapter 10 a15, Chapter 11 a25). A character who has been reacting up to this point has been able to develop an understanding of his or her situation through a situation called *anagnorisis* and can now readjust their activities in a situation defined as *peripetia* and consequently react actively to a situation. Alternatively, a previously active character understands the serious opposing forces they face in the *anagnorisis* and will have to react in advance to the unfolding events, marked by the *peripeteia*. This is the most important turning point, which cannot happen without the *anagnorisis* preparing it. Often, these are combined with the *tragic moment*. This, in turn, involves a situation that occurs unexpectedly for the main character, but is nevertheless probable or explicable for the spectator from the previous course of action, and thus brings about the *peripetia* or supports it in retrospect (Stutterheim and Kaiser 2011, 368; Carrière and Bonitzer 1999, 214–15; Stutterheim 2019, 43–47). It appears forcefully and with serious consequence for the lead character and—for the mind of the spectator—in logic correlation to the events of the action so far (see Freytag 1895, 95).

These and the other constant features relate to our experience of reality, which is shaped by perception as well as by *cultural memory* (see Assmann 2011, 2018; Assmann and Livingstone 2006; Kahneman 2012). *Variable elements* also play a significant role in explicit dramaturgy. They are relevant to the construction of a plot and derive too from tradition: for instance, overture/upbeat, conflict or collision, tragic moments, catastrophe/catharsis, secondary characters, and more. When writing a screenplay, one can chose the form and structure that best support the underlying theme and plot as a way of driving narrative and action. The chosen form of explicit dramaturgy as a combination of constant and variable elements, addresses that part of the human brain that stores experience and accumulated knowledge, which is structural and strategic, as in the *slow thinking* described by Daniel Kahneman (2012). Furthermore, dramaturgy considers how this particular cinematic narrative is going to be based on an inseparable relationship between explicit and implicit levels of such performative narration. Even for the explicit level of structure, i.e. plot construction, one can combine different patterns derived from the tradition of theatre, performative arts, and film. The explicit level of a movie, and hence of its script, addresses *structural slow thinking* (see Kahneman 2012). On the other hand, the implicit level triggers *associative, fast thinking*, which gets entertained by surprises as well as by well-designed aesthetic solutions for those aspects of the story, either connected to the experience and knowledge of the audience, or by activating or imagination. Implicit dramaturgy is inscribed in the visual and sonic design of a movie. Examples can include: colour dramaturgy in *The Ghost Writer* (2010) and *Miami Vice* (1984–1989); visual and acoustic references in *The Shining* (1980); references to tarots, the Holy Grail, and the history of the Cathars in Southern France in *The Fifth Element* (1997); visual references to Arnold Böcklin's *Die Toteninsel* (*Isle of the Dead*), that is San Michele, Venice's cemetery island, or the weather conditions mirroring the state of mind of the protagonist in *Shutter Island* (2010); Maverick's jacket in *Top Gun: Maverick* (2022), to mention just a few.

Dramaturgy reflects on both levels: the structural, explicit level of a narrative-performative work, and its implicit aspects (Rohmer 2000). Thus, either in interaction with a dramaturg or by applying dramaturgical knowledge, a screenwriter can tailor their story efficiently to a theme, the production context, and everything else to consider. As a result of this, they can successfully address their future audience.

36.7 Dramaturgy as Tool for Analysis and Research

According to the argument outlined above, it is evident that dramaturgy can serve analysis effectively—its knowledge derived from practice and philosophical reflection and abstraction, as a sub-discipline of aesthetics. Dramaturgical knowledge allows the detection and investigation of practices, patterns, and particularities of screenwriting and filmmaking. Supported by dramaturgical knowledge, one can analyse a work in regard to its use of film language and its *grammar*. It enables one to *read* and interpret a work. One should study the screenplay as an independent work, even though the creative team have transformed it into a movie. More specifically in this regard, this not only allows a well-argued understanding of the impact of the screenwriter and their creativity or art, but it also allows a closer look at dramaturgical intentions of the screenwriter.

The challenge the researcher faces is to not get immersed in the work but to develop an analytical approach to the screenplay. This enables the researcher to distinguish or compare the screenplay and the final film production. Dramaturgical theory prepares the researcher to investigate and identify how a film is made, in terms of artisanship and artistry. Based on the further differentiation into explicit and implicit dramaturgy (see Rohmer 2000; Stutterheim 2015, 2019, 37–54), one can, for example, identify the relationship between *fabula* and *sujet* or plot and story, between the structural and aesthetic design of a work. This knowledge also supports the identification of whether a performative artwork is linear-causal, that is driven by a hero and their conflict; or epic, that is telling a story caused by external circumstances (see Hegel 2003; Carrière and Bonitzer 1999; Stutterheim 2019); and following the structural concept of an open or closed form (see Eco 1989; Klotz 1980; Szondi 1978, 1987; Stutterheim 2015, 2019, 43–47). With the dramaturgical approach one can also detect the "identity of a conscious procedure and an unconscious production, of a willed action and an involuntary process. In short, the identity of logos and pathos", the core elements of an art work (Rancière 2011, 28).

References

A Midsummer Night's Dream. 1935. Written by Charles Kenyon and Mary C. McCall Jr. Directed by Max Reinhardt and William Dieterle. USA: Warner Bros.

Aristoteles. 2008. *Poetik: Übersetzt und erläutert von Arbogast Schmitt*. Edited by Arbogast Schmitt. Berlin: Akademie-Verlag.

Aristotle, and Abu Bishr Matta Ibn Yūnus. 1911. *The Poetics of Aristotle. Translated from Greek into English and from Arabic into Latin, with a revised text, introduction, commentary, glossary and onomasticon by D. S. Margoliouth*. London: Hodder & Stoughton.

Armstrong, Angus. 1941. "Aristotle's Theory of Poetry." *Greece & Rome* 10 (30): 120–25.

Arnzen, Rüdiger, ed. 2021. *Aristotle's Physics VIII, translated into Arabic by Isḥāq ibn Ḥunayn (9th c.)*. Berlin and Boston: De Gruyter.

Asmuth, Bernhard. 2004. *Dramenanalyse*, 6th ed. Stuttgart: J. B. Metzler.

Assmann, Aleida. 2011. *Cultural Memory and Western Civilization: Functions, Media, Archives*. Cambridge: Cambridge University Press.

Assmann, Jan. 2018. *Communicative and Cultural Memory*. Heidelberg: Propylaeum.

Assmann, Jan, and Rodney Livingstone. 2006. *Religion and Cultural Memory: Ten Studies*. Stanford CA: Stanford University Press.

Averroës. 2000. *Averroes' Middle commentary on Aristotle's Poetics*. Trans. and edited by Charles E. Butterworth. South Bend, IN and London: St. Augustine's Press.
Balázs, Béla. 1926. *Der sichtbare Mensch: Eine Film-Dramaturgie*, 2nd ed. Halle/Saale, Germany: Knapp.
Balázs, Béla. 1936. *The Real Sky-Blue*. London: John Lane The Bodley Head.
Balázs, Béla. 1966. *Filmska kultura*. Ljubljana: Gankarjeva Založba.
Balázs, Béla. 1970. *Theory of the Film: Character and Growth of a New Art*. New York: Dover.
Balázs, Béla, 2001. *Ausgewählte literarische Werke in Einzelausgaben*. Edited by Hanno Loewy. Berlin: Verlag Das Arsenal.
Balázs, Béla. 2013a. *El hombre visible, o la cultura del cine*. Buenos Aires: Cuenco de Plata.
Balázs, Béla. 2013b. *Regimas žmogus, arba Kino kultūra*. Vilnius: Mintis.
Balázs, Béla. 2018. *Bluebeard's Castle*, libretto. Leipzig and Frankfurt am Main: Deutsche Nationalbibliothek.
Balázs, Béla. 2019. *Das stille Städtchen: Drama in 3 Akten (5 Bildern)*. Leipzig and Frankfurt am Main: Deutsche Nationalbibliothek.
Balázs, Béla. 2021. *Der Geist des Films*. Halle/Saale, Germany: Knapp.
Balasz, Bela, and Riefenstahl, Leni. 2010. *Das blaue Licht*. Leipzig: Kinowelt Home Entertainment.
Beilenhoff, Wolfgang, ed. 2005. *Poetika Kino: Theorie und Praxis des Films im russischen Formalismus = Poètika kino*. Frankfurt am Main: Suhrkamp.
Bharata. 2010. *The Nāṭyaśāstra*. New Delhi: Munshiram Manoharlal.
Börne, Ludwig. 1987. "Dramaturgische Blätter (1829). Vorrede." In *Dramaturgische Schriften des 19. Jahrhunderts*, edited by Klaus Hammer, 329–36. Berlin: Henschel Verlag.
Brustein, Robert. 1997. "From 'The Future of an un-American Activity'." In *Dramaturgy in American Theater: A Source Book*, edited by Susan Jonas, Geoffrey S. Proehl, and Michael Lupu, 33–36. London: Harcourt Brace.
Busch, Thomas. 2008. "Chronologische Übersicht zur Textgeschichte." In Aristoteles, *Poetik*, edited by Arbogast Schmitt, xvii–xxviii. Berlin: Akademie-Verlag.
Canudo, Ricciotto. 2017. "The Triumph of the Cinema." In *Early Film Theories in Italy 1896–1922*, edited by Francesco Casetti, Silvio Alovisio, and Luca Mazzei, 66–74. Amsterdam: Amsterdam University Press.
Carrière, Jean-Claude, and Pascal Bonitzer. 1999. *Praxis der Drehbuchschreibens*. Berlin: Alexander Verlag.
Corssen, Stefan. 1998. Max Herrmann und die Anfänge der Theaterwissenschaft: Mit teilweise unveröffentlichten Materialien. Berlin: De Gruyter.
Datta, Ketaki. 2016. "Dramaturgy in Indian Theatre: A Closer View." In *The Routledge Companion to Dramaturgy*, edited by Magda Romanska, 94–98. London and New York: Routledge.
Dhanaṃjaya. 1912. *The Daśarūpa: A Treatise on Hindu dramaturgy*. Trans. and commented by George Christian Otto Haas. New York: Columbia University Press.
Eco, Umberto. 1989 [1962]. *The Open Work*. Cambridge, MA: Harvard University Press.
Eisenstein, Sergei. 2010. "The Dramaturgy of Film Form (The Dialectical Approach to Film Form)". In *Sergei Eisenstein*, edited and trans. by Richard Taylor, 161–80. London: I. B. Tauris.

Eisner, Lotte H. 1994. *The Haunted Screen: Expressionism in the German Cinema and the Influence of Max Reinhardt*. London: Thames and Hudson.
Ėjchenbaum, Boris Michajlovič, Jurij Tynjanov, Boris V. Kazanskij, and K. I. Šutko, eds. 2016. *Poėtika kino: Teoretičeskie raboty 1920-ch gg*. Moskow: Akademičeskij Proekt–Al'ma Mater.
Fiebach, Joachim. 2015. *Welt Theater Geschichte: Eine Kulturgeschichte des Theatralen*. Berlin: Verlag Theater der Zeit.
Field, Syd. 1979. Screenplay. *The Foundations of Screenwriting. A step-by-Step Guide from Concept to Finished Script*. New York: Delta.
Filius, L. S., ed. 1999. *The Problemata Physica Attributed to Aristotle: The Arabic Version of Ḥunain ibn Isḥāq and the Hebrew version of Moses ibn Tibbon*. Leiden, Boston and Cologne: Brill.
Fischer-Lichte, Erika, and Benjamin Wihstutz, eds. 2013. *Performance and the Politics of Space: Theatre and Topology*. New York: Routledge.
Fischer-Lichte, Erika, Doris Kolesch, and Matthias Warstat, eds. 2005. *Metzler Lexikon Theatertheorie*. Stuttgart: Metzler.
Foucault, Michel. 1970. *The Order of Things: An Archaeology of the Human Sciences*. London: Tavistock.
Franz, Michael. 2014. "Dramaturgia: Die Einführung eines neuen Terminus in Lukians Dialog 'Von der Tanzkunst'". In *Der dramaturgische Blick: Potenziale und Modelle von Dramaturgie im Medienwandel*, edited by Christa Hasche, Eleonore Kalisch, and Thomas Weber, 37–49. Berlin: Avinius.
Freksa, Friedrich. 2018 (1909). *Regiebuch zu Sumurun: Eine arabische Nacht*. Leipzig and Frankfurt am Main: Deutsche Nationalbibliothek
Freytag, Gustav. 1895. *Freytag's Technique of the Drama: An Exposition of Dramatic Composition and Art*. Chicago: Griggs.
Freytag, Gustav. 1897. *Die Technik des Dramas*. Leipzig: S. Hirzel.
Friedrich, Hölderlin. 1987. Anmerkungen zum Ödipus 1804. In *Dramaturgische Schriften des 19. Jahrhunderts*, edited by Klaus Hammer, 27–32. Berlin: Henschel Verlag.
Frietsch, Wolfram. 2009. Intersubjektivität und Macht: Eine phänomenologische Untersuchung basierend auf Edmund Husserls "Die Krisis der europäischen Wissenschaften und die transzendentale Phänomenologi" bezogen auf magische Diskursfelder im Umkreis der Ethnologie als Raum "wilden Denkens" in der Kultur. Gaggenau, Germany: Scientia Nova Verlag Neue Wiss.
Gebauer, Gunter, and Christoph Wulf. 1995. *Mimesis, Poiesis, Autopoiesis*. Berlin: Akademie Verlag.
Gellrich, Michelle. 1988. *Tragedy and Theory: The Problem of Conflict Since Aristotle*. Princeton NJ: Princeton University Press.
Gindl-Tatárová, Zuzana. 2008. *Practical Dramaturgy: Praktická Dramaturgia*. Bratislava: Film and Television Faculty VSMU, The Academy of Music and Performing Arts.
Goldstein, Leonard. 1988. *The Social and Cultural Roots of Linear Perspective*. Minneapolis MN: MEP Publications.
Grosz, Wilhelm, and Béla Balász. 2006. *Achtung Aufnahme!!: Tragikomödie*. Frankfurt am Main: Universitätsbibliothek Johann Christian Senckenberg.
Haarmann, Hermann. 1991. *Erwin Piscator und die Schicksale der Berliner Dramaturgie: Nachträge zu einem Kapitel deutscher Theatergeschichte*. Munich: Fink.

Hammer, Klaus, ed. 1968. *Dramaturgische Schriften des 18. Jahrhunderts.* Berlin: Henschel Verlag.
Hammer, Klaus, ed. 1987. *Dramaturgische Schriften des 19. Jahrhunderts.* Berlin: Henschel Verlag.
Hay, Peter. 1983. "American Dramaturgy: A Critical Re-Appraisal." *Performing Arts Journal* 7 (3): 7. https://doi.org/10.2307/3245146.
Hegel, Georg Wilhelm Friedrich. 1971. *Vorlesungen über die Ästhetik I/II.* Stuttgart: Reclam.
Hegel, Georg Wilhelm Friedrich. 2003. *Die Poesie.* Stuttgart: Reclam.
Hennig, Anke. 2013. Cinematicity of Speech and Visibility of Literature: The Poetics of Soviet Film Scripts of the Early Sound Film Era. *Cinematicity in Media History*, 118–132.
Herrmann, Max. 1998. "Das theatralische Raumerlebnis". In *Max Herrmann und die Anfänge der Theaterwissenschaft*, edited by Stefan Corssen, 270–81. Tübingen: Max Niemeyer.
Heuner, Ulf. 1999. *Stefan Corssen: Max Herrmann und die Anfänge der Theaterwissenschaft.* Marburg, Germany: Philipps-Universität Marburg; Schüren.
Hevesy, Iván. 1925. *A filmjáték esztétikája és dramaturgiája.* Budapest: Athanaeum.
Horace [Horatius Flaccus], Quintus. 2002. *Ars Poetica: Die Dichtkunst: Lateinisch/Deutsch.* Trans. and edited by Eckart Schäfer. Stuttgart: Reclam.
Huss, Bernhard, Florian Mehltretter, and Gerhard Regn. 2012. *Lyriktheorie(n) der italienischen Renaissance. Poetics in the Italian Renaissance.* Berlin and Boston: De Gruyter.
Jahjā Ibn-ʿAdī al-Mantiqī, Abū-Zakarījā. 1982. *La grande polémique antinestorienne.* Louvain: Bibliotheca Universitatis Lovanii.
Kahneman, Daniel. 2012. *Thinking, Fast and Slow.* London: Penguin.
Kemal, Salim. 2007. The Philosophical Poetics of Alfarabi, Avicenna and Averroes: The Aristotelian Reception. London: Routledge.
Klotz, Volker. 1980. *Geschlossene und offene Form im Drama.* 13th ed. Munich: Hanser Verlag.
Kueppers, Brigitte. 1980. "Max Reinhardt's Sumurun." *The Drama Review* 24 (1): 75–84. https://doi.org/10.2307/1145297.
Lada-Richards, Ismene. 2007. *Silent Eloquence: Lucian and Pantomime Dancing.* London: Duckworth.
Lessing, Gotthold Ephraim. 2011. "Hamburgische Dramaturgie (1767/68)". Stuttgart: Reclam.
Lidova, Natalia. 2014. "Natyashastra." *Oxford Bibliographies*, 29 September. https://www.oxfordbibliographies.com/view/document/obo-9780195399318/obo-978 0195399318-0071.xml. Accessed 18 August 2022.
Marievskaya, N. E. 2019. "Screenplay Theory: Cinema Is Born in Script." *Journal of Film Arts and Film Studies* 11 (1): 136–42. https://doi.org/10.17816/VGIK11 1136-142.
Matta Ibn Yūnus, Abu Bishr. 1887. "Poetica Aristotelis, Arabice, interprete Abu Bashar vel Bishr Matthaeo Dair-Qonnaensi." In *Analecta Orientalia ad Poeticam Aristoteleam* edited by David Samuel Margoliouth. London: D. Nutt.
Miami Vice. 1984–1989 (5 seasons). Created by Anthony Yerkovich. USA: Michael Mann Produtions, Universal Television.
Muni, Bharata. 2016. *Nāṭyaśāstram: A Treatise on Ancient Indian Dramaturgy and Histrionics.* Varanasi: Chaukhamba.

Nagler, Alois M. 1959. *A Source Book in Theatrical History.* New York: Dover.
Ninotschka. 1939. Written by Melchior Lengyel, Charles Brackett, Billy Wilder, Ernst Lubitsch. Directed by Ernst Lubitsch. USA: Metro-Goldwyn-Mayer.
North by Northwest. 1959. Written by Ernest Lehman. Directed by Alfred Hitchcock. USA: Metro-Goldwin-Mayer.
Plato. 2021. *The Republic.* Vachendorf, Germany: FilRougeViceversa.
Potolsky, Matthew. 2006. *Mimesis.* New York, London: Routledge.
Rabelais, Francois. 2016. *Gargantua and Pantagruel.* Dinslaken, Germany: Anboco.
Rancière, Jacques. 2009. "The Aesthetic Dimension: Aesthetics, Politics, Knowledge." *Critical Inquiry* 36 (1): 1–19. https://doi.org/10.1086/606120.
Rancière, Jacques. 2009. *The Aesthetic Unconscious.* Cambridge, UK: Polity.
Reichel, Peter, ed. 2000. *Studien zur Dramaturgie: Kontexte, Implikationen, Berufspraxis.* Tübingen: Narr.
Rohmer, Ralf. 2000. "'implizite' oder 'versteckte' Dramaturgien: Skizzierung eines wandelbaren Phänomens – Hypothesen zu seiner theaterhistorischen und theatertheoretischen Bestimmung." In *Studien zur Dramaturgie: Kontexte, Implikationen, Berufspraxis*, edited by Peter Reichel, 13–24. Tübingen: Gunther Narr.
Romanska, Magda. 2016a. "Introduction: Dramaturgy: an Overview of the Concept from Poetics to Smash". In *The Routledge Companion to Dramaturgy*, edited by Magda Romanska, 1–15. London: Routledge.
Romanska, Magda, ed. 2016b. *The Routledge Companion to Dramaturgy.* London: Routledge.
Schechner, Richard. 2010. *Performance Theory.* London: Routledge.
Schmitt, Arbogast. 2008a. "Einleitung". In Aristoteles 2008. *Poetik*, edited by Arbogast Schmitt, 45–192. Berlin: Akademie-Verlag.
Schmitt, Arbogast. 2008b. "Kommentar". In Artistoteles 2008. *Poetik*, edited by Arbogast Schmitt, 193–742. Berlin: Akademie-Verlag.
Schmitt, Arbogast. 2008c. "Vorwort". In Artistoteles 2008. *Poetik*, edited by Arbogast Schmitt, i–xiv. Berlin: Akademie-Verlag.
Shklovski, Victor B. n.d. "Die Temperatur des Films". In *FILM. Auge Kunst Sprache.: Filmdebatten der 20er Jahre in Sowjetrussland*, edited by Oksana Bulgakowa. Berlin: Filmkunsthaus Babylon e.v. Schneider.
Shutter Island. 2010. Written by Laeta Kalogridis. Directed by Martin Scorsese. USA: Paramount Pictures.
Stutterheim, Kerstin. 2015. *Handbuch angewandter Dramaturgie: Vom Geheimnis des filmischen Erzählens; Film, TV und Games.* Frankfurt am Main, Bern and Vienna: PL Academic Research.
Stutterheim, Kerstin. 2019. *Modern Film Dramaturgy: An Introduction.* Berlin and New York: Peter Lang.
Stutterheim, Kerstin, and Silke Kaiser. 2011. *Handbuch der Filmdramaturgie: Das Bauchgefühl und seine Ursachen*, 2nd ed. Frankfurt am Main: Peter Lang.
Sumurûn. 1910. Written by Friedrich Freksa. Directed by Max Reinhardt. Deutsche Bioskop GmbH.
Sumurun. 1920. Written by Hanss Kräly and Ernst Lubitsch. Directed by Ernst Lubitsch. Germany: Projections-AG "Union" fuer UFA.
Szatkowski, Janek. 2019. *A Theory of Dramaturgy.* London and New York: Routledge.
Szekfü, András. 2018. "Iván Hevesy and the Revolution of the 'Second Plan'". *Cinema Journal* 57 (3): 54–60.

Szondi, Peter. 1978. Theorie *des modernen Dramas, 1880–1950*. 13th ed. Frankfurt am Main: Suhrkamp.
Szondi, Peter. 1987. *Theory of the Modern Drama: A Critical Edition*. Minneapolis: University of Minnesota Press.
Tally, Robert T. 2013.*Spatiality*. London and New York: Routledge.
The Fifth Element. 1997. Written by Luc Besson and Robert Mark Kamen. France, UK Gaumont, Pinewood Studios.
The Ghost Writer. 2010. Written by Robert Harris and Roman Polanski. Directed by Roman Polanski. France, Germany, UK: R. P. Productions, France 2 Cinéma, Studio Babelsberg.
The Milky Way (La voie lactée). 1969. Written by Luis Buñuel and Jean-Claude Carrière. Directed by Luis Buñuel. France-Italy-West Germany: Greenwich Film Productions.
The Shining. 1980. Written by Diane Johnson and Stanley Kubrick. Directed by Stanley Kubrick. UK, USA: Warner Bros.
The Shop around the Corner. 1940. Written by Samson P. Raphaelson. Directed by Ernst Lubitsch. USA: Metro-Goldwyn-Mayer Studios.
To Be or Not To Be. 1942. Written by Ernst Justus P. Mayer. Directed by Ernst Lubitsch. USA: Romaine Film Corporation.
Top Gun: Maverick. 2022. Written by Ehren Kruger, Eric Warren Singer, and Christopher McQuarrie. Directed by Joseph Kosinski. USA, Canada: Paramount Pictures, Skydance Media, Jerry Bruckheimer Films.
Turkin, Vladimir K. 2007[1938]. Драматургия Кино [*Dramaturgy of the Cinema*]. Reprint. Moscow: VGIK.
Weimann, Robert. 1988. *Shakespeare und die Macht der Mimesis: Autorität u. Repräsentation im elisabethanischen Theater*. Berlin and Weimar: Aufbau-Verlag.
Wöhrmann, Klaus-Rüdiger. 1967. *Hölderlins Wille zur Tragödie*. München, Wilhelm Fink Verlag.

Open Access This chapter is licensed under the terms of the Creative Commons Attribution 4.0 International License (http://creativecommons.org/licenses/by/4.0/), which permits use, sharing, adaptation, distribution and reproduction in any medium or format, as long as you give appropriate credit to the original author(s) and the source, provide a link to the Creative Commons license and indicate if changes were made.

The images or other third party material in this chapter are included in the chapter's Creative Commons license, unless indicated otherwise in a credit line to the material. If material is not included in the chapter's Creative Commons license and your intended use is not permitted by statutory regulation or exceeds the permitted use, you will need to obtain permission directly from the copyright holder.

CHAPTER 37

Screenwriting Pedagogy in the United States: In Search of the Missing Pieces

Paul Joseph Gulino

37.1 Introduction

Between 1900 and 1950, a confluence of elements led to the creation of an extremely effective training system for screenwriters: the studio system. Writers were hired into writing departments and worked on a large number of scripts, supervised by and in collaboration with other writers. The high volume of production created a valuable feedback loop—writers learned from experience, from audience response to their work, from mentors, and from their collaborators. The writing community of this period constituted a repository of practical knowledge of the craft that faded when studios closed their writing departments in the 1950s and vanished by the 1970s when that generation died off. Since the 1970s, film schools and screenwriting manuals have arisen to fill the gap in training, but these approaches have significant blind spots and limitations. A successful film school is one that can recreate in some capacity the feedback loop of the studio system.

37.2 Early Screenwriting Pedagogy

The primary means by which the earliest filmmakers learned the craft of cinematic storytelling was by watching movies—those they created, and those created by their peers and rivals. These filmmakers—and the writers brought

P. J. Gulino (✉)
Chapman University, Orange, CA, USA
e-mail: gulino@chapman.edu

into the process (in the first decade of the twentieth century)—thus learned by experiment and experience. They had their eye on how the public responded to their work, what their rivals in the industry were up to and how the public responded to *that*, and what theater owners were telling them about audience response to what they created. Their paychecks depended on how well they could read these inputs.

Because the films of the 1900–1914 were produced in high volume and distributed quickly (they were mostly only ten to twenty minutes in length— one or two reels of film), a rapid and highly effective feedback loop was established that allowed screenwriters and their studio collaborators to learn from their successes and failures and those of their rivals and undertake any innovations they thought would get them a leg up on the competition in a ferociously competitive marketplace. Frances Marion, one of the most successful screenwriters of the studio era, recalls the learning process this way:

> In my first years with the studios, not only were there no textbooks that might aid me in discovering what were the essentials for the screen story, but, worse yet, there seemed to be no one, not even among those persons most closely concerned with picture production, who had any clear idea of what they were. Producers, directors and writers had to proceed on a rule of thumb basis and to learn through experience. (Marion 1938, 21)

In his 1981 memoir *Moving Pictures*, screenwriter Budd Schulberg described his experience of the feedback loop this way:

> I grew up on the sidewalk conferences outside the theater that followed the previews of pictures still in the process of final editing. My father, his director, film editor, and various assistants would pass around the preview cards on which the audience had written their capsule critiques... There were no film schools in those days. But those sidewalk postmortems offered thorough lessons in practical filmmaking. (Schulberg 1981, 190)

By the 1910s, demand for movies was so strong that production companies began to create writing departments (*stables*) staffed with writers whose job was both to generate scripts (*scenarios*) for production, and to assess various literary properties and newsworthy events for their filmic potential. These communities of professional writers created yet another pedagogical input—peers, i.e., fellow film writers with whom to exchange ideas, gags, and techniques. There were also opportunities for mentorship in writing departments, with junior writers mentored by senior writers as to the ins and outs of the craft before they moved up (or out). Joseph L. Mankiewicz served as supervisor for junior writers at Paramount, after he had cut his teeth writing titles for silent pictures and moving up in the studio to writing screenplays and producing (Stempel 2000, 124–25). Lamar Trotti was mentored by screenwriting veteran Dudley Nichols at Fox at the start of his career (Stempel 2000, 79–80). Ben Hecht teamed up with fellow playwright and screenwriter Charles

MacArthur to run a script "factory", overseeing the work of junior writers, during the 1930s (Norman 2007, 96–97).

By the 1920s, a writer lucky enough to be awarded a contract at a studio was given an opportunity to receive training from top professionals in the business, from peers, from producers in touch with how material is playing with the public, and from the success or failure of films they watched, including films they themselves wrote. Further, due to the constant flow of scriptwriting assignments from studio bosses (who wanted to make sure writers were earning their salaries), such a writer would also experience a considerable amount of practice at the craft.

Thus, the studio system proved a formidable kind of film school. It had its flaws, especially with the staff writers treated as interchangeable parts in a machine, brought in and fired from myriad projects and having their work rewritten and/or mangled. But it created a deep bench of highly proficient and accomplished screenwriters.

The writers who managed to sign with the studios during the 1900–1950 period benefited from one element that writers of later periods lacked: a robust "feeder" system by which they were able to secure a considerable amount of recognition and experience as professional writers even before embarking on screenwriting careers. Many scenario writers hired by production companies and studios in the first decades of the twentieth century had journalism backgrounds (Stempel 2000, 4–5). This made sense, as journalists, like professional screenwriters, wrote stories, had to write them fast, succinctly and on deadline, were on salary, and had to work collaboratively with a boss (editor), who subjected their work to rewrites. Newspapers were thriving during those days, providing a large pool of available writers.

Theater provided another training experience for those who would become screenwriters. Live theater was a thriving money-making industry in the first half of the twentieth century, and when talking pictures arrived in the late 1920s, writers who could manage dialogue were in considerable demand in Hollywood. Writers could also make a living writing short stories throughout those decades, through publication in a large number of magazines. By the 1920s, writers could also cut their teeth in radio drama.

Writers of note tended to work in many of these forms. Frances Marion was a visual artist, wrote short stories and worked as a journalist before writing for films. Budd Schulberg wrote short stories and worked as a journalist. Ben Hecht was a journalist, novelist, and Broadway playwright. Herman Mankiewicz was a journalist, critic, short story writer, and playwright. Samson Raphaelson was a journalist, advertising copy writer and Broadway playwright. Nunnally Johnson published fifty-two short stories in the *Saturday Evening Post* before being hired at Twentieth Century-Fox (Froug 1972, 243).

The first part of the twentieth century was thus rich with opportunities for writers to hone their skills professionally *before* embarking on training in the craft of screenwriting in the studio system. It is worth noting that in a college-level playwriting class that playwright and screenwriter Samson Raphaelson taught in the spring of 1948 at the University of Illinois, out of thirty students, half had already written radio plays and eleven had already sold their writing in some capacity (see Raphaelson 2015).

Given the highly literate nature of the writers who were being fed into the studio training system, and the intensive and effective feedback loop it provided, it should not be surprising that the craft of screenwriting would be practiced at a very a high level during the studio period.

37.3 Post-Studio Interregnum

Studio writing departments were closed in the late 1940s and early 1950s when studios were forced to divest themselves of their theater chains—and thus a guaranteed market for their productions—as a consequence of the 1948 anti-trust decision in *The United States v. Paramount Pictures*. The loss of this training system proved only the first in a wave of challenges for aspiring screenwriters in the 1950s and 1960s. Opportunities for the kind of preliminary writing experience that had fed studio system became rarer. Theater production was in decline, as were short story publications and radio drama. Newspapers were consolidating and laying off reporters. Some who managed to develop professional writing backgrounds made a jump to professional screenwriting with no intermediary training of the kind studios had hitherto provided. William Goldman was a novelist who had to seek out a book on screenplay format in order to figure out how to do his first adaptation for the screen (Brady 1981, 94). Robert Benton and David Newman were journalists before writing *Bonnie and Clyde*. The only real training in screenwriting such writers received was the method used since cinema's infancy: watching movies. Benton and Newman, for example, immersed themselves in European cinema (Stempel, 186). A professional writer making the jump into screenwriting had to rely on any lessons they absorbed—consciously or not—from a lifetime of watching movies, and wherever their imaginations took them. The result was work that tended to be more idiosyncratic and less consistent than that of the previous generation of writers.

It did not help that a more theoretical assault on the craft of screenwriting erupted during the 1960s in the guise of the *auteur* theory, which celebrated directors as the authors of film and banished screenwriters to a shadow existence whose role in the filmmaking process was a dubious one at best. While movies with traditional storytelling characteristics continued to dominate the box office in the United States, the discourse about screenwriting, which had existed since the 1910s in the publication of numerous scenario writing manuals and in regular columns in magazines such as *The Moving Picture World*, and continued on in the studios, had no purchase anywhere. In order to think about a craft, it is first necessary to understand that it is *possible* to think about it.

During the 1950s, the new medium of television provided some training opportunities reminiscent of the studio approach. Instead of a stable of writers, television offered staff writing positions on specific shows, and a writer lucky enough to land a contract on a show could enjoy the one-on-one mentorship from senior writers, collaboration with peers, frequent writing assignments, fast production turnaround that created a feedback loop so vital to learning in the days of the studios. Post-studio screenwriters such as Frank Pierson, Paddy Chayefsky, Woody Allen, Neil Simon, James L. Brooks, and Buck Henry began in television (Brady 1981).

Television had its limitations in training *screenwriters*, though. Staff writers in television were not given the variety of tasks those trained in the studio stables were. A staff writer in television worked with a shorter script length, the programs generally limited to 24 or 45 minutes, using characters and a basic setting already created. This is compared to the demands of the studio system, where writers were handling 90- to 120-minute features with newly invented characters and plots, or those adapted from novels or other media. Television writers also had to work within the constraints of network time slots, commercial interruptions, and sponsor and network restrictions about content. Finally, television writing tended to emphasize dialogue and de-emphasized visual elements, given the small screen size.

Oddly enough, breakdown in the professional training process and the theoretical assault on the craft of screenwriting occurred at precisely a time when, because producers were interested connecting with the "second youth market" of the late 1960s, they were more open to submissions of screenplays by unknowns than in previous periods (Stempel 2000, 190–91).

37.4 The Return of the Screenwriting Manual

In the 1970s, screenwriting manuals started to appear to answer the obvious need for screenwriting pedagogy in the absence of institutional training and in the presence of opportunities for submitting screenplays. For the purposes of this chapter, I will focus on three that have had widespread influence in popular screenwriting discourse.

Syd Fields' *Screenplay: The Foundations of Screenwriting* (1979) had wide influence early in this cycle of publications, advocating what he called the *paradigm*, consisting of beginning, middle and end (corresponding to three acts) and two plot points (marking the end of acts one and two). Although the book contained chapters on creating and building characters and writing dramatic scenes, the bulk of it dealt with structure. The notion of the *three-act structure*, supposedly derived from Aristotle's *Poetics*, became popularized by the book in screenwriting discourse.

In 1992, Christopher Vogler expanded on a memorandum he wrote while employed at Disney Animation and published it as *The Writer's Journey: Mythic Structure for Storytellers and Screenwriters*. Inspired by the work of Joseph Campbell, this was an attempt to demonstrate how Campbell's ideas about the "hero's journey" and Jungian character archetypes set forth in his book on comparative mythology, *The Hero with A Thousand Faces*, could help aspiring screenwriters develop their stories. While this approach retained the three acts, it expanded on what events those acts should contain, numbering twelve in all. Buoyed by its association with Campbell, and Vogler's association with Disney, the book has had widespread influence on screenwriting discourse.

A third highly influential manual was published by Blake Snyder in 2005.[1] This volume, *Save the Cat!*, did Vogler three better, articulating fifteen "beats" in his book. Further, while Vogler claimed his story approach was more a suggestive guideline than an invariable formula, Snyder's claims are more definitive (Snyder 2005, 96).

Positive aspects of learning the craft of screenwriting from books is that it is inexpensive and can give a writer with no exposure to screenwriting other than watching movies a plan by which they can get started. The downside is that there is no feedback loop by which the craft or practice of screenwriting can be refined. Knowledge of certain concepts alone does not result in a capacity to practice the craft effectively any more than knowledge of music theory alone can make someone proficient at playing the flute.

The other downside is that the usefulness of the knowledge gained is constrained by the depth of insight the books provide, and the way they are used by aspiring writers (i.e., will they be viewed as a source of insight or of formulae?) The arguments made by Field are based primarily on his experience as a reader during the 1970s. Vogler served as a reader during the 1980s (in addition to being inspired by Joseph Campbell's work). Snyder's book emerged from his experience successfully navigating the market for spec screenplays in the 1990s. Thus, the main frame of reference of these writers is generally limited to screenplays written long after the end of the studio training period. Further, despite Vogler's assertion that his book (1998) is a "guideline… not a cookbook recipe" and that "it's possible to write good stories that don't exhibit every feature of the Hero's Journey" (237–38), he also refers to it as a "writing manual" and "practical guide" (xi)—guidance that goes on for almost three hundred detailed pages and provides no clues as to the consequences of veering from it.

One noteworthy feature all three of these volumes share is in their approach to the very issue they are known for: structure. Syd Field defines "dramatic structure" as "A LINEAR ARRANGEMENT OF RELATED INCIDENTS, EPISODES OR EVENTS LEADING TO A DRAMATIC RESOLUTION" (Field, 10, all caps in original). Vogler and Snyder provide more details about these incidents, episodes, and events. None of the three books deals explicitly with the other crucial element of story structure—information disclosure to the audience. In doing so, they focus primarily on the story as against the story*telling*, the narrative over the narration, the *fabula* and not the *syuzhet*. The problem with assuming that all information disclosure is linear can perhaps

---

[1] This book became so popular its influence was ruled by critic Peter Suderman in *Slate* in 2013: "Save the Movie! The 2005 screenwriting book that's taken over Hollywood—and made every movie feel the same" (Suderman 2013).

best be illustrated by means of a joke (which is an extremely economical form of storytelling):

> When I die, I want to die peacefully in my sleep, like my grandmother, and not screaming in terror like the passengers in grandma's car.

If we were to tell this story by disclosing the linear arrangement of incidents, episodes, and events, it would be rendered like this:

> My grandmother was driving her car. The car had passengers in it. She fell peacefully asleep while driving. The car crashed. My grandmother was killed without even waking up, but the passengers in the car were wide awake when the crash happened and screamed in terror before they died. When I die, I want to die peacefully in my sleep, like my grandmother, and not screaming in terror like the passengers in her car.

The second telling of the story has a beginning, middle, and end, and all the important component incidents disclosed, but its impact on a reader is vastly different from that derived from the first telling. If the desired outcome is a laugh from the audience, it is unlikely to succeed. One could *restructure* the story, but if that meant simply rearranging the events, it would not lead to any improvement. Only by rearranging the *disclosure* of events is it likely to evoke a laugh.

Tellingly, none of these books discusses dramatic irony, a tool central to considerations about story vs. storytelling, and the wellspring of great films from Ernst Lubitsch to Billy Wilder to Alfred Hitchcock—filmmakers who were either gone or in their twilight when these writers were developing their advice about writing screenplays.

Another limiting characteristic of these three volumes is their assumption that the values of the audience are always in alignment with those of the main character. This will tend to channel writers into a narrow path in which, for example, the main character undergoes an "all is lost" and "dark night of the soul" (Snyder 2005, 70) or "ordeal" (Vogler 1998, 14) at the end of Act II. If the audience is not onboard with the character's main objective, the "all is lost moment" for the *audience* might be when the character *achieves* their objective, rather than fears not getting it. Under this guidance, great films such as *The Apartment* could not have been written. To the extent that these books influence how produced movies are written, aspiring writers studying those movies will conclude that the movies validate the advice in the books, leading to an echo chamber in screenwriting discourse in which crucial aspects of previous knowledge of the craft is lost.

An alternative approach to screenwriting pedagogy emerged in the 1970s in the United States under the influence of František (Frank) Daniel, a writer and producer who was one of the founders of the Czech national film school, FAMU, and later inaugural dean of the American Film Institute and artistic director of the Sundance Institute. He learned the craft of screenwriting by immersing himself in cinema (including American films of the studio era) and through the study of theatrical drama, and he enjoyed the kind of feedback loop of production and exhibition of his own screenplays and films he produced in the Czech film industry, very similar to that enjoyed by writers in the studio system.

Daniel wrote no books in English. His approach was articulated in David Howard's books *The Tools of Screenwriting* (1995, co-authored by Edward Marbley) and *How to Build A Great Screenplay* (2004), and in my own volume, *Screenwriting: The Sequence Approach* (2004). Daniel rejected the notion of "plot points" and developed what might be called an "audience-centered" approach. The first act functions to create a "main tension" in the audience; the second act sustains that tension, and the third act resolves it and explores the consequences of that resolution. Anticipating David Bordwell's linking of constructivist psychology to audience comprehension of a film, Daniel argued that the screenwriter's job is to make the audience keen observers of detail, exploiting its tendency to put clues together and anticipate the direction of the story. Audience engagement and "participation" in the story was central. Daniel also articulated many screenwriting techniques used in the studio period, identifying them with terminology derived from theater or otherwise improvised. Among these is the "sequence" approach to planning and writing a screenplay, which he derived from his understanding of the classical Hollywood approach of writing a multi-reel feature in a way that each reel ("sequence") had its own dramatic integrity.

The advantage of Daniel's "audience-centered" approach over those espousing a particular set of story moments lies in its flexibility. The ways in which a writer can use its various tools and concepts to seize and maintain audience participation in a story is limited only by the writer's imagination. Daniel's approach can also account for the success of the large number of successful films that do not follow the paradigms laid out by advocates of "story-centered" approaches. Finally, its conceptual approach applies to the writing of series as well as feature films; for example, a writer who understands how to create and release tension in an audience can do so within a two-hour feature or across multiple episodes.

Despite their limitations, screenwriting manuals can provide aspiring screenwriters with a crucial first step in learning the craft, notwithstanding the inherent limitations of any particular book, or of book learning generally in the absence of an effective feedback loop.

37.5 The Rise of the Film School

Although courses in screenwriting date back to 1915, when Columbia University offered a course in "Photoplay Composition" (Saccone 2021, 3), it wasn't until the 1960s that film schools started to emerge and play a significant role in the training of film scholars and filmmakers—though not, initially, screenwriters. It was not until the 1970s that veteran writer-producer William Froug arrived at UCLA and built up its screenwriting program (Crane 2013). Frank Daniel was founding director of the American Film Institute in 1969, and established the screenwriting program at Columbia University's Film Division in 1979. USC did not have a graduate screenwriting program till Daniel, by then serving as its dean, established one in 1989 under the direction of David Howard. Chapman University's Film School launched its degrees in screenwriting a decade after that.

The primary instructional vehicle for teaching screenwriting in an academic environment has been the writing workshop, in which student work is read and critiqued by the teacher and fellow students. It is, in effect, an opportunity to revive the studio approach, with its stables of writers and the senior writer instructing the junior writers in the craft—in this case with the teacher serving the role of the senior writer and fellow students the peers.

There are, however, significant differences that make this revival difficult to pull off in practice. For one thing, while the teacher and classmates provide a ready audience for a writer, there is no outside audience—the paying public— to provide feedback. Another involves the roles the students and teachers play. In the studio system, a junior writer was an employee of the studio and was learning on the job. The writer served the needs of the studio (or got fired). The senior writer who offered instruction was the junior writers' boss (and the producers were of course the bosses of all the writers). In contrast, in a writing workshop, it is the students who are, effectively, the bosses. The students (or their parents) hire the teacher to deliver instruction. The teacher serves as more of a highly paid consultant, helping to guide the students to bring their projects to fruition. Whereas in the studio system a senior writer might take over a project and rewrite the work of another writer, in a workshop setting this is strictly forbidden. A teacher can only instruct and advise.

This fact has given rise to an ethos in film schools that was completely unknown in the days of the studio-trained writer: nurturing the writer as a person. The mission of Chapman University's Film School is "to open the minds and nurture the dreams of students, preparing them for a creative life in the film and media arts". The mission of the University of Southern California's School of Cinematic Arts is "to develop and articulate the creative, scholarly and entrepreneurial principles and practices of film, television and interactive media". University of California, Los Angeles "develops outstanding humanistic storytellers, industry leaders and scholars whose diverse, innovative voices enlighten, engage and inspire change for a better world". At New York University: "We prepare and empower students to embark on journeys toward their creative and professional goals by emphasizing the pursuit of knowledge, creative exploration, and personal development". No studio ever paid Nunnally Johnson, Ben Hecht, or Frances Marion to pursue their personal development. They were paid to deliver product that audiences would pay to see. But teachers at a film school, operating without the benefit of a paying public audience, have evolved a very different role.

Further, if a screenwriting instructor is using a screenwriting manual as a text, the instruction may serve simply to reinforce what is in the book, since, in the absence of public audience response, the book itself becomes part of the feedback loop by which writing is judged. This of course leaves the workshop dependent on the quality of the book chosen. Indeed, in a 1996 memorandum to the writing faculty at the University of Southern California, then-chair John Furia, Jr., discouraged the use of Syd Fields' book and any others that used what he described as "formula" approach, as they do not encourage originality.

37.6 Comparing the Craft of Screenwriting Across Eras

Which type of training is more effective—the studio system or the current hodgepodge of academic and book learning? Is it even possible to answer that question?

Screenwriter Budd Schulberg claims to have seen every movie produced by every studio each year during the early 1930s. His assessment: "We saw the godawful (30 percent), the passable (45 percent), the good (15 percent), and the better-than-good to excellent (that happy 10 percent)" (Schulberg 1981, 317). Any such survey in the twenty-first century would properly include the cinema of series/streaming, since this form has largely escaped the peculiar constraints of broadcast network series noted above and are viewed on screens of much bigger size and better quality than traditional television, and is thus comparable to the feature length cinematic form. But the staggering volume of production of series and traditional features precludes the possibility of a single person viewing it all. Further, Schulberg himself died in 2009 and can be of no help offering a direct comparison.

All the practitioners of the studio period are dead. No one can hire Samson Raphaelson and a currently active writer to write a script based on a given premise and compare the two. It may be possible to compare remakes to their original, but these exist in a special relationship with that original work, and the reason they are made is because the original was successful.

Beyond that, it is not easy to articulate what knowledge or rubrics, precisely, the studio system operated under—a relatively easy task in current discourse given the plethora of books and academic programs. A manual from that period, *How to Write and Sell Film Stories* (1938), written by Frances Marion, conveys the lessons on screenwriting she had learned working with Irving Thalberg, according to Marion biographer Cari Beauchamp (1998, 341). Thalberg guided the development of many films as head of production at MGM in the 1920s and 30s, and thus had a wide influence on screenwriting practice during that period. Marion's book does not contain anything like the kind of detailed lists of events or incidents found in Vogler and Snyder and makes no mention of act structure. The closest it comes is:

Plot is the design, pattern or outline of the story action; it is a statement of the problems or obstacles that confront certain specific characters, their reaction to those problems or obstacles, and the result. It is a series of events or situations affected by the characters involved and affecting them, with the situations building up to a climax. It is a string of relevant and dramatic situations, preferably rising out of character and affecting it, and woven together in such sequence and ascending strength as to make an interesting story. (Marion 1938, 51; emphasis in original)

Just as Steven Price has noted a variation in the screenplay format in the various studios in the 1930s (Price 2013, 144–45), Tom Stempel has identified what might be called "house styles" in the storytelling. MGM under Thalberg, for example, privileged the memorable scene over plot, resulting in a more episodic approach. At Fox, the emphasis was on "narrative movement", yielding a "smooth flow". Warner Brothers' stories were "insistent and driving" (Stempel 2000, 78). Ethan Mordden, in *The Hollywood Studios*, described the different experience of the Marx Brothers at two studios. "A Marx Brothers Movie is a series of sketches on a theme [at Paramount]. But a Thalberg movie [at MGM] is a story clearly told" (Mordden 2013, 113).

Knowledge of a craft is one thing, though, and proficiency at a craft is another. Because each story is unique, universal principles guiding their creation are of little use. When to reveal information, when to withhold it, the limitless choices of character and situation make the most effective storytelling strategy a moving target. Frequent practice and a sturdy feedback loop can help a writer recognize certain storytelling situations or patterns and make informed choices based on knowledge of options borne from experience.

One dictum in the screenwriting trade—that it is a visual form of writing—has a long history. "Say it with props. Say it with actions" was a sign that hung over scenario writers' desks during the silent era, according to Scott Eyman (Eyman 1997, 17). Writers trained in the studio system did seem adept at using props, actions, blocking, and other visual elements when approaching the writing of the dramatic scene. In *Screenplay*, Syd Field stresses "A screenplay is a STORY TOLD WITH PICTURES" (1979, 7, all caps in the original) and "[y]ou must find ways to reveal your character's conflicts *visually*" (23) or "reveal them by their actions" (28). Another influential manual of the twenty-first century, *Story*, by Robert McKee, has this emphatic advice on the subject: "'Show, don't tell' is the ultimate creative task: to write in a purely dramatic and visual way, to show a natural world of natural human being behavior, to express the complexity of life *without telling*" (McKee 2006, 370, italics in the original). Such a criterion might provide the basis for a comparison of current screenwriting craft to that of the studio period, focusing on the writing of scenes rather than the broader structural elements discussed above.

Examining two films written about a similar subject, or with similar story objectives, both of which achieved acclaim in their time, might provide insight, however imprecise, on the use of the tools of visual writing (actions, blocking, props, costumes, and atmosphere) to tell a story and reveal character, executed under two different training methods.

37.6.1 Hacksaw Ridge *vs.* Sergeant York

One such comparison can be made between *Hacksaw Ridge* (2016), which was about a conscientious objector from Virginia during World War II, and *Sergeant York* (1941), about a conscientious objector from Tennessee during World War I. Both were based on real individuals, from the same general Southeastern region of the United States. The stories the two films tell is very different, but both contain a succession of three scenes early on with nearly identical story content: the main character encounters a woman and is smitten, reports to his family that he is going to marry her (and she does not know it yet), and then returns to woo her.

Hacksaw Ridge was credited to Robert Schenkkan and Andrew Knight, the former of whom won a Humanitas Prize, a Pulitzer Prize, a Tony, and a WGA Award. He earned a BA in Drama and an MFA in Theatre Arts. Knight is a veteran television writer and producer. The film itself was nominated for Best Picture by the Motion Picture Academy.

Sergeant York was credited to Abem Finkel, Harry Chandlee, Howard Koch, and John Huston, all products of the studio system, with Koch getting preparatory experience as a playwright and radio writer, working with Huston on the latter. The film was nominated for Best Picture and Best Screenplay by the Motion Picture Academy.

A viewing of the comparable scenes reveals that while both employ the use of props and some blocking, the scenes in the 2016 film are generally static and dialogue driven. They also lack much in the way of conflict. The response of characters to conflict is a way of visually revealing the inner lives of those characters. In *Sergeant York,* the writers employ actions, blocking, and additional characters to develop conflict in the scenes. The reactions of other characters to the main character's behavior yield insight into their pre-existing life patterns and relationships and help externalize what is internal. There is even brief use of dramatic irony in the 1941 script.

Based on the criterion of visual writing, the scenes written forty years before Syd Field's *Screenplay* succeed in using props, actions, reactions, blocking, and conflict to reveal character and tell the story with pictures substantially more effectively than the scenes written for the 2016 film.

37.6.2 Sunset Boulevard *vs.* Hacks

Another example may perhaps be even more useful, even though it involves the comparison of the first part of a feature film and a series pilot—in this case the first thirty minutes of *Sunset Boulevard* (1950) and the first thirty minutes (first episode) of *Hacks* (2021). Both involve a young writer in Hollywood who is desperate for a writing job, tries various means to get one, and finally winds up in the employ of an aging female star.

The *Hacks* episode ("There Is No Line"), credited to Lucia Aniello (who also directed), Paul W. Downs and Jen Statsky, won a primetime Emmy for Outstanding Writing for a Comedy Series. All three writers had a decade of experience writing for various television shows prior to *Hacks*. *Sunset Boulevard*, credited to Billy Wilder (who also directed), Charles Brackett, and D.M. Marshman, Jr., won an Oscar for Best Writing, Story and Screenplay. Wilder and Brackett were veterans of the studio training system.

Like the scenes in *Hacksaw Ridge,* those in *Hacks* make little use of blocking, actions, props, or costumes to tell the story with pictures: they are almost entirely dialogue driven. There is well-developed conflict in the scenes that unfold, yet what the characters' reactions to those conflicts reveal about their characters is ambiguous at best. Ava (Hannah Einbinder) is in danger of losing her house due to unemployment, but when her manager Jimmy (Paul W. Downs) offers her a gig as a joke writer for a Las Vegas star Deborah Vance (Jean Smart), she rejects it without even asking any details. Perhaps she has very strict standards? Perhaps she is too vain? Too neurotic? Detached from reality? Or is this the "refusal of the call" espoused by Vogler? Later, she accepts the offer, after spending the night with a delivery man. Perhaps she *is* just neurotic. More perplexing is Jimmy's behavior. Why does he lie to her about a non-existent job offer, then send her to Las Vegas at her own expense for a non-existent job interview? Perhaps he is a sadist? Neurotic? Hoping to be sued? Jimmy's action does create dramatic irony, but it is resolved quickly when Deborah Vance informs Ava there is no job. Equally perplexing is Deborah Vance's action: after conducting the interview for a non-existent job, she hires Ava—not because Ava demonstrated her comedic ability by sharing a joke, but after *Deborah* comes up with a better one. The story eventually gets where it needs to go—Ava working for Deborah. But to get there, the writers rely on seemingly irrational behavior by the three principal characters.

In contrast, the first thirty minutes of *Sunset Boulevard* constitute a master class in visual writing. The scene in which writer Joe Gillis (William Holden) pitches his story to Paramount producer Sheldrake (Fred Clark) is alive with physical action—Joe standing up to give his pitch, then pacing into the rear of the office in time for Betty (Nancy Olsen) to enter (and not see him); her entrance and exit, Sheldrake's retreat to the couch and Joe's pursuit thereto. There are also props—Sheldrake taking a pill with a glass of milk to visually confirm his ulcers, his use of a cigar, the folder containing the reader's report that Betty delivers and that Sheldrake pushes away from himself to reinforce his decision to reject it. The introduction of dramatic irony with Betty's entrance is logical and makes for a memorable introduction a major character. Later, at a golf course, Joe snatches the golf ball from his agent (Lloyd Gough) to make visible his anger and frustration, and finally at the mansion of Norma Desmond (Gloria Swanson), the screenwriters make much use of props (the car, the dead monkey and its bier, the coffin, the caviar and champagne, Norma's massive script) and blocking (Joe's journey up the stairs and to Norma's room, his subsequent retreat, her invitation to him to another room to read the script, Max's rolling out of the refreshments and relighting the room by closing the curtains and turning on a light).

In contrast to the characters in *Hacks,* the actions the characters in *Sunset Boulevard* take are logically motivated and give us insight into their inner lives.

In these two examples, using the visual writing criterion alone, acclaimed writers trained in the studio system outdid the acclaimed writers of the twenty-first century. Of course, these are not the only criteria, and these examples may not be representative or fair. David Bordwell *has* noted a decreased use of blocking in twenty-first century films, which he lays to an increase in the amount of camera movement (Bordwell 2006, 184–5), though none of the twenty-first century scenes discussed here utilized much camera movement, either. Perhaps these particular twenty-first century writers on these particular projects just opted not to write them in a visual way. It is also possible that current screenwriting practice suffers certain limitations because writers are unaware of some of the options available to them that writers trained in the system studio were aware of.

37.7 How to Teach Screenwriting

Writers during the studio era had a wider range of opportunities to gain writing experience and prove themselves through fiction, playwriting, radio writing, and journalism before embarking on training in screenwriting than their current day counterparts have. Once they earned a spot in a studio writing stable, they were given on-the-job training through a rigorous feedback loop. This, combined with the big demand for movies and resulting large number of productions (and thus a great deal of practice), resulted in much inventiveness and innovation. It is not surprising that such a system created a deep bench of highly accomplished screenwriters. That system is gone, though with the vertically integrated monopolies reappearing in the form of the streaming services, it is possible it may return in some form.

Meanwhile, there are workarounds that may help solve the problems that aspiring writers face. Screenwriting manuals are in abundance; these can be used as long as their content is not taken as formulae to be memorized and executed by rote. For the most part, writers currently lack the sort of proving ground provided in the studio era by the publication of short stories or the production of plays. But current digital technology offers the possibility of creating cinematic works that rival the technical quality of feature films and series—something unheard of before a decade ago. Response from festivals and online distribution can create a feedback loop so vital to the successful training of screenwriters during the studio period. Demonstrating one's ability to tell stories cinematically through small scale productions distributed online can and has led to writers obtaining deals with production entities for professional production and distribution. Issa Rae's web series *The Misadventures of*

Awkward Black Girl, for example, led to the launch on HBO of *Insecure* in 2016.

In the academy, there is an opportunity to create that all important feedback loop, utilizing this same technology. The advantages and limitations of the workshop feedback loop have been discussed. But film schools are in a position to launch online channels of their own to distribute dramatic series, for example, to the general public, much like campus radio stations in previous eras could compete with professional radio stations in their area. The key would be for the school to generate consistently high-quality content, something impossible if students—those *learning* to create high-quality content—are in charge, as is currently the case. The only way to get around this is if series generated by film schools was supported by funding. Promising students could apply to write for a campus series and be hired on something of a work-study basis. Teachers with professional writing experience could then serve as head writers collaborating with junior writers (hired students), who would have to deliver professional level content or be fired. The content thus created and distributed could generate feedback from the public otherwise lacking in the academic experience.

References

Brady, John. 1981. *The Craft of the Screenwriter*. New York: Simon & Schuster.
Beauchamp, Cari. 1998. *Without Lying Down: Frances Marion and the Powerful Women of Early Hollywood*. Los Angeles: University of California Press.
Bonnie and Clyde. 1967. Written by David Newman, Robert Benton. Directed by Arthur Penn. USA: Warner Bros. Pictures.
Bordwell, David, 2006, *The Way Hollywood Tells It*. Los Angeles: University of California Press.
Crane, Jennifer. 2013. "Influential UCLA Professor and Producer William Froug Dies at 91." *Daily Bruin*, 3 September. https://dailybruin.com/2013/09/03/influential-ucla-professor-and-producer-william-froug-dies-at-91. Accessed 22 May 2022.
Eyman, Scott. 1997. *The Speed of Sound: Hollywood and the Talkie Revolution 1926–1930*. New York: Simon & Schuster.
Field, Syd. 1979. *Screenplay: The Foundations of Screenwriting*. New York: Bantam Doubleday.
Froug, William. 1972. *The Screenwriter Looks at the Screenwriter*. Hollywood: Silman-James.
Gulino, Paul Joseph. 2004. *Screenwriting: The Sequence Approach. The Hidden Structure of Successful Screenplays*. New York and London: Continuum.
Hacks. 2021–present (3 seasons). Created by Lucia Aniello, Paul W. Downs, and Jen Statsky. USA: First Thought Productions, Paulilu Productions, Fremulon, 3 Arts Entertainment, Universal Television.
Hacksaw Ridge. 2016. Written by Robert Shenkkan and Andrew Knight. Directed by Mel Gibson. USA, Australia: Summit Entertainment, Cross Creek Pictures, Demarest Media, Argent Pictures, IM Global, AI Film, Vendian Entertainment, Kylin Pictures, Pandemonium Films, Permut Presentations Production

Howard, David. 2004. *How to Build a Great Screenplay:* A Master Class in Storytelling for Film. New York: St Martin's Press.
Howard, David, and Edward Marbley. 1995. *The Tools of Screenwriting: A Writer's Guide to the Craft and Elements of a Screenplay.* New York: St Martin's Press.
Insecure. 2016–2021 (5 seasons). Created by Issa Rae and Larry Wilmore. USA: Issa Rae Productions, Hoorae Media, Penny for Your Thoughts Entertainment, 3 Arts Entertainment, HBO Entertainment.
Marion, Frances. 1938. *How to Write and Sell Film Stories.* London: J. Miles.
Mordden, Ethan. 2013. *The Hollywood Studios: House Style in the Golden Age of the Movies.* New York: Knopf.
Norman, Marc. 2007. *What Happens Next: A History of American Screenwriting.* New York: Random House.
Price, Steven. 2013. *A History of the Screenplay.* New York: Palgrave MacMillan.
Raphaelson, Samson. 2015. *The Human Nature of Playwriting.* Tessellate Media. Kindle Edition.
Saccone, Kate. 2021. "Alice Guy Blache at Columbia University: One Hundred Years Later." *Women Film Pioneers Project*, 5 January. https://academiccommons.columbia.edu/doi/10.7916/d8-ef6g-3x82/download. Accessed 22 May 2022.
Schulberg, Budd. 1981. *Moving Pictures: Memories of a Hollywood Prince.* Briarcliff Manor, NY: Stein and Day.
Sergeant York. 1941. Written by Harry Chandlee, Abel Finkel, John Huston, and Howard E. Koch. Directed by Howard Hawks. USA: Warner Bros. Pictures.
Snyder, Blake. 2005. *Save the Cat! The Last Screenwriting Book You'll Ever Need.* Studio City, CA: Michael Wiese Productions.
Stempel, Tom, 2000. *FrameWork: A History of Screenwriting in the American Film*, 3rd ed. Syracuse, NY: First Syracuse University Press.
Suderman, Peter. 2013. "Save the Movie! The 2005 screenwriting book that's taken over Hollywood—and made every movie feel the same." *Slate*, July. https://slate.com/culture/2013/07/hollywood-and-blake-snyders-screenwriting-book-save-the-cat.html. Accessed 22 May 2022.
Sunset Boulevard. 1950. Written by Charles Brackett, Billy Wilder, and D. M. Marshman Jr. USA: Paramount Pictures.
The Apartment. 1960. Written by Billy Wilder and I. A. L. Diamond. Directed by Billy Wilder. USA: The Mirisch Company.
The Misadventures of Awkward Black Girl. 2011–2013 (2 seasons). Created by Issa Rae. USA: Hoorae.
Vogler, Christopher. 1998. *The Writer's Journey: Mythic Structure for Writers*, 2nd ed. Studio City, CA: Michael Wiese Productions.

CHAPTER 38

Screenwriting Manuals and Pedagogy in Italy from the 1930s to the End of the Twentieth Century

Mariapia Comand

38.1 Introduction

This study takes a pedagogical viewpoint to provide a historical excursus into the process of institutionalization and elevation of screenwriting to an academic discipline in Italy over a time span that goes from the 1930s to the end of the twentieth century. Since it covers such a long period of time, it is necessary to select the precise issues and fundamental turning points to focus on. From the multiple methodological possibilities, a historical and cultural analysis was chosen, the aim of which is to pinpoint some junctures in the history of screenwriting within the wider Italian context. Hence, the article will investigate the places, institutions, and figures that made the biggest mark at various historical turning points. It can be assumed that this process went through different impulses and transitional moments depending on the different formative agencies involved, schools of thought, cultural systems of reference, and educational aims, as well as the distinct milieus in which all these elements and aspects took shape and drew their strength.

In the 1930s and 40s, the engine behind the first pedagogical drive—prompted by a mixture of cultural, industrial, and ideological motivations—was the Centro Sperimentale di Cinematografia in Rome and its journal *Bianco e Nero*. Indeed, under the fascist dictatorship, film writing was considered the prime target for ideological control of the medium.

M. Comand (✉)
University of Udine, Udine, Italy
e-mail: mariapia.comand@uniud.it

Between the 1940s and 50s the ideology changed direction. In Italy, the Cold War led to an anti-communist alliance between the governing Christian Democrats, the Vatican, and US influence. All the same, ideology remained a decisive factor in the institutionalization of screenwriting, as demonstrated by the manuals and the educational activities organized at the many film clubs of the time.

Between the 1950s and 70s, the process begun in the 1930s to culturally legitimize screenwriting came to a head: scripts appeared in the catalogues of the smallest as well as the most authoritative Italian publishers, for economic as well as cultural reasons.

In the last decades of the century, screenwriters and trade associations seized the cultural limelight. They began to steer the debate, stepped up to teach screenwriting as a subject, and cemented their professional status once and for all.

As Paolo Russo wrote in 2014: "For 120 years, cinema has captivated us with its tales of dreams, adventures, love stories, and tragedies; thousands of stories that all start from a script. Despite their central role, screenwriting—a creative process, craft, technical skill, and industrial practice—and scripts have rarely received the attention they deserve", going on to say that "the majority of the most traditional critical studies have adopted a historiographical perspective, with a mainly biographic-monographic slant" (2014, 12). The goal of this study is to rise to the challenge and explore new paths. In so doing, it will examine two specific areas: publishing, in particular the manuals, journals, and series that have performed a significant role in the history of Italian screenwriting; and education, in this case looking at the establishment of screenwriting schools and the academic courses on offer.

38.2 Literacy and Ideology in the 1930s and 1940s

In Italy, screenwriting began to gain pedagogical attention in the interwar period. On the one hand, this was the upshot of the affirmation of film culture in Europe (Hagener 2014); on the other, it was the expression of the fascist desire for ideological control over the cinema (Manetti 2012). A third reason must be added to these, namely the advent of talkies—in Italy with the 1930 film *La canzone dell'amore* by Gennaro Righelli—a paradigm shift that prompted the need to draw up a new, shared set of writing principles and regulations. "When films started to talk, the public began to talk back. (…) Hence (…) the need to write for cinema" reads the Italian edition of the film writing guide by Seton Margrave (Margrave 1939, 19). The Italian translation of the book, which met with "almost unanimous approval" at the time (Bruni 2006, 421), reflects the widespread need felt in the film sector and the growing interest in film writing.

In his early 1930s manual, *Come nasce un film* [How a Film Is Born], director Alessandro Blasetti, one of the most authoritative voices of the time, hailed the screenwriter "a true co-author" (Blasetti 1982, 175). Blasetti was the first screenwriting teacher at the first Italian public film school, the CSC–Centro Sperimentale di Cinematografia, set up by the fascist state in the mid-1930s. As can be seen from student Giulio Niederkorn's course programme for the 1935–1936 academic year, screenwriting lessons were coupled with directing lessons: in all, they totalled 16 hours a week. What is more, screenwriting found its way across the whole programme: acting students had to invent details for assigned scenes before they got into the characters' parts; editing and production students had to analyse films from transcripts of "masterpieces" seen on the Moviola.

There is no doubt that fascism's interest in screenwriting was instrumental: following prior appraisal of the scripts, the Direzione Generale di Cinematografia (i.e. the government department for film, established in 1934) advanced large sums of public funding to producers (Ben-Ghiat 2001; Mazzei 2006). Although the drive to provide for professional education has to be seen in a totalitarian light, it did enable unexpected intellectual openings. In particular, the CSC journal *Bianco e Nero*, a film studies periodical that has been published since 1937, played a key role in taking the screenwriting debate to the international level by translating articles by Bela Balàzs (1940, 58–60), Sergei Eisenstein (1939, 174–176), Hans Richter (1939, 106–113), and Werner Kortwich (1941, 30–34) to quote just a few. Umberto Barbaro was a screenwriter and Marxist critic who learned the ropes working for *Cinematografo* journal directed by Blasetti; he was also member of the CSC and of *Bianco e Nero* staff (Brunetta 1969; Genovese 1986). Barbaro played a particularly significant role: as an intellectual, teacher, and professional, he not only imported the lessons of Vsevolod I. Pudovkin by translating his 1926 work *Kinostsenari* (English edition: *The Film Scenario*, 1930), but also wrote the essay/manual *Film: soggetto e sceneggiatura* [Film: Story Outline and Screenplay] (Barbaro 1939). Barbaro's contribution set a milestone in screenwriting culture in Italy, summing up European theories ranging from Balázs' ideas on the story outline and Pudovkin's stimulus on theme, to Eisenstein's observations on conflict, as well as the reflections of Ricciotto Canudo, Sebastiano Arturo Luciani, Germaine Dulac, and others. Within this raft of theory, Barbaro drew up an original pedagogy of film writing, beginning with the theme, which ensures the moral organization of the contents. As he explained, "the story outline is the particular vision, the theme is the conception of the world that it suggests" (Barbaro 1939, 11); he then went on to deal with the hero, conflict, treatment, and finally the audiovisual rendering of the concepts thanks to a wealth of examples taken from the history of the cinema.

The translations of story outlines, publication of full or partial scripts, and in-depth narrative analyses reveal *Bianco e Nero*'s educational aspirations. This is how the journalist and film theorist Renato May motivated the initiative:

The publication of film scripts has been going on for some time. The volume *Successful Film Writing*, edited by Seton Margrave, appeared in London, and has been translated in Italy by Paola Ojetti for Bompiani (…). The trend in France is to put together and publish the full dialogues of the biggest film hits, linked by brief explanations describing the action that the dialogues refer to. Marcel Pagnol even started a series of these books taken from his films. In Italy (…) there have been various special instalments of *Bianco e Nero* entirely dedicated to publishing working documents (…). Therefore, we are looking at a renewal of interest in what is one of the most important phases in making a film, while everywhere there are complaints of unskilled screenwriters in Italy and continuation of the questionable—moreover obsolete in practice and theory—quibbles over whether film is or is not screenwriting. Therefore, the intention behind publishing scripts is above all to offer strictly objective and ample documentation on some typical films that the world of film spectators, critics, and historians have recognized as a typically cinematographic expression of art. (May 1939, 16–17)[1]

While the Centro Sperimentale di Cinematografia and *Bianco e Nero* were the most important actors in the field of education, this does not mean that there were not any other active subjects. Indeed, there were various Italian and foreign manuals for audiovisual production with sections on screenwriting: for example, *Come si fa un film a Hollywood* (English edition: *We Make the Movies*) by Nancy Naumburg was published in Italy by *Cine-Magazzino*—there is no date in the Italian version of the manual but the publication can be traced to the period between 1937 and 1940; or the *Filmindustria* producers' handbook by Raffaello Maggi from 1934. A particularly important volume for our purposes is *Come scrivere e sceneggiare un soggetto cinematografico* [How to Write and Script a Film Story Outline] by Santi Paladino (1943), an extraordinarily complete and precise text that was discovered in the Biblioteca Nazionale Centrale in Florence. For example, he writes about story outlines: "The first draft of the plot usually consists of a short story—from three to five typewritten pages—written in the present tense. It is enough to give a general idea of the story but if the story writer wants to add some of the most important details of the action or some dialogue, the pages can get up to 15 or even more" (Paladino 1943, 12). Paladino then illustrates the characteristics of treatments with an abundance of technical details, specifying that "a normal film is made (…) of 400–900 frames, in turn contained in 100–200 sequences. The order of the sequences gives rise to the so-called treatment. The technical and artistic details of the sequences, divided into the various frames, then give you the screenplay, that is, the last stage of the evolving story outline" (11). Following that, Paladino sets out the precise number of pages that a treatment should consist of, with relation to the duration of the film: "drafting an hour-long project (…) takes a minimum of 100 typewritten pages" (17–18). Next,

---

[1] All translations from the Italian original are the author's own.

he briefly outlines the camera movements, and a film terms glossary. Last, he illustrates the Italian-style script technique in fashion at the time:

> Shots should be described on the left half of the sheet, and as well as indicating the progressive number, these should include an abbreviation of the shot scale and camera angle, the actors' movements and expressions, the scenario details, camera movements, colours, reverse shots, fades, superimposition etc., in short everything concerning the camera. The dialogue, sounds, noises and everything else to do with the soundtrack must be noted on the right half of the sheet, with the name of the characters at the beginning of the sentences of the dialogue. Alongside the name, the out of frame will be indicated in brackets if the person speaking is not captured by the camera. (Paladino, 1943, 39)

Paladino cites a vast range of useful cases to illustrate the general concepts, accompanying the explanations with a series of passages taken from original screenplays (for example, from the films of Mario Camerini). He sets out a practical guide to give any beginner the basic notions to debut in writing for the seventh art. As for the author, it remains a mystery why a journalist without any particular experience of cinema should write such an accurate screenwriting manual and publish it at a time when Italy was being devastated by World War Two.

38.3 The Pedagogy of Screenwriting During the Cold War

The changes that the CSC and *Bianco e Nero* underwent with the passage from fascist dictatorship to the Italian Republic were more in form than substance: the communist Barbaro became a lecturer in screenwriting at the CSC while former fascist Luigi Chiarini was re-appointed as principal editor of *Bianco e Nero* (Bruni et al. 2016, 82). In the post-war period, the journal continued the educational activities that had hitherto set it apart: for example, the Italian edition of the manual by John Howard Lawson *Theory and Technique of Playwriting* (1936) in 1951, and the systematic publication of original screenplays, excerpts from scripts, transcripts, and story outlines.

What had changed immensely was the historical context. The Cold War and the consequential ideological radicalization impacted Italian cinema, which those in power deemed to be under left-wing political influence: screenwriting, that is, the *front line* in controlling film contents, became one of the fields of rivalry between communists and Catholics to gain popular consensus, and therefore, it was heavily hit by censorship. In 1953, a CSC student denounced in the Marxist-leaning journal *Cinema nuovo* how the Centro Sperimentale was awash with "Barnabite college mentality" (Celli 1953, 161), declaring he had dropped out owing to the censorship of a story outline—a crude account of imprisonment set in Rome at the time of its liberation from the Germans—that he had written.

It is significant that the first teaching of screenwriting in universities was of Catholic inspiration. The course was established at the Università Internazionale di Studi Sociali Pro Deo, founded in Rome in 1945 by the Dominican brother Félix Morlion, who had connections with the American Office of Strategic Service (OSS, the forerunner of the CIA) and a reputation as an expert in psychological warfare and propaganda techniques. This university, a Vatican-US anti-communist meeting point (Tommaso Subini 2015), offered a screenwriting option that included specific teaching on this subject.[2] Its goal was to train Christian professionals capable of dealing with media tools and holding forth in public debate. As such, Morlion's strategy included the creation of "Cineforums" (Treveri Gennari 2009, 83), a sort of "confessional" film club (Tosi 1999, 329) where the discussion on topics of current debate after free film viewings was led by especially instructed experts. As Elena Mosconi explains:

> The Dominican's methodology consisted of a short introduction to the film, a group viewing, and a debate led by a preferably secular moderator. The spectators were invited to identify the central topic of the work ("the emotionally charged idea that gives life to the plot") and the way it is expressed in the text, and to point out the most stimulating scenes. It was only at this point that the technical and artistic aspects of the film were tackled, also with the help of experts: screenwriting, frames, set design, acting, photography, soundtrack, etc. Lastly, the debate had to cast light on the moral aspects of the film (…) and perhaps the social ones too. (2018, 156)

One can legitimately presume that the manual titled *Tecnica dello scrittore cinematografico* [Film Writer's Technique] (undated but presumably from the mid-1950s) found at the Biblioteca Nazionale Centrale in Florence was also written in this context and for similar purposes. The author was Giuseppe Rossi Bellicampi, a Catholic journalist who wrote religious texts.[3] The textbook is subdivided into various chapters and sections (entitled "Differenza tra romanzo e soggetto cinematografico" [The difference between a novel and a film story outline], "Gli attori e i personaggi" [Actors and characters], "Il vaglio delle idee nel soggetto cinematografico" [Weighing up story outline ideas], "La sintesi fotografica della narrazione" [The photo board of the story], "L'intreccio della trama ed il movimento dell'azione" [Plot lines and movement of the action] and so on). At the end, there are questions

---

[2] As can be seen from the brochures of 1948–1949 and 1949–1950, now in Bruni et al. 2016, 117.

[3] The manual by Giuseppe Rossi Bellicampi, *Tecnica dello scrittore cinematografico* was published by La Monastica di Vico publishers in Lazio. The text is undated but, considering the films it mentions, in all likelihood it was published in 1955.

for evaluation and self-evaluation of the topics previously addressed. Here is a passage from the section "La funzione sociale del cinema" [The social function of film] as an example:

> Those who approach film writing consciously and seriously and with civil responsibility must not lose sight of the social function of film. Cinema is a double-edged sword and (…) it helps (…) set a good or bad example for the whole population. (…) Most films develop a thesis (…), the characters act as live interpreters of the thesis. The story writer (…) has to be able to stigmatize and strike down falseness and corruption by giving their actions consequences. In the end, the spectator must be convinced that the killer, the violent figure is punished and the actions of the pervert, the immoral character have to arouse (…) the real disgust and disapproval of the public. If (…) the author indulges the character's vices and praises their lack of scruples, then he renders a dreadful service to society, undermining the bases of civil coexistence and upsetting the balance behind people's basically healthy spirit. (Bellicampi 1955?, 19–20)

At the end of the section, we find questions such as: "What is the social function of cinema? Where does film's evocative strength lie? What are the story writer's responsibilities? How should crime be presented? What is a film's thesis? What are the characters' functions with respect to the thesis? What does the spectator have to be convinced of?" (Bellicampi 1955?, 20).

Despite the exasperated ideologies and rigidity of the Cold War, film schools started to build important transnational relations in that same period. *Bianco e Nero* informs us of the international film schools meeting that took place in Paris in 1958 (De Gregorio 1958, 3), at which institutes such as the CSC–Centro Sperimentale di Cinematografia, IDHEC Institut des Hautes Études Cinématographiques (Paris), VGIK-Vserossijskij Gosudarstvenn'ij Institut Kinematografii (Moscow), and the Łódź film school, to quote at least the oldest ones present, discussed teaching issues, in particular about screenwriting. The report in *Bianco e Nero* is a precious historical document that gives us a taste of the pedagogical thinking and policies of the time and reveals the shared opinion that an excessively structured education can "dampen the instinctive talents" of the budding screenwriter. It is preferable to act maieutically, bringing the students to analyse the dynamics of dramaturgy inside and around themselves. As for the tools to provide the aspiring film writer with, the Italian speaker stressed the "dialectics of conflict", the French speaker an "analysis of the essential elements of dramatic construction", and the German speaker highlighted the importance of "pinpointing film's specificity for a comparison with other dramatic genres" (*Il quinto convegno delle scuole di cinema e di televisione*, 1958, 5). Furthermore, the speech by Italian delegate Giorgio Prosperi gives us numerous details on the models and practices used to teach screenwriting at the Centro Sperimentale di Cinematografia in the 1950s: we learn that the theoretical framework was accompanied by history and analysis (analysing classic film scripts), followed by Socratic-style creative practice to develop the student's awareness, while the second year of schooling consisted almost exclusively in the search of a subject for the final directing exercise (Prosperi 1958, 24).

38.4 From Script to Print Between the 1950s and 1970s

Book series devoted to screenwriting started to circulate in the 1950s once the literacy phase was complete. Nevertheless, we should first account for the "legendary"—in the eyes of generations of film lovers—albeit fleeting "Serie Sceneggiature" [Script Series] published by Società Editrice Poligono in the second half of the 1940s (Lorenzo Pellizzari 1999, 9). The project pursued by cinema enthusiasts and professionals close to the future Cineteca Italiana di Milano (including directors Luigi Comencini and Alberto Lattuada) came about in 1945 and wound up within five years. The volumes offered the transcription of films—in particular French films—that had survived bombing in the war and were made available by the Cineteca. The goal behind the operation was to preserve the films, by putting them safely onto paper, so to speak: "to transcribe the films and capture the frames, the group often watched the films together on Moviola, or even (…) studied the films by hand in the kitchens of their homes" (Gimmelli 2020, 515). The handful of titles published included *Entr'acte* by René Clair (Viazzi 1945) and *Vampyr* by Carl Theodor Dreyer (Buzzi and Lattuada 1948).

In the early 1950s, publications of scripts flourished. Even, when they were one-offs undertakings they were the sign of an increasing interest all the same: for example, the journal *Filmcritica* tried to form its own "Testi e sceneggiatura" [Texts and Script] series by publishing the scripts of *Journal d'un curé de campagne* (*Diary of a Country Priest*) by Robert Bresson (1953), *Ace in the Hole* by Billy Wilder (1951, co-written with Lesser Samuels and Walter Newman), and *Limelight* by Charlie Chaplin (1952).

The script series "Dal soggetto al film" [From the Story Outline to the Film], started in 1955, was more significant and complete. The heart and mind behind the initiative was film critic, cineaste, and cultural organizer Renzo Renzi, who had been in 1953 at the centre of a sensational court case before a military tribunal—and duly sentenced—for writing and publishing a story outline entitled *L'armata s'agapò* (on the occupation of Greece by the Italian army) which was judged offensive towards the armed forces. Antonio Costa (2004) maintains that "the notoriety earned on that occasion definitely helped Renzi to obtain approval for the risky project from the publishers Cappelli: so risky that the word screenplay (…) was nowhere to be seen either on the cover or the title page" (456). Indeed, Costa notes, all that appeared on the cover "was always the name of the director alone: as if to say that the book is dedicated to the film as a whole" (2004, 456). Throughout twenty years, the series dealt almost exclusively with Italian cinema, publishing the preparatory materials for the films—the story outline, treatment, and screenplay, at times transcript, other times the original—with the intention of "rummaging through the drawers of screenwriters, directors (…) because (…) those notebooks, which had always been thrown into warehouse basements, hold the secret story (…) of artistic creation", as stated on the back cover of the first issue (Baldelli 1998, 760). Leafing through the volume dedicated to *Senso* by Luchino Visconti (Cavallaro 1955) to get an idea of how the materials were organized, one finds excerpts from the first and second draft of the screenplay, a detailed analysis of the narrative choices made by the screenwriters, the evolution of the script starting from the idea, the initial short story, the extended beat sheet of the first and final versions, interspersed with eye-witness accounts. The "Dal soggetto al film" series marks an important acknowledgement for screenwriting, at the time perceived as a "hopelessly subordinate and obscure" practice, to quote writer Alberto Moravia in the novel *Contempt* (*Il disprezzo* 1999, 39). The Cappelli catalogue also features story outlines and screenplays by Vittorio De Sica, Michelangelo Antonioni, Visconti again, Roberto Rossellini, Federico Fellini, and many more Italian filmmakers. The wealth of materials and information contained in the books offers many possibilities for analysis: for example, we can rebuild the dynamics, routines, and writing rituals or explore the evolution of the scripts from a philological and formal point of view.

The Cappelli series was not an isolated case. In the 1950s, almost all the most important Italian publishers—Mondadori, Rizzoli, Feltrinelli, and Longanesi—started to add scripts to their catalogues. Often, they were Italian titles pushed by the fame of the director, who was almost always the script writer too (as often was the case at this time). A significant series is "Film e discussioni" [Film and Discussions] by Garzanti, headed by director, screenwriter, and writer Pier Paolo Pasolini, which featured nearly all of his scripts starting from *Il Vangelo secondo Matteo* (*The Gospel According to Matthew*) (Gambetti 1964). Garzanti published Pasolini's complete works, including his famous essay "La sceneggiatura come struttura che vuole essere altra struttura" [The Screenplay as a Structure that Wants to Be Another Structure], a structuralist epistemological reflection on film writing that put its mark on screenwriting theory of that period (Pasolini 1965).

There is more than one reason why between the 1950s and 1970s scripts were put into print and proliferated in book shops, often typeset in the form of a book. The first fact to consider is that the upward trend in book publications during this period of clear development in the publishing industry (Ferretti 2004) was inversely proportionate to the trend in box office ticket sales. While from the 1950s to 70s the number of books published increased exponentially, after 1955 box office sales began to plunge.[4] The gap that opened in the book market resulted in a strategy to exploit film's *narrative capital*, that is, the commercial potential of the stories and characters made famous by the big screen, which by no means ended in the movie theatre. Hence,

---

[4] See ISTAT [National Institute of Statistics] data, "Serie storiche 1926–2014 (tavole 8.1 anni e 8.4)" [Historical series 1926–2014, tables 8.1 and 8.4].

presumably, this is the logic behind the impromptu publication of scripts by small publishers, such as the "Collana di studi cinematografici" [Film Studies Series] by Fratelli Bocca in the 1950s, the "…Ciak!" […Lights, Camera!] series by publishers Zibetti in the 1960s, or the "Copioni cinematografici" [Film Scripts] series by the Istituto di Propaganda Libraria in the 1970s. At the start of the 1960s, even producer Goffredo Lombardo, owner of the film production company Titanus, got in on the act with the "Il cinematografo" [The Cinematographer] script series published by FM Edizioni, whose goal, as per the back cover of the volume dedicated to *Divorzio all'italiana* (*Divorce Italian Style*), was to "prove the literary value of the film author's work" (Moscon 1961).

It is important to understand whether the publication of the scripts occurred before or after the film was released. In the case of Pasolini, the documents from the Garzanti archive show that the scripts arrived in the book shops before the films came out in the movie theatres, at once providing and drawing impetus from the launch of the film product.[5]

Einaudi—the most authoritative publisher in Italy at the time, governed by Italy's intellectual aristocracy—also published scripts before the film's cinema release. It started to print scripts in the early 1960s, first of all from Ingmar Bergman's films (1961), and *L'année dernière à Marienbad* (*Last Year at Marienbad*) (1961), continuing with Italian and European auteur cinema and titles by directors Michelangelo Antonioni, Bernardo Bertolucci, Federico Fellini, Jean-Luc Godard, Luis Buñuel, Krzysztof Kieślowski, and more. With the appearance of the Einaudi script catalogue, one can argue that screenwriting finally gained full cultural legitimation.

38.5 Screenwriter-Professors. The 1980s and 1990s

Script publication continued in the 1980s, in journals (*Immagine* and *Segnocinema* stood out in particular) and the publishing field. The Mantua film club's "Casa del Mantegna-Provincia di Mantova" series made its debut in 1984. The first issue included *Sei soggetti per il cinema. Storie inedite di Age e Scarpelli* et al. [Six Film Outlines. Unpublished Stories by Age and Scarpelli et al.] (Circolo del Cinema S. M. Eisenstein 1984), displaying the names of "pure" screenwriters rather than the director/screenwriters pairing on the cover for the first time (Baschiera 2014). From then on, thanks to the scriptwriters who made their works available, hundreds of books were published, mainly on popular Italian films and genre cinema. It marked a turning point for film writers. In the 1980s, they played the leading role in relaunching Italian cinema with the public, by creating and organizing training

---

[5] As we learn from a letter dated 4 August 1965 sent to Pasolini by Paola Dalai at Garzanti, preserved at the Gabinetto G. P. Vieusseux (Fondo Pier Paolo Pasolini, *Serie Corrispondenza*, Aldo Garzanti publishers unit).

opportunities and meetings with the authors. In addition, an award for original and unpublished scripts, the Premio Solinas (an award named after an Italian scriptwriter), was established in the mid-1980s. It soon became one of the main recruitment channels for audiovisual writing professionals—Paolo Sorrentino won it in 1997—as well as an opportunity for debate and training: for instance, in 1994 it hosted the SOURCES scriptwriters' workshop, and two years later it offered advanced training with Bottega Creativa workshops (Nigro 1999). The jury of the Solinas award included some of the biggest names among Italian scriptwriters, such as Suso Cecchi d'Amico, Age and Scarpelli, and Ugo Pirro. Pirro's career is a demonstration of the phase of "industrial reflexivity" (Thornton Caldwell 2008, 14) that screenwriting went through in the last decades of last century: professional screenwriters wanted to put their creative experiences to good use, look at their work through a historical lens to specify the screenwriter's role, and find legitimation as educators.

Multi-award-winning screenwriter Ugo Pirro—Best Screenplay for *A ciascuno il suo* (*We Still Kill the Old Way*) at the Cannes Festival in 1967 as well as two Oscar nominations for Best Screenplay in 1970 with *Il giardino dei Finzi Contini* (*The Garden of the Finzi-Continis*) and *Indagine su un cittadino al di sopra di ogni sospetto* (*Investigation of a Citizen Above Suspicion*)—was one of the first to pursue this direction. He held a great many seminars, starting with a collaboration with Associazione Cinema Democratico [Democratic Cinema Association] (Moscati 1989, 30) in 1981. These seminars provided the basis for the manual *Per scrivere un film* [How to Write a Film] (Pirro [1982] 2002), which shortly afterwards would be joined by the memoirs *Soltanto un nome nei titoli di testa* [Just a Name in the Opening Credits] (Pirro 1998) and *Il cinema della nostra vita* [The Cinema of Our Lives] (Pirro 2001). Pirro built a "narrative of self" (Giddens 1991) with these autobiographical and technical tales, betraying the need to assert his own identity as an artist and that of his discipline. The manual clearly states his aspiration to point public attention to screenwriting and claim its rightful place within the cinema industry: "This book is a report on my experiences as a film writer. It is both an attempt to give an insider's analysis of the screenwriter's work and its for the main part unknown function and to illustrate a possible working method" (Pirro [1982] 2002, 1). The guide follows an inductive method (Caldwell 2008, 36), setting out industrial practices and techniques through personal stories in a logic of self-representation. In the manual and in his writings, Pirro accompanies technical explanations with personal memories. Here is a passage from the memoir *Il cinema della nostra vita*, in which he describes the writer's room he shared with director Elio Petri:

> We sat around a rustic wooden table in the living room, working on the project, heads down, like a pair of office clerks. We got on amazingly well, more than arguing, it was like we were thinking out loud (…). During meetings, Elio fidgeted on his chair so much that he broke it (…) as if he was thinking with his

whole body. (...) This is what we did to write the scenes, the short descriptions, and the dialogue: we sat opposite each other, Elio had the typewriter in front of him, I had a biro in my hand and a pile of sheets that I wrote the script outline on as we gradually defined the structure of the film. We wrote the script the Italian way. The sheet was divided into two columns: on the left (...) as was customary, we described the sets (...), the characters' movements and all of their characteristics; on the right-hand side of the page, [we wrote] the dialogues, the musical effects, and noises. (...) I tried to write the dialogues by hand and then dictate them to him, and he added or cut them out as appropriate. At times, a line could spark an argument or a long silence. Those were the moments when Elio bit his nails to the quick. He lay down on the deck chair in the sun and thought as he smoked. (Pirro 2001, 34–37)

Pirro's manual was followed by other manuals by Age (1990), one of the most important writers of Italian-style comedy, scriptwriter Lucio Battistrada with journalist Massimo Felisatti (1993), and writer Vincenzo Cerami (1996), author of many scripts for Roberto Benigni. They are all manuals in which the authors theorize the practice starting from their personal experiences as authors and artists. In this regard, it is worth quoting the incipit of the volume by Age, which goes through the evolution of the screenwriting profession in Italy:

> For around ten years after the end of the Second World War (...), anyone could write a film script; people came and went, there were no rules. The contracts were extremely lax and at times it was enough just to take part in the odd session to gain the right to put your name on the script with the others. (...) This elasticity gradually came to be adjusted as of the end of the 1950s. The authors started to value their role more and, therefore, to defend it. (...). The press, the media, which had had no idea about the function or importance of screenwriting until the middle of the 1960s (...) started to quote the film writers, even though the quality and role of screenwriting were rarely taken into examination and, if they were, it was only to underline their paucity. Script authors are like lighthouse keepers: everyone sees the light, but no one sees them. (Age 1990, 7–8)

These manuals were usually the upshot of teaching experiences. The main person to pick up the reins from Pirro was Leo Benvenuti, who made a name for himself as a teacher on the ANAC-Associazione Nazionale Autori Cinematografici screenwriting courses in the 1990s (Angeli 2005, 94). The school's students included someone like Umberto Contarello who co-wrote the Oscar-winning *La grande bellezza* (*The Great Beauty*, 2013) with Paolo Sorrentino, and Enzo Monteleone, who penned story and screenplay of *Mediterraneo* (1991), Oscar for Best Foreign Language Film in 1992.

Training initiatives took off in the 1990s, with the opening of the Scuola Holden (a writing school named after the main character of *The Catcher in the Rye* by J. D. Salinger) in Turin in 1994, whose programme hinged wholly around narrative techniques, creative writing, and storytelling. However, what most marked this decade was the encounter with the US culture of screenwriting education. This arrived in Italy thanks to Dino Audino and his publishing house, founded in Rome in 1987, whose goal was to promote a pragmatic conception of writing based on writing models and paradigms, with an eye on audiovisual series as well as cinema. In 1992, Dino Audino launched *Script*, the first specialized screenwriting journal in Italy whose pages hosted and sparked debates, interviews, and analyses, within a new system of reference—that of the screenwriting guru. It was Audino who introduced the guides by the Screenwritings Gurus to the Italian market. The first was *The Writer's Journey* by Chris Vogler (1982), translated into Italian in 1996, followed by the guide by Linda Seger, *Making a Good Script Great* (1987), which came out in Italy in 1997. Dozens of guru manuals would be printed in Italy in the following years.

Again upon the initiative of the *Script* journal in collaboration with RAI state television, the first screenwriters training course with Linda Seger, Dara Marks, Rachel Ballon, Linda Palmer, Cristopher Vogler, and other American script consultants took place in Italy in 1996. This is how Dino Audino motivated his choices:

> To teach the basics of scriptwriting, we had no choice but to turn to the United States. Not because there were no great, albeit ageing scriptwriters in Italy, but because the American movie industry and the US film studies departments have created specific professional figures in the story analysis and dramaturgical structures teaching sector (story analysts, story editors. and history consultants). These are not yet present in our country, but an audiovisual industry like Rai needs them more and more. (Audino 1997, 4)

The last arena to turn screenwriting into a study discipline was that of Italian state universities. As we have seen, the subject was first taught in a Catholic university in the post-war period. Scriptwriting had first entered the study programmes of state universities in the early 1970s (at the University of Parma), but only as a module in the Film History and Film Scriptwriting Technique course (Bruni et al. 2020, 89). Screenwriting first appeared as a standalone subject in state universities in the third millennium: a screenwriting workshop was on the syllabus for the 2002–2003 academic year at the University of Bologna; a specific "Television and Film Writer" course has been on offer at the University of Rome 3 since the early 2000s; and screenwriting was first offered as a course at the University of Udine in 2002–03.

38.6 Conclusions

The process of institutionalization of screenwriting in Italy during the twentieth century was promoted by different agencies, was developed in different environments (different according to the historical phases), and was crossed by tensions of different nature.

In the period of the fascist dictatorship, that is to say between the Thirties and the early Forties, the State centralized cinema activities in Rome, and culturally legitimized cinema by dedicating some public institutions to it (the School of Cinema, CSC and the film studies journal *Bianco e Nero*) in which space was given to the teaching of screenwriting and to the international debate regarding writing for cinema. The short season of neorealism, in the second half of the 1940s, rejects the idea of the screenplay (not the practice), precisely because it represented the phase of censorship and control over contents of films during fascism.

Screenplay is once again at the centre of public attention during the Cold War (especially in the 1950s): in this period the teaching of Screenwriting—which for the first time enters an Italian university, but private and catholic—goes framed in the historical context of the ideological antagonism between communist, catholic, and democratic forces. Republican Italy, therefore, pursued the same pre-war logic of ideological control over the script. However, the 1950s also saw other agencies and forces at play: the publishing industry began publishing series of screenplays, capitalizing the cultural prestige that cinema began to enjoy, prestige destined to grow in the 1960s and 1970s following the influence of the politique des auteurs.

The Eighties and Nineties saw screenwriters and film professionals gaining authority and space through various editorial, educational, and cultural initiatives: film writers published manuals, held scriptwriting courses and instituted awards dedicated to screenwriting, animating a lively public debate. Only at the turn of the third millennium screenplay entered Italian public universities, sanctioning a definitive recognition of screenwriting as a discipline and interest not motivated by instrumental, ideological or economic interests.

References

A ciascuno il suo (*We Still Kill the Old Way*). 1967. Written by Elio Petri and Ugo Pirro. Directed by Elio Petri. Italy: Cemofilm.
Ace in the Hole. 1951. Written by Billy Wilder, Lesser Samuels, and Walter Newman. Directed by Billy Wilder. USA: Paramount Pictures.
Age. 1990. *Scriviamo un film*. Parma: Pratiche.
Age, Suso Cecchi d'Amico, and Leonardo Benvenuti. 1994. *Scrivere per il cinema: seminario di specializzazione su tecniche di sceneggiatura*. Rome: SIAE.
Angeli, Alfredo. 2005. *Rosso Malpelo Schizza Veleno*. Rome: Fazi.
Audino, Dino. 1997. "Editoriale". *Script* 12/13: 4.
Balàzs, Bela. 1940. "Il dialogo." *Bianco e Nero* 2: 58–60.
Baldelli, Pio. 1998. "A proposito di una collana cinematografica." *Letterature moderne* 6: 759–68.
Barbaro, Umberto. 1939. "Film: soggetto e sceneggiatura." *Bianco e Nero* 7: 4–76.
Baschiera, Stefano. 2014. "I registi-sceneggiatori." *Quaderni del CSCI* 10: 63–67.
Battistrada, Lucio and Massimo Felisatti. 1993. *Corso di sceneggiatura*. Milan: Sansoni.
Bellicampi, Giuseppe Rossi. [1955?]. *Tecnica dello scrittore cinematografico*. Vico nel Lazio, Italy: La Monastica.

Ben-Ghiat, Ruth. 2001. *Fascist Modernities. Italy, 1922–1945*, Berkeley-Los Angeles-London: University of California Press.
Bergman, Ingmar. 1961. *Quattro film. Sorrisi di una notte d'estate, Il settimo sigillo, Il posto delle fragole, Il volto*. Turin: Einaudi.
Blakeston, Oswell. 1949. *How to Script. Amateur Films*. London-New York: Focal Press. Italian edition: Blakeston, O. 1952. *La composizione del film: come si fa la sceneggiatura*. Milan: Edizioni del Castello.
Blasetti, Alessandro. 1932. *Come nasce un film*, Rome: Edizioni di Cinematografo.
Blasetti, Alessandro. 1982. *Il cinema che ho vissuto*, edited by Franco Prono. Bari: Dedalo.
Bresson, Robert. 1953. *Diario di un curato di campagna*. Rome: Edizioni Filmcritica.
Brunetta, Gian Piero. 1969. *Umberto Barbaro e l'idea di Neorealismo (1930–1943)*. Padua: Liviana Editrice.
Bruni, David. 2006. "Sceneggiatura e sceneggiatori". In *Storia del cinema italiano, vol. V, 1934–1939*, edited by Orio Caldiron, 413–30. Venice-Rome: Marsilio-Bianco e Nero.
Bruni, David, Antioco Floris, Massimo Locatelli, and Simone Venturini, eds. 2016. *Dallo schermo alla cattedra. La nascita dell'insegnamento universitario e dell'audiovisivo in Italia*. Rome: Carocci.
Bruni, David, Antioco Floris, Massimo Locatelli, and Simone Venturini. 2020. *Il cinema come disciplina. L'università italiana e i media audiovisivi (1970–1990)*. Milan: Mimesis.
Buzzi, Aldo, and Bianca Lattuada, eds, 1948. *Vampyr di Carl Theodor Dreyer*. Milan: Poligono.
Caldwell, John Thornton. 2008. *Production Culture. Industrial Reflexivity and Critical Practice in Film and Television*, Durham, NC: Duke University Press.
Cavallaro, Giovanni Battista, ed. 1955. *Senso di Luchino Visconti*. Bologna: Cappelli.
Celli, Gian. 1953. *Perché un allievo si è dimesso dal centro. Cinema nuovo* 7: 161.
Cerami, Vincenzo. 1996. *Consigli a un giovane scrittore. Narrativa, cinema, teatro, radio*. Milan: Garzanti.
Chaplin, Charlie. 1953. *Luci della ribalta*. Rome: Edizioni Filmcritica.
Circolo del Cinema S. M. Ejzenstejn. 1984. *Sei soggetti per il cinema. Storie inedite di Age e Scarpelli et al*. Mantua, Italy: Casa del Mantegna.
Costa, Antonio. 2004. "Dal soggetto al film, una collana cinematografica." In *Storia del cinema italiano, vol. IX, 1954–1959*, edited by Sandro Bernardi, 456–57, Venice-Rome: Marsilio-Bianco e Nero.
De Gregorio, Domenico. 1958. "Il mese." *Bianco e nero* 7: 3–6.
Divorzio all'italiana (Divorce Italian Style). 1961. Written by Alfredo Giannetti, Ennio De Concini, Pietro Germi, and Agenore Incrocci (uncredited). Italy: Lux Film, Vides Cinematografica, Galatea Film.
Entr'acte. 1924. Written by René Clair and Francis Picabia. Directed by René Clair. France: Les Ballets Suedois.
Ėjzenštejn, Sergej Michajlovič. 1939. "Soggetto e sceneggiatura." *Bianco e nero* 2: 174–76.
Ferretti, Gian Carlo. 2004. *Storia dell'editoria in Italia. 1945–2003*. Turin: Einaudi.
Field, Syd. 1984. *The Screenwriter's Workbook. A Workshop Approach*. New York: Dell. Italian edition: Field, Syd. 1991. *La sceneggiatura. Il film sulla carta*. Milan: Lupetti.
Floris, Antioco, and Francesco Pitassio, eds. 2012. *A scuola di cinema. La formazione nelle professioni dell'audiovisivo*. Udine: Forum.

Gaudenzi, Cosetta. 2020. "Screenwriting." In *Italian Cinema. From the Silent Screen to the Digital Image,* edited by Joseph Luzzi, 292–98. New York-London: Bloomsbury.
Gambetti, Giacomo, ed. 1964. *Il Vangelo secondo Matteo. Un film di Pier Paolo Pasolini.* Milan: Garzanti.
Genovese, Nino, ed. 1986. *Barbaro & Chiarini. I teorici del cinema dietro la macchina da presa.* Messina: De Spectaculus.
Giddens, Antony. 1991. *Modernity and Self-Identity: Self and Society in the Late Modern Age.* Cambridge: Polity Press.
Gimmelli, Gabriele. 2020. *Aldo Buzzi. Tutte le opere.* Milan: La nave di Teseo.
Hagener, Malte, ed. 2014. *Emergence of Film Culture: Knowledge Production, Institution Building and the Fate of the Avant-Garde in Europe*, 1919–1945. New York: Berghahn.
Il giardino dei Finzi Contini (*The Garden of the Finzi-Continis*). 1970. Written by Ugo Pirro and Vittorio Bonicelli. Directed by Vittorio De Sica. Italy, West Germany: Titanus, Documento Film, CCC-Filmkunst.
Il Vangelo secondo Matteo (*The Gospel According to Matthew*). 1964. Written and directed by Pier Paolo Pasolini. Italy, France: Arco Film, Lux Compagnie Cinématographique de France.
Indagine su un cittadino al di sopra di ogni sospetto (*Investigation of a Citizen Above Suspicion*). 1970. Written by Elio Petri and Ugo Pirro. Directed by Elio Petri. Italy: Vera Films.
Journal d'un curé de campagne (*Diary of a Country Priest*). 1953. Written and directed by Robert Bresson. France: UGC.
Kortwich, Werner. 1941. "La sceneggiatura." *Bianco e Nero* 5: 30–34.
L'année dernière à Marienbad (*Last Year at Marienbad*). 1961. Written by Alain Robbe-Grillet. Directed by Alain Resnais. France, Italy: Cocinor, Terra-Film, Cormoran Films, Precitel, Como Films, Argos Films, Les Films Tamara, Cinétel, Silver Films, Cineriz.
La canzone dell'amore (*The Song of Love*). 1930. Written by Giorgio Simonelli and Gennaro Righelli. Directed by Gennaro Righelli. Italy: CINES.
La grande bellezza (*The Great Beauty*). 2013. Written by Umberto Contarello. Directed by Paolo Sorrentino. Italy, France: Indigo Film, Babe Film, Medusa Film, Pathé, France 2 Cinèma.
Lawson, John Howard. 1936. *Theory and Technique of Playwriting.* New York: Putnams. Italian edition: Lawson, J. H. 1951. *Teoria e tecnica della sceneggiatura.* Rome: Bianco e Nero.
Limelight. 1952. Written and directed by Charlie Chaplin. USA: Celebrated Films Corp.
McKee, Robert. 1997. *Story. Substance, Structure, Style and the Principle of Screenwriting.* New York: Harper. Italian edition: McKee, R. 2000. *Story. Contenuti, struttura, stile, principi della sceneggiatura per il cinema e la fiction tv.* Rome: International Forum.
Maggi, Raffaello. 1934. *Filmindustria.* Busto Arsizio, Italy: Pianezza.
Manetti, Daniela. 2012. *Un'arma poderosissima. Industria cinematografica e Stato durante il fascismo 1922–1943.* Milan: Franco Angeli.
Margrave, Seton. 1936. *Successful Film Writing.* London: Methuen. Italian edition: Margrave, S. 1939. *Come si scrive un film.* Milan: Bompiani.

May, Renato. 1939. "Storia e tecnica della sceneggiatura." In *Bianco e Nero* 12: 16–27.
Mazzei, Luca. 2006. "Prima e dopo l'immagine: percorsi tra testo letterario e film nel cinema degli anni '30." In *Sulla carta. Storia e storie della sceneggiatura in Italia*, edited by Mariapia Comand, 71–108. Turin: Lindau.
Mediterraneo. 1991. Written by Enzo Monteleone. Directed by Gabriele Salvatores. Italy: A.M.A. Film, Penta, Silvio Berlusconi Communications, Cecchi Gori Group Tiger Cinematografica.
Moravia, Alberto. 1999 [1954]. *Contempt*, trans. Angus Davidson, New York: New York Review Books.
Mosconi, E. 2018. "Quando il cinema scende in piazza. Forme, funzioni, figure del cineforum cattolico." *Schermi* 3: 157–76.
Moscati, Massimo. 1989. *Manuale di sceneggiatura*. Milan: Mondadori.
Moscon, Giorgio, ed. 1961. *Divorzio all'italiana*. Rome: Edizioni F.M.
Naumburg, Nancy. [1937–1940?] *Come si fa un film a Hollywood*. English ed.: *We Make the Movies*. Rome: ARS.
Nigro, Francesca. 1999. *Nuovissimo vademecum per leggere e scrivere il cinema. Consigli, storie e autori dal Premio Solinas*. Milan: Edizioni Il Castoro.
Paladino, Santi. 1943. *Come scrivere e sceneggiare un soggetto cinematografico*. Rome: Editoriale Arte e Storia.
Pasolini, Pier Paolo. 1965. *La sceneggiatura come "struttura che vuol essere altra struttura"*. In *Empirismo eretico*, 188–97. Milan: Garzanti.
Pellizzari, Lorenzo. 1999. *Poligono e contorni. Marcel Carnè*, edited by Corrado Terzi, 9–37. Cesena, Italy: Il Ponte Vecchio.
Pirro, Ugo. 2002 [1982]. *Per scrivere un film*, 2nd edition. Turin: Lindau.
Pirro, Ugo. 1998. *Soltanto un nome nei titoli di testa. I felici anni Sessanta del cinema italiano*. Turin: Einaudi.
Pirro, Ugo. 2001. *Il cinema della nostra vita*, Turin: Lindau.
Prosperi, Giorgio. 1958. "Incontro internazionale delle scuole di Cinema. L'insegnamento della Sceneggiatura." *Bianco e Nero* 7: 23–28.
Pudovkin, Vsevolod I. 1926. *Kinostsenari*. Moska: Kinospeciat. Italian edition: Pudovkin, Vsevolod I. 1932. *Il soggetto cinematografico*, edited by Umberto Barbaro. Rome: Edizioni d'Italia-CSC. English edition: Pudovkin, Vsevolod I.1930. "The Film Scenario". In *On Film Technique: Three Essays and an address*, trans. Ivor Montagu. London: Gollancz.
Renzi, Renzo. 1953. "L'armata s'agapò." *Cinema nuovo* 4: 73–75.
Richter, Hans. 1939. "Chi scrive lo scenario?" *Bianco e Nero* 2: 106–13.
Robbe-Grillet, Alain. 1961. *L'anno scorso a Marienbad*. Turin: Einaudi.
Russo, Paolo, ed. 2014. *Nero su Bianco. Sceneggiatura e sceneggiatori in Italia*. Monographic issue of *Quaderni del CSCI* 10.
Salinger, J. D. 1951 [1945–1946]. *The Catcher in the Rye*. New York: Little, Brown and Co.
Seger, Linda. 1987. *Making a Good Script Great*. New York: Samuel Franch. Italian edition: Seger, Linda, 1997. *Come scrivere una grande sceneggiatura*. Rome: Dino Audino Editore.
Senso. 1954. Written by Suso Cecchi d'Amico and Luchino Visconti. Directed by Luchino Visconti. Italy: Lux Film.
Subini, Tommaso. 2015. "The Failed Project of a Catholic Neorealism: On Giulio Andreotti, Félix Morlion e Roberto Rossellini." In *Moralizing Cinema Film,*

Catholicism and Power, edited by Daniel Biltereyst and Daniela Treveri Gennari. New York: Routledge.

Tosi, Virgilio. 1999. *Quando il cinema era un circolo: la stagione d'oro dei cineclub (1945–1956)*. Rome: Centro Sperimentale di Cinematografia.

Treveri Gennari, Daniela. 2009. *Post-War Italian Cinema. American Intervention, Vatican Interests*. London: Routledge.

Vampyr. 1932. Written by Christen Jul and Carl Theodor Dreyer. Directed by Carl Theodor Dreyer. Germany: Tobis Filmkunst.

Viazzi, Glauco, ed. 1945. *Entr'acte di René Clair*. Milan: Poligono.

Vogler, Christopher. 1982. *The Writer's Journey: Mythic Structure for Storytellers and Screenwriters*, Studio City: Michael Wiese Production. Italian edition: Vogler, Christopher. 1999. *Il viaggio dell'eroe, La struttura del mito ad uso di scrittori di narrativa e cinema*. Rome: Dino Audino Editore.

Wilder, Billy. 1952. *L'asso nella manica*. Rome: Edizioni Filmcritica.

CHAPTER 39

Screenwriting, Short Film, and Pedagogy

Díóg O'Connell

39.1 Introduction

Far from being a stepping stone to feature film production or a form of film apprenticeship, the Irish short film has become an established and recognised genre in its own right, shifting in its cultural significance at various points in recent history. The absence of a critical mass of feature film production, for cultural, economic and political reasons, for much of the twentieth century in Ireland, situates the short film in a significant space. As a post-colonial country, achieving independence from Britain and establishing the Free State in 1922, film as culture was a casualty of the independent government. It was neither supported nor viewed in cultural terms, rather it was seen as a force for propaganda and information (Gibbons et al. 1988). Ireland, therefore, did not experience a film movement on a par with its European neighbours that can be characterised as national cinema, until the late twentieth century cinema. The one constant, however, in Irish film culture is the short film, with a long history spanning the twentieth century.

This chapter explores the short film in Ireland and how it lends itself as a site of pedagogical practice for screenwriting because of its eclectic formal attributes and its success at a critical and creative level, evidenced through awards and audience response. Raskin's description of the short film as stories that "tell their stories with such remarkable economy [that] take our breath

D. O'Connell (✉)
Institute of Art, Design and Technology, Dublin, Ireland
e-mail: diog.oconnell@iadt.ie

away", and at their best, the audience finds themselves "drawn into their world, caught up in the lives of their characters, moved or amused by the events that unfold, then finally eased out of the fiction once again, feeling profoundly enriched by the experience—all in a matter of five or ten or fifteen minutes" (Raskin 2015, 1), helps frame this analysis. The short film is considered here in its narrative and aesthetic attributes and linked to earlier developments in film history. This chapter establishes connections between silent cinema at the start of the twentieth century and new narrative forms at the start of the twenty-first century, presenting a bridge between early silent cinema and new narrative forms, as bookending yet integrating a key and defining era of film history and evolution. In doing so, this approach reclaims and applies seminal writings in Film Studies, for screenwriting studies today.

The short film in Ireland embedded as a form during the first wave of Irish film (1975–1988)[1] and consolidated in the vacuum between 1987 and 1993 when the Irish Film Board/Screen Ireland) was de-activated in 1986, after a short six-year life. Film Base (1986–2018), an organisation set up to provide training, education and equipment hire as well as support for Irish film-makers in the absence of wider public policy and sustained public finance, took on the role as agitator, campaigning for the re-instatement of the film industry infrastructure. It also became the central portal of short film production. Due to its political activism, short films emerging through Film Base often harnessed experimental narrative forms and channelled challenging representations of key tropes associated with Irish cultural identity. This changed following the re-instatement of the Irish Film Board/Screen Ireland in 1993 and in association with RTÉ (the national broadcaster), supports for short films were more stream-lined, leading to mainstream narrative forms, having "the effect of making the resulting films look much the same in terms of visual style, editing and narrative" (McLoone 2000, 157). This chapter explores short film against this backdrop and in this context while suggesting that the picture painted by McLoone might be more complex, and that short film in Ireland is a key component of Irish film culture.

Against the backdrop of films including *Frankie* (2007, Darren Thornton, writer-director); *New Boy* (2007, Steph Green, writer-director); *The Carpenter and his Clumsy Wife* (2004, Peter Foott, writer-director); *The Door* (2008, Juanita Wilson, writer-director); *35 Aside* (1996, Damian O'Donnell, writer-director); *3 Joes* (1991, Lenny Abrahamson, writer-director); *He Shoots, He Scores* (1995, John Moore, writer-director) and *Jack's Bicycle* (1990, John Moore, writer-director), the aim of this chapter is to scrutinise the nature of Irish short film—its formal attributes, its story telling techniques, its visual style, its provenance as well as its legacy and to explore its potential as a site of pedagogical exploration and experimentation in screenwriting education

---

[1] The first wave of Irish film is spans *Caoineadh Airt O Laoire* (Bob Quinn, 1975) to *Reefer and the Model* (Joe Comerford, 1988) and is regarded as an experimental and challenging period of Irish film Culture.

and training. More design than accident, this selection of films represents a tendency in short film to be the work of a writer-director team, a characteristic of short film outside Ireland also. Given that the short films mentioned here, in all cases, are written and directed by the same person, the short film becomes a useful text in the classroom, to explore the art of screenwriting as form and aesthetic. Rather than strictly appropriating the *blueprint* analogy (Maras 2009, 117), this chapter illustrates how the short film is a central pedagogical tool for screenwriting, when practice and criticism are intricately linked.

39.2 Narrative Aesthetics Explored

Screenwriting manuals feature on the reading lists of most screenwriting courses as a key resource, but one that the student/scriptwriter can follow without instruction. The manual has limited use as a pedagogical tool due to its already clear and instructional style. What screenwriter doesn't have Syd Field's invaluable *Screenplay* (1979) on their book shelf but did they need to sign up to a course in screenwriting to gain access to its content? While theory and practice can have a fractured relationship, how one informs the other has been evolving steadily for some time now. The examination of narrative strategies that place the storytelling medium in its historical context, alongside narrative theory, that explores the engagement between screenwriter/filmmaker, story and spectator, is an emerging space of praxis. The screenwriting manual combined with critical theory of narratology provides a context for practice as an intellectual critical endeavour through close and rigorous scrutiny. For example, the screenwriting manual might detail how to develop a character, how to write backstory and how to reveal subtext, but Edward Branigan's theory of focalization (1998, 101) is a useful method to understand the difference between a character that "sees and hears" and a character that "says and does" (Bordwell 1990, 66). This is just one example of how theory can inform praxis, as a useful pedagogical tool in screenwriting.

Although not a theory of short film narrative, Tom Gunning's seminal text on *cinema of attractions* is a useful framework for exploring the short film narrative in the classroom, as it evolved in cinema history. It is also a useful text in illustrating how early narrative analysis aligns with emerging narratives in a new media space and on new platforms. Gunning defines his concept as "a cinema that displays its visibility, willing to rupture a self-enclosed fictional world for a chance to solicit the attention of the spectator" (Gunning 1997), a solid launching pad for exploring the short film. At first glance, Gunning's emphasis on early film, before 1906, might seem anachronistic. The films he explores predate the Hollywood Studio System and the Classical Realist Text but the elements of classical narrative are already in place, even if classical narrative does not embed until the coming of sound. What connects this era with its descendant a century later is this idea of *attraction*, and often the absence of a *narrative impulse*, so beloved of the screenwriting manual. Referring to very early cinema, Gunning states that the films of George Méliès are not about playing out of the scenario but the scenario is simply a pretext for the staged spectacle, or in the words describing his work, the tricks. In the same historical period, the Lumiere brothers present their narrative to an audience as recorders of actuality, albeit with interventions. Films like *La Sortie de l'Usine Lumière à Lyon* (1895) and *L'arrivée d'un train en gare de La Ciotat* (1895) can be considered closer to the short film of late and narrative forms in the emerging and developing new media platform space, than feature length films of the early-mid twentieth century.

In sitting side by side short form narratives that define new media, for example, the impact *YouTube* and *TikTok* are making on the telling of stories, these early films are useful pedagogical tools to expand the understanding and conception of narrative forms for the screenwriting student today. These films are not centrally about telling a story but rather about presentation, as was the films of the Lumière brothers. To what extent content on new media platforms are narrative forms is a question as valid in the twenty-first century as it has been for varied film narratives in Film Studies for decades. Gunning argues that the narrative elements defining early films were not so much supplanted or disappeared by the consolidation of the classical narrative, but went underground or were subsumed as elements, only to emerge subversively later on in the Hollywood Studios' output. Spectacle in the Musical and distinctive aesthetic in the visual style of some Westerns can be read this way. Gunning sees the short film as a subversion of the narrative form and suggests its resurfacing coincides with fallow periods of film production. In Irish film history, this is evidenced in film productions from the 1970s to 1990s (*Emtigon*, 1970 and *Waterbag*, 1984 writer-director Joe Comerford; *Stephen* (1990 writer-director Johnny Gogan), for example. The short film becomes a way to speak, to address, to look the spectator in the eye, in a contrasting way to the seamless entrapment of classical and mainstream narratives and at key historical moments. The difference, therefore, between the films Tom Gunning discusses and what is produced for new media platforms is not a million miles apart. Exposure to these early narrative forms, therefore, can only enrich the scripting process of new stories and forms a key part of pedagogies.

Tom Gunning's call for a return to the vision of Eisenstein, which inspired his theory of *cinema of attractions* brought on by "a need to rediscover the Utopian promise the cinema offered" (Gunning 2006: 32), which was first discovered by theorists and film-makers in the 1920s in Russia and Walter Benjamin and Siegfried Kracauer in the 1930s, is a useful starting point. Gunning contrasts this approach with "the ideological critique of the cinematic apparatus that had dominated Film Theory post-1960s", favouring "these earlier avant-garde thinkers and practitioners [who] saw revolutionary possibilities (both political and aesthetic) in the novel ways cinema took hold of its spectator" (Gunning 2006, 32). What he was calling for was a curiosity for the range of film practices, and what these narrative strategies do for audience engagement. This chimes very much with the plurality and eclectic nature of the short film, and equally with the emergence of short form narratives on new media platforms.[2] Film Studies, with an over-reliance on ideological analysis and identity frameworks, tended to extinguish the spell of narrative discovery. What Gunning does is seek to reignite the flame of narrative investigation, by re-appropriating "the work of Sergei Eisenstein, both as theorist and as filmmaker, [who] presented an alternative: an excitement about the (then) new possibilities of cinema deriving from the Utopian confluence of modernist practice and political revolution" (Gunning 2006, 32). This is combined with a critique, both ideological and formal, of dominant practices. For Gunning, the concept of the attraction captured the potential energy of cinema's address to the spectator, offering a timely response to understanding the short film in recent times. It brings theory directly into the heart of praxis, an aspiration of film programmes not often realised.

John Moore's *He Shoots, He Scores* (1998) is a film that stretches the film frame in building a story that captures some of the magic that cinema presents as possibilities (Gunning 1997). This 11-minute black and white film is a futuristic, surreal comedy, set in one location where two boys meet by chance encounter, at a bus-stop sometime in the future. Clearly, a nod to Samuel Beckett's *Waiting for Godot* (1952), this film achieves what Gunning desires for film, an experimentation of the form to explore beyond story. In this instance, it leaves it open but expands beyond expectations of realism. An earlier film, 16-mm black and white short film *3 Joes* (1991) by Lenny Abrahamson has all the potential and limitations of a student film, but equally imagined and sitting within a realm of possibilities. Twenty-seven minutes in duration, it is a long short that now might seem laboured and stretched but as a precursor to the later films of Abrahamson as director (*Adam and Paul*, 2004; *Garage*, 2007; *What Richard Did*, 2012; *Room*, 2015; *Normal People*, 2020 and *Conversations with Friends*, 2022), it reveals storytelling as character and observation, focussing on three young men called Joe doing a bit of housework, one summer's morning. Depicting the mundane in subtle comic mode. this film recalls early silent cinema rather than recent classical inspiration, and can also be traced right through Abrahamson's oeuvre, to his most recent television drama, *Conversations with Friends*, where acting and aesthetic stamp his auteur credentials.

Juanita Wilson's *The Door* (2008) also uses the "magical possibilities of cinema" by dodging a classical story to recount an episode in allegorical fashion from the time of the 1986 Chernobyl disaster, an exploration of a father's devastation at the events afflicting his family and the loss of his daughter. Nominated for an academy award, this short film demonstrates a way of telling a story as experience, using the traditional linear format to reveal symbolism, visual and iconic, in the form of the door. While each film adapts

---

[2] New media platforms such as *Vimeo*, *YouTube*, *YouTube Shorts* and *TikTok* have provided another distribution and exhibition outlet for the short film side-stepping the traditional route to audience via the festival circuit, in turn changing narrative practice and audience engagement at a fundamental level.

a narrative style that is on the one hand accessible, the other obscure, they connect and overlap in the lingering visual style that each film imparts. The viewing is an experience rather than a journey, and with experience, rather than journey, there is a truth in recall that transplants the spectator straight back to the initial encounter. This is an achievement of the short film that sets it aside from other narrative forms.

Gunning's understanding and definition of *cinema of attraction* is that it commands spectator attention through provoking, as he describes, visual curiosity, and providing pleasure in the spectacle. This can take the form of sweeping narrative or quirky story. The short film has, in Eisenstein's words, a "freedom from the creation of a diegesis, its accent on direct stimulation" (Gunning 1997, 66), accidently or by design, implementing Eisenstein's theory of dialectic montage. Written and directed by Peter Foott, *The Carpenter and his Clumsy Wife* (2004) is a black comedy about a carpenter who uses his skills to repair what he believes to be his wife's inadequacies, by chopping off her body parts and replacing them with wood carvings. The short format requires an audience engagement in the moment, not necessarily one of *anticipation and recall* which is common in the feature length film. This engagement in the moment takes an emotional and physiological journey, which is less about reason and more about feeling. By the close of the film, the spectator has been put through a number of emotional experiences that challenge the normal expectations around conventional story tropes. A bit like the experience of the *sublime*, having watched the short film, the spectator is left with a transcended narrative experience that might be described as complete, although difficult to explain why. This short was the graduation film of Peter Foott, the director of the 3-part comedy drama series, *The Young Offenders* (2018–2020 BBC/RTÉ) which was a follow-on from the 2016 feature film of the same name. Looking at the short film in this context, many of Gunning's attributes for *cinema of attractions* are evident in the practice of the emerging filmmaker. What Foott transplants from his short film practice to conventional television drama is a connection with the absurd. Evidence of his style, this reveals the short as part of and a stage in his narrative process, rather than the stepping stone sometimes suggested. The short film provides an object or artefact to study storytelling and narrative construction, including plot and character, development or otherwise that starts with the script and is complete in production. These films can be folded into the pedagogies of scriptwriting more readily than the feature film, if explored as ways of doing rather ways of representing, in case study fashion.

Gunning sees changes in shot arrangement, cinematography and editing as not just ways of expressing narrative tensions, but the whole point of the film. This formalist approach, that hooks everything on attraction, is easily appropriated for the short film. In David O'Sullivan's *Moore Street Masala* (2009), a story with social and political resonance in Ireland when economic boom switches to bust is evoked but through the wider filmic references of the Bollywood musical, visual excess and traditional romance narrative. This film pulls together the narrative elements identified by Propp and Eisenstein while making highly localised and cultural references. Similarly, to the earlier examples, and like many of the short films explored here, the pleasure is purely in the viewing, not diminished with repeat visits, most likely enhanced. With the mental recall of the viewing experience, some of the emotions are re-ignited. This is partly due to the intensity of a short temporal narrative, but equally to the arrangement of the narrative strategies mentioned here. By focussing on aesthetics in this way, the screenwriter can be free of the manual and the formula, and for the short film screenwriter, experimentation becomes a means to narrative end, rather than a stepping stone along a career-path.

39.3 NARRATIVE FORM RE-VISITED

In teaching screenwriting through analysing the short film, the experience in the classroom or studio can move quickly beyond a skills-based approach to include history and theory, becoming not only an intellectual engagement with ideas, but also a methodology to explore application. The traditional university approach to the seminar can usefully be appropriated in an art school setting, by engaging the student through the exploration of historical context and shifting narrative forms. The field of study has expanded because of the emergence of new media, shorter form narratives and easier access routes to film archive material. The twenty-first century students' familiarity with these narrative forms ideally places them to draw these connections, in an appropriate pedagogical environment. The discussion below illustrates how basic concepts, such as plot and character, can move beyond a simple descriptive explanation of terms, to the possibilities that narrative presents, when the short film connects with much earlier nascent films. Linking contemporary short film with earlier traditions of silent film, is not new but is timely.

Edwin S. Porter's *The Great Train Robbery* (1903) is one of the key moments in cinema history and the development of the film form, providing all the elements that would go on to form the classical realist text. It combines spectacle and narrative at a pivotal moment in the history of early cinema and was described by Gunning as a "direct assault on the spectator... towards linear narrative" (Gunning 1997, 61). Early film's "ambiguous heritage", which combined presentation and representation, storytelling and spectacle, is particularly useful for short film analysis. Bookending the first hundred years of cinema, *The Great Train Robbery* and *Six Shooter* (2004) reveal how developed, advanced and established film narrative was, quite early on in its history and how little its fundamentals have changed in its first century. Playwright Martin McDonagh's film debut as writer-director about a train encounter between a recently bereaved man (Brendan Gleeson) and a violently angry youth, Kid (Rúaidhrí Conroy) was the winner of the Academy Award for Best Short Film in 2006. Set on a train, where a chance encounter between a number of just bereaved passengers with, unbeknownst to them, Kid who has just killed his mother, this film is simultaneously a homage to cinematic tradition as well as a seamless presentation of classic elements. *The Great Train Robbery* struggled with a depiction in realism prior to the evolution of certain narrative elements, notably characterisation and coherent plot development held together through continuity editing, necessary for suspension of disbelief. *Six Shooter*, although not using much more in the line of narrative strategy, masterfully crafts through highly developed characterisation and seamless plot, a story that without suspension of disbelief is beyond the philosophical underpinning of realism. McDonagh, whose writing for theatre is exacting in form, transfers seamlessly to the short film format, and despite its almost one location, it is a pure film experience. Taking the location of his film, the train, as his stage, he crafts a script that fully utilises what editing and juxtaposition of shots, offer the storyteller.

The Great Train Robbery sees the almost obsolete tableau shot dominate, alongside innovative organisation of shots in the style of cross-cutting and match cuts. Spectator engagement is achieved through strategies of cinematic narration such as framing, editing and type of shot while a very early, if not the earliest, example of characterisation appears in the form of the close up shot. However, the narrative function of this shot is unclear as it is not part of the narrative diegesis and can be edited in at the start or at the end of the film. The close up shot does not acquire a motivating function in the fiction film unless it is integrated within the overall cinematic narration.

However unrefined in its structure and delivery of plot and story, *The Great Train Robbery* is a parallel film to McDonagh's *Six Shooter*; they are films of spectacle and narrative. What *Six Shooter* reveals is the masterful storytelling of Martin McDonagh, and the pleasure for the spectator is in the precision of narrative construction, a fully formed and mature version of the seeds sewn in *The Great Train Robbery*. Ruth Barton notes that *Six Shooter* "abounds with cinephile references, not least to John Ford's 1939 *Stagecoach* and its series of encounters between the law and ideas of respectability" (Barton 2019, 165). However, it is McDonagh's experimentation with the possibilities of form and narrative, that supersede the cultural representational path that Barton highlights, and that makes this film connect across the century. Cross references can be made between the trains as a central hub of story—it is what allows the action take place. In both, exteriors play pivotal plot points—when the bereaved mother in *Six Shooter* throws herself from the moving train and in *The Great Train Robbery* when the driver's assistant is brutally killed by the robbers and thrown off the moving train. In *Six Shooter*, the interior of the train acts as a site of character reveal, almost like the stage but with all the possibilities that editing allows. *The Great Train Robbery*, despite a display for the camera through static framing, is pure film. There is no question of theatrical influences dominating here; this is a narrative compiled of editing. The short film again lends itself as an object and artefact to teaching the budding screenwriter about editing. A screenwriter imagines, in their mind's eye, their story unfolding on screen, as a story assembled through the arranging of pictures. In developing this skill, the fundamentals of editing are studied and understood.

The film is an object or artefact that can be broken down, scenario-like, into its component parts, isolating elements of plot and character for example, and revealing the narrative trade tools of the screenwriter. While both films' essence is in how they are edited, the original idea is conceived scenario-like. While the final film is complete, seamless and coherent, the process of breaking up the parts, and putting back together, is a useful way to introduce experimental writing to the student screenwriter. Barton argues that "*Six Shooter* productively references transnational models of filmmaking to move it outside of a narrow Irish framework" (Barton 2019, 166), something that connects many of these award-winning shorts with the traditions of early cinema, and with the genre of short film.

39.4 Case Study as Method in Pedagogy

This case study approach is not unique. Richard Raskin in *The Art of the Short Fiction Film* (2002) built a discursive frame around the short film in his critical writings and selection of short film material for analysis. In discussing the length of the short film, he taps into what might appear as an inconsequential detail but one that pre-occupies educators in film schools the world over, namely devising the best structure for the film student as a starting point. Length is key to all elements of form and content, impacting on character and plot development for example, as well as all other variations on narrative execution. Less than 10 minutes is defined by Raskin as a short film—for example, John Moore's *He Shoots, He Scores*—whereas 25–40 minutes in Scandinavia is considered a *novellefilm* or in France as the *moyen metrage* (Raskin 2002, 3)—for example, Lenny Abrahamson's *3 Joes*. In describing the *novellefilm*, as "essentially a miniature feature film" and the short film as "an art form in its own right and with a much freer form of storytelling" (Raskin 2002, 3). Richard Raskin's *manifesto* makes three substantive points. Conflict is not necessary for the short film; there is no need for a character arc, and wordless storytelling is a real option for the short film (Raskin 2002, 4). Exploratory, rather than prescriptive, this is a useful starting point for teaching screenwriting for the short film, with narrative tendencies and strategies as a focus point.

In his essay, *The Short Film and Irish Cinema*, Conn Holohan suggests that "[…] short film… can only offer a singular narrative moment, and the relationship of that moment to any wider reality or truth is necessarily tentative, provisional, dependent upon interpretation and insight. It does not sample reality to make it meaningful but transforms reality into something other" (Holohan 2009, 186). The viewer, according to Holohan, translates the vision into a legible interpretation, situating it in its wider context of culture and society, described by Holohan as "the operation of metaphor" (Holohan 2009, 186), resonant of the films discussed above. Recognising the danger of formulaic solutions, these definitions are useful methods in revealing the clear and obvious contradictions a straightjacket brings, while paradoxically giving a structure for analysis, to engage, explore, explain, elaborate and evaluate, stages in a pedagogical approach to teaching screenwriting.

35 Aside (1996) tells the story of Philip, a misfit who is struggling to settle in at his new school. When he is bullied, his mother takes matters into her own hands to sort things out between Philip and his schoolmates. Slotting into the television half-hour, this short is 26 minutes long. Part of a new funding scheme, Short Cuts, supported by RTÉ and Irish Film Board/Screen Ireland in 1994, it provided a pathway for the emergence of a wave of young directors. Serving both audience and director well, Damian O'Donnell followed this production with *East is East* (1999), *Heartlands* (2002) and *Inside I'm Dancing* (2004), three popular and mainstream feature films he directed. John Moore, a graduate of the same college class, followed his writing/directing debut *He Shoots, He Scores* with *Jack's Bicycle* (1996), revealing a shift in direction towards the mainstream. Moore's short film oeuvre lay the groundwork for his highly successful Hollywood career as a director (*Behind Enemy Lines*, 2001; *The Omen*, 2006; *A Good Day to Die Hard*, 2013). Similarly, Oscar-nominated Kirsten Sheridan's experimental graduate film from the National Film School at IADT, *Patterns* (1999), which she wrote and directed, was followed by the Short Cut funded, *The Case of Majella McGinty* (1999), written by Morna Regan and directed by Sheridan, about a little girl who escapes her stressful life by crawling into a suitcase. Sheridan then made Irish Film Board/Screen Ireland supported feature film *Disco Pigs* (2001), also as director. Sheridan illustrates the relationship between the experimental nature of the film school experience, to a more refined conventional approach to feature production that characterised the re-activated Irish Film Board of the 1990s. The bridge between these two approaches is the funded short.

While the Short Cuts scheme ran between 1994 and 2004, lasting ten years, it shifted away from the television format as its initial defining duration, to be replaced eventually by a range of different schemes including the Short Shorts, finally abandoning the television defining length, as Raskin might have predicted. And in this process, it widened the narrative parameters and space for more experimentation. To celebrate the tenth anniversary of the Short Cuts film scheme, Irish Film Board and RTÉ commissioned five new titles for 2004, including *Sunburn* by Jennifer Keegan (director) and Brian Lynch (writer); *Screwback* by Brian O'Malley (writer-director); *Prey Alone* by James Maher (writer-director); *The Wonderful Story of Kelvin Kind* by Ian Power (writer-director); and *Recoil* by Billy McCannon (writer-director). All these films were shorter at between twelve and fifteen minutes, conforming to a shift for reduced duration and yet within the guidelines, producing hugely contrasting work and by default, anticipating a direction short film would later take as digital technology and new platforms evolved and took hold.

The Wonderful Story of Kelvin Kind is a triumph of production design and aesthetic. Its reference world is clearly itself, denying fixed positions for time and space. It is the world of film. Using fully the potential of sound and vision, this might be classified as experimental with a mainstream story. On the other hand, Billy McCannon's *Recoil* is clearly rooted to a space and time, situating its story within Northern Ireland and IRA violence, a very common trope in Irish cinema. It claws at realism, positioning the spectator very much in a real milieu, the Troubles, and because of its conventional storytelling, is hindered in similar ways to its feature length counter-parts about conflict in Northern Ireland. Ian Power's *The Wonderful Story of Kelvin Kind*, in dodging realism, creates cinematic narrative walls that are solid and defining, in an art form tradition. While each film can be taken as a stand-alone case study, what binds them as a unit is Raskin's idea that short films "allow physical objects charged with meaning for their characters to bear important parts of the storytelling. In this way, inner experience and outer objects can be connected" (Raskin 2015: 5). However, in a story so rooted in a complex history outside of its diegesis, the danger is falling into mythic traps. *Recoil* like many Hollywood films before it, attempts to explain a complex political and social context in archetypal figures, in this instance the mother, seen many times before in Irish and Hollywood versions of events. Raskin's paradoxical contention that "short films telling simple stories are most likely to be experienced by viewers as being deep, because they leave a habitable space inside for viewers to enter" (Raskin 2002, 2) sits easily with *The Wonderful Story of Kelvin Kind*, its visual style, sound scape and production design contributing to its complex world. It is in this space that pedagogical screenwriting practice can experiment, encouraging the testing of theories and methods.

The period that follows tracks the next stage in short film evolution in Ireland, a parallel path to what was happening in feature film-making. Darren Thornton, although not a Short Cuts graduate, is an interesting case in point. His short film as a writer-director, *Frankie* (2007) tells the story of a teenage boy on the precipice of fatherhood. Deftly crafted in 12 minutes, it spans the spectrum of national cinema territory—social comment, resonant characters shaped by their environment and in keeping with Irish film culture post-1990s, idiosyncratically characterised by local accent and humour. Thornton's mastering of the narrative structure as defined by David Bordwell, seamless diegesis of space and time, executed through continuity editing, already evident in his television drama *Love is the Drug* (2004), which he co-wrote with Barbara Bergin and Martin Maguire, and a precursor to his feature film production, *A Date for Mad Mary* (2016), as writer and director.

Thornton's path through television drama to feature film, via the short film, as writer and director, is interesting. His command of the genre is evident in his early work. *Frankie* is not a stage in film training or a stepping stone to a career in features, but a bridge between television drama and film, and part of Thornton's film repertoire, generating an audience response as fresh and lively a decade after its construction. Experience in the classroom, teaching students about storytelling and screenwriting, and using *Frankie* as a case study, reveals it as a short film that never loses its impact or its edge with the passage of time. *Frankie* fits snugly into Raskin's typology: causality; choice; consistency;

focus—all working towards a seamless narrative, and this becomes an object and artefact in the classroom, to take apart in all its narrative parts. Despite using the final film as the object, it is the evidence of screenwriting practice that students can learn most about.

Credit to Screen Ireland in its nascent period that it did not saddle itself to one version of the short film. Experimentation and change aptly describes the varied approach to the short film in the last three decades, adapting and changing funding models according to how the film industry was evolving. From the examples explored above, these schemes served emerging filmmakers well, and while it gave them opportunities to develop and hone their craft, it wasn't a means to an end. However, the official line seems to be shifting. According to Screen Ireland's website, the current scheme for funding shorts encourages "strong, original storytelling, visual flair, and production values appropriate to the big screen. It offers an opportunity for producers, directors and writers to work in a professional environment that will bring their experience up to a higher level and can be seen as a potential stepping stone for future full-length film-makers".[3]

The short film has become a reduced entity within Screen Ireland policy and is currently viewed as a stepping stone or training ground for feature production. As film production is torn between the crude dichotomy of culture and industry, the space to experiment and engage in alternative narrative forms is relegated very much to the periphery. This is surprising given the technological fragmentation/explosion that has opened up many possibilities in new media platforms and elides the contribution short film-making has made at key historical moments in Irish film. Referring to vacuum periods in Irish film activity, McLoone noted that "the short became a way in which the whole film community in Ireland kept in touch with the 'raw materials' of film-making and its importance in this regard should not be underestimated" (McLoone 2000: 152).

39.5 Conclusion

The short film is an art form and when analysed formally, aesthetically and narratively, can be absorbed into the pedagogies of screenwriting. In Holohan's words, "explanation must come at another level of discourse or else the act must remain uncanny, an unsettling disturbance of the known world", moving away from representation and realism as a frame of analysis towards metaphor and symbol, "speaking to a reality which is outside of itself, which its brief moment of narrative transformation can only gesture towards" (Holohan 2009, 186). The short film is much more varied, unique, idiosyncratic and

---

[3] A useful platform to gain insight into the wide ranging ideological underpinnings of Irish film is Screen Ireland's website, which illustrates the real tensions between art and industry for any national funding agency. https://www.screenireland.ie/funding/short-film-schemes/focus-shorts (accessed 10 November 2021).

eclectic for the conventional theories of identity politics to be ultimately meaningful. This might explain its absence from the dominant discourses within national cinema.

The narrow framing of the short film as a stepping stone and training ground for emerging film-makers is largely redundant, when the art form is surveyed in both its widest and most focussed imagining. Conceptualised as an art form or a genre, a distinctive narrative with its own evolutionary path and developmental process, it lends itself as both a critical and creative force in the pedagogy of screenwriting. Whether it is conceived as a gag, a moment, a story or an experiment, its pedagogical impetus can perform within the instructional screenwriting programme for challenge-based learning or emerging spaces grappling with the shifting sands of new media platforms. Dusting off the seminal Film Studies texts of Burch and Gunning, that rigorously investigated early cinema forms from the nickelodeons (1905–1915) through primitive cinema (until 1919) and on to the silent era, seems particularly prescient in the light of exploding narrative forms finding new platforms because of transformative technologies. Old knowledge re-imagined can offer a guide and a new light.

As McLoone contends, "if the main purpose of the short is as a vehicle for training and gaining experience in all aspects of film-making—handling actors, pre-production planning, producing and dealing with the business end, post-production and finally distribution and marketing—then in effect the potential of its 'institutional space' is denied" (McLoone 2001, 156). This "institutional space", McLoone argues, should allow for "a more liberating environment for experiment and exploration" (156) in a time when the Irish Film Board/Screen Ireland is promoting a more mainstream approach to all its narrative forms. The short film is not only a pedagogical tool for analysis and appreciation but a narrative form that facilitates experiment and exploration. While it can be stepping stone, for twenty-first century film-makers, it is much more than just this.

References

Joes. 1991. Written and directed by Lenny Abrahamson. Ireland: Temple Films.
Aside. 1996. Written and directed by Damian O'Donnell. Ireland: RTÉ, IFB.
A Date for Mad Mary. 2016. Written and directed by Darren Thornton. Ireland: IFB, Element Pictures.
A Good Day to Die Hard. 2013. Written by Skip Woods. Directed by John Moore. USA: Giant Pictures, TSG Entertainment, Temple Hill Entertainment.
Adam and Paul. 2004. Written by Mark O'Halloran. Directed by Lenny Abrahamson. Ireland: IFB, Element Pictures.
Barton, Ruth. 2019. *Irish Cinema in the Twenty-First Century*. Manchester: Manchester University Press.
Behind Enemy Lines. 2001. Written by David Veloz and Zak Penn. Directed by John Moore. USA: Davis Entertainment.

Bordwell, David. 1990. *Narration in the Fiction Film*. 4th ed. Madison, WI: University of Wisconsin Press.
Branigan, Edward. 1998. *Narrative Comprehension and Film*. 3rd ed. London and New York: Routledge.
Caoineadh Airt O Laoire. 1975. Written by Mairtín Mac Donncha, Seosamh O'Cuaig, and Bob Quinn. Directed by Bob Quinn. Ireland: Cinegael.
Conversations with Friends. 2022. Written by Alice Birch, Mark O'Halloran, Meadhbh McHugh, and Susan Soon He Stanton. Directed by Lenny Abrahamson. Ireland: BBC 3, Screen Ireland, RTÉ
Disco Pigs. 2001. Written by Enda Walsh. Directed by Kirsten Sheridan. Ireland: IFB.
East is East. 1999. Written by Ayub Khan-Din. Directed by Damien O'Donnell. UK: Film 4.
Frankie. 2007. Written and directed by Darren Thornton. Ireland: Screen Ireland.
Garage. 2007. Written by Mark O'Halloran. Directed by Lenny Abrahamson. Ireland: IFB, Element Pictures.
Gibbons, Luke, Kevin Rockett, and John Hill. 1988. *Cinema and Ireland*. London: Routledge.
Gunning, Tom. 1997. "*The Cinema of Attractions: Early Film, Its Spectator and the Avant-Garde*." In *Early Cinema: Space, Frame, Narrative*, edited by Thomas Elsaesser and Adam Barker, 63–70. London: BFI.
Gunning, Tom. 2006. "Attractions: How They Came into the World." In *The Cinema of Attractions Reloaded*, edited by Wanda Strauven, 31–40. Amsterdam: University of Amsterdam Press.
He Shoots, He Scores. 1995. Written and directed by John Moore. Ireland: Film Base.
Heartlands. 2002. Written by Paul Fraser. Directed by Damien O'Donnell. UK, USA: Miramax.
Holohan, Conn. 2009. "The Short Film and Irish Cinema." *Estudios Irlandeses* 4: 148–203.
Holohan, Conn. 2011. "Virtual Cinema Short Films." *Estudios Irlandeses* 6: 191–224.
Inside I'm Dancing. 2004. Written by Christian O'Reilly. Directed by Damien O'Donnell. Ireland: IFB, Studio Canal and Working Title Films.
Jack's Bicycle. 1990. Written and directed by John Moore. Ireland: Film Base.
L'arrivée d'un train en gare de La Ciotat (*Train Pulling into a Station*). 1895. Auguste Lumière, Louis Lumière. France: Société A. Lumière et ses Fils.
La Sortie de l'Usine Lumière à Lyon (*Workers Leaving the Factory*). 1895. Directed by Louis Lumière. France: Société A. Lumière et ses Fils.
Love is the Drug. 2004. Written by Barbara Bergin, Martin Maguire, and Darren Thornton. Directed by Darren Thornton. Ireland: RTÉ.
Maras, Stephen. 2009. *Screenwriting: History, Theory and Practice*. London: Wallflower Press.
McLoone, Martin. 2001. *Irish Film: The Emergence of a Contemporary Cinema*. London: BFI.
Monahan, Barry. 2011. "Short Shorts: A Masala of Musicals—A review." *Estudios Irlandeses* 6: 191–224.
Moore Street Masala. 2009. Written and directed by David O'Sullivan. Ireland: Dye House Films.
New Boy. 2007. Written and directed by Steph Green. Ireland: Screen Ireland.
Normal People. 2020. Written by Sally Rooney. Directed by Lenny Abrahamson. Ireland: RTÉ, Screen Ireland, BBC.

Patterns. 1999. Written and directed by Kirsten Sheridan. Ireland: IADT.
Prey Alone. 2004. Written and directed by James Maher. Ireland: RTÉ, IFB.
Raskin, Richard. 2002. *The Art of the Short Fiction Film: A Shot by Shot Study of Nine Modern Classics*. Jefferson, NC: McFarland.
Raskin, Richard. 2015. "New Theories of the Short Film." *Musicbed Blog*, 8 June. https://musicbed.com/blog/filmmaking/writing/new-theories-of-the-short-film-a-conversation-with-dr-richard-raskin. Accessed 6 July 2022.
Reefer and the Model. 1988. Written by and directed by Joe Comerford. Ireland: Berber Films.
Room. 2015. Written by Emma Donohue. Directed by Lenny Abrahamson. Ireland: Element Pictures.
Six Shooter. 2004. Written and directed by Martin McDonagh. Ireland: Film4 and Screen Ireland.
The Carpenter and his Clumsy Wife. 2004. Written and directed by Peter Foott. Ireland: Vico Films.
The Case of Majella McGinty. 1999. Written by Morna Regan. Directed by Kirsten Sheridan. Ireland: RTÉ, IFB.
The Door. 2008, Written and directed by Juanita Wilson. Ireland: Screen Ireland.
The Great Train Robbery. 1903. Directed by Edwin S. Porter. USA: Edison Manufacturing Company.
The Omen. 2006. Written by David Seltzer. Directed by John Moore. USA: 20th Century Studios.
The Young Offenders. 2018–2020 (3 seasons). Created by Peter Foott. Ireland, UK: BBC, RTÉ
What Richard Did. 2012. Written by Malcolm Campbell. Directed by Lenny Abrahamson. Ireland: Element Pictures.

CHAPTER 40

Screenwriters in the Academy: The Opportunities of Research-Led Practice

Craig Batty

40.1 Introduction

Screenwriting has been part of the university sector for many decades now, but as a part of research cultures within this sector, it is still very new. While many countries still grapple with the concept of creative practice research, the idea of screenwriting as a form of research—or screenplays as research artefacts—is growing. This is especially so as the number of doctoral candidates engaging with screenwriting increases substantially, particularly in countries such as Australia, New Zealand, Ireland, South Africa and the UK, and the flow-on from this as and when these doctoral graduates take up positions in universities. While questions of the form of screenwriting research (e.g. what does a research screenplay look like?) and the process by which it occurs (e.g. how is screenwriting framed as a research practice?) have been explored by myself and others over the past decade (e.g. Batty 2014, 2016; Batty and McAulay 2016; Batty and Taylor 2019), the fundamental question of purpose is largely unexplored: Why would one purposely bring together screenwriting practice and academic research?

In this chapter, then, I map some of the reasons why screenwriters might come into the academy to engage with research, as well as the consequences that can arise from this interaction. Drawing on relevant literature, examples and my own experience as a researcher of screenwriting practice research, I

C. Batty (✉)
University of South Australia, Adelaide, SA, Australia
e-mail: craig.batty@unisa.edu.au

© The Author(s), under exclusive license to Springer Nature Switzerland AG 2023
R. Davies et al. (eds.), *The Palgrave Handbook of Screenwriting Studies*, https://doi.org/10.1007/978-3-031-20769-3_40

explore some of the motivations, experiences and outcomes of screenwriters in the academy. I am particularly interested in how the reciprocity of theory and practice can lead to what I see as productive identity shifts of both practitioners and researchers when engaging in this kind of research.

As I have argued previously, the creative doctorate is an incubator for research-led approaches to expanding knowledge and expanding one's extant practice (Batty and Berry 2016). The doctoral space offers a particularly useful lens to understand the appeal and potential of screenwriting practice research, and this will be emphasised in the chapter. Driven by a scholarly question or proposition, and underpinned by methodological rigour, what happens when doctoral candidates or trained researchers step into an experimental research space and brave the unknown? How open to new understandings, practices and applications might they become? And what does a transition from practitioner to practitioner-researcher look like?

40.2 Scene 1: The Creative Doctorate

First it feels relevant to map a short history of the creative doctorate, especially from an Australian perspective[1] where the largest number of creative doctorates have been awarded internationally. This is where much of the literature on creative practice research has been developed, and because the doctorate is a training space in which practitioner identity shifts occur most frequently and in the most pronounced way (Brew 2001; Finlayson 2012; Simmons and Holbrook 2013; Wilson 2017), it provides a clear site and structure for understanding the affordances of theory–practice interactions.

There has been significant growth in the number of creative doctorates awarded internationally over the past 20 years,[2] particularly in Australia (Evans et al. 2003; Krauth 2011; The Changing PhD 2013)—whose academics are recognised as leaders in creative practice research discourse and methodology (Batty 2019)—but also in the UK, Ireland and more recently in New Zealand and South Africa.[3] These doctorates span a number of creative and professional disciplines, notably architecture, art and design, dance, creative writing, media and screen production, music, and performance and theatre. This has given rise to a significant increase in the literature on creative practice research broadly and the creative doctorate specifically—though the substance of this extant literature is on defining research practices in creative fields (what does

---

[1] While I am British and completed my own screenwriting PhD in the UK, I have lived and worked in Australia since January 2012. It is during this time, especially due to the exposure I have had to leaders in the field of the creative doctorate, that I have built specialised research strength on the creative doctorate broadly, and the screenwriting practice doctorate specifically. I have also supervised and examined 50 creative doctorates.

[2] The creative arts/practice doctorate has been undertaken through a myriad of awards, including the Doctor of Philosophy, Doctor of Creative Arts, Doctor of Creative Industries and Doctor of Visual Arts.

[3] For example, I examined two of the first screenwriting practice PhDs from this country.

it look like?) and ways of undertaking research and supervising doctorates in this relatively new landscape.

Defining texts and key figures in doctoral research practices across creative disciplines include: in architecture, art and design (Allpress et al. 2012; Baker et al. 2009; Barrett and Bolt 2010; Carter 2007; Vaughan 2017); in dance (Phillips et al. 2009; Stock 2009); in creative writing (Brien 2006; Kroll and Harper 2012; Webb 2015); in media and screen production (Batty and Kerrigan 2018; Bell 2006; Knudsen 2003); in music (Draper and Harrison 2011; Harrison 2014); and in performance and theatre (Freeman 2010; Nelson 2013). In Australia, the Government's former Office for Learning and Teaching (OLT) commissioned several studies to enhance understanding of the nature and pedagogy of supporting research degree students in new disciplines and creative fields. These include Blass et al. (2014) and Boud et al. (2014) on building capacity and leadership in new research disciplines; Hamilton et al. (2014) on creative doctorates; Harrison (2014) on music; Phillips et al. (2009) on dance; and et al. (2008, 2012) on creative writing. Other important studies include Frayling (1993) on research in, for and through creative practice; Hope (2016) on the different ways that practice featured in funded UK research projects; the "Florence Principles" (2016) on artistic research; Newbury (1997) on research training and supervision in the arts; and Wilson (2017) on the influence of Australian federal research policy on creative practitioners working in the academy.

The substantive literature on the creative doctorate, nestled within a rapidly growing field of creative practice research, has provided a strong foundation for what I am calling "second generation" creative doctorates. What I mean by this is that questions such as "how is creative practice also a research practice?", which dominated early debates, have been superseded by questions such as "how do we assess quality?", "what is the nature and level of contribution to knowledge?" and "how equipped are creative practitioners as doctoral learners to take their practice into new epistemologies?" (Batty and Holbrook 2017; Simmons and Holbrook 2013). The screenwriting doctorate, a relative newcomer to the creative doctorate landscape,[4] is perhaps able to take on these questions and be poised to set new standards. To clarify, the creative doctorate has been well and truly mapped in Australia, and to some extent the UK, and there is now a critical mass of doctoral-qualified supervisors across all creative practice fields to take their disciplines forward, fully embracing the potential of research to incubate, expand and potentially transform practice—individually, collectively and perhaps also at an industrial level (noting that this would require many people and much buy-in).

---

[4] There are approximately 75 completed screenwriting practice doctorates from around the world, with at least the same number currently in candidature.

40.3 Scene 2: The Screenwriting Practice Doctorate

While much has been written about creative practice research degrees broadly, and creative writing and screen production research degrees specifically, there has been less published about the screenwriting practice research degree. This is despite a growth in the number of candidates undertaking screenwriting practice doctorates around the world. I have published fairly widely on this topic, on my own and with my doctoral candidates and research colleagues, in an attempt to start to define the field and provide methodological scaffolding for future screenwriting researchers—but there is still much that has not been written about, especially in relation to the specific nature of doctoral studies in/through screenwriting practice, and the outcomes of this creative-critical practice.

One area of specific interest is the position of screenwriting between creative writing and screen production. On the one hand, it is a writing practice that has somewhat of an authorial status, despite it being (in industry at least) the result of a long and complex script development process (Batty and Taylor 2021). On the other hand, it is typically a practice dependent upon or aimed towards production—a text in search of itself (McNamara 2018). This dichotomy presents both a challenge and an opportunity for the screenwriting practice doctorate: first, in struggling to define its fabric and function (e.g. what is the purpose of the research-based screenplay? How can this be assessed?); and second, the potential for a particular type of research pedagogy to emerge (e.g. is there a place for the doctoral screenplay in the ecology of script development? How might research be used to answer industry-based questions?). As some of my extant publications try to demonstrate, this point is evident in the literature being published in journals across the fields of creative writing and screen and media production.

One of the issues that arises in both the literature and general discussions of creative doctorates (Batty and Holbrook 2017), and is certainly no stranger to the screenwriting practice doctorate, is something along the lines of "what even is it?". This is where definitions are useful, if not laborious. Further, if we consider an outsider's view of screenwriting practice research—that is, industry itself—the question becomes quite important because unless "they" understand what it can be/look like, there is likely to be no appetite for considering its potential. From my own experience as a doctoral supervisor, I have admitted many screenwriting and script development professionals into candidature, and it was integral to have a shared understanding of the nature of screenwriting practice research—and the outcomes it might provide—from the outset. As I tell all of my candidates, there is no point theorising their practice for theorising sake—it is more important to use the space (and privilege) of research to do something for their practice, to achieve outcomes (as well as outputs) that are meaningful for them personally but also, ideally, for their industry/field. This goes to the heart of defining screenwriting practice research: What it is and how one does it should be determined by what one wants to gain from undertaking it in the first place.

40.4 Scene 3: Defining Screenwriting Practice Research

A practice "in which the screenwriter makes use of the intellectual space offered by the academy and those within it to incubate and experiment with ideas, with the intention that their processes or their screenplays—*or both*—change as a result" (Batty and McAulay 2016), screenwriting as research possesses a critical focus that "often reflects the distinct vision of a single writer-researcher" (Baker 2013, 4). It can also be systematically much more self-reflexive than in the industry, meaning that "the writing is informed more by discipline specific knowledge than by commercial demands or the expectations of wider audiences or readerships" (Baker 2013, 4). In this regard, "screenplays can—and do—use research to underpin their creation (practice-led research); their content and form (research-informed practice); and their critical and industrial contexts (research-led practice)" (Baker et al. 2015, 3).

Research in academic screenwriting might include aspects such as historical, legal and geographic information, but it goes much further than this. This, as Desmond Bell (2008) reminds us, is what all practitioners do as research; this does not make it novel. Screenwriting research, whether framed as *about*, *for* or *through* practice (see Frayling 1993; Hope 2016), is aimed at producing new knowledge on every level. This might comprise:

- narrative techniques that adhere to or expand on existing paradigms (see Batty 2009; Jacey 2010; Taylor 2014);
- the industrial contexts that shape how a screenplay might be developed and pitched (see Street 2015; McMillan 2014);
- the social, cultural and industrial relevance of the script as text (see Sculley 2015; Igelström 2014);
- and the very practice of screenwriting itself (see Hawkins 2013; Sawtell 2016).

Harper and Kroll (2008) argue that writers in the academy are "functioning in multiple ways: practicing as artists; researching their creative process; researching their art form itself; and engaging in practice-led research (in order to discover new knowledge)" (10). Screenwriting that takes place under the guise of creative practice research thus has a different set of goals than that of commercial screenwriting, even if the end goal of the research screenplay is to have it produced (commercially or independently).

The shift towards the creation of screenplay research artefacts mirrors a similar shift that took place in the field of creative writing twenty years ago, and more recently in the discipline of screen production, where subject associations such as the Australian Screen Production Education and Research Association (ASPERA) are building their confidence in defining and articulating the screen works produced by practitioner-academics as research outputs (see Kerrigan et al. 2015; Glisovic et al. 2016). Screenwriting as a mode of research is, I would thus argue, at an important time in history, where understandings of the practice are improving, and case studies of the resultant research artefacts are increasing.

40.5 Scene 4: Screenwriting Research as a Form of Script Development

From an industry perspective, script development is both a creative and a commercial process in which ideas, emotions and personalities combine with and are contested by the practicalities, policies and movements of broadcasters, production companies and financiers to tell a story in the best way possible under the circumstances at the time. Also a social process, where the creative activities of writing and production intersect (Kerrigan and Batty 2016), script development can be viewed as a collaborative endeavour that functions "according to how both the power held and the control wielded by specific participants work against the extent to which parties are willing to collaborate and extend trust to each other" (Macdonald 2013, 77). A "collaborative journey to make the story as good as it can possibly be" (Bloore 2012: 11), it can often be understood as an endeavour underpinned by 'the thorny question of when do you agree to compromise on your vision to 'get the film made'?" (Bloore 2012, 4). At the same time, however, "collaboration should not be seen as a compromise because acceptance of one's peers is the ultimate creative accomplishment" (Kerrigan and Batty 2016, 6). Indeed, screen theorists such as Staiger (2012) argue that because "no script has ever been without multiple causes for its form and style, no event of writing pure and simple (…) studies of script authorship are important for understanding the complex creative process of film-making" (76). I see script development as a central process within this script authorship.

Script development is laden with a strong sense of external industrialisation and individual emotion: constant negotiations are made between the self (ideas, vision) and the screenplay (structures, formulas, conventions), sometimes made more complex by the reality that script development may involve unpaid labour (see Conor 2014, 31–33). In this regard, is it any wonder that there are an increasing number of screenwriters choosing to develop their projects in the academy, particularly for doctorates? A space of "constellations and connections" in which "practices, methods and understandings meet and shape new methodologies [of practice]" (Batty and Berry 2016, 182), the academy can productively function "as a vital incubator for risk taking, reflexivity and fearless critical thinking" (Batty and Berry 2016, 182) for the screenwriter, asking them "to bring multidisciplinary perspectives and creative research strategies to bear on issues and possibilities, and often to think outside the existing boxes" (Cherry and Higgs 2011, 13).

Based on *research* primarily, as opposed to—but most probably for the future benefit of—*professional practice*, this activity might be conceived of as a practice of "academic script development". Situated outside of the industry, yet fully acknowledging that the work created might eventually find a home within it, the screenwriter can take advantage of research-based script development as an activity that "challenges the idea of being in control at all times, creating the possibility for surprise, for the kind of creative disruption […] that precedes innovation" (Cherry and Higgs 2011, 20). Concerned with "improving and/or innovating practice, and by doing so also creating new knowledge about practice drawn from an insider's perspective" (Batty and Berry 2016, 184), script development in the academy thus offers a way of freeing oneself of the shackles of industry to pursue ideas and practices based on personal, philosophical and/or practical research interests that may innovate future work—of both the individual screenwriter and others in the field.

From my experience of supervising this kind of research, this could include new ways of working with particular demographics in collaborative writers' room settings where there might be real or perceived representational issues; methods for drawing attention to character perspective and dramatic tone in relation to important social concerns; the development of hybrid script-novella artefacts that have the dual function of attracting an audience to the story and script development personnel to the screenplay; and playful approaches to script development which focus on theme, metaphor and emotion, as opposed to plotting the character journey. Embedded fieldwork in industry would also be a powerful sell here.

40.6 Scene 5: The Screenplay as a Research Artefact

While the idea of innovating practice through research incubation might sound appealing to some, and indeed in my own experience as a PhD supervisor this has most certainly led to transformations in candidates' practice, there inevitably exists a gap between what is written and what is desired for production (in an industrial context). Indeed, one of the clearest observations I have made over the past decade is that it is hard to find examples of research excellence in screenplays that are also industrially excellent. This usually goes one of two ways: the research rigour has led to work that is conceptually excellent, but at the level of industry is unlikely to appeal or at the level of craft is not strong enough, or the screenplay is very well written and will appeal to industry, but the research content is either incremental (additive, not transformative) or poorly framed. Good examples of works that fill this void are coming into frame, perhaps more so as seasoned practitioners enrol in doctoral programmes, but a problem of screenwriting practice research is that there is still a gap—real or perceived—between work that invites thinking and work that can be produced. This is why the academy has developed its own platforms for publishing screenwriting research works.

Unlike novels, poems and plays—another scripted form that some would argue is not complete until it is performed—screenplays are rarely, if at all, studied as literary artefacts. For the most part, screenplays are [mis?]understood as mere blueprints for film, television and other moving image works, rather than completed texts in and of themselves (see Baker 2013; Baker et al. 2015; Batty and McAulay 2016). A strong and recent argument made by numerous scholars and creative practice researchers is that screenplays are indeed finished creative works in their own right, regardless of their industrial (production) contexts (Batty et al. 2016; Boon 2008; Macdonald 2010). This is especially true in the doctoral space, where the screenplay functions as a major work of scholarship under the guise of creative practice research (see Lee et al. 2016).

Ted Nannicelli argues that scripts can and should be understood as literature, as "ontologically autonomous works" (2013, 135) that are finished texts in and of themselves, and that can be read as such. Using virtual or online fan scripts as a case study, Nannicelli goes on to maintain that it is practitioners (screenwriters) who:

> (...) determine the boundaries of our screenplay concept, that our screenplay concept has changed over time, that we are now in an historical moment when some screenplays are complete, autonomous works, and that we are also now in an historical moment when some people write screenplays with the intention of creating literature while certain communities of readers appreciate them as such. (2013, 135)

For Dallas Baker, creative writing academic whose doctorate was in screenwriting, "collaborative scriptwriting refuses the notion of authorial integrity and disrupts the idea of 'authentic voice', which is often at the heart of the teaching of creative writing. Scriptwriting also displaces the idea that creativity is an internal and individual or solitary process" (2013, 4).

For the practice of screenwriting, it can be difficult to assign "authorship" of ideas, intentions and scholarly investigations to a screenplay when it contains the work of so many others, especially if produced. This is why the screenplay-as-research-artefact with a clear articulation of the screenwriter's role has taken hold within the academy. If we are to study screenwriting practice seriously, then there needs to be an accessible body of work to analyse and discuss. From the perspective of understanding those works' research pursuits, it is arguably essential that alongside the screenplays themselves we need to see writers' research notes, scholarly annotations and/or reflections on the development process. This is not unlike the annotations and supplementary notes on *real-world* screenplays that are available in archives. As Steven Price reminds us:

Only a tiny fraction of the material that screenwriting researchers may be interested in has been published; much of the reminder is either unavailable, available only in a single library collection or simply unknown. Ownership and copyright issues mean that little of this material can be legally disseminated either in digital or in print form, while cuts in funding for libraries and universities threaten both the archives themselves and those who may wish to visit them. (2013, 88)

Price notes that this situation is changing somewhat as the field of "screenwriting studies" has "started to accumulate its materials—its evidence", even if is it "very late in the day, compared to cognate fields such as literary criticism and film studies" (2013, 88). Nevertheless, recent developments in screenwriting studies are shining a light on the screenplay and its potential as a site of study (Nelmes 2010), particularly for the creative practice researcher. But how valuable is the *unproduced* screenplay, and to whom? Published research-led screenplays might be thought of as akin to the *spec script*, "written speculatively by a writer who chooses to do so other than at the behest of a studio or producer as a work for hire" (Corley and Megel 2014, 12). Like spec scripts, while at the time of publication research screenplays might not be seen as industry artefacts per se, there is nothing to say that they cannot be read, and potentially bought, by industry.

Examples of published research screenplays include the thirty that can be found across three special issues of *TEXT: Journal of Writing and Writing Courses* (2013; 2015; 2018). Each of these scripts was written *on spec* within and for the academy, peer reviewed anonymously by practitioner-researchers who understood the research expectations of these works. Like the more recent examples in the journal *Sightlines: Filmmaking in the Academy* (2021; 2022), these scripts were published with accompanying research statements that articulate their background, contribution and significance, and sometimes the methodology under which they were created. While such research *scaffolding* is often contested (see Glisovic et al. 2016; Batty et al. 2018), it is my personal view that such an articulation is necessary so that readers (who might include industry professionals) can grasp what it is that makes these scripts purposeful. Left to fend for themselves, they could be perceived as spurious, aloof, sitting in ivory towers.

As can be seen across these screenplays—some of which are driven by conceptual ideas, some by content- and craft-related questions—the screenplay as a research artefact is a result of a unique creative practice research methodology comprising various methods and techniques that include the act of writing and/or reflecting on that writing. Performing its research *data* symbolically in ways recognisable to its audience (the screenplay reader) (Haseman 2006), the screenplay as research artefact uses its inherent devices— such as form and format, structure, character, theme, setting and dialogue—to *tell* research. Screenplays as research artefacts thus contribute knowledge in their very fabric, and although accompanying notes or research statements necessarily explicate this research, they do so in conversation with the screenplay itself.

40.7 Scene 6: Screenwriters in the Academy

One largely unexplored aspect of screenwriting as research is how screenwriters themselves feel about bringing their practice into the academy, and what impact being in the academy has on the work they then do. As outlined, the various research topics, questions and methods we have examples of—from completed doctorates, and from informal conversations with screenwriters working in the academy—all contribute to knowledge and practice in different ways, spanning theory, history, craft and industry. There really is no one-size-fits-all model. But one thing is clear: bringing research to bear on creative practice leads to an identity shift of some sort. While this is still a gap in screenwriting research, we can draw from other research areas to help us understand what might be happening to screenwriters in the academy.

The first question we might ask is: Why would a screenwriter come into the academy in the first place? What is it that they are looking to achieve? In my experience of the doctoral space in particular, this largely relates to a feeling that industry is stagnant, and screenwriters want more from the creative development process. This relates to the discourse on doctoral education, in particular the notion of contribution: What is the doctorate contributing to the researcher him/herself, not just the field? Some reasons for undertaking a doctorate are intrinsic and individual, and related to personal curiosity and interest, as well as the challenge of producing work at the highest level; other reasons are extrinsic, related to factors such as job prospects, kudos and value in one's family (Wellington 2013, 1492). The notion of a doctorate leading to enhanced job prospects in the screen industry is an interesting one: while there are yet no published studies of this, it would seem reasonable to guess that at this relatively early stage in the life of screenwriting practice research, the most clear-cut examples are those screenwriters and script professionals who are seeking employment in the university sector. In Australia there are several industry professionals who hold doctorates, namely in film-making or creative industries, but to what extent their experience of research has shifted the way they think and practice is yet to be examined.

Writing on the nature and experience of academic research, Angela Brew suggests that, while for some "research is concerned with the generation of skills or knowledge which they conceptualize as external to themselves", and it has little, if anything, to do with their own learning, for others "research questions go beyond the intellectual issues and are carried over into all aspects of life" (Brew 2001, 131–32). Here, in what Brew calls a "journey variation", "there is frequently the idea of a personal journey and an emphasis on the assimilation of research into the researcher's life and understanding" (2001, 132). What does this look like for the screenwriting practice researcher? While at one end of the spectrum, some established practitioners in the academy can feel adrift, frightened and that their extant practice is now worthless, others rise to the challenge and allow the identity shift to take its course, open to the assimilation of a new practitioner-researcher identity (Holbrook et al. 2013; Simmons and Holbrook 2013).

In the broader field of creative writing, there has been much discussion of the experience of and potential for creative practitioners coming into the academy. From their study across Australia, Webb et al. report that "many staff and students feel out of place, or out of their depth, at this level of academic practice", and that "within the wider writing community professional writers and publishers have expressed concerns about the extent to which higher degree training fits graduates to function as professionals" (2008, 7). While this research is 15 years old now, it does replicate some of the observations highlighted about the relatively new field of screenwriting practice research. These experiences are also expressed by Katrina Finlayson, writing at the time as a doctoral candidate: "they [creative writing doctoral candidates] will try on various identities and will most likely experience a prolonged period of uncertainty of self as they explore what it might mean for them to shape an identity as an academic" (2012, 2); and fellow candidate Rachel Le Rossignol: "creative practitioners have a greater distance to travel to reach the place where practice and theory are comfortably integrated" (2014, 1). Le Rossignol takes this further:

> With its 'different gatekeepers', students can already become like 'fish out of water', having to adapt to new discourses, tools, audiences, methods and, indeed, a different logic: add to this the sense that artist-academics are perceived by some as 'lightweights' who must work much harder to achieve regard (Webb et al. 2012, pp.8-9) and the message of lost identity capital is not only made clear, but linked to the very skills and experience which may have earned them a place as a Doctoral candidate. (2014, 4–5)

Like the (limited) doctoral education discourse focussing on creative fields, these sentiments echo the experiences of many candidates who enter the academy from a successful career in industry: imposter syndrome, epistemic rifts, fear of failure, an ability to see what their new identity may be. As Jenny Wilson, who studied a range of creative practitioners working in the academy for her own PhD, reports: "Those who combine the roles of artist, academic and student navigate a complex environment of expectations set by their employing university, their supervising institution and the external art world in which their practice is located" (2014, 199). And while for these people, "the process of doctoral interrogation provided 'more insight' and a greater personal understanding of how research related to their artistic practice" (Wilson 2014, 212–13), still "fears were expressed that locating an artistic career solely within the confines of academia can affect both the identity and practice of the artist" (Wilson 2014, 213–14).

But a core message often reiterated is that these "two worlds" will cohere—"to be a writer, to be a researcher, to be a teacher: to be an early-career creative-writing academic" (Finlayson 2012, 1)—and that for those who are willing to integrate, the possibilities of transgression are to be embraced: "Creative researchers have the choice to remain committed to their writerly identity, to adopt a scholarly identity, or to attempt to integrate both" (Le Rossignol 2014, 8). From my own perspective, I see great value in screenwriters entering the academy, not only for themselves and their own personal and professional development, but also for the academy itself, which is forever in need of new ways of knowing and more creative ways to knowledge production. For coursework students, too, having exposure to industry practitioners who, through research interactions, can innovate rather than merely replicate extant practices, means there is potential for greater risk taking and innovation.

40.8 Conclusion

This chapter has outlined that there are many possibilities of a research-led approach to screenwriting practice, for screenwriters themselves, for the academy and those in it, and ideally also for industry. While the chapter has possibly posed as many questions as it has given answers—pointing to a clear need for more research on screenwriters in the academy—it has hopefully laid some crucial definitional, practical and philosophical foundations for those with a vested interest in this space. It is my real hope that this chapter also serves as an invitation for new screenwriters and industry professionals to engage with the academy, whether for doctoral research or other forms of research partnership, especially in line with my personal wish for more research-excellent-industry-standard screenplays to be produced. Just as the creative arts thesis is full of possibilities, I also see that the nexus of screenwriting researcher and practitioner "is clearly emergent, allegorical, polyvocal and, above all, exciting" (Ravelli et al. 2014, 6).

As someone who has dedicated the last decade to better understanding the nature and outcomes of screenwriting practice research, I am hopeful that others will also be excited by the potential of research-led screenwriting and screenwriters in the academy. To date we have only scratched the surface, and in the context of a shifting university environment that privileges new forms of knowledge and research applications, and greater connections between the academy and industry, there is clear potential for a future of screenwriting where theory and practice intersect in ways we have not yet unleashed.

References

Allpress, Brent, Robyn Barnacle, Lesley Duxbury, L. and Elizabeth Grierson, eds. 2012. *Supervising Practices for Postgraduate Research in Art, Architecture and Design*. Cham: Springer.

Barrett, Estelle, and Barbara Bolt, eds. 2010. *Practice as Research: Approaches to Creative Arts Enquiry*. London: I.B. Tauris.

Baker, Dallas John. 2013. "Scriptwriting as Creative Writing Research: A Preface." *TEXT: Journal of Writing and Writing Courses*, special issue "Scriptwriting as Creative Writing Research" 19: 1–8. https://textjournal.scholasticahq.com/article/28883. Accessed 8 August 2022. https://doi.org/10.52086/001c.28883.

Baker, Su, Brad Buckley, and Giselle Kett. 2009. *Future-Proofing the Creative Arts in Higher Education: Scoping for Quality in Creative Arts Doctoral Programs*. Melbourne: ACUADS.

Baker, Dallas John, Craig Batty, Debra Beattie, and Susan Davis. 2015. "Scriptwriting as a Research Practice: Expanding the Field." *TEXT: Journal of Writing and Writing Courses*, special issue "Scriptwriting as Creative Writing Research II" 29: 1–11. https://textjournal.scholasticahq.com/article/27278. Accessed 8 August 2022. https://doi.org/10.52086/001c.27278.

Batty, Craig. 2009. "When What You Want Is Not What You Need: An Exploration of the Physical and Emotional Journeys Undertaken by a Protagonist in a Mainstream Feature Film." PhD diss., Bangor University, UK.

Batty, Craig. 2014. "Introduction". In *Screenwriters and Screenwriting: Putting Practice into Context*, edited by Craig Batty, 1–7. Basingstoke, UK: Palgrave Macmillan.

Batty, Craig. 2016. "Screenwriting Studies, Screenwriting Practice and the Screenwriting Manual." *New Writing: The International Journal for the Practice and Theory of Creative Writing* 13 (1): 59–70.

Batty, C. 2019. University Management Should Take Creative Practice Research Seriously ... Before it's Too Late. NiTRO, 18 April 2019.

Batty, Craig, and Alec McAulay. 2016. "The Academic Screenplay: Approaching Screenwriting as a Research Practice." *Writing in Practice: The Journal of Creative Writing Research* 2: 1–13.

Batty, Craig, and Allyson Holbrook. 2017. Contributing to Knowledge in Creative Writing Research: What, Where, How? *TEXT: Journal of Writing and Writing Courses, special issue* 44: 1–16.

Batty, Craig, and Marsha Berry. 2016. "Constellations and Connections: The Playful Space of the Creative Practice Research Degree." *Journal of Media Practice* 16 (3): 181–94.

Batty, Craig, and Susan Kerrigan, eds. 2018. *Screen Production Research: Creative Practice as a Mode of Enquiry*. London: Palgrave Macmillan

Batty, Craig, and Stayci Taylor. 2019. "Comedy Writing as Method: Reflections on Screenwriting in Creative Practice Research." *New Writing: The International Journal for the Practice and Theory of Creative Writing* 16 (3): 374–92.

Batty, Craig, and Stayci Taylor, eds. 2021. *Script Development: Critical Approaches, Creative Practices, International Perspectives*. London: Palgrave Macmillan.

Batty, Craig, Leo Berkeley, and Smiljana Glisovic. 2018. "A Morning Coffee in Melbourne: Discussing the Contentious Spaces of Media Practice Research." *Media Practice and Education* 19 (1): 8–17.

Batty, Craig, Louise Sawtell, and Stayci Taylor. 2016. "Thinking Through the Screenplay: The Academy as a Site for Research-Based Script Development." *Journal of Writing in Creative Practice* 9 (1–2): 149–62.

Bell, Desmond. 2006. Creative Film and Media Practice as Research: In Pursuit of that Obscure Object of Knowledge. *Journal of Media Practice* 7 (2): 85–100.

Bell, Desmond. 2008. "Creative Film and Media Practice as Research: In Pursuit of That Obscure Object of Knowledge." *International Journal of Technology Management & Sustainable Development* 7 (2): 85–100.

Blass, E., S. Bertone, J. Luca, C. Standing, R. Adams, H. Borland, and Q. Han, 2014. Developing a Toolkit and Framework to Support New Postgraduate Research Supervisors in Emerging Research Areas. Available at: http://www.olt.gov.au/project-developing-toolkit-and-framework-support-new-postgraduate-researchsupervisors-emerging-re-0. Accessed 19 March 2018.

Bloore, Peter. 2012. *The Screenplay Business: Managing Creativity and Script Development in the Film Industry*. Abingdon: Routledge.

Boon, Kevin Alexander. 2008. *Script Culture and the American Screenplay*. Detroit: Wayne State University Press.

Boud, David, Angela Brew, Robyn Dowling, Margaret Kiley, Janne Malfroy, Jo McKenzie, and Kevin Ryland. 2014. Building Local Leadership for Research Education. Available at: http://www.olt.gov.au/project-building-local-leadership-researcheducation-2011. Accessed 19 June 2018.

Brew, Angela. 2001. *The Nature of Research: Inquiry in Academic Contexts*. Abingdon, UK: Routledge.

Brien, Donna Lee. 2006. Creative Practice as Research: A Creative Writing Case Study. *Media International Australia (Incorporating Culture and Policy)* 118: 53–59.

Carter, Paul. 2007. *Material Thinking: The Theory and Practice of Creative Research*. Melbourne: Melbourne University Press.

Cherry, Nita, and Joy Higgs. 2011. "Researching in Wicked Practice Spaces: Artistry as a Way of Researching the Unknown in Practice". In *Creative Spaces for Qualitative Researching: Living Research*, edited by Joy Higgs, Angie Titchen, Debbie Horsfall, and Donna Bridges, 13–22. Rotterdam: Sense Publishers.

Conor, Bridget. 2014. *Screenwriting: Creative Labor and Professional Practice*. London: Routledge.

Corley, Elisabeth Lewis, and Joseph Megel. 2014. "White Space: An Approach to the Practice of Screenwriting as Poetry". In *Screenwriters and Screenwriting: Putting Practice into Context*, edited by Craig Batty, 11–29. Basingstoke, UK: Palgrave Macmillan.

Draper, Paul, and Scott D. Harrison, 2011. Through the Eye of a Needle: The Emergence of a Practice-led Research Doctorate in Music. *British Journal of Music Education* 28 (1): 87–102.

Evans, Terry, Peter Macauley, Margot Pearson, and Karen Tregenza. 2003. "A brief review of PhDs in creative and performing arts in Australia." Available at: https://dro.deakin.edu.au/articles/conference_contribution/A_brief_review_of_PhDs_in_creative_and_performing_arts_in_Australia/20544660. Accessed 03 January 2022.

Finlayson, Katrina. 2012. "Encounters with Future Selves: Crafting an Identity as a Creative-Writing Academic." *Encounters: Place, Situation, Context* – The Refereed Proceedings of the 17th Conference of the Australasian Association of Writing Programs 2012, 1–9. Geelong, Australia. https://aawp.org.au/wp-content/uploads/2015/03/Finlayson_1.pdf. Accessed 8 August 2022.

Frayling, Christopher. 1993. "Research in Art and Design." *Royal College of Art Research Papers* 1 (1). https://researchonline.rca.ac.uk/384/3/frayling_research_in_art_and_design_1993.pdf. Accessed 8 August 2022.

Freeman, John. 2010. *Blood, Sweat and Theory: Research Through Practice in Performance*. Faringdon: Libri Publishing.

Glisovic, Smiljana, Leo Berkeley, and Craig Batty. 2016. "The Problem of Peer Review in Screen Production: Exploring Problems and Proposing Solutions." *Studies in Australasian Cinema* 10 (1): 5–19.

Hamilton, Jillian, Mandy Thomas, Susan Carson, and Elizabeth Ellison. 2014. *Good Practice Report: Postgraduate Research and Coursework Degrees*. Available at: http://www.olt.gov.au/resource-good-practice-report-postgraduate-researchand-coursework-degrees-2014. Accessed 19 March 2018.

Harrison, S. 2014. *Pro-Active Music Higher Degrees: Promoting, Acting on and Evaluating Quality Teaching and Learning in Music Higher Degrees*. Available at: http://www.olt.gov.au/resource-pro-active-music-higher-degrees. Accessed 19 March 2018.

Harper, Graeme, and Jeri Kroll, eds. 2008. *Creative Writing Studies: Practice, Research and Pedagogy*. Clevedon, UK: Multilingual Matters.

Haseman, Brad. 2006. A Manifesto for Performative Research. Media International Australia, *Incorporating Culture & Policy* 118: 98–106.

Hawkins, Matthew. 2013. "Writing Is Rewriting: Defining the Purpose of Drafts in Feature Film Development in the Collaborative, Micro-Budget Environment." PhD diss., Flinders University, Australia.

Holbrook, Allyson, Beverley Simmons, Jill Scevak, and Janene Budd, J. 2013. *TEXT: Journal of Writing and Writing Courses*, special issue "Higher Degree Research Candidates' Initial Expectations in Fine Art" 22: 1–16. https://textjournal.scholasticahq.com/article/28301. Accessed 9 April 2022. https://doi.org/10.52086/001c.28301.

Hope, Sophie. 2016. "Bursting Paradigms: A Colour Wheel of Practice-Research." *Cultural Trends* 25 (2): 74–86.

Igelström, Ann. 2014. "Narration in the Screenplay Text." PhD diss., Bangor University, UK.

Jacey, Helen. 2010. "Journey to Nowhere: The Writing of Loy and Christopher Vogler's Screenwriting Paradigm." PhD diss., University of the Arts London, UK.

Kerrigan, Susan, and Craig Batty. 2016. "Re-conceptualizing Screenwriting for the Academy: The Social, Cultural and Creative Practice of Developing a Screenplay." *New Writing: The International Journal for the Practice and Theory of Creative Writing* 13 (1): 130–44.

Kerrigan, Susan, Leo Berkeley, Sean Maher, Michael Sergi, and Alison Wotherspoon. 2015. "Screen Production Enquiry: A Study of Five Australian Doctorates." *Studies in Australasian Cinema* 9 (2): 93–109.

Knudsen, Eric. 2003. Doctorate by Media Practice: A Case Study. *Journal of Media Practice* 3 (3): 179–184.

Krauth, Nigel. 2011. Evolution of the exegesis: The radical trajectory of the creative writing doctorate in Australia. *Text: Journal of Writing and Writing Programs*, 15 (1): 1–14.

Kroll, Jeri, and Graeme Harper. 2012. *Research Methods in Creative Writing*. Basingstoke: Palgrave Macmillan.

Lee, Sung-ju Suya, Lomdahl, Anne-Marie, Louise Sawtell, Stephen Sculley, and Stayci Taylor. 2016. "Screenwriting and the Higher Degree by Research: Writing a Screenplay for a Creative Practice PhD." *New Writing: The International Journal for the Practice and Theory of Creative Writing* 13 (1): 85–97.

Le Rossignol, Rachel. 2014. "Maintaining Writerly Identity During the Creative PhD." *Minding The Gap: Writing Across Thresholds and Fault Lines* – The Refereed

Proceedings of the 19th Conference of the Australasian Association of Writing Programs 2014, 1–16. Wellington, New Zealand. http://www.aawp.org.au/wp-content/uploads/2015/05/Le_Rossignol__R.writerly_identity.pdf. Accessed 8 August 2022.

Macdonald, Ian W. 2010. "Editorial." *Journal of Screenwriting* 1 (1): 7–10.

Macdonald, Ian W. 2013. *Screenwriting Poetics and the Screen Idea*. Basingstoke: Palgrave Macmillan.

McMillan, Susan. 2014. "The Screenwriter's Pitch: The Art and Science of Telling and Selling Stories." PhD diss., Bath Spa University, UK.

McNamara, Joshua. 2018. "Decomposing Scripts: Ethnography and Writing About Writing." *Journal of Screenwriting* 9 (1): 103–16.

Nannicelli, Ted. 2013. "The Ontology and Literary Status of the Screenplay: The Case of 'Scriptfic'." *Journal of Literary Theory* 13 (1–2): 135–53.

Nelmes, Jill, ed. 2010. *Analysing the Screenplay*. London: Routledge.

Nelson, Robin. 2013. *Practice as Research in the Arts: Principles, Protocols, Pedagogies, Resistances*. Basingstoke: Palgrave Macmillan.

Newbury, D. 1997. *Research and Practice in the PhD: Issues for Training and Supervision*. Birmingham Institute of Art and Design.

Phillips, Maggi, Cheryl F. Stock, and Kim Vincs. 2009. *Dancing Between Diversity and Consistency: Evaluating Assessment in Postgraduate Studies in Dance*. Available at: http://www.olt.gov.au/project-dancing-between-diversity-ecu-2006. Accessed 19 March 2018.

Price, Steven. 2013. "The Screenplay: An Accelerated Critical History." *Journal of Screenwriting* 4 (1): 87–97.

Ravelli, Louise, Brian Paltridge, and Sue Starfield. 2014. "Introduction." In *Doctoral Writing in the Creative and Performing Arts*, edited by Louise Ravelli, Brian Paltridge, and Sue Starfield, 1–6. Faringdon, UK: Libri Publishing.

Sawtell, Louise. 2016. "The Paperless Screenplay: Writing on, for and with the SCREEN." *Journal of Writing in Creative Practice* 9 (1–2): 33–46.

Sculley, Stephen. 2015. "*Stringer*, Episode 1: A Television Novel." *TEXT: Journal of Writing and Writing Courses*, special issue "Scriptwriting as Creative Writing Research II" 29: 1–30. https://textjournal.scholasticahq.com/article/27281. Accessed 8 August 2022. https://doi.org/10.52086/001c.27281.

Simmons, Beverley, and Allyson Holbrook. 2013. "From Rupture to Resonance: Uncertainty and Scholarship in Fine Art Research Degrees." *Arts and Humanities in Higher Education* 12 (2–3): 204–21.

Staiger, Janet. 2012. "Considering the Script as Blueprint." *Northern Lights: Film & Media Studies Yearbook* 10 (1): 75–90.

Stock, Cheryl F. 2009. Choreographing Research: Supervising the Dancing Thesis. *TEXT: Journal of Writing and Writing Courses (Special Issue 6: Supervising the Creative Arts Research Higher Degree: Towards Best Practice*, 13: 1–15.

Street, Karen Lee. 2015. "The Multiverse of Edgar Allan Poe, C. Auguste Dupin, and the London Monster." PhD diss., University of South Wales.

Taylor, Stayci. 2014. "The Model Screenwriter: A Comedy Case Study." *Minding the Gap* – The Refereed Proceedings of the 19th Conference of the Australasian Association of Writing Programs 2014. Wellington, New Zealand. http://www.aawp.org.au/wp-content/uploads/2015/05/Taylor_S_The_Model_Screenwriter.pdf. Accessed 8 August 2022.

The 'Florence Principles' on the Doctorate in the Arts. 2016. Amsterdam: European League of the Institutes of the Arts. Available at: http://www.elia-artschools.org/userfiles/File/customfiles/1-the-florence-principles20161124105336_20161202112511.pdf. Accessed 20 February 2017.

Vaughan, Laurene, ed. 2017. *Practice-based Design Research*. London: Bloomsbury.

Webb, Jen. 2015. *Researching Creative Writing*. Cambridge: Frontinus Press.

Webb, Jen, Donna Lee Brien, and Sandra Burr. 2012. *Examining doctorates in the creative arts: A guide*. Canberra: Australasian Association of Writing Programs. Available at: http://www.olt.gov.au/project-examination-doctoral-degreescreative-arts-process-practice-and-standards-2010. Accessed 19 March 2018.

Webb, Jennifer, Donna Lee Brien, Axel Bruns, Greg Battye, Jordan Williams, Craig Bolland, and Judith Smith. 2008. *Australian Writing Programs Network: Final Report*. Australian Learning and Teaching Council, Canberra. http://eprints.qut.edu.au/20085/. Accessed 8 August 2022.

Wellington, Jerry. 2013. "Searching for 'Doctorateness'." *Studies in Higher Education* 38 (10): 1490–503.

Wilson, Jenny. 2014. "Artist-Academic as Doctoral Student: Navigating Different Expectations, Frameworks and Identities." In *Doctoral Writing in the Creative and Performing Arts*, edited by Louise Ravelli, Brian Paltridge, and Sue Starfield, 199–218. Faringdon, UK: Libri Publishing.

Wilson, Jenny. 2017. *Artists in the University: Positioning Artistic Research in Higher Education*. Cham: Springer.

Author and Title Index

Numbers
13 Reasons Why, 440
24, 593, 595
27 Dresses, 514
35 Aside, 744, 752

A
Aah, Safdar, 372
Aarseth, Espen, 169, 549
Abbas, K.A. (Khwaja Ahmad), 371–373, 377, 381
Abbate, Fabrizio, 418
Abe, 592
Abell, Catharine, 124
Abrahamson, Lenny, 744, 747, 751
  3 Joes, 744, 747, 751
Abramovic, Marina, 173
Abrams, J.J., 83
A Bridge Too Far, 554
Abū Bishr Mattā ibn Yūnus, 691
A Bug's Life, 574, 575
A ciascuno il suo (*We Still Kill the Old Way*), 735
A Clockwork Orange, 22
Adam, 355, 357
Adam and Paul, 747
A Date for Mad Mary, 753
Adkins, Lisa, 509
Administrativnyy vostorg (*Administrative Ecstasy*), 242
A Doll's House, 301

Adventure, 549
Adventures in the Screen Trade, 554
A filmjáték esztétikája és dramaturgiája (*Aesthetics and Dramaturgy of the Film Play*), 697
Agarrando pueblo, 357
Age, 736
Age and Scarpelli, 734, 735
Agee, James, 7, 137, 140–142, 229
  "Comedy's Greatest Era", 229
Agent Carson, 557
A Good Day to Die Hard, 752
A History of the Screenplay, 214, 220
Ai, Xia, 297, 303, 304, 308, 309
Akbar, Arifa, 173
Akerman, Chantal, 102, 615, 616
al-Ahmar, Nadia, 493
Alaren, Mac, 250
al-Asad, Hafiz, 491
Albani, Cassandra, 415
"A Letter on Theatre" ("Iz 'Pisem o teatre'"), 242
Alexander, 666
Alien, 27
Alien[3], 21–23
Allen, Woody, 713
Almodóvar, Pedro, 495
Al-Nahhat (*The Sculptor*), 493, 496, 500
Al-Saher (*The Mentalist*), 493, 495, 498–500
Alvi, Abrar, 371

Amadeus, 665
A Midsummer Night's Dream, 696
Amirpour, Ana Lily, 358
A Modern Girl, 297, 303
A Most Violent Year, 477
Amrohi, Kamal, 371, 372
An Affair to Remember, 511
Anand, Inder Raj, 372
Andartes, 556
Anderson, David, 578
Anderson, Joseph L., 316, 321
Andreatta, Eleonora (Tinny), 412
Andrés Caicedo: Unos buenos pocos amigos (*Andrés Caicedo: A Few Good Friends*), 351
Andreyev, Leonid, 242
Andronikos of Rhodes, 691
Anfisa, 242
Angeli, Alfredo, 736
Angelitos empantanados o historias para jovencitos [*Angels in the Mud, Or Stories for Young Readers*], 357
Aniello, Lucia, 721
Antoine, André, 245
Antonioni, Michelangelo, 733, 734
Apollinaire, Guillaume, 134, 142, 249
A Postcard, 328
Arata, Masao, 319
Aristotle, 167, 169, 217, 219, 691–693
  Poetics, 691–693, 713
Arlanch, Francesco, 417, 420
Armstrong, Louis, 137
Arnheim, Rudolf, 209
Arrival, 113
Ars Magna Lucis et Umbrae, 96
Artale, Enrico Maria, 423
Arzner, Dorothy, 259
"A Single Isolated Incident", ep. of *Mr. Novak*, 340–343
Asparagus, 579
Astaire, Fred (and Ginger Rogers), 282, 284, 286
A Star is Born, 262
Astruc, Alexandre, 34, 101
  The Birth of a New Avant-Garde: La Caméra-Stylo, 101
Atlantis, 241
Auden, W.H., 137
Audino, Dino, 737

August, John, 76, 471
Aurélia, 120
Auslander, Philip, 173
Averroes, 691
Aviram, Motti, 455
Awlad Adam [*Children of Adam*], 493, 497–500
A Woman Kept Waiting, 328
Aylesworth, Reiko, 595
Azlant, Eddie, 232
Azlant, Edward, 214, 227, 232

B
Bøckman, 183
Bacharach, Burt, 143
Back Street, 298
Badejo, Bolaji, 27
Badger, Clarence, 231
Baker, Sean, 458
  The Florida Project, 458
Balada para niños muertos [*Ballad for dead children*], 351
Balázs, Bela, 99, 697, 727
Baldelli, Pio, 733
Baldwin, James, 479
Ballon, Rachel, 737
Black Mirror: Bandersnatch, 177
Bandra, 379
Banks, Miranda J., 212, 233
Baptista, Tiago, 97
Barbaro, Umberto, 727, 729
Barnet, Belinda, 360
Barnouw, Erik, 335
Baron, Suzanne, 103
Barris, Kenya, 77
Barr, Richard, 534
Barrymore, John, 260
Barthes, Roland, 6, 94, 98, 99
Barton, Ruth, 750, 751
Barzun, Jacques, 142
Baschiera, Stefano, 734
Bataille, Henry, 239
Batchler, Janet, 74
Batchler, Lee, 74
Batman, 123
Batman Forever, 74
Battistrada, Lucio, 736
Batty, Craig, 94, 99, 196

Bauer, Lev, 278
Bauer, Yevgeni, 248
Bazin, André, 95
Beat Saber, 200
Beauchamp, Cari, 234, 271, 718
Beau Revel, 232
Becker, Howard, 78, 80
Beckett, Samuel, 136, 747
   Waiting for Godot, 747
Bednarek, Monika, 153
Beethoven, Ludwig van, 290, 291
Begbie, 112, 117, 119
Behind Enemy Lines, 752
Bellak, George, 338
Belle, 520
Bellicampi, Giuseppe Rossi, 730
Bell, Julia, 185
Ben Casey, 335
Ben-Ghiat, Ruth, 727
Benigni, Roberto, 736
Benjamin, Walter, 136, 365, 378, 746
Benton, Robert, 712
Benvenuti, Leo, 736
Beranger, Clara, 212
Bergin, Barbara, 753
Bergman, Ingmar, 102, 105, 132, 133, 144, 146, 210, 216, 734
   Virgin Spring, 144
Berkeley, Busby, 283
Berlant, Lauren, 368
Berlin, Irving, 284
Bernardi, Joanne, 317
Bern, Vera, 247
Bertin, Pierre, 249
Bertolt Brecht, 365
Bertolucci, Bernardo, 611, 615, 734
Betsey Trotwood, 120
Better Call Saul, 593
Beynon, Gwydion, 401
Bianco e Nero, 727, 729
Bibas, Olivier, 424
Bicycle Thieves, 268
Big, 478
Bigelow, Kathryn, 520
Birthright, 266, 267
Bises, Stefano, 424
Biswas, Anil, 372
Blackburn, Kate, 152
BlacKkKlansman, 609

Black Panther, 469, 477
Blanca, 417
Blasetti, Alessandro, 726
Blast Theory, 168, 173, 180, 186
Bloch, Ernst, 619
Blom, August, 240
Blondie of the Follies, 279
Blood and Sand, 263
Blood and Truth, 545, 557–559
Bloore, Peter, 77, 79
Boal, Augusto, 169–171, 177, 183, 185, 615, 616
Boatman, Michael, 595
Bocca, Fratelli, 734
Böcklin, Arnold, 702
Bøckman, Petter, 183
Boddy, William, 336
Bode, Christoph, 192
Bodyguard, 47, 60–62
Bogart, Humphrey, 114
Bogle, Donald, 337
Boje, David M., 181
Bolter, David, 170
Bonnie and Clyde, 712
Booker, Christopher, 106
Bordwell, David, 105, 716, 722, 753
Borgia, 412, 421
Borowczck, Walerian, 578
Bourdieu, Pierre, 11, 28, 509, 513–516, 521, 523
Bownlow, Kevin, 233
Boyd, Brian, 176
Boyd, Ryan L., 152
Boyens, Philippa, 520
Boys Don't Cry, 476
Boyz n The Hood, 475
Brace, Max, 574
Brackett, Charles, 281, 721
Brackett, Leigh, 520
Braga, Paolo, 415
Brandon, Teena, 592
Branigan, Edward, 26, 745
Braque, Georges, 74
Breaking Bad, 588–593, 596, 600, 601
Brecht, Bertolt, 12, 99, 134, 169–171, 173, 610, 611, 614, 694–696
   The Threepenny Opera, 99, 697
Breen, Richard L., 281
Brennert, Hans, 242, 244, 247

Brera, Guido Maria, 418
Bresson, Robert, 732
　Journal d'un curé de campagne (*Diary of a Country Priest*), 732
Bride Wars, 514
Brik, Osip, 252
Broad City, 593
Brodkin, Herb, 333–336, 338, 339, 345
Bronenosets Potyomkin (*Battleship Potemkin*), 694
Brooklyn, 477
Brooks Barnes, 512
Brooks, James L., 713
Brosnan, Pierce, 123
Brown, Alan, 454, 459, 460
Brown, Noel, 456, 459
Browning, Tod, 350
　Dracula, 350
Browlow, Kevin, 226, 227, 229
　Parade's Gone By, 229
Bruce, Lenny, 592
Bruder, Jessica, 616
Brunetta, Gian Piero, 727
Bruni, David, 726, 737
Bucaccio, Elena, 418, 420
Büchner, Georg, 693
Buckingham, David, 457
Bulane-Hopa, Seipati, 399
Buñuel, Luis, 144, 700, 734
Bunyan, John, 119
　The Pilgrim's Progress, 119
Burch, Noël, 755
Burns, Charles, 358
Bushnell, John, 342, 344
Butch Cassidy and the Sundance Kid, 142
Butheina Awad, 493
Buzzi, Aldo, 732
Bye Bye Africa, 126, 127

C
Cai, Chusheng, 304
Caicedo, Andrés, 9, 349–357, 359–362
Caicedo, Rosario, 349–351
Cain, James M., 217, 219
　The Postman Always Rings Twice, 217
Caldwell, John Thornton, 87, 735
Camerini, Mario, 729

Camille, 263
Campbell, Alan, 262
Campbell, Joseph, 217, 219, 396, 398, 713, 714
　The Hero with a Thousand Faces, 217, 396, 713
Canavan, Gerry, 359
Canudo, Ricciotto, 697, 727
Carey, 596
Carl, 601
Carlborg, Herbert A., 336
Carlotta's Face, 579
Carreras, Michael, 572
Carrière, Jean-Claude, 102–104, 700
　The Secret Language of Film, 103
Car Wash, 478
Casablanca, 113, 118, 265
Cassavetes, John, 112, 349
Cast Away, 56, 57–58
Cavallaro, Giovanni Battista, 733
Cazdyn, Eric, 316, 323, 325
Celli, Gian, 729
Cenni, Francesco, 422
CENTRUM, 462
Cerami, Vincenzo, 736
Cerniglia, Ken, 694
Cervera, Maria, 424
Cesarano, Daniele, 418
Chaffey, Don, 572
Chander, Krishan, 373, 379
Chandlee, Harry, 720
Chandler, Raymond, 136
Chang, Eileen, 299, 306–309
Chan, Pauline, 643, 644, 650–653, 658
　33 Postcards, 643, 644, 650, 652–654, 657–659
Chapin, Anna Alice, 261
Chaplin, Charlie, 229, 267, 300, 732
　Limelight, 732
Chatman, Seymour, 96, 105
Chayefsky, Paddy, 713
Cheng, Xuemei, 297, 308
Cherkasov, Aleksandr Apollinar'yevich, 253
Chester, George Randolph, 263
Chester, Lillian, 263
Chewing Gum, 85
Chewing Gum Dreams, 87
Chiarini, Luigi, 729

"…Ciak!" script series, 734
China Seas, 279
Choose Your Own Adventure books, 546
Chopra, Baldev Raj (B.R.), 371
Christmas of the Comets, 461
Cimino, Michael, 219
   Heaven's Gate, 219
Cine-Magazzino, 728
Cinema (Kino), 247
Cinema nuovo, 729
Cinematografo, 727
Citizen Kane, 7
Clair, René, 732
Clark, Fred, 721
Clash of the Titans, 572
Clements, Paul, 185
Cleopatra, 261
Close Encounters of the Third Kind, 113
C'mon C'mon, 615–618
Cocteau, Jean, 144
Coel, Michaela, 85, 86
Cohen, Nadja, 94
Cohen, Ted, 74
Cohn, Harry, 265
Cole, Joe Robert, 477
Collana di studi cinematografici, 734
Collins, Leroy, 266
Collins, Suzanne, 520
"Colour of Change: Hollywood Race in the Writers Room", 471
Come nasce un film, 726
Comencini, Francesca, 423
Comencini, Luigi, 732
Comerford, Joe, 746
Come scrivere e sceneggiare un soggetto cinematografico, 728
Come si fa un film a Hollywood, 728
Commando, 610
Community for Creative Non-Violence v. Reid, 531
Comoedia, 250
Complex TV, 411
Connery, Sean, 122, 123
Conor, Bridget, 30, 212, 368
   Screenwriting: Creative Labor and Professional Practice, 212
Conroy, Rúaidhrí, 749
Conscience, 298
Contempt, 733

Conversations with Friends, 747
Conway, Shirl, 339
Coogie, 598
Cook, Chrystal Allene, 510
"Copioni cinematografici", 734
Coppola, Francis Ford, 216, 219, 465
   Apocalypse Now, 219
Coppola, William, 216
Corbucci, Claudio, 425
Corbucci, Sergio, 421
Corliss, Richard, 210, 315
   Talking Pictures, 210, 211
Corman, Roger, 349–351
Costa, Antonio, 732
Costa, João Bénard da, 96
Couchman, Jeffrey, 138
   The Night of the Hunter: A Biography of a Film, 138
Count of Buffon, 106
Coxon, Lucinda, 520
Craig, Daniel, 122, 123
Crash, 477
Craven, Wes, 7, 144, 145
   Nightmare on Elm Street, 144
Crémieux, Benjamin, 249
Crimson Peak, 520, 521
Csikzentmihalyi, Mihalyi, 35
Culpeper, Jonathan, 152, 153
Cupid's Puppet, 296, 301, 303
Curtis, Richard, 79, 120, 121, 127
Curtiz, Michael, 265
Cuse, Carlton, 83
Cutting, James E., 47
Cyberpunk 2077, 551

D

Daddy Long Legs, 104
Dafoe, Willem, 611
Daily Express, 546
Dalai, Paola, 734
Dal soggetto al film, 732
d'Amico, Suso Cecchi, 102, 268, 735
Danish Film Institute (Det Danske Filminstitut), 640
Dalton, Tony, 573
Dances, 680
Dances with Wolves, 666, 680
Dancyger, Ken, 105

Daniel, Frank, 29, 694, 715–717
Dan in Real Life, 593
Danny Ross, 336–338
Dardenne, Jean-Pierre, 613
Dardenne, Luc, 613
Dargis, Manohla, 114
Dasarupa (A Treatise on Hindu Dramaturgy), 691, 693
Das blaue Licht, 697
Das Fremde Mädchen (The Foreign Girl), 240
Dassanowsky, Robert, 281
Das Tage-Buch, 246
Davies, Desmond, 572
Davies, Rosamund, 24, 25, 94, 196
da Vinci, Leonardo, 508
Davis, Geena, 507
Dawley, J. Searle, 213
Days of Our Lives, 397
Deadsy, 578
de Croisset, Francis, 245
Dee, Ruby, 338, 340
De Gregorio, Domenico, 731
DeHaan, Dane, 594
Deleuze, Gilles, 548
Della Porta, Giambattista, 96
  De refractione optices parte libri novem, 96
  Magiae naturalis libri XX, 96
Delluc, Louis, 250
del Ruth, Hampton, 230, 231
del Toro, Guillermo, 520
deMille, Beatrice, 261
DeMille, Cecil B., 261, 268, 269, 271
De Mille, William C., 227, 260, 261
  Hollywood Saga, 227
De Niro, Robert, 25, 611
Den okända, 240
Depardieu, Gerard, 611
Deren, Maya, 94
Der Hauptmann von Köpenick (The Capitain of Koepenick), 695
Der letzte Tag (The Last Day), 241
Der Kinematograph, 247
Derleth, August, 354
Der Märtyrer seines Herzens [Martyr of His Heart], 291
Der Student von Prag (The Student from Prague), 241

De Sica, Vittorio, 733
Destino fatal (Tales of Terror), 350
Detroit: Become Human, 551, 555
Deus Ex, 552
De Vere, Alison, 579
Devils, 359, 418, 424
Devitt, Michael, 116
Dewey, Ray, 344
Dhanamjaya, 691
Diamant-Berger, Henri, 245, 247
Diamond, I.A.L., 228
Dickens, Charles, 120, 479
  David Copperfield, 120
Die Feder, 241
Die Toteninsel (Isle of the Dead), 702
Dietrich, Rainer, 192
Die Zappelnde Leinwald (The Flickering Screen), 244
Dinehart, Stephen, 553
Dirty Harry, 609
Disco Elysium, 552
Disco Pigs, 752
Distinction, 514
Divorzio all'italiana (Divorce Italian Style), 734
Dix, Beulah Marie, 212
Dixon, Ivan, 336
Dixon, Steve, 173, 177, 180, 183
Django, 421, 423, 424
Doc, 417
Docter, Pete, 570
Done in Oil, 231
Don Juan, 260
Donner, Carla, 285, 289
Dooley, Kath, 195
Dorian Gray, 475
Dostoevsky, Fyodor, 144
Dowd, Tom, 178
Downs, Paul W., 721
Downton Abbey, 512
Doyle, Arthur Conan, 266
Драматургия Кино (*Dramaturgy of the Cinema*), 694
Dramatists Guild, 11, 529, 534
Dramaturgy of Film Form, 694
Dream, 172, 173
Dreyer, Carl Theodor, 100, 732
Driessen, Paul, 578
Dr. Kildare, 335, 341

Dr. No, 123
Du Bois, W.E.B., 472
Dulac, Germaine, 727
Dupont, Ewald André, 250
Durbin, Deanna, 284
Durrant, Roberta, 392, 393, 400
Dutt, Guru, 371
Duvivier, Julien, 291
Dvořák, Petr, 436

E
Earth vs The Flying Saucers, 574
Eastern Times, 304
East Is East, 752
Edge, 549
Efunsetan's Story, 623, 624, 629, 630, 632–634, 636–639
Efunsetan Aniwura, 624, 629–639
Efunsetan Aniwura: Iyalode of Ibadan, 628, 631
Eikhenbaum, Boris, 95
Einbinder, Hannah, 721
Ein Herr auf Bestellung (*A Gentleman to Order*), 287
Elephant, 441
Elephant Man, 478
Eller, Paul, 251
Elliot, Nils Lindahl, 34
Elskovsleg, 240, 241
Emilia Galotti, 693
Emtigon, 746
Eng, Esther, 298, 306, 308
Enkvist, N.E., 151, 152, 159
Enríquez, Mariana, 358
Entr'acte, 732
Ephron, Nora, 212, 511
  Sleepless in Seattle, 511
Epstein brothers, 271
Epstein, Julius, 265
Epstein, Philip, 265
Esquinca, Bernardo, 358
Estella Marsh, 355, 359
European Broadcasting Union, 463
Eustis, Oskar, 694
Evans, David, 423
Evans, Walker, 137, 140
Ewers, Hanns Heinz, 241
Ex Machina, 113

"Express Stop from Lenox Avenue", ep. of *The Nurses*, 338, 340
Eyes Without a Face, 495
Eyman, Scott, 719

F
Fable, 552
Fahed, Amer, 493
Fairbanks, Douglas, 270
Fairburne, Karl, 554, 555
Fairfax, Marion, 260, 265, 266
Fairouz, 490
Fanon, Frantz, 393
Fantômas, 246
Fargo, 34
Farpões Baldios (*Barbs Wastelands*), 97
Fasoli, Leonardo, 422
Faulkner, William, 136
Faust, 123, 281
Felisatti, Massimo, 736
Fellini, Federico, 144, 733, 734
Ferrell, Rose, 94, 105, 106
Ferri, Gabriele, 170
Feuillade, Louis, 245
Field, Allyson Nadia, 361
Fielding, Henry, 125, 126
  Tom Jones, 125
Field, Syd, 153–155, 217, 219, 608, 664, 665, 693, 713, 714, 718–720, 745
  Screenplay: The Foundations of Screenwriting, 713
Fight Club, 614
Film: soggetto e sceneggiatura, 727
Filmcritica, 732
Filmindia, 373
Filmindustria, 728
Filmkurier, 251
Fincher, David, 614
Fine, Richard, 211, 215
  Hollywood and the Profession of Authorship, 211
Finkel, Abem, 720
First Day, 459
Fisher, Marc, 353
Fish, Stanley, 29
Fitzgerald, F. Scott, 136, 211
  The Last Tycoon, 211

Fleabag, 58
Flee, 579
Florence, Lam, 308
Flusser, Vilém, 189, 192
  Video et Phénoménologie, 189
Fo, Dario, 612
Follows, Stephen, 132
Fontana, Tom, 412
Foott, Peter, 744, 748
  The Carpenter and his Clumsy Wife, 748
Ford, John, 750
Forst, Willi, 280
Fortnite, 462
Foucault, Michel, 81
Four Days of Naples, 554
Four Weddings and a Funeral, 79
Fowler, Gene, 229, 230
Fra Diavolo (The Devil's Brother), 261
FrameWork, 230
Franciscus, James, 340
Franju, Georges, 495
Frankie, 744, 753
Franklin, Luke, 424
Frasca, Gonzalo, 549
Frascella, Lawrence, 511
Freaky Friday, 478
Freddie Krueger, 146
Freeman, Leonard, 343, 345
Freeman, Martin, 58
Freksa, Friedrich, 695
Freytag, Gustav, 692
  Technique of the Drama, 692
Friday the 13th, 535, 536
Friends, 58, 74
Friend, Stacie, 119
From the Manger to the Cross, 228
Frost, Anthony, 185
Froug, William, 717
Fuguet, Alberto, 352, 353, 360
Fukunaga, Cary Joji, 123
Fulcrum, 173
Fumagalli, Armando, 415
Furia, John, 718

G
Gable, Clark, 279
Gad, Urban, 250

Gaiman, Neil, 559
Gambetti, Giacomo, 733
Gandhi, Indira, 378
Gans, Herbert, 473
Ganz, Adam, 25
Garage, 747
García Márquez, Gabriel, 352, 353
Gardini, Gina, 414, 422, 424
Gardner, Howard, 35
Garzanti, Aldo, 733, 734
Gaumont, Léon, 246
Gauntier, Gene, 212, 228, 229
Gaur, Vrajendra, 376
Gay, Andrew Kenneth, 32
Gell-Mann, Murray, 46–47, 53
Generations, 389, 395, 397, 401
Genette, Gérard, 105, 132
Gentleman's Agreement, 476
Ghosh, Nabendu, 371
Ghostbusters, 460
Giarrusso, Vincenzo, 24, 25
Gibson, Angus, 397
Gibson, William, 23
Giddens, Antony, 735
Giger, H.R., 27
Giler, David, 22
Ginzburg, Carlo, 136
Giovanni's Room, 479
Gish, Lillian, 262
Gleeson, Brendan, 749
Glyn, Elinor, 212
God's Stepchildren, 266
Godard, Jean-Luc, 127, 136, 349, 734
Gods and Generals, 666
Godshall, Zack, 615, 618
Goethe, Johann Wolfgang, 101
Gogan, Johnny, 746
Gogol, Nikolai Vasilyevich, 252
Gold Diggers of 1933, 284
Golden Gate Girl, 298
Gold, Judy, 595
Goldman, Jane, 520
Goldmann, Lucien, 615
Goldman, William, 7, 142–144, 554, 712
Goldoni, Carlo, 192
Goldwyn, Samuel, 211, 244
Gomes, Rita Azevedo, 101
Gómez, Felipe, 351, 352

Gomorra: La serie, 422
Gone with the Wind, 137
Goodwin, Richard M., 59
Gossett, Jr., Louis, 338
Gough, Lloyd, 721
Goulding, Edmund, 75, 279
Gourdin-Sangouard, Isabelle, 75
Grand Hotel, 75, 326
Grand Theft Auto, 551
Green, Steph, 744
Greimas, Algirdas Julien, 614
Greve, Julian, 358
Griesemer, James R., 196
Griffith, D.W., 209, 225, 226, 271
Griffiths, Keith, 26
Grotowski, Jerzy, 169, 173, 185
Guattari, Felix, 548
Guerra, Tonino, 102
Gujral, Inder Kumar, 379
Gunning, Tom, 96, 745–749, 755
Guttenberg, Steve, 595
Guy-Blaché, Alice, 296

H
Hacks, 720–722
Hacksaw Ridge, 720, 721
Hageman, Andrew, 359
Hagener, Malte, 726
Hajjo, Al-Laith, 493
Halbwachs, Maurice, 546
Hamburgische Dramaturgie (Hamburg Dramaturgy), 693
Hamilton, Ian, 98, 233
Hamlet, 203
Hamlett, Christina, 455
  Screenwriting for Teens, 455
Handbook of Children's Film and Television, 463
Hanks, Tom, 56, 511
Happy Reunion of Troubled Friends, 299, 305
Hardy, Oliver, 261
Hardy, Thomas, 477
  Jude the Obscure, 477
Harlequin, 192
Haroun, Mahamat-Saleh, 112, 126, 127
  Bye Bye Africa, 112
Harris, Ben, 420, 424

Harryhausen, Ray, 572–574
Harry Potter, 458
Hartley, Steven, 557
Hartmann, Nils, 412, 419
Harwood, Johanna, 122
Hatta, Naoyuki, 320
Hauptmann, Gerhart, 240, 241
Hawas [Obsession], 493, 495, 500
Hayes, Raphael, 336–338
Heartaches, 298
Heartlands, 752
Hearts of Darkness: A Filmmaker's Apocalypse, 465
Heart Strategy, 230
Heat, 665
Hecht, Ben, 134, 136, 271, 710, 711, 717
Hecht, Jessica, 593
Heerman, Victor, 269, 270
Hegel, Georg Wilhelm Friedrich, 693, 694
"He Grabs a Train and Rides", unfilmed ep. of *Mr. Novak*, 343–345
Heine, Heinrich, 693
Hellman, Lillian, 307
Hell on Wheels, 422
He, Luo, 298
Henry, Buck, 713
Hensman, Rohini, 369
Hermansson, Casie, 463
Herrmann, Max, 696, 697
Her Story, 587
Herzog, Werner, 102
He Shoots, He Scores, 744, 747, 751, 752
Hevesy, Iván, 697
Heymann, Werner, 284
High Maintenance, 587, 593
Hill, Walter, 22
Hilmes, Michele, 334
Hirst, Michael, 415
Histoires d'Amérique: Food, Family and Philosophy, 615, 616, 618
Hitchcock, Alfred, 7, 134, 137, 208, 270, 614, 715
Hitchins, Derek, 50
Hoban, Russell, 578
Hocking, Clint, 549
Hodge, John, 119
Hoffenstein, Samuel, 281, 287

Hofmeyer, Harry, 392, 394
Holden, William, 721
Hölderlin, Friedrich, 693
Holger-Madsen, 240
Holländer, Friedrich, 284
Hollander, Tom, 58
Holly, Ellen, 336
The Hollywood Screenwriters, 210
Holmes, Garth, 395
Holohan, Conn, 751, 754
Home Affairs, 400
Honours and Sins, 298
Hopa, Baleka, 399
Hopkins, Adam, 354, 356
Hopkins, Gerard Manley, 142
Horace [Horatius Flaccus], Quintus, 691
  Ars Poetica, 691
Horror Inc. v. Miller, 535
House Number Sixty-six, 298
House of Games, 219
Hou, Yao, 298
Howard, Bronson, 263
Howard, David, 716, 717
  The Tools of Screenwriting, 716
Howard, Luke, 101
Howard, Vince, 343
How to Build a Great Screenplay, 716
How to Write and Sell Film Stories, 718
Huang, Hou, 297
Hudson, Earl, 266
Humphrey, Hal, 342
Hunicke, Robin, 201, 202
Hunt for the Wilderpeople, 458
Hunt, Lester, 125
Hu, Ping, 297, 308
Hurbis-Cherrier, Mick, 155
Hurst, Fannie, 469, 476
Hurwitz, Max, 422
Huston, John, 720

I
I Am a Cat, 319
Ibn Sina (Avicenna), 691
Ibsen, Henrik, 301
Ichikawa, Kon, 321
искусство экрана (*Screen Art lecture series*), 694
Ide, Masato, 328

Identity, 476
If Beale Street Could Talk, 479
Iida, Shinbi, 318, 324
Ikeda, Tadao, 319
Il cinema della nostra vita, 735
"Il cinematografo" script series, 734
Il giardino dei Finzi Contini (*The Garden of the Finzi-Continis*), 735
Ilsa, 118
Il Vangelo secondo Matteo (*The Gospel According to Matthew*), 733
I May Destroy You, 87
Imitation of Life, 476
Immagine, 734
Ince, Thomas, 213, 227, 231–233, 245, 271
Indagine su un cittadino al di sopra di ogni sospetto (*Investigation of a Citizen Above Suspicion*), 735
Indivar, 373
Ingqumbo Yeminyanya (*The Wrath of the Ancestors*), 392–394
Ings, Welby, 26
Insecure, 723
Inside I'm Dancing, 752
Intersexions, 400
In the Heat of the Night, 343
In the Street, 137
Inxeba (*The Wound*), 399
IOU, 168, 173, 174, 176, 186
Ishaq ibn Hunain, 691
Isibaya (*The Kraal*), 401
Isidingo: The Need, 395
I soliti ignoti (*Big Deal on Madonna Street*), 268
It's a Women's World, 298
Itami, Mansaku, 324
It Follows, 594
Itō, Daisuke, 324
Ivens, Joris, 102
  Une Histoire de Vent, 102

J
Jack's Bicycle, 744, 752
Jackson, Felix, 284
Jackson, Siobhan, 33, 34
Jade, Robert, 123
Jagger, Dean, 341

Jaipuri, Hasrat, 373
Jalalabadi, Qamar, 373, 376
James Bond, 122, 123
James, Henry, 138
Jameson, Arthur, 355
Janet Lamb, 336, 337
Jason and the Argonauts, 572
Jenkins, Henry, 167
Jenny Bishop, 338–340
Jentis, Caytha, 595
Jericho, 114
JJ, 594
Jogia, Avan, 594
Johansson, Scarlett, 113
Johnson, Beth, 464
Johnson-Cochran, Dwayne, 469
Johnson, Keith, 169
Johnson, Kristen, 617
Johnson, Nunnally, 211, 225, 711, 717
John-Steiner, Vera, 74
Johnstone, Keith, 170, 171
   Impro, 170
Jones, 126
Jones, Bob, 345
Jordan, A.C., 393, 394
Jordan, Kayla, 152
Journal of Screenwriting, 4, 207
Joyce, Hester, 29
Joyce, James, 138
Jukes, Peter, 420
Jurassic Park, 113

K

Kael, Pauline, 114
Kafka, Franz, 144
Kahneman, Daniel, 702
Kajánková, Lucia, 431, 440–446, 448
Kaling, Mindy, 87
Kallay, Jasmina, 167
Kapoor, Raj, 371
Karen, 596, 597, 599
Karpov, Evtikhy Pavlovich, 173
Kasdan, Lawrence, 520
Kashmiri, Agha Jani, 378
Katzenberg, Jeffrey, 588
Kaufman, George S., 262
Kaul, Mahesh, 372, 380
Kavish, C.L., 373, 382

Kayla (Amy Bailey), 558
Kazantzakis, Nicolas, 612
Keaton, Buster, 229, 263, 270
Keegan, Jennifer, 752
Kemper, Renee, 595
Kentarō Kobayashi (小林 賢太郎,
   Kobayashi Kentarō), 694
Kenworthy, Duncan, 79
Kern, Jerome, 284
Kerr, Alfred, 241
Khanzhonkov, Alexander, 243
Khululeka (Be Free), 395, 397
Kick Ass, 520
Kido, Shirō, 318, 322
Kieślowski, Krzysztof, 734
Kikushima, Ryūzō, 320
Killing Eve, 87
Kim, 593, 596, 597, 599
Kim, John, 183
Kingdom of Heaven, 666, 676
King, Stephen, 460
Kinoshita, Keisuke, 320
Kinostsenari, 727
Kipling, Rudyard, 106, 135
Kircher, Athanasius, 96
Kishi, Matsuo, 317
Klassen, 461–463
Knight, Andrew, 720
Knoller, Noam, 168
Knowlton, Henry, 232
Knudsen, Erik, 32
Kobayashi, Masaru, 318–320
Koch, Howard, 265, 720
Koenitz, Hartmund, 167–171
Kon, Satoshi, 578
Korte, Barbara, 94
Kortwich, Werner, 727
Kousa, Rami, 493
Kovalyov, Igor, 578
Kracauer, Siegfried, 746
Krikowa, Natalie, 459
Ksenofontova, Alexandra, 29, 103
Ksiri, Salam, 493
Kubrick, Stanley, 210
Kwatsha, Linda, 394
Kyōya Collar Shop, 319

L

La casa lobo, 358
Lady from the Blue Lagoon, 298
La estirpe sin nombre (*The Nameless Offspring*), 354, 355, 357, 359, 361
La grande bellezza (*The Great Beauty*), 736
Lai, Man-wai, 297
Lai, Pak-hoi, 298
Lamarque, Peter, 123
Lam, Cho-Cho, 297
Lanc, Zdeněk, 437
Landow, George, 170
Langlois, Henri, 96
L'année dernière à Marienbad (*Last Year at Marienbad*), 734
La Nouvelle revue, 239
La región salvaje, 358
Larkin, Bryan, 557
Larkin, Ruth, 345
L'armata s'agapò, 732
L'arrivée d'un train en gare de La Ciotat (*Train Pulling into a Station*), 746
La Roue (*The Wheel*), 326
"La sceneggiatura come struttura che vuole essere altra struttura", 733
Lasky, Jesse L., 261
La sombra sobre Innsmouth (*The Shadow over Innsmouth*), 354, 355, 357, 359, 361
La sortie de l'usine Lumière à Lyon (*Workers Leaving the Lumière Factory in Lyon*), 746
Lass, Jakob, 33
Last House on the Left, 144
La strada di casa [*The Way Home*], 417
Last Tango in Paris, 114
Last Year at Marienbad, 664
Lattuada, Alberto, 732
Lattuada, Bianca, 732
Laughton, Charles, 138
  Night of the Hunter, 138
Laurel, Brenda, 167, 169–171
Laurel, Stan, 261
Laurent, Lawrence, 341
Lauzen, Martha M., 507
Lavedan, Henri, 239
La Vedette, 239

Lawrence, Carol Munday, 478
Lawrence Taylor, Daniel, 85, 86, 88
Lawson, John Howard, 216, 729
  Theory and Technique of Playwriting and Screenwriting, 216, 729
Lazenby, George, 123
Lazendörfer, Tim, 360
Leaf, Caroline, 578
LeBlanc, Marc, 201, 202
Le Cinéma, 245
Leclerc, Georges-Louis, 106
  Discours sur le Style (*Discourse on Style*), 106
Lediga, Kagiso, 402, 403
Lee, Carl, 338, 340
Lee, Spike, 478, 609
Le Film, 244–246, 249, 250
Le fils (*The Son*), 613
Leigh, Mike, 112, 121, 127, 185
Leise flehen meine Lieder (*Lover Divine*), 280, 291
Le Journal, 240
L'enfant (*The Child*), 613
Leonard, Charles, 185
Leroux, Gaston, 297
Les Cahiers du Mois, 249
Lessing, Gotthold Ephraim, 693, 694
Lester, Gideon, 694
Let Us Now Praise Famous Men, 137–138
Lewis, David, 115, 116, 123
Liebelei (*Flirtation*), 240
Lieber, Jeffrey, 82
Life Magazine, 229
Lightning Ridge: The Land of Black Opals, 655
Likavec, Silvia, 183
Like Water for Chocolate, 352
Lim, Florence, 297
Lindau, Paul, 241
Lindelof, Damon, 83
Li, Pingqian, 304
Little, Natasha, 558
Littleton, Karen, 523
Little Women, 269
Livingston, Paisley, 123, 124
Liz Thorpe, 339
Lloyd, Harold, 229

Lodkina, Alena, 644, 654–656, 658, 659
  Strange Colours, 644, 650, 654–659
Lohengrin, 282
Lokhande, N.M., 369
Lombardo, Goffredo, 734
London Heist, 557, 558
Long Live the Mistress, 299, 306, 307
Lonnie, 338–340
Loos, Anita, 212, 262, 271, 279
Los amantes de Suzie Bloom, 354
Lost, 83
Louvish, Simon, 231, 233
Love Actually, 79, 120
Lovecraft, H.P. (Howard Phillips), 353–355, 357, 360
Love is the Drug, 753
Love Me Tonight, 282, 286
Low and Behold, 615, 618
Lubitsch, Ernst, 695, 715
Luciani, Sebastiano Arturo, 727
Lucian of Samosa, 690
Ludhianvi, Sahir, 377
Lumière brothers, 746
Lunt, Chris, 419
Lupo, Rino, 97
Lury, Karen, 454
Lusuardi, Nicola, 424
Lu Xun, 301
Lynch, Brian, 752
Lynch, David, 131, 358

M
MacArthur, Charles, 136, 711
Macdonald, Ian W., 2, 3, 26, 75, 95, 191, 277, 354, 360, 462
MacDonald, J. Fred, 334
Machen, Arthur, 358
Machon, Josephine, 169
Mack, Max, 241
MacNicholas, Robin, 168
MacPherson, Jeanie, 212, 261, 268, 272
Madden, Richard, 60
Madeline, 355, 359
Madhusudan, 372
Mad Love Mad Fire, 298
Mad Max: Fury Road, 520
Mad Men, 589

Maggi, Raffaello, 728
Magrs, Paul, 185
Maguire, Martin, 753
Maher, James, 752
  Prey Alone, 752
Mahlatsi, Teboho, 397
Maibaum, Richard, 122
Making a Good Script Great, 737
Makino, Masahiro, 319
Makwarela, Phathutshedzo, 401
Malik, Sarita, 86
Mamabolo, Makgano, 400
Mamet, David, 8, 143, 209, 217–219, 271
Manchevski, Milcho, 646, 659
Mandela, Nelson, 389
Manetti, Daniela, 726
Mankiewicz, Herman J., 7, 152, 225, 271, 711
Mankiewicz, Joseph L., 710
Mann, Denise, 82
Manners, 440
Manovich, Lev, 199
Mapes, Victor, 263
Mar, Anna, 248
Maras, Steven, 2, 3, 24, 25, 29, 35, 94, 95, 98, 100, 106, 190, 212, 213
Marcel, Kelly, 520
Margaret, 666
Margrave, Seton, 726
Marion, Frances, 102, 104, 212, 234, 235, 262, 264, 265, 270, 271, 279, 710, 711, 717, 718
Marks, Dara, 737
Marks, Ryan, 557
Marshall, E.G., 337
Marshman, Jr., D.M., 721
Marsh, Obed, 354, 355
Martin, Adrian, 25, 26, 94, 95, 97
Marvelous Mrs. Maisel, 592
Marx, Harpo, 262
Masemola, Warren, 402
Maski, 242
Mason, Sarah Y., 269, 270, 272
Material für Filmschriftsteller [*Material for Film Writers*], 241
Mateus, Marta, 97
Mather, Berkely, 122
Mathis, June, 262, 263, 270, 272

Matsetel, Lodi, 400
Maxa, Jan, 438
Maxu, Weibang, 297
Mayakovsky, Vladimir, 252
Mayer, Carl, 24, 102, 103, 237, 251
Mayolo, Carlos, 349, 351, 357
May, *Renato*, 727–728
Mayr, Brigitte, 102
Mazibuko, Beth, 400
Mazursky, Paul, 349
Mazzei, Luca, 727
McCannon, Billy, 752
   Recoil, 752, 753
McCord, Vera, 263
McCreadie, Marsha, 212
McDonagh, Martin, 749, 750
McGilligan, Patrick, 210
McGonigal, Jane, 183
McKean, Dave, 559
McKee, Robert, 153, 278, 547, 608, 719
McLaren, Norman, 578
McLaverty-Robinson, Andy, 170
McLoone, Martin, 744, 754, 755
McNeil, Claudia, 338, 340
McOndo movement, 353, 360, 362
McRobbie, Angela, 368
Mean Girls, 477
Medici–Masters of Florence, 414–418, 420
Mediterraneo, 736
Meehan, John, 281
Méliès, George, 745
Melodia, Sara, 415, 419
Melville, Herman, 260
Menen, Aubrey, 554
Mercure de France, 249
Meredyth, Bess, 260, 265, 270, 272
Merimée, Prosper, 136
Metz, Christian, 131
Miami Vice, 702
Michaels, Joel B., 350, 356
Micheaux, Oscar, 266, 267, 470
Midge, 592
Midsummer Night's Dream, 172
Mike Deacon, 557
Millard, Kathryn, 25, 26, 32, 36, 94, 167, 194, 197
Miller, Victor, 535

Mills, Mike, 615, 616
Milton, John, 134
   Paradise Lost, 134
Mimura, Shintarō, 324
Minna von Barnhelm, 693
Mittell, Jason, 334, 411
Miyazaki, Hayao, 576, 577
Mizoguchi, Kenji, 319
Mizuki, Yōko, 320
Moayedi, Reza, 57
Moby Dick, 260
Mock, Flora, 350
Modern Women, 299, 305
Modi, Sohrab, 371
Mohammad Lotfi, 493
Moi, Toril, 510, 512, 514, 515, 523
   Appropriating Bourdieu: Feminist theory and Pierre Bourdieu's sociology of culture, 510
Molder, Maria Filomena, 96
Molnár, Ferenc, 281
Moniz, Lúcia, 120
Monroe, Maika, 594
Monteleone, Enzo, 736
Mooney, 458
Moore, Alan, 358
Moore, Henry, 508
Moore, John, 744, 747, 751, 752
Moore, Roger, 123
Moravia, Alberto, 733
Mordden, Ethan, 719
Morgan, Abi, 520
Morlion, Félix, 730
Moroka family, 397
Morris, Errol, 138
Moscon, Giorgio, 734
Mosconi, Elena, 730
Moss, 402
Most Dangerous Game, 591
Motion Picture News, 260
Moving Pictures, 710
Mozart, Wolfgang Amadeus, 290
Mozarts Leben, Lieben und Leiden [Mozart's Life, Love and Suffering], 291
Mr Catty, 184
Mr. Novak, 9, 340–343, 345
Mrs. Doubtfire, 478
Mrs. Hill, 338

Mrs. Maisel, 600
Mrs. Palmer, 337
Mukařovský, Jan, 48
Mukherjee, Debashree, 377
Mukhram Sharma, Pandit, 371
Müller, Fritz, 240
Müller, Heiner, 694
Müllerová, Alena, 441–443, 445, 447, 448
Mumsnet, 512
Mura no hanayome (*The Village Bride*), 326
Murch, Walter, 576
Murder in Harlem, 266
Murnau, Friedrich Wilhelm, 34, 102
  Sunrise, 102
Murphy, J.J., 34, 36, 94, 458
Murray, Janet, 167, 168, 171, 175, 176, 194, 201, 203
Murray, Johnny, 358

N
Nachahmungspoesie (*Imitation*), 692
Naipaul, Vidiadhar Surajprasad, 26
Naked City, 343
Nathan der Weise (*Nathan the Wise*), 693
Nath, Mohinder, 376, 378
National Film School of Denmark, 464
National Heroine, 298
Nāṭyaśāstra (*Science of Drama*), 690
Naumburg, Nancy, 728
Nava, Jorge, 350
  Balada para niños muertos, 350
Navarre, René, 246
Ndamase, Joyce, 392, 394
Ndoda, 389, 399
Nelmes, Jill, 27
Nero, Franco, 421
Neuman, E. Jack, 341, 342, 344, 345
New Boy, 744
Newell, Mike, 79
Newman, David, 712
Newman, Michael Z., 589
Newsome, Carman, 266
Newton, Thandiwe, 64
New Women, 304
New Year's Eve (*Sylvester*), 251

New York Times, 512
Ngai, Sianne, 358
Ngcobo, Kethiwe, 391
Nichols, Dudley, 102
Nichols, Mike, 349
Niederkorn, Giulio, 727
Night of the Hunter, 137
Nigro, Francesca, 735
Ninotchka, 281, 695
Nkwinti, Mntunzima, 399
NLRB v. Hearst Publications, 532
Noche sin fortuna, 359
Noda, Kōgo, 316, 320, 323
Noerdlinger, Henry, 341
Nomadland, 615, 616, 618, 619
Nonceba, 396
Non uccidere (*Thou Shalt Not Kill*), 425
Norimasa, Kaeriyama, 319, 324
Normal People, 747
Norman, Marc, 213–215, 233
Norstein, Yuri, 566, 571, 578
North by Northwest, 700
Northcroft, George J.H., 455, 465
No Time to Die, 123
Notorious, 137
Notting Hill, 79
Novak, 343, 344
Novecento, 611, 612, 615, 617, 618
Nudes, 440
Nwonka, Clive, 86
Nyatasastra, 693

O
Oakland Tribune, 300
O'Bannon, Dan, 27
Obst, Linda, 511
O'Connell, Díóg, 78
O'Connell, Ryan, 593
O'Connolly, Jim, 572
Odd Obsession, 321
O'Donnell, Damian, 744, 752
O'Gorman, Marcel, 581
O'Grady, Alice, 180
Ojo al cine, 349, 352, 353
Old Loves and New, 266
Olivia, 597, 599, 600
Olsen, Nancy, 721
Olsen, Stein Holm, 123

O'Malley, Brian, 752
　Screwback, 752
Omasta, Michael, 103
Once Upon a Time in America, 477
O'Neill, Cecily, 169, 176
One Million Years B.C., 572–574
Operation Black Antler, 180
Opperman, Deon, 395
Orlando, 478
Orson Welles, 7
Ōsaka Elegy, 319
Osanai, Kaoru, 324
Ōshima, Nagisa, 326
Ospina, Luis, 349, 351, 357
Osten, Franz, 371
O'Sullivan, David, 748
　Moore Street Masala, 748
Ozu, Yasujirō, 319, 323

P
Paladino, Santi, 728
Palgrave Handbook of Children's Film and Television, 454
"Palgrave Studies in Screenwriting" book series, 4
Pallant, Chris, 26
Palmer, Linda, 737
Pal, Niranjan, 371
Pandey, Kamlesh, 366
Paolini, Marco, 694
Papaioannou, Spyros, 179
Parasite, 114
Paris-Midi, 239
Parker, Dorothy, 262
Parker, Philip, 26, 30
Parkkinen, Sami, 694
Parn, Priit, 578, 579
Parry, Becky, 462
　Children, Film and Literacy, 462
Pasolini, Pier Paolo, 24, 94, 97, 98, 102, 733, 734
Passchier, Bata, 395
Patrickson, Bronwen, 176
Patterns, 752
Patterson, Frances Taylor, 97
Peele, Jordan, 358
Peer Gynt, 281
Pegas, 242, 247, 249

Peirse, Alison, 79, 464
Pellegrini, Michele, 422, 426
Pellizzari, Lorenzo, 732
Pelo, Riikka, 102
Pennebaker, James, 7, 152, 156, 157, 159, 161
Perry, Eleanor, 212
Per scrivere un film, 735
Pete Butler, 343, 344
Peterson, Bob, 570
Petri, Elio, 735
Petronio, Barbara, 418
Petzold, Christian, 96
Phil, 597
Phillips, Andrea, 178
Picasso, Pablo, 74
Pickford, Mary, 261, 262, 270
Pick, Lupu, 102
Picnic at Hanging Rock, 615
Pierson, Frank, 713
Pinter, Harold, 209
Pirro, Ugo, 735, 736
Piscator, Erwin, 695, 696
Pitt, Suzan, 578, 579
Poetics, 691–693
Police Academy, 595
Poligono, Società Editrice, 732
Popat, Sita, 173, 174, 177
Pope, 168
Porter, Cole, 284
Porter, Edwin S., 749
　The Great Train Robbery, 749, 750
Portrait de la jeune fille en feu, 615, 618, 619
Potter, Anna, 457
Power, Ian, 752
　The Wonderful Story of Kelvin Kind, 752, 753
Prejudice: The Invisible Wall, 340
Prels, Max, 247
President Mulaudzi, 401, 402
President Zondo, 401
Pressburger, Emeric, 136
Preston, Lawrence, 337, 338
Prévert, Jacques, 134
Price, Steven, 2, 24–26, 35, 82, 94, 99, 234, 315, 719
Principal Vane, 341, 342
Prokopová, Alena, 441, 442, 445

Propp, Vladimir, 549, 749
Prosperi, Giorgio, 731, 732
Pryor, Richard, 476
Psycho, 614
Pt. Chandrashekhar, 372
Pudovkin, Vsevolod Illarionovich, 29, 727
Pura sangre [*Pure Blood*], 357
Purvis, Neal, 123
Pu, Shunqing, 296, 301, 303, 305, 308, 309

Q
Queen Sono, 390, 402
!Qué viva la música!, 352, 353, 362
Quinn, Joanna, 578

R
Rabelais, Francois, 692
Rae, Issa, 87, 722
Rafelson, Bob, 8, 218, 219, 349
Rahbani Brothers, 490
Ramaphosa, Cyril, 401
Ramosino, Luisa Cotta, 415, 419
Ramsey, Robert, 83
Rancière, Jacques, 690
Ranft, Joe, 574
Raphaelson, Samson, 711, 718
Rashk, Arjun Dev, 372
Raskin, Richard, 743, 751–753
Ravagli, Maddalena, 422
Raymond, Jon, 75
"Reaching Young Audiences: Serial fiction and cross-media storyworlds for children and young audiences", 454
Red Branch Heroes (*RBH*), 177, 178, 186
Red Branch Heroes (RBH), 178
Red Oaks, 593
Redvall, Eva Novrup, 26, 360
Reich, Andrew, 74
Reichardt, Kelly, 75
Reich, Walter, 25
Reign, April, 470
Reiner, Rob, 144, 460
  Stand by Me, 460

Reinhardt, Gottfried, 281
Reinhardt, Max, 281, 695, 696
Reiniger, Lotte, 578
Reis, António, 104
Reisch, Walter, 135, 279–281, 283–285, 287, 289, 291
Renzi, Renzo, 732
Retrieval, 297
Richie, Donald, 316, 321
Richter, Hans, 727
Rick Blaine, 113, 117–119, 121
Ricky Butler, 343, 344
Ricoeur, Paul, 132
Riefenstahl, Leni, 102
Riggs, Stephanie, 167, 171, 172, 184
Righelli, Gennaro, 726
  La canzone dell'amore [*The Song of Love*], 726
Ring, Carl, 533
Ring v. Spina, 533, 535
Rinne, Kirsi, 3
Risvig, Jonas, 462
Robinson, Casey, 265
Rocha, Paulo, 104
  Mudar de Vida [*Change of Life*], 104
Rogers, Ginger (and Fred Astaire), 282, 284, 286
Rodgers, Jimmie, 345
Rokuhei, Susukita, 316
Roma, 477
Romero, George, 349
Romero Rey, Sandro, 350, 354, 359
Room, 747
Roosevelt, Franklin D., 370
Rose, Frank, 175, 176
Rosenbaum, Jonathan, 97
Rosenberg, Stuart, 349
Rose, Reginald, 334, 335
  Playhouse 90, 335
Rosetta, 613
Rossellini, Roberto, 733
Route 66, 343
Roy, Bimal, 371
Ruggeri, Mario, 418–420
Ruhemann, Andrew, 579
Rumbaut, Rubén G., 476
Rush, Jeff, 105
Russell Micheaux, Alice Burton, 2, 9, 266, 267

Russo, Paolo, vii, 4, 29, 38, 115, 128, 612, 726
Ruttmann, Walter, 102
Ryan, 594, 597, 599
Ryan, Marie-Laure, 168, 170, 175, 178, 183

S
Sabroe, Iben Albinus, 26
Sagar, Ramanand, 372, 373
Sagay, Misan, 520
Sahir Ludhianvi, 376
Sainsbury, Mark, 116
Saints and Sinners, 339
Salinger, J.D., 736
Salmon, Colin, 557
Salter, Brent, 529, 536
Sam Benedict, 341
Samurai Town, 319
Sang, Hu, 299, 306
Saral, Mahendra, 373
Sardou, Victorien, 239
Sarris, Andrew, 210
Sátántangó, 664
Satō, Tadao, 316, 321–324
Saturday Evening Post, 711
Sauchelli, Andrea, 123, 124
Saving Mr. Banks, 520
Sawyer, R. Keith, 28, 36
Scarface, 136
Schechner, Richard, 169, 172, 173, 177
Schefer, Jean Louis, 96
Schell, Jesse, 202
Schenkkan, Robert, 720
Schlager, 281
Schleifer, Ronald, 134
  Modernism and Time: The Logic of Abundance in Literature, Science, and Culture 1880-1930, 134
Schmidt-Gentner, Willy, 284
Schneer, Charles H., 572
Schneider, Ralf, 94
Schnitzler, Arthur, 240, 241, 281
Schopenhauer, Arthur, 693
Schrader, Paul, 98, 106, 612
Schubert, Franz, 280, 290, 291
Schulberg, Budd, 710, 711, 718
Schumacher, Joel, 477, 480

Schundfilme, 240
Schwarzenegger, Arnold, 610
Schweblin, Samanta, 358
Sciamma, Céline, 615, 618
Science magazine, 49
Scorsese, Martin, 612
Scott, Allan, 284
Scott, Felix, 557
Screenwriting: The Sequence Approach, 716
Script magazine (Italy), 737
Script magazine (USA), 266
Secret Story Network (SSN), 181, 183, 186
S'dumo, 389, 392
Segal, Steve, 575, 576
Seger, Linda, 510, 737
Segnocinema, 734
Sei soggetti per il cinema. Storie inedite di Age e Scarpelli et al., 734
Sengupta, Rakesh, 26
Sennett, Mack, 213, 229–232
"The Sennett Screenplays", 231
Senso, 733
Sergeant York, 720
Sergei Mikhailovich, 22, 134, 209, 253, 694, 747–749
  Battleship Potemkin, 22, 727
Serino, Davide, 426
Sermoneta, Alessandro, 418, 420
Sex Education, 441
Sexual Perversity in Chicago, 218
S'gudi S'naysi (It's Good, It's Nice), 389, 392, 393
Shailendra, 373
Shakespeare in Mzansi, 398
Shakespeare, William, 398
Shall We Dance, 282, 286
Sharma, Narendra, 372
Sharpsteen, Ben, 575
Sharp, Tony, 557, 558
Shazam!, 478
Sheng, Qinxian, 299, 305, 308
Sheridan, Kirsten, 752
Sherlock Jr., 140
Sherlock series, 177
Sherlock: The Network, 177
Shindō, Kaneto, 320, 323–329
Shinkai, Makoto, 576

Shipp, Cameron, 229
Shklovsky, Viktor, 176, 252, 694, 699
Shohat, Ella, 114
Shusett, Ronald, 27
Shutter Island, 702
Šifra, Miro, 442
Silliphant, Stirling, 343, 344
Silverstein, Melissa, 507
Simon, Neil, 713
Simonton, Dean, 35
Sine-Fono, 242
Sirk, Douglas, 469, 476
   Imitation of Life, 469
Sister's Tragedy, 297
Sisters of Gion, 319
Six Shooter, 749–751
Skam, 434, 439, 440, 460
Skeggs, Beverley, 509
Skoller, Donald, 100
Sleepless in Seattle, 511
Slide, Anthony, 227
Slide, Tony, 228, 233
Smairi, Majdi, 493
Smart, Jean, 721
Smith, Cecil, 345
Smith, Clark Ashton, 355
Smith, Murray, 114, 115, 122
Smith, Stacy L., 510
Sniper Elite, 554
Sniper Elite 3, 554
Sniper Elite 4, 545, 554–558
Snyder, Blake, 714, 718
Society, 389, 400
Sohn, Peter, 574
Solomon, Stanley J., 26
Soltanto un nome nei titoli di testa [*Just a Name in the Opening Credits*], 735
Song at Midnight, 297
Sophia, 125
Sorrentino, Paolo, 735, 736
Soul, 574, 575
Soul Buddiez, 397
Soul City, 396
Special, 587, 588, 593–597, 599–601
Spies, Adrian, 338–340
Spina, 533
Spinoza, Baruch, 548
Spirit of the Overseas Chinese, 298

Spotnitz, Frank, 414, 415, 420, 424
Srinivasan, M.B., 381
Stagecoach, 750
Stahl, John, 476
Staiger, Janet, 214, 215, 324
Stambler, Bob, 341, 345
Stam, Robert, 114
Star, Susan Leigh, 94, 196
State of the Union, 587
Statsky, Jen, 721
Steemers, Jeanette, 457
Stempel, Tom, 213, 215, 233, 719
Stephen, 746
Sterelny, Kim, 116
Sternberg, Claudia, 24, 94, 98, 152, 154, 163, 208, 215
Sternheim, Julius, 246
Stiller, Mauritz, 240
Stilwell, Robyn, 278
Stir Crazy, 476
Stolz, Robert, 284
Stone, Matthew, 84
Stoppard, Tom, 209
Storaro, Vittorio, 34
Stovepipe Hat, 533
Stranger than Fiction, 125
Strauss Jr., Johann, 280–283, 285, 286, 289, 290
Striving, 340
Stromboli, 654
Suburban Bliss, 395
Suburra–La serie (*Suburra: Blood on Rome*), 414
Sud, Verna, 594
Suffragette, 520
Sullivan, C. Gardner, 213
Sumurûn (*One Arabian Night*), 695
Sunburn, 752
Sunrise, 24
Sunset Blvd., 214, 720–722
Susukita, Rokuhei, 321, 324
Suzie, 592
Svankmajer, Jan, 578
Swanson, Gloria, 721
Sylvestre, 103
Szczepanik, Petr, 36, 220

T
Tales of Terror, 350
Tanaka, Eizō, 319
Tanaka, Jun'ichirō, 316, 317, 321, 322, 324, 325
Tanizaki, Jun'ichirō, 324
Tan, Shaun, 579
Tarantula, 261
Tarkovsky, Andrei, 146
Tarr, Béla, 664
Tati, Jacques, 103
   Monsieur Hulot's Holiday, 103
Taves, Brian, 233
Taylor, Stayci, 94, 99
Taylor, Stephanie, 523
Taylor, William, 338
TBH, 431, 432, 435, 439–441, 444, 446–448
Tecnica dello scrittore cinematografico, 730
Terra Nova, 520
Terrone, Enrico, 117, 125
Tetris, 551
Thabang, 402
Thalberg, Irving, 75, 264, 265, 278, 279, 718, 719
"The Adversary", ep. of *Westworld*, 64–65
That Thing You Do!, 666
The African Queen, 137
The American Weird, 358
The Apartment, 715
The Autobiography of Malcolm X, 219
The Big House, 262
The Birth of a Nation, 225, 226
The Black Dog, 579
The Blockhead (Der Dummkopf), 237
The Blonde Saint, 266
The Bronze Bell, 232
The Call of Youth, 270
The Carpenter and His Clumsy Wife, 744
The Case of Majella McGinty, 752
"The Case of the Inappropriate Alarm Clock (Part 4)", 138
The Catcher in the Rye, 736
The Champ, 262
The Chi, 588–590, 592, 594, 596, 598, 599, 601

The Classical Hollywood Cinema, 214
The Cosby Show, 389
The Curse of Quon Gwon, 295, 300, 296, 308
The Day the Earth Stood Still, 478
The Defenders, 9, 333–338
The Desert Healer, 266
The Dirty Dozen, 511
The Door, 744
The Driver Is Red, 579
The Eagles Mate, 261
The Eddy, 421
The Eleven, 177, 178
The Empire Strikes Back, 520
The Escape, 476
The Fast and the Furious, 518
The Fellowship of the Ring, 666, 668, 669, 672
The Fifth Element, 702
The Film Scenario, 727
The Four Horseman of the Apocalypse, 263
The Fox's Gratitude, 297
The Front Page, 136
The Full Monty, 57–58
The Gay Divorcee, 282
The Ghost Writer, 702
The Girl from Chicago, 266
The Glory of Life, 318
The Goddess, 298
The Godfather, 477
The Good Wife, 595
The Great Day, 270
The Great Waltz, 280–286, 289, 291
The Guardian, 173
The Guild, 587, 593
The Hate U Give, 475, 477
The Henrietta, 263
The Hobbit, 546
The Honorable Beggar, 299, 305
The Hunger Games, 520
The Jim Gaffigan Show, 595
The King of Comedy, 229
The King of Jazz, 285
The King of Kings, 268
The Last of Us Part 2, 551
The Last Performance, 57
The Last Picture Show, 349
The Last Temptation of Christ, 612

The Last Wave, 615
The Line, 200
"The Literary Fact", 48
The Lizzie Bennet Diaries, 177, 587
The Lord of the Rings, 520, 666, 679
The Lost Thing, 579
The Lost World, 266
The Lying Truth, 266
The Marvelous Mrs. Maisel, 588–591, 592–594, 596, 601
The Milky Way, 700
The Mindy Project, 87
The Misadventures of Awkward Black Girl, 587, 593, 723
The Mosquito Coast, 615
The Moving Picture World, 712
The Nameless Offspring, 355
The Nation, 140
The New World, 666
The New York Hat, 271
The Nurses, 9, 338, 340
The Omen, 752
The Only Son, 319
The Other (Der Andere), 241
The Other F Word, 587, 588, 595, 598, 601
The Phantom of the Opera, 297
The Picture of Dorian Gray, 475
The Postman Always Rings Twice, 8, 218, 219
The Princess Bride, 143
"The Prisoner", ep. of *The Defenders*, 338
The Purple Rose of Cairo, 125
The Quiet One, 137
"There Is No Line", ep. of *Hacks*, 721
The Republic, 390, 401, 402
The Return of the King, 666, 673, 680
The Riot Club, 520
The River, 401
The Saphead, 263
The Sea Beast, 260
The Seal of R'lyeh, 354
The Secret World, 358
The Shape of Water, 478
The Shining, 700, 702
The Shop Around the Corner, 137, 696
The Short Film and Irish Cinema, 751
The Sims, 179

The Skin I Live In, 495
The Soul of Black Folks, 472
The Spirit of Utopia, 619
The Stranger, 588, 594, 595, 598, 601
The Ten Commandments, 268
The Tudors, 415
The Two Towers, 666, 668, 669, 671–673
The Untouchables, 219
The Upside, 478
The Valley of Gwangi, 572, 573
The Verdict, 219
The Voorman Problem, 47, 56, 58, 64
The Wire, 589
The Wiz, 478
The Wolves in the Walls, 559
The Writer's Journey: Mythic Structure for Storytellers and Screenwriters, 713, 737
The Young Offenders, 748
Thirty-six Amazons, 298
Thomasson, Amie L., 117, 119
Thomson, David, 27
Thomson v. Larson, 147 F.3d 195 (2d Cir. 1998), 531
Thornton, Darren, 744, 753
Three Modern Women, 304
Thurm, Eric, 589
Thusi, Pearl, 402
Tian, Han, 304
Tieber, Claus, 24, 25, 75, 104, 105, 234
Tinkerbell, 518
Titanic, 281, 665
To Be or Not To Be, 696
Todorov, Tzvetan, 610
Tofts, Darren, 360
Tolstoy, Leo, 144, 252
Tong Sing-to, 298, 308
Top Gun: Maverick, 702
Top Hat, 288
To the Lighthouse, 135
Toure, Nakhane, 399
Towne, Robert, 216
Townsend, Robert, 479
Trainspotting, 112
Tremont, John, 355, 356
Treveri Gennari, Daniela, 730
Trivedi, Chimanlal, 372
Trotti, Lamar, 710

Troy, 666
Truffaut, François, 144
Tu, Guangqi, 305
Turkin, Nikandr, 248
Turkin, Vladimir, 694
Turner, Victor, 176
Tynyanov, Yuri, 48, 254, 694

U

Umthunzi Wentaba (The Mountain's Shadow), 389, 399, 400
Under Fire, 609
Under the E'mei Mountain, 297
Under the Skin, 113
Unending Love, 299, 306
The United States v. Paramount Pictures, 712
Un passo dal cielo (One Step from Heaven), 413
Unsell, Eve, 261, 269
Untouchable, 478
Up, 570

V

Vajda, László, 99
Valentino, Rudolph, 263, 270
Vampyr, 732
Van Horne, Harriet, 339, 340
Vanoye, Francis, 35
Van Sant, Gus, 441
Variety, 269
Varotsis, George, 46, 48, 63
Vašíčková, Dorota, 438, 441, 447
Vemmer, Mogens, 463
Verlaine, Paul, 136
Veronica Mars, 593
Vestnik Kinematografii, 243
Viazzi, Glauco, 732
Vikander, Alicia, 113
Vincent Price, 350
Viola come il mare [Purple Like the Sea], 413
Visconti, Luchino, 733
Vogler, Christopher, 219, 713, 714, 718, 721, 737
von Bartalanffy, Ludwig, 48
von Goethe, Johann Wolfgang, 693

von Hofmannsthal, Hugo, 240
Vorlesungen zur Ästehtik [Lectures on Aesthetics], 693
VR Worlds, 557
Vuelven [Return], 358
Vundla, Mfundi, 397

W

Wada, Natto, 321
Wade, Laura, 520
Wagner, Richard, 282
Waithe, Lena, 592
Waititi, Taika, 458
Wake in Fright, 654
Walker, Michael A., 419
Walk, Wolfgang, 202
WALL-E, 574, 575
Waller-Bridge, Phoebe, 87, 123
Walsh, Fran, 520
Walter White, 589–591, 600
Walton, Kendall, 116, 124
Wan, Hoi-ling, 298, 300, 308
Waterbag, 746
Watson, Mary Ann, 334, 335
Weaver, Sigourney, 27
Weber, Lois, 259, 264, 271, 296
Weiler, Lance, 176
  Sherlock Holmes & the Internet of Things, 176
Weill, Kurt, 137
Weir, Peter, 615
Weitman, Robert, 342
Welles, Orson, 152, 225
  Citizen Kane, 152–157, 160–163, 165, 166
Wells, Paul, 26, 565
Welsh, Irvine, 119
We Make the Movies, 728
West, Nathanael, 211
  The Day of the Locust, 211
Westworld, xxxviii, 47, 54–56, 58–60, 64–68
Wet Straits (Nureta kaikyō), 326
Weyl, Hermann, 46
What Richard Did, 747
When the Streetlights Go On, 591
White, Poppy Cannon, 337
Whitman, Meg, 588

Whole Life Through, 193
Wiene, Robert, 102
Wilder, Billy, 134, 136, 228, 715, 721, 732
   Ace in the Hole, 732
Wilder, Gene, 476
Wilder, Thornton, 694
Wilson, George, 124
Wilson, Juanita, 744, 747
   The Door, 747
Wilson, Rita, 511
Wintersteller, Christina, 25
Witness, 615
Wodehouse, P.G., 136
Wolf, Friedrich, 695, 696
Wollheim, Richard, 125
Women's Home Companion, 228
Women's Monthly, 297
Women and Hollywood blog, 507
Wonder of Women, 260
Wong, Bruce, 298
Wong, Marion E., 9, 266, 267, 295, 296, 300, 301, 308
Woods, Frank E., 225, 226
Woods, Vienna, 286
Woolcott, Alexander, 262
Woolf, Virginia, 135
Woo, Yen Yen Jocelyn, 183
Wreyford, Natalie, 79, 86
Writing Children's Books for Dummies, 455
Writing for children, 455
Wu, Xun, 299

X
X-Men: First Class, 520

Y
Yagi, Yasutarō, 320
Yahya ibn Adi, 691
Yamagami, Itarō, 324, 328
Yamanaka, Sadao, 324
Yarrow, Ralph, 185
Yasumi, Toshio, 320
Yates, Michael, 574
Yelena, Aïcha, 126
Yizo Yizo (It Is the Way It Is), 397
Yoda, Yoshikata, 319
Yorke, John, 570
You Can Say Vagina, 33, 34
Young Master (Botchan), 319

Z
Zanuck, Darryl F., 278
Zappe, Florian, 358
Zepernick, Janet, 463
Zerozerozero, 421, 422
Zhao, Chloé, 615
Zigomar, 327
Zubeck, Robert, 201, 202
Zuckmayer, Carl, 695
Zukal, Josef, 437, 438
Zukor, Adolph, 270
Zuma, Jacob, 401
Zwelinzima, 393, 394

Subject Index

Numbers
1848 revolution, 289
4-D manifolds, 6, 47, 62–63, 67

A
Abbaye de Creteil group, 142
ABC Australia, 459
abstract artefact(s), 117, 118, 123–125, 127, 128
Abu Dhabi Media, 493
Abu Dhabi TV, 493
academic research, 14
Academy Award, 260, 262, 265, 343
Academy Museum, 267
Academy of Motion Picture Arts and Sciences, 226, 260
acculturation, 473, 476
act(s), 12, 599, 700
actant(s), 614, 615
action, 519, 520
Action Role-Playing Game, 548
act of reading, 95
adaptation(s), 9, 226, 251, 319, 320, 322, 391, 479
advertising agencies, 532
affordable fiction, 458, 461
affordances, 171
Africa Film Drama Art (AFDA), 395
African languages, 391
African National Congress (ANC), 389
Africans, 522

agency/agent(s), 113, 176, 390, 396
 human, 111–112
 to address social ills, 396
 to affect change, 404
 intentional, 113, 117, 119, 125, 127
Ahmedabad, 369
alignment, 458
allegiance, 458
All India Trade Union Congress (AITUC), 369
Amazon, 425, 527
American Film Institute, 715
American Film Institute Archives, 511
American film musicals, 9
American independent cinema, 4
anagnorisis, 700, 701
analytical frames, 29
Andheri, 366
Anglocentric bias, 207
Anica, 427
Anica Academy, 427
animatics, 26
animation, 12, 563–573, 575, 576, 578–582
animation toolbox, 12
Annecy Festival, 582
anthology, 324
antitrust, 535
antitrust law, 528, 532, 533, 539
Apartheid system, 8–9, 387, 388, 392
aporia, 692
apparatus, 278

© The Editor(s) (if applicable) and The Author(s), under exclusive license to Springer Nature Switzerland AG 2023
R. Davies et al. (eds), *The Palgrave Handbook of Screenwriting Studies*,
https://doi.org/10.1007/978-3-031-20769-3

Approved Production Contract (APC), 528, 534, 539
Arab, 485
　nationalism, 489
　popular culture, 490
　satellite broadcasting, 490
　television, 492
　television drama, 491
　world, 492
archetype(s), 487, 595, 602, 610, 612
archive(s)/archival, 37, 207, 209, 217–218
　materials, 208
　research, 4, 8, 209, 213
arc(s), 589, 591, 592, 597, 599
Aristotelian drama, 609
Aristotelian paradigm, 592
Art Directors' Association, 371
artefactual entities, 117
art-house cinema, 216
Artists' Manager Basic Agreement (AMBA), 537
art worlds, 78
ASIFA, 582
Asian silent cinema, 8
assimilation, 11, 469, 473
Assistant Film Directors' Association, 371
Association for Revolutionary Cinematography (*Assotsiatsiya revolyutsionnoy kinematografii*, ARK), 253
Association of Art Directors, 382
Association of Film Editors, 371
Association of German Film Authors (*Verband deutscher Filmautoren*), 247
Association of Talent Agencies, 537
Astor Theatre, 260
Atlantique, 421
attractions, 96
audience, 474, 521, 522
audience-centered, 716
audience participation, 173
audio-visual industry, 390
Austria, 240
auteur, 27, 246, 323
auteur theory, 244, 712
authenticity, 422, 491

author, 27, 28, 243
author/audience dynamic, 171
authorship, 2, 6, 10, 73, 80–85, 87–89, 198, 241, 323, 412, 424, 427
autoethnographic, 545
Autorenfilme, 240–241
avant-garde(s), 248, 250, 252
avant-texte, 35

B

Baalbeck International Festival, 489
Ba'athist regime, 490
back-end payments, 536
backstory, 56, 113
barks, 552, 553
BBC, 60
BBC Children's Commissioning, 457
beats, 55–57, 714
behavioural patterns, 50
Bellyfeel Productions, 177
Berlin Dramaturgy, 695
Berliner Ensemble, 694
Berlin Flow, 33
Best Original Screenplay, 262
bible, 418
Big Light, 414
Big Time Film (*Dashidai*), 298
Biograph Company, 260
biographies, 229, 235
Biograph Studios, 261
biopic, 280
black/black people
　audience(s), 395–396
　characters, 388, 391, 397
　children and young adult(s), 389
　depictions, 388
　disadvantage, 389
　educating, 395–396
　emancipation of women, 400
　film industry, 391
　influencing understanding of own experience, 393
　queer, 400
　people in townships, 401
　screenwriters, 10
　South Africans, 9, 388, 398, 402–404
　voice, 388
　women character, 400, 403

blacklist, 212, 537
Black Lives Matter, 470
block universe, 62, 63, 68
blueprint, 6, 289
   see also screenplay as blueprint
Bombay film industry, 375
Bombay Mill Hands Association, 369
Bombay (Mumbai), 369
book series, 732
Boston University, 587
botteghe di scrittura, 27
boundaries, 400
boundary object(s), 24, 25, 27, 45, 196
branching narrative, 556
brane, 63, 68
Brechtian alienation strategy, 611
Brechtian drama, 609
British film industry, 368
British Library, 209
broadcasters, 509
Broadcast Standards, 342, 344, 345
Broadway, 531, 534
brown-face, 232
budgeting, 423

C
Calcutta (Kolkata), 369
Cali, Grupo de, 353, 357
California Talent Agencies Act, 537
caméra-stylo, 34
CA model, 58, 59. See also Cellular Automata (CA)
Canal Plus, 412, 421
Cannes Film Festival, 321
capital, 509, 515
Cappelli, 732
Casa del Mantegna-Provincia di Mantova, 734
Casino Theatre, 695
Catherine Curtis Corporation, 263
Cattleya, 414, 421, 422
causally connected, 596, 598, 601, 602
Cellular Automata (CA), 6, 47, 53–55, 67
cellular automata simulators, 56
Celluloid Ceiling reports, 507
censorship, 240, 327, 729
central question, 591, 597

Centre for the Study of Women in Television and Film, 507
Centro Sperimentale di Cinematografia, 727
Chapman University's Film School, 717
character(s)/characterization, 5, 12, 486, 492, 494, 496–500
   arc, 494. See also arc(s)
   character-driven, 517
   complexity, 590, 594–596
   community of, 60
   development, 7, 495
   flat, 487
   modes, 487
   profiles, 111, 113, 117, 127
   round, 487
Character Artists' Association, 371
characterisation, 486, 497, 498
chick flick(s)/chick's movie(s), 511, 519
childhood, 455, 462
children, 10, 453–465
children's films, 519
Children's Media Foundation, 464
China Film (*Huaying*), 299, 305
China Sound & Silent Film Production, 298
China Sun Motion Picture, 296
Chinese Communist Party, 304
Chinese Exclusion Act, 296
Chinese women screenwriters, 9, 295
choice(s), 589, 594, 600
chronological types of histories, 316
Cine Costume and Make up Artists' Association, 371
Cine Dance Directors' Association, 371
Cine Dancers' Union, 382
Cine Junior Artistes Association, 382
cinemagoers, 512
cinematic competence, 98
cinematic design, 98
cinematic diction, 105
cinematic idea, 26, 95, 97, 106
cinematic rhythm, 105
cinematic style, 101
cinematic tension, 101
cinematic thinking, 94
Cinematic Virtual Reality, 195
cinematic vocation, 100
cinematographic image, 96

Cine Musicians' Association, 382
Cine Production Association, 371
Cineteca Italiana di Milano, 732
Circolo del Cinema S.M. Eisenstein, 734
cisgender, 522
class, 521
classical era, 215
classical Hollywood, 315
classical sound era, 214
class struggle, 617
cliché, 496
cliffhanger, 591, 592, 598, 601, 602
climax, 665
clock of character, 611
co-authorship, 180
Code of Conduct, 538
code switching, 473
co-executive producer/creative producer, 422
cognition, 486
cognitive narratological approaches, 610
cognitive stereotypes, 487
coherence, 598
Cold War, 376
collaboration, 74–77, 79–81, 86, 87, 89, 180, 211
collaborative, 176
collaborative emergence, 36
collectible documents, 553, 555, 556
collective and collaborative practices, 6
collective bargaining, 528
collective behaviour, 47, 53
collective storytelling, 181
colour-coding, 219
Columbia University, 716, 717
comic-book movie(s), 219
coming-of-age stories, 454, 459, 460, 462
commission, 521, 523
commissioners, 412, 457
commissioning editor, 440, 447
commitment, 414
communication, 491
communities, 29, 60
competition law, 528
complementary collaboration, 74
complex/complexity, 48–49
  adaptive system, 46

Complex Systems Theory (CST), 45, 48
  effective, 53
  in screenwriting, 56
  map of complexity sciences, 47
  system(s), 6, 45, 49, 50, 52
complex TV, 607
complicating action, 665
concept, 418
conflict, 487, 498, 614, 700
conspiracy in restraint of trade, 533
contemporary aesthetics, 358
contingent commodities, 434
continuity, 23, 250, 254
continuity script, 214
control, 49
conventions, 78–80, 84–89, 250, 251, 253
conversation, 180
cooperation, 76–80, 87–89
cooperative networks, 80, 81, 85, 87, 89
co-production(s), 12, 643, 644, 647, 650
copyright, 13, 214, 220, 528, 535, 539
Copyright Act (1957), 381, 535
Copyright Act (1976), 531
copyright law, 209, 535
costumes, 228
couleur locale, 501
Courier font, 218
COVID-19 pandemic, 382, 462
Creative Artists Agency (CAA), 536
creative doctorate, 760
creative labour, 368
creative matrix, 26, 30
creative practice research, 759
creative process, 102, 763
creative producer unit, 440, 446
Creative Skillset, 513
creative visions, 436
creative writing, 3, 762
creativity, 28, 427
creativity research, 35
credit, 220, 242
crime, 519
critical analysis, 3, 29, 34
Critical Digital Humanities, 6, 67
critical practice, 3, 29, 32
critics, 520

Cross Media School of Children's
  Fiction, 464
ČT (Česká Televize), 10, 436, 437,
  440–448
cultural backgrounds, 389
cultural industries, 396
cultural legitimation, 734
cultural memory, 702
cultural pluralism, 480
cultural production, 516
cultural sensitivities, 399
cut scenes, 550–553
Czechoslovakia, 36
Czech Republic, 36

D
Dadar, 372, 373
Damascene milieu, 491
dance, 288
Danish Writers Guild, 455
dawn of democracy, 396
decentralized control, 49
decision-makers, 523
découpage, 250
democratic dispensation, 390
denegation, 611
designs, 26
Deutsches Theater, 695
development, 25, 36, 319, 665
developmental arc, 496
development culture, 432
development phase, 422
Devil's Reef, 355
dialogue, 152, 153, 155–163, 165, 166,
  214, 218
dialogue writer, 26
diaspora, 470
diction, 104, 106
diegetic, 278
digital connectivity, 546
digital humanities, 7, 46, 67, 151
digital streaming services, 493
digitized, 210
director's cuts, 12
director's script, 251
Directors Guild of America (DGA), 538,
  539
discourse analysis, 35

discourse(s), 24, 30, 516, 522
discourse-time, 105
discoverable, 556
discrimination, 479
disenfranchisement, 477
Disney, 425, 572, 575
Disney Animation, 713, 714
Dispute Settlement Committee, 380
distaste(s)/distasteful, 511, 514, 521,
  522
distributed, 49
distributed collaboration, 74, 75
distribution companies, 509
diverse/diversity, 470, 522–523
divide between conception and
  execution, 53, 253
division of labour, 371
doctoral candidates, 759
documentaries, 5
documentary filmmaking, 318
dogma, 28
Dogme 95, 33
domain, 6, 25, 27, 28
dominant, 515, 516, 521
dominated, 515, 522
double consciousness, 472
double/dual address, 456
double structured narratives, 105
doxa, 13, 28, 613
DR (Danish public service broadcaster),
  456, 457, 460, 461
  DR Media researchers, 457, 461
  DR Ramasjang, 456, 457
  DR Ultra, 456, 457, 461
drafting, 728
drama, 58, 517, 519
dramatic irony, 715, 721
dramatic structure, 104, 714
dramatists, 528, 529
Dramatists Guild, 528–534, 539
dramaturg(s), 539, 698, 699
dramaturgy, 5, 13, 689, 690, 698–700
drawing, 26
Drehbuch, 220
drug-related subject matter, 344
Dunwich, 354
dynamic suture, 551

E
Eagle Films, 493
early cinema, 323
economic equality, 397
Edison Company, 213, 261
education, 13
educational
  media channels, 396
  programming, 398
  SABC, 395
  setting, 32
Einaudi, 734
Elementary Tetrad, 202
elite, 516
embodied cognition, 50
emergence, 49, 50
emergent behaviour, 62, 68
emergent storytelling, 183
Eminent Authors, 211
Emmy Award, 401, 721
employee, 528, 530, 535
employers of screenwriters, 509
enacting stories, 558
engagement, 176
England, 355
English, 357
epic narration, 691
epic theatre, 365
episodic integrity, 589, 591, 596, 597
epistemological insight, 6
epos, 691
ergodic, 549, 555
ethnicity, 491
ethnographic shift, 431, 443
European(s), 8, 522
European avant-gardes, 237
event ontology, 63
Eve Unsell Photoplay Staff, 263
evolution, 47, 53
executives, 416
experimental screenplays, 249, 250
explanations, 300
explicit dramaturgy, 702
external perspective, 123, 125–128
extra-diegetic, 278, 282

F
fabula, 703, 714

Factories Act (1948), 379
"family" timeslot, 344
Famous Players Film Company, 261
Famous Players-Lasky Corporation, 244, 250
Famous Studios, 373, 382
FAMU, 441, 715
fantasy, 9
feature film, 57
Federation of Western India Cine Employees (FWICE), 371, 382
feedback, 49
feedback loop, 177, 709, 710, 713, 719, 722, 723
"feeder" system, 711
Feltrinelli, 733
female writers, 212, 464. *See also* women screenwriters
femininity, 491
feminist, 509, 521
fictional world, 113, 116, 118, 119, 125–128
fiction films, 5
fictosexuality, 125
field, 6, 28
film criticism, 321
film culture, 726
Film d'Art, 238, 239
film fiction, 300
film history, 228, 231, 315
film idea, 26
Filminute festival, 57
film labour markets, 513
film musicals, 291. *See also* musicals
film philosophy, 34
Film Producers' Guild of India (Producers Guild of India), 381
film scholars, 321
film schools, 13, 709, 711
film screenings, 399
film studios, 213
Film Workers Federation, 382
Film Writers' Association (FWA), 366, 368, 371–373, 375–382
Film Writers' Cooperative Housing Society, 380
filter bubbles, 435
financier, 516, 522
First National, 260, 266

five-act structure, 592
flashback, 497
FM Edizioni, 734
Fogma, 33
Fordist, 215
format, 215, 241, 250, 254
formatting, 22
fractals, 48
France, 239, 247, 250
freelance/freelancing, 13, 340, 471

G
game design document, 201
Game of life rules, 59
games, 7
game studies, 202
game theory, 47
game writing and narrative design, 545
gender, 11, 211, 521–523
gendered habitus, 515
gendered stereotypes, 512
gendered taste, 522
gender inequality, 507
General Systems Theory, 48
genetic criticism, 35
genkō yōshi, 329
Gerasimov Institute of Cinematography (VGIK, now the Russian State University of Cinematography), 694
genre(s), 315, 495, 517, 519, 522
Germany, 240, 246, 247, 250
global audience, 403
global market, 414
"going small" production model, 434
golden age, 333
golden age of television seriality, 411
Golden Line, 493
good taste, 516
gothic fiction, 359
gothic horror, 350, 353
graph theory, 53
Great American Songbook, 284
Great Depression, 370
Great Wall Motion Pictures, 296
group practice, 28, 36
growth cycle model, 59
guide, 729

H
habitus, 509, 515–516, 519, 522, 523
Hamburg's *National Theatre*, 693
handbooks ("how to" manuals), 2, 13
handbooks on screenwriting, 241, 246
happenings and environmental theatre, 173
haptic encounters(s), 12, 624, 626, 629, 631–637, 639, 640
Harry Ransom Center (HRC), 209, 218
Hays Code, 264
HBO Max, 425
head writer(s), 413, 417, 422
Hearst, 532
hero's journey, 219, 713, 714
heterosexual, 522
Heurigen, 291
high concept, 219
high-end drama, 486
hiring, 509
historiography, 207, 317, 321
history of screenwriting, 225, 233, 725
holism, 48
Hollywood, 4, 8, 229, 234, 277, 279, 281, 282, 284, 291, 353, 368, 371, 535, 711
   B movies, 360
   mode(s) of production, 316, 436
   norms, 684
   studios, 746
   studio system, 13. *See also* studio system
Hollywood Ten, 212
homophily, 79, 89
horror, 9, 519
Horror Inc., 535
Hulu, 527
humour, 392, 460
hyper-realist, 613

I
Ida May Park Productions, 263
identity, 389, 472
identity crisis, 400
identity labels, 512
IDHEC (Institute des Hautes Études Cinématographiques), 731
image, 96, 102

image composition, 98
imaginaries, 446
imagined communities, 488
imitation [*Nachahmungspoesie*], 692
immersive/interactive, 167, 175
Immersive Virtual Reality (VR), 7, 190. *See also* Virtual Reality
immigrant, 477
improvisation, 36, 250
improvisational forms of performance, 168
Ince studio, 233
inciting incident, 597, 599, 601, 602
independent contractors, 528, 532, 535, 539
independent web series, 432
index cards, 218
India, 37, 376
India's independence, 381
Indian Motion Picture Employees' Association, 371
Indian Motion Picture Producers' Association (IMPPA), 370, 381
Indian People's Theatre Association (IPTA), 377
Indian Performing Right Society (IPRS), 381
individual producers, 509
industrial contexts, 208
industrial organization, 215
industrial reflexivity, 735
industry, 762
industry insiders, 512
in-game dialogue, 553
innovation, 432
Irish Film Board/Screen Ireland, 78, 744, 752, 755
Innsmouth, 354, 355, 357
Institute on Gender in Media, 507
institutionalization, 725
institutional racism, 342
integrated musical, 285
integration without identification, 336, 338
integrative collaboration, 74
intellectual worker(s), 365, 379
interactive/interactivity, 169
  and immersive media, 7
  screenplay, 190

script, 7
theatre, 186
interface, 202
internal perspective, 125, 127, 128
internal stance, 119
international audience, 415
International Creative Management (ICM), 536
international players, 426
interpretive communities, 28, 29
intertitles, 213, 214, 240, 242
introduction of sound, 214
"invisible" workers, 382
invisible costs, 475
Ireland, 14
Irish cinema, 753
Irish film, 743, 744, 746, 753, 754
iron screenplay, 253
irrealism, 116, 119, 123
I See Media, 493
isiXhosa culture, 393
Istituto di Propaganda Libraria, 734
Italian writers, 29

J
Japanese cinema, 316, 320
Japanese film, 316
Japanese screenwriting, 315
Japan Writers Guild, 327
Jawwy TV, 493
Jogeshwari cave, 375
Joker system, 170
journalism, 711
journals, 726
judgements of taste, 509
Jungian character archetypes, 713

K
Kammerspiele Theatre, 695
Kala Nagar, 379
Keystone Studios, 229
Kim's Threefold World Model, 183
kitchen sink dramas, 519
knowledge, 770

L
labor, 539

labor exemption to antitrust law, 533, 536
labor law, 528, 532, 535
labor union, 538
labour activism, 367, 370
labour movements, 368
landscape of the mind, 615
language, 474
language barrier, 417
LARPs, 183
Lasky company, 270
Lasky Feature Play, 260
Latin American, 359–362
Latin American film history, 361
Latin American literature and cinema, 352
Latin American screenwriting, 354
lattice point(s), 53, 56–58, 64
league of Broadway theatre owners, 532
League of Regional Theatres (LORT), 534
lean management theory, 32
learning and teaching, 32
Lebanese national identity, 11
Lebanese-ness, 486, 488, 493, 494
Lebanon, 485
Left-wing Drama Association, 304
legitimacy, 515
lesbian, 522
Let Toys Be Toys, 512
LGBT, 445
Lianhua Film, 298
Library of Congress, 209, 212, 227, 231–233
libretto, 251, 252
license fees, 533
liminality, 176
linear-causal drama, 692
linear dynamics, 49
linearity, 48
linear scheduling, 435
linear scripts, 7
lingua franca, 421, 424
Linguistic Inquiry and Word Count software (LIWC), 7
linguistic texture, 7
literary, 216
literary author(s), 237–239, 241–244, 249, 252

literary scenario, 251
literary script, 253
literary techniques, 7
literary theory, 48
literature in flux, 24
live action scripted fiction, 454
live anthology drama, 333, 339
liveness, 169
local content, 402
locations, 593, 595
Łódź film school, 731
Lois Weber Productions, 262
London Coliseum, 695
Longanesi, 733
long-distance collaboration, 419
Los Angeles, 350
Los Angeles County Museum of Art, 234
low-budget short, 595
ludologists, 549
ludology, 549
ludonarrative dissonance, 549, 552, 560
Lux Vide, 414–417, 419, 420
lyrics, 284

M

Madras (Chennai), 369
Mahalaxmi, 373
mainstream cinema, 11
main tension, 716
make-belief, 116, 118, 124
male gaze, 495
management of production resources, 418
Mandarin Film Company, 267, 300
manifolds, 62. *See also* 4-D manifolds
manipulation of media objects, 195
Manny Company, 535
manual(s), 11, 13, 30, 32, 278, 453–455, 460, 464, 465, 589, 726
manuscript, 228, 233, 329
Margaret Herrick Library (MHL), 208, 210, 215, 226, 227, 230–231, 270
Margery Wilson Productions, 263
marginalized, 515
Marion Fairfax Productions, 260
market-driven, 509
Marshall Neilan Productions, 260

Marvel, 477
Marx Brothers, 719
Marxist, 609, 617
masculinity, 491
master-scene screenplay/script, 22–24, 30, 215–216, 218, 280, 317
Matunga, 372
MBC4, 493
media industry studies, 432
media literacy, 457
mediating institutions, 536
medieval European theatre and literature, 612
memoirs, 228, 229
memory, 12, 63
memory retention, 63
memory retrieval, 474
men critics, 522
men directors, 521
men screenwriters, 521
meritocratic, 509
metafictional, 116, 125–127
methodology, 767
#MeToo, 470
Metro Pictures, 262
MGM, 75, 210, 215, 261, 265, 342, 344, 718, 719
Micheaux production company, 267
microhistories, 217, 220
micro-narrative, 12, 568–572, 575–577, 580–582
MIDI, 56, 68
migrant film workers, 382
migration, 477
mimesis [imitation], 119–121, 696
mimetic, 119, 608–609
mind-dependent, 117
mind-games, 48
mind-independent, 118
Minimum Basic Agreement (MBA), 528–529, 532, 539
Ministry of Information and Broadcasting, 375
Minkovski diagram, 63
minoritised racial, 508
minority, 469
mirroring, 11, 469
mise en scène, 253
modal realism, 115

Modern Theatre, 695
modularity, 48
Mondadori, 733
Moscow State School of Cinematography, 136
motifs, 323
Motion Picture Academy, 720
Motion Picture Association of America (MPAA), 512
Motion Picture Engineers, 226
Motion Picture Society of India (MPSI), 370
motivation(s), 607, 609, 610, 612, 613, 615
movie studios, 534
moving image, 96, 97, 101
MTV, 493
multiculturalism, 473
multiple-reel films, 239
multi-strand narratives, 58
mumblecore, 33
munshi, 26
musalsalat, 499
Museum of Modern Art, 228
mushaira, 373
music, 101, 102, 104, 277
musicalization, 287
musical number(s), 9, 282–284, 287, 289, 291
musicals, 278. *See also* film musicals
music films, 290
music in screenplays, 291
Mzansi Magic, 401

N
narration, 691, 714
narrative(s), 607, 609, 610, 612–616, 618, 714
 beats, 54
 composition, 613
 construction, 610, 613
 designer, 553, 554, 559, 560
 development, 613
 discourse, 105
 drive, 176, 591, 598
 dynamics, 610
 homeostasis, 48
 possibilities, 200

schema, 26
storyworld, 607
strategy, 610, 612–613, 617–618
structure, 100, 615
style, 225
universe, 192
voice, 105
world, 616
narrativist-ludology, 549
national character, 486, 494, 499, 500
national character stereotypes, 494
National Defence Cinema, 308
National Education Association (NEA), 341
national film and television industry, 390
national film culture, 390
national film history, 316
National Film Preservation Board of the Library of Congress, 268
National Film School in Rome, 13
national film schools, 13
national identity, 488
nationality, 496, 498
National Labor Relations Act (NLRA, 1935), 530, 532
National Labor Relations Board, 530
national on-screen (TV and film) tradition, 390
national othering, 489
national stereotypes, 501
naturalism, 696
navigation, 180
Nazi Germany, 290
Nazi (National Socialist) regime, 280–281, 291
NBC, 344, 345
negotiated narrative, 179, 185
Netflix, 421, 425, 427, 441, 463, 527, 588, 593
network control, 334, 335
network executives, 337
network of relations, 560
network(s), 47, 53, 59, 60, 67
networks analyses, 6
network system, 334–335
neurocinematic, 50
New England, 357
new era of hope, 395
new era of screenplay depictions, 397

New Frontier character dramas, 334
New Hollywood, 215, 216, 219, 349, 664
new media, 527
NewNew, 33
New York, 532, 534
New York League of Theatres, 534
New York University, 717
niche, 593, 595, 602
Nigerian historical drama, 12
Nobel Prize in Literature, 240
nodal navigation, 195
non-binary, 509, 521, 522
non-linear, 547
nonlinear systems/nonlinearity, 47, 49–50
non-narrative texts, 96
Non-Playable Characters (NPC), 550, 552, 556
non-sequential structure, 558
non-writing producers, 415
nostalgia, 491
notes, 230
novel, 520
NRK, 463

O

object problem, 24
one-reelers, 230
online curation, 435, 437
online-only content, 434, 435, 437, 438, 440, 441, 448
online-only formats, 435, 439
ontological insight, 6
ontological status, 112, 115, 124
ontology, 115, 190
ontology of character, 116
ontospace, 63
opera, 462
oral ballad traditions, 25
oral discussion, 211
oral history, 210, 226
oral records, 210
orchestrate, 179
organization, 47
original screenplays, 729
orthodox screenwriting, 28–30
orthodoxy, 28–30, 36, 78, 80, 88

Oscar, 269
#OscarsSoWhite, 470
othering, 501
outlines, 416
outsiderness, 477–478

P

Pacific War, 300
package, 215
packaging, 536, 537
pan-Arab, 488
pan-Arab audience, 11
pan-Arab dramas, 486, 492, 495
paradigm, 601, 713
parametric narration, 105
Paramount, 719, 721
Paramount+, 425
Paramount Decree, 215–216
parasocial relations, 124
partakers, 172
participation, 180
participative, 169
passing, 11, 469
Pathé, 239, 243
pattern formation, 47, 53, 55, 59
payoff, 547
Peabody Award, 342
pedagogical thinking, 731
pedagogy, 743–746, 748, 749, 751–755, 762
performance/installation art, 173
performance directors, 558
performative processes, 167
period film (*jidaigeki*), 324
peripeteia, 700, 701
peri-urban context, 394
personalization, 435
personified, 113
person(s), 112, 114–116, 118, 119
phase line, 64
phase space, 63
phenomenon, 191
pigeonholing, 464
piracy, 209
Pixar, 574–576
plants, 596
platform imaginaries, 435, 436, 446
platformization, 432, 434

platform studies, 432
Plautus Productions, 333
playwright, 230, 528, 535, 539
playwriting, 239
plectics, 46
plexus, 46
plot, 495, 501
plot complexity, 50
plot continuity, 104
plot development, 497
plot point, 278, 716
plots, 486
poetics, 190, 588, 589, 599, 601, 603
point-to-point mapping, 68
polymorphic, 185
popular music, 289
possible worlds theories, 7, 62, 115
Post-Apartheid film and television writing, 8, 392
post-colonial novels, 394
post-feminist, 515
postwar cinema, 318
post-World War II, 233, 318, 320
POV, 598
Practice-as-Research (PAR), 33
Practice-Led-Research (PLR), 33
practitioner, 760
practitioner-researcher, 760
precariat, 367
precarization, 368, 369
predominantly white, 397
Premio Solinas, 735
prescripting, 199
presence, 53, 58, 59
President's Gold Medal, 375
prestige, 588–593, 595
pretence, 114, 116–118, 123, 124
pre-viz software, 26
prewar cinema, 318
prey-predator model, 59
procedural authorship, 199
process drama, 176
process work (forum theatre), 170
producer, 512
producer units, 448
production, 564, 565, 567, 568, 571–582
Production Code, 281
production companies, 501, 509

SUBJECT INDEX 813

production design, 26
production practices, 412
production report, 230
production scheduling, 423
production systems, 426
production values, 589, 593, 595
professional culture, 423
professional organization, 341
professional practice, 427
professional screenwriters, 735
project leader, 446
proletariat, 365
props, 228
protagonist(s), 493, 499
prototype, 25, 34
PSM web series, 433, 434
psychodrama, 36
public financiers, 509
public interest groups, 335
public service, 415, 439, 441, 442
Public Service Media (PSM), 431, 432, 434, 435, 440
public service web series, 435
published screenplays/scripts, 209, 211, 248–251, 732, 734
Publishers Association, 478
publishing, 13
Puo Pha Productions, 400
Pure Film Movement, 317, 324
puzzle, 48

Q

qualitative analysis, 492
quality programming, 335
Quibi, 587, 588, 591

R

race, 521
racial inequality, 337
racial integration, 335
racial politics, 335
racing game, 548
racism, 496, 499
radial graph/radar graph, 65
radio, 532
Radio Writers Guild, 532
RAI, 414

Rai 1, 415
Rai Fiction, 412, 415
rainbow, 219
Ramadan, 486, 492, 499
random layout, 61
Ranjit Studios, 373
reader, 98, 100, 104
reading, 94, 99–101, 103
reading perspective, 107
reading the screenplay, 97, 104
realism, 461, 608
reality television, 492
recognition/identification, 458, 460, 701
recursion/recursive, 49, 52
re-enactment or performative, 185
RED, 79
reframing, 477
Regelpoesie, 691
rehearsals, 230
relationships, 589, 590, 593, 597
remuneration, 414
representation, 470, 496, 498
representation of time, 7
representations of childhood, 456
representation without identification, 343
research artefacts, 759
research cultures, 759
research work, 34
resolution, 595, 597
reversion, 701
revue film, 285
re-writer, 219
rhythm, 94, 95, 100–102, 104–106, 287
rhythmization, 285
rich white men, 521
rights in derivative works, 535
Rizzoli, 733
RKO, 284
role-playing games, 180
romantic comedy, 518, 519
Roop Tara Studios, 373
Royal Shakespeare Company, 172, 186
RTÉ, 744, 752
ruinous presidency, 401
Russia, 242, 247, 251
Russian Formalism, 48
Russian methods, 29

S

SABC Education, 397
SABC television, 388
sandbox, 551, 555
Scandinavian countries, 454, 464
SCAS model, 50, 53. *See also* Screenwriting as a Complex Adaptive System (SCAS)
scenario, 239, 242, 244, 250, 254, 319, 330, 710
 crisis, 244, 245, 248, 252
 fever, 13, 217
 script, 214, 216
scene outlines, 214
scene text, 152–155, 157, 158, 160–163, 165, 166
schemata, 486, 487, 489
science-fiction/Sci-Fi, 519
Screen Actors Guild (SAG-AFTRA), 537
screen adaptation, 393
Screen Australia, 78
screen idea, 3, 25–27, 29, 34–35, 95, 191, 436, 458
Screen Idea Work Group (SIWG), 27, 36, 45, 277, 278, 280
Screen Ireland, 754
screenplay, 2, 4–5, 46, 111, 117–118, 127, 248, 471, 623–626, 628, 630–634, 636, 637, 639, 640
 archives, 217
 as blueprint, 2
 as a popular literary form, 8
 as literature, 213, 249–251
 as material texts, 213
 drafts, 209
 format, 214
 publications, 251
 reader, 93
 reading, 100
 stylistic visual expression, 631
 text, 7, 104
screenplectics, 45, 46, 67
screen production, 762
screenwriter, 2, 113, 127, 131
screenwriter's voice, 100, 106
Screenwriters' Association of India, 9
Screenwriters' Association (SWA), 366
Screenwriters' guilds, 9
Screen Writers Guild, 262, 530
screenwriting, 25, 112, 114, 189, 486, 494, 501, 725, 732
 academic, 763
 academies, 13
 as creative labour, 4
 competitions, 244, 251
 conventions, 246, 250
 department, 242, 244
 discourse, 238–239, 243–250, 252–254
 gurus, 737
 handbooks, 250
 historiography, 8
 manuals, 13, 30, 216, 219, 227, 246, 251, 254, 608–610, 709, 718
 practice research, 759
 process, 2
 research, 35
 schools, 13
 studies, 28, 37, 196, 361
 style, 106
 system, 53
 teacher(s)/teaching, 13, 727
 team, 400
 techniques, 11, 403
 universities, 13
 work, 508
Screenwriting as a Complex Adaptive System (SCAS), 47, 48, 52, 56, 62, 63, 67
Screenwriting Research Network (SRN), 3, 207
script/scripting, 25–27, 190, 231–232, 734
 anthologies, 319
 consultants, 737
 department (*kyakuhonbu*), 321
 development, 4, 22, 216–217, 764
 doctor, 220
 factory, 711
 format, 215
 scouting (*shinario hantingu*), 320
Scuola Holden, 736
Second Circuit Court of Appeals, 535, 539
Second World War, 328
Sediba Spark Program 2005, 398
segmentation, 456, 457
segregation, 513

self-actualisation, 400
self-organization, 49, 53
self-presentation, 491
self-reference, 280
self-referentiality, 50
Sennett collection, 231
Sennett studios, 230, 231
separation of conception and execution, 245, 246, 253
sequence, 716
serial arc, 418
Serial Eyes, 413, 415, 423–425
serial formats, 60
seriality, 425
serialized, 588, 590, 596, 601
serial shows, 58
serial structure, 418
serial writing, 421
setting, 496
setup, 547, 593, 596, 665
sexist, 518
sexuality, 521
shinario sakka (scenario author), 319, 322
Shōchiku Studios, 318
shooting script, 284
short film, 14, 56, 62
short-form, 439, 442, 588, 591, 593–595, 599, 601, 602
short form serialized dramas, 12, 588
short-form series, 587
short stories, 214
showrunner, 99, 100, 412, 423, 442, 446, 448
Shree Sound Studios, 372, 373
silent cinema, 214, 744
silent comedy, 229, 231
silent era, 8, 318, 321, 328
silent film, 225, 226, 228, 233, 234
silent screenwriting, 227, 233, 238
simulation, 183
single address, 456
Sinophone cinema, 295, 296, 300, 308
Sinophone screenplays and films, 307
sit-coms, 57
sketches, 26
Sky, 421
Sky Italia, 412, 424
slow thinking, 702

soap, 462
social class, 513
socialised, 523
social issues drama, 334, 340, 341
social mobility, 389
social realism, 454, 462, 492, 494
social schemata, 494
Society of Audio Visual Engineers, 382
Society of Film Editors, 382
Society of Stage Directors and Choreographers, 531
sociomaterial, 436
socio-political divisiveness, 490
soggetti (treatments), 416, 420
Soul City Institute for Justice, 396
sound, 233, 317, 319
sourcers, 172
South Africa/South African
  audience, 391, 393, 399
  depictions, 387, 392, 396
  Department of Arts, Culture, Science and Technology, 398
  Film and Television section, 396
  fledgling democracy, 388
  government, 395
  Hollywoodization of screenwriting culture, 398
  influencing understanding of own experience, 398
  Interim Constitution (1996), 395
  mainstream, 400
  national identity, 391
  present day, 403
  screens, 395
  screenwriting, 393
  society, 387
  South African Broadcasting Corporation (SABC), 387–388, 391, 398
  television's decentralization, 401
  townships, 392
  transition to democracy, 388, 396
  unemployment, 402
  youth, 399
space of consequences, 63
space of possibilities, 50, 62
spacetime, 63
spaghetti western, 421
spatial, 547

spatial exploration, 195
specialized screenwriting journal, 737
specificity thesis, 209
spec script, 216
spectatorship, 199
spectral layout, 61
speculative imagination, 197
speculative media, 361
stable, 712, 717
stakes, 589, 590, 596
stance (external/internal), 118
stand-alone, 596
Standards and Practices, 343
Star Film, 297, 304
state space, 63
state support, 375
state universities, 737
statistical analysis, 151, 152
step outlines, 218
stereotype(s), 489, 492, 498, 501, 510, 511, 522
stereotypical gendered roles, 517
story [*fabula*], 96, 689
storyboard, 26, 565, 567, 570–577, 580–582
storyboarding, 26, 208
story-centered, 716
story conductor, 183
story conference, 27, 216, 218, 219, 231, 279
story department, 230
storyline, 55, 56, 58
storymaster, 183
storyplexing, 171
story structure, 714
storytelling, 416
story-time, 105
storyworld, 7, 56, 59, 60, 63, 64, 68, 178, 609
streaming, 587–589, 592
streaming platform, 402
strong female character, 519
structure, 589–592, 595, 598–602, 714, 718
structuring principles, 318
student, 588, 602
studio era, 710
studios, 325

studio system, 4, 284, 320, 325, 709.
  See also Hollywood studio system
stylistic visual expression, 631, 633
subjective and collective memory, 546
subjective choices, 509
subtext, 471
sujet [*syuzhet*], 689, 703
summary, 601
Sundance Institute, 716
superhero, 518, 519
super-natural world, 460
Supreme Court, 532
suspension of disbelief, 607, 611
symbolic act, 697
symbolic action [*symbolisches Handeln*], 696
symbolic violence, 510, 516
symplectic(s), 46
synopses, 300
synopsis, 231
synthesis of the orthodoxy, 31
Syria, 485
Syrian identity, 490
Syrian national identity, 11
Syrian-ness, 486, 488, 493, 494
system, 49
system, process and product, 170
systems theory, 47

T
Taft-Hartley Act, 532
talent agents, 536, 539
taste, 508, 516, 521, 523
tastemaker, 516
teaser, 592, 599, 600
teens, 10
teleological types of histories, 316
teleplays, 9
television
  Christmas calendar, 461
  drama, 492
  networks, 538
  playwright, 339
  sitcom, 392
telling stories, 521
template, 601
tension, 101, 716
termination of transfer rights, 535

Text, 6, 94, 98–100, 104, 105
textual, 99
textual analysis, 35
textual cues, 487
theatre, 239, 243, 246–248, 254, 611, 615
Theatre Laboratory, 169
Theatre of the Absurd, 144
Theaterwissenschaftliches Institut (Theatrical-Scientific Institute), 696
theatrical play script, 209
theatrical play text, 214
thematic analysis, 493
thematic integrity, 591, 596
themes, 323, 589, 590
three-act structure, 217, 596, 600–601, 713–714
Threefold World Model for RPGs, 183
thriller, 518, 519, 595, 601
Tik Tok, 33, 463
time, 131
topical clusters, 47, 53
Trade Union Act, 369, 371, 378
trade union conglomerates, 370
trade unions, 367–369
traditional narrative composition, 613
tragedy, 691
tragic moment, 700, 701
training courses, 426, 427
training system, 712
transcripts, 230
transculturality, 646
transcultural screenwriting, 5
transformational arc, 488, 494
   see also arc(s), character arc
transgender, 522
transitory, 471
translations of story outlines, 727
transnational, 12, 462, 486
   cinema, 647, 648
   film, 643–645
   film theory, 647
   projects, 412
   transnational writers' rooms, 10
treatment, 111, 117, 127, 417, 422, 728
Tremont Hall, 355, 356, 359
Triangle, 230
Triangle-Keystone, 213, 230

tropical gothic, 353
Turkish cinema, 368
turning point, 664, 665
TV networks, 9
TV writers, 527
tweens, 10
Twentieth Century-Fox, 711, 719
Twitter, 538
two-column format, 282
twofoldness, 119, 125–127, 611, 612
typists, 219

U
UCLA, 717
UK, 247
UK Film Council, 507
UK film industry, 507
unfilmed screenplays, 9
unionization, 368
Union Minister for Housing, 379
union(s), 320, 382, 528
United States Supreme Court, 530
United Talent Agency (UTA), 536, 538
universal, 244, 261, 284, 602, 610
universality, 434, 612
Universal Pictures, 269
universal truth, 659
universities, 13
University of California, 717
University of Los Angeles, 717
University of Madison-Wisconsin, 210, 215
University of Southern California, 226
University of Southern California's School of Cinematic Arts, 717
Universum Film Aktiengesellschaft (UFA), 695
unreliable narrator, 178
unrepresented, 470
USA, 247, 254

V
Verfremdungseffekte (alienation effect), 611
VGIK-Vserossijskij Gosudarstvenn'ij Institut Kinematografii, 731
Videogames, 12

Viennese Film, 289–291
Virtual Reality, 551, 557, 559. *See also* Immersive VIrtual Reality (VR)
vision, 95, 96, 101, 102, 106
vision du monde, 615, 616
visual
  counterpoint, 694
  form, 97
  language, 397, 403
  story, 106
  storytelling, 94
voice, 83, 84, 105, 106
vote, 395

W

war movies, 519–520
Warner Brothers, 210, 215, 265
web, 587, 602
web series, 10, 431, 433
weird, 9, 353, 358
Wenhua Film Company, 299, 306
Western India Cinematographers Association, 371
Western India Society of Cinematographers, 382
Western India Sound Engineers' Association, 371
white-owned production companies, 391
white space, 215
Wiener Film, 280
William Morris Entertainment (WME), 536
William S. Hart's house, 271
women/women's, 522
  directors, 520
  screenwriters, 4, 11, 229, 234, 520, 522
  cinema, 296
  issues, 519
  screenwriting, 521
  stories, 522
  tastes, 520
  voice, 510
  writing, 510, 523
Women Film Pioneers Project, 272, 296

workers' rights, 379
work for hire, 535, 539
working method, 426
working practices, 420
workshops, 424
worldbuilding, 550, 559, 593
world Cinema, 647
world line, 64
World War I, 238, 239, 243, 244, 247, 250, 369
Writers' guilds, 4, 11, 233
  Writers Guild Italia (WGI), 413, 414
  Writers Guild of America (WGA), 82–83, 212, 368, 527, 529, 530, 535–538
  Writers Guild of America East (WGAE), 527
  Writers Guild of America West (WGAW), 527
  Writers Guild of Great Britain (WGGB), 80
writers' room, 24, 27, 74, 76–78, 80, 83, 411, 431, 440, 441
writing departments (*stables*), 215, 710, 722
writing with light, 34
writing with music, 25
writing workshop, 717

X

xenophobia, 496
Xhosa people, 399

Y

yED, 68
Yoruba, 630
young audiences, 453, 454, 456–459, 461, 463–465
youthful renaissance, 397
youthification, 432, 434
YouTube, 461–463, 587, 602

Z

Zibetti, 734

Printed in the United States
by Baker & Taylor Publisher Services